ACCOUNTING
PRINCIPLES AND APPLICATIONS

ACCOUNTING
PRINCIPLES AND APPLICATIONS
FIFTH EDITION

Horace R. Brock, Ph.D., C.P.A.
Professor of Accounting
College of Business Administration
North Texas State University
Denton, Texas

Charles E. Palmer, D.C.S., C.P.A.
Chairman of the Board
Strayer College
Washington, D.C.

Billie M. Cunningham, Ph.D.
Assistant Professor of Accounting
M.J. Neeley School of Business
Texas Christian University
Fort Worth, Texas

Gregg Division
McGraw-Hill Book Company

New York   Atlanta   Dallas   St. Louis   San Francisco
Auckland   Bogotá   Guatemala   Hamburg   Johannesburg   Lisbon
London   Madrid   Mexico   Montreal   New Delhi   Panama   Paris
San Juan   São Paulo   Singapore   Sydney   Tokyo   Toronto

Sponsoring Editor: **Sherry Cohen**
Editing Supervisor: **Vesta K. Wells**
Design and Art Supervisor: **Caryl Valerie Spinka**
Production Supervisor: **Priscilla Taguer**

Text/Cover Designer: **Delgado Design**
Cover Photographer: **Ken Karp**

Library of Congress Cataloging in Publication Data

Brock, Horace R.
    Accounting: principles and applications.
    Includes index.
    1. Accounting.   I. Palmer, Charles Earl, date.
II. Cunningham, Billie M.   III. Title.
HF5635.B8545   1986   657   84-12592
ISBN 0-07-008260-X

ISBN 0-07-008260-X

C O N T E N T S

PREFACE

In the complex, intensely competitive environment of modern business, accounting plays a vital and constantly expanding role. Management needs a steady stream of timely financial information in order to make sound decisions and effectively control operations. A knowledge of the accounting process and an ability to work with financial information are, therefore, highly important for students who are preparing for a wide range of business careers as well as for students who are planning to enter the field of accounting. The fifth edition of *Accounting: Principles and Applications* has been specially designed to serve the needs of all students who require a well-rounded, comprehensive introduction to accounting. For students whose career objectives call for only one course in accounting, this book provides the necessary understanding of accounting principles and procedures. For students who need a broader knowledge of accounting, this book lays a strong foundation for additional study.

ORGANIZATION AND CONTENT OF THE TEXT

Accounting: Principles and Applications, Fifth Edition has been carefully planned to help students master accounting in a logical and efficient manner. The text material is divided into three parts and moves steadily from basic concepts to more complex and sophisticated topics. Part 1 provides thorough coverage of the fundamentals of financial accounting; Part 2 takes the students into more advanced areas of financial accounting; and Part 3 provides an introduction to managerial accounting.

To reinforce learning, every chapter ends with a summary of the material covered, a discussion of the managerial implications of the material, review questions, managerial questions, exercises, problems, and alternate problems. A business project that appears after Chapter 6 of Part 1 serves as a short built-in practice set. A series of microcomputer problems after Chapter 18 provides a culminating activity for Part 1. A business project that appears after Chapter 36 of Part 2 involves the students in financial analysis and decision-making activities.

The fifth edition of *Accounting: Principles and Applications* retains the characteristics that have made previous editions such an effective learning tool: short units of instruction; a clear, concise writing style; and abundant illustrations. But this edition has also added many new features that will enhance the learning process.

- Increased attention is now given to the underlying concepts and principles of accounting. A new first chapter explains the nature and purpose of accounting and introduces students to generally accepted accounting principles and the role of the Financial Accounting Standards Board and other authoritative bodies in their development. Detailed coverage of generally accepted accounting principles and financial reporting standards appears in Chapter 19. References to appropriate Statements of Financial Accounting Standards and Opinions of the Accounting Principles Board are provided throughout Part 2.

- The coverage of the recording process in Part 1 is now handled in a more concise fashion, and adjustments are introduced earlier.

- Internal control is now stressed throughout Parts 1 and 2, beginning with a discussion of the audit trail in Chapter 4.

- The end-of-chapter material has been expanded to include numerous review questions and exercises. The problems and alternate problems have been substantially revised, and new problems have been added in order to give the instructor more flexibility in making assignments.

- A new chapter on corporate reporting (Chapter 33) provides coverage of consolidated financial statements, supplementary disclosures, and constant-dollar accounting.

- There is a greater emphasis on the analysis and use of accounting data for decision making. For example, the coverage of funds flow analysis and financial statement analysis has been revised and expanded, and a project on financial analysis and decision making has been added to Part 2. Similarly, a new chapter on cost-revenue analysis for decision making (Chapter 44) now appears in Part 3.

- The coverage of depreciation in Chapter 24 has been updated to include the Accelerated Cost Recovery System.
- Present-value analysis has been added to the discussion of the amortization of bond discount and premium in Chapter 31 and the discussion of financial planning in Chapter 46.
- The coverage of computerized accounting systems has been increased and thoroughly revised. A discussion of microcomputer accounting systems for small businesses appears in Chapter 12. Larger-scale systems are explained in Chapter 18.
- Microcomputer problems have been added to give the students practical experience with automated accounting if suitable equipment and software are available.
- A glossary is now provided at the back of the book. This glossary includes definitions of important terms that are presented throughout the text.

APPLICATION ACTIVITIES

Effective application activities are essential to the learning process in accounting. This text provides abundant opportunities for the students to put their knowledge into practice.

Review Questions. The review questions that appear at the end of each chapter are designed to check the students' understanding of key concepts, procedures, and terms covered in the chapter.

Managerial Discussion Questions. The managerial discussion questions serve two purposes. They are intended to stimulate class discussion and to help the students develop an awareness of how management uses accounting data.

Exercises. The exercises given at the end of each chapter are short activities that reinforce important aspects of the material presented in the chapter. Each exercise typically covers one concept or procedure. The exercises are ideal for classroom use as a reinforcement tool, or they may be assigned for homework.

Problems. The problems that appear at the end of each chapter involve the analysis of business transactions and the preparation of financial records and statements. These problems are much broader in scope than the exercises, and cover a variety of concepts and procedures.

Alternate Problems. The alternate problems for each chapter are similar to the regular problems and can be used in several ways. They can be assigned for remedial work, enrichment, review, or makeup work; or they can be used in class as demonstration problems. Still another approach is to assign different sets of problems to different classes.

Business Projects. Two business projects appear in the text. The first project, which is given after Chapter 6 of Part 1, takes the students through a complete one-month accounting cycle for a small service business. The second project, which is presented after Chapter 36 of Part 2, places the students in the role of a loan officer at a bank who must analyze the comparative financial statements of a small but growing software company that wants money to expand its operations. The students must prepare a detailed analysis of the statements, interpret the results, and then recommend a decision to the bank's loan committee.

Microcomputer Problems. A series of microcomputer problems appear after Chapter 18 of Part 1. These problems allow the students to set up an accounting system for a new business, process transactions for the first two months of the firm's operations, handle end-of-period procedures for each month, and then work with computer printouts of the financial statements and other accounting records to analyze financial data.

LEARNING AIDS

A number of learning aids are available for use with the fifth edition of *Accounting: Principles and Applications*. These materials are designed to enhance the effectiveness of the course for the student.

Study Guide and Working Papers. A separate workbook is available for each part of the text. This learning aid includes performance objectives for each chapter, directions for studying the chapter, self-checking questions and exercises that the students can use to evaluate their understanding of the text material, and working papers for

the problems or alternate problems and the business projects.

Practice Sets. There are three practice sets specially designed for use with *Accounting: Principles and Applications*, Fifth Edition.

Brookside Real Estate: A Sole Proprietorship Service Business Practice Set involves a one-month accounting cycle for a real estate agency. Working from source documents, the students record transactions in a combined journal; post to the general ledger and the accounts payaable ledger; prepare banking, payroll, and petty cash records; and perform end-of-period activities. This set can be used after Chapter 14 of Part 1. It is ideal for situations in which the instructor wants to provide intensive experience in handling the daily financial activities of a small office.

Lifestyles Furniture: A Sole Proprietorship Merchandising Business Practice Set is intended for use after Chapter 17 of Part 1. Working from a narrative of transactions, the students perform one month's accounting activities for a retail furniture store. The accounting system of this firm includes special journals and subsidiary ledgers as well as the general journal and the general ledger. A series of management questions is also provided so that students have an opportunity to interpret the accounting records they have prepared.

Champs Inc.: A Corporation Accounting and Financial Statement Analysis Practice Set is designed for use after Chapter 36 of Part 2. Working from a narrative, the students record transactions, prepare financial statements, and handle adjusting and closing procedures for a corporation that operates a chain of sporting goods stores. The general journal and the general ledger are used for the accounting entries. After completing the end-of-period procedures, the students make a detailed comparative analysis of the firm's financial data for several fiscal years and answer interpretive questions.

In addition to the three practice sets described above, users of *Accounting: Principles and Applications,* Fifth Edition may want to consider two other suitable practice sets: *Sight and Sound Electronics* by Stennick and *Skeeter's Pizza Parlor: A Shoebox Accounting Practice Set* by Peterson. Both of these practice sets can be completed manually or on a computer with the assistance of *Microcomputer General Ledger System* by Hamilton, which is described below. The sets include source documents and can be used after Chapter 17 of Part 1.

Microcomputer Software. *Microcomputer General Ledger System* by Hamilton is an easy-to-use software program that will give students hands-on experience with automated accounting. It consists of a combined program and data disk and a user's manual that includes operating instructions, a demonstration problem, and a project for the students to complete. Versions are available for the IBM PC, the Apple II Plus and IIe, and the TRS-80 Model III and Model 4. This software can be used with the microcomputer problems in the text, *Sight and Sound Electronics, Skeeter's Pizza Parlor,* and instructor-prepared problems and projects.

TEACHING AIDS

A variety of helpful teaching aids are available for use with *Accounting: Principles and Applications,* Fifth Edition.

Course Management and Solutions Manuals. There is a separate *Course Management and Solutions Manual* for each part of the text. These manuals include teaching suggestions, sample course schedules, transparency masters for accounting forms, student check sheets that can be duplicated, assignment and testing logs, and a complete key to the questions, exercises, problems, alternate problems, and projects in the text.

Solutions Transparencies. A set of transparencies containing solutions for problem material in the text is also available for each part.

Examination Manual. A comprehensive examination manual includes objective questions, exercises, and problems for every chapter in the text. This material is arranged in a series of chapter-by-chapter achievement tests and can be reproduced in that form; or instructors can treat the manual as a test bank and use it to construct their own tests.

Test Booklets. There is a separate test booklet for each part of the text. Each booklet includes four tests, which contain objective questions, problems, and exercises. Instructors who adopt the program can obtain individual test booklets for all students in their classes free of charge.

Microcomputer Test Bank. This automated test bank includes a wide variety of objective questions for all chapters of the text and is a handy means of producing custom-designed tests for every class. Versions are available for the IBM PC and the Apple II Plus and IIe.

ACKNOWLEDGMENTS

The authors are extremely grateful to the following accounting educators who reviewed the previous edition and provided many helpful suggestions for improvement: Diane B. Birch, Becker Junior College; Jill Burch, the Hickey School of St. Louis; George C. Converse, The Academy for Business Careers; Sharon L. Cook, University of Alaska; Donald R. Davis, Modesto Junior College; Joseph Dorzweiler, Hamilton Business College; Estelle S.

Faier, Metropolitan Technical Community College of Omaha; Donald R. Gaither, Chattanooga State Technical Community College; Beatrice R. Getzen, San Diego Community College (Mesa); Jerome H. Gottleib, Israel Discount Bank and American Institute of Banking (New York); Hope C. Griffin, Glendale Community College; Angela M. Grimaldi, the Stone School; Louis Harmin, Sullivan County Community College; Greg Harpole, Lane Community College; Mary Ann Hatzberger, the Sawyer School at Pawtucket; Mary Jo Jensen, Rutledge Junior College; Joel Katz, Davenport College—Kalamazoo; Thomas V. Kennedy, Manufacturers Hanover Trust Company and American Institute of Banking (New York); Albert C. Loring, Riverside College; Thelma L. Mitchell, Indiana University/Purdue University at Fort Wayne; Norman Muller, Greenfield Community College; Peter Neigler, Monroe Business Institute; Joanne Owens, Draughons Junior College; Vivian A. Pacsy, Monroe Business Institute; George O. Ritchey, Harrisburg Area Community College; Dolores Sorenson, Sierra College; Neal R. VanZante, Midwestern State University; Betty Vergon, Indiana Vocational Technical College at South Bend; and Duane H. White, Royal Business School.

The authors also wish to express their deep appreciation to the following accounting educators who reviewed the manuscript for the present edition, checked solutions, and helped to prepare some of the supplementary items: Susan G. Anderson, Port Side Vocational-Technical School; Diane Birch, Becker Junior College; Jill Burch, the Hickey School of St. Louis; George C. Converse, The Academy for Business Careers; Linda Herrington, Community College of Allegheny County; Mary Jo Jensen, Rutledge Junior College; Susanne Mackey, Anchorage Community College; Vivian A. Pacsy, Monroe Business Institute; Mildred Polisky, formerly of Milwaukee Area Technical College; Mary C. Pretti and Brenda Smith, State Technical Institute of Memphis; Lillian F. Winkler, formerly of the Wheeler School; and William J. Zahurak, Community College of Allegheny County.

Horace R. Brock
Charles E. Palmer
Billie M. Cunningham

PART 1

ACCOUNTING: BASIC PRINCIPLES

CHAPTER

1

Accounting is often called "the language of business." Some people describe accounting as a communication system, and others view it as an information system. Accounting is also defined as an art whose primary purpose is to gather and communicate financial information about an economic or social entity. (A business is an example of an economic entity. A nonprofit hospital is an example of a social entity.) In business the accountant may be considered the interpreter and communicator of financial information about an economic entity.

BASIC CONCEPTS OF ACCOUNTING

THE NEED FOR FINANCIAL INFORMATION

Suppose that a relative leaves you a substantial sum of money and you decide to carry out your lifelong dream of opening a small shop to sell sportswear. You rent space in a local shopping center, purchase fixtures and equipment, purchase goods to sell, hire salespeople, and open the store to customers. Before long you realize that in order to run your business successfully, you will need financial information about it. And to obtain that information, someone must gather data about the firm's financial affairs and analyze the data.

What type of financial information should you have in order to operate your business successfully? At regular intervals you will probably need answers to the following questions.

- How much cash does the business have?
- How much money do customers owe the business?
- What is the cost of the merchandise sold?
- How much did the volume of sales increase?
- What is the amount owed to suppliers?
- How much profit has the firm made?

As your business grows, you will need even more financial information in order to evaluate the firm's performance and make decisions about the future. When an efficient accounting system is in operation, owners and managers can obtain a wide range of useful information quickly. This is why it is so important for a business to have a well-run accounting system directed by a professional accountant.

THE NATURE OF AN ACCOUNTING SYSTEM

An *accounting system* is designed to accumulate data about a firm's financial affairs, classify the data in a meaningful way, and summarize it in periodic reports, which are called *financial statements*. Owners and managers receive much of the information they need from financial statements. The accountant not only establishes the records and procedures that make up the accounting system and supervises the operations of the system but also interprets the resulting financial information. Most owners and managers rely heavily on the judgment and knowledge of the accountant when making financial decisions.

THE ACCOUNTING PROCESS

The purpose of accounting is to provide financial information. In fact, many people call accounting "the language of business" because the results of the accounting process—financial statements—communicate essential information about a business to many concerned individuals and organizations (owners, managers, government agencies, banks, suppliers, and so on).

The accounting process involves recording, classifying, summarizing, interpreting, and communicating financial information about an economic or social entity. An *entity* is something that can be recognized as having its own separate identity, such as an individual, a town, a university, or a business. The term *economic entity* usually refers to a *business*—an organization whose major purpose is to produce a profit for its owners. *Social entities* are nonprofit organizations, such as cities, public schools, and public hospitals.

This book will focus on the accounting process for businesses, but keep in mind that nonprofit organizations need similar financial information. Starting with Chapter 2, the book will describe and illustrate the accounting process. In order to fully understand this process, it is necessary to first understand the environment in which accounting takes place. Therefore, the remainder of this chapter is devoted to a discussion of the following topics.

- The different types of business entities that exist.
- The people and organizations that use the financial information produced by the accounting process.
- The rules or principles that must be followed in the accounting process.
- The different areas of accounting.

DIFFERENT TYPES OF BUSINESS ENTITIES

There are three major legal forms of business entity: the sole proprietorship, the partnership, and the corporation. While the accounting process for all three types of business entity is generally the same, differences in their structures and in the laws that apply to these structures require some differences in the way certain aspects of their financial affairs are accounted for. These specific differences in accounting procedures will be presented in detail later in the book as accounting for the different business structures is discussed. However, for now it will be helpful for you to understand the basic differences in the three types of business entity.

Sole Proprietorships

A *sole proprietorship* is a form of business entity owned by one person. The life of the business ends when the owner is no longer willing or able to keep the firm going. Many small businesses are operated as sole proprietorships.

The owner of a sole proprietorship is legally responsible for the debts and taxes of the business. If, for example, the firm is unable to pay its debts, the creditors (those people, companies, or government agencies to whom the firm owes money) can turn to the owner for payment. The owner may then have to pay the debts of the business from personal savings or other personal resources.

When the time comes to pay income taxes, the owner's income and the income of the business are combined to compute the total tax responsibility of the owner.

While the owner's money and the money of the business may seem to be almost the same, it is very important that the accounting process for the business be limited to the financial transactions of the firm. Remember, accounting deals with financial information about an economic entity. The owner of the business and the business are separate entities. If the owner's personal transactions are mixed up with those of the business, it will be very difficult to measure the performance of the firm. Accountants use the term *separate entity assumption* to describe this idea of separating the accounting process for a business from the accounting process for the personal finances of the owner or owners.

Partnerships

A *partnership* is a form of business entity owned by two or more people. The partnership structure is very common in businesses that offer a professional service, such as law firms, accounting firms, architectural firms, medical practices, and dental practices. At the beginning of the partnership, two or more individuals enter into a contract that outlines each partner's percentage of ownership; what share of the profits each partner will receive; how much each partner will contribute to the business; what duties each partner will perform; how much responsibility each partner will have to creditors and tax authorities for the amounts owed by the business; and other information detailing the rights, obligations, and limitations of each partner. The partners may share equally in the ownership and profits of the business, or they may share in any proportion agreed upon in the contract. When an individual is unwilling or unable to remain a partner, then the partnership dissolves and a new partnership may be formed with the remaining partners or with new partners.

As in a sole proprietorship, the partners are individually, and as a group, responsible for the debts and taxes of the partnership. Their personal bank accounts or other personal resources may be used to pay creditors when the partnership is unable to provide payment. Again, it is important that the accounting process for a partnership be limited to the financial transactions of the firm and not include the personal transactions of the partners.

Corporations

The *corporation* is considerably different from the other forms of business entity—the sole proprietorship and the partnership. The major difference has to do with the ownership of the business. There are *publicly owned* and *privately owned corporations* (often called *closely held corporations*). Anyone can invest in a publicly owned corporation. Shares of stock for such corporations are bought and sold on stock exchanges and in the over-the-counter markets. (*Shares of stock* represent ownership in a corporation and are indicated by stock certificates.) In closely held corporations, ownership is limited to specific individuals, usually family members.

Most large corporations have sold many thousands of shares of stock. Generally each investor's proportion of ownership is determined by the number of shares of stock purchased by that individual as compared with the total number of shares sold by the corporation. For example, assume that Nancy Ling currently owns 250 shares of the Sample Corporation's stock. If the Sample Corporation has issued (sold) 1,000 shares of stock up to this point, Ling has a 25 percent ownership interest in the corporation (250 shares ÷ 1,000 shares = 0.25, or 25%). If the owners of the Sample Corporation have to make a decision by voting, then Ling will have 250 votes (one for each share of stock that she owns). The other owners will have a total of 750 votes.

The corporate form of business entity is unique in that ownership can change through the sale of shares of stock by one individual to another without the firm ending. (Some corporations have new owners daily because their shares are actively traded on stock exchanges.) One of the advantages of a corporation is that it can last forever, whereas the maximum life of a sole proprietorship is the life of its owner. Similarly, a partnership can last only as long as the life span of any of its partners. The death or withdrawal of one partner ends the partnership.

Corporate owners, often called *stockholders* or *shareholders,* are not responsible for the debts or taxes of the corporation. The most money that a stockholder can lose if the corporation is unable to pay its bills is his or her initial investment in the firm—the cost of the shares of stock that were purchased by the stockholder.

The corporate entity, like the sole proprietorship and the partnership, must be accounted for separately from the financial affairs of its owners. This separation is usually easier with a corporation than with a sole proprietorship or a partnership because, in most cases, stockholders do not participate in the day-to-day operations of the business.

Some major characteristics of the three types of business entity are summarized in the table below.

MAJOR CHARACTERISTICS OF DIFFERENT TYPES OF BUSINESS ENTITY

Characteristic	Type of Business Entity		
	Sole Proprietorship	Partnership	Corporation
Ownership	One owner.	Two or more owners.	Several owners (may have many owners, even thousands of owners).
Life of the business	The life of the business ends when the owner dies, is unable to carry on operations, or decides to close the firm.	The life of the business ends when one or more partners withdraw, when a partner dies, or when the partners decide to close the firm.	Corporations can continue forever. Ownership changes through the sale of stock. The life of a corporation ends only when it can no longer pay its creditors and goes bankrupt or when the stockholders vote to liquidate it.
Responsibility for the debts of the business	The owner is responsible for the debts of the firm when the firm is unable to pay.	The partners are responsible individually and jointly for the debts of the firm when the firm is unable to pay.	The stockholders are not responsible for the debts of the firm and can only lose their original investment.

It was mentioned earlier that the results of the accounting process are communicated to many individuals and organizations who are interested in the financial affairs of a business. Who are these individuals and organizations, and why do they want to obtain financial information about a particular firm?

Owners and Managers

Assume again that you inherited some money and opened a small shop that sells sportswear. One user of financial information about the business is obviously you, the owner. The information that you need, and that all owners and managers need, is information that will help you to evaluate the results of your operations and to plan and make decisions for the future. Should you drop long-sleeved pullover sweaters that are not selling well from your product line, or should you just reduce the price to encourage sales? How much money should you spend on advertising? How much should you charge for a new type of denim jacket that you are adding to your product line? How does this year's profit compare with the profit you earned the year before? Should you open a new store? These questions would be difficult to answer without financial information.

Suppliers

Even though your business is a small sole proprietorship, a number of people other than you, the owner, may be interested in its financial affairs. For example, when you first ask for credit from suppliers of goods, they may want financial information in order to assess the ability of your firm to pay its debts. They may also use the data to determine exactly how much credit you should be given.

Banks

What if you decide to ask your bank for a loan so that you can open a new store across town? The bank will want to assure itself that your firm will be in business long enough to pay back the loan. It will also want to be relatively certain that the firm will have enough cash to pay back the loan in a timely fashion (when payments are due). The bank will therefore require that you provide financial information prepared by your accountant and will use this information in determining whether to give you the loan and in setting the terms of the loan.

Tax Authorities

The Internal Revenue Service (IRS) and other tax authorities are interested in financial information about your firm because this information serves to determine the tax base. Income taxes are based on adjusted profit; sales taxes are based on sales income; and property taxes are based on the assessed value of buildings, equipment, and inventory (the goods available for sale). All of this information is provided by the accounting process.

Regulatory Agencies

If a firm is in an industry regulated by a governmental agency, the business may be required to supply financial information to that agency. For example, the Federal Communications Commission may obtain financial information from radio and television stations. Similarly, the Public Utilities Commission may obtain financial information from public utilities companies.

If a firm is a publicly owned corporation, the Securities and Exchange Commission (SEC) will be interested in its financial information. In 1933 and 1934, Congress passed the Securities Act and the Securities Exchange Act in an effort to regulate the financial information that was provided by corporations that traded their stock on stock exchanges and in the over-the-counter markets. This was for the protection of potential investors who, up until that time, could not depend on the fairness of the published financial information of corporations when deciding whether to buy stock. Also, since each firm used its own particular method of accounting, it was difficult for investors to compare the financial information of different companies in order to decide which company's stock to purchase.

The SEC was created to review and oversee the accounting methods of publicly owned corporations. Although the SEC has delegated this job to the accounting profession, the SEC still retains the right to have the final say on any matter of financial accounting by publicly owned corporations. If financial reporting that results from the accounting methods of one of these firms does not meet with the approval of the SEC, the SEC can suspend trading of that company's stock on the stock exchanges.

Customers

In some industries, customers pay special attention to financial information about the firm with which they plan to do business. They may use this information to try to estimate how long the company will be operating. The computer industry is an example of one where customers are concerned about the life of a firm. Before a customer spends a lot of money on a computer, that customer will want to feel reasonably sure that the manufacturer will be around for the next several years to service the computer, replace parts, and provide additional components. Also, the customer will want to be able to purchase programs for that computer as the need arises. If the computer manufacturer goes out of business, it is likely that programmers and software houses will stop writing programs to fit that manufacturer's computer. One way that the customer can estimate the economic health of a company and the likelihood that it will remain in business is by analyzing financial information about the firm.

Employees

Employees may also be interested in having financial information about the business where they work. For example, they may be members of a profit-sharing plan and therefore be very concerned about the financial results of the firm's operations. If a large corporation has employees who belong to a labor union, the union may use financial information about the firm to assess its ability to pay higher wages and benefits when a new contract is negotiated.

From the above discussion and the illustration on page 8, you can see that there are many different types of users of financial information about a business. As you learn about the accounting process, you will begin to understand why financial information is so important to these individuals and organizations and how they can use such information to meet their needs.

GENERALLY ACCEPTED ACCOUNTING PRINCIPLES

As mentioned previously, Congress has given the Securities and Exchange Commission the final say on matters of financial reporting by publicly owned corporations. The SEC has delegated the job of determining proper financial accounting standards to the accounting profession. (However, the SEC has sometimes overridden decisions of the accounting profession.) In accordance with its re-

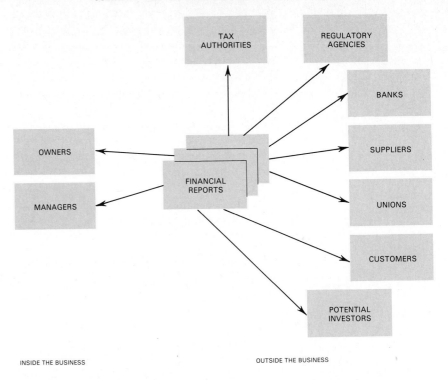

sponsibility, the accounting profession has developed, and continues to develop, a set of *generally accepted accounting principles (GAAPs)*. Some of these principles apply to all types of companies, and some apply only to specific industries or specific situations. Generally accepted accounting principles must be followed by publicly owned companies unless they can demonstrate that if they applied these principles to their affairs the information produced would be misleading.

The Development of Generally Accepted Accounting Principles

Currently, generally accepted accounting principles are developed by a group called the Financial Accounting Standards Board (FASB), which is composed of seven full-time members. The principles established by the FASB are called *Statements of Financial Accounting Standards*. The FASB develops its Statements by using a feedback process, in which interested people and organizations can participate by communicating their opinions to the FASB.

First the FASB writes a *discussion memorandum*, which explains the topic under current consideration. Then public hearings are held where accountants and other interested parties can express their opinions, either orally or in writing. The groups that most consistently offer opinions about proposed FASB statements are the SEC, the American Institute of Certified Public Accountants (AICPA), individual public accounting firms, the American Accounting Association (AAA), and companies with a direct interest in a particular Statement that has been proposed by the FASB.

The AICPA is a national association of professional accountants. It represents accountants in many situations, one of which is in the development of accounting principles. The AAA is a group of accounting educators. Opinions about proposed accounting principles are offered by members of the AAA to the FASB, usually after considerable research has been done about possible effects of a new principle on financial reporting and on other areas of the economy that would be directly or indirectly affected by the proposed principle.

After the FASB holds public hearings about a potential Statement, it prepares a draft of the Statement, called an *exposure draft,* which describes the FASB's proposed solution to the problem being considered. The FASB then receives and evaluates public comment about the exposure draft. Finally, its members vote on the Statement. If four or more of the members approve, the proposed Statement becomes one of the generally accepted accounting principles.

**THE PROCESS USED BY THE FINANCIAL ACCOUNTING STANDARDS BOARD (FASB)
TO DEVELOP GENERALLY ACCEPTED ACCOUNTING PRINCIPLES**

Issues Discussion Memorandum STEP 1	Obtains Responses to Discussion Memorandum STEP 2
Issues Exposure Draft STEP 3	Obtains Responses to Exposure Draft STEP 4

RESPONDENTS

SEC

AICPA

Public Accounting Firms

AAA

Other Interested Parties

FASB

Issues Statement of Principle STEP 5

The Use of Generally Accepted Accounting Principles

To ensure that generally accepted accounting principles are followed by publicly owned corporations, the SEC requires that financial information, in the form of financial statements, be submitted annually by all such companies to the SEC. These financial statements must be *audited* (reviewed) by an accountant who is not on the staff of the firm that issued the statements (an independent certified public accountant). In addition, the statements must include a report by the accountant about the review. (This document is known as the *auditor's report.*)

The purpose of the review is to obtain the objective opinion of a professional accountant from outside the company that the financial statements fairly present the operating results and financial position of the business and that the information was prepared according to generally accepted accounting principles. The financial statements and the auditor's report must be made available to stockholders and potential stockholders of publicly owned corporations. You will learn more about auditing later in this chapter.

Businesses and the environments in which they operate are constantly changing. The economy, technology, and laws change. Therefore, financial information and the methods of presenting that information must change in order to meet the needs of the people who use the information. Generally accepted accounting principles are changed and refined as accountants respond to the changing environment.

THE MAJOR AREAS OF ACCOUNTING

As discussed before, there are many uses to which financial information about businesses can be put. Because of these many uses, because of the large amount of financial information that must be analyzed, and because of reporting requirements imposed by the IRS, the SEC, and other governmental agencies, it has become necessary for accountants to specialize. Accountants usually choose to practice in one of three areas: public accounting, private accounting, or governmental accounting.

Public Accounting

Public accountants belong to firms whose major business is the performance of accounting services for other companies. These firms are called *public accounting firms*. There are three major types of services offered by public accounting firms: auditing, tax accounting, and management advisory services.

Auditing The importance of auditing has already been mentioned in connection with the SEC's financial reporting requirements for publicly owned corporations. Auditors review the financial statements of other companies to assess their fairness and their adherence to generally accepted accounting principles.

In order to be sure that a particular company's financial information is being presented fairly in its statements, the auditor must look not only at the statements themselves but also at how that financial information was obtained. Financial information cannot be presented fairly if some data is missing, invalid, recorded twice, or recorded in the wrong place. In a large company the auditing process can take weeks or months and require a team of auditors working together on the firm's financial data.

Auditors must be *certified public accountants (CPAs)*. The qualifications for becoming a CPA vary somewhat from state to state but usually involve the following types of requirements. The accountant must have earned a certain number of college credits in accounting courses, must have worked a certain number of years under the supervision of a CPA, must have demonstrated a certain level of personal character (for example, cannot be a convicted felon), and must have passed a test called the *Uniform CPA Examination*.

Tax Accounting The tax service offered by public accounting firms involves preparation of the quarterly and annual tax forms that client companies must submit to the IRS and to other tax authorities. This work also includes a number of activities surrounding the preparation of tax forms, such as gathering, classifying, and summarizing the information to be presented in the forms. Another important aspect of tax accounting is to provide advice to client companies about how to plan their financial affairs in order to reduce their taxes in the future without violating the tax laws.

Management Advisory Services The area of management advisory services is a growing one for public accounting firms. This area involves helping client companies improve their information systems or improve their performance. For example, an accounting firm may be hired to improve the efficiency of a specific subsystem in a client company, such as payroll or accounts receivable.

Private Accounting

A private accountant works on the staff of a single business in private industry. Accountants of this type perform a wide range of activities. They have major responsibilities in the area of *financial accounting*—the accumulation of data about a business's financial transactions and the reporting of this data to owners, managers, and other interested parties such as the SEC. Private accountants establish a company's accounting policies, direct its accounting system, prepare its financial statements, interpret its financial information, and provide financial advice to management. These accountants may also prepare tax forms and perform tax planning services for the company. (Generally, small businesses use public accounting firms for their tax form preparation and tax planning work.)

Another important area of responsibility for private accountants is the preparation of internal reports for management, such as the following.

Budgets for sales, expenses, production, and cash.
Reports highlighting the differences between actual amounts and budgeted amounts.
Reports showing detailed information about the costs involved in manufacturing products.
Reports showing the likely financial effects of management decisions such as adding a new product line.

The term *managerial accounting,* or *management accounting,* is normally used to refer to the activities involved in accumulating the data needed for internal reports, analyzing the data, and preparing the reports. Since these reports are strictly for internal use, the SEC has no interest in their content.

An area of growing interest for private accountants is the design of their companies' accounting systems. Increasingly, accounting systems are being viewed as information systems; and modern information-handling techniques and equipment are being used to improve their operations—to achieve greater accuracy, efficiency, and speed. Large and medium-sized companies now make heavy use of computers in their accounting systems; and with the widespread availability of inexpensive microcomputers, many small businesses are now able to automate some of their accounting work. Computers are especially helpful with routine, time-consuming tasks, such as recording, calculating, and summarizing financial data. The goal of accounting systems design is to produce useful financial information as quickly, efficiently, and economically as possible, regardless of whether manual or automated procedures are used.

Some private accountants do *internal auditing* for their companies. The internal auditor reviews the accounting policies, records, and procedures of the firm to make sure that its financial data is being recorded, classified, and summarized properly. Any weaknesses in the system are reported to management along with the internal auditor's recommendations for change.

Jobs in the field of private accounting are highly varied. Large companies normally have extensive accounting departments that employ many accountants, accounting paraprofessionals, and accounting clerks. Most of the accounting personnel in such companies perform specialized activities. For example, some accountants handle only tax work, others concentrate on budgeting and financial planning, and still others devote their time to internal auditing. In a small company there may be a single accountant who performs all of the firm's accounting work with the assistance of several clerical employees. The accountant who is in charge of a business's accounting activities is usually called the *controller*.

Governmental Accounting

Although governmental units are not profit-making entities, they receive and pay out huge amounts of money and must have procedures for recording and managing this money. Agencies of the federal government and of state and local governments employ accountants to keep financial records and prepare financial reports. Those agencies that regulate certain types of businesses or oversee their reporting procedures, such as the SEC, hire accountants to audit the financial statements and records of the businesses under their jurisdiction. The Internal Revenue Service and the Federal Bureau of Investigation have large numbers of accountants on their staffs and use them to uncover possible violations of the law.

PRINCIPLES AND PROCEDURES SUMMARY

Accounting is the process by which financial information about a business is recorded, classified, summarized, and interpreted and then communicated to owners, managers, and other interested parties. All types of businesses need and use financial information. Sole proprietorships, partnerships, and corporations have different structures and operate by different rules, but the financial information needed by each is generally the same. Nonprofit organizations also need similar types of financial information in order to conduct their operations in an efficient manner.

Those firms that sell stock on stock exchanges or in the over-the-counter markets must publish audited financial reports annually, submit these reports to the Securities and Exchange Commission, and make the reports available to stockholders. Such reports must follow generally accepted accounting principles. The SEC has delegated the authority to develop generally accepted accounting principles to the accounting profession. Currently a group called the Financial Accounting Standards Board handles this task.

Because of the different business structures, the need for many different types of financial information, and the complex requirements of tax and regulatory agencies, accountants usually specialize in one of three major areas. Some accountants work for public accounting firms and perform auditing, tax, or management advisory functions. Other accountants work in private industry and set up and supervise accounting systems, prepare financial reports, prepare internal reports, or do internal auditing. Still other accountants work for government agencies. They keep track of public funds and expenditures, or they audit the financial records of businesses and individuals to see whether they are in compliance with regulatory laws, tax laws, and other laws.

MANAGERIAL IMPLICATIONS

The managers of a business must make sure that the firm has an efficient accounting system that produces financial information that is timely, accurate, and fair. Financial statements should be based on generally accepted accounting principles. Internal reports for management need not follow these principles but should provide useful information that will aid in the process of monitoring and controlling operations.

Managers also have a responsibility to actively use the financial information they receive about their firms. When properly studied and interpreted, financial information can help managers to do a more effective job of controlling present operations, making decisions, and planning for the future. The sound use of financial information is essential to good management.

REVIEW QUESTIONS

1. What is the purpose of accounting?
2. Why is accounting often called "the language of business"?
3. What does the accounting process involve?
4. What are the three types of business entity? What are the differences among these types of entity?
5. What is the separate entity assumption, and why is it important in accounting for a business?
6. What types of people or organizations are interested in financial information about a firm, and why are they interested in this information?
7. What are generally accepted accounting principles?
8. Why are generally accepted accounting principles needed?
9. How are generally accepted accounting principles developed?
10. What is the function of the Securities and Exchange Commission in regard to financial reporting?
11. What is the purpose of the Financial Accounting Standards Board?
12. What are the three major areas of accounting?
13. What types of services do public accountants provide?
14. What are the major functions or activities performed by accountants in private industry?

15. What standards must a person meet in order to become a certified public accountant?
16. What is a controller?

MANAGERIAL DISCUSSION QUESTIONS

1. Why is it important for managers to have financial information?
2. Do you think that a manager will obtain enough financial information to control operations effectively if he or she simply reads a set of financial statements once a year? Why or why not?
3. The owner of a small business commented to a friend that he did not see the need for an accounting system in his firm because he closely supervised day-to-day operations and knew exactly what was happening in the business. Would you agree with his statement? Why or why not?
4. This chapter listed a number of questions that the owner or manager of a firm might ask when trying to evaluate the results of the firm's operations and its financial position. If you were an owner or manager, what other questions would you ask in order to judge the firm's performance, control operations, make decisions, and plan for the future?
5. A firm does not have to follow generally accepted accounting principles for internal reporting purposes. Internal reports are therefore designed to meet the needs of management. Why might management still find it useful to study financial reports for the firm that are prepared according to generally accepted accounting principles?
6. The major objective of most businesses is to earn a profit. What other objectives might a business have? How can financial information help management to achieve these objectives?
7. Many business owners and managers are not accountants. Why is it useful for such people to have a basic knowledge of accounting?

In order to provide information to management and others who are interested in the financial affairs of a business, the accountant must have a system for gathering, classifying, summarizing, and reporting data about the firm's transactions—its financial events. In this chapter we will discuss the analysis of transactions and two of the end results of such analysis: the balance sheet and the income statement.

ANALYZING BUSINESS TRANSACTIONS

THE IMPORTANCE OF ACCOUNTING IN BUSINESS

Accountants occupy a vital position in business today because they help managers make decisions. Making the right decisions at the right time is the key to successful business operations.

As we discussed in Chapter 1, managers need full and accurate financial information about a business in order to make the right decisions. This information must be easily available, and it must be up to date. Accountants provide such information by systematically recording financial facts about the business and using these facts to prepare reports.

However, recording and reporting financial information are only two aspects of accounting. In addition, accountants interpret, or explain, the meaning of the information; give advice about financial problems; and assist in the financial planning of future operations. Accountants are able to perform these functions because of the nature of the recording procedure.

The recording procedure includes provisions for classifying and summarizing financial information to facilitate the later reporting and interpreting of this information. Classification allows the accountant to sort out similar data and group like items together for clarity and more efficient use. The classified information is then summarized into financial statements. These statements are reports showing the results of operations for the accounting period and the financial position of the business at the end of the period.

ACCOUNTING BEGINS WITH ANALYSIS

Long before there can be any recording, reporting, or interpreting of financial information, accountants have to analyze every business transaction. A *business transaction* is a financial event that a firm is involved in. It may consist of a purchase, a sale, a receipt or payment of cash, or any other financial happening. The effects of each transaction must be studied in order to know what information to record and where to record it.

Since the accounting process actually begins with an analysis of the transactions of a business, this phase is the natural starting point for a study of accounting. Let us see how the accountant would analyze the transactions of the Gold Medal Fitness Center, a firm that provides a wide range of exercise facilities and classes. This sole proprietorship business is owned by John Scott, a marathon runner, and is managed by Susan Lopez, a former college swimming champion and later a coach. The firm is located in a large office complex, and its facilities include a jogging track, racquetball courts, a swimming pool, and many types of exercise equipment. Scott rented space in the office complex so that business executives, with their current interest in physical fitness, would have easy access to the facilities. However, he also draws customers from all over the community.

To simplify recordkeeping and billing, Scott has given charge accounts to occupants of the office complex and other steady customers. He bills them on a monthly basis for the services they have used during the period. Other customers pay in cash immediately after each exercise class or session.

STARTING A NEW BUSINESS

Let's start from the beginning. Scott obtained the funds to start the business by withdrawing $80,000 from his personal bank account. He deposited the money in a new bank account that he opened in the name of the firm, the Gold Medal Fitness Center. The separate bank account for the firm helps Scott keep his financial interest in the business separate from his personal funds. The establishment of this bank account on November 6, 19X5, was the first transaction of the new firm.

The accountant who helped Scott start a set of accounting records for the business explained that there were two important financial facts to be recorded at the time.

a. The business had $80,000 of property in the form of cash, which was on deposit in the bank.
b. Scott had an $80,000 financial interest in the business, which is called his *equity,* or *capital.*

The firm's position at that time may be expressed in the form of the following simple equation.

GOLD MEDAL FITNESS CENTER

Property	=	Financial Interest
(a) Cash $80,000	=	(b) John Scott, Capital $80,000

The equation *property equals financial interest* reflects the basic fact that in a free enterprise system all property is owned by someone. In this case Scott owns the business because he supplied the property (cash).

RENTING FACILITIES

The first thing that Scott did after setting up the business with his cash investment was to rent facilities. The lease that he signed specified a monthly rent of $5,000 and required that he pay eight months' rent in advance. Scott therefore issued a $40,000 check to cover the rent for December through July. The accountant explained that two facts had to be recorded about this transaction.

c. The firm prepaid (paid in advance) the rent for the next eight months in the amount of $40,000. As a result the firm obtained the right to occupy facilities for an eight-month period. In accounting, this right is considered a form of property.

d. The firm decreased its cash balance by $40,000.

Here is how the firm's financial position looked after this transaction.

GOLD MEDAL FITNESS CENTER

		Property			=	Financial Interest
	Cash	+	Prepaid Rent		=	John Scott, Capital
Beginning investment	(a) $80,000				=	(b) $80,000
(c) Rented facilities			+$40,000			
(d) Paid out cash	−40,000					
New balances	$40,000	+	$40,000		=	$80,000

Notice that the total property remains the same, even though the form of the property has changed. If the rent had not been paid in advance but had been paid for the current month only, it would be considered an expense rather than property. This aspect of accounting will be discussed in more detail in a later chapter.

PURCHASING EQUIPMENT FOR CASH

The manager, Susan Lopez, saw that her first task was to get the fitness center ready for business operations, which were to begin on December 1, 19X5. She bought exercise equipment for $20,000 and paid for it with a check drawn against the firm's bank account. Again, the accountant analyzed the transaction to see what had to be recorded and quickly identified two essential elements.

e. The firm purchased new property (equipment) for $20,000.

f. The firm paid out $20,000 in cash.

Here is the financial position of the business after this transaction was recorded.

GOLD MEDAL FITNESS CENTER

	Property						=	Financial Interest
	Cash	+	Prepaid Rent	+	Equipment		=	John Scott, Capital
Previous balances	$40,000	+	$40,000				=	$80,000
(e) Purchased equipment					+$20,000			
(f) Paid out cash	−20,000							
New balances	$20,000	+	$40,000	+	$20,000		=	$80,000

Although there was again a change in the form of some of the firm's property (cash to equipment), the equation that expresses the change shows that the total value of the property remained the same. Scott's financial interest, or equity, was also unchanged. Again, *property* (Cash, Prepaid Rent, and Equipment) *was equal to financial interest* (John Scott, Capital).

Note carefully that the accountant was recording the financial affairs of the business entity, the fitness center. Scott's personal assets, such as his personal bank account, house, furniture, and automobile, were kept separate from the property of the firm. Nonbusiness property is not included in the accounting records of the business entity.

PURCHASING EQUIPMENT ON CREDIT

Lopez also bought hairdryers, benches and lockers for the locker rooms, and other necessary equipment from Olson, Inc., at a cost of $10,000. Olson, Inc., agreed to allow 60 days for the Gold Medal Fitness Center to pay the bill. This arrangement is sometimes called a *charge account*, or *open-account credit*. Amounts that a business must pay in the future under this agreement are known as *accounts payable*. The companies or individuals to whom the amounts are owed are called *creditors*. This time the accountant's analysis revealed the following basic elements.

g. The firm purchased new property in the form of equipment that cost $10,000.
h. The firm owed $10,000 to Olson, Inc.

This increase in equipment was made without an immediate cash payment because Olson, Inc., was willing to accept a claim against the fitness center's property until the bill was paid. There were then two different financial interests or claims against the firm's property—the creditor's claim (Accounts Payable) and the owner's claim (John Scott, Capital).

Here is how the transaction looked in equation form.

GOLD MEDAL FITNESS CENTER

	Cash	+	Prepaid Rent	+	Equipment	=	Accounts Payable	+	John Scott, Capital
Previous balances	$20,000	+	$40,000	+	$20,000	=			$80,000
(g) Purchased equipment					+10,000				
(h) Incurred a debt							+$10,000		
New balances	$20,000	+	$40,000	+	$30,000	=	$10,000	+	$80,000

Notice that when property values and financial interests increase or decrease, the total of the items on one side of the equation still equals the total on the other side. This happens because there are financial interests, or claims against business property, as soon as the property is purchased. The creditor's claim lasts until the debt is paid. The owner's claim lasts as long as he or she continues to own the business.

PURCHASING SUPPLIES

From her previous experience working at a fitness center, Lopez was able to estimate the amount of supplies that Gold Medal would need to start operations. She therefore placed an order for soap, shampoo, paper towels, and other supplies that had a total cost of $2,000. The company that sold the items, Reliable Supplies Inc., requires cash payments from businesses that are less than six months old. Gold Medal therefore included a check with its order. After analyzing the transaction, the accountant identified the following major elements.

i. The firm purchased supplies that cost $2,000.
j. The firm paid out $2,000 in cash.

Here is how this transaction affected the business's property and financial interests.

GOLD MEDAL FITNESS CENTER

	Cash	+	Supplies	+	Prepaid Rent	+	Equipment	=	Accounts Payable	+	John Scott, Capital
					Property			**=**		**Financial Interests**	
Previous balances	$20,000	+			$40,000	+	$30,000	=	$10,000	+	$80,000
(i) Purchased supplies			+$2,000								
(j) Paid out cash	−2,000										
New balances	$18,000	+	$2,000	+	$40,000	+	$30,000	=	$10,000	+	$80,000

Because of this transaction, the form of the fitness center's property again changed (some cash was exchanged for supplies), but the total value of the property remained the same. Also, Scott's financial interest in the firm (his equity) stayed the same.

PAYING A CREDITOR

Lopez decided to pay $5,000 to Olson, Inc., to reduce the fitness center's debt to that business. This transaction is analyzed as follows.

k. The firm paid out $5,000 in cash.
l. The claim of Olson, Inc., against the firm was reduced by $5,000.

The effect of this transaction on the firm's property and financial interests can be expressed in equation form as shown below.

GOLD MEDAL FITNESS CENTER

	Cash	+	Supplies	+	Prepaid Rent	+	Equipment	=	Accounts Payable	+	John Scott, Capital
					Property			**=**		**Financial Interests**	
Previous balances	$18,000	+	$2,000	+	$40,000	+	$30,000	=	$10,000	+	$80,000
(k) Paid out cash	−5,000										
(l) Reduced a debt									−5,000		
New balances	$13,000	+	$2,000	+	$40,000	+	$30,000	=	$ 5,000	+	$80,000

Accountants use a formal pattern and special accounting terms when they prepare their reports. For example, they refer to property that a business owns as the business's *assets* and to the debts or obligations of the business as its *liabilities*. The owner's financial interest is called *owner's equity, proprietorship,* or *net worth. Owner's equity* is the preferred term and is the term used throughout this book. At regular intervals the accountant for the Gold Medal Fitness Center will show the status of the firm's assets, liabilities, and owner's equity in a formal report called a *balance sheet*. Here is how the firm's balance sheet looked on November 30, 19X5—the day before operations actually began.

GOLD MEDAL FITNESS CENTER
Balance Sheet
November 30, 19X5

Assets		Liabilities and Owner's Equity	
Cash	13,000 00	Liabilities	
Supplies	2,000 00	Accounts Payable	5,000 00
Prepaid Rent	40,000 00	Owner's Equity	
Equipment	30,000 00	John Scott, Capital	80,000 00
		Total Liabilities and	
Total Assets	85,000 00	Owner's Equity	85,000 00

The accountant lists the assets on the left side of the balance sheet and the liabilities and owner's equity on the right side. This arrangement is similar to the equation *property equals financial interests,* which was illustrated earlier. Property was shown on the left side of the equation, and financial interests appeared on the right side. Here are several other important details about the form of the balance sheet.

1. The three-line heading of the balance sheet gives the firm's name (who), the title of the report (what), and the date of the report (when). Every balance sheet heading must contain these three lines.
2. On this form of balance sheet (the account form), the total of the assets always appears on the same horizontal line as the total of the liabilities and owner's equity.
3. When financial statements are handwritten or typed on accounting paper with ruled columns, dollar signs are usually omitted. However, in typewritten financial statements that are not prepared on ruled forms, dollar signs are generally used with the first amount in each column and with each total.
4. A single line is used to show that the figures above it are being added or subtracted. Double lines are used under the final figure in a column or section of a report. If the report is prepared by hand rather than typewritten, lines should always be drawn with a ruler.

The balance sheet illustrated above shows the amount and types of property the business owned, the amount owed to creditors, and the amount of the owner's interest in the firm on November 30, 19X5. This statement therefore gave John Scott a complete picture of the financial position of his business as it was ready to start operations.

THE FUNDAMENTAL ACCOUNTING EQUATION

The word *balance* in the title Balance Sheet has a very special meaning. It serves to emphasize that the total of the figures on the left side of the report equals the total of the figures on the right side. In accounting terms the firm's assets are equal to the total of its liabilities and owner's equity. This equality can be expressed in equation form, as illustrated below. The figures shown are again for the Gold Medal Fitness Center on November 30, 19X5.

$$\text{Assets} = \text{Liabilities} + \text{Owner's Equity}$$
$$\$85,000 = \quad \$5,000 \quad + \quad \$80,000$$

The relationship between assets and liabilities plus owner's equity is called the *fundamental accounting equation*. There are many uses for this equation in accounting work. As a matter of fact, the entire process of analyzing, recording, and reporting business transactions is based on the fundamental equation.

EFFECTS OF REVENUE AND EXPENSES

Shortly after the Gold Medal Fitness Center opened for business on December 1, 19X5, the first customer came for an exercise session. Soon more customers followed. This began a stream of revenue for the business. The result of revenue is an increase in assets. *Revenue, or income,* is the inflow of money or other assets (including claims to money, such as charge accounts) that results from sales of goods or services or from the use of money or property. An *expense,* on the other hand, involves the outflow of money, the use of other assets, or the incurring of a liability. Expenses include the costs of any materials, labor, supplies, and services used in an effort to produce revenue. If there is an excess of revenue over expenses, it represents a profit. Of course, the chance to make profits is the reason that people like John Scott risk their money by investing it in a business. A firm's accounting records show the detailed results of all transactions involving revenue and expenses.

SELLING SERVICES FOR CASH

During the month of December 19X5, the Gold Medal Fitness Center earned a total of $12,200 in revenue from customers who paid cash for exercise classes and sessions. The accountant analyzed this fact in the following manner.

m. The firm received $12,200 in cash for services provided to customers.
n. The owner's equity increased by $12,200 because of this inflow of assets from revenue. (Revenue always increases the owner's equity.)

Accountants prefer to keep the revenue figures separate from the owner's equity figure until the financial statements are prepared. Therefore, the revenue appears in equation form as shown in the table on page 22.

GOLD MEDAL FITNESS CENTER

	Assets				=	Liabilities +		Owner's Equity	
	Cash +	Supplies +	Prepaid Rent +	Equipment =		Accounts Payable +		John Scott, Capital +	Revenue
Previous balances	$13,000 +	$2,000 +	$40,000 +	$30,000 =		$5,000 +		$80,000	
(m) Received cash	+12,200								
(n) Owner's equity increased by revenue									+$12,200
New balances	$25,200 +	$2,000 +	$40,000 +	$30,000 =		$5,000 +		$80,000 +	$12,200

Keeping revenue separate from the owner's equity will help the firm's accountant compute the total revenue much more easily at the end of the month, when the financial reports are prepared.

SELLING SERVICES ON CREDIT

In December 19X5 the Gold Medal Fitness Center also earned $6,100 of revenue from charge account customers. These customers are allowed 30 days to pay. Amounts owed by such customers are known as *accounts receivable*. These accounts represent a new form of asset for the firm—claims for future collection from customers. The accountant's analysis broke the transaction down into the following elements.

o. The firm acquired a new asset, Accounts Receivable, of $6,100.
p. The owner's equity was increased by the revenue of $6,100.

The following equation shows the effects of this transaction.

GOLD MEDAL FITNESS CENTER

	Assets					=	Liabilities +		Owner's Equity	
	Cash +	Accounts Receivable +	Supplies +	Prepaid Rent +	Equipment =		Accounts Payable +		John Scott, Capital +	Revenue
Previous balances	$25,200		$2,000 +	$40,000 +	$30,000 =		$5,000 +		$80,000 +	$12,200
(o) Received new asset		+$6,100								
(p) Owner's equity increased by revenue										+6,100
New balances	$25,200 +	$6,100 +	$2,000 +	$40,000 +	$30,000 =		$5,000 +		$80,000 +	$18,300

COLLECTING RECEIVABLES

By the end of December 19X5, customers who obtained services on credit had paid a total of $5,500 to apply to their accounts. The accountant therefore recognized the following changes.

q. The firm received $5,500 in cash.
r. Accounts Receivable was reduced by $5,500.

These changes affected the equation as follows.

GOLD MEDAL FITNESS CENTER

	Assets					= Liabilities +	Owner's Equity	
	Cash +	Accounts Receivable	+ Supplies +	Prepaid Rent	+ Equipment =	Accounts Payable	+ John Scott, Capital	+ Revenue
Previous balances	$25,200 +	$6,100	+ $2,000	+ $40,000 +	$30,000 =	$5,000 +	$80,000	+ $18,300
(q) Received cash	+5,500							
(r) Accounts receivable reduced		−5,500						
New balances	$30,700 +	$ 600	+ $2,000	+ $40,000 +	$30,000 =	$5,000 +	$80,000	+ $18,300

Notice that revenue is not recorded when cash is collected from charge account customers. In this transaction there is merely a change in the type of asset (from accounts receivable to cash). Revenue was recorded when the sales on credit took place (see Entry p). Notice also that the fundamental accounting equation, *assets equal liabilities plus owner's equity,* holds true, regardless of the changes arising from individual transactions.

PAYING EXPENSES

So far Scott has done very well. His equity has been increased by sizable revenues. However, keeping a business running costs money. When a business has expenses, they reduce owner's equity.

Employees' Salaries

During December 19X5, the first month of operations, the Gold Medal Fitness Center paid $10,100 for employees' salaries. The accountant analyzed this transaction as follows.

s. Cash was reduced by the payment of $10,100 to cover the salaries.
t. The owner's equity was reduced by the $10,100 outflow of assets for the expense.

The accountant prefers to keep expense figures separate from the figures for the owner's capital and the revenue. The effect of the expense for salaries is shown in the equation at the top of page 24. The separate record of expenses is kept for the same reason as the separate record of revenue is kept—to help analyze operations for the period.

Utilities

At the end of December 19X5, the fitness center received a $300 bill for the utilities that it had used during the month. A check was issued to pay the bill immediately. The accountant explained to Scott that this was another business expense and analyzed it as shown on page 24 (see Items u and v).

GOLD MEDAL FITNESS CENTER

	Assets					= Liabilities +		Owner's Equity		
	Cash +	Accounts Receivable +	Supplies +	Prepaid Rent +	Equipment =	Accounts Payable +	John Scott, Capital +	Revenue −	Expenses
Previous balances	$30,700 +	$600 +	$2,000 +	$40,000 +	$30,000 =	$5,000 +	$80,000 +	$18,300	
(s) Paid out cash	−10,100								
(t) Owner's equity reduced by expense									$10,100
New balances	$20,600 +	$600 +	$2,000 +	$40,000 +	$30,000 =	$5,000 +	$80,000 +	$18,300 −	$10,100

u. Cash was reduced by the payment of $300 for utilities.

v. The owner's equity decreased by $300 because of the expense incurred.

After this transaction was recorded, the equation appeared as shown below.

GOLD MEDAL FITNESS CENTER

	Assets					= Liabilities +		Owner's Equity		
	Cash +	Accounts Receivable +	Supplies +	Prepaid Rent +	Equipment =	Accounts Payable +	John Scott, Capital +	Revenue −	Expenses
Previous balances	$20,600 +	$600 +	$2,000 +	$40,000 +	$30,000 =	$5,000 +	$80,000 +	$18,300 −	$10,100
(u) Paid out cash	−300								
(v) Owner's equity reduced by expense									300
New balances	$20,300 +	$600 +	$2,000 +	$40,000 +	$30,000 =	$5,000 +	$80,000 +	$18,300 −	$10,400

THE INCOME STATEMENT

The balance sheet shows the financial condition of a business at a given time. It shows what the business owns and owes, as well as the owner's equity. It does not, however, show the results of business operations, that is, what actually happened to bring about the firm's financial condition. This is the job of another formal accounting report called an *income statement, profit and loss statement,* or *statement of income and expenses. Income statement* is now the most popular term with accountants and is used throughout this book. Here is how the accountant for the Gold Medal Fitness Center would present the results of the firm's first month of operations on an income statement, assuming that there are no further expenses.

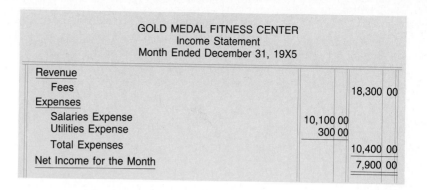

GOLD MEDAL FITNESS CENTER					
Income Statement					
Month Ended December 31, 19X5					
Revenue					
Fees				18,300	00
Expenses					
Salaries Expense	10,100	00			
Utilities Expense	300	00			
Total Expenses				10,400	00
Net Income for the Month				7,900	00

The net income or net loss is reported at the bottom of the income statement. This figure is the difference between the sales price of the services performed or goods sold (revenue) and the cost of the services and goods used (expenses) during a specific period of time. Where there is more revenue than expenses, the result is a *net income*. When expenses are greater than revenue, the result is a *net loss*. In the rare case when revenues and expenses are equal, the firm is said to *break even*. The income statement illustrated above shows a net income because revenue was greater than expenses.

Net income is sometimes called net profit. However, accountants prefer to use net income because it is more precise.

Notice that the three-line heading of the income statement shows who, what, and when. The first line is used for the firm's name (who). The second line gives the title of the report (what). The third line tells the exact period of time covered by the report (when). In the illustration the third line clearly indicates that the income statement reports the results of operations for the single month of December 19X5.

If the income statement covered the three months of January, February, and March, the third line would read, "Three-Month Period Ended March 31, 19X5." The third line of a statement reporting the results of operations for a 12-month period beginning on January 1 and ending on December 31 of the same calendar year would read, "Year Ended December 31, 19X5." In instances where the 12-month reporting period ends on a date other than December 31, the third line of the income statement would identify the period as a fiscal year, for example, "Fiscal Year Ended June 30, 19X5," or "Fiscal Year Ended November 30, 19X5."

Also, note the correct use of single and double lines. This income statement does not have dollar signs because it was prepared on accounting paper with ruled columns. However, dollar signs would be used on a typewritten income statement that is not prepared on a ruled form.

THE BALANCE SHEET

The income statement by itself is meaningful to business owners, managers, and other interested parties. However, it is even more informative when considered in relation to the assets and equities that were involved in earning the revenue. Therefore, the balance sheet is once again prepared to give the details of these assets and equities. The final totals in the fundamental accounting equation supply the figures that are required for preparing a balance sheet for the Gold Medal Fitness Center as of December 31, 19X5.

	Assets				=	Liabilities	+		Owner's Equity		
Cash	+ Accounts Receivable	+ Supplies	+ Prepaid Rent	+ Equipment	=	Accounts Payable	+	John Scott, Capital	+ Revenue	− Expenses	
$20,300 +	$600	+ $2,000	+ $40,000	+ $30,000	=	$5,000	+	$80,000	+ $18,300	− $10,400	

The balance sheet prepared from the figures in the above equation summarizes the assets, liabilities, and owner's equity of the business.

GOLD MEDAL FITNESS CENTER
Balance Sheet
December 31, 19X5

Assets		Liabilities and Owner's Equity		
Cash	20,300 00	Liabilities		
Accounts Receivable	600 00	Accounts Payable		5,000 00
Supplies	2,000 00	Owner's Equity		
Prepaid Rent	40,000 00	John Scott, Capital		
Equipment	30,000 00	Dec. 1, 19X5	80,000 00	
		Net Income for Month	7,900 00	
		John Scott, Capital		
		Dec. 31, 19X5		87,900 00
		Total Liabilities and		
Total Assets	92,900 00	Owner's Equity		92,900 00

The net income of $7,900 shown on the December income statement appears on the balance sheet as an increase in owner's equity. The owner's equity on December 31 is determined by adding the net income for December to the owner's equity that existed on December 1. A net loss would be subtracted. The net income or net loss figure is a connecting link that explains the change in owner's equity during the period. Notice that the income statement is prepared before the balance sheet because the amount of the net income or net loss for the period is needed to compute the owner's equity that appears on the balance sheet at the end of the period. Of course, the balance sheet also shows the types and amounts of property that the business owns (assets) and the amounts owed to creditors (liabilities) on the reporting date.

THE IMPORTANCE OF THE STATEMENTS

Preparing financial statements is one of the accountant's most important jobs. Therefore, all figures must be checked and double-checked to make sure they are accurate. As we discussed in Chapter 1, the figures shown on the balance sheet and the income statement are used by business managers and owners to control current operations and make plans for the future. Creditors, prospective investors, governmental agencies, and many others are also vitally interested in the profits of the business and in the asset and equity structure. Each day millions of business decisions are made on the basis of financial reports.

PRINCIPLES AND PROCEDURES SUMMARY

The accounting process begins with the analysis of business transactions. The accountant analyzes each transaction to determine its effect on the fundamental accounting equation: *assets equal liabilities plus owner's equity*. The balance sheet is a statement that shows the assets, liabilities, and owner's equity on a given date.

Some changes in owner's equity result from revenue, and others result from expenses. These changes are summarized on the income statement. The difference between revenue and expenses is the net income or net loss of the business for the period. The net income or net loss for the period also appears on the balance sheet prepared at the close of the same period. Net income or net loss is the connecting link between the owner's equity at the beginning of the period and the owner's equity at the end of the period.

MANAGERIAL IMPLICATIONS

Accurate and informative financial records and statements are necessary so that business people can make sound decisions. Accounting information helps to determine whether a profit has been made, the amount of the assets on hand, the amount owed to creditors, and the amount of owner's equity. Any well-run and efficiently managed business will have a good accounting system to provide timely and useful information.

REVIEW QUESTIONS

1. What is revenue?
2. What are expenses?
3. What information does the income statement contain?
4. What are assets, liabilities, and owner's equity?
5. What information does the balance sheet contain?
6. What is the fundamental accounting equation?
7. Describe the effects of each of the following business transactions on assets, liabilities, and owner's equity.
   a. Bought equipment on credit.
   b. Paid salaries to employees.
   c. Sold services for cash.
   d. Paid cash to a creditor.
   e. Bought furniture for cash.
   f. Sold services on credit.
8. How is net income determined?
9. What information is contained in the heading of a financial statement?
10. Why does the third line of the heading differ on the balance sheet and the income statement?

11. How does net income affect owner's equity?

MANAGERIAL DISCUSSION QUESTIONS

1. How does an accounting system help managers control operations and make sound decisions?
2. Why should managers be concerned with changes in the amount of creditors' claims against the business?
3. It is reasonable to expect that all new businesses will have a net income from the first month's operations? From the first year's operations?
4. After examining financial data for a monthly period, the owner of a small business expressed surprise that the firm's cash balance had decreased during the month even though there was a substantial net income. Do you think that this owner is right to expect cash to increase whenever there is a net income? Why or why not?

EXERCISES

EXERCISE 2-1   **Completing the accounting equation.** The fundamental accounting equation for several businesses is shown below. Supply the missing amounts.

	Assets	=	Liabilities	+	Owner's Equity
1.	$53,000	=	$12,000	+	$?
2.	$97,000	=	$?	+	$72,000
3.	$?	=	$ 1,500	+	$31,000

EXERCISE 2-2   **Determining accounting equation amounts.** Just before it opened for business, the Speedy Film Processing Laboratory, owned by Patrick Ryan, had the following assets and liabilities. Determine the amounts that would appear in the firm's fundamental accounting equation *(Assets = Liabilities + Owner's Equity).*

ASSETS		LIABILITIES	
Cash	$ 3,500	Loans Payable	$5,000
Laboratory Supplies	600	Accounts Payable	2,100
Laboratory Equipment	24,200		

EXERCISE 2-3   **Determining accounting equation amounts.** The financial data shown below is for the medical practice of Dr. Janet Ross when she began operations on March 1, 19X2. Determine the amounts that would appear in Dr. Ross's fundamental accounting equation *(Assets = Liabilities + Owner's Equity).*

Owes $12,000 to the Craig Equipment Company.
Has $4,250 in cash.
Has medical supplies that cost $850.
Owes $2,300 to the Douglas Furniture Company.
Has medical equipment that cost $21,000.
Has office furniture that cost $5,300.

EXERCISE 2-4   **Preparing a balance sheet for a new firm.** Using the data from Exercise 2-3, prepare a balance sheet for the medical practice of Dr. Janet Ross as of March 1, 19X2, when she opened her office to patients. (Use "Janet Ross, M.D." in the first line of the balance sheet heading.)

EXERCISE 2-5   **Determining the effects of transactions on the accounting equation.** The Tidy Lawn Care Service had the transactions listed below during the month of April 19X1. Show how each transaction would be recorded in the accounting equation. Then compute the totals at the end of the month. The headings to be used in the equation are as follows.

Assets			= Liabilities +		Owner's Equity		
Cash +	Accounts Receiv- able	+ Equipment =	Accounts Payable	+ Paul Lema, Capital	+ Revenue	− Expenses

TRANSACTIONS

1. Paul Lema started the business with a cash investment of $10,000.
2. Purchased equipment for $4,000 on credit.
3. Performed services for $800 in cash.
4. Purchased additional equipment for $2,000 in cash.
5. Performed services for $1,500 on credit.
6. Paid salaries of $1,200 to employees.
7. Received $900 cash from charge account customers.
8. Paid $2,500 to a creditor on account.

EXERCISE 2-6   **Computing net income or net loss.** The Arrow Electronic Service had the following revenue and expenses during the month ended June 30, 19X4. Did the firm earn a net income or incur a net loss for the period? What was the amount?

REVENUE		EXPENSES	
Fees for TV repairs	$4,100	Rent	$ 800
Fees for stereo repairs	1,800	Salaries	2,500
		Telephone	80
		Utilities	120

EXERCISE 2-7   **Computing net income or net loss.** On December 1, 19X1, Ralph Tonelli and Gary Wood opened a law office. During December their firm had the following transactions involving revenue and expenses. Did the firm earn a net income or incur a net loss for the period? What was the amount?

Paid $600 for rent.
Provided services for $550 in cash.
Paid $100 for telephone service.
Paid salaries of $1,800 to employees.
Provided services for $1,200 on credit.
Paid $50 for office cleaning service.

EXERCISE 2-8 **Preparing an income statement.** At the beginning of November 19X5, Ann Lewis started the Lewis Financial Service, a firm that offers advice about investing and managing money. On November 30, 19X5, the accounting records of the business showed the following information. Prepare an income statement for the month of November 19X5.

Cash	$2,900	Fees	$12,900
Accounts Receivable	400	Rent Expense	1,200
Office Supplies	200	Salaries Expense	4,000
Office Equipment	9,000	Telephone Expense	100
Accounts Payable	500		
Ann Lewis, Capital (as of Nov. 1, 19X5)	4,400		

EXERCISE 2-9 **Preparing a balance sheet that includes net income.** Using the information provided in Exercise 2-8, prepare a balance sheet for the Lewis Financial Service as of November 30, 19X5.

EXERCISE 2-10 **Identifying transactions.** The following equation shows the effects of a number of transactions that took place at the Far Horizons Travel Agency during the month of August 19X1. Describe each transaction.

	Assets					=	Liabilities	+		Owner's Equity			
	Cash	+	Accounts Receivable	+	Equipment	=	Accounts Payable	+	Carl Hess, Capital	+	Revenue	−	Expenses
Bal.	$9,000	+	$ 200	+	$20,000	=	$1,000	+	$28,200	+	0	−	0
1.	−500												500
2.			+1,800								+1,800		
3.	−2,000				+2,000								
4.	−300						−300						
5.	+1,200										+1,200		
6.	+700		−700										
7.	−1,100												1,100

EXERCISE 2-11 **Preparing an income statement.** Using the information provided in Exercise 2-10, prepare an income statement for the Far Horizons Travel Agency. This statement should cover the month ended August 31, 19X1. (Assume that the $500 amount was for rent and the $1,100 amount was for salaries.)

EXERCISE 2-12 **Preparing a balance sheet that includes net income.** Using the information provided in Exercise 2-10, prepare a balance sheet for the Far Horizons Travel Agency as of August 31, 19X1.

PROBLEMS

PROBLEM 2-1 **Analyzing the effects of transactions on the accounting equation.** On March 1, 19X1, Ruth Stern established the Scenic Landscaping Service.

Instructions Analyze the following transactions. Then use the equation form to record the changes in property, claims of creditors, and owner's equity. (Use plus, minus, and equal signs.)

1. The owner invested $10,000 in cash to begin the business.
2. Purchased equipment for $6,000 in cash.
3. Purchased $1,000 of additional equipment on credit.
4. Paid $500 in cash to creditors.
5. The owner made an additional investment of $1,500 in cash.

PROBLEM 2-2 **Preparing a balance sheet for a new firm.** David Lee plans to open the Lee Business Systems Company on December 1, 19X5. This firm will develop computer programs for business clients.

Instructions Use the following figures to prepare a balance sheet dated December 1, 19X5. (You will need to compute the owner's equity.)

Cash	$ 4,000
Computers	82,000
Office Furniture	10,000
Accounts Payable	34,000

PROBLEM 2-3 **Analyzing the effects of transactions on the accounting equation.** Joan McNeal is an architect who specializes in developing plans to remodel old buildings. At the beginning of June 19X6, her firm's financial records showed the following assets, liabilities, and owner's equity.

Cash	$ 3,000	Accounts Payable	$ 1,700
Accounts Receivable	2,000	Joan McNeal, Capital	18,300
Office Furniture	6,000	Revenue	5,000
Auto	11,000	Expenses	3,000

Instructions Set up an equation form using the balances given above. Then record the effects of the following transactions in the equation. (Use plus, minus, and equal signs.) Record new balances after each transaction has been entered. Prove the equality of the two sides of the final equation on a separate sheet.

1. Provided services for $1,100 in cash.
2. Paid $150 in cash for a new office chair.
3. Received $700 in cash from credit clients.
4. Paid $100 in cash for telephone service.
5. Sent a $600 check in partial payment of the amount due creditors.
6. Paid salaries of $2,000 in cash.
7. Sent a check for $90 to pay an electric bill.
8. Performed services for $2,000 on credit.
9. Paid $260 in cash for auto repairs.
10. Performed services for $1,500 in cash.

PROBLEM 2-4 **Preparing an income statement and a balance sheet.** The equation on page 32 shows the transactions of the Image Photographic Service during March 19X5. The business is owned by Roy Bates.

				Assets				=	Liabilities	+			Owner's Equity		
	Cash	+	Accts. Rec.	+	Supplies	+	Equip.	=	Accts. Pay.	+	Roy Bates, Capital	+	Revenue	−	Expenses
Balances, Mar. 1	700	+	500	+	300	+	2,000	=	300	+	3,200	+	0	−	0
Paid for utilities	−70														70
New balances	630	+	500	+	300	+	2,000	=	300	+	3,200	+	0	−	70
Sold services on credit			+700										+700		
New balances	630	+	1,200	+	300	+	2,000	=	300	+	3,200	+	700	−	70
Paid telephone bill	−50														50
New balances	580	+	1,200	+	300	+	2,000	=	300	+	3,200	+	700	−	120
Sold services for cash	+1,000												+1,000		
New balances	1,580	+	1,200	+	300	+	2,000	=	300	+	3,200	+	1,700	−	120
Paid salaries	−1,000														1,000
New balances	580	+	1,200	+	300	+	2,000	=	300	+	3,200	+	1,700	−	1,120
Paid for repairs	−75														75
New balances	505	+	1,200	+	300	+	2,000	=	300	+	3,200	+	1,700	−	1,195

Instructions Analyze each transaction carefully. Then prepare an income statement for the month and a balance sheet for March 31, 19X5. List the expenses in detail on the income statement.

ALTERNATE PROBLEMS

PROBLEM 2-1A **Analyzing the effects of transactions on the accounting equation.** On July 1, 19X3, Donna Cole established the Cole Employment Agency.

Instructions Analyze the following transactions. Then record in equation form the changes in property, claims of creditors, and owner's equity. (Use plus, minus, and equal signs.)

1. The owner invested $12,500 in cash to begin the business.
2. Paid $2,200 in cash for the purchase of equipment.
3. Purchased additional equipment for $5,000 on credit.
4. Paid $2,500 in cash to creditors.
5. The owner made an additional investment of $4,000 in cash.

PROBLEM 2-2A **Preparing a balance sheet for a new firm.** Eric Hanson plans to open the Anchor Boat Repair Service on May 1, 19X5. This firm will repair and refinish sailboats.

Instructions Use the following figures to prepare a balance sheet dated May 1, 19X5. (You will need to compute the owner's equity.)

Cash	$ 2,000
Supplies	850
Equipment	19,000
Accounts Payable	5,000

PROBLEM 2-3A **Analyzing the effects of transactions on the accounting equation.** Marie Alda owns the Flair Design Studio. At the beginning of September 19X3, her firm's financial records showed the following assets, liabilities, and owner's equity.

Cash	$1,600	Accounts Payable	$ 500
Accounts Receivable	800	Marie Alda, Capital	4,800
Supplies	500	Revenue	700
Office Furniture	3,000	Expenses	100

Instructions Set up an equation form using the balances given above. Then record the effects of the following transactions in the equation. (Use plus, minus, and equal signs.) Record new balances after each transaction has been entered. Prove the equality of the two sides of the final equation on a separate sheet.

1. Performed services for $200 on credit.
2. Paid $125 in cash for utilities.
3. Performed services for $500 in cash.
4. Paid $50 in cash for office cleaning service.
5. Sent a check for $200 to a creditor.
6. Paid $50 in cash for the telephone bill.
7. Issued checks for $900 to pay salaries.
8. Performed more services for $600 in cash.
9. Purchased additional supplies for $70 on credit.
10. Received $300 from accounts receivable.

PROBLEM 2-4A **Preparing an income statement and a balance sheet.** The following equation shows the transactions of the Spotless Dry Cleaning Service during February 19X5. The business is owned by Mark Owen.

	Assets					=	Liabilities	+	Owner's Equity			
	Cash	+	Accts. Rec.	+	Supplies	+	Equip.	=	Accts. Pay.	+	Mark Owen, Capital	+	Revenue	−	Expenses

	Cash	+	Accts. Rec.	+	Supplies	+	Equip.	=	Accts. Pay.	+	Mark Owen, Capital	+	Revenue	−	Expenses
Balances, Feb. 1	2,500	+	400	+	2,000	+	7,500	=	1,200	+	11,200	+	0	−	0
Paid for utilities	− 250														250
New balances	2,250	+	400	+	2,000	+	7,500	=	1,200	+	11,200	+	0	−	250
Sold services for cash	+1,500												+1,500		
New balances	3,750	+	400	+	2,000	+	7,500	=	1,200	+	11,200	+	1,500	−	250
Paid a creditor	−350								−350						
New balances	3,400	+	400	+	2,000	+	7,500	=	850	+	11,200	+	1,500	−	250
Sold services on credit			+500										+500		
New balances	3,400	+	900	+	2,000	+	7,500	=	850	+	11,200	+	2,000	−	250
Paid salaries	−1,000														1,000
New balances	2,400	+	900	+	2,000	+	7,500	=	850	+	11,200	+	2,000	−	1,250
Paid telephone bill	− 100														100
New balances	2,300	+	900	+	2,000	+	7,500	=	850	+	11,200	+	2,000	−	1,350

Instructions Analyze each transaction carefully. Then prepare an income statement for the month and a balance sheet for February 28, 19X5. List the expenses in detail on the income statement.

The accountant's methods of analyzing transactions and presenting financial information were discussed in Chapter 2. In this chapter we will discuss the way in which the accountant keeps records of the changes that are caused by business transactions. These records are a fundamental part of all accounting systems.

SETTING UP ACCOUNTS

ACCOUNTS FOR ASSETS, LIABILITIES, AND OWNER'S EQUITY

Obviously, accountants do not have time to make up a new equation after every transaction. Instead, they keep separate written records called *accounts* for each asset and liability and for the owner's equity of the business. Another look at the affairs of the Gold Medal Fitness Center will help explain the accountant's recording procedure. When John Scott invested $80,000 on November 6, 19X5, the accountant analyzed the transaction and identified two important facts to be recorded.

a. The business had $80,000 of property in the form of cash deposited in the bank.
b. Scott had an $80,000 financial interest in the business.

The firm's financial position at that time is illustrated by the following equation.

GOLD MEDAL FITNESS CENTER

Property	=	Financial Interest
(a) Cash $80,000	=	(b) John Scott, Capital $80,000

A formal balance sheet for the firm on November 6, 19X5, would have looked like this.

GOLD MEDAL FITNESS CENTER
Balance Sheet
November 6, 19X5

Assets		Owner's Equity	
Cash	80,000	John Scott, Capital	80,000

Scott's financial investment of $80,000 is recorded in an account called John Scott, Capital, which appears on the balance sheet under the heading Owner's Equity. This heading identifies the financial interest of the owner. A second type of financial interest is shown on the balance sheet under the heading Liabilities. This heading identifies amounts that the business owes to creditors. (The Gold Medal Fitness Center has no liabilities on November 6, 19X5.)

The total of the two types of financial interest in a business is equal to the total of the property that the business owns. The various kinds of property are recorded in accounts and are shown on the balance sheet under the heading Assets. For example, the $80,000 in cash from John Scott's investment is recorded in an asset account called Cash.

The relationship between what a business owns and what it owes is best illustrated by the first simple equation that you learned in Chapter 2: *Property = Financial Interest*. When this basic proposition is expanded and classified, it becomes the fundamental accounting equation: *Assets = Liabilities + Owner's Equity*.

Accounts are separate written records of the assets, liabilities, and owner's equity of a business. They are kept so that financial information can be analyzed, recorded, classified, and summarized. As many accounts are set up as are needed to clearly identify the various kinds of property a business owns (assets) and the various types of financial interest in that property (liabilities and owner's equity). The title of each account describes the form of property or financial interest.

One type of account that the accountant might use to analyze and record transactions is called a *T account*. This account consists of two lines, one vertical and one horizontal, which resemble the letter *T*. The title of the account is written on the horizontal (top) line. Increases and decreases in the account are entered on different sides of the vertical line.

Asset Accounts

The location of items in the fundamental accounting equation determines where amounts are recorded in the T accounts. For instance, the accountant for the Gold Medal Fitness Center set up a separate account for the asset Cash. The opening balance of $80,000 (a) is entered on the left side of the account because assets always appear on the left side of the balance sheet and on the left side of the accounting equation. (The plus and minus signs shown below do not normally appear in the accounts. However, they are presented here to help you identify increases and decreases in accounts.)

+	Cash	−
(a) 80,000		

Since increases in assets are recorded on the left side of accounts, decreases are recorded on the right side.

Owner's Equity Accounts

The accountant sets up another account called John Scott, Capital, to record Scott's equity. Because owner's equity always appears on the right side of the balance sheet and the accounting equation, the accountant enters the opening balance of $80,000 (b) on the right side of the John Scott, Capital account.

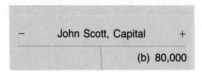

Since the right side of the owner's equity account is used to record increases in owner's equity, the left side must be used to record decreases.

Liability Accounts

Like owner's equity, liabilities always appear on the right side of the balance sheet and the accounting equation. Thus increases in liabilities are recorded on the right side of accounts, and decreases are recorded on the left side. Since the Gold Medal Fitness Center had no liabilities when it was established on November 6, 19X5, the accountant did not set up any liability accounts at that time.

Recording Prepaid Rent

When the Gold Medal Fitness Center rented its facilities, the lease specified that eight months' rent must be paid in advance. Scott issued a check for $40,000 to make the necessary payment. As a result, the firm obtained the right to occupy the facilities for an eight-month period. In accounting, this right is considered property—an asset. Thus the accountant analyzed the transaction as follows.

c. The firm acquired an asset in the form of prepaid rent, totaling $40,000.
d. The firm paid out $40,000 in cash.

To record the prepaid rent (c), the accountant first opened a new asset account called Prepaid Rent and then entered the $40,000 on the left, or increase, side of that account.

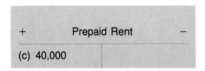

Since the cash payment (d) reduced the firm's cash balance, the accountant recorded the $40,000 on the right, or decrease, side of the Cash account.

Recording a Cash Purchase of Equipment

When the Gold Medal Fitness Center bought exercise equipment for $20,000 in cash, the accountant made the following analysis.

e. The firm purchased new assets in the form of equipment at a cost of $20,000.
f. The firm paid out $20,000 in cash.

To record the purchase of equipment (e), the accountant first opened a new asset account for equipment and then entered the $20,000 on the left, or increase, side.

+	Equipment	−
(e) 20,000		

The payment of $20,000 in cash (f) is entered on the right side of the Cash account because decreases in assets are recorded on the right side.

+	Cash	−
(a) 80,000		(d) 40,000
		(f) 20,000

Recording a Credit Purchase of Equipment

Later, when the business bought hair dryers, benches, lockers, and other necessary equipment for $10,000 on credit from Olson, Inc., the accountant's analysis showed the following effects.

g. The firm purchased new assets in the form of equipment at a cost of $10,000.
h. The firm owed $10,000 as an account payable to Olson, Inc.

As before, the increase in equipment (g) is entered on the left side of the Equipment account.

+	Equipment	−
(e) 20,000		
(g) 10,000		

The accountant opened a new account for the liability Accounts Payable to record the amount owed to Olson, Inc. (h). The $10,000 is entered on the right side of this account because liabilities appear on the right side of the balance sheet and the accounting equation.

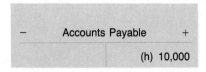

−	Accounts Payable	+
		(h) 10,000

Since the right side of liability accounts is used for increases, the left side is used for decreases.

When the Gold Medal Fitness Center bought supplies for $2,000 in cash, the accountant made the following analysis.

i. The firm purchased new assets in the form of supplies at a cost of $2,000.
j. The firm paid out $2,000 in cash.

To record this purchase of supplies (i), the accountant first opened a new asset account for supplies and then entered the $2,000 on the left, or increase, side.

+	Supplies	−
(i) 2,000		

The payment of $2,000 in cash (j) is entered on the right side of the Cash account because decreases in assets are recorded on the right side of the asset accounts.

+	Cash	−
(a) 80,000		(d) 40,000
		(f) 20,000
		(j) 2,000

The firm's position after this transaction appears in equation form below.

			Property				=	Financial Interests		
Cash	+	Supplies	+	Prepaid Rent	+	Equipment	=	Accounts Payable	+	John Scott, Capital
$18,000	+	$2,000	+	$40,000	+	$30,000	=	$10,000	+	$80,000

A formal balance sheet prepared at this time (November 28, 19X5) shows the following situation.

GOLD MEDAL FITNESS CENTER
Balance Sheet
November 28, 19X5

Assets		Liabilities and Owner's Equity	
Cash	18,000	Liabilities	
Supplies	2,000	Accounts Payable	10,000
Prepaid Rent	40,000	Owner's Equity	
Equipment	30,000	John Scott, Capital	80,000
		Total Liabilities and	
Total Assets	90,000	Owner's Equity	90,000

Recording Payment to a Creditor

On November 30, 19X5, the business paid $5,000 to Olson, Inc., to apply against its debt of $10,000. The accountant made the following analysis of this transaction.

k. The firm paid out $5,000 in cash.
l. The claim of Olson, Inc., against the firm was reduced by $5,000.

The decrease in cash (k) is entered on the right (decrease) side of the Cash account. The decrease in the liability (l) is entered on the left (decrease) side of the Accounts Payable account.

+	Cash	−	−	Accounts Payable	+
(a) 80,000	(d) 40,000		(l) 5,000		(h) 10,000
	(f) 20,000				
	(j) 2,000				
	(k) 5,000				

The transactions already discussed took place in November. They were necessary to prepare the Gold Medal Fitness Center for business on the morning of December 1, 19X5. After these November transactions have been entered in the accounts, the financial position of the firm is the same as the position shown on the balance sheet of November 30, 19X5 (page 20). Notice that this position is represented by the December 1 account balances given below. (The illustration below has been simplified by omitting the individual transactions for November from the accounts. For example, Cash: $80,000 − $40,000 − $20,000 − $2,000 − $5,000 = $13,000.)

	ASSETS SECTION			LIABILITIES SECTION	
+	Cash	−	−	Accounts Payable	+
13,000					5,000

				OWNER'S EQUITY SECTION	
+	Supplies	−	−	John Scott, Capital	+
2,000					80,000

+	Prepaid Rent	−
40,000		

+	Equipment	−
30,000		

ACCOUNTS FOR REVENUE AND EXPENSES

As you learned in Chapter 2, many of the transactions of a business involve revenue and expenses. These items are also recorded in accounts. Let's examine the revenue and expense transactions of the Gold Medal Fitness Center for December to see how they are recorded in the accounts.

Recording Revenue From Services Sold for Cash

During December the business earned a total of $12,200 in revenue from customers who paid cash for exercise classes and sessions. The accountant made the following analysis.

m. The firm received $12,200 in cash.
n. The owner's equity increased by $12,200 because of this inflow of assets from revenue.

The accountant recorded the receipt of cash (m) by entering $12,200 on the left (increase) side of the asset account Cash.

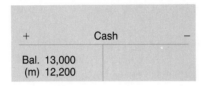

+	Cash	−
Bal. 13,000		
(m) 12,200		

How is the increase in owner's equity recorded? One way would be to record the $12,200 on the right side of the John Scott, Capital account. However, the accountant wants to keep the revenue figures separate from the owner's investment until the end of the month (or until financial reports are prepared). Therefore, the accountant opens a new account called Fees.

Remember that revenue is a subdivision of owner's equity. The accountant uses this subdivision to classify and summarize the various kinds of revenue that a business has. Different accounts are used for different types of revenue. However, at this point in its operations, the Gold Medal Fitness Center needs just one revenue account, which is called Fees. The title of this account describes the specific type of revenue recorded in it.

The accountant entered the $12,200 of revenue (n) on the right side of the Fees account because revenue increases owner's equity and an owner's equity account is increased on the right side.

−	Fees	+
		(n) 12,200

Since the right side of the revenue account is used to record increases, the left side is used to record decreases. (Decreases in a revenue account may be required by corrections, by transfers to other accounts, or by refunds. However, such entries are not required often.)

As noted already, other types of revenue would be recorded in separate accounts. For instance, if the fitness center began to sell a line of exercise clothes, the accountant would set up another revenue account called Sales. The two accounts would be classified under the heading Revenue on the income statement, and the total of their balances would be the total operating revenue of the business for the accounting period.

Recording Revenue From Services Sold on Credit

During December the Gold Medal Fitness Center also earned revenue of $6,100 from charge account customers. The accountant's analysis showed the following effects.

o. The firm obtained a new asset—accounts receivable of $6,100.
p. The owner's equity was increased by the revenue of $6,100.

To record this transaction, the accountant first opened a new asset account called Accounts Receivable and entered the $6,100 increase in assets (o) on the left (increase) side. Then the accountant entered the $6,100 increase in owner's equity (p) on the right (increase) side of the Fees account.

+	Accounts Receivable	–	–	Fees	+
(o) 6,100					(n) 12,200
					(p) 6,100

Recording Receipts From Charge Account Customers

When charge account customers paid a total of $5,500 to apply to their accounts, the accountant made the following analysis.

q. The firm received $5,500 in cash.
r. Accounts Receivable was reduced by $5,500.

Recording this information involved the use of two asset accounts. The accountant entered the $5,500 increase in cash (q) on the left side of the Cash account and the $5,500 decrease in accounts receivable (r) on the right side of the Accounts Receivable account. Notice that there is no revenue from this transaction. The revenue was entered when the sales on credit were recorded (Entry p).

+	Cash	–	+	Accounts Receivable	–
Bal. 13,000			(o) 6,100		(r) 5,500
(m) 12,200					
(q) 5,500					

Recording an Expense for Salaries

Like other firms, the Gold Medal Fitness Center encountered expenses in running its business. The first expense was for employees' salaries of $10,100. The accountant determined that this expense had the following effects.

s. The payment of $10,100 for salaries reduced the asset Cash.

t. The owner's equity was reduced by the $10,100 outflow of assets for the expense.

The reduction in cash (s) is recorded by an entry on the right (decrease) side of the asset account Cash.

+	Cash	−
Bal. 13,000		(s) 10,100
(m) 12,200		
(q) 5,500		

The decrease in owner's equity that results from the expense could be entered on the left (decrease) side of the John Scott, Capital account. However, the accountant prefers to keep expenses separate from the owner's equity until the end of the month (or until financial reports are prepared). Like revenue, expenses are a subdivision of owner's equity. This subdivision is used to classify and summarize the various costs of operating the business.

The recording technique used by the Gold Medal Fitness Center requires the opening of a new account called Salaries Expense. This title describes the specific type of expense recorded in the account. Other kinds of expenses will be recorded in separate accounts, each with its own descriptive title. For instance, the payment of monthly utility bills for the business will be recorded in an account called Utilities Expense. These two accounts are classified under the heading Expenses on the income statement. The total of all such account balances is the total operating expenses of the business for the accounting period.

The accountant enters the $10,100 of salaries (t) on the left side of the Salaries Expense account because expenses decrease owner's equity and an owner's equity account is decreased on the left side. Remember that an increase in an expense brings about a decrease in owner's equity. The plus and minus signs shown in the illustration below indicate the effect on the expense account, not the effect on owner's equity.

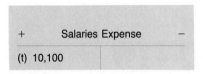

+	Salaries Expense	−
(t) 10,100		

Recording an Expense for Utilities

During December 19X5 the Gold Medal Fitness Center also had an expense of $300 for utilities, which it paid by issuing a check. The accountant made the following analysis of this transaction.

u. The payment of $300 for utilities reduced the asset Cash.
v. The owner's equity was reduced by the $300 outflow of assets for the expense.

The reduction in cash (u) was recorded in the usual way by an entry on the right (decrease) side of the asset account Cash.

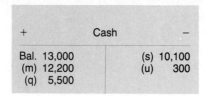

```
    +             Cash            –

Bal.  13,000               (s)  10,100
(m)   12,200               (u)     300
(q)    5,500
```

To record the expense (v), the accountant entered $300 on the left (increase) side of the Utilities Expense account.

```
    +        Utilities Expense    –

(v) 300
```

As you can see, the procedure for recording expenses is the opposite of the procedure for recording revenue. Increases in expenses are recorded on the left side of the accounts because expenses reduce owner's equity. Decreases in expenses are recorded on the right side of the accounts. (Decreases in expenses may result from corrections, transfers to other expense accounts, or refunds. However, such entries are not required often.)

After the December 19X5 transactions of the Gold Medal Fitness Center have been recorded, the account balances are determined. The firm's accounts then appear as illustrated on the next page. Notice that the balances of the various T accounts at the end of December are the same as those shown in equation form on page 26. Once the account balances have been determined, the accountant can use them to prepare the income statement and the balance sheet, as shown on the next page.

An *account balance* is the difference between the amounts recorded on the two sides of an account. It is computed by first adding the figures on each side of the account. Then the smaller total is subtracted from the larger. The result is the account balance. If the total of the figures on the right side is greater than the total on the left side, the balance is recorded on the right side. If the total of the figures on the left side is greater, the balance is recorded on the left side.

For example, the total of the figures on the left side of the fitness center's Cash account on December 31, 19X5, is $30,700. The total of the figures on the right side is $10,400. By using the procedure explained above, the balance of the Cash account is computed as $20,300 ($30,700 − $10,400 = $20,300) and is recorded on the left side of the account. Of course, if an account contains only one amount, that figure is the balance.

Notice that items marked "Bal." are balances carried forward from the November transactions.

ASSETS SECTION

Cash

Bal. 13,000	(s) 10,100
(m) 12,200	(u) 300
(q) 5,500	
20,300	

Accounts Receivable

(o) 6,100	(r) 5,500
600	

Supplies

Bal. 2,000	

Prepaid Rent

Bal. 40,000	

Equipment

Bal. 30,000	

LIABILITIES SECTION

Accounts Payable

	Bal. 5,000

OWNER'S EQUITY SECTION

John Scott, Capital

	Bal. 80,000

Salaries Expense

(t) 10,100	

Utilities Expense

(v) 300	

Fees

	(n) 12,200
	(p) 6,100
	18,300

GOLD MEDAL FITNESS CENTER
Income Statement
Month Ended December 31, 19X5

Revenue		
Fees		18,300 00
Expenses		
Salaries Expense	10,100 00	
Utilities Expense	300 00	
Total Expenses		10,400 00
Net Income for the Month		7,900 00

GOLD MEDAL FITNESS CENTER
Balance Sheet
December 31, 19X5

Assets		Liabilities and Owner's Equity		
Cash	20,300 00	Liabilities		
Accounts Receivable	600 00	Accounts Payable		5,000 00
Supplies	2,000 00	Owner's Equity		
Prepaid Rent	40,000 00	John Scott, Capital		
Equipment	30,000 00	Dec. 1, 19X5	80,000 00	
		Net Income for Month	7,900 00	
		John Scott, Capital		
		Dec. 31, 19X5		87,900 00
		Total Liabilities and		
Total Assets	92,900 00	Owner's Equity		92,900 00

THE RULES OF DEBIT AND CREDIT

Accountants do not say "left side" or "right side" when they talk about making entries in accounts. They use the term *debit* when they refer to an entry on the left side of an account and the term *credit* when they refer to an entry on the right side of an account. For example, accountants increase assets by debiting asset accounts, and they decrease assets by crediting asset accounts. However, accountants increase liabilities by crediting liability accounts and decrease liabilities by debiting liability accounts. The following illustration summarizes the rules for debiting and crediting accounts.

GUIDE FOR DEBITING AND CREDITING

ASSET ACCOUNTS

DEBIT	CREDIT
Enter the original amount on this side. Enter increases on this side.	Enter decreases on this side.

LIABILITY ACCOUNTS

DEBIT	CREDIT
Enter decreases on this side.	Enter the original amount on this side. Enter increases on this side.

OWNER'S EQUITY ACCOUNT

DEBIT	CREDIT
Enter decreases (withdrawals, and so forth) on this side.	Enter the beginning investment on this side. Enter increases (additional investments, and so forth) on this side.

REVENUE ACCOUNTS

DEBIT	CREDIT
Enter decreases in owner's equity through a reduction of revenue (sales returns, allowances, and so forth) on this side.	Enter increases in owner's equity (sales of goods or services) on this side.

EXPENSE ACCOUNTS

DEBIT	CREDIT
Enter decreases in owner's equity through expenses (rent, salaries, utilities, selling expenses, administrative expenses, and so forth) on this side.	Enter increases in owner's equity through a reduction of expenses on this side.

THE DOUBLE-ENTRY SYSTEM

The analysis of each transaction produces at least two effects. The effect of an entry on the debit, or left, side of one account is balanced by the effect of an entry on the credit, or right, side of another account. For this reason, the modern system of accounting is usually called the *double-entry system*. This system involves recording both effects of every transaction in order to present a complete picture. The balancing relationship also explains why both sides of the equations shown in Chapter 2 were always equal.

Since most businesses have many different accounts, it is necessary to set up a system that allows the accounts to be easily identified and located. A *chart of accounts* represents such a system. Each account is given a number as well as a name. The number is assigned on the basis of the type of account. Similar accounts are grouped within a certain block of numbers. For example, asset accounts could be numbered from 100 to 199, liability accounts from 200 to 299, owner's equity accounts from 300 to 399, and so on. These numbers help identify the type of account, no matter where it is in a firm's financial records.

Typically, accounts are numbered in the order that they appear on the financial statements. The balance sheet accounts are listed first and then the income statement accounts, as illustrated in the chart of accounts shown below. This chart of accounts was set up for the Gold Medal Fitness Center by the firm's accountant. Notice that the accounts are not numbered consecutively. For example, the numbering under Assets jumps from 101 to 111 and then to 121, 131, and 141. These gaps are ordinarily left in each block of numbers so that additional accounts may be added when needed.

GOLD MEDAL FITNESS CENTER
Chart of Accounts

Account Number	Account Name
100–199	**ASSETS**
101	Cash
111	Accounts Receivable
121	Supplies
131	Prepaid Rent
141	Equipment
200–299	**LIABILITIES**
202	Accounts Payable
300–399	**OWNER'S EQUITY**
301	John Scott, Capital
400–499	**REVENUE**
401	Fees
500–599	**EXPENSES**
511	Salaries Expense
514	Utilities Expense

As you have seen, the asset, liability, and owner's equity accounts appear on the balance sheet at the end of an accounting period. The balances of these accounts are then carried forward to start the new period. Such accounts are sometimes called *permanent,* or *real, accounts* because they continue from accounting period to accounting period.

In contrast to these permanent accounts are the revenue and expense accounts, which appear on the income statement at the end of an accounting period. Accountants use revenue and expense accounts to classify and summarize changes in owner's equity during the period. Then, as you will see later, the balances of these accounts are transferred to a summary account at the end of the period. In turn, the balance of the summary account is transferred to owner's equity. As a result of this transfer process, the balances of the revenue and expense accounts are zero at the start of the new accounting period. The revenue and expense accounts are therefore called *temporary*, or *nominal*, *accounts*.

PRINCIPLES AND PROCEDURES SUMMARY

Each transaction is analyzed to identify its effects on the fundamental accounting equation (*Assets = Liabilities + Owner's Equity*). Then the effects of each transaction are recorded in the proper accounts. The location of the entries in an account is based on where the item appears in the fundamental equation and on the balance sheet. An increase in an asset is shown on the debit, or left, side of the account because assets appear on the left side of the equation and the balance sheet. The credit, or right, side of an asset account is used to record decreases. In contrast, liabilities appear on the right side of the equation and the balance sheet. Therefore, an increase in a liability is recorded on the credit, or right, side of the account. The opposite side of a liability account is used for recording decreases. Similarly, increases in owner's equity are shown on the credit side of an owner's equity account. Decreases in owner's equity appear on the debit side.

Revenue is recorded by making entries on the credit side of the separate revenue accounts because revenue increases owner's equity. Expenses are recorded on the debit side of the separate expense accounts because expenses decrease owner's equity.

Accounts are arranged in a predetermined order and numbered for handy reference and quick identification. The list of the accounts used by a business is called its chart of accounts. Typically, the accounts are numbered in the order that they appear on the financial statements. The balance sheet accounts come first and are followed by the income statement accounts.

MANAGERIAL IMPLICATIONS

Recording entries in accounts provides an efficient method of gathering data about the financial affairs of a business. From the accounts, the accountant can easily prepare the income statement, which summarizes the revenue and expenses of the business for a specific period of time. The accountant can also use the accounts to prepare the balance sheet, which summarizes the assets, liabilities, and owner's equity of the business on a given date. Owners, managers, creditors, banks, and many others use these statements to make decisions about the business.

REVIEW QUESTIONS

1. What are accounts?
2. What is a chart of accounts?
3. In what order do the accounts appear in the chart of accounts?
4. When a chart of accounts is created, number gaps are left within groups of accounts. Why are these number gaps necessary?
5. The terms *debit* and *credit* are often used in describing the effects of transactions on different accounts. What do these terms mean?
6. Decide whether each of the following types of accounts would normally have a debit balance or a credit balance.
   a. An asset account
   b. A liability account
   c. The owner's capital account
   d. A revenue account
   e. An expense account
7. Accounts are classified as permanent or temporary accounts. What do these classifications mean?
8. Why is Prepaid Rent considered an asset account?
9. Why is the modern system of accounting usually called the double-entry system?
10. How is the balance of an account determined?

MANAGERIAL DISCUSSION QUESTIONS

1. How do the income statement and the balance sheet help management make sound decisions?
2. At any time, how can management find out whether a firm can pay its bills as they become due?
3. If a firm's expenses equal or exceed its revenue, what actions might management take?
4. In discussing a firm's latest financial statements, a manager says that it is the "results on the bottom line" that really count. What does the manager mean?

EXERCISES

EXERCISE 3-1   **Describing the rules of debit and credit.** Complete each of the following statements by using the word *debit* or *credit* wherever appropriate.

1. Asset accounts normally have _____ balances. These accounts increase on the _____ side and decrease on the _____ side.
2. Liability accounts normally have _____ balances. These accounts increase on the _____ side and decrease on the _____ side.
3. The owner's capital account normally has a _____ balance. This account increases on the _____ side and decreases on the _____ side.

4. Revenue accounts normally have _____ balances. These accounts increase on the _____ side and decrease on the _____ side.

5. Expense accounts normally have _____ balances. These accounts increase on the _____ side and decrease on the _____ side.

EXERCISE 3-2 **Identifying account balances.** Indicate whether each of the following accounts would normally have a debit balance or a credit balance.

1. Accounts Payable   5. Equipment
2. Fees   6. Accounts Receivable
3. Cash   7. Salaries Expense
4. Paul Salazar, Capital   8. Supplies

EXERCISE 3-3 **Identifying transactions recorded in T accounts.** The following T accounts show transactions that were recorded at the Heritage Furniture Repair Service, a firm that specializes in restoring antique furniture. The entries for the first transaction are labeled with the letter *a,* the entries for the second transaction are labeled with the letter *b,* and so on. Describe each transaction that took place. These transactions cover the first month of the firm's operations—January 19X2.

Cash			
(a) 40,000		(b) 10,000	
(d) 5,000		(e) 150	
(g) 500		(h) 2,500	

Equipment	
(c) 15,000	

Fees	
	(d) 5,000
	(f) 2,000

Accounts Receivable	
(f) 2,000	(g) 500

Accounts Payable	
	(c) 15,000

Telephone Expense	
(e) 150	

Supplies	
(b) 10,000	

Mark Connors, Capital	
	(a) 40,000

Salaries Expense	
(h) 2,500	

EXERCISE 3-4 **Determining account balances.** Refer to the T accounts illustrated in Exercise 3-3, and determine the balances.

EXERCISE 3-5 **Preparing an income statement.** Using the account balances determined in Exercise 3-4, prepare an income statement for the Heritage Furniture Repair Service. This income statement is for the month ended January 31, 19X2.

EXERCISE 3-6 **Preparing a balance sheet.** Using the account balances determined in Exercise 3-4 and the net income or net loss determined in Exercise 3-5, prepare a balance sheet for the Heritage Furniture Repair Service as of January 31, 19X2.

EXERCISE 3-7 **Setting up T accounts and entering the balances.** The financial data shown below is for the Allen Office Planning Company as of December 1, 19X5. This firm does interior planning and design work for business offices. Set up a T account for each item listed, and enter the balance on the correct side of the account. Write *Bal.* next to the amount of the balance, as shown below.

Cash	$ 10,000
Accounts Receivable	12,000
Equipment	25,000
Accounts Payable	5,000
Lois Allen, Capital	9,000
Fees	130,000
Rent Expense	22,000
Salaries Expense	75,000

```
              Cash
_____
Bal. 10,000    |
```

EXERCISE 3-8 **Analyzing transactions and recording the effects in T accounts.** The Allen Office Planning Company had the following transactions during the month of December 19X5. Analyze these transactions, and then record their effects in the T accounts that you set up in Exercise 3-7.

TRANSACTIONS

1. Collected $8,000 in cash from credit customers.
2. Paid $2,000 for the December rent.
3. Performed services for $14,000 on credit.
4. Paid $3,000 in cash to creditors.
5. Performed services for $11,000 in cash.
6. Paid $7,000 for salaries.

EXERCISE 3-9 **Determining account balances.** Refer to the T accounts that you worked with in Exercise 3-8, and determine the balances.

EXERCISE 3-10 **Preparing an income statement.** Using the account balances determined in Exercise 3-9, prepare an income statement for the Allen Office Planning Company. This income statement is for the year ended December 31, 19X5.

EXERCISE 3-11 **Preparing a balance sheet.** Using the account balances determined in Exercise 3-9 and the net income or net loss determined in Exercise 3-10, prepare a balance sheet for the Allen Office Planning Company as of December 31, 19X5.

EXERCISE 3-12 **Preparing a chart of accounts.** The accounts that will be used by the Timely Personnel Service are shown below. Prepare a chart of accounts for the firm. Classify the accounts by type, arrange them in an appropriate order, and assign suitable account numbers.

Joyce Kline, Capital	Office Supplies	Accounts Payable
Cash	Utilities Expense	Office Equipment
Salaries Expense	Prepaid Rent	Fees
Accounts Receivable	Telephone Expense	

PROBLEMS

PROBLEM 3-1   **Using T accounts to record transactions involving assets, liabilities, and owner's equity.** The following transactions took place at the Logan Tax Advisory Service over a period of several months.

Instructions   Set up T accounts for the accounts listed in parentheses after the transactions. Analyze each transaction carefully. Then record the amounts in the T accounts affected by that transaction. Use plus and minus signs to show increases and decreases in each account.

a. Roy Logan invested $12,500 cash in the business. (Cash and Roy Logan, Capital.)
b. Purchased office furniture for $2,000 in cash. (Office Furniture and Cash.)
c. Bought a microcomputer for $2,450, to be paid in 30 days. (Office Equipment and Accounts Payable.)
d. Purchased a used car for the firm for $5,000 in cash. (Automobile and Cash.)
e. Logan gave his personal library of tax books, valued at $500, to the business. (Library Books and Roy Logan, Capital.)
f. Bought a computer program for $400, to be paid in 60 days. This program will be used in tax planning work. (Software and Accounts Payable.)
g. Paid $2,450 to settle the amount owed on the microcomputer. (Accounts Payable and Cash.)

PROBLEM 3-2   **Using T accounts to record transactions involving assets, liabilities, and owner's equity.** The following transactions occurred at several different businesses and are not related.

Instructions   Analyze each of the transactions. Decide what accounts are affected, and enter the proper titles at the top of a pair of T accounts. Then record the effects of the transaction in the T accounts. Use plus and minus signs before the amounts to show the increases and decreases.

a. Lynn McNair, an owner, made an additional investment of $5,000 in cash.
b. A firm purchased store equipment for $2,500 in cash.
c. A firm sold some surplus office furniture for $200 in cash.
d. A firm purchased an electronic typewriter for $950, to be paid in 60 days.
e. A firm purchased store equipment for $1,000 on credit.
f. Peter Rossi, an owner, withdrew $1,000 of his original cash investment.
g. A firm bought a delivery truck for $8,000 on credit. Payment is due in 90 days.
h. A firm issued a check for $250 to a supplier in partial payment of an open account balance.

PROBLEM 3-3   **Using T accounts to record transactions involving revenue and expenses.** The transactions on page 52 took place at the Rapid Delivery Service.

Instructions   Analyze each of the transactions. Decide what accounts are affected, and enter the proper titles at the top of a pair of T accounts. Then record the effects of the transaction in the T accounts. Use plus and minus signs before the amounts to show the increases and decreases.

a. Sold services for $1,600 in cash.
b. Paid $500 for the month's rent.
c. Sold additional services for $2,000 on credit.
d. Paid $100 for the monthly electric bill.
e. Paid $85 in cash for office cleaning service.
f. Paid $2,000 for salaries.
g. Sold services for $1,500 in cash.
h. Received a $450 bill for repairs to a delivery van used in the business. Payment is due in 30 days.
i. Received a $10 cash refund for an overcharge on the bill for office cleaning service.
j. Paid $65 for the monthly telephone bill.
k. Paid $320 in cash for gasoline for the firm's delivery vans during the month.
l. Sold additional services for $500 on credit.

PROBLEM 3-4   **Using T accounts to record a variety of transactions.** Ellen Gold is a consulting engineer who helps businesses solve air pollution problems and other environmental problems. Transactions and account titles for her firm are shown below and on page 53.

Instructions   Analyze the transactions. Then record each one in the appropriate T accounts. Use plus and minus signs before the amounts to show the increases and decreases. Identify each entry in the T accounts by writing the letter of the transaction next to the entry.

ASSETS	REVENUE
Cash	Fees
Accounts Receivable	
Office Furniture	EXPENSES
Office Equipment	Rent Expense
	Utilities Expense
LIABILITIES	Salaries Expense
Accounts Payable	Telephone Expense
	Miscellaneous Expense
OWNER'S EQUITY	
Ellen Gold, Capital	

a.   Ellen Gold invested $12,000 in cash to start the business.
b.   Paid $700 for one month's rent.
c.   Bought office furniture for $2,500 in cash.
d.   Performed services for $800 in cash.
e.   Paid $135 for the monthly telephone bill.
f.   Sold services for $1,400 on credit.
g.   Purchased a typewriter for $350 and paid $100 cash immediately. The balance is due in 30 days.
h.   Received a bill for $165 for office cleaning service. Payment is due in 30 days.

i. Received $600 from credit clients.
j. Purchased additional office chairs for $400. Received credit terms of 30 days.
k. Paid $2,200 for salaries.
l. Issued a check for $150 in partial payment of the amount owed for office chairs.
m. Performed services for $700 in cash.
n. Issued a check for $160 to pay the utility bill.
o. Performed services for $1,800 on credit.
p. Collected $500 from accounts receivable.
q. Paid $65 of the bill from the office cleaning service that was received previously.
r. Paid $90 to a duplicating service for photocopy work performed during the month.

PROBLEM 3-5 **Preparing financial statements from T accounts.** The accountant for Ellen Gold's firm prepares financial statements at the end of each month.

Instructions Use the figures in the T accounts for Problem 3-4 to prepare an income statement and a balance sheet. (The first line of the statement headings should read Ellen Gold, Consulting Engineer.) Assume that the transactions took place during the month ended June 30, 19X5. Determine the account balances before you start work on the financial statements.

ALTERNATE PROBLEMS

PROBLEM 3-1A **Using T accounts to record transactions involving assets, liabilities, and owner's equity.** The following transactions took place at the Downtown Automotive Repair Service over a period of several months.

Instructions Set up T accounts for the accounts listed in parentheses after the transactions. Analyze each transaction carefully. Then record the amounts in the T accounts affected by that transaction. Use plus and minus signs to show increases and decreases in each account.

a. David Hill invested $20,000 cash in the business. (Cash and David Hill, Capital.)
b. Purchased testing equipment for $1,000 in cash. (Shop Equipment and Cash.)
c. Bought auto parts for $2,200. Payment is due in 30 days. (Auto Parts and Accounts Payable.)
d. Purchased a used tow truck for $8,000 in cash. (Truck and Cash.)
e. Hill gave to the firm his personal set of tools that cost $600. (Shop Equipment and David Hill, Capital.)
f. Bought an office desk and chair for $200. Payment is due in 30 days. (Office Furniture and Accounts Payable.)
g. Paid $850 in cash to apply to the amount owed for auto parts. (Accounts Payable and Cash.)

PROBLEM 3-2A   **Using T accounts to record transactions involving assets, liabilities, and owner's equity.** The following transactions occurred at several different businesses and are not related.

Instructions   Analyze each of the transactions. Decide what accounts are affected, and enter the proper titles at the top of a pair of T accounts. Then record the effects of the transaction in the T accounts. Use plus and minus signs before the amounts to show the increases and decreases.

a. A firm purchased office equipment for $2,000 in cash.
b. Mary Haines, an owner, withdrew $1,500 of the cash she had invested.
c. A firm sold a piece of surplus store equipment for $250 in cash.
d. A firm purchased a used delivery truck for $5,000 in cash.
e. A firm paid $400 in cash to apply against an account owed.
f. A firm purchased office equipment for $450. The amount is to be paid in 60 days.
g. Frank Lazlo, an owner, made an additional investment of $2,500 in cash.
h. A firm paid $150 by check for office equipment that it had previously purchased on credit.

PROBLEM 3-3A   **Using T accounts to record transactions involving revenue and expenses.** The following transactions took place at the Roberts House Painting Service.

Instructions   Analyze each of the transactions. Decide what accounts are affected, and enter the proper titles at the top of a pair of T accounts. Then record the effects of the transaction in the T accounts. Use plus and minus signs before the amounts to show the increases and decreases.

a. Paid $400 for one month's rent.
b. Sold services for $500 in cash.
c. Paid $1,600 for salaries.
d. Sold additional services for $1,800 on credit.
e. Paid $75 for the monthly telephone bill.
f. Paid $380 in cash for repairs to the van that the firm uses to transport its equipment to jobs.
g. Received a $15 cash refund for an overcharge on the bill for repairing the van.
h. Sold services for $600 on credit.
i. Paid $110 for the monthly electric bill.
j. Paid $95 in cash for gasoline for the firm's van during the month.
k. Gave a refund of $100 in cash to a customer because the wrong shade of paint was used. (The customer previously paid cash for the job.)
l. Performed services for $900 in cash.

PROBLEM 3-4A   **Using T accounts to record a variety of transactions.** Linda Santos is a management consultant who helps businesses plan and install electronic office systems. Transactions and account titles for her firm are shown on page 55.

Instructions   Analyze the transactions. Then record each one in the appropriate T accounts. Use plus and minus signs in front of the amounts to show the increases and decreases. Identify each entry in the T accounts by writing the letter of the transaction next to the entry.

ASSETS	REVENUE
Cash	Fees
Accounts Receivable	
Office Equipment	
Automobile	EXPENSES
	Rent Expense
	Utilities Expense
LIABILITIES	Salaries Expense
Accounts Payable	Telephone Expense
	Automobile Expense

OWNER'S EQUITY
Linda Santos, Capital

a. Linda Santos invested $23,000 in cash to set up the business.
b. Paid $600 for one month's rent.
c. Bought a used automobile for the firm for $5,000 in cash.
d. Performed services for $800 in cash.
e. Paid $110 for automobile repairs.
f. Performed services for $1,450 on credit.
g. Purchased office chairs for $600 on credit.
h. Received $700 from credit clients.
i. Paid $300 to reduce the amount owed for the office chairs.
j. Issued a check for $120 to pay the monthly utility bill.
k. Purchased office equipment for $3,000 and paid half of this amount in cash immediately. The balance is due in 30 days.
l. Issued a check for $2,325 to pay salaries.
m. Performed services for $950 in cash.
n. Performed services for $1,675 on credit.
o. Paid $105 for the monthly telephone bill.
p. Collected $750 from accounts receivable.
q. Purchased additional office equipment, and received a bill for $225, due in 30 days.
r. Paid $60 in cash for gasoline for the automobile during the month.

PROBLEM 3-5A **Preparing financial statements from T accounts.** The accountant for the firm owned by Linda Santos prepares financial statements at the end of each month.

Instructions Use the figures in the T accounts for Problem 3-4A to prepare an income statement and a balance sheet. (The first line of the statement headings should read Linda Santos, Management Consultant.) Assume that the transactions took place during the month ended April 30, 19X5. Determine the account balances before you start work on the financial statements.

In the last chapter you learned that the analysis of each transaction is the basis for recording the effects of the transaction in the accounts. In business, accountants keep written records of each analysis for future reference. These records allow the accountants to recheck their work and trace the details of any transaction long after it has happened.

BASIC ACCOUNTING RECORDS

JOURNALS

The analysis of each transaction is kept in a financial record called a *journal*. This record is really a diary of business activities that lists events involving financial affairs—transactions—as they occur. The transactions are entered in *chronological order*—in the order that they happen day by day.

A number of different types of journals are used in business. The one that will be examined in this chapter is the general journal. As we discuss more complex accounting systems and records in later chapters, you will become familiar with other kinds of journals.

THE GENERAL JOURNAL

As its name implies, the *general journal* can be used to record all types of transactions that a business has. To illustrate how transactions are entered in this journal, let us consider again the financial affairs of the Gold Medal Fitness Center.

When the owner, John Scott, invested $80,000 to start the firm, the accountant analyzed the transaction and identified the following effects.

a. The business had $80,000 of property in the form of cash.
b. Scott had an $80,000 financial investment in the business.

Then, using this analysis as a guide, the accountant knew that the transaction should be entered as follows.

a. Debit the Cash account to record the increase in the asset Cash.
b. Credit the John Scott, Capital account to record the new ownership interest.

The accountant's written record of the analysis of the transaction appears in the general journal shown on page 57.

Notice that each page in the general journal is given a number and that the year is recorded at the top of the Date column. The month and day are also written in the Date column on the first line of the first entry. After the first entry the year and month are recorded only when a new page is begun or when either

GENERAL JOURNAL				Page 1	
DATE	DESCRIPTION OF ENTRY	POST. REF.	DEBIT	CREDIT	
19 X5 Nov. 6	Cash		80,000 00		
	John Scott, Capital			80,000 00	
	Beginning investment of owner.				

the year or the month changes. However, the day of each transaction is written in the Date column on the first line of each entry.

The account to be debited is always recorded first in the Description of Entry column. The account title is written close to the left margin, and the debit amount is then entered on the same line in the Debit column.

The account to be credited is always recorded on the line beneath the debit. The account title is indented about half an inch from the left margin. Next the credit amount is entered on the same line in the Credit column.

A brief explanation follows the credit part of the entry. This explanation begins at the left margin of the Description of Entry column so that as much space as possible is available. Explanations should be complete but concise.

Whenever possible, the explanation for a journal entry should include a description of the source of the information contained in the entry. For example, if a check is written to make a payment, the explanation in the journal entry for that transaction should include the check number. Similarly, if goods are purchased on credit, the explanation in the journal entry should show the number of the supplier's invoice (bill). These source document numbers are part of an *audit trail*—a chain of references that makes it possible to trace information about transactions through the accounting process. The audit trail helps the accountant to locate errors in the system. It also helps to prevent fraud because it provides a means of checking the data in a firm's financial records against the original data about the transactions that appears in the source documents.

Account titles are written in the general journal exactly as they appear in the chart of accounts and in the accounts themselves. Use of the exact wording of each account title minimizes the possibility of errors when the figures are transferred to the accounts. (The transfer of information from the general journal to the accounts is the next step in the accounting process and will be discussed later in this chapter.)

Accountants usually leave a blank line between each general journal entry. This separates the transactions and makes them easier to identify and read. Some accountants prefer to use this blank line to number each general journal entry for identification purposes.

Because the accountant writes the transaction analysis in a journal before making any entry in the accounts, a journal is sometimes referred to as a *record of original entry*. The process of recording data in a journal is called *journalizing*. By journalizing first, the accountant knows that all the information about a transaction is recorded in one place before any details can be forgotten.

The journal entries made at the Gold Medal Fitness Center during November provide a good illustration of the techniques that are used to record transactions in the general journal. For example, when the firm paid $40,000 rent in advance for December through July, the accountant analyzed the transaction as follows and then prepared the journal entry shown below.

c. The business acquired a new asset (prepaid rent) at a cost of $40,000.
d. The business paid out $40,000 in cash.

GENERAL JOURNAL					Page 1
DATE	DESCRIPTION OF ENTRY	POST. REF.	DEBIT	CREDIT
19 X5				
Nov. 7	Prepaid Rent		40,000 00	
	Cash			40,000 00
	Paid rent in advance for an eight-month period (December 19X5 through July 19X6), Check 1001.			

Notice the use of the check number in the explanation for the journal entry. This number will form part of the audit trail for the transaction.

When the Gold Medal Fitness Center bought exercise equipment for $20,000 in cash, the accountant made the following analysis and then recorded the journal entry shown below.

e. The business purchased new assets (equipment) at a cost of $20,000.
f. The business paid out $20,000 in cash.

GENERAL JOURNAL					Page 1
DATE	DESCRIPTION OF ENTRY	POST. REF.	DEBIT	CREDIT
19 X5				
Nov. 9	Equipment		20,000 00	
	Cash			20,000 00
	Purchased exercise equipment, Check 1002.			

When the firm bought locker room equipment and other necessary equipment on credit from Olson, Inc., the accountant analyzed the situation as follows and made the journal entry shown on page 59.

g. The business purchased new assets (equipment) at a cost of $10,000.
h. The business owed $10,000 as an account payable to Olson, Inc.

Notice how the audit trail is created for this transaction by listing the supplier's invoice number in the explanation for the journal entry.

GENERAL JOURNAL

Page 1

DATE	DESCRIPTION OF ENTRY	POST. REF.	DEBIT	CREDIT
19 X5				
Nov. 10	Equipment		10,000 00	
	Accounts Payable			10,000 00
	Purchased locker room equipment and other equipment on credit from Olson, Inc., Invoice 2788, payable in 60 days.			

When the firm bought supplies for $2,000 in cash, the accountant analyzed the transaction as follows and then prepared the journal entry shown below.

i. The business purchased new assets (supplies) at a cost of $2,000.
j. The business paid out $2,000 in cash.

GENERAL JOURNAL

Page 1

DATE	DESCRIPTION OF ENTRY	POST. REF.	DEBIT	CREDIT
19 X5				
Nov. 28	Supplies		2,000 00	
	Cash			2,000 00
	Purchased soap, shampoo, paper towels, and other supplies, Check 1003.			

Finally, an analysis of the payment to Olson, Inc., showed the following results. Based on this analysis, the accountant recorded the journal entry shown below.

k. The firm paid out $5,000 in cash.
l. Olson's claim against the firm was reduced by $5,000.

GENERAL JOURNAL

Page 1

DATE	DESCRIPTION OF ENTRY	POST. REF.	DEBIT	CREDIT
19 X5				
Nov. 30	Accounts Payable		5,000 00	
	Cash			5,000 00
	Paid Olson, Inc. on account for Invoice 2788, Check 1004.			

Notice that the debit item is always entered in the general journal first. This is the case even if the accountant happens to consider the credit item first while mentally analyzing the transaction.

You will recall that the Gold Medal Fitness Center officially opened for business on December 1, 19X5, and the following transactions were completed during that month. The journal entries made for these transactions provide a further illustration of the procedures used to record data in the general journal. (Refer to Items m through v in Chapter 3 to review the accountant's analysis of the December transactions.)

1. Sold services for $12,200 in cash.
2. Sold services for $6,100 on credit.
3. Received $5,500 in cash from credit customers to apply to their accounts.
4. Paid $10,100 for salaries.
5. Paid $300 for a utility bill.

The necessary entries in the general journal are shown below. (In actual practice the transactions involving sales and cash received on account would be spread throughout the month and recorded as they occurred. However, for the sake of simplicity, these transactions have been summarized and recorded as of December 31 in the illustration.)

GENERAL JOURNAL				Page 2
DATE	DESCRIPTION OF ENTRY	POST. REF.	DEBIT	CREDIT
19 X5 Dec. 31	Cash		12,200 00	
	Fees			12,200 00
	Sold services for cash.			
31	Accounts Receivable		6,100 00	
	Fees			6,100 00
	Sold services on credit.			
31	Cash		5,500 00	
	Accounts Receivable			5,500 00
	Received cash from credit customers on account.			
31	Salaries Expense		10,100 00	
	Cash			10,100 00
	Paid monthly salaries to employees, Checks 1005–1012.			
31	Utilities Expense		300 00	
	Cash			300 00
	Paid monthly bill for utilities, Check 1013.			

Compound Entries

Each of the journal entries shown so far consists of a single debit and a single credit. However, some transactions require a *compound entry*—a journal entry that contains several debits or several credits. In a compound entry the accountant records all debits first and then records the credits. One point to remember about this type of entry is that no matter how many accounts are involved, the total debits must equal the total credits.

Suppose that the Gold Medal Fitness Center purchases some exercise bicycles for $1,500, gives $500 in cash immediately, and agrees to pay the balance in 30 days. This transaction would be analyzed as follows. Then the accountant would make the compound entry shown below.

1. The asset Equipment is increased by $1,500.
2. The asset Cash is decreased by $500.
3. The liability Accounts Payable is increased by $1,000.

GENERAL JOURNAL				Page 6
DATE	DESCRIPTION OF ENTRY	POST. REF.	DEBIT	CREDIT
19 X5 June 2	Equipment		1,500 00	
	Cash			500 00
	Accounts Payable			1,000 00
	Purchased exercise bicycles on credit from Lewis Inc., Invoice 49621. Issued Check 1587 for a $500 down payment. The balance is payable in 30 days.			

Notice that this compound entry contains equal debits and credits, just as any journal entry should ($1,500 = $500 + $1,000).

LEDGER ACCOUNTS

As you have seen, a journal contains a chronological (day-by-day) record of a firm's transactions. Each entry provides a written analysis of a transaction, showing what accounts should be debited and credited and the amounts involved. With the journal as a guide, the accountant can enter the data about transactions in the accounts that are affected.

Although T accounts are a good device for quickly analyzing the effects of transactions, they are not suitable for use in business as financial records. Instead, business firms keep each account on a printed form that has a heading and several columns. This arrangement makes it possible to record all the necessary data efficiently. The printed forms used for the accounts appear on separate sheets in a book or binder or on separate cards in a tray.

All the accounts together are referred to as a *ledger*. The process of transferring data from a journal to a ledger is known as *posting*. Because this process takes place after the transactions are journalized, a ledger is sometimes called a *record of final entry*.

THE GENERAL LEDGER

One essential type of ledger for every business is the *general ledger*. This ledger is the master reference file for the accounting system because it provides a permanent, classified record of every financial element involved in a firm's operations. Many companies also have other kinds of ledgers that supplement the information in the general ledger. You will become familiar with some of these other ledgers in later chapters, but keep in mind that the general ledger is the main ledger of a business.

Ledger Account Forms

Several different forms are available for general ledger accounts. The simplest, the *standard ledger form,* is really just an expansion of the T account. An example of this form is shown below with some entries posted from the general journal of the Gold Medal Fitness Center for illustrative purposes. The disadvantage of the standard ledger form is that the balance of an account is not known at all times. Instead, whenever this information is needed, someone must calculate the total debits and credits in the account and then determine the balance.

		Cash					No.	101
DATE	EXPLANATION	POST. REF.	DEBIT	DATE	EXPLANATION	POST. REF.	CREDIT	
19 X5 Nov. 6		J1	80,000 00	19 X5 Nov. 7 9		J1 J1	40,000 00 20,000 00	

The accountant for the Gold Medal Fitness Center has decided to use a *balance ledger form* for the business's general ledger accounts. With this form the balance of an account is always available because it is recorded after each entry is posted. The following illustrations show how data about the first transaction of the fitness center—the beginning investment of the owner—was posted from the general journal to the proper general ledger accounts. The posting process will be explained in the next section, but notice the arrangement of columns in the balance ledger form and how the various columns are used.

GENERAL JOURNAL				Page 1
DATE	DESCRIPTION OF ENTRY	POST. REF.	DEBIT	CREDIT

19 X5 Nov. 6	Cash
	    John Scott, Capital
	    Beginning investment of owner.
		101
		301
			80,000 00	80,000 00

		Cash				No. 101
DATE	EXPLANATION	POST. REF.	DEBIT	CREDIT	BALANCE	DR. CR.
19 X5 Nov. 6		J1	80,000 00		80,000 00	Dr.

John Scott, Capital					No.	301

DATE	EXPLANATION	POST. REF.	DEBIT	CREDIT	BALANCE	DR. CR.
19 X5 Nov. 6		J1		80,000 00	80,000 00	Cr.

Posting General Journal Entries to the General Ledger

To understand the posting process, examine the following illustrations. On November 7, 19X5, the accountant for the Gold Medal Fitness Center made an entry in the general journal to record the payment of rent in advance for an eight-month period. Then the accountant posted the data from the journal to the proper accounts in the general ledger. The accountant transferred the debit amount to the Prepaid Rent account and transferred the credit amount to the Cash account.

GENERAL JOURNAL   Page 1

DATE	DESCRIPTION OF ENTRY	POST. REF.	DEBIT	CREDIT
19 X5 Nov. 7	Prepaid Rent		40,000 00	
	Cash			40,000 00
	Paid rent in advance for an eight-month period (December 19X5 through July 19X6), Check 1001.			

Prepaid Rent					No.	131

DATE	EXPLANATION	POST. REF.	DEBIT	CREDIT	BALANCE	DR. CR.
19 X5 Nov. 7		J1	40,000 00		40,000 00	Dr.

Cash					No.	101

DATE	EXPLANATION	POST. REF.	DEBIT	CREDIT	BALANCE	DR. CR.
19 X5 Nov. 6		J1	80,000 00		80,000 00	Dr.
7		J1		40,000 00	40,000 00	Dr.

The procedure used in posting data from a general journal entry like the one shown above is to start with the first account listed in the entry—the account to be debited. The accountant locates the necessary account in the general ledger and then follows these steps.

1. The date is recorded in the Date column of the account.
2. If necessary, a notation explaining the entry is made in the Explanation column. However, routine entries usually do not require an explanation.
3. The number of the journal page is recorded in the Posting Reference (Post. Ref.) column of the account. For example, *J1* is used in the Prepaid Rent account shown on page 63 to indicate that the entry was posted from page 1 of the general journal. The letter *J* in front of the page number is an abbreviation that identifies the general journal.
4. The debit amount is recorded in the Debit column of the account.
5. The balance of the account is determined and then recorded in the Balance column.
6. The type of balance is noted in the last column of the account by entering the abbreviation *Dr.* for debit or *Cr.* for credit.
7. The number of the ledger account is recorded in the Posting Reference (Post. Ref.) column of the journal.

The accountant uses similar steps to post the credit amount from the general journal entry. Once this work is done, the posting process for the transaction is complete and the journal entry includes the numbers of the two ledger accounts that were posted, as shown below.

GENERAL JOURNAL Page 1

DATE	DESCRIPTION OF ENTRY	POST. REF.	DEBIT	CREDIT
19 X5				
Nov. 7	Prepaid Rent	131	40,000 00	
	Cash	101		40,000 00
	Paid rent in advance for an eight-month period (December 19X5 through July 19X6), Check 1001.			

Writing the journal page number in each ledger account and the ledger account number in the journal indicates that the entry has been posted and ensures against posting the same entry twice or not at all. The journal page numbers in the accounts and the account numbers in the journal provide a useful cross-reference when entries must be traced and transactions verified. Like the source document numbers that appear in the explanations for journal entries, posting references are part of the audit trail. Together, all of these references allow the accountant to trace an amount from the ledger to the proper journal entry and then to the source document that contains the original data about the transaction.

After the accountant for the Gold Medal Fitness Center posts all the entries for November and December from the general journal, the firm's general ledger accounts appear as shown on pages 65 and 66. Refer to the journal entries, which are given on pages 57 through 60, and trace the postings carefully.

Cash   No. 101

DATE		EXPLANATION	POST. REF.	DEBIT	CREDIT	BALANCE	DR. CR.
19	X5						
Nov.	6		J1	80,000 00		80,000 00	Dr.
	7		J1		40,000 00	40,000 00	Dr.
	9		J1		20,000 00	20,000 00	Dr.
	28		J1		2,000 00	18,000 00	Dr.
	30		J1		5,000 00	13,000 00	Dr.
Dec.	31		J2	12,200 00		25,200 00	Dr.
	31		J2	5,500 00		30,700 00	Dr.
	31		J2		10,100 00	20,600 00	Dr.
	31		J2		300 00	20,300 00	Dr.

Accounts Receivable   No. 111

DATE		EXPLANATION	POST. REF.	DEBIT	CREDIT	BALANCE	DR. CR.
19	X5						
Dec.	31		J2	6,100 00		6,100 00	Dr.
	31		J2		5,500 00	600 00	Dr.

Supplies   No. 121

DATE		EXPLANATION	POST. REF.	DEBIT	CREDIT	BALANCE	DR. CR.
19	X5						
Nov.	28		J1	2,000 00		2,000 00	Dr.

Prepaid Rent   No. 131

DATE		EXPLANATION	POST. REF.	DEBIT	CREDIT	BALANCE	DR. CR.
19	X5						
Nov.	7		J1	40,000 00		40,000 00	Dr.

Equipment   No. 141

DATE		EXPLANATION	POST. REF.	DEBIT	CREDIT	BALANCE	DR. CR.
19	X5						
Nov.	9		J1	20,000 00		20,000 00	Dr.
	10		J1	10,000 00		30,000 00	Dr.

Accounts Payable   No. 202

DATE	EXPLANATION	POST. REF.	DEBIT	CREDIT	BALANCE	DR. CR.
19 X5						
Nov. 10		J1		10,000 00	10,000 00	Cr.
30		J1	5,000 00		5,000 00	Cr.

John Scott, Capital   No. 301

DATE	EXPLANATION	POST. REF.	DEBIT	CREDIT	BALANCE	DR. CR.
19 X5						
Nov. 6		J1		80,000 00	80,000 00	Cr.

Fees   No. 401

DATE	EXPLANATION	POST. REF.	DEBIT	CREDIT	BALANCE	DR. CR.
19 X5						
Dec. 31		J2		12,200 00	12,200 00	Cr.
31		J2		6,100 00	18,300 00	Cr.

Salaries Expense   No. 511

DATE	EXPLANATION	POST. REF.	DEBIT	CREDIT	BALANCE	DR. CR.
19 X5						
Dec. 31		J2	10,100 00		10,100 00	Dr.

Utilities Expense   No. 514

DATE	EXPLANATION	POST. REF.	DEBIT	CREDIT	BALANCE	DR. CR.
19 X5						
Dec. 31		J2	300 00		300 00	Dr.

As you can see, each ledger account provides a complete running history of the increases and decreases in the item that it represents. When a balance ledger form is used, the account also shows the current balance for the item at all times.

The general ledger accounts are usually arranged so that the balance sheet accounts—assets, liabilities, and owner's equity—come first. The accounts for the income statement come next, with the revenue accounts first, followed by the expense accounts. The numbering system used in the chart of accounts follows the same order. This arrangement speeds the preparation of the income statement and the balance sheet. All figures are found in the general ledger in the order in which they will be presented on the financial statements.

CORRECTING ERRORS IN THE JOURNAL AND THE LEDGER

Sometimes errors are made when recording transactions in the journal. For example, a wrong account title or amount may be used in a journal entry. If the error is discovered before the entry is posted, a correction can be made by neatly crossing out the incorrect item and writing the correct data above it. To ensure honesty and provide a clear audit trail, accountants do not permit erasures in a journal.

If the journal entry that contains an error has already been posted, it is not an acceptable practice to change the entry itself or to change the postings in the ledger accounts. Instead, a *correcting entry* should be journalized and posted. The following example will illustrate the necessary procedure. On August 5, 19X5, an automobile service station purchased some equipment for its repair shop for $800 in cash. By mistake, the person who recorded the transaction debited the Office Equipment account rather than the Shop Equipment account, as shown below.

19 X5					
Aug. 5	Office Equipment	141	800 00	
	Cash	101		800 00
	Purchased equipment, Check 6421.			

The error was not discovered until the beginning of the next month after the data had been posted to the ledger. At that time the following entry was journalized and posted to correct the error. Notice that this entry debits Shop Equipment and credits Office Equipment for $800. Thus it serves to transfer the sum out of the Office Equipment account and into the Shop Equipment account.

19 X5					
Sept. 1	Shop Equipment	151	800 00	
	Office Equipment	141		800 00
	To correct error made in entry of Aug. 5			
	when a purchase of shop equipment			
	was mistakenly recorded as office			
	equipment.			

PRINCIPLES AND PROCEDURES SUMMARY

A journal provides a chronological (day-by-day) record of a firm's transactions. It contains a written analysis of each transaction that occurred. The process of recording transactions in a journal is called journalizing. The general journal is one type of journal that is widely used in business. It has the advantage of being able to accommodate all kinds of transactions that a business may have.

In a general journal entry, the debit portion is always recorded first. Then the credit portion is recorded, and a brief explanation is provided. Whenever possible, the explanations for journal entries should include source document numbers in order to create an audit trail.

Data is transferred from the journal entries to the accounts. This process is called posting. The individual accounts together form a ledger. There are various types of ledgers, but the main ledger for every business is the general ledger. This ledger contains the accounts that are used to prepare the financial statements.

The posting references placed in the journal and the ledger accounts form another part of the audit trail. They serve to cross-reference the entries and make it possible to trace or recheck any transaction in the firm's accounting records.

MANAGERIAL IMPLICATIONS

Business managers should make sure that their firms have efficient procedures for recording transactions. A well-run accounting system provides for prompt and accurate journalizing of all transactions. It also provides for timely and accurate posting of data to the ledger accounts. The information that appears in the financial statements comes from the general ledger. Since management uses this information for decision making, it is essential that the statements be prepared quickly at the end of each period and that they contain the correct figures. The promptness and accuracy of the statements depends heavily on the efficiency of the recording process.

Another characteristic of a well-run accounting system is that it has a strong audit trail. For the sake of accuracy and honesty, the firm should be able to trace amounts through the accounting records and back to their origin—the source documents on which the transactions were first recorded.

REVIEW QUESTIONS

1. What is the purpose of a journal?
2. What procedure is used to record an entry in the general journal?
3. What is the value of having an explanation for each general journal entry?
4. Why is it important that exact account titles be used in the general journal?
5. What is a compound journal entry?
6. What is a ledger?
7. What is the advantage of using a balance ledger form rather than the standard ledger form?
8. What is posting?
9. In what order are accounts arranged in the general ledger? Why?
10. What are posting references? Why are they used?

11. What is an audit trail? Why is it desirable to have an audit trail?
12. How should corrections be made in the general journal and the general ledger?

MANAGERIAL DISCUSSION QUESTIONS

1. Why should management be concerned about the efficiency of a firm's procedures for journalizing and posting transactions?
2. How might a poor set of recording procedures affect the flow of information to management?
3. The owner of a new business recently told his accountant that he could not see the value of having both a journal and a ledger. He felt that it was a waste of effort to enter data about transactions in two different records. How would you explain the value of having both records?
4. Why should management insist that a firm's accounting system have a strong audit trail?

EXERCISES

EXERCISE 4-1 **Identifying the accounts to be used in journal entries.** Selected accounts from the general ledger of the United Office Cleaning Service are shown below. Decide what accounts should be debited and credited when the following transactions are recorded in the general journal. Indicate the numbers of the correct accounts.

ACCOUNTS

101	Cash	301	Kevin Riley, Capital
111	Accounts Receivable	401	Fees
121	Supplies	511	Rent Expense
131	Equipment	514	Salaries Expense
202	Accounts Payable	517	Utilities Expense

TRANSACTIONS

1. Issued a check for $750 to pay the monthly rent.
2. Purchased supplies for $300 on credit.
3. The owner made an additional investment of $5,000 in cash.
4. Collected $800 from credit customers.
5. Performed services for $1,600 in cash.
6. Issued a check for $550 to pay a creditor on account.
7. Purchased some new equipment for $725, and paid for it immediately by giving a check.
8. Provided services for $2,200 on credit.
9. Sent a check for $110 to the utility company to pay the monthly bill.
10. Gave a cash refund of $50 to a customer because of a poor cleaning job. (The customer had previously paid in cash.)

EXERCISE 4-2   **Journalizing transactions involving assets, liabilities, and owner's equity.**
Selected accounts from the general ledger of the Elegant Decorating Service are
shown below. Give the general journal entries that would be made to record the
following transactions. (Be sure to include dates and explanations in these entries
and in the entries for the rest of the exercises.)

ACCOUNTS

101	Cash	141	Automobile
111	Accounts Receivable	202	Accounts Payable
121	Supplies	301	Alice Schmidt, Capital
131	Equipment	401	Fees

511	Rent Expense
514	Salaries Expense
517	Telephone Expense
520	Automobile Expense

TRANSACTIONS FOR SEPTEMBER 19X5

Sept. 1 Alice Schmidt invested $22,000 in cash to start the firm.
       4 Purchased office equipment for $2,500 on credit from Rogers Inc.
         Received Invoice 9823, which is payable in 30 days.
      16 Purchased an automobile that will be used to visit clients. Issued
         Check 1001 for $7,300 in full payment.

EXERCISE 4-3   **Journalizing transactions involving assets, liabilities, and owner's equity.**
Make general journal entries for the following additional transactions of the
Elegant Decorating Service. Use the account titles shown in Exercise 4-2.

TRANSACTIONS FOR SEPTEMBER 19X5

Sept. 20 Purchased supplies for $225. Paid immediately with Check 1002.
      23 Returned damaged supplies, and received a cash refund of $25.
      30 Issued Check 1003 for $2,500 to Rogers Inc. as payment on account
         for Invoice 9823.

EXERCISE 4-4   **Journalizing transactions involving revenue and expenses.** On October 1,
19X5, the Elegant Decorating Service opened for business. Give the general
journal entries that would be made to record the following transactions. Use the
account titles shown in Exercise 4-2.

TRANSACTIONS FOR OCTOBER 19X5

Oct.   1 Issued Check 1004 for $500 to pay the rent for October.
      15 Performed services for $850 in cash.
      22 Issued Check 1005 for $78 to pay the monthly telephone bill.

EXERCISE 4-5   **Journalizing transactions involving revenue and expenses.** Make general
journal entries for the following additional transactions of the Elegant Decorating
Service. Use the account titles shown in Exercise 4-2.

TRANSACTIONS FOR OCTOBER 19X5

Oct. 25 Performed services for $1,600 on credit.
      29 Issued Check 1006 for $65 to pay a bill for gasoline used in the firm's
         automobile during the month.
      31 Issued Check 1007 for $800 to pay employee's monthly salary.

EXERCISE 4-6   **Recording compound entries.** The following transactions took place at the Elegant Decorating Service during November 19X5. Give the general journal entries that would be made to record these transactions. Use a compound entry for each transaction. Refer to Exercise 4-2 for the necessary account titles.

TRANSACTIONS FOR NOVEMBER 19X5

Nov.   5 Performed services for the Alpine Motel for $4,000. This client is paying $1,500 in cash now and will pay the balance in 60 days.
       18 Purchased an electronic calculator for $110 and some supplies for $50 from the same company. Issued Check 1008 for the total.
       23 Received Invoice 2601 for $300 from Kelly's Garage for repairs to the firm's automobile. Issued Check 1009 for half the amount, and have arranged to pay the other half in 30 days.

EXERCISE 4-7   **Recording a correcting entry.** On August 2, 19X4, an employee of the Lawrence Company mistakenly debited the Utilities Expense account rather than the Telephone Expense account when recording a bill of $120 for July telephone service. The error was discovered on August 31. Make a general journal entry to correct the error.

EXERCISE 4-8   **Recording a correcting entry.** On November 15, 19X2, an employee of the Melville Company mistakenly debited the Truck account rather than the Truck Expense account when recording a bill of $465 for repairs. The error was discovered on December 1. Make a general journal entry to correct the error.

PROBLEMS

PROBLEM 4-1   **Recording transactions in the general journal.** The transactions on page 72 took place at the Four Seasons Tennis Center during December 19X1. This firm has indoor courts where customers can play tennis for a fee. It also rents equipment and offers tennis lessons.

Instructions   Analyze each transaction, and record the effects in general journal form. Choose the account titles from the following chart of accounts. Be sure to number the journal page *1* and to write the year at the top of the Date column. Include an explanation for each entry.

	ASSETS		LIABILITIES		EXPENSES
101	Cash	202	Accounts Payable	511	Equipment Repairs Expense
111	Accounts Receivable				
121	Supplies		OWNER'S EQUITY	514	Telephone Expense
141	Equipment			517	Utilities Expense
		301	Steven DeLuca, Capital	520	Salaries Expense
				523	Rent Expense

REVENUE

401   Fees

TRANSACTIONS FOR DECEMBER 19X1

Dec.   1 Issued Check 7921 for $1,200 to pay the December rent.

         5 Sold services for $1,000 in cash.

         5 Sold services for $1,540 on credit.

      10 Paid the November telephone bill of $90 by means of Check 7922.

      11 Received a bill for $85 for equipment repairs. Issued Check 7923 to pay it.

      12 Received $400 on account from credit customers.

      15 Issued Checks 7924–7929 for $2,100 for semimonthly salaries.

      18 Issued Check 7930 for $150 to purchase supplies.

      19 Purchased new tennis rackets for $1,550 on credit from Ward Inc. Received Invoice 4311, payable in 30 days.

      20 Issued Check 7931 for $380 to purchase new nets (Equipment).

      21 Received $525 on account from credit customers.

      21 Returned a damaged net, and received a cash refund of $96.

      22 Sold services for $1,680 in cash.

      22 Sold services for $2,370 on credit.

      26 Issued Check 7932 for $180 to purchase supplies.

      28 Paid the monthly electric bill of $277 by means of Check 7933.

      31 Issued Checks 7934–7939 for $2,100 for semimonthly salaries.

PROBLEM 4-2   **Journalizing and posting transactions.** On August 1, 19X1, Marion Gibbs opened an advertising agency. She plans to use the chart of accounts shown below. The financial activities of her business during the first month of operations are listed on page 73.

Instructions   1. Journalize the transactions. Be sure to number the journal page *1* and to write the year at the top of the Date column. Include an explanation for each entry.

         2. Post to the ledger accounts. Before you start the posting process, open the accounts by entering the titles and numbers in the headings. (Use the order that the accounts follow in the chart of accounts.)

ASSETS

101 Cash
111 Accounts Receivable
121 Supplies
141 Office Equipment
151 Art Equipment

LIABILITIES

202 Accounts Payable

OWNER'S EQUITY

301 Marion Gibbs, Capital

REVENUE

401 Fees

EXPENSES

511 Telephone Expense
514 Salaries Expense
517 Utilities Expense
520 Rent Expense
523 Office Cleaning Expense

Aug.   1   Marion Gibbs invested $28,000 cash in the business.

2   Issued Check 1001 for $850 to pay the August rent for the office.

5   Bought desks and other office furniture for $5,000 from Ross Inc. Received Invoice 3647, payable in 60 days.

6   Issued Check 1002 for $1,800 to purchase equipment for the art department.

7   Bought supplies for $250. Paid with Check 1003.

10   Issued Check 1004 for $85 to pay for office cleaning service.

12   Sold services for $600 in cash and $1,750 on credit. (Use one compound entry.)

15   Returned damaged supplies, and received a cash refund of $30.

18   Bought an electronic typewriter for $900 from Key Office Systems. Received Invoice 562. Issued Check 1005 to make a down payment of $300. The balance is payable in 30 days. (Use one compound entry.)

20   Issued Check 1006 for $2,000 to Ross Inc. as payment on account for Invoice 3647.

26   Sold services for $1,275 on credit.

27   Paid $85 for the monthly telephone bill. Issued Check 1007.

30   Received $700 in cash from credit customers.

30   Sent Check 1008 to pay the monthly utility bill of $120.

30   Issued Checks 1009–1011 for $2,300 to the employees for their monthly salaries.

PROBLEM 4-3   **Auditing journal entries.** All of the journal entries shown below contain errors. They were prepared by an employee of the Robbins Company who does not have an adequate knowledge of accounting.

Instructions   Examine the journal entries carefully to locate the errors. Provide a brief written description of each error.

19	X2			
Feb.	1	Accounts Payable	1,200 00	
		Fees		1,200 00
		Performed services on credit.		
	2	Cash	105 00	
		Telephone Expense		105 00
		Paid for January telephone service, Check 2706.		
	3	Office Equipment	140 00	
		Office Supplies	80 00	
		Cash		250 00
		Purchased a file cabinet and office supplies, Check 2707.		

PROBLEM 4-4   **Preparing a chart of accounts.** The accountant for the Jefferson Dental Laboratory has recommended that the accounts shown below be established in the firm's general ledger.

Instructions   Prepare a chart of accounts for the firm. Classify the accounts by type, arrange them in an appropriate order, and assign suitable account numbers.

ACCOUNTS

Ruth Swenson, Capital	Laboratory Supplies	Utilities Expense
Accounts Receivable	Fees	Accounts Payable
Cash	Salaries Expense	Office Equipment
Rent Expense	Laboratory Equipment	Telephone Expense

ALTERNATE PROBLEMS

PROBLEM 4-1A   **Recording transactions in the general journal.** The transactions on pages 74 and 75 took place at Holiday Bus Tours during October 19X1. This firm provides guided tours to nearby historical sites and also charters its buses to local groups.

Instructions   Analyze each transaction, and record the effects in general journal form. Use the account titles in the following chart of accounts. Be sure to number the journal page *1* and to put the year at the top of the Date column. Include an explanation for each entry.

ASSETS	LIABILITIES	EXPENSES
101 Cash	202 Accounts Payable	511 Rent Expense
111 Accounts Receivable		514 Advertising Expense
131 Office Equipment	OWNER'S EQUITY	517 Telephone Expense
141 Buses		520 Bus Expense
	301 Martin Perez, Capital	523 Salaries Expense
		527 Utilities Expense
	REVENUE	
	401 Fees	

TRANSACTIONS FOR OCTOBER 19X1

Oct. 1 Issued Check 3412 for $1,800 to pay the October rent.
   3 Paid an advertising bill of $250 by means of Check 3413.
   5 Sold services for $2,100 in cash.
   6 Issued Check 3414 for $110 to pay the September telephone bill.
   9 Sold services for $3,400 on credit.
   14 Received a $300 bill for bus repairs. Paid it with Check 3415.
   15 Issued Checks 3416–3421 for $2,650 to pay semimonthly salaries.
   18 Collected $1,300 on account from credit customers.
   21 Paid $100 to purchase an electronic calculator for the office. Issued Check 3422.

24 Sold services for $2,250 on credit.
26 Received $800 in cash from accounts receivable.
27 Sold services for $1,600 in cash.
28 Issued Check 3423 for $75 to give a cash refund to a group because their chartered bus was late. (The group had previously paid in cash.)
29 Paid the October utility bill of $150 with Check 3424.
30 Issued Checks 3425–3430 for $2,650 to pay semimonthly salaries.
31 Issued Check 3431 for $420 to pay a bill for diesel fuel used in the buses.
31 Purchased new desks and chairs for $900 on credit from Wilson Inc. Received Invoice 5861, payable in 30 days.

PROBLEM 4-2A

Journalizing and posting transactions. On July 1, 19X1, Susan Chang opened a data processing service. She plans to use the chart of accounts shown below. The financial activities of the business during the first month of operations are listed below and on page 76.

Instructions

1. Journalize the transactions. Be sure to number the journal page *1* and to write the year at the top of the Date column. Include an explanation for each entry.
2. Post to the ledger accounts. Before you start the posting process, open the accounts by entering the titles and the numbers in the headings. (Use the order that the accounts follow in the chart of accounts.)

ASSETS		LIABILITIES		EXPENSES	
101	Cash	202	Accounts Payable	511	Telephone Expense
111	Accounts Receivable			514	Advertising Expense
121	Supplies		OWNER'S EQUITY	517	Salaries Expense
141	Office Equipment			520	Rent Expense
151	Software	301	Susan Chang, Capital	523	Utilities Expense

REVENUE

401 Fees

TRANSACTIONS FOR JULY 19X1

July
1 Susan Chang invested $30,000 cash in the business.
2 Paid the office rent of $500 with Check 1001.
3 Bought computer equipment for $15,000 on credit from Hill Business Systems. Received Invoice 829. Issued Check 1002 for $5,000 to make a down payment. The balance is payable in 60 days. (Use one compound entry.)
3 Issued Check 1003 for $1,600 to purchase software for the computer.
4 Paid a $100 advertising bill with Check 1004.
5 Issued Check 1005 for $300 to purchase supplies.
8 Sold services for $650 in cash.
11 Sold services for $1,000 on credit.
15 Collected $250 from accounts receivable.

17 Issued Check 1006 for $150 to purchase a supply cabinet.

20 Paid the monthly telephone bill of $95 with Check 1007.

22 Sold services for $500 in cash and $1,200 on credit. (Use one compound entry.)

25 Issued Check 1008 for $3,000 to Hill Business Systems as payment on account for Invoice 829.

30 Issued Check 1009 to pay the monthly utility bill of $170.

31 Issued Checks 1010 and 1011 for $2,000 to the employees for their monthly salaries.

PROBLEM 4-3A **Auditing journal entries.** All of the journal entries shown below contain errors. They were prepared by an employee of the Winfield Company who does not have an adequate knowledge of accounting.

Instructions Examine the journal entries carefully to locate the errors. Provide a brief written description of each error.

19 X3				
May	1	Office Furniture	245 00	
		Accounts Receivable		245 00
		Purchased a desk on credit from Hale Inc., Invoice A636, payable in 30 days.		
	2	Cash	170 00	
		Office Supplies		170 00
		Purchased office supplies, Check 4361.		
	3	Cash	600 00	
		Accounts Receivable	600 00	
		Fees		1,100 00
		Performed services for the Bell Company, which paid half in cash and will pay the balance in 60 days.		

PROBLEM 4-4A **Preparing a chart of accounts.** The accountant for the Drake Television Repair Service has recommended that the accounts shown below be established in the general ledger of this new firm.

Instructions Prepare a chart of accounts for the firm. Classify the accounts by type, arrange them in an appropriate order, and assign suitable account numbers.

ACCOUNTS

Rent Expense	Salaries Expense	Telephone Expense
Fees	Supplies	Michael Drake, Capital
Accounts Receivable	Tools	Accounts Payable
Cash	Truck Expense	Truck

As you already know, the purpose of having journals and ledgers is to gather data that is needed to prepare the financial statements. After an accountant posts all the transactions for the operating period to the ledger accounts, the financial statements are prepared. Because management will use the financial statements to make decisions, the accountant wants to be sure that these reports contain no errors. Before preparing the statements, therefore, the accountant tests the accuracy of the amounts that were recorded during the period.

THE TRIAL BALANCE, ADJUSTMENTS, AND THE WORKSHEET

THE TRIAL BALANCE

One device that accountants use to test the accuracy of the financial records is the *trial balance*. When John Scott started the Gold Medal Fitness Center with a cash investment, we said that property equaled financial interests. Then, using more technical language, we stated that assets equaled liabilities plus owner's equity. Later we saw that every entry on the debit, or left, side of one account is matched by an entry of equal amount on the credit, or right, side of another account. The firm's financial records started with an equality of debits and credits and continued that equality in the recording process. Consequently, it follows that the sum of the debit balances in the general ledger accounts should equal the sum of the credit balances after all transactions have been posted. If the ledger is not *in balance*—that is, if the debit balances do not equal the credit balances—it is clear that an error has been made.

To test the equality of the debits and credits in the general ledger, accountants use the following procedure. First they determine the balance of each account. Then they add the debit and credit balances separately to see if the totals are equal.

FINDING THE BALANCE OF AN ACCOUNT

When the standard ledger form is used for the general ledger accounts, two steps are required to compute the balance of each account. It is necessary first to add the figures on each side of the account and then to subtract the smaller total from the larger total. General ledger accounts in this form are balanced at the end of each year, at any other times when financial statements will be prepared, and whenever the bottom of a ledger sheet is reached and a new sheet must be started.

As you saw in the previous chapter, the Gold Medal Fitness Center uses the balance ledger form for its general ledger accounts. With this form, the balance is determined every time a new entry is posted. Thus the account balances are always available, which speeds up the preparation of the trial balance and the financial statements.

The accountant lists the balances of the general ledger accounts on a trial balance form such as the one shown below. This procedure allows the accountant to see if the total of the debit balances equals the total of the credit balances. The accounts are listed in order by account number, just as they appear in the general ledger. The balance of each account is written in the proper column. Debit balances are entered in the left column, and credit balances are entered in the right column.

Notice that the trial balance illustrated here has a three-line heading that shows who, what, and when. The date is the closing date for the accounting period. Observe, too, that there are no dollar signs in the amount columns. Accountants usually omit dollar signs when they prepare financial statements, schedules, or working papers on ruled forms.

GOLD MEDAL FITNESS CENTER
Trial Balance
December 31, 19X5

ACCT. NO.	ACCOUNT NAME	DEBIT	CREDIT
101	Cash	20,300 00	
111	Accounts Receivable	600 00	
121	Supplies	2,000 00	
131	Prepaid Rent	40,000 00	
141	Equipment	30,000 00	
202	Accounts Payable		5,000 00
301	John Scott, Capital		80,000 00
401	Fees		18,300 00
511	Salaries Expense	10,100 00	
514	Utilities Expense	300 00	
	Totals	103,300 00	103,300 00

The balances shown on the trial balance prepared at the Gold Medal Fitness Center on December 31, 19X5, came from the ledger accounts illustrated on pages 65 and 66 of Chapter 4. The last figure listed in the Balance column of each account is the amount that was recorded on the trial balance. For example, the last figure shown in the Balance column of the Cash account on page 65 is a debit balance of $20,300. This is the balance that was transferred to the firm's trial balance.

When the Debit and Credit columns of the trial balance are equal, the accountant knows that the financial records are in balance. The accountant is also sure that a debit has been recorded for every credit.

If the Debit and Credit columns are not equal, it is clear that an error has been made. The error may be in the trial balance, or it may be in the financial records. The following are some common errors.

1. Adding amounts incorrectly on the trial balance.
2. Posting only half a journal entry. For example, a debit is posted without a credit, or vice versa.

3. Posting both halves of a journal entry as debits or credits. (Two debits or two credits are posted to the ledger, rather than one debit and one credit.)
4. Posting an amount incorrectly from a journal entry.
5. Recording unequal debits and credits in a journal entry.
6. Adding or subtracting amounts incorrectly when determining an account balance.

If the trial balance is out of balance, many accountants use the following procedures to locate the error or errors.

1. Check the arithmetic on the trial balance.
2. Check that the balances of the accounts were correctly transferred from the ledger to the trial balance form.
3. Check the arithmetic used in computing the account balances in the ledger.
4. Check the accuracy of the postings by tracing the amounts recorded in the ledger back to the journal entries.

The arithmetic on the trial balance can be checked for errors by adding the columns again in the opposite direction. That is, if the columns were first added from top to bottom, they should be verified by adding from bottom to top.

Sometimes the accountant can determine the type of error by the amount of the difference involved. For this reason, when the debit and credit totals on the trial balance are not equal, the accountant computes the difference by subtracting the smaller total from the larger total. If the difference is divisible by 9, there may have been a *transposition* ($357 for $375) or a *slide* ($375 for $37.50). If the difference can be divided by 2, the amount of a debit may have been posted as a credit, or a credit posted as a debit.

ERRORS NOT REVEALED BY THE TRIAL BALANCE

The trial balance is very helpful in locating many types of errors. However, it will give no indication that certain other types of errors exist. Examples of such errors are as follows.

1. A transaction could have been omitted.
2. The same transaction could have been recorded more than once.
3. A part of a journal entry could have been posted to the wrong account.
4. There could have been offsetting arithmetic errors in the accounts.
5. There could have been offsetting arithmetic errors in totaling the trial balance columns.

Fortunately, these types of errors do not happen often. The trial balance is therefore a good test of accuracy.

THE WORKSHEET

When the trial balance shows that the general ledger is in balance, the accountant is ready to prepare the financial statements for the period. These statements must be completed as soon as possible if they are to be useful. Therefore, anything that can be done to save time is important. One way that accountants can prepare the financial statements more quickly is by using a form called a *worksheet*.

A very common type of worksheet is shown on pages 88 and 89. Notice that this worksheet contains ten money columns, which are arranged in five sections labeled Trial Balance, Adjustments, Adjusted Trial Balance, Income Statement, and Balance Sheet. Each section includes a Debit column and a Credit column. Also notice that the third line of the worksheet heading shows the period of operations covered by the figures on the worksheet.

The Trial Balance Section

To save time and effort, many accountants combine the trial balance process with the preparation of the worksheet. They list the accounts directly on the worksheet and then transfer the balances from the general ledger to the Debit and Credit columns of the Trial Balance section. After the account balances are recorded on the worksheet, the equality of the debits and credits is proved in the usual manner.

Examine the Trial Balance section of the partial worksheet illustrated below. The accountant for the Gold Medal Fitness Center has added four new accounts to the firm's general ledger: Accumulated Depreciation—Equipment 142, Supplies Expense 517, Rent Expense 520, and Depreciation Expense—Equipment 523. These accounts do not have any balances yet, but they will be needed as other parts of the worksheet are prepared. The accountant has therefore listed them in the Trial Balance section so that they can appear in numeric order with the rest of the general ledger accounts. The use of these new accounts will be explained in the discussion of the Adjustments section of the worksheet that follows.

GOLD MEDAL FITNESS CENTER
Worksheet (Partial)
Month Ended December 31, 19X5

	ACCT. NO.	ACCOUNT NAME	TRIAL BALANCE		ADJUSTMENTS	
			DEBIT	CREDIT	DEBIT	CREDIT
1	101	Cash	20,300 00			
2	111	Accounts Receivable	600 00			
3	121	Supplies	2,000 00			(a)1,250 00
4	131	Prepaid Rent	40,000 00			(b)5,000 00
5	141	Equipment	30,000 00			
6	142	Accumulated Depreciation—Equipment				(c) 500 00
7	202	Accounts Payable		5,000 00		
8	301	John Scott, Capital		80,000 00		
9	401	Fees		18,300 00		
10	511	Salaries Expense	10,100 00			
11	514	Utilities Expense	300 00			
12	517	Supplies Expense			(a)1,250 00	
13	520	Rent Expense			(b)5,000 00	
14	523	Depreciation Expense—Equipment			(c) 500 00	
15		Totals	103,300 00	103,300 00	6,750 00	6,750 00
16						
17						

The Adjustments Section

In many businesses the data in the general ledger accounts at the end of an accounting period does not present a complete picture of the firm's financial affairs even though transactions have been recorded accurately throughout the period. Certain financial changes have occurred within the business as a result of its operations that have not yet been entered in the accounting records. These changes must be recognized and recorded at the end of each accounting period. The Adjustments section of the worksheet is used to assemble such information so that it can be reported in the financial statements. Then, after the statements have been prepared, the information is journalized and posted in order to bring the accounting records up to date.

Most changes in a firm's account balances are caused by transactions between the business and another business or individual. In the case of the Gold Medal Fitness Center, all the changes in its accounts discussed so far were caused by transactions that the firm had with suppliers, customers, the landlord, and employees. These changes were easy to recognize and were therefore journalized and posted as they occurred. However, some changes are not caused by transactions with other businesses or individuals. Instead, they arise from the internal operations of the firm itself. As noted already, it is necessary to recognize and record such changes at the end of each accounting period. The worksheet provides a convenient device for gathering the information and determining the effects of the changes on the accounts involved.

The process of updating accounts at the end of an accounting period for previously unrecorded items that belong to the period is referred to as making *adjustments* or *adjusting entries*. The following examples of adjustments made at the Gold Medal Fitness Center on December 31, 19X5, the end of the business's first month of operations, will provide a more detailed explanation of the process.

Adjustment for Supplies Used On November 28, 19X5, the Gold Medal Fitness Center purchased supplies for $2,000. Some of these supplies were used during December in the course of operations. However, on the December 31 trial balance, the Supplies account still shows a balance of $2,000. In order to present an accurate and complete picture of the firm's financial affairs at the end of December, the accountant must make an adjustment for this item. Otherwise, the asset account Supplies will be overstated because less supplies are actually on hand. Similarly, the firm's expenses will be understated because the cost of supplies used represents an operating expense that has not been recorded.

On December 31, 19X5, the manager of the fitness center made a count of the remaining supplies and found that they totaled $750. This meant that supplies amounting to $1,250 were used during the month ($2,000 − $750 = $1,250). The effects on the firm's accounts are as follows.

1. The Supplies Expense account increases by $1,250.
2. The Supplies account decreases by $1,250.

To recognize these effects, the accountant makes an adjustment on the worksheet that consists of a debit of $1,250 to Supplies Expense and a credit of $1,250 to Supplies, as shown on page 80. Notice that the two parts of the adjustment are labeled (a) in order to identify them for future reference. This procedure is especially helpful when the adjustments are journalized after the financial statements have been prepared.

Adjustment for Expired Rent On November 7, 19X5, the Gold Medal Fitness Center paid $40,000 rent in advance for an eight-month period (December 19X5 through July 19X6). As a result of this transaction, the firm acquired the right to occupy facilities for the specified period. Since this right is considered a form of property, the $40,000 was debited to an asset account called Prepaid Rent. On December 31, 19X5, the firm's trial balance still shows a balance of $40,000 in this account. Yet the fitness center has used up part of its right to occupy the facilities—one month of the prepaid rent has expired.

Since the $40,000 sum covered an eight-month period, the expired rent for December amounts to $5,000 ($\frac{1}{8}$ of $40,000 = $5,000). Thus on December 31 the asset account Prepaid Rent is overstated by $5,000. At the same time the firm's expenses are understated because the $5,000 of expired rent represents an operating expense that has not been recorded. The cost of facilities used is a cost of doing business.

To update the accounts involved, it is necessary to make an adjustment on December 31. The effects of this adjustment are as follows.

1. The Rent Expense account increases by $5,000.
2. The Prepaid Rent account decreases by $5,000.

The accountant enters the adjustment on the worksheet by recording a debit of $5,000 to Rent Expense and a credit of $5,000 to Prepaid Rent. These two figures are labeled (b) in the Adjustments section of the partial worksheet shown on page 80.

Supplies and prepaid rent are known as *prepaid expenses*. They are expense items that are acquired and paid for in advance of their use. As you have seen, at the time of their acquisition, these items represent assets for a business and are therefore recorded in asset accounts. However, as they are used, their cost is transferred to expense accounts by means of adjusting entries at the end of each accounting period.

Other common prepaid expenses are prepaid insurance and prepaid advertising. These items are debited to the asset accounts Prepaid Insurance and Prepaid Advertising when they are acquired. Later the expired cost that applies to each accounting period is debited to Insurance Expense and Advertising Expense and credited to the asset accounts in end-of-period adjusting entries.

Adjustment for Depreciation One other adjustment must be made for the Gold Medal Fitness Center at the end of December 19X5, its first month of operations. On November 9 and 10 the firm purchased equipment at a total cost of $30,000. This equipment was put to use in December when the fitness center opened for business. At the time the equipment was bought, its cost was debited to the asset account Equipment. On December 31, 19X5, the firm's trial balance therefore shows a balance of $30,000 in the Equipment account.

The various items of equipment that were purchased all have an estimated useful life of five years and no expected salvage value after that period. (*Salvage value* means that an item can be sold for additional use or for scrap.) Because long-term assets like the fitness center's equipment help to earn revenue for a business, their cost should be charged to operations (transferred to expense) as they are used during their lives. This is done at the end of each accounting period by means of an adjusting entry. The process of allocating the cost of a long-term asset to operations during its expected useful life is known as *depreciation*.

There are many different ways to determine the amount of depreciation to charge to expense in each accounting period. The method that the accountant for the fitness center has decided on is a very simple and widely used one called the *straight-line method* of depreciation. With this method an equal amount of depreciation is charged off in each accounting period during the asset's useful life.

Since the equipment purchased by the fitness center is expected to have a useful life of five years and no salvage value, its entire cost of $30,000 must be depreciated over the five-year period. The amount of depreciation for December 19X5, the first month of operations, is computed by first converting the asset's useful life from years to months: 5×12 months $= 60$ months. Then the total depreciation to be taken is divided by the total number of months: $30,000 \div 60 = 500$. Thus the amount of depreciation to be charged off for December 19X5 and every other month during the asset's useful life is $500.

As the cost of the equipment is gradually transferred to expense, its *book value* (recorded value) as an asset must be reduced. This procedure cannot be carried out by directly decreasing the $30,000 balance in the asset account Equipment. Generally accepted accounting principles require that the original cost of a long-term asset continue to appear in the asset account until the item is disposed of. Thus another account called Accumulated Depreciation— Equipment is used to keep a record of the total depreciation taken and to reduce the book value of the asset.

Accumulated Depreciation—Equipment is a special type of account called a *contra asset account*. It has a credit balance, which is contrary to the normal balance of an asset account. This credit balance is subtracted from the debit balance of the Equipment account on the balance sheet to report the book value of the asset.

The effects of the adjustment for depreciation at the Gold Medal Fitness Center on December 31, 19X5, are as follows.

1. Depreciation Expense—Equipment increases by $500.
2. Accumulated Depreciation—Equipment increases by $500.

The accountant enters the adjustment on the worksheet by recording a debit of $500 to Depreciation Expense—Equipment and a credit of $500 to Accumulated Depreciation—Equipment. These two figures are labeled (c) on the partial worksheet shown on page 80.

If the fitness center had other kinds of long-term assets, an adjustment for depreciation would be made for each one. Typical long-term assets owned by businesses in addition to equipment are land, buildings, trucks, automobiles, furniture, and fixtures. Of these items, only land is not subject to depreciation.

After the adjustment for depreciation of the equipment is recorded on the worksheet of the fitness center, the Adjustments section is totaled and ruled. The totals of the Debit and Credit columns in this section should be equal. If they are not, the accountant must locate and correct the error or errors before continuing. Examine the partial worksheet on page 80 to see how the Adjustments section was completed.

The Adjusted Trial Balance Section

The next task for the accountant is to prepare an adjusted trial balance on the worksheet. This process involves two steps. First the accountant combines the figures from the Trial Balance section and the Adjustments section to record the updated account balances. Then the accountant makes a final check on the equality of the debits and credits before extending the balances to the financial statement sections.

GOLD MEDAL FITNESS CENTER
Worksheet (Partial)
Month Ended December 31, 19X5

	ACCT. NO.	ACCOUNT NAME	TRIAL BALANCE DEBIT	TRIAL BALANCE CREDIT	ADJUSTMENTS DEBIT	ADJUSTMENTS CREDIT	ADJUSTED TRIAL BALANCE DEBIT	ADJUSTED TRIAL BALANCE CREDIT
1	101	Cash	20,300 00				20,300 00	
2	111	Accounts Receivable	600 00				600 00	
3	121	Supplies	2,000 00			(a)1,250 00	750 00	
4	131	Prepaid Rent	40,000 00			(b)5,000 00	35,000 00	
5	141	Equipment	30,000 00				30,000 00	
6	142	Accumulated Depreciation—Equipment				(c) 500 00		500 00
7	202	Accounts Payable		5,000 00				5,000 00
8	301	John Scott, Capital		80,000 00				80,000 00
9	401	Fees		18,300 00				18,300 00
10	511	Salaries Expense	10,100 00				10,100 00	
11	514	Utilities Expense	300 00				300 00	
12	517	Supplies Expense			(a)1,250 00		1,250 00	
13	520	Rent Expense			(b)5,000 00		5,000 00	
14	523	Depreciation Expense—Equipment			(c) 500 00		500 00	
15		Totals	103,300 00	103,300 00	6,750 00	6,750 00	103,800 00	103,800 00
16								
17								

Refer to the Adjusted Trial Balance section of the partial worksheet shown above. Notice that the balances of the accounts that did not require adjustment have simply been extended to this section from the Trial Balance section. For example, the $20,300 balance of the Cash account that appears in the Debit column of the Trial Balance section was recorded in the Debit column of the Adjusted Trial Balance section without any change.

However, the accountant must recompute the balances of some of the accounts that are affected by adjustments. For example, the Supplies account has a debit balance of $2,000 in the Trial Balance section and shows a credit entry of $1,250 in the Adjustments section. Thus the accountant determines that the updated balance is $750 ($2,000 − $1,250 = $750) and records this amount in the Debit column of the Adjusted Trial Balance section. In a similar manner the accountant finds that Prepaid Rent has an updated balance of $35,000 ($40,000 − $5,000 = $35,000).

When figures must be combined to calculate updated account balances for the adjusted trial balance, the following procedures are used.

1. If an account has a debit balance in the Trial Balance section and there is a debit entry in the Adjustments section, the two amounts are added.
2. If an account has a debit balance in the Trial Balance section and there is a credit entry in the Adjustments section, the credit amount is subtracted.
3. If an account has a credit balance in the Trial Balance section and there is a credit entry in the Adjustments section, the two amounts are added.
4. If an account has a credit balance in the Trial Balance section and there is a debit entry in the Adjustments section, the debit amount is subtracted.

The other accounts affected by adjustments at the Gold Medal Fitness Center (Accumulated Depreciation—Equipment, Supplies Expense, Rent Expense, and Depreciation Expense—Equipment) had no balances when the Trial Balance section of the worksheet was prepared. Thus the accountant just extends the figures shown for these accounts in the Adjustments section to the Adjusted Trial Balance section. For example, the $500 credit entry for Accumulated Depreciation—Equipment in the Adjustments section is recorded as the balance of that account in the Credit column of the Adjusted Trial Balance section.

Once all account balances have been recorded in the Adjusted Trial Balance section, the accountant totals and rules the Debit and Credit columns. Just as with the original trial balance, the adjusted trial balance should have equal debit and credit totals. If these totals are not equal, the accountant must locate the error or errors. It is essential that all figures be correct before they are used to complete the financial statement sections of the worksheet.

The Income Statement and Balance Sheet Sections

The Income Statement and Balance Sheet sections of the worksheet are used to organize the figures needed for these financial reports. For example, in order for the accountant to prepare an income statement, all the revenue and expense account balances must be in one place. It is convenient for the accountant to assemble this information on the worksheet.

The process of completing the financial statement sections is quite simple. Starting at the top of the Adjusted Trial Balance section, the accountant examines each general ledger account in turn. If an account will appear on the balance sheet, the amount is entered in the Balance Sheet section. If an account will appear on the income statement, the amount is entered in the Income Statement section. When amounts are *extended* from the Adjusted Trial Balance section to the statement sections, the accountant must be sure not to enter a debit amount in a credit column or a credit amount in a debit column.

The Balance Sheet Section Remember that the general ledger accounts are numbered according to type in the following sequence: assets, liabilities, owner's equity, revenue, and expenses. The accounts appear on the worksheet in this order. Thus the first five accounts in the Adjusted Trial Balance section of the partial worksheet shown on page 86 are assets. They are extended to the Debit column of the Balance Sheet section. As noted before, the debit amounts continue to appear as debit amounts after they are extended.

The next three accounts in the Adjusted Trial Balance section have credit balances. They are a contra asset account (Accumulated Depreciation—Equipment), a liability account (Accounts Payable), and an owner's equity account (John Scott, Capital). The accountant extends the balances of these accounts to the Credit column of the Balance Sheet section.

GOLD MEDAL FITNESS CENTER
Worksheet (Partial)
Month Ended December 31, 19X5

	ACCT. NO.	ACCOUNT NAME	ADJUSTED TRIAL BALANCE DEBIT	CREDIT	INCOME STATEMENT DEBIT	CREDIT	BALANCE SHEET DEBIT	CREDIT
1	101	Cash	20,300 00				20,300 00	
2	111	Accounts Receivable	600 00				600 00	
3	121	Supplies	750 00				750 00	
4	131	Prepaid Rent	35,000 00				35,000 00	
5	141	Equipment	30,000 00				30,000 00	
6	142	Accumulated Depreciation—Equipment		500 00				500 00
7	202	Accounts Payable		5,000 00				5,000 00
8	301	John Scott, Capital		80,000 00				80,000 00
9	401	Fees		18,300 00		18,300 00		
10	511	Salaries Expense	10,100 00		10,100 00			
11	514	Utilities Expense	300 00		300 00			
12	517	Supplies Expense	1,250 00		1,250 00			
13	520	Rent Expense	5,000 00		5,000 00			
14	523	Depreciation Expense—Equipment	500 00		500 00			
15		Totals	103,800 00	103,800 00	17,150 00	18,300 00	86,650 00	85,500 00
16		Net Income			1,150 00			1,150 00
17					18,300 00	18,300 00	86,650 00	86,650 00
18								
19								

The Income Statement Section All revenue and expense accounts must appear on the income statement. Thus the accountant extends the credit balance of the Fees account to the Credit column of the Income Statement section of the worksheet, as shown above. The last five accounts in the Adjusted Trial Balance section are expense accounts. The accountant extends their debit balances to the Debit column of the Income Statement section.

After all account balances have been transferred from the Adjusted Trial Balance section of the worksheet to the financial statement sections, the accountant totals the Income Statement columns. In the Income Statement columns of the worksheet for the Gold Medal Fitness Center, the debits (expenses) total $17,150 and the credits (revenue) total $18,300.

Next the accountant adds the amounts in the Balance Sheet columns. The debits (assets) total $86,650 and the credits (contra asset, liabilities, and owner's equity) total $85,500. These totals are entered as shown on the partial worksheet above.

Since the Income Statement columns include all revenue and expenses, the totals of these columns are used to determine the net income or net loss. The smaller column total is subtracted from the larger one. In this case the total of the

Credit column ($18,300), which represents the revenue, exceeds the total of the Debit column ($17,150), which represents the expenses. Consequently, there is a net income of $1,150 ($18,300 − $17,150 = $1,150).

The net income causes a net increase in owner's equity as a result of the firm's operations for the month. Thus the amount of net income must be extended to the Balance Sheet section of the worksheet.

The net income is recorded on the worksheet below the total of the Debit column of the Income Statement section and the total of the Credit column of the Balance Sheet section. The words "Net Income" are entered to identify the amount.

After the net income is recorded on the worksheet, the Income Statement and Balance Sheet columns are totaled again. All pairs of columns should then be in balance. The complete worksheet prepared at the Gold Medal Fitness Center on December 31, 19X5, is shown on pages 88 and 89.

If the business had a loss, the accountant would write "Net Loss" on the worksheet and enter the amount in the Credit column of the Income Statement section and the Debit column of the Balance Sheet section.

THE FINANCIAL STATEMENTS

All the figures that the accountant needs to prepare the financial statements are now properly organized on the worksheet. The accounts are even arranged in the order in which they must appear on the income statement and the balance sheet.

The Income Statement

The income statement is prepared directly from the data in the Income Statement section of the worksheet. Compare the income statement for the Gold Medal Fitness Center shown below with the worksheet illustrated on pages 88 and 89.

If the firm had incurred a net loss, the final amount on the income statement would be labeled "Net Loss for the Month."

GOLD MEDAL FITNESS CENTER
Income Statement
Month Ended December 31, 19X5

Revenue		
Fees		18,300 00
Expenses		
Salaries Expense	10,100 00	
Utilities Expense	300 00	
Supplies Expense	1,250 00	
Rent Expense	5,000 00	
Depreciation Expense—Equipment	500 00	
Total Expenses		17,150 00
Net Income for the Month		1,150 00

The Balance Sheet

The accounts listed on the balance sheet are taken directly from the Balance Sheet section of the worksheet. Compare the balance sheet for the Gold Medal Fitness Center given on page 88 with the worksheet on pages 88 and 89.

GOLD MEDAL FITNESS CENTER
Balance Sheet
December 31, 19X5

Assets			
Cash			20,300 00
Accounts Receivable			600 00
Supplies			750 00
Prepaid Rent			35,000 00
Equipment		30,000 00	
Less Accumulated Depreciation		500 00	29,500 00
Total Assets			86,150 00
Liabilities and Owner's Equity			
Liabilities			
Accounts Payable			5,000 00
Owner's Equity			
John Scott, Capital, Dec. 1, 19X5		80,000 00	
Net Income for the Month		1,150 00	
John Scott, Capital, Dec. 31, 19X5			81,150 00
Total Liabilities and Owner's Equity			86,150 00

Notice how the equipment is reported on the balance sheet. Three figures are shown in connection with this item—the original cost of $30,000, the accumulated depreciation of $500, and the book value of $29,500. The book value is computed by subtracting the accumulated depreciation from the original cost. (The book value should not be confused with the market value. The book value is

GOLD MEDAL FITNESS CENTER
Worksheet
Month Ended December 31, 19X5

	ACCT. NO.	ACCOUNT NAME	TRIAL BALANCE DEBIT	TRIAL BALANCE CREDIT	ADJUSTMENTS DEBIT	ADJUSTMENTS CREDIT
1	101	Cash	20,300 00			
2	111	Accounts Receivable	600 00			
3	121	Supplies	2,000 00			(a)1,250 00
4	131	Prepaid Rent	40,000 00			(b)5,000 00
5	141	Equipment	30,000 00			
6	142	Accumulated Depreciation—Equipment				(c) 500 00
7	202	Accounts Payable		5,000 00		
8	301	John Scott, Capital		80,000 00		
9	401	Fees		18,300 00		
10	511	Salaries Expense	10,100 00			
11	514	Utilities Expense	300 00			
12	517	Supplies Expense			(a)1,250 00	
13	520	Rent Expense			(b)5,000 00	
14	523	Depreciation Expense—Equipment			(c) 500 00	
15		Totals	103,300 00	103,300 00	6,750 00	6,750 00
16		Net Income				
17						
18						
19						

simply the portion of the original cost that has not yet been depreciated. The market value may be higher or lower.)

Also notice that the net income for the period ($1,150) is added to Scott's beginning capital ($80,000) in the Owner's Equity section of the balance sheet. The sum of these two figures is Scott's capital at the end of the period ($81,150).

The accountant for the fitness center is now using a type of balance sheet called the *report form*. Unlike the *account form*, which was illustrated previously (see page 26), the report form has the liabilities and owner's equity listed under the assets rather than to the right of them. The report form is widely used because it provides more space for entering account titles and because it is easier to prepare on a typewriter.

JOURNALIZING AND POSTING ADJUSTING ENTRIES

The worksheet is simply a tool that aids the accountant in the preparation of financial statements. Any changes in account balances recorded on the worksheet are not shown in the general journal and the general ledger until the accountant journalizes and posts adjusting entries. The procedure for making adjusting entries in the accounting records is explained in the next chapter.

PRINCIPLES AND PROCEDURES SUMMARY

The trial balance is used to prove the equality of the debits and credits in the general ledger. Accountants must take a trial balance before they prepare the financial statements for a period.

ADJUSTED TRIAL BALANCE		INCOME STATEMENT		BALANCE SHEET		
DEBIT	CREDIT	DEBIT	CREDIT	DEBIT	CREDIT	
20,300 00				20,300 00		1
600 00				600 00		2
750 00				750 00		3
35,000 00				35,000 00		4
30,000 00				30,000 00		5
	500 00				500 00	6
	5,000 00				5,000 00	7
	80,000 00				80,000 00	8
	18,300 00		18,300 00			9
10,100 00		10,100 00				10
300 00		300 00				11
1,250 00		1,250 00				12
5,000 00		5,000 00				13
500 00		500 00				14
103,800 00	103,800 00	17,150 00	18,300 00	86,650 00	85,500 00	15
		1,150 00			1,150 00	16
		18,300 00	18,300 00	86,650 00	86,650 00	17
						18
						19

A worksheet is normally used to save time in preparing the statements. First the trial balance information is recorded on the worksheet. Next any adjustments to account balances are entered. Then an adjusted trial balance is prepared to prove the equality of the debits and credits again. Next the figures needed for the income statement and the balance sheet are organized in the appropriate sections of the worksheet. Then the net income or net loss for the period is determined. Finally the amounts in the Income Statement and Balance Sheet sections of the worksheet are presented in the formal financial reports. After these reports are prepared, the adjustments shown on the worksheet must be recorded in the general journal and the general ledger.

Prepaid expenses are expense items that are acquired and paid for in advance of their use. At the time of their acquisition, these items represent assets and are therefore recorded in asset accounts. As they are used, their cost is transferred to expense by means of adjusting entries at the end of each accounting period.

Depreciation is the process of allocating the cost of a long-term asset to operations over its expected useful life. A portion of the cost of the asset is charged off as an expense at the end of each accounting period during its useful life.

MANAGERIAL IMPLICATIONS

Taking a trial balance helps to pinpoint errors in a firm's accounting records. If serious errors occur repeatedly, management should investigate the reasons. There may be a need to improve the accounting system or to improve the skills or work habits of the employees involved.

The use of a worksheet allows the accountant to prepare financial statements more rapidly. Thus management can obtain necessary information when it is still timely. This information allows management to evaluate the results of operations and the financial position of the business and to make decisions. The more accounts that a firm has in its general ledger, the more useful the worksheet is in speeding up the preparation of the financial statements.

It is important to management that the accountant record appropriate adjustments. Otherwise, the financial statements will not present a complete and accurate picture of the firm's financial affairs.

REVIEW QUESTIONS

1. What is the purpose of the trial balance?
2. If the trial balance shows equal debits and credits, can the accountant be sure that no errors were made in recording transactions? Explain.
3. What are some reasons why a trial balance might not balance?
4. What procedures would an accountant use to locate errors when a trial balance is out of balance?
5. Why is the worksheet prepared?
6. What are adjustments?

7. Why is it necessary to make an adjustment for supplies used?
8. What are prepaid expenses? Give four examples of prepaid expense items.
9. What adjustment would be recorded for expired insurance?
10. What is depreciation?
11. Give three examples of assets that would be subject to depreciation.
12. How does the straight-line method of depreciation work?
13. Why is an accumulated depreciation account used in making the adjustment for depreciation?
14. What is book value?
15. How does a contra asset account differ from a regular asset account?
16. What three amounts are reported for a long-term asset like equipment on the balance sheet?
17. How does a report-form balance sheet differ from an account-form balance sheet?
18. Why is the net income for a period recorded in the Balance Sheet section of the worksheet as well as the Income Statement section?
19. What three amounts appear in the Owner's Equity section of a balance sheet when it is prepared at the end of an accounting period?
20. Why is it necessary to journalize and post adjusting entries even though the data is already recorded on the worksheet?

MANAGERIAL DISCUSSION QUESTIONS

1. How does the worksheet help the accountant to provide management with vital information?
2. Suppose that the president of a company where you work as an accountant questions whether it is really worthwhile for you to spend time making adjustments at the end of each accounting period. How would you explain the value of the adjustments?
3. At the beginning of the current year, the Williams Company purchased a new building and some very expensive new machinery. One of the officers of the firm has asked you whether this is likely to have any effect on the firm's year-end income statement. What answer would you give?
4. A building owned by the Santana Company was recently valued at $350,000 by a real estate expert. The president of the company is questioning the accuracy of the firm's latest balance sheet because it shows a book value of $125,000 for the building. How would you explain this situation to the president?

EXERCISES

EXERCISE 5-1 **Preparing a trial balance.** On June 30, 19X2, the general ledger of the Frosty Air Conditioning Service showed the accounts and balances given on page 92. Prepare a trial balance for the firm. (Assume that every account has the normal debit or credit balance.)

ACCOUNTS

Cash	$8,650	Accounts Payable	$ 1,600
Accounts Receivable	3,100	Frank Nash, Capital	22,650
Supplies	2,500	Fees	5,800
Equipment	7,200	Rent Expense	750
Accum. Depr.—Equip.	1,500	Salaries Expense	2,910
Truck	9,400	Truck Expense	150
Accum. Depr.—Truck	3,200	Telephone Expense	90

EXERCISE 5-2 **Determining the effects of errors on the trial balance.** The following errors occurred in posting amounts from the general journal to the general ledger. Decide whether each error would cause the trial balance to be out of balance or would have no effect on the trial balance.

ERRORS

1. A $650 debit to Cash was posted twice. The credit part of the journal entry was posted only once.
2. A $300 debit to Accounts Receivable was posted to Accounts Payable.
3. A $250 credit to Fees was posted as $520. The debit part of the journal entry was posted correctly as $250.
4. A $1,000 debit to Repairs Expense was posted as $100. The $1,000 credit to Cash in the same journal entry was also posted as $100.
5. A $300 credit to Fees was not posted at all. However, the debit part of the journal entry was posted.
6. A $75 debit to Supplies was posted as a credit. The $75 credit to Cash in the same journal entry was correctly posted as a credit.
7. An entire journal entry, consisting of a $500 debit to Equipment and a $500 credit to Accounts Payable, was not posted.

EXERCISE 5-3 **Determining an adjustment for expired rent.** On May 1, 19X5, the Carlson Company, a new firm, paid $4,800 rent in advance for a six-month period. The accountant debited this sum to the Prepaid Rent account. What adjustment should the accountant record for expired rent on the firm's May 31, 19X5, worksheet?

EXERCISE 5-4 **Determining an adjustment for supplies used.** On May 1, 19X5, the Carlson Company purchased supplies for $950. The accountant debited this sum to the Supplies account. An inventory of supplies at the end of May showed that items costing $510 were on hand. What adjustment should the accountant record for supplies used on the firm's May 31, 19X5, worksheet?

EXERCISE 5-5 **Determining an adjustment for depreciation.** On May 1, 19X5, the Carlson Company purchased some equipment for $6,000. The equipment is expected to have a useful life of five years and no salvage value at the end of that period. The firm will use the straight-line method of depreciation. What adjustment should the accountant record for depreciation on the firm's May 31, 19X5, worksheet?

EXERCISE 5-6   **Determining an adjustment for expired insurance.** On May 1, 19X5, the Carlson Company purchased a two-year insurance policy for $1,440. The accountant debited this sum to the Prepaid Insurance account. What adjustment should the accountant record for expired insurance on the firm's May 31, 19X5, worksheet?

EXERCISE 5-7   **Determining an adjustment for expired advertising.** On May 1, 19X5, the Carlson Company signed a contract with a local radio station for advertising that will extend over a one-year period. The firm paid $960 in advance, and the accountant debited this sum to the Prepaid Advertising account. What adjustment should the accountant record for expired advertising on the firm's May 31, 19X5, worksheet?

EXERCISE 5-8   **Completing the Trial Balance section of a worksheet.** On January 31, 19X3, the general ledger of the Diaz Company showed the following accounts and balances. Prepare the Trial Balance section of the worksheet for this firm. (Assume that every account has the normal debit or credit balance.) The worksheet covers the month of January.

ACCOUNTS

Cash	$ 5,700	Joan Diaz, Capital	$15,760
Accounts Receivable	2,450	Fees	6,100
Supplies	1,800	Rent Expense	600
Prepaid Insurance	2,160	Salaries Expense	2,850
Equipment	12,000	Supplies Expense	-0-
Accum. Depr.—Equip.	4,800	Insurance Expense	-0-
Accounts Payable	900	Depr. Expense—Equip.	-0-

EXERCISE 5-9   **Completing the Adjustments section of a worksheet.** On January 31, 19X5, the accountant for the Diaz Company found that supplies used during the month totaled $740, expired insurance totaled $90, and depreciation totaled $200. Prepare the Adjustments section of the worksheet for this firm.

EXERCISE 5-10   **Completing the Adjusted Trial Balance section of a worksheet.** Refer to your solutions for Exercises 5-8 and 5-9, and use the data to prepare the Adjusted Trial Balance section of the Diaz Company's January 31, 19X3, worksheet.

EXERCISE 5-11   **Completing the Income Statement section of a worksheet.** Refer to your solution for Exercise 5-10, and use the data to prepare the Income Statement section of the Diaz Company's January 31, 19X3, worksheet.

EXERCISE 5-12   **Completing the Balance Sheet section of a worksheet.** Refer to your solutions for Exercises 5-10 and 5-11, and use the data to prepare the Balance Sheet section of the Diaz Company's January 31, 19X3, worksheet.

EXERCISE 5-13   **Preparing an income statement.** Refer to your solution for Exercise 5-11, and use the data to prepare an income statement for the Diaz Company. This income statement should cover the month ended January 31, 19X3.

EXERCISE 5-14   **Preparing a balance sheet.** Refer to your solution for Exercise 5-12, and use the data to prepare a balance sheet for the Diaz Company as of January 31, 19X3.

PROBLEMS

PROBLEM 5-1   **Journalizing, posting, and preparing a trial balance.** Joyce McNab owns and operates Apex Productions, a firm that records radio commercials for clients. On April 1, 19X5, its general ledger had the accounts and balances shown below. During the month of April, the following transactions took place at this firm.

Instructions   1. Set up the general ledger accounts listed below, and enter the April 1 balances. If an account does not have a balance on April 1, simply record the account title and number. (To enter a balance, record the date, write the word "Balance" in the Explanation column, place a check mark in the Post. Ref. column, record the amount in the Balance column, and write "Dr." or "Cr." to identify the type of balance.)
2. Prepare general journal entries to record the April transactions. (Use *4* as the number of the journal page.)
3. Post the journal entries to the general ledger accounts.
4. Prepare a trial balance in the first two columns of a ten-column worksheet. (You can omit the Income Summary account from the trial balance. This account will be explained in Chapter 6 and used in Problem 6-2.)

ACCT. NO.	ACCOUNT NAME	BALANCE
101	Cash	$12,480 Dr.
111	Accounts Receivable	3,500 Dr.
121	Supplies	1,650 Dr.
131	Prepaid Insurance	
141	Equipment	24,000 Dr.
142	Accum. Depr.—Equipment	7,200 Cr.
202	Accounts Payable	2,240 Cr.
301	Joyce McNab, Capital	32,190 Cr.
399	Income Summary	
401	Fees	
511	Rent Expense	
514	Salaries Expense	
517	Telephone Expense	
520	Supplies Expense	
523	Insurance Expense	
526	Depr. Expense—Equipment	

TRANSACTIONS FOR APRIL 19X5

Apr.   1 Issued Check 2356 for $1,200 to pay the monthly rent.
2 Purchased a one-year insurance policy for the business. Issued Check 2357 for $1,680 to pay the entire premium in advance.
5 Issued Check 2358 for $1,240 to pay Wilson Inc., creditor, on account for Invoice 389.

8 Purchased recording tape (supplies) for $580 from Superior Audio Products. Received Invoice 9241, which is payable in 30 days.

14 Sold services for $2,100 in cash.

15 Issued Checks 2359–2361 for $1,640 to pay the semimonthly salaries of the employees.

18 Collected $1,900 from credit clients on account.

22 Sold services for $850 in cash and $4,400 on credit. (Use a compound entry.)

27 Paid the monthly telephone bill of $120 with Check 2362.

29 Sold services for $2,000 on credit.

30 Issued Checks 2363–2365 for $1,640 to pay the semimonthly salaries.

NOTE: Save your working papers for use in Problem 5-2.

PROBLEM 5-2 **Preparing a worksheet and financial statements.** This problem is a continuation of Problem 5-1.

Instructions 1. Record the following adjustments on the worksheet of Apex Productions.
   a. Supplies used during the month, $930.
   b. Expired insurance for the month, $140.
   c. Depreciation for the month, $400.
2. Complete the worksheet.
3. Prepare an income statement for the month ended April 30, 19X5.
4. Prepare a balance sheet as of April 30, 19X5. (Use the report form.)

NOTE: Save your working papers for use in Problem 6-2.

PROBLEM 5-3 **Journalizing, posting, and preparing a trial balance.** Barry Evans, a former professional golfer, has decided to open a school that will provide golf instruction. His chart of accounts is shown below. During June 19X5, the first month of operations, the school had the transactions given on page 96.

Instructions 1. Set up the general ledger accounts listed below.
2. Prepare general journal entries to record the June transactions. (Use *1* as the number of the journal page.)
3. Post the journal entries to the general ledger accounts.
4. Prepare a trial balance for the Evans Golf School in the first two columns of a ten-column worksheet. (You can omit the Income Summary account from the trial balance. This account will be explained in Chapter 6 and used in Problem 6-3.)

ACCOUNTS

101	Cash	399	Income Summary
111	Accounts Receivable	401	Fees
121	Supplies	511	Rent Expense
131	Prepaid Advertising	514	Salaries Expense
141	Equipment	517	Telephone Expense
142	Accum. Depr.—Equipment	520	Supplies Expense
202	Accounts Payable	523	Advertising Expense
301	Barry Evans, Capital	526	Depr. Expense—Equipment

TRANSACTIONS FOR JUNE 19X5

June   1 Barry Evans started the business with a cash investment of $20,000.
        1 Issued Check 1001 for $850 to pay the monthly rent.
        2 Purchased equipment for $6,000 from Delta Products. Received Invoice 9093, payable in 60 days.
        3 Issued Check 1002 for $720 to purchase supplies.
        4 Signed an advertising contract with the local newspaper for a one-year period. Issued Check 1003 for $2,100 to pay the entire amount in advance.
        6 Purchased additional equipment for $1,800. Paid for it immediately by issuing Check 1004.
        9 Performed services for $1,250 on credit.
       15 Issued Checks 1005 and 1006 for $1,100 to pay the semimonthly salaries of the employees.
       17 Performed services for $870 in cash.
       20 Collected $600 on account.
       25 Issued Check 1007 for $85 to pay the monthly telephone bill.
       28 Sent Check 1008 for $3,000 to Delta Products as a payment on account for Invoice 9093.
       29 Performed services for $730 in cash and $550 on credit. (Use a compound entry.)
       30 Issued Checks 1009 and 1010 for $1,100 to pay the semimonthly salaries of the employees.

NOTE: Save your working papers for use in Problem 5-4.

PROBLEM 5-4   **Preparing a worksheet, computing adjustments, and preparing financial statements.** This problem is a continuation of Problem 5-3.

Instructions   1. Prepare the Adjustments section of the worksheet for the Evans Golf School.
        a. Compute and record the adjustment for supplies used during the month. An inventory taken on June 30 showed that supplies costing $570 were on hand.
        b. Compute and record the adjustment for expired advertising for the month. (Calculate the amount on the basis of the full month, not a part of the month.)
        c. Compute and record the adjustment for depreciation for the month. The firm's equipment is estimated to have a useful life of five years and is not expected to have any salvage value. The straight-line method of depreciation will be used. (Calculate the amount of depreciation for June on the basis of the full month, not a part of the month.)
    2. Complete the worksheet.
    3. Prepare an income statement for the month ended June 30, 19X5.
    4. Prepare a balance sheet as of June 30, 19X5. (Use the report form.)

NOTE: Save your working papers for use in Problem 6-3.

Preparing a worksheet, computing adjustments, and preparing financial statements. The Glenview Real Estate Company manages office buildings for property owners. On March 31, 19X4, the firm's general ledger had the accounts and balances shown below.

Instructions

1. Prepare a trial balance in the first two columns of a ten-column worksheet. The worksheet covers the three-month period ended March 31, 19X4.
2. Prepare the Adjustments section of the worksheet.
   a. Compute and record the adjustment for supplies used during the three-month period. An inventory taken on March 31 showed that supplies costing $450 were on hand.
   b. Compute and record the adjustment for expired insurance for the three-month period. On January 2, 19X4, the firm purchased a two-year insurance policy and paid the entire premium of $3,480 in advance.
   c. Compute and record the adjustment for depreciation for the three-month period. The firm's equipment was purchased on January 2, 19X3. At that time the accountant estimated that it would have a useful life of five years. There is no expected salvage value.
3. Complete the worksheet.
4. Prepare an income statement for the three-month period ended March 31, 19X4.
5. Prepare a balance sheet as of March 31, 19X4. (Use the report form.)

ACCT. NO.	ACCOUNT NAME	BALANCE
101	Cash	$11,500 Dr.
111	Accounts Receivable	2,200 Dr.
121	Supplies	1,350 Dr.
131	Prepaid Insurance	3,480 Dr.
141	Equipment	16,800 Dr.
142	Accum. Depr.—Equipment	3,360 Cr.
202	Accounts Payable	1,800 Cr.
301	Marie DeMarco, Capital	13,940 Cr.
401	Fees	46,000 Cr.
511	Rent Expense	4,200 Dr.
514	Salaries Expense	23,600 Dr.
517	Utilities Expense	1,120 Dr.
520	Telephone Expense	850 Dr.
523	Supplies Expense	
526	Insurance Expense	
529	Depr. Expense—Equipment	

ALTERNATE PROBLEMS

PROBLEM 5-1A **Journalizing, posting, and preparing a trial balance.** George Lang owns and operates Omni Pictures, a firm that does commercial photography for advertising agencies. On May 1, 19X7, its general ledger had the accounts and balances shown below. During the month of May the following transactions took place at this firm.

Instructions
1. Set up the general ledger accounts listed below, and enter the May 1 balances. If an account does not have a balance on May 1, simply record the account title and number. (To enter a balance, record the date, write the word "Balance" in the Explanation column, place a check mark in the Post. Ref. column, record the amount in the Balance column, and write "Dr." or "Cr." to identify the type of balance.)
2. Prepare general journal entries to record the May transactions. (Use 5 as the number of the journal page.)
3. Post the journal entries to the general ledger accounts.
4. Prepare a trial balance in the first two columns of a ten-column worksheet. (You can omit the Income Summary account from the trial balance. This account will be explained in Chapter 6 and used in Problem 6-2A.)

ACCT. NO.	ACCOUNT NAME	BALANCE
101	Cash	$10,810 Dr.
111	Accounts Receivable	2,590 Dr.
121	Supplies	1,140 Dr.
131	Prepaid Insurance	
141	Equipment	18,000 Dr.
142	Accum. Depr.—Equipment	4,800 Cr.
202	Accounts Payable	2,400 Cr.
301	George Lang, Capital	25,340 Cr.
399	Income Summary	
401	Fees	
511	Rent Expense	
514	Salaries Expense	
517	Telephone Expense	
520	Supplies Expense	
523	Insurance Expense	
526	Depr. Expense—Equipment	

TRANSACTIONS FOR MAY 19X7

May   1 Issued Check 8921 for $650 to pay the monthly rent.
      2 Sold services for $2,400 on credit.
      4 Purchased a one-year insurance policy for the business. Issued Check 8922 for $1,500 to pay the entire premium in advance.
      9 Collected $890 from credit customers on account.
     12 Purchased film and other supplies for $470 from the Photo Mart. Received Invoice 3710, which is payable in 30 days.
     15 Issued Checks 8923 and 8924 for $1,210 to pay the semimonthly salaries of the employees.
     19 Sold services for $950 in cash.
     24 Issued Check 8925 for $1,400 to pay Howard, Inc., a creditor, for Invoice 631.
     26 Sold services for $500 in cash and $2,100 on credit. (Use a compound entry.)

31 Issued Checks 8926 and 8927 for $1,210 to pay the semimonthly salaries of the employees.

31 Received the monthly telephone bill, and sent Check 8928 for $105 to pay it.

NOTE: Save your working papers for use in Problem 5-2A.

PROBLEM 5-2A

Preparing a worksheet and financial statements. This problem is a continuation of Problem 5-1A.

Instructions

1. Record the following adjustments on the worksheet of Omni Pictures.
   a. Supplies used during the month, $620.
   b. Expired insurance for the month, $125.
   c. Depreciation for the month, $300.
2. Complete the worksheet.
3. Prepare an income statement for the month ended May 31, 19X7.
4. Prepare a balance sheet as of May 31, 19X7. (Use the report form.)

NOTE: Save your working papers for use in Problem 6-2A.

PROBLEM 5-3A

Journalizing, posting, and preparing a trial balance. Carole Wood, a computer programmer, has decided to open a school that will teach business executives how to use microcomputers effectively. Her chart of accounts is shown below. During September 19X7, the first month of operations, the school had the transactions given below and on page 100.

Instructions

1. Set up the general ledger accounts listed below.
2. Prepare general journal entries to record the September transactions. (Use *1* as the number of the journal page.)
3. Post the journal entries to the general ledger accounts.
4. Prepare a trial balance for the Executive Computer School in the first two columns of a ten-column worksheet. (You can omit the Income Summary account from the trial balance. This account will be explained in Chapter 6 and used in Problem 6-3A.)

ACCOUNTS

101	Cash	399	Income Summary
111	Accounts Receivable	401	Fees
121	Supplies	511	Salaries Expense
131	Prepaid Rent	514	Advertising Expense
141	Equipment	517	Telephone Expense
142	Accum. Depr.—Equipment	520	Supplies Expense
202	Accounts Payable	523	Rent Expense
301	Carole Wood, Capital	526	Depr. Expense—Equipment

TRANSACTIONS FOR SEPTEMBER 19X7

Sept. 1 Carole Wood started the business with a cash investment of $45,000.

1 Signed a lease for the necessary facilities for the school. Issued Check 1001 for $7,800 to pay the rent in advance for a six-month period, as specified in the lease.

2 Purchased computers for $22,000 from Micro Products Inc. Received Invoice 4732. Issued Check 1002 for $10,000 as a down payment, and agreed to pay the balance in 60 days. (Use a compound entry.)

3 Issued Check 1003 for $5,000 to purchase desks and chairs.

4 Paid $250 for an advertisement in the business section of the local newspaper to announce the opening of the school. Issued Check 1004.

5 Purchased supplies for $890, and paid for them immediately with Check 1005.

10 Performed services for $1,700 on credit.

15 Issued Checks 1006–1008 for $1,550 to pay the semimonthly salaries of the employees.

19 Performed services for $2,100 in cash.

26 Issued Check 1009 for $600 to pay for some advertisements on the local radio station.

28 Collected $850 on account.

30 Issued Check 1010 for $120 to pay the monthly telephone bill.

30 Performed services for $2,300 in cash.

30 Issued Checks 1011–1013 for $1,550 to pay the semimonthly salaries of the employees.

NOTE: Save your working papers for use in Problem 5-4A.

PROBLEM 5-4A **Preparing a worksheet, computing adjustments, and preparing financial statements.** This problem is a continuation of Problem 5-3A.

Instructions

1. Prepare the Adjustments section of the worksheet for the Executive Computer School.

    a. Compute and record the adjustment for supplies used during the month. An inventory taken on September 30 showed that supplies costing $370 were on hand.

    b. Compute and record the adjustment for expired rent for the month.

    c. Compute and record the adjustment for depreciation for the month. The firm's equipment is estimated to have a useful life of five years and is not expected to have any salvage value. The straight-line method of depreciation will be used. (Calculate the amount of depreciation for September on the basis of the full month, not a part of the month.)

2. Complete the worksheet.

3. Prepare an income statement for the month ended September 30, 19X7.

4. Prepare a balance sheet as of September 30, 19X7. (Use the report form.)

NOTE: Save your working papers for use in Problem 6-3A.

PROBLEM 5-5A **Preparing a worksheet, computing adjustments, and preparing financial statements.** The Northside Animal Hospital is owned and operated by Dr. Peter O'Donnell, a veterinarian. On March 31, 19X3, the hospital's general ledger had the accounts and balances shown on page 101.

Instructions

1. Prepare a trial balance in the first two columns of a ten-column worksheet. The worksheet covers the three-month period ended March 31, 19X3.
2. Prepare the Adjustments section of the worksheet.
   a. Compute and record the adjustment for supplies used during the three-month period. An inventory taken on March 31 showed that supplies costing $800 were on hand.
   b. Compute and record the adjustment for expired insurance for the three-month period. On January 2, 19X3, the hospital purchased a one-year insurance policy and paid the entire premium of $3,120 in advance.
   c. Compute and record the adjustment for depreciation for the three-month period. The hospital's equipment was purchased on January 2, 19X1. At that time the accountant estimated that it would have a useful life of five years. There is no expected salvage value.
3. Complete the worksheet.
4. Prepare an income statement for the three-month period ended March 31, 19X3.
5. Prepare a balance sheet as of March 31, 19X3. (Use the report form.)

ACCT. NO.	ACCOUNT NAME	BALANCE
101	Cash	$ 9,700 Dr.
111	Accounts Receivable	4,200 Dr.
121	Supplies	2,950 Dr.
131	Prepaid Insurance	3,120 Dr.
141	Equipment	33,000 Dr.
142	Accum. Depr.—Equipment	13,200 Cr.
202	Accounts Payable	2,500 Cr.
301	Peter O'Donnell, Capital	19,920 Cr.
401	Fees	37,850 Cr.
511	Rent Expense	4,500 Dr.
514	Salaries Expense	14,000 Dr.
517	Telephone Expense	1,300 Dr.
520	Utilities Expense	700 Dr.
523	Supplies Expense	
526	Insurance Expense	
529	Depr. Expense—Equipment	

6

Once the worksheet and financial statements are completed, the accountant must bring the general ledger up to date by recording the adjusting and closing entries. The purpose of the adjusting entries is to create a permanent record of the adjustments that appear on the worksheet. The closing entries are designed to transfer the results of operations to owner's equity and to prepare the revenue and expense accounts for use in the next period. Since all entries in the general ledger are posted from a journal, the accountant first makes the adjusting and closing entries in the general journal. One final step that the accountant takes at the end of the period is to prepare another trial balance in order to be sure that the general ledger is still in balance.

END-OF-PERIOD PROCEDURES

ADJUSTING ENTRIES

As we discussed in Chapter 5, the worksheet is a tool that helps the accountant to determine the effects of adjustments on account balances and to prepare the financial statements. After the statements are completed, it is necessary to create a permanent record of any changes in account balances that are shown on the worksheet. This is done by recording *adjusting entries* in the general journal and then posting the entries to the general ledger. To see how the process works, let's consider again the financial affairs of the Gold Medal Fitness Center on December 31, 19X5, the end of its first month of operations.

GOLD MEDAL FITNESS CENTER
Worksheet (Partial)
Month Ended December 31, 19X5

	ACCT. NO.	ACCOUNT NAME	TRIAL BALANCE DEBIT	CREDIT	ADJUSTMENTS DEBIT	CREDIT	ADJUSTED TRIAL BALANCE DEBIT	CREDIT
1	101	Cash	20,300 00				20,300 00	
2	111	Accounts Receivable	600 00				600 00	
3	121	Supplies	2,000 00			(a)1,250 00	750 00	
4	131	Prepaid Rent	40,000 00			(b)5,000 00	35,000 00	
5	141	Equipment	30,000 00				30,000 00	
6	142	Accumulated Depreciation—Equipment				(c) 500 00		500 00
7	202	Accounts Payable		5,000 00				5,000 00
8	301	John Scott, Capital		80,000 00				80,000 00
9	401	Fees		18,300 00				18,300 00
10	511	Salaries Expense	10,100 00				10,100 00	
11	514	Utilities Expense	300 00				300 00	
12	517	Supplies Expense			(a)1,250 00		1,250 00	
13	520	Rent Expense			(b)5,000 00		5,000 00	
14	523	Depreciation Expense—Equipment			(c) 500 00		500 00	
15		Totals	103,300 00	103,300 00	6,750 00	6,750 00	103,800 00	103,800 00
16								
17								

When the worksheet for December was prepared, the firm's accountant decided that three adjustments were necessary in order to provide a complete and accurate picture of the fitness center's operating results and financial position. These adjustments were for supplies used, expired rent, and depreciation on the equipment that the business owns. The accountant must now journalize and post each adjustment. The entries are made in the order that the adjustments appear on the worksheet. Thus the accountant begins with the adjustment labeled (a). (Refer to the partial worksheet shown on page 102.)

Adjustment for Supplies Used

The first adjustment listed on the December worksheet involves a debit of $1,250 to Supplies Expense and a credit of $1,250 to the asset account Supplies. This adjustment charges the cost of the supplies used during the month to operations, and it decreases the firm's assets to reflect the amount of supplies actually on hand at the end of the period. The necessary entry in the general journal is shown below.

GENERAL JOURNAL   Page 3

DATE	DESCRIPTION OF ENTRY	POST. REF.	DEBIT	CREDIT
	Adjusting Entries			
19 X5				
Dec. 31	Supplies Expense		1,250 00	
	Supplies			1,250 00
	To record the supplies used during the month.			

Many accountants prefer to separate the adjusting entries from the routine entries that are recorded throughout the accounting period. One common method is to write the heading "Adjusting Entries" in the Description of Entry column of the general journal on the line above the first adjusting entry. This procedure was used by the accountant for the fitness center.

Adjustment for Expired Rent

The second adjustment appearing on the December worksheet involves a debit of $5,000 to Rent Expense and a credit of $5,000 to the asset account Prepaid Rent. Remember that the fitness center paid rent in advance for an eight-month period and therefore gained the right to occupy facilities during the period. At the end of December, after the firm used the facilities for a month, part of that right expired. The adjustment therefore charges the cost of one month's rent to operations, and it decreases the firm's assets. The necessary general journal entry is shown on page 104. (Account numbers appear in this illustration because all the entries have been posted.)

Adjustment for Depreciation

The last adjustment recorded on the December worksheet involves a debit of $500 to Depreciation Expense—Equipment and a credit of $500 to the contra asset account Accumulated Depreciation—Equipment. As we discussed in

Chapter 5, this adjustment charges part of the cost of the equipment to operations and decreases the book value of the equipment. The entry made in the general journal is shown below.

	GENERAL JOURNAL				Page 3
DATE	DESCRIPTION OF ENTRY	POST. REF.	DEBIT	CREDIT	
	Adjusting Entries				
19 X5					
Dec. 31	Supplies Expense	517	1,250 00		
	Supplies	121		1,250 00	
	To record the supplies used during the month.				
31	Rent Expense	520	5,000 00		
	Prepaid Rent	131		5,000 00	
	To record expired rent for the month.				
31	Depr. Expense—Equipment	523	500 00		
	Accum. Depr.—Equipment	142		500 00	
	To record depreciation for the month.				

As soon as all adjusting entries are recorded in the general journal, the accountant posts the data to the general ledger. It is important that the account balances be up to date before the closing entries are made. Refer to the accounts illustrated on pages 108 through 110 to see how the adjusting entries made at the Gold Medal Fitness Center on December 31, 19X5, were posted. Notice that the word "Adjusting" is written in the Explanation column of the accounts to identify these entries.

CLOSING ENTRIES

The next task for the accountant at the end of the period is to record *closing entries*. These entries serve two purposes. They transfer the results of operations (the net income or net loss for the period) to owner's equity, and they reduce the balances of the revenue and expense accounts to zero so that they are ready to receive data for the next period.

The Income Statement section of the worksheet contains the data that the accountant uses to make the closing entries. Refer to the partial worksheet shown on page 105 as you study each closing entry.

The Income Summary Account

A special general ledger account called Income Summary is used to aid in the closing procedure. First the accountant transfers the balances of the revenue and expense accounts to this account. It is credited for the total of the revenue account balances and debited for the total of the expense account balances. Then the accountant transfers the balance of the Income Summary account, which represents the net income or net loss for the period, to the owner's capital account.

GOLD MEDAL FITNESS CENTER
Worksheet (Partial)
Month Ended December 31, 19X5

	ACCT. NO.	ACCOUNT NAME	ADJUSTED TRIAL BALANCE		INCOME STATEMENT		BALANCE SHEET	
			DEBIT	CREDIT	DEBIT	CREDIT	DEBIT	CREDIT
1	101	Cash	20,300 00				20,300 00	
2	111	Accounts Receivable	600 00				600 00	
3	121	Supplies	750 00				750 00	
4	131	Prepaid Rent	35,000 00				35,000 00	
5	141	Equipment	30,000 00				30,000 00	
6	142	Accumulated Depreciation—Equipment		500 00				500 00
7	202	Accounts Payable		5,000 00				5,000 00
8	301	John Scott, Capital		80,000 00				80,000 00
9	401	Fees		18,300 00		18,300 00		
10	511	Salaries Expense	10,100 00		10,100 00			
11	514	Utilities Expense	300 00		300 00			
12	517	Supplies Expense	1,250 00		1,250 00			
13	520	Rent Expense	5,000 00		5,000 00			
14	523	Depreciation Expense—Equipment	500 00		500 00			
15		Totals	103,800 00	103,800 00	17,150 00	18,300 00	86,650 00	85,500 00
16		Net Income			1,150 00			1,150 00
17					18,300 00	18,300 00	86,650 00	86,650 00

As its name implies, the Income Summary account is a device for summarizing the results of operations in the general ledger. It is used only at the end of a period to help with the closing procedure. The transfer of the net income or net loss to the owner's capital account reduces the balance of the Income Summary account to zero, and it remains without a balance until the closing procedure for the next period.

The Income Summary account is classified as a temporary owner's equity account. Other titles sometimes used for this account are Revenue and Expense Summary and Income and Expense Summary.

Transferring Revenue Account Balances

On December 31, 19X5, the worksheet for the Gold Medal Fitness Center shows a credit balance of $18,300 in the Fees account. This balance represents the total revenue for the period. The following general journal entry is now made to close the Fees account.

GENERAL JOURNAL   Page 4

DATE		DESCRIPTION OF ENTRY	POST. REF.	DEBIT	CREDIT
		Closing Entries			
19 X5					
Dec. 31		Fees		18,300 00	
		Income Summary			18,300 00
		To close the revenue account.			

Since the Fees account has a credit balance, it is necessary to debit the account for the same amount in order to close it. The offsetting credit is made to the Income Summary account. The effects of this closing entry are to transfer the total revenue for the period to the Income Summary account and to reduce the balance of the revenue account to zero.

Many accountants prefer to separate the closing entries from other types of journal entries. One common method is to write "Closing Entries" in the Description of Entry column of the general journal on the line above the first closing entry.

Transferring Expense Account Balances

The Income Statement section of the fitness center's worksheet lists five expense accounts and shows that the total of their balances is $17,150. The accountant makes the general journal entry shown on page 107 to close these accounts.

Since the expense accounts have debit balances, it is necessary to credit each account in order to close it. The accountant makes a compound entry in the general journal to accomplish this. The total of the expenses is debited to the Income Summary account, and each expense account is *individually* credited for the amount of its balance. The effects of this closing entry are to transfer the total of the expenses for the period to the Income Summary account and to reduce the balances of the expense accounts to zero.

After the accountant for the fitness center posts the first two closing entries from the general journal to the general ledger, the revenue and expense accounts appear as shown on pages 109 and 110. These accounts have no balances because they have been *closed* to the Income Summary account.

Notice that the accountant has written "Closing" in the Explanation column of the individual revenue and expense accounts to identify clearly the closing entries in the general ledger. Similarly, accountants often make notations in the Explanation column of the Income Summary account to identify entries. For example, all the entries in the Income Summary account shown on page 109 have been identified.

Notice that the Income Summary account now reflects the totals of the Income Statement columns of the worksheet (see page 105). The general journal entry to close the revenue accounts summarized and transferred the data appearing in the Credit column of the Income Statement section. The general journal entry to close the expense accounts summarized and transferred the data appearing in the Debit column of the Income Statement section.

Transferring Net Income or Net Loss to Owner's Equity

The next step in the closing procedure is to transfer the balance of the Income Summary account to the owner's capital account. On December 31, 19X5, the Income Summary account of the Gold Medal Fitness Center had a credit balance of $1,150. This represents the net income for the month (revenue of $18,300 minus expenses of $17,150).

Refer to the worksheet illustrated on page 105. The transfer of net income to owner's equity was shown on the worksheet by entering a pair of counterbalancing figures in the Income Statement Debit column and the Balance Sheet Credit column. An explanatory notation, "Net Income," was written on the worksheet to identify these figures. The accountant now makes an entry in the general journal to record the transfer of the net income, as shown below. This entry involves a debit of $1,150 to the Income Summary account and a credit of $1,150 to John Scott, Capital.

GENERAL JOURNAL   Page 4

DATE	DESCRIPTION OF ENTRY	POST. REF.	DEBIT	CREDIT
	Closing Entries			
19 X5				
Dec. 31	Fees	401	18,300 00	
	Income Summary	399		18,300 00
	To close the revenue account.			
31	Income Summary	399	17,150 00	
	Salaries Expense	511		10,100 00
	Utilities Expense	514		300 00
	Supplies Expense	517		1,250 00
	Rent Expense	520		5,000 00
	Depr. Expense—Equipment	523		500 00
	To close the expense accounts.			
31	Income Summary	399	1,150 00	
	John Scott, Capital	301		1,150 00
	To transfer the net income for the month to the owner's capital account.			

When this entry is posted, the balance of the Income Summary account is reduced to zero and the owner's capital account is increased by the amount of the net income. Refer to the accounts shown on page 109. Notice that the new balance of the John Scott, Capital account agrees with the final amount listed in the Owner's Equity section of the balance sheet for December 31, 19X5.

GOLD MEDAL FITNESS CENTER
Balance Sheet
December 31, 19X5

Assets			
Cash			20,300 00
Accounts Receivable			600 00
Supplies			750 00
Prepaid Rent			35,000 00
Equipment		30,000 00	
Less Accumulated Depreciation		500 00	29,500 00
Total Assets			86,150 00
Liabilities and Owner's Equity			
Liabilities			
Accounts Payable			5,000 00
Owner's Equity			
John Scott, Capital, Dec. 1, 19X5		80,000 00	
Net Income for the Month		1,150 00	
John Scott, Capital, Dec. 31, 19X5			81,150 00
Total Liabilities and Owner's Equity			86,150 00

All the changes resulting from operations during the period are now reflected in the general ledger accounts given below and on pages 109 and 110.

Cash — No. 101

DATE		EXPLANATION	POST. REF.	DEBIT	CREDIT	BALANCE	DR. CR.
19 X5							
Nov.	6		J1	80,000 00		80,000 00	Dr.
	7		J1		40,000 00	40,000 00	Dr.
	9		J1		20,000 00	20,000 00	Dr.
	28		J1		2,000 00	18,000 00	Dr.
	30		J1		5,000 00	13,000 00	Dr.
Dec.	31		J2	12,200 00		25,200 00	Dr.
	31		J2	5,500 00		30,700 00	Dr.
	31		J2		10,100 00	20,600 00	Dr.
	31		J2		300 00	20,300 00	Dr.

Accounts Receivable — No. 111

DATE		EXPLANATION	POST. REF.	DEBIT	CREDIT	BALANCE	DR. CR.
19 X5							
Dec.	31		J2	6,100 00		6,100 00	Dr.
	31		J2		5,500 00	600 00	Dr.

Supplies — No. 121

DATE		EXPLANATION	POST. REF.	DEBIT	CREDIT	BALANCE	DR. CR.
19 X5							
Nov.	28		J1	2,000 00		2,000 00	Dr.
Dec.	31	Adjusting	J3		1,250 00	750 00	Dr.

Prepaid Rent — No. 131

DATE		EXPLANATION	POST. REF.	DEBIT	CREDIT	BALANCE	DR. CR.
19 X5							
Nov.	7		J1	40,000 00		40,000 00	Dr.
Dec.	31	Adjusting	J3		5,000 00	35,000 00	Dr.

Equipment — No. 141

DATE		EXPLANATION	POST. REF.	DEBIT	CREDIT	BALANCE	DR. CR.
19 X5							
Nov.	9		J1	20,000 00		20,000 00	Dr.
	10		J1	10,000 00		30,000 00	Dr.

Accumulated Depreciation—Equipment No. 142

DATE	EXPLANATION	POST. REF.	DEBIT	CREDIT	BALANCE	DR. CR.
19 X5 Dec. 31	Adjusting	J3		500 00	500 00	Cr.

Accounts Payable No. 202

DATE	EXPLANATION	POST. REF.	DEBIT	CREDIT	BALANCE	DR. CR.
19 X5 Nov. 10		J1		10,000 00	10,000 00	Cr.
30		J1	5,000 00		5,000 00	Cr.

John Scott, Capital No. 301

DATE	EXPLANATION	POST. REF.	DEBIT	CREDIT	BALANCE	DR. CR.
19 X5 Nov. 6		J1		80,000 00	80,000 00	Cr.
Dec. 31	Net Income	J4		1,150 00	81,150 00	Cr.

Income Summary No. 399

DATE	EXPLANATION	POST. REF.	DEBIT	CREDIT	BALANCE	DR. CR.
19 X5 Dec. 31	Revenue	J4		18,300 00	18,300 00	Cr.
31	Expenses	J4	17,150 00		1,150 00	Cr.
31	Net Income	J4	1,150 00		–0–	

Fees No. 401

DATE	EXPLANATION	POST. REF.	DEBIT	CREDIT	BALANCE	DR. CR.
19 X5 Dec. 31		J2		12,200 00	12,200 00	Cr.
31		J2		6,100 00	18,300 00	Cr.
31	Closing	J4	18,300 00		–0–	

Salaries Expense No. 511

DATE	EXPLANATION	POST. REF.	DEBIT	CREDIT	BALANCE	DR. CR.
19 X5 Dec. 31		J2	10,100 00		10,100 00	Dr.
31	Closing	J4		10,100 00	–0–	

Utilities Expense
No. 514

DATE	EXPLANATION	POST. REF.	DEBIT	CREDIT	BALANCE	DR. CR.
19 X5 Dec. 31		J2	300 00		300 00	Dr.
31	Closing	J4		300 00	–0–	

Supplies Expense
No. 517

DATE	EXPLANATION	POST. REF.	DEBIT	CREDIT	BALANCE	DR. CR.
19 X5 Dec. 31	Adjusting	J3	1,250 00		1,250 00	Dr.
31	Closing	J4		1,250 00	–0–	

Rent Expense
No. 520

DATE	EXPLANATION	POST. REF.	DEBIT	CREDIT	BALANCE	DR. CR.
19 X5 Dec. 31	Adjusting	J3	5,000 00		5,000 00	Dr.
31	Closing	J4		5,000 00	–0–	

Depreciation Expense—Equipment
No. 523

DATE	EXPLANATION	POST. REF.	DEBIT	CREDIT	BALANCE	DR. CR.
19 X5 Dec. 31	Adjusting	J3	500 00		500 00	Dr.
31	Closing	J4		500 00	–0–	

The example given in this chapter shows the closing process at the end of one month for illustrative purposes. Normally, closing takes place only at the end of the fiscal year.

THE POSTCLOSING TRIAL BALANCE

The accountant wants to avoid having mistakes in the general ledger at the start of the new period. These mistakes may arise from errors made in recording the adjusting and closing entries. If such errors should occur, the general ledger will not balance at the end of the new period and it might be very time-consuming to find the errors. For this reason the accountant prepares a *postclosing trial balance*, or *after-closing trial balance*, as the last step in the end-of-period routine.

Only the accounts with balances are listed on a postclosing trial balance. These are the accounts that remain open at the end of the period—the asset, liability, and owner's capital accounts. If the postclosing trial balance totals are equal, the accountant can safely proceed with the recording of entries for the new period. The postclosing trial balance prepared for the Gold Medal Fitness Center on December 31, 19X5, is shown below.

GOLD MEDAL FITNESS CENTER
Postclosing Trial Balance
December 31, 19X5

ACCT. NO.	ACCOUNT NAME	DEBIT	CREDIT
101	Cash	20,300 00	
111	Accounts Receivable	600 00	
121	Supplies	750 00	
131	Prepaid Rent	35,000 00	
141	Equipment	30,000 00	
142	Accumulated Depreciation—Equipment		500 00
202	Accounts Payable		5,000 00
301	John Scott, Capital		81,150 00
	Totals	86,650 00	86,650 00

Finding and Correcting Errors

The postclosing trial balance, like the trial balance, indicates the existence of certain types of errors in the accounting records. But even if an error is detected, the accountant still must determine where it was made and take steps to correct it. The audit trail aids the accountant in tracing data through the firm's accounting records in order to find errors. Refer to page 78 of Chapter 5 for a discussion of some of the more common errors in accounting records and how they are found and corrected.

THE ACCOUNTING CYCLE

The *accounting cycle* is a series of steps performed during each fiscal period to classify, record, and summarize financial data for a business and produce needed financial information. You learned about the entire accounting cycle as you studied the financial affairs of the Gold Medal Fitness Center during the first month of its operations. The steps of the cycle are listed below.

1. *Analyze transactions*. The data about transactions appears on a variety of source documents—sales slips, purchase invoices, credit memorandums, check stubs, and so on. The accountant must examine the source documents and analyze the data in order to determine the effects of the transactions.
2. *Journalize the data about transactions*. The accountant records the effects of the transactions in one or more journals.
3. *Post the data about transactions*. The accountant transfers the data about transactions from the journal entries to the accounts in one or more ledgers.
4. *Prepare a worksheet*. At the end of each period of operations, the accountant prepares a worksheet. The Trial Balance section of the worksheet is used to prove the equality of the debits and credits in the general ledger. The Adjustments section is used to enter any changes in account balances that may be necessary at the end of the period in order to present a more accurate and complete picture of the firm's financial affairs. The Adjusted Trial Balance section provides a check on the equality of the debits and credits after the

adjustments are combined with the original account balances. The Income Statement and Balance Sheet sections allow the accountant to arrange the data needed for the financial statements in an orderly manner so that the statements can be prepared quickly.

5. *Prepare financial statements*. The accountant prepares financial statements in order to report information to owners, managers, and other interested parties. The income statement shows the results of operations for the period, and the balance sheet shows the financial position of the business as of the end of the period.

6. *Record adjusting entries*. The accountant journalizes and posts adjusting entries in order to create a permanent record of the changes in account balances made on the worksheet when the adjustments for the period were determined.

7. *Record closing entries*. The accountant journalizes and posts closing entries in order to transfer the results of operations to owner's equity and to prepare the revenue and expense accounts for use in the next period. The closing entries reduce the balances of the revenue and expense accounts to zero.

8. *Prepare a postclosing trial balance*. The accountant takes another trial balance to make sure that the general ledger is in balance after the adjusting and closing entries are posted.

9. *Interpret the financial information*. The accountant, owners, managers, and other interested parties must interpret the information shown on the financial statements and other less formal financial reports that may be prepared during the accounting cycle.

The various steps of the accounting cycle are summarized below.

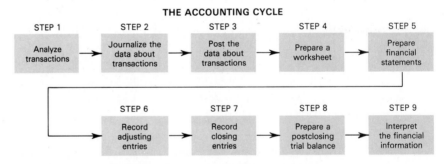

THE ACCOUNTING CYCLE

STEP 1	STEP 2	STEP 3	STEP 4	STEP 5
Analyze transactions	Journalize the data about transactions	Post the data about transactions	Prepare a worksheet	Prepare financial statements

STEP 6	STEP 7	STEP 8	STEP 9
Record adjusting entries	Record closing entries	Prepare a postclosing trial balance	Interpret the financial information

After studying the accounting cycle of the Gold Medal Fitness Center, you have an understanding of how data flows through a simple accounting system for a small business. The data comes into the system by means of source documents; is recorded in the general journal; is posted to the general ledger; is proved, adjusted, and summarized on the worksheet; and is then reported on financial statements. This flow of data is illustrated in the chart shown below.

THE FLOW OF DATA THROUGH A SIMPLE ACCOUNTING SYSTEM

Source Documents → General Journal → General Ledger → Worksheet → Financial Statements

In succeeding chapters of this book, you will become familiar with accounting systems that have more complex records, procedures, and financial statements. However, keep in mind that the steps of the accounting cycle remain the same and the underlying accounting principles also remain the same.

PRINCIPLES AND PROCEDURES SUMMARY

After the worksheet and financial statements are completed, the accountant records adjusting and closing entries and prepares a postclosing trial balance. The Adjustments section of the worksheet provides the data needed for the adjusting entries. Once these entries are journalized and posted, the balances in the general ledger accounts will agree with the figures shown on the worksheet and the financial statements.

The data for the closing entries is taken from the Income Statement section of the worksheet. A special temporary owner's equity account called Income Summary is used in the closing procedure. The balances of the revenue and expense accounts are transferred to this account. Then the balance of the Income Summary account, which represents the net income or net loss for the period, is transferred to the owner's capital account. After the closing entries are posted, the capital account reflects the results of operations for the period and the revenue and expense accounts have zero balances. Thus the revenue and expense accounts are ready to accumulate data for the next period.

A postclosing trial balance is prepared to test the equality of the debit and credit balances in the general ledger after the adjusting and closing entries have been recorded. The postclosing trial balance lists only the accounts that remain open at the end of the period—the asset, liability, and owner's capital accounts.

The accounting cycle consists of a series of steps that are repeated in each fiscal period. These steps are designed to classify, record, and summarize financial data for a business and produce needed financial information.

MANAGERIAL IMPLICATIONS

Management must have timely and accurate financial information in order to control operations and make decisions. Such information can only come from a well-designed and well-run accounting system. Although management is not involved in the details of day-to-day accounting procedures or end-of-period accounting procedures, the efficiency of these procedures has a major effect on the quality and promptness of the financial information that management receives.

REVIEW QUESTIONS

1. What three procedures are performed at the end of each accounting period?
2. Why is it necessary to journalize and post adjusting entries?
3. Where does the accountant obtain the data needed for the adjusting entries?

4. Why does the accountant record closing entries at the end of a period?
5. How is the Income Summary account used in the closing procedure?
6. Where does the accountant obtain the data needed for the closing entries?
7. Why is a postclosing trial balance prepared?
8. What accounts appear on a postclosing trial balance?
9. What is the accounting cycle?
10. Name the steps of the accounting cycle.
11. Briefly describe the flow of data through a simple accounting system.

MANAGERIAL DISCUSSION QUESTIONS

1. Why is it important that a firm's financial records be kept up to date and that management receive the financial statements promptly after the end of each accounting period?
2. What kinds of operating and general policy decisions might be influenced by data on the financial statements?
3. An officer of the Shaw Company recently commented that when he receives the firm's financial statements, he looks at just the bottom line of the income statement—the line that shows the net income or net loss for the period. He said that he does not bother with the rest of the income statement because "it's only the bottom line that counts." He also does not read the balance sheet. Do you think that this manager is correct in the way he uses the financial statements? Why or why not?
4. The president of the Wilson Company is concerned about the firm's ability to pay its debts on time. What items on the balance sheet would help her to assess the firm's debt-paying ability?

EXERCISES

EXERCISE 6-1   **Identifying the accounts to be used in recording transactions.** The transactions given on page 115 took place at the Crossroads Car Wash during June 19X4, its first month of operations. Give the numbers of the accounts to be debited and credited to record each transaction.

ACCOUNTS

101	Cash	401	Fees
121	Supplies	511	Rent Expense
131	Prepaid Insurance	514	Salaries Expense
134	Prepaid Advertising	517	Utilities Expense
141	Equipment	520	Supplies Expense
142	Accum. Depr.—Equip.	523	Insurance Expense
202	Accounts Payable	526	Advertising Expense
301	Joseph Rossi, Capital	529	Depr. Expense—Equip.
399	Income Summary		

TRANSACTIONS

1. Joseph Rossi started the business with a cash investment.
2. Issued a check to pay the monthly rent.
3. Purchased equipment. Issued a check for half the amount as a down payment and agreed to pay the other half in 90 days.
4. Purchased a one-year insurance policy for the business. Issued a check to pay the full amount in advance.
5. Issued a check to purchase supplies.
6. Signed a one-year advertising contract with the local radio station. Issued a check to pay the entire cost in advance.
7. Issued a check to pay the monthly utility bill.
8. Sold services for cash during the month.
9. Issued checks to the employees for their monthly salaries.

EXERCISE 6-2 **Identifying the accounts to be used to make adjusting entries.** At the end of June 19X4, the accountant for the Crossroads Car Wash determined that the following adjusting entries were necessary. Give the numbers of the accounts that should be debited and credited in each of these entries. Use the accounts shown in Exercise 6-1.

ADJUSTING ENTRIES

1. An entry for supplies used.
2. An entry for expired insurance.
3. An entry for expired advertising.
4. An entry for depreciation on the equipment.

EXERCISE 6-3 **Identifying the accounts to be used to make closing entries.** The necessary closing entries for the Crossroads Car Wash at the end of June 19X4 are listed below. Give the numbers of the accounts that should be debited and credited in each of these entries. Use the accounts shown in Exercise 6-1.

CLOSING ENTRIES

1. An entry to close the revenue account.
2. An entry to close the expense accounts.
3. An entry to transfer the net income for the period to owner's equity.

EXERCISE 6-4 **Journalizing an adjusting entry for supplies used.** The worksheet for the Fitzgerald Company shows that it used supplies amounting to $580 during the month of January 19X1. Prepare the adjusting entry for this item that would appear in the firm's general journal.

EXERCISE 6-5 **Journalizing an adjusting entry for expired insurance.** The worksheet of the Fitzgerald Company shows that it had expired insurance of $125 for the month of January 19X1. Prepare the adjusting entry for this item that would appear in the firm's general journal.

EXERCISE 6-6   **Journalizing an adjusting entry for depreciation on trucks.** The worksheet of the Fitzgerald Company shows that it had depreciation of $600 on its trucks for the month of January 19X1. Prepare the adjusting entry for this item that would appear in the firm's general journal.

EXERCISE 6-7   **Journalizing an adjusting entry for depreciation on equipment.** The worksheet of the Fitzgerald Company shows that it had depreciation of $410 on its equipment for the month of January 19X1. Prepare the adjusting entry for this item that would appear in the firm's general journal.

EXERCISE 6-8   **Journalizing an entry to close a revenue account.** The data given below is from the Income Statement section of the worksheet for the Johnson Company. This worksheet covers the month ended March 31, 19X5. Prepare the general journal entry to close the revenue account.

INCOME STATEMENT

ACCOUNT NAME	DEBIT	CREDIT
Fees		$5,800
Rent Expense	$1,000	
Salaries Expense	2,100	
Utilities Expense	190	
Telephone Expense	100	
Supplies Expense	430	
Insurance Expense	160	
Depr. Expense—Equipment	320	
Totals	$4,300	$5,800

EXERCISE 6-9   **Journalizing an entry to close expense accounts.** Refer to the data for the Johnson Company provided in Exercise 6-8. Prepare the general journal entry to close the expense accounts.

EXERCISE 6-10   **Journalizing an entry to transfer net income to owner's equity.** Refer to the data for the Johnson Company provided in Exercise 6-8. Prepare the general journal entry to transfer the net income for the period to owner's equity. (The owner of the business is Laura Johnson.)

EXERCISE 6-11   **Identifying items on the financial statements.** Managers often consult financial statements for specific types of information. Indicate whether each of the following items of information would appear on the income statement or the balance sheet or on both reports. Use *I* for the income statement and *B* for the balance sheet.

1. The cash on hand.
2. The revenue earned during the period.
3. The total assets of the business.
4. The net income for the period.

5. The owner's capital at the end of the period.
6. The supplies on hand.
7. The cost of supplies used during the period.
8. The accounts receivable of the business.
9. The accumulated depreciation on the firm's equipment.
10. The amount of depreciation charged off on the firm's equipment during the period.
11. The original cost of the firm's equipment.
12. The book value of the firm's equipment.
13. The total expenses for the period.
14. The accounts payable of the business.

PROBLEMS

PROBLEM 6-1 **Journalizing the adjusting and closing entries.** The Peters Market Research Agency, owned by Ruth Peters, is employed by large companies to test customer reactions to their products. On January 31, 19X2, the firm's worksheet showed the data about adjustments given below. The balances of the revenue and expense accounts listed in the Income Statement section of the worksheet also appear below.

Instructions
1. Record adjusting entries in the general journal. (Use account titles similar to those illustrated in the text.)
2. Record closing entries in the general journal. (You will need to compute the amount of net income to transfer to owner's equity.)

ADJUSTMENTS

a. Supplies used, $140
b. Expired rent, $750
c. Depreciation on office equipment, $280

REVENUE AND EXPENSE ACCOUNTS

401	Fees	$19,250 Cr.
511	Salaries Expense	10,300 Dr.
514	Utilities Expense	115 Dr.
517	Telephone Expense	235 Dr.
520	Travel Expense	2,230 Dr.
523	Supplies Expense	140 Dr.
526	Rent Expense	750 Dr.
529	Depr. Expense—Office Equipment	280 Dr.

PROBLEM 6-2 **Journalizing and posting the adjusting and closing entries; preparing a post-closing trial balance.** This problem is a continuation of Problems 5-1 and 5-2. It involves end-of-period activities for Apex Productions, a firm that prepares radio commercials for clients.

Instructions 1. Using data from the firm's worksheet, record adjusting entries in the general journal.
2. Post the adjusting entries to the general ledger accounts.
3. Using data from the firm's worksheet, record closing entries in the general journal.
4. Post the closing entries to the general ledger accounts.
5. Prepare a postclosing trial balance as of April 30, 19X5.

PROBLEM 6-3 **Journalizing and posting the adjusting and closing entries; preparing a post-closing trial balance.** This problem is a continuation of Problems 5-3 and 5-4. It involves end-of-period activities for the Evans Golf School.

Instructions 1. Using data from the firm's worksheet, record adjusting entries in the general journal.
2. Post the adjusting entries to the general ledger accounts.
3. Using data from the firm's worksheet, record closing entries in the general journal.
4. Post the closing entries to the general ledger accounts.
5. Prepare a postclosing trial balance as of June 30, 19X5.

PROBLEM 6-4 **Journalizing and posting transactions, preparing a worksheet, and preparing financial statements.** On March 1, 19X6, Gary Roth, a professional musician, started the Good Times Band, a group that will play at weddings, dances, and other social functions. His chart of accounts is shown on page 119, along with the transactions that took place during March.

Instructions 1. Open the general ledger accounts.
2. Record the March transactions in the general journal.
3. Post the journal entries to the general ledger accounts.
4. Prepare a trial balance in the first two columns of a ten-column worksheet.
5. Prepare the Adjustments section of the worksheet.
   a. Compute and record the adjustment for expired insurance. (Assume that a full month of coverage has expired.)
   b. Compute and record the adjustment for depreciation on the equipment. The accountant estimates that the equipment will have a useful life of five years and no salvage value. (Take a full month of depreciation for March.)
   c. Compute and record the adjustment for depreciation on the van. The accountant estimates that the van will have a useful life of three years and a salvage value of $2,000. (In order to compute the total amount of depreciation for the three-year period, subtract the salvage value from the original cost. Take a full month of depreciation for March.)
6. Complete the worksheet.
7. Prepare an income statement for the month ended March 31, 19X6.
8. Prepare a balance sheet as of March 31, 19X6. (Use the report form.)

ACCOUNTS

101	Cash	399	Income Summary
111	Accounts Receivable	401	Fees
121	Prepaid Insurance	511	Rent Expense
131	Equipment	514	Telephone Expense
132	Accum. Depr.—Equipment	517	Salaries Expense
141	Van	520	Advertising Expense
142	Accum. Depr.—Van	523	Insurance Expense
202	Accounts Payable	526	Depr. Expense—Equipment
301	Gary Roth, Capital	529	Depr. Expense—Van

TRANSACTIONS FOR MARCH 19X6

Mar. 1 Gary Roth began the business with a cash investment of $35,000.

1 Issued Check 1001 for $500 to pay the monthly rent.

2 Purchased sound equipment for $6,000. Issued Check 1002 to pay for it immediately.

3 Purchased a van to transport the sound equipment and instruments. (The musicians will use their own instruments.) The total cost of the van is $11,000. Issued Check 1003 for $5,500 as a down payment and agreed to pay the balance in 60 days. Received Invoice 981 from Allen Motors. (Use a compound entry.)

5 Purchased a one-year insurance policy for $1,560. Issued Check 1004 to pay the full amount in advance.

8 Issued Check 1005 for $320 for advertisements that will run in the local newspaper during March.

15 Issued Checks 1006–1013 for $5,100 to pay the semimonthly salaries of the employees.

22 Paid the monthly telephone bill of $80 by means of Check 1014.

27 Issued Check 1015 for $1,500 as a payment on account to Allen Motors for Invoice 981.

31 Performed services for $4,140 in cash and $8,650 on credit during March. (Use a compound entry.)

31 Issued Checks 1016–1023 for $5,100 to pay the semimonthly salaries of the employees.

NOTE: Save your working papers for use in Problem 6-5.

PROBLEM 6-5   **Journalizing and posting the adjusting and closing entries; preparing a post-closing trial balance.** This problem is a continuation of Problem 6-4.

Instructions   1. Record adjusting entries in the general journal.

2. Post the adjusting entries to the general ledger accounts.

3. Record closing entries in the general journal.

4. Post the closing entries to the general ledger accounts.

5. Prepare a postclosing trial balance for the Good Times Band as of March 31, 19X6.

ALTERNATE PROBLEMS

PROBLEM 6-1A

Journalizing the adjusting and closing entries. The Sanitex Commercial Laundry, owned by Thomas Wayne, provides service to hotels, motels, and hospitals. On January 31, 19X6, the firm's worksheet showed the data about adjustments given below. The balances of the revenue and expense accounts listed in the Income Statement section of the worksheet also appear below.

Instructions

1. Record adjusting entries in the general journal. (Use account titles similar to those illustrated in the text.)
2. Record closing entries in the general journal. (You will need to compute the amount of net income to transfer to owner's equity.)

ADJUSTMENTS

a. Supplies used, $1,430
b. Expired insurance, $185
c. Depreciation on machines, $560

REVENUE AND EXPENSE ACCOUNTS

401	Fees	$16,400 Cr.
511	Rent Expense	1,500 Dr.
514	Salaries Expense	8,000 Dr.
517	Utilities Expense	320 Dr.
520	Telephone Expense	105 Dr.
523	Supplies Expense	1,430 Dr.
526	Insurance Expense	185 Dr.
529	Depr. Expense—Machines	560 Dr.

PROBLEM 6-2A

Journalizing and posting the adjusting and closing entries; preparing a postclosing trial balance. This problem is a continuation of Problems 5-1A and 5-2A. It involves end-of-period activities for Omni Pictures, a firm that does commercial photography for advertising agencies.

Instructions

1. Using data from the firm's worksheet, record adjusting entries in the general journal.
2. Post the adjusting entries to the general ledger accounts.
3. Using data from the firm's worksheet, record closing entries in the general journal.
4. Post the closing entries to the general ledger accounts.
5. Prepare a postclosing trial balance as of May 31, 19X7.

PROBLEM 6-3A

Journalizing and posting the adjusting and closing entries; preparing a postclosing trial balance. This problem is a continuation of Problems 5-3A and 5-4A. It involves end-of-period activities for the Executive Computer School.

Instructions

1. Using data from the firm's worksheet, record adjusting entries in the general journal.

2. Post the adjusting entries to the general ledger accounts.
3. Using data from the firm's worksheet, record closing entries in the general journal.
4. Post the closing entries to the general ledger accounts.
5. Prepare a postclosing trial balance as of September 30, 19X7.

PROBLEM 6-4A **Journalizing and posting transactions, preparing a worksheet, and preparing financial statements.** On July 1, 19X8, Craig Miller started the Miller Auto Customizing Service, a firm that will rebuild cars and vans to give them custom features. His chart of accounts is shown below, along with the transactions that took place during July.

Instructions
1. Open the general ledger accounts.
2. Record the July transactions in the general journal.
3. Post the journal entries to the general ledger accounts.
4. Prepare a trial balance in the first two columns of a ten-column worksheet.
5. Prepare the Adjustments section of the worksheet.
   a. Compute and record the adjustment for supplies used. A count made on July 31 showed that supplies costing $700 were on hand.
   b. Compute and record the adjustment for expired rent.
   c. Compute and record the adjustment for expired advertising.
   d. Compute and record the adjustment for depreciation on the equipment. The accountant estimates that the equipment will have a useful life of five years and a salvage value of $1,000. (In order to compute the total amount of depreciation for the five-year period, subtract the salvage value from the original cost. Take a full month of depreciation for July.)
6. Complete the worksheet.
7. Prepare an income statement for the month ended July 31, 19X8.
8. Prepare a balance sheet as of July 31, 19X8. (Use the report form.)

ACCOUNTS

101	Cash	399	Income Summary
111	Accounts Receivable	401	Fees
121	Supplies	511	Salaries Expense
131	Prepaid Rent	514	Utilities Expense
134	Prepaid Advertising	517	Telephone Expense
141	Equipment	520	Supplies Expense
142	Accum. Depr.—Equipment	523	Rent Expense
202	Accounts Payable	526	Advertising Expense
301	Craig Miller, Capital	529	Depr. Expense—Equipment

TRANSACTIONS FOR JULY 19X8

July 1 Craig Miller began the business with a cash investment of $27,000.
     1 Signed a lease for facilities. Issued Check 1001 for $4,800 to pay the rent in advance for six months, as specified in the lease.
     1 Purchased equipment for $3,500. Issued Check 1002 to pay for it immediately.

1 Signed a one-year advertising contract with the local newspaper. Issued Check 1003 for $1,920 to pay the full amount in advance.

4 Purchased supplies for $1,450. Paid for them with Check 1004.

6 Purchased additional equipment for $4,100 from the Lane Company. Received Invoice 5723, payable in 30 days.

15 Issued Checks 1005 and 1006 for $1,200 to pay the semimonthly salaries of the employees.

22 Sent Check 1007 for $75 to pay the monthly telephone bill.

31 Performed services for $2,400 in cash and $3,855 on credit during July.

31 Received the monthly utility bill, which totaled $160. Paid it with Check 1008.

31 Issued Checks 1009 and 1010 for $1,200 to pay the semimonthly salaries of the employees.

NOTE: Save your working papers for use in Problem 6-5A.

PROBLEM 6-5A **Journalizing and posting the adjusting and closing entries; preparing a postclosing trial balance.** This problem is a continuation of Problem 6-4A.

Instructions
1. Record adjusting entries in the general journal.
2. Post the adjusting entries to the general ledger accounts.
3. Record closing entries in the general journal.
4. Post the closing entries to the general ledger accounts.
5. Prepare a postclosing trial balance for the Miller Auto Customizing Service as of July 31, 19X8.

This project will give you an opportunity to apply your knowledge of accounting principles and procedures by handling all the accounting work of the Gold Medal Fitness Center for the month of January 19X6. Assume that you are now the accountant for this firm.

SERVICE BUSINESS ACCOUNTING CYCLE

INTRODUCTION

During January 19X6 the business will use the same records and procedures that you learned about in Chapters 2 through 6. However, the chart of accounts has been expanded as shown below.

GOLD MEDAL FITNESS CENTER
Chart of Accounts

ASSETS		REVENUE	
101	Cash	401	Fees
111	Accounts Receivable		
121	Supplies		EXPENSES
131	Prepaid Rent		
134	Prepaid Insurance	511	Salaries Expense
141	Equipment	514	Utilities Expense
142	Accum. Depr.—Equipment	517	Supplies Expense
		520	Rent Expense
LIABILITIES		523	Depr. Expense—Equipment
		526	Insurance Expense
202	Accounts Payable	529	Advertising Expense
		532	Telephone Expense
OWNER'S EQUITY		535	Maintenance Expense
301	John Scott, Capital		
399	Income Summary		

The transactions for January 19X6 are on pages 124 and 125. Follow the instructions given below and on page 124 in order to complete the project.

INSTRUCTIONS

1. Open the general ledger accounts, and enter the balances for January 1, 19X6. Obtain the necessary figures from the postclosing trial balance prepared on December 31, 19X5, which appears on page 111.

2. Analyze the transactions, and then record them in the general journal. (Use *1* as the number of the first journal page.)
3. Post the transactions to the general ledger accounts.
4. Prepare a trial balance in the first two columns of a ten-column worksheet.
5. Prepare the Adjustments section of the worksheet.
   a. Compute and record the adjustment for supplies used during the month. An inventory taken on January 31 showed that supplies costing $900 were still on hand.
   b. Record the adjustment for expired rent of $5,000 for the month.
   c. Compute and record the adjustment for expired insurance for the month.
   d. Record the adjustment for depreciation of $500 on the equipment for the month.
6. Complete the worksheet.
7. Prepare an income statement for the month ended January 31, 19X6.
8. Prepare a balance sheet as of January 31, 19X6. (Use the report form.)
9. Journalize and post the adjusting entries.
10. Journalize and post the closing entries.
11. Prepare a postclosing trial balance.
12. Interpret the financial information.
    a. Compare the January income statement that you prepared with the December income statement shown on page 87. What changes occurred in total revenue, total expenses, and net income? Did the firm achieve better operating results in January? Explain your answer.
    b. Compare the January 31 balance sheet that you prepared with the December 31 balance sheet shown on page 88. What changes occurred in the total assets, the liabilities, and the owner's ending capital? What changes occurred in cash and accounts receivable? Has there been an improvement in the firm's financial position? Explain your answer.

TRANSACTIONS FOR JANUARY 19X6

Jan. 2 Purchased a one-year insurance policy for $2,280. Issued Check 1014 to pay the full amount in advance.
      4 Purchased supplies for $1,100. Paid for them immediately with Check 1015.
      7 Collected a total of $210 on account from credit customers during the first week of January.
      7 Sold services for $3,070 in cash and $1,530 on credit during the first week of January. (Use a compound entry.)
      9 Returned some supplies that were damaged. Received a cash refund of $100.
     11 Issued Check 1016 for $560 to pay for advertising on the local radio station during the month.
     14 Collected a total of $300 on account from credit customers during the second week of January.
     14 Sold services for $3,560 in cash and $1,790 on credit during the second week of January. (Use a compound entry.)
     16 Issued Check 1017 for $125 to pay for maintenance work on the pool.

18 Purchased supplies for $800 from Ryan Inc. Received Invoice 3392, payable in 30 days.

21 Collected a total of $750 on account from credit customers during the third week of January.

21 Sold services for $3,280 in cash and $1,620 on credit during the third week of January. (Use a compound entry.)

23 Issued Check 1018 for $250 to pay for an advertisement in the local newspaper.

25 Received the monthly telephone bill and paid it with Check 1019 for $110.

26 Issued Check 1020 for $5,000 to Olson Inc. as a payment on account for Invoice 2788.

28 Collected a total of $970 on account from credit customers during the fourth week of January.

28 Sold services for $3,450 in cash and $1,750 on credit during the fourth week of January. (Use a compound entry.)

30 Issued Check 1021 for $170 to pay for cleaning service for the month. (Classify this transaction as maintenance.)

31 Sent Check 1022 for $385 in payment of the monthly bill for utilities.

31 Issued Checks 1023–1030 for $10,100 to pay the monthly salaries of the employees.

31 Sold services for $700 in cash and $350 on credit on January 30 and 31. (Use a compound entry.)

Accounting systems must be designed to meet the needs of individual businesses. The nature of a firm's operations, the volume of transactions it has, the complexity of its transactions, and many other factors help to determine the types of accounting records and procedures that are established for a specific business. One of the goals of the accountant is to design a system that makes the recording of financial data as efficient as possible and that produces needed information quickly and accurately.

ACCOUNTING FOR SALES AND ACCOUNTS RECEIVABLE

THE ACCOUNTING SYSTEM OF A MERCHANDISING BUSINESS

When an accounting system is developed for a firm, one important consideration is the nature of its operations. Different types of businesses have different needs that arise from the nature of their operations. There are three basic types of businesses. A *service business* sells services, a *merchandising business* sells goods that it purchases for resale, and a *manufacturing business* sells goods that it produces.

The Gold Medal Fitness Center, the firm that was described in Chapters 2 through 6, is an example of a service business. It provides exercise facilities and exercise classes to customers, who pay a fee for using the facilities or attending the classes. The firm that we will examine in the next group of chapters, Sports World, is a merchandising business.

Like the Gold Medal Fitness Center, Sports World is a small firm, but it requires a more complex set of financial records and statements because it must account for purchases and sales of goods and for its *merchandise inventory*—the stock of goods that it keeps on hand. Also, the business has a greater number of credit transactions with customers and suppliers.

In order to permit the efficient recording of financial data, the accounting systems of most merchandising businesses include special journals and subsidiary ledgers in addition to the general journal and the general ledger.

Special Journals and Subsidiary Ledgers

A *special journal* is a journal that is used to record only one type of transaction. For example, the *sales journal,* which is discussed in this chapter, is used to record only sales of merchandise on credit. A *subsidiary ledger* is a ledger that contains accounts of a single type. For example, the *accounts receivable ledger,* which is also discussed in this chapter, contains accounts for credit customers.

Generally, merchandising businesses use the following journals and ledgers in their accounting systems.

JOURNALS

Type of Journal	Purpose
Sales Journal	To record sales of merchandise on credit.
Purchases Journal	To record purchases of merchandise on credit.
Cash Receipts Journal	To record the cash received from all sources, including cash sales and cash collected on account from credit customers.
Cash Payments Journal	To record all cash paid out.
General Journal	To record any transaction that does not belong in a special journal, and to record the adjusting and closing entries.

LEDGERS

Type of Ledger	Content
General Ledger	The accounts for the items that appear on the financial statements—assets, liabilities, owner's equity, revenue, and expenses.
Accounts Receivable Ledger	The accounts for credit customers.
Accounts Payable Ledger	The accounts for creditors.

In this chapter and succeeding chapters, you will learn how the accounting systems of merchandising businesses operate and will become familiar with their financial records, procedures, and statements.

THE NEED FOR A SALES JOURNAL

Sports World is a retail merchandising business that sells a variety of sporting goods, including equipment for golf, tennis, racquetball, skiing, fishing, and scuba diving. The firm is a sole proprietorship owned and operated by Lynn Frank, who was formerly a sales manager for a company that manufactures sporting goods. She started Sports World five years ago.

To understand why a sales journal is so useful, consider how credit sales of merchandise made at Sports World would be entered in a general journal and posted to the general ledger as shown on page 128.

As you can see, a great amount of repetition is involved in both journalizing and posting these sales. The four credit sales made on December 1, 19X4, required four separate entries in the general journal and involved four debits to Accounts Receivable, four credits to Sales Tax Payable, four credits to Sales (the firm's revenue account), and four explanations. The posting of twelve items to the three general ledger accounts represents still further duplication of effort. Obviously, this is not an efficient recording procedure for a business that has a substantial number of credit sales each month.

19 X4						
Dec. 1	Accounts Receivable	111	254 40		
	Sales Tax Payable	231		14 40	
	Sales	401		240 00	
	Sold merchandise on credit to Ruth Carr, Sales Slip 3521.				
1	Accounts Receivable	111	84 80		
	Sales Tax Payable	231		4 80	
	Sales	401		80 00	
	Sold merchandise on credit to John Costa, Sales Slip 3522.				
1	Accounts Receivable	111	169 60		
	Sales Tax Payable	231		9 60	
	Sales	401		160 00	
	Sold merchandise on credit to Roy Hess, Sales Slip 3523.				
1	Accounts Receivable	111	76 32		
	Sales Tax Payable	231		4 32	
	Sales	401		72 00	
	Sold merchandise on credit to Janet Bell, Sales Slip 3524.				

Accounts Receivable No. 111

DATE	EXPLANATION	POST. REF.	DEBIT	CREDIT	BALANCE	DR. CR.
19 X4 Dec. 1	Balance	✔			3,262 00	Dr.
1		J12	254 40		3,516 40	Dr.
1		J12	84 80		3,601 20	Dr.
1		J12	169 60		3,770 80	Dr.
1		J12	76 32		3,847 12	Dr.

Sales Tax Payable No. 231

DATE	EXPLANATION	POST. REF.	DEBIT	CREDIT	BALANCE	DR. CR.
19 X4 Dec. 1		J12		14 40	14 40	Cr.
1		J12		4 80	19 20	Cr.
1		J12		9 60	28 80	Cr.
1		J12		4 32	33 12	Cr.

Sales No. 401

DATE	EXPLANATION	POST. REF.	DEBIT	CREDIT	BALANCE	DR. CR.
19 X4 Dec. 1		J12		240 00	240 00	Cr.
1		J12		80 00	320 00	Cr.
1		J12		160 00	480 00	Cr.
1		J12		72 00	552 00	Cr.

A special journal intended only for credit sales provides a more efficient method of recording these transactions. The January credit sales of Sports World appear below in a sales journal to illustrate how such a journal is used. (For the sake of simplicity, the sales journal shown here includes just a limited number of transactions. The firm actually has many more credit sales each month.)

					ACCOUNTS RECEIVABLE	SALES TAX PAYABLE	SALES
DATE		SALES SLIP NO.	CUSTOMER'S NAME	✓	DEBIT	CREDIT	CREDIT
Jan.	2	3601	James Allen		53 00	3 00	50 00
	7	3602	Helen Pace		132 50	7 50	125 00
	10	3603	Anthony Bruno		328 60	18 60	310 00
	14	3604	Marilyn Diaz		80 56	4 56	76 00
	17	3605	David Fisher		42 40	2 40	40 00
	20	3606	Karen Drake		245 92	13 92	232 00
	26	3607	James Allen		100 70	5 70	95 00
	28	3608	John Costa		173 84	9 84	164 00
	31	3609	Ruth Carr		50 88	2 88	48 00

SALES JOURNAL for Month of January 19X5 — Page 1

Notice how the headings and columns in the sales journal speed up the recording process. No account titles are entered, and only one line is needed to record the complete information for each transaction—the date, the sales slip number, the customer's name, the debit to Accounts Receivable, the credit to Sales Tax Payable, and the credit to Sales. In addition, since the sales journal is used for a single purpose, there is no need to enter any explanations. Thus a great deal of repetition is avoided in recording the firm's credit sales.

The use of a sales journal also strengthens the audit trail. All entries for credit sales are grouped together in one place, and the Sales Slip Number column serves as a convenient reference to the source documents that contain the original data about these transactions.

Recording Entries in a Sales Journal

Entries in the sales journal are usually made on a daily basis. In a retail business like Sports World, the data needed for each entry is taken from a copy of the sales slip issued to the customer, as shown on page 130.

Many state and local governments impose a sales tax on retail sales of certain goods and services. Businesses are required to collect this tax from their customers and send it to the proper tax agency at regular intervals. When goods or services are sold on credit, the sales tax is usually recorded at the time of the sale even though it will not be collected immediately. A liability account called Sales Tax Payable is credited for the sales tax charged. Since Sports World is located in a state that has a sales tax on retail transactions, its sales journal includes a Sales Tax Payable Credit column.

Notice how the amounts involved in a credit sale are recorded in the type of sales journal illustrated on page 130. The total owed by the customer is entered in

SPORTS WORLD
365 Broad Street   San Francisco, CA 94107

Qty.	Description	Unit Price	Amount
1	Tennis Racket		50 00
		Sales Tax	3 00
		Total	53 00

DATE	SALESPERSON	AUTH.
1/2/X5	M. Reese	LF

Goods Taken ☒   To Be Delivered ☐

Send to:

Special Instructions:

I authorize this purchase to be charged to my account.

James Allen
Signature

SALES SLIP **3601**

NAME _James Allen_
ADDRESS _216 Lawson Street_
San Francisco, CA 94118

OFFICE COPY

SALES JOURNAL for Month of January 19X5   Page 1

DATE	SALES SLIP NO.	CUSTOMER'S NAME	✓	ACCOUNTS RECEIVABLE DEBIT	SALES TAX PAYABLE CREDIT	SALES CREDIT
Jan. 2	3601	James Allen		53 00	3 00	50 00
7	3602	Helen Pace		132 50	7 50	125 00
10	3603	Anthony Bruno		328 60	18 60	310 00
14	3604	Marilyn Diaz		80 56	4 56	76 00
17	3605	David Fisher		42 40	2 40	40 00
20	3606	Karen Drake		245 92	13 92	232 00
26	3607	James Allen		100 70	5 70	95 00
28	3608	John Costa		173 84	9 84	164 00
31	3609	Ruth Carr		50 88	2 88	48 00

the Accounts Receivable Debit column, the sales tax is entered in the Sales Tax Payable Credit column, and the price of the goods is entered in the Sales Credit column.

Many small retail firms use a sales journal that is similar to the one shown above. However, keep in mind that special journals vary in format according to the needs of individual businesses. Examples of sales journals with different columnar arrangements are presented later in this chapter.

Posting From a Sales Journal

A sales journal not only simplifies the initial recording of credit sales, but also eliminates a great deal of repetition in posting these transactions. When a sales journal is used, it is not necessary to post each credit sale individually to the general ledger accounts that are affected. Instead, summary postings are made at the end of the month after the amount columns of the sales journal are totaled.

In actual practice, before any posting takes place, the accountant proves the equality of the debits and credits recorded in the sales journal by comparing the column totals. The following proof is for the sales journal that is illustrated below. All multicolumn special journals should be proved in a similar manner before their totals are posted.

PROOF OF SALES JOURNAL

Debits

Accounts Receivable Debit Column $1,208.40

Credits

Sales Tax Payable Credit Column $ 68.40
Sales Credit Column   1,140.00
   $1,208.40

After verifying the equality of the debits and credits, the accountant rules the sales journal and posts the column totals to the general ledger accounts involved, as shown below and on page 132. To indicate that the postings have been made, the accountant enters the numbers of the accounts in parentheses under the column totals in the sales journal and enters the abbreviation *S1* in the Post. Ref. column of the accounts. This abbreviation shows that the data was posted from page 1 of the sales journal.

SALES JOURNAL for Month of January 19X5   Page 1

DATE	SALES SLIP NO.	CUSTOMER'S NAME	✓	ACCOUNTS RECEIVABLE DEBIT	SALES TAX PAYABLE CREDIT	SALES CREDIT
Jan. 2	3601	James Allen	✓	53 00	3 00	50 00
7	3602	Helen Pace	✓	132 50	7 50	125 00
10	3603	Anthony Bruno	✓	328 60	18 60	310 00
14	3604	Marilyn Diaz	✓	80 56	4 56	76 00
17	3605	David Fisher	✓	42 40	2 40	40 00
20	3606	Karen Drake	✓	245 92	13 92	232 00
26	3607	James Allen	✓	100 70	5 70	95 00
28	3608	John Costa	✓	173 84	9 84	164 00
31	3609	Ruth Carr	✓	50 88	2 88	48 00
31		Totals		1,208 40	68 40	1,140 00
				(111)	(231)	(401)

Accounts Receivable   No. 111

DATE	EXPLANATION	POST. REF.	DEBIT	CREDIT	BALANCE	DR. CR.
19 X5						
Jan. 1	Balance	✓			1,098 16	Dr.
14		J1		137 80	960 36	Dr.
22		J1		21 20	939 16	Dr.
31		S1	1,208 40		2,147 56	Dr.

Sales Tax Payable						No. 231	
DATE	EXPLANATION	POST. REF.	DEBIT	CREDIT	BALANCE	DR. CR.	
19 X5							
Jan. 14		J1	7 80		7 80	Dr.	
22		J1	1 20		9 00	Dr.	
31		S1		68 40	59 40	Cr.	

Sales						No. 401	
DATE	EXPLANATION	POST. REF.	DEBIT	CREDIT	BALANCE	DR. CR.	
19 X5							
Jan. 31		S1		1,140 00	1,140 00	Cr.	

During the month the individual entries in the sales journal are posted to the customer accounts in the accounts receivable ledger. The check marks in the journal illustrated on page 131 show that these postings have been completed. (The necessary procedure is described in a later section of this chapter.)

Advantages of a Sales Journal

From the example presented here, it is clear that the use of a special journal for credit sales saves time, effort, and recording space. Both the journalizing process and the posting process become more efficient, but the advantage in the posting process is especially significant. If a business like Sports World used the general journal to record 300 credit sales a month, the firm would have to make 900 individual postings to the general ledger—300 to Accounts Receivable, 300 to Sales Tax Payable, and 300 to Sales. With a sales journal the firm makes only three summary postings to the general ledger at the end of each month no matter how many credit sales were entered.

The use of a sales journal and other special journals also allows division of work. In a business with a fairly large volume of transactions, it is essential that several employees be able to record transactions at the same time.

Finally, the sales journal improves the audit trail by bringing together all entries for credit sales in one place and listing them by source document number as well as by date. This makes it easier to trace the details of such transactions.

RECORDING SALES RETURNS AND ALLOWANCES

A sale is entered in the accounting records of a business at the time the goods are sold or the service is provided. If something is wrong with the goods or service, the firm may take back the goods, resulting in a *sales return,* or give the customer a reduction in the price of the goods or service, resulting in a *sales allowance.*

When a return or allowance is related to a credit sale, the normal practice is to issue a document called a *credit memorandum* to the customer rather than giving a cash refund. The credit memorandum states that the customer's account is being reduced by the amount of the return or allowance plus any sales tax that may be involved. A copy of the credit memorandum provides the data needed to enter the transaction in the firm's accounting records.

Depending on the volume of sales returns and allowances that a business has, it may use a general journal to record these transactions or it may use a special sales returns and allowances journal.

General Journal Entries for Sales Returns and Allowances

In a small firm that has a limited number of sales returns and allowances each month, there is no need to establish a special journal for such transactions. Instead, the required entries are made in the general journal, as shown below.

19 X5					
Jan. 14	Sales Returns and Allowances	451	130 00	
	Sales Tax Payable	231	7 80	
	Accounts Receivable/Anthony Bruno	111/✓		137 80
	Accepted a return of defective merchandise, Credit Memorandum 191. The original sale was made on Sales Slip 3603 of Jan. 10.			
22	Sales Returns and Allowances	451	20 00	
	Sales Tax Payable	231	1 20	
	Accounts Receivable/Karen Drake	111/✓		21 20
	Gave an allowance for damaged merchandise, Credit Memorandum 192. The original sale was made on Sales Slip 3606 of Jan. 20.			

These entries were recorded at Sports World for a return of defective merchandise by Anthony Bruno on January 14 and an allowance given to Karen Drake on January 22 for damaged but usable merchandise. Notice that each entry includes a debit to an account called Sales Returns and Allowances for the amount of the return or allowance, a debit to Sales Tax Payable for the amount of sales tax involved, and a credit to Accounts Receivable for the reduction in the sum owed by the customer. (There is also a credit to the customer's account in the accounts receivable ledger, which will be discussed in a later section of this chapter.)

Accountants prefer to use a Sales Returns and Allowances account rather than make a direct debit to the Sales account. This procedure gives a firm a complete record of its sales returns and allowances for each accounting period. Business managers consider this record one of several measures of operating efficiency.

The Sales Returns and Allowances account is referred to as a *contra revenue account* because it has a debit balance, which is contrary to the normal balance for a revenue account. The debit balance of Sales Returns and Allowances is used to reduce the credit balance of the Sales account on the income statement.

A customer who returns goods or receives an allowance in connection with a sale that originally involved sales tax is entitled to a credit for the appropriate amount of the tax as well as a credit for the sales amount. Similarly, the business is not required to pay sales tax to the tax authority for returns and allowances. The reduction in the firm's sales tax liability is entered by debiting the Sales Tax Payable account when the return or allowance is recorded.

Sales Returns and Allowances Journal

In a business that has a substantial number of sales returns and allowances, it is efficient to use a special journal for these transactions. An example of a sales returns and allowances journal is shown below.

SALES RETURNS AND ALLOWANCES JOURNAL for Month of July 19X5 Page 7

DATE	CREDIT MEMO. NO.	CUSTOMER'S NAME	✓	ACCOUNTS RECEIVABLE CREDIT	SALES TAX PAYABLE DEBIT	SALES RET. & ALLOW. DEBIT
July 2	2346	James Doyle	✓	21 20	1 20	20 00
2	2347	Sally Hanson	✓	15 90	90	15 00
30	2451	Thomas Wilenski	✓	63 60	3 60	60 00
31		Totals		1,632 40	92 40	1,540 00
				(111)	(231)	(451)

REPORTING NET SALES

At the end of each accounting period, the balance of the Sales Returns and Allowances account is subtracted from the balance of the Sales account in the Revenue section of the income statement. The resulting figure is the *net sales* for the period.

For example, suppose that the Sales Returns and Allowances account at Sports World contains a balance of $150 at the end of January 19X5, as shown below. Also suppose that the Sales account has a balance of $8,725 at the time. The Revenue section of the firm's income statement would therefore appear as follows.

Revenue

Sales	$8,725.00
Less Sales Returns and Allowances	150.00
Net Sales	$8,575.00

Sales Returns and Allowances   No. 451

DATE	EXPLANATION	POST. REF.	DEBIT	CREDIT	BALANCE	DR. CR.
19 X5						
Jan. 14		J1	130 00		130 00	Dr.
22		J1	20 00		150 00	Dr.

THE NEED FOR AN ACCOUNTS RECEIVABLE LEDGER

A business that extends credit to customers must manage its accounts receivable carefully. The amounts owed by credit customers must be collected promptly in order to provide the steady stream of cash needed for the firm's day-to-day operations. Accounts receivable represent a substantial asset for many businesses, and this asset must be converted into cash in a timely manner. Otherwise, a firm may not be able to pay its bills even though it has a large volume of sales and earns a satisfactory profit.

In order to manage accounts receivable effectively, it is essential to have detailed information about the transactions with credit customers and to know the balances owed by such customers at all times. This is accomplished by setting up an accounts receivable ledger with individual accounts for all credit customers. The accounts receivable ledger is referred to as a subsidiary ledger because it is separate from and subordinate to the general ledger.

The information in the accounts receivable ledger makes it possible to verify that customers are paying their balances on time and that they are within their credit limits. (Many firms assign a credit limit to each customer, based on the financial resources and credit record of the customer.) The accounts receivable ledger also permits a business to answer questions from credit customers easily and quickly. Customers may want to know about their current balances or may feel that the firm has made a billing error, which must be looked into.

USING AN ACCOUNTS RECEIVABLE LEDGER

The accounts for credit customers are kept on ledger sheets or cards. The normal practice is to use a balance ledger form with three money columns, as shown on page 136. Notice that this form does not contain a column for indicating the type of account balance. The balances in the customer accounts are presumed to be debit balances since asset accounts normally have debit balances. However, occasionally there is a credit balance because a customer has overpaid the amount owed or has returned goods that were already paid for. One common procedure for dealing with this situation is to circle the balance in order to show that it is a credit amount.

In a small business like Sports World, the customer accounts are kept in alphabetic order in the accounts receivable ledger. Larger firms and firms that use computers to process their financial data assign an account number to each credit customer and arrange the customer accounts in numeric order within the accounts receivable ledger.

Daily Routine for the Accounts Receivable Ledger

Postings to the accounts receivable ledger are usually made on a daily basis so that the customer accounts can be kept up to date at all times.

Posting a Credit Sale Each credit sale recorded in the sales journal is posted to the appropriate customer's account in the accounts receivable ledger, as shown on page 136.

The date, the sales slip number, and the amount that the customer owes as a result of the transaction are simply transferred from the sales journal to the customer's account. The amount is taken from the Accounts Receivable Debit

SALES JOURNAL for Month of January 19X5   Page 1

DATE	SALES SLIP NO.	CUSTOMER'S NAME	✓	ACCOUNTS RECEIVABLE DEBIT	SALES TAX PAYABLE CREDIT	SALES CREDIT
Jan. 2	3601	James Allen	✓	53 00	3 00	50 00

NAME   James Allen
ADDRESS   216 Lawson Street
          San Francisco, CA 94118   TERMS n/30

DATE	DESCRIPTION	POST. REF.	DEBIT	CREDIT	BALANCE
19 X5					
Jan. 1	Balance	✓			222 60
2	Sales Slip 3601	S1	53 00		275 60

column of the journal and entered in the Debit column of the account. Then the new balance is determined and recorded.

To show that the posting has been completed, a check mark (✓) is entered in the sales journal and the abbreviation *S1* is entered in the Post. Ref. column of the customer's account. (As noted before, this abbreviation identifies page 1 of the sales journal.)

Posting Cash Received on Account In an accounting system that has special journals and subsidiary ledgers, the cash collected from credit customers is first recorded in a cash receipts journal and then posted to the individual customer accounts in the accounts receivable ledger. The account illustrated below shows a posting for cash received on January 6 from James Allen, a credit customer of Sports World. (The necessary entry in the cash receipts journal will be discussed in Chapter 9.)

NAME   James Allen
ADDRESS   216 Lawson Street
          San Francisco, CA 94118   TERMS n/30

DATE	DESCRIPTION	POST. REF.	DEBIT	CREDIT	BALANCE
19 X5					
Jan. 1	Balance	✓			222 60
2	Sales Slip 3601	S1	53 00		275 60
6		CR1		222 60	53 00

Posting a Sales Return or Allowance Whether sales returns and allowances are recorded in the general journal or in a special sales returns and allowances journal, each of these transactions must be posted to the appropriate customer's account in the accounts receivable ledger. The following illustrations show how a return of merchandise at Sports World on January 14 was posted from the general journal to the account of Anthony Bruno, the customer involved.

19 X5					
Jan. 14	Sales Returns and Allowances	451	130 00		
	Sales Tax Payable	231	7 80		
	Accounts Receivable/Anthony Bruno	111/✓			137 80
	Accepted a return of defective merchandise, Credit Memorandum 191. The original sale was made on Sales Slip 3603 of Jan. 10.				

NAME   Anthony Bruno
ADDRESS   9 Glen Road
       San Francisco, CA 94107   TERMS n/30

DATE	DESCRIPTION	POST. REF.	DEBIT	CREDIT	BALANCE
19 X5					
Jan. 10	Sales Slip 3603	S1	328 60		328 60
14	CM 191	J1		137 80	190 80

Because the credit amount in the general journal entry for this transaction required two postings, the accountant has recorded the account number 111 and a check mark in the Post. Ref. column of the journal. The 111 indicates that the amount was posted to the Accounts Receivable account in the general ledger, and the check mark indicates that the amount was posted to the customer's account in the accounts receivable ledger. Notice that the accountant used a diagonal line to separate the two posting references.

End-of-Month Routine for the Accounts Receivable Ledger

The use of an accounts receivable ledger does not eliminate the need for the Accounts Receivable account in the general ledger. This account remains in the general ledger and continues to appear on the balance sheet at the end of each fiscal period. However, the Accounts Receivable account is now considered a *control account*—an account that serves as a link between a subsidiary ledger and the general ledger because its balance summarizes the balances of the accounts in the subsidiary ledger.

At the end of each month, after all the postings have been made from the sales journal, the cash receipts journal, and the general journal to the accounts receivable ledger, the accountant proves the balances in this ledger against the balance of the Accounts Receivable account in the general ledger. First the accountant prepares a *schedule of accounts receivable,* which lists all unpaid balances in the subsidiary ledger. Then the accountant compares the total of the schedule with the balance of the Accounts Receivable account in the general ledger. The two figures should be the same. If they are not, the accountant must locate and correct the error or errors.

Assume that the accounts receivable ledger at Sports World contains the accounts shown below and on pages 139 and 140 on January 31, 19X5. To prepare a schedule of accounts receivable, the firm's accountant examines all the accounts and lists the name of any customer with an unpaid balance and the amount of the balance, as shown on page 140. Then the accountant adds the figures to find the total owed to the business by its credit customers.

NAME James Allen
ADDRESS 216 Lawson Street
San Francisco, CA 94118   **TERMS** n/30

DATE	DESCRIPTION	POST. REF.	DEBIT	CREDIT	BALANCE
19 X5					
Jan. 1	Balance	✓			222 60
2	Sales Slip 3601	S1	53 00		275 60
6		CR1		222 60	53 00
26	Sales Slip 3607	S1	100 70		153 70

NAME Janet Bell
ADDRESS 1069 Warren Street
San Francisco, CA 94116   **TERMS** n/30

DATE	DESCRIPTION	POST. REF.	DEBIT	CREDIT	BALANCE
19 X5					
Jan. 1	Balance	✓			76 32
10		CR1		76 32	–0–

NAME Anthony Bruno
ADDRESS 9 Glen Road
San Francisco, CA 94107   **TERMS** n/30

DATE	DESCRIPTION	POST. REF.	DEBIT	CREDIT	BALANCE
19 X5					
Jan. 10	Sales Slip 3603	S1	328 60		328 60
14	CM 191	J1		137 80	190 80

NAME Ruth Carr
ADDRESS 14 Oak Street
San Francisco, CA 94123   **TERMS** n/30

DATE	DESCRIPTION	POST. REF.	DEBIT	CREDIT	BALANCE
19 X5					
Jan. 1	Balance	✓			254 40
5		CR1		254 40	–0–
31	Sales Slip 3609	S1	50 88		50 88

NAME John Costa
ADDRESS 49 Vista Road
San Francisco, CA 94118
TERMS n/30

DATE		DESCRIPTION	POST. REF.	DEBIT	CREDIT	BALANCE
19 X5						
Jan.	1	Balance	✓			84 80
	12		CR1		84 80	–0–
	28	Sales Slip 3608	S1	173 84		173 84

NAME Marilyn Diaz
ADDRESS 2147 Mission Drive
San Francisco, CA 94112
TERMS n/30

DATE		DESCRIPTION	POST. REF.	DEBIT	CREDIT	BALANCE
19 X5						
Jan.	1	Balance	✓			65 72
	14	Sales Slip 3604	S1	80 56		146 28
	18		CR1		65 72	80 56

NAME Karen Drake
ADDRESS 1026 Barr Street
San Francisco, CA 94131
TERMS n/30

DATE		DESCRIPTION	POST. REF.	DEBIT	CREDIT	BALANCE
19 X5						
Jan.	20	Sales Slip 3606	S1	245 92		245 92
	22	CM 192	J1		21 20	224 72

NAME David Fisher
ADDRESS 147 Fallon Street
San Francisco, CA 94116
TERMS n/30

DATE		DESCRIPTION	POST. REF.	DEBIT	CREDIT	BALANCE
19 X5						
Jan.	1	Balance	✓			137 80
	17	Sales Slip 3605	S1	42 40		180 20
	23		CR1		137 80	42 40

NAME Roy Hess
ADDRESS 611 Tower Drive
San Francisco, CA 94127
TERMS n/30

DATE		DESCRIPTION	POST. REF.	DEBIT	CREDIT	BALANCE
19 X5						
Jan.	1	Balance	✓			169 60

NAME	Helen Pace				TERMS n/30
ADDRESS	10 Station Plaza				
	San Francisco, CA 94107				

DATE		DESCRIPTION	POST. REF.	DEBIT	CREDIT	BALANCE
19 X5						
Jan.	1	Balance	✓			86 92
	7	Sales Slip 3602	S1	132 50		219 42

A comparison of the total of the schedule of accounts receivable prepared at Sports World on January 31, 19X5, and the balance of the Accounts Receivable account in the general ledger shows that the two figures are the same. (Refer to the illustrations presented below.)

SPORTS WORLD
Schedule of Accounts Receivable
January 31, 19X5

CUSTOMER	BALANCE
James Allen	153 70
Anthony Bruno	190 80
Ruth Carr	50 88
John Costa	173 84
Marilyn Diaz	80 56
Karen Drake	224 72
David Fisher	42 40
Roy Hess	169 60
Helen Pace	219 42
Total	1,305 92

Accounts Receivable   No. 111

DATE		EXPLANATION	POST. REF.	DEBIT	CREDIT	BALANCE	DR. CR.
19 X5							
Jan.	1	Balance	✓			1,098 16	Dr.
	14		J1		137 80	960 36	Dr.
	22		J1		21 20	939 16	Dr.
	31		S1	1,208 40		2,147 56	Dr.
	31		CR1		841 64	1,305 92	Dr.

In addition to providing a proof of the subsidiary ledger, the schedule of accounts receivable serves another function. It reports information about the firm's accounts receivable at the end of the month. Management can review the schedule to see exactly how much each customer owes and how much is due the business from all of its credit customers.

RECORDING CREDIT SALES IN A WHOLESALE BUSINESS

The operations of Sports World are typical of those of many *retail businesses*—businesses that sell goods and services directly to individual consumers. In contrast, *wholesale businesses* are manufacturers or distributors of goods that sell to retailers or large consumers such as hotels and hospitals. The basic procedures used by wholesalers to handle sales and accounts receivable are the same as those used by retailers. However, many wholesalers offer cash discounts and trade discounts, which are not commonly found in retail operations.

The procedures that are used in connection with cash discounts are examined in Chapter 9. The handling of trade discounts is described in this section.

List Prices and Trade Discounts

A wholesale business must offer its goods to trade customers at less than retail prices so that the trade customers can resell the goods at a profit. This price adjustment by wholesale businesses often takes the form of *trade discounts,* which are reductions from the *list prices*—the established retail prices. There may be a single trade discount or a series of discounts for each type of goods. The *net price* (list price less all trade discounts) is the amount that the wholesaler records in its sales journal as the sales price of the goods.

The same goods may be offered to different customers at different trade discounts, depending on the size of the order and the costs of selling to the various types of customers.

Computation of a Single Trade Discount Suppose that the list price of some goods is $500 and the trade discount is 40 percent. The amount of the discount is $200, and the net price to be shown on the invoice and recorded in the sales journal is $300.

List price	$500
Less 40% discount	200
Invoice price	$300

Computation of a Series of Trade Discounts If the list price of some goods is $500 and the trade discount is quoted in a series such as 25 and 15 percent, a different net price will result.

List price	$500.00
Less first discount	
(25% of $500)	125.00
Difference	$375.00
Less second discount	
(15% of $375)	56.25
Invoice price	$318.75

Sales Journal Entries

Since sales taxes apply only to retail transactions, a wholesale business does not need to account for such taxes. Its sales journal may therefore be as simple as the one shown on page 142. Notice that this sales journal has a single amount column, and the total of the amount column is posted to the general ledger at the end of the month as a debit to the Accounts Receivable account and a credit to the Sales account. During the month, the individual entries in the sales journal are posted to the customer accounts in the accounts receivable ledger.

SALES JOURNAL for Month of January 19X5   Page 1

DATE	INVOICE NO.	CUSTOMER'S NAME	✓	AMOUNT
Jan. 2	7862	Elmwood Appliance Center	✓	300 00
31	7887	Lee Department Store	✓	1,800 00
31		Total		24,600 00
				(111)
				(401)

Accounts Receivable   No. 111

DATE	EXPLANATION	POST. REF.	DEBIT	CREDIT	BALANCE	DR. CR.
19 X5 Jan. 1	Balance	✓			20,500 00	Dr.
31		S1	24,600 00		45,100 00	Dr.

Sales   No. 401

DATE	EXPLANATION	POST. REF.	DEBIT	CREDIT	BALANCE	DR. CR.
19 X5 Jan. 31		S1		24,600 00	24,600 00	Cr.

Wholesale businesses issue *invoices* to bill their customers for goods. Copies of the invoices are used to enter the transactions in the sales journal.

CREDIT POLICIES

The use of credit is considered to be one of the most important factors in the rapid growth of modern economic systems. Sales on credit are made by large numbers of wholesalers and retailers of goods and by many professional people and service businesses. The assumption is that the volume of both sales and profits will increase if buyers are given a period of a month or more to pay for the goods or services they purchase.

However, the increase in profits that a business expects when it grants credit will be realized only if each customer completes the transaction by paying for the goods or services purchased. If payment is not received, the expected profits become actual losses and the purpose for granting the credit is defeated. Business firms try to protect against the possibility of such losses by investigating a customer's credit record and ability to pay for purchases before allowing any credit to the customer.

Professional people, such as doctors, lawyers, and architects, and owners of small businesses like Sports World usually make their own decisions about granting credit. Such decisions may be based on personal judgment or on reports available from local credit bureaus, information supplied by other creditors, and credit ratings supplied by national firms such as the Dun & Bradstreet Companies, Inc.

Larger businesses maintain a credit department to determine the amounts and types of credit that should be granted to customers. In addition to using credit data supplied by institutions, the credit department may obtain financial statements and related reports from customers who have applied for credit. This information is analyzed to help determine the maximum amount of credit that may safely be granted to each customer and suitable credit terms for the customer. Financial statements that have been audited by certified public accountants are used extensively by credit departments.

Even though the credit investigation is thorough, some accounts receivable become uncollectible. Unexpected business developments, errors of judgment, incorrect financial data, and many other causes may lead to defaults in payments by customers. Experienced managers know that some uncollectible accounts are to be expected in normal business operations and that limited losses indicate that a firm's credit policies are sound. Provisions for such limited losses from uncollectible accounts are usually made in budgets and other financial projections.

Each business must reach its own decisions as to the most desirable credit policies for it to use to achieve maximum sales with minimum losses from uncollectible accounts. A credit policy that is too tight results in a low level of losses at the expense of increases in sales volume that might otherwise be achieved. A credit policy that is too lenient may result in increased sales volume accompanied by a high level of losses. Good judgment based on knowledge and experience must be used to achieve a well-balanced credit policy. This policy must be realistic and yet liberal enough to contribute to increases in profitable sales. However, it must also be conservative enough to hold losses from uncollectible accounts to an acceptable level.

TYPES OF CREDIT SALES

There are many different arrangements for selling goods and services on credit. The most common types of credit sales are described in this section.

Open-Account Credit

The form of credit most commonly offered by professional people and small businesses permits the sale of services or goods to the customer with the understanding that the amount is to be paid at a later date. This type of arrangement is called *open-account credit*. It is usually granted on the basis of personal acquaintance or knowledge of the customer by the professional person or the owner or manager of the business. However, formal credit checks may also be used. The amount involved in each transaction is usually small, and payment is expected within 30 days or on receipt of a monthly statement.

Sports World is an example of a firm that uses the open-account credit arrangement. Under this arrangement, sales transactions are recorded by debits to the Accounts Receivable account and credits to the Sales account. Collections on account are recorded by debits to the Cash account and credits to the Accounts Receivable account.

Business Credit Cards

Many retail businesses, especially large ones such as department store chains, gasoline companies, and car rental companies, provide their own credit cards (sometimes called charge cards or charge plates) to customers who have established credit. The credit card serves as a means of identification and as an indicator that the customer has an account with the issuing firm. Such firms usually have a credit department, which makes a thorough check of each customer before an account is opened and the customer is given the credit card.

The credit card is normally made of plastic, and the name of the customer and the account number assigned are printed on it in raised letters and numbers. Whenever a sale is made, a sales slip is prepared in the usual manner. Then the sales slip and the credit card are placed in a mechanical device that prints the customer's name, account number, and other data on all copies of the sales slip. In addition to the use of the credit card, many businesses require that the sales-clerk contact the credit department by telephone or computer terminal to verify the customer's credit status before completing the transaction.

The credit card sales discussed in this section are similar to the open-account credit sales explained previously. Sales of this type are also referred to as *charge account sales*. They are recorded by debits to the Accounts Receivable account and credits to a revenue account such as Sales. Collections on account are recorded by debits to Cash and credits to Accounts Receivable.

Bank Credit Cards

A very popular method for retailers to provide credit while minimizing or avoiding the risk of losses from uncollectible accounts is to allow customers to use *bank credit cards*. The most widely accepted bank credit cards are Mastercard and Visa. Many banks participate in one or both of these credit card arrangements, and other banks have their own credit cards.

These credit cards are issued to consumers by banks rather than by the businesses that accept the cards in sales transactions. Individuals who want such credit cards must fill out an application form. If an applicant meets the necessary requirements, a plastic card is issued with the name and identifying account number printed in raised characters.

Almost any type of business may participate in these credit card programs by meeting the conditions set by the bank. When a sale is made to a cardholder, the business completes a special sales slip such as the one shown on page 145. This form must be imprinted with data from the customer's bank credit card and then signed by the customer. Many businesses continue to complete their regular sales slips for internal control and other purposes in addition to preparing the special sales slip required by the bank.

When a business makes a sale on the basis of a bank credit card, it acquires an asset that can be converted into cash immediately without responsibility for later collection from the customer. Periodically (preferably each day), the com-

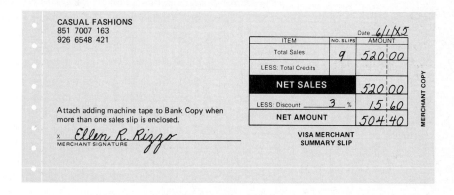

pleted sales slips from the bank credit card sales are totaled. The number of sales slips and the total amount of the sales are recorded on a special deposit form, as illustrated below.

The deposit form, along with the completed sales slips, is presented to the firm's bank in much the same manner as a cash deposit. Depending upon the arrangements that have been made, either the bank will deduct a fee, called a *discount* (usually in the 2½ to 6 percent range), and immediately credit the depositor's checking account with the net amount of the sales or it will credit the depositor's checking account for the full amount of the sales and then deduct the discount at the end of the month. (If the second procedure is used, the total discount for the month will appear on the bank statement.)

The bank has responsibility for collecting from the cardholders. If any amounts are uncollectible, the bank sustains the loss. For the retailer, bank credit card sales are like cash sales. The accounting procedures for such sales are therefore quite similar to the accounting procedures for cash sales, which you will learn about in Chapter 9. If the business is billed once each month for the bank's discount, the total amount involved in the daily deposit of the credit card sales slips is debited to Cash and credited to Sales.

Credit Card Companies

A number of well-known credit cards, such as American Express, Diners Club, and Carte Blanche, are issued by business firms or subsidiaries of business firms that are operated for the special purpose of handling credit card transactions. The individual seeking to become a cardholder must submit an application containing the required information and must pay an annual fee to the credit card company. If the individual's credit references are satisfactory, the credit card is issued. It is normally reissued at one-year intervals so long as the company's credit experience with the cardholder remains satisfactory.

Hotels, restaurants, airline companies, many types of retail stores, and a wide variety of other businesses accept these credit cards. When making sales to cardholders, sellers usually prepare their own sales slip or bill and then complete a special sales slip required by the credit card company. As with the sales slips for bank credit cards, the forms must be imprinted with the identifying data on the customer's card and signed by the customer. (Such sales slips are sometimes referred to as *sales invoices, sales drafts,* or *sales vouchers*. The term used varies from one credit card company to another.)

The effect of such a sale is that the seller acquires an account receivable from the credit card company rather than from the customer. Periodically, the seller summarizes the completed sales slips and submits them to the credit card company, which pays the seller promptly. At approximately one-month intervals, the credit card company bills the cardholders for all sales slips it has acquired during the period. It is the responsibility of the company to collect from the cardholders.

The accounting procedures for sales involving credit card companies are discussed in a later section of this chapter.

Layaway or Will-Call Sales

In a *layaway sale,* or *will-call sale,* the customer makes a deposit on a certain item and the store puts it aside. The customer must pay the rest of the price (usually within a specified time) before taking possession of the goods. A customer who does not complete the payments within the time allowed may legally forfeit the amount that has already been paid. However, in many cases the store refunds the payments made or credits them against other purchases in an effort to retain customer goodwill. Experience with sales of this type indicates that most customers complete their payments and receive the goods.

The accounting procedure for layaway sales is as follows. The sale is recorded when the customer makes the deposit and the merchandise is put aside. Cash is debited for the amount of the deposit, and Accounts Receivable is debited for the balance. The Sales account is credited for the entire price of the item. In effect, the transaction is recorded as a credit sale, on which a part payment has been made. Later payments are recorded as collections on account. When the price of the goods has been paid in full, the goods are given to the customer.

COD Sales

COD (cash on delivery) sales are made to customers without established credit who want goods delivered or shipped to them. The cash is collected from the customer at the time of delivery. If the customer cannot pay, the goods are returned to the seller.

The simplest accounting procedure for such sales is to prepare a sales slip marked ''COD'' to accompany the goods. The delivery person is instructed to collect the amount shown on the sales slip. No entry is made in the Accounts Receivable account. If the customer pays, the transaction is then processed as a cash sale. If the customer does not pay, the sales slip is voided and the merchandise is returned to stock.

ACCOUNTING FOR SALES INVOLVING CREDIT CARD COMPANIES

The procedure used to account for sales made on the basis of credit cards issued by credit card companies is similar to the procedure for recording open-account credit sales. However, an important difference is that the account receivable is with the credit card company, not with the cardholders who buy the goods or services.

There are two basic methods of recording these sales. Businesses that have few transactions with credit card companies normally debit the amounts of such sales to the usual Accounts Receivable account in the general ledger and credit them to the same Sales account that is used for cash sales and other types of credit sales. An individual account for each credit card company is set up in the accounts receivable subsidiary ledger. This method of recording sales that involve credit cards issued by credit card companies is illustrated by the following sales journal entries.

SALES JOURNAL for Month of April 19X5				ACCOUNTS RECEIVABLE		SALES TAX PAYABLE CREDIT	SALES CREDIT	Page 4
DATE	SALES SLIP NO.	CUSTOMER'S NAME	√	DEBIT				
Apr. 2	714	American Express (Ann Walsh)		36 40		1 40	35 00	
9	751	Diners Club (Robert Treat)		43 68		1 68	42 00	

The receipt of payment from a credit card company is recorded in the cash receipts journal, as shown at the top of page 148. Notice that the fees charged by the credit card companies for processing these sales are debited to an account called Discount Expense on Credit Card Sales.

Firms that do a large volume of business with credit card companies may debit all such sales to a special Accounts Receivable From Credit Card Companies account in the general ledger, thus separating this type of receivable from the accounts receivable resulting from open-account credit sales. Another special account called Sales—Credit Card Companies is credited for the revenue from these transactions. The sales journal illustrated on page 148 shows how the necessary entries are made.

Subsidiary ledger accounts may not be needed. Instead, a file is maintained of copies of the periodic summaries submitted to the credit card companies for payment. The total amount of the unpaid summaries in the file at any time should equal the balance of the Accounts Receivable From Credit Card Companies account in the general ledger at the same time.

CASH RECEIPTS JOURNAL for Month of April 19X5

DATE	EXPLANATION	ACCOUNTS RECEIVABLE ✓	ACCOUNTS RECEIVABLE CREDIT	SALES TAX PAYABLE CREDIT	SALES CREDIT	OTHER ACCOUNTS CREDIT — ACCOUNT TITLE	POST REF.	AMOUNT	DISC. EXP. ON CREDIT CARD SALES DEBIT	CASH DEBIT
Apr. 28	American Express (Ann Walsh)		36 40						2 55	33 85
30	Diners Club (Robert Treat)		43 68						3 06	40 62

SALES JOURNAL for Month of July 19X5

DATE	SALES SLIP NO.	CUSTOMER'S NAME	ACCOUNTS RECEIVABLE ✓	ACCOUNTS RECEIVABLE DEBIT	ACCTS. REC.—CREDIT CARD COMPANIES ✓	ACCTS. REC.—CREDIT CARD COMPANIES DEBIT	SALES TAX PAYABLE CREDIT	SALES CREDIT	SALES—CREDIT CARD COMPANIES CREDIT
July 6		Summary of credit card sales/American Express				3,090 00	90 00		3,000 00
10		Summary of credit card sales/Diners Club				2,008 50	58 50		1,950 00
31		Totals				18,952 00	552 00		18,400 00
						(114)	(231)		(404)

CASH RECEIPTS JOURNAL for Month of July 19X5

DATE	EXPLANATION	ACCOUNTS RECEIVABLE ✓	ACCOUNTS RECEIVABLE CREDIT	ACCTS. REC.—CREDIT CARD COMPANIES ✓	ACCTS. REC.—CREDIT CARD COMPANIES CREDIT	SALES TAX PAYABLE CREDIT	SALES CREDIT	DISC. EXP. ON CREDIT CARD SALES DEBIT	CASH DEBIT
July 20	Summary of 7/6/American Express				3,090 00			216 30	2,873 70
25	Summary of 7/10/Diners Club				2,008 50			140 60	1,867 90
31	Totals				16,391 00			1,147 37	15,243 63
					(114)			(592)	(101)

When payments are received from the credit card companies, the entries appear as shown in the cash receipts journal at the bottom of page 148.

PRINCIPLES AND PROCEDURES SUMMARY

In designing an accounting system for a business, the accountant must consider the nature of the firm's operations, the volume of its transactions, and a number of other factors. The accounting systems of most merchandising businesses include special journals and subsidiary ledgers as well as the general journal and the general ledger. The use of these additional journals and ledgers increases the efficiency of the recording function and permits division of labor.

The sales journal is a special journal in which all sales on credit are entered. These transactions are usually recorded on a daily basis. At the end of each month, the sales journal is totaled, proved, and ruled and the column totals are posted to the general ledger. One important advantage of using a sales journal rather than a general journal to record credit sales is that there is no need to post individual entries to the general ledger during the month. A summary posting is made at the end of the month, which saves a great deal of time and effort.

In many areas, retail sales of goods and services are subject to a sales tax. This tax is normally entered when the sale is made so that the firm has the appropriate amount of liability in its financial records. The most efficient way to record the sales tax owed on credit sales is by placing a Sales Tax Payable Credit column in the sales journal.

Sales returns and allowances are usually debited to a contra revenue account. The balance of this account is subtracted from the balance of the Sales account on the income statement in order to show the net sales for the period. If a firm has a substantial number of sales returns and allowances, it is efficient to use a special journal for these transactions. Otherwise, they are entered in the general journal.

Accounts with individual credit customers are kept in a subsidiary ledger called the accounts receivable ledger. Daily postings are made to this ledger from the sales journal, the cash receipts journal, and the general journal or sales returns and allowances journal. The current balance of a customer's account is computed after each posting so that the amount owed is known at all times. At the end of each month, a schedule of accounts receivable is prepared. This schedule is used to prove the subsidiary ledger against the Accounts Receivable account in the general ledger. It also provides a report of the amounts that are due from credit customers.

Credit sales are very common, and many different credit arrangements are used. Each firm must choose the credit policy that suits its needs.

MANAGERIAL IMPLICATIONS

Management must be certain that all sales on credit and other transactions that affect accounts receivable are recorded promptly, efficiently, and accurately. Credit sales are a major source of revenue in many businesses, and accounts receivable represent a major asset. Management needs up-to-date and correct information about both sales and accounts receivable in order to monitor the financial health of the firm.

The use of a sales journal and other special journals saves time and effort and reduces the cost of accounting work. In a retail firm that must handle sales tax, the sales journal and the cash receipts journal also provide a convenient method of recording the amounts owed for this tax. When the data is posted to the Sales Tax Payable account in the general ledger, the firm has a complete and systematic record that speeds the completion of the periodic sales tax return. The firm also has detailed proof of its sales tax figures in case of a tax audit.

Management must select a well-balanced credit policy. This policy should help to increase sales volume but should also keep losses from uncollectible accounts at an acceptable level.

The use of an accounts receivable subsidiary ledger provides management and the credit department with up-to-date information about the balances owed by all customers. This is of special value in controlling credit and collections and in evaluating the effectiveness of credit policies. Since much of the cash needed for day-to-day operations usually comes from accounts receivable, management must keep a close watch on the promptness of customer payments.

REVIEW QUESTIONS

1. Explain how service, merchandising, and manufacturing businesses differ from each other.
2. Why does a small merchandising business like Sports World usually need a more complex set of financial records and statements than a small service business?
3. What is a special journal? Give four examples of special journals.
4. What is a subsidiary ledger? Give two examples of subsidiary ledgers.
5. What type of transaction is recorded in the sales journal?
6. What are the advantages of having a sales journal?
7. Which accounts are kept in the accounts receivable ledger?
8. Why is it useful for a firm to have an accounts receivable ledger?
9. What is a control account? Explain the relationship between the Accounts Receivable account in the general ledger and the customer accounts in the accounts receivable ledger.
10. What is a sales return? What is a sales allowance?
11. Why is a sales return or allowance usually recorded in a special Sales Returns and Allowances account rather than being debited to the Sales account?
12. What kind of account is Sales Returns and Allowances?
13. The sales tax on a credit sale is not collected from the customer immediately. When is this tax usually entered in a firm's accounting records? What account is used to record this tax?
14. How is a multicolumn special journal proved at the end of each month?
15. How are the net sales for an accounting period determined?
16. What purposes does the schedule of accounts receivable serve?

17. How do retail and wholesale businesses differ?
18. What is a trade discount? Why do some firms offer trade discounts to their customers?
19. What is open-account credit?
20. Why are bank credit card sales similar to cash sales for a business?
21. What is the discount on credit card sales? What type of account is used to record this item?
22. When a firm makes a sale involving a credit card issued by a credit card company, does the firm have an account receivable with the cardholder or with the credit card company?
23. What procedure does a business use to collect amounts owed to it for sales involving credit cards issued by credit card companies?
24. What two methods are commonly used to record sales involving credit cards issued by credit card companies?
25. What is a layaway sale? How is this type of sale recorded?
26. What is a COD sale?

MANAGERIAL DISCUSSION QUESTIONS

1. Why is it usually worthwhile for a business to sell on credit even though it will have some losses from uncollectible accounts?
2. How can a firm's credit policy affect its profitability?
3. Why should management insist that all sales on credit and other transactions affecting the firm's accounts receivable be journalized and posted promptly?
4. How can an efficient set of accounting records help management maintain sound credit and collection policies?
5. How does the Sales Returns and Allowances account provide management with a measure of operating efficiency? What problems might be indicated by a high level of returns and allowances?
6. Suppose that you are the accountant for a small chain of clothing stores. Up to now the firm has offered open-account credit to qualified customers but has not allowed the use of bank credit cards. The president of the chain has asked your advice about changing the firm's credit policy. What advantages might there be in eliminating the open-account credit and accepting bank credit cards instead? Do you see any disadvantages?
7. During the past year the Shelton Company has had a very substantial increase in its losses from uncollectible accounts. Assume that you are the newly hired controller of this firm and that you have been asked to find the reason for the increase. What policies and procedures would you investigate?

EXERCISES

EXERCISE 7-1   **Identifying the accounts used to record sales and related transactions.** The transactions given on page 152 took place at the Trailways Shop, a retail business that sells camping equipment. Indicate the numbers of the general ledger accounts that would be debited and credited to record each transaction.

GENERAL LEDGER ACCOUNTS

101	Cash	401	Sales
111	Accounts Receivable	451	Sales Returns and Allowances
231	Sales Tax Payable		

TRANSACTIONS

1. Sold merchandise on credit. The transaction involved sales tax.
2. Received checks from credit customers on account.
3. Accepted a return of merchandise from a credit customer. The original sale involved sales tax.
4. Sold merchandise for cash. The transaction involved sales tax.
5. Gave an allowance to a credit customer for damaged merchandise. The original sale involved sales tax.
6. Provided a cash refund to a customer who returned merchandise. The original sale was made for cash and involved sales tax.

EXERCISE 7-2 **Identifying the journals used for a variety of transactions.** The accounting system of the Trailways Shop includes the journals listed below. Indicate which journal would be used to record each of the following transactions.

JOURNALS

Cash Receipts Journal   Sales Journal
Cash Payments Journal   General Journal
Purchases Journal

TRANSACTIONS

1. Sold merchandise on credit.
2. Accepted a return of merchandise from a credit customer.
3. Paid the monthly rent.
4. Purchased merchandise on credit.
5. Sold merchandise for cash.
6. Collected sums on account from credit customers.
7. Received an additional cash investment from the owner.
8. Issued a check to pay a creditor on account.

EXERCISE 7-3 **Recording credit sales.** The following transactions took place at the Trailways Shop during May 19X3. Indicate how these transactions would be entered in a sales journal like the one shown on page 129.

TRANSACTIONS

May   1   Sold a tent and other items on credit to David Aaron. Issued Sales Slip 1101 for $560 plus sales tax of $28.

        2   Sold a backpack, an air mattress, and other items to Eileen Moore. Issued Sales Slip 1102 for $240 plus sales tax of $12.

        3   Sold a lantern, cooking utensils, and other items to Peter Dawkins. Issued Sales Slip 1103 for $185 plus sales tax of $9.25.

EXERCISE 7-4   **Recording a sales return.** On May 8, 19X3, the Trailways Shop accepted a return of some damaged merchandise from Susan Voss, a credit customer. Issued Credit Memorandum 129 for $73.50, which includes sales tax of $3.50. The original sale was made on Sales Slip 1132 of May 5. Show how the necessary general journal entry would be recorded.

EXERCISE 7-5   **Recording a sales allowance.** On May 21, 19X3, the Trailways Shop gave an allowance to Thomas DeLeon, a credit customer, for some merchandise that was slightly damaged but usable. Issued Credit Memorandum 130 for $10.50, which includes sales tax of $0.50. The original sale was made on Sales Slip 1198 of May 19. Show how the necessary general journal entry would be recorded.

EXERCISE 7-6   **Determining net sales.** On May 31, 19X3, the general ledger of the Trailways Shop contained a balance of $24,580 in the Sales account and a balance of $1,160 in the Sales Returns and Allowances account. What was the amount of net sales for the month?

EXERCISE 7-7   **Preparing the Revenue section of the income statement.** On June 30, 19X3, the general ledger of the Trailways Shop contained a balance of $25,940 in the Sales account and a balance of $1,225 in the Sales Returns and Allowances account. Prepare the Revenue section of the firm's income statement for the month ended June 30, 19X3.

EXERCISE 7-8   **Computing a trade discount.** The Warren Distributing Company, a wholesale firm, made sales with the following list prices and trade discounts. What amount will the firm use to record each sale in the sales journal?

1. List price of $750 and trade discount of 40 percent.
2. List price of $1,200 and trade discount of 40 percent.
3. List price of $360 and trade discount of 30 percent.

EXERCISE 7-9   **Computing a series of trade discounts.** The Asheville Corporation, a wholesale firm, made sales with the following list prices and trade discounts. What amount will the firm use to record each sale in the sales journal?

1. List price of $2,000 and trade discounts of 25 and 15 percent.
2. List price of $1,800 and trade discounts of 25 and 15 percent.
3. List price of $940 and trade discounts of 20 and 10 percent.

PROBLEMS

PROBLEM 7-1   **Recording credit sales in the sales journal and posting the totals to the general ledger.** MicroLand is a retail store that sells microcomputer equipment and software. The firm's credit sales for January 19X1 are listed on page 154 along with the general ledger accounts used to record these sales. (The balance shown is for the beginning of the month.)

Instructions
1. Open the general ledger accounts, and enter the balance of Accounts Receivable for January 1, 19X1.
2. Record the transactions in a sales journal like the one shown on page 129. (Use *1* as the journal page number.)
3. Total, prove, and rule the sales journal as of January 31.
4. Post the column totals from the sales journal to the proper general ledger accounts.

GENERAL LEDGER ACCOUNTS

111	Accounts Receivable	$18,200 Dr.
231	Sales Tax Payable	
401	Sales	

TRANSACTIONS FOR JANUARY 19X1

Jan. 2 Sold a microcomputer system to Goldman and O'Keefe, a law firm. Issued Sales Slip 721 for $4,650 plus sales tax of $186.

5 Sold an electronic spreadsheet program and other software to Ann Ferris. Issued Sales Slip 722 for $595 plus sales tax of $23.80.

9 Sold word processing software and a letter-quality printer to the Drake Insurance Agency. Issued Sales Slip 723 for $1,620 plus sales tax of $64.80.

12 Sold a microcomputer system to Mark Zelinski. Issued Sales Slip 724 for $3,200 plus sales tax of $128.

18 Sold two disk drives and a video monitor to Laura Brown. Issued Sales Slip 725 for $1,150 plus sales tax of $46.

24 Sold three microcomputer systems to the Wagner Real Estate Company. Issued Sales Slip 726 for $9,480 plus sales tax of $379.20.

26 Sold data base management software to Richard McCann. Issued Sales Slip 727 for $295 plus sales tax of $11.80.

31 Sold word processing software to Maria Ramos. Issued Sales Slip 728 for $350 plus sales tax of $14.

PROBLEM 7-2

Journalizing credit sales and sales returns and allowances; posting to the general ledger; reporting sales revenue. The New Directions Furniture Center is a retail store that specializes in modern living room and dining room furniture. The firm's credit sales and sales returns and allowances for March 19X6 are listed on page 155 along with the general ledger accounts used to record these transactions. (The balances shown are for the beginning of March.)

Instructions
1. Open the general ledger accounts, and enter the balances for March 1, 19X6.
2. Record the transactions in a sales journal like the one shown on page 129 and in a general journal. (Use *3* as the page number for the sales journal and *9* as the page number for the general journal.)
3. Post the entries from the general journal.
4. Total, prove, and rule the sales journal as of March 31.
5. Post the column totals from the sales journal.

6. Prepare the heading and the Revenue section of the firm's income statement for the month ended March 31, 19X6.

GENERAL LEDGER ACCOUNTS

111	Accounts Receivable	$2,606 Dr.
231	Sales Tax Payable	1,195 Cr.
401	Sales	
451	Sales Returns and Allowances	

TRANSACTIONS FOR MARCH 19X6

Mar. 1 Sold a living room sofa to Deborah Watson. Issued Sales Slip 1483 for $875 plus sales tax of $43.75.

6 Sold three living room chairs to Robert Kruger. Issued Sales Slip 1484 for $790 plus sales tax of $39.50.

9 Sold a dining room set to Kathleen Ryan. Issued Sales Slip 1485 for $2,600 plus sales tax of $130.

11 Accepted a return of a damaged chair from Robert Kruger. The chair was originally sold on Sales Slip 1484 of March 6. Issued Credit Memorandum 207 for $278.25, which includes sales tax of $13.25.

17 Sold living room tables and bookcases to Henry Chu. Issued Sales Slip 1486 for $2,250 plus sales tax of $112.50.

23 Sold eight dining room chairs to Anita Kovacs. Issued Sales Slip 1487 for $1,600 plus sales tax of $80.

25 Gave Henry Chu an allowance for scratches on his bookcases. Issued Credit Memorandum 208 for $52.50, which includes sales tax of $2.50. The bookcases were originally sold on Sales Slip 1486 of March 17.

27 Sold a living room sofa and four chairs to Victor Chavez. Issued Sales Slip 1488 for $1,840 plus sales tax of $92.

29 Sold a dining room table to Judith Stern. Issued Sales Slip 1489 for $650 plus sales tax of $32.50.

31 Sold a living room modular wall unit to Gary Lawson. Issued Sales Slip 1490 for $1,570 plus sales tax of $78.50.

Note: Save your working papers for use in Problem 7-3.

PROBLEM 7-3   **Posting to the accounts receivable ledger and preparing a schedule of accounts receivable.** This problem is a continuation of Problem 7-2.

Instructions   1. Set up an accounts receivable subsidiary ledger for the New Directions Furniture Center. Open an account for each of the credit customers listed on page 156 and enter the balances as of March 1, 19X6. All of these customers have terms of n/60.

2. Post the individual entries from the sales journal and the general journal prepared in Problem 7-2.

3. Prepare a schedule of accounts receivable for March 31, 19X6.

4. Check the total of the schedule of accounts receivable against the balance of the Accounts Receivable account in the general ledger. The two amounts should be equal.

CREDIT CUSTOMERS

Name	Balance
Victor Chavez	$ 225.50
Henry Chu	
Anita Kovacs	
Robert Kruger	570.00
Gary Lawson	245.00
Kathleen Ryan	
Judith Stern	465.50
Deborah Watson	1,100.00

PROBLEM 7-4

Journalizing credit sales involving trade discounts; posting to the general ledger; reporting sales revenue. The Howard Distributing Company sells toys and games to retail stores. The firm offers a trade discount of 40 percent on toys and 30 percent on games. Its credit sales and sales returns and allowances for June 19X7 are listed below along with the general ledger accounts used to record these transactions. (The balance shown is for the beginning of June 19X7.)

Instructions

1. Open the general ledger accounts, and enter the balance of Accounts Receivable for June 1, 19X7.
2. Record the transactions in a sales journal like the one shown on page 142 and in a general journal. (Use 6 as the page number for the sales journal and 18 as the page number for the general journal.) Be sure to enter each sale at its *net price*.
3. Post the entry from the general journal to the proper general ledger accounts.
4. Total and rule the sales journal as of June 30.
5. Post the column total from the sales journal to the proper general ledger accounts.
6. Prepare the heading and the Revenue section of the firm's income statement for the month ended June 30, 19X7.

GENERAL LEDGER ACCOUNTS

111	Accounts Receivable	$21,750 Dr.
401	Sales	
451	Sales Returns and Allowances	

TRANSACTIONS FOR JUNE 19X7

June   1 Sold toys to the Crown Department Store. Issued Invoice 4576, which shows a list price of $8,800 and a trade discount of 40 percent.

            5 Sold games to the Martin Bookstores. Issued Invoice 4577, which shows a list price of $10,650 and a trade discount of 30 percent.

9 Sold games to the Toy and Game Emporium. Issued Invoice 4578, which shows a list price of $3,520 and a trade discount of 30 percent.

14 Sold toys to the Elway Variety Stores. Issued Invoice 4579, which shows a list price of $12,200 and a trade discount of 40 percent.

18 Accepted a return of all the games shipped to the Toy and Game Emporium because they were damaged in transit. Issued Credit Memorandum 362. The original sale was made on Invoice 4578 of June 9.

22 Sold toys to Wilson's Toy Circus. Issued Invoice 4580, which shows a list price of $8,160 and a trade discount of 40 percent.

26 Sold games to the Crown Department Store. Issued Invoice 4581, which shows a list price of $10,150 and a trade discount of 30 percent.

30 Sold toys to the Rockwell Toy Center. Issued Invoice 4582, which shows a list price of $11,700 and a trade discount of 40 percent.

Note: Save your working papers for use in Problem 7-5.

PROBLEM 7-5 **Posting to the accounts receivable ledger and preparing a schedule of accounts receivable.** This problem is a continuation of Problem 7-4.

Instructions 1. Set up an accounts receivable subsidiary ledger for the Howard Distributing Company. Open an account for each of the credit customers listed below, and enter the balances as of June 1, 19X7. All of these customers have terms of n/45.

2. Post the individual entries from the sales journal and the general journal prepared in Problem 7-4.

3. Prepare a schedule of accounts receivable for June 30, 19X7.

4. Check the total of the schedule of accounts receivable against the balance of the Accounts Receivable account in the general ledger. The two amounts should be equal.

CREDIT CUSTOMERS

Name	Balance
Crown Department Store	$ 7,440
Elway Variety Stores	10,100
Martin Bookstores	
Rockwell Toy Center	
Toy and Game Emporium	4,210
Wilson's Toy Circus	

ALTERNATE PROBLEMS

PROBLEM 7-1A **Recording credit sales in the sales journal and posting the totals to the general ledger.** Bay City Electronics is a retail store that sells consumer electronics products. The firm's credit sales for July 19X1 are listed on page 158 along with the general ledger accounts used to record these sales. (The balance shown is for the beginning of the month.)

Instructions

1. Open the general ledger accounts, and enter the balance of Accounts Receivable for July 1, 19X1.
2. Record the transactions in a sales journal like the one shown on page 129. (Use 7 as the journal page number.)
3. Total, prove, and rule the sales journal as of July 31.
4. Post the column totals from the sales journal to the proper general ledger accounts.

GENERAL LEDGER ACCOUNTS

111	Accounts Receivable	$4,390 Dr.
231	Sales Tax Payable	
401	Sales	

TRANSACTIONS FOR JULY 19X1

July   1   Sold a video cassette recorder and blank cassettes to Lois Robbins. Issued Sales Slip 542 for $845 plus sales tax of $50.70.

6   Sold a stereo system to Patrick McMullen. Issued Sales Slip 543 for $1,750 plus sales tax of $105.

11   Sold a color television set to Kenneth Reed. Issued Sales Slip 544 for $610 plus sales tax of $36.60.

17   Sold a digital record player to Rosemary Dunn. Issued Sales Slip 545 for $390 plus sales tax of $23.40.

23   Sold a stereo cassette deck and speakers to Linda Montez. Issued Sales Slip 546 for $725 plus sales tax of $43.50.

27   Sold a portable color television set to Eric Lindstrom. Issued Sales Slip 547 for $245 plus sales tax of $14.70.

29   Sold a video cassette recorder and blank cassettes to Janet Selby. Issued Sales Slip 548 for $795 plus sales tax of $47.70.

31   Sold a digital clock-radio and a portable cassette player to Vincent DeMassi. Issued Sales Slip 549 for $139 plus sales tax of $8.34.

PROBLEM 7-2A

Journalizing credit sales and sales returns and allowances; posting to the general ledger; reporting sales revenue. The Danville Home Improvement Center sells wall panels, paint, floor tiles, and other items needed for home remodeling jobs. The firm's credit sales and sales returns and allowances for August 19X5 are listed on page 159 along with the general ledger accounts used to record these transactions. (The balances shown are for the beginning of the month.)

Instructions

1. Open the general ledger accounts, and enter the balances for August 1, 19X5.
2. Record the transactions in a sales journal like the one shown on page 129 and in a general journal. (Use 8 as the page number for the sales journal and 24 as the page number for the general journal.)
3. Post the entries from the general journal.
4. Total, prove, and rule the sales journal as of August 31.

5. Post the column totals from the sales journal.
6. Prepare the heading and the Revenue section of the firm's income statement for the month ended August 31, 19X5.

GENERAL LEDGER ACCOUNTS

111	Accounts Receivable	$2,822 Dr.
231	Sales Tax Payable	480 Cr.
401	Sales	
451	Sales Returns and Allowances	

TRANSACTIONS FOR AUGUST 19X5

Aug.   1 Sold kitchen cabinets and floor tiles to Thomas McMurtry. Issued Sales Slip 2875 for $1,300 plus sales tax of $52.

        4 Sold wall panels, ceiling tiles, and other items to Alice Jenkins. Issued Sales Slip 2876 for $2,450 plus sales tax of $98.

        7 Accepted a return of a damaged kitchen cabinet from Thomas McMurtry. Issued Credit Memorandum 431. The item was originally sold for $110 plus sales tax of $4.40 on Sales Slip 2875 of August 1.

     12 Sold paint, wallpaper, and other items to Dominic LaRosa. Issued Sales Slip 2877 for $635 plus sales tax of $25.40.

     16 Sold unpainted bookcases, stain, and varnish to Karen Anderson. Issued Sales Slip 2878 for $920 plus sales tax of $36.80.

     21 Sold wall panels and floor tiles to Carl Kessler. Issued Sales Slip 2879 for $1,785 plus sales tax of $71.40.

     23 Sold light fixtures and ceiling tiles to Dorothy Norman. Issued Sales Slip 2880 for $460 plus sales tax of $18.40.

     25 Gave Carl Kessler an allowance of $104 because of scratches on his wall panels. This amount includes sales tax of $4. Issued Credit Memorandum 432. The wall panels were originally sold on Sales Slip 2879 of August 21.

     27 Sold bathroom cabinets, wall tiles, and light fixtures to Sarah Logan. Issued Sales Slip 2881 for $825 plus sales tax of $33.

     31 Sold wall panels and other items to George Petrovic. Issued Sales Slip 2882 for $1,660 plus sales tax of $66.40.

Note: Save your working papers for use in Problem 7-3A.

PROBLEM 7-3A   **Posting to the accounts receivable ledger and preparing a schedule of accounts receivable.** This problem is a continuation of Problem 7-2A.

Instructions   1. Set up an accounts receivable subsidiary ledger for the Danville Home Improvement Center. Open an account for each of the credit customers listed on page 160, and enter the balances as of August 1, 19X5. All of these customers have terms of n/60.

2. Post the individual entries from the sales journal and the general journal prepared in Problem 7-2A.

3. Prepare a schedule of accounts receivable for August 31, 19X5.

4. Check the total of the schedule of accounts receivable against the balance of the Accounts Receivable account in the general ledger. The two amounts should be equal.

CREDIT CUSTOMERS

Name	Balance
Karen Anderson	$ 270.00
Alice Jenkins	
Carl Kessler	1,024.00
Dominic LaRosa	
Sarah Logan	580.00
Thomas McMurtry	
Dorothy Norman	636.00
George Petrovic	312.00

PROBLEM 7-4A **Journalizing credit sales involving trade discounts; posting to the general ledger; reporting sales revenue.** The Bell Importing Company sells costume jewelry and low-priced watches to retail stores. The firm offers a trade discount of 40 percent on the jewelry and 30 percent on the watches. Its credit sales and sales returns and allowances for October 19X8 are listed below and on page 161 along with the general ledger accounts used to record these transactions. (The balance shown is for the beginning of October 19X8.)

Instructions 1. Open the general ledger accounts, and enter the balance of Accounts Receivable for October 1, 19X8.
2. Record the transactions in a sales journal like the one shown on page 142 and in a general journal. (Use *10* as the page number for the sales journal and *30* as the page number for the general journal.) Be sure to enter each sale at its *net price*.
3. Post the entry from the general journal to the proper general ledger accounts.
4. Total and rule the sales journal as of October 31.
5. Post the column total from the sales journal to the proper general ledger accounts.
6. Prepare the heading and the Revenue section of the firm's income statement for the month ended October 31, 19X8.

GENERAL LEDGER ACCOUNTS

111	Accounts Receivable	$26,150 Dr.
401	Sales	
451	Sales Returns and Allowances	

TRANSACTIONS FOR OCTOBER 19X8

Oct. 1 Sold costume jewelry to the Regal Fashion Centers. Issued Invoice 7653, which shows a list price of $10,200 and a trade discount of 40 percent.

4 Sold watches to the Glen Variety Stores. Issued Invoice 7654, which shows a list price of $12,360 and a trade discount of 30 percent.

10 Sold watches to the Medico Drugstores. Issued Invoice 7655, which shows a list price of $15,640 and a trade discount of 30 percent.

16 Sold costume jewelry to the Marcus Jewelry Store. Issued Invoice 7656, which shows a list price of $4,800 and a trade discount of 40 percent.

22 Sold watches to the Oakdale Department Store. Issued Invoice 7657, which shows a list price of $8,900 and a trade discount of 30 percent.

24 Accepted a return of all the costume jewelry shipped to the Marcus Jewelry Store because the items were damaged in transit. Issued Credit Memorandum 584. The original sale was made on Invoice 7656 of October 16.

27 Sold costume jewelry to the Glen Variety Stores. Issued Invoice 7658, which shows a list price of $16,500 and a trade discount of 40 percent.

31 Sold watches to the Hilton Economy Stores. Issued Invoice 7659, which shows a list price of $18,250 and a trade discount of 30 percent.

Note: Save your working papers for use in Problem 7-5A.

PROBLEM 7-5A

Posting to the accounts receivable ledger and preparing a schedule of accounts receivable. This problem is a continuation of Problem 7-4A.

Instructions

1. Set up an accounts receivable subsidiary ledger for the Bell Importing Company. Open an account for each of the credit customers listed below, and enter the balances as of October 1, 19X8. All of these customers have terms of n/45.

2. Post the individual entries from the sales journal and the general journal prepared in Problem 7-4A.

3. Prepare a schedule of accounts receivable for October 31, 19X8.

4. Check the total of the schedule of accounts receivable against the balance of the Accounts Receivable account in the general ledger. The two amounts should be equal.

CREDIT CUSTOMERS

Name	Balance
Glen Variety Stores	$ 8,650
Hilton Economy Stores	12,200
Marcus Jewelry Store	
Medico Drugstores	
Oakdale Department Store	5,300
Regal Fashion Centers	

Just as the management of a merchandising business must have timely and accurate information about sales and accounts receivable in order to control operations and make decisions, it must also have appropriate information about purchases and accounts payable. Buying needed goods on time, keeping track of the amounts owed to suppliers, and paying invoices promptly so that the firm can maintain a satisfactory credit rating are all vital to successful operations in a merchandising business. Thus the accounting system of a merchandising business should contain records and procedures that permit quick and efficient handling of data about purchases and accounts payable.

ACCOUNTING FOR PURCHASES AND ACCOUNTS PAYABLE

PURCHASING PROCEDURES

Merchandising businesses normally purchase most of their goods on credit under an open-account arrangement. In a large firm there is usually a centralized purchasing department that is responsible for locating suitable suppliers, obtaining price quotations and credit terms, and placing orders.

Whenever a sales department needs goods, it sends the purchasing department a form called a *purchase requisition*, which lists the items that are wanted. The purchase requisition is signed by the manager of the sales department or some other person who is authorized to approve requests for merchandise. The purchasing department selects a supplier that can furnish the necessary goods at an appropriate price and issues a form called a *purchase order* to the supplier. The purchase order specifies exactly what items are required, the quantity, the price quoted, and the agreed credit terms. This form is signed by the firm's purchasing agent or some other employee who has responsibility for approving purchases.

As soon as the goods arrive at the firm, they are examined and a form called a *receiving report* is prepared to show the quantity received and the condition of the goods. The purchasing department then compares the supplier's invoice (bill) with the receiving report and the purchase order. If the invoice contains any errors or if defective goods were received, the purchasing department contacts the supplier and settles the problem.

After the invoice is checked by the purchasing department, it is sent to the accounting department along with copies of the purchase order and the receiving report. The accounting department rechecks the quantities, prices, and extensions on the invoice and then records the purchase. Shortly before the due date of the invoice, the accounting department issues a check to the supplier and records the payment.

In a small firm, purchasing activities are usually handled by a single individual on a part-time basis. This individual may be the owner, a manager, or some other highly responsible member of the staff.

INTERNAL CONTROL OF PURCHASES

Because of the large amounts of money spent to buy goods, most businesses develop careful procedures for the control of purchases and their payment. In Chapter 11 you will learn about the voucher system, a special system that many firms use to achieve this internal control. Essentially, however, whether the voucher system is in use or not, a business should be sure that its control process includes the following safeguards.

1. All purchases are made only after proper authorization has been given in writing.
2. Goods are carefully checked when they are received. Then they are compared with the purchase order and with the invoice received from the supplier.
3. The computations on the invoice are checked for accuracy.
4. Authorization for payment is made by someone other than the person who ordered the goods. This authorization is given only after all the verifications have been made.
5. Still another person writes the check for payment.
6. Prenumbered forms are used for purchase requisitions, purchase orders, and checks. Periodically the numbers of the documents that were issued are verified to make sure that all forms can be accounted for.

One major objective of these procedures is to create written proof that all purchases and payments are properly authorized. Another major objective is to ensure that several different people are involved in the process of buying and receiving goods and making the necessary payments. This division of responsibility provides a system of checks and balances.

In a small firm with a limited number of employees, it may be difficult to achieve as much division of responsibility as is desirable. However, the accountant for such a business tries to design as effective a set of control procedures as the company's resources will allow.

THE MERCHANDISE PURCHASES ACCOUNT

The purchase of goods by a firm is considered a cost of doing business. During each accounting period, the amounts involved in such transactions are debited to a temporary account called Merchandise Purchases. This account and other accounts related to purchases appear just before the expense accounts in the general ledger and are reported on the income statement in a section called Cost of Goods Sold. At the end of the accounting period, Merchandise Purchases and the other related accounts are closed.

THE NEED FOR A PURCHASES JOURNAL

For most merchandising businesses, it is not efficient to enter credit purchases of goods in a general journal. Instead, a special journal called a *purchases journal* is used to record these transactions. To see why a purchases journal is helpful, consider how four credit purchases made by Sports World during the first week of December 19X4 would appear in a general journal. Each entry would involve a separate debit to Merchandise Purchases and a separate credit to Accounts Payable plus a detailed explanation, as shown below.

19X4				
Dec. 1	Merchandise Purchases	501	625 00	
	Accounts Payable	205		625 00
	Purchased merchandise from Prestige Athletic Goods, Invoice 43480, dated Nov. 28, terms 2/10, n/30.			
2	Merchandise Purchases	501	810 00	
	Accounts Payable	205		810 00
	Purchased merchandise from Warren Wholesale Company, Invoice 522, dated Nov. 30, terms n/30.			
4	Merchandise Purchases	501	460 00	
	Accounts Payable	205		460 00
	Purchased merchandise from Active Sporting Goods, Invoice 2389, dated Dec. 1, terms n/30.			
5	Merchandise Purchases	501	1,150 00	
	Accounts Payable	205		1,150 00
	Purchased merchandise from Best Products Corporation, Invoice A7517, dated Dec. 2, terms 2/10, n/30.			

If these transactions were recorded in the general journal, they would also require eight individual postings to general ledger accounts: four postings to Merchandise Purchases and four postings to Accounts Payable.

Merchandise Purchases   No. 501

DATE	EXPLANATION	POST. REF.	DEBIT	CREDIT	BALANCE	DR. CR.
19X4						
Dec. 1		J12	625 00		625 00	Dr.
2		J12	810 00		1,435 00	Dr.
4		J12	460 00		1,895 00	Dr.
5		J12	1,150 00		3,045 00	Dr.

Accounts Payable   No. 205

DATE	EXPLANATION	POST. REF.	DEBIT	CREDIT	BALANCE	DR. CR.
19X4						
Dec. 1	Balance	✓			1,700 00	Cr.
1		J12		625 00	2,325 00	Cr.
2		J12		810 00	3,135 00	Cr.
4		J12		460 00	3,595 00	Cr.
5		J12		1,150 00	4,745 00	Cr.

Clearly, it would be very time-consuming to record purchases of merchandise on credit in this manner each month. A great deal of effort would be wasted in making repetitive journal entries and repetitive postings.

USING A PURCHASES JOURNAL

A special journal intended only for credit purchases of merchandise simplifies and speeds up the recording process for these transactions. Refer to the purchases journal shown below. Notice how the various columns in this journal efficiently organize the data about the firm's credit purchases and make it possible to record each purchase on a single line. In addition, there is no need to enter account titles and explanations.

Recording Entries in a Purchases Journal

Purchases of merchandise on credit must be journalized promptly because it is essential that a business have an up-to-date record of the amounts that it owes to suppliers. Otherwise, the firm might not be able to make payments on time and maintain a good credit rating. Each purchase should therefore be recorded as soon as the supplier's invoice has been verified.

The purchases journal shown below is used by Sports World. Notice that it includes columns for recording the date of the entry, the name of the supplier, the invoice number, the invoice date, the credit terms, and the amount of the purchase. The necessary information is taken from the supplier's invoice. (To the customer this document is a *purchase invoice*. To the supplier it is a *sales invoice*.) An example of an invoice is shown on page 166.

PURCHASES JOURNAL for Month of January 19X5   Page 1

DATE		PURCHASED FROM	INVOICE NO.	INVOICE DATE	TERMS	✓	AMOUNT
Jan.	3	Warren Wholesale Company	649	12/31	n/30		1,200 00
	12	Active Sporting Goods	2453	1/8	n/30		310 00
	17	Best Products Corporation	A7620	1/14	2/10, n/30		245 00
	24	Prestige Athletic Goods	43571	1/20	2/10, n/30		520 00
	28	Miller Distributing Company	845	1/25	n/30		1,130 00
	30	Best Products Corporation	A7694	1/26	2/10, n/30		275 00

The invoice date and the credit terms must be carefully recorded because they determine when payment is due. Some suppliers require payment 30 days after the date of the invoice. These terms are usually expressed as *net 30 days* or *n/30* on the invoice. Other suppliers allow the customer to take a discount of 1 or 2 percent if payment is made within a short period of time, often 10 days. Alternatively, the customer can pay the full amount of the invoice at the end of a longer period, such as 30 days. Credit terms of this type are shown on the invoice as *2% 10 days, net 30 days,* or *2/10, n/30*. Still other suppliers have terms of *net 10 days EOM*, or *n/10 EOM*, which means that the full amount is due 10 days after the end of the month in which the invoice was issued.

The discounts mentioned here are known as *cash discounts*. They are offered by suppliers in order to encourage quick payment of invoices by customers. To the customer this type of price reduction is a *purchase discount*. To the supplier it is a *sales discount*. The accounting treatment of cash discounts is described in Chapter 9.

WARREN WHOLESALE COMPANY
671 Valley Street
Los Angeles, California 90046

SOLD TO: Sports World
365 Broad Street
San Francisco, CA 94107

INV. NO.: **649**

INV. DATE: Dec. 31, 19X4

TERMS: net 30 days

SHIP VIA: Truck prepaid

QUANTITY	ITEM	UNIT PRICE	AMOUNT
10	Power Play Tennis Rackets	$ 25.00	$ 250.00
5	All-Pro Golf Sets	110.00	550.00
5 pr.	Silver Slope Skis	80.00	400.00
			$1,200.00

Keep in mind that the purchases journal is used to record only credit purchases of merchandise. Credit purchases of other items such as equipment and supplies that are to be used in the business and not resold to customers are entered in the general journal.

Posting From a Purchases Journal

The use of a special journal greatly simplifies the posting process for purchases of merchandise on credit. No amounts are posted from the purchases journal to the general ledger during the month. Instead, summary postings are made at the end of this period.

The purchases journal and general ledger accounts shown on page 167 illustrate the necessary procedure. At the end of each month, the accountant for Sports World adds the amounts recorded in the purchases journal, enters the total, and rules the journal. Since there is only one money column, the accountant posts the total as a debit to Merchandise Purchases and a credit to Accounts Payable in the general ledger. Then, to show that the postings were made, the accountant enters the numbers of the accounts below the total of the purchases journal and enters the abbreviation *P1* in the Posting Reference column of the accounts. (This abbreviation indicates that the data was posted from page 1 of the purchases journal.)

For the sake of simplicity, the purchases journal shown on page 167 contains only a limited number of entries. In actual practice Sports World would have many more entries each month. Thus the time saved by making summary postings to the general ledger is even greater than this illustration indicates.

During the month, the individual entries in the purchases journal are posted to the creditor accounts in the accounts payable ledger. The check marks in the

DATE		PURCHASED FROM	INVOICE NO.	INVOICE DATE	TERMS	✓	AMOUNT
Jan.	3	Warren Wholesale Company	649	12/31	n/30	✓	1,200 00
	12	Active Sporting Goods	2453	1/8	n/30	✓	310 00
	17	Best Products Corporation	A7620	1/14	2/10, n/30	✓	245 00
	24	Prestige Athletic Goods	43571	1/20	2/10, n/30	✓	520 00
	28	Miller Distributing Company	845	1/25	n/30	✓	1,130 00
	30	Best Products Corporation	A7694	1/26	2/10, n/30	✓	275 00
	31	Total					3,680 00
							(501)
							(205)

Merchandise Purchases   No. 501

DATE	EXPLANATION	POST. REF.	DEBIT	CREDIT	BALANCE	DR. CR.
19 X5 Jan. 31		P1	3,680 00		3,680 00	Dr.

Accounts Payable   No. 205

DATE	EXPLANATION	POST. REF.	DEBIT	CREDIT	BALANCE	DR. CR.
19 X5 Jan. 1	Balance	✓			1,920 00	Cr.
31		P1		3,680 00	5,600 00	Cr.

journal illustrated above show that these postings have been completed. (The procedure for posting to the accounts payable ledger is discussed in a later section of this chapter.)

Advantages of a Purchases Journal

Every business has certain types of transactions that occur over and over again. A well-designed accounting system includes journals that permit efficient recording of such transactions. In most merchandising firms, purchases of goods on credit take place often enough to make it worthwhile to use a purchases journal. This type of special journal saves time and effort by simplifying the initial entry of purchases and by eliminating repetitive postings to the general ledger. With a one-column purchases journal like the one shown above, no matter how many transactions are recorded each month, it is only necessary to make two summary postings to the general ledger at the end of the month.

The use of a purchases journal along with other special journals also permits the division of accounting work among different employees. Still another advantage of a purchases journal is that it strengthens the audit trail. All purchases of goods on credit are conveniently grouped together in a single journal, and the entry for each purchase clearly shows the number and date of the supplier's invoice—the source document for the transaction.

RECORDING FREIGHT IN

Some purchases are made with the understanding that the buyer will pay the *freight charge*—the cost of shipping the goods from the seller's warehouse. In certain cases the buyer is billed directly by the transportation company for the freight charge and issues a check to that company. In other cases the freight charge is paid by the seller and then shown on the invoice that the buyer receives for the goods. The total of the invoice covers both the price of the goods and the freight charge.

No matter how the billing for a freight charge is handled, the amount involved is debited to an account called Freight In or Transportation In. This is one of several accounts related to purchases, and it appears in the Cost of Goods Sold section of the income statement, where its balance is added to the balance of the Merchandise Purchases account.

When a freight charge is listed on the seller's invoice, the buyer must enter three elements in its accounting records, as indicated by the following example.

Price of goods (to be debited to Merchandise Purchases)	$252
Freight charge (to be debited to Freight In)	12
Total of invoice (to be credited to Accounts Payable)	$264

To record this type of transaction efficiently, it is necessary to use a multi-column purchases journal, such as the one shown below.

PURCHASES JOURNAL for Month of June 19X5   Page 6

DATE	PURCHASED FROM	INVOICE NO.	INVOICE DATE	TERMS	✓	ACCOUNTS PAYABLE CREDIT	MERCH. PURCH. DEBIT	FREIGHT IN DEBIT
June 3	Dantz Company	2596	6/1	n/30		264 00	252 00	12 00

RECORDING PURCHASES RETURNS AND ALLOWANCES

As noted already, in a business with a good system of internal control, new merchandise is examined carefully as soon as it arrives to make sure that it is satisfactory. If the wrong goods were shipped or if any items are damaged or defective, the firm contacts the supplier and arranges to send back the merchandise, which results in a *purchase return,* or to obtain a reduced price, which results in a *purchase allowance.* The supplier then issues a credit memorandum as evidence that credit has been granted for the return or allowance.

Suppose that Sports World receives merchandise from the Warren Wholesale Company on January 3, 19X5, and finds that some goods are damaged. Warren agrees to accept a return of the items and to give credit for them as soon as they arrive back at its warehouse. Meanwhile, Sports World records the full amount of the invoice ($1,200) in its purchases journal. On January 17 Sports World receives a credit memorandum for $50 from Warren and makes an entry in its general journal as shown on page 169.

	19 X5					
	Jan.	17	Accounts Payable/Warren Wholesale Co.	205/✓	50 00	
			Purchases Returns and Allowances	503		50 00
			Received Credit Memorandum 38 for			
			damaged merchandise that was returned.			
			The original purchase was made on			
			Invoice 649 of Dec. 31, 19X4.			

Notice that this entry includes a debit to Accounts Payable and a credit to an account called Purchases Returns and Allowances. (In addition, there is a debit to the creditor's account in the accounts payable ledger, which will be explained in a later section of this chapter.)

Although it would be possible to credit Merchandise Purchases for returns and allowances, accountants prefer to use another account—Purchases Returns and Allowances—in order to have a separate record of these transactions. Purchases Returns and Allowances is referred to as a contra account because it has a credit balance, which is contrary to the normal balance of a cost account. The credit balance of Purchases Returns and Allowances is subtracted from the debit balance of Merchandise Purchases in the Cost of Goods Sold section of the income statement.

A business that has only a few purchases returns and allowances each month records these transactions in a general journal. However, in a firm with a sizable number of purchases returns and allowances, it is more efficient to use a special purchases returns and allowances journal.

DETERMINING THE COST OF PURCHASES

The income statement of a merchandising business contains a section called Cost of Goods Sold. This section combines information about the merchandise inventory at the start of the accounting period, the cost of the purchases made during the period, and the merchandise inventory at the end of the period. The final figure in this section—the cost of goods sold—is used in computing the net income or net loss for the period.

If a business has freight charges, the cost of purchases is reported on the income statement as shown below.

Cost of Goods Sold

Merchandise Inventory, June 1, 19X5		$10,620
Merchandise Purchases	$22,400	
Freight In	550	
Delivered Cost of Purchases	$22,950	
Less Purchases Returns and Allowances	1,710	
Net Delivered Cost of Purchases		21,240
Total Merch. Available for Sale		$31,860
Less Merch. Inventory, June 30, 19X5		13,700
Cost of Goods Sold		$18,160

Notice that the balance of the Merchandise Purchases account ($22,400) and the balance of the Freight In account ($550) are added to find the delivered cost of purchases ($22,950). Then the balance of the Purchases Returns and Allowances account ($1,710) is subtracted to find the net delivered cost of purchases ($21,240).

If a firm does not have any freight charges, the computation of its cost of purchases is simpler. The balance of the Purchases Returns and Allowances account is subtracted from the balance of the Merchandise Purchases account to find the net purchases for the period, as in the following example.

Merchandise Purchases	$3,680	
Less Purchases Returns and Allowances	150	
Net Purchases		$3,530

In Chapter 16 you will see how the complete income statement for a merchandising business is prepared and how the cost of goods sold is used in calculating the results of operations.

THE NEED FOR AN ACCOUNTS PAYABLE LEDGER

It is highly important for a business to pay invoices on time so that it can maintain a good credit reputation with its suppliers. Being able to buy merchandise on credit allows a firm to conduct more extensive operations and use its financial resources more effectively than if it were required to pay cash for all purchases.

The need for prompt payment of invoices makes it essential that businesses keep detailed records of the amounts they owe. The most efficient method of organizing this information is to set up an *accounts payable ledger* with individual accounts for all creditors. (A firm's creditors may include suppliers of equipment and services as well as suppliers of merchandise.)

Each account in the accounts payable ledger contains a complete record of the transactions with a creditor—purchases, payments, and returns and allowances. The balance of the account shows the amount currently owed to the creditor. Like the accounts receivable ledger, the accounts payable ledger is known as a subsidiary ledger because it is separate from and subordinate to the general ledger.

USING AN ACCOUNTS PAYABLE LEDGER

It is common for businesses to keep the accounts for their creditors on ledger sheets or cards that are similar to the one shown on page 171. A balance ledger form with three money columns is usually preferred. In a small firm like Sports World, the creditor accounts are placed in alphabetic order for convenience. Larger firms and firms that use computers for their financial recordkeeping work assign an account number to each creditor and maintain the creditor accounts in numeric order.

Since liability accounts normally have credit balances, all balances in the accounts payable ledger are presumed to be credit balances. However, debit balances may occur from time to time because of an overpayment or a return of goods that were already paid for. One simple method of handling this situation is to circle the balance to show that it is a debit amount.

Daily Routine for the Accounts Payable Ledger

Because of the importance of having up-to-date information about the sums owed to creditors at all times, postings to the accounts payable ledger should be made on a daily basis.

Posting a Credit Purchase Each credit purchase of goods recorded in the purchases journal is posted to the proper creditor's account in the accounts payable ledger, as shown below.

PURCHASES JOURNAL for Month of January 19X5   Page 1

DATE	PURCHASED FROM	INVOICE NO.	INVOICE DATE	TERMS	✓	AMOUNT
Jan. 3	Warren Wholesale Company	649	12/31	n/30	✓	1,200 00

NAME   Warren Wholesale Company
ADDRESS   671 Valley Street
         Los Angeles, CA 90046   **TERMS** n/30

DATE	DESCRIPTION	POST. REF.	DEBIT	CREDIT	BALANCE
19 X5					
Jan. 1	Balance	✓			400 00
3	Invoice 649, 12/31/X4	P1		1,200 00	1,600 00

Notice that the date the transaction was journalized, the invoice number, the date of the invoice, and the amount are transferred from the purchases journal to the creditor's account. The amount is entered in the Credit column of the account. Then the new balance is determined and recorded. To indicate that the posting process has been completed, a check mark (✓) is placed in the purchases journal and the abbreviation *P1* is entered in the Posting Reference column of the creditor's account.

Purchases of equipment and services on credit that appear in the general journal are posted in a similar manner.

19 X5				
Jan. 26	Store Equipment	131	1,450 00	
	Accounts Payable/Chase Company	205/✓		1,450 00
	Purchased new display racks and shelves, Invoice 29668, dated Jan. 21, terms n/60.			

NAME   Chase Company
ADDRESS   8632 Willamette Boulevard
         Eugene, OR 97405   **TERMS** n/60

DATE	DESCRIPTION	POST. REF.	DEBIT	CREDIT	BALANCE
19 X5					
Jan. 26	Invoice 29668, 1/21/X5	J1		1,450 00	1,450 00

Posting Cash Paid on Account In a firm that uses special journals and subsidiary ledgers, the cash paid to creditors is first recorded in a cash payments journal and then posted to the appropriate accounts in the accounts payable ledger. The account illustrated below shows the posting of a payment made by Sports World to one of its creditors on January 12, 19X5. (The necessary entry in the cash payments journal is discussed in Chapter 9.)

NAME	Warren Wholesale Company				
ADDRESS	671 Valley Street				
	Los Angeles, CA 90046				TERMS n/30

DATE	DESCRIPTION	POST. REF.	DEBIT	CREDIT	BALANCE
19 X5					
Jan. 1	Balance	✓			400 00
3	Invoice 649, 12/31/X4	P1		1,200 00	1,600 00
12		CP1	400 00		1,200 00

Posting a Purchase Return or Allowance Whether purchases returns and allowances are first entered in the general journal or in a special purchases returns and allowances journal, these transactions must be posted to the accounts payable ledger. The following illustration shows how a return of damaged merchandise by Sports World was posted from the general journal to the creditor's account.

19 X5				
Jan. 17	Accounts Payable/Warren Wholesale Co.	205/✓	50 00	
	Purchases Returns and Allowances	503		50 00
	Received Credit Memorandum 38 for			
	damaged merchandise that was returned.			
	The original purchase was made on			
	Invoice 649 of Dec. 31, 19X4.			

NAME	Warren Wholesale Company				
ADDRESS	671 Valley Street				
	Los Angeles, CA 90046				TERMS n/30

DATE	DESCRIPTION	POST. REF.	DEBIT	CREDIT	BALANCE
19 X5					
Jan. 1	Balance	✓			400 00
3	Invoice 649, 12/31/X4	P1		1,200 00	1,600 00
12		CP1	400 00		1,200 00
17	CM 38	J1	50 00		1,150 00

Notice that the debit amount in the general journal entry requires two postings—one to the Accounts Payable account in the general ledger and one to the creditor's account in the subsidiary ledger. This double posting is indicated by placing the account number 205 and a check mark in the Posting Reference column of the journal. A diagonal line separates the two posting references.

End-of-Month Routine for the Accounts Payable Ledger

When an accounts payable ledger is used, the Accounts Payable account in the general ledger becomes a control account and serves as a link between the two ledgers. Its balance summarizes the balances of the creditor accounts in the subsidiary ledger.

At the end of each month, after all amounts have been posted from the purchases journal, the cash payments journal, and the general journal to the accounts payable ledger, the balances in this ledger are proved against the balance of the Accounts Payable account in the general ledger. A two-step procedure is followed. First a *schedule of accounts payable* is prepared. This schedule lists all balances owed to creditors. Next the total of the schedule is compared with the balance of the Accounts Payable account in the general ledger. The two figures should be the same.

On January 31, 19X5, the accounts payable ledger of Sports World contained the accounts shown below and on page 174.

NAME	Active Sporting Goods					
ADDRESS	204 Drake Avenue					
	Seattle, WA 98115				TERMS	n/30
DATE	DESCRIPTION	POST. REF.	DEBIT	CREDIT	BALANCE	
19 X5 Jan. 12	Invoice 2453, 1/8/X5	P1		310 00	310 00	

NAME	Best Products Corporation					
ADDRESS	9941 Golden Gate Plaza					
	Oakland, CA 94604				TERMS	2/10, n/30
DATE	DESCRIPTION	POST. REF.	DEBIT	CREDIT	BALANCE	
19 X5 Jan. 1	Balance	✔			1,300 00	
5		CP1	1,300 00		–0–	
17	Invoice A7620, 1/14/X5	P1		245 00	245 00	
22		CP1	245 00		–0–	
30	Invoice A7694, 1/26/X5	P1		275 00	275 00	

NAME	Chase Company					
ADDRESS	8632 Willamette Boulevard					
	Eugene, OR 97405				TERMS	n/60
DATE	DESCRIPTION	POST. REF.	DEBIT	CREDIT	BALANCE	
19 X5 Jan. 26	Invoice 29668, 1/21/X5	J1		1,450 00	1,450 00	

NAME	Miller Distributing Company					
ADDRESS	3183 Pacific Road					
	San Diego, CA 92401				TERMS	n/30

DATE		DESCRIPTION	POST. REF.	DEBIT	CREDIT	BALANCE
19 X5						
Jan.	1	Balance	✓			220 00
	19	CM 72	J1	100 00		120 00
	24		CP1	120 00		–0–
	28	Invoice 845, 1/25/X5	P1		1,130 00	1,130 00

NAME	Prestige Athletic Goods					
ADDRESS	267 Spring Street					
	Denver, CO 80216				TERMS	2/10, n/30

DATE		DESCRIPTION	POST. REF.	DEBIT	CREDIT	BALANCE
19 X5						
Jan.	24	Invoice 43571, 1/20/X5	P1		520 00	520 00
	28		CP1	520 00		–0–

NAME	Warren Wholesale Company					
ADDRESS	671 Valley Street					
	Los Angeles, CA 90046				TERMS	n/30

DATE		DESCRIPTION	POST. REF.	DEBIT	CREDIT	BALANCE
19 X5						
Jan.	1	Balance	✓			400 00
	3	Invoice 649, 12/31/X4	P1		1,200 00	1,600 00
	12		CP1	400 00		1,200 00
	17	CM 38	J1	50 00		1,150 00
	29		CP1	1,150 00		–0–

The schedule of accounts payable illustrated below was prepared from these accounts. A comparison of its total with the balance of the Accounts Payable account in the firm's general ledger shows that the two amounts are equal.

SPORTS WORLD
Schedule of Accounts Payable
January 31, 19X5

CREDITOR	BALANCE
Active Sporting Goods	310 00
Best Products Corporation	275 00
Chase Company	1,450 00
Miller Distributing Company	1,130 00
Total	3,165 00

			POST.				DR.
DATE	EXPLANATION		REF.	DEBIT	CREDIT	BALANCE	CR.
19 X5							
Jan. 1	Balance		✓			1,920 00	Cr.
17			J1	50 00		1,870 00	Cr.
19			J1	100 00		1,770 00	Cr.
26			J1		1,450 00	3,220 00	Cr.
31			P1		3,680 00	6,900 00	Cr.
31			CP1	3,735 00		3,165 00	Cr.

(Accounts Payable — No. 205)

PRINCIPLES AND PROCEDURES SUMMARY

In a firm with a strong system of internal control, there are careful procedures for approving requests for new merchandise, choosing suitable suppliers, placing orders with the suppliers, checking goods after they arrive, verifying invoices, and approving payments. In addition, purchases, payments, and returns and allowances are entered in the firm's accounting records promptly and accurately.

Merchandising businesses normally purchase the majority of their goods on credit. The most efficient way to record such transactions is to use a special purchases journal. With this type of journal, only one line is needed to enter all the data about a credit purchase. Also, the posting process is greatly simplified because no amounts are posted to the general ledger until the end of the month, when summary postings are made. For example, with a one-column purchases journal, the total of all amounts is posted to the general ledger at the end of the month as a debit to Merchandise Purchases and a credit to Accounts Payable.

Some purchases of goods are made with the understanding that the buyer will pay the freight charges. The amounts of these charges are debited to an account called Freight In. If the seller pays the freight charge in advance for the buyer, the sum involved appears on the seller's invoice and must be recorded in the purchases journal along with the price of the goods. In such cases a multicolumn purchases journal is needed.

Returns and allowances on purchases of goods are credited to an account called Purchases Returns and Allowances. These transactions may be recorded in the general journal or in a special purchases returns and allowances journal.

The use of an accounts payable subsidiary ledger helps a firm to keep track of the amounts that it owes to creditors. Postings are made to this ledger on a daily basis. Each credit purchase of goods is posted from the purchases journal, each payment on account is posted from the cash payments journal, and each return or allowance related to a credit purchase is posted from the general journal or the purchases returns and allowances journal. At the end of the month, a schedule of accounts payable is prepared. This schedule lists the balances owed to the firm's creditors and is used in proving the accuracy of the subsidiary ledger. The total of the schedule of accounts payable is compared with the balance of the Accounts Payable account in the general ledger, which serves as a control account. The two amounts should be equal.

Merchandise Purchases, Freight In, and Purchases Returns and Allowances are all temporary accounts that are used to accumulate data about the cost of purchases during an accounting period. These accounts are reported in the Cost of Goods Sold section of the income statement.

MANAGERIAL IMPLICATIONS

Management and the accountant must work together to make sure that there is good internal control of purchasing operations. A carefully designed system of checks and balances must be set up to protect the business against fraud and errors and against excessive investment in merchandise.

The accountant must also make sure that all transactions related to credit purchases of goods are recorded efficiently and that up-to-date information about the amounts owed to creditors is always available. The use of a purchases journal and an accounts payable ledger helps to accomplish these goals.

Maintaining a good credit reputation with suppliers is of great concern to management, and this can only be done when there is a well-run accounting system that pays invoices on time. In addition, a well-run accounting system provides management with information that allows the planning of future cash needs so that sufficient funds are on hand for the payment of suppliers but surplus funds can be invested. Alternatively, if there will be a temporary shortage of funds, management is aware of the problem ahead of time and can arrange a loan or take other measures to handle the situation.

The use of separate accounts for recording purchases of goods, freight charges, and purchases returns and allowances also provides valuable information to management. It makes it possible to analyze all the elements involved in the cost of purchases.

REVIEW QUESTIONS

1. What activities does a purchasing department perform?
2. What is the purpose of each of the following documents?
   a. purchase requisition
   b. purchase order
   c. receiving report
   d. invoice
   e. credit memorandum
3. What are the major safeguards that should be built into a system of internal control for purchases of goods?
4. What type of transaction is recorded in the purchases journal?
5. Explain the advantages of using a purchases journal.

6. Why are the invoice date and terms recorded in the purchases journal?
7. A business has purchased some new equipment for use in its operations and not for resale to customers. Should this transaction be entered in the purchases journal? If not, where should it be recorded?
8. What do the following credit terms mean?
   a. n/30
   b. 2/10, n/30
   c. n/10 EOM
9. Why do some suppliers offer cash discounts?
10. What is the purpose of the Freight In account?
11. Why do accountants prefer to use a Purchases Returns and Allowances account rather than crediting these transactions to the Merchandise Purchases account?
12. On what financial statement do the accounts related to purchases of merchandise appear? In which section of this statement are they reported?
13. How is the net delivered cost of purchases computed?
14. Why is it useful for a business to have an accounts payable ledger?
15. What type of accounts are kept in the accounts payable ledger?
16. What is the relationship of the Accounts Payable account in the general ledger to the accounts payable subsidiary ledger?
17. What is a schedule of accounts payable? Why is it prepared?

MANAGERIAL DISCUSSION QUESTIONS

1. Why should management be concerned about internal control of purchases?
2. How can good internal control of purchases protect a firm from fraud and errors and from excessive investment in merchandise?
3. In what ways would excessive investment in merchandise harm a business?
4. Why should management be concerned about the timely payment of invoices?
5. Why is it important for a firm to maintain a satisfactory credit rating?
6. Suppose that you are the new controller of a small but growing company and you find that the firm has a policy of paying cash for all purchases of goods even though it could obtain credit. The president of the company does not like the idea of having debts, but the vice president thinks that this is a poor business policy that will hurt the firm in the future. The president has asked your opinion. Would you agree with the president or the vice president? Why?

EXERCISES

EXERCISE 8-1   **Identifying the accounts used to record purchases and related transactions.**
The transactions on page 178 took place at the Open Road Bicycle Shop. Indicate

the numbers of the general ledger accounts that would be debited and credited to record each transaction.

GENERAL LEDGER ACCOUNTS

101	Cash	502	Freight In
205	Accounts Payable	503	Purchases Returns
501	Merchandise Purchases		and Allowances

TRANSACTIONS

1. Purchased merchandise for $700. The terms of the supplier's invoice are 2/10, n/30.
2. Returned some damaged merchandise to a supplier and received a credit memorandum for $125.
3. Issued a check for $400 to a supplier as a payment on account.
4. Purchased merchandise for $920 plus a freight charge of $48. The supplier's invoice is payable in 30 days.
5. Received an allowance for some merchandise that was slightly damaged but can be sold at a reduced price. The supplier's credit memorandum is for $50.
6. Purchased merchandise for $330 in cash.

EXERCISE 8-2 **Identifying the journals used to record purchases and related transactions.** The accounting system of the Open Road Bicycle Shop includes the journals listed below. Indicate which journal would be used to record each of the transactions shown in Exercise 8-1.

JOURNALS

Cash Receipts Journal   Sales Journal
Cash Payments Journal   General Journal
Purchases Journal

EXERCISE 8-3 **Recording credit purchases.** The following transactions took place at the Monroe Auto Parts Center during the first week of July 19X1. Indicate how these transactions would be entered in a purchases journal like the one shown on page 165.

TRANSACTIONS

July 1 Purchased batteries for $1,950 from the Russell Corporation. Received Invoice 8621, dated June 27, which has terms of n/30.
3 Purchased mufflers for $575 from the Sterling Company. Received Invoice 441, dated June 30, which has terms of 1/10, n/60.
5 Purchased car radios for $2,820 from Allen Audio Products. Received Invoice 5317, dated July 1, which has terms of 2/10, n/30.

EXERCISE 8-4 **Recording credit purchases involving freight charges.** The transactions listed on page 179 took place at the Hogan Building Supply Company during the first week of March 19X6. Indicate how these transactions would be entered in a purchases journal like the one shown on page 168.

TRANSACTIONS

Mar. 1 Purchased door frames for $3,200 plus a freight charge of $190 from the Argo Corporation. Received Invoice 2586, dated Feb. 26, which has terms of 2/10, n/30.

4 Purchased wallboard for $5,750 plus a freight charge of $260 from the Willis Company. Received Invoice 872, dated March 1, which has terms of n/60.

EXERCISE 8-5 **Recording a purchase return.** On June 5, 19X1, the Elmwood Appliance Center received Credit Memorandum 368 for $980 from the Arrow Corporation. The credit memorandum covered a return of damaged microwave ovens originally purchased on Invoice 5293 of May 16. Show the general journal entry that would be made at Elmwood for this transaction.

EXERCISE 8-6 **Recording a purchase allowance.** On June 23, 19X1, the Elmwood Appliance Center was given an allowance of $100 by the Home Products Company, which issued Credit Memorandum 34. The allowance was for scratches on some refrigerators that were originally purchased on Invoice 986 of June 11. Show the general journal entry that would be made at Elmwood for this transaction.

EXERCISE 8-7 **Determining the cost of purchases.** On May 31, 19X3, the general ledger of Banner Fashions, a clothing store, contained a balance of $16,680 in the Merchandise Purchases account, a balance of $475 in the Freight In account, and a balance of $1,262 in the Purchases Returns and Allowances account. What was the delivered cost of the purchases made during May? What was the net delivered cost of these purchases?

PROBLEMS

PROBLEM 8-1 **Journalizing credit purchases and purchases returns and allowances; posting to the general ledger.** The Dale Photo Mart is a retail store that sells cameras, film, and photographic accessories. The firm's credit purchases and purchases returns and allowances for April 19X5 are listed on page 180 along with the general ledger accounts used to record these transactions. (The balance shown is for the beginning of April.)

Instructions 1. Open the general ledger accounts, and enter the balance of Accounts Payable for April 1, 19X5.
2. Record the transactions in a purchases journal like the one shown on page 165 and in a general journal. (Use *4* as the page number for the purchases journal and *12* as the page number for the general journal.)
3. Post the entries from the general journal to the proper general ledger accounts.
4. Total and rule the purchases journal as of April 30.

5. Post the column total from the purchases journal to the proper general ledger accounts.
6. Compute the net purchases of the firm for the month of April.

GENERAL LEDGER ACCOUNTS

205	Accounts Payable	$3,476 Cr.
501	Merchandise Purchases	
503	Purchases Returns and Allowances	

TRANSACTIONS FOR APRIL 19X5

Apr. 1 Purchased instant cameras for $1,995 from the Janus Company, Invoice 3445, dated March 26; the terms are 30 days net.
      8 Purchased black-and-white film for $347.50 from General Photographic Products, Invoice 11021, dated April 3, net payable in 60 days.
     12 Purchased lenses for $226.30 from the Allied Optical Company, Invoice 2783, dated April 9; the terms are 1/10, n/60.
     18 Received Credit Memorandum 216 for $225 from the Janus Company for defective cameras that were returned. The cameras were originally purchased on Invoice 3445 of March 26.
     20 Purchased color film for $1,064.80 from General Photographic Products, Invoice 11197, dated April 15, net payable in 60 days.
     23 Purchased camera cases for $485 from Houston Leather Goods, Invoice 30138, dated April 18, net due and payable in 45 days.
     28 Purchased disc cameras for $2,469.40 from the Briggs Corporation, Invoice 5072, dated April 24; the terms are 2/10, n/30.
     30 Received Credit Memorandum 1529 for $60 from Houston Leather Goods. The amount is an allowance for slightly damaged but usable goods purchased on Invoice 30138 of April 18.

NOTE: Save your working papers for use in Problem 8-2.

PROBLEM 8-2 **Posting to the accounts payable ledger and preparing a schedule of accounts payable.** This problem is a continuation of Problem 8-1.

Instructions 1. Set up an accounts payable subsidiary ledger for the Dale Photo Mart. Open an account for each of the creditors listed on page 181, and enter the balances as of April 1, 19X5.
2. Post the individual entries from the purchases journal and the general journal prepared in Problem 8-1.
3. Prepare a schedule of accounts payable for April 30, 19X5.
4. Check the total of the schedule of accounts payable against the balance of the Accounts Payable account in the general ledger. The two amounts should be equal.

CREDITORS

Name	Terms	Balance
Allied Optical Company	1/10, n/60	$ 556
Briggs Corporation	2/10, n/30	
General Photographic Products	n/60	2,620
Houston Leather Goods	n/45	300
Janus Company	n/30	

PROBLEM 8-3

Journalizing credit purchases, freight charges, and purchases returns and allowances; posting to the general ledger. The Lexington Office Products Center is a retail business that sells office equipment, furniture, and supplies. Its credit purchases and purchases returns and allowances for September 19X1 are listed below along with the general ledger accounts used to record these transactions. (The balance shown is for the beginning of September.)

Instructions

1. Open the general ledger accounts, and enter the balance of Accounts Payable for September 1, 19X1.
2. Record the transactions in a purchases journal like the one shown on page 168 and in a general journal. (Use 9 as the page number for the purchases journal and 27 as the page number for the general journal.)
3. Post the entries from the general journal to the proper general ledger accounts.
4. Total, prove, and rule the purchases journal as of September 30.
5. Post the column totals from the purchases journal to the proper general ledger accounts.
6. Compute the net delivered cost of the firm's purchases for the month of September.

GENERAL LEDGER ACCOUNTS

205	Accounts Payable	$4,670 Cr.
501	Merchandise Purchases	
502	Freight In	
503	Purchases Returns and Allowances	

TRANSACTIONS FOR SEPTEMBER 19X1

Sept.   3 Purchased desks for $1,980 plus a freight charge of $53 from the Carson Office Furniture Company, Invoice 2431, dated Aug. 29; the credit terms are 30 days net.

7 Purchased electronic typewriters for $2,825 from United Office Machines Inc., Invoice 42917, dated Sept. 2, net due and payable in 60 days.

10 Received Credit Memorandum 165 for $150 from the Carson Office Furniture Company. The amount is an allowance for slightly damaged but usable desks purchased on Invoice 2431 of Aug. 29.

16 Purchased file cabinets for $638.50 plus a freight charge of $31 from the Grant Corporation, Invoice 8066, dated Sept. 11, terms of 30 days net.

20 Purchased electronic desk calculators for $550 from United Office Machines Inc., Invoice 43256, dated Sept. 15, net due and payable in 60 days.

23 Purchased bond paper and copying machine paper for $1,472.30 plus a freight charge of $22 from the Merit Paper Company, Invoice 91648, dated Sept. 18; the terms are 1/10, n/30.

28 Received Credit Memorandum 692 for $110 from United Office Machines Inc. for defective calculators that were returned. The calculators were originally purchased on Invoice 43256 of Sept. 15.

30 Purchased office chairs for $860.20 plus a freight charge of $34 from Business Furniture Inc., Invoice 669, dated Sept. 25, terms of 2/10, n/30.

NOTE: Save your working papers for use in Problem 8-4.

PROBLEM 8-4   **Posting to the accounts payable ledger and preparing a schedule of accounts payable.** This problem is a continuation of Problem 8-3.

Instructions

1. Set up an accounts payable subsidiary ledger for the Lexington Office Products Center. Open an account for each of the creditors listed below, and enter the balance as of September 1, 19X1.
2. Post the individual entries from the purchases journal and the general journal prepared in Problem 8-3.
3. Prepare a schedule of accounts payable for September 30, 19X1.
4. Check the total of the schedule of accounts payable against the balance of the Accounts Payable account in the general ledger. The two amounts should be equal.

CREDITORS

Name	Terms	Balance
Business Furniture Inc.	2/10, n/30	$1,400
Carson Office Furniture Company	n/30	
Grant Corporation	n/30	530
Merit Paper Company	1/10, n/30	2,740
United Office Machines Inc.	n/60	

ALTERNATE PROBLEMS

PROBLEM 8-1A   **Journalizing credit purchases and purchases returns and allowances; posting to the general ledger.** The Alpine Ski Shop is a retail store that sells ski equipment and clothing. The firm's credit purchases and purchases returns and allowances for December 19X2 are listed on page 183 along with the general ledger accounts used to record these transactions. (The balance shown is for the beginning of December.)

Instructions

1. Open the general ledger accounts, and enter the balance of Accounts Payable for December 1, 19X2.
2. Record the transactions in a purchases journal like the one shown on page 165 and in a general journal. (Use *12* as the page number for the purchases journal and *36* as the page number for the general journal.)
3. Post the entries from the general journal to the proper general ledger accounts.
4. Total and rule the purchases journal as of December 31.
5. Post the column total from the purchases journal to the proper general ledger accounts.
6. Compute the net purchases of the firm for the month of December.

GENERAL LEDGER ACCOUNTS

205	Accounts Payable	$5,402 Cr.
501	Merchandise Purchases	
503	Purchases Returns and Allowances	

TRANSACTIONS FOR DECEMBER 19X2

Dec. 1 Purchased ski boots for $1,449.80 from Mountainside Products, Invoice 7256, dated Nov. 28, net payable in 45 days.

6 Purchased skis for $2,785 from Hanover Industries, Invoice 1694, dated Dec. 2; the terms are net 30 days.

9 Received Credit Memorandum 551 for $300 from Mountainside Products for damaged ski boots that were returned. The boots were originally purchased on Invoice 7256 of Nov. 28.

15 Purchased down jackets for $1,187.20 from Winter Fashions Inc., Invoice 869, dated Dec. 11, net due and payable in 60 days.

19 Purchased ski poles for $590 from Hanover Industries, Invoice 1766, dated Dec. 15; the terms are net 30 days.

22 Purchased ski pants for $765 from the Hilton Clothing Company, Invoice 64091, dated Dec. 16; the terms are 1/10, n/60.

28 Received Credit Memorandum 83 for $45 from Hanover Industries for defective ski poles that were returned. The items were originally purchased on Invoice 1766 of Dec. 15.

31 Purchased sweaters for $620 from Century Knit Goods, Invoice 4538, dated Dec. 27; the credit terms are 2/10, n/30.

NOTE: Save your working papers for use in Problem 8-2A.

PROBLEM 8-2A   **Posting to the accounts payable ledger and preparing a schedule of accounts payable.** This problem is a continuation of Problem 8-1A.

Instructions

1. Set up an accounts payable subsidiary ledger for the Alpine Ski Shop. Open an account for each of the creditors listed on page 184, and enter the balances as of December 1, 19X2.

2. Post the individual entries from the purchases journal and the general journal prepared in Problem 8-1A.
3. Prepare a schedule of accounts payable for December 31, 19X2.
4. Check the total of the schedule of accounts payable against the balance of the Accounts Payable account in the general ledger. The two amounts should be equal.

CREDITORS

Name	Terms	Balance
Century Knit Goods	2/10, n/30	
Hanover Industries	n/30	$ 425
Hilton Clothing Company	1/10, n/60	1,250
Mountainside Products	n/45	1,547
Winter Fashions Inc.	n/60	2,180

PROBLEM 8-3A

Journalizing credit purchases, freight charges, and purchases returns and allowances; posting to the general ledger. The Greenhouse is a retail store that sells garden equipment, furniture, and supplies. Its credit purchases and purchases returns and allowances for June 19X8 are listed below along with the general ledger accounts used to record these transactions. (The balance shown is for the beginning of June.)

Instructions

1. Open the general ledger accounts, and enter the balance of Accounts Payable for June 1, 19X8.
2. Record the transactions in a purchases journal like the one shown on page 168 and in a general journal. (Use 6 as the page number for the purchases journal and 18 as the page number for the general journal.)
3. Post the entries from the general journal to the proper general ledger accounts.
4. Total, prove, and rule the purchases journal as of June 30.
5. Post the column totals from the purchases journal to the proper general ledger accounts.
6. Compute the net delivered cost of the firm's purchases for the month of June.

GENERAL LEDGER ACCOUNTS

205	Accounts Payable	$4,485 Cr.
501	Merchandise Purchases	
502	Freight In	
503	Purchases Returns and Allowances	

TRANSACTIONS FOR JUNE 19X8

June   1 Purchased lawn mowers for $2,450 plus a freight charge of $61 from the Glenn Corporation, Invoice 7792, dated May 26, net due and payable in 60 days.

5 Purchased outdoor chairs and tables for $3,185 plus a freight charge of $79 from the Rustic Garden Furniture Company, Invoice 936, dated June 2; the net amount is due in 45 days.

9 Purchased grass seed for $542.80 from Superior Lawn Products, Invoice 21864, dated June 4; the credit terms are 30 days net.

16 Received Credit Memorandum 124 for $100 from the Rustic Garden Furniture Company. The amount is an allowance for scratches on some of the chairs and tables originally purchased on Invoice 936 of June 2.

19 Purchased fertilizer for $428.70 from Superior Lawn Products, Invoice 21937, dated June 15; the credit terms are 30 days net.

21 Purchased garden hoses for $639.50 from the McGill Rubber Company, Invoice 8571, dated June 17, terms of 1/15, n/60.

28 Received Credit Memorandum 322 for $130 from the McGill Rubber Company for damaged hoses that were returned. The goods were purchased on Invoice 8571 of June 17.

30 Purchased lawn sprinkler systems for $1,960 plus a freight charge of $34 from Duval Industries, Invoice 58819, dated June 26; the credit terms are 2/10, n/30.

NOTE: Save your working papers for use in Problem 8-4A.

PROBLEM 8-4A

Posting to the accounts payable ledger and preparing a schedule of accounts payable. This problem is a continuation of Problem 8-3A.

Instructions

1. Set up an accounts payable subsidiary ledger for the Greenhouse. Open an account for each of the creditors listed below, and enter the balances as of June 1, 19X8.

2. Post the individual entries from the purchases journal and the general journal prepared in Problem 8-3A.

3. Prepare a schedule of accounts payable for June 30, 19X8.

4. Check the total of the schedule of accounts payable against the balance of the Accounts Payable account in the general ledger. The two amounts should be equal.

CREDITORS

Name	Terms	Balance
Duval Industries	2/10, n/30	
Glenn Corporation	n/60	$2,265
McGill Rubber Company	1/15, n/60	
Rustic Garden Furniture Company	n/45	1,390
Superior Lawn Products	n/30	830

9

The proper handling and recording of cash receipts and cash payments are of vital concern in all types of businesses—service businesses, merchandising businesses, and manufacturing businesses. Cash is an essential asset for every firm, but it is also the asset that is most easily stolen, lost, or mishandled. Thus, a well-managed business has careful procedures to control cash and to record cash transactions.

ACCOUNTING FOR CASH

THE NATURE OF CASH TRANSACTIONS

In accounting, the term *cash* covers checks, money orders, and funds on deposit in a bank as well as currency and coins. Actually, a very large number of cash transactions in modern business involve checks.

Cash Receipts

The makeup of a firm's cash receipts depends on the nature of its operations. Some retail businesses, like supermarkets, obtain the bulk of their receipts in the form of currency and coins. Other retail businesses receive a large number of checks in addition to currency and coins. For example, a department store obtains checks through the mail from its charge account customers when they pay their monthly bills and receives currency and coins from other customers who pay at the time they buy the goods. Wholesale firms obtain almost all of their cash receipts in the form of checks.

Cash Payments

For the sake of safety and convenience, businesses make the great majority of their payments by check. In a well-managed firm, only a very limited number of transactions that cannot easily be handled by check are paid with currency and coins. Carefully controlled special-purpose funds are set up to take care of payments of this type. For example, a petty cash fund is often used to make small payments for items like postage stamps, delivery charges, and minor purchases of office supplies. Some firms also maintain a travel and entertainment fund to provide employees with cash for business-related travel and entertainment expenses.

INTERNAL CONTROL OVER CASH

Every business should have a system of internal control over cash that is specifically tailored to its needs. The accountant plays a vital role in designing such a system and works with management to establish and monitor the system. In developing internal control procedures for the cash receipts and cash payments of a business, accountants follow certain basic principles.

Control of Cash Receipts

As noted already, cash is the asset that is most easily stolen, lost, or mishandled. Yet cash is essential to carrying on business operations, so every penny received for goods or services must be protected to make sure that funds are available to pay expenses and take care of other obligations. The following precautionary routines are especially important for cash receipts.

1. Only designated employees should be allowed to receive cash, whether it consists of checks and money orders delivered by mail or currency and coins handed over in person. These employees should be carefully chosen for reliability and accuracy and should be carefully trained. In some firms, all employees who handle cash are bonded. (*Bonding* means that the employees are investigated by an insurance company, and if their characters and backgrounds are satisfactory, their employer is given insurance against losses that may occur if they steal or mishandle the firm's cash.)
2. For the sake of safety, cash receipts should be kept in a cash register, a locked cash drawer, or a safe while they are on the premises.
3. A record should be made of all cash receipts as the funds come into the business. Typically, for currency and coins, this record consists of an audit tape in a cash register or duplicate copies of prenumbered sales slips that were issued to the customers. The use of a cash register provides an especially effective means of control because the machine automatically produces a tape showing the amounts entered. This tape is locked inside the register until it is removed by a supervisor.
4. Before a bank deposit is made, the funds should be checked against the record made when the cash was received. The employee who does the checking should not be the one who received or recorded the cash.
5. All cash receipts should be deposited in the bank promptly, preferably every day or even several times a day if very large amounts are involved. The funds should be deposited intact—that is, no cash receipts should be used for payments. The person who makes the bank deposit should not be the one who received and recorded the funds.
6. All transactions involving cash receipts should be entered in the firm's accounting records promptly. The person who makes these entries should not be the one who received the funds or deposited them in the bank.
7. The monthly bank statement should be received and reconciled by someone other than the employees who handled, recorded, and deposited the funds.

One of the advantages of having efficient and speedy procedures for handling and recording cash receipts is that the funds reach the bank sooner. Cash receipts are not kept on the premises for more than a short time, which means that the funds are safer and are quickly available for paying bills owed by the firm.

Control of Cash Payments

The control procedures for cash receipts are only one part of a well-designed system of internal control. There must also be control over payments so that none of the firm's cash is spent without proper authorization or supervision. Obviously, a firm's cash is safe only if there is complete control over incoming and outgoing funds.

Internal control of cash payments can be achieved by adopting the following procedures.

1. All payments should be made by check except for payments from special-purpose cash funds such as a petty cash fund or a travel and entertainment fund. (The use of a petty cash fund is discussed later in this chapter.)
2. No check should be issued without a properly approved bill, invoice, or other document that describes the reason for the payment.
3. Bills and invoices should be approved only by designated personnel. These individuals should be experienced and reliable.
4. Checks should be prepared and recorded in the checkbook or check register by someone other than the person who approves the payments.
5. Still another person should sign and mail the checks to creditors.
6. Prenumbered check forms should be used. Periodically the numbers of the checks that were issued and the numbers of the blank forms remaining should be verified to make sure that all forms can be accounted for.
7. When the bank statement is reconciled each month, the canceled checks should be carefully verified against the record of checks issued that appears in the checkbook or check register. The reconciliation process should be handled by someone other than the person who prepared and recorded the checks.
8. All transactions involving cash payments should be entered promptly in the firm's accounting records. The person who makes these entries should not be the one who issues the checks and records them in the checkbook or check register.

In a small business, it is usually not possible to achieve as much division of responsibility in the handling of cash receipts and cash payments as is recommended here. However, no matter what the size of a firm, efforts should be made to set up effective control procedures for cash.

The subject of internal control will be discussed in more detail in Chapter 11.

THE RECORDING PROCESS FOR CASH RECEIPTS

Most businesses constantly receive and pay out cash. Because these transactions occur so often, every accounting system should be designed to permit quick and efficient recording of cash receipts and cash payments.

The Need for a Cash Receipts Journal

To simplify the recording process for cash receipts, many firms use a special *cash receipts journal*. Like the other special journals, this journal speeds up the initial entry of transactions and eliminates a great deal of repetition in posting. The following example shows why a cash receipts journal is so useful.

On December 1, 19X4, Sports World received two checks on account from credit customers and had cash sales. If the firm recorded these transactions in a general journal, the entries would appear as shown on page 189. Notice that the three transactions require three debits to Cash, two credits to Accounts Receivable, one credit to Sales, and one credit to Sales Tax Payable. Thus, it is necessary to record seven account titles and seven amounts, as well as an explanation for each entry.

DATE		DESCRIPTION OF ENTRY	POST. REF.	DEBIT	CREDIT
19 X4					
Dec.	1	Cash	101	127 20	
		Accounts Receivable/John Costa	111/✓		127 20
		Collected cash on account.			
	1	Cash	101	79 50	
		Accounts Receivable/Karen Drake	111/✓		79 50
		Collected cash on account.			
	1	Cash	101	598 90	
		Sales	401		565 00
		Sales Tax Payable	231		33 90
		Sold merchandise for cash.			

The posting of seven items to the general ledger involves still more duplication of effort. Each amount must be posted individually as shown in the following Cash account. Even in a small business like Sports World, this means numerous postings to Cash and other general ledger accounts throughout each month.

							Cash			No. 101

DATE		EXPLANATION	POST. REF.	DEBIT	CREDIT	BALANCE	DR. CR.
19 X4							
Dec.	1	Balance	✓			3,610 00	Dr.
	1		J12	127 20		3,737 20	Dr.
	1		J12	79 50		3,816 70	Dr.
	1		J12	598 90		4,415 60	Dr.

The use of a special journal saves considerable time and effort in recording cash receipts.

Entering Transactions in the Cash Receipts Journal

The format of the cash receipts journal varies according to the needs of each business. For the sake of efficiency, separate columns are set up for the accounts used most often in recording a firm's cash receipts. In the case of Sports World, there are two major sources of cash receipts—checks that arrive in the mail from credit customers who are making payments on account and currency and coins received from cash sales. Thus, the firm's accountant established for the business the type of cash receipts journal shown on page 190.

Notice that there are separate columns for recording debits to Cash and credits to Accounts Receivable, Sales Tax Payable, and Sales. The Other Accounts Credit section is used for items that do not fit into any of the special columns. The columnar arrangement in this journal greatly simplifies both the initial entry and the posting of cash receipts. Only one line is required for each

DATE	EXPLANATION	✓	ACCOUNTS RECEIVABLE CREDIT	SALES TAX PAYABLE CREDIT	SALES CREDIT	OTHER ACCOUNTS CREDIT ACCOUNT TITLE	POST. REF.	AMOUNT	CASH DEBIT
Jan. 5	Ruth Carr		254 40						254 40
6	James Allen		222 60						222 60
7	Cash sales			91 20	1,520 00				1,611 20
9	Investment					L. Frank, Capital		5,000 00	5,000 00
10	Janet Bell		76 32						76 32
12	John Costa		84 80						84 80
14	Cash sales			117 90	1,965 00	Cash Short or Over		4 50	2,078 40
16	Cash refund					Supplies		25 00	25 00
18	Marilyn Diaz		65 72						65 72
21	Cash sales			126 60	2,110 00				2,236 60
23	David Fisher		137 80						137 80
28	Cash sales			98 40	1,640 00	Cash Short or Over		1 20	1,739 60
31	Cash sales			21 00	350 00				371 00

transaction, and there is no need to record account titles for the majority of transactions. In addition, posting to the accounts that are used most often can be done on a summary basis at the end of the month. The only amounts that require individual posting to the general ledger are the ones that appear in the Other Accounts Credit section.

The procedures for entering the most common types of cash receipts transactions in this journal are described below.

Cash Sales and Sales Taxes At Sports World a cash register is used to record the currency and coins received from cash sales and to store the funds until a bank deposit can be made. As each transaction is entered, the cash register produces a receipt for the customer and records data about the sale and the sales tax on an audit tape locked inside the machine. At the end of the day, when the machine is cleared, it prints the totals of the transactions on the audit tape. Then the manager of the store removes the tape, and a *cash register proof* is prepared. This proof is designed to reconcile the currency and coins actually in the machine with the totals shown on the audit tape. After the cash register proof is completed, it is used to enter the cash sales and sales tax in the cash receipts journal. The currency and coins are placed in the night depository of the firm's bank.

For the sake of simplicity, the cash receipts journal illustrated above shows weekly rather than daily entries for cash sales. Notice how the cash sales for the week ended January 7 were recorded. The amount of sales tax collected ($91.20) was entered in the Sales Tax Payable Credit column, the amount of sales ($1,520) was entered in the Sales Credit column, and the total amount of cash received ($1,611.20) was entered in the Cash Debit column.

Cash Short or Over In making change, some errors are certain to occur. When such errors are made, the cash available for deposit from cash sales is either more or less than the amount listed on the audit tape taken from the cash register. If the amount of cash available for deposit is greater than the amount shown on the tape, cash is said to be *over*. If there is less cash than the tape shows, cash is said to be *short*. In practice, cash tends to be short more often than over, perhaps because customers are more likely to notice and complain if they receive too little change than if they receive too much.

For proper control over cash receipts, amounts short or over should be recorded. Since a net shortage is expected, an expense account called Cash Short or Over is used for this purpose. The amount short or over is determined at the end of each day when the funds in the cash register are proved against the audit tape. Information about the shortage or overage, if any, appears on the cash register proof.

At Sports World, the amount short or over is recorded in the cash receipts journal when the cash sales are entered. The account title Cash Short or Over and the amount are placed in the Other Accounts Credit section of the journal on the same line with the entry for the cash sales.

Refer to the cash receipts journal shown on page 190. The firm had a cash shortage of $4.50 for the week ended January 14. Since Cash Short or Over must be debited for shortages, the amount was circled when it was entered in the Other Accounts Credit section. This procedure shows that the amount is a debit. The cash receipts journal illustrated on page 190 also contains an entry for a cash overage of $1.20 for the week ended January 28. Since Cash Short or Over is credited for overages, this amount is recorded in the Other Accounts Credit section in the normal manner.

If a firm has frequent entries for cash shortages and overages, it may set up a special Cash Short or Over column in its cash receipts journal.

Although errors in making change can be expected, large shortages or overages should be investigated. They may indicate dishonesty or incompetence in handling cash. Similarly, if shortages and overages occur too often, it is wise to investigate the situation.

Cash Received on Account Like most retail businesses that sell on credit, Sports World bills its customers once a month. It sends a *statement of account* showing the transactions with each customer during the month and the balance owed. The customer is expected to pay within 30 days after receiving the statement.

When checks are received from credit customers, the amounts are entered in the cash receipts journal, and then the checks are deposited in the firm's bank account. Refer to the cash receipts journal shown on page 190. The entry made on January 5 is for cash received on account from Ruth Carr. Notice that the amount ($254.40) was recorded in the Accounts Receivable Credit column and the Cash Debit column.

Additional Investment by the Owner Sometimes the owner of a business makes an additional cash investment. For example, on January 9, 19X5, Lynn Frank, the owner of Sports World, invested an additional $5,000 cash because she wanted to start modernizing the store and expanding its product line, and she felt that the business would therefore need extra funds. The entry for this transaction was made by recording the account title Lynn Frank, Capital and the amount in the Other Accounts Credit section of the cash receipts journal and by recording the amount in the Cash Debit column.

At the end of the accounting period, information about the additional investment is reported in the Owner's Equity section of the balance sheet as follows.

Owner's Equity

Lynn Frank, Capital, Jan. 1, 19X5	$48,200
Additional Investment	5,000
Total Investment	$53,200
Net Income for January	1,650
Lynn Frank, Capital, Jan. 31, 19X5	$54,850

Receipt of a Cash Refund Occasionally a firm may receive a cash refund for supplies, equipment, or other assets that were purchased for cash and then returned. For example, on January 16, Sports World obtained a cash refund of $25 for some defective supplies that it returned to the seller. This transaction was recorded in the cash receipts journal as shown on page 190. Notice that the credit to the Supplies account was recorded in the Other Accounts Credit section.

Collection of a Promissory Note and Interest A *promissory note* is a written promise to pay a specified amount of money on a specified date. Most notes also require that interest be paid at a specified rate. Promissory notes serve as the basis for granting credit in certain sales transactions. They are also used in some cases to replace open-account credit when a customer has an overdue balance.

For example, on April 1, 19X5, Sports World accepted the 6-month promissory note shown below from David Shaw, a customer who owed $200. Shaw had asked for an extension of time in which to pay his balance because he was having financial difficulties. Sports World agreed to the arrangement if Shaw would issue a promissory note with annual interest at 9 percent. The note provided more legal protection than Shaw's open account, and the interest gave Sports World some compensation for the delay in receiving the funds that Shaw owed.

$ 200.00   April 1, 19 X5

Six months _____ **AFTER DATE** I **PROMISE TO PAY**

TO THE ORDER OF _____ Sports World _____

Two hundred and no/100 ······························· **DOLLARS**

PAYABLE AT City National Bank

VALUE RECEIVED with interest at 9%

NO. 28 **DUE** October 1, 19X5   *David Shaw*

When the note was obtained, Sports World made the following general journal entry to record the new asset and to remove Shaw's balance from the firm's accounts receivable. The debit part of the entry involves an asset account called Notes Receivable. The credit part involves both the Accounts Receivable account in the general ledger and Shaw's account in the accounts receivable subsidiary ledger.

19 X5				
Apr. 1	Notes Receivable	109	200 00	
	Accounts Receivable/David Shaw	111/✓		200 00
	Received a 6-month, 9% note from			
	David Shaw to replace open account.			

On October 1, 19X5, the due date of the note, Sports World received a check for $209 from Shaw. This sum covered the amount of the note ($200) and the interest owed for the 6-month period ($9). The necessary entry was made in the cash receipts journal, as shown below. Notice that the credits to both Notes Receivable and Interest Income were recorded in the Other Accounts Credit section.

CASH RECEIPTS JOURNAL for Month of October 19X5 Page 10

DATE	EXPLANATION	✓	ACCOUNTS RECEIVABLE CREDIT	SALES TAX PAYABLE CREDIT	SALES CREDIT	OTHER ACCOUNTS CREDIT			CASH DEBIT
						ACCOUNT TITLE	POST. REF.	AMOUNT	
Oct. 1	Collection of note from David Shaw					Notes Receivable	109	200 00	
						Interest Income	491	9 00	209 00

Posting From the Cash Receipts Journal

During the month the amounts recorded in the Accounts Receivable Credit column of the cash receipts journal are posted individually to the appropriate customer accounts in the accounts receivable subsidiary ledger. Similarly, the amounts that appear in the Other Accounts Credit column are posted individually to the proper general ledger accounts. At the end of the month, the cash receipts journal is totaled, proved, and ruled. Then the totals of all columns except the Other Accounts Credit column are posted to the general ledger.

The proof of the cash receipts journal involves comparing the column totals to make sure that the debits and credits recorded during the month are equal.

PROOF OF CASH RECEIPTS JOURNAL

	Debits
Cash Debit column	$13,903.44

	Credits
Accounts Receivable Credit column	$ 841.64
Sales Tax Payable Credit column	455.10
Sales Credit column	7,585.00
Other Accounts Credit column	5,021.70
	$13,903.44

After all posting work was completed at Sports World in January 19X5, the firm's cash receipts journal appeared as shown below.

DATE	EXPLANATION	✓	ACCOUNTS RECEIVABLE CREDIT	SALES TAX PAYABLE CREDIT	SALES CREDIT	OTHER ACCOUNTS CREDIT ACCOUNT TITLE	POST. REF.	AMOUNT	CASH DEBIT
Jan. 5	Ruth Carr	✓	254 40						254 40
6	James Allen	✓	222 60						222 60
7	Cash sales			91 20	1,520 00				1,611 20
9	Investment					L. Frank, Capital	301	5,000 00	5,000 00
10	Janet Bell	✓	76 32						76 32
12	John Costa	✓	84 80						84 80
14	Cash sales			117 90	1,965 00	Cash Short or Over	529	(4 50)	2,078 40
16	Cash refund					Supplies	129	25 00	25 00
18	Marilyn Diaz	✓	65 72						65 72
21	Cash sales			126 60	2,110 00				2,236 60
23	David Fisher	✓	137 80						137 80
28	Cash sales			98 40	1,640 00	Cash Short or Over	529	1 20	1,739 60
31	Cash sales			21 00	350 00				371 00
31	Totals		841 64	455 10	7,585 00			5,021 70	13,903 44
			(111)	(231)	(401)			(X)	(101)

Posting to the Accounts Receivable Ledger In order to keep the accounts receivable subsidiary ledger up to date at all times, amounts are posted to this ledger from the cash receipts journal on a daily basis. Each figure listed in the Accounts Receivable Credit column is transferred to the account of the customer involved. For example, the $254.40 received from Ruth Carr on January 5 was posted to her account in the subsidiary ledger, as shown below. Notice that the posting reference *CR1* was entered in the account to indicate that the data came from page 1 of the cash receipts journal. A check mark (✓) was placed in the journal to show that the amount was posted.

NAME	Ruth Carr				
ADDRESS	14 Oak Street				
	San Francisco, CA 94123				TERMS n/30

DATE	DESCRIPTION	POST. REF.	DEBIT	CREDIT	BALANCE
19 X5					
Jan. 1	Balance	✓			254 40
5		CR1		254 40	–0–
31	Sales Slip 3609	S1	50 88		50 88

Posting to the General Ledger As noted already, the figures listed in the Other Accounts Credit column of the cash receipts journal are posted individually to the general ledger during the month. For example, the entries of $4.50 and $1.20 made on January 14 and 28 were posted to the Cash Short or Over account as shown on page 195. (Notice that the circled amount was posted as a debit.) The abbreviation *CR1* appears in the Post. Ref. column of the account to indicate the source of the entries, and the account number 529 appears in the cash receipts journal to show that the figures were posted.

			POST.				DR.
DATE	EXPLANATION		REF.	DEBIT	CREDIT	BALANCE	CR.

Cash Short or Over — No. 529

DATE	EXPLANATION	POST. REF.	DEBIT	CREDIT	BALANCE	DR. CR.
19 X5						
Jan. 14		CR1	4 50		4 50	Dr.
28		CR1		1 20	3 30	Dr.

The use of a special journal for cash receipts allows the summary posting of amounts to Cash and the other accounts for which there are separate columns in the journal. At the end of each month, the totals of these columns are posted to the general ledger. For example, the totals posted from the cash receipts journal of Sports World to Cash, Accounts Receivable, Sales Tax Payable, and Sales are shown below and on page 196. Refer to the cash receipts journal illustrated on page 194 to trace the postings.

Cash — No. 101

DATE	EXPLANATION	POST. REF.	DEBIT	CREDIT	BALANCE	DR. CR.
19 X5						
Jan. 1	Balance	✓			4,200 00	Dr.
31		CR1	13,903 44		18,103 44	Dr.

Accounts Receivable — No. 111

DATE	EXPLANATION	POST. REF.	DEBIT	CREDIT	BALANCE	DR. CR.
19 X5						
Jan. 1	Balance	✓			1,098 16	Dr.
14		J1		137 80	960 36	Dr.
22		J1		21 20	939 16	Dr.
31		S1	1,208 40		2,147 56	Dr.
31		CR1		841 64	1,305 92	Dr.

Sales Tax Payable — No. 231

DATE	EXPLANATION	POST. REF.	DEBIT	CREDIT	BALANCE	DR. CR.
19 X5						
Jan. 1	Balance	✓			712 40	Cr.
10		CP1	712 40		—0—	
14		J1	7 80		7 80	Dr.
22		J1	1 20		9 00	Dr.
31		S1		68 40	59 40	Cr.
31		CR1		455 10	514 50	Cr.

	Sales						No. 401
DATE	EXPLANATION	POST. REF.	DEBIT	CREDIT	BALANCE	DR. CR.	
19 X5 Jan. 31		S1		1,140 00	1,140 00	Cr.	
31		CR1		7,585 00	8,725 00	Cr.	

The account numbers entered beneath the totals in the journal show that the figures have been posted. Notice that an X is placed below the total of the Other Accounts Credit column to indicate that this amount is not posted.

Accounting for Cash Discounts on Sales

Like most retail firms that provide credit, Sports World allows its customers 30 days in which to pay. However, as noted in Chapter 8, many wholesale firms offer their credit customers an opportunity to deduct 1 or 2 percent from the total of an invoice if they pay within a specified short discount period, usually 10 days. Otherwise, the full amount of the invoice is due at the end of a longer credit period, often 30 days. The purpose of the cash discount is to encourage customers to pay invoices quickly.

If the customer takes the discount, it is entered in the firm's financial records at the time the cash is received. A contra revenue account called Sales Discount is used to record the sum involved. Normally, a separate Sales Discount Debit column is set up in the cash receipts journal to facilitate the entry of these amounts, as shown below.

CASH RECEIPTS JOURNAL for Month of August 19X5 — Page 8

DATE	EXPLANATION	✓	ACCOUNTS RECEIVABLE CREDIT	SALES CREDIT	OTHER ACCOUNTS CREDIT ACCOUNT TITLE	POST. REF.	AMOUNT	SALES DISCOUNT DEBIT	CASH DEBIT
Aug. 1	Wallace Co.	✓	1,650 00					33 00	1,617 00

In the example illustrated here, the Daniels Corporation received a check for $1,617 from the Wallace Company, a credit customer, in payment of an invoice for $1,650 less a 2 percent discount, which amounted to $33.

Notice that three elements must be recorded when a cash receipt involves a sales discount.

1. The amount of the original sale (as a credit to Accounts Receivable).
2. The amount of the discount (as a debit to Sales Discount).
3. The amount of cash received (as a debit to Cash).

At the end of each accounting period, the debit balance of the Sales Discount account appears on the income statement as a deduction from the credit balance of the Sales account. For example, Sales Discount is presented on the income statement of the Daniels Corporation in the following manner.

Revenue		
Sales		$36,480
Less: Sales Returns and Allowances	$1,200	
Sales Discount	565	1,765
Net Sales		$34,715

Advantages of the Cash Receipts Journal

The cash receipts journal offers the same type of advantages as the other special journals. It saves time, effort, and recording space. The use of separate columns for the accounts most often debited and credited in recording cash receipts speeds up the initial entry of these transactions and allows summary postings to the general ledger at the end of each month. The elimination of repetitive posting work is especially important because even a small business may have numerous cash receipts transactions during a month, and individual postings would be very time-consuming.

The use of a cash receipts journal along with other special journals also permits the division of labor among the accounting staff. With this arrangement several employees can enter transactions at the same time. Finally, the cash receipts journal strengthens the audit trail by grouping all transactions involving cash receipts together in one record.

The Change Fund

Retail firms that receive currency and coins from sales made "over the counter" usually maintain a change fund in order to be able to provide change to their customers. The change fund is placed in the cash register at the beginning of each day and is removed at the end of the day when the money in the register is proved. Then the cash receipts for the day are deposited in the bank, and the change fund is stored in a safe or some other secure place overnight.

An asset account called Change Fund is set up for this item. The balance of the account remains at a fixed level unless management decides that there is a need to increase the fund. Accounting entries are made for the change fund only when it is established and if it is increased.

The amount of the change fund depends on the needs of each business. At Sports World, $75 was selected as a suitable amount.

THE RECORDING PROCESS FOR CASH PAYMENTS

As noted already, a good system of internal control requires that payments be made by check. After approval for a payment is received, one employee prepares the check and records it in the checkbook or check register, and another employee journalizes and posts the transaction. Chapter 10 explains the procedures that should be used to issue checks and maintain banking records. The accounting entries for cash payments are discussed in this section.

The Need for a Cash Payments Journal

Unless a business has just a few cash payments each month, the process of recording these transactions in the general journal is very time-consuming. For example, consider the general journal entries shown on page 198, which are for three cash payments made by Sports World on December 1, 19X4. Notice that these entries require the recording of seven account titles, seven amounts, and three explanations.

DATE		DESCRIPTION OF ENTRY	POST. REF.	DEBIT	CREDIT
19 X4					
Dec.	1	Rent Expense	511	700 00	
		Cash	101		700 00
		Paid December rent, Check 3412.			
	1	Accounts Payable/Best Products Corp.	205/✓	550 00	
		Cash	101		539 00
		Purchases Discount	504		11 00
		Paid Invoice A7548 less discount,			
		Check 3413.			
	1	Accounts Payable/Warren Wholesale Co.	205/✓	385 00	
		Cash	101		385 00
		Paid Invoice 601, Check 3414.			

The posting procedure for the three entries involves still more repetition because all seven amounts must be posted individually to the general ledger. Three postings must be made to Cash, two to Accounts Payable, one to Purchases Discount, and one to Rent Expense. The following Cash account illustrates the need for numerous separate postings when the general journal is used for the initial entry of cash payments.

| | | | | | | | | Cash | | | | No. | 101 |

DATE		EXPLANATION	POST. REF.	DEBIT	CREDIT	BALANCE	DR. CR.
19 X4							
Dec.	1	Balance	✓			3,610 00	Dr.
	1		J12		700 00	2,910 00	Dr.
	1		J12		539 00	2,371 00	Dr.
	1		J12		385 00	1,986 00	Dr.

A special *cash payments journal* provides a far more efficient method of recording these transactions.

Entering Transactions in the Cash Payments Journal

The use of a cash payments journal saves a great deal of time and effort in both the journalizing and posting of cash payment transactions. To understand the reasons for this improvement in efficiency, refer to the cash payments journal shown on page 199, which was set up for Sports World. Notice that this journal has separate columns for the accounts that the firm uses most often to record its cash payments—Cash, Accounts Payable, and Purchases Discount. The Other Accounts Debit section allows the entry of items that do not fit into any of the special columns.

DATE	CHECK NO.	EXPLANATION	ACCOUNTS PAYABLE ✓	ACCOUNTS PAYABLE DEBIT	OTHER ACCOUNTS DEBIT ACCOUNT TITLE	POST. REF.	AMOUNT	PURCH. DISCOUNT CREDIT	CASH CREDIT
Jan. 2	3431	January rent			Rent Expense		700 00		700 00
5	3432	Best Products Corp.		1,300 00				26 00	1,274 00
9	3433	Store fixtures			Store Equipment	✓	600 00		600 00
10	3434	Tax remittance			Sales Tax Payable		712 40		712 40
12	3435	Warren Wholesale Co.		400 00					400 00
13	3436	Store supplies			Supplies		375 00		375 00
16	3437	Withdrawal			L. Frank, Drawing		1,200 00		1,200 00
18	3438	Electric bill			Utilities Expense		150 00		150 00
22	3439	Best Products Corp.		245 00				4 90	240 10
23	3440	Telephone bill			Telephone Expense		86 00		86 00
24	3441	Miller Distrib. Co.		120 00					120 00
26	3442	Newspaper ad			Advertising Expense		195 00		195 00
28	3443	Prestige Athletic Goods		520 00				10 40	509 60
29	3444	Warren Wholesale Co.		1,150 00					1,150 00
31	3445	January payroll			Salaries Expense		2,100 00		2,100 00

The special columns eliminate the need to record the same account titles constantly, and they also eliminate the need for individual postings to Cash, Accounts Payable, and Purchases Discount throughout the month. Instead, summary postings can be made to these accounts at the end of each month. Only the amounts in the Other Accounts Debit section require individual postings to the general ledger.

The procedures for making the most common types of entries in the cash payments journal are explained below.

Payments for Expenses Most businesses pay a variety of expenses each month. For example, Sports World issued checks for rent, electricity, telephone service, advertising, and salaries on January 2, 18, 23, 26, and 31. Refer to these entries in the cash payments journal shown above. Notice that the title of the expense account involved and the amount to be debited to this account are recorded in the Other Accounts Debit section. The offsetting credit appears in the Cash Credit column.

Payments on Account Merchandising businesses usually make numerous payments on account to suppliers for goods that were purchased on credit. If no cash discount is involved, the entry in the cash payments journal simply requires a debit to Accounts Payable and a credit to Cash. For example, refer to the entries of January 12, 24, and 29 in the cash payments journal shown above.

When there is a cash discount, three elements must be recorded.

1. The total amount of the purchase (as a debit to Accounts Payable).
2. The amount of the discount (as a credit to Purchases Discount).
3. The amount of cash paid out (as a credit to Cash).

The entries of January 5, 22, and 28 in the cash payments journal of Sports World illustrate the necessary recording procedure for payments on account that involve cash discounts.

Purchases Discount is a contra cost account that appears in the Cost of Goods Sold section of the income statement at the end of each accounting period. The credit balance of Purchases Discount is deducted from the debit balance of Merchandise Purchases on this statement in the following manner.

Merchandise Purchases		$3,680.00
Less: Purchases Returns and Allowances	$150.00	
Purchases Discount	41.30	191.30
Net Purchases		$3,488.70

Cash Purchases of Equipment and Supplies When a firm makes a cash purchase of equipment, supplies, or another asset, the transaction is recorded in the cash payments journal. For example, refer to the entries made on January 9 and 13 in the cash payments journal shown on page 199. These entries are for store fixtures and store supplies that were purchased for cash by Sports World. Notice that the debit part of each entry was recorded in the Other Accounts Debit section.

Payment of Taxes As discussed before, many retail businesses are required to collect sales tax from their customers. This tax must be remitted periodically to the appropriate tax agency, usually on a monthly or quarterly basis. For example, on January 10, 19X5, Sports World issued a check for $712.40 to the state sales tax commission to pay the sales tax owed for December 19X4. The necessary entry is shown in the cash payments journal illustrated on page 199. Notice that the debit to Sales Tax Payable appears in the Other Accounts Debit section.

In addition to sales tax, a firm may be required to pay a variety of other taxes, such as payroll taxes and property taxes. The entries for the payment of payroll taxes are presented in Chapter 14.

Cash Withdrawals by the Owner In sole proprietorships and partnerships, the owners do not receive salaries. To obtain funds for their personal living expenses, they make withdrawals of cash against previously earned profits that have become part of their capital or against profits that are expected in the future. Accountants usually set up a special type of owner's equity account called a *drawing account* to record withdrawals of this type. Only withdrawals that are intended to permanently reduce the owner's investment in the business are recorded in the capital account.

On January 16, a check for $1,200 was issued to Lynn Frank, the owner of Sports World, as a cash withdrawal for personal living expenses. The necessary entry was made in the cash payments journal, as shown on page 199. The amount was debited to the Lynn Frank, Drawing account.

At the end of each accounting period, information about the withdrawals made during the period is reported in the Owner's Equity section of the balance sheet as follows.

Owner's Equity

Lynn Frank, Capital, Jan. 1, 19X5		$48,200
Additional Investment		5,000
Total Investment		$53,200
Net Income for January	$1,650	
Less Withdrawals	1,200	
Net Increase in Owner's Equity		450
Lynn Frank, Capital, Jan. 31, 19X5		$53,650

Payment of Freight Charges Freight charges on purchases of goods can be handled in two different ways. In some cases, the seller pays the freight charge and then lists it on the invoice sent to the buyer. The total that the buyer pays includes both the price of the goods and the shipping cost. When this arrangement is used, the buyer records the freight charge in the purchases journal, as shown on page 168. Another common procedure is to have the buyer pay the transportation company directly when the goods arrive. The buyer issues a check for the freight charge and records it in the cash payments journal as shown below. Freight In is debited.

CASH PAYMENTS JOURNAL for Month of February 19X5   Page 2

			ACCOUNTS PAYABLE		OTHER ACCOUNTS DEBIT			PURCH. DISCOUNT CREDIT	CASH CREDIT
DATE	CHECK NO.	EXPLANATION	✓	DEBIT	ACCOUNT TITLE	POST. REF.	AMOUNT		
Feb. 1	3446	Freight charge			Freight In	502	53 00		53 00

Payment of a Cash Refund When a customer purchases goods for cash and then returns them or receives an allowance, the customer is usually given a cash refund. For example, on March 1, 19X5, Sports World issued a check for $42.40 to a customer who returned a defective item that was previously sold to her for cash. The check covered the price of the item ($40) and the sales tax collected ($2.40). This transaction was entered in the cash payments journal as shown below. Notice that the debits to Sales Returns and Allowances and Sales Tax Payable appear in the Other Accounts Debit section.

CASH PAYMENTS JOURNAL for Month of March 19X5   Page 3

			ACCOUNTS PAYABLE		OTHER ACCOUNTS DEBIT			PURCH. DISCOUNT CREDIT	CASH CREDIT
DATE	CHECK NO.	EXPLANATION	✓	DEBIT	ACCOUNT TITLE	POST. REF.	AMOUNT		
Mar. 1	3462	Cash refund			Sales Ret. and Allow.	451	40 00		
					Sales Tax Payable	231	2 40		42 40

Cash Purchases of Merchandise Although most merchandising businesses buy the bulk of their goods on credit, occasional purchases may be made for cash. These purchases are recorded in the cash payments journal, as shown below.

CASH PAYMENTS JOURNAL for Month of April 19X5   Page 4

| DATE | CHECK NO. | EXPLANATION | | ACCOUNTS PAYABLE DEBIT | OTHER ACCOUNTS DEBIT | | | PURCH. DISCOUNT CREDIT | CASH CREDIT |
					ACCOUNT TITLE	POST. REF.	AMOUNT		
Apr. 1	3479	Purchase of goods			Merch. Purchases	501	350 00		350 00

Payment of a Promissory Note and Interest As discussed already, a promissory note may be issued to settle an overdue account or to obtain goods, equipment, or other property. For example, on June 10, 19X5, Sports World issued a 6-month promissory note for $1,500 to purchase some new store fixtures from the Allen Equipment Company. The note had an interest rate of 10 percent. This transaction was recorded in the general journal of Sports World by debiting Store Equipment and crediting a liability account called Notes Payable, as shown below.

19 X5				
June 10	Store Equipment	131	1,500 00	
	Notes Payable	201		1,500 00
	Issued a six-month, 10% note to the			
	Allen Equipment Co. for the purchase			
	of new store fixtures.			

On December 10, 19X5, Sports World issued a check for $1,575 in payment of the note ($1,500) and the interest ($75) owed to the Allen Equipment Company. This transaction was recorded in the cash payments journal, as illustrated below. Notice that the entry includes a debit to Notes Payable and a debit to Interest Expense. Both of these amounts appear in the Other Accounts Debit section.

CASH PAYMENTS JOURNAL for Month of December 19X5   Page 12

| DATE | CHECK NO. | EXPLANATION | | ACCOUNTS PAYABLE DEBIT | OTHER ACCOUNTS DEBIT | | | PURCH. DISCOUNT CREDIT | CASH CREDIT |
					ACCOUNT TITLE	POST. REF.	AMOUNT		
Dec. 10	3628	Note paid to Allen Equipment Co.			Notes Payable Interest Expense	201 593	1,500 00 75 00		1,575 00

Posting From the Cash Payments Journal

During the month the figures in the Accounts Payable Debit column of the cash payments journal are posted individually to the accounts payable subsidiary ledger, and the figures in the Other Accounts Debit column are posted individually to the general ledger. At the end of the month, the cash payments journal is totaled, proved, and ruled. Then the totals of all columns except the Other Accounts Debit column are posted to the general ledger. The proof of the cash payments journal is prepared as shown below. The column totals are compared to be sure that the debits and credits in the journal are equal.

PROOF OF CASH PAYMENTS JOURNAL

	Debits
Accounts Payable Debit column	$3,735.00
Other Accounts Debit column	6,118.40
	$9,853.40

	Credits
Purchases Discount Credit column	$ 41.30
Cash Credit column	9,812.10
	$9,853.40

The cash payments journal of Sports World for January 19X5 appears as shown below after all posting is completed.

CASH PAYMENTS JOURNAL for Month of January 19X5   Page 1

DATE	CHECK NO.	EXPLANATION	ACCOUNTS PAYABLE ✓	ACCOUNTS PAYABLE DEBIT	OTHER ACCOUNTS DEBIT ACCOUNT TITLE	POST. REF.	AMOUNT	PURCH. DISCOUNT CREDIT	CASH CREDIT
Jan. 2	3431	January rent			Rent Expense	511	700 00		700 00
5	3432	Best Products Corp.	✓	1,300 00				26 00	1,274 00
9	3433	Store fixtures			Store Equipment	131	600 00		600 00
10	3434	Tax remittance			Sales Tax Payable	231	712 40		712 40
12	3435	Warren Wholesale Co.	✓	400 00					400 00
13	3436	Store supplies			Supplies	129	375 00		375 00
16	3437	Withdrawal			L. Frank, Drawing	302	1,200 00		1,200 00
18	3438	Electric bill			Utilities Expense	517	150 00		150 00
22	3439	Best Products Corp.	✓	245 00				4 90	240 10
23	3440	Telephone bill			Telephone Expense	520	86 00		86 00
24	3441	Miller Distrib. Co.	✓	120 00					120 00
26	3442	Newspaper ad			Advertising Expense	514	195 00		195 00
28	3443	Prestige Athletic Goods	✓	520 00				10 40	509 60
29	3444	Warren Wholesale Co.	✓	1,150 00					1,150 00
31	3445	January payroll			Salaries Expense	523	2,100 00		2,100 00
31		Totals		3,735 00			6,118 40	41 30	9,812 10
				(205)		(X)		(504)	(101)

Posting to the Accounts Payable Ledger   If a firm is to have current information about the amounts that it owes to creditors, the accounts payable ledger must be kept up to date at all times. For this reason, the figures in the Accounts Payable Debit column of the cash payments journal are posted on a daily basis to the appropriate accounts in the accounts payable subsidiary ledger.

The account for the Best Products Corporation given below shows the posting of a $1,300 payment to this creditor on January 5. To indicate that the data came from page 1 of the cash payments journal, the abbreviation *CP1* was entered in the Post. Ref. column of the account. A check mark (✓) in the journal shows that the sum was posted.

NAME	Best Products Corporation					
ADDRESS	9941 Golden Gate Plaza					
	Oakland, CA 94604				TERMS	2/10, n/30

DATE		DESCRIPTION	POST. REF.	DEBIT	CREDIT	BALANCE
19 X5						
Jan.	1	Balance	✓			1,300 00
	5		CP1	1,300 00		–0–
	17	Invoice A7620, 1/14/X5	P1		245 00	245 00
	22		CP1	245 00		–0–
	30	Invoice A7694, 1/26/X5	P1		275 00	275 00

Posting to the General Ledger Each amount listed in the Other Accounts Debit column of the cash payments journal must be posted individually to the general ledger during the month. For example, the entry of January 2 in the cash payments journal of Sports World was posted to the Rent Expense account, as shown below. Again, the abbreviation *CP1* is placed in the account to indicate the source of the data. The account number 511 is entered in the cash payments journal to show that the amount has been posted.

				Rent Expense			No. 511

DATE		EXPLANATION	POST. REF.	DEBIT	CREDIT	BALANCE	DR. CR.
19 X5							
Jan.	2		CP1	700 00		700 00	Dr.

At the end of each month, summary postings are made to Cash and the other general ledger accounts for which there are separate columns in the cash payments journal. The following illustrations show the posting of the column totals to Cash, Accounts Payable, and Purchases Discount at Sports World on January 31. Trace these postings from the cash payments journal given on page 203.

				Cash			No. 101

DATE		EXPLANATION	POST. REF.	DEBIT	CREDIT	BALANCE	DR. CR.
19 X5							
Jan.	1	Balance	✓			4,200 00	Dr.
	31		CR1	13,903 44		18,103 44	Dr.
	31		CP1		9,812 10	8,291 34	Dr.

Accounts Payable						No. 205
DATE	EXPLANATION	POST. REF.	DEBIT	CREDIT	BALANCE	DR. CR.
19 X5						
Jan. 1	Balance	✓			1,920 00	Cr.
17		J1	50 00		1,870 00	Cr.
19		J1	100 00		1,770 00	Cr.
26		J1		1,450 00	3,220 00	Cr.
31		P1		3,680 00	6,900 00	Cr.
31		CP1	3,735 00		3,165 00	Cr.

Purchases Discount						No. 504
DATE	EXPLANATION	POST. REF.	DEBIT	CREDIT	BALANCE	DR. CR.
19 X5						
Jan. 31		CP1		41 30	41 30	Cr.

The account numbers are placed beneath the totals in the cash payments journal to indicate that the amounts have been posted. An X is entered below the total of the Other Accounts Debit column to show that this figure is not posted.

Advantages of the Cash Payments Journal

The cash payments journal provides the same kind of benefits as the cash receipts journal and the other special journals.

1. It simplifies and speeds up both the journalizing and posting of cash payments.
2. It permits division of labor because several members of the accounting staff can record transactions in different special journals at the same time.
3. It improves the audit trail because all cash payments are grouped together in one record and are listed by check number.

THE PETTY CASH FUND

Although bills should be paid only by check and only after proper authorization has been given for the payment, it is not practical to make every payment by check. There are times when small expenditures must be made with currency and coins. For example, if $1.25 is needed to send a package to a customer quickly, it is not efficient to wait until the proper approval has been obtained and a check is written. Most businesses find it convenient to pay such small expense items from a *petty cash fund.*

Establishing the Fund

To set up a petty cash fund, a check is written to the order of the person who will be in charge of the fund—usually the office manager, the cashier, or a secretary. The check is cashed, and the money is placed in a safe or a locked cash box to be used for payments as needed. The entry to record the check establishing the petty cash fund involves a debit to an asset account called Petty Cash Fund. This entry is made in the cash payments journal, as shown below. The amount of the fund depends on the needs of each business. At Sports World, $100 was chosen as an appropriate sum for the petty cash fund.

CASH PAYMENTS JOURNAL for Month of May 19X5   Page 5

DATE	CHECK NO.	EXPLANATION	✓	ACCOUNTS PAYABLE DEBIT	OTHER ACCOUNTS DEBIT ACCOUNT TITLE	POST. REF.	AMOUNT	PURCH. DISCOUNT CREDIT	CASH CREDIT
May 1	3501	Establish petty cash fund			Petty Cash Fund	105	100 00		100 00

Making Payments From the Fund

Each payment from the petty cash fund is usually limited to some relatively small amount, such as $15. When a payment is made from the fund, a form called a *petty cash voucher* is prepared. The petty cash vouchers are numbered in sequence and are dated as they are used. When a payment is made, the amount is entered on the voucher, the purpose of the expenditure is noted, and the account to be charged is identified. The person receiving payment is asked to sign the voucher as a receipt, and the person in charge of the petty cash fund initials the voucher to indicate that it has been checked for completeness.

A petty cash voucher issued to record the payment of $8.75 for office supplies is shown below.

PETTY CASH VOUCHER 1

NOTE: This form must be filled out in ink or typewritten.

DESCRIPTION OF EXPENDITURE	ACCOUNT TO BE CHARGED	AMOUNT
Office Supplies	Supplies 129	8 75
	TOTAL	8 75

RECEIVED

THE SUM OF ___Eight___ ------------------------- DOLLARS AND ___75/100___ CENTS

SIGNED _a. C. abbott_ DATE 5|3|X5 APPROVED BY _M. A._ DATE 5|3|X5
Delta Office Supply Co.

The Petty Cash Analysis Sheet

A memorandum record of petty cash transactions is made on an *analysis sheet*. (Sometimes analysis sheets are kept in a *petty cash book*.) Cash put in the fund is listed in the Receipts column, and cash paid out is listed in the Payments column. Special columns are set up for items that occur frequently, such as Supplies, Delivery Expense, and Miscellaneous Expense. An Other Accounts Debit column is provided for accounts that are not involved in petty cash transactions often. The petty cash analysis sheet prepared at Sports World during the month of May 19X5 is shown on page 207.

DATE	VOU. NO.	EXPLANATION	RECEIPTS	PAYMENTS	DISTRIBUTION OF PAYMENTS				
					SUP. DEBIT	DEL. EXP. DEBIT	MISC. EXP. DEBIT	OTHER ACCOUNTS DEBIT	
								ACCOUNT TITLE	AMOUNT
May 1	—	Establish fund	100 00						
3	1	Office supplies		8 75	8 75				
5	2	Delivery service		12 50		12 50			
10	3	Withdrawal		15 00				L. Frank, Drawing	15 00
14	4	Postage stamps		10 00			10 00		
19	5	Delivery service		9 25		9 25			
25	6	Window washing		14 00			14 00		
28	7	Store supplies		7 50	7 50				

Replenishing the Fund

At the end of each month (or sooner if the fund runs low), the petty cash fund is replenished so that there will be an adequate amount of money on hand to meet anticipated needs. The total of the vouchers for payments from the fund plus the cash on hand should always equal the amount of the fund—$100 in this case.

The first step in replenishing the fund is to total each column on the petty cash analysis sheet. A check is then written for an amount sufficient to restore the petty cash fund to its original balance. The amount of this check is recorded in the cash payments journal. The petty cash analysis sheet indicates the accounts to be debited when the check is entered in the cash payments journal. The column totals for May at Sports World showed the following information.

ACCOUNTS

Supplies	$16.25
Delivery Expense	21.75
Miscellaneous Expense	24.00
Lynn Frank, Drawing	15.00
	$77.00

The reimbursement check for $77 is issued to the person in charge of the petty cash fund and is recorded in the cash payments journal, as shown below.

DATE	CHECK NO.	EXPLANATION	ACCOUNTS PAYABLE		OTHER ACCOUNTS DEBIT			PURCH. DISCOUNT CREDIT	CASH CREDIT
			✓	DEBIT	ACCOUNT TITLE	POST. REF.	AMOUNT		
May 31	3519	Replenish petty cash fund			Supplies	129	16 25		
					L. Frank, Drawing	302	15 00		
					Delivery Expense	532	21 75		
					Miscellaneous Expense	591	24 00		77 00

It is important to note that the petty cash analysis sheet is not a record of original entry and the figures are not posted from it to the general ledger accounts. The expenditures made from the petty cash fund are recorded in the cash payments journal only when the fund is replenished. The amounts are posted to the general ledger from the cash payments journal.

The reimbursement check is entered on the petty cash analysis sheet, and the sheet is balanced and ruled as shown below.

PETTY CASH ANALYSIS SHEET for Month of May 19X5   PAGE 1

								DISTRIBUTION OF PAYMENTS		
					SUP. DEBIT	DEL. EXP. DEBIT	MISC. EXP. DEBIT	OTHER ACCOUNTS DEBIT		
DATE	VOU. NO.	EXPLANATION	RECEIPTS	PAYMENTS				ACCOUNT TITLE	AMOUNT
May 1	—	Establish fund	100 00						
3	1	Office supplies		8 75	8 75				
5	2	Delivery service		12 50		12 50			
10	3	Withdrawal		15 00				L. Frank, Drawing	15 00
14	4	Postage stamps		10 00			10 00		
19	5	Delivery service		9 25		9 25			
25	6	Window washing		14 00			14 00		
28	7	Store supplies		7 50	7 50				
31	—	Totals	100 00	77 00	16 25	21 75	24 00		15 00
31	—	Balance on hand		23 00					
			100 00	100 00					
31	—	Balance on hand	23 00						
31	—	Replenish fund	77 00						
31	—	Carried forward	100 00						

The balance of $100 will be brought forward on the first line of the petty cash analysis sheet for June. The amount will be entered in the Receipts column. A dash will be placed in the Voucher Number column, and ''Brought Forward'' will be used as the explanation.

Internal Control of the Petty Cash Fund

Whenever there is valuable property or cash to protect, the accountant must establish safeguards. Petty cash is no exception. The following principles of internal control are usually applied to petty cash.

1. The petty cash fund is used only for payments of a minor nature that cannot conveniently be made by check.
2. The amount of money set aside for the fund does not exceed an approximate amount needed to cover 1 month's payments from the fund.
3. The check to establish the fund is made out to the person in charge of the fund—never to the order of Cash.
4. The person in charge of the fund has sole control of the money and is the only one authorized to make payments from the fund.
5. The money for the petty cash fund is kept in a safe, a locked cash box, or a locked drawer.
6. All payments made from the fund are covered by petty cash vouchers signed by the persons who received the money. The vouchers show the details of the payments and thus provide an audit trail for the fund.

PRINCIPLES AND PROCEDURES SUMMARY

All businesses, whether they are large or small, should have a system of internal control for cash. This system is intended to protect funds from theft and mishandling and to make sure that there are accurate records of cash receipts and cash payments.

The use of special journals leads to a more efficient recording process for cash transactions. The cash receipts journal and cash payments journal contain separate columns for the accounts that a firm uses most often to enter its cash transactions. The provision of these columns eliminates a great deal of repetition in both the initial recording and the posting of cash receipts and cash payments. Much of the posting work can be done on a summary basis at the end of each month.

In business, cash payments should be made by check. However, minor payments are often made in currency and coins through a petty cash fund. A petty cash voucher is prepared for each payment and signed by the person receiving the money. The person who is in charge of the fund keeps a petty cash analysis sheet as a record of the expenditures made. The fund is replenished periodically, with a check drawn for the sum that was spent. At this time, an entry is made in the cash payments journal to record the debits to the accounts involved.

MANAGERIAL IMPLICATIONS

Cash is an essential asset, and it must be carefully safeguarded against loss and theft. Management and the accountant must therefore work together to make sure that a firm has an effective set of controls for cash receipts and cash payments. These controls should be built into all procedures for handling and recording cash.

After a suitable control system has been established, management and the accountant must monitor the system to see that it functions properly and is not abused. Because cash is so vital to business operations, the control system should be checked periodically to be sure that it is working as intended.

Management and the accountant must also set up procedures that will ensure the quick and efficient recording of cash transactions. In order to make day-to-day decisions properly, management needs current information about the firm's cash position.

REVIEW QUESTIONS

1. What does the term *cash* mean in business?
2. Describe the major controls for cash receipts.
3. Explain what *bonding* means.
4. Describe the major controls for cash payments.
5. What are the advantages of using special journals for cash receipts and cash payments?

6. How are postings made to the Cash account from the cash receipts journal and the cash payments journal each month?

7. How are amounts posted from the Accounts Receivable Credit column of the cash receipts journal? from the Other Accounts Credit column? Are the totals of these columns posted? If so, how?

8. How are amounts posted from the Accounts Payable Debit column of the cash payments journal? from the Other Accounts Debit column? Are the totals of these columns posted? If so, how?

9. How are cash shortages and overages recorded? What type of account is Cash Short or Over?

10. What entry is made to record an additional cash investment by the owner of a sole proprietorship business? What journal is used?

11. What is a promissory note? Under what circumstances might a firm receive a promissory note?

12. What entry is made to record the collection of a promissory note and interest? What journal is used?

13. Why do some wholesale businesses offer cash discounts to their customers?

14. How does a firm record a check received on account from a customer when a cash discount is involved? What journal is used?

15. What type of account is Sales Discount? How is this account presented on the income statement?

16. What is a change fund?

17. What entry is made to record a cash withdrawal for personal living expenses by the owner of a sole proprietorship business? What journal is used?

18. On which financial statement are withdrawals by the owner reported?

19. How does a firm record a payment on account to a creditor when a cash discount is involved? What journal is used?

20. What type of account is Purchases Discount? How is this account presented on the income statement?

21. Why would a business use a petty cash fund?

22. What is the purpose of the petty cash voucher? the petty cash analysis sheet?

23. When are petty cash expenditures entered in a firm's accounting records?

24. When is the petty cash fund replenished?

25. Describe the major controls for petty cash.

MANAGERIAL DISCUSSION QUESTIONS

1. Why should management be concerned about achieving effective internal control over cash receipts and cash payments?

2. How does management benefit when cash transactions are recorded quickly and efficiently?

3. Why do some companies require that all employees who handle cash be bonded?

4. Why is it a good practice for a business to make all payments by check except for minor payments from a petty cash fund?

5. The new accountant for the Asheville Hardware Center, a large retail store, found the following weaknesses in the firm's cash-handling procedures. How

would you explain to management why each of these procedures should be changed?

a. No cash register proof is prepared at the end of each day. The amount of money in the register is considered the amount of cash sales for the day.

b. Small payments are sometimes made from the currency and coins in the cash register. (The store has no petty cash fund.)

c. During busy periods for the firm, cash receipts are sometimes kept on the premises for several days before a bank deposit is made.

d. When funds are removed from the cash register at the end of each day, they are placed in an unlocked office cabinet until they are deposited.

e. The person who makes the bank deposits also records them in the checkbook, journalizes cash receipts, and reconciles the bank statement.

EXERCISES

EXERCISE 9-1 **Identifying the accounts used to record a variety of transactions.** The transactions below and on page 212 took place at the Home Electronics Center, a retail store. Indicate the numbers of the general ledger accounts that would be debited and credited to record each transaction.

GENERAL LEDGER ACCOUNTS

101	Cash	401	Sales
109	Notes Receivable	451	Sales Ret. and Allow.
111	Accounts Receivable	491	Interest Income
121	Supplies	501	Merchandise Purchases
131	Equipment	503	Purchases Ret. and Allow.
201	Notes Payable	504	Purchases Discount
205	Accounts Payable	511	Rent Expense
231	Sales Tax Payable	514	Cash Short or Over
301	Gary Ward, Capital	591	Interest Expense
302	Gary Ward, Drawing		

TRANSACTIONS

1. Issued a check for $750 to pay the monthly rent.
2. Purchased supplies for $280 on credit.
3. The owner invested an additional $12,000 cash in the business.
4. Had cash sales of $4,200 plus sales tax of $168.
5. Purchased merchandise for $1,650. The supplier's invoice is payable in 30 days.
6. Accepted a 2-month promissory note for $400 from a credit customer to settle an overdue account. Interest will be paid at a rate of 10 percent.
7. Returned damaged merchandise to a supplier and received a credit memorandum for $150.
8. Purchased new store equipment for $5,000 and issued a 4-month promissory note to the dealer. Interest will be paid at a rate of 12 percent.
9. Sold merchandise for $600 on credit plus sales tax of $24.

10. Issued a check for $1,960 to a creditor on account. The payment is for an invoice of $2,000 less a cash discount of $40.
11. Purchased merchandise for $720 in cash.
12. Collected a $500 promissory note plus interest of $15.
13. Accepted a return of defective merchandise originally sold on credit. Issued a credit memorandum for $78 to the customer. This amount includes $75 for the goods and $3 for the sales tax.
14. Issued a check for $1,722 to pay a $1,680 promissory note plus interest of $42.
15. Had cash sales of $5,950 plus sales tax of $238. There was a cash shortage of $6.
16. Issued a check for $1,000 to the owner as a cash withdrawal for personal use.
17. Collected $2,300 from credit customers on account.
18. Issued a check for $649 to remit sales tax to the state sales tax authority.
19. Issued a check for $170 to purchase supplies.
20. Received a cash refund of $25 for damaged supplies that were returned. The supplies were originally purchased for cash.

EXERCISE 9-2 **Identifying the journals used to record a variety of transactions.** The accounting system of the Home Electronics Center includes the journals listed below. Indicate which journal would be used to record each of the transactions given in Exercise 9-1.

JOURNALS

Cash receipts journal   Sales journal
Cash payments journal   General journal
Purchases journal

EXERCISE 9-3 **Recording cash receipts.** The following transactions took place at the Madison Shoe Store during the first week of September 19X1. Indicate how these transactions would be entered in a cash receipts journal like the one shown on page 190.

TRANSACTIONS

Sept.   1 Had cash sales of $1,400 plus sales tax of $56. There was a cash overage of $2.
2 Collected $180 on account from Joyce Levine, a credit customer.
3 Had cash sales of $1,250 plus sales tax of $50.
4 Angela Ruiz, the owner, made an additional cash investment of $7,000.
5 Had cash sales of $1,600 plus sales tax of $64. There was a cash shortage of $5.

EXERCISE 9-4 **Recording cash payments.** The transactions on page 213 took place at the Madison Shoe Store during the first week of September 19X1. Indicate how these transactions would be entered in a cash payments journal like the one shown on page 199.

Sept.   1   Issued Check 3805 for $600 to pay the monthly rent.

       1   Issued Check 3806 for $1,220 to the Voss Company, a creditor, on account.

       2   Issued Check 3807 for $2,500 to purchase new equipment.

       2   Issued Check 3808 for $496 to remit sales tax to the state sales tax authority.

       3   Issued Check 3809 for $686 to the Hale Company, a creditor, on account for an invoice of $700 less a cash discount of $14.

       4   Issued Check 3810 for $590 to purchase merchandise.

       5   Issued Check 3811 for $750 as a cash withdrawal for personal use by Angela Ruiz, the owner.

EXERCISE 9-5   **Computing cash discounts.** During the second week of September 19X1, the Madison Shoe Store paid the following invoices to creditors within the discount period. Determine the amount of the cash discount on each invoice and the amount paid to the creditor.

1. An invoice for $550 with terms of 2/10, n/30.
2. An invoice for $1,260 with terms of 1/15, n/60.
3. An invoice for $725 with terms of 2/10, n/30.

EXERCISE 9-6   **Recording sales discounts.** On May 1, 19X4, the Lawrence Corporation, a wholesale firm, collected cash on account from the following customers who took the permitted discount of 2 percent. Indicate how each of these transactions would be entered in a cash receipts journal like the one shown on page 196.

TRANSACTIONS

1. Received $431.20 from Morgan Fashions for an invoice of $440 less a cash discount of $8.80.
2. Received $637 from Lawson Apparel for an invoice of $650 less a cash discount of $13.

EXERCISE 9-7   **Recording the receipt of a promissory note.** On April 1, 19X6, the Hart Company accepted a 2-month promissory note for $800 from John Lucas, a credit customer, to settle his overdue account. The note has an interest rate of 12 percent. Show the general journal entry that would be made to record this transaction at the Hart Company.

EXERCISE 9-8   **Recording the collection of a promissory note and interest.** On June 1, 19X6, the Hart Company received a check from John Lucas in payment of his $800 promissory note plus interest of $16. Indicate how this transaction would be recorded in a cash receipts journal like the one shown on page 190.

EXERCISE 9-9   **Recording the issuance of a promissory note.** On January 10, 19X1, the Kendall Company purchased new warehouse equipment for $15,000 from the Ferranti Corporation and issued a 3-month promissory note with interest at 10 percent. Show the general journal entry that would be made to record this transaction at the Kendall Company.

EXERCISE 9-10   **Recording the payment of a promissory note and interest.** On April 10, 19X1, the Kendall Company issued Check 6638 to the Ferranti Corporation to pay its $15,000 promissory note plus interest of $375. Indicate how this transaction would be recorded in a cash payments journal like the one shown on page 199.

EXERCISE 9-11   **Recording the establishment of a petty cash fund.** On January 2, 19X8, the Loomis Company issued Check 1297 for $75 to establish a petty cash fund. Indicate how this transaction would be recorded in a cash payments journal like the one shown on page 199.

EXERCISE 9-12   **Recording the replenishment of a petty cash fund.** On January 31, 19X8, the Loomis Company issued Check 1344 to replenish its petty cash fund. An analysis of the payments from the fund showed the following totals: Supplies, $21; Delivery Expense, $18; and Miscellaneous Expense, $15. Indicate how this transaction would be recorded in a cash payments journal like the one shown on page 199.

EXERCISE 9-13   **Reporting sales revenue.** On March 31, 19X5, the general ledger of the Mansfield Company contained the following account balances: Sales, $36,550; Sales Returns and Allowances, $1,700; and Sales Discount, $490. Prepare the Revenue section of the firm's income statement for the month ended March 31, 19X5.

EXERCISE 9-14   **Reporting the cost of purchases.** On November 30, 19X2, the general ledger of the Sato Company contained the following account balances: Merchandise Purchases, $28,800; Purchases Returns and Allowances, $2,340; and Purchases Discount, $275. Show how the firm's cost of purchases would be reported in the Cost of Goods Sold section of its income statement for the month ended November 30, 19X2.

EXERCISE 9-15   **Reporting changes in owner's equity.** The accounting records of the Continental Art Gallery show that the owner, Susan Norris, had capital of $51,000 on June 1, 19X1, and made withdrawals totaling $1,800 during the month. The firm earned a net income of $3,320 for the period. Prepare the Owner's Equity section of its balance sheet as of June 30, 19X1. (There was no additional investment during the period.)

PROBLEMS

PROBLEM 9-1   **Journalizing cash receipts; posting to the general ledger.** The Video Shack is a retail store that sells blank and prerecorded videocassettes. The firm's cash receipts for February 19X5 are listed below along with the general ledger accounts used to record these transactions.

Instructions
1. Open the general ledger accounts, and enter the balances as of February 1, 19X5.
2. Record the transactions in a cash receipts journal like the one shown on page 190. (Use 2 as the page number.)
3. Post the individual entries from the Other Accounts Credit section of the cash receipts journal to the proper general ledger accounts.
4. Total, prove, and rule the cash receipts journal as of February 28.
5. Post the column totals from the cash receipts journal to the proper general ledger accounts.

GENERAL LEDGER ACCOUNTS

101	Cash	$ 4,960 Dr.
109	Notes Receivable	350 Dr.
111	Accounts Receivable	1,025 Dr.
121	Supplies	610 Dr.
231	Sales Tax Payable	295 Cr.
301	Kevin Walsh, Capital	34,000 Cr.
401	Sales	
491	Interest Income	
514	Cash Short or Over	

TRANSACTIONS FOR FEBRUARY 19X5

Feb. 3 Collected $125 from David Weiss, a credit customer, on account.
     5 Received a cash refund of $30 for damaged supplies.
     7 Had cash sales of $2,140 plus sales tax of $107 during the first week of February. There was a cash shortage of $5.
     9 Kevin Walsh, the owner, invested an additional $5,000 cash in the business.
    12 Received $95 from Janet Peters, a credit customer, in payment of her account.
    14 Had cash sales of $1,760 plus sales tax of $88 during the second week of February. There was a cash overage of $2.
    16 Collected $210 from Karen Stone, a credit customer, to apply toward her account.
    19 Received a check from Douglas Moore to pay his $350 promissory note plus interest of $7.
    21 Had cash sales of $1,620 plus sales tax of $81 during the third week of February.
    25 Joseph Vario, a credit customer, sent a check for $145 to pay the balance he owes.
    28 Had cash sales of $1,980 plus sales tax of $99 during the fourth week of February. There was a cash shortage of $3.

PROBLEM 9-2 **Journalizing cash payments and recording petty cash; posting to the general ledger.** The cash payments of the Regal Jewelry Store, a retail business, for July

19X1 are listed below and on page 217 along with the general ledger accounts used to record these transactions.

Instructions
1. Open the general ledger accounts, and enter the balances as of July 1, 19X1.
2. Record all payments by check in a cash payments journal like the one shown on page 199. (Use 7 as the page number.)
3. Record all payments from the petty cash fund on a petty cash analysis sheet like the one shown on page 207. (Use 7 as the sheet number.)
4. Post the individual entries from the Other Accounts Debit section of the cash payments journal to the proper general ledger accounts.
5. Total, prove, and rule the petty cash analysis sheet as of July 31. Then record the replenishment of the fund and the final balance on the sheet.
6. Total, prove, and rule the cash payments journal as of July 31.
7. Post the column totals from the cash payments journal to the proper general ledger accounts.

GENERAL LEDGER ACCOUNTS

101	Cash	$12,240 Dr.
105	Petty Cash Fund	
121	Supplies	530 Dr.
201	Notes Payable	700 Cr.
205	Accounts Payable	4,460 Cr.
231	Sales Tax Payable	980 Cr.
302	Helen Shaw, Drawing	
451	Sales Returns and Allowances	
504	Purchases Discount	
511	Delivery Expense	
514	Miscellaneous Expense	
520	Rent Expense	
523	Salaries Expense	
526	Telephone Expense	
591	Interest Expense	

TRANSACTIONS FOR JULY 19X1

July 1 Issued Check 1421 for $600 to pay the monthly rent.

2 Issued Check 1422 for $980 to remit sales tax to the state tax commission.

3 Issued Check 1423 for $575 to the Digital Watch Company, a creditor, in payment of Invoice 8680 of June 5.

4 Issued Check 1424 for $100 to establish a petty cash fund. (After journalizing this transaction, be sure to enter it on the first line of the petty cash analysis sheet.)

5 Paid $15 from the petty cash fund for office supplies, Petty Cash Voucher 1.

7 Issued Check 1425 for $721 to the Savoy Corporation in payment of a $700 promissory note and interest of $21.

8 Paid $10 from the petty cash fund for postage stamps, Petty Cash Voucher 2.

10 Issued Check 1426 for $130 to a customer as a cash refund for a defective watch that was returned. (The original sale was made for cash.)

12 Issued Check 1427 for $78 to pay the monthly telephone bill.

14 Issued Check 1428 for $1,225 to Gem Importers, a creditor, in payment of Invoice 36892 of July 6 ($1,250) less a cash discount ($25).

15 Paid $9.25 from the petty cash fund for delivery service, Petty Cash Voucher 3.

17 Issued Check 1429 for $175 to make a cash purchase of store supplies.

20 Issued Check 1430 for $686 to Designer Chains Inc., a creditor, in payment of Invoice 5113 of July 12 ($700) less a cash discount ($14).

22 Paid $12 from the petty cash fund for a personal withdrawal by Helen Shaw, the owner, Petty Cash Voucher 4.

25 Paid $15 from the petty cash fund to have the store windows washed, Petty Cash Voucher 5.

27 Issued Check 1431 for $890 to Jewel Creations, a creditor, in payment of Invoice 656 of June 30.

30 Paid $11.75 from the petty cash fund for delivery service, Petty Cash Voucher 6.

31 Issued Check 1432 for $1,750 to pay the monthly salaries of the employees.

31 Issued Check 1433 for $1,500 to Helen Shaw, the owner, as a withdrawal for personal use.

31 Issued Check 1434 for $73 to replenish the petty cash fund. (Foot the columns of the petty cash analysis sheet in order to determine the accounts that should be debited and the amounts involved.)

PROBLEM 9-3   **Journalizing sales, cash receipts, and sales discounts; posting to the general ledger.** Allegro Products is a wholesale business that sells musical instruments. The transactions involving sales and cash receipts that the firm had during May 19X3 are listed on page 218 along with the general ledger accounts used to record these transactions.

Instructions   1. Open the general ledger accounts, and enter the balances as of May 1, 19X3.
2. Record the transactions in a one-column sales journal, a cash receipts journal like the one shown on page 196, and a general journal. (Use 5 as the page number for each of the special journals and 15 as the page number for the general journal.)
3. Post the entries from the general journal to the proper general ledger accounts.
4. Total, prove, and rule the special journals as of May 31.
5. Post the column totals from the special journals to the proper general ledger accounts.
6. Prepare the heading and the Revenue section of the firm's income statement for the month ended May 31, 19X3.

GENERAL LEDGER ACCOUNTS

101	Cash	$4,100 Dr.
109	Notes Receivable	
111	Accounts Receivable	5,250 Dr.
401	Sales	
451	Sales Returns and Allowances	
452	Sales Discount	

TRANSACTIONS FOR MAY 19X3

May 1 Sold merchandise for $1,850 to the Harmony Music Center. Issued Invoice 9321 with terms of 2/10, n/30.

3 Received a check for $715.40 from the Symphony Shop in payment of Invoice 9319 of April 24 ($730) less a cash discount ($14.60).

5 Sold merchandise for $635 in cash to a new customer who has not yet established credit.

8 Sold merchandise for $2,420 to Bob's Music Store. Issued Invoice 9322 with terms of 2/10, n/30.

10 The Harmony Music Center sent a check for $1,813 in payment of Invoice 9321 of May 1 ($1,850) less a cash discount ($37).

15 Accepted a return of damaged merchandise from Bob's Music Store. Issued Credit Memorandum 408 for $350. The original sale was made on Invoice 9322 of May 8.

19 Sold merchandise for $5,170 to the Music Emporium. Issued Invoice 9323 with terms of 2/10, n/30.

23 Collected $1,480 from the Classic Guitar Shop for Invoice 9320 of April 25.

26 Accepted a 2-month promissory note for $2,600 from Webb's Music World in settlement of its overdue account. The note has an interest rate of 12 percent.

28 Received a check for $5,066.60 from the Music Emporium in payment of Invoice 9323 of May 19 ($5,170) less a cash discount ($103.40).

31 Sold merchandise for $4,495 to Music Makers Inc. Issued Invoice 9324 with terms of 2/10, n/30.

PROBLEM 9-4   **Journalizing sales, cash receipts, and sales tax; posting to the general ledger.** During October 19X7, the Majestic Antique Shop, a retail firm, had the transactions involving sales and cash receipts that are listed on page 219. The general ledger accounts used to record these transactions are also on page 219.

Instructions   1. Open the general ledger accounts, and enter the balances as of October 1, 19X7.

2 Record the transactions in a sales journal like the one shown on page 129, a cash receipts journal like the one shown on page 190, and a general journal. (Use *10* as the page number for each of the special journals and *30* as the page number for the general journal.)

3. Post the entries from the general journal and from the Other Accounts Credit section of the cash receipts journal to the proper general ledger accounts.

4. Total, prove, and rule the special journals as of October 31.
5. Post the column totals from the special journals to the proper general ledger accounts.

GENERAL LEDGER ACCOUNTS

101	Cash	$ 2,492.50 Dr.
109	Notes Receivable	
111	Accounts Receivable	1,535.10 Dr.
231	Sales Tax Payable	
301	John Valenza, Capital	45,600.00 Cr.
401	Sales	
451	Sales Returns and Allowances	
514	Cash Short or Over	

TRANSACTIONS FOR OCTOBER 19X7

Oct. 1 Received a check for $262.50 from Thomas DeWitt to pay his account.

3 Sold a table on credit for $665 plus sales tax of $33.25 to Karen Cole, Sales Slip 3972.

5 John Valenza, the owner, invested an additional $7,000 cash in the business in order to expand operations.

6 Had cash sales of $1,780 plus sales tax of $89 during the period October 1–6. There was a cash shortage of $5.

8 Sold chairs on credit for $930 plus sales tax of $46.50 to Patrick O'Connor, Sales Slip 3973.

11 Accepted a 2-month promissory note for $525 from Donald Hall to settle his overdue account. The note has an interest rate of 10 percent.

13 Had cash sales of $1,960 plus sales tax of $98 during the period October 8–13.

15 Collected $315 on account from Janet Massi.

19 Sold a lamp on credit for $240 plus sales tax of $12 to Denise Richards, Sales Slip 3974.

20 Had cash sales of $1,650 plus sales tax of $82.50 during the period October 15–20. There was a cash shortage of $2.25.

23 Granted an allowance to Denise Richards for scratches on the lamp that she bought on Sales Slip 3974 of Oct. 19. Issued Credit Memorandum 156 for $21, which includes a price reduction of $20 and sales tax of $1.

25 Leon Roth sent a check for $432.60 to pay the balance he owes.

27 Had cash sales of $2,155 plus sales tax of $107.75 during the period October 22–27.

29 Sold a cabinet on credit for $590 plus sales tax of $29.50 to Janet Massi, Sales Slip 3975.

31 Had cash sales of $720 plus sales tax of $36 during the period October 29–31. There was a cash overage of $1.10.

Note: Save your working papers for use in Problem 9-5.

PROBLEM 9-5   **Posting to the accounts receivable ledger and preparing a schedule of accounts receivable.** This problem is a continuation of Problem 9-4.

Instructions   1. Set up an accounts receivable ledger for the Majestic Antique Shop. Open an account for each of the customers listed below, and enter the balances as of October 1, 19X7. All of these customers have terms of n/30.
2. Post the individual entries from the sales journal, the cash receipts journal, and the general journal prepared in Problem 9-4.
3. Prepare a schedule of accounts receivable for October 31, 19X7.
4. Check the total of the schedule of accounts receivable against the balance of the Accounts Receivable account in the general ledger. The two amounts should be the same.

CREDIT CUSTOMERS

Name	Balance
Karen Cole	
Thomas DeWitt	$262.50
Donald Hall	525.00
Janet Massi	315.00
Patrick O'Connor	
Denise Richards	
Leon Roth	432.60

PROBLEM 9-6   **Journalizing purchases, cash payments, and purchase discounts; posting to the general ledger.** The Runners Emporium is a retail store that sells jogging shoes and clothes. Transactions involving purchases and cash payments that the firm had during June 19X2 are listed on page 221 along with the general ledger accounts used to record these transactions.

Instructions   1. Open the general ledger accounts, and enter the balances in these accounts as of June 1, 19X2.
2. Record the transactions in a one-column purchases journal, a cash payments journal like the one shown on page 199, and a general journal. (Use 6 as the page number for each of the special journals and 18 as the page number for the general journal.)
3. Post the entries from the general journal and from the Other Accounts Debit section of the cash payments journal to the proper accounts in the general ledger.
4. Total, prove, and rule the special journals as of June 30.
5. Post the column totals from the special journals to the general ledger accounts.
6. Show how the firm's cost of purchases would be reported on its income statement for the month ended June 30, 19X2.

GENERAL LEDGER ACCOUNTS

101	Cash	$ 9,830 Dr.
131	Equipment	14,000 Dr.
201	Notes Payable	
205	Accounts Payable	1,220 Cr.
501	Merchandise Purchases	
503	Purchases Returns and Allowances	
504	Purchases Discount	
511	Rent Expense	
514	Telephone Expense	
517	Salaries Expense	

TRANSACTIONS FOR JUNE 19X2

June 1 Issued Check 5680 for $725 to pay the monthly rent.

3 Purchased merchandise for $1,100 from Ames Athletic Shoes, Invoice 674, dated May 30; the terms are 2/10, n/30.

5 Purchased new store equipment for $1,500 from the Wynn Company, Invoice 29076, dated June 4, net payable in 30 days.

7 Issued Check 5681 for $690 to the Outdoor Clothing Company, a creditor, in payment of Invoice 3324 of May 9.

8 Issued Check 5682 for $1,078 to Ames Athletic Shoes, a creditor, in payment of Invoice 674 of May 30 ($1,100) less a cash discount ($22).

12 Purchased merchandise for $850 from Mitchell Sportswear, Invoice 4992, dated June 9, net due and payable in 30 days.

15 Issued Check 5683 for $95 to pay the monthly telephone bill.

18 Received Credit Memorandum 324 for $265 from Mitchell Sportswear for defective goods that were returned. The original purchase was made on Invoice 4992 of June 9.

21 Purchased new store equipment for $4,000 from the Kraus Company. Issued a 3-month promissory note with interest at 11 percent.

23 Purchased merchandise for $2,250 from Marathon Products, Invoice 9127, dated June 20; terms of 2/10, n/30.

25 Issued Check 5684 for $530 to Mitchell Sportswear, a creditor, in payment of Invoice 4761 of May 28.

28 Issued Check 5685 for $2,205 to Marathon Products, a creditor, in payment of Invoice 9127 of June 20 ($2,250) less a cash discount ($45).

30 Purchased merchandise for $910 from Fleet Running Shoes, Invoice 37413, dated June 26; the terms are 1/10, n/30.

30 Issued Check 5686 for $1,800 to pay the monthly salaries of the employees.

PROBLEM 9-7 **Journalizing purchases, freight charges, cash payments, and purchase discounts; posting to the general ledger.** During April 19X5, the Hilton Rug Mart, a retail firm, had the transactions involving purchases and cash payments that are listed below and on page 223. The general ledger accounts used to record these transactions appear below.

Instructions

1. Open the general ledger accounts, and enter the balances as of April 1, 19X5.
2. Record the transactions in a purchases journal like the one shown on page 168, a cash payments journal like the one shown on page 199, and a general journal. (Use *4* as the page number for each of the special journals and *12* as the page number for the general journal.)
3. Post the entries from the general journal and from the Other Accounts Debit section of the cash payments journal to the proper general ledger accounts.
4. Total, prove, and rule the special journals as of April 30.
5. Post the column totals from the special journals to the proper general ledger accounts.

GENERAL LEDGER ACCOUNTS

101	Cash	$18,945 Dr.
121	Supplies	710 Dr.
201	Notes Payable	
205	Accounts Payable	9,560 Cr.
501	Merchandise Purchases	
502	Freight In	
503	Purchases Returns and Allowances	
504	Purchases Discount	
511	Rent Expense	
514	Utilities Expense	
517	Salaries Expense	

TRANSACTIONS FOR APRIL 19X5

Apr.
1 Issued Check 7231 for $1,940 to Superior Floor Coverings, a creditor, in payment of Invoice 56325 of March 3.

2 Issued Check 7232 for $1,200 to pay the monthly rent.

6 Purchased carpeting for $4,450 from Rosedale Mills, Invoice 827, dated April 3; terms of 2/10, n/30.

6 Issued Check 7233 for $61 to the Ace Trucking Company to pay the freight charge on goods received from Rosedale Mills.

8 Purchased store supplies for $370 from the Reiss Company, Invoice 2440, dated April 6, net amount due in 30 days.

11 Issued Check 7234 for $4,361 to Rosedale Mills, a creditor, in payment of Invoice 827 of April 3 ($4,450) less a cash discount ($89).

14 Purchased carpeting for $3,700 plus a freight charge of $42 from Waverly Products, Invoice 4953, dated April 11, net due and payable in 30 days.

17 Gave a 2-month promissory note for $5,500 to the McManus Corporation, a creditor, to settle an overdue balance. The note bears interest at 12 percent.

21 Purchased area rugs for $2,800 from Northland Crafts, Invoice 677, dated April 18; the terms are 2/10, n/30.

22 Issued Check 7235 for $180 to pay the monthly utility bill.

24 Received Credit Memorandum 41 for $300 from Northland Crafts for a damaged rug that was returned. The original purchase was made on Invoice 677 of April 18.

25 Issued Check 7236 for $1,650 to make a cash purchase of merchandise.

26 Issued Check 7237 for $2,450 to Northland Crafts, a creditor, in payment of Invoice 677 of April 18 ($2,800) less a return ($300) and a cash discount ($50).

27 Purchased hooked rugs for $4,100 plus a freight charge of $56 from the Blue Ridge Company, Invoice 8631, dated April 23, net payable in 45 days.

28 Issued Check 7238 for $2,120 to Waverly Products, a creditor, in payment of Invoice 4811 of March 30.

30 Issued Check 7239 for $2,600 to pay the monthly salaries of the employees.

Note: Save your working papers for use in Problem 9-8.

PROBLEM 9-8   **Posting to the accounts payable ledger and preparing a schedule of accounts payable.** This problem is a continuation of Problem 9-7.

Instructions   1. Set up an accounts payable ledger for the Hilton Rug Mart. Open an account for each of the creditors listed below, and enter the balance as of April 1, 19X5.
2. Post the individual entries from the purchases journal, the cash payments journal, and the general journal prepared in Problem 9-7.
3. Prepare a schedule of accounts payable for April 30, 19X5.
4. Check the total of the schedule of accounts payable against the balance of the Accounts Payable account in the general ledger. The two amounts should be the same.

CREDITORS

Name	Balance	Terms
Blue Ridge Company		n/45
McManus Corporation	$5,500	1/10, n/30
Northland Crafts		2/10, n/30
Reiss Company		n/30
Rosedale Mills		2/10, n/30
Superior Floor Coverings	1,940	n/30
Waverly Products	2,120	n/30

ALTERNATE PROBLEMS

PROBLEM 9-1A   **Journalizing cash receipts; posting to the general ledger.** The Sound Center is a retail store that sells stereo equipment, records, and tapes. The firm's cash receipts for February 19X1 are listed below along with the general ledger accounts used to record these transactions.

Instructions

1. Open the general ledger accounts, and enter the balances as of February 1, 19X1.
2. Record the transactions in a cash receipts journal like the one shown on page 190. (Use 2 as the page number.)
3. Post the individual entries from the Other Accounts Credit section of the cash receipts journal to the proper general ledger accounts.
4. Total, prove, and rule the cash receipts journal as of February 28.
5. Post the column totals from the cash receipts journal to the proper general ledger accounts.

GENERAL LEDGER ACCOUNTS

101	Cash	$ 2,320 Dr.
109	Notes Receivable	600 Dr.
111	Accounts Receivable	1,570 Dr.
141	Equipment	19,785 Dr.
231	Sales Tax Payable	469 Cr.
301	Marion Stein, Capital	42,500 Cr.
401	Sales	
491	Interest Income	
514	Cash Short or Over	

TRANSACTIONS FOR FEBRUARY 19X1

Feb. 2 Marion Stein, the owner, invested an additional $7,500 cash in the business.

4 Received $416 from Susan Howell, a credit customer, on account.

7 Had cash sales of $3,325 plus sales tax of $133 during the first week of February. There was a cash overage of $1.

10 Collected $152 from Paul Antonovich, a credit customer, in payment of his account.

13 Received a check from Alice Mason to pay her $600 promissory note plus interest of $15.

14 Had cash sales of $2,550 plus sales tax of $102 during the second week of February.

17 Received a cash refund of $385 for some defective store equipment that was returned to the dealer. (The equipment was originally bought for cash.)

20 Carl Ericson, a credit customer, sent a check for $232 to pay the balance he owes.

21 Had cash sales of $2,100 plus sales tax of $84 during the third week of February. There was a cash shortage of $4.

24 Collected $541 from Jean Ashe, a credit customer, in payment of her account.

28 Had cash sales of $2,600 plus sales tax of $104 during the fourth week of February. There was a cash shortage of $6.

PROBLEM 9-2A

Journalizing cash payments and recording petty cash; posting to the general ledger. The cash payments of the International Gift Bazaar, a retail business, for September 19X4 are listed below and on page 226 along with the general ledger accounts used to record these transactions.

Instructions

1. Open the general ledger accounts, and enter the balances as of September 1, 19X4.
2. Record all payments by check in a cash payments journal like the one shown on page 199. (Use 9 as the page number.)
3. Record all payments from the petty cash fund on a petty cash analysis sheet with special columns for Delivery Expense and Miscellaneous Expense. (Use 9 as the sheet number.)
4. Post the individual entries from the Other Accounts Debit section of the cash payments journal to the proper general ledger accounts.
5. Total, prove, and rule the petty cash analysis sheet as of September 30. Then record the replenishment of the fund and the final balance on the sheet.
6. Total, prove, and rule the cash payments journal as of September 30.
7. Post the column totals from the cash payments journal to the general ledger.

GENERAL LEDGER ACCOUNTS

101	Cash	$10,765 Dr.
105	Petty Cash Fund	
141	Equipment	21,500 Dr.
201	Notes Payable	840 Cr.
205	Accounts Payable	3,985 Cr.
231	Sales Tax Payable	672 Cr.
302	Peter Chen, Drawing	
451	Sales Returns and Allowances	
504	Purchases Discount	
511	Delivery Expense	
514	Miscellaneous Expense	
520	Rent Expense	
523	Salaries Expense	
526	Telephone Expense	
591	Interest Expense	

TRANSACTIONS FOR SEPTEMBER 19X4

Sept. 1 Issued Check 934 for $672 to remit sales tax to the state tax commission.

2 Issued Check 935 for $850 to pay the monthly rent.

4 Issued Check 936 for $75 to establish a petty cash fund. (After journalizing this transaction, be sure to enter it on the first line of the petty cash analysis sheet.)

5 Issued Check 937 for $1,176 to Vantage Glassware, a creditor, in payment of Invoice 56793 of Aug. 28 ($1,200) less a cash discount ($24).

6 Paid $10.50 from the petty cash fund for delivery service, Petty Cash Voucher 1.

9 Purchased store equipment for $500. Paid immediately with Check 938.

11 Paid $8 from the petty cash fund for office supplies, Petty Cash Voucher 2. (Charge to Miscellaneous Expense.)

13 Issued Check 939 for $485 to the Nichols Company, a creditor, in payment of Invoice 7925 of Aug. 15.

14 Issued Check 940 for $57 to a customer as a cash refund for defective merchandise that was returned. (The original sale was made for cash.)

16 Paid $15 from the petty cash fund for a personal withdrawal by Peter Chen, the owner, Petty Cash Voucher 3.

18 Issued Check 941 for $92 to pay the monthly telephone bill.

21 Issued Check 942 for $735 to Far Eastern Imports, a creditor, in payment of Invoice 1822 of Sept. 13 ($750) less a cash discount ($15).

23 Paid $12 from the petty cash fund for postage stamps, Petty Cash Voucher 4.

24 Issued Check 943 for $854 to the Stanley Corporation in payment of an $840 promissory note and interest of $14.

26 Issued Check 944 for $620 to Pacific Ceramics, a creditor, in payment of Invoice 3510 of Aug. 29.

27 Paid $9 from the petty cash fund for delivery service, Petty Cash Voucher 5.

28 Issued Check 945 for $1,200 to Peter Chen, the owner, as a withdrawal for personal use.

29 Paid $13.50 from the petty cash fund to have a typewriter repaired, Petty Cash Voucher 6.

30 Issued Check 946 for $1,900 to pay the monthly salaries of the employees.

30 Issued Check 947 for $68 to replenish the petty cash fund. (Foot the columns of the petty cash analysis sheet in order to determine the accounts that should be debited and the amounts involved.)

PROBLEM 9-3A **Journalizing sales, cash receipts, and sales discounts; posting to the general ledger.** The Dawson Medical Supply Company is a wholesale business. Transactions involving sales and cash receipts that the firm had during August 19X7 are listed on page 227 along with the general ledger accounts used to record these transactions.

Instructions
1. Open the general ledger accounts, and enter the balances as of August 1, 19X7.
2. Record the transactions in a one-column sales journal, a cash receipts journal like the one shown on page 196, and a general journal. (Use 8 as the page number for each of the special journals and 24 as the page number for the general journal.)
3. Post the entries from the general journal to the proper general ledger accounts.

4. Total, prove, and rule the special journals as of August 31.

5. Post the column totals from the special journals to the proper general ledger accounts.

6. Prepare the heading and the Revenue section of the firm's income statement for the month ended August 31, 19X7.

GENERAL LEDGER ACCOUNTS

101	Cash	$ 6,340 Dr.
109	Notes Receivable	
111	Accounts Receivable	10,100 Dr.
401	Sales	
451	Sales Returns and Allowances	
452	Sales Discount	

TRANSACTIONS FOR AUGUST 19X7

Aug.   1 Received a check for $2,695 from the Harris Pharmacy in payment of Invoice 8277 of July 21 ($2,750) less a cash discount ($55).

2 Sold merchandise for $7,480 to United Drugstores. Issued Invoice 8279 with terms of 2/10, n/30.

4 Accepted a 3-month promissory note for $4,500 from the Hillside Clinic to settle its overdue account. The note has an interest rate of 11 percent.

7 Sold merchandise for $9,345 to Wayne Memorial Hospital. Issued Invoice 8280 with terms of 2/10, n/30.

11 Collected $7,330.40 from United Drugstores for Invoice 8279 of August 2 ($7,480) less a cash discount ($149.60).

14 Sold merchandise for $1,750 in cash to a new customer who has not yet established credit.

16 Wayne Memorial Hospital sent a check for $9,158.10 in payment of Invoice 8280 of August 7 ($9,345) less a cash discount ($186.90).

22 Sold merchandise for $3,130 to the Leslie Drug Mart. Issued Invoice 8281 with terms of 2/10, n/30.

24 Received a check for $2,500 from Grant Medical Center to pay Invoice 8278 of July 23.

26 Accepted a return of damaged merchandise from the Leslie Drug Mart. Issued Credit Memorandum 311 for $210. The original sale was made on Invoice 8281 of August 22.

31 Sold merchandise for $6,370 to Lane County Hospital. Issued Invoice 8282 with terms of 2/10, n/30.

PROBLEM 9-4A   **Journalizing sales, cash receipts, and sales tax; posting to the general ledger.** During April 19X1, Fiesta Fashions, a retail store, had the transactions involving sales and cash receipts that are on pages 228 and 229. The general ledger accounts used to record these transactions are also on page 228.

Instructions   1. Open the general ledger accounts, and enter the balances as of April 1, 19X1.

2. Record the transactions in a sales journal like the one shown on page 129, a cash receipts journal like the one shown on page 190, and a general journal. (Use *4* as the page number for each of the special journals and *12* as the page number for the general journal.)
3. Post the entries from the general journal and from the Other Accounts Credit section of the cash receipts journal to the proper general ledger accounts.
4. Total, prove, and rule the special journals as of April 30.
5. Post the column totals from the special journals to the proper general ledger accounts.

GENERAL LEDGER ACCOUNTS

101	Cash	$ 3,186.40 Dr.
109	Notes Receivable	
111	Accounts Receivable	1,441.00 Dr.
231	Sales Tax Payable	
301	Anita Ramos, Capital	32,650.00 Cr.
401	Sales	
451	Sales Returns and Allowances	
514	Cash Short or Over	

TRANSACTIONS FOR APRIL 19X1

Apr. 1 Sold a blazer, slacks, and shirts on credit to Roger Dumont for $267 plus sales tax of $13.35, Sales Slip 3415.

4 Nancy Green sent a check for $411.50 to pay the balance she owes.

6 Had cash sales of $5,290 plus sales tax of $264.50 during the period April 1–6. There was a cash overage of $3.

8 Accepted a return of a damaged shirt from Roger Dumont. Issued Credit Memorandum 3208 for $26.25, which covers the price of the item ($25) and sales tax ($1.25). The original sale was made on Sales Slip 3415 of April 1.

10 Collected $389.70 on account from John McCray.

13 Had cash sales of $4,515 plus sales tax of $225.75 during the period April 8–13. There was a cash shortage of $7.

16 Sold a suede coat on credit to Joan Murray for $170 plus sales tax of $8.50, Sales Slip 3416.

18 Anita Ramos, the owner, invested an additional $5,000 cash in the business in order to expand operations.

20 Had cash sales of $3,920 plus sales tax of $196 during the period April 15–20.

22 Sold slacks and sweaters on credit to Maureen O'Casey for $310 plus sales tax of $15.50, Sales Slip 3417.

24 Accepted a 2-month promissory note for $466 from George Garrett to settle his overdue account. The note has an interest rate of 12 percent.

27 Had cash sales of $4,840 plus sales tax of $242 during the period April 22–27. There was a cash shortage of $2.50.

29 Received a check for $173.80 from Max Palevski to pay his account.

30 Sold a leather jacket and blouses on credit to Nancy Green for $220 plus sales tax of $11, Sales Slip 3418.

30 Had cash sales of $1,510 plus sales tax of $75.50 for April 29 and 30.

Note: Save your working papers for use in Problem 9-5A.

PROBLEM 9-5A **Posting to the accounts receivable ledger and preparing a schedule of accounts receivable.** This problem is a continuation of Problem 9-4A.

Instructions
1. Set up an accounts receivable ledger for Fiesta Fashions. Open an account for each of the customers listed below, and enter the balances as of April 1, 19X1. All of these customers have terms of n/30.
2. Post the individual entries from the sales journal, the cash receipts journal, and the general journal prepared in Problem 9-4A.
3. Prepare a schedule of accounts receivable for April 30, 19X1.
4. Check the total of the schedule of accounts receivable against the balance of the Accounts Receivable account in the general ledger. The two amounts should be the same.

CREDIT CUSTOMERS

Name	Balance
Roger Dumont	
George Garrett	$466.00
Nancy Green	411.50
John McCray	389.70
Joan Murray	
Maureen O'Casey	
Max Palevski	173.80

PROBLEM 9-6A **Journalizing purchases, cash payments, and purchase discounts; posting to the general ledger.** The Top-Value Appliance Center is a retail store that sells a variety of household appliances. Transactions involving purchases and cash payments that the firm had during December 19X8 are listed on page 230 along with the general ledger accounts used to record these transactions.

Instructions
1. Open the general ledger accounts, and enter the balances as of December 1, 19X8.
2. Record the transactions in a one-column purchases journal, a cash payments journal like the one shown on page 199, and a general journal. (Use *12* as the page number for each of the special journals and *36* as the page number for the general journal.)
3. Post the entries from the general journal and from the Other Accounts Debit section of the cash payments journal to the proper general ledger accounts.
4. Total, prove, and rule the special journals as of December 31.
5. Post the column totals from the special journals to the proper general ledger accounts.
6. Show how the firm's cost of purchases would be reported on its income statement for the month ended December 31, 19X8.

GENERAL LEDGER ACCOUNTS

101	Cash	$22,850 Dr.
131	Equipment	31,000 Dr.
201	Notes Payable	
205	Accounts Payable	1,900 Cr.
501	Merchandise Purchases	
503	Purchases Returns and Allowances	
504	Purchases Discount	
511	Rent Expense	
514	Telephone Expense	
517	Salaries Expense	

TRANSACTIONS FOR DECEMBER 19X8

Dec.   1 Purchased merchandise for $3,200 from Allied Home Products, Invoice 76595, dated November 28; the terms are 2/10, n/30.

2 Issued Check 1563 for $1,400 to pay the monthly rent.

4 Purchased new store equipment for $6,500 from the Blair Company. Issued a 2-month promissory note with interest at 10 percent.

6 Issued Check 1564 for $3,136 to Allied Home Products, a creditor, in payment of Invoice 76595 of November 28 ($3,200) less a cash discount ($64).

10 Purchased merchandise for $4,450 from the Wagner Corporation, Invoice 9113, dated December 7; terms of 2/10, n/30.

13 Issued Check 1565 for $120 to pay the monthly telephone bill.

15 Issued Check 1566 for $4,361 to the Wagner Corporation, a creditor, in payment of Invoice 9113 of December 7 ($4,450) less a cash discount ($89).

18 Purchased merchandise for $5,900 from the United Appliance Company, Invoice 47283, dated December 16; the terms are 3/10, n/30.

20 Purchased new stockroom equipment for $2,000 from Storage Systems Inc., Invoice 536, dated December 17, net payable in 45 days.

21 Issued Check 1567 for $1,900 to Logan Industries, a creditor, in payment of Invoice 8713 of November 23.

22 Purchased merchandise for $2,650 from the Scovill Corporation, Invoice 36131, dated December 19, net due in 30 days.

24 Issued Check 1568 for $5,723 to the United Appliance Company, a creditor, in payment of Invoice 47283 of December 16 ($5,900) less a cash discount ($177).

28 Received Credit Memorandum 821 for $450 from the Scovill Corporation for damaged goods that were returned. The original purchase was made on Invoice 36131 of December 19.

31 Issued Check 1569 for $2,700 to pay the monthly salaries of the employees.

PROBLEM 9-7A   **Journalizing purchases, freight charges, cash payments, and purchase discounts; posting to the general ledger.** During January 19X4, the Lewis Tile Store, a retail firm, had the transactions involving purchases and cash payments that are listed below and on page 232. The general ledger accounts used to record these transactions also appear below.

Instructions

1. Open the general ledger accounts, and enter the balances as of January 1, 19X4.
2. Record the transactions in a purchases journal like the one shown on page 168, a cash payments journal like the one shown on page 199, and a general journal. (Use *1* as the page number for each of the journals.)
3. Post the entries from the general journal and from the Other Accounts Debit section of the cash payments journal to the proper general ledger accounts.
4. Total, prove, and rule the special journals as of January 31.
5. Post the column totals from the special journals to the proper general ledger accounts.

GENERAL LEDGER ACCOUNTS

101	Cash	$14,890 Dr.
121	Supplies	545 Dr.
201	Notes Payable	
205	Accounts Payable	6,695 Cr.
501	Merchandise Purchases	
502	Freight In	
503	Purchases Returns and Allowances	
504	Purchases Discount	
511	Rent Expense	
514	Utilities Expense	
517	Salaries Expense	

TRANSACTIONS FOR JANUARY 19X4

Jan. 2 Issued Check 675 for $850 to pay the monthly rent.
   4 Issued Check 676 for $2,170 to Artistic Tiles Inc., a creditor, in payment of Invoice 4398 of December 6.
   7 Purchased vinyl floor tiles for $3,640 from the Sterling Corporation, Invoice 925, dated January 4; terms of 2/10, n/30.
   7 Issued Check 677 for $42 to the Rapid Express Company to pay the freight charge on goods received from the Sterling Corporation.
   10 Purchased store supplies for $410 from the Lopez Company, Invoice 1883, dated January 9, net due and payable in 30 days.
   12 Issued Check 678 for $3,567.20 to the Sterling Corporation, a creditor, in payment of Invoice 925 of January 4 ($3,640) less a cash discount ($72.80).
   15 Purchased acoustical ceiling tiles for $4,200 plus a freight charge of $51 from Hamilton Products, Invoice 3925, dated January 11, net amount payable in 30 days.
   18 Gave a 3-month promissory note for $2,800 to Carter Industries, a creditor, to settle an overdue balance. The note bears interest at 11 percent.
   22 Purchased ceramic wall tiles for $1,350 from the Decorative Tile Company, Invoice 77651, dated January 19; the terms are 2/10, n/30.

23 Issued Check 679 for $165 to pay the monthly utility bill.

25 Received Credit Memorandum 212 for $130 from the Decorative Tile Company for damaged goods that were returned. The original purchase was made on Invoice 77651 of January 19.

26 Issued Check 680 for $910 to make a cash purchase of merchandise.

27 Issued Check 681 for $1,195.60 to the Decorative Tile Company, a creditor, in payment of Invoice 77651 of January 19 ($1,350) less a return ($130) and a cash discount ($24.40).

29 Purchased vinyl floor tiles for $3,850 plus a freight charge of $44 from the Montvale Corporation, Invoice 2155, dated January 26; terms of 1/10, n/30.

29 Issued Check 682 for $1,725 to Hamilton Products, a creditor, in payment of Invoice 3843 of December 31.

31 Issued Check 683 for $1,900 to pay the monthly salaries of the employees.

Note: Save your working papers for use in Problem 9-8A.

PROBLEM 9-8A   **Posting to the accounts payable ledger and preparing a schedule of accounts payable.** This problem is a continuation of Problem 9-7A.

Instructions   1. Set up an accounts payable ledger for the Lewis Tile Store. Open an account for each of the creditors listed below, and enter the balances as of January 1, 19X4.

2. Post the individual entries from the purchases journal, the cash payments journal, and the general journal prepared in Problem 9-7A.

3. Prepare a schedule of accounts payable for January 31, 19X4.

4. Check the total of the schedule of accounts payable against the balance of the Accounts Payable account in the general ledger. The two amounts should be the same.

CREDITORS

Name	Balance	Terms
Artistic Tiles Inc.	$2,170	n/30
Carter Industries	2,800	1/10, n/30
Decorative Tile Company		2/10, n/30
Hamilton Products	1,725	n/30
Lopez Company		n/30
Montvale Corporation		1/10, n/30
Sterling Corporation		2/10, n/30

The proper handling of cash receipts and cash payments requires the use of a checking account. When a new business is established, one of the first activities that management must perform is to open a checking account for the firm at a local bank. The checking account provides a safe means of storing cash receipts and an efficient method of making cash payments. This chapter explains the procedures that are used to prepare bank deposits, issue checks, maintain a record of checking account activities, and reconcile the monthly bank statement.

BANKING PROCEDURES AND RECONCILIATIONS

MAKING BANK DEPOSITS

In a firm that has a good system of internal control, cash receipts are deposited often. Keeping substantial amounts of cash on the premises for long periods of time is a dangerous practice. For this reason many businesses make a daily bank deposit, and some make two or three deposits a day. In addition to safeguarding cash, frequent bank deposits provide a steady flow of funds for the payment of expenses and other obligations.

THE DEPOSIT SLIP

A form called a *deposit slip,* or a *deposit ticket,* must be prepared for each bank deposit. These forms are usually provided to the depositor by the bank in which the account is maintained and are usually preprinted with the assigned account number. The deposit slip shown on page 234 was completed at Sports World for a deposit made on June 1, 19X5.

Notice the series of numbers preprinted along the lower edge of the deposit slip. The same series of numbers is also preprinted along the bottom of the checks that Sports World uses (see the illustration on page 238). A special kind of type called *magnetic ink character recognition (MICR) type* that can be "read" by machines is used for the preprinted numbers.

Numbers of this nature contain codes that are used in sorting and routing checks and deposit slips. The first half of the series shown on the checks and deposit slips provided to Sports World, 1210 8640, identifies the Federal Reserve District and the bank. In this system, which was set up by the American Bankers Association, the first pair of numbers (12) indicates that the firm's bank is located in the twelfth Federal Reserve District, and the second pair (10) is a routing number used in the processing of the document. The numbers 8640 identify the City National Bank. The next part of the series, 80 00 42269, is the number that the bank gave to the account of Sports World.

CHECKING ACCOUNT DEPOSIT

	DOLLARS	CENTS
CURRENCY	545	00
COIN	13	75

DATE *June 1, 19X5*

CHECKS List each separately		
1 *11–8182*	120	40
2 *11–8182*	215	00
3 *11–5216*	85	60
4 *11–5216*	140	00
5 *11–7450*	230	25
6 *11–7450*	90	00
7		
8		
9		
10		
11		
12		
13		

ENTER ADDITIONAL CHECKS ON OTHER SIDE.

SPORTS WORLD
365 BROAD STREET
SAN FRANCISCO, CA 94107

BANK COPY

DEPOSITOR COPY

CITY NATIONAL BANK
SAN FRANCISCO, CA 94107

TOTAL FROM OTHER SIDE OR ATTACHED LIST	

Checks and other items are received for deposit subject to the terms and conditions of this bank's collection agreement.

TOTAL	1,440.00

⑈1210⑈8640⑈ ⑈80⑈00 42269⑈

Banks prefer to use deposit slips and checks encoded with these special numbers so that the documents can be processed rapidly and efficiently by computers and other electronic devices. Documents that are not encoded must be handled manually outside the regular processing. This is a slow and costly procedure with much greater possibility of error.

Deposit slips for checking accounts are usually prepared on multicopy sets of forms. The name of the depositor is either preprinted or handwritten on the deposit slip. (Notice that the deposit slip used by Sports World has the firm's name preprinted.)

The current date is written on the deposit slip (June 1, 19X5, in this case). The total value of the paper money is entered opposite the word *currency,* and the total value of the coins is written opposite the word *coin.* Checks and money orders presented for deposit are listed individually on the deposit slip. Some banks require that, in addition to the amount, an identification number be entered for each check or money order. The identification number is taken from the top part of the fraction that appears in the upper right corner of each document. For example, the number 11-8640 would be taken from the check shown on page 238. This identification number is known as the *ABA (American Bankers Association) transit number.*

PREPARING THE DEPOSIT

Preparing a bank deposit involves sorting the currency and coins by denomination and endorsing all checks that are to be deposited as well as filling out the deposit slip. When the items are delivered to the bank, a receipt is obtained as proof of the deposit.

Sorting Currency and Coins

Currency to be deposited should be sorted by denomination, with the smallest denomination on top of the pile. If there is a large amount of currency, the bank may require that the bills be placed in currency bands. These bands are either obtained from the bank or they are simply made from strips of blank paper. If there is a large number of coins of any one denomination, they should be packaged in coin wrappers provided by the bank. The name of the depositor is written or stamped on each currency band and each coin wrapper to identify the source of the funds and avoid the possibility of error.

Endorsing Checks

Each check to be deposited must be *endorsed*. This is the legal process by which the *payee* (the person or firm to whom the check is payable) transfers ownership of the check to the bank. The reason for transferring ownership is to give the bank the legal right to collect payment from the *drawer,* or *payor* (the person or firm that issued the check). In the event that the check cannot be collected, the endorser guarantees payment to all subsequent holders.

There are several forms of endorsement that are in common use. Individuals often use a *blank endorsement*. This endorsement consists of the signature of the payee written on the back of the check, preferably at the left end (the perforated end that was torn away from the stub). A check that has a blank endorsement can be further endorsed by the bearer (anyone into whose hands it should fall by intentional transfer or through loss).

A *full endorsement* is much safer. The payee indicates, as part of the endorsement, the name of the person, firm, or bank to whom the check is to be payable. Only the person, firm, or bank named in the full endorsement can transfer it to someone else.

The most appropriate form of endorsement for business purposes is the *restrictive endorsement,* which limits further use of the check to a stated purpose. Usually, the purpose is deposit in the firm's bank account. For maximum safety and speedy handling, Sports World, like most businesses, uses a rubber stamp to make a restrictive endorsement.

All three types of endorsement are illustrated below.

Blank Endorsement	Full Endorsement	Restrictive Endorsement
Lynn Frank 80-00-42269	PAY TO THE ORDER OF CITY NATIONAL BANK SPORTS WORLD 80-00-42269	PAY TO THE ORDER OF CITY NATIONAL BANK FOR DEPOSIT ONLY SPORTS WORLD 80-00-42269

Handling Postdated Checks

Occasionally a business will receive a *postdated check,* which is a check dated some time in the future. The drawer of such a check may not have sufficient funds in the bank to cover the check but expects to make a deposit to cover the amount before the check is presented for payment. A check of this type should not be deposited before its date. If it is deposited and payment is then refused by the drawer's bank, it becomes a dishonored check. The issuing or accepting of postdated checks is not considered a proper business practice.

Once the deposit has been prepared, it should be delivered promptly to the bank. In most businesses the owner or an employee takes the deposit to the bank during regular banking hours. This person usually gets a stamped duplicate copy of the deposit slip from the teller as a receipt for the funds.

Some firms make deposits by mail because of the distance to the bank, the inconvenience and loss of time caused by the travel involved, or other reasons. For such depositors, the bank may provide special deposit slips and envelopes preaddressed to the mail teller of the bank. After the deposit is recorded, the bank usually sends a receipt by mail to the depositor.

Because Sports World is a retail business that receives cash throughout the day, its bank deposit is prepared at the end of the day. The manager of the store carries the deposit to the bank in a locked bag. Since the bank is not open, he places the bag in the night depository at the door of the bank. The bag slides down a chute into the bank vault for safekeeping overnight. Then, at his convenience during banking hours the next day, the manager visits the bank, unlocks the bag, makes the deposit in the usual manner, and takes the bag back to the store for reuse.

The bank may acknowledge receipt of a deposit in a variety of ways. Many banks issue a machine-printed receipt form indicating the date and amount of money received. This method is widely used for mail deposits and deposits made in automatic teller machines. However, the most common method is for the bank teller to stamp and return one copy of the multicopy deposit slip form. In this way, the depositor obtains a receipt copy with all the details of the deposit. This copy is kept on file for a period of time as proof of the deposit in case it is needed.

MAKING PAYMENTS BY CHECK

As discussed already, a strong system of internal control requires that all payments be made by check except those that are made from a carefully controlled special-purpose cash fund such as a petty cash fund. Certain rules must be followed when preparing checks so that the checks are valid and cannot be altered easily. The correct procedures for issuing checks are discussed in this section.

Authorized Signatures

To be valid, a check must have an authorized signature. For example, at Sports World only Lynn Frank, the owner, is authorized to sign checks for the business. When the firm first opened its checking account, the signature card shown on page 237 was completed.

A *signature card* names any persons who will sign checks drawn on the account and provides a sample of their signatures. This card serves as a contract between the depositor and the bank. It authorizes the bank to make payments from the depositor's account on checks that have an authorized signature.

Larger firms than Sports World may provide for two signatures on each check. This is an excellent control procedure and is particularly appropriate when the owner or owners are not actively involved in management. The advantage of this procedure is that it requires cash payments to be approved by two persons and thereby lessens the possibility of fraud or misuse of the company's funds.

CITY NATIONAL BANK

CHECKING ACCOUNT
AGREEMENT WITH   Sports World

    365 Broad Street
ADDRESS San Francisco, CA 94107   PHONE 555-5678

The undersigned certifies that he or she, as sole proprietor, is doing business under the name of _Sports_
World _____, an unincorporated trade name, that no person other than the undersigned has any interest in said business except as employee and that the following employees, whose signatures appear below, are hereby authorized to sign checks and endorse negotiable instruments in my name and/or in said trade name. Such authority is to continue until written notice to the contrary from the undersigned shall have been received by you.

Witness my hand and seal this the ___26th___ day of ___November___ , 19 _X0_

                          Proprietor ___Lynn Frank___ (L. S.)
                                         (Signature)
Lynn Frank _____ will sign ___Lynn Frank___

(Employee) _____ will sign _____

DATE OPENED Nov. 26, 19X0 _____ INITIAL DEPOSIT ___$ 6,000___

OFFICER ACCEPTING _R Sadowski_ _____ ACCOUNT NO. 80-00-42269

Provisions are sometimes made authorizing any two of several responsible officers or employees to sign checks for the firm. This assures that checks can be issued in the absence of one or more of the authorized signers.

Preparing Standard Checks

A *check* is a written order signed by an authorized person (the *drawer*) instructing a bank (the *drawee*) to pay a specific sum of money to a designated person or firm (the *payee*). Such a check is *negotiable,* which means that ownership of the check can be transferred to another person or firm. As you have already seen, the payee endorses a check to transfer it to a third party.

Many small firms like Sports World use a standard checkbook provided by the bank to business depositors. This type of checkbook contains checks with stubs, as shown on page 238. Several checks appear on each page, and they are perforated for easy removal when they are used. The stubs remain in the checkbook so that they can serve as a record of the firm's checking account activities. The amount of each check issued and each deposit made is entered on the appropriate stub along with the current balance of the account. Both the checks and the stubs are usually prenumbered as a control measure.

Standard checks are normally prepared by hand. Ink must be used to guard against unauthorized changes in the amount or the name of the payee. Similarly, entries on the check stubs are made in ink to prevent later alterations in that data.

There are a number of procedures that should be followed in writing a check. For example, in a standard checkbook, the check stub should always be filled out first. Otherwise, it might be forgotten. The stub is important because it contains information that is needed for future reference. Notice that on the first check stub illustrated on page 238 the opening balance of $5,600 for June is at

Stub No. 3503:

NO. 3503	BAL. BRO'T FOR'D 5,600 00
June 1, 19X5	
Bay Real Estate	
TO ORDER OF	
Rent for June	
FOR	
TOTAL	5,600 00
AMOUNT THIS CHECK	700 00
BALANCE	4,900 00

Check No. 3503:

Sports World
365 Broad Street
San Francisco, CA 94107

No. 3503

June 1, 19X5   11-8640/1210

Pay to the order of _Bay Real Estate_ _____ $700 00/100

Seven hundred and 00/100 _____ Dollars

CITY NATIONAL BANK
SAN FRANCISCO, CA 94107

Lynn Frank

⑆1210⑈8640⑆ ⑈80⑈00 42269⑈

Stub No. 3504:

NO. 3504	
June 2, 19X5	1,440 00
Chase Company	
TO ORDER OF	
Invoice 29954	
FOR	
TOTAL	6,340 00
AMOUNT THIS CHECK	1,960 00
BALANCE	4,380 00

Check No. 3504:

Sports World
365 Broad Street
San Francisco, CA 94107

No. 3504

June 2, 19X5   11-8640/1210

Pay to the order of _Chase Company_ _____ $1,960 00/100

One thousand nine hundred sixty and 00/100 Dollars

CITY NATIONAL BANK
SAN FRANCISCO, CA 94107

Lynn Frank

⑆1210⑈8640⑆ ⑈80⑈00 42269⑈

---

the top, next to the words *Balance Brought Forward*. The amount of the first check, $700, is written next to the words *Amount This Check*. It is then subtracted from the total to obtain the new balance of $4,900. The rest of the details recorded on the stub are the date (June 1, 19X5), the name of the payee (Bay Real Estate), and the purpose of the payment (rent for June).

Once the stub is completed, the check portion is filled out. The date, the name of the payee, and the amount in figures and words are written very carefully. A line is drawn to fill any empty space after the payee's name and after the amount in words. When all the data is entered on the check, it should be examined for accuracy before it is signed and sent out.

The second check stub illustrated above shows the deposit of $1,440 that Sports World made on June 1. Before the second check was written, this deposit was added to the balance appearing at the bottom of the first stub ($4,900 + $1,440). The total of $6,340 was then entered on the second stub. When payment was made to the Chase Company, the rest of the check stub and the check itself were prepared in the manner described previously.

Look again at the checks illustrated, and notice how the amounts are expressed. The amount of each check is written in figures in the space to the right of the dollar sign following the name of the payee. Special care must be taken to write the figures clearly so that they can be read easily. The dollar amount of the check is restated in words on the line below the name of the payee. The writing should begin at the extreme left of the space provided in order to prevent the insertion of additional words. The cents amount is usually shown as a fraction of a dollar. Thus, 15 cents is written as $\frac{15}{100}$. If the check is for an even dollar amount, $\frac{00}{100}$ or $\frac{no}{100}$ is written. (On a typewritten check, the form used is 22/100 or no/100.) The cents amount is usually separated from the dollar amount by the word *and*. It is customary to draw a line from the fraction to the word *Dollars* in order to fill the empty space.

If through error the amount expressed in figures is not the same as the amount in words, the bank will pay the amount written in words or will return the check unpaid.

Notice the numbers printed on the bottom of each check. This is another example of the MICR type discussed earlier in the chapter. The first bank to receive the check after it has been issued will encode the amount of the check in the same type in the lower right corner. The check (and similar deposit slips) can then be handled automatically by electronic devices (called *magnetic character readers*) through regular banking procedures. Checks that are not encoded with the bank number, the account number, and the check amount must be processed manually outside regular procedures.

Preparing Voucher Checks

Rather than using standard checks provided by the bank, many businesses have their own checks printed on special forms that can easily be typed. Each of these forms usually consists of two parts: the check itself and an attached section that is used to give explanatory information such as the amount, number, and date of the invoice being paid. The payee removes the section with the explanatory information before depositing the check. An example of a check form of this type is shown below. (Sports World stopped using standard checks at the beginning of August 19X5.)

Sports World
365 Broad Street
San Francisco, CA 94107

No. 3601   11-8640
                1210

August 4   , 19 X5

Pay to the order of   Star-Herald Papers-------------------- $ 300.00

Three hundred and no/100------------------------------DOLLARS

                                                Sports World

CITY NATIONAL BANK
SAN FRANCISCO, CA 94107   *Lynn Frank*
                                 AUTHORIZED SIGNATURE

⑆1210⑈8640⑆ ⑈80⑈00 42269⑈

Sports World, San Francisco, CA 94107   DETACH BEFORE DEPOSITING

July advertising, Invoice 27641 of 7/31/X5 $300

The explanatory section of the check is known as a *remittance advice*, or *voucher*, and the complete form is usually referred to as a *voucher check*. To facilitate typing, voucher checks are not bound into a checkbook. Instead, they are on loose forms, often arranged in a carbon set so that a copy is made when the check is prepared. The copy is kept as a record of the payment and serves as the basis for the necessary accounting entry. Since there are no check stubs when voucher checks are used, a check register is maintained to keep track of all checks issued, all deposits made, and the current balance of the checking account.

Today, many firms use computer systems to prepare their checks. Voucher checks on continuous forms are placed inside a printer, which is part of the system. The central processing unit of the computer supplies the necessary data about each payment to be made, and the printer automatically enters the data on the voucher checks. When the checks are completed, they are removed from the printer and detached from each other. The checks are then signed. In a large company that issues hundreds or thousands of checks at one time, a check-signing machine may be used to reproduce the authorized signature on all checks.

Voiding Checks

When a check is prepared, no alterations or erasures can be made. If there is an error, the check must be voided and a new one issued. The original check is voided by writing the word *VOID* across its face in large letters and tearing off the signature line. The voided check is then filed so that it can be accounted for. (When the canceled checks for the month are returned with the bank statement, the voided check is placed with them. In this way, the firm is able to maintain a complete file of the checks that were used. Such a practice is important for control purposes.)

The fact that a check has been voided is noted on the appropriate check stub or in the check register.

Check Protectors

When checks are prepared by hand or typed, some firms use a machine called a *check protector* to help prevent fraudulent changes. The check protector imprints the amount in a distinctive type and perforates the check paper under the type.

RECONCILING THE BANK STATEMENT

Once a month the bank sends each individual or firm that has a checking account a statement of the deposits received and the checks paid. A typical bank statement is illustrated on page 241. Enclosed with the bank statement are *canceled checks*—the checks that the bank paid during the month. The depositor may also receive debit memorandums for special bank charges, credit memorandums for special amounts paid into the account, or other papers that have a bearing on the account balance.

Usually, there is a difference between the ending balance shown on the bank statement and the balance shown in the depositor's checkbook and Cash account. The depositor must determine why the difference exists and bring the two sets of records into agreement. This process is known as *reconciling the bank statement*.

The Bank Statement

The bank statement illustrated on page 241 is typical of those issued by many banks. Notice that it provides a day-by-day listing of all checking account transactions that took place during the month. A code, which is explained at the bottom of the form, identifies any transactions that do not involve checks or deposits. For example, the letters *DM* are used to indicate a debit memorandum and the letters *SC* are used to indicate a service charge. The last column of the bank statement shows the balance of the account at the beginning of the period, after each transaction was recorded, and at the end of the period.

Canceled Checks

Any checks paid by the bank during the month are sent to the depositor with the bank statement. Banks cancel these checks by stamping the word *PAID* across the face of each one. For the depositor, canceled checks serve as proof of payment and are therefore filed after the reconciliation process is completed.

Credit Memorandums

Banks prepare a form called a *credit memorandum* to explain any amount other than a deposit that is added to a checking account. For example, when a note receivable is due, a firm may have its bank collect the note from the maker and place the proceeds in its checking account. The bank lists the amount collected on the next bank statement and encloses a credit memorandum to show the details of the transaction.

Debit Memorandums

When a bank deducts any amount other than a paid check from a depositor's account, it issues a form called a *debit memorandum* and encloses it with the next bank statement. Service charges and dishonored checks are items that are often covered by a debit memorandum.

Bank service charges vary a great deal, but some common service charges are for account maintenance, new checkbooks, the use of a night depository, and the collection of a promissory note or another negotiable instrument. The bank uses a debit memorandum to notify the depositor of the type and amount of each service charge.

An example of a debit memorandum is shown below. This form was sent to Sports World to explain a deduction of $125 made from its account for a dishonored check. The check itself was also returned by the bank. (Dishonored checks are discussed in the next section.)

DEBIT	Sports World		CITY NATIONAL BANK
	365 Broad Street		
	San Francisco, CA 94107		
	80-00-42269	DATE June 25, 19X5	
	NSF Check — Thomas Hunt		125 00
			APPROVED
			W. E. H

Dishonored Checks

Sometimes a check that has been deposited is returned and subtracted from the depositor's account. This occurs when the bank on which the check was drawn has refused to honor it, normally because there are not sufficient funds in the drawer's account to cover the check. (The bank usually stamps the letters *NSF* for "Not Sufficient Funds" on the check.) Such a check is said to be *dishonored*. The depositor's records must be adjusted (by means of a journal entry) to reflect the dishonored check. It is also necessary to correct the balance shown in the checkbook.

After a firm is notified of a dishonored check by its bank, it must contact the drawer in order to arrange for collection. The drawer may instruct the firm to redeposit the check on a certain date after it places the necessary funds in its account. The firm's records are again adjusted when the check is redeposited.

BANK RECONCILIATION— ILLUSTRATIVE CASE

Immediately after the bank statement is received, it should be reconciled with the firm's financial records. The following example will illustrate the reconciliation process.

Bank Balance

On July 1, 19X5, Sports World received the bank statement shown on page 241. This statement covers the firm's checking account transactions for the month of

June and contains an ending balance of $6,056.72. The accountant's first action is to compare this amount with the cash balance that appears in the firm's records.

Book Balance of Cash

An examination of the Cash account in the firm's general ledger reveals a balance of $8,288.15 on June 30 after postings have been made from the cash receipts journal and the cash payments journal. This amount, which is shown below, is called the *book balance of cash*. The latest stub in the firm's checkbook also contains the same figure.

			POST. REF.	DEBIT	CREDIT	BALANCE	DR. CR.
DATE		EXPLANATION					
19 X5							
June	1	Balance	✓			5,600 00	Dr.
	30		CR6	20,625 00		26,225 00	Dr.
	30		CP6		17,936 85	8,288 15	Dr.

Cash   No. 101

Reasons for Difference in Balances

Since the difference between the bank balance and the book balance may be due to errors made by either the bank or the depositor, the reconciliation process must be undertaken at once. Errors in the firm's records should be corrected immediately. Errors made by the bank should be called to its attention at the earliest possible time. (Many banks require that errors in the bank statement be reported within a short period of time, usually ten days.)

If no errors have been made in the calculation of the bank balance or the book balance, there are four basic reasons why the balances may not agree.

1. There may be *outstanding checks*—checks that have been written and entered in the firm's cash payments journal but have not been paid by the bank and charged to the depositor's account before the end of the month.
2. There may be a *deposit in transit*—a deposit that has been recorded in the firm's cash receipts journal but has reached the bank too late to be included in the bank statement for the current month.
3. The bank may have deducted service charges or other items that have not yet been entered in the firm's records.
4. The bank may have credited the firm's account for the collection of a promissory note or for other items that have not yet been entered in the firm's records.

Differences stemming from the first two causes listed above require no entries in the firm's records. However, they must be considered in the reconciliation process. Then, the next bank statement must be checked to make sure that the outstanding checks and deposits in transit have been picked up in the bank records. Differences arising from the next two causes must be corrected by making entries in the firm's records so that these records will reflect the increases or decreases of cash.

In addition to the differences already discussed, there are other differences that occur less often. The bank may have made an arithmetic error, given credit to the wrong depositor, or charged a check against the wrong depositor's account. Similarly, a check may have been entered in the firm's records at an amount different from the amount for which it was actually written, or it may not have been entered at all.

Steps in the Reconciliation Process

There are several steps that should be followed in reconciling a bank statement.

Step 1 The canceled checks and debit memorandums sent by the bank are compared with the deductions listed on the bank statement. As noted already, debit memorandums explain any amounts paid from the account other than checks.

Two debit memorandums were enclosed with the bank statement that Sports World received for the month of June. The first debit memorandum covered a check for $125 from Thomas Hunt, a customer, that the bank could not collect because there were not sufficient funds in Hunt's account. This *NSF check,* as it is called, was deducted from the account of Sports World because the firm had endorsed it, deposited it, and received credit for it. (The debit memorandum for Hunt's check is shown on page 242.)

The second debit memorandum was for a monthly service charge of $10 that the firm pays for the use of the bank's night depository. Refer to the bank statement illustrated on page 241 to see how the NSF check and the service charge were reported by the bank on this statement.

Step 2 The canceled checks are arranged in numeric order so that they can be compared with the entries in the checkbook and the cash payments journal. In making this comparison, the accountant verifies the amount of each check and the check number. (Any differences between the canceled checks and the entries in the cash payments journal must be corrected in the general journal.) The endorsement on each canceled check should be examined to make sure that it agrees with the name of payee.

In verifying the canceled checks, the accountant for Sports World found that a $400 check was mistakenly deducted from the firm's account on June 29. The check was issued by another business, Sports Arena, and should have been charged to the account of that firm. The accountant immediately notified the bank of the error and returned the check to the bank. Sports World should receive credit for $400 on the next bank statement.

While comparing the canceled checks with the entries in the checkbook and the cash payments journal, the accountant listed the numbers and amounts of any outstanding checks. This list included Check 3519 for $127.56, Check 3520 for $300, Check 3521 for $101.01, and Check 3523 for $375.

Step 3 The deposits shown on the bank statement are compared with the deposits recorded in the checkbook and the daily receipts that appear in the cash receipts journal. In the case of Sports World, the bank statement agrees with the firm's records except for an amount of $2,600 for the receipts of June 30. The money was placed in the bank's night depository on June 30 but was not actually deposited until the following day, July 1. The accountant made a note of the $2,600 as a deposit in transit. When the next bank statement arrives, it will be checked to see that the bank has included this deposit in its records.

Step 4 The final step is to prove that all differences between the bank balance and the book balance are accounted for. This is done by preparing a formal *bank reconciliation statement,* such as the one shown below. Banks often provide a preprinted reconciliation form on the back of the bank statement, but most businesses use analysis paper and set up the reconciliation statement in the following manner.

SPORTS WORLD
Bank Reconciliation Statement
June 30, 19X5

Balance on bank statement		$6,056.72
Additions:		
Deposit of June 30 in transit	$2,600.00	
Check incorrectly charged to account	400.00	3,000.00
Deductions for outstanding checks:		$9,056.72
Check 3519 of June 25	$ 127.56	
Check 3520 of June 28	300.00	
Check 3521 of June 29	101.01	
Check 3523 of June 30	375.00	
Total outstanding checks		903.57
Adjusted bank balance		$8,153.15
Balance in books		$8,288.15
Deductions:		
NSF check	$ 125.00	
Bank service charge	10.00	135.00
Adjusted book balance		$8,153.15

Notice that there are two main sections in the reconciliation statement. The upper section starts with the ending balance on the bank statement ($6,056.72). To this amount are added any items that increase the bank balance, such as the deposit in transit of $2,600 and the $400 check that was incorrectly charged to the firm's account. The accountant adds these two amounts to the bank balance, which results in a new total of $9,056.72. Then, from this total he subtracts items that decrease the bank balance, such as the four outstanding checks. After the subtraction, there is an adjusted bank balance of $8,153.15.

The second section of the reconciliation statement starts with the balance in the books ($8,288.15 from the Cash account). To this balance, any increases not yet entered in the firm's records are added, such as the proceeds from a note collected by the bank. Sports World did not have any such items during June.

Next, items that were deducted by the bank but are not yet shown in the firm's records must be subtracted from the previous book balance. There are two items of this type—the NSF check of $125 and the bank service charge of $10. Subtracting these amounts from the original book balance results in an adjusted book balance of $8,153.15. The adjusted bank balance and the adjusted book balance agree, as they always should at the end of the reconciliation process.

Adjusting the Financial Records

Items in the second section of the reconciliation statement require entries in the firm's financial records to correct the Cash account balance and the checkbook balance. In the case of Sports World, two entries must be made, as shown in the general journal illustrated below. The first entry is for the NSF check from Thomas Hunt, a credit customer. Notice that the debit part of this entry charges the amount of the check back to the Accounts Receivable account in the general ledger and Hunt's account in the accounts receivable subsidiary ledger. The second entry is for the bank service charge, which is debited to Miscellaneous Expense. Both entries involve a credit to Cash because the effect of the two items is to decrease the Cash account balance.

19 X5					
July	1	Accounts Receivable/Thomas Hunt	111/✓	125 00	
		Cash	101		125 00
		To record NSF check returned by bank.			
	1	Miscellaneous Expense	591	10 00	
		Cash	101		10 00
		To record bank service charge for June.			

After these entries are posted, the Cash account appears as shown below. Notice that the balance of $8,153.15 agrees with the adjusted book balance on the reconciliation statement.

Cash   No. 101

DATE		EXPLANATION	POST. REF.	DEBIT	CREDIT	BALANCE	DR. CR.
19 X5							
June	1	Balance	✓			5,600 00	Dr.
	30		CR6	20,625 00		26,225 00	Dr.
	30		CP6		17,936 85	8,288 15	Dr.
July	1		J7		125 00	8,163 15	Dr.
	1		J7		10 00	8,153 15	Dr.

The checkbook balance is also corrected at this point. A notation is made on the latest check stub to explain the decreases in the balance.

Sometimes the bank reconciliation process reveals an error in the firm's financial records. For example, on October 3, 19X5, when the accountant for Sports World compared the canceled checks for September with the entries in the firm's cash payments journal and checkbook, he found that Check 3628 of September 21, which was issued to pay for advertising, had been recorded incorrectly. The entries in the firm's records indicated the amount as $245, but the canceled check and the bank statement showed that the sum was actually $240. The accountant listed the error of $5 on the bank reconciliation statement as an addition to the book balance of cash. After the reconciliation process was completed, he made the following entry in the general journal to correct the error.

19 X5					
Oct.	3	Cash	101	5 00	
		Advertising Expense	514		5 00
		To correct error in entry for Check 3628			
		of September 21.			

The accountant also added the $5 to the checkbook balance on the latest check stub and made an explanatory notation there.

INTERNAL CONTROL OF BANKING ACTIVITIES

Accountants usually recommend that the following measures be taken to achieve internal control over banking activities.

1. Access to the checkbook should be restricted to a few designated employees. When not in use, the checkbook should be kept in a locked drawer or cabinet.
2. Prenumbered check forms should be used. Periodically, the numbers of the checks that were issued and the numbers of the blank forms remaining should be verified to make sure that all forms can be accounted for.
3. Before checks are signed, they should be examined by a person other than the one who prepared them. They should be matched against the approved invoices or other payment authorizations.
4. The person who prepares the checks and records them in the checkbook should not be the one who mails them to the payees.
5. The monthly bank statement should be received and reconciled by someone other than the employees who handled, recorded, and deposited the cash receipts and issued the checks.
6. All deposit receipts, canceled checks, voided checks, and bank statements should be filed for future reference. This creates a strong audit trail for the checking account.

PRINCIPLES AND PROCEDURES SUMMARY

The use of a checking account is essential if a business is to store its cash receipts safely and make cash payments efficiently. For the sake of security, cash receipts should be deposited daily or even several times a day when very large sums are involved. For maximum control over outgoing cash, all payments should be made by check except those that are made from carefully controlled special-purpose cash funds such as a petty cash fund.

Check writing requires careful attention to details. If a standard checkbook is used, the stub should be completed before the check so that it will not be forgotten. The stub provides the information needed to journalize the payment.

Voucher checks are now widely used in business because they offer several advantages. They can easily be typed or used in a computer system, and they contain an explanatory section that identifies the payment for the creditor.

As soon as the monthly bank statement is received, it should be reconciled with the cash balance shown in the firm's financial records. Usually, differences arise because of deposits in transit, outstanding checks, and bank service charges. However, many factors can lead to a lack of agreement between the bank balance and the book balance. Some differences may require that the firm's records be adjusted after the bank statement is reconciled.

MANAGERIAL IMPLICATIONS

Because a checking account plays such a vital role in the handling of cash receipts and cash payments, management must make sure that the account is maintained properly. Management should work with the accountant to establish suitable controls over all of the firm's banking activities—depositing funds, issuing checks, recording checking account transactions, and reconciling the monthly bank statement.

Having accurate, up-to-date information about the checking account is highly important. In order to pay obligations on time, management must be constantly aware of the firm's cash position so that it can anticipate any shortage of funds and make arrangements to deal with the situation. Conversely, if the firm has more funds on deposit than it needs for current use, management may want to arrange for a temporary investment of the excess amount in order to earn interest.

REVIEW QUESTIONS

1. Why must the payee endorse a check before depositing it?
2. Describe the different types of endorsement. Which type is most appropriate for a business to use?
3. What is a postdated check? When should this kind of check be deposited?
4. What purpose does a signature card serve?
5. What is the advantage of requiring two signatures on a check?
6. Why are MICR numbers printed on deposit slips and checks?
7. Define the term *check*.
8. What type of information is entered on a check stub? Why should a check stub be prepared before the check is written?
9. What is a voucher check?
10. Why would a check be voided? What procedure is used to void a check?
11. What information is shown on the bank statement?
12. Why is a bank reconciliation prepared?

13. Explain the meaning of the following terms.

    a. Canceled check   d. Debit memorandum
    b. Outstanding check   e. Credit memorandum
    c. Deposit in transit   f. Dishonored check

14. What is the book balance of cash?
15. Give some reasons why the bank balance and the book balance of cash may differ?
16. Why are journal entries sometimes needed after the bank reconciliation statement is prepared?
17. What procedures are used to achieve internal control over banking activities?

MANAGERIAL DISCUSSION QUESTIONS

1. Why would management be concerned about having accurate information about the firm's cash position available at all times?
2. Many banks now offer a variety of computer services to clients. Why is it not advisable for a firm to pay its bank to complete the reconciliation procedure at the end of each month?
3. Assume that you are the newly hired controller at the Norton Company, and you have observed the following banking procedures in use at the firm. Would you change any of these procedures? Why or why not?
    a. A blank endorsement is made on all checks that will be deposited.
    b. The checkbook is kept on the top of a desk at all times so that it will be handy.
    c. The same person prepares bank deposits, issues checks, and reconciles the bank statement.
    d. The reconciliation process usually takes place two or three weeks after the bank statement is received.
    e. The bank statement and the canceled checks are thrown away after the reconciliation process is completed.
    f. As a shortcut in the reconciliation process, there is no attempt to compare the endorsements on the back of the canceled checks with the names of the payees shown on the face of these checks.

EXERCISES

EXERCISE 10-1   **Analyzing bank reconciliation items.** During the bank reconciliation process at the Judd Electronics Company, the items listed below and on page 250 were found to be causing a difference between the bank statement and the firm's records. Indicate whether each item will affect the bank balance or the book balance when the bank reconciliation statement is prepared.

1. An outstanding check.
2. A bank service charge.

3. A check issued by another firm that was charged to Judd's account by mistake.
4. A deposit in transit.
5. A debit memorandum for a dishonored check.
6. A credit memorandum for a promissory note that the bank collected for Judd.
7. An error found in Judd's records, which involves the amount of a check. The firm's checkbook and cash payments journal indicate $220 as the amount, but the canceled check itself and the listing on the bank statement show that $230 was the actual sum.

EXERCISE 10-2 **Determining the accounting entries to be made after a bank reconciliation.** Indicate which of the items listed in Exercise 10-1 would require an accounting entry after the bank reconciliation process is completed.

EXERCISE 10-3 **Determining an adjusted bank balance.** On November 2, 19X4, the Santorelli Corporation received a bank statement containing a balance of $14,920 as of October 31. The firm's records showed $14,362 as the book balance of cash on October 31. The following items were found to be causing the difference between the two balances. Prepare the adjusted bank balance section of the firm's bank reconciliation statement.

- A bank service charge of $12.
- A deposit in transit of $857.
- A debit memorandum for an NSF check of $300.
- Three outstanding checks: Check 4107 for $129, Check 4109 for $65, and Check 4110 for $1,533.

EXERCISE 10-4 **Determining an adjusted book balance of cash.** Use the data from Exercise 10-3 to prepare the adjusted book balance section of the bank reconciliation statement for the Santorelli Corporation. Make sure that this balance agrees with the adjusted bank balance computed in Exercise 10-3.

EXERCISE 10-5 **Journalizing a bank service charge.** Prepare a general journal entry to record the Santorelli Corporation's bank service charge of $12 for October. Use November 2, 19X4, as the date of the entry.

EXERCISE 10-6 **Journalizing a dishonored check.** Prepare a general journal entry to record the NSF check of $300 that the Santorelli Corporation received with its October bank statement. The check was issued by Roy Haines, a credit customer of the firm. Use November 2, 19X4, as the date of the entry.

EXERCISE 10-7 **Preparing a bank reconciliation statement.** On April 3, 19X7, the Ross Building Supply Company received a bank statement containing a balance of $22,635 as of March 31. The firm's records showed $23,129 as the book balance of cash on March 31. The items listed on page 251 were found to be causing the difference between the two balances. Prepare a bank reconciliation statement for the firm as of March 31, 19X7.

- Two outstanding checks: Check 6823 for $710 and Check 6824 for $57.
- A credit memorandum for a $2,000 noninterest-bearing note receivable that the bank collected for the firm.
- A debit memorandum for $7, which covers the bank's collection fee for the note.
- A deposit in transit of $1,240.
- A check for $89 issued by another firm that was mistakenly charged to Ross's account.
- A debit memorandum for an NSF check of $1,925 issued by the Ames Construction Company, a credit customer.

EXERCISE 10-8   **Journalizing entries resulting from a bank reconciliation.** Refer to the bank reconciliation statement prepared in Exercise 10-7, and determine which items should be journalized. Prepare general journal entries for these items. Use April 3, 19X7, as the date of the entries. (The firm charges all bank fees to Miscellaneous Expense.)

PROBLEMS

PROBLEM 10-1   **Preparing a bank reconciliation statement and journalizing entries to adjust the cash balance.** On May 2, 19X1, Monet Florists received its April bank statement. Enclosed with the bank statement, shown on page 252, was a debit memorandum for $40, which covered an NSF check issued by Gail Reese, a credit customer. The firm's checkbook contained the following information about deposits made and checks issued during April. The balance of the Cash account and the checkbook on April 30 was $3,972.

TRANSACTIONS FOR APRIL 19X1

Apr.	1 Balance	$6,089
	1 Check 244	100
	3 Check 245	300
	5 Deposit	350
	5 Check 246	275
	10 Check 247	2,000
	17 Check 248	50
	19 Deposit	150
	22 Check 249	9
	23 Deposit	150
	26 Check 250	200
	28 Check 251	18
	30 Check 252	15
	30 Deposit	200

Instructions   1. Prepare a bank reconciliation statement for the firm as of April 30, 19X1.
2. Record general journal entries for any items on the bank reconciliation statement that must be journalized. Date the entries May 2, 19X1.

PROBLEM 10-2 **Preparing a bank reconciliation statement and journalizing entries to adjust the cash balance.** On July 31, 19X5, the balance in the checkbook and the Cash account of the Simon Company was $11,549. The balance shown on the bank statement on the same date was $11,782.05.

- The firm's records indicate that an $879.60 deposit dated July 30 and a $476.80 deposit dated July 31 do not appear on the bank statement.
- A service charge of $4.50 and a debit memorandum of $80 covering an NSF check have not yet been entered in the firm's records. (The check was issued by John Pell, a credit customer.)
- The checks listed below were issued but have not yet been paid by the bank.

Check 864 for $110.50   Check 870 for $576.30
Check 865 for $11.60   Check 871 for $77.35
Check 868 for $238.20   Check 873 for $145.00

- A credit memorandum shows that the bank has collected a $500 note receivable and interest of $15 for the firm. These amounts have not yet been entered in the firm's records.

Instructions 1. Prepare a bank reconciliation statement for the firm as of July 31, 19X5.
2. Record general journal entries for any items on the bank reconciliation statement that must be journalized. Date the entries August 4, 19X5.

PROBLEM 10-3 **Correcting errors revealed by a bank reconciliation.** During the bank reconciliation process at the McKenzie Corporation on February 3, 19X6, the two errors described below and on page 253 were discovered in the firm's records.

- The checkbook and the cash payments journal indicated that Check 8512 of January 7 was issued for $79 to pay for a truck repair. However, examination of the canceled check and the listing on the bank statement showed that the actual amount of the check was $77.

- The checkbook and the cash payments journal indicated that Check 8529 of January 23 was issued for $101 to pay a telephone bill. However, examination of the canceled check and the listing on the bank statement showed that the actual amount of the check was $110.

Instructions
1. Prepare the adjusted book balance section of the firm's bank reconciliation statement. The book balance as of January 31 was $19,451. The errors listed above are the only two items that affect the book balance.
2. Prepare general journal entries to correct the errors. Date the entries February 3, 19X6. Check 8512 was debited to Truck Expense on January 7, and Check 8529 was debited to Telephone Expense on January 23.

ALTERNATE PROBLEMS

PROBLEM 10-1A **Preparing a bank reconciliation statement and journalizing entries to adjust the cash balance.** On March 3, 19X1, the Nakos Towing Service received its February bank statement from the Peoples National Bank. Enclosed with the bank statement, shown on page 254, was a debit memorandum for $56, which covered an NSF check issued by the Central Taxi Company, a credit customer. The firm's checkbook contained the following information about deposits made and checks issued during February. The balance of the Cash account and the checkbook on February 28 was $8,311.

TRANSACTIONS FOR FEBRUARY 19X1

Feb.	1 Balance	$6,500
	1 Check 421	100
	3 Check 422	10
	3 Deposit	500
	6 Check 423	225
	10 Deposit	410
	11 Check 424	200
	15 Check 425	75
	21 Check 426	60
	22 Deposit	730
	25 Check 427	4
	25 Check 428	20
	27 Check 429	35
	28 Deposit	900

Instructions
1. Prepare a bank reconciliation statement for the firm as of February 28, 19X1.
2. Record general journal entries for any items on the bank reconciliation statement that must be journalized. Date the entries March 3, 19X1.

```
                              PEOPLES NATIONAL BANK

     NAKOS TOWING SERVICE                 ACCOUNT NO. 110-624-0
     401 BELL STREET
     CLEVELAND, OH 44106                  PERIOD ENDING  FEB 28, 19X1

          CHECKS                DEPOSITS        DATE           BALANCE

                                               19X1
     AMOUNT BROUGHT FORWARD                     JAN 31        6,500.00

                                  500.00+      FEB  4        7,000.00
                                               FEB  6        6,900.00
       100.00-                    410.00+      FEB 11        7,100.00
       200.00-       10.00-                    FEB 15        6,875.00
       225.00-                                 FEB 19        6,815.00
        60.00-                                 FEB 23        7,545.00
                                  730.00+      FEB 25        7,521.00
        20.00-        4.00-                     FEB 28        7,461.25
         3.75-SC     56.00-DM
```

Preparing a bank reconciliation statement and journalizing entries to adjust the cash balance. On June 30, 19X5, the balance in the Haig Company's checkbook and Cash account was $6,418.59. The balance shown on the bank statement on the same date was $7,542.03.

- The firm's records indicate that a deposit of $944.07 made on June 30 does not appear on the bank statement.
- A service charge of $14.34 and a debit memorandum of $120 covering an NSF check have not yet been entered in the firm's records. (The check was issued by Paul Gibbs, a credit customer.)
- The following checks were issued but have not yet been paid by the bank.

  Check 533 for $148.95
  Check 535 for $97.50
  Check 536 for $425.40

- A credit memorandum shows that the bank has collected a $1,500 note receivable and interest of $30 for the firm. These amounts have not yet been entered in the firm's records.

Instructions
1. Prepare a bank reconciliation statement for the firm as of June 30, 19X5.
2. Record general journal entries for any items on the bank reconciliation statement that must be journalized. Date the entries July 2, 19X5.

PROBLEM 10-3A **Correcting errors revealed by a bank reconciliation.** During the bank reconciliation process at the Moore Company on May 2, 19X5, the two errors described below and on page 255 were discovered in the firm's records.

- The checkbook and the cash payments journal indicated that Check 1240 of April 10 was issued for $350 to make a cash purchase of supplies. However, examination of the canceled check and the listing on the bank statement showed that the actual amount of the check was $305.

- The checkbook and the cash payments journal indicated that Check 1247 of April 18 was issued for $166 to pay a utility bill. However, examination of the canceled check and the listing on the bank statement showed that the actual amount of the check was $186.

Instructions

1. Prepare the adjusted book balance section of the firm's bank reconciliation statement. The book balance as of April 30 was $8,563. The errors listed above are the only two items that affect the book balance.

2. Prepare general journal entries to correct the errors. Date the entries May 2, 19X5. Check 1240 was debited to Supplies on April 10, and Check 1247 was debited to Utilities Expense on April 18.

Every business should have a well-planned system of internal control to ensure accuracy, honesty, and efficiency in the handling of its resources and the recording of its transactions. The exact control procedures used vary somewhat according to the size of a firm and the nature of its operations. However, all systems of internal control are based on certain fundamental principles. This chapter discusses the underlying principles of internal control and presents the voucher system, a widely used method of controlling liabilities and payments in medium-sized and large companies.

INTERNAL CONTROL AND THE VOUCHER SYSTEM

THE NEED FOR INTERNAL CONTROL

Losses to American business from employee carelessness, inaccuracy, and dishonesty are estimated to total billions of dollars a year. No business is immune from this hazard, and to ignore it may mean the difference between a profitable operation and complete failure. That is why accountants recommend that all firms, no matter what their size, establish internal control procedures. These procedures are designed to protect the resources and financial records of a business. However, they also benefit the employees because they limit the temptation to steal or misuse assets and because they pinpoint responsibility, which prevents suspicion from falling on honest employees.

GENERAL PRINCIPLES OF INTERNAL CONTROL

From the discussion up to this point, it is clear that an *internal control system* has three basic purposes: to safeguard assets, to achieve efficient processing of transactions, and to ensure the accuracy and reliability of financial records. The system should be organized and operated so that the work of one person provides a check on the work of another, with minimum duplication of effort. If a business has enough employees to permit the necessary separation of duties, a strong system of internal control can be established. If the number of employees is small, internal control will be weaker and will have to be supplemented by more careful supervision from the owner or manager of the firm.

In previous chapters, you learned about a variety of procedures that are used to control purchases, cash receipts, cash payments, petty cash, and banking activities. Accountants follow certain general principles in developing these control procedures and other control procedures.

1. No one person should be in complete charge of any important business transaction. Two or more employees should be assigned to every major

operation, and the work of one should be planned so that it will be checked against the work of the other at some point in the routine.

2. The people who handle cash and other valuable assets should not be the same as those who have responsibility for recording the assets.

3. Every employee should be trained to do his or her job and should also understand why the job or procedure is to be performed in the specified manner.

4. Only capable and experienced personnel of demonstrated reliability should be assigned to key positions in the internal control system. Unannounced changes in these assignments are also desirable. Annual vacations should be required for each employee, and his or her regular work should be performed by other employees during vacations.

5. All transactions should be backed by adequate documentation.

6. Prenumbered forms should be used for documents produced within the business, such as purchase orders, sales invoices, and checks.

7. The business should maintain a strong audit trail by providing references to source documents in accounting entries, cross-referencing the entries that appear in different records, and keeping documents on file for a specified period of time. In this way, every transaction can be traced through the accounting system to its origin.

8. Whenever appropriate, the controls built into forms, records, and operating routines should be supplemented by electronic or mechanical devices in order to provide maximum protection. For example, cash registers, cashier cages, and locked storerooms make theft or mishandling of assets more difficult.

9. Management should review and evaluate the established system of internal control periodically to make sure that it is operating as planned and continues to provide adequate safeguards.

10. Periodically, management should also have the company's public accounting firm assess the effectiveness of the internal control procedures that are being used. As an outsider, the public accounting firm can provide a more detached evaluation; and because of its broad experience, it is better able to locate weaknesses and design improved procedures.

THE VOUCHER SYSTEM

The *voucher system* is a method of controlling liabilities and cash payments that is based on the use of a form called a *voucher*. This form is prepared to authorize the payment of all obligations, and no check can be issued without a properly approved voucher that is backed by suitable documentation. The voucher is the focal point for a series of tight controls that are built into the system.

This method of internal control is most appropriate for medium-sized and large businesses. The amount of paperwork involved and the number of different individuals required to carry out the procedures correctly make it difficult for a small business to use the voucher system. Also, because the owner of a small firm normally supervises day-to-day operations very closely, there is less need for as elaborate a set of controls as the voucher system provides.

| Controls Involved in a Voucher System | The following controls are usually built into a voucher system. Some of these controls have already been discussed in connection with purchases and cash payments. |

1. No liabilities are incurred without prior authorization. For example, a properly approved purchase order is required for each credit purchase of merchandise.
2. All payments are made by check, except for payments made from carefully controlled special-purpose cash funds such as a petty cash fund.
3. No check is issued without a properly approved voucher to authorize payment.
4. Vouchers are required to set up and replenish cash funds used within the business as well as to cover bills and invoices received from outside parties.
5. All bills and invoices are carefully verified before they are approved for payment.
6. Only designated employees who are experienced and responsible are allowed to approve bills and invoices for payment.
7. Approved bills and invoices are attached to the corresponding vouchers in order to provide supporting documentation.
8. The accounting entries for vouchers and payments are made by someone other than the person who approves the payments.
9. Still another person signs the checks and mails them to creditors.
10. All paid vouchers are kept on file for a specified period of time along with the supporting documentation.

OPERATING THE VOUCHER SYSTEM

A simple system of control over liabilities and cash payments usually works effectively in a small firm like Sports World. However, a larger business with more complex activities requires a more elaborate set of control procedures. The Style Clothing Store, the firm used in this chapter to illustrate the operations involved in the voucher system, is an example of such a business.

The Style Clothing Store is a retail firm owned by two partners: Linda Hanson and Steven Casey. It sells a broad line of casual clothes to both men and women. Hanson was previously sole proprietor, but she formed a partnership with Casey in order to obtain more capital and expand the firm's activities.

Before the new partnership was established on February 1, 19X1, the firm's public accountant recommended that the voucher system be used. She outlined the advantages of this system to Hanson and Casey, and they decided to adopt it.

Preparing and Approving Vouchers

As noted already, the voucher system requires that a voucher be prepared and approved before any obligation is paid or before any sum is used to set up or replenish a cash fund for the business. Vouchers are often numbered consecutively. However, the accountant for the Style Clothing Store has suggested that the firm use a two-part number—the number to the left of the dash representing the month and the number to the right showing the sequence within the month. Thus, Voucher 2-01 identifies the first voucher prepared in February.

Voucher 2-01 was issued on February 1, 19X1, to authorize a payment of $1,250 to the Fisher Realty Company for the monthly rent on the store. Two other vouchers prepared on February 1 were Voucher 2-02 for $100 issued to the cashier, Robert Gallo, to establish a change fund, and Voucher 2-03 for $75 issued to the office clerk, Susan Bates, to establish a petty cash fund. Specific employees were named as the payees of these two vouchers in order to pinpoint responsibility for the change fund and the petty cash fund. The next voucher issued by the firm, Voucher 2-04, which authorizes payment of an invoice for merchandise, provides a good illustration of the procedures used to prepare and approve vouchers.

On February 1, 19X1, the Style Clothing Store received an invoice for goods purchased on credit from Valley Wholesale Clothiers. The first step in handling this transaction was to check the accuracy of the invoice. The clerk who opened the mail used a rubber stamp to place a verification block on the invoice, as shown below. Then she passed the invoice along to Steven Casey, the partner in charge of store operations. He compared the quantities listed on the invoice with the quantities that appear on a receiving report filled out when the shipment arrived. Since the figures matched, he placed a check mark next to each quantity on the invoice and entered his initials in the appropriate area of the verification block.

Casey then gave the invoice to Linda Hanson, who compared it with a copy of the purchase order originally issued to the supplier. She examined the invoice to see that the prices listed did not exceed those specified when the order was placed. She checked off each unit price on the invoice and entered her initials in the verification block to show that the prices charged were correct. Finally, the office clerk, Susan Bates, checked the computations on the invoice. She multi-

VALLEY WHOLESALE CLOTHIERS
123 PONCE DE LEON AVENUE
ATLANTA, GEORGIA 30308

Invoice No. R-47651

SOLD TO Style Clothing Store
246 Main Street
Greenville, SC 29610

Date February 1, 19X1

Customer's Order No. 1-34

Terms 2/10, n/30

QUANTITY	DESCRIPTION OF ITEMS	PER UNIT	AMOUNT
✓ 20	Corduroy Suits D-4786	✓ $45.00	✓$ 900.00
✓ 8 pr.	Denim Jeans P-537	✓ 12.50	✓ 100.00
✓ 1	Denim Jacket R-258	✓ 20.14	✓ 20.14
			✓$1,020.14
		Less 20%	✓ 204.03
			✓ 816.11
		Less 10%	✓ 81.61
			✓$ 734.50

VERIFICATIONS
QUANTITIES RECEIVED — S.C.
PRICES CHARGED — L.H.
EXTENSIONS & TOTAL — S.B.

plied the quantity of each item by its unit price to verify the extensions. Then she added the extensions and calculated the trade discounts to verify the total. She placed a check mark next to each amount on the invoice as she found it to be correct and entered her initials in the verification block when she was finished. At that point, the invoice appeared as shown on page 259.

The same careful verification procedure is used for all bills and invoices received by the business. Of course, if an error is discovered, it is reported to the creditor immediately so that a correction can be made.

Once a bill or invoice is found to be accurate, it provides the basis for preparing a voucher to authorize payment when due. The voucher shown below (2-04) was issued for the invoice from Valley Wholesale Clothiers. After this voucher was prepared by the accounting clerk at the Style Clothing Store, the verified invoice was attached to it and the two documents were given to Casey, the partner in charge of store operations. Casey compared the invoice and the voucher and then signed the voucher to approve payment.

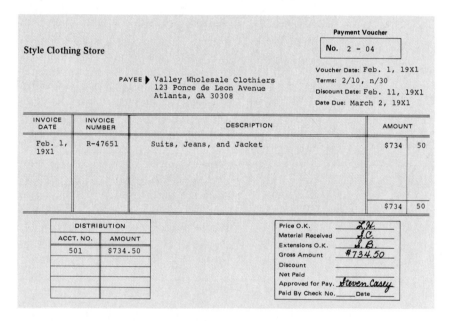

Notice that the Distribution section of the voucher shows the number (501) of the account to be debited (Merchandise Purchases) and the amount ($734.50). This information is used in making an accounting entry for the voucher. No account to be credited is specified because vouchers are normally credited to Accounts Payable. (However, it is sometimes necessary to credit additional accounts. In this case, it is customary to enter all debits and credits in the Distribution section of the voucher.)

Recording and Filing Unpaid Vouchers

After a voucher is approved, it is entered in an accounting record called the *voucher register*. Then if the voucher is not payable immediately, it is placed in a file of unpaid vouchers according to its due date. The file of unpaid vouchers thus represents the accounts payable of the business, and no formal accounts payable subsidiary ledger is needed.

When a voucher is due for payment, a check is issued for the amount involved. This sum is recorded on the voucher along with the check number and the date. (Notice that the voucher shown on page 260 has space for this information in the lower right corner.) The payment of the voucher is entered in an accounting record called the *check register*.

Vouchers that have been paid are stamped "Paid" and then placed in a paid vouchers file, usually in numerical order. However, in some cases, paid vouchers are filed according to the name of the payee to permit easier reference and help avoid duplication of payment.

Division of responsibility must be carefully planned by a firm if its voucher system is to provide the desired amount of control. At the Style Clothing Store, one person (the accounting clerk) prepares the voucher, a second person (Casey) approves the voucher, a third person (the office clerk) prepares the check, and a fourth person (Hanson) signs the check and mails it.

USING THE VOUCHER REGISTER

After vouchers are prepared and approved, they are entered in the voucher register in numerical order. This record provides a detailed listing of the vouchers issued each month and indicates the accounts that should be debited and credited for the transactions involved.

The completed voucher register of the Style Clothing Store for February 19X1 is shown on pages 262 and 263. Notice that it contains space for entering the date and number of each voucher, the name of the payee, and the debit and credit amounts. For the sake of efficiency, there are separate columns for the accounts that are used most often to record the firm's vouchers. This speeds up the initial entry of the vouchers and permits summary postings at the end of the month. Debits and credits to accounts used less often are placed in the Other Accounts section. Columns are also provided for recording the date each voucher is paid and the number of the check issued for the payment.

When entries are made in the voucher register, the amount of each voucher is credited to Accounts Payable. However, some transactions also require credits to other accounts. For example, refer to the entry for Voucher 2-14 in the voucher register of the Style Clothing Store. This voucher was issued for the net pay of Susan Bates, the office clerk, for the semimonthly period ended February 15. The total of her salary ($400) was debited to Office Salaries Expense. To record the taxes withheld from this sum, $28 was credited to FICA Tax Payable and $45 was credited to Employee Income Tax Payable. The net amount due Bates ($327) was credited to Accounts Payable. (For the sake of simplicity, the voucher register illustrated here does not include the payroll amounts for all employees of the Style Clothing Store.)

On February 28, Vouchers 2-27 and 2-28 were issued in favor of Linda Hanson and Steven Casey, the owners, for cash withdrawals for personal use. The voucher register entries show that the amounts were debited to Linda Han-

	DATE	VOU. NO.	PAYABLE TO	PAID DATE	CHECK NO.	ACCTS. PAYABLE CREDIT	FICA TAX PAY. CREDIT	EMPL. INC. TAX PAY. CREDIT
1	Feb. 1	2-01	Fisher Realty Co.	2/1	101	1,250 00		
2	1	2-02	Robert Gallo	2/1	102	100 00		
3	1	2-03	Susan Bates	2/1	103	75 00		
4	1	2-04	Valley Wholesale Clothiers	2/10	108	734 50		
5	3	2-05	Graham Paper Co.			189 50		
6	5	2-06	Office Suppliers			57 75		
7	9	2-07	Kelly & Smith, Attys.			200 00		
8	10	2-08	G. Thompson, CPA			75 00		
9	10	2-09	Burke Clothing Co.	2/19	114	5,240 00		
10	10	2-10	Southern Express Co.	2/11	109	56 35		
11	10	2-11	Fashions, Inc.	2/19	115	4,937 00		
12	10	2-12	Fast Truckers	2/11	110	82 50		
13	12	2-13	Moore Insurance Agency			240 00		
14	15	2-14	Susan Bates	2/15	111	327 00	28 00	45 00
15	15	2-15	Robert Gallo	2/15	112	359 80	30 80	49 40
16	15	2-16	Alfred White	2/15	113	326 70	27 30	36 00
17	18	2-17	Better Box Co.			95 00		
18	25	2-18	Greenville Water Co.			12 50		
19	25	2-19	State Utilities Co.			157 25		
20	27	2-20	Valley Wholesale Clothiers			3,465 00		
21	27	2-21	Central Telephone Co.			76 75		
22	28	2-22	Star-Herald Papers			329 75		
23	28	2-23	Jiffy Delivery Co.			245 00		
24	28	2-24	Susan Bates	2/28	116	327 00	28 00	45 00
25	28	2-25	Robert Gallo	2/28	117	359 80	30 80	49 40
26	28	2-26	Alfred White	2/28	118	326 70	27 30	36 00
27	28	2-27	Linda Hanson	2/28	119	400 00		
28	28	2-28	Steven Casey	2/28	120	375 00		
29	28	2-29	Susan Bates	2/28	121	57 05		
30								
31	28		Totals			20,477 90	172 20	260 80
						(205)	(221)	(222)

son, Drawing, and Steven Casey, Drawing. In a partnership, there are separate capital accounts and drawing accounts for each partner.

During the month, all entries in the Other Accounts section of the voucher register are posted individually to the appropriate accounts in the general ledger. At the end of the month, the voucher register is totaled, proved, and ruled. Then the totals of all columns except the columns in the Other Accounts section are posted to the general ledger.

In a firm that uses the voucher system, there is no need for a purchases journal. The voucher register contains columns that permit the recording of purchases of merchandise on credit.

USING THE CHECK REGISTER

In the accounting system of Sports World, the accounts to be debited for expenditures are recorded in the cash payments journal when the checks are issued. In

MERCH. PURCH. DEBIT	FREIGHT IN DEBIT	STORE SUP. DEBIT	OTHER ACCOUNTS			
			ACCOUNT TITLE	POST. REF.	DEBIT	CREDIT
			Rent Expense	542	1,250 00	
			Change Fund	106	100 00	
			Petty Cash Fund	105	75 00	
734 50						
		189 50				
			Office Supplies	125	57 75	
			Professional Services Expense	554	200 00	
			Professional Services Expense	554	75 00	
5,240 00						
	56 35					
4,937 00						
	82 50					
			Prepaid Insurance	126	240 00	
			Office Salaries Expense	551	400 00	
			Sales Salaries Expense	521	440 00	
			Sales Salaries Expense	521	390 00	
		95 00				
			Utilities Expense	543	12 50	
			Utilities Expense	543	157 25	
3,465 00						
			Other Office Expenses	553	76 75	
			Advertising Expense	522	329 75	
			Delivery Expense	532	245 00	
			Office Salaries Expense	551	400 00	
			Sales Salaries Expense	521	440 00	
			Sales Salaries Expense	521	390 00	
			Linda Hanson, Drawing	301	400 00	
			Steven Casey, Drawing	311	375 00	
	12 55	13 45	Advertising Expense	522	12 00	
			Office Supplies	125	19 05	
14,376 50	151 40	297 95			6,085 05	
(501)	(506)	(129)			(X)	

the voucher system used by the Style Clothing Store, the function of classifying expenditures is performed by the voucher register. The actual payment of cash is always made to settle a specific voucher that was previously recorded in the voucher register as an account payable. Therefore, each check issued under the voucher system results in a debit to Accounts Payable and a credit to Cash. (If the payment is for goods purchased on credit, it may also require a credit to Purchases Discount.) The necessary entry is made in the check register, which takes the place of a cash payments journal.

The check register used by the Style Clothing Store is shown on page 264. Notice that it provides space for recording the date, check number, payee's name, voucher number, and amount of each payment. The checks are entered in numerical order. (This type of check register is an accounting record and should not be confused with the type of check register that some firms use as a memorandum record for their banking activities.)

CHECK REGISTER for Month of February 19X1   Page   1

DATE	CHECK NO.	PAYABLE TO	VOU. NO.	ACCTS. PAYABLE DEBIT	PURCH. DISCOUNT CREDIT	CASH CREDIT
Feb. 1	101	Fisher Realty Co.	2-01	1,250 00		1,250 00
1	102	Robert Gallo	2-02	100 00		100 00
1	103	Susan Bates	2-03	75 00		75 00
10	108	Valley Wh. Clothiers	2-04	734 50	14 69	719 81
28	119	Linda Hanson	2-27	400 00		400 00
28	120	Steven Casey	2-28	375 00		375 00
28	121	Susan Bates	2-29	57 05		57 05
28		Totals		18,334 40	268 23	18,066 17
				(205)	(512)	(101)

The first three entries in the check register of the Style Clothing Store cover the payment of Vouchers 2-01, 2-02, and 2-03 on February 1. These entries simply involve a debit to Accounts Payable and a credit to Cash. However, the entry made on February 10 for the payment of Voucher 2-04 also includes a credit to Purchases Discount. This voucher was issued when the firm received an invoice from Valley Wholesale Clothiers for goods purchased on credit.

The Style Clothing Store uses the procedure described in Chapter 9 to handle cash discounts on purchases. Invoices are recorded at their total price. If discounts are taken, the amounts are credited to Purchases Discount and shown on the income statement as a reduction in the cost of purchases.

In accordance with this procedure, the full amount of the invoice from Valley Wholesale Clothiers ($734.50) was used in preparing a voucher, even though the invoice had terms of 2/10, n/30. Thus the entry in the voucher register included a credit of $734.50 to Accounts Payable for the invoice.

Since payment was made by the necessary date, the firm was able to take the 2 percent cash discount, which amounted to $14.69 ($734.50 × .02). A check for $719.81 ($734.50 − $14.69) was therefore issued to Valley Wholesale Clothiers. Refer to the entry in the check register of the Style Clothing Store to see how this payment was recorded. The full amount of the invoice ($734.50) was debited to Accounts Payable to close out the liability that was previously set up in the voucher register entry. The amount of the discount ($14.69) was credited to Purchases Discount, and the amount actually paid ($719.81) was credited to Cash.

At the end of each month, the check register is totaled, proved, and ruled. Then the totals are posted to the general ledger accounts indicated in the column headings.

PREPARING A SCHEDULE OF VOUCHERS PAYABLE

As noted already, no accounts payable subsidiary ledger is maintained in firms that use the voucher system. The file of unpaid vouchers takes the place of this ledger. At the end of each month, a *schedule of vouchers payable* is prepared from the items in the file. This schedule provides a listing of all amounts owed for unpaid vouchers, as shown below.

STYLE CLOTHING STORE
Schedule of Vouchers Payable
February 28, 19X1

Voucher Number	Payable to	Amount
2-05	Graham Paper Company	$ 189.50
2-06	Office Suppliers	57.75
2-07	Kelly & Smith, Attorneys	200.00
2-08	G. E. Thompson, CPA	75.00
2-13	Moore Insurance Agency	240.00
2-17	Better Box Company	95.00
2-18	Greenville Water Company	12.50
2-19	State Utilities Company	157.25
2-20	Valley Wholesale Clothiers	3,465.00
2-21	Central Telephone Company	76.75
2-22	Star-Herald Papers	329.75
2-23	Jiffy Delivery Company	245.00
	Total	$5,143.50

After it is prepared, the schedule should be checked against the entries in the voucher register to be certain that it includes all vouchers that have not been marked "Paid." Then the total of the schedule should be compared with the balance of the Accounts Payable account in the general ledger to make sure that the two figures are equal.

On February 28, 19X1, the Accounts Payable account at the Style Clothing Store appeared as shown below. The $3,000 posted from the general journal on February 1 represents liabilities from Linda Hanson's sole proprietorship business that the partnership took over when it began operations. The next two amounts are totals posted from the voucher register and the check register at the end of the month. (These entries are identified by the abbreviations *VR* and *CR* in the Post. Ref. column.) Notice that the final balance of the account ($5,143.50) agrees with the total of the schedule of vouchers payable.

\multicolumn{4}{l}{Accounts Payable}			No. 205	
DATE	EXPLANATION	POST. REF.	DEBIT	CREDIT	BALANCE	DR. CR.
19X1 Feb. 1		J1		3,000 00	3,000 00	Cr.
28		VR1		20,477 90	23,477 90	Cr.
28		CR1	18,334 40		5,143 50	Cr.

TRANSACTIONS REQUIRING SPECIAL TREATMENT

As long as invoices are received, verified, vouchered, and paid in the normal manner, businesses using the voucher system can efficiently handle a large volume of transactions. However, the procedures are rather rigid, and certain infrequent transactions may be awkward to record. Here are some typical examples.

Partial Payments

After a voucher has been prepared for the full amount of an invoice, a firm may decide to pay in two or more installments. For instance, suppose that the Style Clothing Store bought furniture and fixtures costing $4,000 on April 4, 19X1, and Voucher 4-08 was prepared to cover the purchase. Being short of cash at the end of April, the firm arranged to pay only half the amount at that time and to pay the other half at the end of May.

In this case, the original voucher (4-08) is canceled by issuing two new vouchers (4-33 and 4-34). The new vouchers are recorded in the voucher register separately, each entry involving a credit of $2,000 to the Accounts Payable account in the usual manner. However, each entry also involves a debit of $2,000 to Accounts Payable, which is recorded in the Other Accounts Debit column to cancel the original voucher. (The original debit of $4,000 to the Furniture and Fixtures account is not affected.) The cancellation is noted in the Date column of the Paid section of the voucher register on the line where Voucher 4-08 (the original voucher) was recorded, and the new voucher numbers are entered in the Check Number column, as illustrated below.

VOUCHER REGISTER for Month of April 19X1										Page 3
			PAID		ACCTS.	OTHER ACCOUNTS				
DATE	VOU. NO.	PAYABLE TO	DATE	CHECK NO.	PAYABLE CREDIT	ACCOUNT TITLE	POST. REF.	DEBIT	CREDIT	
Apr. 4	4-08	Office Suppliers	Canc.	V4-33 V4-34	4,000 00	Furniture and Fixtures	131	4,000 00		
30	4-33	Office Suppliers	4/30	208	2,000 00	Accounts Payable	205	2,000 00		
30	4-34	Office Suppliers			2,000 00	Accounts Payable	205	2,000 00		

The first new voucher (4-33) is paid at the end of April (right away), and the second new voucher (4-34) is filed for payment at the end of May.

Notes Payable

The Style Clothing Store owes $10,000 to the First National Bank on a 9 percent 60-day note, dated February 1, 19X1. When the note becomes due on April 2, a voucher must be prepared to authorize payment of $10,150 (the $10,000 face value of the note plus $150 interest). By means of an entry in the voucher register, Notes Payable—Bank is debited for $10,000, Interest Expense is debited for $150, and Accounts Payable is credited for $10,150. Then a check for $10,150 is issued and entered in the check register to settle the obligation. The entry in the voucher register is shown on page 267.

Another recording problem involving notes payable might arise after a voucher has been prepared for an invoice in the normal manner. Suppose that the

| DATE | VOU. NO. | PAYABLE TO | PAID | | ACCTS. PAYABLE CREDIT | OTHER ACCOUNTS | | | |
			DATE	CHECK NO.		ACCOUNT TITLE	POST. REF.	DEBIT	CREDIT
Apr. 2	4-04	First Nat'l Bank	4/2	204	10,150 00	Notes Pay.—Bank	201	10,000 00	
						Interest Expense	591	150 00	

firm arranges to issue a note payable to the supplier as a means of postponing payment. The amount owed is no longer an account payable. Therefore, a general journal entry is made debiting Accounts Payable (thus canceling the original voucher) and crediting Notes Payable—Trade. When the time comes for payment, a new voucher is prepared for the note (plus interest, if any).

Purchases Returns and Allowances

If the Style Clothing Store receives goods that are unsatisfactory for some reason, either the items are returned to the supplier or they are kept and an allowance is obtained from the supplier. In either case, the amount finally owed to the supplier is less than the amount of the original invoice. If the original invoice has already been vouchered, the accounting records must be adjusted.

For example, suppose that on March 2 the Style Clothing Store receives an invoice for $750 for goods purchased from Madison Wholesalers. Voucher 3-05 is prepared for the invoice. Then, on March 8, an allowance of $50 is made by the supplier to cover damage in transit. The revised amount owed for the invoice is therefore $700.

Method 1 On March 8, when the allowance is made, a new voucher can be issued crediting Accounts Payable for $700, the revised amount. Accounts Payable is also debited for $750 to cancel the original voucher (3-05), and Purchases Returns and Allowances is credited for $50. The entry in the voucher register for the new voucher (3-12) would appear as shown below. A notation is also made on the line for Voucher 3-05 to indicate that it has been canceled by Voucher 3-12.

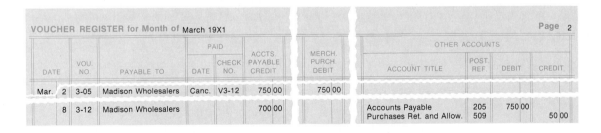

| DATE | VOU. NO. | PAYABLE TO | PAID | | ACCTS. PAYABLE CREDIT | MERCH. PURCH. DEBIT | OTHER ACCOUNTS | | | |
			DATE	CHECK NO.			ACCOUNT TITLE	POST. REF.	DEBIT	CREDIT
Mar. 2	3-05	Madison Wholesalers	Canc.	V3-12	750 00	750 00				
8	3-12	Madison Wholesalers			700 00		Accounts Payable	205	750 00	
							Purchases Ret. and Allow.	509		50 00

Method 2 Some accountants use a simpler method for handling this type of adjustment. Since the voucher register for March was not closed and posted before the allowance was agreed upon, the original entry can be corrected by

making a notation for the $50 allowance on the same line, as shown below. The notation is circled to indicate that it represents a reduction in the firm's accounts payable and its cost of purchases.

VOUCHER REGISTER for Month of March 19X1							OTHER ACCOUNTS				Page 2
			PAID		ACCTS. PAYABLE CREDIT	MERCH. PURCH. DEBIT					
DATE	VOU. NO.	PAYABLE TO	DATE	CHECK NO.			ACCOUNT TITLE	POST REF.	DEBIT	CREDIT	
Mar. 2	3-05	Madison Wholesalers			(50 00) 750 00	(50 00) 750 00					
31		Totals			(50 00) 19,980 00	(50 00) 15,960 00			5,000 00	2,000 00	
					(205)	(501)			(X)	(X)	

The adjustment is recorded on the original voucher, and when the invoice becomes due, payment is made for the net amount. At the end of the month, the figures that are circled in each column of the voucher register are totaled separately from the original figures. The $50 item illustrated is posted as a debit to Accounts Payable and a credit to Purchases Returns and Allowances, thereby accomplishing the same result as the first method. Note, however, that the second method can be used only if the revision is made before the voucher register has been closed for the month.

RECORDING PURCHASE DISCOUNTS LOST

The procedures described in Chapters 8 and 9 for recording purchases and cash discounts are very commonly used. However, there is a disadvantage that may make them undesirable if a good system of internal control is to be developed. If, due to inefficiency, a discount is not taken because an invoice is not paid promptly, the accounting records will not reveal the loss of the discount. To overcome this shortcoming, many accountants prefer to record vouchers for purchases in such a way that discounts not taken will stand out for investigation, while discounts taken are not separately stated in the records.

Under this procedure, purchase invoices are recorded in the voucher register *net of discount;* that is, the amount used for the entry is the invoice price minus the cash discount that may be taken. If the invoice is paid within the discount period, the check is drawn for the exact amount of the original voucher. On the other hand, if the invoice is paid too late to take the discount, the total amount of the invoice must be paid. This sum will be larger than the amount of the original voucher. The difference is recorded in the check register by debiting an account called Discount Lost. The balance of this account is presented in the Cost of Goods Sold section of the income statement as an addition to the balance of Merchandise Purchases.

To illustrate how this procedure for recording purchases and cash discounts works, assume that the Style Clothing Store uses the procedure. On February 1, when the firm receives the invoice for a purchase of $734.50 from Valley Wholesale Clothiers with terms of 2/10, n/30, the invoice is recorded in the voucher register at the net amount ($734.50 − $14.69 = $719.81), as shown below.

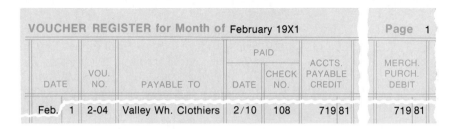

VOUCHER REGISTER for Month of February 19X1						Page 1
			PAID		ACCTS.	MERCH.
DATE	VOU. NO.	PAYABLE TO	DATE	CHECK NO.	PAYABLE CREDIT	PURCH. DEBIT
Feb. 1	2-04	Valley Wh. Clothiers	2/10	108	719 81	719 81

When payment is made within the discount period, it is recorded as follows.

CHECK REGISTER for Month of February 19X1						Page 1
DATE	CHECK NO.	PAYABLE TO	VOU. NO.	ACCTS. PAYABLE DEBIT	DISCOUNT LOST DEBIT	CASH CREDIT
Feb. 10	108	Valley Wh. Clothiers	2-04	719 81		719 81

If the payment is made too late to take the discount, the amount of discount lost is recorded in the check register and management's attention will immediately be directed to this failure. The check register entry shown below reflects the lost discount.

CHECK REGISTER for Month of February 19X1						Page 1
DATE	CHECK NO.	PAYABLE TO	VOU. NO.	ACCTS. PAYABLE DEBIT	DISCOUNT LOST DEBIT	CASH CREDIT
Feb. 20	116	Valley Wh. Clothiers	2-04	719 81	14 69	734 50

PRINCIPLES AND PROCEDURES SUMMARY

Internal control is important for every business, no matter what its size. Each step in the accounting process of a firm should be planned to ensure accuracy, honesty, and efficiency. An essential technique for achieving these goals is to divide responsibility so that every major accounting routine involves two or more employees and the work of one person can be checked against that of another person. In addition to division of responsibility, accountants use a number of other widely recognized techniques to design internal control procedures for a business.

The voucher system is used by many medium-sized and large firms to control their liabilities and cash payments. A voucher is prepared for every expenditure and then approved. The voucher is entered in the voucher register and then placed with other approved vouchers in an unpaid vouchers file. This file takes the place of an accounts payable subsidiary ledger. When a check is issued to pay the voucher, an entry is recorded in the check register and a notation is made in the voucher register. The voucher is then transferred to a paid vouchers file. At the end of each month, a schedule of vouchers payable is prepared.

Certain transactions such as purchases returns and allowances, partial payments, and notes payable may require special treatment when they are recorded under the voucher system.

In some firms, purchases are recorded net of discount. Then, if payments are not made within the discount period, the discounts lost will stand out for investigation.

MANAGERIAL IMPLICATIONS

Because of its nature, cash is easily lost, stolen, or misused. The protection of cash and other assets is vital to successful business operations and should be a major concern of management. Only a well-planned system of internal control can provide the necessary safeguards, and management must work with the accountant to establish and maintain such a system. Aside from protecting assets, a good system of internal control produces other important benefits. It helps to ensure efficient processing of transactions and accurate preparation of financial records, to prevent liabilities from being incurred without proper authorization, and to protect honest employees from suspicion by pinpointing responsibility.

The voucher system is invaluable to management because of the tight control it provides over liabilities and cash payments. Every transaction is carefully recorded, checked, and documented. Responsibility is clear and definite all along the line.

REVIEW QUESTIONS

1. Why is there a need for internal control over business operations?
2. Division of responsibility is one of the most important principles of internal control. How is this principle put into practice?
3. What is the voucher system?
4. Why is the voucher system more appropriate for medium-sized and large businesses than small businesses?
5. What is the purpose of a voucher?
6. A number of different controls are built into the voucher system. Briefly describe five of these controls.
7. What steps are usually followed in verifying an invoice before a voucher is prepared?
8. What is the purpose of the voucher register?
9. What ledger does the unpaid vouchers file replace?

10. What is the purpose of the check register?
11. What information is presented on the schedule of vouchers payable?
12. Under the voucher system, how is the balance of the Accounts Payable account in the general ledger proved at the end of each month?
13. What types of transactions often require special treatment in the voucher system?
14. What is the purpose of recording invoices net of discount?
15. When an invoice that was recorded net of discount is paid after the discount period has ended, what accounts are debited and credited in the check register entry?
16. How is the Discount Lost account presented on the income statement?

MANAGERIAL DISCUSSION QUESTIONS

1. Assume that you are the newly hired controller of the Gilbert Company and have suggested that the firm adopt the voucher system. The president has asked you to provide a brief analysis of the advantages and disadvantages of this system. How would you respond?
2. The personnel manager of the Gilbert Company is concerned that the employees will view the installation of the voucher system as a sign of mistrust. How can this system be explained to the employees as providing benefits to them as well as to the business?
3. How can the management of a firm avoid unnecessary red tape as a by-product of its search for adequate internal controls?
4. In a small business there may be only one or two experienced and reliable employees capable of assuming key positions in an internal control system. Is it impractical to introduce internal controls in this situation? Why or why not?
5. How can the management of a firm establish internal control over the liabilities that are incurred?

EXERCISES

EXERCISE 11-1 **Identifying the accounts used to record transactions in the voucher register.** The vouchers listed on page 272 were prepared at the Oakville Appliance Center during the month of January 19X1. Indicate the numbers of the general ledger accounts that would be debited and credited to record each transaction in the voucher register.

GENERAL LEDGER ACCOUNTS

101	Cash	501	Merchandise Purchases
121	Store Supplies	502	Freight In
131	Store Equipment	504	Purchases Discount
141	Delivery Truck	511	Rent Expense
205	Accounts Payable	514	Salaries Expense
221	FICA Tax Payable	517	Telephone Expense
222	Employee Income Tax Payable	520	Truck Expense

TRANSACTIONS

1. Prepared Voucher 1-01 for $850 owed to the Falk Real Estate Company for the monthly rent on the store.
2. Prepared Voucher 1-02 for $377.60 owed to the Briggs Corporation for a purchase of store supplies; the terms are n/30.
3. Prepared Voucher 1-03 for $79.25 owed to the Central Telephone Company for the monthly telephone bill.
4. Prepared Voucher 1-04 for $2,000 owed to the United Appliance Corporation for a purchase of merchandise; the terms are 2/10, n/30.
5. Prepared Voucher 1-05 for $930 owed to the Roberts Corporation for a purchase of new display shelves for the store; the terms are n/45.
6. Prepared Voucher 1-06 for $1,862 owed to the Mead Distributing Company for a purchase of merchandise ($1,800) and a freight charge ($62); the terms are n/30.
7. Prepared Voucher 1-07 for $495 owed to the DeCarlo Service Station for repairs to the firm's delivery truck; the terms are n/15.
8. Prepared Voucher 1-08 for $729 owed to David Selby, an employee, for his net pay. His total salary for the month was $900. His deductions were $63 for FICA tax and $108 for federal income tax.

EXERCISE 11-2   **Identifying the accounts used to record transactions in the check register.** The following payments were made at the Oakville Appliance Center during the month of January 19X1. Indicate the numbers of the general ledger accounts that would be debited and credited to record each transaction in the check register. (Obtain the account numbers and information about the vouchers being paid from Exercise 11-1. Assume that the firm records invoices at their total price in the voucher register.)

TRANSACTIONS

1. Issued Check 4901 for $850 to pay Voucher 1-01.
2. Issued Check 4902 for $79.25 to pay Voucher 1-03.
3. Issued Check 4903 for $1,960 to pay Voucher 1-04 ($2,000) less a cash discount ($40).
4. Issued Check 4904 for $729 to pay Voucher 1-08.

EXERCISE 11-3   **Preparing a schedule of vouchers payable.** Use the information in Exercises 11-1 and 11-2 to prepare a schedule of vouchers payable for the Oakville Appliance Center as of January 31, 19X1.

EXERCISE 11-4   **Recording an invoice net of discount.** On May 8, 19X3, the Willis Company purchased merchandise from the O'Dell Corporation and received Invoice 5112 for $650. The terms were 2/10, n/30. Willis records invoices net of discount. Show how the entry for the purchase from O'Dell would appear in general journal form.

EXERCISE 11-5   **Recording payment of an invoice before the end of the discount period.** Assume that the Willis Company paid the O'Dell Corporation for Invoice 5112 on May 17, 19X3, and took the cash discount. (Refer to Exercise 11-4 for information about the purchase and how it was recorded.) Show how the entry for the payment to O'Dell would appear in general journal form.

EXERCISE 11-6 **Recording payment of an invoice after the end of the discount period.** Assume that the Willis Company paid the O'Dell Corporation for Invoice 5112 on June 7, 19X3, and was not able to take the cash discount. (Refer to Exercise 11-4 for information about the purchase and how it was recorded.) Show how the entry for the payment to O'Dell would appear in general journal form.

PROBLEMS

PROBLEM 11-1 **Recording transactions in the voucher register and the check register.** Transactions that the Sunrise Health Food Store had during the first two weeks of March 19X3 are listed below and on page 274 along with selected accounts from the firm's general ledger.

Instructions 1. Record the transactions in a voucher register like the one shown on pages 262 and 263 and a check register like the one shown on page 264. This firm enters invoices at their total price.
2. Foot and prove the voucher register and the check register.

GENERAL LEDGER ACCOUNTS

101	Cash	302	Ruth McCabe, Drawing
121	Store Supplies	501	Merchandise Purchases
123	Office Supplies	502	Freight In
131	Store Equipment	504	Purchases Discount
141	Office Equipment	511	Rent Expense
205	Accounts Payable	514	Utilities Expense

TRANSACTIONS FOR MARCH 1–15, 19X3

Mar. 1 Prepared Voucher 3-01 for $1,585 owed to Natural Products Inc. for a purchase of merchandise; the terms are 2/10, n/30.
2 Prepared Voucher 3-02 for $600 owed to the Kahn Real Estate Corporation for the monthly rent on the store. Paid the voucher by Check 1225.
4 Prepared Voucher 3-03 for $150 owed to Kee Business Systems for office file cabinets. Paid the voucher by Check 1226.
5 Prepared Voucher 3-04 for $730 owed to the Walsh Company for a purchase of merchandise; the terms are 2/10, n/30.
5 Prepared Voucher 3-05 for $26 owed to Continental Trucking Inc. for a freight charge on a purchase of merchandise. Paid the voucher by Check 1227.
7 Prepared Voucher 3-06 for $295 owed to the Curtis Paper Company for store supplies; the terms are n/30.
9 Issued Check 1228 to pay Voucher 3-01 less the cash discount of 2 percent.

11 Prepared Voucher 3-07 for $136 owed to the Atlantic Power Company for electricity. Paid the voucher by Check 1229.

12 Prepared Voucher 3-08 for $1,492 owed to the Harvest Corporation for a purchase of merchandise ($1,440) and a freight charge ($52); the terms are n/30.

14 Issued Check 1230 to pay Voucher 3-04 less the cash discount of 2 percent.

15 Prepared Voucher 3-09 for $800 for a cash withdrawal by the owner for personal use. Paid the voucher by Check 1231.

PROBLEM 11-2 **Recording transactions in the voucher register and the check register; preparing a schedule of vouchers payable.** Transactions that occurred at the Toy Bazaar, a retail business, during August 19X1 are listed below and on page 275 along with selected accounts from the firm's general ledger.

Instructions 1. Record the transactions in a voucher register like the one shown on pages 262 and 263, a check register like the one shown on page 264, and a general journal. This firm enters invoices at their total price.
2. Total, prove, and rule the voucher register and the check register.
3. Prepare a schedule of vouchers payable. Obtain the necessary information from the voucher register.

GENERAL LEDGER ACCOUNTS

101	Cash	502	Freight In
121	Store Supplies	503	Purchases Returns and Allowances
123	Office Supplies	504	Purchases Discount
131	Store Equipment	511	Sales Salaries Expense
141	Office Equipment	514	Advertising Expense
201	Notes Payable	517	Rent Expense
205	Accounts Payable	520	Office Salaries Expense
221	FICA Tax Payable	523	Telephone Expense
222	Employee Income Tax Payable	526	Utilities Expense
501	Merchandise Purchases		

TRANSACTIONS FOR AUGUST 19X1

Aug. 1 Prepared Voucher 8-01 for $900 owed to the Jordan Realty Company for the monthly rent. Paid the voucher by Check 1101.

2 Purchased office equipment for $1,900 from the Micro Systems Company, giving a noninterest-bearing 30-day note.

3 Prepared Voucher 8-02 for $55 owed to the ABC Supply Company for office supplies; the terms are n/30.

4 Prepared Voucher 8-03 for $500 owed to the York Company for building new fixtures in the store; the terms are n/30. (Debit Store Equipment.)

5 Prepared Voucher 8-04 for $188 owed to the Mountain Trucking Company for freight on merchandise purchased.

6 Paid Voucher 8-04 by Check 1102.

8 Prepared Voucher 8-05 for $1,000 owed to the Chan Toy Company for a purchase of merchandise; the terms are 2/10, n/30.

9 Purchased a used cash register for $500 from the Town Equipment Company; the terms are $200 cash with the balance due in 30 days. Vouchers 8-06 and 8-07 were prepared for the two installments. Issued Check 1103 for $200 to pay Voucher 8-06.

10 Prepared Voucher 8-08 for $3,000 owed to the Bates Toy Corporation for a purchase of merchandise; the terms are 2/10, n/30.

12 Prepared Voucher 8-09 for $145 owed to the Marsh Company for store supplies; the terms are n/30.

15 Received a credit memorandum for $100 from the Bates Toy Company for a return of damaged merchandise. (Make a circled entry in the voucher register over the entry for Voucher 8-08.)

16 Issued Check 1104 to pay Voucher 8-05 less the 2 percent discount.

18 Prepared Voucher 8-10 for $80 owed to the *Weekend News* for advertising. Paid the voucher by Check 1105.

19 Prepared Voucher 8-11 for $156.40 owed to the Mountain Trucking Company for freight on merchandise purchased.

20 Issued Check 1106 to pay Voucher 8-11.

20 Issued Check 1107 to pay Voucher 8-08 less the return and the 2 percent discount.

25 Prepared Voucher 8-12 for $2,150 owed to Electronic Games Inc. for a purchase of merchandise; the terms are 2/10, n/30.

27 Prepared Voucher 8-13 for $166 owed to City Utilities for electricity used in the store during the month. Paid the voucher by Check 1108.

28 Prepared Voucher 8-14 for $74 owed to the Central Telephone Company for telephone service during the month. Paid the voucher by Check 1109.

31 Prepared Voucher 8-15 for $1,900 note payable of August 2 owed to the Micro Systems Company. Paid the voucher by Check 1110.

31 Prepared Voucher 8-16 for John Perry, the salesclerk, for his salary of $900 less $63 deducted for FICA tax and $85.40 deducted for income tax. Paid the voucher by Check 1111. Prepared Voucher 8-17 for Mary Hernandez, the office clerk, for her salary of $880 less $61.60 deducted for FICA tax and $87.20 deducted for income tax. Paid the voucher by Check 1112.

PROBLEM 11-3   **Recording an invoice at its total price and net of discount.** On March 1, 19X1, City Retailers purchased merchandise from the Marino Corporation. The total invoice price was $2,000, and the terms were 2/10, n/30.

Instructions   1. Record the purchase made by City Retailers in general journal form assuming:
   a. City Retailers records purchases at the total invoice price.
   b. City Retailers records purchases at the net invoice price.
   2. Suppose that City Retailers paid the invoice on March 9. Record the payment in general journal form, assuming:
   a. City Retailers recorded the purchase at the total invoice price.
   b. City Retailers recorded the purchase at the net invoice price.

3. Suppose that City Retailers paid the invoice on March 30 (after the discount period). Record the payment in general journal form, assuming:
   a. City Retailers recorded the purchase at the total invoice price.
   b. City Retailers recorded the purchase at the net invoice price.

ALTERNATE PROBLEMS

PROBLEM 11-1A

Recording transactions in the voucher register and the check register. Transactions that the Salem Medical Supply Company had during the first two weeks of September 19X5 are listed below and on page 277 along with selected accounts from the firm's general ledger.

Instructions

1. Record the transactions in a voucher register like the one shown on pages 262 and 263 and a check register like the one shown on page 264. This firm enters invoices at their total price.
2. Foot and prove the voucher register and the check register.

GENERAL LEDGER ACCOUNTS

101	Cash	302	Paul Lund, Drawing
121	Prepaid Insurance	501	Merchandise Purchases
123	Office Supplies	502	Freight In
131	Warehouse Equipment	504	Purchases Discount
141	Office Equipment	511	Rent Expense
205	Accounts Payable	514	Utilities Expense

TRANSACTIONS FOR SEPTEMBER 1–15, 19X5

Sept.
1 Prepared Voucher 9-01 for $3,240 owed to United Hospital Products for a purchase of merchandise; the terms are 2/10, n/30.

2 Prepared 9-02 for $900 owed to Reed Business Properties Inc. for the monthly rent. Paid the voucher by Check 3710.

3 Prepared Voucher 9-03 for $625 owed to the Kelso Corporation for new storage bins for the warehouse. Paid the voucher by Check 3711.

6 Prepared Voucher 9-04 for $5,400 owed to Dow Medical Equipment for a purchase of merchandise; the terms are 2/10, n/30.

6 Prepared Voucher 9-05 for $136 owed to the Interstate Trucking Company for a freight charge on a purchase of merchandise. Paid the voucher by Check 3712.

8 Prepared Voucher 9-06 for $1,260 owed to the Ramos Insurance Agency for a 1-year insurance policy.

9 Issued Check 3713 to pay Voucher 9-01 less the cash discount of 2 percent.

10 Prepared Voucher 9-07 for $128 owed to the Consumers Power Company for electricity. Paid the voucher by Check 3714.

12 Prepared Voucher 9-08 for $2,173 owed to the Allen Drug Company for a purchase of merchandise ($2,100) and a freight charge ($73); the terms are 1/10, n/30.

14 Prepared Voucher 9-09 for $1,000 for a cash withdrawal by the owner for personal use. Paid the voucher by Check 3715.

15 Issued Check 3716 to pay Voucher 9-04 less the cash discount of 2 percent.

PROBLEM 11-2A **Recording transactions in the voucher register and the check register; preparing a schedule of vouchers payable.** Transactions that occurred at the Columbus Hardware Center, a retail business, during August 19X7 are listed below and on page 278 along with selected accounts from the firm's general ledger.

Instructions 1. Record the transactions in a voucher register like the one shown on pages 262 and 263, a check register like the one shown on page 264, and a general journal. This firm enters invoices at their total price.

2. Total, prove, and rule the voucher register and the check register.

3. Prepare a schedule of vouchers payable. Obtain the necessary information from the voucher register.

GENERAL LEDGER ACCOUNTS

101	Cash	502	Freight In
121	Store Supplies	503	Purchases Returns and Allowances
123	Office Supplies	504	Purchases Discount
131	Store Equipment	511	Sales Salaries Expense
141	Office Equipment	514	Advertising Expense
201	Notes Payable	517	Rent Expense
205	Accounts Payable	520	Office Salaries Expense
221	FICA Tax Payable	523	Telephone Expense
222	Employee Income Tax Payable	526	Utilities Expense
501	Merchandise Purchases		

TRANSACTIONS FOR AUGUST 19X7

Aug. 1 Prepared Voucher 8-01 for $700 in rent owed to the Apex Real Estate Company. Paid the voucher by Check 5201.

2 Purchased office equipment for $800 from the Hogan Office Products Company, giving a noninterest-bearing 30-day note.

3 Prepared Voucher 8-02 for $125 owed to the Hogan Office Products Company for office supplies; the terms are n/30.

4 Prepared Voucher 8-03 for $500 owed to Town Woodworking for building new fixtures in the store; the terms are n/30. (Debit Store Equipment.)

5 Prepared Voucher 8-04 for $136.65 owed to the Madison Trucking Company for freight on merchandise purchased.

6 Paid Voucher 8-04 by Check 5202.

8 Prepared Voucher 8-05 for $2,500 of merchandise purchased from the General Hardware Company; the terms are 2/10, n/30.

9 Purchased a used cash register for $500 from Argo Business Machines; the terms are $250 cash with the balance due in 30 days. Vouchers 8-06 and 8-07 were prepared for the two installments. Issued Check 5203 for $250 to pay Voucher 8-06.

10 Prepared Voucher 8-08 for $3,000 owed to the Tester Hardware Company for merchandise; the terms are 2/10, n/30.

12 Prepared Voucher 8-09 for $100 owed to the Kell Supply Company for store supplies; the terms are n/30.

15 Received a credit memorandum for $100 for damaged merchandise that was returned to the Tester Hardware Company. (Make a circled entry in the voucher register over the entry for Voucher 8-08.)

16 Issued Check 5204 to pay Voucher 8-05 less the 2 percent discount.

18 Prepared Voucher 8-10 for $45 owed to the *Daily Herald* for advertising. Paid the voucher by Check 5205.

19 Prepared Voucher 8-11 for $231.40 owed to the Madison Trucking Company for freight on merchandise purchased.

20 Issued Check 5206 to pay Voucher 8-11.

20 Issued Check 5207 to pay Voucher 8-08 less the return and the 2 percent discount.

25 Prepared Voucher 8-12 for merchandise costing $2,150 purchased from the General Hardware Company; the terms are 2/10, n/30.

27 Prepared Voucher 8-13 for $133 owed to City Utilities for electricity used during the month. Issued Check 5208 to pay the voucher.

28 Prepared Voucher 8-14 for $91.60 owed to the Central Telephone Company for telephone service during the month. The voucher was paid by Check 5209.

31 Prepared Voucher 8-15 for the $800 note payable of August 2 owed to the Hogan Office Products Company. Issued Check 5210 to pay the voucher.

31 Prepared Voucher 8-16 for Frank Sims, the salesclerk, for his salary of $800 less $56 deducted for FICA tax and $80 deducted for income tax. Paid the voucher by Check 5211. Prepared Voucher 8-17 for Mary Cole, the office clerk, for her salary of $860 less $60.20 for FICA tax and $96.40 deducted for income tax. Paid the voucher by Check 5212.

PROBLEM 11-3A

Recording an invoice at its total price and net of discount. On April 10, 19X1, the Ames Department Store purchased merchandise from the Gross Company. The total invoice price was $1,600, and the terms were 3/20, n/60.

Instructions

1. Record the purchase made by Ames in general journal form, assuming:
   a. Ames records purchases at the total invoice price.
   b. Ames records purchases at the net invoice price.
2. Suppose that Ames paid the invoice on April 28. Record the payment in general journal form, assuming:
   a. Ames recorded the purchase at the total invoice price.
   b. Ames recorded the purchase at the net invoice price.
3. Suppose that Ames paid the invoice on June 7 (after the discount period). Record the payment in general journal form, assuming:
   a. Ames recorded the purchase at the total invoice price.
   b. Ames recorded the purchase at the net invoice price.

CHAPTER

12

Most small businesses have just a few employees and can devote only a limited amount of time to the preparation of accounting records. To serve the needs of these businesses, accountants have developed certain types of record systems that have special time-saving and labor-saving features but still produce all the necessary financial information for management. Three examples of such systems are discussed in this chapter.

SMALL BUSINESS RECORD SYSTEMS

SYSTEMS INVOLVING THE COMBINED JOURNAL

The *combined journal* provides the cornerstone for a simple yet effective accounting system in many small firms. As its name indicates, this journal combines features of the general journal and the special journals in a single record.

If a small business has enough transactions to make the general journal difficult to use but too few transactions to make it worthwhile to set up special journals, the combined journal offers a solution. It has many of the advantages of the special journals but provides the simplicity of a single journal. Like the special journals, the combined journal contains separate money columns for the accounts used most often to record a firm's transactions. This speeds up the initial entry of transactions and permits summary postings at the end of the month. Most transactions can be recorded on a single line, and the need to write account titles is minimized.

Other Accounts columns allow the recording of transactions that do not fit into any of the special columns. These columns are also used for entries that would normally appear in the general journal, such as adjusting and closing entries.

Some small firms just use a combined journal and a general ledger in their accounting systems. Others need one or more subsidiary ledgers in addition to the general ledger.

Designing a Combined Journal

To function effectively, a combined journal must be designed to meet the specific needs of a firm. For a new business, the accountant first studies the proposed operations and develops an appropriate chart of accounts. Then the accountant decides which accounts are likely to be used often enough in recording daily transactions to justify special columns in the combined journal.

Consider the combined journal, shown on pages 280 and 281, which belongs to the Plaza Cleaning Shop, a small retail business that provides dry-cleaning service. In designing this journal before the firm opened, the accountant established a Cash section with debit and credit columns because he knew that the business would constantly be receiving cash from customers and paying out cash for expenses and other obligations. The accountant also set up Accounts Receivable and Accounts Payable sections with debit and credit columns because he knew that the firm was planning to offer credit to qualified customers and would make credit purchases of supplies and other items.

After further analysis, the accountant realized that the business would have numerous entries for the sale of services, the payment of employee salaries, and the purchase of supplies. The accountant therefore established columns for recording credits to Sales, debits to Salaries Expense, and debits to Supplies. Finally, the accountant set up an Other Accounts section in the combined journal to take care of transactions that cannot be entered in the special columns.

Recording Transactions in the Combined Journal

The combined journal shown below and on page 281 contains the January 19X5 transactions of the Plaza Cleaning Shop. Notice that most of these transactions require only a single line to record and involve the use of just the special columns. The entries for major types of transactions are explained on page 281.

COMBINED JOURNAL for Month of January 19X5

	DATE	CHECK NO.	EXPLANATION	CASH DEBIT	CASH CREDIT	✓	ACCOUNTS RECEIVABLE DEBIT	ACCOUNTS RECEIVABLE CREDIT
1	Jan. 3	842	Rent for month		900 00			
2	5		David Levine			✓	60 00	
3	6		United Chemicals Inc.					
4	7		Cash sales	1,150 00				
5	7	843	Payroll		520 00			
6	10		Marion Brown	45 00		✓		45 00
7	12		Pacific Products Corporation					
8	13		Thomas Nolan	70 00		✓		70 00
9	14		Cash sales	1,385 00				
10	14	844	Payroll		520 00			
11	17		Joyce Miller			✓	55 00	
12	18		Alvarez Company					
13	19	845	Telephone service		82 00			
14	20		Carl Janowski	64 00		✓		64 00
15	20		Dorothy Russell			✓	33 00	
16	21		Cash sales	1,270 00				
17	21	846	Payroll		520 00			
18	24		Ace Plastic Bags					
19	25		Roger DeKoven			✓	56 00	
20	26	847	Bell Corporation		230 00			
21	28		Cash sales	1,100 00				
22	28	848	Payroll		520 00			
23	30		Note issued for purchase of					
24			cleaning equipment					
25	31		Leslie Stewart			✓	41 00	
26	31		Totals	5,084 00	3,292 00		245 00	179 00
27				(101)	(101)		(111)	(111)
28								

Payment of Expenses During January, the Plaza Cleaning Shop issued checks to pay three kinds of expenses: rent, telephone service, and employee salaries. Notice how the payment of the monthly rent on January 3 was recorded in the combined journal. Since there is no special column for Rent Expense, the debit part of this entry appears in the Other Accounts section. The offsetting credit appears in the Cash Credit column. The payment of the monthly telephone bill on January 19 was recorded in a similar manner. However, when employee salaries were paid on January 7, 14, 21, and 28, both parts of the entries could be made in special columns. Because the firm has a weekly payroll period, the accountant set up a separate column in the combined journal for debits to Salaries Expense.

Sales on Credit On January 5, 17, 20, 25, and 31, the Plaza Cleaning Shop sold services on credit. The necessary entries were made in two special columns of the combined journal—the Accounts Receivable Debit column and the Sales Credit column.

Page 1

✓	ACCOUNTS PAYABLE DEBIT	ACCOUNTS PAYABLE CREDIT	SALES CREDIT	SUPPLIES DEBIT	SALARIES EXPENSE DEBIT	OTHER ACCOUNTS ACCOUNT TITLE	POST. REF.	OTHER ACCOUNTS DEBIT	OTHER ACCOUNTS CREDIT	
						Rent Expense	511	900 00		1
			60 00							2
✓		210 00		210 00						3
			1,150 00							4
					520 00					5
										6
✓		90 00		90 00						7
										8
			1,385 00							9
					520 00					10
			55 00							11
✓		600 00				Equipment	131	600 00		12
						Telephone Expense	514	82 00		13
										14
			33 00							15
			1,270 00							16
					520 00					17
✓		145 00		145 00						18
			56 00							19
✓	230 00									20
			1,100 00							21
					520 00					22
						Equipment	131	1,500 00		23
						Notes Payable	201		1,500 00	24
			41 00							25
	230 00	1,045 00	5,150 00	445 00	2,080 00			3,082 00	1,500 00	26
	(202)	(202)	(401)	(121)	(517)			(X)	(X)	27
										28

Cash Sales Entries for the firm's weekly cash sales were recorded on January 7, 14, 21, and 28. Again, special columns were used—the Cash Debit column and the Sales Credit column.

Cash Received on Account When the Plaza Cleaning Shop collected cash on account from credit customers on January 10, 13, and 20, the transactions were entered in the Cash Debit column and the Accounts Receivable Credit column.

Purchases of Supplies on Credit Because the firm's combined journal includes a Supplies Debit column and an Accounts Payable Credit column, all purchases of supplies on credit can be recorded in special columns. Refer to the entries made on January 6, 12, and 24.

Purchases of Equipment on Credit On January 18, the Plaza Cleaning Shop bought some store equipment on credit. Since there is no special column for equipment, the debit part of the entry was made in the Other Accounts section. The offsetting credit appears in the Accounts Payable Credit column.

Payments on Account Any payments made on account to creditors are recorded in two special columns—Accounts Payable Debit and Cash Credit, as shown in the entry of January 26.

Issuance of a Promissory Note On January 30, the Plaza Cleaning Shop purchased new cleaning equipment and issued a promissory note to the seller. Notice that both the debit to Equipment and the credit to Notes Payable had to be recorded in the Other Accounts section.

Posting From the Combined Journal

One of the advantages of the combined journal is that it simplifies the posting process. All amounts in the special columns can be posted to the general ledger on a summary basis at the end of the month. Only the figures that appear in the Other Accounts section require individual postings to the general ledger during the month. Of course, if the firm has subsidiary ledgers, individual postings must also be made to these ledgers.

Daily Postings The procedures followed at the Plaza Cleaning Shop will illustrate the techniques used to post from the combined journal. Each day any entries appearing in the Other Accounts section are posted to the proper accounts in the general ledger. For example, refer to the combined journal shown on pages 280 and 281. The five amounts listed in the Other Accounts Debit and Credit columns were posted individually during the month. The account numbers recorded in the Post. Ref. column of the journal show that the postings have been made.

Because the Plaza Cleaning Shop has subsidiary ledgers for accounts receivable and accounts payable, individual postings were also made on a daily basis to these ledgers. As each amount was posted, a check mark was placed in the Accounts Receivable or Accounts Payable section of the combined journal.

End-of-Month Postings At the end of the month, the combined journal is totaled, proved, and ruled. Then the totals of the special columns are posted to the general ledger.

Proving the combined journal involves a comparison of the column totals to make sure that the debits and credits are equal. The following procedure is used.

PROOF OF COMBINED JOURNAL

	Debits
Cash Debit Column	$ 5,084
Accounts Receivable Debit Column	245
Accounts Payable Debit Column	230
Salaries Expense Debit Column	2,080
Supplies Debit Column	445
Other Accounts Debit Column	3,082
	$11,166

	Credits
Cash Credit Column	$ 3,292
Accounts Receivable Credit Column	179
Accounts Payable Credit Column	1,045
Sales Credit Column	5,150
Other Accounts Credit Column	1,500
	$11,166

After the combined journal is proved, all column totals except those in the Other Accounts section are posted to the appropriate general ledger accounts. As each total is posted, the account number is entered beneath the column in the journal, as shown on pages 280 and 281. Notice that an X is used to indicate that the column totals in the Other Accounts section are not posted.

Typical Uses of the Combined Journal

The combined journal is used most often in small professional offices and small service businesses. It is less suitable for merchandising businesses but is sometimes used in firms of this type if they are very small and have only a limited number of transactions.

Professional Offices The combined journal may be ideal to record the transactions that occur in a professional office, such as the office of a doctor, lawyer, accountant, or architect. However, special journals are more efficient if transactions become very numerous or are too varied.

Service Businesses The use of the combined journal to record the transactions of the Plaza Cleaning Shop has already been illustrated. The combined journal may be advantageous for a small service business, provided that the volume of transactions does not become excessive and the nature of the transactions does not become too complex.

Merchandising Businesses The combined journal may be used by a merchandising business, but only if the firm is quite small and has a very limited number and variety of transactions involving few accounts. However, even for a small merchandising business, the use of special journals may prove more advantageous.

Disadvantages of the Combined Journal

If the variety of transactions is so great that many different accounts are required, the combined journal will not work well. Either the accountant will have to set up so many columns that the journal will become unwieldy, or it will be necessary to record so many transactions in the Other Accounts columns that little efficiency will result. As a general rule, if the transactions of a business are numerous enough to merit the use of special journals, any attempt to substitute the combined journal is a mistake. Remember that each special journal can be designed for maximum efficiency in recording transactions.

ONE-WRITE SYSTEMS

The *one-write*, or *pegboard*, *system* is another type of record system designed to increase the efficiency of accounting work in small businesses and small professional offices. This system allows the preparation of several records at the same time without rewriting the data. It is used most often for accounts payable, accounts receivable, and payroll—areas where there are many repetitive transactions that must be entered in several different records.

The illustration shown on page 285 indicates how a one-write system for accounts receivable operates. This system is intended to handle sales on credit, cash received on account, and sales returns and allowances. It permits a transaction to be simultaneously journalized, posted to the customer's account, and recorded on the statement of account that will be sent to the customer at the end of the month.

A flat writing board called a *pegboard* is used to hold the records that will be prepared. First, the journal page is placed on the board. Then, the ledger sheet for the customer is positioned over the journal page, and the customer's statement of account is placed on top of the ledger sheet. The forms are arranged so that the first unused line of each is over the first unused line of the previous record. A clamp at one side of the board keeps the forms securely in place. (Some boards of this type have pegs along the sides to hold the forms—hence, the use of the term "pegboard.")

When an entry is made on the form at the top of the pegboard, the data is reproduced on all the other forms at the same time. This is accomplished by having carbon paper between the forms or by using forms that are printed on NCR (no carbon required) paper, which is chemically treated to allow the transfer of entries from one sheet to another.

One-write systems can save a substantial amount of time and effort in the preparation of accounting records in small businesses and small professional offices.

PEGBOARD: Holds forms in place.

JOURNAL: Journal sheet is placed on bottom.

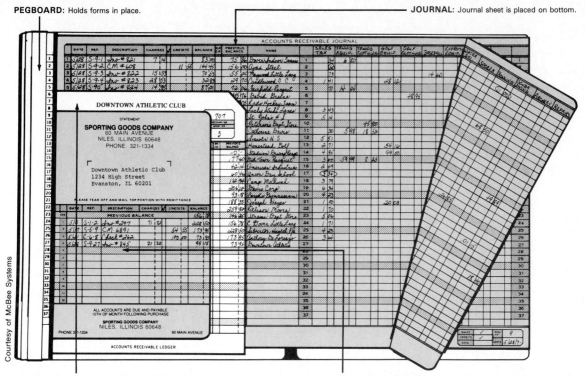

LEDGER ACCOUNT: First customer's account is placed in position. First unused line of account is positioned over first unused line of journal.

STATEMENT OF ACCOUNT: Customer's statement of account is positioned on pegboard so that the first unused line of the statement is on top of writing line to be used on ledger account.

MICROCOMPUTER ACCOUNTING SYSTEMS

Microcomputer accounting systems offer the greatest opportunity for efficient preparation of financial records in small firms. Because of their relatively low prices and ease of use, these systems are spreading rapidly. Not only do they save considerable time and effort by performing many tasks automatically, but they provide management with a wider range of information more quickly than manual accounting systems.

Components of a Microcomputer System

Computers are classified by the size of their internal memory and by their cost. The computers with the smallest memories and the least expensive prices are known as *microcomputers*. The typical microcomputer system used in business consists of a central processing unit and several input and output devices.

The *central processing unit* (CPU) is the heart of the system. It contains the internal memory of the system; handles arithmetic operations, such as addition, subtraction, multiplication, and division; performs logic operations, such as comparing two numbers to see which one is greater; and controls the activities of all parts of the system. *Input devices* are used to enter instructions and data into the system. *Output devices* provide the information that results from the processing of data. The chart on page 286 shows how the various parts of a microcomputer system relate to each other.

A MICROCOMPUTER SYSTEM

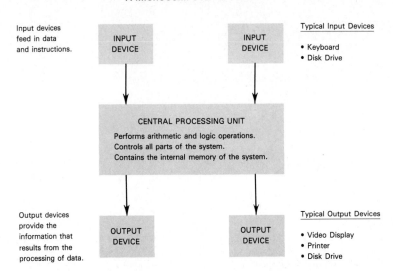

Input devices feed in data and instructions.

INPUT DEVICE

INPUT DEVICE

Typical Input Devices
• Keyboard
• Disk Drive

CENTRAL PROCESSING UNIT
Performs arithmetic and logic operations.
Controls all parts of the system.
Contains the internal memory of the system.

Output devices provide the information that results from the processing of data.

OUTPUT DEVICE

OUTPUT DEVICE

Typical Output Devices
• Video Display
• Printer
• Disk Drive

MAGNETIC DISK

Courtesy Nashua Corporation

Most microcomputer systems used in business have at least two input devices—a keyboard and a disk drive. The *keyboard* is a typewriter-like device that allows the operator to enter data and communicate with the system. The *disk drive* reads the contents of a magnetic disk and transfers the instructions or data on the disk to the central processing unit. One common type of magnetic disk is shown in the margin. It can store more than 1 million characters of data in the form of magnetized spots and can easily hold all the general ledger accounts of a small business. This type of magnetic disk is known as a *flexible disk* or *floppy disk* because it is made of a flexible plastic material. A *hard disk,* which is made of metal, can store an even greater amount of data.

There are also a number of different types of output devices. While a microcomputer system is running, the operator can view data on a device called a *video display terminal,* or *monitor,* which resembles a television set. In order to obtain a printed copy of the results of processing, such as a journal or financial statements, a device known as a *printer* is used. Another form of output is information recorded on a magnetic disk by a disk drive. (Disk drives can enter data on disks as well as read data from the disks.)

In microcomputer accounting systems, the ledgers are stored on magnetic disks and updated whenever new transactions are recorded. Magnetic disks provide *secondary* or *external memory* for the system. They supplement the *primary* or *internal memory* of the system, which is located in the central processing unit.

A photograph of a microcomputer system is on page 287.

Microcomputer Programs

A microcomputer cannot perform accounting work or, in fact, accomplish any task without a set of detailed instructions called a *program.* Every program is written in a language that the machine can understand and gives step-by-step directions for handling the procedures involved. Programs that are designed to run on microcomputer systems are usually kept on magnetic disks so that they are available for use whenever necessary.

MICROCOMPUTER EQUIPMENT

Video Display

Printer

Central
Processing
Unit

Disk Drive

Keyboard

Courtesy of International Business Machines Corporation

Computer equipment is often referred to as *hardware,* and programs are known as *software*. Very few small businesses write their own accounting software or hire a programmer to do this type of work for them. The time required and the cost involved would be too great. Instead, most small businesses purchase ready-made software from computer stores or software companies. One of the reasons why microcomputer accounting systems have been able to spread rapidly is that so much moderately priced, easy-to-use software is available. Some of the areas covered by this software are general ledger and financial reporting, accounts payable, accounts receivable, payroll, financial planning and analysis, tax planning, purchasing, inventory control, and billing.

Specialized accounting software is available for professional offices, such as medical, dental, and legal offices, and for various types of businesses, such as insurance agencies and real estate agencies.

Advantages of a Microcomputer Accounting System

Microcomputer accounting systems offer a number of significant advantages for small businesses and small professional offices.

1. Microcomputers can handle many tasks automatically, which saves a great deal of time and effort. After transactions are entered by the operator, the

system can automatically produce a printed journal, post to the ledger accounts, prepare a trial balance, and prepare financial statements. This is an automated version of the one-write principle.

2. Microcomputers function with a very high degree of accuracy—with much more accuracy than human beings. Of course, the data entered into the system must be correct in order to achieve accurate results.

3. When microcomputers are used, accounting work can be performed more quickly and management can obtain financial information in a more timely fashion.

4. A microcomputer accounting system can produce a broader range of reports more easily. For example, many accounts payable programs provide reports showing an age analysis of the accounts, a preview of the checks that must be issued to pay amounts owed during the next month, and a listing of any cash discounts lost during the past month.

Disadvantages of a Microcomputer Accounting System

As useful as microcomputer accounting systems are, they also have some disadvantages.

1. It may be difficult to achieve division of responsibility. In small firms, a single employee often handles accounting work on the microcomputer and is in complete charge of all journals, ledgers, and payroll records, as well as the billing of customers, the issuance of purchase orders to suppliers, and the preparation of checks for creditors and employees.

2. The possibility of covering up dishonesty is greater. Accounting data that is recorded on magnetic disks can easily be altered without leaving evidence of the change.

3. Accounting records are more vulnerable to loss or destruction when they are stored on disks. The data can easily be erased by accident or intentionally destroyed by an angry employee. (A safeguard against this problem is to prepare a duplicate copy of all disks that contain accounting data and keep the copies in a separate locked file away from the original disks.)

4. The software that is chosen will determine the format of the accounting records and the procedures to be used in the accounting system. If ready-made software is obtained, it is not possible to custom-tailor the records and procedures to the specific needs of a business.

Computerized accounting systems that are used by medium-sized and large businesses are discussed in Chapter 18.

PRINCIPLES AND PROCEDURES SUMMARY

In a small business or small professional office that has a limited number of transactions and uses few accounts, the combined journal can provide the foundation for a simple yet effective accounting system. This journal unites the functions of the various special journals and the general journal into one record. It offers many of the time-saving and labor-saving features of the special journals but also has the flexibility of the general journal. However, even in a small business, a combined journal is not efficient if transactions are too numerous or varied.

One-write systems can also help small firms by allowing them to make entries in several different records at the same time. The records are aligned on a pegboard, and the use of carbon paper or specially treated forms permits data recorded on the top form to be reproduced on all the other forms. One-write systems are used most often in areas such as accounts payable, accounts receivable, and payroll, where there are many repetitive transactions that must be entered in a number of different records.

Microcomputer systems offer small businesses and small professional offices the greatest potential for saving time and effort in their accounting work. Because these systems perform many tasks automatically and operate with a very high degree of accuracy, they can provide more efficiency than a manual accounting system.

MANAGERIAL IMPLICATIONS

When a small firm is established, management should give careful attention to the type of accounting system that will be used. Ease of operation, efficiency, and the ability to supply adequate information on time are all essential. No matter how small a business is, management still needs accurate and timely information in order to control operations properly and make intelligent decisions. Because of limited financial resources, small businesses cannot afford the costly mistakes that may result from information that is late, insufficient, or incorrect.

Small firms that are already operating should review their accounting systems periodically. If the business has expanded, it may need to revise its records and procedures. Even if a firm has not outgrown its present accounting system, management may want to explore the possibility of computerization. The firm's accountant can help management to weigh the potential benefits of this change against the investment that would have to be made in microcomputer equipment and programs.

REVIEW QUESTIONS

1. What is a combined journal?
2. How does an accountant determine which special columns to establish in a combined journal?
3. What types of entries are recorded in the Other Accounts columns of the combined journal?
4. What posting procedure is used for the combined journal?
5. How is the combined journal proved at the end of each month?
6. What advantages does the combined journal offer?
7. What are the disadvantages of the combined journal?
8. What types of firms would find the combined journal most suitable for their operations?

9. How does a one-write system operate?
10. What areas of accounting are most suitable for a one-write system?
11. Describe the functions of the central processing unit of a microcomputer.
12. What is an input device? Give two examples of input devices used in microcomputer systems.
13. What is an output device? Give three examples of output devices used in microcomputer systems.
14. Where are ledger accounts stored in a microcomputer accounting system?
15. What is a program?
16. How do most small firms obtain their accounting software?
17. What are the major advantages of a microcomputer accounting system?
18. What are the major disadvantages of a microcomputer accounting system?

MANAGERIAL DISCUSSION QUESTIONS

1. What aspects of business operations should the management of a small firm consider when deciding whether to use a combined journal or special journals?
2. What major factors would management want to evaluate before making a decision to purchase a microcomputer for the firm's accounting work?
3. Why might the management of a small but growing company decide to convert to a computerized accounting system even though the present manual system is still adequate?
4. Why should the management of a small business consult the firm's accountant before buying any accounting software?

EXERCISES

EXERCISE 12-1 **Determining the entries to be made in a combined journal.** Roger Chang, an architect, uses a combined journal with the money columns shown below to record his transactions. Indicate which columns would be used to enter each of the transactions listed on page 291.

COLUMNS OF COMBINED JOURNAL

a. Cash Debit
b. Cash Credit
c. Accounts Receivable Debit
d. Accounts Receivable Credit
e. Fees Credit
f. Office Supplies Debit
g. Salaries Expense Debit
h. Automobile Expense Debit
i. Other Accounts Debit
j. Other Accounts Credit

TRANSACTIONS

1. Collected $2,000 on account from clients for work performed on credit last month.
2. Purchased office supplies for $89 in cash.
3. Issued a check for $500 to pay the monthly rent.
4. Purchased a new typewriter for $620 in cash.
5. Performed services for $875 in cash.
6. Paid $38 for gasoline and oil used in the firm's automobile.
7. Issued a check for $230 to pay the weekly salary of the office assistant.
8. Completed a job and issued a bill for $1,500 to the client. The amount is payable in 30 days.
9. Issued a check for $78 to pay the monthly telephone bill.
10. Purchased office supplies for $110 on credit.

EXERCISE 12-2 **Determining the entries to be made in a combined journal.** The following additional transactions occurred at the architectural practice of Roger Chang. Indicate which columns in the firm's combined journal would be used to record these transactions. (Refer to the columns listed in Exercise 12-1.)

TRANSACTIONS

1. Purchased some computerized drafting equipment for $3,000. Paid $1,000 in cash immediately and issued a two-month promissory note for the balance.
2. Issued a check for $1,500 to Roger Chang as a withdrawal for personal use.
3. Received a bill for $350 for repairs to the firm's automobile. The amount is payable in 30 days.
4. Issued a check for $110 to a creditor on account.
5. Completed a job for a client. Received $1,300 immediately and billed the client for another $1,000, which is payable in 45 days.

EXERCISE 12-3 **Establishing a combined journal.** The AAA Equipment Repair Service will open for business soon to repair commercial heating and air-conditioning systems. The firm will use a combined journal to record its transactions. Based on the following information, decide what money columns should be placed in the firm's combined journal.

▪ The business will perform most of its work on credit.
▪ There will be many purchases of parts and other supplies. Most of these purchases will be made on credit.
▪ The firm will operate two vans to transport parts and equipment to its jobs.
▪ Salaries will be paid weekly to the four employees.

PROBLEMS

PROBLEM 12-1 **Recording transactions in a combined journal.** Ralph Conti is an interior designer who operates his own business. The transactions that the firm had during June 19X5 are listed on pages 292 and 293 along with the general ledger accounts used to record these transactions.

Instructions 1. Enter the transactions in a combined journal with the following money columns: Cash Debit and Credit, Accounts Receivable Debit and Credit, Fees Credit, Salaries Expense Debit, Office Supplies Debit, Automobile Expense Debit, and Other Accounts Debit and Credit.

2. Total, prove, and rule the combined journal.

GENERAL LEDGER ACCOUNTS

101	Cash	511	Rent Expense
111	Accounts Receivable	514	Salaries Expense
121	Office Supplies	517	Utilities Expense
131	Office Equipment	520	Telephone Expense
141	Automobile	523	Automobile Expense
302	Ralph Conti, Drawing	526	Entertainment Expense
401	Fees		

TRANSACTIONS FOR JUNE 19X5

June   1   Issued Check 343 for $500 to pay the monthly rent.

3 Collected $1,900 from the Pace Company, a client, for work performed on credit during May.

4 Purchased office supplies for $46.25. Paid for them with Check 344.

4 Provided services for $350 in cash.

5 Issued Check 345 for $220 to pay the weekly salary of the office assistant.

8 Purchased a new desk and chair for the office. Paid for them immediately with Check 346 for $385.

9 Issued Check 347 for $67.10 to pay the monthly telephone bill.

10 Issued Check 348 for $36 to pay for gasoline and oil used in the firm's automobile.

11 Completed a job for the Summit Hotel and sent a bill for $2,100. The amount is payable in 30 days.

12 Issued Check 349 for $220 to pay the weekly salary of the office assistant.

15 Issued Check 350 for $31.40 to pay for a purchase of office supplies.

17 Received $500 from James Hunt, a client, for work performed on credit during May.

18 Issued Check 351 for $123 to pay for repairs to the firm's automobile.

18 Provided services for $400 in cash.

19 Issued Check 352 for $220 to pay the weekly salary of the office assistant.

22 Received a bill for $131.25 from the American Express Company for credit card charges and paid it with Check 353. The charges were for entertainment of clients at business lunches.

23 Issued Check 354 for $86 to pay the monthly electric bill.

25 Completed a job for the Embassy Club and sent a bill for $1,750. The amount is payable in 30 days.

26 Issued Check 355 for $220 to pay the weekly salary of the office assistant.

29 Issued Check 356 for $32 to pay for gasoline used in the firm's automobile.

30 Issued Check 357 for $21 to replenish the petty cash fund. An analysis of the petty cash vouchers shows that $9.20 was spent for office supplies and $11.80 was spent for entertainment.

30 Issued Check 358 for $1,800 to the owner as a cash withdrawal for personal use.

PROBLEM 12-2

Recording transactions in a combined journal. On April 1, 19X7, Dr. Sharon Doyle established her medical practice. The transactions that occurred during the first month of operations are listed below and on page 294 along with the accounts used to record these transactions.

Instructions

1. Enter the transactions in a combined journal with the following money columns: Cash Debit and Credit, Accounts Receivable Debit and Credit, Fees Credit, Salaries Expense Debit, Office Supplies Debit, Medical Supplies Debit, and Other Accounts Debit and Credit.

2. Total, prove, and rule the combined journal.

GENERAL LEDGER ACCOUNTS

101	Cash	203	Accounts Payable
111	Accounts Receivable	301	Sharon Doyle, Capital
121	Office Supplies	302	Sharon Doyle, Drawing
123	Medical Supplies	511	Rent Expense
131	Office Furniture	514	Salaries Expense
141	Medical Equipment	517	Telephone Expense
151	Automobile	520	Utilities Expense
201	Notes Payable	523	Automobile Expense

TRANSACTIONS FOR APRIL 19X7

Apr. 1 Sharon Doyle deposited $17,000 to open a checking account for her medical practice at the First National Bank.

1 Signed a lease for a suite of offices at the Medical Arts Building and issued Check 101 for $850 to pay the first month's rent.

1 Purchased office furniture from the Scott Company for $3,200. The amount is payable in 45 days.

2 Purchased medical equipment from Medtec Products for $6,800. Paid $2,500 immediately with Check 102, and issued a 3-month promissory note for the balance.

3 Purchased office supplies for $76.25. Paid for them with Check 103.

4 Issued Check 104 for $273.50 to buy medical supplies.

5 Purchased a used automobile for the practice from Ross Motors. Issued Check 105 for $2,000 as a down payment and agreed to pay the balance of $3,000 in ten monthly installments of $300 each.

8 Billed $500 to Robert Klein, a patient, for surgery. The amount is due in 30 days.

10 Purchased medical supplies for $71.50. Paid for them with Check 106.

12 Received $1,260 from patients for services performed for cash during the week of April 8–12.

12 Issued Check 107 for $680 to pay the weekly salaries of the office staff.

15 Issued Check 108 for $25.40 to purchase office supplies.

16 Billed $475 to Gail Smith, a patient, for surgery. The amount is due in 30 days.

17 Billed $550 to Richard Nye, a patient, for surgery. The amount is due in 30 days.

18 Issued Check 109 for $86.25 to purchase medical supplies.

19 Received $1,640 from patients for services performed for cash during the week of April 15–19.

19 Issued Check 110 for $680 to pay the weekly salaries of the office staff.

22 Billed $500 to Ann McLouth, a patient, for surgery. The amount is due in 30 days.

25 Issued Check 111 for $81.75 to pay the monthly electric bill.

26 Received $1,590 from patients for services performed for cash during the week of April 22–26.

26 Issued Check 112 for $680 to pay the weekly salaries of the office staff.

29 Issued Check 113 for $98.50 to pay the monthly telephone bill.

29 Received a check for $500 from Robert Klein, a patient, to settle his account.

30 Issued Check 114 for $37.25 to purchase office supplies.

30 Received a bill totaling $139.30 for gasoline and minor repairs for the automobile. Issued Check 115 to pay the bill.

30 Received $325 from patients for services performed for cash during April 29 and 30.

30 Issued Check 116 for $2,000 to Sharon Doyle as a cash withdrawal for personal use.

ALTERNATE PROBLEMS

PROBLEM 12-1A **Recording transactions in a combined journal.** Paul DeWitt operates his own management consulting firm. The transactions that the firm had during July 19X1 are listed on page 295 along with the general ledger accounts used to record these transactions.

Instructions   1. Enter the transactions in a combined journal with the following money columns: Cash Debit and Credit, Accounts Receivable Debit and Credit, Fees Credit, Salaries Expense Debit, Office Supplies Debit, Travel and Entertainment Expense Debit, and Other Accounts Debit and Credit.

2. Total, prove, and rule the combined journal.

GENERAL LEDGER ACCOUNTS

101	Cash	401	Fees
111	Accounts Receivable	511	Rent Expense
121	Office Supplies	514	Salaries Expense
131	Furniture	517	Utilities Expense
141	Equipment	520	Telephone Expense
302	Paul DeWitt, Drawing	523	Travel and Entertainment Expense

TRANSACTIONS FOR JULY 19X1

July 1 Received $2,400 from the Dobbs Company, a client, for work performed on credit during June.

2 Issued Check 571 for $650 to pay the monthly rent.

3 Purchased office supplies for $74.30. Paid for them with Check 572.

5 Provided services for $500 in cash.

5 Issued Check 573 for $235 to pay the weekly salary of the office assistant.

8 Purchased an electronic typewriter for the office. Paid for it immediately with Check 574 for $760.

9 Issued Check 575 for $92.30 to pay the monthly electric bill.

11 Issued Check 576 for $408 to pay for airline tickets and hotel accommodations for a business trip.

12 Completed a job for the Travis Corporation and sent a bill for $3,000. The amount is payable in 30 days.

12 Issued Check 577 for $235 to pay the weekly salary of the office assistant.

15 Issued Check 578 for $29.70 to pay for a purchase of office supplies.

16 Received $1,200 from the Leeds Company, a client, for work performed on credit during June.

17 Issued Check 579 for $62.50 for car rental charges incurred when traveling to a client's plant.

19 Provided services for $300 in cash.

19 Issued Check 580 for $235 to pay the weekly salary of the office assistant.

22 Received a bill for $124.60 from the Diners Club for credit card charges and paid it with Check 581. The charges were incurred for entertainment of clients at business lunches.

24 Completed a job for the Hull Corporation and sent a bill for $1,600. The amount is payable in 30 days.

25 Issued Check 582 for $73 to pay the monthly telephone bill.

26 Issued Check 583 for $235 to pay the weekly salary of the office assistant.

29 Issued Check 584 for $59.40 for car rental charges incurred when traveling to a client's headquarters.

31 Issued Check 585 for $24 to replenish the petty cash fund. An analysis of the petty cash vouchers shows that $12.10 was spent for office supplies and $11.90 was spent for entertainment.

31 Issued Check 586 for $2,100 to the owner as a cash withdrawal.

PROBLEM 12-2A **Recording transactions in a combined journal.** On May 1, 19X8, Sandra Collins established her legal practice. The transactions that occurred during the first month of operations are listed below and on page 297 along with the accounts used to record these transactions.

Instructions

1. Enter the transactions in a combined journal with the following money columns: Cash Debit and Credit, Accounts Receivable Debit and Credit, Fees Credit, Salaries Expense Debit, Office Supplies Debit, Automobile Expense Debit, and Other Accounts Debit and Credit.
2. Total, prove, and rule the combined journal.

GENERAL LEDGER ACCOUNTS

101	Cash	203	Accounts Payable
111	Accounts Receivable	301	Sandra Collins, Capital
121	Office Supplies	302	Sandra Collins, Drawing
131	Law Library	511	Rent Expense
135	Furniture	514	Salaries Expense
141	Equipment	517	Telephone Expense
145	Automobile	520	Utilities Expense
201	Notes Payable	523	Automobile Expense

TRANSACTIONS FOR MAY 19X8

May 1 Sandra Collins deposited $20,000 to open a checking account for her legal practice at the City National Bank.

   1 Signed a lease for a suite of offices at the Lincoln Building and issued Check 101 for $900 to pay the first month's rent.

   1 Purchased office furniture for $5,000 from Hogan Products. Paid $2,000 immediately with Check 102 and issued a 3-month promissory note for the balance.

   2 Purchased law books for $870 from the Monroe Company. The amount is due in 30 days.

   3 Issued Check 103 for $74.30 to buy office supplies.

   4 Purchased a typewriter for $550 from the Delta Corporation. The amount is payable in 30 days.

   5 Bought an $8,000 automobile from Santini Motors for use in the practice. Issued Check 104 for $3,000 as a down payment. The balance is due in ten monthly installments of $500 each.

   8 Billed $350 to Charles Emory, a client, for professional services. The amount is payable in 30 days.

   9 Purchased an electronic desk calculator for $70. Paid for it immediately with Check 105.

  12 Received $1,410 from clients for professional services performed for cash during the week of May 8–12.

  12 Issued Check 106 for $560 to pay the weekly salaries of the office staff.

  15 Purchased office supplies for $51.80. Paid for them with Check 107.

  15 Billed $300 to Marie Fasio, a client, for professional services. The amount is payable in 30 days.

17 Issued Check 108 for $27.40 for gasoline and oil used in the firm's automobile.

18 Billed $400 to the Video Mart, a client, for professional services. The amount is payable in 30 days.

19 Received $1,120 from clients for professional services performed for cash during the week of May 15–19.

19 Issued Check 109 for $560 to pay the weekly salaries of the office staff.

22 Issued Check 110 for $74.35 to pay the monthly telephone bill.

23 Billed $650 to the Webb Company, a client, for professional services. The amount is payable in 30 days.

26 Received $1,270 from clients for professional services performed for cash during the week of May 22–26.

26 Issued Check 111 for $560 to pay the weekly salaries of the office staff.

29 Issued Check 112 for $106.30 for gasoline and minor repairs for the firm's automobile.

30 Issued Check 113 for $89.20 to pay the monthly electric bill.

31 Issued Check 114 for $870 to pay the Monroe Company, a creditor, on account.

31 Received $535 from clients for professional services performed for cash during May 29–31.

31 Issued Check 115 for $1,900 to Sandra Collins as a cash withdrawal for personal use.

In the discussion of accounting records up to this point, there has been no detailed treatment of salary and wage payments to employees. A consideration of payroll accounting would have interrupted the coverage of general accounting principles and procedures. Also, payroll accounting, including the related payroll taxes and tax returns, is so important that it requires special attention and extended treatment. Such coverage is provided in this chapter and the next chapter.

PAYROLL COMPUTATIONS, RECORDS, AND PAYMENT

OBJECTIVES OF PAYROLL WORK

The primary objective of payroll work is to compute the wages or salaries due employees and to pay these amounts promptly. Another objective is to classify employee wages and salaries properly and to charge these amounts to the appropriate expense accounts. Until the mid-1930s, payroll accounting involved few other considerations. However, since then the correct computation, payment, and reporting of taxes has become a major objective of payroll work.

In 1935 the federal Social Security Act was passed. Under the terms of this legislation and related funding legislation, it became necessary for businesses to withhold a social security tax from employee earnings, to make their own tax contributions to the social security system, and to keep detailed records of employee earnings. The withholding of federal income tax, which started in 1943, and the enactment of income tax withholding plans by a number of states also added to payroll recordkeeping work. The wage and hour provisions of the federal Fair Labor Standards Act of 1938 (as amended) affected the computation of earnings. The various state worker's compensation insurance laws are a further concern in payroll accounting because they require careful classification of payroll amounts according to the type of work done by employees. The provisions of each law are discussed in greater detail in the paragraphs that follow.

The Social Security System

The federal Social Security Act has been amended several times and is likely to be further amended. The present social security system has two principal parts. The first, discussed in this chapter, consists of the old-age, survivors, and disability insurance program and the hospital insurance program (Medicare). This part of the system is financed entirely by the federal government through taxes levied under the Federal Insurance Contributions Act (FICA). The second part, discussed in Chapter 14, is the federal unemployment insurance program. This part is financed jointly by the federal government and the states through taxes levied under the Federal Unemployment Tax Act (FUTA) and the corresponding state unemployment tax laws. Changes occur in the rates and base figures more often than in the methods of computation. Learn the methods, and then always be sure to use the latest rates and bases.

Coverage Most employers and employees are covered by the social security system. Agricultural workers, domestic workers, and most self-employed persons are covered under special provisions. Railroad workers have a separate program of their own and are therefore exempt. Employees of state and local governments and of certain religious and nonprofit organizations are also exempt but may choose to be covered. Only ordinary business employers and employees that are covered by the system are considered here.

Benefits Insured workers may claim retirement benefits after they retire at age 62 or later. Disability benefits for insured workers are the same as old-age insurance benefits would be if the disabled worker were already 65 and retired. In each case, the amount of benefits depends upon the average indexed earnings of the insured person. Besides retirement and disability benefits, the system makes available hospital insurance benefits for people who are 65 or over and are covered by social security. Further details about benefits, including survivors' benefits, may be obtained from the government publication *Your Social Security* or from district offices of the Social Security Administration (which are listed in telephone directories under United States Government: Department of Health and Human Services).

Identification Numbers Each employer and each employee must obtain an identification number, because millions of employers and employees are covered by the social security system. These numbers help ensure that proper credits for taxes paid are given in cases in which there may be more than one person or company with the same name. Social security records are stored in computers, and the use of identification numbers makes it easier to handle the tremendous volume of entries that must be recorded each year.

The Fair Labor Standards Act

The Fair Labor Standards Act of 1938 (as amended) applies only to firms engaged directly or indirectly in interstate commerce. This federal statute, which is often referred to as the Wage and Hour Law, fixes a minimum hourly rate of pay and maximum hours of work per week to be performed at the regular rate. As of this writing, the minimum hourly rate of pay is $3.35 and the maximum number of hours at the employee's regular hourly rate is 40. Hours worked in excess of 40 in any week must be paid for at an overtime rate of at least one and a half times the regular hourly rate of pay. (This overtime rate is called *time and a half*.) Many employers who are not covered by the federal law pay time and a half for overtime because of union contracts or simply as a good business practice.

The Fair Labor Standards Act requires covered employers to maintain records for each employee to show that the provisions of the law have been followed. No particular form is specified for these records, but they should indicate the name and address of the employee, date of birth, hours worked each day and week, wages paid at the regular rate, and overtime premium wages. Similar information is required for employees subject to the FICA (social security) tax previously discussed. One record for each employee ordinarily serves both purposes.

Worker's Compensation Insurance

All the states have laws covering worker's compensation insurance. These laws require employers to pay for insurance that will reimburse employees for losses suffered from job-related injuries or will compensate their families if death occurs in the course of their employment. Benefits are paid directly to the injured workers or to their survivors.

ILLUSTRATIVE CASE—THE KENT NOVELTY COMPANY

The first step in payroll work is to determine the gross amount of wages or salary earned by each employee. There are a number of common ways of paying employees. Some workers are paid at a stated rate per hour, and their gross pay depends on the number of hours they work. This method is called the *hourly-rate basis*. Other workers are paid an agreed amount for each week or month or other period. This arrangement is called the *salary basis*.

The Kent Novelty Company is used in this chapter and the next to illustrate typical payroll procedures and records. This firm, which is owned by Howard Mason, produces a variety of novelty items and sells them by mail. It is staffed by three production workers and a production supervisor, who are paid weekly on the hourly-rate basis, and by an office clerk, who is paid a weekly salary. The employees are subject to FICA tax and federal income tax withholding. Mason manages the company himself and withdraws a portion of the profits from time to time to take care of his personal living expenses. Because he is the owner of a sole proprietorship business, his drawings are not treated as salary or wages.

The Kent Novelty Company is subject to FICA tax and to federal and state unemployment insurance taxes. Since the mail-order business involves interstate commerce, the firm is also subject to the Fair Labor Standards Act. In addition, the business is required by state law to carry worker's compensation insurance.

DETERMINING GROSS PAY FOR HOURLY EMPLOYEES

To determine the gross pay earned by an employee on an hourly-rate basis, it is necessary to know the rate of pay and the number of hours the employee has worked during the payroll period.

Hours Worked

There are various methods of keeping track of the hours worked by each employee. At the Kent Novelty Company, the production supervisor keeps a weekly time sheet on which she enters the number of hours worked each day by each shop employee. At the end of the week, the office clerk uses this record to prepare the payroll.

If the time sheet system is used in a larger firm, each supervisor keeps a record of the time worked by the employees under his or her supervision. More often, however, a larger business uses a time clock for employees who are paid on an hourly basis. Each employee has a time card and inserts it in the time clock to record the time of arrival and the time of departure. The payroll clerk collects the cards at the end of the week, determines the hours worked by each employee, multiplies the number of hours by the proper rate, and computes the gross pay.

Gross Pay

Suppose that the time sheet kept at the Kent Novelty Company during the week ended January 7, 19X5, shows that the first employee, Peter Brown, worked 40 hours. His rate of pay is $8 an hour. His gross pay of $320 is found by multiplying 40 hours by $8.

The second employee, George Dunn, has worked 44 hours. Four of these hours are overtime. Thus, they must be paid for at Dunn's regular rate ($5) plus a premium rate of one-half of his regular rate ($5 × 0.50 = $2.50 premium rate). Dunn's gross pay is calculated as follows.

Total time × regular rate:	44 hours × $5	$220
Overtime premium:	4 hours × $2.50	10
Gross pay		$230

This method is the one specified under the Wage and Hour Law and is therefore the one used in the illustrations. Another method, which gives the same gross pay, uses the steps shown below.

Regular time earnings:	40 hours × $5	$200
Overtime earnings:	4 hours × $7.50	30
Gross pay		$230

The second method quickly answers the employee's question, "How much more did I earn by working overtime than I would have earned for only 40 hours of work?" The employer, however, is more concerned with the amount of premium the firm could have saved if all the hours had been paid for at the regular rate. The first method gives this information.

The third employee, Carol Rosen, worked 40 hours. Her hourly rate is $6.25. Her gross pay is therefore $250 (40 × $6.25). The fourth employee, Rita Sanchez, is the supervisor. She worked 40 hours, and her rate of pay is $10 per hour. Thus, her gross pay is $400 (40 × $10).

DEDUCTIONS FROM GROSS PAY REQUIRED BY LAW

There are two principal deductions from employees' gross pay that are required by federal law—FICA (social security) tax and income tax withholding. These deductions are explained below and on succeeding pages.

FICA Tax

The taxes required by the Federal Insurance Contributions Act are levied in an equal amount on both the employer and the employee. Since, as was previously mentioned, rates and bases change often, a hypothetical rate and base are used in this discussion. We will assume that a tax rate of 7 percent is applied to a base consisting of the first $38,000 of wages paid to an employee during the calendar year. Wages in excess of the base amount (called *tax-exempt wages*) are not taxed. If an employee works for more than one employer during the year, the FICA tax is deducted on the current base by each employer. The excess tax, if any, is later refunded to the employee by the government or applied to payment of his or her federal income tax for the year.

Although, technically, there are two separate rates for (1) old age, survivors, and disability insurance and (2) hospital insurance, they are generally combined into one rate and referred to simply as *social security tax,* or *FICA tax.* The latter term is used in this textbook.

In the following examples, the FICA tax is deducted from the gross pay of each employee of the Kent Novelty Company at the assumed rate of 7 percent on the first $38,000 earned during the calendar year. The amount to be deducted can be computed either by multiplying the taxable wages by the FICA rate or by referring to tax tables available from the government and from commercial sources, such as office supply stores.

Tax Computed by the Percentage Method When the employee's FICA tax is computed by the percentage method, the employer multiplies the taxable wages by the tax rate and rounds the answer to the nearest penny. The FICA taxes to be deducted by the Kent Novelty Company, based on the gross pay previously calculated and a tax rate of 7 percent, are shown below.

Employee	Gross Pay	Tax Rate	FICA Tax
Peter Brown	$320	7%	$22.40
George Dunn	230	7%	16.10
Carol Rosen	250	7%	17.50
Rita Sanchez	400	7%	28.00
Total			$84.00

Tax Determined From Tax Table FICA taxes on wages can be determined from the Social Security Employee Tax Table in *Circular E,* the *Employer's Tax Guide,* which is published by the Internal Revenue Service. At the assumed 7 percent rate, the FICA tax due on the $320 of wages earned by Peter Brown would amount to $22.40. This is the same amount that was calculated by using the percentage method. The table shows FICA tax of $21 on wages of $300 and $1.40 on wages of $20. These two tax amounts are added as shown below to find the FICA tax to be withheld.

WAGES	FICA TAX
On $300	$21.00
On 20	1.40
On $320	$22.40

Federal Income Tax Withholding

A substantial portion of the federal government's revenue comes from the income tax on individuals. Many rules and regulations are used in determining the amount of federal income tax that each person must pay. Also keep in mind that rates, rules, and regulations change often. The rates used in this text are for illustrative purposes only. In actual practice, a current edition of the Internal Revenue Service's *Circular E* would be consulted for up-to-date rates and other information.

Most taxpayers are on a pay-as-you-go basis. This means that the federal income tax due from a person earning a salary or wages must be withheld by the employer and paid to the government periodically—at the same time that FICA taxes are paid. At the end of each year, the employee files a tax return. If the amount withheld does not cover the amount of income tax due, the employee pays the balance. If too much has been withheld, the employee will receive a refund.

Claiming Withholding Exemptions and Allowances The amount of federal income tax a person must pay depends on the amount of income, the number of personal exemptions and withholding allowances, and marital status. The matter of exemptions and allowances is a technical subject that cannot be fully explored here. In brief, a person is ordinarily entitled to one exemption for himself or herself, one for a spouse (unless the spouse also works and claims an exemption), and one for each dependent for whom the person provides more than half the support during the year. A person may also be entitled to a special withholding allowance; to withholding allowances based on various tax credits, if eligible; and to other withholding allowances based on itemized deductions and alimony, if any.

Employees claim the number of exemptions and withholding allowances to which they are entitled by completing an *Employee's Withholding Allowance Certificate, Form W-4*. This form is filed with the employer. Peter Brown's Form W-4 is illustrated on pages 304 and 305. Because of the highly individual and complex nature of the withholding allowances based on tax credits, itemized deductions, and alimony, they are not considered here.

If an employee fails to file a Form W-4, the employer must withhold federal income tax from the employee's wages as though there were no exemptions or allowances. If the number of exemptions or allowances decreases, the employee must file a new Form W-4 within 10 days. If the number of exemptions or allowances increases, the employee may file an amended certificate.

If the employee desires, he or she may use Form W-4 to instruct the employer to withhold a specified amount of income tax each payroll period above the amount required by law. This reduces the possibility that a balance may be due when the individual files the yearly income tax return.

Computing Income Tax Withholding There are several methods that can be used to compute the amount of federal income tax to be withheld from an employee's earnings. However, all except one require cumbersome computations. The exception is the *wage-bracket table method,* which involves the use of tables to determine the amount of tax. The simplicity of this method explains why it is used almost universally. *Circular E,* the *Employer's Tax Guide,* contains withholding tables for weekly, biweekly, semimonthly, monthly and daily or miscellaneous payroll periods for single and married persons. Sections of the

Department of the Treasury—Internal Revenue Service

Employee's Withholding Allowance Certificate

OMB No. 1545–0010

1 Type or print your full name	2 Your social security number
Peter Brown	_324-76-1245_

Home address (number and street or rural route)

24 Oak Street

City or town, State, and ZIP code

Manchester, NH 03104

3 Marital Status	☐ Single ☒ Married
	☐ Married, but withhold at higher Single rate
	Note: If married, but legally separated, or spouse is a nonresident alien, check the Single box.

4 Total number of allowances you are claiming (from line F of the worksheet on page 2) . . . . | |

5 Additional amount, if any, you want deducted from each pay . . . . | $ |

6 I claim exemption from withholding because (see instructions and check boxes below that apply):

  a ☐ Last year I did not owe any Federal income tax and had a right to a full refund of **ALL** income tax withheld, **AND**

  b ☐ This year I do not expect to owe any Federal income tax and expect to have a right to a full refund of

    ALL income tax withheld. If both a and b apply, enter the year effective and "EXEMPT" here . . ▶ | Year |

  c If you entered "EXEMPT" on line 6b, are you a full-time student? . . . . ☐ Yes ☐ No

Under the penalties of perjury, I certify that I am entitled to the number of withholding allowances claimed on this certificate, or if claiming exemption from withholding, that I am entitled to claim the exempt status.

Employee's signature ▶ _Peter Brown_   Date ▶ _January 26_ , 19_X1_

7 Employer's name and address (Employer: Complete 7, 8, and 9 only if sending to IRS)	8 Office code	9 Employer identification number

-------------------- Detach along this line. Give the top part of this form to employer; keep the lower part for your records. --------------------

Privacy Act and Paperwork Reduction Act Notice.—If you do not give your employer a certificate, you will be treated as a single person with no withholding allowances as required by IRC sections 3402(l) and 3401(e). We ask for this information to carry out the Internal Revenue laws of the United States. We may give the information to the Dept. of Justice for civil or criminal litigation and to the States and the District of Columbia for use in administering their tax laws.

Purpose.—The law requires that you complete Form W-4 so that your employer can withhold Federal income tax from your pay. Your Form W-4 remains in effect until you change it or, if you entered "EXEMPT" on line 6b above, until February 15 of next year. By correctly completing this form, you can fit the amount of tax withheld from your wages to your tax liability.

If you got a large refund last year, you may be having too much tax withheld. If so, you may want to increase the number of your allowances on line 4 by claiming any other allowances you are entitled to. The kinds of allowances, and how to figure them, are explained in detail below.

If you owed a large amount of tax last year, you may not be having enough tax withheld. If so, you can claim fewer allowances on line 4, or ask that an additional amount be withheld on line 5, or both.

If the number of withholding allowances you are entitled to decreases to less than you are now claiming, you must file a new W-4 with your employer within 10 days.

The instructions below explain how to fill in Form W-4. **Publication 505** contains more information on withholding. You can get it from most IRS offices.

For more information about who qualifies as your dependent, what deductions you can take, and what tax credits you qualify for, see the Form 1040 Instructions.

Line-By-Line Instructions

Fill in the identifying information in boxes 1 and 2. If you are married and want tax withheld at the regular rate for married persons, check "Married" in box 3. If you are married and want tax withheld at the higher Single rate (because both you and your spouse work, for example), check the box "Married, but withhold at higher Single rate" in box 3.

Line 4 of Form W-4

Total number of allowances.—Use the worksheet on page 2 to figure your allowances. Add the number of allowances for each category explained below. Enter the total on line 4.

If you are single and hold more than one job, you may not claim the same allowances with more than one employer at the same time. If you are married and both you and your spouse are employed, you may not both claim the same allowances with both of your employers at the same time. To have the highest amount of tax withheld, claim "0" allowances on line 4.

A. Personal allowances.—You can claim the following personal allowances:

1 for yourself, 1 if you are 65 or older, and 1 if you are blind.

If you are married and your spouse either does not work or is not claiming his or her allowances on a separate W-4, you may also claim the following allowances: 1 for your spouse, 1 if your spouse is 65 or older, and 1 if your spouse is blind.

B. Special withholding allowance.—Claim the special withholding allowance if you are single and have one job **or** you are married, have one job, and your spouse does not work. You may still claim this allowance so long as the total wages earned on other jobs by you or your spouse (or both) is 10% or less of the combined total wages. Use this special withholding allowance only to figure your withholding. Do not claim it when you file your return.

C. Allowances for dependents.—You may claim one allowance for each dependent you will be able to claim on your Federal income tax return.

Note: If you are not claiming any deductions or credits, skip D and E, add lines A, B, and C, enter the total on line F and carry the total over to line 4 of W-4.

Before you claim allowances under D and E, total your non-wage taxable income (interest, dividends, self-employment income, etc.) and subtract this amount from estimated deductions you would otherwise enter in D1. If your non-wage income is greater than the amount of estimated deductions, you cannot claim any allowances under D. Moreover, you should take one-third of the excess (non-wage income over estimated deductions) and add this to the appropriate "A" value in Table 1 if determining allowances under E.

D. Allowances for estimated deductions.—If you expect to itemize deductions, you can claim additional withholding allowances. See Schedule A (Form 1040) for deductions you can itemize.

You can also count deductible amounts you pay for (1) alimony (2) qualified retirement contributions including Keogh (H.R. 10) plans (3) moving expenses (4) employee business expenses (Part I of Form 2106) (5) the deduction for two-earner married couples, (6) net losses shown on Schedules C, D, E, and F (Form 1040), the last line of Part II of Form 4797, and the net operating loss carryover, (7) penalty on early withdrawal of savings, and (8) direct charitable contributions. **Note:** Check with your employer to see if any tax is being withheld on moving expenses or IRA contributions. Do not include these amounts if tax is not being withheld; otherwise, you may be underwithheld. For details see **Publication 505.**

The deduction allowed two-earner married couples is 10% of the lesser of $30,000 or the qualified earned income of the spouse with the lower income. Once you have determined these deductions, enter the total on line D1 of the worksheet on page 2 and figure the number of withholding allowances for them.

E. Allowances for estimated tax credits.—If you expect to take credits like those shown on lines 41 through 48 on the 1982 Form 1040 (child care, residential energy, etc.), use the table on the top of page 2 to figure the number of additional allowances you can claim. Include the earned income credit if you are not receiving advance payment of it, and any excess FICA tax withheld. Also, if you expect to income average, include the amount of the reduction in tax because of averaging when using the table.

Line 5 of Form W-4

Additional amount, if any, you want deducted from each pay.—If you are not having enough tax withheld from your pay, you may ask your employer to withhold more by filling in an additional amount on line 5. Often married couples, both of whom are working, and persons with two

Form **W-4**

or more jobs need to have additional tax withheld. You may also need to have additional tax withheld because you have income other than wages, such as interest and dividends, capital gains, rents, alimony received, etc. Estimate the amount you will be underwithheld and divide that amount by the number of pay periods in the year. Enter the additional amount you want withheld each pay period on line 5.

Line 6 of Form W–4

Exemption from withholding.—You can claim exemption from withholding only if last year you did not owe any Federal income tax and had a right to a refund of all income tax withheld, **and** this year you do

not expect to owe any Federal income tax and expect to have a right to a refund of all income tax withheld. If you qualify, check boxes 6a and b, write the year exempt status is effective and "EXEMPT" on line 6b, and answer Yes or No to the question on line 6c.

If you want to claim exemption from withholding next year, you must file a new W–4 with your employer on or before February 15 of next year. If you are not having Federal income tax withheld this year, but expect to have a tax liability next year, the law requires you to give your employer a new W–4 by December 1 of this year. If you are covered by FICA, your employer must withhold social security tax.

You may be fined $500 if you file, with no reasonable basis, a W–4 that results in less tax being withheld than is properly allowable. In addition, criminal penalties apply for willfully supplying false or fraudulent information or failing to supply information requiring an increase in withholding.

Your employer must send to IRS any W–4 claiming more than 14 withholding allowances **or** claiming exemption from withholding if the wages are expected to usually exceed $200 a week. The employer is to complete boxes 7, 8, and 9 only on copies of the W–4 sent to IRS.

Table 1—For Figuring Your Withholding Allowances For Estimated Tax Credits and Income Averaging (Line E)

Estimated Salaries and Wages from all Sources	Single Employees (A)	Single Employees (B)	Head of Household Employees (A)	Head of Household Employees (B)	Married Employees (When Spouse not Employed) (A)	Married Employees (When Spouse not Employed) (B)	Married Employees (When Both Spouses are Employed) (A)	Married Employees (When Both Spouses are Employed) (B)
Under $15,000	$ 100	$160	$ 50	$160	$ 80	$120	$ 0	$120
15,000–25,000	150	250	0	250	90	180	360	180
25,001–35,000	200	320	0	320	130	260	840	230
35,001–45,000	390	370	0	370	180	340	1,590	260
45,001–55,000	1,120	370	0	370	250	360	2,300	350
55,001–65,000	2,150	370	670	370	560	370	3,130	350
Over 65,000	3,320	370	1,640	370	1,110	370	4,000	370

Worksheet to Figure Your Withholding Allowances to be Entered on Line 4 of Form W–4

A Personal allowances . . . . ▶ | **A** _____

B Special withholding allowance (not to exceed 1 allowance—see instructions on page 1) . . . . . ▶ | **B** _____

C Allowances for dependents . . . . ▶ | **C** _____

If you are not claiming any deductions or credits, skip lines D and E.

D Allowances for estimated deductions:

  1 Enter the total amount of your estimated itemized deductions, alimony payments, qualified retirement contributions including Keogh (H.R. 10) plans, deduction for two-earner married couples, business losses including net operating loss carryovers, moving expenses, employee business expenses, penalty on early withdrawal of savings, and direct charitable contributions for the year . . . . ▶ | **1** $ _____

  2 If you do not plan to itemize deductions, enter $500 on line D2. If you plan to itemize, find your total estimated salaries and wages amount in the left column of the table below. (Include salaries and wages of both spouses.) Read across to the right and enter the amount from the column that applies to you. Enter that amount on line D2 . . . ▶ | **2** $ _____

Estimated salaries and wages from all sources:	Single and Head of Household Employees (only one job)	Married Employees (one spouse working and one job only)	Employees with more than one job or Married Employees with both spouses working¹
Under $15,000	. . $2,800	. . $3,900	. . 40%
15,000–35,000	. . 2,800	. . 3,900	. . 23% of estimated salaries and wages
35,001–50,000	. . 9% of estimated salaries and wages	. . 3,900	. . 20%
Over $50,000	. . 11%	. . 8% of estimated salaries and wages	. . 18%

  3 Subtract line D2 from line D1 (But not less than zero) . . . . ▶ | **3** $ _____

D _____

  4 Divide the amount on line D3 by $1,000 (increase any fraction to the next whole number). Enter here . . ▶

E Allowances for estimated tax credits and income averaging: use Table 1 above for figuring withholding allowances

  1 Enter estimated tax credits, excess FICA tax withheld, and tax reduction from income averaging and tax withheld on interest and dividends . . . . $ _____

  2 Enter the column (A) amount for your salary range and filing status (single, etc.) However, enter 0 if you claim 1 or more allowances on line D4. $ _____

  3 Subtract line 2 from line 1 (If zero or less, do not complete lines 4 and 5) . . . . $ _____

  4 Find the column (B) amount for your salary range and filing status . . . . $ _____

  5 Divide line 3 by line 4. Increase any fraction to the next whole number. This is the maximum number of withholding allowances for estimated tax credits and income averaging. Enter here . . . . ▶ | **E** _____

  Example: A taxpayer who expects to file a Federal income tax return as a single person estimates annual wages of $12,000 and tax credits of $650. The $12,000 falls in the wage bracket of under $15,000. The value in column (A) is 100. Subtracting this from the estimated credits of 650 leaves 550. The value in column (B) is 160. Dividing 550 by 160 gives 3.4. Since any fraction is increased to the next whole number, show 4 on line E.

F Total (add lines A through E). Enter total here and on line 4 of Form W–4 . . . . ▶ | **F** _____

¹ If you earn 10% or less of your total wages from other jobs or one spouse earns 10% or less of the couple's combined total wages, you can use the "Single and Head of Household Employees (only one job)" or "Married Employees (one spouse working and one job only)" table, whichever is appropriate.

☆U.S. GOVERNMENT PRINTING OFFICE   E I #52-1074467

SINGLE Persons—WEEKLY Payroll Period

And the wages are—		And the number of withholding allowances claimed is—										
At least	But less than	0	1	2	3	4	5	6	7	8	9	10
		The amount of income tax to be withheld shall be—										
$135	$140	$17.80	$14.10	$10.50	$7.40	$4.70	$2.00	$0	$0	$0	$0	$0
140	145	18.70	15.10	11.40	8.20	5.40	2.70	0	0	0	0	0
145	150	19.70	16.00	12.40	9.00	6.10	3.40	.70	0	0	0	0
150	160	21.10	17.50	13.80	10.20	7.20	4.40	1.70	0	0	0	0
160	170	23.00	19.40	15.70	12.10	8.80	5.80	3.10	.40	0	0	0
170	180	24.90	21.30	17.60	14.00	10.40	7.30	4.50	1.80	0	0	0
180	190	27.00	23.20	19.50	15.90	12.20	8.90	5.90	3.20	.50	0	0
190	200	29.40	25.10	21.40	17.80	14.10	10.50	7.40	4.60	1.90	0	0
200	210	31.80	27.20	23.30	19.70	16.00	12.40	9.00	6.00	3.30	.60	0
210	220	34.20	29.60	25.20	21.60	17.90	14.30	10.60	7.50	4.70	2.00	0
220	230	36.60	32.00	27.40	23.50	19.80	16.20	12.50	9.10	6.10	3.40	.80
230	240	39.00	34.40	29.80	25.40	21.70	18.10	14.40	10.70	7.70	4.80	2.20
240	250	41.40	36.80	32.20	27.60	23.60	20.00	16.30	12.60	9.30	6.20	3.60
250	260	43.80	39.20	34.60	30.00	25.50	21.90	18.20	14.50	10.90	7.80	5.00
260	270	46.20	41.60	37.00	32.40	27.80	23.80	20.10	16.40	12.80	9.40	6.40
270	280	48.90	44.00	39.40	34.80	30.20	25.70	22.00	18.30	14.70	11.00	7.90
280	290	51.80	46.40	41.80	37.20	32.60	28.00	23.90	20.20	16.60	12.90	9.50
290	300	54.70	49.10	44.20	39.60	35.00	30.40	25.80	22.10	18.50	14.80	11.20
300	310	57.60	52.00	46.60	42.00	37.40	32.80	28.10	24.00	20.40	16.70	13.10
310	320	60.50	54.90	49.40	44.40	39.80	35.20	30.50	25.90	22.30	18.60	15.00
320	330	63.40	57.80	52.30	46.80	42.20	37.60	32.90	28.30	24.20	20.50	16.90
330	340	66.50	60.70	55.20	49.60	44.60	40.00	35.30	30.70	26.10	22.40	18.80
340	350	69.70	63.60	58.10	52.50	47.00	42.40	37.70	33.10	28.50	24.30	20.70
350	360	72.90	66.70	61.00	55.40	49.80	44.80	40.10	35.50	30.90	26.30	22.60
360	370	76.10	69.90	63.90	58.30	52.70	47.20	42.50	37.90	33.30	28.70	24.50
370	380	79.30	73.10	66.90	61.20	55.60	50.00	44.90	40.30	35.70	31.10	26.50
380	390	82.50	76.30	70.10	64.10	58.50	52.90	47.40	42.70	38.10	33.50	28.90
390	400	85.70	79.50	73.30	67.20	61.40	55.80	50.30	45.10	40.50	35.90	31.30
400	410	88.90	82.70	76.50	70.40	64.30	58.70	53.20	47.60	42.90	38.30	33.70
410	420	92.10	85.90	79.70	73.60	67.40	61.60	56.10	50.50	45.30	40.70	36.10
420	430	95.30	89.10	82.90	76.80	70.60	64.50	59.00	53.40	47.80	43.10	38.50
430	440	98.60	92.30	86.10	80.00	73.80	67.70	61.90	56.30	50.70	45.50	40.90
440	450	102.30	95.50	89.30	83.20	77.00	70.90	64.80	59.20	53.60	48.00	43.30
450	460	106.00	98.90	92.50	86.40	80.20	74.10	67.90	62.10	56.50	50.90	45.70
460	470	109.70	102.60	95.70	89.60	83.40	77.30	71.10	65.00	59.40	53.80	48.30
470	480	113.40	106.30	99.10	92.80	86.60	80.50	74.30	68.20	62.30	56.70	51.20
480	490	117.10	110.00	102.80	96.00	89.80	83.70	77.50	71.40	65.20	59.60	54.10
490	500	120.80	113.70	106.50	99.40	93.00	86.90	80.70	74.60	68.40	62.50	57.00
500	510	124.50	117.40	110.20	103.10	96.20	90.10	83.90	77.80	71.60	65.50	59.90
510	520	128.20	121.10	113.90	106.80	99.70	93.30	87.10	81.00	74.80	68.70	62.80
520	530	131.90	124.80	117.60	110.50	103.40	96.50	90.30	84.20	78.00	71.90	65.70
530	540	135.60	128.50	121.30	114.20	107.10	100.00	93.50	87.40	81.20	75.10	68.90
540	550	139.30	132.20	125.00	117.90	110.80	103.70	96.70	90.60	84.40	78.30	72.10
550	560	143.00	135.90	128.70	121.60	114.50	107.40	100.30	93.80	87.60	81.50	75.30
560	570	146.70	139.60	132.40	125.30	118.20	111.10	104.00	97.00	90.80	84.70	78.50
570	580	150.40	143.30	136.10	129.00	121.90	114.80	107.70	100.60	94.00	87.90	81.70
580	590	154.10	147.00	139.80	132.70	125.60	118.50	111.40	104.30	97.20	91.10	84.90
590	600	157.80	150.70	143.50	136.40	129.30	122.20	115.10	108.00	100.80	94.30	88.10
600	610	161.50	154.40	147.20	140.10	133.00	125.90	118.80	111.70	104.50	97.50	91.30
610	620	165.20	158.10	150.90	143.80	136.70	129.60	122.50	115.40	108.20	101.10	94.50
620	630	168.90	161.80	154.60	147.50	140.40	133.30	126.20	119.10	111.90	104.80	97.70
630	640	172.60	165.50	158.30	151.20	144.10	137.00	129.90	122.80	115.60	108.50	101.40
640	650	176.30	169.20	162.00	154.90	147.80	140.70	133.60	126.50	119.30	112.20	105.10
650	660	180.00	172.90	165.70	158.60	151.50	144.40	137.30	130.20	123.00	115.90	108.80
660	670	183.70	176.60	169.40	162.30	155.20	148.10	141.00	133.90	126.70	119.60	112.50
		37 percent of the excess over $670 plus—										
$670 and over		185.50	178.40	171.30	164.20	157.10	149.90	142.80	135.70	128.60	121.50	114.40

tables for single and married persons paid weekly are illustrated above and on page 307.

After the proper table has been chosen, the first step in using the table is to find the line that covers the amount of wages the employee earned. Follow across this line until you reach the column corresponding to the number of withholding allowances claimed. The amount shown at this point in the table is the income

MARRIED Persons—WEEKLY Payroll Period

And the wages are—		And the number of withholding allowances claimed is—										
At least	But less than	0	1	2	3	4	5	6	7	8	9	10
		The amount of income tax to be withheld shall be—										
$310	$320	$46.20	$41.40	$37.50	$33.70	$29.80	$26.00	$22.50	$19.50	$16.40	$13.40	$10.70
320	330	48.70	43.80	39.50	35.70	31.80	28.00	24.10	21.10	18.00	14.90	12.10
330	340	51.20	46.30	41.50	37.70	33.80	30.00	26.10	22.70	19.60	16.50	13.50
340	350	53.70	48.80	44.00	39.70	35.80	32.00	28.10	24.30	21.20	18.10	15.00
350	360	56.20	51.30	46.50	41.70	37.80	34.00	30.10	26.30	22.80	19.70	16.60
360	370	58.70	53.80	49.00	44.20	39.80	36.00	32.10	28.30	24.40	21.30	18.20
370	380	61.20	56.30	51.50	46.70	41.90	38.00	34.10	30.30	26.40	22.90	19.80
380	390	63.70	58.80	54.00	49.20	44.40	40.00	36.10	32.30	28.40	24.60	21.40
390	400	66.20	61.30	56.50	51.70	46.90	42.10	38.10	34.30	30.40	26.60	23.00
400	**410**	68.70	63.80	**59.00**	54.20	49.40	44.60	40.10	36.30	32.40	28.60	24.80
410	420	71.20	66.30	61.50	56.70	51.90	47.10	42.30	38.30	34.40	30.60	26.80
420	430	73.70	68.80	64.00	59.20	54.40	49.60	44.80	40.30	36.40	32.60	28.80
430	440	76.20	71.30	66.50	61.70	56.90	52.10	47.30	42.50	38.40	34.60	30.80
440	450	78.70	73.80	69.00	64.20	59.40	54.60	49.80	45.00	40.40	36.60	32.80
450	460	81.60	76.30	71.50	66.70	61.90	57.10	52.30	47.50	42.70	38.60	34.80
460	470	84.70	78.80	74.00	69.20	64.40	59.60	54.80	50.00	45.20	40.60	36.80
470	480	87.80	81.90	76.50	71.70	66.90	62.10	57.30	52.50	47.70	42.90	38.80
480	490	90.90	85.00	79.00	74.20	69.40	64.60	59.80	55.00	50.20	45.40	40.80
490	500	94.00	88.10	82.10	76.70	71.90	67.10	62.30	57.50	52.70	47.90	43.10
500	510	97.10	91.20	85.20	79.20	74.40	69.60	64.80	60.00	55.20	50.40	45.60
510	520	100.20	94.30	88.30	82.30	76.90	72.10	67.30	62.50	57.70	52.90	48.10
520	530	103.30	97.40	91.40	85.40	79.50	74.60	69.80	65.00	60.20	55.40	50.60
530	540	106.40	100.50	94.50	88.50	82.60	77.10	72.30	67.50	62.70	57.90	53.10
540	550	109.50	103.60	97.60	91.60	85.70	79.70	74.80	70.00	65.20	60.40	55.60
550	560	112.60	106.70	100.70	94.70	88.80	82.80	77.30	72.50	67.70	62.90	58.10
560	570	116.00	109.80	103.80	97.80	91.90	85.90	80.00	75.00	70.20	65.40	60.60
570	580	119.40	112.90	106.90	100.90	95.00	89.00	83.10	77.50	72.70	67.90	63.10
580	590	122.80	116.30	110.00	104.00	98.10	92.10	86.20	80.20	75.20	70.40	65.60
590	600	126.20	119.70	113.10	107.10	101.20	95.20	89.30	83.30	77.70	72.90	68.10
600	610	129.60	123.10	116.50	110.20	104.30	98.30	92.40	86.40	80.40	75.40	70.60
610	620	133.00	126.50	119.90	113.40	107.40	101.40	95.50	89.50	83.50	77.90	73.10
620	630	136.40	129.90	123.30	116.80	110.50	104.50	98.60	92.60	86.60	80.70	75.60
630	640	139.80	133.30	126.70	120.20	113.70	107.60	101.70	95.70	89.70	83.80	78.10
640	650	143.20	136.70	130.10	123.60	117.10	110.70	104.80	98.80	92.80	86.90	80.90
650	660	146.60	140.10	133.50	127.00	120.50	113.90	107.90	101.90	95.90	90.00	84.00
660	670	150.20	143.50	136.90	130.40	123.90	117.30	111.00	105.00	99.00	93.10	87.10
670	680	153.90	146.90	140.30	133.80	127.30	120.70	114.20	108.10	102.10	96.20	90.20
680	690	157.60	150.50	143.70	137.20	130.70	124.10	117.60	111.20	105.20	99.30	93.30
690	700	161.30	154.20	147.10	140.60	134.10	127.50	121.00	114.40	108.30	102.40	96.40
700	710	165.00	157.90	150.80	144.00	137.50	130.90	124.40	117.80	111.40	105.50	99.50
710	720	168.70	161.60	154.50	147.40	140.90	134.30	127.80	121.20	114.70	108.60	102.60
720	730	172.40	165.30	158.20	151.10	144.30	137.70	131.20	124.60	118.10	111.70	105.70
730	740	176.10	169.00	161.90	154.80	147.70	141.10	134.60	128.00	121.50	115.00	108.80
740	750	179.80	172.70	165.60	158.50	151.40	144.50	138.00	131.40	124.90	118.40	111.90
750	760	183.50	176.40	169.30	162.20	155.10	147.90	141.40	134.80	128.30	121.80	115.20
760	770	187.20	180.10	173.00	165.90	158.80	151.60	144.80	138.20	131.70	125.20	118.60
770	780	190.90	183.80	176.70	169.60	162.50	155.30	148.20	141.60	135.10	128.60	122.00
780	790	194.60	187.50	180.40	173.30	166.20	159.00	151.90	145.00	138.50	132.00	125.40
790	800	198.30	191.20	184.10	177.00	169.90	162.70	155.60	148.50	141.90	135.40	128.80
800	810	202.00	194.90	187.80	180.70	173.60	166.40	159.30	152.20	145.30	138.80	132.20
810	820	205.70	198.60	191.50	184.40	177.30	170.10	163.00	155.90	148.80	142.20	135.60
820	830	209.40	202.30	195.20	188.10	181.00	173.80	166.70	159.60	152.50	145.60	139.00
830	840	213.10	206.00	198.90	191.80	184.70	177.50	170.40	163.30	156.20	149.10	142.40
840	850	216.80	209.70	202.60	195.50	188.40	181.20	174.10	167.00	159.90	152.80	145.80
850	860	220.50	213.40	206.30	199.20	192.10	184.90	177.80	170.70	163.60	156.50	149.40
		37 percent of the excess over $860 plus—										
$860 and over		222.40	215.30	208.10	201.00	193.90	186.80	179.70	172.60	165.50	158.30	151.20

tax to be withheld. For example, Rita Sanchez has two withholding allowances and earned $400 for the week. In the section of the table for married persons paid weekly that appears above, the appropriate line is the one covering wages between $400 and $410. On this line, under the column headed ''2,'' the amount of tax is given as $59. The amount of federal income tax to be withheld from each of the other hourly employees of the Kent Novelty Company is obtained in a similar manner from the sections of the weekly wage-bracket withholding tables illustrated on pages 306 and 307. The results are summarized below.

Employee	Gross Pay	Marital Status	Withholding Allowances	Income Tax to Be Withheld
Peter Brown	$320	Married, wife works	1	$ 43.80
George Dunn	230	Single	1	34.40
Carol Rosen	250	Single with dependents	3	30.00
Rita Sanchez	400	Married with dependent	2	59.00
Total				$167.20

Other Deductions Required by Law

Some states require that state income tax be withheld from employees. The principles and procedures are similar to those already explained for federal income tax withholding. Of course, the appropriate state withholding tables or tax rates must be used.

In certain states, unemployment tax or disability tax must also be deducted from employees' wages. The amounts to be deducted are determined by applying the specified rates to taxable wages as defined in the law. The procedures involved in such deductions are similar to those that have already been illustrated.

For the sake of simplicity, we will assume that no other deductions are required by law from the wages of the hourly employees of the Kent Novelty Company.

DEDUCTIONS FROM GROSS PAY NOT REQUIRED BY LAW

Many kinds of deductions not required by law are made by agreement between the employee and the employer. For example, a specified deduction from the earnings of an employee may be made at the end of each payroll period for group life insurance or group medical insurance. Employers often pay part of the cost of such programs.

Company retirement plans may be financed entirely by the employer or by the employee and employer jointly. In the latter case, employee contributions are usually based on the wages or salary earned and are usually deducted at the end of each payroll period.

In some cases, employees ask to have amounts deducted from their earnings and deposited in a bank or a company credit union, or accumulated and used to buy United States savings bonds, shares of stock, or other investments. The employee signs an authorization for such deductions and may change this authorization or withdraw it at any time. Employees who have received advances from their employers or who have bought merchandise from the firm often repay such debts through payroll deductions. When employees belong to a union, the contract between the employer and the union may specify that union dues be deducted from employee wages.

These and other possible payroll deductions increase the payroll record-keeping work but do not involve any new principles or procedures. They are handled in the same way as the required deductions for FICA and income taxes, which have been discussed in detail.

DETERMINING GROSS PAY FOR SALARIED EMPLOYEES

A salaried employee earns an agreed sum of money for each payroll period, whether it is weekly, biweekly, semimonthly, or monthly. The office clerk at the Kent Novelty Company is paid a weekly salary.

Hours Worked

Many salaried workers are covered by the provisions of the Wage and Hour Law that deal with maximum hours and overtime premium pay. The employer should keep a time record for all salaried workers of this type to make sure that their hourly earnings meet the legal requirements. (Generally, salaried employees who hold supervisory or managerial positions are not subject to such requirements and are known as *exempt employees*.)

Gross Pay

During the first week of January, Ellen West, the office clerk at the Kent Novelty Company, worked her regular schedule of 40 hours. Therefore, no overtime premium is involved and her agreed salary of $200 is her gross pay for the week.

DEDUCTIONS FROM GROSS PAY

Regardless of the method of paying an employee, FICA tax is deducted at the end of each payroll period until the base amount of earnings for the calendar year is reached. For Ellen West this tax is 7 percent of $200 for the week, or $14.

West is not married and claims only one personal exemption for federal income tax withholding purposes. The amount of income tax to be withheld from her earnings is found by referring to the weekly wage-bracket withholding table illustrated on page 306. Her gross pay of $200 is included in the line that reads "At least $200, but less than $210." Under the column for one withholding allowance, $27.20 is shown as the amount of income tax to be deducted.

RECORDING PAYROLL INFORMATION FOR EMPLOYEES

Payroll personnel must compute employee earnings and deductions accurately and promptly so that the net amounts can be paid at the scheduled times. After the computations are made, the payroll information for the period is entered in a record called a *payroll register*.

The Payroll Register

The payroll register illustrated on pages 310 and 311 shows information about the earnings and deductions of Kent's five employees for the weekly period ended January 7, 19X5. Each employee's name, withholding allowances, marital status, and regular rate can be entered in the register in advance to save time in payroll preparation. From the completed time records, the hours worked each day are entered in the register, along with the total and overtime hours for the week. Gross pay computations are made in the manner previously described and are entered in the Earnings section. These amounts are classified according to regular and overtime premium earnings. The sum of the earnings is entered in the Total column.

NAME	INC. TAX ALLOW.	MARITAL STATUS	HOURS BY DAYS							HOURS WORKED		REGULAR RATE	EARNINGS		
			S	M	T	W	T	F	S	TOTAL	OVER-TIME		REGULAR	OVERTIME PREMIUM	TOTAL
Brown, Peter	1	M		8	4	8	8	8	4	40		8.00 per hr.	320 00		320 00
Dunn, George	1	S		8	8	8	8	8	4	44	4	5.00 per hr.	220 00	10 00	230 00
Rosen, Carol	3	S		8	8	8	4	8	4	40		6.25 per hr.	250 00		250 00
Sanchez, Rita	2	M		8	8	4	8	8	4	40		10.00 per hr.	400 00		400 00
West, Ellen	1	S		8	8	8	8	8		40		200.00 per wk.	200 00		200 00
													1,390 00	10 00	1,400 00

The next two columns of the payroll register are used only when an employee has earnings that are tax exempt (above $7,000 for FUTA and above the assumed base of $38,000 for FICA). This information comes from the Cumulative Total column of the employee's individual earnings record. (See the illustration on page 313. This record is explained in a later section.)

The FICA tax and federal income tax withholdings are determined as previously described. These figures are entered in the appropriate columns of the Deductions section of the payroll register. Any other deductions are recorded with a proper explanation in the Other column. Then the deductions for each employee are subtracted from the gross pay to find the net amount owed to the employee. This figure is recorded in the Net Amount column. The last two columns of the payroll register are used to classify employee earnings as office salaries or shop wages.

When the payroll information for all employees has been entered in the payroll register, the columns are totaled as shown. The accuracy of the register should be proved at this point, before the payroll is paid. This proof is accomplished by cross-footing—adding and subtracting the column totals across the register. The total of the Regular Earnings column plus the total of the Overtime Premium column should equal the total of the Total Earnings column. The total of the Total Earnings column minus the totals of the Deductions columns should equal the total of the Net Amount column. For the payroll register shown above and on page 311, this proof would be expressed in the following way: $1,390.00 + $10.00 = $1,400.00; $1,400.00 − $98.00 − $194.40 = $1,107.60.

Once the payroll register has been checked for accuracy, the payroll information is entered in the firm's accounting records. The column totals from the payroll register supply all the necessary figures.

If there were several salaried employees at the Kent Novelty Company, the firm might use separate payroll registers for these employees and the hourly employees. However, since Kent has only one salaried employee, the earnings and deductions of all employees are recorded in the same payroll register.

January 7 19X5   Paid January 9, 19X5

TAX-EXEMPT WAGES		DEDUCTIONS			PAID		DISTRIBUTION	
FICA	FUTA	FICA TAX	INCOME TAX	OTHER	NET AMOUNT	CHECK NO.	OFFICE SALARIES	SHOP WAGES
		22 40	43 80		253 80	4725		320 00
		16 10	34 40		179 50	4726		230 00
		17 50	30 00		202 50	4727		250 00
		28 00	59 00		313 00	4728		400 00
		14 00	27 20		158 80	4729	200 00	
		98 00	194 40		1,107 60		200 00	1,200 00

THE ACCOUNTING ENTRY FOR PAYROLL

The gross pay of the employees should be charged to the appropriate expense accounts. For the production workers at the Kent Novelty Company, this account is entitled Shop Wages Expense. For the office clerk, the correct account is Office Salaries Expense. Separate liability accounts are used for each type of deduction made from the employees. A liability account is also used to record the amount of net pay due, since the accounting entry for the payroll is made before the employees are actually paid. This account is called Salaries and Wages Payable.

The entry made in Kent's general journal to record the January 7 payroll is shown below after posting has been completed.

19 X5					
Jan.	7	Office Salaries Expense	517	200 00	
		Shop Wages Expense	611	1,200 00	
		FICA Tax Payable	221		98 00
		Employee Income Tax Payable	222		194 40
		Salaries and Wages Payable	225		1,107 60
		Employee earnings, deductions, and net pay for the week ended January 7, 19X5.			

PAYING THE PAYROLL

Some businesses, particularly small firms, pay their employees in cash. However, most businesses prefer to make such payments by check. The canceled check provides a record of the payment and the employee's endorsement serves as a receipt. The use of checks avoids the inconvenience of obtaining the cash and putting it in pay envelopes and also eliminates the risk involved in handling large amounts of currency. Another convenient and safe method of paying employees, which is gaining popularity, is the direct-deposit method.

Paying in Cash

When the payroll is to be paid in cash, one check is prepared for the total amount of net pay owed to the employees. Then this check is cashed, and the firm obtains bills and coins of suitable denominations so that the correct net pay amount can be inserted in the pay envelope of each worker. The pay envelope usually has an information block printed on it. This area is used to enter the earnings, deductions, and net pay for the period. The employees may be asked to sign a receipt or to sign on their lines in the payroll register as evidence that the pay was received.

Paying by Check

When employees are paid by check, an individual check is prepared for each worker. The check number is entered in the Check Number column of the payroll register on the same line as the employee's other information. (See the payroll register illustrated on pages 310 and 311.) Information about the employee's gross earnings, deductions, and net pay is usually shown on a stub of the payroll check. The employee detaches the stub and keeps it as a record of his or her payroll data for the period.

Of course, the payroll check is issued to the employee for the net pay amount. The effect of the payments is to decrease the Salaries and Wages Payable account and to decrease the Cash account. Thus, after the checks are prepared, the amounts are recorded in the cash payments journal by debiting Salaries and Wages Payable and crediting Cash.

Payroll checks may be drawn on the firm's regular bank account or on a separate payroll bank account. If a separate payroll bank account is used, one check is usually drawn on the regular bank account for the net amount of wages and salaries payable and deposited in the payroll bank account. This check is entered in the cash payments journal as a debit to Salaries and Wages Payable and a credit to Cash. Since individual checks totaling this amount are immediately issued from the payroll bank account, this account never has a balance. Thus it does not appear on the financial statements.

Paying by Direct Deposit

A method of paying employees that is becoming more common is the direct-deposit method. Under this method, a firm has its bank transfer the net pay of each employee from its own account to the employee's personal checking account. The employee receives a statement showing his or her earnings, deductions, and net pay for the period and the date when the net pay was deposited.

INDIVIDUAL EARNINGS RECORDS

At the beginning of each year, or when a new employee is hired during the year, an *individual earnings record* (sometimes called a *compensation record*) is set up for each worker. This record contains the employee's name, address, social security number, date of birth, number of withholding allowances claimed, rate of pay, and any other information that may be needed. The details for each pay period are posted to the employee's individual earnings record from the payroll register. The record for Peter Brown illustrated on page 313 shows the data for the first payroll in January.

Note that the details shown in this record include the payroll date (entered in the Week Ended column), the date paid, the hours worked, the earnings (broken down into regular earnings and overtime premium earnings as indicated in the

NAME Peter Brown					**RATE** $8 per hour			**SOC. SEC. NO.** 324-76-1245				
ADDRESS 24 Oak Street, Manchester, NH 03104								**DATE OF BIRTH** Jan. 23, 1958				
WITHHOLDING ALLOWANCES 1								**MARITAL STATUS** Married				

PAYROLL NO.	DATE		HOURS WORKED		EARNINGS				DEDUCTIONS				
	WK. END.	PAID	TOT. HRS.	O.T. HRS.	REGULAR AMOUNT	OVERTIME PREMIUM AMOUNT	TOTAL AMOUNT	CUMU-LATIVE TOTAL	FICA TAX	INCOME TAX	OTHER	NET PAY
1	1/7	1/9	40		320 00		320 00	320 00	22 40	43 80		253 80

payroll register), each deduction, and the net pay. One item is not obtained from the payroll register—the cumulative total. This amount is the employee's year-to-date gross pay. It is computed whenever a payroll entry is made in an earnings record.

The individual earnings records are usually totaled monthly and at the end of each calendar quarter. In this way, they provide information needed in making tax payments and filing tax returns, as described in the next chapter.

COMPLETING JANUARY PAYROLLS

In order to complete the January payrolls for the Kent Novelty Company, assume that all employees worked the same number of hours a week during the month as they did in the first week. Thus, they also had the same earnings, deductions, and net pay each week.

Journal Entries

As explained already, a general journal entry is made to record the payroll for all employees of the Kent Novelty Company. Since we are assuming an identical payroll for each week of the month, the four weekly payrolls require entries similar to the one shown on page 311.

Postings to Ledger Accounts

The entries for the weekly payrolls at Kent are posted from the general journal to the payroll accounts in the general ledger. At the end of January, these accounts appear as shown below and on page 314.

	Office Salaries Expense						No. 517
DATE	EXPLANATION	POST. REF.	DEBIT	CREDIT	BALANCE	DR. CR.	
19X5							
Jan. 1	Balance	✓			9,600 00	Dr.	
7		J12	200 00		9,800 00	Dr.	
14		J12	200 00		10,000 00	Dr.	
21		J12	200 00		10,200 00	Dr.	
28		J12	200 00		10,400 00	Dr.	

Shop Wages Expense   No. 611

DATE		EXPLANATION	POST. REF.	DEBIT		CREDIT		BALANCE		DR. CR.
19	X5									
Jan.	1	Balance	✓					54,400	00	Dr.
	7		J12	1,200	00			55,600	00	Dr.
	14		J12	1,200	00			56,800	00	Dr.
	21		J12	1,200	00			58,000	00	Dr.
	28		J12	1,200	00			59,200	00	Dr.

FICA Tax Payable   No. 221

DATE		EXPLANATION	POST. REF.	DEBIT		CREDIT		BALANCE		DR. CR.
19	X5									
Jan.	7		J12			98	00	98	00	Cr.
	14		J12			98	00	196	00	Cr.
	21		J12			98	00	294	00	Cr.
	28		J12			98	00	392	00	Cr.

Employee Income Tax Payable   No. 221

DATE		EXPLANATION	POST. REF.	DEBIT		CREDIT		BALANCE		DR. CR.
19	X5									
Jan.	7		J12			194	40	194	40	Cr.
	14		J12			194	40	388	80	Cr.
	21		J12			194	40	583	20	Cr.
	28		J12			194	40	777	60	Cr.

Salaries and Wages Payable   No. 225

DATE		EXPLANATION	POST. REF.	DEBIT		CREDIT		BALANCE		DR. CR.
19	X5									
Jan.	7		J12			1,107	60	1,107	60	Cr.
	9		CP12	1,107	60			—0—		
	14		J12			1,107	60	1,107	60	Cr.
	16		CP12	1,107	60			—0—		
	21		J12			1,107	60	1,107	60	Cr.
	23		CP12	1,107	60			—0—		
	28		J12			1,107	60	1,107	60	Cr.
	30		CP12	1,107	60			—0—		

As previously mentioned, the earnings and deductions of each employee are posted to an individual earnings record. At the end of each month, the postings to these records for the period can be checked against the amounts posted to the payroll accounts in the general ledger. Each earnings record is totaled for the month. Then a list is made of the column totals for gross earnings, for each deduction, and for net pay, usually on a calculator. The totals from the earnings records shown on the calculator tape are compared with the current month's postings to the corresponding general ledger accounts. Any differences are found and corrected.

The individual earnings record for Peter Brown at the end of January is shown below. The record for each of the other employees of the Kent Novelty Company is similar. The calculator tapes that are also illustrated below list the total earnings, deductions, and net pay entered in the individual earnings records during January.

EARNINGS RECORD FOR 19X5

NAME Peter Brown RATE $8 per hour SOC. SEC. NO. 324-76-1245
ADDRESS 24 Oak Street, Manchester, NH 03104 DATE OF BIRTH Jan. 23, 1958
WITHHOLDING ALLOWANCES 1 MARITAL STATUS Married

PAYROLL NO.	DATE		HOURS WORKED		EARNINGS				DEDUCTIONS			NET PAY
	WK. END.	PAID	TOT. HRS.	O.T. HRS.	REGULAR AMOUNT	OVERTIME PREMIUM AMOUNT	TOTAL AMOUNT	CUMU-LATIVE TOTAL	FICA TAX	INCOME TAX	OTHER	NET PAY
1	1/7	1/9	40		320 00		320 00	320 00	22 40	43 80		253 80
2	1/14	1/16	40		320 00		320 00	640 00	22 40	43 80		253 80
3	1/21	1/23	40		320 00		320 00	960 00	22 40	43 80		253 80
4	1/28	1/30	40		320 00		320 00	1,280 00	22 40	43 80		253 80
	January				1,280 00		1,280 00		89 60	175 20		1,015 20

Gross Earnings	FICA Tax Payable	Income Tax Payable	Net Pay
.00 *	.00 *	.00 *	.00 *
1,280 .00	89 .60	175 .20	1,015 .20
920 .00	64 .40	137 .60	718 .00
1,000 .00	70 .00	120 .00	810 .00
1,600 .00	112 .00	236 .00	1,252 .00
800 .00	56 .00	108 .80	635 .20
5,600 .00 *	392 .00 *	777 .60 *	4,430 .40 *

Compare the calculator tapes with the postings to the general ledger accounts shown on pages 313 and 314. Notice that the total gross pay recorded in the earnings records equals the sum of the debits to Office Salaries Expense and

Shop Wages Expense during January. Similarly, the totals for FICA tax payable and employee income tax payable on the calculator tapes (which represent the amounts from the individual earnings records) agree with the postings to the general ledger accounts for these items. With the following proof completed, the records are ready for the payroll transactions of the next month.

PROOF OF POSTINGS TO PAYROLL ACCOUNTS

Earnings:	Office Salaries Expense	517	$ 800.00	
	Shop Wages Expense	611	4,800.00	$5,600.00 (Dr.)
Deductions:	FICA Tax Payable	221		$ 392.00 (Cr.)
	Employee Income Tax Payable	222		777.60 (Cr.)
Net Pay:	Salaries and Wages Payable	225		4,430.40 (Cr.)
				$5,600.00 (Cr.)

RECORDING THE LIABILITY FOR UNPAID SALARIES AND WAGES

In many cases, it is not possible for the employer to pay all salaries and wages in the accounting period in which they are earned. As a result, there are amounts owed to employees at the end of the period. These are called *accrued salaries and wages payable*. When the total amount is large enough to be important, the accountant should make an adjusting entry at the end of the period to record the fact that the expense has been incurred and the liability exists. The adjusting entry appears first on the worksheet and is then journalized and posted.

At the end of the annual accounting period on January 31, 19X5, the accountant for the Kent Novelty Company determined that the firm had the following accrued amounts for employee earnings: salary of $80 owed to the office clerk and wages of $468 owed to the production workers. These amounts covered Monday, January 30, and Tuesday, January 31. After recording the necessary adjustments on the worksheet, the accountant made the general journal entries shown below. These entries allow the firm to report the correct expenses on the income statement and the correct liabilities on the balance sheet.

19	X5					
Jan.	31	Office Salaries Expense	517	80 00		
		Salaries and Wages Payable	225		80 00	
		Salary accrued for January 30 and 31.				
	31	Shop Wages Expense	611	468 00		
		Salaries and Wages Payable	225		468 00	
		Wages accrued for January 30 and 31.				

Each adjusting entry consists of a debit to the appropriate expense account and a credit to Salaries and Wages Payable. Note that only the gross pay is recorded as an expense and as a liability. No recognition is given to the withholding amounts because the withholdings are not technically made until the employees are paid.

PRINCIPLES AND PROCEDURES SUMMARY

The main objective of payroll work is to compute the wages or salaries owed to employees and to pay these amounts promptly. Other important objectives are the proper classification of wages and salaries so that they are charged to the appropriate expense accounts and the proper computation, payment, and reporting of tax amounts.

The employer is required to withhold at least two taxes from the employee's pay: the employee's FICA tax and federal income tax. Instructions for computing the amount of each of these taxes are provided by the government to the employer. Other required deductions may be made for state and city income taxes. Many employees also have voluntary deductions that are made by agreement between the employee and the employer.

The employer keeps a record of the employees' earnings, deductions, and net pay for each payroll period in a payroll register. Information from this record is used to prepare a payroll entry in the general journal. At the beginning of each year, the employer sets up individual earnings records for the employees. The amounts that appear in the payroll register are posted to the individual earnings records throughout the year so that the firm can have detailed payroll information available for each employee.

MANAGERIAL IMPLICATIONS

Management must be very careful that a firm's payroll procedures and records comply with the provisions of federal, state, and local laws. If the business is covered by the Fair Labor Standards Act, its payments to employees must meet the minimum wage and overtime pay requirements of that law. Similarly, care should be taken that tax withholdings are made from employee earnings in accordance with any laws that apply to the business.

Wages and salaries form a large part of the operating expenses of most firms. Thus, an adequate set of payroll records is also essential as an aid to management in controlling expenses. These records pinpoint the labor cost for each area of the business by showing management exactly what amounts have been spent for sales salaries, office salaries, and factory wages. These records also indicate how much of the amount spent in each area was for overtime. Although overtime is fully justified in many cases, it may also be a sign of inefficiency. Large or frequent expenditures for overtime should therefore be investigated.

To prevent errors and fraud, management should make sure that the payroll records are audited carefully and that payroll procedures are evaluated periodically. The overstatement of hours worked and the issuance of checks to nonexistent employees are common types of fraud in the payroll area. Management must be alert to the potential for dishonesty in this area.

REVIEW QUESTIONS

1. What are the two major parts of the social security system?
2. How is each part of the social security system financed?
3. How does the Fair Labor Standards Act affect the wages paid by many firms?
4. What is time and a half?
5. Under the Fair Labor Standards Act, what information must covered employers keep for each employee in their payroll records?
6. What is the purpose of worker's compensation insurance?
7. How are earnings determined when employees are paid on the hourly-rate basis?
8. How does the salary basis differ from the hourly-rate basis of paying employees?
9. What two deductions from employee earnings are required by federal law?
10. Give four examples of deductions from employee earnings that are not required by law but are sometimes made by agreement between the employee and the employer.
11. What two methods can be used in determining the amount of FICA tax to withhold from an employee's gross pay?
12. What publication of the Internal Revenue Service provides information about the current federal income tax rates and the procedures that employers should use to withhold this tax?
13. What is the simplest method for finding the amount of federal income tax to deduct from an employee's gross pay?
14. What factors determine how much federal income tax an employee owes?
15. What are the three methods of paying employees?
16. How is a payroll bank account used?
17. How does the direct-deposit method of paying employees operate?
18. What is the purpose of the payroll register?
19. What information does an individual earnings record contain?
20. What adjusting entry is made for accrued wages at the end of an accounting period?

MANAGERIAL DISCUSSION QUESTIONS

1. Why should management make sure that a firm has an adequate set of payroll records?
2. How can detailed payroll records aid management in controlling expenses?
3. Why should management carefully check the amount being spent for overtime?
4. The new controller for the Ellis Company, a manufacturing firm, has suggested to management that the business change from paying the factory employees in cash to paying them by check. What reasons would you offer to support this suggestion?

EXERCISES

EXERCISE 13-1   **Computing gross pay.** The hourly rates of four employees of the Vernon Company are shown below along with the hours that these employees worked during one week. Determine the gross pay of each employee.

EMPLOYEE NO.	REGULAR HOURLY RATE	HOURS WORKED
1	$6.00	38
2	7.60	40
3	6.50	40
4	8.20	35

EXERCISE 13-2   **Computing regular earnings, overtime premium, and gross pay.** During one week four production employees of the Quinn Manufacturing Company worked the number of hours shown below. All of these employees receive overtime pay at one and a half times their regular hourly rate for any hours worked beyond 40 in a week. Determine the regular earnings, overtime premium, and gross pay for each employee.

EMPLOYEE NO.	REGULAR HOURLY RATE	HOURS WORKED
1	$9.00	43
2	8.40	47
3	7.80	45
4	9.50	44

EXERCISE 13-3   **Computing FICA tax withholdings.** At the end of December 19X5, the four employees of the Keystone Data Processing Service received the monthly salaries listed below. Determine the amount of FICA tax to be withheld from each employee's gross pay for December. The year-to-date earnings of the employees as of November 30 are also shown below. Assume a 7 percent FICA rate and a base of $38,000 for the calendar year.

EMPLOYEE NO.	DECEMBER SALARY	YEAR-TO-DATE EARNINGS THROUGH NOVEMBER 30
1	$2,500	$27,500
2	3,250	35,750
3	1,825	20,075
4	2,260	24,860

EXERCISE 13-4   **Determining federal income tax withholdings.** Data about the marital status, withholding allowances, and weekly salaries of the four office workers at the Judd Insurance Agency are listed on page 320. Use the tax tables on pages 306 and 307 to find the amount of federal income tax to be deducted from each employee's gross pay.

EMPLOYEE NO.	MARITAL STATUS	WITHHOLDING ALLOWANCES	WEEKLY SALARY
1	S	1	$240
2	M	3	375
3	S	2	220
4	M	1	330

EXERCISE 13-5   **Computing employee earnings.** During the week ended May 7, 19X5, the three employees of the DePalma TV Repair Service worked the hours shown below at the specified hourly rates. The firm pays overtime at one and a half times the regular hourly rate for any hours worked beyond 40 in a week. Determine the regular earnings, overtime premium, and gross pay for each employee. Also determine the totals for all employees.

EMPLOYEE NO.	REGULAR HOURLY RATE	HOURS WORKED
1	$7.20	47
2	6.60	42
3	7.50	44

EXERCISE 13-6   **Computing employee deductions.** Data about the marital status and withholding allowances of the three employees of the DePalma TV Repair Service are listed below. Find the FICA tax, federal income tax, and total deductions for each employee for the week ended May 7, 19X5. Also compute the totals for all employees. Obtain the gross pay for each employee from your solution to Exercise 13-5. Assume a 7 percent FICA rate, and consider all earnings taxable. To determine the amount of federal income tax, refer to the tax tables on pages 306 and 307.

EMPLOYEE NO.	MARITAL STATUS	WITHHOLDING ALLOWANCES
1	M	4
2	S	1
3	M	2

EXERCISE 13-7   **Computing net pay.** Determine the net pay of each of the three employees of the DePalma TV Repair Service for the week ended May 7, 19X5. Also determine the total net pay for all employees. Obtain the necessary data from your solutions to Exercises 13-5 and 13-6.

EXERCISE 13-8   **Journalizing the payroll.** Prepare a general journal entry to record the weekly payroll of the DePalma TV Repair Service on May 7, 19X5. Obtain the necessary amounts from your solutions to Exercises 13-5, 13-6, and 13-7. The firm uses the following payroll accounts.

221 FICA Tax Payable
222 Employee Income Tax Payable
225 Wages Payable
517 Wages Expense

EXERCISE 13-9 **Journalizing the payroll.** On April 30, 19X1, the payroll register of the Carlton Distributing Company showed the following totals for the month: earnings, $8,470; FICA tax, $592.90; income tax, $1,016.40; and net pay, $6,860.70. Of the total earnings, $6,120 was for the sales staff and $2,350 was for the office employees. Prepare a general journal entry to record the monthly payroll of the firm on April 30, 19X1. The firm uses the following payroll accounts.

221	FICA Tax Payable	511	Sales Salaries Expense
222	Employee Income Tax Payable	531	Office Salaries Expense
225	Salaries Payable		

EXERCISE 13-10 **Journalizing an adjustment for accrued salaries.** On December 31, 19X8, the end of the annual accounting period at the Simon Company, the firm owed salaries of $1,765 to its employees. These salaries will not be paid until January 4, 19X9. Prepare a general journal entry to record the adjustment for the firm's accrued salaries. The company uses the following payroll accounts.

221 FICA Tax Payable
222 Employee Income Tax Payable
225 Salaries Payable
514 Salaries Expense

PROBLEMS

PROBLEM 13-1 **Preparing a payroll register and journalizing the payroll.** The Lawrence Medical Testing Laboratory has four employees and pays them on an hourly basis. During the week ended January 7, 19X5, these employees worked the number of hours shown on page 322. Information about their hourly rates, marital status, and withholding allowances also appears on page 322.

Instructions
1. Enter the basic payroll information for each employee in a payroll register. Record the employee's name, number of withholding allowances, marital status, total and overtime hours, and regular hourly rate. Consider any hours worked beyond 40 in the week as overtime hours.
2. Compute the regular earnings, overtime premium, and total earnings for each employee. Enter the figures in the payroll register.
3. Compute the amount of FICA tax to be withheld from each employee's total earnings. Assume a 7 percent FICA rate. Enter the figures in the payroll register.
4. Determine the amount of federal income tax to be withheld from each employee's total earnings. Use the tax tables on pages 306 and 307. Enter the figures in the payroll register.
5. Compute the net pay of each employee, and enter the figures in the payroll register.
6. Total and prove the payroll register.
7. Prepare a general journal entry to record the payroll for the week ended January 7, 19X5. The firm's payroll accounts include Wages Payable and Wages Expense.

EMPLOYEE	HOURS WORKED	REGULAR HOURLY RATE	MARITAL STATUS	WITHHOLDING ALLOWANCES
Robert Katz	44	$9.30	M	4
Joan McNally	42	8.20	S	1
Frank Oliveri	36	8.50	S	2
Marion Parks	46	9.00	M	1

PROBLEM 13-2   **Preparing a payroll register and journalizing the payroll.** Richard Gomez operates the Dade Lawn Care Service. He has three employees and pays them on an hourly basis. During the week ended July 21, 19X1, his employees worked the number of hours shown below. Information about their hourly rates, marital status, and withholding allowances also appears below.

Instructions   1. Enter the basic payroll information for each employee in a payroll register. Record the employee's name, number of withholding allowances, marital status, total and overtime hours, and regular hourly rate. Consider any hours worked beyond 40 in the week as overtime hours.
2. Compute the regular earnings, overtime premium, and total earnings for each employee. Enter the figures in the payroll register.
3. Compute the amount of FICA tax to be withheld from each employee's total earnings. Assume a 7 percent FICA rate. Enter the figures in the payroll register.
4. Determine the amount of federal income tax to be withheld from each employee's total earnings. Use the tax tables on pages 306 and 307. Enter the figures in the payroll register.
5. Compute the net pay of each employee, and enter the figures in the payroll register.
6. Total and prove the payroll register.
7. Prepare a general journal entry to record the payroll for the week ended July 21, 19X1. The firm's payroll accounts include Wages Payable and Wages Expense.

EMPLOYEE	HOURS WORKED	REGULAR HOURLY RATE	MARITAL STATUS	WITHHOLDING ALLOWANCES
Peter DeSalvo	43	$7.50	M	3
Thomas Kane	38	6.40	S	1
Susan Ross	45	7.20	M	2

PROBLEM 13-3   **Computing and recording an adjustment for accrued wages.** When the annual accounting period ended on December 31, 19X7, at the Urban Delivery Service, the firm owed wages for two days of work to its four employees. These wages will not be paid until January 19X8.

Instructions   1. Compute the total amount of accrued wages. Use the data given on page 323. No overtime is involved.
2. Prepare a general journal entry to record the accrued wages on December 31, 19X7.

EMPLOYEE	HOURS WORKED ON DEC. 30 AND 31	REGULAR HOURLY RATE
James Barry	16	$6.50
Alice Beck	14	6.80
Glen Larson	12	7.30
Joyce McGill	16	6.60

ALTERNATE PROBLEMS

PROBLEM 13-1A

Preparing a payroll register and journalizing the payroll. The Royce Film Processing Laboratory has four employees and pays them on an hourly basis. During the week ended January 21, 19X5, these employees worked the number of hours shown below. Information about their hourly rates, marital status, and withholding allowances also appears below.

Instructions

1. Enter the basic payroll information for each employee in a payroll register. Record the employee's name, number of withholding allowances, marital status, total and overtime hours, and regular hourly rate. Consider any hours worked beyond 40 in the week as overtime hours.
2. Compute the regular earnings, overtime premium, and total earnings for each employee. Enter the figures in the payroll register.
3. Compute the amount of FICA tax to be withheld from each employee's total earnings. Assume a 7 percent FICA rate. Enter the figures in the payroll register.
4. Determine the amount of federal income tax to be withheld from each employee's total earnings. Use the tax tables on pages 306 and 307. Enter the figures in the payroll register.
5. Compute the net pay of each employee, and enter the figures in the payroll register.
6. Total and prove the payroll register.
7. Prepare a general journal entry to record the payroll for the week ended January 21, 19X5. The firm's payroll accounts include Wages Payable and Wages Expense.

EMPLOYEE	HOURS WORKED	REGULAR HOURLY RATE	MARITAL STATUS	WITHHOLDING ALLOWANCES
Judith Abrams	43	$9.40	M	3
Keith O'Dell	46	8.80	M	4
Donna Shaw	36	8.60	S	1
Paul Zachary	42	9.10	S	2

PROBLEM 13-2A

Preparing a payroll register and journalizing the payroll. Eileen Patrick operates the Greenfield Catering Service. She has three employees and pays them on an hourly basis. During the week ended June 14, 19X1, her employees worked the number of hours shown on page 324. Information about their hourly rates, marital status, and withholding allowances also appears on page 324.

Instructions

1. Enter the basic payroll information for each employee in a payroll register. Record the employee's name, number of withholding allowances, marital status, total and overtime hours, and regular hourly rate. Consider any hours worked beyond 40 in the week as overtime hours.

2. Compute the regular earnings, overtime premium, and total earnings for each employee. Enter the figures in the payroll register.

3. Compute the amount of FICA tax to be withheld from each employee's total earnings. Assume a 7 percent FICA rate. Enter the figures in the payroll register.

4. Determine the amount of federal income tax to be withheld from each employee's total earnings. Use the tax tables on pages 306 and 307. Enter the figures in the payroll register.

5. Compute the net pay of each employee, and enter the figures in the payroll register.

6. Total and prove the payroll register.

7. Prepare a general journal entry to record the payroll for the week ended June 14, 19X1. The firm's payroll accounts include Wages Payable and Wages Expense.

EMPLOYEE	HOURS WORKED	REGULAR HOURLY RATE	MARITAL STATUS	WITHHOLDING ALLOWANCES
Ruth Adams	42	$7.40	M	2
Lynn Brown	35	6.50	S	1
Joseph Corso	44	7.00	M	1

PROBLEM 13-3A **Computing and recording an adjustment for accrued wages.** When the annual accounting period ended on January 31, 19X8, at the Circle Clothing Store, the firm owed wages for three days of work to its four employees. These wages will not be paid until February, after the start of the new accounting period.

Instructions

1. Compute the total amount of accrued wages. Use the data given below. No overtime is involved.

2. Prepare a general journal entry to record the accrued wages on January 31, 19X8.

EMPLOYEE	HOURS WORKED ON JAN. 29, 30, AND 31	REGULAR HOURLY RATE
Anna Alvarez	24	$6.00
Mark Dillon	18	5.80
Jennifer Reed	24	5.50
Carl Wyzanski	21	5.90

Businesses are required by law to act as collection agents for the FICA tax and the income tax due from employees. Firms must deduct, account for, and transmit these taxes to the government. They are also responsible for paying unemployment taxes and reporting employee earnings to the government. This chapter explains how the accountant makes tax payments and files the required tax returns and reports.

PAYROLL TAXES, DEPOSITS, AND REPORTS

CHANGES IN TAX RATES AND BASES

In recent years, frequent and substantial changes have been made in the social security (FICA) and federal unemployment (FUTA) taxes. The rates have increased, and the maximum amount of taxable wages has risen. Businesses must always be sure to use the latest rates and bases and follow the latest regulations. *Circular E,* the *Employer's Tax Guide,* and other publications of the Internal Revenue Service are intended to help employers keep informed about current developments and requirements.

DEPOSIT OF FICA TAXES AND INCOME TAXES WITHHELD

Generally, federal income taxes withheld from employee earnings and FICA taxes (both the employee and employer shares) are deposited in a Federal Reserve Bank or other authorized financial institution. Most commercial banks are authorized to receive such deposits. The employer enters the amount of the deposit on a preprinted government form, which must be included with a check for the taxes that are due. This form is the Federal Tax Deposit, Form 8109. The frequency of deposits is determined by the amount owed.

If at the end of the quarter the total undeposited taxes are less than $500, no deposit is required. The taxes may be paid to the Internal Revenue Service when Form 941 is filed (see page 330), or they may be deposited by the end of the following month.

If at the end of any month of the quarter the total undeposited taxes for the quarter are $500 or more but less than $3,000, the taxes must be deposited within 15 days after the end of the month. If the taxes are less than $500, they may be carried over to the next month within the quarter.

If at the end of any eighth-monthly period (approximately one-eighth of a month) the total undeposited taxes for the quarter amount to $3,000 or more, they must be deposited within three banking days after the end of the eighth-monthly period. An eighth-monthly period ends on the 3d, 7th, 11th, 15th, 19th, 22d, 25th, and last day of any month. (Local holidays observed by authorized financial institutions, Saturdays, Sundays, and legal holidays are not counted as banking days.)

Employer's FICA Tax

Since a business pays the FICA tax at the same rate and on the same taxable wages as its employees, the amount of tax the firm owes is usually the same as that deducted from the employees. However, small differences can occur due to rounding off individual tax deductions. Some firms handle this situation by matching the amount deducted from the employees when making the tax deposit. Any final difference is settled on the quarterly tax return, Form 941.

In the case of the Kent Novelty Company, all salaries and wages paid during the week of January 7, 19X5 were subject to FICA tax. At the assumed rate of 7 percent, the firm therefore owed $98 as its share of the FICA tax ($1,400 × .07). This is exactly the same as the amount withheld from employee earnings for FICA tax. (Refer to the total of the FICA Tax column in the payroll register illustrated on page 311.)

Because the Kent Novelty Company keeps its accounting records on the accrual basis, its expense and liability for the employer's FICA tax are recorded in the general journal at the end of each payroll period, as shown below. The amount of the tax is debited to an account called Payroll Taxes Expense and credited to FICA Tax Payable, the same liability account used to record the employees' contribution. (The entry illustrated here also involves the employer's expense and liabilities for unemployment taxes, which are discussed in a later section of this chapter.)

19X5				
Jan. 7	Payroll Taxes Expense	543	127 40	
	FICA Tax Payable	221		98 00
	Federal Unemployment Tax Payable	223		11 20
	State Unemployment Tax Payable	224		18 20
	Employer's payroll taxes for the week ended January 7, 19X5.			

Deposit of January Taxes

At the end of January 19X5, the accounting records of the Kent Novelty Company contained the following information about tax deductions from employee earnings and the employer's FICA tax for the month.

Employees' FICA Tax Deducted	$ 392.00
Employees' Federal Income Tax Deducted	777.60
Employer's FICA Tax	392.00
Total	$1,561.60

Since the total taxes owed at the end of January exceed $500 but are less than $3,000, the amount must be deposited in an authorized bank by February 15, 19X5. Kent makes the necessary payment by writing a check to the depository bank, which in this case is the Security National Bank. The transaction is entered in the cash payments journal, as shown on page 327. Notice that

FICA Tax Payable is debited for $784 and Employee Income Tax Payable is debited for $777.60 to record the decrease in these two liabilities. Cash is credited for the total amount of the deposit, $1,561.60.

			ACCOUNTS PAYABLE		OTHER ACCOUNTS DEBIT			PURCH. DISCOUNT CREDIT	CASH CREDIT
DATE	CHECK NO.	EXPLANATION	✓	DEBIT	ACCOUNT TITLE	POST. REF.	AMOUNT		
Feb. 14	4810	Deposit of Jan. taxes			FICA Tax Payable	221	784 00		
					Empl. Inc. Tax Pay.	222	777 60		1,561 60

CASH PAYMENTS JOURNAL for Month of February 19X5 — Page 2

As mentioned already, the deposit must be accompanied by a properly filled out Federal Tax Deposit, Form 8109. When this machine-readable form is processed, the amount paid is credited to the employer by the Internal Revenue Service. The Form 8109 filed in February by the Kent Novelty Company is shown below. This form covers the payment of the January FICA taxes and federal income tax withholdings owed by the firm.

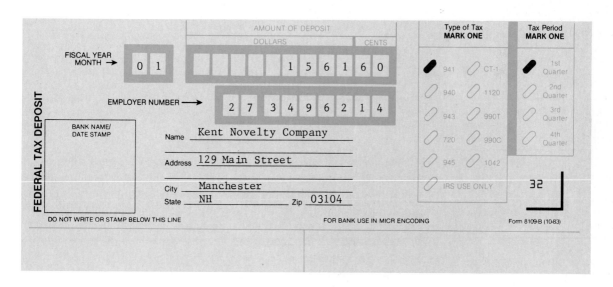

February Payroll Records

There were four weekly payroll periods in February for the Kent Novelty Company. To simplify the example, assume that each hourly employee worked the same number of hours each week as in January and had the same gross pay and deductions. Assume also that the office clerk, Ellen West, earned her regular salary and had the same deductions as in January. The individual earnings records for the employees were posted and proved against the payroll accounts in the general ledger as previously described. Then a tax deposit form was prepared and the taxes deposited in the bank. Finally, an entry was made in the cash payments journal to record the deposit.

March Payroll Records

In March, the Kent Novelty Company had five weekly payroll periods, making a total of 13 weekly periods for the quarter. Assume again that the earnings and deductions of the employees were the same for each week as in January and February. The firm therefore owed a total of $1,952 for March FICA taxes and federal income tax withholdings. The necessary tax deposit was made before the due date of April 15 and recorded in the cash payments journal.

Quarterly Summary of Earnings Records

At the end of each calendar quarter, the individual earnings records are totaled for the quarter. This involves adding the monthly totals in the Earnings, Deductions, and Net Pay sections of each employee's record. The sums are placed on the line for the appropriate quarter. The cumulative total of the employee's earnings is also entered on this line. The record for Peter Brown, completely posted and summarized for the first quarter, is illustrated on the next page.

The quarterly totals for each employee of the Kent Novelty Company, taken from the individual earnings records, are shown below.

Employee	Total Earnings	FICA Tax	Income Tax
Peter Brown	$ 4,160	$ 291.20	$ 569.40
George Dunn	2,990	209.30	447.20
Carol Rosen	3,250	227.50	390.00
Rita Sanchez	5,200	364.00	767.00
Ellen West	2,600	182.00	353.60
Totals	$18,200	$1,274.00	$2,527.20

EMPLOYER'S QUARTERLY FEDERAL TAX RETURN

During the month following the end of each calendar quarter (April, July, October, and January), most employers must file with the Internal Revenue Service a tax report called the Employer's Quarterly Federal Tax Return, Form 941. This tax report provides information about the total wages and other employee earnings subject to federal income tax withholding, the total wages and tips subject to FICA tax, the total of the taxes owed for each of the deposit periods in the quarter, and the total of the deposits made by the employer. In effect, Form 941 serves as a verification of the employer's compliance with the applicable laws.

Schedule for Filing Form 941

Form 941 must be filed quarterly by all employers subject to federal income tax withholding, FICA tax, or both, with certain exceptions as specified in *Circular E*. The due date for the return and any tax payment due is the last day of the month following the end of each calendar quarter. If all taxes were deposited during the calendar quarter, the employer may file the return by the 10th day of

EARNINGS RECORD FOR 19X5

NAME Peter Brown   **RATE** $8 per hour   **SOC. SEC. NO.** 324-76-1245

ADDRESS 24 Oak Street, Manchester, NH 03104   **DATE OF BIRTH** Jan. 23, 1958

WITHHOLDING ALLOWANCES 1   **MARITAL STATUS** Married

PAYROLL NO.	DATE WK. END.	DATE PAID	HOURS WORKED TOT. HRS.	HOURS WORKED O.T. HRS.	EARNINGS REGULAR AMOUNT	EARNINGS OVERTIME PREMIUM AMOUNT	EARNINGS TOTAL AMOUNT	CUMULATIVE TOTAL	DEDUCTIONS FICA TAX	DEDUCTIONS INCOME TAX	DEDUCTIONS OTHER	NET PAY
1	1/7	1/9	40		320 00		320 00	320 00	22 40	43 80		253 80
2	1/14	1/16	40		320 00		320 00	640 00	22 40	43 80		253 80
3	1/21	1/23	40		320 00		320 00	960 00	22 40	43 80		253 80
4	1/28	1/30	40		320 00		320 00	1,280 00	22 40	43 80		253 80
	January				1,280 00		1,280 00		89 60	175 20		1,015 20
1	2/4	2/6	40		320 00		320 00	1,600 00	22 40	43 80		253 80
2	2/11	2/13	40		320 00		320 00	1,920 00	22 40	43 80		253 80
3	2/18	2/20	40		320 00		320 00	2,240 00	22 40	43 80		253 80
4	2/25	2/27	40		320 00		320 00	2,560 00	22 40	43 80		253 80
	February				1,280 00		1,280 00		89 60	175 20		1,015 20
1	3/3	3/5	40		320 00		320 00	2,880 00	22 40	43 80		253 80
2	3/10	3/12	40		320 00		320 00	3,200 00	22 40	43 80		253 80
3	3/17	3/19	40		320 00		320 00	3,520 00	22 40	43 80		253 80
4	3/24	3/25	40		320 00		320 00	3,840 00	22 40	43 80		253 80
5	3/31	3/31	40		320 00		320 00	4,160 00	22 40	43 80		253 80
	March				1,600 00		1,600 00		112 00	219 00		1,269 00
	First Quarter				4,160 00		4,160 00	4,160 00	291 20	569 40		3,299 40

the second month following the end of the quarter. The accountant for the Kent Novelty Company prepared the business's Form 941 for the first quarter of 19X5 as shown on page 330.

Completing Form 941

Much of the data needed to complete Form 941 is obtained from the quarterly summary of earnings records illustrated on page 328. The top of Form 941 shows the employer's name and identification number. The total of the wages and other employee earnings subject to withholding ($18,200) is entered on Line 2, and the total income tax withheld ($2,527.20) is entered on Line 3. Since there is no adjustment of income tax to be reported on this return, the amount of $2,527.20 is also entered on Line 5.

The total of the wages subject to FICA taxes ($18,200) is reported on Line 6. This amount is multiplied by 14 percent, which represents the combined rate (7 percent × 2) for both the employer and the employees. The result is $2,548, the total amount of FICA taxes due. (When taxable tips are reported,

Form **941**		**Employer's Quarterly Federal Tax Return**		OMB No. 1545-0029
Department of the Treasury Internal Revenue Service		▶ For Paperwork Reduction Act Notice, see page 2.		

			T	
			FF	
			FD	
			FP	
			I	
			T	

Your name, address, employer identification number, and calendar quarter of return. (If not correct, please change.)

▶

Name (as distinguished from trade name)
Howard Mason
Trade name, if any
Kent Novelty Company
Address and ZIP code
129 Main Street, Manchester, NH 03104

Date quarter ended
MAR 31, 19X5
Employer identification number
27-3496214

If address is different from prior return, check here ▶

Record of Federal Tax Liability
(Complete if line 13 is $500 or more)

If you made eighth-monthly deposits using the 95% rule, check here . . . . ▶ ☐

If you are a first-time 3-banking-day depositor, check here . . . . ▶ ☐

See the instructions under rule 4 on page 4 for details.

Date wages paid		Tax liability
Day		
First month of quarter	1st through 3rd . . . A	
	4th through 7th . . B	
	8th through 11th . . C	390.40
	12th through 15th . . D	
	16th through 19th . . E	390.40
	20th through 22nd . . F	
	23rd through 25th . . G	390.40
	26th through last . . H	390.40
I	Total . . . . . ▶	1,561.60
Second month of quarter	1st through 3rd . . . I	
	4th through 7th . . J	390.40
	8th through 11th . . K	
	12th through 15th . . L	390.40
	16th through 19th . . M	
	20th through 22nd . . N	390.40
	23rd through 25th . . O	
	26th through last . . P	390.40
II	Total . . . . . ▶	1,561.60
Third month of quarter	1st through 3rd . . . Q	
	4th through 7th . . R	390.40
	8th through 11th . . S	
	12th through 15th . . T	390.40
	16th through 19th . . U	390.40
	20th through 22nd . . V	
	23rd through 25th . . W	390.40
	26th through last . . X	390.40
III	Total . . . . . . ▶	1,952.00
IV	Total for quarter (add lines I, II, and III)	5,075.20

If you are not liable for returns in the future, write "FINAL" . . . . ▶

Date final wages paid . . . . ▶

1	Number of employees (except household) employed in the pay period that includes March 12th (complete first quarter only) . . . . . ▶	5	
2	Total wages and tips subject to withholding, plus other employee compensation . . . . . ▶	18,200	00
3	Total income tax withheld from wages, tips, pensions, annuities, sick pay, gambling, etc. . ▶	2,527	20
4	Adjustment of withheld income tax for preceding quarters of calendar year . . . . . . ▶	-0-	
5	Adjusted total of income tax withheld	2,527	20
6	Taxable FICA wages paid: $ 18,200 00 × 14% (.14) equals tax	2,548	00
7 a	Taxable tips reported: $ × 7% (.07) equals tax	-0-	
b	Tips deemed to be wages (see instructions): $ × 7% (.07) equals tax	-0-	
8	Total FICA taxes (add lines 6, 7a, and 7b) . . .	2,548	00
9	Adjustment of FICA taxes (see instructions) . ▶	-0-	
10	Adjusted total of FICA taxes	2,548	00
11	Total taxes (add lines 5 and 10) . . . . ▶	5,075	20
12	Advance earned income credit (EIC) payments, if any	-0-	
13	Net taxes (subtract line 12 from line 11). This must equal line IV	5,075	20
14	Total deposits for quarter, including any overpayment applied from a prior quarter, from your records . ▶	5,075	20
15	Undeposited taxes due (subtract line 14 from line 13). Enter here and pay to Internal Revenue Service . ▶	-0-	
16	If line 14 is more than line 13, enter overpayment here ▶ $ and check if to be: ☐ Applied to next return, or ☐ Refunded.		

Under penalties of perjury, I declare that I have examined this return, including accompanying schedules and statements, and to the best of my knowledge and belief it is true, correct, and complete.

Signature ▶ *Howard Mason* Title ▶ **Owner** Date ▶ **4/25/X5**

Please file this form with your Internal Revenue Service Center (see instructions on "Where to File"). Form **941**

<hr />

they are entered on Line 7. The tips are subject to the employee's FICA tax, but the employer is not required to pay any FICA tax on tips.)

Since Kent's employees had no taxable tips, the figure of $2,548 shown on Line 6 is also recorded on Line 8. Similarly, since there were no adjustments that relate to FICA taxes, the amount of $2,548 is entered on Line 10 as the adjusted total of FICA taxes. (Sometimes the rounding of figures causes a minor difference between the amount of FICA taxes computed on the quarterly wages and the amount of FICA taxes deposited. When this occurs, the difference is entered on Line 9 as an adjustment in order to bring the total FICA taxes due into agreement with the total tax deposits made during the quarter and reported on Form 941.)

The sum of the adjusted total of federal income tax withheld ($2,527.20), which appears on Line 5, and the adjusted total of FICA taxes ($2,548), which appears on Line 10, is the total of the taxes for the quarter. This figure, $5,075.20, is recorded on Line 11. Since there were no advance earned income credit payments, a zero is placed on Line 12, and the amount shown on Line 11 is entered on Line 13 as the net taxes for the quarter.

If Line 13 is $500 or more, as is the case with the Form 941 for the Kent Novelty Company, the section labeled Record of Federal Tax Liability must be completed. This section appears on the left side of the form and is used to show the firm's liability for federal income withheld and FICA tax (both employee and employer shares) after each wage payment and at the end of each month during the quarter. The total tax liability for the quarter is entered on Line IV. This amount and the amount on Line 13 must be equal.

The total of the deposits made during the quarter ($5,075.20) is recorded on Line 14 and then subtracted from the net taxes for the quarter ($5,075.20) on Line 13. Since the two figures are the same, there are no undeposited taxes due and a zero is recorded on Line 15.

If any taxes are owed when Form 941 is completed, a check is issued to the Internal Revenue Service for the amount due or a deposit is made, depending on the sum involved.

If the employer has not deducted enough taxes from the employees, the firm must make up any difference. This increases the charge to the firm's Payroll Taxes Expense account. Although the employer is supposed to remit excess collections, small overages resulting from rounding off individual deductions are often absorbed in the Payroll Taxes Expense account.

WAGE AND TAX STATEMENTS

After the end of a year, employers must give each employee a Wage and Tax Statement, Form W-2, which contains information about the employee's earnings and tax withholdings for the year. Form W-2 must be issued by January 31 of the next year. (If an employee leaves the firm before the end of the year, the employer may provide Form W-2 at any time up to January 31 of the next year. However, if the employee asks for Form W-2 sooner, it must be issued within 30 days after the request or after the final wage payment, whichever is later.)

There are two basic types of Form W-2. One is used in areas that have no state and local tax withholdings, and thus it shows only deductions for federal income tax and FICA (social security) tax. The other type of Form W-2 is used in areas with state and local tax withholdings and therefore reports these deductions as well as the deductions for federal income tax and FICA tax.

The information for Form W-2 is obtained from the individual earnings records after they have been posted and summarized for the year. The type of earnings record used by the Kent Novelty Company shows earnings and deductions for the first six months on the front of the record. (Information for the second quarter is identical to that for the first quarter, which is illustrated on page 329.) The reverse side of the earnings record contains information for the third and fourth quarters and also provides a line for entering yearly totals for each item.

Most large employers use computers to keep their payroll records. The Internal Revenue Service encourages these employers to file the data for the Forms W-2 on magnetic tape or disks.

Assume that the individual earnings records for the employees of the Kent Novelty Company show the following totals for the year. (Notice that none of the employees earned more than the assumed tax base of $38,000 during the year. Therefore, all wages and salaries paid were subject to FICA tax.)

Employee	Total Earnings	FICA Tax	Income Tax
Peter Brown	$16,640.00	$1,164.80	$ 2,277.60
George Dunn	11,960.00	837.20	1,788.80
Carol Rosen	13,000.00	910.00	1,560.00
Rita Sanchez	20,800.00	1,456.00	3,068.00
Ellen West	10,400.00	728.00	1,414.40
Totals	$72,800.00	$5,096.00	$10,108.80

Wage and Tax Statements are sometimes referred to as withholding statements. The one for Peter Brown is illustrated below. (For purposes of this discussion, state and local tax considerations have been omitted.)

1 Control number 22222 OMB No. 1545-0008		For Official Use Only	
2 Employer's name, address, and ZIP code	3 Employer's identification number 27-3496214	4 Employer's State number 531-2977-0
Kent Novelty Company 129 Main Street Manchester, NH 03104	5 Stat employee □ Deceased □ Legal rep. □ 942 emp. □ Subtotal □ Void □	
	6 Allocated tips	7 Advance EIC payment
8 Employee's social security number 324-76-1245	9 Federal income tax withheld $2,277.60	10 Wages, tips, other compensation $16,640.00	11 Social security tax withheld $1,164.80
12 Employee's name (first, middle, last) Peter Brown	13 Social security wages $16,640.00	14 Social security tips
24 Oak Street Manchester, NH 03104	16 *	
	17 State income tax	18 State wages, tips, etc.	19 Name of State
15 Employee's address and ZIP code	20 Local income tax	21 Local wages, tips, etc.	22 Name of locality

Form **W-2 Wage and Tax Statement**   Copy A For Social Security Administration   Department of the Treasury
* See Instructions for Forms W-2 and W-2P   Internal Revenue Service

If there is a state income tax in addition to the federal income tax, six copies of Form W-2 are prepared. Three are given to the employee, who must attach one to his federal income tax return, attach one to his state income tax return, and keep the other for his records. The employer keeps one copy for the firm's records, sends one to the state tax department, and sends one to the Social Security Administration with the annual Transmittal of Income and Tax Statements, Form W-3, which is described next. If there is a city or county income tax as well as the state tax, the firm must prepare additional copies of Form W-2.

ANNUAL TRANSMITTAL OF INCOME AND TAX STATEMENTS

After filing the last quarterly return for the year on Form 941, the employer must also prepare a Transmittal of Income and Tax Statements, Form W-3. This form must be submitted with all Forms W-2 for the employees to the Social Security Administration. Form W-3 is due by February 28 following the end of the calendar year. The Social Security Administration processes the Forms W-2, records the employees' FICA wages, and sends the employees' FICA and income tax information to the Internal Revenue Service.

Form W-3 reports the total FICA wages; total FICA tax withheld; total wages, tips, and other compensation; total federal income tax withheld; and other information. These totals must be the same as those reported on the Forms W-2 submitted and on the quarterly Forms 941 for the year. The Forms W-2 allow the government to identify the employees from whom federal income tax and FICA tax were withheld during the year and to make sure that the totals withheld agree with the amounts remitted by the employer. A completed Form W-3 for the Kent Novelty Company appears below.

The filing of Form W-3 marks the end of the routine procedures needed to account for payrolls and for FICA taxes and federal income tax withholdings.

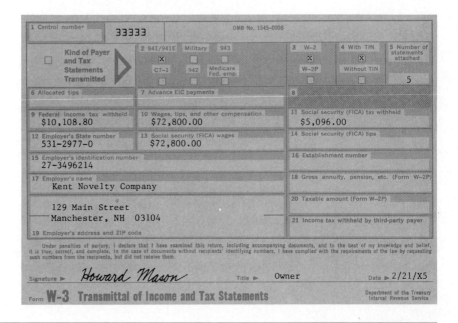

UNEMPLOYMENT INSURANCE

Protection of workers against the risks of unemployment is the second major part of the social security program. The taxes, records, and reports that are required by federal and state unemployment insurance regulations are discussed in this section.

Coverage

The basic unemployment legislation of 1935 imposed a direct payroll tax on certain employers to provide funds for an unemployment insurance program. Under the Federal Unemployment Tax Act (FUTA), an "employer" usually includes any person or organization that (1) pays wages of $1,500 or more during any calendar quarter in the current or preceding calendar year, or (2) employs 1 or more persons, on at least some portion of 1 day, in each of 20 or more calendar weeks during the current or preceding taxable year. Employers who qualify as exempt organizations under Section 501(c)(3) of the Internal Revenue Code (such as nonprofit schools and institutions) are not subject to the FUTA tax. Beginning in 1978, coverage was extended to agricultural and domestic service employees in certain situations.

Benefits

Before receiving unemployment benefits, a worker who loses his or her job must register with the state employment office and must accept any satisfactory position in his or her field of work that is offered. If, after a waiting period (one week in most cases), work cannot be found, the state pays the unemployed person a specified weekly amount designed to help relieve the financial problems resulting from a period of temporary unemployment. The length of time that state unemployment benefits are paid varies from state to state but is normally about 26 weeks. However, the unemployed person must actively look for work during this period and accept a suitable job, if one becomes available.

In 1972, because of high rates of unemployment, an extended federal-state unemployment compensation benefits program was instituted to help those unemployed persons whose regular state unemployment benefits were used up. Under certain conditions, the regular state benefits can be extended for a period of about 13 weeks. Other measures of an emergency nature have been taken occasionally to provide additional extensions of unemployment benefits in states having unusually severe conditions of unemployment.

Taxes

Under the original act, a gross tax amounting to 3 percent of the first $3,000 paid each covered worker during the calendar year was levied on the employer by the federal government. The act was further designed to encourage the states to provide their own unemployment insurance programs. Special provisions permitted employers to deduct a credit of as much as 90 percent of the 3 percent federal tax for payments made to states with approved plans. Employers can take advantage of these provisions because each state has set up an approved unemployment insurance program.

The gross FUTA tax has been changed a number of times. At this writing, it is 3.5 percent. Similarly, the base wages subject to the tax have been increased in several stages to the current $7,000.

Since the maximum credit deductible by employers from their FUTA tax for payments made to state unemployment compensation plans is still 2.7 percent

(90 percent of 3 percent), only the remaining 0.8 percent of the FUTA tax is actually paid to the federal government.

In addition to the tax on the employer, a few states also levy an unemployment tax on the employee. This tax is determined by the employer at the rate and on the base required by the state law. The amount is sent to the appropriate state agency at the specified time and in the specified manner. The handling of this tax is similar in principle to the handling of the employee's FICA tax, which was discussed previously.

Experience Ratings

One of the purposes of the unemployment insurance program is to stabilize employment and reduce unemployment. Firms that provide steady employment are granted a lower state tax rate under an *experience-rating*, or *merit-rating, system*. With this system, a business may take a credit against the FUTA tax as though it paid at the normal state rate (to a maximum of 2.7 percent). Hence, the firm may pay as little as a fraction of 1 percent to the state instead of the usual 3.5 to 4 percent without a favorable experience rating. Penalty rates as high as 6 to 7.5 percent may be levied in some states if a firm has a poor record of providing steady employment.

Accounting Entries

Firms like the Kent Novelty Company that use the accrual basis of accounting usually record federal and state unemployment taxes at the end of each payroll period when they record the employer's share of the FICA tax. For example, on January 7, 19X5, Kent makes the general journal entry shown below. Notice that the unemployment taxes are debited to Payroll Taxes Expense and credited to two liability accounts called Federal Unemployment Tax Payable and State Unemployment Tax Payable.

Since the total employee earnings of $1,400 for the January 7 payroll period are subject to unemployment taxes, the FUTA tax of 0.8 percent is computed as follows: $1,400 \times 0.008 = 11.20. The SUTA tax, which the firm pays at a rate of 1.3 percent because of its favorable employment record, is determined in a similar manner: $1,400 \times 0.013 = 18.20.

19 X5						
Jan.	7	Payroll Taxes Expense	543	127 40		
		FICA Tax Payable	221		98 00	
		Federal Unemployment Tax Payable	223		11 20	
		State Unemployment Tax Payable	224		18 20	
		Employer's payroll taxes for the week				
		ended January 7, 19X5.				

STATE UNEMPLOYMENT TAX

Employers subject to state unemployment tax (SUTA) laws must file returns and pay the tax on a quarterly basis. The individual state forms differ in detail, but they generally include information similar to the information required under FUTA. The state limits for taxable wages are usually the same as those of FUTA.

Taxable Wages	The employer obtains the information concerning the taxable wages paid from the individual employee earnings records in the same way that the data for Form 941 was compiled at the Kent Novelty Company. In some quarters, the data for unemployment tax and FICA tax may be identical. For example, in the first calendar quarter, the amount of wages subject to state unemployment tax at the Kent Novelty Company is the same as the taxable wages reported on Form 941. However, in later quarters, the amounts will differ. Keep in mind that the base of taxable wages used for computing each employee's FICA tax is much higher than that used for unemployment tax. In this text, we are assuming a base of $38,000 for FICA tax, while the base for unemployment tax is $7,000.

Payment of Taxes	The SUTA tax is usually due by the last day of the month following the end of the calendar quarter, and the amount owed must be paid at that time. For example, in April, the Kent Novelty Company must pay its tax for the first quarter of the year and file the proper return with the required information concerning employees and their taxable wages.

During the first calendar quarter of 19X5, the Kent Novelty Company paid wages totaling $18,200 to its five employees (see the summary on page 337). No employee had cumulative earnings in excess of $7,000. Therefore, all wages paid were subject to the state unemployment tax. Assume that the Kent Novelty Company has earned a favorable experience rating and that its SUTA rate is 1.3 percent. At this rate, on the taxable wages of $18,200 paid during the first quarter, the total unemployment tax due the state is $236.60.

The firm issues a check payable to the proper tax collection authority, such as the State Division of Employment Security, for the amount of the tax due ($236.60) and sends the check with the tax return. The entry to record the transaction is made in the cash payments journal, as shown below. State Unemployment Tax Payable is debited, and Cash is credited.

CASH PAYMENTS JOURNAL for Month of April 19X5   Page 4

DATE	CHECK NO.	EXPLANATION	ACCOUNTS PAYABLE ✓	ACCOUNTS PAYABLE DEBIT	OTHER ACCOUNTS DEBIT ACCOUNT TITLE	POST. REF.	AMOUNT	PURCH. DISCOUNT CREDIT	CASH CREDIT
Apr. 20	4932	Tax for first quarter			State Unempl. Tax Payable	224	236 60		236 60

The same procedure is followed in later quarters. The taxable wages are determined from the data in the individual earnings records. Note that in the earnings record for Peter Brown, illustrated on page 329, there is a Cumulative Total column showing the year-to-date wages. This column is used to find out when the tax exemption point is reached. Thus, the record would show that Peter Brown reached the $7,000 maximum for unemployment tax with his wages for the week ended June 2. The tax-exempt wages for each employee for FICA tax and unemployment tax are entered in the columns of the payroll register provided for that purpose (see page 311).

When preparing state unemployment returns at the end of each quarter, the accountant examines the individual earnings records to determine the taxable wages. Then the accountant computes the state unemployment tax to be paid. The necessary data for the Kent Novelty Company for each quarter of 19X5 is shown below.

Quarter Ended	Taxable Wages	SUTA Tax Paid
March 31	$18,200	$236.60
June 30	13,480	175.24
September 30	3,320	43.16
December 31	–0–	–0–
Totals	$35,000	$455.00

FEDERAL UNEMPLOYMENT TAX

The tax levied under the Federal Unemployment Tax Act (FUTA) is paid only by the employer in a manner similar to the unemployment taxes levied by the various states. The relationship between the federal and state programs was discussed earlier in this chapter.

FUTA Tax Deposits

As already noted, at this writing, the FUTA tax rate is 3.5 percent of the first $7,000 of annual wages paid to each employee who is covered by the law. FUTA taxes must be deposited in a Federal Reserve Bank or other authorized financial institution, and must be accompanied by a preprinted tax form—the Federal Tax Deposit, Form 8109. The employer must compute the amount of the FUTA tax liability on a quarterly basis and deposit any amount due by the last day of the first month following the end of the calendar quarter.

To determine if a deposit must be made for any of the first three quarters, the employer multiplies that part of the first $7,000 of each employee's wages paid during the quarter by 0.8 percent. If the total tax owed for the quarter and any undeposited tax from a prior quarter amount to more than $100, the sum must be deposited by the last day of the first month following the quarter. If the amount is $100 or less, it need not be deposited but must be added to the amount subject to deposit for the next quarter.

The schedule on page 328 shows that the total earnings of the Kent Novelty Company's five employees for the first calendar quarter of 19X5 amounted to $18,200. Since no employee had earnings of as much as $7,000, the entire $18,200 was subject to FUTA tax computed at the rate of 0.8 percent. The resulting tax of $145.60 was deposited on April 21, 19X5. The check issued by the firm was accompanied by a properly completed Federal Tax Deposit, Form 8109, and was recorded in the cash payments journal as illustrated on page 338.

DATE	CHECK NO.	EXPLANATION	ACCOUNTS PAYABLE		OTHER ACCOUNTS DEBIT			PURCH. DISCOUNT CREDIT	CASH CREDIT
			✓	DEBIT	ACCOUNT TITLE	POST. REF.	AMOUNT		
Apr. 21	4933	Deposit for first quarter			Fed. Unempl. Tax Payable	223	145 60		145 60

The Kent Novelty Company made another deposit of FUTA tax on July 22, 19X5. This deposit was for the second quarter of the year when the firm paid taxable wages of $13,480 and therefore owed FUTA tax of $107.84 ($13,480 × 0.008). No further deposits were needed during the year because the firm's FUTA liability for the third quarter was only $26.56 ($3,320 × 0.008) and no taxable wages were paid in the fourth quarter.

The net federal unemployment tax for the year is reported on the Employer's Annual Federal Unemployment Tax Return, Form 940. After computing the net tax, the employer subtracts all the amounts deposited during the year. If the remainder is more than $100, the entire sum must be deposited by January 31. If the net tax for the year minus any deposits is $100 or less, it may be deposited or it may be paid with Form 940 by January 31.

Filing Form 940

Each employer covered by FUTA must file a Form 940 and pay any tax due for the year by the following January 31. The information for this return comes partly from the individual earnings records and partly from copies of the state unemployment tax returns that the employer has filed during the year. The Form 940 prepared at the Kent Novelty Company for the calendar year 19X5 is shown on page 339.

Computing Credit for State Unemployment Tax

Notice that Kent's Form 940 lists contributions of $455 for state unemployment tax and indicates that the required sum was actually paid. This data about the state tax appears on lines A and B at the top of Form 940. The figure of $455 reflects the firm's experience rating of 1.3 percent.

Computing Taxable Wages

The first part of Form 940 requires a listing of the total payments to employees during the calendar year less any payments exempt from taxation. The difference between these two amounts is the total taxable FUTA wages. As the Form 940 illustrated on page 339 shows, the Kent Novelty Company made total payments of $72,800 to its employees during 19X5. Tax-exempt wages for the year amounted to $37,800, leaving $35,000 taxable. (This is easily proved, since the Kent Novelty Company had five employees, all of whom earned more than $7,000 during the calendar year.)

The gross federal tax based on $35,000 of taxable wages at the required 3.5 percent rate is $1,225. However, Kent earned a maximum credit of $945 (1.3 percent actually paid to the state + 1.4 percent credit = 2.7 percent maximum

Form **940**		**Employer's Annual Federal Unemployment (FUTA) Tax Return**	OMB No. 1545-0028

Department of the Treasury
Internal Revenue Service

▶ For Paperwork Reduction Act Notice, see page 2.

19--

	T
	FF
	FD
	FP
	I
	T

Name (as distinguished from trade name)

Calendar Year **19X5**

If incorrect, make any necessary change. ▶

Howard Mason

Trade name, if any

Employer identification number

Kent Novelty Company

27-3496214

Address and ZIP code

129 Main Street, Manchester, NH 03104

A Did you pay all required contributions to your State unemployment fund by the due date of Form 940? . . . . [X] Yes [ ] No

If you check the "Yes" box, enter amount of contributions paid to your State unemployment fund . . . . ▶ $ **455** | 00

B Are you required to pay contributions to only one State? . . . . [X] Yes [ ] No

If you checked the "Yes" box, (1) Enter the name of the State where you are required to pay contributions . . . . ▶ **New Hampshire**

(2) Enter your State reporting number(s) as shown on State unemployment tax return . . . . . . ▶ **531-2977-0**

PART I.—Computation of Taxable Wages and Credit Reduction (To Be Completed by All Taxpayers)

1	Total payments (including exempt payments) during the calendar year for services of employees	1	**72,800** 00
2	Exempt payments. (Explain each exemption shown, attaching additional sheets if necessary) ▶ _____	Amount paid	
3	Payments for services in excess of $7,000. Enter only the excess over the first $7,000 paid to individual employees exclusive of exempt amounts entered on line 2. Do not use State wage limitation	3 **37,800** 00	
4	Total exempt payments (add lines 2 and 3)	4	**37,800** 00
5	**Total taxable wages** (subtract line 4 from line 1). (If any portion is exempt from State contributions, see instructions)▶	5	**35,000** 00
6	Credit reduction for unpaid advances to the States listed. Enter the wages included on line 5 above for each State and multiply by the rate shown.		

(a) AR _____ x.006	(g) MI _____ x.006	(m) VT _____ x.006
(b) CT _____ x.007	(h) MN _____ x.006	(n) WV _____ x.006
(c) DE _____ x.006	(i) NJ _____ x.006	Outside the U.S.
(d) DC _____ x.011	(j) OH _____ x.006	(o) PR _____ x.006
(e) IL _____ x.007	(k) PA _____ x.006	(p) VI _____ x.006
(f) KY _____ x.003	(l) RI _____ x.006	

7 Total credit reduction (add lines 6(a) through 6(p) and enter on line 2, Part II or line 4, Part III) . . . . . ▶ | 7 |

PART II.—Tax Due or Refund (Complete If You Checked the "Yes" Boxes in Both Items A and B Above)

1	FUTA tax. Multiply the wages on line 5, Part I, by .008 and enter here	1	**280** 00
2	Enter amount from line 7, Part I	2	**-0-**
3	**Total FUTA tax** (add lines 1 and 2)	3	**280** 00
4	Less: Total FUTA tax deposited for the year from your records	4	**253** 44
5	**Balance due** (subtract line 4 from line 3—if over $100, see Part IV instructions). Pay to IRS . ▶	5	**26** 56
6	**Overpayment** (subtract line 3 from line 4). Check if to be: [ ] Applied to next return, or [ ] Refunded . ▶	6	

PART III.—Tax Due or Refund (Complete If You Checked the "No" Box in Either Item A or Item B Above. Also complete Part V)

1	Gross FUTA tax. Multiply the wages on line 5, Part I, by .035	1	
2	Maximum credit. Multiply the wages on line 5, Part I, by .027	2	
3	Enter the smaller of the amount on line 11, Part V, or line 2, Part III .	3	
4	Enter amount from line 7, Part I	4	
5	**Credit allowable** (subtract line 4 from line 3)	5	
6	Total FUTA tax (subtract line 5 from line 1)	6	
7	Less: Total FUTA tax deposited for the year from your records	7	
8	**Balance due** (subtract line 7 from line 6—if over $100, see Part IV instructions). Pay to IRS . ▶	8	
9	**Overpayment** (subtract line 6 from line 7). Check if to be: [ ] Applied to next return, or [ ] Refunded . ▶	9	

PART IV.—Record of Quarterly Federal Tax Liability for Unemployment Tax (Do not include State liability)

Quarter	First	Second	Third	Fourth	Total for Year
Liability for quarter	145.60	107.84	26.56		280.00

If you will not have to file returns in the future, write "Final" here (see general instruction "Who Must File") . . . . ▶

Under penalties of perjury, I declare that I have examined this return, including accompanying schedules and statements, and to the best of my knowledge and belief, it is true, correct, and complete, and that no part of any payment made to a State unemployment fund claimed as a credit was or is to be deducted from the payments to employees.

Date ▶ **1/25/X5**   Signature ▶ *Howard Mason*   Title (Owner, etc.) ▶ **Owner**

Form **940**

credit × \$35,000 = \$945). Thus, the amount owed the federal government is \$280 (\$35,000 × 0.008). This sum appears in the second part of Form 940 on Lines 1 and 3. The total tax deposited during the year is given on Line 4, and any balance due appears on Line 5.

Reporting FUTA Tax Liability

In the fourth part of Form 940, the employer records the liability for federal unemployment tax during the year. Kent owed FUTA tax of \$145.60 for the first quarter, \$107.84 for the second quarter, and \$26.56 for the third quarter. Since only the first two amounts were deposited, the firm's Form 940 shows a balance of \$26.56 due on Line 5 of Part II. Kent issued a check for this amount and enclosed it with the tax return.

WORKER'S COMPENSATION INSURANCE

Employers required by state law to carry worker's compensation insurance generally pay an estimated premium in advance. Then, after the end of the year, they pay an additional premium (or receive credit for overpayment) based on an audit of their payroll amounts for the year. The rate of the insurance premium varies with the risk involved in the work performed. Therefore, it is important to have employees classified properly according to the kind of work they do and to summarize labor costs according to the insurance premium classifications.

For the purpose of this insurance rating, there are only two different work classifications at the Kent Novelty Company: office work and shop work. The premium rates are \$0.20 per \$100 for office work and \$3.20 per \$100 for shop work. Based on employee earnings for the previous year, the Kent Novelty Company paid an estimated premium of \$2,000 on January 15, 19X5. This premium was paid in advance to cover the year 19X5. A check was issued to the insurance company for the necessary amount. The accountant then made an entry in the cash payments journal debiting Worker's Compensation Insurance Expense and crediting Cash.

At the end of 19X5, the accountant analyzed the payroll data for that year and applied the proper rates to determine the actual premium. As a result of this analysis, the accountant found that a balance was owed for the worker's compensation insurance.

Classification	Payroll	Rate	Premium
Office Work	\$10,400.00	\$0.20/\$100	\$ 20.80
Shop Work	62,400.00	\$3.20/\$100	1,996.80
Totals	\$72,800.00		\$2,017.60
Less Estimated Premium Paid			2,000.00
Balance of Premium Due			\$ 17.60

The final balance due the insurance company, \$17.60, is paid by check and entered in the cash payments journal as a debit to Worker's Compensation Insurance Expense and a credit to Cash.

INTERNAL CONTROL OVER PAYROLL OPERATIONS

Accountants usually recommend that the following procedures be used to achieve internal control over payroll operations.

1. Only highly responsible, well-trained employees should be involved in payroll operations.
2. Payroll records should be kept in locked files, and the employees who work with them should be cautioned to maintain confidentiality about pay rates and other information in the records.
3. No new employees should be added to the payroll system without written authorization from management. Similarly, no changes in employee pay rates should be made without written authorization from management.
4. No changes should be made in an employee's withholding allowances without obtaining a properly completed and signed Form W-4 from the employee.
5. No voluntary deductions should be made from employee earnings without obtaining a signed authorization from the employee involved.
6. The payroll checks should be examined by someone other than the person who prepares them. Each check should be compared with the entry for the employee in the payroll register.
7. The person who prepares the payroll checks should not be the one who distributes them to the employees.
8. The monthly statement for the payroll bank account should be received and reconciled by someone other than the person who prepares the payroll checks.
9. Prenumbered forms should be used for the payroll checks. Periodically, the numbers of the checks issued and the numbers of the unused checks should be verified to make sure that all checks can be accounted for.
10. All authorization forms for adding new employees to the payroll system, changing pay rates, and making voluntary deductions should be kept on file. Similarly, all Forms W-4 should be retained.

PRINCIPLES AND PROCEDURES SUMMARY

Employers serve as collection agents for the FICA tax and federal income tax withheld from employee earnings and must remit these amounts, together with the employer's FICA tax, to the government as required by law. These taxes must be deposited in an authorized bank if they amount to a certain sum. The schedule for deposits varies according to the sums involved. A Federal Tax Deposit, Form 8109, is prepared and submitted with each deposit.

At the end of each calendar quarter, the employer must file a quarterly tax return on Form 941 reporting taxable wages paid to employees during the quarter, the federal income tax withheld, and FICA taxes. Any balance of taxes due must be paid with this return or deposited.

By the end of January, each employee must be given a Wage and Tax Statement, Form W-2, showing his or her earnings for the year and deductions for FICA tax and income tax. The employer prepares an annual Transmittal of Income and Tax Statements, Form W-3, and files it together with copies of the Forms W-2 issued to the employees.

Unemployment insurance protects workers against the financial problems of temporary unemployment. It is administered by the various state governments. Taxes for this insurance are paid by the employers to both the state and federal governments. However, a few states also levy unemployment insurance tax on employees.

State unemployment tax returns differ in detail but usually require a list of employees, their social security numbers, and the taxable wages paid. An Employer's Annual Federal Unemployment Tax Return, Form 940, must be filed each January for the preceding calendar year. It shows the total wages paid, the amount of taxable wages, and the FUTA tax owed for the year. As of this writing, the gross tax is 3.5 percent of the first $7,000 paid each employee during the calendar year. Credit of up to 2.7 percent against the gross tax is allowed for unemployment tax paid under state plans or waived because of state experience ratings.

Employers may be required under state law to carry worker's compensation insurance. Ordinarily, an estimated premium is paid at the beginning of each year. A final settlement is made with the insurance company on the basis of an audit of the payroll after the end of the year. Premiums vary according to the type of work performed by each employee.

MANAGERIAL IMPLICATIONS

Management must make sure that payroll taxes are computed properly and paid on time. It is also essential that payroll tax returns and forms be prepared accurately and filed promptly in order to avoid penalties imposed by law. The payroll and accounting records must allow the preparation of these reports in an efficient manner.

Managers should be familiar with the various types of payroll taxes in order to understand their impact on operating costs. In many businesses, the expense for payroll taxes amounts to a sizable sum. It is especially helpful for managers to be knowledgeable about the regulations concerning unemployment tax in their states because a favorable experience rating can substantially reduce this tax.

REVIEW QUESTIONS

1. Who pays the FICA tax?
2. How can an employer keep informed about changes in the rates and bases for the FICA and FUTA taxes?
3. What factor determines how often deposits of federal income tax withheld and FICA tax are made?

4. What government form is prepared to accompany deposits of federal taxes?
5. Where are deposits of federal taxes made?
6. What is the purpose of Form 941? How often must it be filed?
7. What happens if the employer fails to deduct enough federal income tax or FICA tax from employee earnings?
8. What is the purpose of Form W-2? When must it be issued? To whom is it sent?
9. What is the purpose of Form W-3? When must it be issued? To whom is it sent?
10. Why was the unemployment insurance system established?
11. How do jobless workers obtain unemployment benefits?
12. Who pays the FUTA tax? Who pays the SUTA tax?
13. How do the FUTA and SUTA taxes relate to each other?
14. What is the purpose of Form 940? How often is it filed?
15. How do experience ratings affect SUTA taxes?
16. Who pays for worker's compensation insurance?
17. When is the premium for worker's compensation insurance usually paid?
18. Why is it important for firms that purchase worker's compensation insurance to classify wages according to the type of work employees perform?

MANAGERIAL DISCUSSION QUESTIONS

1. Why should management be concerned about the accuracy and promptness of payroll tax deposits and payroll tax returns?
2. What is the significance to management of the experience-rating system used to determine the employer's tax under the state unemployment insurance laws?
3. The Harris Company recently discovered that a payroll clerk had issued checks to nonexistent employees for several years and cashed the checks himself. The firm does not have any internal control procedures for its payroll operations. What specific controls might have led to the discovery of this fraud more quickly or discouraged the payroll clerk from even attempting the fraud?

EXERCISES

EXERCISE 14-1   **Determining when to deposit federal income tax withheld and FICA tax.** The amounts of federal income tax withheld and FICA tax (both employee and employer shares) shown on page 344 were owed by different businesses on the specified dates. In each case, decide whether the firm is required to deposit the sum in an authorized financial institution. If a deposit is necessary, give the date by which it should be made.

1. Total taxes of $620 owed on January 31, 19X1.
2. Total taxes of $5,100 owed on February 7, 19X1.
3. Total taxes of $380 owed on March 31, 19X1.
4. Total taxes of $440 owed on April 30, 19X1.

EXERCISE 14-2   **Journalizing a deposit of federal income tax withheld and FICA tax.** After the Chan Company paid its employees on May 15, 19X5, the firm's general ledger showed a balance of $1,674 in the FICA Tax Payable account and a balance of $1,388 in the Employee Income Tax Payable account. On May 16, 19X5, the business issued Check 879 to deposit the taxes owed in the Wayne National Bank. Record this transaction in general journal form.

EXERCISE 14-3   **Computing the employer's payroll taxes.** At the end of the weekly payroll period on May 28, 19X6, the payroll register of the Highland Manufacturing Company showed employee earnings of $21,900. Determine the firm's payroll taxes for the period. Use an assumed FICA rate of 7 percent, the FUTA rate of 0.8 percent, and the SUTA rate of 2.7 percent. Consider all earnings subject to FICA tax and $16,500 subject to FUTA and SUTA taxes.

EXERCISE 14-4   **Journalizing the employer's payroll taxes.** Prepare a general journal entry to record the payroll taxes of the Highland Manufacturing Company for the weekly period ended May 28, 19X6. Obtain the necessary amounts from your solution to Exercise 14-3.

EXERCISE 14-5   **Determining when to deposit FUTA tax.** The following amounts of FUTA tax were owed by different businesses on the specified dates. In each case, decide whether the firm is required to deposit the sum in an authorized financial institution. If a deposit is necessary, give the date by which it should be made.

1. FUTA tax of $250 owed on March 31, 19X1.
2. FUTA tax of $90 owed on June 30, 19X1.
3. FUTA tax of $75 owed on December 31, 19X1.

EXERCISE 14-6   **Journalizing a deposit of FUTA tax.** On March 31, 19X4, the Federal Unemployment Tax Payable account in the general ledger of the Forest Company showed a balance of $273. This represents the FUTA tax owed for the first quarter of the year. On April 25, 19X4, the firm issued Check 1187 to deposit the amount owed in the Lee National Bank. Record this transaction in general journal form.

EXERCISE 14-7   **Computing the SUTA tax to be reported on the quarterly tax return.** On April 20, 19X7, the Cavallo Trucking Company prepared its state unemployment tax return for the first quarter of the year. The firm had taxable wages of $43,200. Because of a favorable experience rating, Cavallo pays SUTA tax at a rate of 1.6 percent. How much SUTA tax did the firm owe for the quarter?

EXERCISE 14-8   **Journalizing the payment of SUTA tax.** On June 30, 19X4, the State Unemployment Tax Payable account in the general ledger of the Hilltop Motel showed a balance of $342. This represents the SUTA tax owed for the second quarter of the year. On July 21, 19X4, the business issued Check 5625 to the state unemployment insurance fund. Record this payment in general journal form.

EXERCISE 14-9   **Computing the FUTA tax to be reported on the annual tax return.** On January 24, 19X2, the Sadowski Automotive Repair Service prepared its Employer's Annual Federal Unemployment Tax Return, Form 940 for the year 19X1. During 19X1, the business paid total wages of $93,600 to its four employees. Of this amount, $28,000 was subject to FUTA tax. Using a rate of 0.8 percent, determine the FUTA tax owed for 19X1 and the balance due on January 24, 19X2 when Form 940 was filed. A deposit of $187.20 was made during the year.

EXERCISE 14-10   **Computing the estimated premium on worker's compensation insurance.** The Delmar Manufacturing Company estimates that its office employees will earn $40,000 next year and its factory employees will earn $210,000. The firm pays the following rates for worker's compensation insurance: $0.15 per $100 of wages for the office employees and $3.50 per $100 of wages for the factory employees. Determine the estimated premium for each group of employees and the total estimated premium for the business for next year.

PROBLEMS

PROBLEM 14-1   **Computing and recording the employer's payroll taxes.** The payroll register of the World Travel Agency showed total employee earnings of $1,080 for the week ended April 7, 19X1.

Instructions

1. Compute the employer's payroll taxes for the period. Use an assumed rate of 7 percent for the employer's share of the FICA tax, and use 0.8 percent for FUTA tax and 2.7 percent for SUTA tax. All earnings are taxable.
2. Prepare a general journal entry to record the employer's payroll taxes for the period.

PROBLEM 14-2   **Preparing Form 941.** During the month following the end of each calendar quarter, an employer is required by law to file Form 941, the Employer's Quarterly Federal Tax Return. Assume that the World Travel Agency, owned by Patrick Sullivan, received the required form from the Internal Revenue Service for the second quarter of 19X1. A payroll summary for the quarter appears on page 346.

The firm prepared the required tax deposit forms and issued checks as follows during the quarter.

a. Federal Tax Deposit, Form 8109, $1,099.24, paid on May 14, 19X1.
b. Federal Tax Deposit, Form 8109, $1,160.93, paid on June 13, 19X1.

PAYROLL SUMMARY

Date Wages Paid	Total Earnings	FICA Tax Deducted	Income Tax Withheld
Apr. 7	$ 1,080	$ 75.60	$ 119.88
14	1,120	78.40	124.32
21	1,150	80.50	127.65
28	990	69.30	119.79
	$ 4,340	$ 303.80	$ 491.64
May 5	$ 1,050	$ 73.50	$ 116.55
12	1,230	86.10	138.99
19	1,190	83.30	124.95
26	1,160	81.20	132.24
	$ 4,630	$ 324.10	$ 512.73
June 2	$ 980	$ 68.60	$ 116.62
9	1,060	74.20	117.66
16	1,140	79.80	140.22
23	1,090	76.30	122.08
30	1,210	84.70	143.10
	$ 5,480	$ 383.60	$ 639.68
Totals	$14,450	$1,011.50	$1,644.05

Instructions

1. On July 14 the firm issued Check 3918 to deposit the federal income tax withheld and the FICA tax (both employee and employer shares) for the third month (June). In general journal form, record issuance of the check.

2. Complete Form 941 in accordance with the discussions in the textbook and the instructions on the form itself. Use the assumed 14 percent total FICA rate in computations. Use 3415 Broad Street, Denver, Colorado 80215 as the business's address and 57-0202745 as the employer's identification number. Date the form July 27, 19X1. The owner will sign it.

PROBLEM 14-3 **Determining federal and state unemployment taxes; preparing Form 940.**
Certain transactions and procedures relating to federal and state unemployment taxes are given below and on page 347 for the Erie Fashion Center, a retail store owned by Helen Thomas. The firm's address is 1616 Drake Street, Buffalo, New York 14214. The employer's identification number is 57-0202746. Carry out the procedures as instructed in each of the following steps.

Instructions

1. Compute the state unemployment insurance tax owed for the quarter ended March 31, 19X1. This information will be shown on the employer's quarterly report to the state agency that collects SUTA tax. The Erie Fashion Center has received a favorable experience rating and therefore pays only a 2 percent state unemployment tax rate. The employee earnings for the first quarter are shown on page 347. All earnings are subject to SUTA tax.

EARNINGS SUMMARY

Social Security Number	Name of Employee	Total Earnings
251–07–4400	Robert Anton	$ 1,840.00
586–22–1401	Alice Bates	1,841.00
247–15–3302	John Cortez	1,840.00
322–08–9903	Ruth DeMaio	2,196.00
333–11–8504	Joseph Lang	2,007.50
538–13–4905	Donna Reese	1,900.00
Total		$11,624.50

2. On April 29, 19X1, the firm issued Check 2745 for the amount you computed in Instruction 1. Record the transaction in general journal form.

3. Complete Form 940, the Employer's Annual Federal Unemployment Tax Return. Assume that all wages have been paid and that all quarterly payments have been submitted to the state as required. The payroll information for 19X1 appears below. The required federal tax deposit of $188.33 was made on July 14, 19X1, using Form 8109. Date the unemployment tax return January 22, 19X2. The owner will sign it.

PAYROLL SUMMARY

Quarter Ended	Total Wages Paid	Wages Paid in Excess of $7,000	State Unemployment Tax Paid
Mar. 31	$11,624.50	-0-	$232.49
June 30	11,916.50	-0-	238.33
Sept. 30	11,400.00	-0-	228.00
Dec. 31	11,500.00	$4,441.00	141.18
Totals	$46,441.00	$4,441.00	$840.00

4. On January 22, 19X2, the firm issued Check 2917 for the amount shown on Line 5 of Part II of Form 940. In general journal form, record issuance of the check.

PROBLEM 14-4 **Computing and recording the premium for worker's compensation insurance.** On January 31, 19X5, the Atlas Chemical Company issued a check to pay its estimated premium for worker's compensation insurance for the year.

Instructions 1. Use the following information to compute the estimated premium for 19X5.

CLASSIFICATION	AMOUNT OF ESTIMATED WAGES	INSURANCE RATES
Office Work	$ 35,000	$0.18/$100
Factory Work	180,000	$4.00/$100

2. Check 4561 was issued to pay the estimated premium. Record the transaction in general journal form.
3. On January 20, 19X6, an audit of the firm's payroll records for 19X5 showed that it had actually paid wages of $36,400 to its office employees and wages of $178,500 to its factory employees. Compute the actual premium for the year and the balance due the insurance company or the credit due the firm.

PROBLEM 14-5 **Computing and recording unemployment taxes and the premium for worker's compensation insurance.** The Pacific Landscaping Service has four employees. The following table shows their cumulative earnings through June 19X7 and their July wages.

Employee	Cumulative Earnings Through June	July Wages
Brian McDuff	$5,520	$920
Carol Slater	4,725	825
George Warren	4,500	750
Diane Zeleski	4,200	700

Instructions
1. Assuming that the four employees had earnings in August and September equal to their July wages, compute the amount of state unemployment tax that the firm would owe on the wages for the third quarter of the year. Use 2.7 percent as the tax rate. (Consider $7,000 as the maximum taxable wages for each employee for the calendar year.)
2. In general journal form, make the entry on October 10 to record the firm's payment of the state unemployment tax when the return for the third quarter is filed.
3. Compute the federal unemployment tax due through June at the rate of 0.8 percent on the first $7,000 paid each employee.
4. On July 28 Check 1175 was issued to deposit the FUTA tax for the first and second quarters. Make an entry in general journal form to record the tax deposit.
5. Compute the federal unemployment tax due for the third quarter. Indicate by a general journal entry or a statement whether a deposit of this tax is necessary.
6. On January 4, 19X7, the firm paid the estimated premium for worker's compensation insurance for 19X7. This premium was based on an expected payroll of $36,000 and a premium rate of $3 per $100 of wages.
   a. In general journal form, make the entry to record issuance of Check 741 to pay the estimated premium on January 4, 19X7.
   b. Compute the balance due based on the firm's actual payroll for the year, which totaled $37,890. Then make an entry in general journal form to record the issuance of Check 992 for the amount on January 18, 19X8.

PROBLEM 14-1A

Computing and recording the employer's payroll taxes. The payroll register of the Glen Car Rental Agency showed total employee earnings of $940 for the week ended July 7, 19X1.

Instructions

1. Compute the employer's payroll taxes for the period. Use an assumed rate of 7 percent for the employer's share of the FICA tax, and use 0.8 percent for FUTA tax and 2.7 percent for SUTA tax. All earnings are taxable.
2. Prepare a general journal entry to record the employer's payroll taxes for the period.

PROBLEM 14-2A

Preparing Form 941. During the month following the end of each calendar quarter, an employer is required to file Form 941, the Employer's Quarterly Federal Tax Return. Assume that the Glen Car Rental Agency, owned by Paul Stewart, received the required form from the Internal Revenue Service for the third quarter of 19X1. A payroll summary for the quarter appears below.

The firm prepared the required tax deposit forms and issued checks as follows.

a. Federal Tax Deposit, Form 8109, $923.38, was paid on August 13, 19X1.
b. Federal Tax Deposit, Form 8109, $908.87, was paid on September 14, 19X1.

PAYROLL SUMMARY

Date Wages Paid	Total Earnings	FICA Tax Deducted	Income Tax Withheld
July 7	$ 940	$ 65.80	$ 95.62
14	980	68.60	99.69
21	940	65.80	95.62
28	960	67.20	97.65
	$ 3,820	$267.40	$ 388.58
Aug. 4	$ 920	$ 64.40	$ 93.58
11	940	65.80	95.62
18	940	65.80	95.62
25	960	67.20	97.65
	$ 3,760	$263.20	$ 382.47
Sept. 1	$ 980	$ 68.60	$ 99.69
8	940	65.80	95.62
15	960	67.20	97.65
22	940	65.80	95.62
29	920	64.40	93.58
	$ 4,740	$331.80	$ 482.16
Totals	$12,320	$862.40	$1,253.21

Instructions

1. On October 13 the firm issued Check 5790 to deposit the federal income tax withheld and the FICA tax (both employee and employer shares) for the third month (September). In general journal form, record issuance of the check.

2. Complete Form 941 in accordance with the discussions in this chapter and the instructions on the form itself. Use the assumed 14 percent total FICA rate in computations. Use the following address for the company: 1111 Glen Drive, Green Bay, Wisconsin 54303. Use 57-0202222 as the employer identification number. Date the return October 30, 19X1. The owner will sign it.

PROBLEM 14-3A

Determining federal and state unemployment taxes; preparing Form 940. Certain transactions and procedures relating to federal and state unemployment taxes are given below and on page 351 for the Consumer Electronics Mart, a retail store owned by Marcia Rubin. The firm's address is 128 University Drive, Kansas City, Missouri 64120. The employer's identification number is 57-6161611. Carry out the procedures as instructed in each of the following steps.

Instructions

1. Compute the state unemployment insurance tax owed on the employees' wages for the quarter ended March 31, 19X1. This information will be shown on the employer's quarterly report to the state agency that collects SUTA tax. The Consumer Electronics Mart has received a favorable experience rating and therefore pays only a 1.5 percent state unemployment tax rate. The employee earnings for the first quarter are given below. All earnings are subject to SUTA tax.

EARNINGS SUMMARY

Social Security Number	Name of Employee	Total Earnings
444–00–1234	Ralph Alda	$ 1,625
444–09–4325	Eileen Burns	2,400
333–01–3456	Daniel Field	1,800
333–09–5431	Susan Garrett	2,800
222–02–4567	Eric Swenson	2,130
222–09–7531	Marie Vargas	2,800
111–03–5678	Stanley Wood	2,050
		$15,605

2. On April 28, 19X1, the firm issued Check 9619 for the amount you computed in Instruction 1. Record the issuance of the check in general journal form.

3. Complete Form 940, the Employer's Annual Federal Unemployment Tax Return. Assume that all wages have been paid and that all quarterly payments have been submitted to the state as required. The payroll information for 19X1 appears on page 351. The required federal tax deposit forms and checks were submitted as follows: a deposit of $124.84 on April 21, a deposit of $137.60 on July 22, and a deposit of $129.56 on October 21. Date the unemployment tax return January 28, 19X2. The owner will sign it.

PAYROLL SUMMARY

Quarter Ended	Total Wages Paid	Wages Paid in Excess of $7,000	State Unemployment Tax Paid
Mar. 31	$15,605.00	-0-	$234.08
June 30	17,200.00	-0-	258.00
Sept. 30	17,500.00	$ 1,305.00	242.93
Dec. 31	19,100.00	19,100.00	-0-
Totals	$69,405.00	$20,405.00	$735.01

4. In general journal form, record issuance of Check 9748 for $129.56 to deposit the FUTA tax due for the third quarter. This deposit was made on October 21, 19X1.

PROBLEM 14-4A   **Computing and recording the premium for worker's compensation insurance.** On January 28, 19X3, the Apex Printing Company issued a check to pay its estimated premium for worker's compensation insurance for the year.

Instructions   1. Use the following information to compute the estimated premium for 19X3.

CLASSIFICATION	AMOUNT OF ESTIMATED WAGES	INSURANCE RATES
Office Work	$ 22,000	$0.15/$100
Shop Work	140,000	$3.10/$100

2. Check 1823 was issued to pay the estimated premium. Record the transaction in general journal form.
3. On January 22, 19X4, an audit of the firm's payroll records for 19X3 showed that it had actually paid wages of $23,500 to its office employees and wages of $139,100 to its shop employees. Compute the actual premium for the year and the balance due the insurance company or the credit due the firm.

PROBLEM 14-5A   **Computing and recording unemployment taxes and the premium for worker's compensation insurance.** The table given below shows cumulative earnings of the four employees of the Artistic Ceramics Company at the end of June, September, and December, 19X6.

	Cumulative Earnings		
Employee	Through June	Through September	Through December
Joanne Casey	$4,800	$7,200	$ 9,600
David Marshak	5,480	8,720	11,960
Lois Seldin	3,900	5,850	7,800
Richard Tate	-0-	1,800	4,500

Instructions

1. Compute the amount of state unemployment tax that would be due on the wages paid by the firm for the third quarter of the year. Use 2.7 percent as the tax rate. Consider $7,000 as the tax base for each employee for the year.

2. In general journal form, make the entry on October 12 to record payment of the state unemployment tax when the return for the third quarter is filed.

3. Compute the federal unemployment tax due through June at the rate of 0.8 percent on the first $7,000 paid each employee.

4. Assume that Check 516 was issued on July 22 to deposit the FUTA tax for the first and second quarters. Make an entry in general journal form to record the tax deposit.

5. Compute the federal unemployment tax due for the third quarter. Indicate by a general journal entry or a statement whether a deposit is necessary.

6. On January 5, 19X6, the firm paid the estimated premium for worker's compensation insurance for 19X6. The estimated premium was based on an expected payroll of $33,000 and a premium rate of $2.75 per $100 of wages.

   a. In general journal form, make the entry to record issuance of Check 349 to pay the estimated premium on January 5, 19X6.

   b. Compute the balance due for the worker's compensation insurance premium based on the actual payroll for the year. Then make an entry in general journal form to record the issuance of Check 783 for the amount due on January 20, 19X7.

In Chapter 5 you learned that certain adjustments must be made to accounts at the end of each fiscal period so that the income statement will include all revenue and expense items that apply to the current period. In this way, the expenses of the period are matched against the revenues that they helped to produce. Because the matching principle is at the heart of financial reporting today, this chapter provides detailed coverage of the techniques used to adjust the accounts so that they accurately reflect the operations of each period.

ACCRUALS AND DEFERRALS

THE ACCRUAL BASIS
The procedure that most nearly attains the objective of matching revenues and expenses of specific fiscal periods is called the *accrual basis* of accounting. Under the accrual basis, all revenues and all expenses are recognized on the income statement for the applicable period, regardless of when the cash related to the transactions is received or paid.

Revenue is normally recognized when a sale is completed, which is usually when title to the goods passes to the customer or when the service is provided. This occurs even though accounts receivable resulting from sales on credit are not collected immediately. Similarly, the costs related to purchases of merchandise are recorded when the purchases are made—that is, when title to the goods passes to the buyer—regardless of the actual time of payment for the goods. The proper recognition of operating and nonoperating expenses requires that each expense item be assigned to the period in which it helped to earn revenue for the business, even though the item may be paid for in an earlier or later period. Some expense items like rent and utilities are clearly associated with a specific period, but others are more difficult to assign.

Transactions involving revenue and expense items sometimes occur before the period to which they actually relate. For example, insurance premiums are normally paid in advance, and the coverage often extends over several periods. In other cases, the transaction involving a revenue or expense item may not take place until after the period to which the item applies. For example, employees may work during December but not be paid for this work until January of the next year.

Because there is a difference between the time that certain items are recorded in the accounts and the time that they are actually realized or used, it is necessary to examine each account balance at the end of a fiscal period to see if it contains amounts of revenues or expenses that should be allocated to other periods. It is impossible to present an accurate picture of the financial position of a business or the results of its operations for the period until all pertinent information has been recorded and until the *mixed accounts* (accounts that contain elements of both assets and expenses or both liabilities and revenue) have been analyzed. Adjusting entries are usually needed to ensure that the revenue and expense accounts will contain amounts relating only to the current period and that the asset and liability accounts will reflect amounts properly classified as assets and liabilities.

PREPARATION OF THE WORKSHEET

The procedures used at Sports World at the end of its fiscal year on December 31, 19X8, will illustrate typical adjustments that are made in order to provide an accurate financial picture for an operating period. Remember that Sports World is a retail merchandising business that sells a wide range of sporting goods. Transactions that the firm had during 19X5 were discussed in Chapters 7 through 10. Sports World moved to a larger store and greatly expanded its operations in 19X6. To handle the increased complexity and variety of transactions, the accountant developed a new chart of accounts for the firm.

As a basis for the discussion of adjustments, look at the trial balance of Sports World, which has been entered in the first two amount columns of the worksheet on page 355. Notice that some accounts have no balances in the Trial Balance columns. All of these accounts will be used when the adjustments are made.

Additional pairs of debit and credit columns with the following headings are provided on the worksheet: Adjustments, Adjusted Trial Balance, Income Statement, and Balance Sheet. (See the complete worksheet illustrated on pages 390 and 391.)

As discussed in Chapter 5, the amounts of the adjustments for a period are recorded in the Adjustments section of the worksheet. A letter is used to identify the debit and credit parts of each adjusting entry. After recording all adjustments on the worksheet, the accountant totals the two columns in the Adjustments section to check the equality of the debits and credits. Then the accountant combines the amounts in the Adjustments section with the amounts originally recorded in the Trial Balance section. The resulting figures are entered in the Adjusted Trial Balance section as another verification of equality. Finally, the accountant extends all figures to the proper columns of the Income Statement and Balance Sheet sections and completes the worksheet.

The worksheet is a highly useful device for assembling data about a firm's adjustments and organizing the information that will appear on the financial statements.

RECORDING THE LOSS FROM UNCOLLECTIBLE ACCOUNTS ON THE WORKSHEET

Some of the accounts receivable that result from credit sales are never collected because the customers become bankrupt or for other reasons. The loss from uncollectible accounts represents an operating expense for a business and should be matched against the revenue recorded when the sales were made. Often, however, the specific uncollectible accounts are not known until later periods. To

	ACCT. NO.	ACCOUNT NAME	TRIAL BALANCE DEBIT	TRIAL BALANCE CREDIT
1	101	Cash	15,300 00	
2	105	Petty Cash Fund	100 00	
3	107	Change Fund	200 00	
4	109	Notes Receivable	800 00	
5	111	Accounts Receivable	24,000 00	
6	112	Allowance for Uncollectible Accounts		50 00
7	116	Interest Receivable		
8	121	Merchandise Inventory	63,000 00	
9	131	Supplies	4,835 00	
10	133	Prepaid Insurance	3,120 00	
11	135	Prepaid Interest	225 00	
12	141	Store Equipment	8,900 00	
13	142	Accumulated Depreciation—Store Equipment		3,200 00
14	151	Office Equipment	2,750 00	
15	152	Accumulated Depreciation—Office Equipment		980 00
16	201	Notes Payable—Trade		2,000 00
17	203	Notes Payable—Bank		9,000 00
18	205	Accounts Payable		6,500 00
19	216	Interest Payable		
20	221	FICA Tax Payable		938 00
21	223	Employee Income Tax Payable		804 00
22	225	Federal Unemployment Tax Payable		22 00
23	227	State Unemployment Tax Payable		60 00
24	229	Salaries Payable		
25	231	Sales Tax Payable		6,600 00
26	301	Lynn Frank, Capital		75,314 00
27	302	Lynn Frank, Drawing	30,000 00	
28	401	Sales		422,000 00
29	451	Sales Returns and Allowances	7,400 00	
30	491	Interest Income		136 00
31	493	Miscellaneous Income		366 00
32	501	Merchandise Purchases	248,500 00	
33	502	Freight In	3,300 00	
34	503	Purchases Returns and Allowances		2,700 00
35	504	Purchases Discount		4,900 00
36	511	Sales Salaries Expense	71,300 00	
37	514	Advertising Expense	6,900 00	
38	517	Supplies Expense		
39	520	Cash Short or Over	75 00	
40	523	Delivery Expense	1,200 00	
41	526	Depreciation Expense—Store Equipment		
42	529	Insurance Expense		
43	532	Cleaning Service Expense	1,800 00	
44	535	Rent Expense	12,000 00	
45	538	Utilities Expense	2,550 00	
46	541	Office Salaries Expense	16,200 00	
47	544	Payroll Taxes Expense	7,705 00	
48	547	Office Expense	390 00	
49	550	Professional Services Expense	1,100 00	
50	553	Telephone Expense	1,320 00	
51	556	Loss From Uncollectible Accounts		
52	559	Depreciation Expense—Office Equipment		
53	591	Interest Expense	600 00	
		Totals	535,570 00	535,570 00

permit the matching of the expense for uncollectible accounts with the sales revenue for the current period, accountants have developed several methods for estimating the amount of loss that will be incurred. This amount is recorded as an adjustment at the end of the period.

At Sports World, the estimated loss from uncollectible accounts is calculated as a percent of the net credit sales for the year. The rate used is based on the firm's past experience with uncollectible accounts and the accountant's assessment of current business conditions. For 19X8, the accountant estimates that three-tenths of a percent (0.3 percent) of the firm's net credit sales of $190,000 will result in uncollectible accounts of $570 ($190,000 $\times$ 0.003 = $570). This estimated loss is recorded in the Adjustments section of the year-end worksheet, as shown below. An expense account called Loss From Uncollectible Accounts is debited for the sum and a contra asset account called Allowance for Uncollectible Accounts is credited. The figures are labeled (a) to identify the two parts of the entry for future reference.

ACCT. NO.	ACCOUNT NAME	TRIAL BALANCE		ADJUSTMENTS	
		DEBIT	CREDIT	DEBIT	CREDIT
112	Allowance for Uncollectible Accounts		50 00		(a)570 00
556	Loss From Uncollectible Accounts			(a)570 00	

Notice that Allowance for Uncollectible Accounts has a credit balance of $50 in the Trial Balance section of the worksheet. When the estimate of the loss from uncollectible accounts is based on sales, the exact amount of loss calculated for each period is credited to this account. Any remaining balance from previous periods is not considered when recording the adjustment.

Loss From Uncollectible Accounts appears in the Operating Expenses section of the income statement. Allowance for Uncollectible Accounts is reported in the Assets section of the balance sheet, where its balance is deducted from the balance of Accounts Receivable. The resulting figure is the estimated collectible amount of the firm's accounts receivable.

In later periods, whenever the account of a specific customer becomes uncollectible, it must be written off. A general journal entry is made debiting Allowance for Uncollectible Accounts and crediting Accounts Receivable and the customer's account in the accounts receivable subsidiary ledger. Notice that the expense account Loss From Uncollectible Accounts is not involved in this entry. It is used only when the end-of-period adjustment is recorded and is not affected by the later writeoff of individual accounts that have been identified as uncollectible.

The balance of Allowance for Uncollectible Accounts is reduced throughout the fiscal year as customer accounts are written off.

As discussed in Chapter 5, most businesses have long-term assets that require an end-of-period adjustment for depreciation. These assets are often referred to as *property, plant, and equipment* and include such items as buildings, trucks, automobiles, machinery, furniture, fixtures, and office equipment. Land is the only long-term asset that is not subject to depreciation.

Remember that *depreciation* is the process of allocating the cost of a long-term asset to operations during its expected *useful life*—the number of years that the asset will be used in the business. This process involves the gradual transfer of acquisition cost to expense. Depreciation is recorded on the worksheet at the end of each fiscal period by a debit to a depreciation expense account and a credit to an accumulated depreciation account (a contra asset account).

There are a number of different methods for calculating yearly depreciation. Sports World uses the *straight-line method* for the two types of long-term assets that it owns: store equipment and office equipment. With this method, an equal amount of depreciation is taken in each year of the asset's expected useful life.

To apply the straight-line method, the accountant first determines the useful life and estimates the *salvage value*—the amount that the asset can be sold for when the firm disposes of it at the end of its useful life. The cost less the salvage value is known as the *depreciable base* of the asset. This sum is divided by the number of years in the asset's useful life to find the amount of yearly depreciation, as shown in the following formula.

$$\frac{\text{Depreciable Base}}{\text{Useful Life}} = \text{Yearly Depreciation}$$

or

$$\frac{\text{Cost} - \text{Salvage Value}}{\text{Useful Life}} = \text{Yearly Depreciation}$$

Depreciation of Store Equipment

At the beginning of January 19X6, when Sports World moved to a larger store, it purchased new store equipment for $8,900. The balance of the Store Equipment account reflects this acquisition cost. Since the firm's accountant assigned a useful life of 5 years to the items and a salvage value of $900, the yearly depreciation is $1,600.

$$\frac{\$8,900 \text{ (cost)} - \$900 \text{ (salvage value)}}{5 \text{ years (useful life)}} = \$1,600 \text{ (yearly depreciation)}$$

The necessary adjustment for store equipment appears on the 19X8 worksheet as shown on page 358. The two parts of the entry are labeled (*b*).

Depreciation of Office Equipment

At the beginning of 19X6, Sports World also purchased new office equipment. The balance of the Office Equipment account shows that the items had a total cost of $2,750. The assigned useful life is 5 years, and the estimated salvage value is $300. Based on this data, the yearly depreciation is calculated as $490.

$$\frac{\$2,750 \text{ (cost)} - \$300 \text{ (salvage value)}}{5 \text{ years (useful life)}} = \$490 \text{ (yearly depreciation)}$$

The adjustment for office equipment is labeled (*c*) on the 19X8 worksheet illustrated below.

ACCT. NO.	ACCOUNT NAME	TRIAL BALANCE		ADJUSTMENTS	
		DEBIT	CREDIT	DEBIT	CREDIT
142	Accumulated Depreciation—Store Equipment		3,200 00		(b)1,600 00
152	Accumulated Depreciation—Office Equipment		980 00		(c)490 00
526	Depreciation Expense—Store Equipment			(b)1,600 00	
559	Depreciation Expense—Office Equipment			(c)490 00	

RECORDING ACCRUED AND PREPAID ITEMS ON THE WORKSHEET

Many expense items clearly belong to a particular fiscal period. They are paid for and used during that period and appear in the accounts at the end of the period. However, as mentioned previously, some expense items involve a more complex situation because they are paid for and recorded in one period but not fully used until a later period. Other expense items are used in one period but not paid for and recorded until a later period. When these situations occur, adjustments must be made so that the financial statements for the period will show all expenses related to the firm's current operations—no more and no less. Similar adjustments may also be required for revenue items so that the financial statements will accurately reflect the income earned during the period.

Accrued Expenses

Accrued expenses are expense items that relate to the current period but have not yet been paid for and do not yet appear in the accounts. On December 31, 19X8, Sports World has three accrued expense items that require adjustments: accrued salaries, accrued payroll taxes, and accrued interest on notes payable. Because accrued expenses involve amounts that must be paid in the future, the necessary adjustment for each item consists of a debit to an expense account and a credit to a liability account.

Accrued Salaries All full-time sales and office employees at Sports World are paid semimonthly—on the fifteenth and the last day of each month. Hence, the trial balance prepared on December 31, 19X8, reflects the correct salaries expense for these employees for the year. However, the firm also has several part-time salesclerks who are paid weekly. On December 31, 19X8, salaries totaling $400 are owed to these employees and have not been recorded, because they are not due for payment until January 3, 19X9. Since the expense for these salaries properly belongs to 19X8, the accountant makes an adjustment debiting Sales Salaries Expense and crediting Salaries Payable for $400. This entry appears on the worksheet shown on page 359, where it is labeled (*d*).

ACCT. NO.	ACCOUNT NAME	TRIAL BALANCE DEBIT	TRIAL BALANCE CREDIT	ADJUSTMENTS DEBIT	ADJUSTMENTS CREDIT
229	Salaries Payable				(d)400 00
511	Sales Salaries Expense	71,300 00		(d)400 00	

Accrued Payroll Taxes As of December 31, 19X8, the accounts of Sports World include all payroll taxes owed on the salaries of the firm's full-time employees. However, the employer's payroll taxes on the accrued salaries of the part-time salesclerks have not been recorded. An examination of the firm's payroll records shows that the entire $400 of accrued salaries is subject to the employer's share of the FICA tax, and $250 is subject to FUTA tax and SUTA tax. With an assumed rate of 7 percent for FICA tax and rates of 0.8 percent for FUTA tax and 2 percent for SUTA tax, the accrued payroll taxes for the period are computed as follows.

$$
\begin{aligned}
\text{FICA tax: } \$400 \times 0.07 &= \$28 \\
\text{FUTA tax: } \$250 \times 0.008 &= 2 \\
\text{SUTA tax: } \$250 \times 0.02 &= \underline{5} \\
\text{Total accrued payroll taxes} &= \underline{\underline{\$35}}
\end{aligned}
$$

The accountant records the necessary adjustment for accrued payroll taxes on the worksheet by debiting Payroll Taxes Expense for $35 and crediting FICA Tax Payable for $28, Federal Unemployment Tax Payable for $2, and State Unemployment Tax Payable for $5. The four amounts are labeled (e) on the worksheet shown below.

ACCT. NO.	ACCOUNT NAME	TRIAL BALANCE DEBIT	TRIAL BALANCE CREDIT	ADJUSTMENTS DEBIT	ADJUSTMENTS CREDIT
221	FICA Tax Payable		938 00		(e)28 00
225	Federal Unemployment Tax Payable		22 00		(e)2 00
227	State Unemployment Tax Payable		60 00		(e)5 00
544	Payroll Taxes Expense	7,705 00		(e)35 00	

Not all businesses make an adjustment for accrued payroll taxes because the taxes are not legally owed until the salaries are paid to the employees. However, in order to match revenue and expenses as closely as possible, some accountants prefer to record the expense for accrued payroll taxes at the end of the fiscal period, even though it is not technically necessary to do so. The accountant for Sports World uses this approach.

Accrued Interest on Notes Payable On December 1, 19X8, Sports World issued a 2-month note for $2,000 with interest at 12 percent to a creditor. At the time, the amount of the note was recorded in the Notes Payable—Trade account, but no entry was made for the interest, which will be paid when the note matures on February 1, 19X9. However, the interest expense is actually incurred day by day and should be apportioned to each fiscal period involved in order to obtain a complete and accurate picture of expenses. At the end of the fiscal year on December 31, 19X8, the accountant for Sports World therefore makes an adjustment for 1 month of accrued interest on the trade note payable.

The amount of accrued interest to record is determined by using the interest formula Principal $\times$ Rate $\times$ Time, as shown below. The principal is the amount of the note ($2,000); the rate is 12 percent, which is expressed as the fraction $\frac{12}{100}$; and the time is 1 month, which is expressed as the fraction $\frac{1}{12}$.

$$\$2,000 \times \tfrac{12}{100} \times \tfrac{1}{12} = \$20$$

The adjustment consists of a debit to Interest Expense and a credit to a liability account called Interest Payable. This entry is labeled (f) on the firm's worksheet, as shown below.

ACCT. NO.	ACCOUNT NAME	TRIAL BALANCE		ADJUSTMENTS	
		DEBIT	CREDIT	DEBIT	CREDIT
216	Interest Payable				(f)20 00
591	Interest Expense	600 00		(f)20 00	

Other Accrued Expenses Accrued property taxes represent another common accrued expense item. Many businesses are subject to property taxes imposed by state and local governments and find it necessary to accrue some of these taxes at the end of the fiscal period.

Prepaid Expenses

Prepaid, or *deferred, expenses* are expense items that are paid for and recorded in advance of their use. Often a portion of the item remains unused at the end of the fiscal period and is therefore applicable to future periods. Because of the nature of these items, many businesses treat them as assets when they are paid for and initially recorded. At the end of each fiscal period, an adjustment is made to transfer the cost of the portion used during the period from the asset account to an expense account. Sports World uses this approach in handling the three prepaid expense items that it has: supplies, prepaid insurance, and prepaid interest on notes payable.

Supplies Used At Sports World, store supplies are purchased in fairly large quantities and are debited to the asset account Supplies. On December 31, 19X8, when the trial balance was prepared, this account had a balance of $4,835. However, an inventory of the supplies taken on that date showed that items costing $610 were actually on hand. This means that items costing $4,225 were used during the year ($4,835 − $610 = $4,225). To charge the cost of the supplies used to the current year's operations, and to avoid overstating the firm's assets, the accountant makes an adjustment debiting Supplies Expense and crediting Supplies for $4,225. This adjustment is labeled (g) on the firm's worksheet, as shown below.

ACCT. NO.	ACCOUNT NAME	TRIAL BALANCE		ADJUSTMENTS	
		DEBIT	CREDIT	DEBIT	CREDIT
131	Supplies	4,835 00			(g)4,225 00
517	Supplies Expense			(g)4,225 00	

Sports World purchases office supplies in very small quantities and debits them directly to an expense account called Office Expense. This account is also used to record the cost of other minor items needed for the office, such as postage stamps. The amount of office supplies is too limited to warrant handling as a prepaid expense item.

Expired Insurance On April 1, 19X8, Sports World purchased a 1-year insurance policy for $3,120 and paid the full premium in advance. The amount was debited to the asset account Prepaid Insurance. On December 31, 19X8, this account still has a balance of $3,120, but the insurance coverage for 9 months has expired. The accountant must therefore make an adjustment to charge the cost of the expired insurance to operations and to decrease the firm's assets so that they reflect only the insurance coverage that still remains. This is done by debiting Insurance Expense and crediting Prepaid Insurance for $2,340 ($\frac{9}{12}$ of the original premium of $3,120). The necessary adjustment is labeled (h) on the firm's worksheet, as shown below.

ACCT. NO.	ACCOUNT NAME	TRIAL BALANCE		ADJUSTMENTS	
		DEBIT	CREDIT	DEBIT	CREDIT
133	Prepaid Insurance	3,120 00			(h)2,340 00
529	Insurance Expense			(h)2,340 00	

Prepaid Interest on Notes Payable On November 1, 19X8, Sports World borrowed money from its bank and gave a 3-month note for $9,000, bearing interest at 10 percent. The bank deducted the entire amount of interest ($225) in advance, and the firm therefore received $8,775. This transaction was recorded by debiting Cash for $8,775, debiting an asset account called Prepaid Interest for $225, and crediting Notes Payable—Bank for $9,000.

By the end of the fiscal year on December 31, 19X8, 2 months had passed since the note was issued to the bank and only 1 month remained until the maturity date of February 1, 19X9. Thus, two-thirds of the prepaid interest should properly be recorded as an expense for 19X8. To accomplish this, the accountant makes an adjustment debiting Interest Expense and crediting Prepaid Interest for $150 ($\frac{2}{3}$ of $225). The required adjustment is labeled (*i*) on the firm's worksheet, as shown below.

ACCT. NO.	ACCOUNT NAME	TRIAL BALANCE		ADJUSTMENTS	
		DEBIT	CREDIT	DEBIT	CREDIT
135	Prepaid Interest	225 00			(i)150 00
591	Interest Expense	600 00		(f)20 00 (i)150 00	

Other Prepaid Expenses Prepaid rent, prepaid advertising, and prepaid taxes are other common prepaid expense items. When these items are initially paid for, the amounts are debited to asset accounts—Prepaid Rent, Prepaid Advertising, and Prepaid Taxes. At the end of each fiscal period, an adjustment is made to transfer the portion that expired during the period from the asset account to an expense account. For example, the adjustment for expired rent would consist of a debit to Rent Expense and a credit to Prepaid Rent.

Alternative Method Some businesses use a different method to handle prepaid expense items. When they pay for the item, they debit its cost to an expense account. At the end of each fiscal period, they make an adjustment to transfer the unexpired portion from the expense account to an asset account. For example, suppose that a firm using this method purchases a 1-year insurance policy on August 1, 19X8, and pays the full premium of $1,200 in advance. The transaction is recorded by debiting Insurance Expense and crediting Cash for $1,200. At the end of the firm's fiscal year on December 31, 19X8, the insurance coverage for 5 months has expired and the coverage for 7 months remains. The firm therefore makes an adjustment debiting Prepaid Insurance and crediting Insurance Expense for $700, which is the cost of the unexpired insurance ($\frac{7}{12}$ of $1,200).

No matter which method is used to handle prepaid expenses, the same figures will be reported on the financial statements at the end of each fiscal period.

Accrued Income

Accrued income is income that has been earned but not yet received and recorded. If at the time the trial balance is prepared, there is any item of this nature, an adjustment is necessary so that the income statement will include all the income that belongs to the current period. The appropriate revenue account must be credited to increase its balance even though the amount will not be collected until a later period. The offsetting debit may be to an asset account or a liability account, depending on the item involved. At the end of its fiscal year on December 31, 19X8, Sports World had two types of accrued income—accrued interest on notes receivable and accrued commission on sales tax.

Accrued Interest on Notes Receivable Interest-bearing notes receivable are usually recorded at their face value when obtained and are carried in the accounting records at this value until they are collected. The interest income is recorded when it is received, which is normally when the note is settled at maturity. However, the interest is actually earned day by day throughout the time that the note is held. Therefore, at the end of a fiscal period, any accrued interest that has been earned but not recorded should be recognized by means of an adjustment.

On November 1, 19X8, Sports World accepted a 4-month, 12 percent note for $800 from a customer with an overdue balance. The interest is due on March 1, 19X9, when the note is paid. However, the interest for 2 months (November and December) represents income for 19X8. This amount is calculated by using the interest formula discussed previously: Principal × Rate × Time = Interest.

$$\$800 \times \tfrac{12}{100} \times \tfrac{2}{12} = \$16$$

To record the interest income of $16 earned in 19X8 but not yet received, the accountant makes an adjustment debiting an asset account called Interest Receivable and crediting a revenue account called Interest Income. The two parts of the entry are labeled (*j*) on the worksheet shown below.

ACCT. NO.	ACCOUNT NAME	TRIAL BALANCE DEBIT	TRIAL BALANCE CREDIT	ADJUSTMENTS DEBIT	ADJUSTMENTS CREDIT
116	Interest Receivable			(j)16 00	
491	Interest Income		136 00		(j)16 00

Accrued Commission on Sales Tax Sports World is located in a state that imposes a sales tax on retail sales. Businesses collect this tax from customers and remit it to a state agency on a quarterly basis. The sales tax law allows the firms to keep 2 percent of the tax money if they file the quarterly tax return and pay the net amount due promptly. On December 31, 19X8, Sports World owed sales tax of $6,600 for the fourth quarter of the year. The tax will be paid on schedule in

January 19X9, and the permitted commission of $132 will be deducted at that time ($6,600 × 0.02 = $132).

Because the commission represents income earned in 19X8, the accountant for Sports World makes the following adjustment on the year-end worksheet. The amount is debited to Sales Tax Payable and credited to a revenue account called Miscellaneous Income. The two parts of the entry are labeled (*k*).

ACCT. NO.	ACCOUNT NAME	TRIAL BALANCE		ADJUSTMENTS	
		DEBIT	CREDIT	DEBIT	CREDIT
231	Sales Tax Payable		6,600 00	(k)132 00	
493	Miscellaneous Income		366 00		(k)132 00

The effect of this adjustment is to decrease the firm's liability for the sales tax owed and to increase its income to reflect the commission that has been earned but not yet taken.

Unearned Income

Some businesses have *unearned,* or *deferred, income*—income that is received before it is earned. Under the accrual basis of accounting, any portion of a firm's income that has been received but not earned during a fiscal period should not be reported on the income statement prepared for the period. The amount should be reported as income only when it is earned in a succeeding period. Since there are no unearned income items at Sports World, an example from another type of business is presented here.

Unearned Subscription Income for a Publisher Magazine publishers obtain subscriptions in advance, often several years in advance. When a publisher first receives income from subscriptions, it is unearned; and the subscriptions represent a liability because the publisher has an obligation to provide the magazines during the specified period of time. As the magazines are sent to the subscribers, the income is gradually earned and the liability decreases.

To illustrate the accounting treatment of unearned subscription income, let us consider the operations of an imaginary publisher, the Briggs Corporation. Assume that this firm starts a new magazine called *Computer Trends* at the beginning of 19X8. Whenever subscriptions are received during the year, the amounts are debited to Cash and credited to a liability account called Unearned Subscription Income. At the end of 19X8, this liability account has a balance of $225,000. An examination of the firm's records shows that $100,000 of the balance applies to subscriptions for the current year and has therefore been earned in 19X8. The accountant makes an adjustment to transfer the earned amount from the liability account to a revenue account. This adjustment involves a debit to Unearned Subscription Income and a credit to Subscription Income for $100,000, as shown on the worksheet on page 365.

ACCT. NO.	ACCOUNT NAME	TRIAL BALANCE		ADJUSTMENTS	
		DEBIT	CREDIT	DEBIT	CREDIT
241	Unearned Subscription Income		225,000 00	(a)100,000 00	
411	Subscription Income				(a)100,000 00

After the adjustment is journalized and posted, the Unearned Subscription Income account has a balance of $125,000, which represents subscriptions that apply to future periods. This amount appears as a liability on the balance sheet prepared for December 31, 19X8. The balance of $100,000 in the Subscription Income account appears as revenue from operations on the 19X8 income statement.

Other Unearned Income Items In addition to magazine publishers, many other types of business and professional firms receive unearned income. For example, management fees, rental income, legal fees, architectural fees, construction fees, and advertising income are often obtained in advance. The normal practice in each case is to record the unearned income in a liability account when it is first received and then transfer the earned amount to a revenue account at the end of the fiscal period.

Alternative Method There is an alternative method for handling unearned income. Under this method, the funds are initially recorded in a revenue account. At the end of each fiscal period, the balance of the revenue account is analyzed, and any income that is still unearned is transferred to a liability account. For example, if unearned subscription income is treated in this manner, it is credited to the Subscription Income account when it is obtained. The end-of-period adjustment consists of a debit to Subscription Income and a credit to Unearned Subscription Income for the remaining unearned amount.

No matter which method is used to handle unearned income, the same figures will appear on the financial statements at the end of the period.

RECORDING ENDING MERCHANDISE INVENTORY ON THE WORKSHEET

In a merchandising business like Sports World, there is one additional account that must be updated in order to present an accurate financial picture for the period—the Merchandise Inventory account. When the trial balance is taken at the end of the period, this account still shows the beginning inventory. Before the financial statements are prepared, its balance must be updated to reflect the ending inventory for the period. Because this change is recorded in the financial statement sections of the worksheet rather than in the Adjustments section, the necessary procedure is described in Chapter 16.

SPORTS WORLD
Worksheet (Partial)
Year Ended December 31, 19X8

	ACCT. NO.	ACCOUNT NAME	TRIAL BALANCE DEBIT	CREDIT	ADJUSTMENTS DEBIT	CREDIT	ADJUSTED TRIAL BALANCE DEBIT	CREDIT
1	101	Cash	15,300 00				15,300 00	
2	105	Petty Cash Fund	100 00				100 00	
3	107	Change Fund	200 00				200 00	
4	109	Notes Receivable	800 00				800 00	
5	111	Accounts Receivable	24,000 00				24,000 00	
6	112	Allow. for Uncollectible Accounts		50 00		(a)570 00		620 00
7	116	Interest Receivable			(j)16 00		16 00	
8	121	Merchandise Inventory	63,000 00				63,000 00	
9	131	Supplies	4,835 00			(g)4,225 00	610 00	
10	133	Prepaid Insurance	3,120 00			(h)2,340 00	780 00	
11	135	Prepaid Interest	225 00			(i)150 00	75 00	
12	141	Store Equipment	8,900 00				8,900 00	
13	142	Accum. Depreciation—Store Equipment		3,200 00		(b)1,600 00		4,800 00
14	151	Office Equipment	2,750 00				2,750 00	
15	152	Accum. Depreciation—Office Equipment		980 00		(c)490 00		1,470 00
16	201	Notes Payable—Trade		2,000 00				2,000 00
17	203	Notes Payable—Bank		9,000 00				9,000 00
18	205	Accounts Payable		6,500 00				6,500 00
19	216	Interest Payable				(f)20 00		20 00
20	221	FICA Tax Payable		938 00		(e)28 00		966 00
21	223	Employee Income Tax Payable		804 00				804 00
22	225	Fed. Unempl. Tax Payable		22 00		(e)2 00		24 00
23	227	State Unempl. Tax Payable		60 00		(e)5 00		65 00
24	229	Salaries Payable				(d)400 00		400 00
25	231	Sales Tax Payable		6,600 00	(k)132 00			6,468 00
26	301	Lynn Frank, Capital		75,314 00				75,314 00
27	302	Lynn Frank, Drawing	30,000 00				30,000 00	
28	401	Sales		422,000 00				422,000 00
29	451	Sales Returns and Allowances	7,400 00				7,400 00	
30	491	Interest Income		136 00		(j)16 00		152 00
31	493	Miscellaneous Income		366 00		(k)132 00		498 00
32	501	Merchandise Purchases	248,500 00				248,500 00	
33	502	Freight In	3,300 00				3,300 00	
34	503	Purchases Returns and Allowances		2,700 00				2,700 00
35	504	Purchases Discount		4,900 00				4,900 00
36	511	Sales Salaries Expense	71,300 00		(d)400 00		71,700 00	
37	514	Advertising Expense	6,900 00				6,900 00	
38	517	Supplies Expense			(g)4,225 00		4,225 00	
39	520	Cash Short or Over	75 00				75 00	
40	523	Delivery Expense	1,200 00				1,200 00	
41	526	Depr. Expense—Store Equipment			(b)1,600 00		1,600 00	
42	529	Insurance Expense			(h)2,340 00		2,340 00	
43	532	Cleaning Service Expense	1,800 00				1,800 00	
44	535	Rent Expense	12,000 00				12,000 00	
45	538	Utilities Expense	2,550 00				2,550 00	
46	541	Office Salaries Expense	16,200 00				16,200 00	
47	544	Payroll Taxes Expense	7,705 00		(e)35 00		7,740 00	
48	547	Office Expense	390 00				390 00	
49	550	Professional Services Expense	1,100 00				1,100 00	
50	553	Telephone Expense	1,320 00				1,320 00	
51	556	Loss From Uncollectible Accounts			(a)570 00		570 00	
52	559	Depr. Expense—Office Equipment			(c)490 00 (f)20 00		490 00	
53	591	Interest Expense	600 00		(i)150 00		770 00	
		Totals	535,570 00	535,570 00	9,978 00	9,978 00	538,701 00	538,701 00

After all adjustments are entered on the worksheet, an adjusted trial balance must be prepared. This task involves combining the original trial balance figures and the adjustments in order to determine the updated account balances for the period. The columns of the adjusted trial balance are then totaled to make sure that the debits and credits are equal. The partial worksheet illustrated on page 366 shows the adjusted trial balance for Sports World on December 31, 19X8.

Notice that the balances of the accounts that did not require adjustment have simply been extended to the Adjusted Trial Balance section from the Trial Balance section. For example, the $15,300 balance of the Cash account that appears in the Debit column of the Trial Balance section was recorded in the Debit column of the Adjusted Trial Balance section without any change.

When figures must be combined to calculate updated account balances, the following procedures are used.

1. If an account has a debit balance in the Trial Balance section and there is a debit entry in the Adjustments section, the two amounts are added. For example, the original debit balance of $71,300 for Sales Salaries Expense and the adjustment of $400 were added to find the updated balance of $71,700.
2. If an account has a debit balance in the Trial Balance section and there is a credit entry in the Adjustments section, the credit amount is subtracted. For example, the adjustment of $4,225 for Supplies was subtracted from the original debit balance of $4,835 to find the updated balance of $610.
3. If an account has a credit balance in the Trial Balance section and there is a credit entry in the Adjustments section, the two amounts are added. For example, the original credit balance of $50 for Allowance for Uncollectible Accounts and the adjustment of $570 were added to find the updated balance of $620.
4. If an account has a credit balance in the Trial Balance section and there is a debit entry in the Adjustments section, the debit amount is subtracted. For example, the adjustment of $132 for Sales Tax Payable was subtracted from the original credit balance of $6,600 to find the updated balance of $6,468.

PRINCIPLES AND PROCEDURES SUMMARY

The accrual basis of accounting requires that all revenue and expenses of a fiscal period be matched and reported on the income statement of the period to determine the net income or net loss. Typically, certain adjustments must be made to the revenue and expense accounts at the end of the period in order to make sure that they correctly reflect amounts that apply to the current period and do not include amounts that pertain to other periods. Provisions for the expense for uncollectible accounts and the expense for depreciation are common examples of such adjustments. Other typical adjustments of expense accounts involve accrued expenses and prepaid expenses.

Accrued expenses represent expense items that have been incurred or used but not yet paid or recorded. Prepaid, or deferred, expenses represent expense items that have been recorded but not yet incurred or used. A firm may also have adjustments involving accrued income and unearned income. Accrued income is income that has been earned but not yet recorded. Unearned, or deferred, income is income that has not yet been earned but has been received and recorded.

MANAGERIAL IMPLICATIONS

The matching process is necessary if managers are to know the true revenue, expenses, and net income or net loss of a period. If accrued and deferred items were not adjusted, the financial statements would be incomplete and misleading; and they would therefore be of no help in evaluating operations. Since adjustments tend to increase or decrease net income or net loss, managers should be familiar with the procedures and underlying assumptions used by their firm's accountant to handle accruals and deferrals.

REVIEW QUESTIONS

1. What is the purpose of the accrual basis of accounting?
2. Under the accrual basis, when is revenue from sales normally recognized?
3. Under the accrual basis, when are the costs related to purchases of goods normally recorded?
4. Under the accrual basis, when are operating and nonoperating expenses normally recognized?
5. Why must the accounts be examined carefully at the end of a fiscal period before financial statements are prepared?
6. What are mixed accounts?
7. Why should the estimated expense for uncollectible accounts be recorded before the losses from these accounts actually occur?
8. What adjustment is made to record the estimated expense for uncollectible accounts?
9. What is depreciation?
10. What types of assets are subject to depreciation? Give three examples of such assets.
11. Explain the meaning of the following terms that relate to depreciation.
    a. Salvage value
    b. Depreciable base
    c. Useful life
    d. Straight-line method
12. What adjustment is made for depreciation on office equipment?
13. What is an accrued expense? Give three examples of items that often become accrued expenses.
14. What adjustment is made to record accrued salaries?
15. What is a prepaid expense? Give three examples of prepaid expense items.
16. How is the cost of an insurance policy recorded when the policy is purchased?

17. What adjustment is made to record expired insurance?
18. What is the alternative method of handling prepaid expenses?
19. What is accrued income? Give an example of an item that might produce accrued income.
20. What adjustment is made for accrued interest on a note receivable?
21. What is unearned income? Give two examples of items that would be classified as unearned income.
22. How is unearned subscription income recorded when it is received?
23. What adjustment is made to record the subscription income earned during a period?
24. What is the alternative method of handling unearned income?

MANAGERIAL DISCUSSION QUESTIONS

1. Assume that you are the newly hired controller for the Bradshaw Company, a wholesale firm that sells most of its goods on credit. You have found that the business does not make an adjustment for estimated uncollectible accounts at the end of each year. Instead, the expense for uncollectible accounts is recorded during the year as individual accounts are identified as bad debts. Would you recommend that the firm continue its present accounting treatment of uncollectible accounts? Why or why not?

2. On July 1, 19X5, the Roland Company rented a portion of its warehouse to another business for a 1-year period and received the full amount of $4,200 in advance. At the end of Roland's fiscal year on December 31, 19X5, the firm's income statement showed $2,100 as rental income. The other $2,100 appeared in the liabilities section of the firm's balance sheet as unearned rental income. The owner, James Roland, felt that the entire sum should have been reported on the income statement as income because all the cash was received in 19X5. How would you explain to Roland why the accountant's treatment of the $4,200 was correct?

3. Some firms initially record the cost of an insurance policy as an expense and then make an adjustment at the end of the fiscal year to transfer the unexpired amount to an asset account. Does this method produce different financial results from the method used by Sports World? Explain.

4. Why is it important for management to understand the accounting methods used to report data on the firm's financial statements?

EXERCISES

EXERCISE 15-1   **Determining an adjustment for uncollectible accounts.** During the year 19X1, the Raymond Company had net credit sales of $850,000. Past experience shows that 0.9 percent of the firm's net credit sales result in uncollectible accounts. What adjustment for uncollectible accounts should be recorded on the firm's worksheet for the year ended December 31, 19X1? Indicate the accounts that should be debited and credited and the amount.

EXERCISE 15-2   **Recording a purchase of equipment.** On January 2, 19X1, the Rizzoli Auto Service Center, a new firm, purchased equipment for $26,000 in cash. In general journal form, show the entry that would be made to record this transaction.

EXERCISE 15-3   **Determining an adjustment for depreciation on equipment.** The equipment purchased by the Rizzoli Auto Service Center for $26,000 on January 2, 19X1, has an estimated useful life of 5 years and an estimated salvage value of $3,500. What adjustment for depreciation should be recorded on the firm's worksheet for the year ended December 31, 19X1? Indicate the accounts that should be debited and credited and the amount.

EXERCISE 15-4   **Determining an adjustment for accrued wages.** On December 31, 19X1, the McConnell Toy Company owed wages of $5,200 to its factory employees, who are paid weekly. What adjustment for accrued factory wages should be recorded on the firm's worksheet for the year ended December 31, 19X1? Indicate the accounts that should be debited and credited and the amount.

EXERCISE 15-5   **Determining an adjustment for accrued payroll taxes.** On December 31, 19X1, the McConnell Toy Company owed the employer's FICA tax on the entire $5,200 of accrued wages for its factory employees and owed FUTA and SUTA taxes on $1,400 of the accrued wages. Assume that the firm is subject to the following tax rates: 7 percent for FICA, 0.8 percent for FUTA, and 2.7 percent for SUTA. What adjustment for accrued payroll taxes should be recorded on the firm's worksheet for the year ended December 31, 19X1? Indicate the accounts that should be debited and credited and the amounts.

EXERCISE 15-6   **Determining an adjustment for accrued interest on a note payable.** On December 31, 19X1, the Notes Payable account at the Orion Manufacturing Company had a balance of $1,500. This represented a 3-month, 12 percent note issued on November 1. What adjustment for accrued interest on the note payable should be recorded on the firm's worksheet for the year ended December 31, 19X1? Indicate the accounts that should be debited and credited and the amount.

EXERCISE 15-7   **Recording a purchase of supplies.** On January 2, 19X1, the Valdez Word Processing Service purchased magnetic disks, paper, and other supplies for $800 in cash. In general journal form, show the entry that would be made to record this transaction. (Assume that Valdez uses the same method of recording supplies as Sports World.)

EXERCISE 15-8   **Determining an adjustment for supplies used.** On December 31, 19X1, an inventory of supplies at the Valdez Word Processing Service showed that items costing $190 were on hand. The Supplies account had a balance of $800. What adjustment for supplies used should be recorded on the firm's worksheet for the year ended December 31, 19X1? Indicate the accounts that should be debited and credited and the amount.

EXERCISE 15-9 **Recording a payment for an insurance policy.** On August 1, 19X1, the Ryan Company paid a premium of $3,240 in cash for a 2-year insurance policy. In general journal form, show the entry that would be made to record this transaction. (Assume that Ryan uses the same method of recording insurance premiums as Sports World.)

EXERCISE 15-10 **Determining an adjustment for expired insurance.** On December 31, 19X1, an examination of the insurance records at the Ryan Company showed that coverage for a period of 5 months had expired on the 2-year policy purchased for $3,240. What adjustment for expired insurance should be recorded on the firm's worksheet for the year ended December 31, 19X1? Indicate the accounts that should be debited and credited and the amount.

EXERCISE 15-11 **Recording a payment for advertising purchased in advance.** On April 1, 19X1, the Harbor Seafood Restaurant signed a 1-year advertising contract with a local radio station and issued a check for $1,920 to pay the total amount owed. In general journal form, show the entry that would be made to record this transaction.

EXERCISE 15-12 **Determining an adjustment for expired advertising.** On December 31, 19X1, the accountant for the Harbor Seafood Restaurant found that the firm had 3 months left on the 1-year advertising contract for $1,920 that it had signed with a local radio station. What adjustment for expired advertising should be recorded on the firm's worksheet for the year ended December 31, 19X1? Indicate the accounts that should be debited and credited and the amount.

EXERCISE 15-13 **Recording a payment of interest in advance.** On December 1, 19X1, the Discount Camera Center borrowed $10,000 from its bank in order to expand its operations. The firm issued a 4-month, 12 percent note for $10,000 to the bank and received $9,600 in cash because the bank deducted the interest for the entire period in advance. In general journal form, show the entry that would be made to record this transaction.

EXERCISE 15-14 **Determining an adjustment for prepaid interest on a note payable.** On December 31, 19X1, the Prepaid Interest account at the Discount Camera Center had a balance of $400. This amount represented the interest deducted in advance on a 4-month note issued by the firm to its bank on December 1. What adjustment for prepaid interest should be recorded on the firm's worksheet for the year ended December 31, 19X1? Indicate the accounts that should be debited and credited and the amount.

EXERCISE 15-15 **Determining an adjustment for accrued interest on a note receivable.** On December 31, 19X1, the Notes Receivable account at the Carroll Company had a balance of $4,800, which represented a 6-month, 10 percent note issued by a customer on August 1. What adjustment for accrued interest on the note receivable should be recorded on the firm's worksheet for the year ended December 31, 19X1? Indicate the accounts that should be debited and credited and the amount.

EXERCISE 15-16   **Determining an adjustment for the accrued commission on sales tax.** On December 31, 19X1, the Sales Tax Payable account at the Lee Shoe Store had a balance of $645. This represented the sales tax owed for the fourth quarter of 19X1. The firm is scheduled to send the amount to the state sales tax agency on January 15, 19X2. At that time, the firm will deduct a commission of 2 percent of the tax due, as allowed by state law. What adjustment for the accrued commission on the sales tax should be recorded on the firm's worksheet for the year ended December 31, 19X1? Indicate the accounts that should be debited and credited and the amount.

EXERCISE 15-17   **Recording the receipt of unearned subscription income.** During the week ended January 7, 19X1, the Kovacs Publishing Company received $12,000 from customers for subscriptions to its magazine *Modern Business*. In general journal form, show the entry that would be made to record this transaction. (The Kovacs Publishing Company uses the same method of recording unearned subscription income as the Briggs Corporation.)

EXERCISE 15-18   **Determining an adjustment for earned subscription income.** On December 31, 19X1, the Unearned Subscription Income account at the Kovacs Publishing Company had a balance of $845,600. An analysis of this amount showed that $430,000 represented income for the current year (19X1) and the rest pertained to future years. What adjustment for earned income should be recorded on the firm's worksheet for the year ended December 31, 19X1? Indicate the accounts that should be debited and credited and the amount.

EXERCISE 15-19   **Recording the receipt of unearned rental income.** On September 1, 19X1, the Hart Real Estate Company rented a commercial building that it owns to a new tenant and received $15,000 in advance to cover the rent for 6 months. In general journal form, show the entry that would be made to record this transaction.

EXERCISE 15-20   **Determining an adjustment for earned rental income.** On December 31, 19X1, the Unearned Rental Income account at the Hart Real Estate Company had a balance of $15,000, which represented rent paid in advance on September 1 for a 6-month period. What adjustment for earned rental income should be recorded on the firm's worksheet for the year ended December 31, 19X1? Indicate the accounts that should be debited and credited and the amount.

PROBLEMS

PROBLEM 15-1 **Journalizing transactions involving prepaid expenses, unearned income, and other items.** On July 1, 19X7, Janet Linz, an attorney, established her own legal practice. Selected accounts and transactions of the firm are given below.

Instructions Record the transactions in general journal form. Omit explanations. (Assume that the firm treats prepaid expenses as assets initially and treats unearned income as a liability initially.)

ACCOUNTS

101	Cash	203	Accounts Payable
121	Supplies	241	Unearned Legal Fees
123	Prepaid Rent	401	Legal Fees
125	Prepaid Insurance	520	Supplies Expense
127	Prepaid Interest	523	Rent Expense
131	Furniture	526	Insurance Expense
141	Equipment	591	Interest Expense
201	Notes Payable		

TRANSACTIONS FOR JULY 1–5, 19X7

July   1 Signed a lease for a suite of offices and issued Check 101 for $4,500 to pay the rent in advance for 6 months.

1 Borrowed money from the Security National Bank by issuing a 4-month, 10 percent note for $6,000. Received $5,800 because the bank deducted the interest in advance.

1 Signed an agreement with the Maxwell Company to act as its legal counsel for a year. Received the entire fee of $1,800 in advance.

1 Purchased office equipment for $3,200 from the Apex Corporation. Issued a 2-month, 12 percent note in payment.

1 Purchased a 1-year insurance policy and issued Check 102 for $840 to pay the entire premium.

3 Purchased office furniture for $5,900 from the Harris Company. Issued Check 103 for $3,900 and agreed to pay the balance in 60 days.

5 Purchased office supplies for $430 and paid for them with Check 104.

PROBLEM 15-2 **Recording adjustments on a worksheet.** On July 31, 19X7, after one month of operations, the general ledger of Janet Linz, attorney, contained the accounts and balances shown on page 374.

Instructions 1. Prepare a partial worksheet with the following sections: Trial Balance, Adjustments, and Adjusted Trial Balance.

2. Use the data about the firm's accounts and balances to complete the Trial Balance section.

3. Enter the adjustments described on page 374 in the Adjustments section. Identify each adjustment with the appropriate letter.

4. Complete the Adjusted Trial Balance section.

ACCOUNTS AND BALANCES

101	Cash	$12,100 Dr.
111	Accounts Receivable	650 Dr.
121	Supplies	430 Dr.
123	Prepaid Rent	4,500 Dr.
125	Prepaid Insurance	840 Dr.
127	Prepaid Interest	200 Dr.
131	Furniture	5,900 Dr.
132	Accum. Depr.—Furniture	
141	Equipment	3,200 Dr.
142	Accum. Depr.—Equipment	
201	Notes Payable	9,200 Cr.
203	Accounts Payable	2,000 Cr.
211	Interest Payable	
241	Unearned Legal Fees	1,800 Cr.
301	Janet Linz, Capital	12,610 Cr.
401	Legal Fees	4,000 Cr.
511	Salaries Expense	1,600 Dr.
514	Utilities Expense	110 Dr.
517	Telephone Expense	80 Dr.
520	Supplies Expense	
523	Rent Expense	
526	Insurance Expense	
529	Depr. Expense—Furniture	
532	Depr. Expense—Equipment	
591	Interest Expense	

ADJUSTMENTS

a. On July 31, an inventory of supplies showed that items costing $380 were on hand. Record an adjustment for the supplies used during July.

b. On July 1, the firm paid $4,500 in advance for 6 months' rent. Record an adjustment for the expired rent for July.

c. On July 1, the firm purchased a 1-year insurance policy for $840. Record an adjustment for the expired insurance for July.

d. On July 1, the firm paid $200 interest in advance on a 4-month note that it issued to its bank. Record an adjustment for the portion of the interest that should be considered an expense for July.

e. On July 3, the firm purchased office furniture for $5,900. The furniture is expected to have a useful life of 5 years and a salvage value of $500. Record an adjustment for depreciation on the furniture for July. (Compute the depreciation for a full month.)

f. On July 1, the firm purchased office equipment for $3,200. The equipment is expected to have a useful life of 5 years and a salvage value of $800. Record an adjustment for depreciation on the equipment for July.

g. On July 1, the firm issued a 2-month, 12 percent note for $3,200. Record an adjustment for the accrued interest for July.

h. On July 1, the firm received a legal fee of $1,800 in advance for a 1-year period. Record an adjustment for the amount earned during July.

PROBLEM 15-3 **Recording adjustments on a worksheet.** The Plant Emporium is a retail store that sells plants, soil, and decorative pots. On December 31, 19X5, the firm's general ledger contained the accounts and balances shown below.

Instructions
1. Prepare the Trial Balance section of a ten-column worksheet. The worksheet should cover the year ended December 31, 19X5.
2. Enter the adjustments described on page 376 in the Adjustments section. Identify each adjustment with the appropriate letter.
3. Complete the Adjusted Trial Balance section.

ACCOUNTS AND BALANCES

101	Cash	$ 4,700 Dr.
111	Accounts Receivable	3,100 Dr.
112	Allowance for Uncollectible Accounts	52 Cr.
121	Merchandise Inventory	11,800 Dr.
131	Supplies	1,200 Dr.
133	Prepaid Advertising	960 Dr.
141	Store Equipment	7,000 Dr.
142	Accum. Depr.—Store Equipment	1,300 Cr.
151	Office Equipment	1,600 Dr.
152	Accum. Depr.—Office Equipment	280 Cr.
201	Notes Payable	5,000 Cr.
203	Accounts Payable	1,750 Cr.
211	Interest Payable	
221	FICA Tax Payable	430 Cr.
223	Employee Income Tax Payable	390 Cr.
225	Federal Unemployment Tax Payable	25 Cr.
227	State Unemployment Tax Payable	83 Cr.
229	Salaries Payable	
231	Sales Tax Payable	850 Cr.
301	Peter Dall, Capital	25,711 Cr.
302	Peter Dall, Drawing	20,000 Dr.
401	Sales	83,600 Cr.
451	Sales Returns and Allowances	1,100 Dr.
491	Miscellaneous Income	49 Cr.
501	Merchandise Purchases	46,400 Dr.
502	Freight In	500 Dr.
503	Purchases Returns and Allowances	430 Cr.
504	Purchases Discount	370 Cr.
511	Rent Expense	6,000 Dr.
514	Telephone Expense	590 Dr.
517	Salaries Expense	14,100 Dr.
520	Payroll Taxes Expense	1,270 Dr.
523	Supplies Expense	
526	Advertising Expense	
529	Depr. Expense—Store Equipment	
532	Depr. Expense—Office Equipment	
535	Loss From Uncollectible Accounts	
591	Interest Expense	

ADJUSTMENTS

a. During 19X5, the firm had net credit sales of $35,000. The accountant estimates that 0.6 percent of these sales will result in uncollectible accounts. Record an adjustment for the expected loss from uncollectible accounts for the year.

b. On December 31, 19X5, an inventory of the supplies showed that items costing $350 were on hand. Record an adjustment for the supplies used during the year.

c. On October 1, 19X5, the firm signed a 6-month advertising contract for $960 with a local newspaper and paid the full amount in advance. Record an adjustment for the expired advertising for the year.

d. On January 2, 19X4, the firm purchased store equipment for $7,000. At that time, the equipment was estimated to have a useful life of 5 years and a salvage value of $500. Record an adjustment for depreciation on the store equipment for 19X5.

e. On January 2, 19X4, the firm purchased office equipment for $1,600. At that time, the equipment was estimated to have a useful life of 5 years and a salvage value of $200. Record an adjustment for depreciation on the office equipment for 19X5.

f. On November 1, 19X5, the firm issued a 3-month, 12 percent note for $5,000. Record an adjustment for the accrued interest on this note for the fiscal year 19X5.

g. On December 31, 19X5, the firm owed salaries of $200 that will not be paid until 19X6. Record an adjustment for the accrued salaries for the fiscal year 19X5.

h. On December 31, 19X5, the firm owed the following payroll taxes on the accrued salaries of $200: the employer's FICA tax (7 percent), FUTA tax (0.8 percent), and SUTA tax (2.7 percent). Record an adjustment for the accrued payroll taxes for 19X5.

i. On December 31, 19X5, the firm owed sales tax of $850 for the fourth quarter of the year. This amount will be paid to the state sales tax agency in January 19X6. At that time, the firm will deduct a commission of 2 percent of the tax due. Record an adjustment for the accrued commission on the sales tax for the fourth quarter of 19X5.

Note: Save your worksheet for use in Problem 16-1.

PROBLEM 15-4   **Recording adjustments on a worksheet.** The Nutri-Products Company is a distributor of nutritious snack foods like granola bars. On December 31, 19X3, the firm's general ledger contained the accounts and balances shown on page 377.

Instructions   1. Prepare the Trial Balance section of a ten-column worksheet. The worksheet should cover the year ended December 31, 19X3.

2. Enter the adjustments described on pages 377 and 378 in the Adjustments section of the firm's worksheet. Identify each adjustment with the appropriate letter.

3. Complete the Adjusted Trial Balance section.

ACCOUNTS AND BALANCES

101	Cash	$ 15,300 Dr.
109	Notes Receivable	4,000 Dr.
111	Accounts Receivable	17,600 Dr.
112	Allowance for Uncollectible Accounts	210 Cr.
116	Interest Receivable	
118	Merchandise Inventory	43,000 Dr.
121	Supplies	5,200 Dr.
123	Prepaid Insurance	2,700 Dr.
131	Office Equipment	3,900 Dr.
132	Accum. Depr.—Office Equipment	1,400 Cr.
141	Warehouse Equipment	14,000 Dr.
142	Accum. Depr.—Warehouse Equipment	4,800 Cr.
201	Notes Payable	15,000 Cr.
205	Accounts Payable	6,100 Cr.
211	Interest Payable	
221	FICA Tax Payable	840 Cr.
223	Employee Income Tax Payable	720 Cr.
225	Federal Unemployment Tax Payable	13 Cr.
227	State Unemployment Tax Payable	20 Cr.
229	Salaries Payable	
301	Gary Smith, Capital	55,267 Cr.
302	Gary Smith, Drawing	28,000 Dr.
401	Sales	330,000 Cr.
451	Sales Returns and Allowances	5,000 Dr.
491	Interest Income	50 Cr.
501	Merchandise Purchases	175,000 Dr.
502	Freight In	3,000 Dr.
503	Purchases Returns and Allowances	4,600 Cr.
504	Purchases Discount	3,400 Cr.
511	Rent Expense	18,000 Dr.
514	Telephone Expense	1,100 Dr.
517	Salaries Expense	80,000 Dr.
520	Payroll Taxes Expense	6,500 Dr.
523	Supplies Expense	
526	Insurance Expense	
529	Depr. Expense—Office Equipment	
532	Depr. Expense—Warehouse Equipment	
535	Loss From Uncollectible Accounts	
591	Interest Expense	120 Dr.

ADJUSTMENTS

a. During 19X3, the firm had net credit sales of $280,000. Past experience indicates that 0.5 percent of these sales should result in uncollectible accounts. Record an adjustment for the expected loss from uncollectible accounts for the year.

b. On August 1, 19X3, the firm received a 6-month, 12 percent note for $4,000 from a customer with an overdue balance. Record an adjustment for accrued interest on this note for 19X3.

c. On December 31, 19X3, an inventory of the supplies showed that items costing $600 were on hand. Record an adjustment for the supplies used.

d. On May 1, 19X3, the firm purchased a 1-year insurance policy for $2,700. Record an adjustment for the expired insurance for the year.

e. On January 2, 19X1, the firm purchased office equipment for $3,900. At that time, the equipment was estimated to have a useful life of 5 years and a salvage value of $400. Record an adjustment for depreciation for 19X3.

f. On January 2, 19X1, the firm purchased warehouse equipment for $14,000. At that time, the equipment was estimated to have a useful life of 5 years and a salvage value of $2,000. Record an adjustment for depreciation for 19X3.

g. On November 1, 19X3, the firm issued a 4-month, 11 percent note for $15,000. Record an adjustment for the accrued interest on this note for 19X3.

h. On December 31, 19X3, the firm owed salaries of $2,500 that will not be paid until 19X4. Record an adjustment for the accrued salaries for 19X3.

i. On December 31, 19X3, the firm owed the employer's FICA tax (7 percent) on $2,500 of accrued salaries, FUTA tax (0.8 percent) on $500 of accrued salaries, and SUTA tax (1.2 percent) on $500 of accrued salaries. Record an adjustment for the accrued payroll taxes for 19X3.

Note: Save your worksheet for use in Problem 16-2.

ALTERNATE PROBLEMS

PROBLEM 15-1A **Journalizing transactions involving prepaid expenses, unearned income, and other items.** On September 1, 19X6, Kevin Doyle, a former college professor, established the Management Skills Company, a firm that will work with large corporations to provide courses for their executives in areas like computer literacy, time management, and human relations. Selected accounts and transactions of the firm are given below and on page 379.

Instructions Record the transactions in general journal form. Omit explanations. (Assume that the firm treats prepaid expenses as assets initially and treats unearned income as a liability initially.)

ACCOUNTS

101	Cash	131	Furniture	401	Course Fees
121	Supplies	141	Equipment	520	Supplies Expense
123	Prepaid Rent	201	Notes Payable	523	Rent Expense
125	Prepaid Advertising	203	Accounts Payable	526	Advertising Expense
127	Prepaid Interest	241	Unearned Course Fees	591	Interest Expense

TRANSACTIONS FOR SEPTEMBER 1–5, 19X6

Sept. 1 Signed a lease for an office and issued Check 101 for $2,100 to pay the rent in advance for 6 months.

  1 Signed an agreement with the Webster Corporation to provide courses at its headquarters during the months of September, October, and November. Received the entire fee of $9,000 in advance.

1 Borrowed money from the Madison National Bank by issuing a 3-month, 12 percent note for $7,500. Received $7,275 because the bank deducted the interest in advance.

1 Purchased office furniture for $2,800 from Lane Office Systems. Issued a 2-month, 9 percent note in payment.

1 Signed a 6-month advertising contract for $1,200 with a business magazine. Issued Check 102 to pay the entire amount in advance.

3 Purchased videotape equipment and other equipment needed for the courses for $4,500 from the Ward Company. Issued Check 103 for $2,500 and agreed to pay the balance in 60 days.

5 Purchased office supplies for $370 and paid for them with Check 104.

PROBLEM 15-2A   **Recording adjustments on a worksheet.** On September 30, 19X6, after 1 month of operations, the general ledger of the Management Skills Company contained the accounts and balances shown below.

Instructions

1. Prepare a partial worksheet with the following sections: Trial Balance, Adjustments, and Adjusted Trial Balance.

2. Use the data about the firm's accounts and balances to complete the Trial Balance section.

3. Enter the adjustments described on page 380 in the Adjustments section. Identify each adjustment with the appropriate letter.

4. Complete the Adjusted Trial Balance section.

ACCOUNTS AND BALANCES

101	Cash	$14,500 Dr.
121	Supplies	370 Dr.
123	Prepaid Rent	2,100 Dr.
125	Prepaid Advertising	1,200 Dr.
127	Prepaid Interest	225 Dr.
131	Furniture	2,800 Dr.
132	Accum. Depr.—Furniture	
141	Equipment	4,500 Dr.
142	Accum. Depr.—Equipment	
201	Notes Payable	10,300 Cr.
203	Accounts Payable	2,000 Cr.
211	Interest Payable	
241	Unearned Course Fees	11,000 Cr.
301	Kevin Doyle, Capital	3,365 Cr.
401	Course Fees	
511	Salaries Expense	800 Dr.
514	Telephone Expense	60 Dr.
517	Entertainment Expense	110 Dr.
520	Supplies Expense	
523	Rent Expense	
526	Advertising Expense	
529	Depr. Expense—Furniture	
532	Depr. Expense—Equipment	
591	Interest Expense	

ADJUSTMENTS

a. On September 30, an inventory of the supplies showed that items costing $320 were on hand. Record an adjustment for the supplies used during September.

b. On September 1, the firm paid $2,100 in advance for 6 months' rent. Record an adjustment for the expired rent for September.

c. On September 1, the firm signed a 6-month advertising contract for $1,200 and paid the full amount in advance. Record an adjustment for the expired advertising for September.

d. On September 1, the firm paid $225 interest in advance on a 3-month note that it issued to its bank. Record an adjustment for the portion of the interest that should be considered an expense for September.

e. On September 1, the firm purchased office furniture for $2,800. The furniture is expected to have a useful life of 5 years and a salvage value of $400. Record an adjustment for depreciation on the furniture for September.

f. On September 3, the firm purchased equipment for $4,500. The equipment is expected to have a useful life of 5 years and a salvage value of $600. Record an adjustment for depreciation on the equipment for September. (Compute the depreciation for a full month.)

g. On September 1, the firm issued a 2-month, 9 percent note for $2,800. Record an adjustment for the accrued interest for September.

h. During September, the firm received fees of $11,000 in advance. An analysis of the firm's records shows that $3,500 applies to services provided in September and the rest pertains to future months. Record an adjustment for the amount earned during September.

PROBLEM 15-3A

Recording adjustments on a worksheet. The Toy Palace is a retail store that sells toys, games, and bicycles. On December 31, 19X8, the firm's general ledger contained the accounts and balances shown below and on page 381.

Instructions

1. Prepare the Trial Balance section of a ten-column worksheet. The worksheet should cover the year ended December 31, 19X8.

2. Enter the adjustments described on pages 381 and 382 in the Adjustments section. Identify each adjustment with the appropriate letter.

3. Complete the Adjusted Trial Balance section.

ACCOUNTS AND BALANCES

101	Cash	$ 6,900 Dr.
111	Accounts Receivable	5,300 Dr.
112	Allowance for Uncollectible Accounts	80 Cr.
121	Merchandise Inventory	34,500 Dr.
131	Supplies	2,900 Dr.
133	Prepaid Advertising	1,320 Dr.
141	Store Equipment	8,200 Dr.
142	Accum. Depr.—Store Equipment	1,440 Cr.
151	Office Equipment	2,100 Dr.
152	Accum. Depr.—Office Equipment	360 Cr.

201	Notes Payable	8,000 Cr.
203	Accounts Payable	2,150 Cr.
211	Interest Payable	
221	FICA Tax Payable	1,480 Cr.
223	Employee Income Tax Payable	1,260 Cr.
225	Federal Unemployment Tax Payable	32 Cr.
227	State Unemployment Tax Payable	110 Cr.
229	Salaries Payable	
231	Sales Tax Payable	2,450 Cr.
301	Marie Testa, Capital	28,380 Cr.
302	Marie Testa, Drawing	25,000 Dr.
401	Sales	246,800 Cr.
451	Sales Returns and Allowances	4,300 Dr.
491	Miscellaneous Income	148 Cr.
501	Merchandise Purchases	125,200 Dr.
502	Freight In	1,700 Dr.
503	Purchases Returns and Allowances	1,260 Cr.
504	Purchases Discount	2,140 Cr.
511	Rent Expense	30,000 Dr.
514	Telephone Expense	1,070 Dr.
517	Salaries Expense	42,300 Dr.
520	Payroll Taxes Expense	3,800 Dr.
523	Supplies Expense	
526	Advertising Expense	1,500 Dr.
529	Depr. Expense—Store Equipment	
532	Depr. Expense—Office Equipment	
535	Loss From Uncollectible Accounts	
591	Interest Expense	

ADJUSTMENTS

a. During 19X8, the firm had net credit sales of $110,000. The accountant estimates that 0.7 percent of these sales will result in uncollectible accounts. Record an adjustment for the expected loss from uncollectible accounts for the year.

b. On December 31, 19X8, an inventory of the supplies showed that items costing $700 were on hand. Record an adjustment for the supplies used during the year.

c. On September 1, 19X8, the firm signed a 6-month advertising contract for $1,320 with a local newspaper and paid the full amount in advance. Record an adjustment for the expired advertising for the year.

d. On January 2, 19X7, the firm purchased store equipment for $8,200. At that time, the equipment was estimated to have a useful life of 5 years and a salvage value of $1,000. Record an adjustment for depreciation on the store equipment for 19X8.

e. On January 2, 19X7, the firm purchased office equipment for $2,100. At that time, the equipment was estimated to have a useful life of 5 years and a salvage value of $300. Record an adjustment for depreciation on the office equipment for 19X8.

f. On October 1, 19X8, the firm issued a 4-month, 11 percent note for $8,000. Record an adjustment for the accrued interest on this note for 19X8.

g. On December 31, 19X8, the firm owed salaries of $500 that will not be paid until 19X9. Record an adjustment for the accrued salaries for 19X8.

h. On December 31, 19X8, the firm owed the employer's FICA tax (7 percent) on $500 of accrued salaries, FUTA tax (0.8 percent) on $125 of accrued salaries, and SUTA tax (2.4 percent) on $125 of accrued salaries. Record an adjustment for the accrued payroll taxes for 19X8.

i. On December 31, 19X8, the firm owed sales tax of $2,450 for the fourth quarter of the year. This amount will be paid to the state sales tax agency in January 19X9. At that time, the firm will deduct a commission of 2 percent of the tax due. Record an adjustment for the accrued commission on the sales tax for the fourth quarter of 19X8.

Note: Save your worksheet for use in Problem 16-1A.

PROBLEM 15-4A **Recording adjustments on a worksheet.** Valley Forge Furniture is a retail store that sells reproductions of colonial furniture. On December 31, 19X4, the firm's general ledger contained the accounts and balances shown below and on page 383.

Instructions 1. Prepare the Trial Balance section of a ten-column worksheet. The worksheet should cover the year ended December 31, 19X4.

2. Enter the adjustments described on page 383 in the Adjustments section. Identify each adjustment with the appropriate letter.

3. Complete the Adjusted Trial Balance section.

ACCOUNTS AND BALANCES

101	Cash	$ 13,600 Dr.
109	Notes Receivable	2,000 Dr.
111	Accounts Receivable	18,200 Dr.
112	Allowance for Uncollectible Accounts	180 Cr.
116	Interest Receivable	
118	Merchandise Inventory	84,000 Dr.
121	Supplies	4,900 Dr.
123	Prepaid Insurance	3,000 Dr.
131	Store Equipment	5,500 Dr.
132	Accum. Depr.—Store Equipment	1,960 Cr.
141	Warehouse Equipment	12,100 Dr.
142	Accum. Depr.—Warehouse Equipment	4,240 Cr.
201	Notes Payable	12,000 Cr.
205	Accounts Payable	16,100 Cr.
211	Interest Payable	
221	FICA Tax Payable	910 Cr.
223	Employee Income Tax Payable	780 Cr.
225	Federal Unemployment Tax Payable	36 Cr.
227	State Unemployment Tax Payable	117 Cr.
229	Salaries Payable	
301	Ann Kerr, Capital	76,187 Cr.
302	Ann Kerr, Drawing	30,000 Dr.

401	Sales	445,000 Cr.
451	Sales Returns and Allowances	11,000 Dr.
491	Interest Income	80 Cr.
501	Merchandise Purchases	270,000 Dr.
502	Freight In	5,000 Dr.
503	Purchases Returns and Allowances	7,600 Cr.
504	Purchases Discount	4,400 Cr.
511	Rent Expense	24,000 Dr.
514	Telephone Expense	1,200 Dr.
517	Salaries Expense	78,000 Dr.
520	Payroll Taxes Expense	6,900 Dr.
523	Supplies Expense	
526	Insurance Expense	
529	Depr. Expense—Store Equipment	
532	Depr. Expense—Warehouse Equipment	
535	Loss From Uncollectible Accounts	
591	Interest Expense	190 Dr.

ADJUSTMENTS

a. During 19X4, the firm had net credit sales of $340,000. Past experience indicates that 0.9 percent of these sales should result in uncollectible accounts. Record an adjustment for the expected loss from uncollectible accounts for the year.

b. On September 1, 19X4, the firm received a 6-month, 12 percent note for $2,000 from a customer with an overdue balance. Record an adjustment for accrued interest on this note for 19X4.

c. On December 31, 19X4, an inventory of supplies showed that items costing $1,100 were on hand. Record an adjustment for the supplies used during the year.

d. On June 1, 19X4, the firm purchased a 1-year insurance policy for $3,000. Record an adjustment for the expired insurance for the year.

e. On January 2, 19X2, the firm purchased store equipment for $5,500. At that time, the equipment was estimated to have a useful life of 5 years and a salvage value of $600. Record an adjustment for depreciation on the store equipment for 19X4.

f. On January 2, 19X2, the firm purchased warehouse equipment for $12,100. At that time, the equipment was estimated to have a useful life of 5 years and a salvage value of $1,500. Record an adjustment for depreciation on the warehouse equipment for 19X4.

g. On November 1, 19X4, the firm issued a 3-month, 10 percent note for $12,000. Record an adjustment for the accrued interest on this note for 19X4.

h. On December 31, 19X4, the firm owed salaries of $1,800 that will not be paid until 19X4. Record an adjustment for the accrued salaries for 19X4.

i. On December 31, 19X4, the firm owed the employer's FICA tax (7 percent) on $1,800 of accrued salaries, FUTA tax (0.8 percent) on $375 of accrued salaries, and SUTA tax (2.4 percent) on $375 of accrued salaries. Record an adjustment for the accrued payroll taxes for 19X3.

Note: Save your worksheet for use in Problem 16-2A.

After determining the end-of-period adjustments and recording them on the worksheet, the accountant must complete the worksheet and prepare the financial statements. These procedures should be carried out as quickly and efficiently as possible because management needs timely information about the results of operations and the financial position of the business.

THE WORKSHEET AND THE FINANCIAL STATEMENTS

ENTERING ADJUSTMENTS ON THE WORKSHEET

Chapter 15 presented the end-of-period adjustments made at Sports World on December 31, 19X8, so that revenues and expenses for the year can be properly matched and net income can be correctly stated. The eleven adjustments are listed below according to the letters used to identify them on the worksheet. The illustration on page 366 shows how these adjustments were entered in the Adjustments section of the worksheet and how the columns of the Adjustments section were then totaled to make sure that the debits and credits were equal. The number of the page on which each adjustment is discussed appears below in parentheses.

a. Estimated loss from uncollectible accounts for the year (pages 354 and 356).
b. Depreciation of store equipment (pages 357 and 358).
c. Depreciation of office equipment (pages 357 and 358).
d. Accrued salaries (pages 358 and 359).
e. Accrued payroll taxes (pages 359 and 360).
f. Accrued interest on notes payable (page 360).
g. Supplies used (page 361).
h. Expired insurance (page 361).
i. Prepaid interest transferred to expense (page 362).
j. Accrued interest on notes receivable (page 363).
k. Accrued commission on sales taxes (pages 363 and 364).

COMPLETING THE ADJUSTED TRIAL BALANCE SECTION

After recording the adjustments, the accountant prepared the Adjusted Trial Balance section of the worksheet. This was done by combining the figures in the Adjustments section with the original trial balance figures. Then the accountant totaled the Adjusted Trial Balance columns to prove the equality of the debits and credits in the updated balances. The partial worksheet on page 366 shows how the Adjusted Trial Balance section appeared after it was completed.

The next step in the preparation of the worksheet is to record the ending merchandise inventory for the period in the financial statement columns. Remember that *merchandise inventory* is the stock of goods that a business has on hand for sale to customers.

An asset account for merchandise inventory is kept in the general ledger. However, during a fiscal period, all purchases of goods are debited to the cost account Merchandise Purchases and all sales of goods are credited to the revenue account Sales. No entries are made in the Merchandise Inventory account. Thus, when the trial balance is prepared at the end of the period, this account still shows the beginning inventory for the period.

To determine the amount of the ending inventory, a careful count is made of the goods on hand at the end of the period. Then the total cost of the items is computed. This figure must be recorded on the worksheet so that the financial statements will reflect the ending inventory.

The trial balance prepared at Sports World on December 31, 19X8, shows a balance of $63,000 for the Merchandise Inventory account. This balance represents the stock of goods on January 1, 19X8, the beginning of the fiscal year. However, a count taken on December 31, 19X8, indicates that the items on hand at the end of the year total $64,000.

The amount of the ending inventory is determined as follows. First, the quantity of each type of goods that the firm has in stock is listed on a form called an *inventory sheet*. Next, the quantity is multiplied by the unit cost to find the total cost of the item. Then, the totals for all the different items on hand are added to find the cost of the entire inventory. A portion of an inventory sheet prepared at Sports World is illustrated below.

SPORTS WORLD
Inventory Sheet

SHEET NO. 10

DATE December 31, 19X8

QUANTITY	DESCRIPTION	UNIT COST	TOTAL
20	Power Play Tennis Rackets	$25.00	$ 500.00
10	Champion Tennis Rackets	40.00	400.00
25	Grand Slam Tennis Rackets	30.00	750.00
6 pr.	Silver Slope Skis	80.00	480.00
5 pr.	Continental Skis	75.00	375.00
3 pr.	Alpine Racing Skis	90.00	270.00
	Total Inventory		$64,000.00

Counted by *a. s.*   Priced by *m. H.*   Checked by *P. R.*

Merchandise Inventory is the one account that appears on both the income statement and the balance sheet. On the income statement, the figures for the beginning and ending inventory are combined with information about the purchases made during the period to determine the cost of goods sold, as shown below. On the balance sheet, the ending inventory is reported as an asset.

Cost of Goods Sold		
Merchandise Inventory, Jan. 1, 19X8		$ 63,000.00
Merchandise Purchases	$248,500.00	
Freight In	3,300.00	
Delivered Cost of Purchases	$251,800.00	
Less Purchases Ret. and Allow.	$2,700.00	
Purchases Discount	4,900.00	7,600.00
Net Delivered Cost of Purchases		244,200.00
Total Merch. Available for Sale		$307,200.00
Less Merch. Inventory, Dec. 31, 19X8		64,000.00
Cost of Goods Sold		$243,200.00

Notice how the merchandise inventory figures are used in the Cost of Goods Sold section of the income statement. The beginning inventory and the net delivered cost of purchases are added to find the total merchandise available for sale during the period. Then the ending inventory is subtracted from the total merchandise available for sale to find the cost of goods sold for the period.

In order to present the correct information about merchandise inventory on the financial statements, the following procedure is used on the worksheet. (This procedure is illustrated on the partial worksheet shown below.)

1. The beginning inventory ($63,000) is charged to the cost of goods sold by placing it in the Debit column of the Income Statement section.
2. The ending inventory ($64,000) is recorded as a reduction in the cost of goods sold by placing it in the Credit column of the Income Statement section.
3. The ending inventory ($64,000) is recorded as an asset by placing it in the Debit column of the Balance Sheet section.

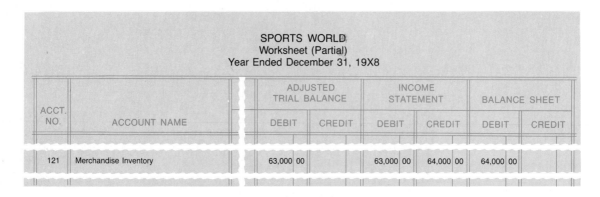

SPORTS WORLD
Worksheet (Partial)
Year Ended December 31, 19X8

ACCT. NO.	ACCOUNT NAME	ADJUSTED TRIAL BALANCE		INCOME STATEMENT		BALANCE SHEET	
		DEBIT	CREDIT	DEBIT	CREDIT	DEBIT	CREDIT
121	Merchandise Inventory	63,000 00		63,000 00	64,000 00	64,000 00	

After the merchandise inventory figures are entered on the worksheet, the accountant can complete the financial statement sections.

PREPARING THE BALANCE SHEET SECTION

When the chart of accounts is established for a business, blocks of numbers are assigned to the various types of accounts. In the case of Sports World, the following numbers are used for the accounts that appear on the balance sheet: 100–199 for asset accounts, 200–299 for liability accounts, and 300–399 for owner's equity accounts. Thus, it is easy to identify the account balances that should be recorded in the Balance Sheet section of the worksheet; and these balances are simply extended from the Adjusted Trial Balance section. The only exception is the balance of the Merchandise Inventory account. As a result of the procedure described on page 386, the ending inventory already appears in the Debit column of the Balance Sheet section. The amount shown for Merchandise Inventory in the Adjusted Trial Balance section is the beginning inventory, which is not transferred because it will not be reported on the balance sheet.

With the one exception just noted, the balances of all accounts numbered 100–399 that appear in the Debit column of the Adjusted Trial Balance section are carried over to the Debit column of the Balance Sheet section. Similarly, the balances of all accounts numbered 100–399 that appear in the Credit column of the Adjusted Trial Balance section are extended to the Credit column of the Balance Sheet section.

SPORTS WORLD
Worksheet (Partial)
Year Ended December 31, 19X8

ACCT. NO.	ACCOUNT NAME	ADJUSTED TRIAL BALANCE		BALANCE SHEET	
		DEBIT	CREDIT	DEBIT	CREDIT
101	Cash	15,300 00		15,300 00	
105	Petty Cash Fund	100 00		100 00	
107	Change Fund	200 00		200 00	
109	Notes Receivable	800 00		800 00	
111	Accounts Receivable	24,000 00		24,000 00	
112	Allowance for Uncollectible Accounts		620 00		620 00
116	Interest Receivable	16 00		16 00	
121	Merchandise Inventory	63,000 00		64,000 00	
131	Supplies	610 00		610 00	
133	Prepaid Insurance	780 00		780 00	
135	Prepaid Interest	75 00		75 00	
141	Store Equipment	8,900 00		8,900 00	
142	Accum. Depreciation—Store Equipment		4,800 00		4,800 00
151	Office Equipment	2,750 00		2,750 00	
152	Accum. Depreciation—Office Equipment		1,470 00		1,470 00
201	Notes Payable—Trade		2,000 00		2,000 00
203	Notes Payable—Bank		9,000 00		9,000 00
205	Accounts Payable		6,500 00		6,500 00
216	Interest Payable		20 00		20 00
221	FICA Tax Payable		966 00		966 00
223	Employee Income Tax Payable		804 00		804 00
225	Federal Unemployment Tax Payable		24 00		24 00
227	State Unemployment Tax Payable		65 00		65 00
229	Salaries Payable		400 00		400 00
231	Sales Tax Payable		6,468 00		6,468 00
301	Lynn Frank, Capital		75,314 00		75,314 00
302	Lynn Frank, Drawing	30,000 00		30,000 00	

PREPARING THE INCOME STATEMENT SECTION

In the chart of accounts used by Sports World, the numbers 400–499 are assigned to the revenue accounts and the numbers 500–599 are assigned to the cost and expense accounts. Thus, all accounts in these two number blocks will appear on the income statement, and their balances should be extended from the Adjusted Trial Balance section of the worksheet to the Income Statement section, as shown below.

SPORTS WORLD
Worksheet (Partial)
Year Ended December 31, 19X8

ACCT. NO.	ACCOUNT NAME	ADJUSTED TRIAL BALANCE		INCOME STATEMENT	
		DEBIT	CREDIT	DEBIT	CREDIT
121	Merchandise Inventory			63,000 00	64,000 00
401	Sales		422,000 00		422,000 00
451	Sales Returns and Allowances	7,400 00		7,400 00	
491	Interest Income		152 00		152 00
493	Miscellaneous Income		498 00		498 00
501	Merchandise Purchases	248,500 00		248,500 00	
502	Freight In	3,300 00		3,300 00	
503	Purchases Returns and Allowances		2,700 00		2,700 00
504	Purchases Discount		4,900 00		4,900 00
511	Sales Salaries Expense	71,700 00		71,700 00	
514	Advertising Expense	6,900 00		6,900 00	
517	Supplies Expense	4,225 00		4,225 00	
520	Cash Short or Over	75 00		75 00	
523	Delivery Expense	1,200 00		1,200 00	
526	Depr. Expense—Store Equipment	1,600 00		1,600 00	
529	Insurance Expense	2,340 00		2,340 00	
532	Cleaning Service Expense	1,800 00		1,800 00	
535	Rent Expense	12,000 00		12,000 00	
538	Utilities Expense	2,550 00		2,550 00	
541	Office Salaries Expense	16,200 00		16,200 00	
544	Payroll Taxes Expense	7,740 00		7,740 00	
547	Office Expense	390 00		390 00	
550	Professional Services Expense	1,100 00		1,100 00	
553	Telephone Expense	1,320 00		1,320 00	
556	Loss From Uncollectible Accounts	570 00		570 00	
559	Depr. Expense—Office Equipment	490 00		490 00	
591	Interest Expense	770 00		770 00	

Notice that in addition to the balances of the revenue, cost, and expense accounts, the Income Statement section contains the figures for the beginning and ending merchandise inventory. These amounts appear as a result of the procedure described on page 386 and will be used in preparing the Cost of Goods Sold section of the income statement.

COMPLETING THE WORKSHEET

Once all the necessary account balances have been entered in the financial statement sections of the worksheet, the net income or net loss for the period is determined and the worksheet is completed. The first step is to total the debits and credits in the Income Statement section.

Refer to the worksheet shown on pages 390 and 391. When the columns of the Income Statement section are added, the debits total $455,170 and the credits total $494,250. Since the credits exceed the debits, the difference of $39,080 represents net income for the period. This figure is entered in the Debit column so that the two columns will balance. Then the final total of each column ($494,250) is recorded on the worksheet.

Because the net income belongs to the owner and represents an increase in equity, it is also entered in the Credit column of the Balance Sheet section, as explained in Chapter 5. Then, the debits and credits in the Balance Sheet section are added, and the totals are recorded above the net income line (to make it easier to find any errors that may occur). In this case, the total of the Debit column is $147,531 and the total of the Credit column is $108,451. The difference between the two totals is $39,080, which is the same as the net income for the year. (The difference should always be equal to the net income or net loss for the period.)

Next, the final totals of the Balance Sheet columns, including the net income, are determined and entered. In this case, each total is $147,531 and the two columns therefore balance. The last step is to rule all money columns to show that the worksheet has been completed.

PREPARING THE FINANCIAL STATEMENTS

All the information needed to prepare the financial statements is now assembled on the worksheet. The figures required to present the results of operations for the period are contained in the Income Statement section, and the figures required to report the financial position of the business on the last day of the period are available in the Balance Sheet section.

The accountant for Sports World prepares three financial statements at the end of each fiscal period: an income statement, a statement of owner's equity, and a balance sheet. The income statement and the balance sheet are arranged in a *classified* format; that is, revenues, expenses, assets, and liabilities are divided into groups of similar accounts and a subtotal is given for each group. This more elaborate method of presenting financial information makes the statements more meaningful to readers and is widely used.

THE CLASSIFIED INCOME STATEMENT

The classified income statement shown on page 393 reports the results of operation at Sports World during the fiscal year ended December 31, 19X8. Notice that there are various sections that identify revenues by source and expenses by type. The term *multiple-step income statement* is sometimes used to describe this form of income statement because several subtotals and totals are computed before the net income is presented. The simpler type of income statement that lists all revenues in one section and all expenses in another section is known as a *single-step income statement* because just one computation is necessary to determine the net income—the total of the expenses is subtracted from the total of the revenues. (An example of a single-step income statement appears on page 87.)

SPORTS WORLD
Worksheet
Year Ended December 31, 19X8

	ACCT. NO.	ACCOUNT NAME	TRIAL BALANCE DEBIT	TRIAL BALANCE CREDIT	ADJUSTMENTS DEBIT	ADJUSTMENTS CREDIT
1	101	Cash	15,300 00			
2	105	Petty Cash Fund	100 00			
3	107	Change Fund	200 00			
4	109	Notes Receivable	800 00			
5	111	Accounts Receivable	24,000 00			
6	112	Allowance for Uncollectible Accounts		50 00		(a)570 00
7	116	Interest Receivable			(j)16 00	
8	121	Merchandise Inventory	63,000 00			
9	131	Supplies	4,835 00			(g)4,225 00
10	133	Prepaid Insurance	3,120 00			(h)2,340 00
11	135	Prepaid Interest	225 00			(i)150 00
12	141	Store Equipment	8,900 00			
13	142	Accum. Depreciation—Store Equipment		3,200 00		(b)1,600 00
14	151	Office Equipment	2,750 00			
15	152	Accum. Depreciation—Office Equipment		980 00		(c)490 00
16	201	Notes Payable—Trade		2,000 00		
17	203	Notes Payable—Bank		9,000 00		
18	205	Accounts Payable		6,500 00		
19	216	Interest Payable				(f)20 00
20	221	FICA Tax Payable		938 00		(e)28 00
21	223	Employee Income Tax Payable		804 00		
22	225	Federal Unemployment Tax Payable		22 00		(e)2 00
23	227	State Unemployment Tax Payable		60 00		(e)5 00
24	229	Salaries Payable				(d)400 00
25	231	Sales Tax Payable		6,600 00	(k)132 00	
26	301	Lynn Frank, Capital		75,314 00		
27	302	Lynn Frank, Drawing	30,000 00			
28	401	Sales		422,000 00		
29	451	Sales Returns and Allowances	7,400 00			
30	491	Interest Income		136 00		(j)16 00
31	493	Miscellaneous Income		366 00		(k)132 00
32	501	Merchandise Purchases	248,500 00			
33	502	Freight In	3,300 00			
34	503	Purchases Returns and Allowances		2,700 00		
35	504	Purchases Discount		4,900 00		
36	511	Sales Salaries Expense	71,300 00		(d)400 00	
37	514	Advertising Expense	6,900 00			
38	517	Supplies Expense			(g)4,225 00	
39	520	Cash Short or Over	75 00			
40	523	Delivery Expense	1,200 00			
41	526	Depr. Expense—Store Equipment			(b)1,600 00	
42	529	Insurance Expense			(h)2,340 00	
43	532	Cleaning Service Expense	1,800 00			
44	535	Rent Expense	12,000 00			
45	538	Utilities Expense	2,550 00			
46	541	Office Salaries Expense	16,200 00			
47	544	Payroll Taxes Expense	7,705 00		(e)35 00	
48	547	Office Expense	390 00			
49	550	Professional Services Expense	1,100 00			
50	553	Telephone Expense	1,320 00			
51	556	Loss From Uncollectible Accounts			(a)570 00	
52	559	Depr. Expense—Office Equipment			(c)490 00 (f)20 00	
53	591	Interest Expense	600 00		(i)150 00	
54		Totals	535,570 00	535,570 00	9,978 00	9,978 00
55		Net Income				
56						

ADJUSTED TRIAL BALANCE		INCOME STATEMENT		BALANCE SHEET		
DEBIT	CREDIT	DEBIT	CREDIT	DEBIT	CREDIT	
15,300 00				15,300 00		1
100 00				100 00		2
200 00				200 00		3
800 00				800 00		4
24,000 00				24,000 00		5
	620 00				620 00	6
16 00				16 00		7
63,000 00		63,000 00	64,000 00	64,000 00		8
610 00				610 00		9
780 00				780 00		10
75 00				75 00		11
8,900 00				8,900 00		12
	4,800 00				4,800 00	13
2,750 00				2,750 00		14
	1,470 00				1,470 00	15
	2,000 00				2,000 00	16
	9,000 00				9,000 00	17
	6,500 00				6,500 00	18
	20 00				20 00	19
	966 00				966 00	20
	804 00				804 00	21
	24 00				24 00	22
	65 00				65 00	23
	400 00				400 00	24
	6,468 00				6,468 00	25
	75,314 00				75,314 00	26
30,000 00				30,000 00		27
	422,000 00		422,000 00			28
7,400 00		7,400 00				29
	152 00		152 00			30
	498 00		498 00			31
248,500 00		248,500 00				32
3,300 00		3,300 00				33
	2,700 00		2,700 00			34
	4,900 00		4,900 00			35
71,700 00		71,700 00				36
6,900 00		6,900 00				37
4,225 00		4,225 00				38
75 00		75 00				39
1,200 00		1,200 00				40
1,600 00		1,600 00				41
2,340 00		2,340 00				42
1,800 00		1,800 00				43
12,000 00		12,000 00				44
2,550 00		2,550 00				45
16,200 00		16,200 00				46
7,740 00		7,740 00				47
390 00		390 00				48
1,100 00		1,100 00				49
1,320 00		1,320 00				50
570 00		570 00				51
490 00		490 00				52
770 00		770 00				53
538,701 00	538,701 00	455,170 00	494,250 00	147,531 00	108,451 00	54
		39,080 00			39,080 00	55
		494,250 00	494,250 00	147,531 00	147,531 00	56

The different sections of the classified income statement are explained below. Refer to the illustration on page 393 to see how each section is arranged.

Operating Revenue

The first section of the classified income statement contains the revenue from operations for the period—the revenue that is earned from the normal activities of the business. Other income is presented separately in a later section. In the case of Sports World, all operating revenue comes from sales of merchandise. The first figure listed in this section is therefore the total sales. Notice that the amount of sales returns and allowances is deducted to find the net sales for the period. (Because Sports World is a retail firm, it does not offer sales discounts to its customers. If it did, the sales discounts would also be treated as a deduction from the total sales.)

Cost of Goods Sold

The Cost of Goods Sold section combines the figures for the beginning and ending inventory with all the figures related to purchases in order to determine the cost of the merchandise that was sold during the period.

Gross Profit on Sales

The gross profit on sales is the difference between the net sales and the cost of goods sold. This figure is highly important because all operating expenses will be deducted from it. Obviously, if a business is to earn a net income, the gross profit on sales must be great enough to more than cover the operating expenses.

Operating Expenses

Operating expenses are expenses that arise from the normal activities of a business. On the income statement prepared for Sports World, these expenses are divided into two groups, and a subtotal is shown for each group. The selling expenses include all expenses that are directly related to the sale and delivery of goods. The general and administrative expenses cover rent, utilities, the salaries of office employees, and other expenses that are necessary to the conduct of business operations but are not directly connected with the sales function.

Net Income or Net Loss From Operations

The total of the operating expenses for the period is deducted from the gross profit on sales to determine the net income or net loss from operations. Keeping operating and nonoperating income separate makes it possible to appraise the true operating efficiency of the firm.

Other Income

Any income that is earned from nonoperating sources is reported in the Other Income section. At Sports World, small amounts of nonoperating income were obtained in 19X8 from interest on notes receivable and from the commission deducted from sales taxes.

Other Expenses

Any expenses that are not directly connected with operations appear in the Other Expenses section. A common expense of this type is interest on notes payable or a mortgage payable.

Net Income or Net Loss for the Period

The final total on the income statement shows the combined results of all types of revenue and expenses. If this amount is a net loss, it is placed in parentheses.

SPORTS WORLD
Income Statement
Year Ended December 31, 19X8

Operating Revenue				
Sales				$422,000.00
Less Sales Returns and Allowances				7,400.00
Net Sales				$414,600.00
Cost of Goods Sold				
Merchandise Inventory, Jan. 1, 19X8			$ 63,000.00	
Merchandise Purchases		$248,500.00		
Freight In		3,300.00		
Delivered Cost of Purchases		$251,800.00		
Less Purchases Ret. and Allow.	$2,700.00			
Purchases Discount	4,900.00	7,600.00		
Net Delivered Cost of Purchases			244,200.00	
Total Merch. Available for Sale			$307,200.00	
Less Merch. Inventory, Dec. 31, 19X8			64,000.00	
Cost of Goods Sold				243,200.00
Gross Profit on Sales				$171,400.00
Operating Expenses				
Selling Expenses				
Sales Salaries Expense		$ 71,700.00		
Advertising Expense		6,900.00		
Supplies Expense		4,225.00		
Cash Short		75.00		
Delivery Expense		1,200.00		
Depr. Expense—Store Equipment		1,600.00		
Total Selling Expenses			$ 85,700.00	
General and Administrative Expenses				
Insurance Expense		$ 2,340.00		
Cleaning Service Expense		1,800.00		
Rent Expense		12,000.00		
Utilities Expense		2,550.00		
Office Salaries Expense		16,200.00		
Payroll Taxes Expense		7,740.00		
Office Expense		390.00		
Professional Services Expense		1,100.00		
Telephone Expense		1,320.00		
Loss From Uncollectible Accounts		570.00		
Depr. Expense—Office Equipment		490.00		
Total Gen. and Admin. Expenses			46,500.00	
Total Operating Expenses				132,200.00
Net Income From Operations				$ 39,200.00
Other Income				
Interest Income		$ 152.00		
Miscellaneous Income		498.00		
Total Other Income			$ 650.00	
Other Expenses				
Interest Expense			770.00	
Net Nonoperating Expense				120.00
Net Income for Year				$ 39,080.00

The *statement of owner's equity* reports the changes that have occurred in the owner's financial interest during the fiscal period. This statement is prepared before the balance sheet so that the amount of the ending capital is available for presentation on the balance sheet. The following statement of owner's equity was completed at Sports World for the year ended December 31, 19X8.

SPORTS WORLD
Statement of Owner's Equity
Year Ended December 31, 19X8

Capital, Jan. 1, 19X8	$ 75,314
Net Income for Year	39,080
Total	$114,394
Less Withdrawals	30,000
Capital, Dec. 31, 19X8	$ 84,394

Because the owner made no additional investments during the period, all the information needed for the statement of owner's equity appears on the worksheet. The balance shown for the capital account in the Balance Sheet section of the worksheet is listed as the beginning capital ($75,314) on the statement of owner's equity. To this figure is added the net income for the period ($39,080), also taken from the worksheet. The amount of withdrawals ($30,000) is obtained from the balance of the drawing account in the Balance Sheet section of the worksheet. This amount is subtracted on the statement of owner's equity to find the ending capital ($84,394).

If the owner made additional investments during the period, it is necessary to consult the capital account in the general ledger before preparing the statement of owner's equity. This account provides information about the beginning capital and the amounts invested.

THE CLASSIFIED BALANCE SHEET

The classified balance sheet shown on page 395 reports the financial position of Sports World on December 31, 19X8, the end of its fiscal year. This type of balance sheet divides the various assets and liabilities into groups, as explained below and on page 396.

Current Assets

The first section of the classified balance sheet lists the *current assets,* which consist of cash, items that will normally be converted into cash within one year, and items that will be used up within one year. These items are usually listed in order of liquidity—ease of conversion into cash. Current assets are vital to a firm's survival because they provide the funds needed to pay bills and meet expenses.

SPORTS WORLD
Balance Sheet
December 31, 19X8

Assets

Current Assets

Cash			$ 15,300.00
Petty Cash Fund			100.00
Change Fund			200.00
Notes Receivable			800.00
Accounts Receivable		$24,000.00	
Less Allowance for Uncollectible Accounts		620.00	23,380.00
Interest Receivable			16.00
Merchandise Inventory			64,000.00
Prepaid Expenses			
Supplies		$ 610.00	
Prepaid Insurance		780.00	
Prepaid Interest		75.00	1,465.00
Total Current Assets			$105,261.00

Plant and Equipment

Store Equipment	$8,900.00		
Less Accumulated Depreciation	4,800.00	$ 4,100.00	
Office Equipment	$2,750.00		
Less Accumulated Depreciation	1,470.00	1,280.00	
Total Plant and Equipment			5,380.00
Total Assets			$110,641.00

Liabilities and Owner's Equity

Current Liabilities

Notes Payable—Trade	$ 2,000.00
Notes Payable—Bank	9,000.00
Accounts Payable	6,500.00
Interest Payable	20.00
FICA Tax Payable	966.00
Employee Income Tax Payable	804.00
Federal Unemployment Tax Payable	24.00
State Unemployment Tax Payable	65.00
Salaries Payable	400.00
Sales Tax Payable	6,468.00
Total Current Liabilities	$ 26,247.00

Owner's Equity

Lynn Frank, Capital	84,394.00
Total Liabilities and Owner's Equity	$110,641.00

| Plant and Equipment | The next section of the classified balance sheet shows the firm's *plant and equipment*—property that will be used for a long time in the conduct of business operations. Managers must keep a close watch on these assets because they usually represent a very sizable investment and may therefore be difficult and costly to replace.

Notice that three amounts are reported for each item of plant and equipment. The original cost, the accumulated depreciation, and the book value. For the store equipment owned by Sports World, the original cost is $8,900, the accumulated depreciation is $4,800, and the book value is $4,100. Remember that the book value of an item bears no relation to the market value. It is simply the portion of the original cost that has not been depreciated yet. |

Plant and Equipment

The next section of the classified balance sheet shows the firm's *plant and equipment*—property that will be used for a long time in the conduct of business operations. Managers must keep a close watch on these assets because they usually represent a very sizable investment and may therefore be difficult and costly to replace.

Notice that three amounts are reported for each item of plant and equipment. The original cost, the accumulated depreciation, and the book value. For the store equipment owned by Sports World, the original cost is $8,900, the accumulated depreciation is $4,800, and the book value is $4,100. Remember that the book value of an item bears no relation to the market value. It is simply the portion of the original cost that has not been depreciated yet.

Current Liabilities

The third section of the classified balance sheet lists *current liabilities*—the debts that must be paid within one year. These items are usually presented in order of priority of payment. Since the firm's credit reputation depends upon prompt settlement of its debts, management must make sure that funds are available when these obligations become due.

Long-Term Liabilities

Following current liabilities on the classified balance sheet are *long-term liabilities*—debts of the business due more than a year in the future. Although repayment of these obligations may not be due for several years, management must make sure that periodic interest is paid promptly. A mortgage payable, notes payable that extend for more than a year, and loans payable that extend for more than a year are common types of long-term liabilities. (Sports World had no long-term liabilities on December 31, 19X8.)

Owner's Equity

Because the accountant for Sports World prepares a statement of owner's equity, the firm's balance sheet simply shows the ending capital in the Owner's Equity section. The separate statement of owner's equity reports all information about the changes that occurred in the owner's financial interest during the period.

PRINCIPLES AND PROCEDURES SUMMARY

As soon as all adjustments have been entered on the worksheet, the accountant completes the worksheet and prepares the financial statements. The first step is to combine the figures in the Trial Balance section with the adjustments in order to obtain an adjusted trial balance. Next, the ending merchandise inventory is recorded on the worksheet. Then each item in the Adjusted Trial Balance columns is extended to the appropriate financial statement section of the worksheet.

When all figures in the Adjusted Trial Balance section have been transferred, the Income Statement columns are totaled and the net income or net loss is determined. The amount of net income or net loss is then entered in the Balance Sheet section. At this point, the total debits must equal the total credits in the Balance Sheet columns.

Next, financial statements are prepared from the information on the worksheet. The format of these statements can vary, but many firms prepare classified statements because they provide more meaningful information to readers.

A classified income statement for a merchandising business usually includes the following sections: operating revenue, cost of goods sold, gross profit on sales, operating expenses, net income from operations, other income, other expenses, and net income for the period. To make the income statement even more useful, operating expenses may be broken down into several categories, such as selling expenses and general and administrative expenses.

On a classified balance sheet, the assets and liabilities are arranged in groups. Assets are usually presented in two groups—current assets and plant and equipment. Liabilities are also divided into two groups—current liabilities and long-term liabilities.

Current assets consist of cash, items that will normally be converted into cash within one year, and items that will be used up within one year. Plant and equipment consists of property that will be used for a long time in the operations of the business. Current liabilities are debts that must be paid within one year, whereas long-term liabilities are due more than a year in the future.

In addition to the income statement and the balance sheet, a statement of owner's equity may be prepared to provide detailed information about the changes in the owner's financial interest during the period. Otherwise, this data is presented in the Owner's Equity section of the balance sheet.

MANAGERIAL IMPLICATIONS

Managers are keenly interested in receiving timely financial statements, especially the periodic income statement, which shows the results of operations. The worksheet is a very useful device for gathering data about adjustments and for preparing the income statement. Managers are also interested in prompt preparation of the balance sheet because it shows the financial position of the business at the end of the fiscal period.

As soon as the statements are available, managers must carefully study the figures in order to evaluate the firm's operating efficiency and financial strength. A common technique is to compare the data shown on the current statements with the data from previous statements. This procedure places the current amounts in perspective and reveals trends that have developed. In large firms, comparison with the published financial reports of other companies in the same industry is also highly useful.

Classified financial statements are prepared so that managers and others can more easily draw meaningful conclusions from the information on the statements. However, managers must understand the nature and significance of the groupings in order to obtain the proper value from these statements.

REVIEW QUESTIONS

1. How does the worksheet help the accountant to prepare financial statements more efficiently?
2. What is merchandise inventory?

3. How is the amount of the ending merchandise inventory determined?
4. What entries are made for merchandise inventory in the financial statement sections of the worksheet?
5. What types of accounts appear in the Income Statement section of the worksheet?
6. What types of accounts appear in the Balance Sheet section of the worksheet?
7. What are classified financial statements?
8. What is the purpose of the income statement?
9. Explain the difference between a single-step income statement and a multiple-step income statement.
10. What is the gross profit on sales?
11. How is net income from operations determined?
12. What is the difference between operating revenue and other income?
13. What are operating expenses?
14. Which section of the income statement contains information about the purchases made during the period and the beginning and ending merchandise inventory?
15. What is the purpose of the balance sheet?
16. What are current assets? Give four examples of items that would be considered current assets.
17. What is plant and equipment? Give two examples of items that would be considered plant and equipment.
18. How do current liabilities and long-term liabilities differ?
19. What is the advantage of having classified financial statements?
20. What information is provided by the statement of owner's equity?

MANAGERIAL DISCUSSION QUESTIONS

1. Why is it important to compare the financial statements of the current year with those of prior years?
2. Should a manager be concerned if the balance sheet shows a large increase in current liabilities and a large decrease in current assets? Explain your answer.
3. The latest income statement prepared at the Wilkes Company shows that net sales increased by 10 percent over the previous year and selling expenses increased by 25 percent. Do you think that management should investigate the reasons for the increase in selling expenses? Why or why not?
4. Why is it useful for management to compare a firm's financial statements with financial information from other companies in the same industry?
5. For the last two years, the income statement of the Fashion Clothing Center, a large retail store, has shown a substantial increase in the merchandise inventory. Why might management be concerned about this development?
6. The Anderson Company had an increase in sales and net income during its last fiscal year, but cash decreased and the firm was having difficulty paying its bills by the end of the year. What factors might cause a shortage of cash even though a firm is profitable?

EXERCISES

EXERCISE 16-1 **Classifying income statement items.** The accounts shown below appear on the worksheet of the Mayville Appliance Store. Indicate the section of the classified income statement where each account will be reported.

SECTIONS OF CLASSIFIED INCOME STATEMENT

A. Operating Revenue   C. Operating Expenses   E. Other Expenses
B. Cost of Goods Sold   D. Other Income

ACCOUNTS

1. Merchandise Purchases   5. Merchandise Inventory   8. Sales Ret. and Allow.
2. Salaries Expense   6. Interest Income   9. Utilities Expense
3. Sales   7. Freight In   10. Purchases Discount
4. Interest Expense

EXERCISE 16-2 **Classifying balance sheet items.** The accounts shown below appear on the worksheet of the Mayville Appliance Store. Indicate the section of the classified balance sheet where each account will be reported.

SECTIONS OF CLASSIFIED BALANCE SHEET

A. Current Assets   C. Current Liabilities   E. Owner's Equity
B. Plant and Equipment   D. Long-Term Liabilities

ACCOUNTS

1. Sales Tax Payable   5. Accounts Payable   8. Prepaid Insurance
2. Cash   6. Store Supplies   9. Delivery Van
3. John Cortez, Capital   7. Mortgage Payable   10. Accounts Receivable
4. Building

EXERCISE 16-3 **Reporting operating revenue.** The worksheet of the Variety Gift Shop contains the revenue, cost, and expense accounts listed below. Prepare the heading and Operating Revenue section of the firm's income statement for the year ended December 31, 19X5.

ACCOUNTS

401	Sales	$77,000 Cr.
451	Sales Returns and Allowances	2,400 Dr.
501	Merchandise Purchases	36,000 Dr.
502	Freight In	750 Dr.
503	Purchases Returns and Allowances	840 Cr.
504	Purchases Discount	610 Cr.
511	Rent Expense	7,200 Dr.
514	Utilities Expense	1,330 Dr.
517	Advertising Expense	1,400 Dr.
520	Salaries Expense	18,000 Dr.
523	Payroll Taxes Expense	1,670 Dr.
526	Depreciation Expense—Equipment	500 Dr.

EXERCISE 16-4   **Reporting the cost of goods sold.** The Variety Gift Shop had a merchandise inventory that amounted to $14,000 on January 1, 19X5, and $16,000 on December 31, 19X5. Use this data and the data in Exercise 16-3 to prepare the Cost of Goods Sold section of the firm's income statement for the year ended December 31, 19X5.

EXERCISE 16-5   **Reporting the gross profit on sales.** Determine the gross profit on sales that should be reported on the income statement of the Variety Gift Shop for the year ended December 31, 19X5. Use the data from your solutions to Exercises 16-3 and 16-4.

EXERCISE 16-6   **Reporting operating expenses.** Prepare the Operating Expenses section of the Variety Gift Shop's income statement for the year ended December 31, 19X5. Obtain the necessary data from Exercise 16-3. (The firm does not divide its operating expenses into selling and administrative expenses.)

EXERCISE 16-7   **Reporting the net income from operations.** Determine the net income from operations that should be reported on the income statement of the Variety Gift Shop for the year ended December 31, 19X5. Use the data from your solutions to Exercises 16-5 and 16-6.

EXERCISE 16-8   **Preparing a classified income statement.** The worksheet of the Midtown Shoe Center contains the revenue, cost, and expense accounts listed below. Prepare a classified income statement for this firm for the year ended December 31, 19X8. The merchandise inventory amounted to $27,000 on January 1, 19X8, and $25,200 on December 31, 19X8. (The expense accounts numbered 511 through 517 represent selling expenses and those numbered 531 through 546 represent general and administrative expenses.)

ACCOUNTS

401	Sales	$124,000 Cr.
451	Sales Returns and Allowances	3,100 Dr.
491	Miscellaneous Income	110 Cr.
501	Merchandise Purchases	51,000 Dr.
502	Freight In	900 Dr.
503	Purchases Returns and Allowances	1,500 Cr.
504	Purchases Discount	800 Cr.
511	Sales Salaries Expense	22,000 Dr.
514	Store Supplies Expense	1,100 Dr.
517	Depreciation Expense—Store Equipment	800 Dr.
531	Rent Expense	6,000 Dr.
534	Utilities Expense	1,400 Dr.
537	Office Salaries Expense	10,000 Dr.
540	Payroll Taxes Expense	2,500 Dr.
543	Depreciation Expense—Office Equipment	200 Dr.
546	Loss From Uncollectible Accounts	320 Dr.
591	Interest Expense	260 Dr.

EXERCISE 16-9   **Preparing a statement of owner's equity.** The worksheet of the Midtown Shoe Center contains the owner's equity accounts listed below. Use this data and the net income determined in Exercise 16-8 to prepare a statement of owner's equity for the year ended December 31, 19X8. There were no additional investments made during the period.

ACCOUNTS

301	Elaine Price, Capital	$30,060 Cr.
302	Elaine Price, Drawing	21,000 Dr.

EXERCISE 16-10   **Preparing a classified balance sheet.** The worksheet of the Midtown Shoe Center contains the asset and liability accounts listed below. (The balance of the Notes Payable account consists of notes that are due within a year.) Prepare a balance sheet dated December 31, 19X8. Obtain the ending capital for the period from the statement of owner's equity completed in Exercise 16-9.

ACCOUNTS

101	Cash	$ 5,500 Dr.
107	Change Fund	100 Dr.
111	Accounts Receivable	2,700 Dr.
112	Allowance for Uncollectible Accounts	380 Cr.
121	Merchandise Inventory	25,200 Dr.
131	Store Supplies	950 Dr.
133	Prepaid Interest	90 Dr.
141	Store Equipment	5,100 Dr.
142	Accum. Depr.—Store Equipment	800 Cr.
151	Office Equipment	1,600 Dr.
152	Accum. Depr.—Office Equipment	200 Cr.
201	Notes Payable	2,700 Cr.
203	Accounts Payable	1,800 Cr.
216	Interest Payable	30 Cr.
231	Sales Tax Payable	1,240 Cr.

PROBLEMS

PROBLEM 16-1   **Completing a worksheet and preparing classified financial statements.** This problem is a continuation of Problem 15-3.

Instructions   1. A physical count of the goods on hand at the Plant Emporium on December 31, 19X5, showed a total merchandise inventory of $13,000. Make the necessary entries for merchandise inventory in the financial statement sections of the worksheet.
2. Complete the worksheet.
3. Prepare a classified income statement for the year ended December 31, 19X5. (The firm does not divide its operating expenses into selling and administrative expenses.)

4. Prepare a statement of owner's equity for the year ended December 31, 19X5. (No additional investments were made during the period.)

5. Prepare a classified balance sheet as of December 31, 19X5. (All notes payable are due within a year.)

Note: Save your worksheet for use in Problem 17-1.

PROBLEM 16-2 **Completing a worksheet and preparing classified financial statements.** This problem is a continuation of Problem 15-4. It involves end-of-period work for the Nutri-Products Company.

Instructions
1. A physical count of the goods on hand at the Nutri-Products Company on December 31, 19X3, showed a total merchandise inventory of $42,000. Make the necessary entries for merchandise inventory in the financial statement sections of the worksheet.

2. Complete the worksheet.

3. Prepare a classified income statement for the year ended December 31, 19X3. (The firm does not divide its operating expenses into selling and administrative expenses.)

4. Prepare a statement of owner's equity for the year ended December 31, 19X3. (No additional investments were made during the period.)

5. Prepare a classified balance sheet as of December 31, 19X3. (All notes payable are due within a year.)

Note: Save your worksheet for use in Problem 17-2.

PROBLEM 16-3 **Preparing classified financial statements.** The Micro Circuits Company distributes electronic components to computer manufacturers. The adjusted trial balance data given on page 403 is from the firm's worksheet for the year ended December 31, 19X7. A physical count of the goods on hand at that date showed an ending merchandise inventory of $56,000.

Instructions
1. Prepare a classified income statement for the year ended December 31, 19X7. (The expense accounts numbered 511 through 515 represent warehouse expenses, those numbered 521 through 527 represent selling expenses, and those numbered 531 through 549 represent general and administrative expenses.)

2. Prepare a statement of owner's equity for the year ended December 31, 19X7. (No additional investments were made during the period.)

3. Prepare a classified balance sheet as of December 31, 19X7. (The mortgage and the loans extend for more than a year.)

ALTERNATE PROBLEMS

PROBLEM 16-1A **Completing a worksheet and preparing classified financial statements.** This problem is a continuation of Problem 15-3A. It involves end-of-period work for the Toy Palace. The necessary instructions appear on page 404.

MICRO CIRCUITS COMPANY
Worksheet (Partial)
Year Ended December 31, 19X7

Acct. No.	Account Name	Adjusted Trial Balance	
		Debit	Credit
101	Cash	$ 6,775	
105	Petty Cash Fund	100	
109	Notes Receivable	2,700	
111	Accounts Receivable	13,625	
112	Allowance for Uncollectible Accounts		1,250
121	Merchandise Inventory (Jan. 1)	58,500	
123	Warehouse Supplies	690	
126	Office Supplies	330	
129	Prepaid Insurance	1,800	
141	Land	9,000	
151	Building	42,000	
152	Accum. Depr.—Building		12,000
153	Warehouse Equipment	8,000	
154	Accum. Depr.—Warehouse Equipment		3,600
155	Delivery Equipment	11,500	
156	Accum. Depr.—Delivery Equipment		4,400
157	Office Equipment	5,000	
158	Accum. Depr.—Office Equipment		2,250
201	Notes Payable		4,800
203	Accounts Payable		10,500
206	Interest Payable		120
251	Mortgage Payable		14,000
253	Loans Payable		3,000
301	Ruth Newman, Capital (Jan. 1)		99,410
302	Ruth Newman, Drawing	31,500	
401	Sales		418,400
451	Sales Returns and Allowances	4,300	
491	Interest Income		370
501	Merchandise Purchases	192,600	
502	Freight In	3,200	
503	Purchases Returns and Allowances		1,860
504	Purchases Discount		2,540
511	Warehouse Wages Expense	47,400	
513	Warehouse Supplies Expense	1,525	
515	Depr. Expense—Warehouse Equipment	1,200	
521	Sales Salaries Expense	64,800	
523	Travel and Entertainment Expense	5,125	
525	Delivery Wages Expense	21,000	
527	Depr. Expense—Delivery Equipment	2,200	
531	Office Salaries Expense	17,400	
533	Office Supplies Expense	750	
535	Insurance Expense	1,300	
537	Utilities Expense	2,400	
539	Telephone Expense	1,380	
541	Payroll Taxes Expense	13,500	
543	Property Taxes Expense	1,150	
545	Loss From Uncollectible Accounts	1,200	
547	Depr. Expense—Building	2,000	
549	Depr. Expense—Office Equipment	750	
591	Interest Expense	1,800	
	Totals	$578,500	$578,500

1. A physical count of the goods on hand at the Toy Palace on December 31, 19X8, showed a total merchandise inventory of $36,000. Make the necessary entries for merchandise inventory in the financial statement sections of the worksheet.

2. Complete the worksheet.

3. Prepare a classified income statement for the year ended December 31, 19X8. (The firm does not divide its operating expenses into selling and administrative expenses.)

4. Prepare a statement of owner's equity for the year ended December 31, 19X8. (No additional investments were made during the period.)

5. Prepare a classified balance sheet as of December 31, 19X8. (All notes payable are due within a year.)

Note: Save your worksheet for use in Problem 17-1A.

PROBLEM 16-2A   **Completing a worksheet and preparing classified financial statements.** This problem is a continuation of Problem 15-4A.

Instructions   1. A physical count of the goods on hand at Valley Forge Furniture on December 31, 19X4, showed a total merchandise inventory of $83,000. Make the necessary entries for merchandise inventory in the financial statement sections of the worksheet.

2. Complete the worksheet.

3. Prepare a classified income statement for the year ended December 31, 19X4. (The firm does not divide its operating expenses into selling and administrative expenses.)

4. Prepare a statement of owner's equity for the year ended December 31, 19X4. (No additional investments were made during the period.)

5. Prepare a classified balance sheet as of December 31, 19X4. (All notes payable are due within a year.)

Note: Save your worksheet for use in Problem 17-2A.

PROBLEM 16-3A   **Preparing classified financial statements.** High-Grade Products distributes automobile parts to service stations and repair shops. The adjusted trial balance data given on page 405 is from the firm's worksheet for the year ended December 31, 19X1. A physical count of the goods on hand at that date showed an ending merchandise inventory of $62,000.

Instructions   1. Prepare a classified income statement for the year ended December 31, 19X1. (The expense accounts numbered 511 through 515 represent warehouse expenses, those numbered 521 through 525 represent selling expenses, and those numbered 531 through 551 represent general and administrative expenses.)

2. Prepare a statement of owner's equity for the year ended December 31, 19X1. (No additional investments were made during the period.)

3. Prepare a classified balance sheet as of December 31, 19X1. (The mortgage and the long-term notes extend for more than a year.)

HIGH-GRADE PRODUCTS
Worksheet (Partial)
Year Ended December 31, 19X1

Acct. No.	Account Name	Adjusted Trial Balance Debit	Adjusted Trial Balance Credit
101	Cash	$ 43,000	
105	Petty Cash Fund	200	
109	Notes Receivable	5,000	
111	Accounts Receivable	50,600	
112	Allowance for Uncollectible Accounts		1,400
116	Interest Receivable	100	
121	Merchandise Inventory (Jan. 1)	65,200	
123	Warehouse Supplies	1,150	
126	Office Supplies	300	
129	Prepaid Insurance	1,820	
141	Land	7,500	
151	Building	46,000	
152	Accum. Depr.—Building		7,200
153	Warehouse Equipment	9,400	
154	Accum. Depr.—Warehouse Equipment		4,800
155	Office Equipment	4,200	
156	Accum. Depr.—Office Equipment		1,520
201	Notes Payable—Short-Term		7,000
203	Accounts Payable		29,500
206	Interest Payable		150
251	Notes Payable—Long-Term		5,000
253	Mortgage Payable		10,000
301	Carl Furjanic, Capital (Jan. 1)		163,510
302	Carl Furjanic, Drawing	32,000	
401	Sales		495,100
451	Sales Returns and Allowances	3,700	
491	Interest Income		240
501	Merchandise Purchases	219,000	
502	Freight In	4,400	
503	Purchases Returns and Allowances		5,780
504	Purchases Discount		4,120
511	Warehouse Wages Expense	53,600	
513	Warehouse Supplies Expense	2,400	
515	Depr. Expense—Warehouse Equipment	1,200	
521	Sales Salaries Expense	75,100	
523	Travel Expense	11,500	
525	Delivery Expense	18,200	
531	Office Salaries Expense	42,000	
533	Office Supplies Expense	560	
535	Insurance Expense	4,400	
537	Utilities Expense	3,000	
539	Telephone Expense	1,590	
541	Payroll Taxes Expense	15,300	
543	Building Repairs Expense	1,350	
545	Property Taxes Expense	6,200	
547	Loss From Uncollectible Accounts	1,290	
549	Depr. Expense—Building	1,800	
551	Depr. Expense—Office Equipment	760	
591	Interest Expense	1,500	
	Totals	$735,320	$735,320

At the end of each fiscal period, the accountant is concerned about preparing the worksheet and financial statements quickly so that management can obtain the information it needs about the results of operations and the financial position of the business. After this work is done, the accountant must make adjusting and closing entries to complete the financial records for the period. Then, to be sure that the general ledger is still in balance, the accountant prepares a postclosing trial balance.

ADJUSTING AND CLOSING PROCEDURES

JOURNALIZING THE ADJUSTING ENTRIES

The worksheet shows the accounts to be adjusted and the amounts involved. Thus, once the financial statements have been prepared, the accountant uses the data on the worksheet to record adjusting entries in the general journal. These entries are essential if the firm is to have a complete and accurate record of its financial affairs for the period.

Each adjusting entry in the general journal should contain a detailed explanation of how the amount was arrived at. The explanation should be sufficient to allow another person, such as an auditor, to easily understand what was done and why. For example, notice the explanation given in the adjusting entry shown below. This entry was made at Sports World for the estimated loss from uncollectible accounts (Adjustment *a* on the worksheet).

		Adjusting Entries (Adjustment a)			
19 X8					
Dec. 31	Loss From Uncollectible Accounts	556	570 00		
	Allowance for Uncollectible Accounts	112		570 00
	To record estimated loss from			
	uncollectible accounts for 19X8, based			
	on 0.3% of net credit sales of $190,000.			

The next two adjusting entries recorded at Sports World were for depreciation of store equipment and office equipment. These entries appear on page 407. In each case, the explanation refers the reader to a schedule on which the computations are based. This schedule shows the various types of equipment owned, the dates that the items were purchased, their estimated useful lives, their estimated salvage value, and the yearly depreciation charges. Separate schedules are kept for the store equipment and the office equipment.

The rest of the adjusting entries made at Sports World on December 31, 19X8, are illustrated on pages 407 and 408. Notice that the identifying letter used

		(Adjustment b)			
Dec.	31	Depr. Expense—Store Equipment	526	1,600 00	
		Accum. Depr.—Store Equipment	142		1,600 00
		To record depreciation for 19X8, as shown by schedule in file.			
		(Adjustment c)			
	31	Depr. Expense—Office Equipment	559	490 00	
		Accum. Depr—Office Equipment	152		490 00
		To record depreciation for 19X8, as shown by schedule in file.			
		(Adjustment d)			
	31	Sales Salaries Expense	511	400 00	
		Salaries Payable	229		400 00
		To record accrued salaries of part-time salesclerks for December 28–31.			
		(Adjustment e)			
	31	Payroll Taxes Expense	544	35 00	
		FICA Tax Payable	221		28 00
		Federal Unemployment Tax Payable	225		2 00
		State Unemployment Tax Payable	227		5 00
		To record accrued payroll taxes on accrued salaries for December 28–31:			

FICA tax 7% of $400   = $28
FUTA tax 0.8% of $250 =   2
SUTA tax 2% of $250   =   5
     Total $35

		(Adjustment f)			
	31	Interest Expense	591	20 00	
		Interest Payable	216		20 00
		To record accrued interest on a two-month, 12% trade note payable dated Dec. 1, 19X8:			

$$\$2{,}000 \times \frac{12}{100} \times \frac{1}{12} = \$20$$

		(Adjustment g)			
	31	Supplies Expense	517	4,225 00	
		Supplies	131		4,225 00
		To record supplies used during 19X8.			
		(Adjustment h)			
	31	Insurance Expense	536	2,340 00	
		Prepaid Insurance	126		2,340 00
		To record expired insurance on a one-year policy purchased for $3,120 on April 1, 19X8.			
		(Adjustment i)			
	31	Interest Expense	591	150 00	
		Prepaid Interest	127		150 00
		To record transfer of ⅔ of prepaid interest of $225 to expense for a three-month, 10% note payable issued to the bank on Nov. 1, 19X8.			

		(Adjustment j)			
Dec.	31	Interest Receivable	116	16 00	
		Interest Income	491		16 00
		To record accrued interest earned			
		on a four-month, 12% note receivable			
		dated Nov. 1, 19X8:			

$$\$800 \times \frac{12}{100} \times \frac{2}{12} = \$16$$

		(Adjustment k)			
	31	Sales Tax Payable	231	132 00	
		Miscellaneous Income	493		132 00
		To record accrued commission earned			
		on sales tax owed for fourth quarter			
		of 19X8:			
		Sales Tax Payable $6,600			
		Commission Rate × .02			
		Commission Due $132.00			

for each adjustment on the worksheet appears above the corresponding entry in the general journal.

Trace the data about the adjustments from the worksheet shown on pages 390 and 391 to the journal entries.

POSTING THE ADJUSTING ENTRIES

The next step in the end-of-period routine is to post the adjusting entries from the general journal to the general ledger accounts involved. This task should be completed promptly because the account balances must be up to date before the closing entries are made. The posting procedure used is the same as the one described in Chapter 6. For example, refer to the account shown below, which reflects the posting of the debit part of Adjustment *d* from the general journal illustrated on page 407.

		Sales Salaries Expense					No. 511
DATE	EXPLANATION	POST. REF.	DEBIT	CREDIT	BALANCE	DR. CR.
19 X8						
Dec. 31	Balance	✓			71,300 00	Dr.
31	Adjusting	J25	400 00		71,700 00	Dr.

Notice that the word "Adjusting" has been recorded in the Explanation column of the account. This identifies the nature of the entry and distinguishes it from the entries for transactions that occurred during the fiscal period. (For the sake of simplicity, the account shown here contains only the balance on December 31 prior to the adjustment. The entries made at the end of each semimonthly payroll period throughout the year have been omitted.)

After all adjusting entries are posted, the balances of the general ledger accounts should match the amounts shown in the Adjusted Trial Balance section of the worksheet (pages 390 and 391). In the case of Sales Salaries Expense, the updated balance is $71,700.

JOURNALIZING THE CLOSING ENTRIES

The worksheet is the source of the data for the general journal entries required to close the temporary accounts—the revenue, cost, and expense accounts. Each balance appearing in the Income Statement section of the worksheet is closed to the Income Summary account. The following four-step procedure is used.

1. Set up the ending inventory by debiting Merchandise Inventory for the specified amount. Debit the revenue accounts and the other temporary accounts with credit balances to close them. Credit the Income Summary account for the total.
2. Debit the Income Summary account for the total of the beginning inventory, the cost and expense account balances, and the debit balances of other temporary accounts. Credit each account individually to close it.
3. Transfer the balance of the Income Summary account, which represents the net income or net loss for the period, to the owner's capital account. If there is a net income, debit the Income Summary account and credit the capital account. If a net loss was incurred, debit the capital account and credit the Income Summary account.
4. Transfer the balance of the owner's drawing account to the owner's capital account. Debit the capital account and credit the drawing account.

The closing procedure is described in detail in the next sections.

Step 1: Recording Ending Inventory and Closing the Revenue Accounts

Refer to the Income Statement section of the completed worksheet for Sports World, which appears on pages 390 and 391. Six items are listed in the Credit column of this section. The accountant makes the first closing entry by debiting each account for the amount shown and crediting Income Summary for the total, $494,250. This entry, which is illustrated below, provides a record of the ending merchandise inventory and closes the revenue accounts and other temporary accounts with credit balances.

		Closing Entries			
19 X8					
Dec. 31	Merchandise Inventory	121	64,000 00		
	Sales	401	422,000 00		
	Interest Income	491	152 00		
	Miscellaneous Income	493	498 00		
	Purchases Returns and Allowances	503	2,700 00		
	Purchases Discount	504	4,900 00		
	Income Summary	399		494,250 00	
	To set up the ending merchandise inventory and to close the revenue accounts and other temporary accounts with credit balances.				

Step 2:
Closing the Cost and Expense Accounts

Refer again to the worksheet illustrated on pages 390 and 391. The Debit column of the Income Statement section shows the amounts for the beginning merchandise inventory, the cost and expense accounts, and the other temporary accounts with debit balances. The accountant records the second closing entry by debiting Income Summary for the total of these items, $455,170, and crediting each account for the balance listed, as shown below. The purpose of this entry is to charge the beginning inventory to the current period's operations and to close the cost and expense accounts and other temporary accounts with debit balances.

Dec.	31	Income Summary	399	455,170 00	
		Merchandise Inventory	121		63,000 00
		Sales Returns and Allowances	451		7,400 00
		Merchandise Purchases	501		248,500 00
		Freight In	502		3,300 00
		Sales Salaries Expense	511		71,700 00
		Advertising Expense	514		6,900 00
		Supplies Expense	517		4,225 00
		Cash Short or Over	520		75 00
		Delivery Expense	523		1,200 00
		Depr. Expense—Store Equipment	526		1,600 00
		Insurance Expense	529		2,340 00
		Cleaning Service Expense	532		1,800 00
		Rent Expense	535		12,000 00
		Utilities Expense	538		2,550 00
		Office Salaries Expense	541		16,200 00
		Payroll Taxes Expense	544		7,740 00
		Office Expense	547		390 00
		Professional Services Expense	550		1,100 00
		Telephone Expense	553		1,320 00
		Loss From Uncollectible Accounts	556		570 00
		Depr. Expense—Office Equipment	559		490 00
		Interest Expense	591		770 00
		To close the beginning merchandise inventory, the cost and expense accounts, and other temporary accounts with debit balances.			

Step 3:
Closing the Income Summary Account

The effect of the first two closing entries is to transfer the results of operations for the period to the Income Summary account. After this data is posted, the balance of the Income Summary account will represent the net income or net loss for the period. Since the entire net income or net loss in a sole proprietorship belongs to the owner, the third closing entry made in this type of business transfers the net income or net loss to the owner's capital account.

In the case of Sports World, there is a net income of $39,080 for the fiscal year 19X8. The Income Summary account is therefore debited for $39,080, and the Lynn Frank, Capital account is credited, as shown below.

Dec.	31	Income Summary	399	39,080 00	
		Lynn Frank, Capital	301		39,080 00
		To transfer the net income for 19X8 to the owner's capital account.			

This entry closes the Income Summary account; and it remains closed until it is used in the end-of-period routine for the next year.

**Step 4:
Closing the Drawing
Account**

The final step in the closing process for a sole proprietorship is to transfer the balance of the owner's drawing account to the owner's capital account. In the case of Sports World, the required entry involves a debit to Lynn Frank, Capital and a credit to Lynn Frank, Drawing for $30,000, as shown below. This entry closes the drawing account and updates the capital account so that its balance will agree with the ending capital reported on the statement of owner's equity and the balance sheet.

Dec. 31	Lynn Frank, Capital	301	30,000 00	
	Lynn Frank, Drawing	302		30,000 00
	To close the owner's drawing account.			

POSTING THE CLOSING ENTRIES

The closing entries are posted from the general journal to the general ledger in the usual manner. This process reduces the balances of the temporary accounts to zero, as shown in the following example.

Sales Salaries Expense — No. 511

DATE	EXPLANATION	POST. REF.	DEBIT	CREDIT	BALANCE	DR. CR.
19 X8						
Dec. 31	Balance	✓			71,300 00	Dr.
31	Adjusting	J25	400 00		71,700 00	Dr.
31	Closing	J26		71,700 00	–0–	

The word "Closing" is recorded in the Explanation column of each account involved to identify the nature of these entries.

PREPARING A POSTCLOSING TRIAL BALANCE

As soon as the closing entries have been posted, a postclosing trial balance should be prepared to make sure that the general ledger is in balance. Only the accounts that are still open—the asset and liability accounts and the owner's capital account—appear on the postclosing trial balance. The amounts shown should match those reported on the balance sheet. For example, compare the postclosing trial balance illustrated on page 412 with the balance sheet illustrated on page 395.

Of course, if the postclosing trial balance shows that the general ledger is out of balance, the error or errors must be located. Then, correcting entries must be journalized and posted. It is essential that the general ledger be in balance before any transactions are recorded for the new fiscal period.

SPORTS WORLD
Postclosing Trial Balance
December 31, 19X8

ACCT. NO.	ACCOUNT NAME	DEBIT	CREDIT
101	Cash	15,300 00	
105	Petty Cash	100 00	
107	Change Fund	200 00	
109	Notes Receivable	800 00	
111	Accounts Receivable	24,000 00	
112	Allowance for Uncollectible Accounts		620 00
116	Interest Receivable	16 00	
121	Merchandise Inventory	64,000 00	
131	Supplies	610 00	
133	Prepaid Insurance	780 00	
135	Prepaid Interest	75 00	
141	Store Equipment	8,900 00	
142	Accumulated Depreciation—Store Equipment		4,800 00
151	Office Equipment	2,750 00	
152	Accumulated Depreciation—Office Equipment		1,470 00
201	Notes Payable—Trade		2,000 00
203	Notes Payable—Bank		9,000 00
205	Accounts Payable		6,500 00
216	Interest Payable		20 00
221	FICA Tax Payable		966 00
223	Employee Income Tax Payable		804 00
225	Federal Unemployment Tax Payable		24 00
227	State Unemployment Tax Payable		65 00
229	Salaries Payable		400 00
231	Sales Tax Payable		6,468 00
301	Lynn Frank, Capital		84,394 00
	Totals	117,531 00	117,531 00

PREPARING THE ACCOUNTS FOR THE NEXT PERIOD

After the balances of the revenue, cost, and expense accounts have been reduced to zero by means of the closing entries, the same ledger sheets can be used to record data for the new fiscal year. However, some accountants prefer to rule these accounts as shown below before entering transactions for the new period. Other accountants prefer to set up new ledger sheets for the revenue, cost, and expense accounts each year. The prior year's ledger sheets are kept in a permanent file.

The ledger sheets for the asset and liability accounts and the owner's capital account need not be ruled if the balance ledger form is used. The balances in

		Supplies Expense					No. 517	
DATE		EXPLANATION	POST. REF.	DEBIT	CREDIT	BALANCE	DR. CR.	
19 X8 Dec. 31		Adjusting	J25	4,225 00		4,225 00	Dr.	
	31	Closing	J26		4,225 00	—0—		

these accounts at the end of one period simply become the beginning balances for the next period.

REVERSING ENTRIES

Certain adjustments made in the current period may lead to recording problems in the new period. Many accountants follow a policy of reversing adjustments of this nature at the start of the new period in order to avoid difficulties later. The necessary entries, which are known as *reversing entries,* are first made in the general journal and then posted to the general ledger.

Adjustment *d* recorded at Sports World provides a good illustration of why reversing entries can be helpful. On December 31, 19X8, the firm owed salaries of $400 to its part-time salesclerks. Since the salaries will not be paid until January 19X9, the accountant made an adjustment debiting Sales Salaries Expense and crediting Salaries Payable for $400 on the December 31 worksheet. This adjustment allowed the amount to be charged as an expense during the correct fiscal year and to be presented accurately as a liability at the end of the period. After the financial statements were prepared, the accountant journalized and posted the adjustment for accrued salaries expense along with the firm's other adjustments.

On January 3, 19X9, when the weekly payroll period for the part-time salesclerks ends, a total of $600 is owed to these employees for salaries. However, only $200 of the $600 amount pertains to the current year. A busy employee who is journalizing the payroll might easily overlook the fact that $400 of the sum was recorded as accrued salaries expense at the end of the previous year. Even if the employee recognizes the item as being related to Adjustment *d,* the situation is complicated because it is necessary to consult the end-of-period records for 19X8 and then properly divide the expense and liability involved between the two fiscal years. This is a time-consuming procedure, and it can easily lead to errors.

A simple method of avoiding such problems is to make reversing entries before recording any transactions for the new period. Each reversing entry is the exact opposite of the related adjusting entry. The account credited in the adjusting entry is now debited, and the account debited in the adjusting entry is now credited. For example, the accountant at Sports World debited Salaries Payable and credited Sales Salaries Expense for $400 to reverse Adjustment *d,* as shown below. (Notice that the reversing entry is dated as of the start of the new fiscal year—January 1, 19X9.)

			Reversing Entries				
19	X9						
Jan.	1	Salaries Payable		229	400 00		
		Sales Salaries Expense		511		400 00	
		To reverse Adjusting Entry d made on Dec. 31, 19X8.					

This entry guards against any later oversight, eliminates the need for checking old records, and makes it unnecessary to divide the amount of salaries between the two fiscal years when the payroll is recorded on January 3, 19X9.

After the reversing entry is posted, the Salaries Payable account has a zero balance and the Sales Salaries Expense account has a credit balance of $400, as shown below. Thus, the entry for the $600 of salaries owed to the part-time salesclerks can be made in the normal manner at the end of the payroll period on January 3, 19X9.

Salaries Payable — No. 229

DATE		EXPLANATION	POST. REF.	DEBIT	CREDIT	BALANCE	DR. CR.
19 X8							
Dec.	31	Adjusting	J25		400 00	400 00	Cr.
19 X9							
Jan.	1	Reversing	J1	400 00		–0–	

Sales Salaries Expense — No. 511

DATE		EXPLANATION	POST. REF.	DEBIT	CREDIT	BALANCE	DR. CR.
19 X8							
Dec.	31	Balance	✓			71,300 00	Dr.
	31	Adjusting	J25	400 00		71,700 00	Dr.
	31	Closing	J26		71,700 00	–0–	
19 X9							
Jan.	1	Reversing	J1		400 00	400 00	Cr.

The credit balance of $400 in the Sales Salaries Expense account partially offsets the debit of $600 posted from the payroll entry of January 3. The result is a debit balance of $200, which represents the correct amount of expense for 19X9. (See the illustration below.) Since the Salaries Payable account has no balance after the reversing entry is posted, there is no problem when the payroll is recorded on January 3. Once the posting of the payroll entry is made, this account contains the correct amount of liability.

Sales Salaries Expense — No. 511

DATE		EXPLANATION	POST. REF.	DEBIT	CREDIT	BALANCE	DR. CR.
19 X8							
Dec.	31	Balance	✓			71,300 00	Dr.
	31	Adjusting	J25	400 00		71,700 00	Dr.
	31	Closing	J26		71,700 00	–0–	
19 X9							
Jan.	1	Reversing	J1		400 00	400 00	Cr.
	3		J2	600 00		200 00	Dr.

Not all adjustments cause later recording problems and should therefore be reversed. Normally, the adjustments requiring reversal are accrued expense items that will involve future payments of cash and accrued income items that will involve future receipts of cash. Thus, there is no need to reverse adjustments for uncollectible accounts, depreciation, and prepaid expenses. (Adjustments for prepaid expenses do not require reversal if these items are initially recorded as assets, as is done at Sports World. However, when prepaid expense items are initially treated as expenses, the end-of-period adjustments for these items must be reversed.)

At Sports World, there are four adjustments that require reversal as of January 1, 19X9. The reversing entry for the first of these adjustments—accrued salaries expense—has already been illustrated. The next adjustment that must be reversed is the one for accrued payroll taxes expense. The necessary entry, which is shown below, allows the firm to avoid recording problems on January 3, 19X9, when the employer's payroll taxes on the salaries of the part-time sales-clerks must be journalized.

Jan.	1	FICA Tax Payable	221	28 00	
		Federal Unemployment Tax Payable	225	2 00	
		State Unemployment Tax Payable	227	5 00	
		Payroll Taxes Expense	544		35 00
		To reverse Adjusting Entry e made on			
		Dec. 31, 19X8.			

The third adjustment that requires reversal is the one for accrued interest expense. This adjustment covered one month of interest on a 2-month, 12 percent trade note payable for $2,000 that was issued on December 1, 19X8. The $20 of interest that applied to 19X8 was recorded by debiting Interest Expense and crediting Interest Payable. The reversing entry shown below prevents recording difficulties when the note is paid on February 1, 19X9.

Jan.	1	Interest Payable	216	20 00	
		Interest Expense	591		20 00
		To reverse Adjusting Entry f made on			
		Dec. 31, 19X8.			

In addition to the three adjustments for accrued expense items, Sports World had two adjustments for accrued income items at the end of 19X8. The first of these items was accrued interest income on a note receivable. Since the firm will obtain cash for the note and the interest in the new fiscal year, the adjustment must be reversed.

Remember that Sports World accepted a 4-month, 12 percent note for $800 from a customer on November 1, 19X8. The interest of $16 for November and December 19X8 was recorded in an adjusting entry that debited Interest Receivable and credited Interest Income. This adjustment is reversed as shown below in order to eliminate any difficulties in recording the receipt of the interest when the note is paid on March 1, 19X9.

Jan.	1	Interest Income	491	16 00	
		Interest Receivable	116		16 00
		To reverse Adjusting Entry j made on			
		Dec. 31, 19X8.			

After the reversing entry is posted, the Interest Receivable account has a zero balance and the Interest Income account has a debit balance of $16, as shown below. When the firm receives a check for $832 in payment of the note and the interest on March 1, 19X9, the transaction can be recorded in the normal manner—by debiting Cash for $832, crediting Notes Receivable for $800, and crediting Interest Income for $32. The $16 debit balance of the Interest Income account partially offsets the credit posting of $32 on March 1. The resulting credit balance of $16 represents the correct amount of interest income on the note for 19X9.

Interest Receivable — No. 116

DATE		EXPLANATION	POST. REF.	DEBIT	CREDIT	BALANCE	DR. CR.
19 X8							
Dec.	31	Adjusting	J25	16 00		16 00	Dr.
19 X9							
Jan.	1	Reversing	J1		16 00	–0–	

Interest Income — No. 491

DATE		EXPLANATION	POST. REF.	DEBIT	CREDIT	BALANCE	DR. CR.
19 X8							
Dec.	31	Balance	✓			136 00	Cr.
	31	Adjusting	J25		16 00	152 00	Cr.
	31	Closing	J26	152 00		–0–	
19 X9							
Jan.	1	Reversing	J1	16 00		16 00	Dr.
Mar.	1		CR3		32 00	16 00	Cr.

The second accrued income item that Sports World had at the end of 19X8 was an accrued commission on the sales tax collected during the fourth quarter. Since no cash will be received in January 19X9 when the sales tax return is filed, there is no need to reverse the adjustment made for the accrued commission.

| The Need for Reversing Entries | It is not essential that a firm record reversing entries at the start of a new fiscal period. However, many accountants follow this practice because it simplifies the handling of transactions related to prior adjustments that occur in the new period and therefore helps to eliminate errors. |

REVIEW OF THE ACCOUNTING CYCLE

Typical accounting procedures, records, and statements for merchandising businesses have now been discussed in detail. Chapters 15 through 17 presented the end-of-period activities for businesses of this type. Earlier chapters focused on the day-to-day recording process in merchandising businesses. Underlying the various procedures described are the steps of the accounting cycle, which are performed in each fiscal period to classify, record, and summarize financial data and produce needed financial information. These steps are reviewed below.

1. *Analyze transactions*. The data about transactions comes into an accounting system on a variety of source documents—sales slips, purchase invoices, credit memorandums, check stubs, and so on. Each document must be examined to analyze the transaction and determine its financial effects.
2. *Journalize the data about transactions*. The effects of each transaction are recorded in the appropriate journal. Most merchandising businesses use a number of special journals as well as the general journal.
3. *Post the data about transactions*. The data about each transaction is transferred from the journal entries to the accounts in one or more ledgers. Typically, a merchandising business has several subsidiary ledgers in addition to the general ledger.
4. *Prepare a worksheet*. At the end of each period of operations, a worksheet is prepared. The Trial Balance section of the worksheet is used to prove the equality of the debits and credits in the general ledger. The Adjustments section is used to enter any changes in account balances that may be necessary at the end of the period in order to present a more accurate and complete picture of the firm's financial affairs. The Adjusted Trial Balance section provides a check on the equality of the debits and credits after the adjustments are combined with the original account balances. The Income Statement and Balance Sheet sections allow the accountant to arrange the data needed for the financial statements in an orderly manner so that the statements can be prepared quickly.
5. *Prepare financial statements*. A set of formal financial statements is prepared to report information to owners, managers, and other interested parties.
6. *Record adjusting entries*. Adjusting entries are journalized and posted in order to create a permanent record of the changes in account balances that were made on the worksheet when the adjustments were determined.
7. *Record closing entries*. Closing entries are journalized and posted in order to transfer the results of operations to owner's equity and to prepare the revenue, cost, and expense accounts for use in the next period. The closing entries reduce the balances of the temporary accounts to zero.
8. *Prepare a postclosing trial balance*. Another trial balance is taken to make sure that the general ledger is still in balance after the adjusting and closing entries have been posted.

9. *Interpret the financial information.* The accountant, owners, managers, and other interested parties must interpret the information shown on the financial statements and other less formal financial reports that may be prepared. This information is used to evaluate the results of operations and the financial position of the business and to make decisions.

In addition to the steps listed here, some firms record reversing entries, as discussed on pages 413 through 417 of this chapter.

The chart shown below illustrates the flow of data through an accounting system that uses special journals and subsidiary ledgers. Notice that the system is composed of several smaller areas or subsystems that perform specialized functions.

- The accounts receivable area records transactions involving sales and cash receipts and maintains the accounts with credit customers. This area also handles the billing of credit customers.
- The accounts payable area records transactions involving purchases and cash payments and maintains the accounts with creditors. This area also issues checks to pay the firm's obligations.
- The general ledger and financial reporting area records transactions that do not belong in the special journals such as credit purchases of plant and equipment,

THE FLOW OF FINANCIAL DATA THROUGH AN ACCOUNTING SYSTEM THAT HAS SPECIAL JOURNALS AND SUBSIDIARY LEDGERS

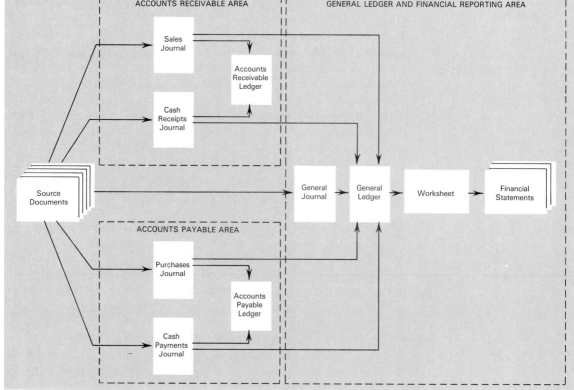

maintains the general ledger accounts, carries out the end-of-period procedures, and prepares financial statements. This area is the focal point for the accounting system because the results of all the firm's transactions eventually flow into the general ledger; and, of course, the general ledger provides the data that is presented on the financial statements.

PRINCIPLES AND PROCEDURES SUMMARY

When the year-end worksheet and financial statements have been completed, adjusting entries are recorded in the general journal and posted to the general ledger. The data for these entries comes from the Adjustments section of the worksheet. The next step in the end-of-period procedure is to journalize and post closing entries from the data in the Income Statement section of the worksheet. Then, to make sure that the general ledger is still in balance after the adjusting and closing entries have been posted, a postclosing trial balance is prepared.

At the beginning of each new fiscal period, many accountants follow the practice of reversing certain adjustments that were made in the previous period. This is done to avoid recording problems with transactions related to the adjustments that will occur in the new period.

Only adjusting entries for accrued expenses and accrued income need be considered in the reversing process. Furthermore, only those accrued expense and income items that will involve future payments and receipts of cash are likely to cause difficulties later and should therefore be reversed.

The use of reversing entries is optional, but these entries save time, promote efficiency, and help to achieve a proper matching of revenue and expenses in each fiscal period. When reversing entries are recorded, there is no need to examine each transaction to see whether a portion applies to a past period and then divide the amount of the transaction between the two periods.

MANAGERIAL IMPLICATIONS

Although management is not directly involved in carrying out the end-of-period procedures, the efficiency of these procedures should be of concern to management. Correct adjusting entries must be made if all revenue and expense items are to be recorded and matched in the appropriate period. Similarly, both the adjusting and closing processes must be handled properly if the firm's financial records are to contain complete and accurate information about its affairs during the fiscal year.

The promptness of the closing entries is also important. The sooner the financial records are closed for the old period, the sooner the recording of transactions for the new period can begin. Any significant lag between the time that transactions occur and the time that they are recorded can lead to serious problems. For example, information that management may need on a daily or weekly basis, such as the firm's cash position, will not be available or will not be up to date.

The efficiency of the adjusting and closing procedures also has an effect on the annual audit by the company's public accounting firm. Audits of financial records are greatly speeded up by good end-of-period procedures. For example, detailed explanations in the general journal make it easy for an auditor to understand and check the adjusting entries.

REVIEW QUESTIONS

1. Why is it necessary to journalize and post adjusting entries if the amounts of the adjustments already appear on the worksheet?
2. Why should detailed explanations be provided for all adjusting entries when they are recorded in the general journal?
3. Briefly explain the four steps in the closing procedure for a sole proprietorship merchandising business.
4. Describe the entry that would be made at the Bell Company to close the Income Summary account in each of the following cases. (The owner of the firm is Janet Bell.)
   a. There is a net income of $35,000.
   b. There is a net loss of $12,000.
5. After closing entries are posted, which of the following types of accounts will have zero balances?
   a. Asset accounts
   b. Revenue accounts
   c. Owner's drawing account
   d. Liability accounts
   e. Income Summary account
   f. Cost and expense accounts
   g. Owner's capital account
6. What is the purpose of the postclosing trial balance?
7. What types of accounts appear on the postclosing trial balance?
8. Why are reversing entries helpful?
9. What types of adjustments are reversed?
10. On December 31, 19X1, the Chan Company made an adjusting entry debiting Interest Receivable and crediting Interest Income for $30 of accrued interest. What reversing entry would be recorded for this item as of January 1, 19X2?
11. Various adjustments made at the Smith Company are listed below. Which ones should be reversed?
   a. An adjustment for the estimated loss from uncollectible accounts
   b. An adjustment for depreciation on equipment
   c. An adjustment for accrued salaries expense
   d. An adjustment for accrued payroll taxes expense
   e. An adjustment for accrued interest expense
   f. An adjustment for supplies used
   g. An adjustment for expired insurance
   h. An adjustment for accrued interest income
12. Name the steps of the accounting cycle.

MANAGERIAL DISCUSSION QUESTIONS

1. Why should management be concerned about the efficiency of the end-of-period procedures?
2. Why is it important that the closing process be completed promptly?

EXERCISES

EXERCISE 17-1

Recording an adjusting entry for uncollectible accounts. During the year 19X5, the Ricardo Company had net credit sales of $360,000. Past experience indicates that 0.5 percent of the firm's net credit sales result in uncollectible accounts. Show the adjusting entry that should be made for uncollectible accounts in the general journal on December 31, 19X5. Include a detailed explanation. (Assume that this item is Adjustment *a* on the firm's worksheet. Assign letters to the firm's other adjusting entries in sequence.)

EXERCISE 17-2

Recording an adjusting entry for depreciation on equipment. When the Ricardo Company started operations on January 2, 19X3, it purchased equipment for $42,000. This equipment has an estimated useful life of five years and an estimated salvage value of $4,000. Show the adjusting entry that should be made in the general journal on December 31, 19X5 to record the depreciation for 19X5. Include a detailed explanation.

EXERCISE 17-3

Recording an adjusting entry for accrued salaries. On December 31, 19X5, the Ricardo Company owed salaries of $340 to its office employees for December 29–31. These salaries will not be paid until January 4, 19X6. Show the adjusting entry that should be made for accrued salaries in the general journal on December 31, 19X5. Include a detailed explanation.

EXERCISE 17-4

Recording an adjusting entry for accrued payroll taxes. On December 31, 19X5, the Ricardo Company owed the employer's FICA tax on the entire $340 of accrued salaries for its office employees and owed FUTA and SUTA taxes on $125 of the accrued salaries. Assume that the firm is subject to the following tax rates: 7 percent for FICA, 0.8 percent for FUTA, and 2 percent for SUTA. Show the adjusting entry that should be made for accrued payroll taxes in the general journal on December 31, 19X5. Include a detailed explanation.

EXERCISE 17-5

Recording an adjusting entry for accrued interest on a note payable. On December 31, 19X5, the Notes Payable account at the Ricardo Company had a balance of $6,000. This represented a 4-month, 11 percent note issued on October 1, 19X5. Show the adjusting entry that should be made for accrued interest on the note payable in the general journal on December 31, 19X5. Include a detailed explanation.

EXERCISE 17-6   **Recording an adjusting entry for supplies used.** At the end of 19X5, the Ricardo Company had supplies on hand totaling $1,450. The balance of the Supplies account was $3,770. Show the adjusting entry that should be made in the general journal on December 31, 19X5 to record the supplies used during 19X5. Include a detailed explanation.

EXERCISE 17-7   **Recording an adjusting entry for expired insurance.** On September 1, 19X5, the Ricardo Company purchased a one-year insurance policy for $2,700. Show the adjusting entry that should be made for expired insurance in the general journal on December 31, 19X5. Include a detailed explanation.

EXERCISE 17-8   **Recording an adjusting entry for accrued interest on a note receivable.** On December 31, 19X5, the Notes Receivable account at the Ricardo Company had a balance of $1,500. This represented a 6-month, 10 percent note issued by a customer with an overdue balance on November 1. Show the adjusting entry that should be made for accrued interest on the note receivable in the general journal on December 31, 19X5. Include a detailed explanation.

EXERCISE 17-9   **Recording an entry to close the revenue accounts.** On December 31, 19X1, the Income Statement section of the worksheet for the Sanders Company contained the information given below. Show the entry that should be made in the general journal to set up the ending merchandise inventory, close the revenue accounts, and close the other temporary accounts with credit balances.

	INCOME STATEMENT	
	Debit	Credit
Merchandise Inventory	$ 38,000	$ 40,000
Sales		245,000
Sales Returns and Allowances	4,100	
Sales Discount	3,300	
Interest Income		100
Merchandise Purchases	125,000	
Freight In	1,700	
Purchases Returns and Allowances		1,900
Purchases Discount		2,200
Rent Expense	8,400	
Utilities Expense	2,100	
Telephone Expense	1,300	
Salaries Expense	65,000	
Payroll Taxes Expense	5,150	
Supplies Expense	1,600	
Depreciation Expense	2,400	
Interest Expense	350	
Totals	$258,400	$289,200

EXERCISE 17-10   **Recording an entry to close the cost and expense accounts.** Refer to the data given in Exercise 17-9 for the Sanders Company on December 31, 19X1. Show

the entry that should be made in the firm's general journal to close the beginning merchandise inventory, the cost and expense of accounts, and the other temporary accounts with debit balances.

EXERCISE 17-11 **Recording an entry to close the Income Summary account.** Refer to the data given in Exercise 17-9 for the Sanders Company on December 31, 19X1. Compute the net income or net loss for the year. Then show the entry that should be made in the firm's general journal to close the Income Summary account. The owner of the firm is Karen Sanders.

EXERCISE 17-12 **Recording an entry to close the drawing account.** The Karen Sanders, Drawing account had a balance of $26,000 on December 31, 19X1. Show the entry that should be made in the general journal to close this account.

EXERCISE 17-13 **Recording reversing entries.** Examine the adjusting entries made in Exercises 17-1 through 17-8, and determine which ones should be reversed. Show the reversing entries that should be recorded in the general journal as of January 1, 19X6. Include appropriate explanations.

PROBLEMS

PROBLEM 17-1 **Journalizing adjusting, closing, and reversing entries.** This problem is a continuation of Problem 16-1. Obtain all necessary data from the worksheet prepared for the Plant Emporium.

Instructions 1. Record adjusting entries in the general journal as of December 31, 19X5. Use 25 as the first journal page number. Include explanations for the entries.
2. Record closing entries in the general journal as of December 31, 19X5. Include explanations.
3. Record reversing entries in the general journal as of January 1, 19X6. Include explanations.

PROBLEM 17-2 **Journalizing adjusting, closing, and reversing entries.** This problem is a continuation of Problem 16-2. Obtain all necessary data from the worksheet prepared for the Nutri-Products Company.

Instructions 1. Record adjusting entries in the general journal as of December 31, 19X3. Use 25 as the first journal page number. Include explanations for the entries.
2. Record closing entries in the general journal as of December 31, 19X3. Include explanations.
3. Record reversing entries in the general journal as of January 1, 19X4. Include explanations.

PROBLEM 17-3 **Journalizing adjusting and reversing entries.** The data given on page 424 concerns adjustments to be made at the Vincent Company.

Instructions
1. Record the necessary adjusting entries in the general journal as of December 31, 19X1. Use 25 as the first journal page number. Include explanations.
2. Record reversing entries in the general journal as of January 1, 19X2. Include explanations.

ADJUSTMENTS

a. On September 1, 19X1, the firm signed a lease for a warehouse and paid rent of $8,400 in advance for a 6-month period. Make an adjusting entry for the expired rent for 19X1.

b. On December 31, 19X1, an inventory of the supplies showed that items costing $920 were on hand. The balance of the Supplies account was $5,560. Make an adjusting entry for the supplies used during 19X1.

c. A depreciation schedule for the firm's equipment shows that a total of $3,900 should be charged off as depreciation for 19X1. Make an adjusting entry for this amount.

d. On December 31, 19X1, the firm owed salaries of $2,200 that will not be paid until January 19X2. Make an adjusting entry for the accrued salaries for 19X1.

e. On December 31, 19X1, the firm owed the employer's FICA tax (7 percent) on $2,200 of accrued salaries, FUTA tax (0.8 percent) on $600 of accrued salaries, and SUTA tax (2.7 percent) on $600 of accrued salaries. Make an adjusting entry for the accrued payroll taxes for 19X1.

f. On November 1, 19X1, the firm received a 4-month, 10 percent note for $2,700 from a customer with an overdue balance. Make an adjusting entry for the accrued interest on the note receivable.

PROBLEM 17-4

Preparing a worksheet and classified financial statements; recording end-of-period entries. The Universal Software Center is a retail firm that sells computer programs for home and business use. On December 31, 19X7, its general ledger contained the accounts and balances shown on page 425.

Instructions
1. Prepare the Trial Balance section of a ten-column worksheet. The worksheet should cover the year ended December 31, 19X7.
2. Enter the adjustments described on pages 425 and 426 in the Adjustments section. Identify each adjustment with the appropriate letter.
3. Complete the worksheet. The ending merchandise inventory was $34,000.
4. Prepare a classified income statement for the year ended December 31, 19X7. (The firm does not divide its operating expenses into selling and administrative expenses.)
5. Prepare a statement of owner's equity for the year ended December 31, 19X7. (No additional investments were made during the period.)
6. Prepare a classified balance sheet as of December 31, 19X7. (All notes payable are due within a year.)
7. Record adjusting entries in the general journal as of December 31, 19X7. Use 25 as the first journal page number. Omit explanations.

8. Record closing entries in the general journal as of December 31, 19X7. Omit explanations.
9. Record reversing entries in the general journal as of January 1, 19X8. Omit explanations.

ACCOUNTS AND BALANCES

101	Cash	$ 6,800 Dr.
111	Accounts Receivable	13,600 Dr.
112	Allowance for Uncollectible Accounts	40 Cr.
121	Merchandise Inventory	31,000 Dr.
131	Supplies	2,380 Dr.
133	Prepaid Insurance	1,020 Dr.
141	Equipment	17,000 Dr.
142	Accum. Depr.—Equipment	5,600 Cr.
201	Notes Payable	3,500 Cr.
205	Accounts Payable	2,900 Cr.
211	Interest Payable	
221	FICA Tax Payable	280 Cr.
223	Employee Income Tax Payable	240 Cr.
225	Federal Unemployment Tax Payable	15 Cr.
227	State Unemployment Tax Payable	37 Cr.
229	Salaries Payable	
301	John Dillon, Capital	46,070 Cr.
302	John Dillon, Drawing	25,000 Dr.
401	Sales	256,000 Cr.
451	Sales Returns and Allowances	4,800 Dr.
501	Merchandise Purchases	159,000 Dr.
502	Freight In	1,800 Dr.
503	Purchases Returns and Allowances	3,500 Cr.
504	Purchases Discount	2,300 Cr.
511	Rent Expense	7,200 Dr.
514	Telephone Expense	1,082 Dr.
517	Salaries Expense	46,000 Dr.
520	Payroll Taxes Expense	3,700 Dr.
523	Supplies Expense	
526	Insurance Expense	
529	Depr. Expense—Equipment	
532	Loss From Uncollectible Accounts	
591	Interest Expense	100 Dr.

ADJUSTMENTS

a. During 19X7, the firm had net credit sales of $115,000. Past experience indicates that 0.6 percent of these sales should result in uncollectible accounts. Record an adjustment for the expected loss from uncollectible accounts for the year.
b. On December 31, 19X7, an inventory of the supplies showed that items costing $550 were on hand. Record an adjustment for the supplies used during the year.

c. On June 1, 19X7, the firm purchased a one-year insurance policy for $1,020. Record an adjustment for expired insurance for the year.

d. On January 2, 19X5, the firm purchased equipment for $17,000. At that time, the equipment was estimated to have a useful life of five years and a salvage value of $3,000. Record an adjustment for depreciation on the equipment for 19X7.

e. On September 1, 19X7, the firm issued a 6-month, 12 percent note for $3,500. Record an adjustment for the accrued interest on this note.

f. On December 31, 19X7, the firm owed salaries of $800 that will not be paid until 19X8. Record an adjustment for the accrued salaries for 19X7.

g. On December 31, 19X7, the firm owed the employer's FICA tax (7 percent) on $800 of accrued salaries, FUTA tax (0.8 percent) on $250 of accrued salaries, and SUTA tax (2 percent) on $250 of accrued salaries. Record an adjustment for the accrued payroll taxes.

ALTERNATE PROBLEMS

PROBLEM 17-1A

Journalizing adjusting, closing, and reversing entries. This problem is a continuation of Problem 16-1A. Obtain all necessary data from the worksheet prepared for the Toy Palace.

Instructions

1. Record adjusting entries in the general journal as of December 31, 19X8. Use *25* as the first journal page number. Include explanations for the entries.
2. Record closing entries in the general journal as of December 31, 19X8. Include explanations.
3. Record reversing entries in the general journal as of January 1, 19X9. Include explanations.

PROBLEM 17-2A

Journalizing adjusting, closing, and reversing entries. This problem is a continuation of Problem 16-2A. Obtain all necessary data from the worksheet prepared for Valley Forge Furniture.

Instructions

1. Record adjusting entries in the general journal as of December 31, 19X4. Use *25* as the first journal page number. Include explanations for the entries.
2. Record closing entries in the general journal as of December 31, 19X4. Include explanations.
3. Record reversing entries in the general journal as of January 1, 19X5. Include explanations.

PROBLEM 17-3A

Journalizing adjusting and reversing entries. The data given on page 427 concerns adjustments to be made at the Jorganson Company.

Instructions

1. Record the necessary adjusting entries in the general journal as of December 31, 19X5. Use *25* as the first journal page number. Include explanations.
2. Record reversing entries in the general journal as of January 1, 19X6. Include explanations.

ADJUSTMENTS

a. On August 1, 19X5, the firm signed a one-year advertising contract with a trade magazine and paid the entire amount—$3,000—in advance. Make an adjusting entry for the expired advertising for 19X5.

b. On December 31, 19X5, an inventory of the supplies showed that items costing $750 were on hand. The balance of the Supplies account on December 31 was $3,490. Make an adjusting entry for the supplies that were used during 19X5.

c. A depreciation schedule for the firm's equipment shows that a total of $2,630 should be charged off as depreciation for 19X5. Make an adjusting entry for this amount.

d. On December 31, 19X5, the firm owed salaries of $1,600 that will not be paid until January 19X6. Make an adjusting entry for the accrued salaries for 19X5.

e. On December 31, 19X5, the firm owed the employer's FICA tax (7 percent) on $1,600 of accrued salaries, FUTA tax (0.8 percent) on $450 of accrued salaries, and SUTA tax (2.4 percent) on $450 of accrued salaries. Make an adjusting entry for the accrued payroll taxes for 19X5.

f. On October 1, 19X5, the firm received a 6-month, 12 percent note for $2,200 from a customer with an overdue balance. Make an adjusting entry for the accrued interest on the note receivable.

PROBLEM 17-4A

Preparing a worksheet and classified financial statements; recording end-of-period entries. The Speedway Cycle Center is a retail firm that sells motorcycles, parts, and accessories. On December 31, 19X2, its general ledger contained the accounts and balances shown on page 428.

Instructions

1. Prepare the Trial Balance section of a ten-column worksheet. The worksheet should cover the year ended December 31, 19X2.

2. Enter the adjustments described on pages 428 and 429 in the Adjustments section. Identify each adjustment with the appropriate letter.

3. Complete the worksheet. The ending merchandise inventory for 19X2 was $58,000.

4. Prepare a classified income statement for the year ended December 31, 19X2. (The firm does not divide its operating expenses into selling and administrative expenses.)

5. Prepare a statement of owner's equity for the year ended December 31, 19X2. (No additional investments were made during the period.)

6. Prepare a classified balance sheet as of December 31, 19X2. (All notes payable are due within a year.)

7. Record adjusting entries in the general journal as of December 31, 19X2. Use 25 as the first journal page number. Omit explanations.

8. Record closing entries in the general journal as of December 31, 19X2. Omit explanations.

9. Record reversing entries in the general journal as of January 1, 19X3. Omit explanations.

ACCOUNTS AND BALANCES

101	Cash	$ 11,560 Dr.
111	Accounts Receivable	33,120 Dr.
112	Allowance for Uncollectible Accounts	110 Cr.
121	Merchandise Inventory	55,000 Dr.
131	Supplies	4,050 Dr.
133	Prepaid Insurance	1,740 Dr.
141	Equipment	22,900 Dr.
142	Accum. Depr.—Equipment	7,200 Cr.
201	Notes Payable	4,000 Cr.
205	Accounts Payable	5,920 Cr.
211	Interest Payable	
221	FICA Tax Payable	470 Cr.
223	Employee Income Tax Payable	395 Cr.
225	Federal Unemployment Tax Payable	25 Cr.
227	State Unemployment Tax Payable	60 Cr.
229	Salaries Payable	
301	Mark Murphy, Capital	77,180 Cr.
302	Mark Murphy, Drawing	32,000 Dr.
401	Sales	435,000 Cr.
451	Sales Returns and Allowances	8,200 Dr.
501	Merchandise Purchases	270,000 Dr.
502	Freight In	3,000 Dr.
503	Purchases Returns and Allowances	5,900 Cr.
504	Purchases Discount	3,800 Cr.
511	Rent Expense	12,000 Dr.
514	Telephone Expense	1,830 Dr.
517	Salaries Expense	78,200 Dr.
520	Payroll Taxes Expense	6,290 Dr.
523	Supplies Expense	
526	Insurance Expense	
529	Depr. Expense—Equipment	
532	Loss From Uncollectible Accounts	
591	Interest Expense	170 Dr.

ADJUSTMENTS

a. During 19X2, the firm had net credit sales of $310,000. Past experience indicates that 1.5 percent of these sales should result in uncollectible accounts. Record an adjustment for the expected loss from uncollectible accounts for the year.

b. On December 31, 19X2, an inventory of the supplies showed that items costing $935 were on hand. Record an adjustment for the supplies used during the year.

c. On March 1, 19X2, the firm purchased a one-year insurance policy for $1,740. Record an adjustment for expired insurance for the year.

d. On January 2, 19X0, the firm purchased equipment for $22,900. At that time, the equipment was estimated to have a useful life of five years and a salvage value of $4,900. Record an adjustment for depreciation on the equipment for 19X2.

e. On November 1, 19X2, the firm issued a 5-month, 12 percent note for $4,000. Record an adjustment for the accrued interest on this note.

f. On December 31, 19X2, the firm owed salaries of $1,300 that will not be paid until 19X3. Record an adjustment for the accrued salaries for 19X2.

g. On December 31, 19X2, the firm owed the employer's FICA tax (7 percent) on $1,300 of accrued salaries, FUTA tax (0.8 percent) on $200 of accrued salaries, and SUTA tax (2.2 percent) on $200 of accrued salaries. Record an adjustment for the accrued payroll taxes.

Large and medium-sized businesses make extensive use of computers in their accounting systems. Computers not only permit the quick and efficient processing of substantial numbers of transactions with a very high degree of accuracy, but they can produce a wide range of detailed financial reports at short intervals. This expanded reporting capability is especially important because it provides management with the kind of financial information that is needed to effectively plan and control operations in a large organization. Chapter 12 discussed the use of microcomputers by small businesses to automate their accounting work. This chapter examines the types of computerized accounting systems commonly found in large and medium-sized firms.

COMPUTERIZED ACCOUNTING SYSTEMS

MAINFRAME COMPUTERS AND MINICOMPUTERS

Microcomputers are able to handle the accounting activities of most small businesses in a satisfactory manner, but they do not have enough internal memory and speed to process the transactions of a large or medium-sized firm in an efficient and timely fashion. These firms therefore use mainframe computers or minicomputers to complete the bulk of their accounting work—the day-to-day recording of transactions, the maintenance of ledger accounts and other essential accounting records, and the preparation of financial reports and statements. Microcomputers are sometimes used in such firms by individual accountants to perform analytical tasks like making cash flow projections or evaluating alternative budget plans, but they do not have the capacity to handle the operations of a large-scale accounting system.

Computers are usually divided into categories according to the size of their internal memory, their speed in processing data, and their cost. The models with the largest internal memory, the fastest processing speed, and the highest price are known as *mainframe computers*. Because these computers sell for very substantial sums—usually several hundred thousand dollars to several million dollars—they are only cost-effective in large businesses that have a high volume of data to be processed. The illustration on page 431 shows a mainframe system, which consists of a central processing unit and many input and output devices. Notice that this equipment fills an entire room.

Minicomputers offer less internal memory and less speed than mainframe computers, but they are still very powerful machines. In fact, they have as much processing capacity as mainframe computers did in the 1960s. The advantage of minicomputers is that they are considerably less expensive than mainframe computers. Most models sell for $30,000 to $100,000, which makes them affordable by medium-sized businesses. A minicomputer system is shown on page 431.

Minicomputers are also used by many large businesses in decentralized operations—departments, branch offices, branch stores, factories, and warehouses. The minicomputers may function independently of the firm's mainframe

A MAINFRAME COMPUTER SYSTEM

Courtesy of Burroughs Corporation

A MINICOMPUTER SYSTEM

Courtesy of Digital Equipment Corporation

computer at headquarters, or they may serve as terminals transmitting data over telephone lines to the mainframe computer for processing and receiving needed information. Often, minicomputers in decentralized locations handle some processing tasks themselves and pass along more complex tasks to the mainframe computer. This type of arrangement is usually referred to as a *distributed processing system* because much of the firm's data processing work is distributed around the company rather than being confined to a single computer center. The chart shown on page 432 illustrates a distributed processing system.

All computer systems contain a central processing unit, input devices, and output devices. However, mainframe systems usually operate with many input and output devices, whereas minicomputer systems make use of just a few such

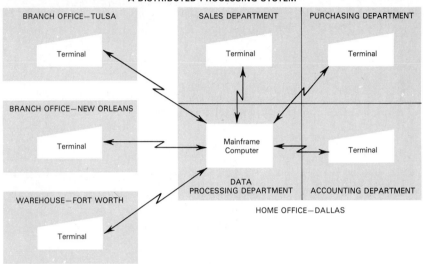

A DISTRIBUTED PROCESSING SYSTEM

BRANCH OFFICE—TULSA — Terminal

BRANCH OFFICE—NEW ORLEANS — Terminal

WAREHOUSE—FORT WORTH — Terminal

SALES DEPARTMENT — Terminal

PURCHASING DEPARTMENT — Terminal

Mainframe Computer

DATA PROCESSING DEPARTMENT

ACCOUNTING DEPARTMENT — Terminal

HOME OFFICE—DALLAS

devices. Compare the examples of the two types of systems that are shown on page 431.

Central Processing Unit

As its name implies, the *central processing unit (CPU)* is the part of the computer system where data is actually processed. The CPU contains the internal memory of the system, an arithmetic/logic unit, and a control unit. The *internal memory* provides temporary storage for data that is being processed and for the programs (instructions) that are being used to handle the data. The *arithmetic/ logic unit* makes calculations and performs logic operations such as comparing two numbers to see which one is greater. The *control unit* manages the activities of all components of the system. For example, it directs the flow of data from the input devices to the CPU and from the CPU to the output devices. It also moves data from one section of the CPU to another.

Input Devices

The data to be processed by a computer system is known as *input*. This data is fed into the system through *input devices*. With a mainframe computer or a minicomputer, it is possible to enter data directly by means of a terminal that has a keyboard. However, when accounting data is involved, the most common practice is to first transfer the data from source documents to an input medium such as magnetic tape, magnetic disks, or punched cards and then use a tape drive, disk drive, or card reader to feed the data in. If source documents contain either numbers printed in a special machine-readable typeface or a bar code, the data can be entered into the system by an optical scanner.

Output Devices

The information that results from the processing of data by a computer system is referred to as *output*. A variety of *output devices* are available for use with mainframe computers and minicomputers, and each produces a different form of output. For example, the video display of a terminal shows information on a televisionlike screen. A printer provides a *hard copy*—a printed copy—of the information. A tape drive records the information on magnetic tape, and a disk drive records it on a magnetic disk. (Tape drives and disk drives are both input and output devices.)

External Memory

MAGNETIC DISKS

Courtesy of NCR Corporation

In firms that use mainframe computers and minicomputers, the ledgers and other essential files with accounting data are kept on magnetic tapes or magnetic disks. These tapes or disks provide *external memory* for the system—storage outside the central processing unit. When transactions are to be processed, the appropriate files are placed in tape drives or disk drives so that the CPU can obtain the necessary data from them.

A set of magnetic disks, called a *disk pack,* is shown in the margin. These disks, which are made of metal and are therefore known as *hard disks,* can hold files containing millions of characters of data. Some minicomputers use another type of magnetic disk, which is made of plastic and called a *flexible disk* or *floppy disk,* to store accounting files. (An illustration of a flexible disk appears on page 286.)

THE COMPONENTS OF A COMPUTER SYSTEM

CENTRAL PROCESSING UNIT

Internal Memory

INPUT DEVICE

Control Unit

OUTPUT DEVICE

Arithmetic/Logic Unit

———▶ Data Flow
- - - ▶ Control

LARGE-SCALE COMPUTERIZED ACCOUNTING SYSTEMS

The large-scale accounting systems that are built around mainframe computers and minicomputers must be carefully designed to take maximum advantage of the capabilities of the equipment but also to minimize the possibility of fraud and human error. Procedures, forms, and job responsibilities must be planned so that they allow efficient processing of financial data yet include strong controls.

| Systems Design | Large companies usually have a sizable staff of data processing specialists. Among these employees are systems analysts who work with the managers of the accounting department and other departments to design suitable automated procedures, records, reports, and controls. When accounting activities are to be automated, a systems analyst studies the manual procedures, consults with the accounting staff about needed improvements, develops specifications for the new procedures, and then communicates the information to a programmer, who writes the necessary instructions for the computer. After the automated procedures are installed, the systems analyst may be asked to update or improve them from time to time. |

A medium-sized business may have one or more staff members who can handle systems analysis and design tasks, or it may need to hire an outside consultant for this work. Many large public accounting firms now employ specialists in computerized accounting systems who can plan suitable procedures for a client and also help the client to install the procedures.

Programming

In order to accomplish any activity, a computer must have a set of detailed instructions called a *program*. The program breaks down a procedure into a series of very small steps and tells the computer what data to use for each step, what tasks to perform with the data—for example, what calculations to make, where to place the partially or fully processed data, and so on. Programs are written in a language that the computer can understand, such as COBOL or BASIC.

A large company usually has a number of programmers on its data processing staff, and these people write the programs for any accounting procedures and other procedures that the company decides to automate. A medium-sized business may have one or more employees who do programming, may hire an outside programmer, or may purchase ready-made programs from a software firm.

Operations

Mainframe computers are usually operated by a centralized data processing department that handles work for all segments of the company including the accounting department. The magnetic tapes or disks containing the ledger accounts and other essential accounting files are therefore kept in the data processing department and updated by that department.

As transactions occur, the source documents related to them (invoices, credit memorandums, and so on) are verified, analyzed, and coded by the accounting department and then sent to the data processing department. The coding usually consists of entering appropriate account numbers so that the amounts shown on the source documents can be charged to the proper general ledger and subsidiary ledger accounts. When the data processing department receives the source documents, it transfers the data to a computer input medium such as magnetic tape, magnetic disks, or punched cards. The input data is then fed into the computer system, which updates the ledger accounts and produces a printed journal or transaction listing. The journal or transaction listing is sent to the accounting department as a record of the transactions that were processed.

In addition to updating the ledgers and preparing journals, the computer system is used to bill customers, issue checks to creditors, calculate and record the payroll, issue payroll checks, prepare certain tax forms such as the yearly wage and tax statements for employees (Form W-2), and prepare a wide variety of financial reports and statements.

Notice that under the arrangement described here the accounting department sends input in the form of source documents to the data processing department and receives completed output—journals, reports, statements, and so on. The accounting department does not handle the recording function. This arrangement frees the accounting staff from many repetitive clerical tasks and allows more time for analyzing, planning, and controlling financial operations.

A medium-sized firm with a minicomputer may also place it in a centralized data processing department and have that department perform work for the accounting department and all other segments of the company.

An alternative arrangement used in some large businesses is to decentralize data processing operations by giving each department a minicomputer and having the individual departments handle much of their own recordkeeping work and report preparation. The minicomputers are linked to a mainframe computer in the data processing department, which still performs certain high-volume jobs that require powerful equipment. The minicomputers also communicate certain types of information to the mainframe system in order to update various centralized files that are kept by the data processing department for the company as a whole. (See the chart on page 432 for an example of a decentralized, or distributed, processing system.)

Controls

Because fraud and human error can have a disastrous effect on a large-scale computerized accounting system, carefully designed controls must be built into the system. Several widely used control techniques are discussed in another section of this chapter.

Personnel

The data processing department of a large firm with a mainframe computer usually has a staff consisting of managers, systems analysts, programmers, computer operators, data entry clerks, and tape or disk librarians. This staff not only handles the daily activities of the system but helps users such as the accounting department to automate new applications and update or improve existing applications. A medium-sized firm with a minicomputer will normally have a more limited data processing staff.

CONTROL TECHNIQUES

Manual accounting systems contain records that can be visually checked by accounting personnel. Furthermore, unless a firm is very small, several people are usually involved in each part of the accounting system, which allows for separation of duties and the checking of one person's work with another's work. These characteristics facilitate the detection of errors and minimize opportunities for fraud. Computerized accounting systems, however, keep records on machine-readable media such as magnetic tapes and disks and process data within the electronic circuitry of the equipment. In addition, a relatively small number of employees may effectively control an entire company's data processing activities, including the preparation of accounting records, the billing of customers, the issuance of checks to creditors and employees, and the preparation of payroll records. Under these circumstances, the task of detecting errors and preventing fraud is considerably more difficult.

To preserve the integrity of a computerized accounting system, accountants and data processing specialists have developed a variety of control techniques. These techniques fall into four basic categories: separation of functions; physical controls over equipment, programs, and files; input-output controls; and program controls.

Of course, no amount of control can guarantee absolute accuracy and honesty in a computerized accounting system. Moreover, too many controls will lead to an overly expensive, inflexible system that operates very slowly. An appropriate balance must therefore be maintained between the need to build barriers against fraud and errors and the need to keep costs at a reasonable level and ensure timely processing of transactions.

Separation of Functions

In a well-managed data processing department, systems analysis and programming are separated from computer operations. The employees who plan the computerized procedures and write the programs are not allowed to run the equipment and handle the tapes or disks that contain the programs and data files. Similarly, the employees who run the equipment and handle the tapes or disks with the programs and data files are not permitted to see the planning documents for the procedures and the coding for the programs. The idea behind this separation of functions is to prevent any individual from having both a detailed knowledge of the procedures and programs and access to the equipment and the tapes or disks on which the programs and data files are recorded. The combination of detailed knowledge and physical access greatly increases the possibility of fraudulent changes in programs and files.

Another precautionary measure is to give custody of the tapes or disks with the programs and data files to a librarian who is not involved in computer operations. This employee issues the tapes or disks only as they are needed for jobs and stores them in a locked room when they are not in use.

Of course, if a firm has very few data processing employees, it is not possible to achieve as much separation of functions as is desirable.

Physical Controls

There are a variety of physical controls that should be used with mainframe and minicomputer systems.

- The room where the equipment is located should be kept locked, and only authorized personnel should be allowed to enter it.
- The tapes or disks that contain the programs and data files should be placed in a locked storage room and should be in the care of a librarian who is not involved in computer operations. The librarian should release programs and files only to computer operators just before they must run specific jobs, and the programs and files should be returned promptly after the jobs are completed. The librarian should maintain a log showing which programs and files are issued, the date and time of withdrawal and return, and the signature of each computer operator involved.

- The documents that contain specifications for the computerized procedures and coding for the programs should be kept in locked files.
- When a computer system has terminals, each authorized user should be given a password that must be entered before gaining access to programs and files that are in the system. As an added precaution, programs and files in sensitive areas such as accounts payable and payroll should have their own special passwords.
- The computer system should automatically make a record of all attempted usage at terminals, whether the effort is unsuccessful or successful. The record should indicate what time the attempt was made and from which terminal.

Input-Output Controls

Certain precautionary routines can be followed to make sure that all input data submitted to the computer center on source documents is processed and that no transactions are intentionally or unintentionally added or omitted. These routines often involve the use of control totals for input and output.

Before each batch of documents is submitted to the computer center, various totals are manually calculated for the batch. For example, the number of documents might be counted and the dollar total of all the transactions contained in the batch might be determined. When the data from the batch is run by the computer system, the program directs the system to make a count of the transactions being processed and the total dollar amount. At the end of the job, the system prints out the totals that it has accumulated. These amounts are compared with the totals calculated from the input data on the source documents.

Other control procedures are used to ensure that the computer operator does not tamper with output. For example, all checks are either printed on prenumbered forms or given sequential numbers by the system. After the checks are taken from the printer and separated from each other, a supervisor examines them to make sure that there are no gaps in the numbers. This practice guards against removal of any checks by the computer operator.

Program Controls

Certain types of controls can be written into programs to identify incorrect or fraudulent data. Two common examples are discussed below.

- Programs can be designed to locate and call attention to invalid code numbers such as account numbers, employee numbers, and stock numbers. For the sake of security, most programs of this type are written in such a way that they will not process the transaction until a valid code number is entered.
- Programs can also be designed to check the reasonableness of amounts. For instance, a payroll program may be written so that it identifies employees whose hours worked or total earnings for a pay period exceed amounts that have been designated as reasonable. The computer prints out a report showing the names of such employees and the figures involved. The data processing department verifies the amounts with the managers of the departments where these people work before any checks are issued.

EDP AUDITING

Because of their nature, large-scale computerized accounting systems cannot be audited effectively by simply using traditional audit procedures. In response to this situation, public accounting firms and internal auditors have developed a set of techniques for which the term *EDP auditing* is often used. (EDP is an abbreviation for electronic data processing.)

EDP auditing not only involves checking sample input and output from the system but actually uses the computer to assess the efficiency and accuracy of the system in processing transactions and the quality of the controls that have been established. Special audit programs are widely used to assist in this work.

MICROCOMPUTERS AS ANALYTICAL TOOLS

Although microcomputers are not powerful enough to process transactions and prepare accounting records in large and medium-sized businesses, they are increasingly being used by accountants in such firms for analytical activities. The development of electronic spreadsheet programs has turned the microcomputer into a highly valuable tool for financial analysis. Budgeting, tax planning, cash flow projections, and cost-revenue analysis are just a few areas where microcomputers can provide significant help to accountants.

PRINCIPLES AND PROCEDURES SUMMARY

Manual processing of accounting data is too slow, cumbersome, and labor-intensive for most large and medium-sized businesses today. Mainframe computers and minicomputers provide a means for such firms to record a very high volume of transactions with great speed and accuracy and prepare a wide range of detailed financial reports.

A computer system in a large or medium-sized business may operate under a centralized or decentralized arrangement. When a centralized arrangement is used, the data processing department handles the recordkeeping work and report preparation for the accounting department and all other segments of the company. The accounting department sends input in the form of source documents to the data processing department and receives completed journals, reports, statements, and other output. With a decentralized arrangement, the accounting department and other departments have their own minicomputers and carry out many of their own recordkeeping activities. However, the mainframe computer in the data processing department is still used for complex and high-volume jobs. The minicomputers also transmit certain types of data to the mainframe computer so that the data can be placed in centralized files.

The detection of errors and the prevention of fraud are more difficult in a computerized accounting system than in a manual accounting system. For this reason, carefully designed controls must be built into a computerized accounting system. These controls fall into four basic categories: separation of functions; physical controls over equipment, programs, and files; input-output controls; and program controls.

Although microcomputers are not suitable for processing transactions in large and medium-sized businesses, they can serve as valuable analytical tools for accountants in such firms when they are used with electronic spreadsheet programs.

MANAGERIAL IMPLICATIONS

Computers have had a very strong impact on accounting work in large and medium-sized businesses. Because computers now handle the recording process in these firms, the accounting staff is able to spend more time analyzing, planning, and controlling financial operations. For management, this shift in focus has meant that the accounting staff can provide a greater amount of analytical information for use in decision making.

Management is also in a better position to monitor the financial performance of all segments of the organization because a computerized accounting system can produce a broad range of detailed reports at short intervals. This is highly important in a large business, which may have many branches located at a distance from headquarters.

However, the strong reporting capability of computerized accounting systems can also present problems. Management may be overwhelmed with too much information and with information that is not useful. The accounting staff must work closely with management to make sure that appropriate financial reports are being produced and that management understands the reports.

The accounting staff must also be alert to necessary changes in the computerized accounting system as the firm grows and its operations expand. Management may require new types of information, and there may be a need to change the procedures for handling transactions and to revise the controls used in the system.

REVIEW QUESTIONS

1. How do mainframe computers and minicomputers differ from each other?
2. What is a distributed processing system?
3. Explain the purpose of each of the following components of a computer system:
   a. Input device
   b. Central processing unit (CPU)
   c. Output device
4. Name the three sections of the CPU. What functions does each section perform?
5. What is input?
6. Name three input devices that are often used with mainframe and minicomputer systems.
7. What is output?
8. Describe three forms of output from mainframe and minicomputer systems, and name the devices that produce the output.
9. What is external memory?
10. In a manual accounting system, the ledger accounts are normally kept on sheets of paper in a binder or bound book. What media are used for the ledger accounts in large-scale computerized accounting systems?

11. What tasks does a systems analyst perform?
12. What is a program?
13. How do large companies obtain their programs? medium-sized companies?
14. When a firm has a centralized computer system, what department handles the recording of transactions and the maintenance of the files with the ledger accounts?
15. Why is it more difficult to detect errors and prevent fraud in a computerized accounting system than in a manual accounting system?
16. What are the four basic types of controls that are used in large-scale computerized accounting systems?
17. How is separation of functions achieved in a data processing department?
18. Describe two common types of program controls.
19. What is EDP auditing?
20. How are microcomputers used in large and medium-sized businesses?

MANAGERIAL DISCUSSION QUESTIONS

1. What benefits does management receive from a computerized accounting system?
2. Why is a computerized accounting system especially helpful to the management of a large business with branch operations?
3. If many accounting procedures can be handled by computers, why are trained accountants in greater demand than ever?
4. Why is it important for an accountant in a firm that has a computerized accounting system to understand the basic operations of the system even though the data processing department handles the preparation of accounting records?

MICRO-COMPUTER PROBLEMS

These problems are designed for use with *Microcomputer General Ledger System* by Stephen S. Hamilton, a software program published by Gregg/McGraw-Hill.

PROBLEM 1

Using the computer to set up an accounting system and record transactions.
Modern Images is a small sole proprietorship service business that does photographic work for advertising agencies. The firm was established on August 1, 19X6. Its chart of accounts is shown below along with transactions that the business had during the month of August.

Instructions

1. Open the Vital Statistics File at the computer. (The necessary directions for carrying out this step and all other steps listed here are given in the *User's Manual* for *Microcomputer General Ledger System*.)
2. Open the chart of accounts at the computer. (All accounts had zero balances on August 1, 19X6.)
3. Print the chart of accounts.
4. Open the general ledger accounts at the computer.
5. Analyze the transactions listed below, and determine the numbers of the accounts to be debited and credited and the amounts that are involved.
6. Record the transactions at the computer. (Use the General Journal Program.)
7. Post the transactions at the computer. (Use the General Journal Program.)
8. Print the general journal.
9. Prepare a trial balance at the computer, and print it. (Use the trial balance option of the Financial Statements Program.) Make sure that the trial balance has equal debit and credit totals. If it does not, recheck your work to find the error or errors, record and post correcting entries, and then prepare a new trial balance.

GENERAL LEDGER ACCOUNTS

101	Cash	302	Gary Ross—Drawing
111	Accounts Receivable	399	Income Summary
121	Photographic Supplies	401	Fees
123	Office Supplies	511	Rent Expense
131	Prepaid Rent	514	Utilities Expense
151	Equipment	517	Telephone Expense
152	Accum. Depr.—Equipment	520	Salaries Expense
155	Office Furniture	523	Photographic Supplies Expense
156	Accum. Depr.—Office Furniture	526	Office Supplies Expense
201	Accounts Payable	529	Depr. Expense—Equip.
203	Notes Payable	532	Depr. Expense—Office Furn.
205	Interest Payable	901	Interest Expense
301	Gary Ross—Capital		

TRANSACTIONS FOR AUGUST 19X6

Aug.   1   Gary Ross invested $25,000 in cash to start the business.

          1   Signed a lease for a studio and issued Check 101 for $1,650 to pay the rent in advance for three months.

1 Purchased office furniture for $2,400 and issued a 3-month, 12 percent note in payment.

2 Purchased photographic and darkroom equipment for $8,000. Issued Check 102 for $5,000 and agreed to pay the balance in 60 days.

4 Purchased photographic supplies for $1,500. The amount is due in 30 days.

5 Purchased office supplies for $280 and issued Check 103 to pay for them immediately.

9 Performed services for $350 in cash.

10 Returned some defective office supplies and received a cash refund of $15.

15 Issued Check 104 for $500 to pay the semimonthly salary of an employee.

17 Performed services for $200 in cash.

24 Issued Check 105 for $65 to pay the monthly telephone bill.

28 Issued Check 106 for $800 to the owner as a withdrawal for personal use.

29 Issued Check 107 for $106 to pay the monthly electric bill.

31 Billed $1,400 to customers for services performed on credit during August. The terms are n/30.

31 Issued Check 108 for $500 to pay the semimonthly salary of the employee.

Note: If your instructor has assigned Problem 2, save the data from Problem 1 that is on your disk.

PROBLEM 2   **Using the computer to complete end-of-period work.** This problem is a continuation of Problem 1. Problem 2 involves the preparation of financial statements and the handling of adjusting and closing procedures for Modern Images at the end of its monthly accounting period on August 31, 19X6. The adjustments to be made are shown below. The data from Problem 1 must be on your disk in order to complete the necessary work.

Instructions   1. Determine the numbers of the accounts to be debited and credited in the adjusting entries and the amounts involved.

2. Delete the journal entries for the August transactions from your disk. Do this work at the computer. (Use the edit function of the General Journal Program.) Be sure that you have a printout of the journal entries for the August transactions before you delete them.

3. Record the adjusting entries at the computer. (Use the General Journal Program.)

4. Post the adjusting entries at the computer. (Use the General Journal Program.)

5. Print the general journal page with the adjusting entries.

6. Prepare an adjusted trial balance at the computer and print it. (Use the trial balance option of the Financial Statements Program.) If the adjusted trial balance is not in balance, find your error or errors, record and post correcting entries, and then prepare a new adjusted trial balance.

7. Prepare an income statement at the computer and print it. (Use the option for a service business income statement in the Financial Statements Program.)
8. Prepare a ratio report at the computer and print it. (Use the ratio report option of the Financial Statements Program.)
9. Determine the numbers of the accounts to be debited and credited in the closing entries and the amounts involved.
10. Delete the adjusting entries from your disk. Do this work at the computer. (Use the edit function of the General Journal Program.) Be sure that you have a printout of the adjusting entries before you delete them.
11. Record the closing entries at the computer. (Use the General Journal Program.)
12. Post the closing entries at the computer. (Use the General Journal Program.)
13. Print the general journal page with the closing entries.
14. Prepare a postclosing trial balance at the computer and print it. (Use the trial balance option of the Financial Statements Program.) If the postclosing trial balance is not in balance, find your error or errors, record and post correcting entries, and then prepare a new postclosing trial balance.
15. Prepare a balance sheet at the computer and print it. (Use the balance sheet option of the Financial Statements Program.)

ADJUSTMENTS

a. On August 1, the firm paid rent of $1,650 in advance for a 3-month period. Record an adjustment for the expired rent for August.
b. An inventory of the photographic supplies taken on August 31 showed that items costing $1,310 were on hand. Record an adjustment for the photographic supplies used during August.
c. An inventory of the office supplies taken on August 31 showed that items costing $245 were on hand. Record an adjustment for the office supplies used during August.
d. On August 1, the firm issued a 3-month, 12 percent note payable for $2,400. Record an adjustment for the accrued interest for August.
e. On August 2, the firm purchased equipment for $8,000. This equipment is expected to have a useful life of 5 years and a salvage value of $1,400. It will be depreciated on a straight-line basis. Record an adjustment for the depreciation for August.
f. On August 1, the firm purchased office furniture for $2,400. This furniture is expected to have a useful life of 5 years and a salvage value of $300. It will be depreciated on a straight-line basis. Record an adjustment for depreciation for August.

Note: If your instructor has assigned Problem 3, save the data from Problems 1 and 2 that is on your disk.

PROBLEM 3   **Using the computer to record transactions.** This problem is a continuation of Problems 1 and 2. It involves the recording of transactions for the second month of operations at Modern Images. The data from Problems 1 and 2 must be on your disk in order to complete the necessary work.

Instructions
1. Analyze the September transactions listed below. Determine the accounts to be debited and credited, and the amounts involved.
2. Delete the closing entries for August from your disk. Do this work at the computer. (Use the edit function of the General Journal Program.) Be sure that you have a printout of the closing entries before you delete them.
3. Record the September transactions at the computer. (Use the General Journal Program.)
4. Post the September transactions at the computer. (Use the General Journal Program.)
5. Print the general journal.
6. Prepare a trial balance at the computer and print it. (Use the trial balance option of the Financial Statements Program.) Make sure that the trial balance has equal debit and credit totals. If it does not, recheck your work to find the error or errors, record and post correcting entries, and then prepare a new trial balance.

TRANSACTIONS FOR SEPTEMBER 19X6

Sept. 2 Issued Check 109 for $1,500 to pay a creditor on account.
       4 Performed services for $250 in cash.
       7 Purchased some special color film for $75, and paid for it immediately with Check 110.
      10 Received $300 in cash from clients for work performed on credit during August.
      15 Issued Check 111 for $500 to pay the semimonthly salary of the employee.
      17 Performed services for $400 in cash.
      19 Issued Check 112 for $18 to purchase some office supplies.
      22 Issued Check 113 for $100 as a partial refund to a client who was not satisfied with a set of photographs. The client previously paid in cash.
      24 Issued Check 114 for $72 to pay the monthly telephone bill.
      26 Received $900 in cash from clients for work performed on credit during August.
      28 Issued Check 115 for $109 to pay the monthly electric bill.
      29 Issued Check 116 for $800 to the owner as a withdrawal for personal use.
      30 Billed $2,200 to clients for services performed on credit during September. The terms are n/30.
      30 Issued Check 117 for $500 to pay the semimonthly salary of the employee.

Note: If your instructor has assigned Problem 4, save the data from Problems 1 through 3 that is on your disk.

PROBLEM 4 **Using the computer to complete end-of-period work.** This problem is a continuation of Problems 1 through 3. Problem 4 involves the preparation of financial statements and the handling of adjusting and closing procedures for Modern Images at the end of its monthly accounting period on September 30, 19X6. The adjustments to be made are shown below. The data from Problems 1 through 3 must be on your disk in order to complete the necessary work.

Instructions Follow Steps 1 through 15 that are given in Problem 2. However, in Step 2 delete the journal entries for the September transactions from your disk. After you complete Step 15, print the ledger accounts. (Use the General Ledger Program to obtain the printout.)

ADJUSTMENTS

a. Record an adjustment for the expired rent for September. Refer to Problem 2 to obtain the necessary information.

b. An inventory of the photographic supplies taken on September 30 showed that items costing $1,165 were on hand. Record an adjustment for the photographic supplies used during September.

c. An inventory of the office supplies taken on September 30 showed that items costing $238 were on hand. Record an adjustment for the office supplies used during September.

d. Record an adjustment for the interest on the note payable that accrued during September. Refer to Problem 2 to obtain the necessary information.

e. Record an adjustment for depreciation on the equipment for September. Refer to Problem 2 to obtain the necessary information.

f. Record an adjustment for depreciation on the office furniture for September. Refer to Problem 2 to obtain the necessary information.

Note: Save your computer printouts from Problems 1 through 4 for use in Problem 5.

PROBLEM 5 **Interpreting the information on computer printouts.** This problem is a continuation of Problems 1 through 4. Problem 5 involves analysis of the financial records and statements that you prepared for the first two months of operations at Modern Images. Use your computer printouts to complete this work.

Instructions 1. Compare the results of operations for August and September. Comment on the changes in total revenues, total expenses, and net income or net loss. Explain whether a favorable or unfavorable trend seems to be developing in regard to the operating results.

2. Compare the financial position of the business at the end of August with the end of September. Comment on the changes in total assets, total liabilities, and owner's equity. Explain whether the firm is in a stronger or a weaker financial position as of September 30.

3. The owner started the business with a cash investment of $25,000 on August 1. Determine how much cash the firm had on August 31 and on September 30.

4. The balance of the Accounts Payable account represents a debt that must be paid at the beginning of October. Determine if the firm has enough cash on hand to cover this debt. If so, determine how much cash will be left over for operating expenses and other obligations after this debt is paid.

5. Based on past experience with similar businesses, the accountant for Modern Images estimates that 80 percent of the outstanding accounts receivable on September 30 will be collected during the next month. Determine how much cash this will bring into the firm during October.

6. The owner made an investment of $25,000 when he began the firm on August 1. Determine how much the owner's capital has increased or decreased as of September 30. Discuss which major factors caused the change in the amount of capital.

ACCT
2 →

PART 2

FINANCIAL ACCOUNTING: BASIC PRINCIPLES

In Part 1 you learned how accounting procedures are used to properly record business transactions in a sole proprietorship. You also learned how to prepare an income statement and a balance sheet to reflect the net income or net loss of a business and to show its financial condition. These accounting procedures and financial statements are based on accounting principles and rules that have come to be generally accepted. In Part 2 you will gain an understanding of generally accepted accounting principles and financial reporting standards. You will also become familiar with the application of accounting principles and procedures to the operations of partnerships and corporations.

ACCOUNTING PRINCIPLES AND REPORTING STANDARDS

THE NEED FOR GENERALLY ACCEPTED ACCOUNTING PRINCIPLES

In a sole proprietorship, adherence to proper accounting rules is important even though the owner is usually deeply involved in the firm's activities and is the person primarily interested in its financial affairs. However, creditors, suppliers, and others must also be able to rely on the financial statements prepared for a sole proprietorship. When the business is a partnership or a corporation, it is even more important that operations be properly accounted for because it is very likely that the owners will not be intimately involved in the activities of the firm. Generally accepted accounting principles make financial statements meaningful and useful, regardless of the type of business organization.

The various needs for reliable financial information can be satisfied only if there are rules, procedures, and principles of accounting that are generally accepted and used. If each company made up its own rules, there could be no basis for comparing the earnings and financial position of different firms. Even the records and reports of a particular company could not be compared for different periods unless accounting principles were applied consistently. In addition, users of the financial statements would probably be misinformed and misled.

This chapter discusses generally accepted accounting principles and the basic assumptions, concepts, and modifying conventions that underlie them. In addition, the chapter describes how accounting principles are developed and put into use. Later chapters examine in detail the application of generally accepted accounting principles.

THE SOURCES OF GENERALLY ACCEPTED ACCOUNTING PRINCIPLES

Many of today's accounting principles were developed over a period of years in response to the changing needs for business reports. The process has worked very much like this. A particular procedure is devised by an accountant as a solution to a specific problem. Then other accountants find the procedure suitable for their problems and start to use it. Eventually, the procedure may become widely used and may be recognized by the professional accountants, accounting writers, and organizations that are responsible for developing generally accepted accounting principles. Other accounting principles have resulted from a decision by an authoritative rule-making body to select one of several alternative methods being used in practice. In still other cases, rule-making bodies have developed standards on the basis of logic or deductive reasoning because there were no clearly defined practices being used to account for certain types of transactions or events.

Accounting principles, or standards, that have "authoritative support" in this country are developed through a cooperative effort between the private (business) sector and the public (governmental) sector of the economy. Currently, the main bodies involved are the Securities and Exchange Commission (SEC) in the public sector and the Financial Accounting Standards Board (FASB) in the private sector.

The SEC

In 1934 the Securities and Exchange Commission was set up to administer the Securities Act of 1933 and the Securities Exchange Act of 1934. Among other powers, the SEC has authority to define accounting terms and to prescribe accounting principles. The SEC also determines the form and content of accounting reports filed by companies under its jurisdiction. Since all publicly held companies (those whose stocks are traded in the organized securities markets) and all companies with more than a specified number of shareholders (owners) are subject to SEC regulations, the SEC is a dominant force in accounting. However, historically, the SEC has used these powers rather sparingly, preferring to let the accounting profession develop acceptable accounting principles and financial reporting standards.

Since 1937 the SEC has issued over 200 *Accounting Series Releases* (ASRs) giving its preferences or requirements on various accounting matters. Some, but not all, of these releases prescribe accounting principles to be followed. In one of the releases (ASR 150, issued in 1973), the SEC stated that it would view the pronouncements of the Financial Accounting Standards Board as having "authoritative support." In addition, the release said that generally the SEC would rely on the FASB's pronouncements as the proper accounting principles to be followed by companies under the SEC's jurisdiction. Even though the SEC does rely on the private sector to take the lead in developing accounting principles, the SEC is still responsible for setting the rules for the financial statements filed with it.

The FASB and Its Predecessors

The Financial Accounting Standards Board is the result of efforts by the private sector, especially the American Institute of Certified Public Accountants (AICPA), to develop an organization responsible for formulating financial accounting standards. A brief review of the predecessors of the FASB will help you understand its structure and functions.

From 1939 through 1959, the American Institute of Certified Public Accountants issued a series of *Accounting Research Bulletins* through its Committee on Accounting Procedure. In these bulletins the committee tried to give practical solutions to a number of current problems. While the opinions were not mandatory, most members of the AICPA followed them.

In 1959 the Committee on Accounting Procedure was disbanded. A new body, called the Accounting Principles Board (APB), was formed to issue authoritative statements on accounting principles. The APB existed until 1973 and issued 31 *Opinions*. If members of the AICPA did not follow these opinions, they were required to justify the principles they chose. If the principles could not be justified, members were subject to sanctions by the AICPA. These sanctions had the effect of discrediting members and included, at the extreme, expulsion. Obviously, the APB opinions had a major impact on accounting practices.

In addition to the opinions, the APB issued four *Statements*, which did not have the same binding effect as the opinions. Statement No. 4, issued in 1970, was entitled *Basic Concepts and Accounting Principles Underlying Financial Statements of Business Enterprises*. This statement was a comprehensive listing of basic assumptions, postulates, and principles of accounting that were generally accepted at the time. One other publication of the AICPA should be mentioned. Since 1947 its research department has conducted annual surveys to determine the accounting and reporting practices of some 600 representative corporations. The results of each survey are provided in a publication called *Accounting Trends and Techniques in Published Corporate Annual Reports*.

In 1972 the AICPA, the American Accounting Association, the National Association of Accountants, the Financial Executives Institute, and the Financial Analysts Federation jointly established the Financial Accounting Standards Board (FASB). The FASB is responsible for developing financial accounting standards and principles. By having groups other than the AICPA involved, the organizations that formed the FASB hoped that its rulings would have wide support in the economy.

The FASB receives its funding from the Financial Accounting Foundation. The organizations that set up the FASB choose the trustees of the Financial Accounting Foundation. These trustees are responsible for general oversight of the foundation and for securing financial support through contributions from the private sector. (No governmental funds are used.) More important, the trustees select the seven members of the Financial Accounting Standards Board. The board members, who develop and issue accounting pronouncements, are full-time employees who generally have distinguished accounting backgrounds.

The authoritative pronouncements of the FASB are known as *Statements of Financial Accounting Standards*. Through 1983 the FASB had issued almost 100 statements. As previously pointed out, the Securities and Exchange Commission recognizes these pronouncements as authoritative. The AICPA gives these statements additional support by requiring that its members make sure that the companies whose statements they audit follow the accounting and reporting standards specified in the FASB statements. Any departures from these standards must be justified. Thus the pronouncements of the FASB automatically become generally accepted accounting principles.

One of the FASB's most important projects is called the "conceptual framework project." This project has been under way for a number of years and is expected to last for several more years. Its aim is to develop a series of documents that will provide a theoretical framework for financial accounting. These documents will, among other things, perform the following functions.

1. Define the objectives of accounting.
2. Identify users of financial reports and the uses made of these reports.
3. Develop the best possible definition of financial elements such as assets, liabilities, revenues, and expenses.
4. Establish the form and content of financial statements.
5. Develop measurement standards for income and other items.

The documents produced by the conceptual framework project should lead to more logical and concise accounting principles and reporting standards.

To some extent, the conceptual framework project reflects the suggestion by a number of accountants that accounting principles should be arrived at deductively. This means that rules should be based on observations of the general needs and uses of financial accounting. The following steps might be involved in the deductive process.

Step 1: Identify the users of financial reports.
Step 2: Define what uses are made of financial reports.
Step 3: Determine what kinds of accounting information best serve these uses.
Step 4: Define basic assumptions about the society in which business exists and about the nature of business activities and functions.
Step 5: Develop broad principles, standards, or guides for providing the information needed, based on the assumptions that have been made.
Step 6: Develop detailed rules and procedures for implementing the broad principles.

Although completion of the conceptual framework project is expected to require several years, much of the work has been done. Later in this chapter we shall examine the conclusions that have been reached about the identity of the users of financial reports, the uses made of these reports, the objectives of the reports, the types of information that best serve the needs of the users, and the qualitative characteristics of financial reports.

Other Organizations

Other organizations have also played an important role in developing accounting principles. The Executive Committee of the American Accounting Association published "A Tentative Statement of Accounting Principles Underlying Corporate Financial Statements" in *The Accounting Review* for June 1936. The association has issued revised statements in 1941, 1948, and 1957, with several supplements between the last two revisions. In 1966 a special research committee of the association published a study entitled *A Statement of Basic Accounting Theory*. About half the members of the association are teachers of accounting, and a number of them have written textbooks and articles dealing with accounting principles. Thus, in a variety of ways, the association has been able to stimulate the acceptance of the principles it has developed and perfected over the years.

As early as 1900, the New York Stock Exchange began requiring corporations whose stock and bonds it listed to publish annual reports. Later, quarterly reports were required, and in 1933 the Exchange insisted upon independent audits for all corporations that applied to have their securities listed.

Government regulatory agencies have prescribed detailed systems of accounting for various public utilities, including the railroad industry and the electric power industry. Such agencies are more concerned with regulation, however, than with the development of accounting principles. Similarly, federal income tax requirements have had an impact on financial accounting even though it is not usually necessary that financial accounting practices and tax accounting practices be the same.

THE PRESENT FRAMEWORK OF ACCOUNTING PRINCIPLES

The rules of accounting that you have already learned and that you will study in the remaining chapters of this textbook are embodied in what is known today as the *historical-cost framework* of accounting. There are a number of ideas underlying this framework. Some accountants refer to all of these ideas as accounting *principles;* other accountants refer to them as accounting *concepts.* The exact term one uses for them is immaterial; the ideas involved are the important elements. For the convenience of discussion, we shall separate the ideas into four categories: (1) users and uses of financial reports, (2) underlying assumptions, (3) general principles or concepts, and (4) modifying conventions.

Users and Uses of Financial Reports

Financial reports provide information that is important to many different users. However, because some of these users, such as management, tax authorities, and regulatory agencies have access to the specific information they need from the firm's records, the FASB has concluded that financial reporting rules should concentrate on providing information that is helpful to present and potential investors and creditors in making investment and credit decisions.

In its conceptual framework project, the FASB has also concluded that the information investors and creditors need is information that will help them assess the likelihood of receiving a future cash flow, the amount of such a cash flow, and the time that the cash flow may be received. This conclusion is based on the idea that investors and creditors expect to receive a cash flow directly or indirectly from the business entity, either through the distribution of the company's earnings or through the disposal of their interests for cash. Thus financial report users look for information about profits and about the firm's economic resources (its assets), the claims against those assets (liabilities and owner's equity), and the changes in those assets and in the claims against them. Of course, information about profits appears on the income statement, and information about assets, liabilities, and owner's equity is provided by the balance sheet. Certain analyses of the financial statements also supply meaningful data about the results of operations and the financial condition of a business. (The analysis of financial statements is discussed in Chapters 35 and 36 of this textbook.)

Qualitative Characteristics of Financial Reports

The FASB has concluded that the information given in financial statements should have several *qualitative characteristics.*

Usefulness Obviously, financial information must be useful to statement readers. Otherwise, there is no reason to include it. Usefulness is a rather broad and all-inclusive term and embraces most of the other qualitative characteristics described here.

Relevance The information shown in the statements must be appropriate for, and have a bearing on, the decisions to be made by the users.

Reliability The information shown in the statements must be dependable, that is, free from error and also free from any bias on the part of the preparer.

Verifiability Financial information is said to be verifiable if it can be reviewed by accountants outside the company, and these accountants arrive at the same conclusions as the preparers of the statements. Verifiability usually implies that there are documents such as checks, invoices, and contracts that provide supporting evidence for the statements and that are available for examination.

Neutrality The information shown in the statements should not favor one group of users over another group. It should be prepared in such a way that it is helpful to all groups.

Understandability The information must be presented in a manner that is clear and understandable by readers. However, in preparing financial statements, it is assumed that users have a basic knowledge of business and economics and that they will devote an appropriate amount of time to studying and analyzing the statements.

Timeliness Financial information must be presented in the statements quickly enough to be useful in making related decisions.

Comparability The financial statements for a company must be prepared on a basis that permits comparison with the financial statements of other firms and also with similar data of the company for other periods.

Completeness Financial statements are considered complete if all information that would have a material impact on the decisions of users is presented. Obviously, however, financial statements cannot include every item of information about a company because the cost would be prohibitive and some of the data would not be relevant.

Underlying Assumptions

In applying the present body of accounting theory, accountants have used several assumptions about the economy, business enterprises, and business activities that make accounting principles meaningful. We will refer to these assumptions as (1) the separate entity assumption, (2) the going concern assumption, (3) the stable monetary unit assumption, (4) the objectivity assumption, and (5) the periodicity of income assumption.

Separate Entity Accounting records are kept for a particular business organization. It is assumed that the firm is an entity separate from other businesses and even separate from its owners and creditors. Transactions are recorded in relation to their effects on the business entity. Financial statements summarize these effects for owners, managers, and others. The accounting equation (assets equal liabilities plus owner's equity) expresses the concept concisely.

It is easy to understand the difference between the business entity and its owners in the case of a corporation such as General Motors because the accounting concept of separation agrees with the legal facts. However, the separate entity concept in accounting applies equally to a sole proprietorship or a partnership, even though owners of these types of businesses may be legally liable for all debts of the business and for actions carried out on behalf of the business.

Going Concern (Continuity of Existence) When periodic financial reports are prepared for a business, it is generally assumed that the firm is a going concern and will continue to operate indefinitely. This assumption permits carrying forward a portion of the cost of assets that will be used in future periods. If accountants could not assume that the activities of each business entity would continue into the future, they would have to try to estimate the current value of assets in case of immediate liquidation.

Stable Monetary Unit Accounting records are kept in terms of money. It is convenient for accountants to assume that the value of money is stable or that changes in its value are not great enough to affect the recorded financial data. The costs of assets purchased many years ago are therefore added to the costs of assets recently purchased, and a total dollar amount is reported.

As a matter of fact, the value of money *has* changed substantially in recent years. For this reason, many people have questioned the validity of the assumption that money is a stable measure of value. However, until recently, accounting organizations have been reluctant to give effect to changes in the value of the dollar. In the past few years, research committees of the American Accounting Association and a research study sponsored by the American Institute of Certified Public Accountants have suggested that this problem should be recognized and perhaps be reflected in the financial statements or in supplementary statements. In addition, the FASB and the SEC require that certain larger companies disclose the impact that price-level changes would have on their financial statements.

Objectivity Users of financial reports have a right to expect that the statements are objective—that they are unbiased and fair to all parties. In addition, users are entitled to assume that the statements are based on verifiable evidence rather than on opinions. In accounting this is taken to mean that two competent accountants who look at the same evidence would arrive at the same conclusion. However, the concepts of objectivity and verifiability do not eliminate the factor of judgment from accounting. For example, estimates of the useful lives of plant and equipment, selection of depreciation methods, and estimates of salvage value are all largely subjective decisions. These decisions affect the computation of depreciation expense for each fiscal period. Subjective judgments must also be made in many other cases.

Periodicity of Income Accountants realize that the final and correct results of a firm's operations cannot actually be determined until the business has ceased to exist. Only when all assets have been sold and all liabilities settled is it known for certain what is left for the owners and whether they have experienced a gain or a loss. However, owners, managers, and others need some idea of operating results at short intervals. Accountants must therefore have techniques for interim determination of values so that financial statements can be prepared at least yearly for all businesses and as often as monthly for many firms. The accrual basis of accounting is widely used because it allows accountants to provide financial information for each year or other fiscal period.

If yearly statements (or statements prepared at other intervals during the life of the business) are to have validity, it must be assumed that the nature of a firm's activities is such that they do, in fact, lend themselves to reasonable periodic income determination.

General Principles or Concepts

In deciding how a transaction should be recorded and how its effects should be reported on the financial statements, accountants must keep in mind several basic accounting principles or concepts that serve as guides.

Cost Basis Business transactions are, almost without exception, recorded on the basis of cost, that is, for an amount of money determined through dealings in the market between the business and outsiders. Assets are carried at cost until they are used. At that time, the cost (or an appropriate part of it) is charged against revenue. Cost is preferred to some possible alternatives, such as appraisal value, because cost, when determined in an ''arm's length'' transaction (a transaction with outsiders), is an objective, verifiable measure of economic value. In recent years the cost principle has come under severe criticism. Many people have pointed out that the high rate of inflation throughout the world makes original costs meaningless. Both the FASB and the SEC have recognized this problem by requiring certain large companies to disclose the impact of inflation on their financial statements.

Realization Since accounting reports today focus on the measurement of income for the fiscal period, one critical problem is the determination of the period in which to record revenue and to report it on the income statement. Revenue represents the inflow of new assets resulting from the sale of goods or services. Thus, as a general rule, revenue is recognized when a sale is made or a service is provided to an outsider. It is at this time that revenue is *realized*—new assets are created in the form of money or in the form of claims against others. Thus accountants usually say that revenue should not be recognized until it has been realized.

The realization principle has been the subject of much criticism. For example, it is argued by many people, including some accountants, that if a company owns shares of stock in another corporation and those shares are traded on a stock exchange, the quoted market value of the stock should be recorded in the accounts and any increase in value should be recognized as income. However, under the realization principle, no income is recognized until the increase is realized through sale or exchange. (However, a decrease in value might be recognized under our present accounting principles.)

The argument usually given for insistence on the realization principle is that an increase in value might be eliminated by a later decrease in value before the asset is sold. Also, the realization principle ensures that objective, verifiable evidence underlies the accounting records.

There are a number of important exceptions to the general rule that revenue is recognized at the time of sale. One exception involves accounting for installment sales, which is discussed in Chapter 22. In an installment sale, the difference between the selling price and the cost of the merchandise may be credited to a deferred income account at the time of sale. Part of the deferred income is recognized as revenue whenever a collection is made on the installment account receivable. This method should be used only when it is not possible to estimate losses from defaults on installments.

Another exception to the realization principle that is interesting, but seldom encountered, involves commodities for which there is an assured price and few costs to be incurred in getting the items to market. In this case the revenue may be recognized at the time the commodity is produced. The best example of the recording of revenue when production is completed has historically been in connection with the mining of gold. For many years in this country, gold had a guaranteed market at a fixed price with few after-production costs. Thus the immediate recognition of revenue at the time of production was justified.

Still another, and more complex, exception to the realization principle for reporting revenue is the *percentage-of-completion basis* for measuring income on long-term construction contracts. For example, a contractor may build a bridge that requires three years to complete. It is not logical to wait until the bridge is entirely finished and report all income in the year of completion. Instead, each year a portion of the estimated profit may be recorded as earned. The profit recorded is based on the portion of the estimated total costs for the project incurred during that year.

Still other businesses, especially service firms such as those operated by physicians, attorneys, and accountants, record revenues only when cash is received. This procedure is followed for federal income tax purposes and because of high losses on the outstanding bills owed by patients or clients.

By far the greatest number of businesses follow the general rule that revenue is recognized at the time a sale is made, rather than when cash from the sale is actually received.

Matching Costs With Revenue If income is to be properly measured, revenues must be matched against the expired costs incurred in earning those revenues. This is sometimes referred to as matching effort and accomplishment. To achieve matching, the accountant seeks systematic, rational approaches for determining the period in which costs should be charged against revenues.

Some costs, such as manufacturing costs, can easily be identified with specific products. It is customary to treat these costs as inventory costs and charge them to cost of goods sold when the products are sold. Some other costs, such as office salaries, do not clearly benefit future periods and are charged as expenses when they are incurred. Still other costs benefit many future periods. The accountant therefore seeks to estimate the periods benefited and to charge the costs as expenses during the periods involved. For example, the cost of a store building is depreciated over its estimated useful life.

Many of the controversial questions in accounting involve determining the period or periods in which a cost should be charged as an expense.

The Accrual Basis Inherent in the realization principle and the matching principle is the *accrual principle*. As you have already seen in Part 1, sometimes a transaction occurs in one period but the cash involved is not received or paid out until a later period. Under the accrual principle, transactions are recorded in the period in which they occur, rather than in the period when the cash inflow or outflow takes place. For example, suppose that employees work in December but are not paid until January of the following year. Their earnings should be recorded as an expense in December, and the amount owed to them at the end of December should be shown as a liability on the December 31 balance sheet. Similarly, if a firm purchases office supplies in December and uses only a portion of them in that month, the cost should be allocated so that the part used is treated as an expense and the part still on hand is reported as an asset.

Consistency The need for consistent application of a given accounting procedure from one period to the next in a particular company was mentioned previously. Any lack of consistency would result in financial reports that are not comparable with earlier reports and are therefore misleading.

However, the consistency rule does not mean that no changes in accounting principles or methods can be made. If the application of another accounting method would clearly give a fairer presentation of earnings or financial position, it is proper to change to the new method. Detailed rules have been developed for reporting the effects of the change so that statement users are completely informed.

Full Disclosure It is necessary to disclose all information that might affect the statement user's interpretation of the profitability and financial position of a business. This must be done either in the actual financial statements or in footnotes to the statements. In recent years there have been numerous lawsuits by statement users against certified public accountants and against companies issuing financial statements. The lawsuits have charged that the statements of these companies did not disclose facts that would have influenced investor decisions. As a result, accountants are very careful to include enough information so that the informed reader can obtain a complete and accurate picture. The financial reports issued by large companies usually include a thorough explanation of the accounting principles and methods that have been used in preparing the statements. The SEC has long maintained that the key element of financial reporting is full disclosure.

Modifying Conventions

Although the basic accounting principles and underlying assumptions provide a means for analyzing each business transaction to determine its proper treatment in the accounts, a number of practical considerations have come to be accepted as limiting or modifying the application of the general principles. Among the most important of these "modifying conventions" are materiality, conservatism, and industry practice.

Materiality *Materiality* concerns the significance of an item in relation to the particular situation of which it is a part. An item of a certain dollar amount might be material in a small company and thus would have to be disclosed. However, the same amount might not be significant in a larger firm and could therefore be combined with other figures or be presented in a different manner on the statements.

Although no hard-and-fast rules for judging materiality have been laid down, an item is usually compared with the firm's net income and with total owner's equity in deciding whether it is material. It is generally accepted that a deviation from normal accounting principles is permissible if the amount is immaterial. For example, a business that has sales of $10,000,000 a year might buy a small tool with a useful life of three years for $50. Practicality dictates that this item be charged as an expense rather than recorded as an asset and then depreciated over its useful life. The amount of this transaction is immaterial in such a large business. Although this is an extreme example, it indicates the concept involved.

Conservatism Accountants have long followed a doctrine of conservatism. Assets are understated rather than overstated if any question exists. Recognition of income is deferred until it is realized, and losses and expenses are recognized as soon as they occur.

Although this doctrine is still basically accepted by most accountants, an increasing number concede that undue conservatism in the present may make for a lack of conservatism in the future. For example, if too much of the cost of an asset is charged as depreciation expense in the present period, the firm's net income will be conservatively reported and the book value of the asset will be conservatively stated. But in later years, during which the asset still performs useful services, the depreciation expense will be understated and the net income will be correspondingly overstated, which is not conservative. Increased accuracy of valuation and timing has come to be more important to many accountants than the old-style conservatism.

Industry Practice Sometimes accounting practices have become acceptable in certain industries although not generally acceptable in other industries. These exceptions are often created because of tax laws, regulatory requirements, or high risk involved. For example, in the public utility industry, it has been customary for many years to capitalize, as part of asset costs, all interest expense incurred on money borrowed to build a power plant during the period that the plant is being constructed. Until recently, this practice has not been generally followed in other industries. It has developed in the public utility industry because interest capitalization is permitted by regulatory agencies for rate-making purposes.

THE IMPACT OF ACCOUNTING PRINCIPLES, ASSUMPTIONS, AND MODIFYING CONVENTIONS

Throughout the remainder of this book, you will find many references to accounting principles, assumptions, and modifying conventions. A thorough knowledge of these concepts will help you to understand how individual transactions are accounted for and why they are handled in a specific way. Often the accountant is faced with new or unusual transactions that give rise to accounting questions that do not appear to have simple solutions. Almost invariably the accountant will fall back on the concepts discussed in this chapter in deciding how to handle the transaction. Thus an understanding of this chapter is essential to an understanding of complex accounting issues.

PRINCIPLES AND PROCEDURES SUMMARY

Some of the most important ideas underlying accounting are the cost principle, the realization principle, the matching principle, the accrual principle, the consistency principle, and the full disclosure principle. There are also certain assumptions that have an important influence on accounting. These are the separate entity assumption, the going concern assumption, the stable monetary unit assumption, the objectivity assumption, and the periodicity of income assumption.

In order to obtain greater uniformity and improve reliability, accounting organizations, especially the American Institute of Certified Public Accountants, have taken an active role in developing accounting principles. The ever-increasing interest of government, stockholders, analysts, creditors, and economists in financial reports ensures that there will be continuing progress in the search for accounting principles that will make the reports more meaningful and reliable. Never in the history of accounting has there been such a large and diverse group interested in accounting principles and financial reporting standards. This has led to the formation of the Financial Accounting Standards Board, a private-sector group whose specific task is the development of accounting principles and financial reporting standards. In addition, the federal government plays a role in these matters through the Securities and Exchange Commission, which is the government agency responsible for the reporting standards used by publicly held corporations.

MANAGERIAL IMPLICATIONS

Financial statements are of great importance in managerial decision making. Thus management should understand the basic principles that underlie financial statements. Of particular importance in large firms is the need for comparability between statements so that the management of one firm can compare the results of its operations with those of its competitors. Comparisons of this type are made possible only by the existence of a body of basic accounting concepts, assumptions, principles, and standards that are applied by all businesses.

REVIEW QUESTIONS

1. How do accounting principles originate?
2. Explain the role of the Securities and Exchange Commission (SEC) in developing accounting principles.
3. What are *Accounting Series Releases*?
4. Why was the Financial Accounting Standards Board (FASB) formed?
5. Describe the organization of which the FASB is a part.
6. What is the FASB's conceptual framework project? Why is it important?
7. In what way, if any, are the FASB and the SEC related?
8. Who does the FASB define as the users of financial reports? Why is this important?
9. In this chapter, nine qualitative characteristics of financial reports were discussed. In your opinion, which of these characteristics is most important? Why?
10. Explain what is meant by the cost basis of accounting?
11. What is the major strength of, or argument for, the cost basis?
12. Define the term *realization*. Why is the realization concept used?
13. Name three exceptions to the cost basis of accounting.
14. Explain the matching concept.
15. Why is the accrual basis generally required as the proper basis for measuring income?
16. Explain the separate entity assumption.
17. What is the going concern assumption? Explain how this assumption is important to the cost basis of accounting.
18. Is the assumption of a stable monetary unit valid? If not, why is it still used?
19. What is meant by the term *periodicity of income*?
20. How does materiality affect day-to-day accounting?
21. What is the conservatism convention? What potential problems are created by this convention?

MANAGERIAL DISCUSSION QUESTIONS

1. Why must management understand the principles, concepts, and assumptions underlying a firm's financial statements?
2. How can the element of personal judgment, which is involved in such matters as selection of depreciation methods and estimates of salvage value and useful life, be minimized to preserve the objectivity of an accounting system?
3. Why might management argue that the historical-cost framework should be abandoned?
4. The management of a firm suggests that all financial statements of debtors report "the current value of assets." What objection do you see to this procedure? What benefits do you see in this procedure?

5. Suppose that you are employed as an accountant. An officer of the firm where you work asks why you use generally accepted accounting principles and where these rules come from. Explain the sources of generally accepted accounting principles and the reasons for using them.

EXERCISES

EXERCISE 19-1   **Accounting for prepaid insurance.** The Briggs Corporation paid insurance premiums of $60,000 on December 1, 19X1. These premiums covered a three-year period beginning on that date. What amount should Briggs show as insurance expense for the year 19X1? What accounting principles, concepts, or assumptions support your answer?

EXERCISE 19-2   **Accounting for a building construction contract.** The Gallo Construction Company signed a contract with a customer on July 1, 19X2. The contract called for the construction of a new building to begin on or before December 31, 19X2, and to be completed by December 31, 19X3. The contract price was $1,400,000, and Gallo estimated that the building would cost $1,000,000. No work was begun in 19X2. How much income from the project should Gallo report in 19X2? Why?

EXERCISE 19-3   **Accounting for an increase in the value of an inventory item.** George Mendez buys and sells real estate. On December 31, 19X2, his inventory of property included a tract of undeveloped land for which he had paid $450,000. The fair market value of the land was $600,000 at that date. How much income should Mendez report for 19X2 in connection with this land. Why?

EXERCISE 19-4   **Accounting for small tools.** The Taylor Company purchased several hundred small tools during 19X2 at a total cost of $2,100. Some of the tools were expected to last for a few weeks, some for several months, and some for several years. Taylor's income for 19X2 will be about $1,500,000. How should Taylor account for the small tools in order to be theoretically correct? As a practical matter, how should Taylor account for these tools? Why?

EXERCISE 19-5   **Accounting for personal withdrawals from a business.** Leo Stern is the sole proprietor of a hardware store. Stern's accountant insists that he keep a detailed record of all amounts of money and merchandise that he takes out of the business for his personal use. Why? (In this exercise and all the exercises that follow, name any accounting principles, concepts, or assumptions that support the practice being described.)

EXERCISE 19-6   **Accounting for the inventory of supplies.** At the end of each fiscal period, the accountant for the Marlow Company requires that a careful inventory be made of the office supplies and that the amount on hand be reported as an asset and the amount used during the period be reported as an expense. Why?

EXERCISE 19-7 **Accounting for equipment with no salvage value.** Three years ago the O'Brien Company purchased a machine for $100,000. The machine is expected to have no salvage value. Nevertheless, O'Brien continues to keep the asset's cost in its accounting records and to depreciate the asset over its ten-year useful life, which will include the next seven years. Why?

EXERCISE 19-8 **Accounting for an increase in land value.** On January 14 of last year, the Carlson Company purchased some land for $20,000 on which it planned to construct an office building. At the end of the year, the land had increased in value to $26,000. Nevertheless, Carlson recognized no income as a result of the increase in value. Why?

EXERCISE 19-9 **Accounting for an estimate of uncollectible accounts.** The Van Ness Company has decided to charge off as a loss a portion of its accounts receivable that it estimates will be uncollectible. The accounts involved resulted from the current year's sales. What is the reason for this practice?

EXERCISE 19-10 **Accounting for advertising costs.** The Hudson Company charges off the cost of all newspaper advertising in the year it is incurred even though the advertising probably results in some sales in later years. Why?

EXERCISE 19-11 **Accounting for a charge-off of insurance premiums.** The Goldberg Company's net income is about $1,000,000 a year. The company follows the practice of charging to expense all property insurance premiums when paid. Last year approximately $1,200 of these premiums represented amounts applicable to future years. What is the reason for this practice?

EXERCISE 19-12 **Accounting for research and development costs.** The Stanley Corporation charges all of its research and development costs to expense when incurred. Why?

EXERCISE 19-13 **Accounting for warranties.** The DeMaio Company sells refrigerators. It grants all customers a 12-month warranty, agreeing to make necessary repairs within the following 12-month period free of charge. At the end of each year, the company estimates the total cost to be incurred during the next period under the warranties for appliances sold during the current period and charges that amount to expense, crediting a liability account. Why?

EXERCISE 19-14 **Accounting for litigation that is pending.** At the end of last year, the Stewart Corporation was engaged in defending itself against several major lawsuits. If any of these lawsuits is lost, it would cause a major financial hardship for the corporation. The auditors insisted that the corporation include some discussion of the lawsuits in footnotes to its financial reports. Why?

PROBLEMS

PROBLEM 19-1

Applying various accounting principles and concepts. The accounting treatment or statement presentation of various items is discussed below. The items pertain to different businesses and are unrelated.

Instructions

Indicate in each case whether or not the item has been handled in accordance with generally accepted accounting principles. If so, indicate which of the basic concepts has been followed. If not, indicate which concept has been violated and tell how the item should have been recorded or presented.

1. Included on the balance sheet of the Swift Cleaning Shop is the personal automobile of Martin Webb, the owner.
2. The Fitzgerald Manufacturing Company makes furniture. The cost of a particular chair is $35. However, when the inventory figures are computed for the balance sheet, the amount used for this chair is $68, the normal selling price.
3. On December 1, 19X2, the Ridge Mining Company purchased some highly specialized, custom-made equipment for $400,000. Since the equipment is of no use to anyone else and has no resale value, it is shown on the December 31, 19X2, balance sheet at $1.
4. On December 31, 19X1, the Canfield Corporation valued its inventory according to an acceptable accounting method. On December 31, 19X2, the inventory was valued by a different but also acceptable method, and on December 31, 19X3, the inventory was valued by the method that was used in 19X1.
5. Each year the Evergreen Company values its investments in land at the current market price.
6. In 19X3 the Lomax Corporation had sales of $8 million, all on credit. Statistics of the company for prior years show that losses from uncollectible accounts are equal to about 1 percent of sales each year. However, the Lomax Corporation charges off part of its accounts receivable as a loss only when a specific account is found to be uncollectible.
7. The Sanders Company owns office equipment that was purchased seven years ago. It is still carried in the firm's accounting records at the original cost. No depreciation has ever been taken on the equipment.

PROBLEM 19-2

Reconstructing an income statement to reflect proper accounting principles. The income statement shown on page 466 was sent by Susan Curtis, the owner of the Curtis Audio Center, to several of her creditors who had asked for financial statements. The business is a sole proprietorship that sells record players, tape decks, speakers, and other audio equipment. An accountant for one of the creditors looked over the income statement and found that it did not conform to generally accepted accounting principles.

Instructions

Prepare an income statement for the Curtis Audio Center in accordance with generally accepted accounting principles.

CURTIS AUDIO CENTER
Income Statement
Year Ended December 31, 19X1

Cash Collected From Customers		$460,000
Cost of Goods Sold		
Merchandise Inventory, Jan. 1	$ 50,000	
Payments to Creditors	290,000	
	$340,000	
Less Merchandise Inventory, Dec. 31	55,000	
Cost of Goods Sold		285,000
Gross Profit on Sales		$175,000
Expenses		
Salary to Owner	$ 18,000	
Salaries to Employees	54,000	
Depreciation Expense	17,500	
Income Tax of Owner	12,200	
Payroll Taxes Expense	8,800	
Advertising and Other Selling Expenses	15,000	
Repairs Expense	6,000	
Office Expense	18,000	
Insurance Expense	3,000	
Interest Expense	8,000	
Utility and Telephone Expenses	6,000	
Legal and Audit Expenses	2,000	
Miscellaneous Expense	19,000	
Total Expenses		187,500
Net Loss From Operations		($ 12,500)
Increase in Appraised Value of Land During Year		10,000
Net Loss for Year		($ 2,500)

The following additional information was made available by Curtis.

1. On December 31, 19X1, the accounts receivable from customers total $22,000. On January 1, 19X1, the receivables totaled $18,000.
2. No effort has been made to charge off worthless accounts. An analysis shows that probably $900 of the accounts receivable on December 31, 19X1, will never be collected.
3. The beginning and ending merchandise inventories were valued at their estimated selling price. The actual cost of the ending inventory is estimated to be $33,000, and the actual cost of the beginning inventory was estimated at $30,000.
4. On December 31, 19X1, suppliers of merchandise are owed $29,000, while on January 1, 19X1, they were owed $26,000.
5. The owner paid herself a salary of $1,500 a month from the business's funds and charged this amount to an account called Salary to Owner.

6. The owner also withdrew cash from the firm's bank account in order to pay herself $5,000 interest on her capital investment. This amount was charged to Interest Expense.

7. A check for $12,200 to cover the owner's personal income tax for the previous year was issued from the firm's bank account.

8. Depreciation on assets was computed at 10 percent of the gross profit. An analysis of assets showed that the original cost of the equipment and fixtures totaled $40,000. Their estimated useful life is 10 years with no salvage value. The building had a cost of $75,000. Its useful life is expected to be 25 years with no salvage value.

9. Included in Repairs Expense was a $3,000 payment on December 22 for paving a new parking lot.

10. The increase in land value was based on an appraisal by a qualified real estate appraiser.

ALTERNATE PROBLEMS

PROBLEM 19-1A   **Applying various accounting principles and concepts.** The accounting treatment or statement presentation of various items is discussed below. The items pertain to different businesses and are unrelated.

Instructions   Indicate in each case whether or not the item has been handled in accordance with generally accepted accounting principles. If so, indicate which of the basic concepts has been followed. If not, indicate which concept has been violated and tell how the item should have been recorded or presented.

1. The Dodd Company manufactured some machinery for its own use at a cost of $45,000. The lowest bid price from an outsider was $52,000. The company recorded the machinery at $45,000.

2. At the beginning of the year 19X1, the Elmwood Company bought a building for $100,000. At the end of 19X1, the building's value was appraised at $105,000. Since there was an increase in value, the company did not record depreciation on the building.

3. The balance sheet of the Summit Sporting Goods Store reports prepaid insurance at $300, the cash value of the policy on the date when the statement is prepared. The prepaid insurance consists of the last year of a three-year fire insurance policy that originally cost $1,500.

4. The assets listed in the accounting records of the World Travel Agency include the residence of Gail Sims, the owner of the business.

5. On December 31, 19X1, the accounts receivable of the Anderson Company include $500 owed by Earl Haines, who is in the county jail on charges of passing bad checks. The owner of the Anderson Company writes off the amount because he feels certain that the debt will not be paid, even though Haines insists that he will pay after he gets out of jail and obtains a job.

6. The machinery of the Paragon Manufacturing Company has a depreciated cost of $60,000. However, the machinery could not be sold for more than

$25,000 today. The owner thinks that the machinery should nevertheless be reported on the balance sheet at $60,000.

7. The Valley Hotel owns certain land purchased about 40 years ago for $10,000. Elizabeth Ford, the owner, thinks that since the price level today is almost three times the price level at the time the land was purchased, the balance of the account for this asset should be increased to reflect the price-level change.

PROBLEM 19-2A **Reconstructing an income statement to reflect proper accounting principles.** The income statement shown below was prepared by Gary Morgan, the owner of Morgan's Sand and Surf Shop. The business is a sole proprietorship that sells beachwear, surfboards, and skin-diving equipment. An accountant who looked at the income statement told Morgan that it does not conform to generally accepted accounting principles.

Instructions Prepare an income statement in accordance with generally accepted accounting principles.

MORGAN'S SAND AND SURF SHOP
Income Statement
Year Ended December 31, 19X4

Cash Receipts From Customers		$265,000
Cost of Goods Sold		
Merchandise Inventory, Jan. 1	$ 24,000	
Payments to Suppliers	200,000	
	$224,000	
Less Merchandise Inventory, Dec. 31	30,000	
Cost of Goods Sold		194,000
Gross Profit on Sales		$ 71,000
Operating Expenses		
Salaries Expense	$ 42,000	
Insurance Expense	1,400	
Payroll Taxes Expense	4,600	
Repairs Expense	1,000	
Supplies and Other Office Expenses	6,000	
Advertising and Other Selling Expenses	10,000	
Utilities Expense	2,000	
Interest Expense	3,000	
Total Expenses		70,000
Net Income From Operations		$ 1,000
Increase in Market Value of Store Equipment		3,200
Net Income for Year		$ 4,200

The following additional information is made available by Morgan.

1. On December 31, 19X4, accounts receivable from customers total $15,500. On January 1, 19X4, the receivables totaled $20,000.
2. On December 31, 19X4, accounts receivable amounting to $800 were expected to be uncollectible.
3. On December 31, 19X4, accounts payable owed to suppliers are $21,000. On January 1, 19X4, the outstanding accounts payable were $12,000.
4. Included in Salaries Expense is $6,000 that Morgan withdrew for his personal use.
5. Included in Interest Expense is $1,200 that Morgan withdrew as interest on his capital investment.
6. Miscellaneous repairs of $500 were charged to the Store Equipment account during the year. No new equipment was purchased.
7. Morgan explains that since the estimated value of his store equipment has increased by $3,200 during the year, no depreciation expense was recorded. The store equipment has a total cost of $33,000 and a total estimated useful life of 10 years with no salvage value.

Checks are not the only kind of written order or promise to pay that may be used in financing and settling business transactions. Promissory notes, drafts, and trade acceptances are also sometimes used, especially for larger transactions and for obligations that extend for a longer time than the typical open-account credit period. These documents usually have the characteristics of negotiable instruments.

NOTES PAYABLE AND INTEREST

NEGOTIABLE INSTRUMENTS

The law dealing with negotiable instruments is a part of the Uniform Commercial Code, which has been adopted by the legislatures of all the states. This law specifies that in order to be negotiable, instruments must meet the following requirements.

1. They must be in writing and must be signed by the *maker* (or drawer).
2. They must contain an unconditional promise or order to pay a definite amount of money.
3. They must be payable either on demand or at a future time that is fixed or that can be determined.
4. They must be payable to the order of a specific person or to the bearer.
5. If addressed to a drawee, they must clearly name or identify that person.

The checks illustrated in Chapter 10 were negotiable instruments because they met all these requirements. The promissory note shown below also meets all the requirements of negotiability.

$ 3,000.00	Greenville, S.C. March 18 ___ 19 X2
Ninety days ___ AFTER DATE We ___ PROMISE TO PAY	
TO THE ORDER OF Columbia Equipment Company	
Three Thousand and 00/100 ___ DOLLARS	
PAYABLE AT City National Bank	
VALUE RECEIVED PLUS INTEREST AT THE RATE OF 12 PERCENT PER ANNUM	
	Style Clothing Store
NO. 1 ___ DUE June 16, 19X2	Linda Hanson

A note is merely written evidence of a debt. The note illustrated on page 470 is a promise by the Style Clothing Store to pay $3,000 to the Columbia Equipment Company in 90 days. It is negotiable for the following reasons.

1. It is in writing and signed by the maker (Linda Hanson for the Style Clothing Store).
2. It is an unconditional promise to pay a definite sum.
3. It is payable on a date that can be determined exactly.
4. It is payable to a party named in the instrument.

The note also specifies that interest at the rate of 12 percent a year must be paid at maturity. However, this provision is not needed for negotiability, and some notes may not bear interest.

The amount shown on the note ($3,000) is called the *principal, face value,* or *face amount.* The total that must be paid when the note becomes due (the principal plus the interest) is known as the *maturity value.* In the note illustrated on page 470, the maturity value is not specified.

Interest-Bearing Note Given in Purchase of an Asset

The interest-bearing note issued by the Style Clothing Store was created under the following circumstances. On March 18 Style purchased furniture and store fixtures for $3,000 from the Columbia Equipment Company. Columbia agreed to allow the store 90 days in which to pay for the goods if the store would issue a promissory note bearing interest at 12 percent a year. Columbia worked out this arrangement so that the Style Clothing Store could pay for the goods later, but it also wanted as much legal protection as possible for itself.

Recording the Issuance of the Note The Style Clothing Store records this transaction in its accounting records by making a general journal entry, as shown below. This entry involves a debit to Furniture and Fixtures and a credit to Notes Payable—Trade.

19 X2				
Mar. 18	Furniture and Fixtures	131	3,000 00	
	Notes Payable—Trade	201		3,000 00
	Issued a 90-day, 12% note for store furnishings bought from Columbia Equipment Company.			

No entry is made for the interest at the time the note is given. The interest will be recorded later.

Maturity Date When the note payable becomes due, the Columbia Equipment Company will ask its bank to collect the funds. Obviously, the Style Clothing Store needs to keep a record of the date that payment is due so that it can have enough money available to cover the amount owed. It is therefore important to determine the maturity date of the note immediately. This is done by counting the number of days from the date the note was issued. (The issue date itself is not counted.) For example, a 30-day note issued on January 1 matures 30 days after January 1—on January 31. The following steps are needed to find the maturity date of a 30-day note issued on January 15.

1. Determine the number of days the note will run in the month of issue. In this case, it will run for 16 days in January (31 − 15). 16 days

2. Subtract the number of days the note will run in the month of issue from the total time for which the note was issued. In this case, the remaining time is 14 days (30 − 16). Thus, the note will run for 14 days in February. 14 days

3. Prove the computations. Add the previous figures together to see whether they equal the total period of the note in days: 16 days + 14 days = 30 days. <u>30 days</u>

  Since the note must run 14 days in February, the maturity date is February 14. More than two months may be involved if the time period of the note is longer. For example, the note issued on March 18 to the Columbia Equipment Company was for 90 days. The steps needed to find its maturity date are as follows.

1. Determine the number of days the note will run in the month of issue. In this case it will run for 13 days in March (31 − 18).

2. Add to that number the total days in the following months until within one month of the total time period.

Number of days in April	30 days
Number of days in May	31 days
Total number of days from the issue date to the end of May	74 days

3. Determine the number of days the note will run in the month in which it matures. In this case the note will run for 16 days in June (90 − 74). Thus, the maturity date is June 16. 16 days

4. Prove the computations. Add the previous figures together to see whether they equal the total period of the note in days: 74 days + 16 days = 90 days. <u>90 days</u>

  Sometimes the period of a note is described in months instead of days. For example, the note issued to the Columbia Equipment Company might have been for three months rather than for 90 days. When the period is defined in months, the maturity date is determined by counting ahead to the same date the following month or months. Three months from March 18 is June 18, regardless of the fact that March and May have 31 days and April has 30. No count of the actual days is required.

  If a note is issued at the end of a month, there may be no actual date corresponding to the theoretical due date. In that event the note falls due on the first day of the following month. For example, a six-month note given on August 30 would be due on February 30. However, since there is no February 30, the note is due on March 1.

When a firm grants credit by accepting a promissory note, it must wait for payment and thus forego the use of money during the credit period. The party receiving the credit postpones payment and has the use of the money during the credit period. Since the use of money is a valuable privilege, creditors almost always charge debtors for it. *Interest* is the name given to the price charged for the use of money or credit.

The interest specified in a credit transaction is accounted for separately. It is recorded as interest expense by the debtor and as interest income by the creditor. The following section describes how the interest on a note payable is computed and recorded.

Interest Calculations

The amount of interest for any time period can be determined by using this formula.

$$\text{Interest} = \text{Principal} \times \text{Interest Rate} \times \text{Time in Years}$$

The time period is indicated by a fraction. The exact number of days the note is to run is generally used as the numerator, and 360 is used as the denominator. (Although most years have 365 days, 360 is used for convenience. This 360-day period is referred to as the "bankers' year.") The 90-day term of the Style Clothing Store's note is therefore expressed as $\frac{90}{360}$ of a year.

If we apply the interest formula to the promissory note issued by the Style Clothing Store to the Columbia Equipment Company, we will find that the interest on $3,000 for 90 days at 12 percent is $90.

$$\text{Interest} = \$3,000 \times 0.12 \times \frac{90}{360}$$

$$\text{Interest} = \$90$$

Shortcut Interest Calculations If interest is at the rate of 6 percent and the credit period is 60 days, the 6 percent, 60-day method of calculation can be used. This method operates as follows.

$$\text{Interest} = \text{Principal} \times \text{Rate} \times \text{Time}$$

$$\text{Interest} = \text{Principal} \times 0.06 \times \frac{60}{360}$$

$$\text{Interest} = \text{Principal} \times \frac{6}{100} \times \frac{60}{360}$$

$$\text{Interest} = \text{Principal} \times \frac{\cancel{6}}{100} \times \frac{\cancel{60}}{\cancel{360}}$$

$$\text{Interest} = \text{Principal} \times \frac{1}{100} = \text{Principal} \times 0.01$$

A quick way of multiplying any figure by 0.01 is simply to move the decimal point two places to the left. Thus interest at 6 percent for 60 days is computed by moving the decimal point two places to the left in the principal amount. For example, interest at 6 percent for 60 days on $800 is $8.

$$\$800 \times 0.01 = \$8$$

Since interest is in direct proportion to rate and time, the shortcut method can also be used to determine interest where the rate is more or less than 6 percent or where the time is more or less than 60 days. For example, interest at 6 percent for 75 days on $1,200 can be computed as follows.

Interest at 6% for 60 days $(0.01 \times \$1,200)$ = $12

Interest at 6% for $\underline{15}$ days $\left(\dfrac{15}{60} = \dfrac{1}{4} \text{ of } \$12\right)$ = $\underline{\quad 3}$

Interest at 6% for $\underline{75}$ days = $\underline{\underline{\$15}}$

Similarly, interest at 12 percent for 90 days on $3,000 is determined as shown below.

Interest at 6% for 60 days $(0.01 \times \$3,000)$ = $30

Interest at 12% for 60 days $(2 \times \$30)$ = $\underline{\quad 60}$

Interest at 12% for 90 days $\left(1\dfrac{1}{2} \times \$60\right)$ = $\underline{\underline{\$90}}$

Such calculations are shortcuts in some cases. However, in other cases they may become so involved that it is simpler and more accurate to use the regular formula. With the widespread availability of electronic calculators today, the 6 percent, 60-day method is no longer commonly used.

Payment of the Note and Interest

On the maturity date, June 16, the Style Clothing Store pays the Columbia Equipment Company the $3,000 principal of the note and the $90 interest. The effect of this transaction is shown in general journal form below.

19 X2				
June 16	Notes Payable—Trade	201	3,000 00	
	Interest Expense	591	90 00	
	Cash	101		3,090 00

PARTIAL PAYMENT OF A NOTE PAYABLE

If only partial payment of a note is made at its maturity, a check is prepared for the amount that is being paid. This amount is endorsed on the note by the payee, or the old note is canceled and a new one is issued for the balance due.

If there is no agreement to the contrary, a noninterest-bearing note that is not paid at maturity begins at that time to bear interest at a rate established by law in each state. It continues to do so until it is paid.

RENEWING A NOTE PAYABLE

Sometimes the firm that has issued a note asks for an extension of time in which to pay. If the note payable is renewed for another period of time, no additional accounting entries are required. The usual accounting entry is made when the note is paid on the deferred maturity date.

DISCOUNTING A NOTE PAYABLE AT THE BANK

Business firms often borrow money from banks and sign notes payable as evidence of the debts. Banks invariably charge interest on loans. Like the interest on the note payable to the Columbia Equipment Company, the interest on a bank loan may be paid at maturity. In many cases, however, the bank deducts the interest in advance, and the borrower receives only the difference between the face amount of the note and the interest on it to maturity. This arrangement, which is called *discounting*, works in the following way.

Suppose that the Style Clothing Store arranges to borrow $5,000 at 14 percent from its bank on April 30 by discounting a 30-day note payable. The interest is calculated according to the formula given earlier.

$$\text{Interest} = \$5,000 \times 0.14 \times \frac{30}{360}$$

$$\text{Interest} = \$58.33$$

The bank deducts the $58.33 interest from the $5,000 face amount of the note and the Style Clothing Store receives the difference, which is $4,941.67. The firm will probably have the bank deposit this amount in its checking account.

Recording the Issuance of the Note

The effect of this transaction is shown below in general journal form. Notes Payable—Bank is credited because the accountant wishes to distinguish notes payable to banks from notes payable to businesses. Cash is debited for the amount of cash actually received, and Interest Expense is debited for the amount of interest that was deducted.

19 X2					
Apr. 30	Cash	101	4,941 67	
	Interest Expense	591	58 33	
	Notes Payable—Bank	203		5,000 00

Paying the Note

The maturity date of the Style Clothing Store's note is May 30. (Since it is dated April 30, there are no days to run in April.) The firm prepares a check for $5,000 on May 30 to pay the note. The accountant debits Notes Payable—Bank and credits Cash to record the payment. Since the interest was deducted in advance by the bank and was recorded at the time the note was issued, no further entry for it is required. Only the face amount of the note is paid at maturity.

NOTES PAYABLE REGISTER					
DATE OF ENTRY	PAYEE	WHERE PAYABLE		DATE OF NOTE	TIME TO RUN
19 X2				19 X2	
Mar. 18	Columbia Equipment Co.	City National Bank		Mar. 18	90 days
Apr. 30	City National Bank	City National Bank		Apr. 30	30 days

NOTES PAYABLE REGISTER

If many notes payable are issued, it may be convenient to keep a record of the details by maintaining a *notes payable register*. This record shows the important information about each note payable on a single line. The information includes the date of the note, the payee, where the note is payable, the time it is to run, its maturity date, its face amount, and the interest rate and amount of interest, if any. At the end of each accounting period, a *schedule of notes payable* can be prepared by listing the unpaid notes that appear in the notes payable register. The total must agree with the total of the Notes Payable account(s) in the general ledger, as though proving to a control account.

The two notes issued in March by the Style Clothing Store are entered in a notes payable register as illustrated above.

In the form shown here, the notes payable register is a memorandum record. However, it can also be designed for use as a book of original entry from which postings are made to the ledger accounts. If the notes payable register is used in this way, the entry for the issuance of a note that is recorded in the register takes the place of a journal entry. The posting of the transaction is done directly from the register. The Style Clothing Store does not have enough notes payable to use the register as a book of original entry.

NOTES PAYABLE AND INTEREST EXPENSE ON THE STATEMENTS

Notes payable represent obligations of the business. Thus they appear on the balance sheet as liabilities. As explained earlier, the Style Clothing Store has set up separate accounts called Notes Payable—Trade and Notes Payable—Bank. Both of these accounts are shown on the balance sheet. Notes due within one year are usually classified as current liabilities, and notes due in more than one year are classified as long-term liabilities. The notes presented in this chapter are current liabilities. Long-term liabilities are discussed in Chapter 31.

Interest expense usually appears on the income statement as a nonoperating expense. It is listed under Other Expense, and it is deducted from the figure for Net Income From Operations, as shown below.

Net Income From Operations	$9,675.25	
Other Expense		
Interest Expense		125.30
Net Income	$9,549.95	

YEAR	J	F	M	A	M	J	J	A	S	O	N	D	FACE AMOUNT OF NOTE	RATE	AMOUNT	DATE PAID	REMARKS
					MATURITY DATE									INTEREST			
19X2					16								3,000 00	12%	90 00		
19X2				30									5,000 00	14%	58 33		Discounted

INTERNAL CONTROL OF NOTES PAYABLE

The accountant must carefully control notes payable. Only a very limited number of specifically approved persons should be allowed to issue and sign notes payable on behalf of the firm. This is necessary to ensure that the company's credit is properly used. For example, there have been many instances in which a large number of persons in a firm were authorized to sign notes payable and an employee has used this means to borrow funds for his or her personal use.

All notes payable should be recorded in the notes payable register immediately. Responsibility for prompt payment should be delegated to a specific employee to make certain that the notes are paid on time. Late payment not only endangers the company's credit rating, but it can be costly because many notes contain penalty provisions for late payment. All paid notes should be marked "canceled" and properly receipted at the time of payment. They should then be retained in the company's files for a reasonable period of time.

PRINCIPLES AND PROCEDURES SUMMARY

Notes payable can be noninterest-bearing, but usually they do bear interest. When a note is given for the purchase of an asset, the amount is credited to a notes payable account and debited to an asset account. At the maturity date, a check is prepared for payment of the note and the interest. Only the principal is debited to the Notes Payable account when the payment is recorded. The interest is debited to the Interest Expense account, and the entire amount to be paid—principal and interest—is credited to Cash.

When money is borrowed from a bank and a note is given to the bank, the bank may deduct the interest in advance (discount the note), giving the borrower only the difference between the principal of the note and the interest on it. In this case Notes Payable—Bank is credited for the principal, Interest Expense is debited for the interest, and Cash is debited for the difference (the cash actually received from the bank). This entry is made when the note is issued.

If a business issues many notes, it may keep a notes payable register. Notes payable appear as a liability on the balance sheet. Interest expense is usually classified as a nonoperating expense on the income statement.

MANAGERIAL IMPLICATIONS

Managers must be aware of opportunities to finance operations through the use of short-term notes payable that temporarily provide cash. Sources of such funds include suppliers (through credit extension) and banks. For funds secured through bank loans, the discounting of notes payable results in a higher effective interest rate than that shown on the face of each note. Since the interest is deducted in advance, the borrower does not have the use of all the funds indicated on the face of the note.

Managers must also be familiar with the Uniform Commercial Code if they are to understand the rights and obligations involved in notes payable commitments.

The authority to sign notes payable on behalf of the company should be restricted to a very limited number of persons. Care must be taken that all notes payable are paid on time and that they are securely filed after payment.

REVIEW QUESTIONS

1. What are the requirements that must be met in order for a document to be negotiable?
2. What is meant by the term *face amount* of a note? By the term *principal?*
3. What is the reason that most notes bear interest?
4. What is the "bankers' year"?
5. What is meant by discounting a note payable?
6. When a note payable is discounted, is the maturity value greater than the face value? Explain.
7. Explain the 6 percent, 60-day method of computing interest.
8. If a note dated March 31 is due three months from date, on what date must the note be paid?
9. Explain how the maturity value of a note is computed.
10. Explain how partial payment of a note payable is accounted for.
11. What types of information about a note are recorded in a notes payable register?
12. Explain how the discounting of a note payable is recorded in the general journal.
13. Would you prefer to *(a)* borrow $1,000 from a bank, signing a one-year note bearing interest at 12 percent, or *(b)* have the bank discount your $1,000 one-year note at 12 percent? Explain.
14. Explain how a notes payable register could be used as a book of original entry.
15. How are notes payable shown on the balance sheet?
16. Do you think notes payable are likely to occur in connection with the purchase of merchandise inventory? The purchase of equipment? The borrowing of money?
17. Under what circumstances would partial payment of a note payable be likely to occur?

18. Assume that you are an accountant who is auditing the financial records of a client that has notes payable outstanding. What aspects of the internal control of the notes payable do you think you might be primarily concerned about?

19. Explain why it is important that a record be kept of the due dates of all notes payable.

MANAGERIAL DISCUSSION QUESTIONS

1. Why might managers use outside sources of funds for their business operations? How do they acquire these funds?

2. Of what benefit to managers is the notes payable register?

3. Suppose that you work for a company that often discounts notes payable at the bank. The bank's current discount rate is 12 percent. A member of your company's board of directors suggests that the effective interest rate is more than 12 percent because the company does not have the use of the amount of money shown on the face of the note that is being discounted. Comment on this argument.

4. What would be the benefit of using the notes payable register as a book of original entry?

5. Why should management be familiar with the Uniform Commercial Code's provisions about notes?

EXERCISES

EXERCISE 20-1   **Determining the due dates of notes.** Find the due date of each of the following notes.

1. A note dated June 12, 19X1, due one year from date.
2. A note dated July 13, 19X2, due in 120 days.
3. A note dated January 31, 19X3, due three months from date.

EXERCISE 20-2   **Determining the maturity value of notes.** Compute the maturity value for each of the following notes.

1. A note payable with a face amount of $2,400, dated April 10, 19X1, due in 60 days, bearing interest at 12 percent.
2. A note payable with a face amount of $1,800, dated May 12, 19X1, due in three months, bearing interest at 14 percent.

EXERCISE 20-3   **Recording the issuance of notes payable.** Give the entries in general journal form to record the issuance of each of the notes described in Exercise 20-2.

EXERCISE 20-4   **Recording the payment of notes.** Give the entries in general journal form to record the issuance of a check in payment of each of the notes described in Exercise 20-2.

EXERCISE 20-5 **Recording the issuance of notes payable.** During 19X4, the Smithers Company borrowed money at the First National Bank on two occasions.

1. On June 3, the company borrowed $8,000, giving a 60-day, 12 percent note.
2. On August 12, the company discounted at 14 percent a $3,000, 90-day note payable.

Give the entries in general journal form to record the issuance of each of the above notes.

EXERCISE 20-6 **Recording the payment of notes.** Give the entries in general journal form to record the issuance of a check in payment of each of the notes described in Exercise 20-5.

EXERCISE 20-7 **Recording a note given for a purchase of equipment.** On December 1, 19X4, the Amos Company purchased a microcomputer (office equipment) for $4,200, signing a 90-day, 12 percent note for the entire purchase price. Give the entry in general journal form to record this transaction.

EXERCISE 20-8 **Recording the payment of a note.** Give the entry in general journal form to record the issuance of a check in payment of the note described in Exercise 20-7.

EXERCISE 20-9 **Determining the due dates and maturity value of notes.** Find the due date and the maturity value of each of the following notes.

1. A 60-day note for $12,000, bearing interest at 13 percent, dated September 19, 19X2.
2. A note with a face value of $825, bearing interest at 14 percent, dated August 31, 19X2, and due six months from date.

EXERCISE 20-10 **Recording the payment of notes.** Give the entries in general journal form to record the issuance of a check in payment of each of the notes described in Exercise 20-9.

PROBLEMS

PROBLEM 20-1 **Computing interest on notes payable.** The notes listed below were issued by several businesses. Find the interest due.

1. Compute the total interest on each of the following notes, using the interest formula method. Show all calculations.
   a. A $680 note at 14 percent for 90 days.
   b. A $1,856.80 note at 12 percent for six months.
   c. A $31,890 note at 13.5 percent for 75 days.
2. Compute the total interest on each of the following notes, using the 6 percent, 60-day method. Show all calculations.
   a. A $800 note at 9 percent for 90 days.
   b. A $2,908.50 note at 10 percent for 60 days.
   c. A $14,000 note at 12 percent for 45 days.

PROBLEM 20-2 **Computing the discount on notes payable.** Find the discount on the following noninterest-bearing notes. Show all calculations.

1. An $8,000 note, dated June 3, 19X2, discounted at 12.5 percent for 60 days.
2. A $4,500 note, dated Dec. 12, 19X2, discounted at 13 percent for 40 days.
3. A $32,600 note, dated Dec. 4, 19X2, discounted at 11.5 percent for 75 days.

PROBLEM 20-3 **Recording the discounting and payment of notes payable.** Make the following entries.

1. Give the entries in general journal form to record the discounting of each of the notes payable described in Problem 20-2.
2. Give entries in general journal form to record payment of each of the notes payable described in Problem 20-2.

PROBLEM 20-4 **Recording transactions involving notes payable.** Give the general journal entry to record each of the following transactions.

1. On September 3, 19X1, the Gray Company issued a 90-day, 14 percent note for $6,348.75 in connection with a purchase of factory equipment.
2. On November 18, 19X1, the Gray Company borrowed money from the Merchants State Bank by discounting its own $10,000 note payable. The bank charged a discount rate of 12.75 percent on this noninterest-bearing note. The note matures in three months.
3. The Gray Company paid the September 3 note when it became due.
4. The Gray Company paid the November 18 note when it became due.

PROBLEM 20-5 **Using a notes payable register and recording notes payable transactions.** Robert Santos operates a business that manufactures parts for computers. He makes large purchases of equipment in order to keep improving the efficiency of his operations and to stay competitive in a rapidly changing market. As a result of these equipment purchases, there are numerous transactions involving notes payable. Santos maintains a notes payable register to help him keep track of due dates and interest payments. Selected accounts used by the business are given on page 482. Transactions involving notes payable that took place during the month of July 19X1 follow.

Instructions

1. Enter the following notes in a notes payable register with columns as shown on pages 476 and 477 of the text. Compute and enter the maturity date and interest, if any, when recording each note. Use July 1, 19X1, as the date of the entries.
   a. A note issued to the Wilenski Equipment Company on May 24, 19X1, for $7,000, payable in two months without interest. (This note and all others in this problem are payable at the First State Bank.)
   b. A note issued to United Distributors on May 28, 19X1, for $9,000, due in 60 days with interest at 12 percent.
2. Analyze each of the July transactions, and make the necessary entry or entries. Use a general journal and a notes payable register. (Keep in mind that this firm uses the notes payable register as a memorandum record and not as a book of original entry.)

ACCOUNTS

101	Cash	201	Notes Payable—Trade
131	Factory Equipment	203	Notes Payable—Bank
133	Delivery Equipment	205	Accounts Payable
141	Land	591	Interest Expense

TRANSACTIONS FOR JULY 19X1

July   9 Purchased factory equipment from the Wilson Company and issued a note for $12,000 for three months with interest at 14 percent.

16 Purchased delivery equipment from the Lewis Auto Company; Invoice 888, dated July 16, 19X1. The initial payment of $4,000 was made by Check 701. A $4,000 note due in six months with interest at 14 percent was given to cover the balance of the purchase price.

18 Issued a 90-day, 12 percent note for $5,000 to Lake Realty in payment for land to be used by the company.

23 A 50-day note for $1,500, bearing interest at 9 percent, was given to the Delta Manufacturing Company for factory equipment that was previously purchased on credit.

24 Renewed a $7,000 note dated May 24 that is owed to the Wilenski Equipment Company and was due today. Gave a new note for 60 days with interest at 12 percent. (No journal entry is required. Make a notation in the notes payable register.)

26 Discounted an $8,000 note payable at the First State Bank. The bank deducted a 12 percent discount charge for the 120-day loan.

28 Paid half of the note due United Distributors today and all of the interest owed by Check 745. Issued a new note for $4,500 payable in 60 days with interest at 12 percent. (Make a notation of the cash payment and the renewal note opposite the original note in the Remarks column of the notes payable register. Then enter the new note in the register.)

ALTERNATE PROBLEMS

PROBLEM 20-1A   **Computing interest on notes payable.** The notes listed below were issued by several businesses. Find the interest due.

1. Compute the total interest on each of the following notes, using the interest formula method. Show all calculations.
   a. A $945 note at 13 percent for 120 days.
   b. A $1,346.70 note at 12 percent for four months.
   c. A $43,567 note at 12.5 percent for 80 days.

2. Compute the total interest on each of the following notes, using the 6 percent, 60-day method. Show all calculations.
   a. An $800 note at 12 percent for 120 days.
   b. A $1,348.20 note at 9 percent for 90 days.
   c. A $13,400 note at 8 percent for 45 days.

PROBLEM 20-2A **Computing the discount on notes payable.** Find the discount on the following noninterest-bearing notes. Show all calculations.

1. A $950 note, dated May 1, 19X1, discounted at 13.5 percent for 90 days.
2. A $1,050 note, dated Aug. 1, 19X1, discounted at 9.5 percent for 45 days.
3. An $845 note, dated Dec. 4, 19X1, discounted at 10.5 percent for 90 days. (19X2 was not a leap year.)

PROBLEM 20-3A **Recording the discounting and payment of notes payable.** Make the following entries.

1. Give the entries in general journal form to record the discounting of each of the notes payable described in Problem 20-2A.
2. Give the entries in general journal form to record payment on the due date of each of the notes payable described in Problem 20-2A.

PROBLEM 20-4A **Recording transactions involving notes payable.** Give the general journal entry to record each of the following transactions.

1. On May 5, 19X3, the Bates Company issued a 120-day, 15 percent note for $7,568.34 in connection with a purchase of an automobile.
2. On June 8, 19X3, the Bates Company discounted its own 90-day, noninterest-bearing note with a principal amount of $4,000 at the First National Bank. The bank charged a discount rate of 13 percent.
3. The Bates Company paid the May 5 note on its due date.
4. The Bates Company paid the note discounted on June 8 on its due date.

PROBLEM 20-5A **Using a notes payable register and recording notes payable transactions.** Quick Clean is a chain of dry-cleaning stores owned and operated by Susan McConnell and Paul Rossi. The owners have decided to start a program of modernization and expansion to increase efficiency, reduce operating costs, and increase sales. Since the funds for this program will come partly from their own cash reserves but mostly from notes payable, the partners have decided to set up a notes payable register. This memorandum record will help them maintain control over the due dates and interest payments. Selected accounts used by the business are given on page 484. Transactions involving notes payable that took place during the month of December 19X1 follow.

Instructions 1. Enter the following notes in a notes payable register with columns as shown on pages 476 and 477 of the text. Compute and enter the maturity date and interest, if any, when recording each note. Use December 1, 19X1, as the date of the entries.
   a. A note issued to the Warner Equipment Company on November 1, 19X1, for $5,000, due in 45 days without interest. (This note and all others in this problem are payable at the First National Bank.)
   b. A note issued to the Warner Equipment Company on November 1, 19X1, for $10,000, due in 60 days with interest at 9 percent.
2. Analyze each of the December transactions and make the necessary entry or entries. Use a general journal and a notes payable register. (Keep in mind that

this firm uses the notes payable register as a memorandum record and not as a book of original entry.)

ACCOUNTS

101	Cash	201	Notes Payable—Trade
131	Cleaning Equipment	203	Notes Payable—Bank
133	Delivery Equipment	205	Accounts Payable
141	Land	591	Interest Expense

TRANSACTIONS FOR DECEMBER 19X1

Dec. 1 Purchased additional cleaning equipment from the Warner Equipment Company and issued a note for $8,000 for 90 days with interest at 9 percent.

8 Purchased a used delivery truck from the Lang Truck Sales Company, Invoice 857, dated December 8, 19X1. The initial payment of $3,000 was made by Check 316 on this date. A $3,000 note due in six months with interest at 12 percent was given to cover the balance of the purchase price.

10 Issued a 60-day, 13 percent note for $4,500 to Davis Realty Inc. in payment for land to be used as a parking area for one of the dry-cleaning stores.

11 Issued a 30-day note for $1,250 with interest at 12 percent to the Cleaners Supply Company in order to obtain an extension of credit on an overdue account payable.

16 Renewed the $5,000 note dated November 1, which was due today. Gave to the Warner Equipment Company a new note for 30 days with interest at 9 percent. (No journal entry is required. Make a notation in the notes payable register.)

18 Borrowed $5,000 from the First National Bank on a 120-day note with interest at 14 percent. The note was discounted at the bank.

20 Purchased two dry-cleaning machines from the Apex Cleaning Equipment Company and issued a $10,000 90-day note with interest at 9 percent.

30 Borrowed $5,000 from the First National Bank for 60 days with interest at 14 percent payable at maturity.

31 Paid half of the note due the Warner Equipment Company today and the interest, by Check 331. Issued a new note for $5,000 payable in 45 days with interest at 9 percent. (Make a notation of the cash payment and the renewal note opposite the original note in the Remarks column of the notes payable register. Then enter the new note in the register.)

CHAPTER 21

Some firms accept promissory notes from customers. For example, a customer may be allowed to use a promissory note to finance a purchase of goods. A note that a firm obtains with a customer's written promise to pay in the future is called a note receivable.

NOTES RECEIVABLE AND DRAFTS

NOTES RECEIVABLE

A note receivable is usually interest-bearing. However, it can be noninterest-bearing if the parties involved prefer it that way. The methods used to determine maturity dates and interest due on notes receivable are the same as those used for notes payable, which were explained in the previous chapter. Of course, the entries needed to record notes receivable in a firm's accounting records are different from those used to record notes payable.

A firm may accept a note receivable from a customer at the time of a sale or when extending credit on a past-due account. The procedures for handling notes receivable can be understood from the following typical example.

NONINTEREST-BEARING NOTE RECEIVED

Suppose that John Dow has an overdue balance of $300 in his account with the Style Clothing Store. On April 8, 19X2, Dow offers to give the firm a 30-day, noninterest-bearing note to obtain an extension of time in which to pay. The Style Clothing Store agrees to this arrangement because the note provides stronger evidence of the debt in case legal action becomes necessary.

Receipt of the Note

The Style Clothing Store records the receipt of Dow's note in the general journal, as shown below. Notice that a new asset account called Notes Receivable is debited for $300, and Accounts Receivable/John Dow is credited for $300. The credit part of the entry is recorded as Accounts Receivable/John Dow because it must be posted in two places.

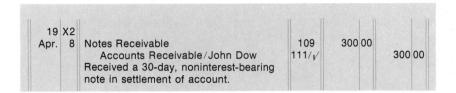

19 X2				
Apr. 8	Notes Receivable	109	300 00	
	Accounts Receivable/John Dow	111/✓		300 00
	Received a 30-day, noninterest-bearing			
	note in settlement of account.			

1. The Accounts Receivable control account must be credited in the general ledger.
2. The account with John Dow must be credited in the accounts receivable subsidiary ledger.

As a result of this *double-posting procedure,* the total of the balances in the subsidiary ledger will remain equal to the balance of the Accounts Receivable control account in the general ledger.

Maturity Date

Dow's note, which was issued on April 8, matures on May 8. The maturity date is computed as follows.

Days the note will run in April: $30 - 8 = 22$	22 days
Days to maturity in May: $30 - 22 = 8$	8 days
Total period of the note	30 days

Collection of the Note

When Dow pays the note at maturity, an entry will be made in the cash receipts journal. This entry will consist of a debit to Cash and a credit to Notes Receivable. Dow's note will then be marked "Paid" and returned to him.

INTEREST-BEARING NOTE RECEIVED

Most firms are willing to meet customers more than halfway to make sales and to retain goodwill. However, a customer who does not settle a bill within the credit period originally agreed upon can usually expect to pay interest on the amount owed in order to receive an extension of credit. Thus promissory notes issued under such conditions are normally interest-bearing. Assume that the Style Clothing Store agrees to accept a 60-day, 8 percent note for $400 from Alice Morgan to cover her past-due account. The note is dated April 14, 19X2.

Receipt of the Note

When the firm receives the note, an entry is made in the general journal. This entry involves a debit to Notes Receivable for $400 and a credit to Accounts Receivable/Alice Morgan for $400.

Maturity Date

The maturity date of Morgan's note is June 13. This date is determined as shown below.

Days the note will run in April: $30 - 14 = 16$	16 days
Days the note will run in May	31 days
Total days to the end of May	47 days
Days in June to maturity: $60 - 47 = 13$	13 days
Total period of the note	60 days

Calculation of Interest

The interest on $400 for 60 days at 8 percent is computed by using the standard interest formula.

$$\text{Interest} = \$400 \times 0.08 \times \frac{60}{360}$$

$$\text{Interest} = \$5.33$$

Collection of the Note

Morgan's payment of the note on the maturity date will include the $400 face amount of the note plus $5.33 interest. Thus the maturity value of the note is $405.33. The Style Clothing Store records the collection of the note by debiting Cash for the total amount, crediting Notes Receivable for $400, and crediting Interest Income for $5.33, as illustrated below in general journal form.

19 X2					
June 13	Cash	101	405 33		
	Notes Receivable	109		400 00	
	Interest Income	491		5 33	
	Collection of Alice Morgan's note.				

PARTIAL COLLECTION OF A NOTE

Suppose that Alice Morgan offers to pay half her note if the Style Clothing Store will renew the balance for an additional 30 days at 8 percent interest. Ordinarily, any payment made on a note is applied first to the interest due. The remaining amount is then applied to the principal owed. In this case, Morgan is paying the interest to maturity of the original note, $5.33, plus half the principal of the note, $200, for a total of $205.33. The entry to record the transaction consists of a debit to Cash for the total, a credit to Notes Receivable for $200, and a credit to Interest Income for $5.33, as shown below in general journal form.

19 X2					
June 13	Cash	101	205 33		
	Notes Receivable	109		200 00	
	Interest Income	491		5 33	
	Collection of part of Alice Morgan's note.				

The original note may be endorsed or receipted in part by the Style Clothing Store to reflect the partial payment. Or the firm may cancel the first note and obtain a new note for the remaining balance from Alice Morgan.

NOTE NOT COLLECTED AT MATURITY

If a note is not paid at maturity, the note is said to be *dishonored*. It is not proper to carry the amount of a dishonored note in the Notes Receivable account. Suppose that Alice Morgan dishonors the note that she issued to the Style Clothing Store. The firm must transfer the balance that she owes so that it is again a part of accounts receivable. This is done by making the general journal entry shown on page 488. Notice that both the Accounts Receivable control account in the general ledger and Morgan's account in the accounts receivable ledger must be debited. Since Morgan now owes the original balance of $400 plus $5.33 interest on the note, each of these accounts is debited for $405.33. The offsetting credits are to Notes Receivable for the face amount of the note ($400) and to Interest Income for the interest ($5.33).

	19 X2					
June	13	Accounts Receivable/Alice Morgan	111/✓	405 33		
		Notes Receivable	109		400 00	
		Interest Income	491		5 33	
		To charge back Alice Morgan's				
		dishonored note plus interest due				
		on it to maturity.				

After an interest-bearing note is dishonored, interest continues to run on the note. The interest charged is at a rate specified by law, which in most cases is higher than the original rate shown on the note. However, the parties may agree on a rate different from the statutory rate. A note usually calls for payment by the maker of all attorney's fees and other costs incurred by the holder that result from nonpayment of the note when due.

NOTES RECEIVED AT THE TIME OF SALE

The notes from Dow and Morgan were obtained when past-due accounts were extended. The Style Clothing Store does not engage in a type of business in which notes are ordinarily received at the time of sale. If the firm receives an occasional note when a sale is made, the transaction is recorded in the general journal as follows.

	19 X2				
June	5	Notes Receivable	109	250 00	
		Sales	401		250 00
		Received 90-day, 12% note from			
		Donald Springer on sale of			
		merchandise.			

If it is common for a business to receive notes from customers at the time of sale, the accountant will provide a special column in the sales journal for debiting Notes Receivable. In this way the total of the notes can be posted to the general ledger in one amount at the end of each month.

DISCOUNTING A NOTE RECEIVABLE

One of the advantages of a note receivable over an open account is that the holder of the note can borrow on it by discounting it at a bank. The bank accepts the note and charges interest on its maturity value at a specified rate for the number of days remaining until maturity. The bank deducts this *discount charge* in advance, and the seller receives the *net proceeds* (the maturity value less the discount charge). The bank usually credits the net proceeds to the firm's checking account.

NONINTEREST-BEARING NOTE DISCOUNTED

Suppose that the Style Clothing Store has to raise cash to meet an obligation at the end of April. The owners decide to discount a 60-day noninterest-bearing note receivable for $500 that the firm obtained from Peter Ross on April 3. The note is payable on June 2. The Style Clothing Store turns the note over to the City National Bank for discounting on April 18. The bank's discount rate is 12 percent. This transaction must be examined carefully because of new elements involved.

Review of the Record Prior to Discounting

The Style Clothing Store received the note on April 3. The amount of the note ($500) was debited to the asset account Notes Receivable in a general journal entry. The accountant then determined the maturity date, which is June 2.

Calculating the Discount and the Proceeds

The method used to determine the discount and the proceeds on the note receivable is similar to that described for a discounted note payable. The steps are as follows.

1. Determine the maturity value of the note. Since the note from Peter Ross is noninterest-bearing, its maturity value is the same as its face amount—$500.

2. Determine the number of days in the discount period (the number of days from the discount date to the maturity date).

Days the note will run in April: 30 − 18 = 12	12 days
Days the note will run in May	31 days
Days the note will run in June to maturity	2 days
Total discount period	45 days

3. Determine the amount of discount to be charged by the bank. This is found by applying the regular interest formula (Interest = Principal × Rate × Time) as shown below. Notice that the time used is the discount period of 45 days.

Discount = Maturity Value × Discount Rate × Discount Period

$$\text{Discount} = \$500 \times 0.12 \times \frac{45}{360}$$

Discount = $7.50

4. Determine the proceeds—the amount to be received from the bank. This amount is the maturity value of the note less the amount of the discount: $500 − $7.50 = $492.50.

Recording the Discounting of the Note

When the computations are completed, the Style Clothing Store records the discounting of the note. The effect of this entry is illustrated below in general journal form.

19 X2						
Apr. 18	Cash		101	492 50		
	Interest Expense		591	7 50		
	Notes Receivable Discounted		110		500 00	
	Discounted Peter Ross's note.					

Notice that two debits are involved—one to Cash for the proceeds ($492.50) and one to Interest Expense for the amount of the discount ($7.50). Also notice that the principal of the note ($500) is credited to a new account called Notes Receivable Discounted rather than to the Notes Receivable account. This credit entry in Notes Receivable Discounted offsets the amount carried as an asset in the Notes Receivable account.

NOTES RECEIVABLE DISCOUNTED—A CONTINGENT LIABILITY

When a note receivable is discounted, it must be endorsed. If the maker of the note does not pay it at maturity, the holder (the bank) can then obtain payment from the endorser. Hence the endorser (in this case, the Style Clothing Store) has a possible, or *contingent,* liability. This fact was recorded in the firm's accounting records by crediting Notes Receivable Discounted. On the balance sheet, the balance of Notes Receivable Discounted is deducted from the balance of Notes Receivable. The difference represents the notes receivable still held, which amount to $750 for the Style Clothing Store.

Notes Receivable	$1,250	
Less Notes Receivable Discounted	500	$750

A more commonly used procedure is to show only the net undiscounted notes on the balance sheet and to include a footnote to the financial statements indicating the amount of discounted notes receivable on which the company has a contingent liability.

DISCOUNTED NONINTEREST-BEARING NOTE PAID AT MATURITY

At the maturity date, the holder of the discounted note presents it to the maker for payment. If Peter Ross pays the note when the bank presents it to him, the Style Clothing Store has no further contingent liability. At that time the firm makes the following general journal entry to remove the liability.

19 X2						
June	2	Notes Receivable Discounted	110	500 00		
		Notes Receivable	109		500 00	
		To close out the asset and the contingent liability upon payment by Peter Ross of his note, which we had discounted at the bank.				

DISCOUNTED NONINTEREST-BEARING NOTE DISHONORED AT MATURITY

If Ross dishonors his note by failing to pay it at maturity, the bank may file a formal protest through a notary public. The Style Clothing Store then has to pay the bank the maturity value of the note plus the protest fee charged by the notary public. (Banks often deduct this amount from the firm's checking account and send a debit memorandum with the dishonored note and the protest form.) Assuming that the protest fee is $10 in this case, the resulting entry is a debit to Accounts Receivable/Peter Ross for $510 and a credit to Cash for $510. Notice that the total of the maturity value and the protest fee ($510)—not merely the amount due on the dishonored note—is charged to the Accounts Receivable control account in the general ledger and the customer's account in the subsidiary ledger.

One more entry is required to complete the record of this transaction. By paying the dishonored note, the Style Clothing Store has removed the contingent liability that was set up when the note was discounted. To eliminate the liability from the firm's accounting records, an entry must be made in the general journal debiting Notes Receivable Discounted and crediting Notes Receivable.

After paying the dishonored note, the Style Clothing Store would probably contact the maker of the note and then turn the note over to an attorney for collection if payment is not received at once.

INTEREST-BEARING NOTE DISCOUNTED

The owners of the Style Clothing Store now decide to increase the firm's available cash by discounting a note received from Lois Norman on April 17. The principal is $600, the note runs for 60 days, and the interest rate is 10 percent. The maturity date of the note is June 16.

Review of the Record Prior to Discounting

On April 17 when the Style Clothing Store obtained the note, the Notes Receivable account was debited and Accounts Receivable/Lois Norman was credited.

Calculating the Discount

On May 2 the Style Clothing Store arranges to discount Norman's note at the bank at 12 percent. The discount and the proceeds on the note are computed as shown below.

1. Determine the maturity value of the note. Since this is an interest-bearing note, its maturity value is found by adding the face amount ($600) and the interest for 60 days at 10 percent ($10). Thus the maturity value of the note is $610.
2. Determine the number of days in the discount period. By counting the days from the discount date to the maturity date, the accountant finds that the discount period is 45 days.

Days the note will run in May: 31 − 2 = 29	29 days
Days the note will run in June to maturity	16 days
Total discount period	45 days

3. Determine the amount of the discount. The bank will levy its charge of 12 percent on the maturity value ($610) for the discount period (45 days). Putting these figures into the interest formula Discount = Maturity Value × Discount Rate × Discount Period, the accountant finds the discount as follows.

$$\text{Discount} = \$610 \times 0.12 \times \frac{45}{360}$$

$$\text{Discount} = \$9.15$$

4. Determine the proceeds. The amount to be received from the bank is $600.85, the maturity value minus the discount charge ($610 − $9.15).

The discounting of the note receivable is recorded at the Style Clothing Store as shown below in general journal form. This time the entry consists of a debit to Cash and two credits—one to Notes Receivable Discounted and the other to Interest Income.

19 X2				
May 2	Cash	101	600 85	
	Notes Receivable Discounted	110		600 00
	Interest Income	491		85
	Discounted Lois Norman's note.			

The credit to Interest Income of $0.85 represents the $10 total interest determined in computing the maturity value, less the discount of $9.15 charged by the bank. If the proceeds had been less than the face amount of the note, the difference would have been debited to Interest Expense.

DISCOUNTED INTEREST-BEARING NOTE PAID AT MATURITY

If Lois Norman pays the note at the maturity date, the Style Clothing Store cancels the contingent liability that was set up at the time the note was discounted. It debits $600 to Notes Receivable Discounted and credits the same amount to Notes Receivable.

DISCOUNTED INTEREST-BEARING NOTE DISHONORED AT MATURITY

If Lois Norman dishonors the note at the maturity date, the Style Clothing Store must pay the maturity value (the face amount of the note plus the interest) and any protest fee to the bank. The firm charges the entire sum to the Accounts Receivable control account in the general ledger and Norman's account in the subsidiary ledger. An entry is also made to remove the contingent liability by debiting Notes Receivable Discounted and crediting Notes Receivable for the face amount of the note.

NOTES RECEIVABLE REGISTER

If a firm has many notes receivable, it may be convenient to set up a *notes receivable register*. This record has somewhat the same form as the notes payable register discussed in the previous chapter. Information recorded in the notes

NOTES RECEIVABLE REGISTER

DATE OF ENTRY	MAKER	WHERE PAYABLE	DATE OF NOTE	TIME TO RUN	YEAR	J	F	M	A	M	J	J	A	S	O	N	D
									MATURITY DATE								
19 X2			19 X2														
Apr. 3	Peter Ross	City National Bank	Apr. 3	60 days	19X2						2						
8	John Dow	First National Bank	8	30 days	19X2					8							
14	Alice Morgan	State Trust Co.	14	60 days	19X2						13						
17	Lois Norman	City National Bank	17	60 days	19X2						16						

receivable register includes the date of the note, the maker, where the note is payable, the time it is to run, the maturity date, the face amount, and the rate and amount of interest, if any. Columns are also provided to record the dates on which notes have been discounted and the banks that are holding the notes. The four notes received by the Style Clothing Store during the month of April (used in the previous examples) are shown in the notes receivable register illustrated below.

NOTES RECEIVABLE AND INTEREST INCOME ON THE STATEMENTS

The Notes Receivable account is a current asset and appears on the balance sheet, usually just below the accounts for cash items. Interest Income is shown on the income statement as other (nonoperating) income. It is listed below Net Income From Operations and added to it. The expense that arises from bank charges on discounted notes is shown in the Interest Expense account. This account also appears below the Net Income From Operations but is deducted. The final sections of an income statement for a firm that has received and paid interest might look like this.

Net Income From Operations	$12,500
Other Income	
Interest Income	125
Total Income	$12,625
Other Expense	
Interest Expense	200
Net Income	$12,425

DRAFTS

A *draft* is a written order that requires the person or business firm addressed to pay a stated sum of money to another person or firm or to the bearer. An ordinary check is one form of draft. Two others are bank drafts and commercial drafts.

Bank Drafts

A *bank draft* is a check written by a bank that orders another bank—one in which it has funds on deposit—to pay the indicated amount to a specified person or business firm. Since a bank draft is more readily accepted than an individual's check, a person may use a bank draft to pay a debt to an out-of-town supplier with whom credit has not been established.

Page 1

FACE AMOUNT OF NOTE	INTEREST		DISCOUNTED		DATE PAID	REMARKS
	RATE	AMOUNT	BANK	DATE		
500 00	None		City National Bank	Apr. 18		
300 00	None				May 8	
400 00	8%	5 33			June 13	
600 00	10%	10 00	City National Bank	May 2		

Another type of draft is called a *cashier's check*. This form of draft is prepared by a bank official. It orders the bank to pay the specified amount from its own funds. Like a bank draft, a cashier's check offers greater protection to a creditor than an individual's check. For this reason, cashier's checks are sometimes used to pay bills.

The purchase of a bank draft or cashier's check is recorded by debiting the account payable that the draft is intended to settle, debiting an expense account for the bank service charge, and crediting Cash. The business issues one of its own checks to the bank to cover the amount of the draft or cashier's check and the amount of the service charge.

For example, suppose that a bill for $525 is to be settled by sending the creditor a bank draft instead of a regular check. The bank imposes a service charge of $1 for the draft. The effect of the entry required for the payment (Check 479) is shown here in general journal form.

19 X2				
May 15	Accounts Payable/Dale Company	205/✓	525 00	
	Collection and Exchange Expense	559	1 00	
	Cash	101		526 00

Commercial Drafts

A *commercial draft* is issued by a person or business firm to order another person or firm to pay a specified sum of money at once or at a determinable later date. This instrument is used to take care of special shipment and collection problems.

A *sight draft* is a commercial draft that is payable on presentation. It is honored by payment. No accounting entry (other than a memorandum notation) is made for the issuance of a sight draft. If the draft is honored, the transaction is recorded as a cash receipt.

Sight drafts may be used for collecting accounts receivable, especially past-due accounts. A draft is usually sent for collection to the customer's bank. If the customer does not honor the draft, his credit standing at the bank may be injured. Thus a debtor is more likely to honor a draft than a collection letter.

It is also possible to ship goods with a sight draft in order to obtain cash on delivery. In this situation, a business paper called a *bill of lading* is sent to a bank near the customer. A sight draft is attached to the bill of lading. The customer must pay the draft to the bank before getting the bill of lading, which is needed to obtain the goods. The collecting bank sends the money, less its collection fee, to the firm that issued the draft. When the funds arrive, the firm records the transaction as a cash sale and debits an expense account for the collection fee. Transmitting a sight draft with a bill of lading is a common practice when shipments are made to customers with poor credit ratings or to new customers who have not yet established credit.

A *time draft* differs from a sight draft in that a period of time is allowed for payment. The maturity date of a time draft may be stated in several different ways.

1. It may be a date specified in the draft.

2. It may be a specified number of days after the date of the draft.
3. It may be a specified number of days after acceptance of the draft.

A time draft requires no accounting entry (other than a memorandum notation) when it is issued. If the person upon whom the instrument is drawn agrees to honor it at maturity, he indicates his agreement by writing "accepted" on the face of the draft, signing it, and dating it. He then records the accepted draft in his accounting records as a note payable and returns it to the drawer, who enters it in his accounting records as a note receivable.

TRADE ACCEPTANCES

A *trade acceptance* is a special form of commercial time draft that arises out of the sale of goods and has this fact noted on its face. The original transaction may be recorded in the same manner as a sale on credit. When the draft has been accepted, it is accounted for as a promissory note. Merchants have found that they have fewer credit losses on trade acceptances than on open-account transactions. Trade acceptances can also be discounted. An example of a trade acceptance is shown below.

INTERNAL CONTROL OF NOTES RECEIVABLE

Drafts are essentially checks and must be handled just as carefully, and since notes receivable are negotiable, they have many of the same characteristics as checks. Thus, the internal control procedures that are devised for these instruments must treat them as almost equivalent to cash items. Authority to accept notes must be delegated to specific persons. All notes received must be entered promptly in the notes receivable register and stored securely in a safe or fireproof vault to which access is carefully controlled. In addition, the actual notes on hand must be verified periodically and compared with the amounts shown in the notes receivable register.

Just prior to a note's maturity, its maker should be informed of the approaching due date and the amount owed. If payment is not received on the due date, the maker should be contacted immediately by a responsible person to find out what is happening. Management should review all past-due notes promptly and take necessary steps, including legal action if appropriate.

PRINCIPLES AND PROCEDURES SUMMARY

Notes receivable, like notes payable, may be interest-bearing or noninterest-bearing. Some firms obtain notes receivable when they extend past-due accounts since the notes give more legal protection than open accounts. When a firm receives a note in this situation, it debits Notes Receivable and credits the Accounts Receivable control account and the individual customer's account. When the note is paid, the firm debits Cash and credits Notes Receivable. If the note is interest-bearing, the interest received is credited to the Interest Income account. If the note is dishonored (not paid at maturity), the amount becomes an account receivable again. The face value of the note plus the interest is debited to the Accounts Receivable control account and the customer's account. Notes Receivable and Interest Income are credited.

It is a common practice in certain types of businesses to accept notes at the time sales are made. If a firm has many such transactions, it would probably set up a special column in its sales journal for debits to Notes Receivable.

A note receivable may be discounted at a bank prior to maturity. In this case, the bank will deduct interest at its discount rate for the time remaining to maturity. The firm discounting the note will debit Cash for the proceeds. Since the note becomes a contingent liability, the amount will be credited to Notes Receivable Discounted. The interest is recorded as a debit to Interest Expense or as a credit to Interest Income, according to the circumstances.

Bank drafts, commercial drafts, and trade acceptances are other types of negotiable instruments sometimes used in business.

MANAGERIAL IMPLICATIONS

Managers should be aware of the possibilities of using negotiable instruments in connection with sales on credit. These instruments are especially useful when cash is short. Notes due some time in the future can be discounted to raise funds for current operations. In some cases, past-due accounts can be converted into notes receivable. The notes give more legal protection to the creditor and are more likely to be collected. Because notes and drafts are negotiable, internal control procedures must be developed to safeguard them.

REVIEW QUESTIONS

1. How does a note receivable differ from an account receivable?
2. What general ledger and subsidiary ledger accounts must be debited and credited when a note receivable is accepted from a customer in settlement of an account receivable?
3. How, if at all, does computation of the maturity value of a note receivable differ from that for a note payable?
4. Explain how partial collection of a note receivable is accounted for.
5. What is a dishonored note?
6. What is meant by discounting a note receivable?

7. Explain how to compute the proceeds from discounting a note receivable.
8. Why is a discounted note receivable considered to be a contingent liability?
9. How are discounted notes receivable shown in the financial statements?
10. What is a protest fee?
11. Explain how to account for a discounted note receivable that is dishonored by the maker.
12. What is a draft?
13. Explain a cashier's check.
14. What is a commercial draft?
15. Explain a sight draft.
16. How does a time draft differ from a sight draft?
17. What is a trade acceptance?
18. When a bank discounts a client's note receivable, why is the discount based on the maturity value of the note?
19. Why is the difference between the face amount of a note receivable and the amount received from discounting the note recorded as interest income or expense? Can you think of another way to record the interest income and/or expense?
20. How might a sight draft be used in carrying on a business? Why is a sight draft used?
21. How are trade acceptances used?

MANAGERIAL DISCUSSION QUESTIONS

1. As a manager, would you consider a note received at the time of sale of merchandise to be as collectible as a note received in exchange for a further extension of credit? Explain.
2. As a manager, why would you insist that dishonored notes receivable be charged back to the Accounts Receivable control account?
3. How can notes receivable be used by management as a means of acquiring cash?
4. How do negotiable instruments help firms sell goods on credit and obtain important legal safeguards?
5. Why would management insist that a record be kept of all dishonored notes?
6. Assume that you are a member of the internal audit staff at the Wagner Corporation. A review of office practices that you were asked to make indicates that notes receivable are kept in an unlocked file cabinet in the treasurer's office. If you were writing a memorandum to management, how would you evaluate this procedure? Would you recommend any changes? If so, what changes?

EXERCISES

EXERCISE 21-1   **Recording the receipt of a note for a past-due account.** On January 12, 19X1, the Aaron Merchandising Company received a 90-day note receivable for $1,200 from John Duncan, a customer whose account was past due. The note bears interest at 14 percent. Give the entry in general journal form that Aaron would make to record receipt of the note.

EXERCISE 21-2   **Recording the discounting of a note receivable.** On February 2, 19X1, the Aaron Merchandising Company discounted the Duncan note described in Exercise 21-1 at the Second State Bank. The bank charged a discount rate of 15 percent. Give the entry in general journal form to record this transaction in Aaron's accounting records.

EXERCISE 21-3   **Recording the payment of a discounted note by the maker.** Assume that Duncan paid the note described in Exercises 21-1 and 21-2 when it became due and that the Second State Bank notified the Aaron Merchandising Company of the payment. Give the entry required (if any) by Aaron.

EXERCISE 21-4   **Recording the dishonoring of a discounted note by the maker.** Assume that Duncan dishonored the note described in Exercises 21-1 and 21-2 when it became due. At the due date the Second State Bank charged the account of the Aaron Merchandising Company for the maturity value of Duncan's note, plus a protest fee of $12.50. Give the entry in general journal form that Aaron would make to record the dishonoring of the note.

EXERCISE 21-5   **Payment of a previously dishonored note by the maker.** Assume that ten days after dishonoring his note, as described in Exercise 21-4, Duncan paid the Aaron Merchandising Company all amounts due. The sum received by Aaron included interest at 14 percent (on the maturity value and the protest fee) from the due date of the note until the payment date. Give the entry in general journal form that Aaron would make to record this transaction.

EXERCISE 21-6   **Computing the maturity value of notes receivable.** Find the maturity value of each of the following notes receivable.

1. A 90-day note, dated February 10, 19X1, with a face value of $10,200, bearing interest at 12 percent.
2. A three-month note, dated January 18, 19X1, with a face value of $820, bearing interest at 13 percent.

EXERCISE 21-7   **Computing the proceeds from a discounted note receivable.** Assume that the 90-day note described in Part 1 of Exercise 21-6 was discounted at a bank on March 1, 19X1. The bank charged a discount rate of 13 percent. Compute the net proceeds.

EXERCISE 21-8   **Recording the discounting of a note receivable.** Give the entry in general journal form to be made by the firm that discounted the note described in Exercise 21-7.

EXERCISE 21-9   **Computing the proceeds from a discounted note receivable.** Assume that the three-month note described in Part 2 of Exercise 21-6 was discounted at a bank on April 1, 19X1. The bank charged a discount rate of 12 percent. Compute the net proceeds.

EXERCISE 21-10   **Recording the discounting of a note receivable.** Give the entry in general journal form to be made by the firm that discounted the note described in Exercise 21-9.

PROBLEMS

PROBLEM 21-1   **Computing interest and maturity value.** The notes received by the Chang Sales Company during 19X1 are summarized below. Find the total interest and the maturity value of each note. Show all computations.

CHANG SALES COMPANY
Summary of Notes Received

Date	Face Amount	Period	Interest Rate
Jan. 22	$ 700	3 months	9%
Mar. 5	3,400	60 days	10.5%
July 8	1,000	45 days	8%
Sept. 15	2,400	3 months	12%

PROBLEM 21-2   **Computing and recording the discount on notes receivable.** On February 1, 19X1, the Chang Sales Company discounted the January 22 note described in Problem 21-1 at the First National Bank. The bank's discount charge was 12 percent. On October 1, 19X1, the firm discounted the September 15 note at a rate of 13 percent. (February had 28 days in 19X1.)

Instructions   1. For each of the two notes, find the discount charged by the bank. Show all computations.
2. Give the entries in general journal form to record the discounting of the two notes.

PROBLEM 21-3   **Computing the proceeds from discounted notes receivable.** The notes receivable held by the Williams Company on January 1, 19X2, are summarized below. On January 2, 19X2, Williams discounted all of these notes at the Third National Bank at a discount rate of 12.5 percent. Find the net proceeds that the firm received from discounting each note. (19X2 was not a leap year.)

Note No.	Date	Face Amount	Period	Interest Rate
64	July 1, 19X1	$6,000	1 year	14%
69	Sept. 4, 19X1	$1,800	6 months	12%
80	Dec. 1, 19X1	$1,340	60 days	13%

PROBLEM 21-4 **Recording the receipt, discounting, and payment of notes receivable.** On October 14, 19X1, the Lombardi X-Ray Company received a 90-day, 10 percent interest-bearing note from the Bayside Medical Group in settlement of Bayside's past-due account of $2,250. On November 5 Lombardi discounted this note at the First State Bank. The bank charged a discount rate of 14 percent. On January 15 Lombardi received notice from the bank that Bayside had paid the note and the interest.

Instructions 1. Give the entries in general journal form that Lombardi would make to record all the transactions involving the note from Bayside.
  2. Assume that when the note became due, Bayside failed to pay it. The bank notified Lombardi on January 15 and charged Lombardi's account for the maturity value of the note plus a $7.50 protest fee. Give the entries in general journal form that Lombardi would make to record the default by the maker of the note.

PROBLEM 21-5 **Using a notes receivable register and recording notes receivable transactions.** Because the King Lumber Company deals with many small builders and remodelers that are in a weak financial position, it often acquires notes receivable as a safety measure. King uses a notes receivable register as a memorandum record to maintain control over the numerous notes it handles. The notes outstanding on March 31, 19X1, are as follows. All the notes are payable at the Republic National Bank unless otherwise specified.

- A $2,400, 12 percent, 6-month note from David Adams, dated January 10.
- A $2,000, 10 percent, 90-day note from Alice McVay, dated January 15. (This note was discounted at the Republic National Bank on February 1, 19X1.)
- A $3,000, 8 percent, 90-day note from the Bell Construction Company, dated January 18. (This note was also discounted at the Republic National Bank on February 1, 19X1.)
- A $1,350, noninterest-bearing, 60-day note from Carl Swanson, dated February 7, payable at the Madison Bank.
- A $2,200, 12 percent, 45-day note from Devon Contractors, dated February 25.
- A $4,800, 7 percent, 120-day note from Ryan Home Builders, dated March 20, payable at the Commercial Bank.

The notes receivable transactions listed on page 501 took place during April 19X1.

Instructions 1. Enter the notes outstanding on March 31, 19X1, in a notes receivable register like the one shown on pages 492 and 493 of this chapter.
  2. Using a general journal, record the notes receivable transactions for April. The required accounts are listed below.
  3. Enter data in the notes receivable register where appropriate.

ACCOUNTS

101	Cash	111	Accounts Receivable
109	Notes Receivable	491	Interest Income
110	Notes Receivable Discounted	591	Interest Expense

TRANSACTIONS FOR APRIL 19X1

Apr. 2 Accepted a 60-day noninterest-bearing note for $1,800, dated today, from Warren Builders, as an extension of credit on its overdue account receivable.

5 Discounted the 6-month note from David Adams for $2,400 at the Commercial Bank. The note is dated January 10. The discount rate set by the bank is 14 percent.

8 Carl Swanson's 60-day note, dated February 7, 19X1, was due today. He gave a check for $650 and a new note for $700 due in 90 days with interest at 12 percent. (Record the amount received in the general journal. Make appropriate comments in the Remarks section of the notes receivable register opposite the entry for the original note, and record the new note on the next open line.)

11 Devon Contractors dishonored its note for $2,200, dated February 25, 19X1, which was due today with interest at 12 percent.

15 Received notice that Alice McVay's 90-day, $2,000 note, dated January 15, 19X1, was dishonored today. This note was discounted at the Republic National Bank on February 1, 19X1. The bank charged the checking account of the King Lumber Company for the maturity value of the note plus a protest fee ($5). (Record the charge-back by the bank in the general journal. Also record in the general journal the termination of the contingent liability for the discounted note.)

16 Accepted a 90-day, 10 percent note for $2,600 from James Miller as an extension of credit on his past-due account receivable.

18 Received notice from the bank that the Bell Construction Company paid its note of January 18, 19X1, which was discounted.

19 Discounted the $4,800 note from Ryan Home Builders, dated March 20, 19X1, at the First National Bank. The discount rate was 13 percent.

ALTERNATE PROBLEMS

PROBLEM 21-1A **Computing interest and maturity value.** The notes received by the O'Leary Manufacturing Company during 19X2 are summarized below. Find the total interest and the maturity value of each note. Show all computations.

O'LEARY MANUFACTURING COMPANY
Summary of Notes Received

Date	Face Amount	Period	Interest Rate
Jan. 18	$2,000	90 days	12%
Jan. 30	1,000	1 month	10%
May 18	1,300	90 days	13%
July 10	825	4 months	10.5%
Oct. 16	425	45 days	9.75%

PROBLEM 21-2A   **Computing and recording the discount on notes receivable.** On June 7, 19X2, the O'Leary Manufacturing Company discounted the May 18 note described in Problem 21-1A at the University State Bank. The bank's discount charge was 12 percent. On August 9, 19X2, the firm discounted the July 10 note at a rate of 13 percent.

Instructions   1. For each of the two notes, find the discount charged by the bank. Show all computations.
2. Give the entries in general journal form to record the discounting of the two notes.

PROBLEM 21-3A   **Computing the proceeds from discounted notes receivable.** The notes receivable held by the Rodriquez Company on July 1, 19X2, are summarized below. On July 3, 19X2, Rodriquez discounted all of these notes at the First National Bank at a discount rate of 13 percent. Find the net proceeds received from discounting each note. (19X2 was not a leap year.)

Note No.	Date of Note	Face Amount	Period	Interest Rate
11	Feb. 12, 19X2	$10,830	1 year	12%
14	Mar. 11, 19X2	$ 1,600	6 months	11%
21	June 1, 19X2	$ 1,920	90 days	12%

PROBLEM 21-4A   **Recording the receipt, discounting, and payment of notes receivable.** On July 18, 19X2, the Eli Corporation received a 75-day, 9 percent interest-bearing note from the Myers Company in settlement of Myers' past-due account of $1,333. On July 31 Eli discounted this note at the American National Bank. The bank charged a discount rate of 14 percent. On October 3 Eli received notice that Myers had paid the note and the interest on the due date.

Instructions   1. Give the entries in general journal form that Eli would make to record each of the transactions involving the note from Myers.
2. Assume that when the note became due, Myers failed to pay it. The bank notified Eli on October 3 and charged Eli's account for the maturity value of the note plus a $10 protest fee. Give the entries in general journal form that Eli would make to record the default by the maker of the note.

PROBLEM 21-5A   **Using a notes receivable register and recording notes receivable transactions.** The Ahmad Supply Company sells equipment, tools, and supplies to small oil-drilling firms. Some of these firms have tight financial resources, and Ahmad therefore obtains notes receivable from such customers for the sake of safety. Ahmad uses a notes receivable register as a memorandum record to maintain control over all the notes it handles. The notes the firm has outstanding on June 30, 19X1, are as follows. All the notes are payable at the First State Bank.

▪ A $9,000, 9 percent, 120-day note from the Star Drilling Company, dated March 20. (This note was discounted at the First State Bank on March 30.)

- A $1,000, 10 percent, 8-month note from the Walsh Company, dated May 8.
- A $4,500, 11 percent, 60-day note from Century Oil and Gas, dated May 14.
- A $2,000, noninterest-bearing, 30-day note from the Davis Corporation, dated June 20.

The notes receivable transactions listed below took place during July 19X1.

Instructions
1. Enter the notes outstanding on June 30, 19X1, in a notes receivable register like the one shown on pages 492 and 493 of this chapter.
2. Using a general journal, record the notes receivable transactions for July. The required accounts are listed below.
3. Enter data in the notes receivable register where appropriate.

ACCOUNTS

101	Cash	111	Accounts Receivable
109	Notes Receivable	491	Interest Income
110	Notes Receivable Discounted	591	Interest Expense

TRANSACTIONS FOR JULY 19X1

July   2 Accepted a 30-day, 11 percent note for $1,500, dated today, from the Regal Oil Company, as an extension of credit on its overdue account receivable.

  5 Discounted the Davis Corporation's 30-day, $2,000 note at the First State Bank. This note was received on June 20. The discount rate charged by the bank was 12.5 percent.

13 Received payment from Century Oil and Gas for its $4,500 note of May 14, plus the interest due.

19 Received notice that the Star Drilling Company refused to pay the First State Bank for its note of March 20, which was discounted at the bank on March 30. The bank charged the checking account of the Ahmad Supply Company for the maturity value of the note plus a protest fee ($5). (Record the charge-back by the bank in the general journal. Also record in the general journal termination of the contingent liability for the discounted note.)

20 Received notice from the First State Bank that the Davis Corporation paid its note of June 20, which was discounted on July 5.

22 Discounted at the First State Bank the $1,000 note from the Walsh Company dated May 8. The bank charged a discount rate of 12.5 percent.

CHAPTER 22

Whenever there are credit transactions, some people fail to pay their obligations. Businesses try to keep their bad debt losses to a minimum by carefully extending credit and by diligently collecting accounts. However, such losses will occur, and they must be considered an expense of doing business on credit. As you learned previously, two methods are generally used for recognizing losses from uncollectible accounts. This chapter discusses in detail the valuation or adjustment of receivables to reflect losses that result from customers not paying their bills. It will also examine the special problems arising from installment sales.

ACCOUNTS RECEIVABLE AND UNCOLLECTIBLE ACCOUNTS

RECORDING LOSSES WHEN THEY OCCUR—THE DIRECT CHARGE-OFF METHOD

A firm that extends credit to a customer expects to collect the amount owed in full. If a customer does not pay the account when due, a loss has occurred. The firm may carry the account in its financial records until the account has definitely become uncollectible. At that time the firm must formally recognize the balance owed as a loss.

Suppose that the Style Clothing Store had elected to follow this procedure and that Gary Lane, a customer, left town without paying his account balance of $75. After exhausting all possibilities of finding Lane and collecting from him, the Style Clothing Store would write off the account as a bad debt by the journal entry shown below. Notice that the amount involved is debited to an expense account called Loss From Uncollectible Accounts. Other widely used titles for this type of account are Bad Debts Expense and Uncollectible Accounts Expense.

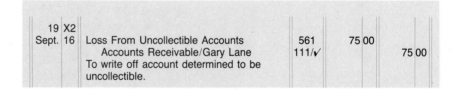

19 X2				
Sept. 16	Loss From Uncollectible Accounts	561	75 00	
	Accounts Receivable/Gary Lane	111/✓		75 00
	To write off account determined to be uncollectible.			

This method of recording uncollectible accounts is often referred to as the *direct charge-off method*. After the accounts known to be uncollectible have been written off, the new balance of Accounts Receivable represents the total of all customer accounts except those that the firm knows are uncollectible. However, it is also likely that other customer accounts will not be collectible, so the balance in the Accounts Receivable account is probably greater than the amount that will actually be obtained from customers.

PROVIDING FOR LOSSES BEFORE THEY OCCUR—THE ALLOWANCE METHOD

Instead of waiting until a particular account proves uncollectible and then recording the loss, it is possible to anticipate losses from uncollectible accounts and to provide for them in the period when the sales are made. By doing so, the seller can match the estimated expense for uncollectible accounts against the revenue that the firm has earned during the same accounting period. This is a logical procedure because the expense for uncollectible accounts is related to the sales transactions from which the accounts receivable resulted. In addition, the amount shown on the balance sheet for accounts receivable will more nearly reflect the amount that will ultimately be collected. The practice of providing for losses from uncollectible accounts before specific accounts become uncollectible is often referred to as the *allowance method*. The Style Clothing Store uses this method.

In order to record the expense for uncollectible accounts and the sales revenue in the same accounting period, the accountant must estimate the losses likely to result from the accounts receivable that have not been collected at the end of the period. There are three common ways of estimating the amount of loss from uncollectible accounts. These techniques are based on the following procedures.

1. Taking a percentage of the net credit sales for the period.
2. Classifying the accounts receivable into age groups at the end of the period, and taking a percentage of each group.
3. Taking a percentage of the total accounts receivable outstanding at the end of the period.

Percentage of Credit Sales

A business that has been operating for a number of years may be able to determine an average ratio of losses from uncollectible accounts to credit sales. It can then use this ratio in estimating future losses. To be accurate, the ratio should be based on net credit sales—total credit sales minus the sales returns and allowances on these sales. However, when sales returns and allowances are few, businesses usually base their estimated losses from uncollectible accounts on total credit sales because this figure is more easily computed.

In some businesses it may be difficult to determine the amount of credit sales. In other businesses the relationship between cash sales and credit sales may remain constant. These businesses may need to base the ratio of losses from uncollectible accounts on total sales, including cash sales. However, as a general rule, only the credit sales should be used because there is no loss on cash sales. Since the Style Clothing Store has relatively few sales returns and allowances, its losses from uncollectible accounts are based on total credit sales.

A new firm may use the experience of other firms in the same line of business in making its estimate. Suppose, for example, that the Style Clothing Store relies on the experience of its predecessor, which was operated for a number of years by Linda Hanson before she formed a partnership with Steven Casey and Janet Miller. Using the data from prior years, the accountant estimates that three-tenths of one percent (0.003) of the firm's credit sales will result in uncollectible accounts. Suppose also that during the partnership's first year of operation $200,000 of sales are made on credit. The store's estimated loss from uncollectible accounts is determined by applying the percentage to the credit sales

$(0.003 \times \$200,000 = \$600)$. The estimated loss from uncollectible accounts for the period is therefore $600. The entry to record this estimate is shown in general journal form below. (The adjustment is actually entered on the worksheet first and is later recorded in the general journal along with the other adjusting entries.)

19 X2				
Jan. 31	Loss From Uncollectible Accounts	561	600 00	
	Allowance for Uncollectible Accounts	112		600 00
	To record estimated bad debt losses for the fiscal year, based on 0.3% of credit sales of $200,000.			

The effect of the debit part of the entry is to charge the estimated loss from uncollectible accounts against the operations of the period. As a result of the credit part of the entry, Allowance for Uncollectible Accounts (sometimes called Allowance for Bad Debts) reflects the estimated shrinkage in the asset accounts receivable. Allowance for Uncollectible Accounts is called a *valuation account* because it literally revalues or reappraises the accounts receivable in the light of reasonable expectations. It is shown on the balance sheet as a deduction from accounts receivable (as illustrated on page 510).

Note that when the estimate of the loss from uncollectible accounts is based on sales, the primary emphasis is on charging as an expense the credit losses that apply to the sales of the period. It is through this process that the accounts receivable can be reported at their expected realizable value. However, valuation is of secondary concern. In other words, the matching principle is being emphasized when the loss from uncollectible accounts is based on sales.

Aging the Accounts Receivable

A procedure called *aging the accounts receivable* can be used as a guide in estimating probable losses from uncollectible accounts. This procedure involves setting up a schedule on which each account receivable is listed by name and

STYLE CLOTHING STORE
Schedule of Accounts Receivable by Age
January 31, 19X2

ACCOUNT WITH	BALANCE	CURRENT	PAST DUE—DAYS		
			1–30	31–60	OVER 60
Lois Adams	125 00	125 00			
Ralph Ames	60 00			45 00	15 00
Irene Ashe	47 50	25 00	22 50		
William Avant	73 00	50 00			23 00
John Zeller	110 00	80 00	30 00		
Totals	12,500 00	9,500 00	1,575 00	850 00	575 00

balance owed. The accountant then analyzes the data in the accounts to determine the age of the various amounts that make up each balance. The column headings of the schedule allow the accountant to classify the amounts according to how long they have been outstanding. The headings may be Current (within the allowed credit period), Past Due 1–30 Days, Past Due 31–60 Days, and Past Due Over 60 days. When a firm breaks down each customer's total debt in this way, it gains a picture of the relative currency of its receivables.

The longer an account is past due, the less likely it is to be collected. For example, past experience at the Style Clothing Store might indicate that 50 percent of the accounts more than 60 days past due will be uncollectible, whereas the figures for the other age groups are 25 percent for accounts 31–60 days past due, 10 percent for accounts 1–30 days past due, and 1 percent for the current accounts. By applying these percentages to the totals shown on the schedule of accounts receivable by age, the accountant estimates the loss from uncollectible accounts for the period as follows.

Over 60 days past due	$0.50 \times \$ \quad 575.00 = \$287.50$
31–60 days past due	$0.25 \times \quad 850.00 = \quad 212.50$
1–30 days past due	$0.10 \times \quad 1,575.00 = \quad 157.50$
Current	$0.01 \times \quad 9,500.00 = \quad 95.00$
Total estimated loss from uncollectible accounts	$752.50

Allowance for Uncollectible Accounts should then be *adjusted to the needed balance* of $752.50. For example, suppose that Allowance for Uncollectible Accounts has a credit balance of $200 on January 31, prior to adjustment. The account must be credited for $552.50 to bring the balance up to $752.50. The following entry is made in the general journal to record this adjustment.

19 X2				
Jan. 31	Loss From Uncollectible Accounts	561	552 50	
	Allowance for Uncollectible Accounts	112		552 50
	To record adjustment of allowance account			
	to needed balance of $752.50, based on			
	aging of accounts receivable.			

On the other hand, suppose that Allowance for Uncollectible Accounts has a debit (deficiency) balance of $50 (from writing off specific accounts, as discussed later). It would then be necessary to credit the account for $802.50 ($50 + $752.50) in order to bring the balance up to $752.50. Whatever the amount, the adjusting entry consists of a debit to Loss From Uncollectible Accounts and a credit to Allowance for Uncollectible Accounts, as previously illustrated.

Note that when the provision for uncollectible accounts is based on the age of the accounts receivable, the primary concern is the proper valuation of the accounts receivable on the balance sheet. The amount charged as an expense is of secondary concern.

Predetermined Percentage of Accounts Receivable

In some cases it is possible to estimate the necessary balance of Allowance for Uncollectible Accounts by applying a single rate, based on past experience, to the total accounts receivable. For example, a firm may estimate that normally one-half of 1 percent (0.005) of the balance of the Accounts Receivable account will be uncollectible, and it may adjust Allowance for Uncollectible Accounts to that amount. If this procedure is followed, the emphasis is again on valuation of the accounts receivable on the balance sheet.

RECORDING ACTUAL UNCOLLECTIBLE AMOUNTS

As you have seen, under the system of providing for losses before they occur, Loss From Uncollectible Accounts is debited and Allowance for Uncollectible Accounts credited for the estimated amount of loss. Then, when a particular account proves uncollectible, it is written off. The amount owed is debited to Allowance for Uncollectible Accounts. The offsetting credit is to the Accounts Receivable control account in the general ledger and the customer's account in the subsidiary ledger. Suppose that the Style Clothing Store determines that the account of Ralph Ames with a balance of $60 is uncollectible. The accountant writes off the account by making the following entry in the general journal.

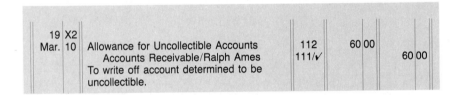

19 X2				
Mar. 10	Allowance for Uncollectible Accounts	112	60 00	
	Accounts Receivable/Ralph Ames	111/✓		60 00
	To write off account determined to be uncollectible.			

Notice that when losses are provided for in advance, the write-off of a particular customer's account does not involve an entry in Loss From Uncollectible Accounts. The expense has already been recorded by means of the adjustment for estimated uncollectible accounts made at the end of the period in which the sale took place.

Normally, Allowance for Uncollectible Accounts will have a credit (excess) balance. However, if the losses written off are greater than those estimated in previous accounting periods, Allowance for Uncollectible Accounts may show a debit (deficiency) balance until the current adjustment is recorded. If the amount of the estimated loss is based on sales, the existence of the debit balance will not affect the amount of the adjustment. However, if the estimated loss is based on accounts receivable, it will be necessary to credit Allowance for Uncollectible Accounts for an amount sufficient to eliminate the debit balance and replace it with the desired credit balance. This means that the adjustment will be greater than the estimated loss from uncollectible accounts for the period.

In other words, if the estimate of the loss is based on sales, do not consider an existing balance in Allowance for Uncollectible Accounts when determining the amount of the adjustment. If, however, the estimate of the loss is based on accounts receivable, consider any existing balance in Allowance for Uncollectible Accounts when computing the adjustment. In this case, after the adjustment is made, the resulting balance of the allowance account should be the amount of accounts receivable estimated to be uncollectible.

COLLECTING AN ACCOUNT THAT WAS WRITTEN OFF

Occasionally an account written off as uncollectible is later collected, in whole or in part. Remember that Gary Lane's account for $75 was written off under the direct charge-off method by a debit to Loss From Uncollectible Accounts and a credit to Accounts Receivable/Gary Lane. Suppose that the account is collected in full several months later. Since Lane's account has already been written off, the general journal entry shown below must be made to reverse the write-off. Then the cash received is recorded in the cash receipts journal by debiting Cash and crediting Accounts Receivable/Gary Lane.

19 X2				
Nov. 10	Accounts Receivable/Gary Lane	111/✓	75 00	
	Loss From Uncollectible Accounts	561		75 00
	To reverse entry dated Sept. 16 writing off this account, which was collected in full today.			

Some accountants prefer to record the amount recovered as a credit to an account called Uncollectible Accounts Recovered, especially when the money is received in a later period than the one in which the write-off was made. The debit part of this entry involves the Accounts Receivable control account in the general ledger and the customer's account in the subsidiary ledger to make sure that all pertinent facts relating to the customer's debt are recorded and can be used for future credit purposes. The collection of the money is recorded in the cash receipts journal in the usual way as a debit to Cash and a credit to Accounts Receivable and the customer's account. The Uncollectible Accounts Recovered account is shown on the income statement under Other Income.

When a firm uses the allowance method to provide for losses, the recovery of an account previously charged off as uncollectible also requires an entry in the general journal to reverse the write-off. For example, the recovery of the $60 balance owed by Ralph Ames is recorded in the general journal as shown below. Notice that Accounts Receivable/Ralph Ames is debited and Allowance for Uncollectible Accounts is credited in the reversal process.

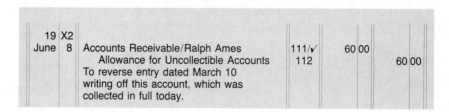

19 X2				
June 8	Accounts Receivable/Ralph Ames	111/✓	60 00	
	Allowance for Uncollectible Accounts	112		60 00
	To reverse entry dated March 10 writing off this account, which was collected in full today.			

An entry in the cash receipts journal is then made in the usual way to record the collection of the account receivable.

If the amount recovered represents only part of the balance written off, the reversal entry is used to restore *only the amount actually collected* unless the firm is almost certain that the remainder will be paid. For example, if Ralph Ames pays only $40 on his $60 balance, the reversal entry in the general journal will be for the smaller amount unless the firm is reasonably sure the additional $20 will be paid.

OTHER RECEIVABLES AND BAD DEBT LOSSES

Just as accounts receivable may result in bad debt losses, so notes receivable and other receivables may prove uncollectible. Losses from uncollectible notes receivable and other receivables may be recorded as they occur, or they may be estimated and provided for ahead of time in the manner previously described for accounts receivable. The same accounts—Loss From Uncollectible Accounts and Allowance for Uncollectible Accounts—can be used for losses from all types of receivables.

EXPENSE ON THE INCOME STATEMENT

Loss From Uncollectible Accounts appears among the operating expenses on the income statement. If the function of giving credit and collecting accounts rests in the sales department, it is classified as a selling expense. However, in most businesses, the credit function is separated from the sales function. For these businesses, Loss From Uncollectible Accounts is usually shown as a general or administrative expense. Some businesses show Loss From Uncollectible Accounts as a deduction from sales revenue on the income statement.

ALLOWANCE FOR UNCOLLECTIBLE ACCOUNTS ON THE BALANCE SHEET

If Allowance for Uncollectible Accounts is used, the balance in this account at the end of the period represents the amount of accounts receivable estimated to be uncollectible. In preparing the balance sheet, the accountant therefore deducts the balance of Allowance for Uncollectible Accounts from the balance of the Accounts Receivable account, as shown below. The difference is considered the net value of the asset. In this case the net value of the firm's accounts receivable is $11,747.50

ASSETS

Current Assets		
Cash		$10,000.000
Accounts Receivable	$12,500.00	
Less Allowance for Uncollectible Accounts	752.50	11,747.50

RECOGNIZING THE EFFECT OF POTENTIAL CASH DISCOUNTS

As explained earlier, cash discounts are sometimes allowed for prompt payment of invoices. If the accounts receivable listed on the balance sheet are subject to cash discounts, the total collected may be somewhat less than the invoice amounts recorded. For example, suppose that a credit sale is recorded by debiting Accounts Receivable for $150. However, if terms such as 2/10, n/30 are allowed, the debt may be settled with the payment of $147 within 10 days.

In some cases the approximate amount of the discounts that can be taken by customers is shown on the balance sheet so that anyone studying the statement will have fair notice of this possibility. However, in most cases, people using the financial statements are expected to know the normal terms of sale in the industry involved. Therefore, it is usually not considered necessary to list the possible sales discounts.

INSTALLMENT SALES PROCEDURES

A special type of receivable is found in businesses that sell on an installment basis. Installment sales are common among retailers of furniture, jewelry, and major household appliances. The usual arrangement is for the customer to make a down payment and then pay the balance in installments over the period of time called for in the contract.

Generally accepted accounting principles require installment sales to be recorded exactly like any other sales on credit—except in unusual circumstances. However, some small retailers use an installment basis of accounting for such sales. They do this because the procedure is permitted for tax purposes, and they prefer to have only one set of records for financial accounting and tax accounting purposes. The installment basis of accounting allows the profit on installment sales to be deferred until the cash is actually received.

To see how this accounting procedure works, suppose that on September 1, 19X1, a store sells a color television set on the installment plan to George Lee for a price of $500. Lee pays $50 as a down payment and another $150 in three $50 installments during the first year. He pays the remaining $300 in six installments of $50 each during the second year. The set originally cost the store $300.

1. At the time of the sale on September 1, 19X1, the transaction is recorded by an entry debiting Installment Accounts Receivable—19X1/George Lee for the total obligation ($500), crediting Merchandise Inventory for the cost of the item sold ($300), and crediting Deferred Gross Profit on 19X1 Installment Sales for the deferred income from the transaction ($200). (A 40 percent rate of gross profit is assumed for all installment sales in 19X1.)

19	X1				
Sept.	1	Installment Accounts Receivable—19X1/			
		George Lee	114/✓	500 00	
		Merchandise Inventory	121		300 00
		Deferred Gross Profit on 19X1			
		Installment Sales	411		200 00
		Made installment sale; deferred			
		income is at 40% rate based on selling			
		price of appliance; Contract X1-310.			

2. The cash received for the down payment results in a debit to Cash and a credit to Installment Accounts Receivable—19X1/George Lee. Later receipts are handled in the same way. (For simplicity, the necessary entries are shown here in general journal form.)

19X1			101	50 00	
Sept. 1	Cash				
	Installment Accounts Receivable—				
	19X1/George Lee		114/√		50 00
	Down payment at time of sale.				

Oct. 1	Cash		101	50 00	
	Installment Accounts Receivable—				
	19X1/George Lee		114/√		50 00
	Collections in October.				

Nov. 1	Cash		101	50 00	
	Installment Accounts Receivable—				
	19X1/George Lee		114/√		50 00
	Collections in November.				

Dec. 1	Cash		101	50 00	
	Installment Accounts Receivable—				
	19X1/George Lee		114/√		50 00
	Collections in December.				

3. At the end of the year in which the sale is made, a portion of the deferred income must be recognized. A rate of gross profit is determined for the year and is applied to collections on the installment sales of that year. For example, assuming a 40 percent rate of gross profit, the amount of income to be recognized in 19X1 for the sale to George Lee is $80. Remember that Lee makes four payments of $50 each that year ($50 \times 4 \times 0.40 = $200 \times 0.40 = $80). The journal entry is shown below. Notice that Deferred Gross Profit on 19X1 Installment Sales is debited and an account called Realized Gross Profit on 19X1 Installment Sales is credited.

19X1				
Dec. 31	Deferred Gross Profit on 19X1			
	Installment Sales	411	80 00	
	Realized Gross Profit on 19X1			
	Installment Sales	421		80 00
	To record realized income of 40% of $200			
	collections on 19X1 sales.			

4. The rate of gross profit determines the amount of deferred income to be recognized at the end of each year during the period of collection, which may

extend over several years. In this instance the customer made six monthly payments of $50 each to complete the contract in 19X2. Using the 40 percent gross profit rate again, this results in income of $120 to be recognized in 19X2 ($50 × 6 × 0.40 = $300 × 0.40 = $120).

	19 X2				
Dec.	31	Deferred Gross Profit on 19X1			
		Installment Sales	411	120 00	
		Realized Gross Profit on 19X1			
		Installment Sales	421		120 00
		To record realized income of 40% of $300			
		collections on 19X1 sales.			

RECORDING DEFAULTS ON INSTALLMENT SALES

If a customer defaults on the payments required by an installment contract, the seller may be able to recover the merchandise and put it back into inventory at its current wholesale value. The gain or loss is recognized and recorded at this point. The exact amount to be recorded is determined by the cost and revenue figures in the records. The balance still owed by the customer must, of course, be removed from the Installment Accounts Receivable account. The remaining deferred income must also be removed from the Deferred Gross Profit on Installment Sales account.

Consider again George Lee, who agreed to pay for the $500 television set on an installment basis. Suppose that he made the $50 down payment and the three periodic payments totaling $150 during the first year but failed to make the payments required in the second year. Assume further that the seller repossessed the television set on February 2, 19X2, and appraised its value at $125. The entry to record the repossession is shown below. Deferred Gross Profit on 19X1 Installment Sales is debited for $120 to eliminate the deferred income that will not be realized. Merchandise Inventory—Repossessed Goods is debited for $125, the current wholesale value of the television set. Loss From Defaults is debited for $55, the amount of loss on the sale. These debits are offset by a credit of $300 to Installment Accounts Receivable—19X1/George Lee, which closes out the customer's balance.

	19 X2				
Feb.	2	Deferred Gross Profit on 19X1			
		Installment Sales	411	120 00	
		Merch. Inventory—Repossessed Goods	122	125 00	
		Loss From Defaults	461	55 00	
		Installment Accounts Receivable—			
		19X1/George Lee	114/✓		300 00
		To record repossession of appliance and			
		loss on default.			

If the television set had not been recovered, the loss would have been $125 greater, or $180. Thus, it would be necessary to debit Loss From Defaults for $180. The other parts of the final entry would be a debit of $120 to Deferred Gross Profit on 19X1 Installment Sales and a credit of $300 to Installment Accounts Receivable—19X1/George Lee.

19 X2					
Feb. 2	Deferred Gross Profit on 19X1				
	Installment Sales	411	120 00		
	Loss From Defaults	461	180 00		
	Installment Accounts Receivable—				
	19X1/George Lee	114/✓		300 00	
	To record default on installment contract;				
	merchandise not repossessed.				

INTERNAL CONTROL OF ACCOUNTS RECEIVABLE

For most companies, Accounts Receivable represents one of the largest assets on the balance sheet. Because of the way in which accounts receivable arise—the delivery of merchandise or services to customers—and because accounts receivable are expected to be converted into cash, internal control is very important.

This control originates with appropriate delegation of authority for approving the extension of credit and an insistence that all credit be properly approved. Detailed procedures must be established to make certain that all sales are properly recorded and that customers' accounts are correctly charged. In addition, every effort must be made to separate the functions of recording the accounts receivable transactions, preparing bills or statements for customers, mailing the bills or statements, and processing the cash received from the customers. This division of responsibility is necessary to make it more difficult for an employee to steal or misuse the company's cash or merchandise and then cover up what was done by making improper entries in the accounts receivable records.

To ensure efficient collection of accounts receivable, customers should be billed regularly and the accounts receivable balances should be aged often. Using the data from the age analysis, management should quickly identify and monitor slow-paying accounts. When accounts are past due, management should promptly investigate the situation and take appropriate action. The responsibility for authorizing charge-offs of uncollectible accounts should only be delegated to selected individuals, and all charge-offs should be approved in writing. Even after accounts have been written off, efforts should be continued to collect them.

Control procedures that apply to the accounts receivable that arise from regular credit sales also apply to accounts receivable from installment sales. However, there are some additional considerations related to installment sales. Installment notes must be carefully controlled and safeguarded. Procedures must be established for assuring that prompt payment of all installments is received when the installments become due. To control the repossession of goods sold on installment contracts, a firm must develop procedures that will ensure the proper recording, handling, and resale of the repossessed items.

PRINCIPLES AND PROCEDURES SUMMARY

When credit is extended to customers, uncollectible accounts will inevitably occur. Before receivables can be accurately presented on the balance sheet and net income can be properly measured, the accounts must be studied for possible adjustment to reflect such losses. The losses can be recorded as particular accounts become uncollectible, or an estimate of probable losses can be recorded before they occur.

The estimate of losses from uncollectible accounts may be determined by taking a certain percentage of credit sales. This percentage is usually based on past experience. The adjustment for the estimated losses is debited to Loss From Uncollectible Accounts and credited to Allowance for Uncollectible Accounts.

The estimate may also be based on an analysis of the age of the accounts receivable. A different percentage for credit losses is applied to each age group, and the resulting amounts are added together. Then Allowance for Uncollectible Accounts is adjusted to the proper balance, and the same amount is charged to Loss From Uncollectible Accounts. The adjustment is made in the same way when the estimate of bad debt losses is computed by applying a single rate to the total accounts receivable..

Under the allowance method, when an account actually becomes worthless, it is written off by a debit to Allowance for Uncollectible Accounts and a credit to Accounts Receivable and to the customer's account in the subsidiary ledger.

Installment sales usually involve a down payment and additional periodic payments on the balance owed. Special accounts are maintained to record all details. The sales price is usually accounted for in the same way as with other sales on credit. However, some retailers use the installment basis of accounting. In the latter case, income is recognized only as the accounts are collected. The overall gross profit rate, determined in the year the sale is made, is applied to collections each year to determine the amount of income recognized.

MANAGERIAL IMPLICATIONS

It is essential that managers keep informed about the losses from uncollectible accounts. This enables them to determine the effectiveness of the credit policies used by their firms, especially with regard to profitability. Managers must weigh the cost of losses against the effects of tighter credit policies on sales volume.

Managers should insist that estimated losses from uncollectible accounts be charged against the revenue of the period in which the sales are made in order to get a proper matching of revenues and expenses. This allows a more accurate determination of net income or net loss.

REVIEW QUESTIONS

1. Explain the direct charge-off method for recording losses from uncollectible accounts.

2. Under what condition would the direct charge-off method be appropriate?
3. What is the major weakness of the direct charge-off method?
4. Name three approaches to measuring uncollectible accounts when the allowance method is used.
5. What is meant by aging the accounts receivable?
6. Explain the purposes of estimating losses from uncollectible accounts and using the allowance method for recording uncollectible accounts.
7. Under the allowance method, what entry is made when a specific customer's account becomes uncollectible?
8. Assuming that the direct charge-off method is used, what entry is made when a firm collects an account that was previously written off?
9. Explain how to treat the collection of an account receivable that was previously written off if the allowance method is used.
10. Under what circumstances would it be logical to base the estimate of uncollectible accounts on gross credit sales rather than on net credit sales?
11. Why is Allowance for Uncollectible Accounts sometimes referred to as a valuation account?
12. If a company is primarily interested in matching expenses and revenues each period, would it base its estimate of uncollectible accounts on sales or on accounts receivable? Explain.
13. Suppose that the estimate of uncollectible accounts is based on credit sales and that Allowance for Uncollectible Accounts has a debit balance before the adjustment is made. Explain how this situation is handled.
14. How would an accountant show Loss From Uncollectible Accounts on the income statement? Explain.
15. What is an installment sale?
16. Is the installment sales method customarily allowed under generally accepted accounting principles? Explain.
17. What types of businesses are likely to use the installment basis of accounting?
18. What is the essential feature of the installment basis of accounting?
19. How are defaults recorded under the installment method?
20. How are repossessed goods recorded under the installment method?
21. If the installment method is not customarily allowed under generally accepted accounting principles, why is it used?
22. Are the effects of potential cash discounts on accounts receivable usually shown on the balance sheet? Why or why not?

MANAGERIAL DISCUSSION QUESTIONS

1. How do managers appraise the effectiveness of a firm's credit policies?
2. What are the advantages of using an analysis of the accounts receivable by age as a guide in estimating losses from uncollectible accounts?
3. Why would managers wish to use the allowance method for recording uncollectible accounts instead of the direct charge-off method?

4. Why is an account receivable that was charged off as uncollectible reinstated if it is later collected?
5. Why would managers wish to use the installment method of accounting?
6. In the Anchor Company, the credit function is delegated to the sales department. In most cases the firm's salespeople are authorized to approve credit for customers. Comment on the desirability of this procedure.

EXERCISES

EXERCISE 22-1 **Recording losses under the direct charge-off method.** The Lone Star Company uses the direct charge-off method to record uncollectible accounts. On July 29, 19X1, the company learned that Alan Shaw, a customer who owed $380, had been declared bankrupt and that no part of the debt was collectible. Give the general journal entry to write off the account.

EXERCISE 22-2 **Recording the collection of an account previously written off under the direct charge-off method.** On January 8, 19X2, the Lone Star Company received a check for $60 and a letter from the bankruptcy official handling the affairs of Alan Shaw. The letter stated that the $60 represented a final distribution of Shaw's assets to his creditors. Give the general journal entry that would be made to partially reverse the write-off recorded in Exercise 22-1.

EXERCISE 22-3 **Estimating and recording uncollectible accounts on the basis of total net sales.** On December 31, 19X1, certain account balances at the Rogers Company were as follows before end-of-year adjustments.

Accounts Receivable	$ 500,000
Allowance for Uncollectible Accounts	3,000 (Debit)
Sales	12,000,000
Sales Returns and Allowances	50,000

A further examination of the business's records showed that cash sales during the year amounted to $1,200,000 and credit sales amounted to $10,800,000. Of the sales returns and allowances, $10,000 came from cash sales and $40,000 came from credit sales. Assume that the Rogers Company bases its estimate of losses from uncollectible accounts on 0.3 percent of total net sales. Compute the estimated amount of losses for 19X1, and give the general journal entry to record the provision for uncollectible accounts.

EXERCISE 22-4 **Estimating and recording uncollectible accounts on the basis of net credit sales.** Assume that the Rogers Company bases its estimate of losses from uncollectible accounts on 0.4 percent of net credit sales. Compute the estimated amount of losses for 19X1, and give the general journal entry to record the provision for uncollectible accounts. Obtain any data that you need for the computation from Exercise 22-3.

EXERCISE 22-5   **Estimating and recording uncollectible accounts on the basis of accounts receivable.** Assume that the Rogers Company bases its estimate of losses from uncollectible accounts on 1.1 percent of accounts receivable. Compute the estimated amount of losses for 19X1, and give the general journal entry to record the provision for uncollectible accounts. Obtain any data that you need for the computation from Exercise 22-3.

EXERCISE 22-6   **Recording the collection of an account previously written off under the allowance method.** The Schmidt Company uses the allowance method to record uncollectible accounts. On January 1, 19X3, its general ledger showed a balance of $1,220,000 for Accounts Receivable and a credit balance of $12,000 for Allowance for Uncollectible Accounts. Assume that on January 8, 19X3, Sam Cole, whose account for $600 had been charged off in 19X1, sent a check to Schmidt for $600 in payment, along with an apology for having been so late. Give the entries in general journal form to reverse the previous write-off of Cole's account and record the receipt of his check.

EXERCISE 22-7   **Recording actual uncollectible amounts under the allowance method.** On February 8, 19X3, the Schmidt Company decided that the $800 account of Jean Gray was worthless and should be written off. Give the general journal entry to record the charge-off.

EXERCISE 22-8   **Recording the collection of an account previously written off under the allowance method.** On July 10, 19X3, Jean Gray paid $800 to the Schmidt Company in settlement of her account, which was charged off on February 8 (see Exercise 22-7). Give the entries in general journal form to reverse the previous write-off of Gray's account and to record the receipt of her check.

EXERCISE 22-9   **Recording sales under the installment method.** In January 19X1 the Richards Company sold appliances on the installment plan for $20,000. The appliances cost $12,000. Give the entry in general journal form to record these sales, using the installment method.

EXERCISE 22-10   **Recording collections and the recognition of income earned under the installment method.** During 19X1 the Richards Company collected $9,000 in cash on the installment sales made in January (see Exercise 22-9). Record in general journal form the receipt of the cash and the recognition of the income from these collections.

EXERCISE 22-11   **Recording a sale under the installment method.** On January 2, 19X1, the Decorative Furniture Store sold goods to Ray Short for $1,000 on the installment plan. The goods had cost Decorative $600. Give the entry in general journal form to record this sale, using the installment method.

EXERCISE 22-12   **Recording collections and the recognition of income earned under the installment method.** During 19X1 Ray Short paid $620 cash, including the down payment, for the goods he purchased from the Decorative Furniture Store (see

Exercise 22-11). Give the entries in general journal form to record the collections and the income realized in 19X1.

EXERCISE 22-13 **Recording a default and a repossession under the installment method.** Ray Short defaulted on January 2, 19X2, and the Decorative Furniture Store repossessed the goods it had sold him (see Exercises 22-11 and 22-12). At the date of repossession, the goods had a value of $700. Give the entry in general journal form to record the default and the repossession in 19X2.

PROBLEMS

PROBLEM 22-1 **Recording uncollectible accounts under the direct charge-off method.** The Bayer Company records losses from uncollectible accounts as they occur. Selected transactions for 19X1 are described below. The accounts involved are Notes Receivable, Accounts Receivable, and Loss From Uncollectible Accounts.

Instructions Record each transaction in general journal form.

TRANSACTIONS FOR 19X1

Feb. 12 The account receivable of Alan Scott, amounting to $98, is determined to be uncollectible and is to be written off.

Mar. 20 Because of the death of Joan Harris, her note receivable amounting to $300 is considered uncollectible and is to be written off.

June 4 Received $45 from Alan Scott in partial payment of his account, which was written off on February 12. The cash obtained has already been recorded in the cash receipts journal. There is doubt that the balance of Scott's account will be collected.

July 9 Received $53 from Alan Scott to complete the payment of his account, which was written off on February 12. The cash obtained has already been recorded in the cash receipts journal.

Aug. 14 The account receivable of Robert West, amounting to $80, is determined to be uncollectible and is to be written off.

Sept. 18 Received $100 from the estate of Joan Harris as part of the settlement of her affairs. This amount is applicable to the note receivable written off on March 20. The cash obtained has already been recorded in the cash receipts journal.

PROBLEM 22-2 **Estimating and recording uncollectible accounts on the basis of sales.** The Plano Feed Company sells farm supplies at both wholesale and retail. The company has found that there is a higher rate of uncollectible accounts from retail credit sales than from wholesale credit sales. Plano computes its estimated loss from uncollectible accounts at the end of each year. The amount is based on the two rates of loss that the firm has developed from experience. Thus a separate computation must be made for each source of sales. The firm uses the percentage of credit sales method.

As of December 31, 19X1, Accounts Receivable has a balance of $186,700, and Allowance for Uncollectible Accounts has a debit balance of $36.20. The following table provides a breakdown of the credit sales for the year 19X1 and the estimated rates of loss.

CREDIT SALES		ESTIMATED
CATEGORY	AMOUNT	RATE OF LOSS
Wholesale	$908,000	0.6%
Retail	274,300	1.1%

Instructions

1. Compute the estimated amount of loss from uncollectible accounts for each of the two categories of credit sales for the year.
2. Prepare an adjusting entry in general journal form to provide for the losses before they occur. (Use Loss From Uncollectible Accounts.)
3. Show how Accounts Receivable and Allowance for Uncollectible Accounts should appear on the balance sheet of the Plano Feed Company as of December 31, 19X1.
4. On January 30, 19X2, the account receivable of Roy Carter, amounting to $283, is determined to be uncollectible and is to be written off. Record the transaction in general journal form.
5. On June 13, 19X2, the attorneys for the Plano Feed Company turned over a check for $283 that they obtained from Roy Carter in settlement of his account, which was written off on January 30. The money has already been entered in the cash receipts journal. Make an entry in general journal form to cancel the original write-off.

PROBLEM 22-3

Estimating and recording uncollectible accounts on the basis of accounts receivable. The schedule of accounts receivable by age shown below was prepared for the Garcia Company at the end of the fiscal year on December 31, 19X1.

GARCIA COMPANY
Schedule of Accounts Receivable by Age
December 31, 19X1

ACCOUNT WITH	BALANCE	CURRENT	PAST DUE—DAYS		
			1–30	31–60	OVER 60
Anton, Janet	180 00	180 00			
Ardath, Robert	210 00		150 00	60 00	
Aston, Thomas	104 00				104 00
Baltus, Ida	80 00	80 00			
Barton, Leslie	62 00	42 00	20 00		
Bender, Harold	225 00	85 00	100 00	40 00	
Benson, Mary	48 00			32 00	16 00
(All Other Accounts)	10,748 00	9,075 00	1,050 00	360 00	263 00
Totals	11,657 00	9,462 00	1,320 00	492 00	383 00

Instructions 1. Compute the estimated uncollectible accounts at the end of the year using these rates.

Current	1%
1–30 days past due	3%
31–60 days past due	8%
Over 60 days past due	20%

2. As of December 31, 19X1, there is a debit balance of $64.12 in Allowance for Uncollectible Accounts. Compute the amount of the adjustment for estimated losses from uncollectible accounts that must be made as part of the adjusting entries.

3. In general journal form, record the adjustment for the estimated losses. (Use Loss From Uncollectible Accounts.)

4. On February 10, 19X2, the account receivable of Ruth Hall, amounting to $108, was recognized as uncollectible. Record this write-off in the general journal.

5. On June 12, 19X2, a check for $50 was received from John Casey to apply on his account, which was written off on November 8, 19X1, as uncollectible. Record the cancellation of the previous write-off in the general journal. The cash obtained has already been entered in the cash receipts journal.

6. Suppose that instead of aging the accounts receivable, the company estimated the uncollectible accounts to be simply 3 percent of the total accounts receivable on December 31. Give the general journal entry to record the adjustment for estimated losses from uncollectible accounts. Assume that Allowance for Uncollectible Accounts has a debit balance of $103.60 before the adjusting entry.

PROBLEM 22-4 **Using different methods to estimate uncollectible accounts.** The balances of selected accounts of the Huang Company on December 31, 19X1, are given below. (Credit sales amounted to $2,810,000. The returns and allowances on these sales totaled $60,000.)

Accounts Receivable	$ 316,500
Allowance for Uncollectible Accounts	380 (credit)
Sales	3,450,000
Sales Returns and Allowances	75,000

Instructions 1. Compute the amount to be charged to Loss From Uncollectible Accounts under each of the following different sets of assumptions.

    a. Uncollectible accounts are estimated to be 0.4 percent of net credit sales.

    b. Uncollectible accounts are estimated to be 0.3 percent of total net sales.

    c. Experience has shown that about 2½ percent of the accounts receivable are uncollectible.

2. Suppose that Allowance for Uncollectible Accounts has a debit balance of $380 instead of a credit balance, but all other account balances remain the same. Compute the amount to be charged to Loss From Uncollectible Accounts under each of the assumptions listed in Part 1.

PROBLEM 22-5 **Using the installment method.** The Sound Center is a retail store that deals in stereo equipment. Some of its larger sales are made on the installment plan. A number of these transactions for the years 19X1 to 19X3 are summarized below. The rate of gross profit on installment sales is 33⅓ percent.

Instructions Record the transactions in general journal form. Use the account titles that appear in the text.

TRANSACTIONS FOR 19X1

Aug. 15 Sold stereo equipment for $600 on the installment plan to George McNeill. He gave $75 cash as a down payment. The Sound Center paid $400 for the equipment.

25 Sold stereo equipment for $420 on the installment plan to Joyce Rosen. She gave $65 cash as a down payment. The equipment cost the Sound Center $280.

Dec. 31 During the remainder of 19X1, McNeill paid an additional $125 on his installment account and Rosen paid an additional $110 on her account. (Record as a combined summary entry on December 31.)

31 Recorded the income realized on collections of 19X1 installment sales.

TRANSACTIONS FOR 19X2

Dec. 31 During 19X2 McNeill paid $70 on his installment account, and Rosen paid $200 on her account.

31 Recorded the income realized in 19X2 on collections of 19X1 installment sales.

TRANSACTION FOR 19X3

Jan. 25 McNeill defaulted on his contract, and his stereo equipment was repossessed. It had a $50 wholesale value on this date.

ALTERNATE PROBLEMS

PROBLEM 22-1A **Recording uncollectible accounts under the direct charge-off method.** The Fairmont Company records losses from uncollectible accounts as they occur. Selected transactions for 19X1 are described below. The accounts involved in these transactions are Notes Receivable, Accounts Receivable, and Loss From Uncollectible Accounts.

Instructions Record each transaction in general journal form.

TRANSACTIONS FOR 19X1

Jan. 15 The account receivable of Aaron Davis, amounting to $96, is determined to be uncollectible and is to be written off.

Mar. 20 Because of the death of Paul O'Grady, his note receivable amounting to $250 is considered uncollectible and is to be written off.

June 4 Received $40 from Aaron Davis in partial payment of his account, which was written off on January 15. The cash obtained has already been recorded in the cash receipts journal. There is doubt that the balance of Davis's account will be collected.

July 17 Received $56 from Aaron Davis to complete payment of his account, which was written off on January 15. The cash obtained has already been recorded in the cash receipts journal.

Sept. 24 Received $105 from the estate of Paul O'Grady as part of the settlement of his affairs. This amount is applicable to the note receivable written off on March 20. The cash obtained has already been recorded in the cash receipts journal.

Sept. 30 The account receivable of Helen Hart, amounting to $75, is determined to be uncollectible and is to be written off.

PROBLEM 22-2A **Estimating and recording uncollectible accounts on the basis of sales.** The U-Build Company sells building materials on credit and records sales in three separate revenue accounts. The company's experience has been that each sales category has a different rate of losses from uncollectible accounts. Thus the total that the company charges off for these losses at the end of each accounting period is based on three computations (one computation for each revenue account). The firm uses the percentage of credit sales method.

As of December 31, 19X1, Accounts Receivable has a balance of $234,550 and Allowance for Uncollectible Accounts has a credit balance of $2,860. The following table provides a breakdown of the credit sales for the year 19X1 and the estimated rates of loss.

CREDIT SALES		
		ESTIMATED
CATEGORY	AMOUNT	RATE OF LOSS
Plumbing	$625,000	0.9%
Electrical	470,000	1.4%
Hardware	138,000	2.0%

Instructions
1. Compute the estimated amount of losses from uncollectible accounts for each of the three categories of credit sales for the year.
2. Prepare an adjusting entry in general journal form to provide for the losses before they occur. (Use Loss From Uncollectible Accounts.)
3. Show how Accounts Receivable and Allowance for Uncollectible Accounts should appear on the balance sheet of the U-Build Company as of December 31, 19X1.
4. On February 17, 19X2, the account receivable of Linda Ellis, amounting to $344, is determined to be uncollectible and is to be written off. Record this transaction in the general journal.
5. On May 15, 19X2, the attorneys for the U-Build Company turned over a check for $344 that they obtained from Linda Ellis in settlement of her account, which was written off on February 17. The money has already been recorded in the cash receipts journal. Make an entry in the general journal to cancel the original write-off.

PROBLEM 22-3A   **Estimating and recording uncollectible accounts on the basis of accounts receivable.** The schedule of accounts receivable by age shown below was prepared for the Fashion Clothing Store at the end of the firm's fiscal year on July 31, 19X2.

FASHION CLOTHING STORE
Schedule of Accounts Receivable by Age
July 31, 19X2

| ACCOUNT WITH | BALANCE | CURRENT | PAST DUE—DAYS | | |
			1–30	31–60	OVER 60
Armad, John	127 00	63 00	64 00		
Bates, Steven	236 00	111 00	90 00	35 00	
Cline, Judith	98 00	98 00			
Derr, Allen	19 00	19 00			
Everett, Linda	316 00			208 00	108 00
Foley, Ann	74 00	29 00	45 00		
Gorin, Charles	197 00	68 00	92 00		37 00
Hayes, Frank	252 00	114 00	138 00		
Ivan, Thomas	132 00			132 00	
Jones, Ellen	59 00		59 00		
(All Other Accounts)	5,637 00	2,932 00	1,874 00	453 00	378 00
Totals	7,147 00	3,434 00	2,362 00	828 00	523 00

Instructions   1. Compute the estimated uncollectible accounts at the end of the fiscal year using these rates.

Current	1%	31–60 days past due	10%
1–30 days past due	4%	Over 60 days past due	20%

2. On June 30, 19X2, there is a debit balance of $113.50 in Allowance for Uncollectible Accounts. Compute the amount of the adjustment for estimated losses from uncollectible accounts that must be made as part of the adjusting entries.

3. In general journal form, record the adjustment for the estimated losses. (Use Loss From Uncollectible Accounts.)

4. On July 18, 19X2, the account receivable of Thomas Ivan, amounting to $132, was recognized as uncollectible because of his serious illness. Record this write-off in the general journal.

5. On August 2, 19X2, a check for $100 was received from Donna Ryan to apply on her account, which was written off on April 19, 19X1, as uncollectible. Record the cancellation of the previous write-off in the general journal. The cash obtained has already been entered in the cash receipts journal.

6. Suppose that instead of aging the accounts receivable, the store estimated the uncollectible accounts to be simply 5 percent of the total accounts receivable on July 31. Give the general journal entry to record the adjustment for estimated losses from uncollectible accounts. Assume that Allowance for Uncollectible Accounts has a credit balance of $62.50 before the adjusting entry.

PROBLEM 22-4A   **Using different methods to estimate uncollectible accounts.** The balances of selected accounts of the Murphy Company on December 31, 19X3, are given below. (Credit sales were $13,100,000. Returns and allowances on these sales were $69,200.)

Accounts Receivable	$ 1,480,000
Allowance for Uncollectible Accounts	4,200 (credit)
Sales	16,700,000
Sales Returns and Allowances	90,400

Instructions   1. Compute the amount to be charged to Loss From Uncollectible Accounts under each of the following different assumptions.
   a. Uncollectible accounts are estimated to be 0.25 percent of net credit sales.
   b. Uncollectible accounts are estimated to be 0.2 percent of total net sales.
   c. Experience has shown that about 1.75 percent of the accounts receivable will prove worthless.
2. Suppose that Allowance for Uncollectible Accounts has a debit balance of $4,200 instead of a credit balance, but all other account balances remain the same. Compute the amount to be charged to Loss From Uncollectible Accounts under each of the assumptions listed in Part 1.

PROBLEM 22-5A   **Using the installment method.** Tarak Appliances is a retail store that sells household appliances and equipment. Small items are sold for cash or on open account to approved credit customers. Major appliances are sometimes sold for cash but are usually sold on the installment plan. Some installment sales transactions that Tarak had with one customer during the years 19X4 to 19X6 are summarized below. Tarak's rate of gross profit on installment sales is 40 percent.

Instructions   Record the transactions in general journal form.

TRANSACTIONS FOR 19X4

July   2 Sold a refrigerator for $1,000 on the installment plan to Steven Perry. He made a down payment of $75 and agreed to pay $25 on the first day of each month thereafter, beginning August 1, 19X4. Tarak paid $600 for the refrigerator.

Aug.   1 Received a check for $25 from Perry as the first monthly payment.

Dec.   31 Recorded the portion of the deferred income on the installment sale to Perry that was earned during 19X4. (Assume that Perry made all the required monthly payments in 19X4.)

TRANSACTION FOR 19X5

Dec.   31 Recorded the portion of the deferred income on the installment sale to Perry that was earned during 19X5. (Again assume that Perry made all the required monthly payments.)

TRANSACTION FOR 19X6

Mar.   15 Repossessed the refrigerator because Perry failed to make any payments in 19X6. On its return, the refrigerator had an appraised value of $180 and was placed in Tarak's inventory.

CHAPTER

23

Information about merchandise inventory must be reported on the financial statements at the end of each accounting period. In Part 1 you saw how a small business valued its inventory in order to provide the necessary data for the financial statements. Larger firms use more complex methods for inventory valuation. Such methods are discussed in this chapter.

MERCHANDISE INVENTORY

IMPORTANCE OF INVENTORY VALUATION

Merchandise Inventory is the one account that appears on both the balance sheet and the income statement. Its valuation is important because in many businesses it represents the asset with the largest dollar amount. At the same time, inventory valuation directly affects the amount of net income or net loss reported for the accounting period.

If other items remain the same, the larger the ending inventory valuation, the lower the cost of goods sold and the higher the reported net income (or the lower the reported net loss). The smaller the ending inventory valuation, the higher the cost of goods sold and the lower the reported net income (or the higher the reported net loss). Thus determining the proper accounting value of inventory is vital.

In most businesses the merchandise inventory at the end of each accounting period is determined by actually counting the number of units of each type of goods on hand and multiplying that number by the appropriate cost per item. This process is known as *taking a physical inventory,* and it is the approach we will use in this chapter. However, in some types of businesses, especially manufacturing businesses, it is desirable to know *at all times* the number of units and the total cost of each item. The procedure used to gain this information is known as the *perpetual inventory procedure.* Perpetual inventory records are discussed in a later chapter.

INVENTORY COSTING METHODS

In Part 1 the merchandise inventory of the businesses discussed was valued at the purchase cost of the items on hand. In such small firms, the valuation of inventory is a relatively simple matter. The stock of merchandise is limited, and the manager is in direct daily contact with operations. Thus the inventory valuation can be based on the specific identification of merchandise, as shown on the inventory sheet on page 527.

```
                    MODERN CLEANING SHOP
                        Inventory Sheet
                     Accessories Department

                                              DATE   February 28, 19X2

  QUANTITY              DESCRIPTION              UNIT COST          TOTAL

  600 sets   Assorted hangers, 8 in set          $1.00         $  600.00
     35      Hat racks                            2.00             70.00
     38      Tie racks                            2.50             95.00
     20      Shoe racks                           3.00             60.00
     62      Shoeshine kits                       2.25            139.50
     18      3-suit garment bags,
             plastic                               .75             13.50
     40      2-suit garment bags,
             plastic                               .40             16.00
     10      Mothproofing spray cans              .60              6.00

             Total inventory                                  $1,000.00
```

Specific Identification Method

As noted previously, it may be possible to keep a record of the purchase price of each item in inventory and therefore to determine the exact cost of the specific merchandise sold. Automobile dealers, art dealers, and merchants who deal with items having a large unit cost or with one-of-a-kind items may account for their inventory by the *specific identification method*. However, this method is not practical for a business such as the Style Clothing Store, where hundreds of similar items of relatively small unit value—such as shirts, blouses, and sweaters—are carried in the inventory. Furthermore, the purchase cost of many types of items may change during the accounting period. Fortunately, accountants can consider several other costing methods in their search for the best one to apply to each business situation.

Average Cost Method

Instead of keeping a record of the cost of each item purchased, it is possible to average the cost of all like items available for sale during the period. This average cost can then be used to value the ending inventory. To understand how the *average cost method* works, study the following analysis of purchases of a certain brand and quality of shirts during the fiscal year of February 1, 19X1, to January 31, 19X2.

Explanation	No. of Units	Unit Cost	Total Cost
Beginning Inventory, Feb. 1, 19X1	100	$6.00	$ 600.00
Purchases:			
Feb. 27, 19X1	50	6.50	325.00
April 20, 19X1	100	7.00	700.00
Oct. 15, 19X1	75	7.50	562.50
Jan. 10, 19X2	75	8.00	600.00
Total Merchandise Available for Sale	400		$2,787.50
Average Cost ($2,787.50 ÷ 400)		$6.9688	
Ending Inventory, Jan. 31, 19X2	125	6.9688	871.10
Cost of Goods Sold	275	6.9688	$1,916.40

Note that the computation begins with the number of units, unit cost, and total cost of the beginning inventory. To these figures are added the amounts of all purchases made during the period. The sum of the units in the beginning inventory and the units purchased represents the total units available for sale. The total cost of the beginning inventory is added to the total cost of each lot purchased to obtain the total cost of the units available for sale. This total cost, $2,787.50, is then divided by the total number of units available to find the average unit cost ($2,787.50 ÷ 400 = $6.9688). The value of the ending inventory is established by multiplying the number of units on hand by the average unit cost (125 × $6.9688 = $871.10). The cost of goods sold can then be easily determined by subtracting the value of the ending inventory from the total value of the merchandise available for sale ($2,787.50 − $871.10 = $1,916.40). The procedure just described is sometimes referred to as the *weighted average method* because it considers both the number of units in each purchase and the unit purchase price in computing a weighted average cost per unit.

The average cost method of inventory valuation is relatively simple to use, but it reflects the limitations of any procedure that involves average figures. The unit cost cannot be related to any tangible unit or lot of merchandise, and it does not reveal price changes as clearly as might be desired. In highly competitive businesses that are subject to significant price and style changes, it is desirable to have a more specific and revealing method of cost determination. Two other popular methods of valuation are the first in, first out method and the last in, first out method.

First In, First Out Method

In most businesses, merchants naturally try to sell their oldest items first. Thus the merchandise on hand at any given time is usually the latest bought. The *first in, first out method* of inventory valuation (usually referred to as FIFO) parallels this physical flow of inventory. The cost of the ending inventory is computed by referring to the cost of the latest purchases.

Using the figures from the previous example, the cost of the ending inventory of 125 units is $975 under the FIFO pricing method, as shown below.

EXPLANATION	NO. OF UNITS	UNIT COST	TOTAL COST
From Purchase of Jan. 10, 19X2	75	$8.00	$600.00
From Purchase of Oct. 15, 19X1	50	7.50	375.00
Ending Inventory, Jan. 31, 19X2	125		$975.00

The cost of goods sold is then found by subtracting the value of the ending inventory from the total value of the merchandise available for sale, which was previously computed ($2,787.50 − $975.00 = $1,812.50).

Actually, the FIFO method attempts to approximate the results of the specific identification method, even though large and varied stocks of merchandise are involved. While it does not identify specific items, it does distinguish between recent and earlier purchases of stock so that the inventory valuation will reflect the most recent price levels. This means that the cost of goods sold will reflect the costs applicable to the oldest goods handled during the period. In a time of rising prices, the difference in the cost of goods sold may have a significant impact on the net income to be reported. For example, there is a difference of $103.90 between the average cost method and the FIFO method in the costing of the 275 shirts sold during the period.

Cost of Goods Sold (Average Cost Method)	$1,916.40
Cost of Goods Sold (FIFO Method)	1,812.50
Difference	$ 103.90

Last In, First Out Method

While the FIFO method will result in a more favorable profit picture under the circumstances just discussed, many accountants, owners, and managers hesitate to use it. They believe that the current cost of merchandise should be matched as closely as possible to current sales dollars. They say that failure to do this means ignoring the ultimate day of reckoning, when inventory has to be replaced at higher costs. The system of valuation that they consider more conservative and realistic is the *last in, first out (LIFO) method*.

The LIFO method of inventory pricing assumes that the most current costs of merchandise purchased should be charged to the cost of goods sold. Thus the value assigned to the inventory still on hand is the cost of the oldest merchandise available during the period. Using the figures from the previous example, the value of the 125 shirts on hand at the end of the period is $762.50. The amount is determined as follows.

EXPLANATION	NO. OF UNITS	UNIT COST	TOTAL COST
From Beginning Inventory, Feb. 1, 19X1	100	$6.00	$600.00
From Purchase of Feb. 27, 19X1	25	6.50	162.50
Ending Inventory, Jan. 31, 19X2	125		$762.50

The cost of goods sold is computed by subtracting $762.50 from the previously established value of the merchandise available for sale ($2,787.50 − $762.50 = $2,025.00). It is apparent that in a time of rising prices, the relatively lower inventory valuation under the LIFO method tends to increase the reported cost of goods sold and decrease the reported net income.

Obviously, the LIFO method of determining inventory costs does not match the actual physical flow of merchandise in most businesses. It is merely a procedure developed for charging the current costs of goods against current sales prices.

Comparing the Results of Inventory Costing Methods

The different results obtained from the use of the average cost, FIFO, and LIFO inventory methods can be seen in the illustration on page 530. (The analysis of purchases is the same as the one shown on page 527.)

Notice that the ending inventory valuation of the same 125 shirts ranges from a low of $762.50 when the LIFO method is used to a high of $975 when the FIFO method is used. The average cost method gives a figure in between (as is almost always the case) of $871.10. Subtracting the ending inventory valuation

COMPARISON OF RESULTS OF INVENTORY COSTING METHODS

Explanation	Units	Unit Cost	Total Cost	Inventory Valuation	Cost of Goods Sold
Beginning Inventory, Feb. 1, 19X1	100	$6.00	$ 600.00		
Purchases:					
Feb. 27, 19X1	50	6.50	325.00		
April 20, 19X1	100	7.00	700.00		
Oct. 15, 19X1	75	7.50	562.50		
Jan. 10, 19X2	75	8.00	600.00		
Total Merchandise Available for Sale	400		$2,787.50		
1. Average Cost Method					
Average Cost per Unit		$6.9688			
Valuation of Ending Inventory	125	6.9688		$871.10	
Cost of Goods Sold					$1,916.40
2. First In, First Out Method					
From Purchase of Jan. 10	75	$8.00	$ 600.00		
From Purchase of Oct. 15	50	7.50	375.00		
Valuation of Ending Inventory				$975.00	
Cost of Goods Sold					$1,812.50
3. Last In, First Out Method					
From Beginning Inventory, Feb. 1	100	$6.00	$ 600.00		
From Purchase of Feb. 27	25	6.50	162.50		
Valuation of Ending Inventory				$762.50	
Cost of Goods Sold					$2,025.00

in each case from the total cost of merchandise available for sale, $2,787.50, gives a high cost of goods sold of $2,025 with the LIFO method and a low cost of goods sold of $1,812.50 with the FIFO method. The average cost method usually gives a figure in between ($1,916.40 in this situation).

Since price trends are a vital element in any inventory valuation, remember these basic rules. In a period of rising prices, the LIFO method results in a higher reported cost of goods sold and a lower reported net income than the FIFO method. In a period of falling prices, the LIFO method results in a lower reported cost of goods sold and a higher reported net income than the FIFO method. Whatever direction prices take, the average cost method results in a reported net income somewhere between the amounts obtained with FIFO and LIFO.

A business cannot change its inventory valuation method at will from one period to the next in order to report the amount of net income it prefers. Once the firm adopts a method, it should use that method consistently from one period to the next. If the managers of a business want to change the method of inventory valuation, they should refer to specific authoritative guides that spell out in detail how the change should be treated on the financial statements. These rules are beyond the scope of this text. For federal income tax purposes, a business must obtain permission from the Director of Internal Revenue before making a change in inventory methods. Although a firm can generally use one accounting method for financial accounting purposes and another for federal income tax purposes, the firm must use the LIFO method for financial accounting if that method is adopted for tax purposes.

COST OR MARKET, WHICHEVER IS LOWER

The methods of inventory valuation discussed so far have been based on cost. However, as you learned in Chapter 19, accountants generally believe that the asset valuation used on the balance sheet should be conservative and should not overstate the asset values. If the market price of an inventory item declines, the merchant will probably have trouble selling it at the usual increase, or markon, above original cost. If the price decline is especially severe, the merchant may even have to sell the item at a loss. Consequently, accountants prefer to value inventory according to the rule of *cost or market, whichever is lower*. As the name of this rule suggests, when the price of an item is below its original purchase cost, the accountant values it at market price instead of cost in order to reflect the lower current value in the firm's financial records.

The market price for the purpose of applying the rule can be described as the price at which the item could be bought (at the inventory date) through the usual channels and in the usual quantities. In some cases, current market prices are quoted in trade publications. In other cases, a recent purchase may give a price that is reasonably close to the current market price. In still other circumstances, the firm's regular suppliers can provide quotations for use in valuing the goods. There are two major ways of applying the lower of cost or market rule. The first is to apply it item by item. The second is to use the total cost and the total market value.

Lower of Cost or Market by Items

If the lower of cost or market rule is to be applied item by item, the cost is determined for each item in the inventory according to one of the acceptable methods (specific identification, average cost, FIFO, or LIFO). Current market price is also determined for each item. Then the basis of valuation (the lower figure) is selected. Finally, the quantity on hand of the item is multiplied by the valuation amount to obtain the total value at the lower of cost or market. The lower value figures for all items are added to determine the value of the inventory as a whole. The application of this rule is illustrated below with assumed figures for two stock items (A and B).

Description	Quantity	Unit Price Cost	Unit Price Market	Valuation Basis	Lower of Cost or Market
Item A	100	$1.00	$1.10	Cost	$100.00
Item B	200	1.50	1.20	Market	240.00
Inventory Valuation—Lower of Cost or Market by Items					$340.00

Lower of Total Cost or Total Market

Under another method of applying the rule of the lower of cost or market, the total cost and the total market value of the entire inventory are computed. The lower of these total figures is then used as the inventory valuation.

| | | Unit Price | | Total | Total |
Description	Quantity	Cost	Market	Cost	Market
Item A	100	$1.00	$1.10	$100.00	$110.00
Item B	200	1.50	1.20	300.00	240.00
				$400.00	$350.00
Inventory Valuation—Lower of Total Cost or Total Market					$350.00

This procedure gives a somewhat less conservative inventory valuation than the item-by-item method if the prices of some items have risen while others have declined. However, advocates of this method justify it on the ground that the total inventory figure is the one that should be presented conservatively. If the market value of the inventory as a whole has not declined below cost, then no adjustment is made and the cost value is presented on the statements.

Lower of Cost or Market by Groups

A variation on the method discussed above involves classifying inventory items by groups or departments and determining the lower of total cost or total market according to these classifications. The lower figure (cost or market) for each group is added to the lower figures for the other groups to obtain the total inventory valuation. Assuming that Items A and B in the preceding example make up Group 1 and that Items C and D make up Group 2, the basic computations required for the group total method are as shown below.

| | | Unit Price | | Total | Total |
Description	Quantity	Cost	Market	Cost	Market
Group 1					
Item A	100	$1.00	$1.10	$100.00	$110.00
Item B	200	1.50	1.20	300.00	240.00
Totals—Group 1				$400.00	$350.00*
Group 2					
Item C	30	$ .70	$ .60	$ 21.00	$ 18.00
Item D	150	.60	.80	90.00	120.00
Totals—Group 2				$111.00*	$138.00

*Lower Figures

In this case, market ($350) is the lower basis for valuation of the items in Group 1, and cost ($111) is the lower basis for valuation of the items in Group 2.

The combined value of Groups 1 and 2 is $461 ($350 + $111). Compare this valuation with the figures obtained from the two other methods that are shown below.

	Lower of Cost or Market by Items			Lower of Total Cost or Total Market		
					Valued at	
Item	Basis	Valuation		Item	Cost	Market
A	Cost	$100		A	$100	$110
B	Market	240		B	300	240
C	Market	18		C	21	18
D	Cost	90		D	90	120
		$448			$511	$488*

*Lower Figure

Valuation according to lower of total cost or total market by groups is a method that produces middle-of-the-road figures. It does not reflect individual fluctuations, as the lower of cost or market by items method does. But it also does not lump together as many value variations as the grand total cost or market figures do. The final choice of one of the three methods will depend on many factors, including the size and variety of the stock of merchandise, the margin of profit on which the business operates, practices in the industry, and the firm's future plans for expansion. Usually, however, the lower of cost or market by items is used.

INVENTORY ESTIMATION PROCEDURES

Sometimes the managers of a business want to know the approximate cost of its inventory without taking a physical count and applying one of the costing procedures. For example, if a fire occurs, the firm will need to know the cost of the goods destroyed in order to provide data for insurance and income tax purposes. Similarly, a department manager in a retail store may be permitted to have only a certain amount of money tied up in inventory. Therefore, the manager must be able to estimate the cost of the department's inventory at any time. Two common techniques for estimating inventory are the gross profit method and the retail method.

Gross Profit Method

The *gross profit method* of estimating inventory assumes that the rate of gross profit on sales is about the same from period to period. It also assumes that the ratio of cost of goods sold to net sales is relatively constant. The procedure can be illustrated as follows. Assume that a company's entire merchandise inventory is destroyed by fire June 26, 19X1, but that its accounting records are preserved. An analysis of the company's income statements for the two preceding years shows that the gross profit rate has been 40 percent of net sales (or that the cost of goods sold has been 60 percent of net sales). The records for the current year provide the following figures.

Inventory (at cost), Jan. 1, 19X1	$ 40,000
Net Purchases (Jan. 1 to June 26, 19X1)	120,000
Net Sales (Jan. 1 to June 26, 19X1)	210,000

The first step is to estimate the cost of goods sold for the period of January 1 to June 26. Since sales were $210,000 and the ratio of cost of goods sold to net sales is assumed to be 60 percent, the estimated cost of goods sold is computed as follows: $0.60 \times \$210,000 = \$126,000$.

The second step is to determine the cost of goods available for sale. This computation is shown below.

Beginning Inventory	$ 40,000
Net Purchases	120,000
Cost of Goods Available for Sale	$160,000

The final step is to compute the estimated ending (destroyed) inventory by subtracting the estimated cost of goods sold ($126,000) from the cost of goods available for sale ($160,000), as shown below.

Cost of Goods Available for Sale	$160,000
Estimated Cost of Goods Sold	126,000
Estimated Ending Inventory	$ 34,000

Retail Method of Inventory Pricing

Another method of estimating inventories, widely used by retailers, is called the *retail method*. Under this method, inventory is classified into groups of items that have about the same rate of markon. (*Markon* is the difference between the cost and the initially established retail price of merchandise.)

The beginning inventory is valued both at cost and at retail. At the time merchandise is purchased, it is recorded at cost and its retail value is determined. The retail value of all merchandise available for sale is obtained by adding the retail value of the beginning inventory and the retail value of the new merchandise purchased. Sales are recorded at their retail price in the usual manner. When the total of sales at retail is subtracted from the total retail value of the merchandise available for sale, the difference is the retail value of the ending inventory. This amount is multiplied by the cost ratio (Total Available for Sale at Cost ÷ Total Available for Sale at Retail) to give the approximate cost of the ending inventory. Using assumed figures, the calculations involved in the application of the retail method of inventory pricing are shown on page 535.

In practice, the application of the retail method of inventory pricing is not quite as simple as this example suggests. Records must be kept of further price increases—*markups*—above the original markons, as well as of markup cancellations. Records must also be kept of *markdowns* below the original markon and of markdown cancellations. When all this information is assembled, the resulting calculations can yield an inventory valuation that will approximate the lower of

	Cost	Retail
Beginning Inventory	$ 4,900	$ 7,500
Merchandise Purchases	60,000	90,000
Freight	100	
Total Merchandise Available for Sale	$65,000	$97,500
Less Sales		79,200
Ending Inventory Priced at Retail		$18,300

$$\text{Cost Ratio} = \frac{\$65,000}{\$97,500} = 66\frac{2}{3}\%$$

Conversion to Approximate Cost:

Ending Inventory at Retail × Cost Ratio	$18,300	
	×0.6667	
Ending Inventory at Cost		$12,200
Cost of Goods Sold ($65,000 − $12,200)		$52,800

cost or market. The requirements of the retail inventory method are discussed in more detail in intermediate-level accounting textbooks.

When there are many merchandise items of small unit value, as is often the case in retail stores, the retail method of inventory pricing permits a firm to determine the approximate cost of its ending inventory from the financial records. Thus the firm does not have to take a physical inventory. In turn, the ease of determining the inventory value makes it possible for the firm to prepare financial statements easily and often.

Many retail stores take a periodic inventory at retail values, using the sales price marked on the merchandise. Then the physical inventory at retail is converted to cost by applying the cost ratio. This is done in the way that the ending retail inventory computed in the previous example was reduced to cost. The Style Clothing Store uses this method of valuation because of its simplicity and because of the firm's need to have inventory values available often.

INTERNAL CONTROL OF INVENTORIES

The degree of physical control over inventories must be appropriate for the nature of the goods involved. For example, the type of control system used for an inventory containing small, valuable, easily disposed of items such as jewelry would be greatly different from that used for an inventory made up of lumber. The former would require far more elaborate safeguards than the latter.

Merchandise purchases should be controlled through a voucher system or a similar mechanism. The removal of merchandise from a company's warehouse or premises should only be made on the basis of such documents as sales invoices and shipping orders. A physical inventory should be taken periodically (at least annually) to verify the goods on hand. The procedures used for the physical inventory should include not only techniques that are designed to produce accurate original counts but also techniques for spot-checking the accuracy of the counts. Similarly, the unit cost figures used in computing the inventory should be verified through spot checks. If the company is having an audit performed by outside auditors, it is customary for a member of the auditor's staff to observe the physical counting process.

PRINCIPLES AND PROCEDURES SUMMARY

There are several inventory costing methods. The specific identification method uses the actual purchase price of the specific items in inventory. The average cost method uses the average of the cost of all like items available for sale during the period for valuing the ending inventory. The first in, first out (FIFO) method develops the cost of the ending inventory from the cost of later purchases. The last in, first out (LIFO) method develops the cost of the ending inventory from the cost of earlier purchases. In a period of rising prices, the LIFO method will result in a lower reported net income than the FIFO method. In a period of falling prices, the LIFO method will result in a higher reported net income. The average cost method will always give a result between the two.

Not all inventory valuation is based on the purchase cost. The rule of cost or market, whichever is lower, is the most conservative method available. It can be applied to individual items in the inventory, to groups of items, or to the inventory as a whole.

The gross profit method of estimating inventory involves estimating the cost of goods sold by applying a historical cost ratio to the sales of the current period. The estimated cost of goods sold is then subtracted from the cost of goods available for sale to arrive at the estimated ending inventory.

The retail method of inventory pricing uses the retail selling price of the items remaining. The retail value of the inventory is multiplied by the cost ratio of the current period to reach the approximate cost. An estimate of the inventory approximating the lower of cost or market can be obtained by fully considering markups, markup cancellations, markdowns, and markdown cancellations.

MANAGERIAL IMPLICATIONS

Because inventory makes up a large part of the assets of most businesses, it must be carefully controlled. The inventory costing method chosen by management must be one that is practical, reliable, and as simple as possible to apply. Inventory valuation is very important in computing federal income tax because the value placed on the inventory determines the net income reported. For example, in times of rising prices, the LIFO method is a means of lowering the income tax by charging off a higher cost of goods sold.

The gross profit method of estimating inventory is an especially valuable tool for approximating the cost of an inventory. It is used in preparing budgets when a physical count cannot be made, and it is used in verifying the reasonableness of the inventory computed under an actual physical count.

Management should consider the retail method of inventory pricing as a means of estimating the cost of goods on hand at any given time. This estimate is especially important in retail businesses where department managers have inventory budgets—specified amounts they are allowed to tie up in inventory. Such managers generally need to know often, sometimes weekly, the amount of inventory they have on hand.

REVIEW QUESTIONS

1. Why does the ending merchandise inventory amount appear on both the balance sheet and the income statement?
2. What is a physical inventory?
3. Explain what is meant by perpetual inventory.
4. Explain the specific identification method of inventory valuation.
5. Is the specific identification method of inventory valuation suitable for a retail grocery store? Why or why not?
6. Explain the assumption underlying the FIFO method. Does this generally agree with the physical flow of merchandise?
7. If prices are rising, will an inventory be higher under the LIFO method or the FIFO method? Explain.
8. What is meant by the term *market* as it is used in the lower of cost or market method of inventory valuation?
9. If a business uses the lower of cost or market method of inventory valuation, how is cost determined?
10. Explain how the lower of cost or market method is applied on a group basis.
11. Is the value of an inventory likely to be lower if the lower of cost or market method is applied on an item-by-item basis, on a group basis, or to the inventory as a whole? Why or why not?
12. Explain the gross profit method of estimating inventories.
13. Suggest two situations in which it might be desirable to estimate inventories without a physical count.
14. Define the term *markon*.
15. Define the term *markdown*.
16. Describe how the cost of an ending inventory is estimated under the retail method.

MANAGERIAL DISCUSSION QUESTIONS

1. Why would management be interested in using the LIFO method of inventory valuation during a period of rising prices?
2. In order to achieve better control over its investment in inventory, the management of a retail store wishes to get an estimate of the cost of inventory at the close of business each week. Outline a procedure to obtain this estimate without actually taking a physical count.
3. Why must management provide for strict control over a firm's inventory?
4. The purchasing manager of a retail store has suggested that the company should maintain a perpetual inventory. The controller opposes this sugges-

tion. In your opinion, on what basis does the controller probably oppose the idea?

5. In what special situations are inventory estimation procedures extremely useful?

6. Why do managers instruct their sales personnel to sell the oldest merchandise first?

7. The manager of a retail store has grown concerned about the time taken to count the merchandise on hand each quarter. She argues that too much time is spent on this activity, with a resulting high cost. She suggests that the company need not take a physical inventory at all but could rely on the retail inventory estimation procedure to arrive at the cost of the inventory. Respond to this argument.

EXERCISES

EXERCISE 23-1   **Using the average cost method of inventory valuation.** Information about the O'Brien Company's inventory of one item during 19X1 is given below. If the firm uses the average cost method, what will be the cost of its ending inventory?

	NO. OF UNITS	UNIT COST
Beginning Inventory, Jan. 1, 19X1	50	$160
Purchases:		
March 19X1	40	162
July 19X1	45	164
November 19X1	30	168
Ending Inventory, Dec. 31, 19X1	35	

EXERCISE 23-2   **Using the FIFO method of inventory valuation.** If the O'Brien Company uses the FIFO method, what will be the cost of its ending inventory? Obtain the necessary data from Exercise 23-1.

EXERCISE 23-3   **Using the LIFO method of inventory valuation.** If the O'Brien Company uses the LIFO method, what will be the cost of its ending inventory? Obtain the necessary data from Exercise 23-1.

EXERCISE 23-4   **Comparing the results of the average cost, FIFO, and LIFO methods.** Do the following work for the O'Brien Company. Obtain the necessary data from your solutions to Exercises 23-1, 23-2, and 23-3.

1. Determine the cost of goods sold under each of the three methods.
2. Arrange the inventory amounts from highest to lowest, and compute the differences between the amounts under each of the three valuation methods.

EXERCISE 23-5   **Using the lower of cost or market method on an item-by-item basis.** The following information concerns four items that the Fischer Company has in its inventory. Two of these items are in the hardware department, and two are in the household goods department. What is the valuation of the ending inventory if the firm uses the lower of cost or market method and applies it on an item-by-item basis?

	Quantity	Unit Cost	Market Value
Hardware			
Item A	300	$30	$32
Item B	220	40	39
Household Goods			
Item Y	600	42	50
Item Z	480	20	14

EXERCISE 23-6 **Using the lower of total cost or total market method.** If the Fischer Company uses the lower of cost or market method and applies it on the basis of total cost and total market, what is the valuation of the ending inventory? Obtain the necessary data from Exercise 23-5.

EXERCISE 23-7 **Using the lower of cost or market method on a group basis.** If the Fischer Company uses the lower of cost or market method and applies it to inventory groups, what is the valuation of the ending inventory? Obtain the necessary data from Exercise 23-5.

EXERCISE 23-8 **Estimating inventory cost under the gross profit method.** Use the following data to compute the estimated inventory cost for the Sanchez Company under the gross profit method.

   Average Gross Profit Rate: 45% of Sales
   Inventory on January 1 (at cost): $60,000
   Purchases From January 1 to Date of Inventory Estimate: $382,000
   Net Sales for Period: $790,000

EXERCISE 23-9 **Estimating inventory cost under the gross profit method.** Assume the same data as in Exercise 23-8, except that the Sanchez Company has a gross profit rate of 48 percent. Compute the estimated cost of the ending inventory.

EXERCISE 23-10 **Estimating inventory cost under the retail method.** Based on the following data, compute the estimated cost of the ending inventory at the Rand Company. Use the retail method.

	COST	RETAIL
Beginning Inventory	$ 40,000	$ 72,000
Purchases	179,000	324,000
Freight	1,000	
Sales		350,000

PROBLEMS

PROBLEM 23-1   **Computing inventory costs under different valuation methods.** The following data concerns inventory and purchases at the Khori Company.

Inventory, Jan.	1	1,800 units at $4.00
Purchases, Jan.	8	1,400 units at $4.20
	Jan. 16	1,200 units at $4.24
	Jan. 24	1,400 units at $4.30
Inventory, Jan.	31	1,820 units

Instructions   Determine the cost of the ending inventory on January 31 under each of the following methods: (1) average cost method, (2) first in, first out (FIFO) method, and (3) last in, first out (LIFO) method. (When using the average cost method, compute the unit cost to four decimal places.)

PROBLEM 23-2   **Computing inventory costs under different valuation methods and applying the lower of cost or market rule.** The following data pertains to Model A home computers that were in the inventory of the Vela Electronics Center during the first six months of 19X1.

Inventory, Jan.	1	22 units at $108
Purchases, Jan.	31	16 units at $102
	Mar. 10	20 units at $97
	May 19	20 units at $95
Inventory, June	30	14 units

Instructions   1. Determine the cost of the inventory on June 30 and the cost of goods sold for the six-month period ending on that date under each of the following valuation methods: *(a)* FIFO, *(b)* LIFO, and *(c)* average cost. (When using the average cost method, compute the unit cost to the nearest cent.)
2. Assume that the replacement cost of each unit on June 30, 19X1, is $96.80. Using the lower of cost or market rule, find the inventory amount under each of the methods given in Part 1.

PROBLEM 23-3   **Applying the lower of cost or market rule by different methods.** The following data concerns inventory at Elkin Products Inc.

	Quantity	Unit Cost	Market Value
Boat Department			
Model T	8	$1,560	$1,800
Model U	7	1,840	1,800
Model W	10	1,360	1,380
Motor Department			
Model A	6	1,380	1,404
Model B	3	1,780	1,760
Model C	5	1,406	1,388

Instructions Determine the amount that the company should report as the inventory valuation at cost or market, whichever is lower. Use each of the following three valuation methods.

1. Lower of cost or market for each item separately.
2. Lower of total cost or total market.
3. Lower of total cost or total market by departments.

PROBLEM 23-4 **Estimating inventory by the gross profit method.** In 19X1 the rate of gross profit on sales at the King Company was 39.9 percent, and in 19X2 the rate was 40.1 percent. At the end of 19X3, the auditor found the following data in the records of the company.

Sales		$1,000,000
Cost of Goods Sold:		
Inventory, Jan. 1, 19X3	$120,000	
Purchases	600,000	
Total Merchandise Available for Sale	$720,000	
Less Inventory, Dec. 31, 19X3	190,000	
Cost of Goods Sold		530,000
Gross Profit on Sales		$ 470,000

Inquiry by the auditor revealed that employees of the King Company had estimated the inventory on December 31, 19X3, instead of taking a complete physical count.

Instructions Using the gross profit method of inventory estimation, verify the reasonableness (or lack of reasonableness) of the inventory estimate made by the company's employees.

PROBLEM 23-5 **Estimating inventory by the retail method.** The Eli Company uses the retail method of inventory pricing. As of December 31, 19X1, the firm's records disclosed the following figures about the beginning inventory for the year, the merchandise purchases made during the period, the total merchandise available, and the total sales.

	ACTUAL COST	RETAIL SALES PRICE
Beginning Inventory, Jan. 1, 19X1	$ 8,000	$ 11,200
Merchandise Purchases During 19X1	72,640	100,800
Total Merchandise Available for Sale	$80,640	$112,000
Total Sales During 19X1 = $98,000		

Instructions
1. Compute the retail value of the ending merchandise inventory as of December 31.
2. Compute the approximate cost of the ending merchandise inventory as of December 31.
3. Compute the cost of goods sold during 19X1.

ALTERNATE PROBLEMS

PROBLEM 23-1A **Computing inventory costs under different valuation methods.** The following data concerns inventory and purchases at the Nichols Company.

Inventory, June	1	150 units at $8.00
Purchases, June	6	200 units at $8.10
	June 14	150 units at $8.40
	June 24	100 units at $8.50
Inventory, June 30		162 units

Instructions Determine the cost of the ending inventory on June 30 under each of the following methods: (1) average cost method, (2) first in, first out (FIFO) method, and (3) last in, first out (LIFO) method. (When using the average cost method, compute the unit cost to four decimal places.)

PROBLEM 23-2A **Computing inventory costs under different valuation methods and applying the lower of cost or market rule.** The following data pertains to Model J insulated doors that were in the inventory of the Building Supply Company during 19X2.

Inventory, Jan.	1	70 units at $42.00
Purchases, Jan.	10	50 units at $42.50
	July 18	75 units at $40.00
	Aug. 12	80 units at $43.30
Inventory, Dec.	31	82 units

Instructions 1. Determine the cost of the inventory on December 31 and the cost of goods sold for the year ending on that date under each of the following valuation methods: *(a)* FIFO, *(b)* LIFO, and *(c)* average cost. (When using the average cost method, compute the unit cost to the nearest cent.)

2. Assume that the replacement cost of each unit on December 31, 19X1, is $41.90. Using the lower of cost or market rule, find the inventory amount under each of the methods given in Part 1.

PROBLEM 23-3A **Applying the lower of cost or market rule by different methods.** The following data concerns inventory at the Harley Electronics Corporation.

	Quantity	Unit Cost	Market Value
Record Department			
Stock No. 101	250	$ 3.00	$ 3.20
Stock No. 102	400	4.40	4.20
Stock No. 103	370	2.00	2.10
Turntable Department			
Stock No. 401	4	170.00	182.00
Stock No. 402	2	410.00	400.00
Stock No. 403	5	153.00	144.00

Instructions Determine the amount to be reported as the inventory valuation at cost or market, whichever is lower, under each of these methods.

1. Lower of cost or market for each item separately.
2. Lower of total cost or total market.
3. Lower of total cost or total market by departments.

PROBLEM 23-4A **Estimating inventory by the gross profit method.** In 19X0 the rate of gross profit on sales at the Kelso Company was 26.2 percent, and in 19X1 the rate was 24.8 percent. At the end of 19X2, the income statement of the company included the following information.

Sales		$820,000
Cost of Goods Sold:		
Inventory, Jan. 1, 19X2	$ 60,000	
Purchases	604,000	
Total Merchandise Available for Sale	$664,000	
Less Inventory, Dec. 31, 19X2	94,000	
Cost of Goods Sold		570,000
Gross Profit on Sales		$250,000

Investigation revealed that employees of the company had not taken an actual physical count of the inventory on December 31, 19X2. Instead, they had merely estimated the inventory.

Instructions Using the gross profit method of inventory estimation, verify the reasonableness (or lack of reasonableness) of the ending inventory shown on the income statement.

PROBLEM 23-5A **Estimating inventory by the retail method.** The January 1 inventory of the Chu Company had a cost of $18,000 and had a retail value of $24,500. During January merchandise was purchased for $8,840 and marked to sell for $11,500. Freight on purchases during January totaled $160. January sales totaled $11,200.

Instructions
1. Compute the retail value of the ending inventory as of January 31.
2. Compute the approximate cost of the ending inventory.
3. Compute the cost of goods sold during January.

Housing and equipping a modern business enterprise for efficient operation often calls for a large investment in property. This chapter explains the accounting procedures and records needed to keep track of the purchase, use, and disposition of property, plant, and equipment—often referred to as fixed assets, or long-lived assets. In addition, the accounting treatment of intangible assets such as patents and copyrights, which have no physical characteristics, is examined.

PROPERTY, PLANT, AND EQUIPMENT; INTANGIBLE ASSETS

PROPERTY, PLANT, AND EQUIPMENT

The category of assets known as property, plant, and equipment includes both *real property* and *tangible personal property*. Among the real property holdings of business enterprises are land, land improvements, buildings, and other structures attached to the land. Tangible personal property consists of machinery, equipment, furniture, and fixtures. Property, plant, and equipment does not include assets not being used in the active conduct of business operations. For example, land purchased for a future building site or land being held for investment would be classified as "other assets" or as "investments," not as property, plant, and equipment. Similarly, intangible assets are not classified as property, plant, and equipment, but separately as "intangible assets."

Three aspects of accounting for property, plant, and equipment are examined in this chapter.

1. The acquisition of these assets.
2. The transfer of the costs of these assets to expense through depreciation or depletion.
3. The disposition of these assets through retirement, sale, or a trade-in for new assets.

ACQUISITION OF PROPERTY, PLANT, AND EQUIPMENT

Items of property, plant, and equipment are usually acquired by purchase. Under the voucher system, a voucher is prepared to authorize payment for an asset. This results in a debit to the appropriate asset account and a credit to Accounts Payable. The voucher is paid in the usual manner, at which time Accounts Payable is debited and Cash is credited.

The total cost of an asset may actually be made up of several elements, each of which must be debited to the account for that asset. The general rule is that the acquisition cost of an asset includes the net price paid the seller, all transportation and installation costs, and the cost of any adjustments or modifications needed to prepare the asset for use. (A cash discount taken for prompt payment of an invoice for an asset should be credited to the asset account rather than to Purchases Discount. The credit to the asset account can be recorded in the general journal with an offsetting debit to Accounts Payable if a voucher was previously recorded for the gross amount of the invoice.)

Suppose that the Style Clothing Store purchases an office machine at a price of $337.50 *FOB (free on board)* the factory (which means that the buyer pays for transportation from the factory). The freight bill is $36.25. When the machine arrives, the firm decides to have extra features installed on it locally, at a net cost of $26.25. At what cost is the machine entered in the Office Equipment account?

The seller's invoice is the first amount to be debited to the Office Equipment account. The transportation charge paid by the Style Clothing Store is part of the cost of the machine and should also be debited to that account. The cost of the changes made to the machine before it is suitable for the intended use is a further charge to the asset account. When all these charges have been posted to the Office Equipment account, the total acquisition cost of the machine will be $400, as shown below.

Net amount paid to seller	$337.50
Freight	36.25
Minor changes in operating features	26.25
Total acquisition cost of machine	$400.00

In the case of land purchased for a building site, the acquisition cost of the land should include the net costs (less salvage) of removing unwanted buildings and of grading and draining the land. The costs of installing permanent walks or roadways, curbing, gutters, and drainage facilities should be capitalized as Land Improvements, subject to depreciation. Some companies that buy land in advance of its use capitalize taxes and other carrying charges as part of the land's cost up to the time the property is used for business purposes.

When items of property, plant, and equipment are constructed by the company for its own use, interest costs incurred on borrowed funds during the construction period are capitalized.[1] The amount capitalized is the interest deemed to apply to the average amount of accumulated costs during the period. If funds have been borrowed specifically for construction, the rate paid on those funds should be used in determining the amount capitalized. If funds are not borrowed for that specific purpose, the rate used is usually the average rate paid on all borrowed funds during the period. The amount of interest capitalized cannot, however, exceed the actual interest costs incurred during the period.

For example, assume that a new warehouse is being constructed by the Gordon Company. During the year the average amount of funds invested in the construction in progress was $2,180,000. The company had borrowed $1,500,000 specifically for use on the project, with interest paid on this loan at the rate of 11 percent. The remaining average investment of $680,000 was financed from other sources. The average rate paid by the firm on its other borrow-

---

[1]"Capitalization of Interest Cost," *Statement of Financial Accounting Standards, No. 34* (Stamford, Conn.: Financial Accounting Standards Board, 1979).

ings, which totaled $5,000,000, was 12½ percent. The interest to be capitalized and thus to become part of the building's cost is $250,000.

Interest on specific borrowing for project (11% × $1,500,000)	$165,000
Interest on balance of average investment (12½% × $680,000)	85,000
Total	$250,000

If the company's total interest paid on funds other than those borrowed specifically for the construction project had been only $65,000, the total amount capitalized would have been limited to $230,000 ($165,000 + $65,000).

COST OF USING PROPERTY, PLANT, AND EQUIPMENT

Several obvious costs are incurred in using assets. These costs include repairs, maintenance, insurance, and taxes. However, there are also hidden costs. Assets such as buildings and machines do not last forever. Their inevitable wearing out through use in a firm's operations must be taken into account as an additional expense of doing business. Other types of assets such as natural resources are also used up in the course of a firm's operations. Two technical terms are commonly used by accountants to distinguish the nature of the expense involved. *Depreciation* is the name given to the allocation of the costs of assets created by human effort, such as buildings and equipment. The allocation of the costs of natural resources, such as minerals, to the units produced is referred to as *depletion*. In addition, the costs of intangible assets are transferred to expense through *amortization*, which is discussed later in this chapter. Depreciation and depletion are explained in detail in the following pages.

Depreciation

As noted above, *depreciation* is the term used in accounting to describe the periodic transfer of acquisition cost to expense for assets such as buildings, machinery, equipment, furniture, and fixtures. Land is not depreciated because it is assumed that land has an infinite life. Four widely used methods of spreading depreciation expense over the useful life of an asset are described later in this chapter.

Depletion

Natural resources, such as timber, oil, and minerals, are physically removed from the land in the process of production. Their cost is part of the expense of carrying on such operations. As explained already, *depletion* is the term used to describe this expense. Methods for computing depletion for financial accounting and tax purposes are discussed later in this chapter.

RECORDING DEPRECIATION, DEPLETION, AND AMORTIZATION

Assets subject to depreciation or depletion are recorded at acquisition cost. They are generally carried at this figure as long as they remain in use. (Of course, later additions or partial dispositions require an adjustment of the acquisition cost figure.)

At the end of each accounting period, the current depreciation or depletion is debited to an appropriate expense account and credited to an accumulated depreciation or accumulated depletion account. For example, assume that a business has plant buildings that cost $100,000 and that an annual depreciation charge of $5,000 is to be recorded for these buildings. Assume also that the business owns a mineral deposit that cost $200,000 and that depletion on it for the current year is $15,000. These current-year expenses for depreciation and depletion appear on the worksheet as adjustments and are later recorded in the general journal as illustrated below.

19 X1					
Dec. 31	Depreciation Expense—Plant Buildings	571	5,000 00		
	Accumulated Depr.—Plant Buildings	142		5,000 00	
	To record depreciation of plant				
	buildings for the year.				
31	Depletion Expense—Mineral Deposit	584	15,000 00		
	Accumulated Depl.—Mineral Deposit	155		15,000 00	
	To record depletion of mineral deposit				
	for the year.				

Assume that this is the first year of use for both assets. The balance sheet presentation at the end of the year is as follows.

Property, Plant, and Equipment

Plant Buildings	$100,000	
Less Accumulated Depreciation	5,000	$ 95,000
Mineral Deposit	$200,000	
Less Accumulated Depletion	15,000	185,000

The accumulated depreciation or depletion accounts are *contra asset accounts*. Their credit balances, which are opposite to the normal asset account balances, reflect the amount of acquisition cost that has been transferred to expense. Thus they permit a more accurate representation of the cost applicable to the remaining life of each asset involved. The difference between the acquisition cost shown in the asset account and the balance of the contra account is the book value, or *net book value,* of the asset. In the examples shown above, the plant buildings have a book value of $95,000 and the mineral deposit has a book value of $185,000.

Because of the importance of depreciation, the following information must be shown on the financial statements or in their accompanying notes.

1. The depreciation expense for the period.
2. The balances of the major classes of depreciable assets, by nature or by function.
3. The accumulated depreciation.
4. A general description of the method or methods used in computing depreciation.[2]

---

[2]"Disclosure of Depreciable Assets and Depreciation," *Opinions of the Accounting Principles Board, No. 12* (New York: American Institute of Certified Public Accountants, 1967), par. 02.

METHODS OF COMPUTING DEPRECIATION

As previously explained, the cost of certain tangible assets is spread over their useful lives through periodic depreciation charges to an expense account and corresponding credits to a contra asset account commonly referred to as an accumulated depreciation account. The total amount charged to the expense account must not exceed the total cost of the asset less any net salvage value that the asset is expected to have at the end of its useful life. In determining the net salvage value, estimated removal costs are deducted from expected proceeds of sale.

Four methods of depreciation that are widely used for financial accounting purposes are described here: straight-line, declining-balance, sum-of-the-years'-digits, and units-of-output. (Certain other methods are also used occasionally.) In addition, the accelerated cost recovery system (ACRS), which is used for federal income tax purposes, is examined.

Straight-Line Method

The *straight-line method* (first presented in Chapter 5) is, because of its simplicity, the most widely used method of computing depreciation. Under this method the same amount of depreciation is recorded for each year or other accounting period over the useful life of the asset. To obtain the annual depreciation, the acquisition cost less the expected net salvage value is divided by the expected life in years. This is expressed by the following formula.

$$\frac{\text{Acquisition Cost} - \text{Net Salvage Value}}{\text{Useful Life in Years}} = \text{Annual Depreciation}$$

Suppose that an office machine purchased by the Style Clothing Store at a total cost of $400 is expected to be used for five years and to have a net salvage value of $40 at the end of that time. The result of these figures is the following equation.

$$\frac{\$400 - \$40}{5} = \frac{\$360}{5} = \$72 \text{ Annual Depreciation}$$

If the firm records depreciation at the end of each fiscal year, $72 is debited to Depreciation Expense—Office Equipment and credited to Accumulated Depreciation—Office Equipment. The monthly amount of the depreciation charge on the office equipment is $\frac{1}{12}$ of $72, or $6. Depreciation on a newly acquired asset is usually computed to the nearest month. For example, if the asset had been purchased on September 5, 19X1, depreciation of $30 (5 months × $6) would be recorded for the company's fiscal year ended January 31, 19X2.

Declining-Balance Method

Under the *declining-balance method* of depreciation, the accountant applies an appropriate percentage to the book value of an asset at the beginning of each year to obtain the depreciation charge for that year. In the past the percentage allowable for income tax purposes on new depreciable personal property (and therefore widely used by business firms) was twice the rate of the straight-line method. (This is called the *double-declining-balance method*.) For assets purchased after 1981, the declining-balance method has been eliminated by the accelerated cost recovery system for income tax purposes. However, the procedure is still sometimes used for financial accounting purposes.

When the straight-line method is applied to the Style Clothing Store's office machine (which has an expected useful life of five years), the yearly depreciation is ⅕, or 20 percent, of the cost minus the net salvage value. The double-declining-balance rate allowable on the same item is twice 20 percent, or 40 percent. (Under tax regulations, the salvage value is ignored when the declining-balance method is used. It is also usually ignored for financial accounting purposes.)

In the first year, the acquisition cost of $400 is multiplied by 40 percent to give a depreciation expense of $160 for that year. The book value at the beginning of the second year is $240 ($400 − $160), and the depreciation expense for the second year is $96 (40 percent of $240). The depreciation of the office machine under the declining-balance method for the five years of its useful life can be illustrated as follows.

DEPRECIATION BY DECLINING-BALANCE METHOD

Year	Beginning Book Value	Rate	Deprecia- tion for Year	Deprecia- tion to Date
1	$400.00	40%	$160.00	$160.00
2	240.00	40%	96.00	256.00
3	144.00	40%	57.60	313.60
4	86.40	40%	34.56	348.16
5	51.84	40%	20.74	368.90

Ending Book Value = $31.10

Although no salvage value is used in computing the annual depreciation, there remains at the end of the five years a book value of $31.10—only slightly less than the estimated salvage value of $40 used under the straight-line method.

Sum-of-the-Years'-Digits Method

Under the *sum-of-the-years'-digits method* of depreciation, a fractional part of the depreciable cost of an asset is charged to expense each year. The denominator of the fraction is always the "sum of the years' digits." This amount is found by simply adding together the numbers representing the years of the asset's useful life. For example, the digits for a machine expected to have a useful life of five years are 1, 2, 3, 4, and 5. Thus the sum of the years' digits is 1 + 2 + 3 + 4 + 5, or 15. The numerator for any year is the number of years remaining in the useful life of the asset. Thus for the first year the fraction is ⁵⁄₁₅, for the second year it is ⁴⁄₁₅, and so on. The fraction is applied to the acquisition cost minus the net salvage value. In the example of the office machine discussed before, these amounts are $400 − $40, or $360.

The table on page 550 applies the sum-of-the-years'-digits method to the office machine owned by the Style Clothing Store. The table also compares this method of depreciation with the two methods previously illustrated. Note that both the declining-balance method and the sum-of-the-years'-digits method give higher depreciation charges in the early years of the asset's life and lower charges in the later years. These two methods are sometimes called *accelerated methods*.

	Sum-of-the-Years'-Digits Method			Depreciation by Other Methods	
Year	Fraction	Cost Minus Salvage	Depreciation for Year	Declining Balance	Straight Line
1	5/15	$360.00	$120.00	$160.00	$ 72.00
2	4/15	360.00	96.00	96.00	72.00
3	3/15	360.00	72.00	57.60	72.00
4	2/15	360.00	48.00	34.56	72.00
5	1/15	360.00	24.00	20.74	72.00
Total Depreciation—5 years			$360.00	$368.90	$360.00
Net Book Value at End of 5 Years			$ 40.00	$ 31.10	$ 40.00

Units-of-Output Method

In some situations the useful life of an asset is related more directly to units of work performed by the asset than to the passage of time. In such cases, depreciation can be calculated at a certain rate for each unit of output. The expense for any time period is then determined by multiplying the rate for each unit by the number of units produced. This method of computing depreciation is called the *units-of-output method*.

For example, suppose that a firm purchases a metal stamping press for $11,000. The press is expected to have a useful life of 1,000,000 stamping impressions and a net salvage value of $1,000 at the end of its useful life. The rate for each stamping is $10,000 ($11,000 − $1,000) divided by 1,000,000, or $0.01. If 50,000 stampings are produced during a period, the depreciation charge is 50,000 × $0.01, or $500.

DEPRECIATION FOR FEDERAL INCOME TAX PURPOSES

Prior to 1981 the depreciation methods allowed for federal income tax purposes were generally the same as those discussed above for financial accounting purposes. For example, depreciable personal property was generally depreciated by the straight-line method, the double-declining-balance method, or the sum-of-the-years'-digits method. Assets acquired prior to 1981 continue to be depreciated for tax purposes by the method originally selected when they were acquired; however, a switch from the double-declining-balance method to the straight-line method is allowed without permission from the Internal Revenue Service.

Assets acquired after 1981 are not subject to ''depreciation'' for federal income tax purposes. Instead, their cost is ''recovered'' through the accelerated cost recovery system (ACRS). Under this method each asset automatically falls into a certain class, and the costs of all assets in that class are charged to expense through a standard formula. For example, all items of personal property belong to one of the following four groups.

- The 3-Year Class: This group includes primarily automobiles and other light transportation equipment.
- The 5-Year Class: This group contains almost all other personal property, including office furniture, fixtures, and equipment; factory equipment and machinery; warehouse equipment; and so on.
- The 10-Year Class: This group contains a very small number of specified assets and will seldom be encountered.
- The 15-Year Class: This group includes public utility property with a life greater than 25 years. Also, buildings are generally recorded on a 15-year basis.

As previously pointed out, the costs for each class of assets are charged off on a specified basis. For example, assets in the 5-year class are charged to expense on the basis of the following formula.

Year	Percent of Cost Charged Off
1	15
2	22
3	21
4	21
5	21

There are special rules concerning the charge-off in the year of acquisition and the year of disposition of an asset.

Instead of using the ACRS, a firm can adopt the units-of-output method of depreciation for income tax purposes if that method is appropriate. Also, a firm can elect to use the straight-line method rather than the ACRS, but only on an extended-life basis. For example, assets in the 5-year ACRS class may be depreciated over either 12 or 25 years.

Obviously, the ACRS is designed to encourage companies to invest in productive business property by permitting a rapid charge-off of costs, with a resulting tax saving, in the early years of the assets' lives. However, the ACRS is clearly not suitable as a means of matching the costs of assets with the revenues generated by those assets. Thus it is not acceptable for financial accounting purposes.

DEPLETION

For financial accounting purposes, the amount to be charged for depletion of property such as oil, a mineral, or metal is based on cost. However, for federal income tax purposes, the depletion can also be computed as a percentage of gross income (sales price) from the product sold. (In some cases, income from oil and gas production is not subject to statutory depletion.) The cost depletion and percentage depletion methods are discussed here.

Depletion for Financial Accounting Purposes

Cost depletion is determined in a manner very similar to depreciation determined by the units-of-output method. The total cost of the mineral deposit is divided by the estimated number of units in the deposit to give the depletion cost for each unit of the mineral extracted. For example, suppose a firm purchases a clay pit that is estimated to contain 500,000 tons of extractable clay suitable for making brick. The firm pays $25,000 for the clay pit. The depletion cost for each ton of clay is $0.05 ($25,000 ÷ 500,000 tons). If the firm extracts 60,000 tons of this clay in a particular year, the depletion will be $3,000 (60,000 × $0.05).

Depletion for Federal Income Tax Purposes

For federal income tax purposes, the depletion to be deducted is the larger of cost depletion or percentage depletion. Cost depletion for tax purposes is computed in the same way as it is for financial accounting purposes (see the discussion above). However, the amount of cost depletion computed for each purpose will generally differ because the costs capitalized for financial accounting and tax purposes are not identical. In addition, if percentage depletion is taken on the tax return, in a year the amount taken will reduce the cost on which cost depletion is based in future years.

Percentage depletion is basically a percentage of the gross income from the sale of minerals from a property. The percentage to be used is specified in the tax law for each type of mineral. However, the amount computed by applying the specified percentage to the gross income is limited to 50 percent of the net income from the property.

To illustrate this computation, assume that cost depletion on the clay pit previously discussed is the same for federal income tax purposes as it is for financial accounting purposes. Also assume that the 60,000 tons of clay produced were sold at an average price of $5 a ton and that the net income before depletion from the operation is $80,000. Further assume that the allowable percentage depletion rate is 7½ percent. When this percentage is applied to the gross income, the resulting tentatively allowable percentage depletion is $22,500 ($300,000 × 0.075). Since this amount is well below the net income limit of $40,000 on percentage depletion (50 percent of $80,000), the percentage depletion for the year is $22,500. This figure is larger than the cost depletion, which was computed as $3,000, so the amount deductible on the firm's federal income tax return will be $22,500.

Percentage depletion is not limited by the mineral property's cost. Thus, over a period of time, the percentage depletion taken may exceed the original cost of the property. It is obvious, therefore, that percentage depletion may provide a substantial tax benefit. However, percentage depletion is not available for some firms, usually large oil- and gas-producing companies.

DISPOSITION OF AN ASSET

Assets that are no longer useful to a business are usually disposed of. They may be sold, traded in, or scrapped. Sometimes useful assets are also sold so the company can purchase better assets. When an asset is disposed of, the following steps are taken to enter the facts in the firm's financial records.

1. The accountant records depreciation to the date of disposition.
2. The accountant closes out the appropriate amounts in the asset account and the related accumulated depreciation account, records the proceeds realized, and determines and records the gain or loss if any.

The accounting entries necessary to record the sale of an asset under various conditions are illustrated by the following example. A firm has a $400 office machine like the one owned by the Style Clothing Store. The firm has recorded depreciation on the straight-line basis for three years at $72 a year, for a total of $216. Six months later (3½ years after the purchase) management decides to sell the machine. The first thing the accountant must do is record depreciation up to the date of the sale. The amount to be recorded is $36 for the six months following the last year in which depreciation was recorded. This amount is debited to Depreciation Expense—Office Equipment and credited to Accumulated Depreciation—Office Equipment.

The Office Equipment account has a debit balance of $400 representing the acquisition cost. The accumulated depreciation account now has a credit balance of $252 ($216 + $36). The book value is $148 ($400 − $252).

Sale at Book Value

Suppose first that the sale is made on credit for an amount equal to the book value of $148. The accountant must do the following.

1. Record the new account receivable of $148 on the books.
2. Close out the balance of $252 in the accumulated depreciation account.
3. Close out the cost of $400 in the asset account.

In the general journal, all these details can be handled in one compound entry, as shown below. Since the sale is for the book value, there is no gain or loss to be recorded.

19 X1					
July 31	Accounts Receivable	111	148 00	
	Accumulated Depr.—Office Equipment	133	252 00	
	Office Equipment	132		400 00
	Sale of calculator (No. 0–1234)			
	at book value.			

Sale Above Book Value

Suppose that the agreed sales price is $175, which is $27 above the book value. Accounts Receivable is debited for $175. The accumulated depreciation account is debited for $252, and the asset account is credited for $400, as before. To complete the entry, a new account, called Gain on Sale of Equipment, is credited for $27, as shown below.

19 X1					
July 31	Accounts Receivable	111	175 00	
	Accumulated Depr.—Office Equipment	133	252 00	
	Office Equipment	132		400 00
	Gain on Sale of Equipment	495		27 00
	Sale of calculator (No. 0–1234) at gain.			

The $27 gain represents, of course, the difference between the sales price of $175 and the book value of $148. It is shown on the income statement as an item of income, usually under the heading Other Income.

Sale Below Book Value

Suppose that the sales price is $125. Compared with the book value of $148, this price represents a loss of $23. Accounts Receivable is debited for the agreed price of $125. The accumulated depreciation account is debited for its balance of $252, and the asset account is credited for $400, as previously explained. A new account called Loss on Sale of Equipment is debited for $23. This general journal entry appears below.

19 X1				
July 31	Accounts Receivable	111	125 00	
	Accumulated Depr.—Office Equipment	133	252 00	
	Loss on Sale of Equipment	595	23 00	
	Office Equipment	132		400 00
	Sale of calculator (No. 0–1234) at loss.			

The loss is shown on the income statement, usually under the heading Other Expenses. Many companies record both gains and losses on sales of assets in a single account that is entitled Gains and Losses on Sales of Assets. If losses exceed gains, the balance is shown on the income statement under Other Expenses. If gains exceed losses, the balance is shown under Other Income.

TRADE-IN OF AN ASSET

Businesses often trade in existing equipment when they purchase new equipment. This type of transaction must be recorded in two steps. First, the accountant records the depreciation on the old asset up to the date of the trade-in. Then the trade-in and the purchase are recorded. Two methods are frequently used to record trade-ins. These are referred to as the *income tax method* and the *fair market value method*.

The Income Tax Method

For many years the federal tax laws have provided that when an asset used in business is traded in for a similar asset, no gain or loss is to be recorded on the transaction. The cost of the new asset is assumed to be the book value (cost minus accumulated depreciation) of the old asset plus the cash amount paid. This procedure is also required in financial accounting when "productive assets" are exchanged at a gain for similar assets.[3] (However, a loss resulting from an exchange of productive assets for similar assets must be recognized.)

Under the income tax method, the accountant must do the following.

1. Credit the asset account for the cost of the old asset traded in.

---

[3]"Accounting for Nonmonetary Transactions," *Opinions of the Accounting Principles Board, No. 29* (New York: American Institute of Certified Public Accountants, 1973), par. 21.

2. Close out the amount in the accumulated depreciation account that covers the old asset.
3. Record the cash payment to be made (as a credit to Accounts Payable if the voucher system is used).
4. Record the new asset at the sum of the cash to be paid plus the book value of the old asset.

The following example illustrates this procedure. A firm trades in a programmable calculator that originally cost $750. Depreciation of $500 was recorded to the date of trade-in, which leaves a book value of $250. The calculator is traded in for a new model having a list price and fair market value of $900. The seller offers an allowance of $300 on the old calculator against the purchase price of the new $900 model. In effect, the trade-in of the old calculator produces a gain of $50 ($300 trade-in allowance less $250 book value) for the purchaser of the new calculator. But that gain is not recognized. Under the procedure outlined above, the accountant must do the following.

1. Remove the cost of the old asset, $750, from the asset account.
2. Remove the applicable depreciation of $500 from the accumulated depreciation account.
3. Record the $600 cash to be paid ($900 cost minus $300 allowance) by crediting Accounts Payable.
4. Record the new calculator in the financial records at $850, which is the sum of the $600 cash to be paid and the $250 book value of the old calculator traded in ($750 cost minus $500 depreciation to date).

The necessary entry, in general journal form, appears below.

19 X1					
Oct. 31	Office Equipment	132	850 00		
	Accumulated Depr.—Office Equipment	133	500 00		
	Office Equipment	132		750 00	
	Accounts Payable	205		600 00	
	Trade-in of old calculator (No. 0–1360)				
	for new machine (No. 0–1395).				

If the seller of the new equipment had made an allowance of only $150 on the trade-in, the purchaser would have realized a loss of $100 ($250 book value less $150 trade-in allowance received). Under *APB Opinion No. 29*, this kind of loss must be recorded, as shown in the next section. However, for income tax purposes no loss would be recorded; instead the new equipment would have a "tax basis" of $1,000—the total of the book value of the old asset ($250) and the amount of cash paid for the new asset ($750). In spite of the requirements of *APB Opinion No. 29* to record all losses on trade-ins, many businesses continue to use the income tax method. They do so on the ground that such losses are usually immaterial. They also want to avoid duplicate recordkeeping. If the income tax method is used in this case, the exchange is recorded as follows.

	19	X1							
	Oct.	31	Office Equipment	132	1,000	00			
			Accumulated Depr.—Office Equipment	133	500	00			
			Office Equipment	132			750	00	
			Accounts Payable	205			750	00	
			Trade-in of old calculator (No. 0–1360)						
			for new machine (No. 0–1395).						

The Fair Market Value Method

As already mentioned, under *APB Opinion No. 29,* if the book value of the old asset exceeds the amount of trade-in allowance received, the new asset should be recognized at its fair market value and the loss should be recognized. The accountant must do the following.

1. Credit the asset account for the cost of the old asset traded in.
2. Close out the amount of depreciation in the accumulated depreciation account.
3. Record the cash payment to be made.
4. Record the new asset at its fair market value (its cash purchase price).
5. Record a loss equal to the difference between the trade-in allowance received and the book value of the old asset.

Assume that this procedure is followed in the second example given under the income tax method. A trade-in allowance of $150 is received on an old asset with a book value of $250. Thus there is a loss of $100 ($250 − $150).

As previously pointed out, the income tax method must be used (no gain recognized), when the trade-in allowance exceeds the book value of the asset traded in.

	19	X1							
	Oct.	31	Office Equipment	132	900	00			
			Accumulated Depr.—Office Equipment	133	500	00			
			Loss on Sale of Equipment	595	100	00			
			Office Equipment	132			750	00	
			Accounts Payable	205			750	00	
			Trade-in of old calculator (No. 0–1360)						
			for new machine (No. 0–1395).						

INTANGIBLE ASSETS

In addition to property, plant, and equipment, many businesses have *intangible assets.* With the exception of computer software, these assets have no physical characteristics.

Assets Classified as Intangible Assets

The major types of intangible assets are patents, copyrights, franchises, trademarks, brand names, organization costs, computer software, and goodwill.

A *patent* represents an exclusive right given by the U.S. Patent Office to manufacture and sell an invention for a period of 17 years from the date of the grant. A patent cannot be renewed, but its life can be extended beyond the original life by a new patent for improvements and changes. Rights accruing from a patent can be assigned, sold, or controlled by the owner.

A *copyright* is the exclusive right granted by the federal government to produce, publish, and sell a literary or artistic work for a period of years. The term of a copyright issued prior to 1978 is 28 years, with the possibility of renewing the copyright for another 47 years. For works registered after 1977, the law is quite complex, but for many of these works, the copyright period lasts for the author's lifetime plus 50 years after the author's death.

Two types of *franchises* are obtained by businesses. The first type is a right granted by a governmental unit for the franchise holder to provide services to the public within the unit's jurisdiction—for example, the exclusive right given to a bus company to operate a bus service in a city. The second type of franchise is an exclusive dealership or an exclusive arrangement between a manufacturer and a dealer or distributor.

Trademarks, trade names, and *brand names* are used to build consumer acceptance, preference, and loyalty for the products of a company. To aid in protecting trademarks and trade names against infringement, they can be registered with the U.S. Patent Office. Trademarks, trade names, and brand names are property rights that businesses can sell to others.

Organization costs include such items as legal fees, corporate charter costs, and expenses for the services of persons who make plans, obtain finances, and carry out other activities necessary to organize a company.

Computer software consists of programs of all types used in computer operations. Computer software may be purchased from outside vendors or may be developed within a company for its own use.

Goodwill represents the value of a business in excess of the value of its identifiable assets. It arises because the profits of the business are greater than normal for the assets employed.

ACQUISITION OF INTANGIBLE ASSETS

Intangible assets may be produced or developed by a firm, or they may be purchased from other parties. A general rule is that only if a firm actually purchases intangible assets from outside parties should they appear in the accounts of the firm.[4] Costs incurred internally to develop intangible assets should be charged to expense. For example, research and development costs must be charged to expense when they are incurred even though the work performed may result in the development of useful and valuable patents or processes.[5] Similarly, costs incurred to develop computer programs should be charged to expense.

AMORTIZATION OF COSTS OF INTANGIBLE ASSETS

Most intangible assets have limited legal and economic (useful) lives. Their acquisition costs should be charged to expense over the shorter of the two lives. *Amortization* is the term used in accounting to describe the process of transferring the acquisition costs of intangible assets to expense.

---

[4]"Intangible Assets," *Opinions of the Accounting Principles Board, No. 17* (New York: American Institute of Certified Public Accountants, 1970), par. 24.
[5]"Accounting for Research and Development Costs," *Statement of Financial Accounting Standards, No. 2* (Stamford, Conn.: Financial Accounting Standards Board, 1974), par. 12.

There are fewer methods for calculating the amount of amortization of intangible assets than for calculating depreciation. The straight-line method is the one commonly used, although the units-of-output method is appropriate in some situations. The sum-of-the-years'-digits method and the declining-balance method are not used to amortize the costs of intangible assets because these methods have never been allowed for federal income tax purposes. As pointed out already, in computing amortization, the shorter of the legal life or the economic life should be used. In no case, however, should the amortization period be more than 40 years.

The periodic amortization is debited to an expense account entitled Amortization (of the specific intangible asset involved) and, by custom, is credited directly to the asset account. The balance in the asset account is thus the book value. For example, assume that a firm purchased a patent for $34,000 and that the patent's estimated economic life is only 5 years even though it has 15 years of legal life remaining at the date of purchase. Thus the amount to be amortized each year is $6,800 ($\frac{1}{5}$ of $34,000). The adjusting entry to record the amortization is shown below.

19 X1					
Dec. 31	Amortization of Patents	538	6,800 00	
	Patents	158		6,800 00
	To record amortization of patent for the year.			

The balance sheet will show Patents at the book value of $27,200 ($34,000 − $6,800). If the same amount of amortization is recorded during the second year, the Patents account will be reported at the end of that year at a book value of $20,400 ($27,200 − $6,800).

INTERNAL CONTROL OF PROPERTY, PLANT, AND EQUIPMENT

The internal control of property, plant, and equipment centers on physical safeguards. Regardless of the size of a business or the nature of the assets it owns, certain procedures are standard.

1. Procedures should be established so that all purchases of assets are made with adequate justification and only after proper authorization is received.
2. Each asset should be given an identification number and clearly marked with this number (usually with decals or paint) to assist in keeping track of the asset and to facilitate a periodic physical inventory. In addition, each asset should be engraved with the identification number in the event the asset is stolen or lost and later recovered.
3. An asset register or other record should be kept. This record should include the name or description of each asset, the date of acquisition, the purchase price, and the physical location of the asset. Other appropriate information may also be a part of this record.

4. A single individual should be assigned responsibility for each asset's safe-keeping, maintenance, and operation.

5. A physical inventory of the assets should be taken periodically and the actual count compared with the asset records. If any assets are missing, a list should be prepared, and the responsible individuals should be contacted in order to locate the items.

6. Procedures should be established for authorizing asset retirements, sales, other dispositions, and replacements.

The internal control of intangible assets usually presents no problem because most of these assets have no physical existence and thus no need for physical safeguards. This is not, however, true for computer software. Disks, tapes, and other items that contain computer programs must be handled in the same way as property, plant, and equipment. Careful protection is also required for any secret formulas or plans on which patented products are based. In addition, companies that own such intangible assets as patents, copyrights, and trademarks must be alert to infringement and must take prompt legal action to enforce their rights.

PRINCIPLES AND PROCEDURES SUMMARY

Property, plant, and equipment are those tangible assets (including real and personal property) used in carrying on a company's business operations. Depending on the nature of the assets, depreciation or depletion must be included as a current expense. Through these expense charges, the cost of each asset is spread over its useful or legal life.

Four widely used methods of computing depreciation are the straight-line method, the declining-balance method, the sum-of-the-years'-digits method, and the units-of-output method. For federal income tax purposes, depreciation on assets acquired prior to 1981 is computed by one of the above methods. However, with assets acquired after 1981, depreciation has been replaced by the accelerated cost recovery system (ACRS) for federal income tax purposes. Depletion is based on cost for financial accounting purposes, and the cost of the asset is charged to expense on the basis of each unit produced. For federal income tax purposes, depletion is generally based on a percentage of gross income from production.

Items of property, plant, and equipment are disposed of in various ways. They can be sold, scrapped, or traded in for other assets. At the time of sale or trade-in, the depreciation must be brought up to date. If a loss results from either a sale or a trade-in, it must be determined and recorded. Gains from sales are recorded, but gains from trade-ins are not.

Except for computer software, intangible assets have no physical characteristics. They, too, are recorded at cost, but are recorded only if they have been acquired from outside parties. Costs incurred internally to develop intangible assets are charged to expense. The acquisition costs of intangible assets are amortized over the shorter of their legal or economic (useful) lives. Amortization is normally recorded on the straight-line basis, but amortization on the units-of-output basis may sometimes be appropriate.

MANAGERIAL IMPLICATIONS

Property, plant, and equipment involve large sums of money. Managers must therefore establish effective control systems for these assets and make sure that proper records are kept of all transactions connected with them. Managers must also understand the differences between the depreciation methods that are used for financial accounting purposes and those used for federal income tax purposes. To assure that the business selects appropriate depreciation methods for financial accounting purposes, managers must be aware of the varying impact of the different methods on net income. And to evaluate the tax implications of proposed asset purchases intelligently, managers should know how different classes of assets are treated under the accelerated cost recovery system. Managers must also study the methods to be used for recording sales or trade-ins of assets because the results obtained from the different methods affect reported net income and taxes differently.

REVIEW QUESTIONS

1. What type of assets are included in the category property, plant, and equipment?
2. Distinguish between real property and personal property.
3. Name the most common items that make up the cost of factory equipment.
4. What is meant by the term *capitalized costs?*
5. A company purchases some land on which are located several old buildings. The land is bought as the location for a new factory, so the existing buildings must be razed. Explain how to account for the purchase price and the cost of razing the old buildings.
6. Explain how depreciation, depletion, and amortization differ and how they are similar.
7. What account is debited and what account is credited to record depreciation on office equipment?
8. Is depreciation for federal income tax purposes the same as depreciation for financial accounting purposes? Explain.
9. Would the depreciation in the first year of an asset's life be greater under the straight-line method or under the declining-balance method?
10. What information relating to the use of property, plant, and equipment must be shown on a firm's financial statements or in accompanying notes?
11. Explain how straight-line depreciation is computed.
12. Explain how salvage value is treated in computing depreciation under the straight-line, sum-of-the-years'-digits, and declining-balance methods.
13. What method is used to compute depletion on a mineral deposit for financial accounting purposes?
14. Explain how percentage depletion is computed.
15. What is an intangible asset?
16. Distinguish between the economic (useful) life of a patent and its legal life. Which is used in computing amortization?

17. Under the income tax method, what will be the cost assigned to a new asset acquired through the trade-in of an old asset?
18. Explain the income tax method for recording trade-ins of assets.
19. Explain the fair market value method for recording trade-ins of assets.
20. Can the total depletion taken on a mineral deposit for tax purposes exceed the capitalized cost of the deposit? Explain.
21. Define the term *accelerated methods*. Which depreciation methods are commonly included in this category?

MANAGERIAL DISCUSSION QUESTIONS

1. Assume that you are an accountant at a manufacturing company. One of the executives of the firm has asked you why some items of property have more than doubled in value but are still recorded at original cost. What explanation would you give for this situation?
2. Explain why a company might find one method of depreciation more advantageous than another for financial accounting purposes.
3. Suppose that you are on the controller's staff at a company. You have suggested that a specific individual be assigned responsibility for each item of property, plant, and equipment owned by the company. A department manager has objected, saying that this is not necessary. Defend your position.
4. Why is percentage depletion advantageous to a company?
5. Why should management insist that a firm's intangible assets be amortized over their economic (useful) lives rather than over their legal lives?
6. Under generally accepted accounting principles, all costs incurred for research and development are charged to expense as they are incurred. An officer of your company has expressed concern over this requirement. What reasons can you give for it?
7. Assume that you have recently accepted employment as the accountant for a small company. You find that there is no record identifying individual items of property, plant, and equipment, and you propose to establish an asset register and to mark all items with an identifying decal. An officer of the firm opposes this as an unnecessary waste of effort. Defend your proposal.

EXERCISES

EXERCISE 24-1   **Determining the elements that make up the cost of an asset.** The following costs were incurred by the Larson Company in connection with the construction of a new office building.

Cost of land and old buildings (the buildings have an estimated value of $20,000)	$120,000
Cost to demolish old buildings	18,000
Cost to construct new office building	920,000

1. What is the capitalized cost of the land?
2. What is the capitalized cost of the new building?

EXERCISE 24-2   **Determining the elements that make up the cost of an asset.** The following costs related to a new computer were incurred by the Rockwell Corporation.

Invoice price	$60,000
Discount allowed for cash payment	(1,000)
Transportation costs	600
Installation costs	800

What is the capitalized cost of the computer?

EXERCISE 24-3   **Recording depreciation.** For the year 19X1, the Simpson Company had depreciation totaling $2,600 on its office equipment. Give the general journal entry to record the depreciation on December 31, 19X1.

EXERCISE 24-4   **Computing depreciation under the straight-line method.** Regal Products acquired an asset on January 2, 19X1, at a capitalized cost of $46,000. The asset's useful life is five years, and its salvage value is estimated to be $1,000. Compute the depreciation on this asset for each of its first two years under the straight-line method.

EXERCISE 24-5   **Computing depreciation under the declining-balance method.** Compute the depreciation on the asset described in Exercise 24-4 for each of its first two years under the declining-balance method.

EXERCISE 24-6   **Computing depreciation under the sum-of-the-years'-digits method.** Compute the depreciation on the asset described in Exercise 24-4 for each of its first two years under the sum-of-the-years'-digits method.

EXERCISE 24-7   **Computing depreciation under the units-of-output method.** The Coronado Corporation purchased 20 automobiles for its sales department on July 1, 19X2, at a total cost of $180,000. The firm's practice is to operate automobiles for 40,000 miles, at which point they are traded in. At that time, they usually have a trade-in value equal to about 40 percent of their original cost. The automobiles purchased in 19X2 were operated for a total of 240,000 miles during that year. Compute the depreciation on these automobiles for 19X2, using the units-of-output method.

EXERCISE 24-8   **Computing amortization of patent cost.** The O'Malley Company purchased a patent for $6,000. At the time of purchase, the remaining legal life of the patent was 24 years. Its estimated useful life was only 4 years, however. Compute amortization on the patent for the first year it was owned by O'Malley.

EXERCISE 24-9   **Computing depreciation of ore property cost.** The Rostelli Company developed a mine in 19X2. Capitalized costs were $600,000. It is estimated that the mine will produce ore for 15 years before being completely exhausted. The total amount of ore to be recovered is estimated at 720,000 tons. During 19X2, 61,000 tons were produced. Compute the depletion for the year.

EXERCISE 24-10 **Computing percentage depletion of oil income.** The Johnson Company qualifies for percentage depletion. During 19X1 a lease the firm owns produced 36,000 barrels of oil, which sold for $30 a barrel. Operating expenses on the lease were $160,000. Compute the percentage depletion on the property for 19X1. (The percentage depletion rate for oil production is 15 percent.)

EXERCISE 24-11 **Computing percentage depletion of oil income.** Assume the same facts as in Exercise 24-10, except that operating expenses in 19X1 were $980,000. Compute the percentage depletion for 19X1.

EXERCISE 24-12 **Recording the sale of an asset at less than book value.** The O'Rourke Company owns a truck that cost $36,000. The firm took depreciation of $16,000 on the truck up to the date of its sale. Give the general journal entry to record the sale of the truck for $14,000.

EXERCISE 24-13 **Recording the sale of an asset for more than book value.** Assume the same facts as in Exercise 24-12, except that the truck was sold for $22,000. Give the general journal entry to record the sale.

EXERCISE 24-14 **Recording straight-line depreciation.** On January 2, 19X1, The Chavez Company purchased some construction equipment for $120,000. Its estimated useful life was 30 years. During a period of 5 years, depreciation of $4,000 was recorded on the item each December 31. On July 1, 19X6, the company traded in this construction equipment for new equipment, which had a value of $150,000. The company paid $60,000 in cash and was given a trade-in allowance of $90,000 on the old equipment. Compute the depreciation on the old equipment for the period January 1–July 1, 19X6, and make a general journal entry to record the amount.

EXERCISE 24-15 **Recording the trade-in of an asset under the income tax method.** Give the general journal entry needed on July 1, 19X6, to record the trade-in described in Exercise 24-14 (after considering the depreciation recorded in that exercise). Use the income tax method to account for the trade-in.

EXERCISE 24-16 **Recording the trade-in of an asset under the fair market value method.** Give the general journal entry needed on July 1, 19X6, to record the trade-in described in Exercise 24-14 (after considering the depreciation recorded in that exercise). Use the fair market value method to account for the trade-in.

PROBLEMS

PROBLEM 24-1 **Determining the costs to be capitalized for acquisitions of assets.** On June 12, 19X3, the Slocum Company purchased a site for a new apartment complex for $150,000. Two existing houses, with a total appraised value of $35,000, had to be razed at a cost of $3,500. Salvage proceeds from the razing of the houses were $4,200. Other costs incurred in connection with the acquisition were $450 for legal fees, $10 for a permit to raze the buildings, and $50 for recording fees and taxes. After the houses were razed, the following additional costs were incurred.

- $2,200 for leveling the lot
- $3,200 to the city for paving the street alongside the lot
- $1,500,000 for construction of the building
- $9,200 for paving the parking lot
- $2,500 for installation of fences around the project

Instructions
1. Compute the capitalized costs of *(a)* the land, *(b)* the building, and *(c)* the land improvements.
2. Assume that the Slocum Company borrowed $1,000,000 specifically to finance the building's construction and that during 19X1 the company paid interest of $50,000 on this loan. The company's other borrowings for the year averaged $2,000,000, and the average interest rate was 13 percent. The average balance of construction in progress during 19X1 was $600,000. What amount of interest will be capitalized in 19X1 as part of the building's cost?

PROBLEM 24-2 **Using different depreciation methods and comparing the results.** On January 2, 19X1, the Hancock Company purchased some new equipment for $73,000. The equipment had an estimated useful life of eight years and an estimated salvage value of $4,000.

Instructions Prepare a schedule showing the annual depreciation and accumulated depreciation for each of the first three years of the asset's life under *(a)* the straight-line method, *(b)* the sum-of-the-years'-digits method, and *(c)* the double-declining-balance method.

PROBLEM 24-3 **Using the straight-line and units-of-output methods of depreciation.** The Jarman Corporation purchased a large truck for $60,000 on January 2, 19X2. The truck's estimated useful life is six years or 300,000 miles. The estimated salvage value is $6,000. During 19X2 the truck was operated 68,000 miles, and in 19X3 it was operated 49,000 miles.

Instructions Compute each year's depreciation for 19X2 and 19X3.

1. Use the straight-line method.
2. Use the units-of-output method.

PROBLEM 24-4 **Computing depletion for financial accounting and tax purposes.** The Easton Mining Company paid $175,000 for mineral rights in 19X7. Additional exploration and development costs totaled $56,000. An estimated total of 100,000 tons of ore will be extracted. During 19X8, 16,000 tons were produced and sold at $100 a ton. Operating expenses (other than depletion) were $1,000,000. The allowable percentage depletion for federal income tax purposes is 10 percent.

Instructions 1. Compute the depletion to be taken for financial accounting purposes in 19X8.

2. Assume that the same costs are capitalized for financial accounting and tax purposes. Compute the depletion allowed for tax purposes in 19X8.
3. Assume the same facts as above, except that the operating expenses were $1,400,000 in 19X8 instead of $1,000,000. Compute the depletion allowed for tax purposes in 19X8.

PROBLEM 24-5 **Recording asset trade-ins and sales.** The transactions listed below occurred at the Willis Hardware Store during the year 19X5.

Instructions 1. Give the entries in general journal form to record the two exchange transactions.
    a. Use the income tax method.
    b. Use the fair market value method.
2. Give the entries in general journal form to record the sale of the forklift truck.
    a. Assume that the sales price was $6,800.
    b. Assume that the sales price was $5,080.

TRANSACTIONS FOR 19X5

Mar. 13 Exchanged a typewriter (Office Equipment) that had cost $742 on May 10, 19X1, four years earlier. The useful life of the old asset was originally estimated at six years and the salvage value at $166. The new typewriter received in exchange had a sales price of $810. Willis gave up the old typewriter and paid $595 in cash. The new machine was estimated to have a life of eight years and a salvage value of $100. Depreciation on the old machine was last recorded on December 31, 19X4, on the straight-line basis.

June 28 Exchanged a pickup truck (Delivery Equipment) for a new one that had a sales price of $10,400. Received a trade-in allowance of $3,000 on the old truck, which had been purchased for $8,800 on March 24, 19X3, two years before. The life of the old truck was originally estimated at four years and the salvage value at $2,000. Depreciation was last recorded on December 31, 19X4, on the straight-line basis. The life of the new truck was estimated to be four years, and it was estimated to have a salvage value of $3,000.

July 30 Sold a forklift truck (Warehouse Equipment) for cash. The forklift truck was purchased on January 4, 19X2, for $9,000 and was depreciated on the straight-line basis, using an estimated life of eight years and an estimated salvage value of $1,800. Depreciation was last recorded on December 31, 19X4.

PROBLEM 24-6 **Recording asset trade-ins and sales.** The Alonzo Company purchased four identical machines on January 2, 19X1, paying $600 cash for each. The useful life of each machine is expected to be five years, and the salvage value at the end of that time is estimated to be $100 for each machine. The company uses the straight-line method of depreciation. Selected transactions involving the machines are listed on page 566. The necessary accounts for recording these transactions are also given on page 566.

Instructions	1. Record the transactions in general journal form.
	2. Assume that the income tax method is to be used, and record the trade-in of Machine 4 on August 29, 19X4, under that method.

ACCOUNTS

101	Cash
141	Machinery
142	Accumulated Depreciation—Machinery
495	Gain on Sale of Machinery
541	Depreciation Expense—Machinery
595	Loss on Sale of Machinery
597	Fire Loss on Machinery

TRANSACTIONS FOR 19X1

Jan. 2 Paid $600 each, in cash, for four machines.
Dec. 31 Recorded depreciation for the year on the four machines.

TRANSACTIONS FOR 19X2

Apr. 1 Machine 1 was destroyed by fire. No insurance was carried.
Dec. 31 Recorded depreciation for the year on the three remaining machines.

TRANSACTIONS FOR 19X3

Aug. 31 Sold Machine 2 for $400 cash.
Dec. 31 Recorded depreciation for the year on the two remaining machines.

TRANSACTIONS FOR 19X4

June 4 Machine 3 was traded in for a similar machine with a $700 list price and fair market value. A trade-in allowance of $300 was received. The balance was paid in cash.
Aug. 29 Machine 4 was traded in for a similar machine with a $720 list price and fair market value. A trade-in allowance of $150 was received. The balance was paid in cash. (Use the fair market value method in recording this transaction.)

PROBLEM 24-7   **Recording intangible assets and research and development costs.** Selected accounts of the Futura Electronics Company are listed below.

Cash
Patents
Computer Software
Research and Development Expense
Amortization of Patents
Amortization of Computer Software

The following are some transactions and events that took place at the company during 19X1.

- Made cash expenditures of $60,000 for research and development costs related to a new patent. This patent was developed in March 19X1 in the company's laboratory.

- Made cash expenditures of $32,385 in June 19X1 for company personnel to develop computer programs that are to be used in the company's research activities.
- Purchased a patent for $30,000 in cash on August 1, 19X1. The patent is to be used in the company's operations.
- Purchased a completed software program for $7,200 in cash from a computer software supply firm on September 1, 19X1. The program is to be used in the company's inventory control system.

The company has discovered that it is impossible to estimate accurately the useful life of computer software, so it has adopted an arbitrary policy of amortizing all such costs over a period of 36 months, beginning with the month of acquisition. Similarly, the company has adopted the practice of amortizing all patents over a period of 60 months, beginning with the month of purchase or acquisition.

Instructions
1. Record the transactions for 19X1 in general journal form.
2. Record amortization of the intangible assets for the year ended December 31, 19X1.

ALTERNATE PROBLEMS

PROBLEM 24-1A **Determining the costs to be capitalized for acquisitions of assets.** On February 12, 19X1, the Murphy Company purchased a site for a new office building for $1,354,000. An existing building with a fair market value of $60,000 had to be razed to clear the site. The cost of demolishing the building was $41,000, and salvage proceeds of $4,500 were received. The Murphy Company paid $1,500 in legal fees related to the purchase, $150 in recording fees, and $50 for a permit to raze the old building. After the old building was razed, the following additional costs were incurred.

- $5,000 for purchase of fill dirt to level the lot
- $1,500 for leveling of the lot
- $6,400 for paving of the street and installation of curbing and gutters
- $9,860,000 for construction of the building
- $31,000 for paving of the parking area
- $6,700 for installation of concrete flood drainage ditches at the back of the property
- $500 to the city for inspection of the completed building

Instructions
1. Compute the capitalized costs of (a) the land, (b) the building, and (c) the land improvements.
2. Assume that the Murphy Company borrowed $7,000,000 to finance construction of the building. During 19X1 Murphy paid interest of $800,000 on the construction loan. The company's other loans averaged $14,000,000 for the year, and the average interest rate was 12 percent. The average balance of construction in progress during 19X1 was $5,800,000. What amount of interest will be capitalized in 19X1 as part of the building's cost?

PROBLEM 24-2A

Using different depreciation methods and comparing the results. The Gluckman Company purchased a new machine on January 2, 19X1, for $60,000. It is expected to have a useful life of five years and a salvage value of $4,500.

Instructions

Prepare a schedule showing the annual depreciation and accumulated depreciation for each of the first three years of the asset's life under (1) the straight-line method, (2) the sum-of-the-years'-digits method, and (3) the double-declining-balance method.

PROBLEM 24-3A

Using the straight-line and units-of-output methods of depreciation. On January 2, 19X3, the Borman Company purchased factory equipment for $32,000. The equipment had an estimated useful life of six years or 5,400 units of product and an estimated salvage value of $950. Actual production for the first three calendar years was 19X3, 275 units; 19X4, 800 units; and 19X5, 1,120 units.

Instructions

Compute each year's depreciation for 19X3, 19X4, and 19X5.

1. Use the straight-line method.
2. Use the units-of-output method.

PROBLEM 24-4A

Computing depletion for financial accounting and tax purposes. The Miller Energy Corporation had total capitalized depletable costs of $50,000 on an oil lease. It was estimated at the beginning of production that 500,000 barrels of oil were recoverable. During the first year of operation, 20,000 barrels were produced and sold at $30 a barrel. Operating expenses, other than depletion, totaled $400,000. The production is eligible for percentage depletion for federal income tax purposes. The depletion rate for oil is 15 percent.

Instructions

1. Compute the depletion to be taken for financial accounting purposes during the first year.
2. Assume that the same costs were capitalized for financial accounting and tax purposes. Compute the depletion allowed for tax purposes in the first year.
3. Assume the same facts as above, except that the operating expenses were $540,000 instead of $400,000. Compute the depletion allowed for tax purposes in the first year.

PROBLEM 24-5A

Recording asset trade-ins and sales. The transactions listed on page 569 occurred at the Haines Distributing Company during the year 19X3.

Instructions

1. Give the entries in general journal form to record the two exchange transactions.
   a. Use the income tax method.
   b. Use the fair market value method.
2. Give the entries in general journal form to record the sale of the automobile.
   a. Assume that the sales price was $4,000.
   b. Assume that the sales price was $7,000.

TRANSACTIONS FOR 19X3

Apr. 29 Exchanged a copying machine (Office Equipment) that had cost $600 on March 2, 19X1, two years earlier. The useful life of the old asset was originally estimated at eight years and the salvage value at $50. The new copying machine had a sales price of $780. Haines gave up the old machine and paid $610 in cash. The new machine was estimated to have a life of eight years and a salvage value of $100. Depreciation on the old machine was last recorded on December 31, 19X2, on the straight-line basis.

July 23 Exchanged an automobile (Automotive Equipment) for a new one that had a sales price of $9,200. Received a trade-in allowance of $3,400 on the old automobile, which had been purchased for $7,800 on May 28, 19X1, two years earlier. The life of the old automobile was originally estimated at four years, the salvage value at $2,400. Depreciation was last recorded on December 31, 19X2, on the straight-line basis. The life of the new automobile was estimated to be four years, and it was estimated to have a salvage value of $3,400.

Aug. 27 Sold an automobile (Automotive Equipment) for cash. The automobile was purchased on January 8, 19X1, for $9,000 and was depreciated on the straight-line basis, using an estimated life of four years and an estimated salvage value of $3,000. Depreciation was last recorded on December 31, 19X2.

PROBLEM 24-6A

Recording asset trade-ins and sales. The Stevens Company purchased four identical machines on January 2, 19X1, paying $555 cash for each. The useful life of each machine is expected to be six years, and the salvage value at the end of that time is estimated to be $75 for each machine. The company uses the straight-line method of depreciation. Selected transactions involving the machines are listed below and on page 570. The necessary accounts for recording these transactions are also given below.

Instructions

1. Record the transactions in general journal form.
2. Assume that the income tax method is to be used, and record the trade-in of Machine 4 on July 31, 19X4, under that method.

ACCOUNTS

101	Cash
141	Machinery
142	Accumulated Depreciation—Machinery
495	Gain on Sale of Machinery
541	Depreciation Expense—Machinery
595	Loss on Sale of Machinery
597	Loss on Stolen Machinery

TRANSACTIONS FOR 19X1

Jan. 2 Paid $555 each, in cash, for four machines.

Dec. 31 Recorded depreciation for the year on the four machines.

TRANSACTIONS FOR 19X2

Mar. 31 Machine 1 was stolen. No insurance was carried.

Dec. 31 Recorded depreciation for the year on the three remaining machines.

TRANSACTIONS FOR 19X3

Sept. 30 Sold Machine 2 for $356 cash.

Dec. 31 Recorded depreciation for the year on the two remaining machines.

TRANSACTIONS FOR 19X4

Apr. 30 Machine 3 was traded in for a similar machine with a list price and fair market value of $610; paid cash, less a $310 trade-in allowance.

July 31 Machine 4 was traded in for a similar machine with a list price and fair market value of $620; paid cash, less a $182 trade-in allowance. (Use the fair market value method in recording this transaction.)

PROBLEM 24-7A **Recording intangible assets and research and development costs.** Selected accounts of the Webster Manufacturing Company are listed below.

Cash
Product Formulas
Computer Software
Research and Development Expense
Amortization of Product Formulas
Amortization of Computer Software

The following are some transactions and events that took place at the company during 19X1.

▪ On March 1, 19X1, the company paid $180,000 to an independent laboratory to purchase product formulas. These formulas are expected to have a useful life of 60 months.

▪ During the year the company made cash expenditures of $150,000 in its research laboratories. It is estimated that $90,000 of this amount relates to a formula that was patented on August 1, 19X1, and is expected to be of benefit for six years. The remaining research and development expenditures were used in unsuccessful efforts to develop products.

▪ On August 24, 19X1, the company paid $24,000 in cash to purchase certain computer programs. The programs have an estimated useful life of 48 months.

Instructions 1. Record the transactions for 19X1 in general journal form.

2. Record amortization of the intangible assets for the year ended December 31, 19X1.

Most businesses are subject to a variety of taxes. It is therefore necessary for a firm to have orderly procedures to account for taxes, to pay the required amounts on schedule, and to file the proper tax forms with government agencies. In many cases, especially when the federal income tax is involved, it is possible to plan business activities and transactions in such a way as to legitimately reduce the tax burden. This chapter discusses some of the major types of taxes that businesses must pay and examines tax procedures that are typically used.

BUSINESS TAXES

TYPES OF TAXES

By far the most important tax for corporations is the *federal income tax,* which is levied on their taxable income. Corporate taxable income is measured in much the same way as net income for financial accounting purposes and is examined further in Chapter 30. Sole proprietorships and partnerships do not pay federal income tax. The net income from a sole proprietorship is combined with the owner's income from other sources and with the owner's deductions of all types. Thus there is no federal income tax on the owner's business income *per se,* but only on the owner's total taxable income. Similarly, no federal income tax is levied on the net income of a partnership. Instead, the partners include their individual shares of the firm's net income when they determine the total taxable income on their personal income tax returns. Although a partnership does not directly pay income tax, it is required to file an information return with the federal government showing its revenue and expenses for the tax year and the distribution of its net income or loss among the partners.

In addition to federal income tax, corporations are subject to state and local income taxes in many areas and to franchise taxes. Most states require corporations to pay an annual *franchise tax* in order to carry on operations within the state.

One of the costs associated with the ownership of business assets such as inventory, property, plant, and equipment is *property taxes*. These taxes, levied by state and local government units, are based on the value of the assets. In addition to property taxes, a firm may be required to pay a number of other taxes, such as *excise taxes* and *retail license fees.* Most retail concerns are also required to collect *sales taxes* from their customers and remit the sales taxes to the state or local government.

In previous chapters you learned how a business deducts social security and income taxes from employee earnings and how it accounts for the payroll taxes that it must pay. You also learned how a business adapts its accounting records to keep track of retail sales taxes collected from customers. Because employee tax deductions and the employer's payroll taxes were discussed in detail in Chapters

13 and 14, they are not covered again here. However, there is a further discussion of sales taxes. In the case of retail sales taxes, a firm's responsibility does not end with collection of the necessary amounts. Appropriate information must be recorded, tax returns must be prepared and submitted, and the tax money must be sent to the proper government agency at regular intervals. The procedures needed to comply with these additional sales tax requirements are discussed here.

INCOME TAXES

As pointed out already, the federal government levies an income tax directly on the net income of corporations. The net income from a sole proprietorship or a partnership is taxed as part of the owner's or partners' income although no income tax is levied on the sole proprietorship or the partnership as a separate entity. Measurement of the net income that is subject to taxation from a business carried on by an individual or a partnership is very similar to measurement of net income for financial accounting purposes, which was discussed in all the preceding chapters of this text. However, business income is only one of many factors entering into an individual's taxable income. Salaries and wages, dividends, interest, rents, royalties, gains and losses from sales of assets, and a host of other types of income not related to operating a business are taxable. Similarly, many expenses completely unrelated to business activities are allowed as deductions in arriving at the individual's taxable income. For example, medical expenses, certain types of personal taxes, interest on personal indebtedness, charitable contributions, contributions to certain retirement plans, losses from thefts and casualties, and hundreds of other nonbusiness expenses may be deductible in arriving at an individual's taxable income.

To further complicate the federal income tax calculation, there are numerous special provisions that make some types of income completely tax-free and that apply different rates to different types of income. Other provisions allow all or a part of some types of expenditures to be offset directly against the tax liability. Even for business activities, there are tax accounting rules that differ widely from those used in financial accounting. You saw two of these differences in the immediately preceding chapter: percentage depletion may be allowed on income from production of natural resources, and accelerated cost recovery is taken in place of depreciation on assets purchased since 1981. There are hundreds of other special rules of this sort—most of them intended to achieve social or economic goals—that completely distort the accounting concept of income.

Obviously, a knowledge of the income tax laws is important to the management of any type of business. As a matter of fact, many business decisions are made largely on the basis of the income tax results. The reason is obvious if one stops to consider that federal income tax rates for individuals go as high as 50 percent, while for corporations the rates go as high as 46 percent. In a book such as this, it is clearly impossible to examine in detail the vast number of rules involved in the federal income tax laws. One who expects to advance in the business world must, however, have a basic understanding of income tax laws and procedures and must be able to recognize those business decisions that should be made only after obtaining advice from competent tax experts. The importance of the federal income tax in business decisions cannot be overemphasized.

Most states and some local governmental units also assess income taxes on individuals and on corporations. State and local income tax laws are usually patterned after the federal laws and often specify that the taxable income computed for federal income tax purposes be used as the basis for calculating the state or local tax.

PROPERTY TAXES

Property taxes are often called *ad valorem taxes* because they are levied on the value of the property taxed. (*Ad valorem* is a Latin term meaning ''according to the value.'') The actual amount of tax to be paid depends on two basic factors: the *value* of the property for tax purposes and the tax *rate* applied to that value.

Taxable Property

Some jurisdictions tax only real property; others tax both real and personal property. Real property includes land and buildings or other structures attached to the land. All other property is classified as personal property. It includes such items as machinery and equipment, furniture and fixtures, and intangible assets.

The value of property for tax purposes almost always differs from the value entered in a firm's accounting records. Accounting records typically use cost or cost less depreciation or amortization. The assessed value of property for tax purposes is usually related to the property's current market value on the assessment date. The basis for the assessed value of property for tax purposes can be total market value (100 percent), but more often it is some percentage of market value (for example, 60 percent).

Assessment and Collection of Property Taxes

In some jurisdictions, public officials appraise real property to determine the assessed value for tax purposes. In others, property owners place a value on their own real property. This value is subject to review and change by a public official or board before the tax rate is applied. Personal property values are often assessed by the owner of the items. (Property owners who are required to set the value of their own property should investigate local customs in establishing these values. Substantial inequities can occur in the assessment of property value for tax purposes.)

Tax Rate

The tax rate is often established by the taxing body after the total assessed value of the property subject to tax has been determined. The taxing body estimates the amount of revenue needed from property taxes and then sets a tax rate that will yield the desired amount of tax revenue when applied to the total assessed value.

The same property can be taxed simultaneously by a number of government units (for example, a city, a county, a school district, and a water supply district). Each taxing authority can determine the tax rate required to raise the revenue it needs.

In many cases, each taxing authority assesses property and levies a tax, and the taxpayer must pay each authority separately. In other cases, a single agency levies and usually collects the taxes for all the units and distributes the proper amount to each authority. The illustration below is of a tax notice that shows real property taxed by several authorities but payment made to only one agency. (A *mill* is a thousandth part of a dollar, or $0.001.)

COUNTY OF GREENVILLE CITY OF GREENVILLE	**TAX NOTICE 19X1**		**N⍛** 7940		
RECEIPT for your taxes for **19X1**, as itemized below. In accordance with law.	Ward THREE		ITEMIZED TAXES		
BRYAN CLEMMONS, Sheriff and Ex-Officio Tax Collector.	Page No. 742			TAXPAYERS COLUMN TAXES PAYABLE	HOMESTEAD EXEMPTION COLUMN
Per _____ Deputy.	ASSESSED VALUATION			$5,250.00	
	State Tax	5.75 Mills		30.19	
NAME AND ADDRESS OF TAXPAYER	•County Tax	28.50 Mills		149.63	
	Sewer CS1	1.70 Mills		8.93	
	Rural Lighting	3.00 Mills		15.75	
	Garbage				
⌐ ¬ Vanderbilt Garage Company 620 Magnolia Avenue Greenville, State 11111 ⌙ ⌎	Acreage	2¢ per Acre			
	PAY LAST AMOUNT IN		THIS COLUMN ▼		
	TOTAL			$204.50	
	INTEREST				
	PENALTY				
DESCRIPTION OF PROPERTY	TOTAL				
Lot 94 Magnolia Subdivision					

Assessment and Payment Dates

The assessed value of property is established at a certain date for each tax jurisdiction, often before the tax rate is established. Thus some time ordinarily elapses between the assessment date and the date on which the tax bills are sent to the taxpayers. Taxes due must then be paid by a specified date. Late payments incur penalties and interest charges. (In some jurisdictions, discounts are allowed for early payment of taxes.)

Accounting for Property Taxes

The accountant in charge of a company's records and procedures for taxes must do the following.

1. Determine the correct amount of tax due and pay it in time to avoid penalties and interest charges.
2. Prepare and file any tax forms that may be required.
3. Enter the tax in the firm's financial records.
4. Charge the tax in the appropriate accounting period or periods as an expense on the income statement. Show the correct amount of tax payable or prepaid on the balance sheet.

Computing the tax liability and completing the appropriate tax returns requires a thorough knowledge of the various tax laws and regulations that apply to the business. Payment of taxes due is handled within the usual disbursement routines used by the business.

As might be supposed, there are several procedures for accounting for taxes, for assigning them as expenses in different accounting periods, and for presenting them on the firm's balance sheet. Generally, however, the most acceptable procedure for recording property taxes is that of a monthly accrual in the firm's financial records during each fiscal period of the taxing authority that levied the taxes. The financial records will then show the appropriate accrual or prepayment at any closing date.[1] The discussion of property tax accounting in the remainder of this chapter follows the treatment advocated here. These procedures are illustrated in detail in later sections of the chapter.

OTHER TAXES AND LICENSES

Most businesses are subject to a host of other taxes levied by state and local governments in addition to property taxes. Some of these charges are actually for licenses or permits, but they are usually classified under the general heading of taxes on the financial statements. For example, states typically require every person or firm doing business as a retailer to obtain a retail license from the state tax commission. In the state where the Style Clothing Store operates, the license must be obtained prior to June 30 for the following fiscal year of the state, starting July 1 (or before the opening of any new business). The license fee is $50 for a firm that consists of one retail store. Higher fees are charged if a firm has additional outlets, with a maximum of $150 for each outlet over 30. Similarly, license fees may be required by city or county governments for the right to carry on business or to sell specified commodities, such as cigarettes or alcoholic beverages. In addition, taxes are now sometimes levied as penalties, such as a tax on the use of natural-gas-fired furnaces. As already noted, corporations are usually required by a state to pay a franchise tax for the right to conduct their operations in the state. Sometimes states also charge similar taxes called *unincorporated business taxes* to sole proprietorships and partnerships. Thus the range of taxes is almost limitless.

Most fees for licenses, permits, and similar items are immaterial in amount and are therefore customarily charged to expense when they are paid or when the statement is received from the taxing authority. If the amounts are material, however, as in the case of state franchise taxes levied on corporations, they may be accrued in the same way as property taxes.

ILLUSTRATION: THE STYLE CLOTHING STORE

The Style Clothing Store is subject to several taxes, which are recorded in an expense account called Taxes and Licenses. The most important tax is the property tax assessed against personal property and real estate. (The Style Clothing Store owns no real estate, but it does have merchandise inventory and other personal property.) In addition to property tax, the store must pay an annual state retail license fee of $50, as previously mentioned, an annual city license fee of $20, and an annual state fee of $32 for a permit to sell cigarettes. (The store has a cigarette vending machine for the use of customers and employees.)

To provide complete information about the individual taxes without having a different ledger account for each one, the firm uses an *analysis ledger sheet*. Notice that the Taxes and Licenses account illustrated on page 576 contains separate analysis columns to record the details of all the taxes paid. The three

---

[1]Committee on Accounting Procedure, *Accounting Research and Terminology Bulletin, Final Edition* (New York: American Institute of Certified Public Accountants, 1961), Chapter 10, sec. A, par. 10.

columns on the right (Debit, Credit, and Balance) provide space for the regular postings and the resulting total balance. The columns on the left provide space for entering the individual taxes. The account number is 555, but subcode numbers—555.1 and 555.2—are assigned to Property Taxes and Other Taxes. If any individual tax other than property taxes was significant, a separate column could be added for that tax. The following entry shows how the columns are used.

PROP. TAXES DR. 555.1	OTHER TAXES DR. 555.2	DATE	EXPLANATION	POST. REF.	DEBIT	CREDIT	BALANCE	DR. CR.
			Taxes and Licenses					No. 555
	50 00	19 X1 June 30	Retail License	VR5	50 00		50 00	Dr.

Assume that the fiscal year for property taxes is July 1 to the following June 30. Also assume that the tax is levied on the assessed value of the real estate, the merchandise inventory, and other personal property on June 30, the last day of the taxing entity's fiscal year. (Many of the technical tax provisions are omitted from the following discussion so that the basic procedural steps are clear. Also keep in mind that procedures vary widely from state to state. Those described here illustrate only one situation.)

In the state where the Style Clothing Store operates, an information return reporting the value of personal property and real estate on June 30 must be filed by each property owner on or before August 31. Then the state tax commission, which administers the tax, adjusts the assessed valuation to what it considers necessary, applies the tax rate, and sends a tax bill in December. This bill is payable on or before December 31. If payment is made after that date, there is a penalty.

In the first year of its partnership operations, the Style Clothing Store submits the required information for property taxes as of June 30. The store starts recording a proportionate amount of these taxes each month, beginning July 1 (the start of the state's fiscal year for property taxes). However, the firm will not know the exact amount due until it receives the tax bill in December. To make the monthly accruals prior to receiving the tax bill, the accountant must estimate the total of the property taxes due for the year and convert it to monthly amounts.

Assume that the accountant estimates the firm's total property taxes for the year as $1,920, or $160 a month. The accountant then records $160 each month (beginning with July) in a journal entry debiting Taxes and Licenses and crediting Property Taxes Payable. The entry made on July 31 is shown below.

19 X1 July 31	Taxes and Licenses	555.1	160 00	
	Property Taxes Payable	235		160 00
	To record estimated property taxes for month of July.			

A similar entry for the estimated property taxes payable is made each month from July through November. By November the total amount in the Property Taxes Payable account will have increased to $800 (5 months × $160). Suppose that in December the actual tax bill shows total taxes due of $1,990 ($70 more than the estimate of $1,920). At this point, the actual tax liability is known and can be recorded. The Property Taxes Payable account is credited for $1,190 to increase it from its present balance of $800 to the actual liability of $1,990. Since the $1,190 applies to December and future months, it is debited to an asset account called Prepaid Taxes. (Note that the term *prepaid* does not, in this case, mean literally "paid in advance." It means that the recorded cost applies to future months. Some accountants prefer to use the title Deferred Property Taxes Expense rather than Prepaid Taxes.) The entry for December is shown below.

19 X1					
Dec. 10	Prepaid Taxes	128	1,190 00	
	Property Taxes Payable	235		1,190 00
	To record balance of property taxes payable as determined on receipt of tax bill.			

At the end of each month, beginning in December and continuing through June, $170 ($1,190 ÷ 7 months) is transferred to the expense account Taxes and Licenses. By June 30 the total cost of the prepaid property taxes will thus have been charged to expense. The journal entry to be made each month is shown below.

19 X1					
Dec. 31	Taxes and Licenses	555.1	170 00	
	Prepaid Taxes	128		170 00
	To transfer to expense the December portion of the prepaid property taxes.			

The new asset, Prepaid Taxes, is shown on the balance sheet on December 31 as $1,020. It represents the tax cost that applies to the future months of January through June (6 months × $170 = $1,020). When the tax bill is actually paid in December, the payment is debited to Property Taxes Payable. In July the same cycle of entries starts over again—monthly estimates through November, then actual figures for December through June.

Statement
Presentation

Let us see how the various tax items that have been discussed appear in the financial records of the Style Clothing Store at the end of the first year of operations, January 31, 19X2. The three ledger accounts involved are Prepaid Taxes, Property Taxes Payable, and Taxes and Licenses. They are shown on page 578 with all entries posted and the balances determined as of January 31.

Prepaid Taxes — No. 128

DATE	EXPLANATION	POST. REF.	DEBIT	CREDIT	BALANCE	DR. CR.
19 X1 Dec. 10		J12	1,190 00		1,190 00	Dr.
31		J12		170 00	1,020 00	Dr.
19 X2 Jan. 31		J1		170 00	850 00	Dr.

Property Taxes Payable — No. 235

DATE	EXPLANATION	POST. REF.	DEBIT	CREDIT	BALANCE	DR. CR.
19 X1 July 31		J7		160 00	160 00	Cr.
Aug. 31		J8		160 00	320 00	Cr.
Sept. 30		J9		160 00	480 00	Cr.
Oct. 31		J10		160 00	640 00	Cr.
Nov. 30		J11		160 00	800 00	Cr.
Dec. 10		J12		1,190 00	1,990 00	Cr.
Dec. 31		VR16	1,990 00		–0–	

Taxes and Licenses — No. 555

PROP. TAXES DR. 555.1	OTHER TAXES DR. 555.2	DATE	EXPLANATION	POST. REF.	DEBIT	CREDIT	BALANCE	DR. CR.
	50 00	19 X1 June 30	State Retail License	VR5	50 00		50 00	Dr.
160 00		July 31		J7	160 00		210 00	Dr.
160 00		Aug. 31		J8	160 00		370 00	Dr.
	20 00	Sep. 24	City License	VR9	20 00		390 00	Dr.
160 00		Sep. 30		J9	160 00		550 00	Dr.
160 00		Oct. 31		J10	160 00		710 00	Dr.
160 00		Nov. 30		J11	160 00		870 00	Dr.
	32 00	Dec. 12	State Cigarette Sales Permit	VR14	32 00		902 00	Dr.
170 00		Dec. 31		J12	170 00		1,072 00	Dr.
170 00		19 X2 Jan. 31		J1	170 00		1,242 00	Dr.
1,140 00	102 00							

SALES AND EXCISE TAXES

Sales and excise taxes imposed by city and state governments vary. However, there is sufficient similarity in accounting for them to make a study of the most typical provisions an informative starting point.

City and State Sales Taxes

Many cities and states impose a tax on retail sales. The tax is collected by the merchant making the sales. This type of tax may be levied on all retail sales, but often certain items are exempt. In most cases the amount of the sales tax is stated separately and then added to the retail price of the merchandise.

The merchant is required to make periodic reports (usually monthly) to the taxing authority and to pay the tax money due at the same time. In some cases the government allows the merchant to retain part of the tax as compensation for collecting it. The procedures for filing a state sales tax return are discussed in a later section of this chapter.

Federal Excise Taxes

The federal government levies an excise tax (which is simply another sales tax) on certain kinds of merchandise, such as automobile tires and petroleum products. This tax is passed on to the consumer by the retailer. Normally, the retailer pays the tax to the manufacturer, who assumes responsibility for preparing quarterly tax returns and sending the tax money to the federal government.

Preparing the State Sales Tax Return

The procedures to be followed at the time a typical sales tax return must be filed are similar to those used by the Style Clothing Store at the end of July 19X1, when it filed the monthly sales tax return with the tax commissioner of the state where it is located. The firm's sales are subject to a 3 percent state sales tax.

At the end of each month, after the accounts have all been posted, the accountant for the Style Clothing Store prepares the sales tax return. (In some states the sales tax return is filed quarterly rather than monthly.) The information required for the monthly return comes from the accounting data of the current month. Three accounts are involved: Sales Tax Payable, Sales, and Sales Returns and Allowances. To highlight the data needed, only the July postings are shown in the ledger accounts illustrated below.

Sales Tax Payable   No. 231

DATE		EXPLANATION	POST. REF.	DEBIT	CREDIT	BALANCE	DR. CR.
19X1 July	31		S6		537 00	537 00	Cr.
	31		CR6		282 00	819 00	Cr.
	31		J7	16 50		802 50	Cr.

Sales   No. 401

DATE		EXPLANATION	POST. REF.	DEBIT	CREDIT	BALANCE	DR. CR.
19X1 July	31		S6		17,900 00	17,900 00	Cr.
	31		CR6		9,400 00	27,300 00	Cr.

Sales Returns and Allowances   No. 452

DATE		EXPLANATION	POST. REF.	DEBIT	CREDIT	BALANCE	DR. CR.
19X1 July	31		J7	550 00		550 00	Dr.

Using these figures as a basis, the accountant determines the amount of the firm's taxable gross sales for July as follows:

Cash Sales	$ 9,400
Credit Sales	17,900
Total Sales	$27,300
Deduct Sales Returns and Allowances	550
Taxable Gross Sales for July	$26,750

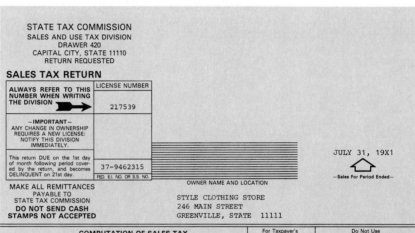

STATE TAX COMMISSION
SALES AND USE TAX DIVISION
DRAWER 420
CAPITAL CITY, STATE 11110
RETURN REQUESTED

SALES TAX RETURN

ALWAYS REFER TO THIS NUMBER WHEN WRITING THE DIVISION ➤	LICENSE NUMBER 217539

—IMPORTANT—
ANY CHANGE IN OWNERSHIP REQUIRES A NEW LICENSE: NOTIFY THIS DIVISION IMMEDIATELY.

This return DUE on the 1st day of month following period covered by the return, and becomes DELINQUENT on 21st day.

37-9462315
FED. E.I. NO. OR S.S. NO.

JULY 31, 19X1
—Sales For Period Ended—

MAKE ALL REMITTANCES PAYABLE TO STATE TAX COMMISSION
DO NOT SEND CASH
STAMPS NOT ACCEPTED

OWNER NAME AND LOCATION

STYLE CLOTHING STORE
246 MAIN STREET
GREENVILLE, STATE 11111

COMPUTATION OF SALES TAX	For Taxpayer's Use	Do Not Use This Column
1. TOTAL Gross proceeds of sales or Gross Receipts (to include rentals)	$26,750.00	
2. Add cost of personal property Purchased on a RETAIL LICENSE FOR RESALE but USED BY YOU or YOUR EMPLOYEES, Including GIFTS and PREMIUMS	–0–	
3. USE TAX—Add cost of personal property purchased outside of STATE for your use, storage or consumption	–0–	
4. Total (Lines 1, 2 and 3)	$26,750.00	
5. LESS ALLOWABLE DEDUCTIONS (Must be itemized on reverse side)	–0–	
6. Net taxable total (Line 4 minus Line 5)	$26,750.00	
7. Sales and Use Tax Due (3% of Line 6)	$ 802.50	
8. LESS TAXPAYER'S DISCOUNT—(Deductible only when amount of Tax due is not delinquent at time of payment) ➤ IF LINE 7 IS LESS THAN $100.00 —DEDUCT 3% IF LINE 7 IS $100.00 BUT LESS THAN $1,000.00 —DEDUCT 2% IF LINE 7 IS $1,000.00 OR MORE —DEDUCT 1%	$ 16.05	
9. NET AMOUNT OF TAX PAYABLE (Line 7 minus Line 8)	$ 786.45	
Add the following penalty and interest if return or remittance is late 10. Specific Penalty: 25% of tax _ _ _ _ _ _ _ _ _ $ _ 11. Interest: ½ of 1% per month from due date until paid. $ _ TOTAL PENALTY AND INTEREST ➤		
12. TOTAL TAX, PENALTY AND INTEREST	$ 786.45	
13. Subtract credit memo No.		
14. TOTAL AMOUNT DUE (IF NO SALES MADE SO STATE)	$ 786.45	

I certify that this return, including the accompanying schedules or statements, has been examined by me and is to the best of my knowledge and belief, a true and complete return, made in good faith, for the period stated, pursuant to the provisions of the Code of Laws 19X1, and Acts Amendatory Thereto.

URGENT—SEE THAT LICENSE NUMBER IS ON RETURN

Division Use Only

Linda Hanson
Signature

Partner _____ August 5, 19X1
Owner, partner or title _____ Date

Return must be signed by owner, or if corporation, authorized person.

The 3 percent sales tax on the gross sales of $26,750 amounts to $802.50. In the state where the Style Clothing Store is located, a retailer who files the sales tax return on time and who pays the tax when it is due is entitled to a discount. The discount is intended to compensate the retailer, at least in part, for acting as a collection agent for the tax. The discount rate depends on the amount of tax to be paid. On amounts between $100 and $1,000, the rate is 2 percent of the tax due. For the Style Clothing Store in July, the discount amounts to $16.05 ($802.50 × 0.02). With the discount deducted, the net tax due is $786.45 ($802.50 − $16.05), as shown on page 580.

The firm prepares a voucher for the net sales tax due and sends a check with the sales tax return. The voucher calls for a debit to Sales Tax Payable (for $786.45 in this case). After the amount of the payment is posted, the balance in the account should be equal (or very nearly equal) to the discount. In this case it is equal, as shown below. (Slight differences can arise because the tax collected at the time of the sale is determined by a bracket method that can give results slightly more or less than the final computations on the tax return.)

	Sales Tax Payable					No. 231	
DATE	EXPLANATION	POST. REF.	DEBIT	CREDIT	BALANCE	DR. CR.
19 X1						
July 31		S6		537 00	537 00	Cr.
31		CR6		282 00	819 00	Cr.
31		J7	16 50		802 50	Cr.
Aug. 5		VR7	786 45		16 05	Cr.

The remaining balance in the firm's Sales Tax Payable account, $16.05, is transferred to an account called Miscellaneous Income by a general journal entry. This entry consists of a debit to Sales Tax Payable and a credit to Miscellaneous Income, as shown below.

19 X1				
Aug. 5	Sales Tax Payable	231	16 05	
	Miscellaneous Income	493		16 05
	To transfer remaining balance in Sales Tax Payable account to a revenue account.			

Recording Sales Tax in the Sales Account

In some states, retailers can credit the entire sales price plus tax to the Sales account. Then, at the end of each month or quarter, they must remove from the Sales account the amount of tax included and transfer that amount to the Sales Tax Payable account. For example, assume that during January 19X5 a retailer whose sales are all taxable sells merchandise for a total price of $10,920, including a 4 percent tax. The entry to record these sales is summarized in general journal form below.

	19 X5				
	Jan. 31	Accounts Receivable	111	10,920 00	
		Sales	401		10,920 00
		To record total sales and sales tax collected during month.			

At the end of the month, the retailer must transfer the sales tax from the Sales account to the Sales Tax Payable account. The first step in the transfer process is to determine the amount of tax involved. The sales tax payable is computed as follows.

$$
\begin{aligned}
\text{Sales} + \text{Tax} &= \$10,920 \\
100\% \text{ of Sales} + 4\% \text{ of Sales} &= \$10,920 \\
104\% \text{ of Sales} &= \$10,920 \\
\text{Sales} &= \frac{\$10,920}{1.04} \\
\text{Sales} &= \$10,500 \\
\text{Tax} = \$10,500 \times 0.04 &= \$420
\end{aligned}
$$

The firm then makes the following entry to transfer the liability from the Sales account.

	19 X5				
	Jan. 31	Sales	401	420 00	
		Sales Tax Payable	231		420 00
		To transfer sales tax payable from Sales account to liability account.			

Recording Federal Excise Tax

As previously explained, some businesses are subject to federal excise tax. They account for the excise tax in much the same manner as they account for the state sales tax. A separate column is set up in the cash receipts journal and the sales journal to record the excise tax liability on sales. At the end of each month, the totals of these columns are posted to a liability account called Excise Tax Payable in the general ledger.

A firm that owes more than $100 of federal excise tax in any month must deposit the tax due in an authorized bank on or before the last day of the following month. (If the amount of tax for any calendar month in a calendar quarter exceeds $2,000, the tax due must be deposited twice a month during the next calendar quarter.) The firm prepares a voucher debiting the Excise Tax Payable account and crediting Accounts Payable for the amount due. Finally, the firm issues a check and sends it to the bank with a Tax Deposit Form 504 (a form similar to the one used for social security tax).

If the excise tax for the month is $100 or less, it is sent with the Quarterly Federal Excise Tax Return, Form 720. This form must be filed within the month following the end of each calendar quarter. Because retailers usually pay their excise taxes to the manufacturers of the goods, details of the quarterly return are not examined here.

TAX CALENDAR

By now it has become obvious that there are a considerable number of tax returns to file and tax payments to make. You have studied payroll taxes, sales and excise taxes, and property taxes. You have also seen that corporations must file income tax returns. The accountant must keep up with all these tax responsibilities and must make sure that they are taken care of promptly and correctly. Tax calendars are used to remind accountants of important tax dates throughout the year.

A *tax calendar* should be prepared for each business. It should show the dates before which each tax item must receive attention. It should also indicate the form numbers of any tax returns that must be filed. The calendar should be checked periodically so that required tax information can be assembled carefully without any last-minute rush.

The January and February portion of the tax calendar for the Style Clothing Store is shown below.

STYLE CLOTHING STORE
TAX CALENDAR

Jan. 20 State Sales Tax Return for December; Form ST-3
      31 State Unemployment Tax Return, quarter ended Dec. 31; Form UCE-101
      31 Employer's Annual Federal Unemployment Tax Return (previous year); Form 940
      31 Employer's Quarterly Federal Tax Return, quarter ended Dec. 31; Form 941
      31 Wage and Tax Statements to each employee for previous year; Form W-2
      31 Transmittal of Income and Tax Statements (previous year); Form W-3
Feb. 15 Deposit of FICA Taxes and Income Tax Withheld for January; Form 8109
      20 State Sales Tax Return for January; Form ST-3

PRINCIPLES AND PROCEDURES SUMMARY

Many kinds of taxes are paid by businesses. Among the most important are federal, state, and local income taxes. Corporations must pay income taxes directly on their net income. Sole proprietorships and partnerships are not subject to income taxes, but the net income from these businesses must be included in the taxable income of the owner or partners. Net income for tax purposes is measured in a way similar to that used to measure net income for financial accounting purposes, but there are major differences. Examples of such differences are the percentage depletion that may be allowed on income from production of natural resources and the accelerated cost recovery system that is used for assets purchased since 1981. Sometimes tax rules reflect social or economic goals.

Property taxes are levied by various state and local government units, including cities, counties, school districts, and water supply districts. The same property can be subject to several taxing authorities. Sometimes, one agency collects the entire tax and distributes it to the participating units. The accountant's job in connection with property taxes is twofold. First, the accountant must determine the amount of tax due, make sure that it is paid on time, and prepare any necessary tax forms. Second, the accountant must record the tax as an expense in the appropriate accounting period and show prepayments or accrued tax liabilities properly on the balance sheet.

Since tax bills are often presented many months after the valuation of the property on which they are based, an estimate of the tax for the year is made. The monthly portion of this estimate is debited to a tax expense account and credited to a tax liability account. When the actual bill is received, the liability and expense accounts must be adjusted to reflect the correct figure, if it is different from the estimate.

Many states and cities impose sales taxes that must be collected by retail merchants from their customers. Although these taxes vary from area to area, they are typically a certain percent of the retail price of each item sold. The total tax collected is sent to the taxing authority, usually monthly or quarterly. In some localities, merchants are given a discount on the sales tax in order to partially compensate them for acting as collection agents.

MANAGERIAL IMPLICATIONS

It is important that managers understand how taxes affect the operations and profits of their businesses. Often good tax planning can substantially reduce the tax burden. It is not necessary that managers know all the detailed rules about income taxes and other taxes, but it is essential that they have a basic understanding of the effect of taxes on different types of transactions and that they use the expertise of tax specialists in order to keep the firm's tax burden to the lowest legal level. Tax planning is highly useful for sole proprietorships and partnerships as well as corporations. Even though sole proprietorships and partnerships are not directly subject to income taxes, they should do tax planning because the net income from their operations is included in the taxable income of the owner or partners.

Managers should investigate the property tax structure of an area before opening a business there. They must also watch changes in tax structure and rates in order to be able to gauge the effects on the firm's costs and profits. It is especially important that managers be familiar with local property valuation customs to make sure that the firm's property taxes are fair.

Managers of retail businesses must make sure that sales taxes are properly charged to customers and collected. They must also be sure that taxes are accurately entered in the firm's records and promptly sent to the taxing authorities along with any required reports. Sellers are, of course, liable for any undercollection of taxes. This situation can be avoided with an efficient control system.

Tax calendars provide a means of making sure that all tax returns and tax payments are submitted on time.

REVIEW QUESTIONS

1. Does an unincorporated business pay an income tax? Explain.
2. In general, how does taxable income for an individual differ from that of a corporation?
3. What is an *ad valorem* tax?
4. In the case of a corporation, is net income for financial accounting purposes exactly the same as net income for tax purposes? Explain.
5. Explain what is meant by assessment date and payment date.
6. What is a *mill?*
7. Over what fiscal period should a business accrue its property taxes?
8. Name three types of taxes, other than payroll taxes, that might be paid by a corporation.
9. Why are taxes such as the fees for retail store licenses and other licenses and permits usually charged to expense when paid instead of being spread over the period to which the payment applies?
10. What is an analysis ledger sheet? Why is it used?
11. How is the property tax rate determined by a taxing authority?
12. What is the purpose of the discount allowed by some states on the sales taxes collected and remitted by merchants?
13. Does a retailer generally have responsibility for remitting federal excise taxes to the government and filing the return? Explain.
14. In a particular state, the sales tax rate is 5 percent of sales. The retailer is allowed to record both the selling price and the tax in the same account. Explain how to compute the sales tax due when this method is used.
15. What is a tax calendar?
16. What is a retail license fee?
17. Why is the prepaid property taxes account sometimes debited when the property tax bill is received during the year?

MANAGERIAL DISCUSSION QUESTIONS

1. How can the managers of a firm help assure that all taxes are paid and all returns filed on or before the due dates?
2. Assume that an officer in a company where you work has suggested that in order to reduce the property tax on merchandise, the company should reduce its inventory to the lowest possible level on the assessment date. Explain what the officer means.

3. Why might management wish to record both sales and sales taxes in the same account?

4. How do various common business taxes affect a firm's costs and profits? What can management do about these taxes?

5. Why can't a taxing authority set the property tax rate at the time it determines the appraised value of the property under its jurisdiction?

6. Assume that you are the chief accountant at a company and that the president has asked you to prepare a report for her summarizing the reasons why the firm should use the same accounting methods for financial accounting and tax purposes and the reasons why it should use different methods. What reasons would you give in your report?

7. Suppose that a manager in your company has suggested that the firm should not hire an expert to advise it on tax matters and to file tax returns. He states that tax matters are merely procedural in nature and all that is required is the ability to read tax form instructions. Comment on this idea.

EXERCISES

EXERCISE 25-1 **Computing property tax rates.** A village government needs to raise $500,000 from property taxes. The total assessed value of its property is $41,000,000. What tax rate (expressed in mills) should the village government levy to yield the desired amount of taxes if it is assumed that 1 percent of the sum levied will never be collected?

EXERCISE 25-2 **Recording estimated property taxes.** The Pactor Company, which uses the calendar year as its accounting period, is located in a taxing unit that has a fiscal year ending on June 30. The company's total property taxes were $4,800 during the fiscal year ended June 30, 19X1. For the fiscal year beginning July 1, 19X1, the company estimates that its taxes will be increased by 6 percent. Give the general journal entry to record estimated property taxes on July 31, 19X1, assuming that the assessed value of the firm's property has not changed during the past year.

EXERCISE 25-3 **Recording estimated property taxes.** Assume the same facts as in Exercise 25-2. Give the general journal entries to record estimated property taxes on August 31, September 30, October 31, November 30, and December 31, 19X1.

EXERCISE 25-4 **Closing the expense account for property taxes.** Assume the same facts as in Exercises 25-2 and 25-3. Give the general journal entry on December 31, 19X1, to close the expense account for property taxes, assuming that $400 per month was recorded as expense from January through June.

EXERCISE 25-5 **Recording the receipt of a tax bill.** Assume the same facts as in Exercises 25-2, 25-3, and 25-4. On January 12, 19X2, the Pactor Company received a property tax bill for $5,200, which covers the taxing entity's fiscal year ending June 30, 19X2. Give the general journal entry to record receipt of the tax bill by Pactor.

EXERCISE 25-6 **Recording the expense for property taxes.** Assume the same facts as in Exercises 25-2 through 25-5. Give the general journal entry that would be made at the Pactor Company on January 31, 19X2, to record its property tax expense for the month.

EXERCISE 25-7 **Recording the remittance of sales tax.** The Stern Company is located in a state with a sales tax rate of 5 percent. During January 19X1 the firm had gross taxable sales of $92,000 and returns on taxable sales of $2,000. The balance of the Sales Tax Payable account at the end of the month was $4,462. The company is required to remit all sales taxes collected, but in no event must the amount paid be less than 5 percent of net taxable sales. Give the entry in general journal form to record remittance of the tax due. (Also make an entry to adjust the Sales Tax Payable account if necessary.)

EXERCISE 25-8 **Recording the remittance of sales tax when a discount is allowed.** Assume the same facts as in Exercise 25-7 but that the retailer is entitled to a discount of 2 percent on the amount of the sales tax due. Give the entries in general journal form to record the remittance of the tax due and to transfer the discount to revenue. (Also make an entry to adjust the Sales Tax Payable account if necessary.)

EXERCISE 25-9 **Computing the sales tax due.** All sales at the Lopez Company are subject to a 6 percent sales tax. The firm records both sales and sales tax in the same account. On November 30, 19X1, the balance of the Sales account was $91,874.60. What is the amount of the sales tax due on that date?

EXERCISE 25-10 **Computing the sales tax due and recording its remittance.** The balances of certain accounts at the McVay Company on January 31, 19X2, were as follows: Sales, $187,610.90; Sales Returns and Allowances, $2,080.90; and Sales Tax Payable, $9,180.38. All of the McVay Company's net sales are subject to a 5 percent sales tax. The retailer must remit monthly the larger of 5 percent of net taxable sales or the amount of tax collected. Give the entry in general journal form to record remittance of the sales tax payable on January 31, 19X2. (Also make an entry to adjust the Sales Tax Payable account if necessary.)

EXERCISE 25-11 **Computing and recording estimated property taxes.** The Vanderclute Company, which began business in its newly constructed building on March 1, 19X1, is located in a city that has a fiscal year beginning September 1. The city's property tax is levied on the basis of assessed property values as of September 1 of each year. The assessed value of Vanderclute's property on September 1, 19X1, was $2,000,000, and the estimated tax rate for the fiscal year was 175 mills per $100 of assessed value. Give the general journal entry on September 30, 19X1, to record Vanderclute's estimated property taxes for September.

EXERCISE 25-12 **Recording estimated property taxes.** Using the facts given for the Vanderclute Company in Exercise 25-11, make the general journal entry to record the firm's estimated property taxes on October 31, 19X1.

EXERCISE 25-13 **Recording the receipt of a tax bill and the adjustment of the expense account for property taxes.** On November 30, 19X1, the Vanderclute Company received its tax bill for the year beginning September 1, 19X1. The statement was for $3,600. Give the entries to record receipt of the tax bill and to adjust the property tax expense account on November 30, 19X1.

EXERCISE 25-14 **Recording the payment of property taxes.** On December 31, 19X1, the Vanderclute Company paid one-half of the tax bill described in Exercise 25-13. Give the entry in general journal form to record this payment.

EXERCISE 25-15 **Recording the expense for property taxes.** Based on the information provided in Exercises 25-11 through 25-14, give the general journal entry that would be made at the Vanderclute Company to record property tax expense on January 31, 19X2.

PROBLEMS

PROBLEM 25-1 **Estimating and recording property taxes.** The Good Times Shop operates on a calendar-year basis. The taxing authority of the city and county in which Good Times is located operates on a fiscal year that runs from July 1 to June 30. On January 1, 19X2, the Prepaid Taxes account of Good Times contains a balance of $720, representing the prepaid property taxes through June 30, 19X2. The entries made during 19X2 in connection with property taxes are listed below.

Instructions In general journal form, record the necessary entries, using these accounts: Cash 101, Prepaid Taxes 128, Property Taxes Payable 235, Taxes and Licenses 555.

ENTRIES FOR 19X2

Jan. 31 Recorded the January tax expense.

June 30 Recorded the June tax expense. (The tax expense was recorded monthly from January through May.)

July 31 Recorded the estimated July tax expense. The estimate of the total taxes for the taxing authority's fiscal year beginning July 1, 19X2, is based on a proposed assessed value of $40,000 and an assumed tax rate of 36 mills.

Aug. 31 Recorded the estimated August tax expense.

Sept. 10 Recorded the tax bill of $1,600 received for July 1, 19X1, to June 30, 19X2.

      30 Recorded the September tax expense.

Oct. 16 Recorded payment of the tax bill of $1,600.

     31 Recorded the October tax expense.

PROBLEM 25-2 **Recording sales, sales returns and allowances, and sales tax.** The Marcus Jewelry Store is located in a state that imposes a sales tax. On June 30, 19X1, a study of the sales slips and credit slips revealed the facts shown on the next page about sales, sales returns, and sales tax for June.

Instructions Record each of the facts in general journal form.

1. Credit sales for the month of June were $208,790.20. There was a 5 percent state sales tax on all these sales.
2. Cash sales for June totaled $31,820. There was a 5 percent state sales tax on all these sales.
3. Some goods sold for cash were returned, and the customers were given a cash refund of $109 plus the 5 percent sales tax.
4. Some goods sold for $385.70 on account were returned, and the customers were given credit for the sales price plus the 5 percent sales tax.

PROBLEM 25-3 **Computing and recording sales tax amounts.** During January 19X1 the Vanguard Computer Store had total sales of $364,610.80 and sales returns and allowances of $3,217.40. At the end of January, the Sales Tax Payable account showed a balance of $18,052.13. The sales tax rate is 5 percent. However, the state sales tax agency allows the firm a discount of 2½ percent of the gross amount of the sales tax due.

Instructions
1. Make the calculations that are required in preparing the sales tax return.
   a. The taxable gross sales for January.
   b. The total sales tax due.
   c. The amount of the discount given the firm.
   d. The amount of the sales tax to be paid to the state tax agency.
2. Show the following in general journal form (omitting explanations).
   a. The entry required to record payment of the net sales tax to the state tax agency.
   b. The entry required to transfer the discount to the Miscellaneous Income account and close the Sales Tax Payable account for January.

PROBLEM 25-4 **Computing and recording sales tax due when a discount is involved.** The Arnold Home Center must collect a sales tax on all its sales. The tax of 5 percent is added to the retail selling price, and the entire amount (sales plus tax) is credited to the Sales account. Similarly, when merchandise is returned by customers, the entire return, both retail selling price and tax, is debited to the Sales Returns and Allowances account. On March 31, 19X1, at the time the quarterly sales tax return is filed, the firm's accounts include the following balances: Sales, $485,467.28, and Sales Returns and Allowances, $2,855.68. The firm is allowed to deduct 2 percent of the sales tax due as a discount to help cover its collection expense.

Instructions
1. Compute the amount of the sales tax on the net sales.
2. Prepare a general journal entry to transfer the gross amount of the sales tax from the Sales account to the Sales Tax Payable account and from the Sales Returns and Allowances account to the Sales Tax Payable account.
3. Prepare a general journal entry to transfer the discount from the Sales Tax Payable account to the Miscellaneous Income account.
4. Prepare a general journal entry to record payment of the net sales tax due.

ALTERNATE PROBLEMS

PROBLEM 25-1A **Estimating and recording property taxes.** The Gates Company estimates its 19X1 property taxes on the basis of a proposed property value assessment of $8,000 and a tax rate of 60 mills. The taxing authority operates on a calendar-year basis. The tax bill is usually received in September and must be paid by November 30 to avoid a penalty. The entries made during 19X1 in connection with property taxes are listed below.

Instructions In general journal form, record the required entries, using these accounts: Cash 101, Prepaid Taxes 128, Property Taxes Payable 235, and Taxes and Licenses 555.

ENTRIES FOR 19X1

Jan. 31 Recorded the estimated January tax expense.
Feb. 28 Recorded the estimated February tax expense.
Sept. 15 Recorded receipt of the tax bill for $524. (Estimated property taxes were recorded monthly from January through August.)
  30 Recorded the September tax expense.
Nov. 25 Recorded payment of the tax bill of $524.
  30 Recorded the November tax expense.
Dec. 31 Recorded the December tax expense.

PROBLEM 25-2A **Recording sales, sales returns and allowances, and sales tax.** The Laval Office Supply Store is located in a state that imposes a sales tax. On May 31, 19X1, a study of the sales slips and credit slips revealed the facts shown below about sales, sales returns, and sales tax for May.

Instructions Record each of the facts in general journal form.

1. Credit sales for the month of May were $155,609.10. There was a 4 percent state sales tax on all these sales.
2. Cash sales for May totaled $3,455.40. There was a 4 percent state sales tax on all these sales.
3. Some goods sold for cash were returned, and the customer was given a cash refund for the amount of the sale, $45.40, plus the 4 percent sales tax.
4. Some goods sold for $890.80 on account were returned, and the customers were given credit for the sales price plus the 4 percent sales tax.

PROBLEM 25-3A **Computing and recording sales tax amounts.** During April 19X1 the Kobe Department Store had total sales of $565,400 and sales returns and allowances of $4,600. At the end of April, the Sales Tax Payable account showed a balance of $16,822.18. The sales tax rate is 3 percent. However, the state sales tax agency allows the firm a discount of 3 percent of the gross amount of the sales tax due.

Instructions 1. Make the calculations that are required in preparing the sales tax return.
  a. The taxable gross sales for April.
  b. The total sales tax due.

c. The amount of the discount given the firm.

d. The amount of the sales tax to be paid to the state tax agency.

2. Show the following in general journal form (omitting explanations).

a. The entry required to record payment of the net sales tax to the state tax agency.

b. The entry required to transfer the discount to the Miscellaneous Income account and to close the Sales Tax Payable account for April.

PROBLEM 25-4A **Computing and recording the sales tax due when a discount is involved.** The Alonzo Gift Store must collect a sales tax on all its sales. The tax, 4 percent of the retail selling price, is credited to the Sales account along with the actual amount of the sale. Similarly, when merchandise is returned by customers, the entire return, both retail selling price and tax, is debited to the Sales Returns and Allowances account. On March 31, 19X1, at the time the quarterly sales tax return is filed, the firm's accounts include the following balances: Sales, $114,240.50, and Sales Returns and Allowances, $1,354.60. The firm is allowed to deduct 3 percent of the sales tax due as a discount to help cover the expense of collecting it.

Instructions 1. Compute the amount of the sales tax on the net sales.

2. Prepare a general journal entry to transfer the gross amount of the sales tax from the Sales account to the Sales Tax Payable account and from the Sales Returns and Allowances account to the Sales Tax Payable account.

3. Prepare a general journal entry to transfer the discount from the Sales Tax Payable account to the Miscellaneous Income account.

4. Prepare a general journal entry to record payment of the net sales tax due.

In the last several chapters, you have become familiar with the financial records of the Style Clothing Store, a partnership. You have seen that the routine accounting procedures for a partnership differ very little from those of a sole proprietorship. In this chapter and the next chapter, you will learn more about the accounting procedures that must be followed when a partnership is formed and when changes in the partners' capital accounts take place.

PARTNERSHIP ORGANIZATION

THE NATURE OF PARTNERSHIPS

In a partnership, two or more persons join together under a written or oral contract as co-owners of a business. The partnership form of organization is widely used in small service businesses and in professional fields such as accounting, law, and medicine, where individuals are closely identified with the services provided. In previous years the rules of conduct of many professional organizations, such as the American Institute of Certified Public Accountants, and the rules of conduct of state regulatory boards and commissions for those professions did not allow practitioners to form corporations. As a result, professional people have historically often joined together in partnerships to pool their talents and abilities. Many small merchandising and manufacturing businesses are also operated as partnerships.

The partnership form of organization has several distinguishing features that are most important in deciding whether to adopt it.

- A partnership permits a pooling of the skills, abilities, and financial resources of two or more individuals.
- Each partner has unlimited liability for the debts of the partnership. This characteristic enhances the credit standing of the firm, but it can be a distinct danger to the individual partners. In most states it is possible for some partners to have limited liability under certain closely regulated conditions. The liability of these partners is limited to their capital investment in the partnership. In such cases, state laws normally require that there be one partner who has unlimited liability. The partners who have limited liability are prohibited from taking an active part in the management of the business and from having their names in the partnership's title. Because of the present nature of the federal income tax laws, limited partnerships have become commonplace as "tax shelters" in some industries such as oil and gas exploration and real estate investment and development.
- A partnership lacks continuity. If one partner dies or is incapacitated, the existing partnership is terminated. If a partner transfers his or her interest to another person, the existing partnership must be dissolved and the business can

be continued only after a new partnership is formed. Of course, the formation of the new entity depends on the ability of the new partners to agree to work together.

- No federal income tax is levied on the net income of a partnership as such. However, the partners must include their shares of the firm's profits when calculating taxable income on their personal income tax returns.

FORMATION OF A PARTNERSHIP

Linda Hanson had owned and operated a clothing store for a number of years. Her business had prospered, but success had also brought some problems. For one thing, competition had increased and customers were demanding a larger assortment of merchandise. For the Style Clothing Store to maintain its competitive position in the rapidly expanding community, Hanson would have to expand the store and carry a bigger and more varied stock. This would, however, require a large sum of money.

Hanson was borrowing all the funds the bank would lend her. Even with this help, however, she was finding it difficult to keep up with bills while adding to her stock and offering credit to her customers. As her accountant and her banker explained, the Style Clothing Store needed more *working capital*. (The current assets of a business are its working capital. However, sometimes this term is used to refer to what is more exactly termed *net working capital*—the excess of current assets over current liabilities.)

Hanson decided to remedy her lack of capital by seeking to form a partnership with another person. In the words of the Uniform Partnership Act adopted by most states, "A partnership is an association of two or more persons to carry on, as co-owners, a business for profit." By forming a partnership with a person who would contribute financial resources, Hanson could carry out her plans for expansion. Furthermore, she knew that a good partner would also assume a substantial share of the growing managerial responsibility. For example, the new person might take charge of purchasing and selling while she concentrated on administration and financial management.

Hanson learned that an acquaintance, Steven Casey, was interested in owning a business. Casey had been employed as a salesperson for a clothing store in another city. He had recently inherited some money, and he wanted to use it to go into business for himself. Hanson and Casey arranged a meeting to explore the possibility of pooling their resources.

Hanson prepared a balance sheet to show the assets, liabilities, and owner's equity of her business as of the date set for the meeting with Casey. This balance sheet appears on page 594.

After their discussion, Hanson and Casey agreed to form a partnership. They decided that a partnership would be a mutually profitable arrangement.

DETERMINING THE VALUE OF NET ASSETS

Linda Hanson offered to contribute the assets of the Style Clothing Store (other than the small cash balance) to the new partnership, which would also assume the liabilities of her firm. Steven Casey agreed to invest cash equal to the value of Hanson's contribution—that is, to the value of the net assets (assets minus liabil-

STYLE CLOTHING STORE
Balance Sheet
January 31, 19X1

Assets

Cash		$ 350.00
Accounts Receivable	$10,800.00	
Less Allowance for Uncollectible Accounts	300.00	10,500.00
Merchandise Inventory		39,000.00
Total Assets		$49,850.00

Liabilities and Owner's Equity

Liabilities	
Notes Payable—Bank	$20,000.00
Accounts Payable	3,000.00
Total Liabilities	$23,000.00
Owner's Equity	
Linda Hanson, Capital	26,850.00
Total Liabilities and Owner's Equity	$49,850.00

ities) of the Style Clothing Store. However, the determination of the exact value of Hanson's net assets raised certain questions that had to be resolved. For example, Casey pointed out that some of the accounts receivable might not be collectible. Any resulting loss should be borne by Hanson, not by the partnership. On the other hand, Hanson noted that the inventory was worth more than the amount shown in the financial records of the firm because prices had gone up since the goods were acquired. Obviously, any gain under these circumstances should belong entirely to Hanson. The prospective partners decided to seek professional advice from a public accountant and from their personal lawyers.

The public accountant examined the records of the Style Clothing Store to make an independent verification of the values shown on the firm's balance sheet. He recommended that $800 of the accounts receivable be regarded as uncollectible, rather than the $300 shown on the January 31 balance sheet. This meant that the customers' accounts transferred to the partnership should be valued at $10,000 instead of $10,500. The accountant also checked the inventory and recommended that the book value be increased by $1,000 to reflect higher current prices. The merchandise inventory should thus be valued at $40,000 instead of $39,000 when the transfer takes place.

Further examination of the firm's financial records by the accountant revealed that the liabilities were properly recorded. Accounts payable amounted to $3,000 and notes payable to the bank amounted to $20,000. One note for $10,000 at 12 percent had 60 days to run. The other note, for $10,000 at 13 percent, had 90 days to run. By special arrangement with the bank, the Style Clothing Store's interest on both notes had been paid up to the date on which the balance sheet was prepared.

Since the assets of the Style Clothing Store were to be transferred to the new partnership at amounts different from those shown on the balance sheet on page 594, it became necessary to adjust the book value of Linda Hanson's equity in the business.

Two entries were made in the general journal to record the adjustment of the asset accounts involved. At that time Allowance for Uncollectible Accounts contained a balance of $300, showing that this amount was considered uncollectible. However, the balance had to be increased to $800 to reflect the valuation given by the accountant. Hanson had to bear the loss by having her owner's equity reduced by the difference ($500).

In the second adjustment, the inventory was increased by $1,000, and Hanson received the benefit of the gain. This adjustment required a debit to Merchandise Inventory and a credit to Linda Hanson, Capital. The two entries to revalue the assets are made in the general journal as shown below.

19 X1					
Jan. 31	Linda Hanson, Capital	301	500 00		
	Allowance for Uncollectible Accounts	112		500 00
	To record additional uncollectible accounts prior to transferring accounts to the new partnership.			
31	Merchandise Inventory	121	1,000 00	
	Linda Hanson, Capital	301		1,000 00
	To record valuation of merchandise inventory before transferring it to the new partnership.			

Notice that since the temporary accounts in the general ledger had already been closed, these adjustments were made directly to the Linda Hanson, Capital account rather than to revenue and expense accounts. The withdrawal of the cash balance by Hanson and the resulting decrease in her equity were recorded by a debit to her capital account and a credit to Cash. After these journal entries were posted to the general ledger accounts, a trial balance contained the amounts shown below.

STYLE CLOTHING STORE
Trial Balance
January 31, 19X1

Accounts Receivable	$10,800	
Allowance for Uncollectible Accounts		$ 800
Merchandise Inventory	40,000	
Notes Payable—Bank		20,000
Accounts Payable		3,000
Linda Hanson, Capital		27,000
Totals	$50,800	$50,800

Observe that the balance of the Linda Hanson, Capital account is now $27,000. This reflects the adjustments that were made to revalue the assets of the firm and to withdraw the cash.

THE PARTNERSHIP AGREEMENT

To avoid any future misunderstanding about the terms of their arrangement, Hanson and Casey had their lawyers draw up a written contract, called a *partnership agreement* or *articles of copartnership*. Both partners signed the agreement, and each received a signed copy. Another copy was provided for the partnership records. The major provisions of the partnership agreement were as follows.

Name, Location, and Nature of the Business

The name of the new business was to be the Style Clothing Store. It was to be located in rented premises at the address specified in the agreement. The store would sell men's and women's clothing at retail and would specialize in sportswear and casual clothes.

Starting Date of Agreement

The agreement was to be effective on February 1, 19X1, at which time the store would open for business in its new location. The agreement was to run until the partnership was terminated either by the death of one of the partners or by mutual consent. (The lawyers explained that a partnership has a limited life. It ends with the death or withdrawal of any partner.)

Fiscal Year

The partners agreed that their fiscal year would begin on February 1 and end on the following January 31. This date was chosen not only because the partnership was to begin on February 1 but also because January 31 was a time of low inventory and light business activity. This meant it would be easy to take a physical inventory and close the accounting records then.

Names of the Partners

The partners were Linda Hanson and Steven Casey. Both were residents of the city of Greenville in a southern state. (Another partner, Janet Miller, was admitted to the firm later, as you will learn in Chapter 27.)

Amounts of Capital to Be Contributed

Hanson was to contribute the assets and liabilities of her sole proprietorship business. She was to receive credit for the amount of her net capital, $27,000, as shown previously on the trial balance. Casey was to contribute $27,000 in cash.

Rights and Duties of Each Partner

Each partner is to devote his or her full time to the operation of the business. Hanson will concentrate on administration, financial management, and advertising. Casey will handle purchasing and selling. Their lawyers explained that a legal characteristic of any partnership is known as *mutual agency*. This means that either partner can make valid contracts for the business and can otherwise conduct its affairs.

Method of Distributing Profits and Losses

The agreement specifies exactly how the profits and losses of the firm will be divided between the partners. (This aspect of the agreement is discussed in the next chapter.)

Accounting Records	The agreement provides that Hanson is to be in charge of the accounting records. She is to keep records on the accrual basis according to generally accepted accounting principles.			

Accounting Records

The agreement provides that Hanson is to be in charge of the accounting records. She is to keep records on the accrual basis according to generally accepted accounting principles.

Drawings by the Partners

In order to have the funds needed to meet living expenses, each partner can withdraw a limited amount from the business each month as part of his or her share of the expected profits for the year.

Dissolution or Liquidation

If one of the partners should die, the accounting records must be closed at the end of that month and the firm's profits to that date must be distributed. The surviving partner can, at his or her option, either pay the amount of the deceased partner's investment to the person's estate and continue the business or liquidate the business and pay the balance of the deceased partner's capital account to the estate. If the partners decide to liquidate the business, Hanson will be in charge of the liquidation process.

Other Provisions

The partners could have included any other items pertinent to the business operation at the time they drew up their contract.

DISSOLVING THE SOLE PROPRIETORSHIP

Once a definite legal and financial understanding had been reached between Hanson and Casey, it was time to terminate the affairs of the Style Clothing Store as a sole proprietorship. Only one entry was needed to close out the adjusted balances of all the accounts in the proprietorship's general ledger. This entry is shown below. Note that it debited Allowance for Uncollectible Accounts, all the liability accounts, and the Linda Hanson, Capital account; and it credited all the asset accounts.

19 X1				
Jan. 31	Allowance for Uncollectible Accounts	112	800 00	
	Notes Payable—Bank	203	20,000 00	
	Accounts Payable	205	3,000 00	
	Linda Hanson, Capital	301	27,000 00	
	Accounts Receivable	111		10,800 00
	Merchandise Inventory	121		40,000 00
	To close all accounts upon dissolution of the proprietorship business.			

The general ledger accounts of the proprietorship are illustrated on pages 598 and 599. The first balances shown are those that appear on the balance sheet prepared on January 31, 19X1 (see page 594). The journal entries to adjust the asset accounts, the entry for the withdrawal of cash, and the final entry closing out all the remaining balances were posted to these accounts. This completed the work on the proprietorship records.

Cash   No. 101

DATE		EXPLANATION	POST. REF.	DEBIT	CREDIT	BALANCE	DR. CR.
19 X1 Jan.	31	Balance	√			350 00	Dr.
	31		CP3		350 00	–0–	

Accounts Receivable   No. 111

DATE		EXPLANATION	POST. REF.	DEBIT	CREDIT	BALANCE	DR. CR.
19 X1 Jan.	31	Balance	√			10,800 00	Dr.
	31		J1		10,800 00	–0–	

Allowance for Uncollectible Accounts   No. 112

DATE		EXPLANATION	POST. REF.	DEBIT	CREDIT	BALANCE	DR. CR.
19 X1 Jan.	31	Balance	√			300 00	Cr.
	31		J1		500 00	800 00	Cr.
	31		J1	800 00		–0–	

Merchandise Inventory   No. 121

DATE		EXPLANATION	POST. REF.	DEBIT	CREDIT	BALANCE	DR. CR.
19 X1 Jan.	31	Balance	√			39,000 00	Dr.
	31		J1	1,000 00		40,000 00	Dr.
	31		J1		40,000 00	–0–	

Notes Payable—Bank   No. 203

DATE		EXPLANATION	POST. REF.	DEBIT	CREDIT	BALANCE	DR. CR.
19 X1 Jan.	31	Balance	√			20,000 00	Cr.
	31		J1	20,000 00		–0–	

Accounts Payable   No. 205

DATE		EXPLANATION	POST. REF.	DEBIT	CREDIT	BALANCE	DR. CR.
19 X1 Jan.	31	Balance	√			3,000 00	Cr.
	31		J1	3,000 00		–0–	

	Linda Hanson, Capital				No. 301	
DATE	EXPLANATION	POST. REF.	DEBIT	CREDIT	BALANCE	DR. CR.
19 X1 Jan. 31	Balance	✓			26,850 00	Cr.
31		J1	500 00		26,350 00	Cr.
31		J1		1,000 00	27,350 00	Cr.
31		CP3	350 00		27,000 00	Cr.
31		J1	27,000 00		–0–	

OPENING THE PARTNERSHIP RECORDS

A new set of accounting records covering the operations of the partnership was then opened. In setting up records for a new business, the accountant should make a *memorandum entry* in the general journal. This entry should indicate the name of the business, the name of the proprietor or partners, and any other pertinent introductory information. The memorandum entry to set up the accounting records for Hanson and Casey's partnership is shown below.

19 X1 Feb. 1	On this date, a partnership was formed between Linda Hanson and Steven Casey to carry on a retail clothing business under the name of the Style Clothing Store, according to the terms of the partnership agreement effective this date.					

Notice the reference to the partnership agreement. The accountant needs to consult this document from time to time. It provides guidance on questions about the partners' original investments, the division of profits, and other matters.

Investment of Hanson

Linda Hanson's investment consisted of her equity in her former business. The partnership assumed the revalued assets and the liabilities. Hanson's capital account was credited for the difference between the two amounts. The facts were recorded in the general journal of the new partnership, as shown below.

19 X1 Feb. 1	Accounts Receivable	111	10,800 00	
	Merchandise Inventory	121	40,000 00	
	Allowance for Uncollectible Accounts	112		800 00
	Notes Payable—Bank	203		20,000 00
	Accounts Payable	205		3,000 00
	Linda Hanson, Capital	301		27,000 00
	Investment of Linda Hanson.			

Notice that the gross balances of both Accounts Receivable and Allowance for Uncollectible Accounts were entered in the records of the partnership. This was necessary because all the individual customers' balances in the accounts receivable subsidiary ledger were transferred to the partnership. Since the Accounts Receivable account in the general ledger must agree with the subsidiary ledger, the gross amount must be entered in the control account. Allowance for Uncollectible Accounts was transferred to the partnership at its revised balance of $800. Thus the net value of the accounts receivable in the records of the partnership was $10,000 ($10,800 − $800), the amount agreed on.

However, when a sole proprietorship transfers items of plant and equipment to a partnership, only the net agreed-on value of these assets is recorded in the partnership accounts. The accumulated depreciation accounts begin with a zero balance in the partnership.

Investment of Casey

Steven Casey's investment consisted of cash in the same amount as Hanson's equity. The receipt of the $27,000 was recorded in the cash receipts journal.

CASH RECEIPTS JOURNAL for Month of **February 19X1**   Page 1

		OTHER ACCOUNTS CREDIT			
DATE	EXPLANATION	ACCOUNT TITLE	POST. REF.	AMOUNT	CASH
Feb. 1	Investment of Steven Casey	Steven Casey, Capital	311	27,000 00	27,000 00

Opening Balance Sheet

The accountant immediately posted the opening entries to record the investments made by the two partners. Of course, the debit to Cash to record Casey's investment was posted only at the end of the month as part of the total of the Cash column in the cash receipts journal.

Linda Hanson, Capital   No.   301

DATE	EXPLANATION	POST. REF.	DEBIT	CREDIT	BALANCE	DR. CR.
19 X1 Feb. 1	Beginning Investment	J1		27,000 00	27,000 00	Cr.

Steven Casey, Capital   No.   311

DATE	EXPLANATION	POST. REF.	DEBIT	CREDIT	BALANCE	DR. CR.
19 X1 Feb. 1	Beginning Investment	CR1		27,000 00	27,000 00	Cr.

With these initial entries and postings, the accounting records of the Style Clothing Store as a partnership were formally opened.

The accountant also prepared a balance sheet at this time to reflect the status of the assets, liabilities, and owners' equity at the start of the new partnership venture. This balance sheet is illustrated below. As you have already learned, the balance sheet of a partnership is in the same form as that for a sole proprietorship except that each partner's equity is shown in a separate capital account in the Owners' Equity section.

STYLE CLOTHING STORE
Balance Sheet
February 1, 19X1

Assets

Cash		$27,000.00
Accounts Receivable	$10,800.00	
Less Allowance for Uncollectible Accounts	800.00	10,000.00
Merchandise Inventory		40,000.00
Total Assets		$77,000.00

Liabilities and Owners' Equity

Liabilities		
Notes Payable—Bank	$20,000.00	
Accounts Payable	3,000.00	
Total Liabilities		$23,000.00
Owners' Equity		
Linda Hanson, Capital	27,000.00	
Steven Casey, Capital	27,000.00	
Total Owners' Equity		54,000.00
Total Liabilities and Owners' Equity		$77,000.00

PRINCIPLES AND PROCEDURES SUMMARY

In a partnership, two or more persons join together as co-owners of a business. Each partner has unlimited liability for the partnership's debts, except in the case of limited partners. A partnership does not have continuity, but terminates on the death or incapacity of a partner. A partnership interest can be transferred only with the approval of the other partners, and even then the existing partnership must be terminated and a new one must be formed. A partnership does not pay federal income tax, but the partners are taxed on their shares of the profits from the partnership.

It is important that the agreement about a partnership's operation be in writing. This will mean fewer chances for possible misunderstanding later. Partnership agreements typically provide for the amounts of capital to be contributed, the rights and duties of each partner, the method of distributing profits and losses, the accounting methods, and the fiscal year to be used. In the case of the partnership of Hanson and Casey, one partner contributed the assets and liabilities of her business and received credit for the difference. The other partner contributed cash equal to the first partner's investment.

The value at which contributed assets are to be entered in the accounting records of the partnership is a matter of agreement between the partners. If the values agreed on are different from those shown in the accounting records of the prior business, the records of the prior business are adjusted before being finally closed.

The accounting records of the new partnership are opened with a memorandum entry in the general journal. Then the partners' investments are entered in their capital accounts.

MANAGERIAL IMPLICATIONS

The partnership form of business offers many advantages to the sole proprietor who needs more capital, managerial assistance, or technical help. It is extremely important, however, that individuals who enter into a partnership have a clear understanding about the duties, obligations, rights, and responsibilities of each partner. These points must be clearly and thoroughly covered in a written partnership agreement. Consultation with a lawyer and an accountant is advisable at every stage of the negotiations.

REVIEW QUESTIONS

1. Why have so many partnerships been formed by persons in the professions?
2. Explain the liability that a general partner has for the debts of a partnership.
3. What is a limited partner?
4. Does a partnership continue to exist after the death of a partner? Explain.
5. Does a partnership pay federal income tax? Explain.
6. Why does revaluation usually take place when noncash assets are transferred to a partnership?
7. How are revaluation gains or losses handled in the accounting records of a sole proprietorship when the firm's assets are being transferred to a partnership?
8. Why should partners have a written partnership agreement?
9. List several items that are commonly included in a partnership agreement.
10. What is the nature of the memorandum entry made in the general journal when a partnership is formed?
11. Is Allowance for Uncollectible Accounts brought forward from the general ledger of a sole proprietorship when the firm's assets and liabilities are being transferred to a partnership? Why?
12. Is Accumulated Depreciation brought forward from the general ledger of a sole proprietorship when the firm's assets and liabilities are being transferred to a partnership? Why?

13. How does the balance sheet of a partnership differ from that of a sole proprietorship?
14. Why have limited partnerships become so popular in recent years?
15. What is net working capital?
16. Give some reasons why a sole proprietor might seek partners.
17. What is meant by the term *partnership agreement* or *articles of copartnership*?
18. When a sole proprietorship is transformed into a partnership, are the balances of all asset and liability accounts brought forward to the new financial records? Explain.

MANAGERIAL DISCUSSION QUESTIONS

1. The owner of a business is considering establishing a partnership with two other persons to carry on the firm. What are some of the disadvantages of the partnership form of organization that she should consider?
2. Explain why it is essential that an owner who is thinking about transferring his existing business assets to a partnership should have all the assets appraised or evaluated before the transfer.
3. Why should partners have a written partnership agreement?
4. From a managerial viewpoint, why is it advisable to bring forward to the financial records of a new partnership both the total of Accounts Receivable and the balance of Allowance for Uncollectible Accounts?
5. Assume that you are the controller for a sole proprietorship business and that the owner tells you that he is considering forming a partnership with two other individuals who would be limited partners. Explain any weaknesses you see in this arrangement from the viewpoint of your employer.

EXERCISES

EXERCISE 26-1 **Recording the revaluation of accounts receivable.** Paul Kelly operates a sole proprietorship business that sells computer software. Kelly has agreed to transfer his assets and liabilities to a partnership. The balances of selected accounts in his general ledger before revaluation are shown below.

Accounts Receivable	$61,000	
Allowance for Uncollectible Accounts		$ 1,200
Merchandise Inventory	78,300	
Furniture and Fixtures	16,407	
Accumulated Depreciation		3,710
Paul Kelly, Capital		182,532

The agreed values of the assets are Accounts Receivable (net), $58,300; Merchandise Inventory, $82,680; and Furniture and Fixtures (net) $30,000. All revenue and expense accounts have been closed. Give the general journal entry to record the revaluation of Paul Kelly's accounts receivable.

EXERCISE 26-2 **Recording the revaluation of merchandise inventory.** Using the data from Exercise 26-1, give the general journal entry to record the revaluation of Paul Kelly's merchandise inventory.

EXERCISE 26-3 **Recording the revaluation of furniture and fixtures.** Using the data from Exercise 26-1, give the general journal entry to record the revaluation of Kelly's furniture and fixtures.

EXERCISE 26-4 **Computing the amount of capital after the revaluation of assets.** What is the balance of Paul Kelly's capital account after the asset revaluations recorded in Exercises 26-1, 26-2, and 26-3?

EXERCISE 26-5 **Determining the accounts that will be transferred to a partnership.** What account(s) and balance(s) related to accounts receivable will be shown in the general ledger of the partnership after the assets are transferred from Paul Kelly's sole proprietorship? (Refer to Exercise 26-1.)

EXERCISE 26-6 **Determining the accounts that will be transferred to a partnership.** What account(s) and balance(s) related to furniture and fixtures will be shown in the general ledger of the partnership after the assets are transferred from Paul Kelly's sole proprietorship? (Refer to Exercises 26-1 and 26-3.)

EXERCISE 26-7 **Recording a cash investment by a partner.** Assume that Lynn Farmer invests an amount of cash equal to the balance of the capital invested by Paul Kelly. Prepare an entry, in general journal form, to record Farmer's investment. (Refer to the solution to Exercise 26-4 for the amount of Kelly's capital.)

EXERCISE 26-8 **Preparing the owners' equity section of a partnership balance sheet.** Using the data from Exercises 26-1 through 26-7, prepare the owners' equity section of the balance sheet as it would appear just after formation of the partnership of Kelly and Farmer. The firm will be called the Superior Software Center.

EXERCISE 26-9 **Recording the revaluation of accounts receivable.** The general ledger of a business owned by John Farantino included the following accounts before he transferred his assets to a partnership: Accounts Receivable, $32,684 (Dr.) and Allowance for Uncollectible Accounts, $3,268 (Cr.). The partners have agreed that the collectible accounts should be valued at $31,042. Give the general journal entry to record the revaluation.

EXERCISE 26-10 **Recording the withdrawal of an asset before formation of a partnership.** Rosa Rodriquez owns a business whose assets and liabilities are to be transferred to a new partnership. Rodriquez and her new partners agree that an automobile previously used in the business is unneeded and that Rodriquez should retain it for personal use. The balances of the accounts related to this asset are Automobile, $12,600, and Accumulated Depreciation, $6,400. Give the general journal entry to record the withdrawal of the automobile from the business by Rodriquez.

PROBLEMS

PROBLEM 26-1 **Recording the formation of a partnership.** Keith Larson operates a small shop that sells ski equipment and ski clothing. His postclosing trial balance on December 31, 19X1, is as follows.

OLYMPIC SKI SHOP
Postclosing Trial Balance
December 31, 19X1

Account Name	Debits	Credits
Cash	$ 1,500	
Accounts Receivable	7,000	
Allowance for Uncollectible Accounts		$ 500
Merchandise Inventory	21,500	
Furniture and Equipment	13,500	
Accumulated Depreciation		10,000
Accounts Payable		2,000
Keith Larson, Capital		31,000
Totals	$43,500	$43,500

Larson plans to enter into a partnership with Joyce DeVoe, effective January 1, 19X2. Profits and losses will be shared equally. Larson is to transfer the assets and liabilities of his store to the partnership, after revaluation as agreed. DeVoe will invest cash equal to Larson's investment after revaluation. The agreed values are Accounts Receivable (net), $6,200; Merchandise Inventory, $22,400; and Furniture and Equipment (net), $5,600.

Instructions In general journal form, give the entries that will be needed to record formation of the partnership in the partnership's accounting records.

PROBLEM 26-2 **Recording the dissolution of a sole proprietorship and the formation of a partnership.** Ruth Roy operates a laundry that provides services to restaurants, hotels, and motels. Financial data for the firm as of December 31, 19X1, is given on page 606. Roy has agreed to enter into a partnership with Joseph Lema, effective January 1, 19X2. The new firm will be called the Ajax Commercial Laundry. Profits and losses will be shared equally. Roy is to transfer the assets and liabilities of her firm to the partnership, at the values agreed on. Lema will invest cash that is equal to Roy's investment after revaluation.

Instructions 1. Give the general journal entries to revalue the assets of the Roy Commercial Laundry and to close out the accounts on December 31, 19X1.
2. Give the memorandum entry in the general journal to record formation of the partnership that will operate the Ajax Commercial Laundry.

3. Give the general journal entry to record Roy's investment in the partnership on January 1, 19X2.
4. Give the general journal entry to record Lema's investment in the partnership on January 1, 19X2.

	BALANCES SHOWN IN ROY'S RECORDS		VALUE AGREED ON BY PARTNERS
Assets Transferred			
Cash		$ 1,600	$ 1,600
Accounts Receivable	$ 1,000		
Allowance for Uncollectible Accounts	100	900	800
Laundry Equipment	$20,000		
Accumulated Depreciation	6,000	14,000	12,000
Building	$24,000		
Accumulated Depreciation	4,000	20,000	16,000
Land		2,000	13,400
Total Assets		$38,500	$43,800
Liabilities and Owner's Equity Transferred			
Accounts Payable		2,000	2,000
Ruth Roy, Capital		$36,500	$41,800

PROBLEM 26-3

Recording the formation of a partnership and preparing a partnership balance sheet. Ahmed Almassi operates the AA Electronics Center, a small retail store that sells calculators, radios, cassette players, and other electronic products. His postclosing trial balance on December 31, 19X1, is given on page 607. Almassi reached an agreement with Stanley Bell to form a partnership, effective January 1, 19X2. Profits and losses will be shared equally, and each partner is to devote at least 90 percent of his time to the business. The arrangement will continue for five years. The new name of the store will be A & B Electronics.

Almassi is to transfer the assets of his firm to the partnership at agreed values as follows: Cash, as shown in the accounting records; Accounts Receivable (net), $8,200; Merchandise Inventory, $43,600; and Delivery Truck, $6,600. The partnership is to assume Almassi's liabilities. He is to receive credit for his net investment as adjusted. Bell will invest cash that is equal to Almassi's net investment.

Instructions

1. Adjust and close the accounting records of the AA Electronics Center on December 31, 19X1, as follows.
   a. Prepare general journal entries adjusting the assets to the agreed values. (The entry to revalue the delivery truck should be made by crediting the accumulated depreciation account.)
   b. Prepare a general journal entry dissolving the sole proprietorship.
2. Record the following in general journal form.
   a. The opening memorandum entry for the partnership.
   b. Almassi's investment in the partnership.
   c. Bell's investment in the partnership.

3. Prepare a balance sheet for the partnership (A & B Electronics) at the beginning of its operations on January 1, 19X2.

AA ELECTRONICS CENTER
Postclosing Trial Balance
December 31, 19X1

Account Name	Debit	Credit
Cash	$ 900	
Accounts Receivable	8,400	
Allowance for Uncollectible Accounts		$ 400
Merchandise Inventory	42,000	
Delivery Truck	7,600	
Accumulated Depreciation		600
Accounts Payable		2,200
Ahmed Almassi, Capital		55,700
Totals	$58,900	$58,900

ALTERNATE PROBLEMS

PROBLEM 26-1A

Recording the formation of a partnership. Rona Gill operates a retail store that sells garden tools and supplies. Her postclosing trial balance on December 31, 19X5, is as follows.

GREEN THUMB GARDEN CENTER
Postclosing Trial Balance
December 31, 19X5

Account Name	Debits	Credits
Cash	$ 6,000	
Accounts Receivable	28,000	
Allowance for Uncollectible Accounts		$ 2,000
Merchandise Inventory	85,000	
Furniture and Equipment	27,000	
Accumulated Depreciation		20,000
Accounts Payable		8,000
Rona Gill, Capital		116,000
Totals	$146,000	$146,000

Gill plans to enter into a partnership with George Pappas, effective January 1, 19X6. Profits and losses will be shared equally. Gill is to transfer the assets and liabilities of her store to the partnership, after revaluation as agreed. Pappas will invest cash equal to Gill's investment after revaluation. The agreed values are Accounts Receivable (net), $25,800; Merchandise Inventory, $88,400; and Furniture and Equipment (net), $12,000.

Instructions In general journal form, give the entries that will be needed to record formation of the partnership in the partnership's accounting records.

PROBLEM 26-2A **Recording dissolution of a sole proprietorship and the formation of a partnership.** David Lang operates a small store that specializes in running shoes and other types of athletic shoes. His postclosing trial balance as of December 31, 19X1, is given below. Lang has agreed to enter into a partnership with Susan Shaw, effective January 1, 19X2. The new firm will be called the Mercury Athletic Shoe Center. Profits and losses are to be shared equally. Lang will transfer the assets and liabilities of his store to the partnership at agreed values. These values are Accounts Receivable (net), $12,400; Merchandise Inventory, $44,800; and Furniture and Equipment (net), $11,200. Lang will receive credit for his net investment as adjusted. Shaw is to invest cash that is equal to Lang's net investment.

Instructions 1. Give the general journal entries to revalue the assets of the Lang Shoe Store and to close out the accounts on December 31, 19X1.
2. Give the memorandum entry in the general journal to record formation of the partnership that will operate the Mercury Athletic Shoe Center.
3. Give the general journal entry to record Lang's investment in the partnership on January 1, 19X2.
4. Give the general journal entry to record Shaw's investment in the partnership on January 1, 19X2.

LANG SHOE STORE
Postclosing Trial Balance
December 31, 19X1

Account Name	Debit	Credit
Cash	$ 3,000	
Accounts Receivable	14,000	
Allowance for Uncollectible Accounts		$ 1,000
Merchandise Inventory	43,000	
Furniture and Equipment	27,000	
Accumulated Depreciation		20,000
Accounts Payable		4,000
David Lang, Capital		62,000
Totals	$87,000	$87,000

PROBLEM 26-3A **Recording the formation of a partnership and preparing a partnership balance sheet.** Marsha Rosen owns a small fabric shop with a growing clientele. In order to obtain additional capital needed for expansion, she entered into a partnership agreement with Alice Perry, effective January 1, 19X2, for the operation of the Fashion Fabric Shop. The partnership agreement is to continue indefinitely. Profits and losses will be divided equally. Each partner is to devote full time to the business, except for an annual three-week vacation. Rosen has rented the building, furniture, and fixtures. Her postclosing trial balance as of December 31, 19X1, is shown below.

Rosen will transfer the assets of her business. However, one $200 account receivable is thought to be uncollectible, and the partners agreed to set up an Allowance for Uncollectible Accounts account for this sum. The merchandise inventory is to be transferred at an agreed value of $36,000. The partnership will take over Rosen's liabilities, and she is to receive credit for her net investment as adjusted. Perry will invest cash that is equal to Rosen's net investment.

Instructions

1. Adjust and close the accounting records of Rosen's Fabric Shop on December 31, 19X1, as follows.
   a. Prepare general journal entries adjusting the assets to the agreed values.
   b. Prepare a general journal entry to dissolve the sole proprietorship.
2. Record the following in general journal form.
   a. The opening memorandum entry for the partnership.
   b. Rosen's investment in the partnership.
   c. Perry's investment in the partnership.
3. Prepare a balance sheet for the partnership (the Fashion Fabric Shop) at the beginning of its operations on January 1, 19X2.

ROSEN'S FABRIC SHOP
Postclosing Trial Balance
December 31, 19X1

Account Name	Debit	Credit
Cash	$ 4,400	
Accounts Receivable	8,400	
Merchandise Inventory	40,000	
Accounts Payable		$ 3,200
Marsha Rosen, Capital		49,600
Totals	$52,800	$52,800

CHAPTER 27

The major differences between the accounting procedures required for a partnership and those for a sole proprietorship relate to the partners' capital accounts. In this chapter we shall examine two major topics affecting capital accounts—the division of profits and losses and the admission of a new partner into the business.

PARTNERSHIPS: PROFIT DIVISION AND EQUITY ACCOUNTING

PARTNER'S CAPITAL ACCOUNT

You learned about the initial contribution of cash or other assets by a partner in Chapter 26. If a partner makes additional investments at a later date, these amounts are credited to the partner's capital account. Withdrawals that are intended to reduce the invested capital permanently are recorded directly as debits to the partner's capital account.

PARTNER'S DRAWING ACCOUNT

Owners and partners of businesses need funds with which to pay their living expenses. They can obtain these funds from their businesses by making current withdrawals against anticipated profits. A drawing account is set up for each partner to record such withdrawals.

The partnership agreement for the Style Clothing Store specified that Linda Hanson could withdraw up to $600 each month and Steven Casey up to $575 each month. The withdrawals are recorded in the cash payments journal by a credit to Cash and a debit to the drawing accounts. The debits are then posted individually from the Other Accounts Debit section of the journal to each partner's drawing account in the general ledger. Thus if Hanson and Casey withdraw the specified amounts each month for 12 months, on January 31, 19X2, Hanson's drawing account will have a debit balance of $7,200 and Casey's will have a debit balance of $6,900.

Instead of withdrawing a lump sum periodically, partners may have the accountant for the business pay their personal bills with business checks. This is not a sound practice because it leads to confusion between business transactions and personal ones. If the practice is followed, however, each check written to pay a personal bill must be charged to the appropriate partner's drawing account by an entry in the cash payments journal. If such entries occur often, special columns may be set up in the cash payments journal for the drawing accounts. Under this system, only one posting to each drawing account will be required at the end of the month.

Although a partner's current withdrawals are not subject to payroll taxes or income tax withholding, they are sometimes called salary. The term *salary* is not completely accurate, but it will be used in this book to conform to common practice. Nonetheless, such withdrawals should *not* be considered expenses of the partnership. Furthermore, they do not represent withdrawals of invested capital. Therefore, they should not be debited directly to the capital accounts of the partners involved but should instead be charged to the drawing accounts.

DIVISION OF PARTNERSHIP PROFITS

Once the net income or net loss from the operations of the period is determined, it is transferred from the Income Summary account to the partners' capital accounts. If no other method for the division of net income or net loss is specified in the partnership agreement, it is divided equally between the partners. For example, if the net income of $19,800 earned by the Style Clothing Store in the first year of its operations is to be divided equally, the credit balance in the Income Summary account is transferred to the partners' capital accounts by the following general journal entry.

19X2				
Jan. 31	Income Summary	399	19,800 00	
	Linda Hanson, Capital	301		9,900 00
	Steven Casey, Capital	311		9,900 00
	To record equal distribution of net income for the year.			

At the end of each fiscal year, the drawing accounts are closed into the partners' capital accounts. Assume that Hanson's drawing account contains a debit balance of $7,200 and Casey's drawing account contains a debit balance of $6,900 at the end of the first year's operations. The following general journal entries are made to close the two partners' drawing accounts into their capital accounts on January 31, 19X2.

19X2				
Jan. 31	Linda Hanson, Capital	301	7,200 00	
	Linda Hanson, Drawing	302		7,200 00
	To close drawing account.			
31	Steven Casey, Capital	311	6,900 00	
	Steven Casey, Drawing	312		6,900 00
	To close drawing account.			

Notice that the closing procedure illustrated is almost the same as for a sole proprietorship. The single difference is that there are two drawing accounts and two capital accounts, one for each partner.

Again assume that Hanson and Casey agreed to divide net income and net losses equally. However, suppose that the store experiences a net loss of $15,000 instead of a net income of $19,800 from the first year's operations. The entries to transfer the balances of the Income Summary account and the drawing accounts to the capital accounts are shown below.

	19 X2				
Jan.	31	Linda Hanson, Capital	301	7,500 00	
		Steven Casey, Capital	311	7,500 00	
		Income Summary	399		15,000 00
		To distribute net loss for the year.			
	31	Linda Hanson, Capital	301	7,200 00	
		Linda Hanson, Drawing	302		7,200 00
		To close drawing account.			
	31	Steven Casey, Capital	311	6,900 00	
		Steven Casey, Drawing	312		6,900 00
		To close drawing account.			

Notice that in the preceding examples there was *no connection* between the partners' drawings and the division of net income. Each partner withdrew the maximum amount permitted under the agreement. The net income or net loss was then divided equally. It is important to remember that the withdrawals of cash are *not of themselves a division of net income*. They are instead drawings in anticipation of net income that will be divided according to the profit-sharing agreement.

PROFIT-SHARING AGREEMENT

Hanson and Casey discussed the question of profit sharing when they were outlining the provisions to be included in their partnership agreement. They did not feel that an equal division of the net income was satisfactory for their particular circumstances. They sought the advice of their lawyers and their accountant to help them work out a fair arrangement.

Hanson and Casey agreed that each would devote full time to the business. Hanson felt that her longer experience in the trade should entitle her to a larger share of the profits. Casey acknowledged Hanson's superior skill and ability, and he conceded that the new business would greatly benefit from Hanson's good reputation and established clientele.

Casey's primary concern was for his capital investment. He planned to leave his entire original capital invested indefinitely and thought he might even add to it. Thus if Hanson made any permanent withdrawals of capital, Casey wanted to be sure that his proportionately larger investment would be considered in the division of net income.

The consultants recommended a combination plan for profit distribution. They pointed out that both partners' interests would be fairly protected under the following arrangement.

1. Salary allowances of $7,200 to Hanson and $6,900 to Casey will be paid each year.
2. Interest at 9 percent will be allowed to each partner on the balance of his or her capital account at the beginning of the year.

3. The remainder of the net income will be divided in the ratio of 75 percent to Hanson and 25 percent to Casey.

The partners agreed to accept this plan, with the understanding that it might later be changed. Let us analyze each part of the plan to identify the purpose and effect on the partners' interests.

Salary Allowance

The salary allowance provision gave a slight advantage to Hanson to compensate for her greater experience in store operation. The difference was small because both partners were to devote full time to the firm and because Casey too had considerable experience in the clothing business. (Under other conditions there might have been a greater difference in the salary allowance provision.)

There is no necessary connection between the salary allowance (as a step in the distribution of net income) and the limit on withdrawals of cash for the partners' current living expenses during the year. However, the two are often the same (as they were in the Hanson and Casey agreement), although there are *vital differences in the purpose and the recording of the items*. The entry for the salary allowances is made regardless of the amount of net income or net loss for the period.

Interest on Capital

Payment of interest at 9 percent on the balance of each partner's capital account at the beginning of the year gives special consideration to the partner who maintains the larger permanent balance in his or her capital account. The interest allowance is also recorded regardless of the amount of net income earned or net loss incurred during the period.

Allocation Ratio for Remainder

The ratio of 75 percent to Hanson and 25 percent to Casey for the remaining net income or net loss was intended to compensate Hanson for the value of her outstanding reputation in the community and the established clientele of the Style Clothing Store.

PUTTING THE PLAN INTO OPERATION

Now let us see how the combination plan works, taking one section at a time. Remember that the profit division is made at the end of the year. It transfers the balance of the Income Summary account to the partners' capital accounts. Assume that the drawing accounts have been debited month by month during the year for the cash withdrawals made by the partners and that they total $7,200 for Hanson and $6,900 for Casey.

Salary Allowance

The first step in dividing net income or net loss is to record the salary allowances of $7,200 to Hanson and $6,900 to Casey. The general journal entry to record these allowances is shown below.

19 X2						
Jan.	31	Income Summary	399	14,100 00		
		Linda Hanson, Capital	301		7,200 00	
		Steven Casey, Capital	311		6,900 00	
		To record agreed salary allowances.				

Interest on Capital

The partners' capital accounts at the beginning of the fiscal year (when the business was established) were Linda Hanson, Capital, $27,000; Steven Casey, Capital, $27,000. At 9 percent interest on each account for the year, the interest allowance is $2,430 ($27,000 × 0.09) for each partner. This allowance is recorded in the general journal as follows.

19 X2				
Jan. 31	Income Summary	399	4,860 00	
	Linda Hanson, Capital	301		2,430 00
	Steven Casey, Capital	311		2,430 00
	To record agreed interest allowance			
	of 9% on beginning capital balances.			

Allocation of Remainder

After the entries to record the salary and interest allowances have been posted, the balance remaining in the Income Summary account will be allocated in the agreed ratio to the partners' drawing accounts. The procedures followed at this point depend on whether there was a net income or a net loss and on its amount. These procedures are illustrated in the following paragraphs.

Profit Greater Than Salaries and Interest Assume that at the end of the fiscal year, the Income Summary account shows a net income of $19,800 after all revenues and expenses are transferred to it. Then the entries are made for the salary allowances ($14,100) and the interest allowances ($4,860). These entries reduce the balance of the Income Summary account to $840, as shown below.

	Income Summary				No.	399
DATE	EXPLANATION	POST. REF.	DEBIT	CREDIT	BALANCE	DR. CR.
19 X2						
Jan. 31	Net Income	✓			19,800 00	Cr.
31	Salary Allowances	J1	14,100 00		5,700 00	Cr.
31	Interest Allowances	J1	4,860 00		840 00	Cr.

The credit balance of $840 is divided in the ratio of 75 to 25 between Hanson and Casey, as specified in the partnership agreement. The entry to close the Income Summary account transfers $630 as a credit to Hanson's capital account and $210 as a credit to Casey's capital account, as shown below.

19 X2				
Jan. 31	Income Summary	399	840 00	
	Linda Hanson, Capital	301		630 00
	Steven Casey, Capital	311		210 00
	To distribute balance of summary			
	account 75% to Hanson and			
	25% to Casey.			

After this journal entry is posted, the Income Summary account is closed. This account and the partners' capital accounts are shown below.

Income Summary   No. 399

DATE		EXPLANATION	POST. REF.	DEBIT	CREDIT	BALANCE	DR. CR.
19 X2							
Jan.	31	Net Income	✓			19,800 00	Cr.
	31	Salary Allowances	J1	14,100 00		5,700 00	Cr.
	31	Interest Allowances	J1	4,860 00		840 00	Cr.
	31	Balance 75%: 25% to Partners	J1	840 00		–0–	

Linda Hanson, Capital   No. 301

DATE		EXPLANATION	POST. REF.	DEBIT	CREDIT	BALANCE	DR. CR.
19 X2							
Jan.	31	Balance	✓			27,000 00	Cr.
	31	Salary Allowance	J1		7,200 00	34,200 00	Cr.
	31	Interest Allowance	J1		2,430 00	36,630 00	Cr.
	31	75% of Balance of Income Summary	J1		630 00	37,260 00	Cr.

Steven Casey, Capital   No. 311

DATE		EXPLANATION	POST. REF.	DEBIT	CREDIT	BALANCE	DR. CR.
19 X2							
Jan.	31	Balance	✓			27,000 00	Cr.
	31	Salary Allowance	J1		6,900 00	33,900 00	Cr.
	31	Interest Allowance	J1		2,430 00	36,330 00	Cr.
	31	25% of Balance of Income Summary	J1		210 00	36,540 00	Cr.

The final step is to close the balances of the partners' drawing accounts into their permanent capital accounts. The necessary journal entries are illustrated below.

19 X2					
Jan.	31	Linda Hanson, Capital	301	7,200 00	
		Linda Hanson, Drawing	302		7,200 00
		To close drawing account.			
	31	Steven Casey, Capital	311	6,900 00	
		Steven Casey, Drawing	312		6,900 00
		To close drawing account.			

Operating Loss Now assume the opposite situation—that the Style Clothing Store suffers a net loss of $15,000 for the first year's operation. The Income Summary account shows this amount as a debit balance after all revenues and expenses have been transferred to it. Even though a loss has occurred, the allowances for salaries and interest must still be made in accordance with the partnership agreement, as in the previous example. The debits of $14,100 for the salary allowances and $4,860 for the interest allowances increase the debit balance of the summary account to $33,960, as shown below.

		Income Summary					No.	399
DATE	EXPLANATION	POST. REF.	DEBIT	CREDIT	BALANCE	DR. CR.		
19 X2								
Jan. 31	Net Loss	✓			15,000 00	Dr.		
31	Salary Allowances	J1	14,100 00		29,100 00	Dr.		
31	Interest Allowances	J1	4,860 00		33,960 00	Dr.		

The debit balance of $33,960 must be divided between Hanson and Casey according to the 75 to 25 ratio specified in the partnership agreement. The entry to close the Income Summary account thus results in a debit of $25,470 to Hanson's capital account and a debit of $8,490 to Casey's capital account. The journal entry to close the summary account is given below.

19 X2				
Jan. 31	Linda Hanson, Capital	301	25,470 00	
	Steven Casey, Capital	311	8,490 00	
	Income Summary	399		33,960 00
	To close debit balance of summary			
	account to partners' capital accounts			
	in ratio of 75:25.			

After this entry is posted, the Income Summary account and the partners' capital accounts appear as shown below and on page 617.

		Income Summary					No.	399
DATE	EXPLANATION	POST. REF.	DEBIT	CREDIT	BALANCE	DR. CR.		
19 X2								
Jan. 31	Net Loss	✓			15,000 00	Dr.		
31	Salary Allowances	J1	14,100 00		29,100 00	Dr.		
31	Interest Allowances	J1	4,860 00		33,960 00	Dr.		
31	Balance 75%: 25% to							
	Partners	J1		33,960 00	–0–			

Linda Hanson, Capital   No. 301

DATE		EXPLANATION	POST. REF.	DEBIT	CREDIT	BALANCE	DR. CR.
19 X2							
Jan.	31	Balance	✓			27,000 00	Cr.
	31	Salary Allowance	J1		7,200 00	34,200 00	Cr.
	31	Interest Allowance	J1		2,430 00	36,630 00	Cr.
	31	75% of Balance of Income Summary	J1	25,470 00		11,160 00	Cr.

Steven Casey, Capital   No. 311

DATE		EXPLANATION	POST. REF.	DEBIT	CREDIT	BALANCE	DR. CR.
19 X2							
Jan.	31	Balance	✓			27,000 00	Cr.
	31	Salary Allowance	J1		6,900 00	33,900 00	Cr.
	31	Interest Allowance	J1		2,430 00	36,330 00	Cr.
	31	25% of Balance of Income Summary	J1	8,490 00		27,840 00	Cr.

The drawing account balances are then closed into the permanent capital accounts, as follows.

19 X2					
Jan.	31	Linda Hanson, Capital	301	7,200 00	
		Linda Hanson, Drawing	302		7,200 00
		To close drawing account.			
	31	Steven Casey, Capital	311	6,900 00	
		Steven Casey, Drawing	312		6,900 00
		To close drawing account.			

Profit Less Than Salary and Interest Allowances Now assume that the operations of the Style Clothing Store for the year resulted in a net income of only $5,000. The net income appears as a credit balance in the Income Summary account after all the revenues and expenses have been closed into it. The later debits of $14,100 for salary allowances and $4,860 for interest, totaling $18,960, change the balance in the Income Summary account to a debit of $13,960 ($18,960 − $5,000). Distributing this in the 75 to 25 ratio results in a debit to Hanson's capital account of $10,470 and a debit to Casey's capital account of $3,490, with an offsetting credit to the Income Summary account. When the journal entry is posted to the permanent capital accounts, there is a resulting decrease in each partner's equity. The drawing accounts are closed into the capital accounts in the normal way.

PARTNERSHIP EQUITY ON THE STATEMENTS

Once the net income or net loss distribution is completed, the financial statements can be prepared. The firm's accountant should present complete financial information but should not clutter the statements with too many details.

Showing Profit Distribution on the Income Statement

The final figure on the income statement for a sole proprietorship is the amount of net income or net loss. On the income statement for a partnership, a schedule is added below this final figure to show the distribution of the net income or net loss to the partners. This portion of the income statement for the Style Clothing Store appears as follows, assuming a net income of $19,800 for the year.

Net Income for Year			$19,800

Distribution of Net Income	Hanson	Casey	Total
Salary Allowance	$ 7,200	$6,900	$14,100
Interest Allowance	2,430	2,430	4,860
Remainder in 75:25 Ratio	630	210	840
Totals	$10,260	$9,540	$19,800

Showing the Results on the Balance Sheet

As a general rule, only the final balances of the partners' capital accounts are shown on the balance sheet. A separate *statement of partners' equities* summarizes the changes that have taken place in the capital accounts during the year. As shown in the illustration below, the statement of partners' equities contains the beginning capital of each partner, additional investments during the year, each partner's share of the net income or net loss, withdrawals, and ending capital.

STYLE CLOTHING STORE
Statement of Partners' Equities
Year Ended January 31, 19X2

	Hanson Capital	Casey Capital	Total Capital
Capital Balances, Feb. 1, 19X1	-0-	-0-	-0-
Investment During Year	$27,000	$27,000	$54,000
Net Income for Year	10,260	9,540	19,800
Totals	$37,260	$36,540	$73,800
Less Withdrawals During Year	7,200	6,900	14,100
Capital Balances, Jan. 31, 19X2	$30,060	$29,640	$59,700

ADMITTING A NEW PARTNER

Existing partners may decide to take in a new partner. When a new partner is admitted, a new partnership results and the old one is dissolved. (The dissolution of a partnership is a legal and financial matter and may have no noticeable effect on the operations of the business.)

Before the admission of the new partner is recorded in the accounting records, two steps should be taken.

1. The accounting records should be closed as of the date preceding the new partnership, and the net income or net loss of the period should be recorded and transferred to the partners' capital accounts in the usual manner.
2. Assets and liabilities should be revalued at amounts agreed on by the old partners and the new partner. This is done in the same way that the values of sole proprietorship accounts are adjusted when they are transferred to a partnership. The gain or loss resulting from revaluation is allocated to the capital accounts of the old partners in their profit and loss ratio. Then the admission of the new partner is recorded.

The procedures for recording the admission of a new partner can be illustrated as follows. Assume that Hanson and Casey have decided to admit a third partner, Janet Miller, as of August 1, 19X1. The accounting records of the firm are therefore closed on July 31, 19X1. At that point Hanson has a capital balance of $28,500, and Casey has a capital balance of $27,500. The assets and liabilities are then revalued as agreed on with Miller, and the resulting gain or loss is allocated to the capital accounts.

Purchase of an Interest

One way to join an existing partnership is to buy a portion of an old partner's share for an agreed sum. (Of course, the prospective partner must have the approval of the old partners.) The money or other consideration passes directly from the purchaser to the old partner and does not appear in the accounting records of the partnership.

Suppose that Hanson sells half her interest in the business to Miller for $15,000. The $15,000 is paid by Miller directly to Hanson. In the accounting records of the partnership, the transfer of half of Hanson's capital account balance to Miller is recorded by a debit to Hanson's capital account for $14,250 and a credit to Miller's capital account for the same amount.

The amount paid by the new partner is not necessarily the same as the amount credited to that person's capital account. In the case of the Style Clothing Store, Miller paid $15,000 but was credited with only $14,250. The price paid is a matter of bargaining between the parties involved, because the value of the interest is a matter of opinion and because circumstances affect the willingness of the buyer and seller to trade at any particular price.

With the admission of the new partner, the old partnership comes to an end and a new one comes into being. The partners should therefore draw up a new partnership agreement that covers all the usual topics.

Investment of Assets by a New Partner

A prospective partner may invest money or other property to obtain admission to the partnership while the old partners continue to participate. The new partner's investment, share of the business, and share of the net income or net loss are matters to be settled among the partners. They are specified in the partnership agreement for the new organization.

Instead of buying part of Hanson's interest, suppose that Miller invests cash in the business. There are several different methods for recording her investment in the partnership.

New Partner Given Credit for Amount Invested Assume that Hanson, Casey, and Miller agreed that Miller would receive a one-third interest in the capital of the store on investing cash in an amount equal to one-third of the total capital in the new partnership. Hanson and Casey, whose capital amounts totaled $56,000 ($28,500 + $27,500), owned two-thirds of the business. Therefore, Miller's one-third must equal $28,000 ($56,000 ÷ 2 = $28,000 = ⅓ interest). Miller invested $28,000, and her capital account was credited for this amount. The partners further agreed that all future profits and losses would be split equally among them and that there would be no salary or interest allowances.

Miller received credit for the amount of cash she invested in the business. However, a new partner can invest more or less than book value for a share of ownership. (The *book value* is the person's share of the total owners' equity after investment.)

Bonus to Old Partners Suppose Miller had agreed to invest $34,000 in cash for a one-third interest. The $34,000 investment would first be recorded in the usual way by a debit to Cash and a credit to Janet Miller, Capital.

After the recording of Miller's investment, the total owners' equity would amount to $90,000 (Hanson, $28,500; Casey, $27,500; Miller, $34,000). Although Miller's capital account should ultimately show a credit balance equal to only one-third of the total equity, $30,000, she would have paid more than this amount. One method of adjusting Miller's capital account to the desired balance of $30,000 would be to allow a bonus to the old partners. In this case Miller's capital would be reduced to $30,000 by a debit of $4,000. The $4,000 difference would be credited to the capital accounts of Hanson and Casey in the old 75 to 25 profit ratio. After the posting of this entry, Miller's capital account balance would reflect one-third of the total owners' equity, as agreed (⅓ × $90,000 = $30,000). Hanson's capital account would show $31,500 ($28,500 + $3,000), and Casey's capital account would show $28,500 ($27,500 + $1,000).

Goodwill to Old Partners Miller may be reluctant to receive credit for less than she actually invested. Another way of treating Miller's investment involves the recording of goodwill.

Miller's investment of $34,000 cash is recorded in the usual way. If Miller's capital account balance is to remain at $34,000, the total equity of the partnership must be three times that amount, or $102,000. The $12,000 difference ($102,000 − $90,000) is recorded in the accounting records as an intangible asset called *goodwill*. The amount is allocated between the old partners in the 75 to 25 ratio by the following entry.

19 X1							
Aug.	1	Goodwill	191	12,000	00		
		Linda Hanson, Capital	301			9,000	00
		Steven Casey, Capital	311			3,000	00
		To set up goodwill on admission of new partner.					

After this entry is posted, the total equity will be $102,000 (Hanson, $37,500; Casey, $30,500; Miller, $34,000). Miller's capital account reflects her one-third share, as agreed.

Bonus to New Partner The incoming partner may also invest less than the book value of his or her interest. For example, Miller may be given a one-third interest for investing only $25,000. After the $25,000 investment is recorded in the usual way, the new total of the owners' equity is $81,000 ($56,000 + $25,000). Miller's $25,000 investment is less than one-third of $81,000. A bonus of $2,000 can be credited to the new partner to increase her capital account to one-third of $81,000, or $27,000. The credit to the Janet Miller, Capital account for $2,000 is offset by debits to the original partners' capital accounts, allocated in the profit and loss ratio of the old partnership. The effect of this procedure on the capital account balances is as follows.

	PREVIOUS BALANCE		CHANGE		NEW BALANCE
Linda Hanson, Capital	$28,500	−	$1,500	=	$27,000
Steven Casey, Capital	27,500	−	500	=	27,000
Janet Miller, Capital	25,000	+	2,000	=	27,000
Total Owners' Equity	$81,000	+	-0-	=	$81,000

Goodwill to New Partner Suppose the old partners are reluctant to have their capital accounts reduced under the bonus method. In this case their agreement to give Miller a one-third share can be satisfied by increasing her capital balance by the appropriate amount and by debiting Goodwill. The combined capital of the old partners, $56,000, is equal to two-thirds of the total equity of the new partnership. Thus $28,000 must be the value of a one-third share. The difference between Miller's cash contribution and the $28,000 ($28,000 − $25,000 = $3,000) is recorded as goodwill in a journal entry, as shown below.

19 X1					
Aug.	1	Goodwill	191	3,000 00	
		Janet Miller, Capital	321		3,000 00
		To set up goodwill and increase new partner's capital to one-third of total owners' equity.			

After this entry is posted, the total equity is $84,000 (Hanson, $28,500; Casey, $27,500; Miller, $28,000). Miller's capital account shows a one-third interest, as agreed.

PRINCIPLES AND PROCEDURES SUMMARY

Investments by a partner are credited to the partner's capital account. Permanent withdrawals of capital are charged to this account. Temporary withdrawals are debited to a drawing account. At the end of the fiscal period, the Income Summary account is closed into the capital accounts, and the drawing accounts are also closed into the capital accounts.

The division of partnership profits and losses can be arranged in any manner agreed on by the partners. Allowances for salaries and interest are made whether the partnership has a profit or a loss. Any balance remaining in the Income Summary account is then divided as agreed.

A new partner is admitted to an established partnership in either of two ways. The new partner may purchase an interest from an old partner, in which case no cash comes into the business. Or the new partner may invest cash or other property, in which case the person may put in more or less than the share of equity agreed to. If the new partner invests more, a bonus may be allowed to the old partners, or goodwill may be recorded and credited to their capital accounts. A new partner who invests less than the agreed share of the total equity may receive credit for a bonus from the capital accounts of the old partners or may have goodwill credited to his or her capital account.

MANAGERIAL IMPLICATIONS

Partners must give serious consideration to the profit and loss distribution formula to make sure that each pertinent factor is properly considered. Before admitting new partners, the old partners must carefully study the advantages and disadvantages of the bonus and goodwill methods. The new profit and loss agreement that results may produce long-term effects different from those expected or intended.

REVIEW QUESTIONS

1. How do the capital accounts of a partnership differ from those of a sole proprietorship?
2. Are partners' salaries considered to be expenses of the partnership? Explain.
3. What account is debited for payment of a partner's salary?
4. In the absence of an agreement to the contrary, how are the profits and losses of a partnership divided?
5. Explain how the net income of a partnership is allocated if it is less than the salary and interest allowances.
6. What information is shown on the statement of partners' equities?
7. Assume that a partnership agreement provides that salaries of different amounts are to be allowed the three partners and that the balance of the Income Summary account is to be allocated equally to the partners. There is a net loss for the year. Discuss how this situation is handled.
8. Why should the assets and liabilities of an existing partnership be revalued at the time of the admission of a new partner?
9. If one partner sells, with the approval of the other partners, a fractional share of her interest in the firm to a new partner, how is the sale recorded in the accounting records of the partnership?

10. Under what circumstances would a bonus to the old partners be recorded at the time of admission of a new partner?
11. What is goodwill?
12. How does goodwill arise at the time of the admission of a new partner?
13. The existing capital of a partnership is $100,000. A new partner is to be admitted by investing $75,000 and is to receive a one-third interest in the partnership. Describe two ways in which the investment might be recorded.
14. Why might a partner prefer to have his investment for a partnership interest recorded by the goodwill method rather than the bonus method?
15. The two partners in a certain firm usually pay their personal bills by writing checks on the bank account of the business. Is this a good business practice? Explain. How should such payments be recorded?
16. Name some factors that commonly affect the profit-sharing agreement among partners.
17. Why does the sale of a share of one partner's capital interest not affect the capital accounts of any of the other original partners?

MANAGERIAL DISCUSSION QUESTIONS

1. Two partners in a new firm failed to make an agreement about how their profits and losses would be divided. At the end of the first year, one partner argued that the division should be based on the balance of the capital accounts. The other argued that there should be an equal division. Which partner was correct? What advice would you give partners about the importance of a definite agreement about the division of profits and losses?
2. If salaries are not treated as partnership expenses, why are they included in partnership agreements?
3. What factors must be weighed when prospective partners attempt to devise a fair profit-sharing agreement?
4. The partnership agreement between two partners specifies that one partner shall be allowed a monthly drawing of $1,000 and the other a monthly drawing of $600. The agreement does not mention salary allowances for the partners. At the end of the year, one partner maintains that a drawing is the same as a salary allowance. Comment on this.
5. Why do partners usually make periodic withdrawals of funds against anticipated profits?
6. Under what circumstances would the members of an existing partnership offer a bonus to a prospective new partner in the firm? Why would a prospective new partner be required to offer a bonus to the old partners in order to obtain admission to the firm?

EXERCISES

EXERCISE 27-1   **Computing the division of a profit with no salaries or interest considered.**
The partnership agreement of Diane Lane and Richard Berry does not indicate

how profits and losses will be shared. The net income of their firm for the year ended December 31, 19X1, was $56,450. How will this amount be divided, assuming that Lane's capital balance before the current year's net income is $104,000 and Berry's capital balance is $52,000?

EXERCISE 27-2 **Computing the division of a profit adequate to cover salaries.** Janet Baker and Marie Conti are partners who share profits and losses in the ratio of 75 and 25 percent. Their partnership agreement provides that each of them will be paid a salary of $10,000, which is to be deducted in arriving at the distribution of profits and losses. Assume that the salaries were withdrawn during 19X1 and were charged to the drawing accounts of the partners. The Income Summary account had a credit balance of $58,000 at the end of the year. What amount of net income or net loss will be allocated to each partner?

EXERCISE 27-3 **Computing the division of a profit inadequate to cover salaries.** The partnership agreement of Brian McKay and Thomas Black provides the following distribution of profits and losses. McKay will receive a salary of $30,000 and Black will receive a salary of $24,000; the balance of the profits and losses will be divided equally. Assume that the salaries were withdrawn during 19X1 and charged to the drawing accounts of the partners. The balance of the Income Summary account shows a net income of $48,000 at the end of the year. How much of the net income will be allocated to each partner?

EXERCISE 27-4 **Computing the division of profit inadequate to cover salaries.** Assume the same facts as in Exercise 27-3, except that the balance of the Income Summary account shows a net income of $16,000. How much of the net income will be allocated to each partner?

EXERCISE 27-5 **Computing the division of a loss with salaries considered.** Assume the same facts as in Exercise 27-3, except that the balance of the Income Summary account shows a net loss of $12,000. How much of the net loss will be allocated to each partner?

EXERCISE 27-6 **Computing the division of a profit with salaries and interest considered.** David Simon and Carol Tate are partners who share profits and losses in the following manner. Simon receives a salary of $20,000, and Tate receives a salary of $30,000. Both partners also receive 10 percent interest on their capital as of the beginning of the year. The balance of any remaining profits or losses is divided equally. The beginning capital amounts for 19X2 were Simon, $100,000, and Tate, $125,000. At the end of the year, the partnership had a net income of $67,000. How much of the net income will be allocated to each partner?

EXERCISE 27-7 **Computing the revaluation of partnership assets.** Peter Allen and George Velonich are partners who share profits and losses in the ratio of 60 and 40 percent. In December 19X1 they decided to admit a new partner. At that time the balances of their capital accounts were $100,000 for Allen and $150,000 for

Velonich. The two existing partners and the new partner agreed that before the new partner is admitted, certain assets should be revalued. These assets include merchandise inventory, carried at $84,000, to be revalued at $80,000, and a building with a book value of $45,000, to be revalued at $110,000. What will be the capital balances of the two existing partners after the revaluation is made?

EXERCISE 27-8 **Determining capital balances after the sale of part of an interest.** Irene Weber and Sandra Hart are partners who share profits and losses in the ratio of 60 and 40 percent. The balances of their capital accounts are Weber, $80,000, and Hart, $100,000. With Hart's agreement, Weber sells one-half of her interest in the partnership to Frank DeSilva for $75,000. What will be the capital account balances of the three partners after this sale?

EXERCISE 27-9 **Determining capital balances after the admission of a partner with a bonus to the old partners.** Ben Chandler and Wayne Hill are partners who share profits and losses in the ratio of 55 and 45 percent. On January 31, 19X2, the balances of their capital accounts were $80,000 for Chandler and $85,000 for Hill. At this date they admitted Robert Ellis to the partnership under the following conditions. Ellis is to invest $100,000 and will receive a one-third interest in the partnership. The bonus method is to be used to record the admission. What will be the capital account balances of the three partners after Ellis is admitted?

EXERCISE 27-10 **Determining capital balances after the admission of a partner with goodwill to the old partners.** Assume the same facts as in Exercise 27-9, except that the goodwill method is to be used to record the investment. What will be the capital agcount balances of the three partners after Ellis is admitted?

EXERCISE 27-11 **Determining capital balances after the admission of a partner with a bonus to the new partner.** James O'Mara and Paul Nathan are partners who share profits and losses in the ratio of 40 and 60 percent. The balances of their capital accounts on December 31, 19X1, were $75,000 for O'Mara and $85,000 for Nathan. At that date they admitted Eileen Scott to the partnership, giving her a one-third interest in return for her cash investment of $70,000. What will be the capital account balances of the three partners after Scott's investment if the bonus method is used to record her admission?

EXERCISE 27-12 **Determining capital balances after the admission of a partner with goodwill to the new partner.** Assume the same facts as in Exercise 27-11, except that the goodwill method is used to record the investment. What will be the capital account balances of the three partners after Scott is admitted?

PROBLEMS

PROBLEM 27-1 **Recording the allocation of profit to partners.** The partnership of Thomas Petty and Chen Ling operates a retail store called the Eastern Gift Bazaar. During the year ended December 31, 19X2, the business earned a net income of

$62,000. Under the terms of the partnership agreement, Petty is authorized to withdraw $1,000 a month and Ling $800 a month in anticipation of profits. For 19X2 each partner has withdrawn the maximum amount, which has been charged to his drawing account. By agreement, net income is to be distributed two-thirds to Petty and one-third to Ling.

Instructions
1. In general journal form, record the entry to transfer the net income to the capital accounts of the partners.
2. Give the general journal entries needed to close each partner's drawing account to his capital account.

PROBLEM 27-2 **Recording the allocation of profit and preparing the statement of partners' equities.** Donna Mason and Ralph Rossi own the Nautilus Seafood Restaurant. Their partnership agreement provides for allowances for salaries of $12,000 a year for Mason and $9,600 for Rossi and interest of 10 percent on each partner's invested capital at the beginning of the year. The remainder of the net income is to be distributed equally between the two partners. On January 1, 19X1, the capital account balances were Mason, $24,000, and Rossi, $56,000. The net income for 19X1 was $41,000.

Instructions
1. Prepare the general journal entry dated December 31, 19X1, to record the agreed allowances for salaries.
2. Prepare the general journal entry to record the agreed allowances for interest.
3. Prepare the general journal entry to record the distribution of the remaining balance of the net income.
4. Prepare the general journal entries to close the drawing accounts into the capital accounts, assuming that the allowed salaries were withdrawn during the year.
5. Prepare a schedule showing the distribution of net income to the partners as it would appear on the income statement of the Nautilus Seafood Restaurant.
6. Prepare a statement of partners' equities showing the changes that took place in the partners' capital accounts during the year.

PROBLEM 27-3 **Computing and recording the allocation of profit to partners.** The partnership agreement of Rex Hall and Eva Cruz, owners of the Lincoln Data Processing Service, provides that net income and net losses for the year are to be divided as follows.

	HALL	CRUZ
Monthly salary	$1,000	$1,500
Interest on beginning capital balance	9%	9%
Ratio for division of remainder	60%	40%

The balances of the capital accounts as of January 1, 19X1, were $100,000 for Hall and $80,000 for Cruz. During 19X1 both partners withdrew their monthly salary allowances, and the withdrawals were charged to the drawing accounts.

Instructions Give the general journal entries on December 31, 19X1, necessary to record the net income or net loss distribution and to close the drawing accounts into the partners' capital accounts under each of the following independent conditions.

1. The net income for the year is $81,600, as shown by the balance in the Income Summary account after all revenues and expenses have been closed into it.
2. The net income for the year is $14,000.
3. The net loss for the year is $8,000.

PROBLEM 27-4 **Recording the sale of a partner's interest and the investment of a new partner.** George Laski and Donald Bates own the Jiffy Dry Cleaning Service. They would like to expand their operations into suburban areas and, in anticipation of this, have offered Nora McCann an interest in the partnership for a payment by her of $30,000 in cash. The capital account balances for Laski and Bates on January 1, 19X1, are Laski, $45,000, and Bates, $35,000. Net income or net loss is shared equally.

Instructions Give the entries in general journal form to record the admission of McCann to the partnership on January 1, 19X1, under each of the following independent conditions.

1. McCann pays Laski for one-half of Laski's interest in the partnership.
2. McCann receives credit for the actual amount invested in the firm.
3. McCann acquires a one-fourth interest, a bonus being allowed.
4. McCann acquires a one-fourth interest, goodwill being recorded.
5. McCann acquires a one-third interest, a bonus being allowed.
6. McCann acquires a one-third interest, goodwill being recorded.

PROBLEM 27-5 **Recording the sale of a partner's interest and the investment of a new partner.** Ruth Sterling and Joanne Taylor are partners in the Executive Employment Agency. The balances of their capital accounts on January 2, 19X1, were Sterling, $30,000, and Taylor, $40,000. The partners agree to admit Anna Ulman to the partnership.

Instructions Give the entries in general journal form to record the admission of Ulman under each of the following independent conditions.

1. Sterling sells one-half of her interest to Ulman for $22,000 in cash.
2. Taylor sells one-half of her interest to Ulman for $16,000 in cash.
3. Ulman invests $30,000 in the business for a one-fourth interest under the bonus method.
4. Ulman invests $30,000 in the business for a one-fourth interest under the goodwill method.

ALTERNATE PROBLEMS

PROBLEM 27-1A **Recording the allocation of profit to partners.** The Rural Wood Company is a woodworking shop organized as a partnership by Carl Metz and Peter Carey. The partners have agreed that Metz can withdraw $1,000 a month and Carey $1,500 a month in anticipation of profits. Net income and net losses are to be distributed

60 percent to Metz and 40 percent to Carey. For the year ended December 31, 19X1, the partnership has earned a net income of $18,600. The drawing accounts of the partners indicate that each withdrew the maximum amount authorized.

Instructions
1. In general journal form, give the entry required to transfer the net income to the capital account of each partner.
2. Give the general journal entries required to close each partner's drawing account into his capital account.

PROBLEM 27-2A **Recording the allocation of profit and preparing the statement of partners' equities.** John Murphy and Linda Cole own the Gourmet Food Emporium. Their partnership agreement provides for salary allowances of $18,000 for Murphy and $14,000 for Cole and interest of 9 percent on each partner's invested capital at the beginning of the year. The remainder of the net income is to be distributed 40 percent to Murphy and 60 percent to Cole. On January 1, 19X1, the capital account balances were Murphy, $80,000, and Cole, $100,000. The net income for 19X1 was $68,000.

Instructions
1. Prepare the general journal entry dated December 31, 19X1, to record the agreed allowances for salaries.
2. Prepare the general journal entry to record the agreed allowances for interest.
3. Prepare the general journal entry to record the distribution of the remaining balance of the net income.
4. Prepare the general journal entries to close the drawing accounts into the capital accounts, assuming that Murphy had drawings of $18,000 and Cole had drawings of $15,000 during the year.
5. Prepare a schedule showing the distribution of net income to the partners as it would appear on the income statement of the Gourmet Food Emporium.
6. Prepare a statement of partners' equities showing the changes that took place in the partners' capital accounts during the year.

PROBLEM 27-3A **Computing and recording the allocation of profit to partners.** The partnership agreement of Robert Weiss and Janice Ward, owners of the Holiday Travel Service, provides that the net income and net losses for the year are to be divided as follows.

	WEISS	WARD
Monthly salary	$1,400	$1,800
Interest on beginning capital balance	10%	10%
Ratio for division of remainder	70%	30%

The balances of the capital accounts as of January 1, 19X1, were $40,000 for Weiss and $50,000 for Ward. During 19X1 both partners withdrew their monthly salary allowances, and the withdrawals were charged to the drawing accounts.

Instructions Give the general journal entries on December 31, 19X1, necessary to record the net income or net loss distribution and to close the drawing accounts into the partners' capital accounts under each of the following independent conditions.

1. The net income for the year is $48,000, as shown by the balance in the Income Summary account after all revenues and expenses have been closed into it.
2. The net income for the year is $4,000.
3. The net loss for the year is $6,000.

PROBLEM 27-4A

Recording the sale of a partner's interest and the investment of a new partner. Steven Lazlo and Michael Dunn own the Madison Financial Advisory Service. On January 1, 19X2, their capital accounts show balances of $40,000 for Lazlo and $20,000 for Dunn. At that date the partners agree to admit Claire Kiley, a tax planning specialist, as a partner in the business. Kiley is to pay $20,000 under the conditions described below. The ratio for dividing net income or net loss between the existing partners is Lazlo, one-third, and Dunn, two-thirds.

Instructions

In general journal form, give the entries to record the admission of Kiley to the partnership on January 1, 19X2, under each of the following independent conditions.

1. Kiley pays Lazlo for one-half of Lazlo's interest.
2. Kiley receives credit for the actual amount invested in the firm.
3. Kiley acquires a one-third interest in the equity, a bonus being allowed.
4. Kiley acquires a one-third interest in the equity, goodwill being recorded.
5. Kiley acquires a one-fifth interest in the equity, a bonus being allowed.
6. Kiley acquires a one-fifth interest in the equity, goodwill being recorded.

PROBLEM 27-5A

Recording the sale of a partner's interest and the investment of a new partner. Mary O'Dell and Susan Avery are partners in the Plaza Health Club and Exercise Studio. The balances of their capital accounts on July 1, 19X2, were O'Dell, $104,000, and Avery, $86,000. The partners agree to admit Lois Clark to the partnership.

Instructions

Give the entries in general journal form to record the admission of Clark under each of the following independent conditions.

1. O'Dell sells 40 percent of her interest to Clark for $71,000 in cash.
2. Avery sells one-half of her interest to Clark for $38,000 in cash.
3. Clark invests $80,000 in the business for a one-fourth interest in the partnership under the bonus method.
4. Clark invests $55,000 in the business for a one-fourth interest in the partnership under the goodwill method.

Up to this point, you have studied the operations of two different types of businesses—a sole proprietorship and a partnership. Now we turn to another important form of business organization—the corporation. This chapter discusses the basic characteristics of the corporation and explains how corporations are formed. Later chapters cover various aspects of corporate operations and the accounting procedures connected with them.

CHARACTERISTICS AND FORMATION OF A CORPORATION

LEGAL ASPECTS OF A CORPORATION

The organization and operation of the sole proprietorship form of business was explained in Part 1 of this book. The partnership form was covered in the presentation of the Style Clothing Store in the last two chapters. Thousands of sole proprietorships and partnerships operate successfully, but these popular forms of organization do not meet the needs of all businesses. James Duncan is an example of a person who must explore other possible forms of business organization to solve his problems.

Duncan has been operating the Duncan Chair Company, a retail store, for a number of years on a modest scale as a sole proprietorship. The business currently sells chairs that are used on patios and lawns, but Duncan has decided to enlarge the line of products to include several types of lawn furniture. He anticipates a substantially increased sales volume and higher profits resulting from the increase in volume and from a greater efficiency of operations. In order to expand his activities, Duncan needs more operating capital to remodel the store and buy new fixtures, to acquire much larger inventories, and to extend more credit to customers.

Several of Duncan's friends are willing to invest as partners in his business, but he has put off a decision because he has some doubts about this arrangement. Although he needs the extra funds, he does not want to share operating control of the firm with people who know nothing about the business. Also, he does not wish to go further in debt.

Duncan's prospective backers have some doubts, too. They don't mind risking the money they invest, but they don't want to be responsible for the debts of the business. Although they don't mind letting Duncan run the business, they do want to have some voice in general policy. They would also like to be assured of a reasonable and regular return on their money.

After several exploratory discussions, Duncan and his friends decide to consult a lawyer who specializes in business law and taxation. The lawyer suggests that the group consider forming a *corporation* to carry on the operations of the expanded business.

| Structure of a Corporation | Under the corporate plan, a *corporate charter* must be obtained from the state. As a corporation, the firm would be a legal entity separate from its owners. In exchange for their investment, the owners of the firm—known as *shareholders* or *stockholders*—would receive *shares of stock*. The owners could then participate in stockholders' meetings, elect a board of directors, and vote on certain questions of basic corporate policy. |

The directors would formulate general operating policies and be responsible for seeing that the activities of the corporation were carried on. They would select officers and other top management personnel to handle everyday operations. The officers would hire employees and would make the day-to-day decisions necessary to operate the business.

The top management of a corporation might consist of the president, one or more vice presidents, a secretary, and a treasurer. (The top accounting official might be called the controller or chief accountant.) As the firm grows, there might be a need for several layers of management, including division managers, department heads, and supervisors. The levels would depend on the nature and complexity of the firm's operations.

CHARACTERISTICS OF A CORPORATION

The lawyer points out to Duncan and his friends that the corporate form of organization—unlike the partnership form—would overcome their objections to investing and would provide other important advantages.

Limited Liability of Owners

As stockholders, Duncan and his associates would have no personal liability for the corporation's debts. In the event of liquidation, the corporation's creditors must look to the assets of the firm to satisfy their claims, not to the owners' personal property. (Usually, however, lending institutions require major stockholders in small corporations to personally guarantee repayment of loans made to the corporation.)

Owners Are Not Agents

The stockholders of a corporation are not empowered to act for the firm. Instead, the board of directors controls the corporation, and the corporate officers are in direct charge of operations. If Duncan were elected president by the board, he would have full responsibility for and control of operations. The other stockholders could, however, express their views at stockholders' meetings and might elect one or more of their number to membership on the board.

Continuous Existence

Potential investors are interested in knowing that operations continue indefinitely. The life of a corporation is not affected by the death, disability, or withdrawal of individual stockholders. (Any of these events would terminate a sole proprietorship or partnership.)

Transferability of Ownership Rights

The owners can sell their shares of stock without consulting or obtaining the consent of other stockholders. Thus Duncan's friends would be free to shift their investments if a better opportunity came along, provided they could find buyers for their shares.

| Legal Basis | The corporation is a special form of organization created by law. As previously mentioned, it is a legal entity separate from its stockholders. It can own property, be a party to contracts, sue and be sued in the courts, and otherwise carry on the business activities defined in its charter. Thus the corporate form of organization allows the owners to do anything they may reasonably wish to do as individuals and yet gives them personal immunities, such as limited liability, not obtainable in a sole proprietorship or a partnership. |

| Corporate Income Tax | Since the corporation is a creation of law, it is subject to certain formalities, regulations, and taxes that are not applied to sole proprietorships and partnerships. For instance, a corporation's profits are subject to federal income tax. Profits paid to stockholders in the form of dividends are taxed a second time as part of the personal income of the recipients. (Under certain conditions and where there are relatively few stockholders, a corporation can choose not to pay the corporate income tax but instead be treated for tax purposes in much the same way as a partnership.) |

State and local governments can also levy an income tax on corporations. In addition, most states require corporations to pay an annual franchise tax for the privilege of carrying on business in the state.

FORMING A CORPORATION

When Duncan and his friends express their desire to organize a corporation, the lawyer explains the steps to be taken. (Requirements and procedures differ from state to state, but those listed below are typical.)

1. Three or more persons must apply to the designated state officer (usually the secretary of state) for a charter permitting the proposed corporation to do business.
2. When issued, the charter specifies the exact name, length of life (state laws often provide for unlimited life), rights and duties, and scope of operations of the corporation. The charter also sets forth the classes of stock and number of shares in each class that can be issued in exchange for money, property, or services.
3. The stockholders elect a board of directors. The board then selects officers, who hire employees and begin operating the business.
4. The capital stock issued by the corporation appears on its balance sheet as part of the owners' equity, which is usually called *stockholders' equity*.

TYPES OF STOCK

The decision about the classes of stock and number of shares must be made before the charter application is filed. The lawyer for Duncan and his friends therefore suggests that the parties consider the various possibilities.

| One Class | If there is only one class of stock, each share carries the same rights and privileges. In general, these rights are as follows. |

1. The right to attend stockholders' meetings.
2. The right to vote in the election of directors and on certain other matters.

3. The right to receive dividends as declared by the board of directors.
4. The right to inspect the corporation's financial records and other records for proper purposes at certain times and places.
5. The right to purchase a proportionate amount of any new stock issued at a later date.

Common Stock

When several classes of stock exist, one class is usually designated *common stock*. This stock normally has all the general rights and privileges, although other classes of stock may enjoy certain preferences over it.

Preferred Stock

One or more classes of stock may have certain preferred claims on the corporation's profits or on its assets in case of liquidation, or they may carry other special preferences that set them apart from the common stock. This kind of stock is known as *preferred stock*. In receiving special preferences, the owners of preferred stock may lose some of their general rights, such as the right to vote.

Liquidation Preferences on Preferred Stock The terms of issue of preferred stock usually provide that in case of liquidation the preferred stockholders have a prior claim on assets. Often a *liquidation value* is assigned to the preferred stock. This means that after the creditors have been paid their claims, the preferred stockholders are paid the specified liquidation value for each share before any assets are distributed to common stockholders. The liquidation value of preferred stock is extended to include any cumulative dividends that may not have been paid. (Cumulative dividends are explained in another section of this chapter.) Because of its importance to users of financial statements, the total amount of liquidation preference on all preferred stock should be shown in the Stockholders' Equity section of the balance sheet.[1]

Convertible Preferred Stock Often preferred stock gives its owners the right to convert their shares into common stock after a specified date. The *conversion ratio,* the number of shares of common stock into which a share of preferred stock can be converted, is specified in the stock certificate. The conversion privilege may help to overcome the reluctance that many investors have to purchasing preferred stock because this type of stock has a fixed dividend rate and its value usually does not increase significantly even though the corporation may be quite profitable.

To better understand the conversion right, assume that a corporation has outstanding 100,000 shares of 12 percent, $25 par value preferred stock that may be converted into common stock at the rate of three shares of common stock for each share of preferred stock surrendered. The conversion privilege is exercisable on or after January 1, 19X9. Owners of the preferred stock may then exchange any or all of their shares for common stock at the stated ratio. Thus, a preferred stockholder with 600 shares could obtain 1,800 shares of common stock by means of the conversion process.

---

[1] "Liquidation Preferences of Preferred Stock," *Opinions of the Accounting Principles Board, No. 10* (New York: American Institute of Certified Public Accountants, 1966), pars. 10 and 11.

Callable Preferred Stock Preferred stock may also be *callable*; that is, the issuing corporation retains the right to repurchase the shares from the stockholders at a specified price. The call price is usually substantially greater than the original issue price. The rights are effective after some specified date. Callable stock gives a corporation greater flexibility in controlling its capital structure.

The following example will illustrate the call feature. Assume that on July 12, 19X1, a corporation issued 50,000 shares of 14 percent, $40 par value preferred stock at $40 a share. The issue terms give the corporation the right to call any part of the preferred stock at any time after December 31, 19X8, for $56 a share.

DIVIDENDS TO STOCKHOLDERS

The right to receive a portion of the corporation's profits is obviously one of the major incentives for investment. Therefore, Duncan's associates give careful thought to their positions under different types of dividend privileges. Stockholders receive part of a corporation's profits in the form of dividends only when the board of directors declares a dividend. The board has almost complete discretion, especially on common stock, in deciding whether to declare a dividend and how much it will be.

Dividends on Preferred Stock

One of the privileges often accorded preferred stock is a priority with respect to dividends. The exact nature of the priority is established by the preferred stock contract for each issue.

1. If the preferred stock is *cumulative* as to dividends, its owners must receive the stated dividend for both the current year and any prior years in which the stated dividend was not paid before the common stockholders can receive any dividends.
2. If the preferred stock is *noncumulative,* its stated dividend for a particular year must be paid in that year before dividends can be paid to common stockholders. However, if no dividends are declared in one year, the next year represents a fresh start. This type of stock has no continuing rights to dividends for the year in which none were declared.
3. Preferred stock is *nonparticipating* unless otherwise stated on the stock certificate. When the stock is nonparticipating, the preferred stockholders receive only the dividend amount specified on the stock certificate.
4. Preferred stock may be *participating*, in which case preferred stockholders receive the regular preferred dividend and may also participate in additional dividends with the common stockholders.

Dividends on Common Stock

Dividends on common stock are paid only after dividend requirements for preferred stock have been met. The fewer the dividend privileges enjoyed by the preferred stockholders, the greater the dividends that the common stockholders can receive, especially in prosperous years.

VALUES OF CAPITAL STOCK

Any experienced lawyer or financial adviser would quickly point out that a purely theoretical consideration of the pros and cons of different types of dividends has only limited usefulness. Even percentage rates (such as 10 percent) or stated dollar amounts of dividends (such as $5 a share) have little significance unless the amount invested or the value of the stock is known. A number of different terms are used in referring to the value of capital stock. These terms are discussed below.

Par Value

Par value is a figure selected by the organizers of the corporation to be assigned to each share of stock for accounting purposes. The par value, if any, is specified in the charter. It is often $100 or $50, but it may be any amount, such as $5, $1, or even less than $1 a share. When a $100 par value preferred stock (without specified extra privileges) is said to have a 12 percent dividend rate, a return of $12 a year is meant.

Stated Value

Laws in many states permit stock to be issued without par value. This type of stock is called *no-par value* stock. In such cases the board of directors of the corporation may assign a *stated value* to the stock. When a stated value is established for no-par value stock, this figure is the amount credited to the capital stock account for each share issued. The stated value serves much the same purpose as par value. When no-par value stock does not have a stated value, it is customary to credit the entire proceeds from the sale of the stock to the capital stock account.

CAPITAL STOCK ON THE BALANCE SHEET

As shown in the following illustration, the Stockholders' Equity section of the corporate balance sheet usually includes information that identifies the classes of stock, the number of shares authorized and issued for each class, their par value, and any special privileges carried by the stock.

Stockholders' Equity

Preferred Stock (12% cumulative, participating, $100 par value, 1,000 shares authorized)	
At Par Value (500 shares issued)	$50,000
Common Stock (no-par value, with stated value of $25, 4,000 shares authorized)	
At Stated Value (1,000 shares issued)	25,000
Total Stockholders' Equity	$75,000

COMPARISON OF DIVIDEND PROVISIONS

Having supplied the basic background information about corporate stock financing to Duncan and his associates, the lawyer explains the effects of the various plans, privileges, and values of stock, using specific figures for each of the alternatives.

Plan A—Only Common Stock Issued

Assume that a corporation has only one class of stock—common stock. Assume also that 2,500 shares at $100 par value were authorized and that all 2,500 shares authorized were issued and remain outstanding.

Situation 1 The dividend declared by the board of directors depends on the corporate earnings and the need to keep profits (called *retained earnings*) for use in the business. A 6 percent dividend would amount to $15,000 a year (2,500 shares × $100 par value × 0.06).

Situation 2 Of course, the board has the right to *pass* the dividend (not pay it) or to declare a smaller dividend if conditions so warrant ($7,500, or 3 percent, instead of $15,000, for instance). If the board does declare a smaller dividend, the stockholders have to be content with the amount. Similarly, stockholders may be fortunate enough to receive a larger dividend if the directors see fit to declare one.

Plan B—Common and Preferred Stock Issued

The uncertainty of dividends described in Plan A is a risk of stock ownership that cannot be entirely avoided. However, preferred stock offers advantages that are attractive to certain types of investors. Assume that a corporation has both preferred and common stock issued and outstanding as follows.

Preferred Stock (12%, $100 par value, 500 shares)	$ 50,000
Common Stock (no-par value, stated value of $50, 4,000 shares)	200,000
Total Capital Stock	$250,000

Situation 1 If the board of directors decides to distribute $17,000, the preferred stockholders will get first consideration. The owners of the 500 shares outstanding will receive a total of $6,000 (500 shares × $100 par value × 0.12), or $12 a share. This will leave $11,000 ($17,000 − $6,000) to be distributed to the common stockholders, who will receive $2.75 a share ($11,000 ÷ 4,000 shares).

Situation 2 If there is only $9,500 to distribute, the preferred stockholders will receive their full 12 percent, or $6,000, and the remaining $3,500 will allow a return of only $0.875 a share on the common stock ($3,500 ÷ 4,000 shares).

Situation 3 If there is only $4,000 to distribute, the preferred stockholders will receive it all—$8 a share ($4,000 ÷ 500). The remaining amount of dividends owed on the preferred stock ($4 a share) will not be paid since the stock is noncumulative. The common stockholders will receive nothing.

Plan C—Common and Cumulative Preferred Stock Issued

When business conditions are poor, preferred stockholders have a better chance for a return than do common stockholders. However, the preferred stockholders' chances can be further improved if the preferred stock is cumulative. Under this privilege the $4 balance owed on each share of the 12 percent dividend remaining unpaid (discussed in the last paragraph) will be carried forward as a continuing claim into future periods.

Situation 1 If the board of directors has $9,000 to distribute in the next year and the preferred stock is cumulative, the preferred stockholders collect the $2,000 (500 × $4) in arrears, plus the regular dividend of $6,000 (500 ×

$100 × 0.12). This leaves only $1,000, or $0.25 a share, for the common stock-holders.

In preparing financial statements, the total and the per-share amounts of cumulative preferred dividends not previously paid should be shown either on the face of the balance sheet or in footnotes to the statements.[2]

Situation 2 Of course, in good years the common stockholders may enjoy very substantial gains. This time, suppose that the directors decide to distribute $36,000. If there is no balance owed to the preferred stockholders because of the cumulative privilege and if their stock is not participating, they will receive only the regular $6,000 (500 × $100 × 0.12). The balance of $30,000 will be divided among the common stockholders. The result will be a dividend of $7.50 a share ($30,000 ÷ 4,000)—a return of 15 percent on the $50 stated value, greater than the 12 percent return received by the preferred stockholders.

Plan D—Common and Cumulative Participating Preferred Stock Issued

Investors may be induced to purchase preferred stock in a corporation, even if present earnings and dividends are low, through the use of participating preferred stock. Under this plan the preferred stockholder receives the regular specified dividend and then shares in any additional dividends with the common stock-holders, as provided by the terms of the preferred stock contract.

The exact terms of participation vary, but one common arrangement calls for the preferred stockholders to receive a dividend rate equal to that provided to the common stockholders. The preferred stockholders are first paid their regular specified dividend. Then common stockholders are paid a dividend at the same rate as the specified rate on the preferred stock. Any remaining dividends to be distributed will be allocated between the two classes of stockholders so that each receives the same rate. This is sometimes referred to as *participating simply*.

Suppose that in the preceding example the 500 shares of preferred stock carried the participating privilege (12 percent, $100 par value, cumulative, participating preferred). In order to distribute $30,000 or 15 percent to the owners of the 4,000 shares of common stock, as just described in Situation 2 of Plan C, provision must be made for a 15 percent return to the preferred stockholders. The latter will receive a regular 12 percent dividend and a further participating dividend of 3 percent, totaling $1,500, as follows.

To Preferred Stock

12% Contract Rate (500 shares × $100 par value × 0.12)	$ 6,000
3% Participation (500 shares × $100 par value × 0.03)	1,500
15% Total to Preferred	$ 7,500

To Common Stock

15% (4,000 × $50 stated value × 0.15)	30,000
Total Dividends Paid	$37,500

Thus for the common stockholders to receive $30,000, a total dividend of $37,500 would have to be declared in order to meet the contractual demand that

---

[2]Ibid.

preferred stockholders receive the same dividend rate as common stockholders.

Other types of participation formulas for preferred stock are also used by some corporations.

FINANCING WITH BONDS

Besides obtaining funds through issuing common and preferred stock, corporations can obtain part of their funds by issuing bonds. *Bonds* are long-term liabilities of the corporation rather than stockholders' equity. They ordinarily carry a fixed rate of interest that may be somewhat lower than the dividend rate for preferred stock. In addition, interest paid on bonds is deductible in computing the federal income tax, while dividends are not deductible.

In practice, the funds for investment in corporate assets are raised through varying combinations of common stock, preferred stock, and bonds. Let us see how a typical combination financial structure might affect the rate of return earned on common stock under circumstances comparable to Situation 2 of Plan C. Suppose that total capital of $250,000 has been raised by the sale of the following securities.

100 Bonds (10% interest, $1,000 par value)	$100,000
500 Shares of Preferred Stock (12%, $100 par value)	50,000
2,000 Shares of Common Stock (no-par value, stated value of $50)	100,000
Total Capital	$250,000

Assume that the company had a net income of $55,000 before bond interest and before income taxes and that the company plans to distribute all net income. The amount available for distribution to stockholders, $36,000, is computed as shown below. (Assume a hypothetical income tax rate of 20 percent.)

Net Income From Operations	$55,000
Less Bond Interest ($100,000 × 0.10)	10,000
Net Income Before Income Taxes	$45,000
Less Income Taxes (assumed rate of 20%)	9,000
Net Income After Income Taxes	$36,000

If the company plans to distribute all available net income to stockholders, the $36,000 is allocated as follows.

To Preferred Stock	
500 Shares, 12% Contract Rate (500 × $100 par value × 0.12)	$ 6,000
To Common Stock	
2,000 Shares, Balance ($36,000 − $6,000)	30,000
	$36,000

The common stockholders in this combination plan now enjoy a return of $15 a share, or 30 percent, on the $50 stated value. The favorable outcome is due to the fact that the company's profits are higher than the contract rate of interest on the bonds and the rate paid as dividends on the preferred stock. This situation is called *trading on the equity*. In lean years such financing may be dangerous from the investors' standpoint because the prior fixed claim of bond interest expense may leave little or nothing for dividends to the stockholders. Moreover, even when the firm operates at a loss, the bondholders' interest must be paid in full.

INCORPORATING A SOLE PROPRIETORSHIP

Now that Duncan and his associates have a knowledge of the usual alternatives in corporate financing, they devise a capital structure to meet their specific needs. Based on capital requirements of $700,000, the prospective owners decide to use two classes of stock, preferred and common, as shown below.

Preferred Stock (12%, $100 par value, noncumulative and nonparticipating, 2,000 shares)	$200,000
Common Stock (no-par value, stated value of $50, 10,000 shares)	500,000
Total Capital Stock	$700,000

Stock will be issued to Duncan in payment for the net assets of the Duncan Chair Company. Stock will also be sold to Duncan's friends who have agreed to go into the venture with him. Duncan will be president of the new corporation.

The lawyer completes the application for a corporate charter for the new firm, to be known as the Duncan Lawn Furniture Corporation. On December 31, 19X1, when the charter is received, the accounting records are set up and a memorandum entry is made in the general journal. This entry, shown below, gives the details of the authorized capital stock.

19 X1		
Dec. 31	The Duncan Lawn Furniture Corporation has been organized to market furniture and to carry on all necessary and convenient related activities. It is authorized to issue 10,000 shares of no-par value common stock ($50 stated value) and 2,000 shares of $100 par value 12% preferred stock that is noncumulative and nonparticipating.	

For permanent reference, the data relating to each authorized class of stock is entered on a separate ledger sheet. The information for the Duncan Lawn Furniture Corporation might be recorded at the top of the ledger sheets as shown below and on page 640.

Common Stock
No-Par Value
($50 Stated Value) 10,000 Shares Authorized   No. 301

DATE	EXPLANATION	POST. REF.	DEBIT	CREDIT	BALANCE	DR. CR.

		Preferred Stock 12% Noncumulative, Nonparticipating $100 Par Value, 2,000 Shares Authorized					No. 311
DATE	EXPLANATION	POST. REF.	DEBIT	CREDIT	BALANCE	DR. CR.	

The accounting records of the new corporation are now ready for transactions, including stock issues, to be recorded as they occur. However, before the Duncan Lawn Furniture Corporation can take over the assets and liabilities of the Duncan Chair Company, the values shown in that firm's accounting records must be examined and possibly adjusted to reflect the true current value of each item owned by the sole proprietorship. The situation is similar to that of a sole proprietor revaluing assets before entering into a partnership (see Chapter 26).

REVALUATION OF ASSETS

The postclosing trial balance of December 31, 19X1—the date the sole proprietorship is being terminated—serves as the starting point for the revaluation process. Duncan is interested in getting as much for his business as he can. The corporation wants to be sure that it is getting true value for its payment. Consequently, both parties will examine every account balance with extreme care in an effort to establish complete and fair values.

DUNCAN CHAIR COMPANY
Postclosing Trial Balance
December 31, 19X1

ACCT. NO.	ACCOUNT NAME	DEBIT	CREDIT
101	Cash	5,000 00	
111	Accounts Receivable	9,000 00	
121	Merchandise Inventory	22,000 00	
140	Land	10,000 00	
141	Building	40,000 00	
142	Accumulated Depreciation—Building		8,000 00
143	Equipment and Fixtures	10,000 00	
144	Accum. Depr.—Equipment and Fixtures		6,000 00
202	Accounts Payable		9,600 00
301	James Duncan, Capital		72,400 00
	Totals	96,000 00	96,000 00

At this stage, any gain or loss resulting from an adjustment or revaluation of assets will cause a corresponding increase or decrease in Duncan's capital. (If the business being incorporated were a partnership, the same procedures would be followed, except that the gain or loss resulting from the revaluation of the assets would be divided among the partners in their profit-sharing ratio.)

Accounts Receivable

The first asset about which there are some reasonable doubts is accounts receivable. Duncan has previously used the direct charge-off method, so there is no Allowance for Uncollectible Accounts account in his general ledger. It is estimated that only $8,000 of the $9,000 shown in the Accounts Receivable account will be collected. The revised estimate of the value of the account indicates an expected loss of $1,000. This loss is charged to a new account called Gain or Loss on Asset Revaluation. A corresponding credit is made to Allowance for Uncollectible Accounts since it is not known at this time just which accounts may prove uncollectible. The revaluation is formally recorded in the general journal of the Duncan Chair Company, as shown below.

19 X1						
Dec. 31	Gain or Loss on Asset Revaluation	409	1,000	00		
	Allowance for Uncollectible Accounts	112			1,000	00
	To reduce book value of accounts receivable by setting up an allowance for uncollectible accounts.					

Of course, the gain or loss resulting from revaluing each asset could be entered directly in the owner's capital account, as illustrated in Chapter 26. However, when a number of revaluations are to be recorded, it is easier to use a Gain or Loss on Asset Revaluation account to assemble and summarize the changes. The net gain or loss is then transferred to the capital account of the owner of a sole proprietorship or is divided among the co-owners of a partnership according to their profit and loss ratio.

Inventory

Some of the items carried in the inventory will not be useful in the operations of the new corporation and will have to be sold for less than their original cost. The merchandise is restated at its estimated value of $20,000 in the accounting records of the proprietorship by a general journal entry debiting Gain or Loss on Asset Revaluation and crediting Merchandise Inventory for $2,000, the amount of the expected loss.

Land

The value of land has generally risen in the area where Duncan's property is located. Expert appraisers estimate that the current market value of Duncan's land is $15,000 rather than the $10,000 shown in the accounting records. A general journal entry is made debiting Land for $5,000 and crediting Gain or Loss on Asset Revaluation for that amount.

Building

Building costs have also risen, and the current market value of Duncan's building is appraised at $36,000. The proprietorship records show that the building cost $40,000 and that the Accumulated Depreciation—Building account has a balance of $8,000. This leaves a book value of only $32,000. To increase the book value to the appraised value of $36,000, the Building account is debited for $4,000 and the Gain or Loss on Asset Revaluation account is credited for that amount. The necessary general journal entry is shown below.

19 X1					
Dec. 31	Building	141	4,000 00	
	Gain or Loss on Asset Revaluation	409		4,000 00
	To increase book value of building to			
	estimated current market value.			

Equipment and Fixtures

It is further estimated that the equipment and fixtures have a value of $4,000. The accounting records show a cost of $10,000 and accumulated depreciation of $6,000, which leaves a book value of $4,000. Thus no adjustment is required in the value of the equipment and fixtures.

REVALUATION ACCOUNT

When the four revaluation entries have been posted, the Gain or Loss on Asset Revaluation account has a credit balance of $6,000, as shown below.

| | Gain or Loss on Asset Revaluation | | | | No. | 409 |

DATE	EXPLANATION	POST. REF.	DEBIT	CREDIT	BALANCE	DR. CR.
19 X1						
Dec. 31		J12	1,000 00		1,000 00	Dr.
31		J12	2,000 00		3,000 00	Dr.
31		J12		5,000 00	2,000 00	Cr.
31		J12		4,000 00	6,000 00	Cr.

    Since the Duncan Chair Company is a sole proprietorship, the entire gain or loss on asset revaluation belongs to the owner, James Duncan. Therefore, the net gain of $6,000 is now transferred to his capital account by a general journal entry debiting Gain or Loss on Asset Revaluation and crediting James Duncan, Capital. The balance of Duncan's capital account is now $78,400. This figure represents the net assets after revaluation (assets of $88,000 minus liabilities of $9,600 equals capital of $78,400).

    If the Duncan Chair Company had been a partnership, the balance of the Gain or Loss on Asset Revaluation account would have been divided among the partners in their profit-sharing ratio.

TRANSFER OF ASSETS AND LIABILITIES TO THE CORPORATION

Once the asset revaluations are entered in the proprietorship records and the resulting gain or loss is transferred to the owner's capital account, the next step is to transfer the assets and liabilities to the corporation. This is done by making a compound entry in the general journal, as shown on page 643. The entry debits an account receivable from the new corporation for the net value of the assets; debits Allowance for Uncollectible Accounts, the accumulated depreciation accounts, and Accounts Payable; and credits the asset accounts.

	19 X1					
	Dec. 31	Receivable From Duncan Lawn				
		Furniture Corporation	113	78,400 00		
		Allowance for Uncollectible Accounts	112	1,000 00		
		Accum. Depr.—Building	142	8,000 00		
		Accum. Depr.—Equipment and Fixtures	144	6,000 00		
		Accounts Payable	202	9,600 00		
		Cash	101		5,000 00	
		Accounts Receivable	111		9,000 00	
		Merchandise Inventory	121		20,000 00	
		Land	140		15,000 00	
		Building	141		44,000 00	
		Equipment and Fixtures	143		10,000 00	
		To transfer the proprietorship assets and liability to the new corporation.				

RECEIPT OF STOCK FROM THE CORPORATION

The new Duncan Lawn Furniture Corporation proposes to issue shares of its stock for the revalued net assets of the Duncan Chair Company, and Duncan has agreed to accept such stock in payment. Preferred stock is issued at par for $40,000 of the assets (400 shares of stock at $100 par value). An additional 768 shares of no-par value common stock with a stated value of $50 a share are issued for the balance of the assets, $38,400. The entry for the receipt of this stock in the accounting records of the proprietorship is shown below.

	19 X1				
	Dec. 31	Common Stock of Duncan Lawn			
		Furniture Corporation	114	38,400 00	
		Preferred Stock of Duncan Lawn			
		Furniture Corporation	115	40,000 00	
		Receivable From Duncan Lawn			
		Furniture Corporation	113		78,400 00
		To record receipt of 768 shares of common stock (at $50 a share) and 400 shares of preferred stock at par ($100 a share) in payment for net assets of Duncan Chair Company.			

DISTRIBUTION OF STOCK TO THE PROPRIETOR

At this point all but three of the proprietorship's accounts have been closed. The remaining open accounts are the two asset accounts representing the two kinds of stock received from the corporation and the James Duncan, Capital account. The final entry, shown on page 644, records the distribution of stock to Duncan and closes all remaining accounts. This entry brings the proprietorship business to an end.

19 X1					
Dec. 31	James Duncan, Capital	301	78,400 00		
	Common Stock of Duncan Lawn				
	Furniture Corporation	114		38,400 00	
	Preferred Stock of Duncan Lawn				
	Furniture Corporation	115		40,000 00	
	To record distribution to				
	Duncan of the stock paid for the				
	net assets of the Duncan Chair				
	Company, completing the liquidation				
	of the proprietorship.				

ACQUISITION OF ASSETS AND LIABILITIES BY THE CORPORATION

The acquisition of the assets and liabilities of the Duncan Chair Company is now recorded in the accounting records of the Duncan Lawn Furniture Corporation, and an entry is made of the stock issued in payment. Identical account titles are used in setting up this acquisition in the corporation's records, and the same amounts are used—with two exceptions. The former accumulated depreciation accounts are not entered in the corporation's records. Instead, the related assets are recorded at their book value. The following two accounts are affected.

1. Building, recorded at $36,000 ($44,000 − $8,000)
2. Equipment and Fixtures, recorded at $4,000 ($10,000 − $6,000)

However, note that Accounts Receivable (a control account) and Allowance for Uncollectible Accounts are both shown in the corporation's records. The balance of Accounts Receivable must be recorded in full because it is not yet known which customers' accounts will prove to be uncollectible, and all the individual accounts in the subsidiary ledger have been transferred to the corporation. The control account balance must agree with the total of the balances in the accounts receivable subsidiary ledger. Allowance for Uncollectible Accounts continues to reflect the estimate that $1,000 of the accounts receivable will not be paid.

The entry made in the general journal of the new corporation records the assets and liabilities taken over and acknowledges a liability to the proprietorship

19 X1				
Dec. 31	Cash	101	5,000 00	
	Accounts Receivable	111	9,000 00	
	Merchandise Inventory	121	20,000 00	
	Land	140	15,000 00	
	Building	141	36,000 00	
	Equipment and Fixtures	143	4,000 00	
	Allowance for Uncollectible Accounts	112		1,000 00
	Accounts Payable	202		9,600 00
	Due to Duncan Chair Company	203		78,400 00
	To record the assets and liability			
	taken over from the Duncan Chair			
	Company for which capital stock			
	is to be issued.			

for the amount of the net assets. This record, which is shown on page 644, follows the memorandum opening entry that was explained previously.

ISSUANCE OF STOCK

To complete the purchase of the Duncan Chair Company, stock is issued as agreed—400 shares of common stock at $50 a share and 768 shares of preferred stock at par, $100 a share. This entry is made in the general journal, as shown below.

19 X1				
Dec. 31	Due to Duncan Chair Company	203	78,400 00	
	Common Stock	301		38,400 00
	Preferred Stock	311		40,000 00
	To record issuance of stock in payment for net assets of the Duncan Chair Company; 768 shares of common stock at $50 a share; 400 shares of preferred stock at par ($100).			

ORGANIZATION COSTS

Bringing a new corporation into existence involves a variety of expenses, such as legal fees, charter fees to the state, and the costs of preparing stock certificates. These expenses are ordinarily paid soon after the corporation receives its charter. They are charged to an intangible asset account, usually called Organization Costs. This account is set up initially as an asset because it is a necessary cost of bringing the corporation into existence, rather than an operating expense.

It has often been argued that since organization costs are incurred to benefit the corporation over its entire life, they should be carried indefinitely on the balance sheet as an intangible asset and should be charged off only when the corporation is liquidated. However, since organization costs would have no sales value if the corporation were to liquidate, accountants follow the conservative practice of charging the amount off to expense over a period of several years.

Generally accepted accounting principles permit organization costs to be amortized over a period of up to 40 years.[3] However, these costs are often charged off over a 5-year period. This period is commonly used because, for federal income tax purposes, organization costs can be amortized over a period of not less than 60 months (5 years). The procedure will be illustrated in Chapter 30.

Suppose that the Duncan Lawn Furniture Corporation incurred organization costs totaling $1,000. Suppose also that these costs were paid on December 31, immediately after the corporation acquired the assets and liabilities of the proprietorship business. In general journal form, this transaction would be recorded as shown on page 646.

---

[3]"Accounting for Intangible Assets," *Opinions of the Accounting Principles Board, No. 17* (New York: American Institute of Certified Public Accountants, 1970), pars. 28 and 29.

19 X1					
Dec. 31	Organization Costs	191	1,000 00		
	Cash	101		1,000 00
	To record payment of legal fees,				
	charter fee, and engraving cost of				
	stock certificates incurred to				
	organize corporation.				

BALANCE SHEET IMMEDIATELY AFTER ORGANIZATION

Immediately following the organization of the Duncan Lawn Furniture Corporation, a balance sheet is prepared. This balance sheet reflects the acquisition of the Duncan Chair Company by the issuance of stock and the payment of organization costs. The following statement summarizes the firm's financial position before operations begin and will serve as a valuable basis for later comparisons.

DUNCAN LAWN FURNITURE CORPORATION
Balance Sheet
December 31, 19X1

Assets

Current Assets		
Cash		$ 4,000
Accounts Receivable	$ 9,000	
Less Allowance for Uncollectible Accounts	1,000	8,000
Merchandise Inventory		20,000
Total Current Assets		$32,000
Property, Plant, and Equipment		
Land	$15,000	
Building	36,000	
Equipment and Fixtures	4,000	
Total Property, Plant, and Equipment		55,000
Intangible Assets		
Organization Costs		1,000
Total Assets		$88,000

Liabilities and Stockholders' Equity

Current Liabilities		
Accounts Payable		$ 9,600
Stockholders' Equity		
Preferred Stock (12%, $100 par value,		
2,000 shares authorized)		
At Par Value (400 shares issued)	$40,000	
Common Stock (no-par value, stated value of $50,		
10,000 shares authorized)		
At Stated Value (768 shares issued)	38,400	
Total Stockholders' Equity		78,400
Total Liabilities and Stockholders' Equity		$88,000

PRINCIPLES AND PROCEDURES SUMMARY

A corporation is organized under state law to carry on activities permitted by its charter. Ownership is evidenced by shares of stock. Stockholders owning voting stock elect a board of directors, which selects officers who hire employees and direct the operations of the business.

Stock may have a par value specified in the charter. If it does not have a specified par value, it is called no-par value stock. The directors may assign to no-par value stock a stated value, which is used for accounting purposes. Preferred stockholders enjoy certain privileges, often including priority in the distribution of dividends. Cumulative and participating provisions may give further advantage to the preferred stockholders, and the preferred stock may be convertible into shares of common stock.

Corporate assets can be bought with funds obtained from the sale of bonds as well as the sale of various types of stock. Common stockholders may benefit when preferred stock or bonds are issued and profits are greater than required for paying the interest on the bonds or the dividends on the preferred shares.

When a new corporation receives its charter, a memorandum entry is usually made in the general journal setting forth the details relating to each class of authorized stock. In turn, separate general ledger accounts are set up for each class of stock authorized, and the data pertaining to each is recorded in the general ledger for future reference.

When a sole proprietorship or a partnership is to incorporate, the accountant's first step is to adjust and close the accounting records of the old business. Asset accounts are adjusted to reflect current values. The gain or loss resulting from the asset revaluations is transferred to the owner's capital account or to the capital accounts of the partners in their profit-sharing ratio.

If an existing business is being purchased by the new corporation, the values of the assets and liabilities being assumed are recorded in the corporation's general journal. The excess of the assets over the liabilities represents the amount that the corporation owes to the former owner or owners. This balance can be paid in stock, in cash, or in other property.

Certain costs are usually incurred in organizing a corporation. These organization costs are ordinarily paid by the corporation. They are charged to an intangible asset account and amortized to expense over a few years' time.

MANAGERIAL IMPLICATIONS

It is essential that the individuals who are setting up a new firm have a clear idea of the nature of a corporation, its rights and limitations, and how the corporation differs from other forms of business organization in order to select the most suitable form for their firm. For example, these individuals should know that the corporation is a separate legal entity apart from its owners, that it has continuous existence regardless of changes in ownership, and that owners have limited liability and are free to dispose of their stock without consulting other stockholders. The organizers of a new firm should also understand the corporation's potential obligations with reference to the payment of taxes and the regulation of operations. High taxes and stringent regulations may make it unprofitable, if not impossible, to operate as intended.

Gains and losses on assets being transferred to a corporation should be recognized in the accounting records of the sole proprietorship or partnership from which the assets are being transferred. These gains or losses rightly belong to the proprietor or to the partners in proportion to their profit-sharing ratio. It is also essential to corporate management that assets be realistically valued so that the true measure of their worth can be made and so that the corporation's profitability can be properly computed and evaluated.

REVIEW QUESTIONS

1. What is a corporate charter?
2. Who are the shareholders of a corporation?
3. What is meant by the statement that shareholders have limited liability?
4. If a shareholder in a corporation dies, will the corporation continue to exist? Explain.
5. Compare the transferability of shares of stock in a corporation with the transferability of a partner's interest in a partnership.
6. What is a corporate franchise tax?
7. If there is only one class of stock, what are the rights of the shareholders? What is this class of stock called?
8. How does preferred stock differ from common stock?
9. What is meant by the term *liquidation preferences*?
10. What are dividends?
11. What is cumulative preferred stock?
12. What is convertible preferred stock?
13. What is callable preferred stock?
14. How does par value differ from stated value?
15. What is participating preferred stock?
16. How do bonds differ from stock?
17. Suggest one major advantage to a corporation in issuing bonds rather than issuing preferred stock. Suggest one disadvantage.
18. What are organization costs? How are they accounted for?
19. How are organization costs classified on the balance sheet?
20. What is meant by the term *trading on the equity*?

MANAGERIAL DISCUSSION QUESTIONS

1. What legal characteristics and limitations of a corporation are of special importance to its management?
2. Would management generally expect to pay a higher rate or a lower rate of dividends on preferred stock than the rate of interest necessary on bonds? Explain.

3. Why would management be interested in issuing no-par value stock?
4. A group of individuals is planning to form a corporation. Explain in general terms the usual steps necessary to do this.
5. Why is the difference between preferred stock and common stock important to management?
6. Why should the management of a corporation be concerned about the realistic valuation of assets transferred to the firm?
7. Assume that the management of a corporation in which you are employed as an accountant has been discussing various means of raising additional capital needed for expansion of the business. The treasurer argues that the issuance of bonds payable is the most logical approach because the interest is deductible on the corporation's federal income tax return. What reasons can you give for opposing the use of bonds?

EXERCISES

EXERCISE 28-1 **Computing the dividend per share on one class of stock.** The Maxwell Corporation has only one class of stock. There are 100,000 shares outstanding. During 19X1 the corporation's net income after taxes was $297,000. The policy of the corporation is to declare dividends equal to 40 percent of its net income. Anthony Bruno owns 620 shares of the stock. How much will Bruno receive as a dividend on his shares?

EXERCISE 28-2 **Computing the dividend per share on noncumulative preferred stock.** The Bernard Corporation has outstanding 10,000 shares of noncumulative, 15 percent, $60 par value preferred stock and 100,000 shares of no-par value common stock. During 19X1 the corporation paid dividends of $72,000. What amount will be paid on each share of preferred stock? What amount will be paid on each share of common stock?

EXERCISE 28-3 **Computing the dividend per share on noncumulative preferred stock.** Assume the same facts about the stock of the Bernard Corporation as in Exercise 28-2. During 19X2 the corporation paid dividends of $108,000. How much will be paid on each share of preferred stock? How much will be paid on each share of common stock?

EXERCISE 28-4 **Computing the dividend per share on noncumulative preferred stock.** Assume the same facts about the stock of the Bernard Corporation as in Exercises 28-2 and 28-3. During 19X3 the corporation paid dividends of $420,000. How much will be paid on each share of preferred stock? How much will be paid on each share of common stock?

EXERCISE 28-5 **Computing the dividend per share on cumulative preferred stock.** The Chilton Corporation has outstanding 30,000 shares of 14 percent, $50 par value cumulative preferred stock and 100,000 shares of no-par value common stock.

During 19X1 the corporation distributed dividends of $125,000. What amount will be paid on each share of preferred stock? What amount will be paid on each share of common stock?

EXERCISE 28-6   **Computing the dividend per share on cumulative preferred stock.** Assume the same facts about the stock of the Chilton Corporation as in Exercise 28-5. During 19X2 the corporation paid dividends of $225,000. What amount will be paid on each share of preferred stock?

EXERCISE 28-7   **Computing the dividend per share on cumulative preferred stock.** Assume the same facts about the stock of the Chilton Corporation as in Exercises 28-5 and 28-6. During 19X3 the corporation distributed dividends of $480,000. What amount will be paid on each share of preferred stock?

EXERCISE 28-8   **Computing the dividend per share on participating preferred stock.** The DeVito Corporation has outstanding 10,000 shares of 15 percent, $50 par value noncumulative, participating preferred stock and 100,000 shares of $10 par value common stock. Under the terms of the preferred stock, dividends paid in excess of the basic preference rate will be distributed as follows. The common stock will receive a dividend up to 15 percent of par value. Any additional dividends will be shared equally (on a percentage basis) between the preferred and common stock. During 19X1 the corporation paid dividends of $80,000. What amount will be paid on each share of preferred stock? What amount will be paid on each share of common stock?

EXERCISE 28-9   **Computing the dividend per share on participating preferred stock.** Assume the same facts about the stock of the DeVito Corporation as in Exercise 28-8 except that the dividends total $255,000. How much will be paid on each share of preferred stock? How much will be paid on each share of common stock?

EXERCISE 28-10   **Computing the conversion of preferred stock into common stock.** The Bellows Corporation has outstanding 50,000 shares of $30 par value preferred stock, issued at an average price of $32 a share. The preferred stock is convertible into common stock at the rate of one-half share of common stock for each share of preferred stock. Louise Jackson owns 400 shares of the preferred stock. During the current year she decides to convert 200 shares into common stock. How many shares of common stock will she receive?

EXERCISE 28-11   **Computing the deduction for bond interest when determining income taxes.** The McConnell Corporation has the following bonds and stock outstanding.

Bonds Payable, 12%	$ 500,000
Preferred Stock, noncumulative, 15%,	
$10 par value, 10,000 shares	100,000
Common Stock, no-par value, with	
stated value of $10,	
100,000 shares	1,000,000

Assume that the corporation had a net income of $480,000 before bond interest and before taxes. Its income tax rate is 20 percent. What is its net income after taxes?

EXERCISE 28-12   **Determining the dividends available for payment after income taxes.** Assume the same facts about the McConnell Corporation as in Exercise 28-11. In addition, assume that the corporation distributes as dividends all of its net income after taxes. What is the total amount that will be paid to the preferred stockholders? What is the total amount that will be paid to the common stockholders?

EXERCISE 28-13   **Determining the stock to be issued for the assets of a sole proprietorship.** Ruth Jenson, the owner of a sole proprietorship firm, is planning to incorporate her business. Her capital account has a balance of $164,000 after revaluation of the assets. Her cash account totals $16,000. She will receive 14 percent, $20 par value preferred stock with a total par value equal to the cash transferred. The balance of her capital is to be exchanged for shares of $10 par value common stock with a total par value equal to the remaining capital. How many shares of preferred stock should be issued to Jenson? How many shares of common stock should be issued to Jenson?

EXERCISE 28-14   **Determining the minimum amortization of organization costs.** The Fernandez Corporation was formed in January 19X2. Organization costs of $2,800 were incurred. What is the least amount of organization costs to be amortized for the year 19X2?

EXERCISE 28-15   **Determining the amortization of organization costs for federal income tax purposes.** Assume the same facts as in Exercise 28-14. The Fernandez Corporation wishes to amortize an amount of organization costs equal to the largest amount that can be charged off on its federal income tax return. How much will Fernandez amortize for 19X2?

PROBLEMS

PROBLEM 28-1   **Computing dividends on different types of preferred stock.** The Cole Corporation has issued and has outstanding 2,000 shares of $75 par value common stock and 2,000 shares of $50 par value 8 percent preferred stock. The board of directors voted to distribute $3,000 as dividends in 19X1, $10,000 in 19X2, and $51,000 in 19X3.

Instructions   Compute the total dividend and the dividend for each share paid to preferred stockholders and common stockholders each year under the following assumed situations.

Case A: The preferred stock is nonparticipating and noncumulative.
Case B: The preferred stock is cumulative and nonparticipating.
Case C: The preferred stock is participating and noncumulative. Under terms

of the preferred stock contract, in any one year the regular 8 percent dividend is paid to preferred stockholders. Then common stockholders are paid a 8 percent dividend. Finally, all remaining dividends are shared between preferred and common stockholders in proportion to their equity.

PROBLEM 28-2   **Computing dividends when there is cumulative preferred stock outstanding.** This problem consists of two parts.

1. A portion of the Stockholders' Equity section of the Marino Corporation's balance sheet as of December 31, 19X2, appears below. Dividends have not been paid for the year 19X1. There has been no change in the number of shares of stock issued and outstanding during 19X1 or 19X2. Assume that the board of directors of the corporation declared a dividend of $15,000 after completing operations for the year 19X2.

Stockholders' Equity

Preferred Stock (10% cumulative, $50 par value, 20,000 shares authorized)	
At Par Value (4,000 shares issued)	$200,000
Common Stock ($25 par value, 35,000 shares authorized)	
At Par Value (10,000 shares issued)	250,000

Instructions
a. Compute the total amount of the dividend to be distributed to the preferred stockholders.
b. Compute the amount of the dividend to be paid on each share of preferred stock.
c. Compute the total amount of the dividend available to be distributed to the common stockholders.
d. Compute the amount of the dividend to be paid on each share of common stock.
e. Compute the amount of dividends in arrears (if any) that the preferred stockholders may expect from future declarations of dividends.
f. Compute the amount of dividends in arrears (if any) that the common stockholders may expect from future declarations of dividends.

2. Assume that after operations for 19X2 are completed, the board of directors declares a dividend of $84,000 instead of $15,000. Use the information given in Part 1 in solving this part.

Instructions
a. Compute the total amount of the dividend to be distributed to the preferred stockholders.
b. Compute the amount of the dividend to be paid on each share of preferred stock.
c. Compute the total amount of the dividend available to be distributed to the common stockholders.
d. Compute the amount of the dividend to be paid on each share of common stock.

e. Compute the amount of dividends in arrears (if any) that the preferred stockholders may expect from future declarations of dividends.

f. Compute the amount of dividends in arrears (if any) that the common stockholders may expect from future declarations of dividends.

PROBLEM 28-3

Preparing the Stockholders' Equity section of the balance sheet. The High-Tech Leisure Corporation was organized for the purpose of producing video games. It has been authorized to issue 20,000 shares of 11 percent noncumulative, nonparticipating preferred stock with a par value of $100 and 50,000 shares of no-par value common stock with a stated value of $50.

Instructions

Prepare the Stockholders' Equity section of the corporation's balance sheet as it will appear after issuance of 12,000 shares of the preferred stock and 18,000 shares of the common stock. Assume that the preferred stock was sold at par value and the common stock at stated value.

PROBLEM 28-4

Comparing alternative forms of corporate financing. The Wallace Corporation produces exercise equipment for use in homes and health clubs. In 19X1 it earned a net income (after taxes) of $35,000. Part of its capital structure on December 31, 19X1, is shown below. The corporation has an expansion plan costing $120,000. It is considering raising funds through *(a)* issuing 2,000 additional shares of common stock at $60 a share or *(b)* issuing $120,000 of 12 percent bonds payable. Assume that additional corporate income will be taxed at a rate of 30 percent and that the bond interest can be deducted in computing the income tax.

Stockholders' Equity

Common Stock ($100 par value, 10,000 shares authorized)
  At Par Value (4,000 shares outstanding) $400,000

Instructions

1. Assume that the expansion would result in increased revenue (before taxes) of $30,000. Show the effects on net income per share of common stock if the financing is carried out under each of the proposed methods.

2. Assume that the expansion would result in increased revenue (before taxes) of only $10,000. Show the effects on net income per share of common stock if the financing is carried out under each of the methods.

PROBLEM 28-5

Revaluing the assets of a sole proprietorship and recording its incorporation. Gary Hull has been operating the Hull Music Center, a retail store selling records and tapes, as a sole proprietorship. The postclosing trial balance shown on page 654 was prepared after the firm's accounting records were closed at the end of its fiscal year on December 31, 19X1.

Hull and three friends have decided to form the Hull Corporation and take over the operation of the Hull Music Center on December 31, 19X1. The accounts receivable are to be revalued at $4,400, merchandise inventory at $50,000, and equipment at $2,100. Hull is to receive 200 shares of Hull Corporation preferred stock at par value ($100) and sufficient $50 par value shares of common stock to cover his adjusted net investment.

HULL MUSIC CENTER
Postclosing Trial Balance
December 31, 19X1

Acct. No.	Account Name	Debit	Credit
101	Cash	$ 6,000	
111	Accounts Receivable	4,750	
112	Allowance for Uncollectible Accounts		$ 250
121	Merchandise Inventory	51,000	
131	Equipment	2,900	
132	Accumulated Depreciation—Equipment		1,100
202	Accounts Payable		3,300
301	Gary Hull, Capital		60,000
	Totals	$64,650	$64,650

Instructions

1. Open general ledger accounts for the Hull Music Center, and record the December 31 balances.

2. Give the general journal entries necessary to record the following events. As each entry is made, post it to the appropriate accounts.

   a. Revaluing the accounts and transferring the net gain or loss on asset revaluation to the Gary Hull, Capital account. Use an account called Gain or Loss on Asset Revaluation 409. Begin the entries on journal page 12.

   b. Transferring the proprietorship's revalued assets and liabilities to the corporation. Set up an account called Receivable From Hull Corporation 113.

   c. Receiving stock from the Hull Corporation: 200 shares of $100 par value preferred stock at par and common stock of $50 par value to settle the Receivable From Hull Corporation account. Set up the accounts Common Stock of Hull Corporation 114 and Preferred Stock of Hull Corporation 115.

   d. Distributing stock to Gary Hull. (After this entry is posted, all the proprietorship accounts should be closed.)

3. In the corporation's general journal, record a memorandum entry describing its formation on December 31, 19X1. The corporation is authorized to issue 2,000 shares of $50 par value common stock and 1,000 shares of $100 par value 12 percent preferred stock that is noncumulative and nonparticipating.

4. Record general journal entries as of December 31 to show the takeover of the assets and liabilities of the proprietorship and the issuance of stock in payment to Gary Hull (Certificates C-1 and P-1). Use the same account titles that the proprietorship used for assets and liabilities. Also use the following new account titles: Due to Hull Music Center 203, Common Stock 301, and Preferred Stock 311.

   (**Note:** Save your working papers for use in Problem 28-6.)

PROBLEM 28-6 **Recording the issuance of stock by a corporation and preparing the opening balance sheet.** This problem is a continuation of Problem 28-5. In addition to the transactions of the Hull Corporation that you recorded in Problem 28-5, the transactions shown on page 655 took place on December 31, 19X1.

Instructions	1. Prepare general journal entries to record the transactions.
	2. Prepare the opening balance sheet as of January 1, 19X2, for the Hull Corporation.

TRANSACTIONS FOR DECEMBER 31, 19X1

1. Cash was received from Kevin O'Shea for the purchase of capital stock, and the stock was issued as follows.
   Common stock, 100 shares at $50 a share.
   Preferred stock, 70 shares at $100 a share.
2. Gary Hull was issued 15 shares of common stock to pay for his services in organizing the corporation. It was agreed that $750 is a fair value for his services. (Debit Organization Costs 191.)

PROBLEM 28-7 **Recording organization costs.** A group of investors recently formed the Childcraft Corporation, which manufactures educational toys.

Instructions 1. Record in general journal form the selected transactions shown below that occurred during the first month of the Childcraft Corporation's existence.
2. What disposition should be made of the balance in the Organization Costs account of the Childcraft Corporation?

TRANSACTIONS FOR JANUARY 19X2

Jan. 5 Issued 200 shares of $20 par value common stock to the promoters for their work in forming the corporation.
      8 Issued 90 shares of $20 par value common stock to an attorney for his work in organizing the corporation.
      8 Paid the secretary of state a fee of $50 to obtain the corporation's charter.

ALTERNATE PROBLEMS

PROBLEM 28-1A **Computing dividends on different types of preferred stock.** The Burke Corporation has issued and has outstanding 10,000 shares of $50 par value common stock and 1,000 shares of $100 par value 13 percent preferred stock. The board of directors voted to distribute $4,000 as dividends in 19X1, $12,000 in 19X2, and $81,000 in 19X3.

Instructions Compute the total dividend and the dividend for each share paid to preferred stockholders and common stockholders each year under the following assumed situations.
Case A: The preferred stock is nonparticipating and noncumulative.
Case B: The preferred stock is cumulative and nonparticipating.
Case C: The preferred stock is participating and noncumulative. Under terms of the preferred stock contract, in any one year the regular 13 percent dividend is paid to preferred stockholders. Then common stockholders are paid a 13 percent dividend. Finally, all remaining dividends

are shared between preferred and common stockholders in proportion to their equity.

PROBLEM 28-2A   **Computing dividends when there is cumulative preferred stock outstanding.** This problem consists of two parts.

1. A portion of the Stockholders' Equity section of the Sadowski Corporation's balance sheet as of December 31, 19X5, appears below. Dividends have not been paid for the years 19X3 and 19X4. There has been no change in the number of shares of stock issued and outstanding during these years. Assume that the board of directors of the Sadowski Corporation declares a dividend of $13,900 after completing operations for the year 19X5.

Stockholders' Equity

Preferred Stock (11% cumulative, $100 par value, 1,000 shares authorized)	
At Par Value (700 shares issued)	$ 70,000
Common Stock (no-par value, with stated value of $50, 5,000 shares authorized)	
At Stated Value (3,000 shares issued)	150,000

Instructions
   a. Compute the total amount of the dividend to be distributed to the preferred stockholders.
   b. Compute the amount of the dividend to be paid on each share of preferred stock.
   c. Compute the total amount of the dividend available to be distributed to the common stockholders.
   d. Compute the amount of the dividend to be paid on each share of common stock.
   e. Compute the amount of dividends in arrears (if any) that the preferred stockholders may expect from future declarations of dividends.
   f. Compute the amount of dividends in arrears (if any) that the common stockholders may expect from future declarations of dividends.

2. Assume that the board of directors of the Sadowski Corporation declares a dividend of $42,900 instead of $13,900 after operations of the year 19X5 are completed. Use the information given in Part 1 in solving this part.

Instructions
   a. Compute the total amount of the dividend to be distributed to the preferred stockholders.
   b. Compute the amount of the dividend to be paid on each share of preferred stock.
   c. Compute the total amount of the dividend available to be distributed to the common stockholders.
   d. Compute the amount of the dividend to be paid on each share of common stock.
   e. Compute the amount of dividends in arrears (if any) that the preferred stockholders may expect from future declarations of dividends.
   f. Compute the amount of dividends in arrears (if any) that the common stockholders may expect from future declarations of dividends.

PROBLEM 28-3A   **Preparing the Stockholders' Equity section of the balance sheet.** The Electronic Media Corporation was organized for the purpose of producing magnetic disks for microcomputers. It has been authorized to issue 10,000 shares of 12 percent noncumulative, nonparticipating preferred stock with a par value of $50 and 60,000 shares of no-par value common stock with a stated value of $35.

Instructions   Prepare the Stockholders' Equity section of the corporation's balance sheet as it would appear after issuance of 7,500 shares of the preferred stock and 20,000 shares of the common stock. Assume that the preferred stock was sold at par value and the common stock at stated value.

PROBLEM 28-4A   **Comparing alternative forms of corporate financing.** A group of individuals is forming a corporation to produce active sportswear such as jogging clothes. Two possible financing plans are being considered.

1. The issuance of 6,000 shares of no-par value common stock at $50 a share, which will bring in $300,000.
2. The issuance of 2,000 shares of no-par value common stock for $200,000 and the issuance of 10 percent bonds payable at a par value of $100,000.

Instructions   Assume an income tax rate of 20 percent. Compute the net income or net loss for each share of common stock under each financing method if the net income, before interest and taxes, for the first year is as follows.

1. $45,000
2. $6,000

PROBLEM 28-5A   **Revaluing the assets of a sole proprietorship and recording its incorporation.** Ross Ayers and David Lewis are equal partners in A and L Motors, which sells used cars and operates an automobile repair service. Net income and losses are shared equally. Lewis expresses a desire to retire from the business. Therefore, Ayers joins with Marie Velez, Ralph Velez, and Sharon Neimer to form a corporation to be known as the Economy Motors Corporation, for the purpose of continuing the business's activities.

The new corporation is authorized to issue 1,000 shares of $100 par value 12 percent preferred stock that is noncumulative and nonparticipating and 2,000 shares of no-par value common stock with a stated value of $50 a share. It is mutually agreed that the accounting records of A and L Motors will be closed on December 31, 19X1, that Ayers and Lewis will each be permitted to withdraw $10,000 in cash, that certain assets will be revalued, and that Economy Motors Corporation will then take over all remaining assets and assume all liabilities. In payment for the business, the Economy Motors Corporation will issue 200 shares of preferred stock to Ayers and 200 shares of preferred stock to Lewis, plus a sufficient number of shares of common stock to each partner to equal the balance of his capital account. Any amount of less than $50 that remains in either account will be paid in cash. The balance sheet accounts of A and L Motors as of December 31, 19X1, are shown on the postclosing trial balance on page 658.

Instructions   1. Open general ledger accounts for A and L Motors, and record the December 31, 19X1, balances.

A AND L MOTORS
Postclosing Trial Balance
December 31, 19X1

Acct. No.	Account Name	Debit	Credit
101	Cash	$ 24,050	
111	Accounts Receivable	12,720	
112	Allowance for Uncollectible Accounts		$ 2,120
121	Parts and Accessories Inventory	12,750	
122	Used Car Inventory	62,700	
140	Land	12,000	
141	Building	33,000	
142	Accumulated Depr.—Building		13,870
143	Repair Equipment	8,720	
144	Accumulated Depr.—Repair Equipment		2,170
202	Accounts Payable		17,860
301	Ross Ayers, Capital		64,960
302	David Lewis, Capital		64,960
	Totals	$165,940	$165,940

2. Record in general journal form the withdrawal in cash of $10,000 each by Ayers and Lewis. Begin the entries for this problem on journal page 12. As each entry is recorded, post it to the appropriate general ledger accounts.

3. Record the following revaluations of assets. Open an account called Gain or Loss on Asset Revaluation 409 to reflect all changes in values.
   a. The accounts receivable are estimated to have a book value of $8,600.
   b. The parts and accessories inventory has a current value of $10,950.
   c. The land has an appraised value of $20,000.
   d. The building has an appraised value of $24,000.
   e. The repair equipment has an appraised value of $7,100.

4. Record the entry to transfer the net gain or loss to the partners' capital accounts. Divide it equally between the accounts.

5. Record the withdrawal of equal amounts of cash by Ayers and Lewis to round off their capital accounts so that they can be closed by the receipt of stock as agreed.

6. Record the entry to transfer the assets and liabilities of A and L Motors to the corporation. Open a new account—Receivable From Economy Motors Corporation 113.

7. Record receipt of the number of shares of preferred and common stock required to pay for A and L Motors under the terms of the agreement. Open accounts for Common Stock of Economy Motors Corporation 114 and Preferred Stock of Economy Motors Corporation 115.

8. Record the distribution of the shares of preferred and common stock to the partners. After this entry is posted, all accounts of A and L Motors should be closed.

9. In the corporation's general journal, record a memorandum entry describing its formation on December 31, 19X1.
10. Record general journal entries as of December 31 to show the takeover of the assets and liabilities of the partnership and the issuance of stock in payment to Ayers (Certificates C-2 and P-2) and Lewis (Certificates C-1 and P-1). Use the same account titles that the partnership used for assets and liabilities. Also use the following new account titles: Due to A and L Motors 203, Common Stock 301, and Preferred Stock 311.
(**Note:** Save your working papers for use in Problem 28-6A.)

PROBLEM 28-6A **Recording the issuance of stock by a corporation and preparing the opening balance sheet.** This is a continuation of Problem 28-5A. In addition to the transactions of the Economy Motors Corporation that you recorded in Problem 28-5A, the transactions shown below took place on December 31, 19X1.

Instructions 1. Prepare general journal entries to record the transactions.
2. Prepare the opening balance sheet as of January 1, 19X2, for the Economy Motors Corporation.

TRANSACTIONS ON DECEMBER 31, 19X1

1. Cash was received as follows from purchasers of capital stock, and the stock was issued. (Use a separate entry for the dealings with each investor.)
Marie Velez, 50 shares of preferred stock at $100 a share and 100 shares of common stock at $50 a share.
Ralph Velez, 50 shares of preferred stock at $100 a share and 100 shares of common stock at $50 a share.
Sharon Neimer, 200 shares of preferred stock at $100 a share.
2. Organization expenses of $1,500 were paid in cash. (Debit Organization Costs 191.)

PROBLEM 28-7A **Recording organization costs.** A group of investors recently formed the Harvest Corporation, which produces natural food products.

Instructions 1. Record in general journal form the selected transactions shown below that occurred during the first month of the Harvest Corporation's existence.
2. What disposition should be made of the balance in the Organization Costs account of the Harvest Corporation?

TRANSACTIONS FOR JANUARY 19X1

Jan. 4 Issued 100 shares of $100 par value common stock to the promoters for their work in forming the corporation.
9 Issued 60 shares of $100 par value common stock to an attorney for his work in organizing the corporation.
13 Paid the secretary of state a fee of $50 to obtain the corporation's charter.

CHAPTER 29

The records needed by a business vary with the nature of its activities and the form of its organization. The accounting records of a typical corporation include most of the accounts, journals, and ledgers that you have been studying. However, corporations must keep some additional records. These records are discussed in the present chapter.

CAPITAL STOCK TRANSACTIONS; CORPORATE RECORDS

CORPORATE RECORDS

The type of owners' equity (stockholders' equity) that a corporation has requires more elaborate recording than that needed for owner's equity in a sole proprietorship or partnership. Not only does the corporation have to keep detailed records of the stockholders' equity, but it must also keep special corporate records such as minutes of meetings of stockholders and directors, corporate bylaws, stock certificate books, stock ledgers, and stock transfer records. These corporate records and procedures will be explained by tracing the various steps followed by the newly organized Duncan Lawn Furniture Corporation as it issues stock.

ARTICLES OF INCORPORATION

A number of provisions in the approved articles of incorporation (corporate charter) relate to the firm's capital structure. It is apparent that the nature and extent of the owners' equity will be directly affected by the authority granted or limitations imposed with regard to the following items.

1. The types and amounts of capital stock authorized.
2. The nature of the business.
3. The property to be acquired.
4. The powers of the corporation.
5. The names, addresses, and investment pledges of the incorporators.

Items 2, 3, and 4 are customarily stated in broad terms in order to give the corporation flexibility in changing the nature of its activities to take advantage of new business opportunities.

The articles of incorporation of the Duncan Lawn Furniture Corporation include the following provisions concerning each of the items listed above.

1. Capital stock authorized. Total authorized capital stock consists of 10,000 shares of no-par value common stock with a stated value of $50 and 2,000

shares of $100 par value 12 percent preferred stock that is noncumulative and nonparticipating.

2. Nature of the business. The firm is to sell lawn furniture.

3. Property to be acquired. The corporation may acquire whatever property is necessary or convenient for carrying out corporate purposes.

4. Powers of the corporation. The corporation is granted power to do whatever is appropriate in conducting the stated business activities and purposes. No length of life is specified.

5. Incorporators. The incorporators and the number of shares they agree to purchase (common stock at $50, preferred stock at par value) are shown below.

	COMMON STOCK	PREFERRED STOCK
James Duncan	800 shares	400 shares
Robert Novak	200 shares	200 shares
Mary Fields	200 shares	200 shares

ISSUING STOCK TO THE INCORPORATORS

The first stock issued by the corporation includes the 768 shares of common stock and 400 shares of preferred stock allowed to James Duncan in payment for the assets and liabilities of the Duncan Chair Company. Now Duncan must buy 32 more shares of common stock at $50 a share to fulfill his agreement as one of the original incorporators.

Suppose he purchases the remaining 32 shares on January 2, 19X2, paying cash. This receipt would ordinarily be recorded in the corporation's cash receipts journal. However, to simplify the illustration, we will show the issuance of stock through general journal entries. The entry of December 31, 19X1, that was made to record the original stock issue is repeated first for reference. It is followed by the entry for the issuance of the 32 additional shares of common stock to Duncan on January 2.

19 X1					
Dec. 31	Due to Duncan Chair Company	203	78,400 00		
	Common Stock (768 shares)	301		38,400 00	
	Preferred Stock (400 shares)	311		40,000 00	
	To record issuance of stock in payment for net assets of Duncan Chair Company: common stock at $50 a share and preferred stock at par ($100).				

19 X2					
Jan. 2	Cash	101	1,600 00		
	Common Stock (32 shares)	301		1,600 00	
	To record issuance of stock to James Duncan at $50 a share—balance of purchase agreed to as original incorporator.				

The other two incorporators, Robert Novak and Mary Fields, have each agreed to purchase 200 shares of common stock at $50 a share and 200 shares of preferred stock at par value, $100 a share. On January 2, 19X2, they pay the corporation the agreed amounts. The entries for the stock issued to them are shown in general journal form below.

19 X2						
Jan.	2	Cash	101	30,000 00		
		Common Stock (200 shares)	301		10,000 00	
		Preferred Stock (200 shares)	311		20,000 00	
		To record issuance of stock to Robert Novak, one of the original incorporators: common stock at $50 a share and preferred stock at par ($100).				
	2	Cash	101	30,000 00		
		Common Stock (200 shares)	301		10,000 00	
		Preferred Stock (200 shares)	311		20,000 00	
		To record issuance of stock to Mary Fields, one of the original incorporators: common stock at $50 a share and preferred stock at par ($100).				

ISSUING ADDITIONAL STOCK

Two other people interested in the new corporation, John Valdez and Alice Hill, each agreed to buy 100 shares of common stock at $50 a share. Valdez comes to the firm's office on January 2 with checks to cover both pledges. The two blocks of stock are then issued as shown in the following general journal entries.

19 X2					
Jan.	2	Cash	101	5,000 00	
		Common Stock (100 shares)	301		5,000 00
		To record issuance of common stock to John Valdez at $50 a share.			
		Cash	101	5,000 00	
		Common Stock (100 shares)	301		5,000 00
		To record issuance of common stock to Alice Hill at $50 a share.			

MEETING OF THE STOCKHOLDERS

Immediately following the issuance of stock on January 2, the first stockholders' meeting is held. The stockholders present and the number of shares of voting stock owned are shown on page 663. Only common stockholders have voting rights in this corporation.

Note that although Alice Hill is not present in person, she is able to vote her stock by executing a proxy and giving it to John Valdez. A *proxy* is an authorization that permits someone else to vote on behalf of a stockholder. Particularly in large corporations, it is a common practice for stockholders who cannot attend stockholders' meetings to give their proxies to people who will be present. The management of a corporation often obtains enough proxies to control the vote in the stockholders' meeting. Occasionally rival factions will each seek proxies and a *proxy fight* develops to decide which slate of directors will be elected.

STOCKHOLDERS OF
DUNCAN LAWN FURNITURE CORPORATION

Name	Shares
James Duncan	800
Robert Novak	200
Mary Fields	200
John Valdez	100
Proxy from Alice Hill to John Valdez	100

Adoption of Bylaws

The first act of the stockholders is the adoption of a proposed set of *bylaws* to serve as a guide for the general operations of the corporation. Bylaws must be consistent with the corporation's charter. They usually include provisions that define the following items.

1. The time, place, and nature of the meetings of stockholders and directors.
2. The number of directors and officers and the method of electing them.
3. The duties of directors, officers, and committees.
4. The rules governing the conduct of meetings and other activities.
5. The fiscal year to be used by the corporation.
6. The method for changing the bylaws.

The bylaws of the Duncan Lawn Furniture Corporation include the following initial provisions.

1. A five-member board of directors is to be elected at the first meeting of the stockholders and annually thereafter on the third Saturday in February. Vacancies occurring between annual elections are to be filled by a vote of the remaining members of the board.
2. Each director's compensation for attending a regular or special meeting of the board is $100. No additional payment will be made for meetings of the executive committee, which is composed of the president, vice president, and secretary-treasurer.
3. The officers of the corporation are to be a president, a vice president, and a secretary-treasurer.
4. Additional common stock may be issued at not less than $50 a share, with a stated value of $50 a share.
5. Additional preferred stock may be issued at not less than $100 (par value) a share.
6. The fiscal year is the calendar year, ending December 31.

Election of Board of Directors

The five initial stockholders are unanimously elected to serve as the first board of directors.

MEETING OF THE BOARD OF DIRECTORS

As soon as the stockholders' meeting is adjourned, the five directors present hold the first meeting of the new board of directors. The board unanimously elects the following officers.

OFFICERS OF
DUNCAN LAWN FURNITURE
CORPORATION

President	James Duncan
Vice President	Robert Novak
Secretary-Treasurer	Mary Fields

Annual salaries are set for the officers, who are expected to devote full time to the business: Duncan, president, $20,000; Novak, vice president, $15,000; and Fields, secretary-treasurer, $15,000. (Salaries are purposely being kept low at this point in order to control expenses and provide maximum funds for other needs.) The board now instructs the officers to remodel the store, purchase a larger and more varied inventory of goods, and hire additional salespeople.

MINUTE BOOK

To keep accurate and complete records of all meetings of stockholders and directors, the corporation maintains a minute book. In the *minute book,* actions taken, directives issued, directors elected, officers elected, and all other matters discussed are formally reported. The chief accountant should study the minutes of each meeting to determine if any of the actions taken concern records and payments for which the accountant is responsible. Decisions noted in the minute book about salaries for officers, authorizations to purchase assets, and declarations of dividends may affect accounting records and procedures.

STOCK CERTIFICATE BOOKS

Capital stock issued by a corporation is in the form of a stock certificate. A separate series of stock certificates must be prepared for each class of stock. Therefore, the Duncan Lawn Furniture Corporation has one series for common stock and one for preferred stock.

A corporation that expects to issue relatively few stock certificates may have them prepared in books. Each certificate is numbered consecutively and attached to a stub from which it is separated at the time of issuance. The certificate indicates the class of stock and the number of shares. If the stock is preferred, the essence of the preferred stock contract is printed on the certificate itself. Certificates become valid when they are properly signed by corporate officers and have the corporate seal affixed to them.

Certificate and Stub Illustrated

The first common stock certificate of the Duncan Lawn Furniture Corporation is issued to James Duncan for 768 shares. The illustration on page 665 shows the certificate and stub as they appear just before the certificate is detached. (The lower section of the stub is used when stock is transferred. This procedure is explained and illustrated shortly.)

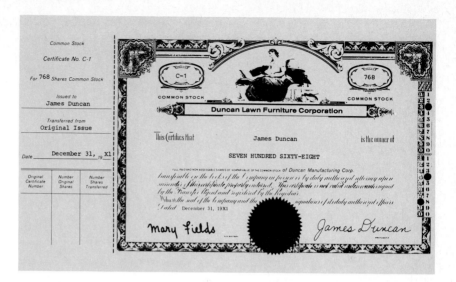

Stubs for Other Issues of Common Stock

As each additional block of shares of common stock is issued, the pertinent information is first recorded on the prenumbered stub. Then a certificate is filled out, detached, and delivered to the purchaser. Certificates C-2 through C-6 are issued to Duncan, Novak, Fields, Valdez, and Hill for the shares previously described. The stubs have the necessary information filled in.

Stubs for Issues of Preferred Stock

Three blocks of preferred stock are issued to the three incorporators. A separate set of stock certificates is used for the preferred stock. These certificates are also bound in a stock certificate book, and each certificate is attached to a prenumbered stub. The procedures for issuing preferred stock are the same as those for issuing common stock. The stub is completed first. Then the certificate is filled in and detached.

CAPITAL STOCK LEDGER AND PROCEDURES

It is important for the corporation or for an agent acting in its behalf to keep careful records of the number of shares of stock issued and of the names and addresses of the stockholders. This information is needed when dividend checks are mailed, when official notices of stockholders' meetings are sent out, when proxies are solicited, and at other times. The record also serves as a check against the possibility of issuing more stock than is authorized by the corporation's charter.

In order to maintain the required information about stockholders, the corporation or its agent sets up a *capital stock ledger,* or *stockholders' ledger,* for each class of stock issued. Within this ledger there is a sheet for each stockholder with the person's name and address, the dates of transactions affecting his or her stock holdings, the certificate numbers, and the number of shares involved in each transaction. The balance shows the number of shares held. The same ledger sheets may also include a record of dividend payments. The ledger sheet set up for the preferred stock of the Duncan Lawn Furniture Corporation owned by James Duncan is illustrated below. Similar capital stock ledger sheets are maintained for the common stockholders.

CAPITAL STOCK LEDGER—PREFERRED

Sheet No. 1   Name: James Duncan   Address: 714 Oak Lane, Greenville, SC 29609

DIVIDENDS PAID			TRANSFERRED FROM OR TO		POST. REF.	CERT. NOS.	RECORD OF SHARES		
DATE	CHECK NO.	AMOUNT	DATE	NAME			SHARES ISSUED	SHARES SURREND.	BALANCE
			19 X1 Dec. 31	Original Issue	J12	P-1	400		400

In all the transactions illustrated so far, the stockholders have acquired their stock directly from the issuing corporation. However, once a quantity of stock has been issued, new stockholders are likely to obtain their shares by purchasing them from owners who want to sell all or part of their holdings. The corporation receives no money in such a transaction. The buyer pays the seller, and the stock is transferred to the new owner in the records of the corporation. A special journal called the *capital stock transfer journal* is used to record the transaction, which is then posted to the stockholders' ledger. One of these journals is maintained for each class of stock issued by the corporation, and all transfers involving that class of stock are recorded in it. (This type of journal is illustrated in a later section of the present chapter.)

Stock Assignment Form

In order to transfer ownership of shares of stock, an *assignment* must be made in proper legal form, and the stock certificate must be surrendered for cancellation. For convenience an assignment form is usually printed on the back of each stock certificate. Suppose James Duncan agrees to sell 200 shares of his preferred stock to Tina Serrano on February 15, 19X2. He completes the assignment form on the reverse side of his stock certificate, P-1, as shown below.

For value received_____I_____hereby sell, assign and transfer unto

Tina Serrano

179 Laurel Street, Greenville, SC 29609

---------------------- TWO HUNDRED ---------------------- *Shares of the Capital Stock represented by the within Certificate, and do hereby irrevocably constitute and appoint*

Mary Fields

_____ Attorney, to transfer the said stock on the books of the within-named Company with full power of substitution in the premises.

Dated, February 15, 19X2

James Duncan

In Presence of: Peter Smith

NOTICE: THE SIGNATURE TO THIS ASSIGNMENT MUST CORRESPOND WITH THE NAME AS WRITTEN UPON THE FACE OF THE CERTIFICATE, IN EVERY PARTICULAR, WITHOUT ALTERATION OR ENLARGEMENT, OR ANY CHANGE WHATEVER.

Capital Stock Transfer Journal Entry

When Certificate P-1 with the completed stock assignment form is presented to the corporation, a new certificate is issued to James Duncan for the 200 shares (of the original 400 shares) he still retains. A new certificate is also issued to Tina Serrano for the 200 shares she has purchased from him. However, before the new certificates are issued, an entry is made in the preferred stock transfer journal of the Duncan Lawn Furniture Corporation, as shown in the illustration below.

PREFERRED STOCK TRANSFER JOURNAL								Page 1	
DATE	SURREND. BY	√	CERT. NO.	NO. OF SHARES	TRANSFER. TO	√	CERT. NO.	NO. OF SHARES
19 X2 Feb. 15	James Duncan	√	P-1	400	James Duncan	√	P-4	200
					Tina Serrano	√	P-5	200

Issuance of New Certificates

The surrendered Certificate P-1 is canceled. The stock certificate stub may have this fact noted on it, or the canceled certificate may be permanently attached to the stub. New certificates for this preferred stock are issued, and the appropriate information is entered on their stubs, as shown in the illustrations below.

Preferred Stock

Certificate No. P-4

For __200__ Shares Preferred Stock

Issued to
James Duncan

Transferred from
James Duncan

Date _____ February 15, 19 X2

Original Certificate Number	Number Original Shares	Number Shares Transferred
P-1	400	200

Preferred Stock

Certificate No. P-5

For __200__ Shares Preferred Stock

Issued to
Tina Serrano

Transferred from
James Duncan

Date _____ February 15, 19 X2

Original Certificate Number	Number Original Shares	Number Shares Transferred
P-1	400	200

Posting to the Capital Stock Ledger

From the information entered in the preferred stock transfer journal, postings are made to the capital stock ledger sheets that are affected. A new sheet is established for Tina Serrano because she is a new shareholder. Then a record of the cancellation of Certificate P-1 and the issuance of new Certificate P-4 is noted on the ledger sheet for James Duncan. After these postings are made, the sheets for Serrano and Duncan in the corporation's capital stock ledger appear as illustrated on page 668.

CAPITAL STOCK LEDGER—PREFERRED

Sheet No. 1   **Name:** James Duncan   **Address:** 714 Oak Lane, Greenville, SC 29609

DIVIDENDS PAID			TRANSFERRED FROM OR TO		POST. REF.	CERT. NOS.	RECORD OF SHARES		
DATE	CHECK NO.	AMOUNT	DATE	NAME			SHARES ISSUED	SHARES SURREND.	BALANCE
			19 X1 Dec. 31	Original Issue	J12	P-1	400		400
			19 X2 Feb. 15	Tina Serrano (200 sh.)	PST1	P-1		400	–0–
			Feb. 15	James Duncan	PST1	P-4	200		200

CAPITAL STOCK LEDGER—PREFERRED

Sheet No. 4   **Name:** Tina Serrano   **Address:** 179 Laurel Street, Greenville, SC 29609

DIVIDENDS PAID			TRANSFERRED FROM OR TO		POST. REF.	CERT. NOS.	RECORD OF SHARES		
DATE	CHECK NO.	AMOUNT	DATE	NAME			SHARES ISSUED	SHARES SURREND.	BALANCE
			19 X2 Feb. 15	James Duncan	PST1	P-5	200		200

TRANSFER AGENT AND REGISTRAR

The directors of the Duncan Lawn Furniture Corporation expect the firm to have relatively few stockholders and only infrequent transactions affecting its capital stock. They decide, therefore, that the business will keep its own stock records.

However, corporations whose stock is widely held and actively traded ordinarily do not keep their own stockholder records. Instead, they turn the responsibility for these records over to a transfer agent and a registrar. The bank that is to serve as a transfer agent is often chosen because of its nearness to the stock exchange or the market in which the corporation's stock is expected to be traded. The same bank may also be appointed registrar.

Transfer Agent

The *transfer agent* receives the stock certificates being surrendered with the assignment forms indicating to whom new certificates should be issued. The agent cancels the old certificates, issues the new ones, and makes the necessary entries in the capital stock ledger. When required to do so by the corporation, the agent also prepares lists of stockholders who should receive dividend payments, notices, and other items. The agent may also prepare and mail the dividend checks.

Registrar

The *registrar* accounts for all the stock issued by the corporation and makes sure that the corporation does not issue more shares than are authorized. The registrar receives from the transfer agent all the canceled certificates and all the new certificates issued. The new certificates must be countersigned by the registrar before they are valid.

Once the business is launched and its relative success and prospects can be evaluated, investors may feel that its stock is actually worth more or less than par value. For example, if the corporation produces very attractive profits even in the early stages of its operations, investors may understandably be willing to pay more than par value to become stockholders. Similarly, if the dividend rate on an issue of preferred stock is higher than the rate that could be earned on other investments with similar risk, investors may be willing to pay more than par value for the preferred stock. The amount paid in excess of par value for securities is called a *premium*.

Suppose that Linda Levy offers to pay a premium of $10 a share, which means a price of $110 a share, for 200 shares of the 12 percent, $100 par value preferred stock of the Duncan Lawn Furniture Corporation. Suppose also that the corporation accepts her offer. Here is how the transaction would be recorded in general journal form.

19 X2					
Mar.	2	Cash	101	22,000 00	
		Preferred Stock (200 shares)	311		20,000 00
		Paid-in Capital in Excess of Par			
		Value of Preferred Stock	315		2,000 00
		To record issuance of preferred stock to			
		Linda Levy for $110 a share.			

In the Stockholders' Equity section of the balance sheet shown below, the amount of the new account, called Paid-in Capital in Excess of Par Value of Preferred Stock, is added to the par value of the shares issued to show the total paid in by that class of stockholder. (The account title might also be Premium on Preferred Stock or some other name.)

Stockholders' Equity
Preferred Stock (12%, $100 par value,
    2,000 shares authorized)
      At Par Value (1,000 shares issued) $100,000
      Paid-in Capital in Excess of Par Value   2,000 $102,000

Although most states prohibit the issuance of stock at a *discount,* or less than par value, this procedure is permitted in a few states. Corporations sometimes sell their stock at a discount as an inducement to hesitant investors. The technique for recording the sale of stock at a discount is illustrated on page 670. In this example 50 shares of $100 par value common stock are issued for $90 a share. Thus the total discount is $500 (50 shares × $10).

When presenting items in the Stockholders' Equity section of the balance sheet, the discount is shown as a deduction from the amount credited to the related stock account. The difference indicates the amount paid in by that class of

19 X5				
May 6	Cash	101	4,500 00	
	Discount on Common Stock	306	500 00	
	Common Stock	301		5,000 00
	To record issuance of 50 shares of $100			
	par value common stock at $90 a			
	share.			

stockholder. If both premiums and discounts occur in sales of the same class of stock, the premiums are added and the discounts deducted separately. The two figures are not combined. For example, assume that the corporation in the above example had already issued 350 shares of common stock at a total premium of $2,000. The Stockholders' Equity section of the balance sheet would appear as follows after issuance of the 50 shares at a discount.

Stockholders' Equity

Common Stock ($100 par value,
   1,000 shares authorized)
    At Par Value (400 shares issued) $40,000
    Paid-in Capital in Excess of Par Value   2,000 $42,000

   Less Discount on Common Stock   500 $41,500

In states where stock can be issued at a discount, the stockholder may have a *contingent liability* to pay the amount of the discount if the corporation needs the funds to pay its creditors.

STATED VALUE FOR NO-PAR VALUE STOCK

No-par value stock provides several theoretical advantages over stock with par value. These advantages are as follows.

1. No-par value stock can be issued for whatever it will bring, without considering premium or discount. This eliminates the contingent liability that might exist if the stock were sold at a discount.
2. The stock buyer is not misled into thinking that a par value amount represents the actual value of the stock. For no-par value stock, the purchaser must be the judge of its worth.
3. The value of no-par value stock issued for property is determined according to the market value of the property received, not according to the par value of the stock issued in payment. This reduces the possibility of issuing stock with a recorded value of more than the property received. Stock issued in excess of the value of property received is sometimes called *watered stock*.

Despite these theoretical advantages, true no-par value stock has not been widely used. In most cases a stated value is set by the board of directors, and this stated value has come to be treated as though it were par value. The stated value is credited to the capital stock account, and any excess received over stated value is treated as a premium.

As you know, the board of directors of the Duncan Lawn Furniture Corporation set a stated value of $50 a share for the no-par value common stock at the time the firm was organized. Assume that the firm's prospects appear bright and that a new investor pays $52 a share for 400 shares of common stock. This transaction would be recorded in general journal form as follows.

19 X2				
Mar. 8	Cash	101	20,800 00	
	Common Stock (400 shares)	301		20,000 00
	Paid-in Capital in Excess of Stated			
	Value of Common Stock	305		800 00
	To record issuance of 400 shares of common stock to Susan Lang at $52 a share (stated value $50 a share).			

Note the credit of $800 to the Paid-in Capital in Excess of Stated Value of Common Stock account (400 shares × $2 a share). On the balance sheet, this item is added to the amount in the Common Stock account to show the total paid by common stockholders.

Some prospective stockholders may not be able to pay immediately for the securities they want to buy. These investors are asked to sign a subscription contract in which they agree to buy the stock at a certain price, to pay for it in accordance with a fixed plan, and to receive the stock when payment is completed. The payment may be due in a single amount at a future date or in installments over a period of time. Such an arrangement gives the corporation a receivable from the subscriber and an obligation to hold enough stock to issue when the subscription is paid in full.

Receipt of Subscriptions

Suppose the Duncan Lawn Furniture Corporation receives a subscription from Doris Martin to purchase 200 shares of common stock at $50 a share (the stated value) and a subscription from Lewis Nichols to buy 200 shares of preferred stock at $110 a share. These subscriptions are recorded as shown on page 672.

Notice that separate subscriptions receivable accounts are used for each class of stock. It is convenient to use the separate accounts in this case because the subscription contract for each type of stock may call for a different payment plan. In the example given here, the common stock is to be paid for in full on the first of the following month. The preferred stock subscription is payable in five monthly installments, beginning on the first day of the following month. Both receivables are shown as current assets on the balance sheet.

Separate accounts must also be kept for the subscribed stock because the corporation has agreed to hold enough stock to issue to the subscribers when they

19X2					
Apr.	1	Subscriptions Receivable—Common	114	10,000 00	
		Common Stock Subscribed (200			
		shares)	302		10,000 00
		To record subscription from Doris Martin			
		to buy 200 shares of common stock			
		at stated value of $50 a share.			
	1	Subscriptions Receivable—Preferred	115	22,000 00	
		Preferred Stock Subscribed (200			
		shares)	312		20,000 00
		Paid-in Capital in Excess of Par			
		Value of Preferred Stock	315		2,000 00
		To record subscription from Lewis Nichols			
		to buy 200 shares of $100 par value			
		preferred stock at $110 a share.			

have paid their contracts in full. Until this time the subscribed accounts are presented in the Stockholders' Equity section of the balance sheet as additions to the same class of stock issued. For example, immediately after the receipt of Nichols' stock subscription, the preferred stock listing in the Stockholders' Equity section appears as shown below.

Stockholders' Equity

Preferred Stock (12%, $100 par value,		
2,000 shares authorized)		
At Par Value (1,000 shares issued)	$100,000	
Subscribed (200 shares)	20,000	
Paid-in Capital in Excess of Par Value	4,000	$124,000

Collection of Subscriptions and Issuance of Stock

The collection of subscriptions and the issuance of stock under these two plans works out as follows.

Single Cash Payment When Martin pays her $10,000 subscription in full on May 1, 19X2, 200 shares of common stock are issued to her. The cash received for this transaction is normally recorded in the cash receipts journal. However, for illustrative purposes, the transaction is shown below in general journal form, followed by an entry to record the issuance of the stock.

19X2					
May	1	Cash	101	10,000 00	
		Subscriptions Receivable—Common	114		10,000 00
		To record receipt of Doris Martin's			
		subscription in full.			
	1	Common Stock Subscribed (200 shares)	302	10,000 00	
		Common Stock (200 shares)	301		10,000 00
		To record issuance of 200 shares of			
		common stock to Doris Martin.			

When these entries have been posted, the Subscriptions Receivable—Common account with Doris Martin is closed and the Common Stock Subscribed account is also closed. The net effect of this series of transactions is to increase the corporation's Cash account by $10,000 and to increase its Common Stock account by the same amount.

Installment Payments Nichols agreed to pay his preferred stock subscription in five monthly installments. If he lives up to his contract, he will pay $4,400 in cash each month for five months, beginning May 1. Each collection will be debited to Cash and credited to Nichols' Subscriptions Receivable—Preferred account. When he makes his final payment, the stock will be issued to him. In general journal form, the collection of the final installment and the issuance of the stock would be recorded as shown below.

19 X2					
Sept.	1	Cash	101	4,400 00	
		Subscriptions Receivable—Preferred	115		4,400 00
		To record receipt of final installment from Lewis Nichols on his stock subscription.			
	1	Preferred Stock Subscribed (200 shares)	312	20,000 00	
		Preferred Stock (200 shares)	311		20,000 00
		To record issuance of 200 shares of preferred stock to Lewis Nichols.			

With the posting of these last entries, the Subscriptions Receivable—Preferred account with Nichols and the Preferred Stock Subscribed account are closed. This series of transactions has resulted in an increase in Cash of $22,000. This amount is offset by a $20,000 increase in the Preferred Stock account for 200 shares sold to Nichols and a $2,000 increase in the Paid-in Capital in Excess of Par Value of Preferred Stock account.

TREATMENT OF DEFAULTS ON STOCK SUBSCRIPTIONS

Not every stock subscriber pays in full according to the contract. What is done about subscriptions that are paid only in part? The answer depends on the action permitted under state law and on the corporation's policy. Among the procedures that may be used are the following.

1. Issuing the amount of stock actually paid for and canceling the balance of the subscription.
2. Retaining the amount paid but issuing no stock, canceling the balance of the subscription, and canceling the entire amount of subscribed stock.
3. Refunding the entire amount paid by the subscriber, canceling the entire subscription, and canceling the entire amount of subscribed stock.
4. Reselling the subscribed stock to another person and refunding the amount paid to the original subscriber after subtracting any costs or losses on the resale.

Each of these default procedures has a significantly different effect on the interests of the corporation and the subscriber. The specifics of defaults are beyond the scope of this course. They are examined in intermediate accounting textbooks.

RECORDS OF STOCK SUBSCRIPTIONS

The corporation needs two special records to keep track of stock subscriptions: the subscription book and the subscribers' ledger.

Subscription Book

The *subscription book* is a listing of stock subscriptions that have been received. This book is used to record the names and addresses of the subscribers, the number of shares they have agreed to buy, and the amounts and times of payment. The subscription book may consist of the actual stock subscription contracts.

Subscribers' Ledger

A separate subsidiary ledger, the subscribers' ledger, is maintained. The *subscribers' ledger* contains an account receivable for each subscriber. This account is debited for the total amount of the original subscription and credited as payments are made by the subscriber to the corporation. No new principles are involved here. The balances of the individual subscriber accounts are summarized by a subscriptions receivable control account in the general ledger.

TREASURY STOCK

Treasury stock is a corporation's own capital stock that has been reacquired. The reacquired stock must have been previously paid for in full and issued to a stockholder in order to be considered treasury stock. Any class or type of stock can be reacquired as treasury stock. No dividends, voting rights, or liquidation preferences apply to this stock.

Reacquisition of a corporation's own capital stock can occur in several different ways. Some examples follow.

1. Donation of the stock to the corporation by a stockholder.
2. Receipt of the stock by the corporation in settlement of a debt that is owed to it.
3. Purchase of the stock by the corporation in exchange for cash or property. (Some states limit the purchase of treasury stock to a total purchase price not in excess of retained earnings.)

There are a number of special accounting procedures involved in the purchase and resale of treasury stock by the corporation. These procedures are explained below.

Purchased Treasury Stock—Cost Basis

When a corporation purchases its own stock, which will probably be reissued at a later date, the transaction is usually recorded at cost. Treasury Stock is debited for the amount paid, and Cash or some other asset account, or a liability account, is credited for the entire amount involved. For example, a preferred share reacquired at $105 in cash after being issued at $100 par value is recorded by a debit to Treasury Stock—Preferred and a credit to Cash, both for $105. (Separate treasury stock accounts are set up as needed for each class of stock.) On the balance sheet, the cost of the reacquired stock is deducted from the sum of all items in the Stockholders' Equity section, as illustrated below.

Stockholders' Equity

Preferred Stock (9%, $100 par value, 10,000 shares authorized)	
At Par Value (200 shares issued, of which one share has been reacquired as treasury stock)	$ 20,000
Common Stock ($20 par value, 5,000 shares authorized)	
At Par Value (2,000 shares issued)	40,000
Total Capital Stock	$ 60,000
Retained Earnings	42,000
	$102,000
Deduct Treasury Stock, Preferred (one share at cost)	105
Total Stockholders' Equity	$101,895

Suppose the share of stock reacquired at $105 is later sold for $108. The entry at the time of sale would be recorded as shown below.

19 X1					
Nov.	1	Cash	101	108 00	
		Treasury Stock—Preferred	319		105 00
		Paid-in Capital From Treasury Stock Transactions—Preferred	317		3 00
		To record sale at $108 of a share of preferred treasury stock purchased at $105.			

Assume that another share of treasury stock previously reacquired at $105 was later sold for only $90. Assume further that this is a share of $100 par value preferred stock originally issued at a premium of $10 a share. The entry required to record the sale includes a number of elements, as shown below.

19 X1					
Nov.	2	Cash	101	90 00	
		Paid-in Capital From Treasury Stock Transactions—Preferred	317	3 00	
		Paid-in Capital in Excess of Par Value of Preferred Stock	315	10 00	
		Retained Earnings	381	2 00	
		Treasury Stock—Preferred	319		105 00
		To record sale at $90 of a share of preferred treasury stock purchased at $105 that had been issued originally at $110.			

Note that Cash is debited for the amount received ($90) and Treasury Stock—Preferred is credited for the amount paid ($105). The difference is absorbed to the extent that credit balances are available. First, Paid-in Capital From Treasury Stock Transactions—Preferred is debited for any amount up to the balance of the account. Second, Paid-in Capital in Excess of Par Value of Preferred Stock is debited up to the amount of the premium received on the issuance of that particular share of stock—in this case $10. Third, the remaining balance is debited to Retained Earnings.

It is usually impossible to determine the exact original issue price for a specific share of stock. In that case the Paid-in Capital in Excess of Par Value of Preferred Stock account is debited for the average amount that applies to each share of outstanding preferred stock being reacquired.

For the example just given, if there had been a large enough balance in the Paid-in Capital From Treasury Stock Transactions—Preferred account to absorb the $15 loss on the resale of the treasury stock (purchased at $105, sold at $90), the entire loss would have been debited to that account. In this case no debits would have been made to Paid-in Capital in Excess of Par Value of Preferred Stock or to Retained Earnings.

Donated Treasury Stock

A corporation may reacquire shares of its own stock by donation under various circumstances. Since the treasury stock in this case is obtained without cost, no entry in dollar amounts is made at the time of acquisition. Only a memorandum entry is made in an appropriate treasury stock account to record the number of shares donated. If the donated treasury stock is later sold, the amount received is debited to Cash and credited to Donated Capital From Treasury Stock Transactions.

REDEMPTION OF PREFERRED STOCK

The terms of a preferred stock issue may give the corporation the right to "call" the stock for redemption and retirement. The *call price* may be a single specified amount for each share, or it may vary depending on the length of time the stock has been outstanding. Also, the corporation may purchase its own preferred stock on the open market with the intent of permanently retiring the shares. Historically, there has been a great deal of argument among accountants over the appropriate way to account for the retirement of preferred stock. However, *Opinion No. 6* of the Accounting Principles Board clarifies the practices to be followed in accounting for the retirement of either preferred or common stock. The practices are summarized here.[1]

1. If the repurchase price is less than the par value or stated value, the excess should be credited to a paid-in capital account (such as Paid-in Capital From Retirement of Preferred Stock). The stock account is then debited for the par value or stated value.
2. Any excess may be charged first against any previous paid-in capital arising from previous retirements and from net "gains" on sales of treasury stock of the same issue.

---

[1]"Status of Accounting Research Bulletins," *Opinions of the Accounting Principles Board, No. 6* (New York: American Institute of Certified Public Accountants, 1965), par. 12.

3. Any remaining excess may next be charged on an average-per-share basis against other paid-in capital in excess of par value accounts for the same issue.

4. Any remaining balance would be charged against Retained Earnings.

As an alternative, *Opinion No. 6* provides that the entire excess of repurchase price over par value may be charged against Retained Earnings in recognition of the fact that a corporation can always capitalize retained earnings for such purposes. For example, if a $75 par value preferred share originally issued at $80 is redeemed for $85, the following entry can be used to record the transaction.

19 X1					
Oct.	1	Preferred Stock (1 share)	311	75 00	
		Paid-in Capital in Excess of Par Value			
		of Preferred Stock	315	5 00	
		Retained Earnings	381	5 00	
		Cash	101		85 00
		To record redemption of one share of			
		$75 par value preferred stock originally			
		issued at $80.			

Redemption of preferred stock for less than the original issue price is discussed in Chapter 30.

PRINCIPLES AND PROCEDURES SUMMARY

The accounting records of a typical corporation include the usual journals and ledgers kept by any firm. In addition, corporations must keep special records. These records include minute books, stockholders' ledgers, stock certificate books, and stock transfer records.

The corporate charter specifies the types and amounts of capital stock authorized. The bylaws serve as guides for the general operations of the firm, which must be consistent with the charter provisions.

When capital stock is transferred, the seller completes the assignment form printed on the back of each stock certificate and surrenders the certificate for cancellation. New certificates are issued to the persons to whom the stock is transferred. A capital stock transfer journal is used to record the transactions, which are posted to the appropriate stockholders' sheets in the capital stock ledger. A corporation whose stock is more actively traded will usually employ a bank as its transfer agent (to keep the records of stock transfers) and its registrar (to account for all the stock issued by the corporation).

When stock is issued at a premium (more than par value), Cash is debited for the total amount received, the capital stock account is credited for the par value, and the premium is credited to Paid-in Capital in Excess of Par Value or a similar account.

In a few states, stock may also be issued at a discount (less than par value) although most state laws prohibit this. Again, Cash is debited for the total, the capital stock account is credited for par value, and the discount is debited to a discount on stock account. No-par value stock is often given a stated value, which serves the same purpose in accounting as does a par value.

Stock can be paid for and issued in a single transaction. It can also be subscribed for first, then paid for and issued at a later date. To record stock subscriptions, a corporation sets up a special subsidiary ledger, called a subscribers' ledger, with a separate account receivable for each subscriber. The individual accounts receivable are controlled by a Subscriptions Receivable account in the general ledger. The stock is issued when the subscription price has been fully paid. Sometimes subscribers fail to pay all the necessary installments on their subscriptions. Those who default on their payments may be treated in various ways according to state law and the policy of the corporation.

Treasury stock is stock that has been fully paid for, issued, and then reacquired by the corporation. Normally, treasury stock that has been purchased is recorded at cost.

Preferred stock may sometimes be redeemed and canceled by the issuing corporation. The capital stock account is debited for the par value, Cash is credited for the amount paid, and some other stockholders' equity account or accounts will be debited or credited for the difference.

MANAGERIAL IMPLICATIONS

Corporate management must be certain that it has adequate records to comply with legal requirements and to keep track of stockholder transactions. The bylaws and charter provisions of the corporation must be carefully followed, and minutes must be kept of all meetings of directors and stockholders. Actions of the board of directors, as reported in the corporate minutes, often have accounting effects that must be recognized and acted upon.

Management must be sure that capital stock issues are properly accounted for. State laws regarding the issuance of stock at a discount must be carefully observed. Management must also be fully informed about state laws concerning stock subscriptions and defaults and must be sure that the accounting records fully reflect all information relating to such transactions. The accounting records must also provide full data on treasury stock because of the detailed laws in most states that relate to such stock.

REVIEW QUESTIONS

1. Name five provisions commonly included in the articles of incorporation.
2. When par value stock is issued, what amount is credited to the capital stock account?
3. What is a proxy?
4. What is a proxy fight?
5. What are the bylaws of a corporation?
6. How are members of the board of directors of a corporation chosen?
7. Explain the purpose of the minute book.

8. Describe the information contained on a stock certificate.
9. What is a stock certificate book?
10. Explain the nature of a capital stock ledger.
11. What is an assignment of stock?
12. Describe the information contained in a capital stock transfer journal.
13. What functions are served by the transfer agent?
14. What role does the registrar serve?
15. How does a premium on stock arise?
16. Is a discount on stock a usual occurrence? Explain.
17. A corporation issues no-par value stock with a stated value of $1.50 a share at $28 a share. How is the transaction recorded?
18. How is the issuance of no-par value stock for cash usually recorded?
19. What is a stock subscription?
20. If there is a default on a stock subscription, what disposition is made of amounts previously paid in?
21. What is treasury stock?
22. How is the purchase of treasury stock recorded?
23. How is donated treasury stock accounted for?
24. A corporation "calls" its preferred stock and retires this stock. How is the purchase and retirement accounted for?

MANAGERIAL DISCUSSION QUESTIONS

1. Why would the management of a corporation seek to control votes at the stockholders' meeting?
2. Why must the management and directors of a corporation be fully informed about laws and regulations affecting corporations? How can they find out what they need to know?
3. How do you think the directors of the Duncan Lawn Furniture Corporation reached their decision to set the stated value of the no-par value common stock at $50?
4. Why would the management of a corporation be willing to sell its stock on a subscription basis, considering all the recordkeeping involved?
5. Why would the management of a corporation consider using corporate funds to purchase the firm's own outstanding stock?
6. Why would both management and stock subscribers be interested in the state laws that deal with defaulting subscribers?
7. The management of the O'Riley Corporation wishes to know why its common stock held as treasury stock should not be shown on the balance sheet as an asset since the stock has a ready market value. Explain.

EXERCISES

EXERCISE 29-1   **Recording the issuance of stock at par value.** The Ferris Corporation issued 2,000 shares of $10 par value common stock and 300 shares of 15 percent, $50 par value preferred stock for cash at par value. Give the entry in general journal form to record the issuance of the stock.

EXERCISE 29-2 **Recording the issuance of stock at a premium.** The Gorman Corporation issued 500 shares of its $20 par value common stock for cash at $31 a share. Give the entry in general journal form to record the issuance of the stock.

EXERCISE 29-3 **Recording the issuance of stock at a discount.** The Hickman Corporation operates in a state in which stock can be sold at a discount. The firm issued 2,000 shares of its $20 par value common stock for cash at $19.20 a share. Give the entry in general journal form to record the issuance of the stock.

EXERCISE 29-4 **Recording the issuance of no-par value common stock for more than the stated value.** The Ibriham Corporation issued 580 shares of its no-par value common stock (stated value, $2) for cash at $2.90 a share. Give the entry in general journal form to record the issuance of the stock.

EXERCISE 29-5 **Recording the receipt of a subscription for common stock.** On June 1, 19X2, the Jalinski Corporation received a subscription from Linda Kelso for 1,000 shares of its $25 par value common stock at a price of $30 a share. Give the entry in general journal form to record receipt of the subscription.

EXERCISE 29-6 **Recording the collection of a payment on a subscription.** Linda Kelso made a payment of $7.50 a share on the stock subscription described in Exercise 29-5. The cash was received on the date of the subscription. The balance is to be paid on July 1, 19X2. Give the entry in general journal form to record the collection of the payment made on the date of the subscription.

EXERCISE 29-7 **Recording the collection of the balance due on a subscription and the issuance of the stock.** Assume the same facts as in Exercises 29-5 and 29-6. On July 1, 19X2, Linda Kelso paid the balance due on her common stock subscription, and the stock was issued to her. Give the entries in general journal form to record the collection of the payment and the issuance of the stock.

EXERCISE 29-8 **Recording the purchase of treasury stock.** On August 1, 19X1, the LeMoyne Corporation repurchased 500 shares of its outstanding $50 par value common stock. The purchase price was $95 a share. The stock was originally issued at $55 a share. Give the entry in general journal form to record the purchase of the treasury stock.

EXERCISE 29-9 **Recording the resale of treasury stock for more than the purchase price.** On September 18, 19X1, the LeMoyne Corporation sold 100 shares of the treasury stock that it purchased on August 1, 19X1 (see Exercise 29-8). The sales price was $102 a share. Give the entry in general journal form to record the resale of the treasury stock.

EXERCISE 29-10 **Recording the resale of treasury stock for less than the purchase price.** Assume the same facts as in Exercises 29-8 and 29-9. On October 24, 19X1, the

LeMoyne Corporation sold an additional 200 shares of the treasury stock purchased on August 1, 19X1. The sales price was $74 a share. Give the entry in general journal form to record the resale of the treasury stock.

EXERCISE 29-11 **Recording the purchase and retirement of preferred stock.** The Martino Corporation has outstanding 10,000 shares of 12 percent, $20 par value preferred stock issued at $24 a share. On October 12, 19X1, the corporation "called" 1,000 shares of the stock at $30 a share and retired them. Give the entry in general journal form to record the purchase and retirement of the preferred stock.

PROBLEMS

PROBLEM 29-1 **Recording the acquisition of assets for stock and the payment of organization costs.** The Majestic Art Gallery, Inc., was formed on January 2, 19X2, to take over the operations of a sole proprietorship business owned by Ellen Moore. The assets and liabilities to be transferred to the corporation are as follows.

Cash	$ 1,800
Accounts Receivable	9,500
Merchandise Inventory	42,000
Furniture and Equipment	6,000
Notes Payable	2,000
Accounts Payable	4,000

The corporation is to issue to Moore sufficient shares of $20 par value 12 percent preferred stock to cover the amount of cash and accounts receivable transferred. The corporation will also issue sufficient shares of no-par value, $50 stated value common stock to cover the remainder of the net assets transferred. In addition, Moore is to be issued 20 shares of common stock in payment for her $1,000 fee for organizing the corporation.

Instructions In general journal form, record the following transactions of the corporation on January 2, 19X2.

1. The acquisition of the assets and liabilities by the corporation and the liability to Moore.
2. The issuance of preferred and common shares to Moore for the net assets transferred.
3. The issuance of 20 shares of common stock to Moore for organizing the corporation.

PROBLEM 29-2 **Recording the issuance of stock for cash and establishing the capital stock ledger.** The Vista Corporation was organized to market high-quality cameras, lenses, and other photographic equipment. The firm is authorized to issue 20,000 shares of no-par value common stock with a stated value of $25 a share and 20,000 shares of 14 percent noncumulative and nonparticipating preferred stock with a par value of $50 a share. The shares of stock sold for cash are shown on page 682.

STOCK SOLD FOR CASH
COMMON STOCK ISSUED AT $25

800 shares—Paul Fazio (Certificate C-1)
1,700 shares—Stanley Hayes (Certificate C-2)
2,000 shares—Ann McGill (Certificate C-3)
1,500 shares—Donald Peters (Certificate C-4)

PREFERRED STOCK ISSUED AT $50

500 shares—Joyce Barry (Certificate P-1)
800 shares—Lois Durant (Certificate P-2)
1,500 shares—Paul Fazio (Certificate P-3)
1,000 shares—Aaron Gold (Certificate P-4)

Instructions 1. Record in general journal form the receipt of cash in payment for the shares of stock listed above and the issuance of the stock on January 2, 19X1. Use a single entry.
2. Prepare the common and preferred capital stock ledger sheets for the individual stockholders, and post the above entry to the sheets.

(Note: Save all papers for use in Problem 29-3.)

PROBLEM 29-3 **Recording stock transfers.** This is a continuation of Problem 29-2. The same data applies. Use the capital stock ledger sheets already prepared.

Instructions 1. Prepare a common stock transfer journal, and record the transfer required by the sale of 850 shares of common stock by Stanley Hayes (Certificate C-2) to Eric Olson on March 14, 19X1. Certificate C-5 was issued to Hayes and Certificate C-6 to Olson. Open an account for Olson. Post to the capital stock ledger.
2. Prepare the general journal entry required to record the issuance on June 8, 19X1, of 300 shares of common stock, paid in cash at stated value, to Eric Olson (Certificate C-7). Post to the capital stock ledger.
3. Prepare a preferred stock transfer journal, and record the transfer of 200 shares of the preferred stock issued to Lois Durant (Certificate P-2) to John Ramos on June 18, 19X1. Certificate P-5 was issued to Durant and Certificate P-6 to Ramos. Open an account for Ramos. Post to the capital stock ledger.
4. Prepare the general journal entry on July 16, 19X1, to record the issuance of 200 shares of preferred stock to Aaron Gold, paid in cash at par value (Certificate P-7). Post to the capital stock ledger.
5. From the capital stock ledgers, prepare a list of the common stockholders and a list of the preferred stockholders and show the number of shares of each type of stock owned by each stockholder.

PROBLEM 29-4 **Recording stock subscriptions.** Blue Ribbon Auto Dealers, Inc., was organized on January 2, 19X1, to operate a chain of used-car lots. The firm is authorized to issue 20,000 shares of $20 par value common stock and 9,000 shares of $50 par value 13 percent preferred stock. The preferred stock is noncumulative and nonparticipating. Selected transactions that took place during January 19X1 are shown on page 683.

Instructions   1. Set up the following general ledger accounts.

        101   Cash
        114   Subscriptions Receivable—Common Stock
        115   Subscriptions Receivable—Preferred Stock
        301   Common Stock
        302   Common Stock Subscribed
        305   Paid-in Capital in Excess of Par Value—Common
        311   Preferred Stock
        312   Preferred Stock Subscribed
        315   Paid-in Capital in Excess of Par Value—Preferred

2. Record the transactions listed below in general journal form, and post them to the general ledger accounts.
3. Prepare the Stockholders' Equity section of a balance sheet for Blue Ribbon Auto Dealers, Inc., as of January 31, 19X1.

TRANSACTIONS FOR JANUARY 19X1

Jan.   2 The corporation received its corporate charter. (Make a memorandum entry.)

       3 Issued 1,000 shares of common stock for cash at $20 a share to John DeLorenzo (Certificate C-1).

       3 Issued 500 shares of preferred stock for cash at $50 a share to Lynn Hodges (Certificate P-1).

     10 Issued 200 shares of common stock for cash at $21 a share to Mark LaSalle (Certificate C-2).

     10 Received a subscription for 500 shares of common stock at $21 a share from Janet Thompson, payable in two installments due in 5 and 15 days.

     14 Received a subscription for 400 shares of preferred stock at $52 a share from George Wesley, payable in two installments due in 10 and 20 days.

     15 Received payment of a stock subscription installment due from Janet Thompson (one-half of purchase price—see the January 10 transaction).

     24 Received payment of a stock subscription installment due from George Wesley (one-half of purchase price—see the January 14 transaction).

     25 Received the balance due on the stock subscription of January 10 from Janet Thompson. Issued the stock (Certificate C-3).

PROBLEM 29-5   **Recording treasury stock purchases and stock subscriptions.** As of December 31, 19X2, the stockholders' equity of Classic Home Furnishings Inc. consisted of common stock (no-par value, $50 stated value, 50,000 shares authorized), 4,000 shares issued ($200,000), and preferred stock (14 percent cumulative, nonparticipating, $20 par value, 25,000 shares authorized), 4,000 shares issued ($80,000). Selected stock transactions that took place during 19X3 are shown on page 684.

Instructions
1. Analyze each of the stock transactions, and record it in general journal form. Use account titles similar to those in the text.
2. Open a general ledger for the accounts listed in the general journal entries. Record the December 31, 19X2, balances given.
3. Post the general journal entries to the general ledger.
4. Prepare the Stockholders' Equity section of the balance sheet for Classic Home Furnishings Inc. as of April 30, 19X3.

TRANSACTIONS FOR 19X3

Jan. 15 Received cash from Eileen Collins for 200 shares of common stock at $52 a share and issued the stock.

Mar. 3 Received cash from Ralph Rodino for 500 shares of preferred stock at $23 a share and issued the stock.

Apr. 15 Rita Chang subscribed to 1,000 shares of preferred stock at $24 a share, paying $12,000 in cash today. The balance is to be paid in cash on May 15.

18 Stewart McNab subscribed to 400 shares of common stock at $53 a share, paying $10,600 in cash today. The balance is to be paid on May 18.

25 The corporation purchased from Ralph Rodino, at $23.50 a share, 50 shares of its own preferred stock for cash. The stock was originally issued at $23 a share. Record the purchase on the cost basis. (Use the Treasury Stock—Preferred 319 account.)

29 The corporation purchased 100 shares of its own common stock for $54 a share, in cash, from Eileen Collins. The stock was originally issued at $52 a share. Record the purchase on the cost basis. (Use the Treasury Stock—Common 309 account.)

PROBLEM 29-6 **Recording treasury stock transactions and the retirement of preferred stock.** The Star Corporation, a manufacturer of sporting goods, has 9,000 shares of 11 percent, $50 par value preferred stock and 8,000 shares of $50 par value common stock outstanding on January 1, 19X2. Preferred stock was issued at $52 a share and common stock at $55 a share. Selected transactions that took place during 19X2 are shown below.

Instructions
1. Give the entries in general journal form to record the transactions listed. Use the cost method to record all treasury stock transactions. (Omit explanations to save time.)
2. Prepare the Stockholders' Equity section of the balance sheet after the transaction of October 13. (The corporation is authorized to issue 20,000 shares of preferred stock and 30,000 shares of common stock.) Assume that the ending balance of Retained Earnings is $285,600.

TRANSACTIONS FOR 19X2

Jan. 17 The corporation repurchased on the open market 100 shares of its own common stock at $56 a share to be held as treasury stock.

Apr. 12 The corporation repurchased on the open market 150 shares of its own common stock at $57 a share to be held as treasury stock.

May 23 The corporation repurchased 200 shares of its own preferred stock at $55 a share and retired them.

July 26 The corporation sold, at $57 a share, the treasury stock that was acquired on January 17.

Oct. 13 The corporation sold 50 shares, for $56.50 a share, of the treasury stock acquired on April 12.

ALTERNATE PROBLEMS

PROBLEM 29-1A **Recording the acquisition of assets for stock and the payment of organization costs.** Western Leather Goods, Inc., was formed on June 1, 19X1, to take over the operations of a sole proprietorship business owned by Joseph Diaz. The assets and liabilities to be transferred to the corporation by Diaz are as follows.

Cash	$ 3,000
Accounts Receivable	16,000
Merchandise Inventory	44,000
Equipment	8,000
Notes Payable	6,000
Accounts Payable	5,000

The corporation is to issue sufficient shares of $50 par value 13 percent preferred stock to cover the cash that Diaz transferred. The corporation will also issue sufficient shares of $20 par value common stock to cover the remainder of the net assets transferred. In addition, the directors feel that Diaz's work and expenses in organizing the corporation are worth $800 and that he should therefore receive 40 shares of common stock as reimbursement.

Instructions In general journal form, record the following transactions of the corporation on June 1, 19X1.

1. The acquisition of the assets and liabilities by the corporation and the liability to Diaz.
2. The issuance of the shares to Diaz for the net assets transferred.
3. The issuance of 40 shares of common stock to Diaz for organizing the corporation.

PROBLEM 29-2A **Recording the issuance of stock for cash and establishing the capital stock ledger.** The Ace Manufacturing Corporation was formed for the purpose of producing digital watches. It is authorized to issue 40,000 shares of no-par value common stock with a stated value of $50 a share and 50,000 shares of 13 percent noncumulative and nonparticipating preferred stock with a par value of $25 a share. The shares of stock sold for cash are shown below and on page 686.

STOCK SOLD FOR CASH
COMMON STOCK ISSUED AT $50

6,000 shares—Daniel Costa (Certificate C-1)
3,000 shares—Louise Hart (Certificate C-2)
3,000 shares—Susan Miller (Certificate C-3)
3,000 shares—Patrick O'Leary (Certificate C-4)

2,000 shares—Daniel Costa (Certificate P-1)
1,000 shares—Louise Hart (Certificate P-2)
1,000 shares—Susan Miller (Certificate P-3)
1,000 shares—Patrick O'Leary (Certificate P-4)

Instructions

1. Record in general journal form the receipt of cash in payment for the shares of stock listed and the issuance of the stock on March 1, 19X1. Use a single entry.
2. Prepare the common and preferred capital stock ledger sheets for the individual stockholders, and post the above entry to the sheets.

(Note: Save all papers for use in Problem 29-3A.)

PROBLEM 29-3A

Recording stock transfers. This is a continuation of Problem 29-2A. The same data applies. Use the capital stock ledger sheets already prepared.

Instructions

1. Prepare a common stock transfer journal, and record the transfer required by the sale of 1,000 shares of common stock by Daniel Costa (Certificate C-1) to Gary Reed on June 15, 19X1. Certificate C-5 was issued to Costa and Certificate C-6 to Reed. Open an account for Reed. Post to the capital stock ledger.
2. Prepare the general journal entry required to record the issuance on July 1, 19X1, of 500 shares of common stock, paid in cash at stated value, to Susan Miller (Certificate C-7). Post to the capital stock ledger.
3. Prepare a preferred stock transfer journal, and record the transfer of 500 shares of the preferred stock issued to Patrick O'Leary (Certificate P-4) to Kathleen O'Leary on August 1, 19X1. Certificate P-5 was issued to Patrick O'Leary and Certificate P-6 to Kathleen O'Leary. Open an account for Kathleen O'Leary. Post to the capital stock ledger.
4. Prepare the general journal entry required to record the issuance on August 15, 19X1, of 250 shares of preferred stock to David Wallace, paid in cash at par value (Certificate P-7). Post to the capital stock ledger.
5. From the capital stock ledgers, prepare a list of the common stockholders and a list of the preferred stockholders and show the number of shares of each type of stock owned by each stockholder.

PROBLEM 29-4A

Recording stock subscriptions. The Melody Corporation was organized on July 1, 19X1, to manufacture musical instruments. The firm is authorized to issue 20,000 shares of $50 par value common stock and 9,000 shares of $50 par value 12 percent preferred stock that is nonparticipating and noncumulative. Selected transactions that took place during July 19X1 are shown on page 687.

Instructions

1. Set up the following general ledger accounts.

101 Cash
114 Subscriptions Receivable—Common Stock
115 Subscriptions Receivable—Preferred Stock
301 Common Stock
302 Common Stock Subscribed

305   Paid-in Capital in Excess of Par Value—Common
311   Preferred Stock
312   Preferred Stock Subscribed
315   Paid-in Capital in Excess of Par Value—Preferred

2. Record the transactions listed below in general journal form, and post them to the general ledger accounts.

3. Prepare the Stockholders' Equity section of a balance sheet for the Melody Corporation, as of July 31, 19X1.

TRANSACTIONS FOR JULY 19X1

July   1 The corporation received its charter. (Make a memorandum entry.)

        1 Issued 300 shares of common stock for cash at $50 a share to Alice Clayton (Certificate C-1).

        2 Issued 250 shares of preferred stock for cash at par value to Jacob Green (Certificate P-1).

        5 Issued 150 shares of common stock for cash at $52 to Frank Oliva (Certificate C-2).

      10 Received a subscription for 200 shares of common stock at $53 a share from Diane Norris, payable in two installments due in 10 and 20 days.

      12 Received a subscription for 100 shares of preferred stock at $52 a share from Richard Selby, payable in two installments due in 15 and 30 days.

      20 Received payment of a stock subscription installment due from Diane Norris (one-half of the purchase price—see the July 10 transaction).

      27 Received payment of a stock subscription installment due from Richard Selby (one-half of the purchase price—see the July 12 transaction).

      30 Received the balance due on the stock subscription of July 10 from Diane Norris. Issued the stock (Certificate C-3).

PROBLEM 29-5A **Recording treasury stock purchases and stock subscriptions.** As of December 31, 19X2, the Trade Winds Corporation, a manufacturer of sailboats, had stockholders' equity that consisted of common stock ($20 stated value, 30,000 shares authorized), 600 shares issued ($12,000), and preferred stock (14 percent, noncumulative, nonparticipating, $80 par value, 12,000 shares authorized), 1,000 shares issued ($80,000). Selected stock transactions that took place during 19X3 are listed on page 688.

Instructions 1. Analyze each of the stock transactions, and record it in general journal form. Use account titles similar to those in the text.

2. Open a general ledger for the accounts listed in the general journal entries. Record the December 31, 19X2, balances given.

3. Post the general journal entries to the general ledger.

4. Prepare the Stockholders' Equity section of the balance sheet of the Trade Winds Corporation as of June 30, 19X3.

TRANSACTIONS FOR 19X3

Jan. 20 Received cash from Sharon Rogers for 100 shares of preferred stock at par and issued the stock.

Feb. 12 Received cash from John Schiller for 100 shares of common stock at $21 a share and issued the stock.

Mar. 10 Received cash from Hugh McManus for 200 shares of preferred stock at $81 a share and issued the stock.

Apr. 1 Gail Dobbs subscribed to 50 shares of preferred stock at $78 a share, paying $2,000 in cash today. The balance is to be paid in cash on July 1.

May 15 Alan Bernstein subscribed to 200 shares of common stock at $19 a share, paying $1,800 in cash today. The balance is to be paid in cash on July 15.

June 5 The corporation purchased 10 shares of its own preferred stock for cash from Robert Bailey at $80 a share. The stock was originally sold and issued at par. Record the purchase on the cost basis. (Use the Treasury Stock—Preferred 319 account.)

30 The corporation purchased 20 shares of its own common stock for cash from Helen Dwight at $20 a share. The stock was originally sold and issued at $21 a share. Record the purchase on the cost basis. (Use the Treasury Stock—Common 309 account.)

PROBLEM 29-6A **Recording treasury stock transactions and the retirement of preferred stock.** Denim Fashions Inc., a manufacturer of clothing, has 2,000 shares of 11 percent, $40 par value preferred stock and 6,000 shares of $50 par value common stock outstanding on January 1, 19X1. The common stock was issued at par. The preferred stock was issued at $42 a share. Selected transactions that took place during 19X1 are listed below.

Instructions 1. Give the entries in general journal form to record the listed transactions. Use the cost method to record all treasury stock transactions. (Omit explanations to save time.)

2. Prepare the Stockholders' Equity section of the balance sheet after the transaction of September 19. (The corporation is authorized to issue 20,000 shares of preferred stock and 30,000 shares of common stock.) Assume that the ending balance of Retained Earnings is $417,500.

TRANSACTIONS FOR 19X1

Feb. 5 The corporation repurchased on the open market 30 shares of its own common stock at $80 a share, to be held as treasury stock.

May 4 The corporation repurchased on the open market 70 shares of its own common stock at $82 a share, to be held as treasury stock.

July 2 The corporation paid $46 a share to redeem and retire 25 shares of its own preferred stock.

Aug. 21 The corporation sold for $86 a share the treasury stock that was acquired on February 5.

Sept. 19 The corporation sold 20 shares, at $80 a share, of the treasury stock acquired on May 4.

The successful operation of a corporation is of vital concern to a number of groups—stockholders, managers and employees, creditors, and the community where the firm is located. For example, the stockholders hope that profits will justify the declaration of dividends or result in an increased value for their stock. Various governmental units are also interested because the corporation's income represents a potential source of revenue through taxes. This chapter explains how accountants determine the corporation's net income, record estimated income taxes due, show the results on the statements, and distribute profits to stockholders.

CORPORATION EARNINGS AND CAPITAL TRANSACTIONS

DETERMINING CORPORATE NET INCOME

The matching of normal and recurring expenses with revenues by time periods, preferably on the accrual basis, is handled in a corporation's accounting records according to the same principles and procedures used for other types of businesses. The net income or net loss is determined by subtracting expenses from revenue. Ultimately, the results of operations are described in summary form on the firm's periodic income statements. Certain items of revenue or expense require special consideration. These are known as *extraordinary, nonrecurring items.*

Current Operating Concept

Some accountants argue that judgment must be used in selecting the items to present on the income statement. They say significant amounts representing *prior period adjustments* (primarily corrections of errors of previous periods), gains or losses on the sale of assets not held for resale, and losses from casualties such as fire might mislead statement users if these items are included on the income statement. This view, called the *current operating concept*, holds that only normally recurring items of profit and loss should appear on the income statement. Nonrecurring gains and losses should be credited or debited directly to the Retained Earnings account. However, the current operating concept has little authoritative support today.

The All-Inclusive Concept

Some accountants maintain that *every item* of profit or loss—for example, even corrections of prior years' errors—should be included on the income statement. This view is known as the *historical* or *all-inclusive concept*. The generally accepted position today is a modified all-inclusive approach, which holds that almost all items of profit and loss should be reported on the income statement but that in some cases the income statement should be divided into two distinct parts. The first part of the income statement should report the income arising from ordinary, recurring operations. The second part should report gains or losses arising from extraordinary, nonrecurring items. These gains or losses are added to or subtracted from the net income from operations in order to arrive at the final net income figure.

However, very few items meet the requirements specified in *Opinion No. 30* of the Accounting Principles Board to qualify as extraordinary items. Those requirements are as follows.

> Extraordinary items are events and transactions that are distinguished by their unusual nature *and* by the infrequency of their occurrence. Thus, *both* of the following criteria should be met to classify an event or transaction as an extraordinary item:
>
> (a) *Unusual nature*—the underlying event or transaction should possess a high degree of abnormality and be of a type clearly unrelated to, or only incidentally related to, the ordinary and typical activities of the entity, taking into account the environment in which the entity operates.
>
> (b) *Infrequency of occurrence*—the underlying event or transaction should be of a type that would not reasonably be expected to recur in the foreseeable future, taking into account the environment in which the entity operates.[1]

Under this concept almost no gains or losses are entered directly in the Retained Earnings account. The major items affecting profit and loss to be entered in the Retained Earnings account are prior period adjustments—mainly corrections of errors made in prior periods.[2] However, settlement in the current period of lawsuits or other litigation initiated in a prior period is not a prior period correction and is therefore not treated as an adjustment of Retained Earnings.[3]

A hypothetical income statement reflecting extraordinary gains and losses is illustrated on page 691. Notice that the gross amount of each extraordinary item of gain or loss is shown and the related effect on income taxes is offset against it so that the item is reported "net of taxes." Some accountants prefer to show only the net amount and to indicate the gross amount and the tax effect in a parenthetical note.

NET INCOME AND INCOME TAXES

At the end of the fiscal period, a worksheet is prepared for a corporation in much the same manner as for a sole proprietorship or a partnership. After the trial balance has been recorded on the worksheet, adjustments have been entered, and the adjusted amounts have been extended to the Income Statement and Balance Sheet sections, the debit and credit columns of the Income Statement section are totaled. Then the income tax on the net difference is estimated and recorded, along with the net income remaining after the tax. The amount of income tax due is estimated rather than waiting for the tax return to be prepared so that completion of the corporation's financial statements will not be delayed at the end of the period.

Estimating the Tax

The estimate of the income tax is based not only on the corporation's income but also on the tax rates in force at the time, the type of income involved, the tax

---

[1] "Reporting the Results of Operations," *Opinions of the Accounting Principles Board, No. 30* (New York: American Institute of Certified Public Accountants, 1973), par. 20.

[2] "Reporting the Results of Operations," *Opinions of the Accounting Principles Board, No. 9* (New York: American Institute of Certified Public Accountants, 1966), par. 23.

[3] "Prior Period Adjustments," *Statement of Financial Accounting Standards, No. 16* (Stamford, Conn.: Financial Accounting Standards Board, 1977), par. 10.

BRISTOL CORPORATION
Income Statement
Year Ended December 31, 19X1

Revenues		
Sales	$1,738,730	
Other Operating Revenues	9,670	
Total Revenues		$1,748,400
Costs and Expenses		
Cost of Goods Sold	$ 766,480	
Research and Development Expense	45,650	
Depreciation Expense	42,420	
Branch Expense and Commissions	430,330	
Selling, Advertising, General, and		
Administrative Expenses	184,140	
Other Operating Expenses	1,160	
Total Costs and Expenses		1,470,180
Net Income From Operations Before Income Taxes		$ 278,220
Income Taxes Applicable to Operating Income		131,552
Net Income From Operations After Income Taxes		$ 146,668

Extraordinary Gains and Losses			
Add Gain on Condemnation of			
Land by City	$10,000		
Less Federal Taxes on Gain	3,000	$ 7,000	
Deduct Tornado Loss on Building	$ 8,000		
Less Federal Tax Reduction	3,840	4,160	
Excess of Extraordinary Gains Over Losses			2,840
Net Income for Year			$ 149,508

credits available, and other factors. As pointed out in Chapter 25, federal income tax rates are changed periodically by Congress. As of this writing, the rates are as follows.

On the first $25,000 of taxable income, 15 percent
On the next $25,000 of taxable income, 18 percent
On the next $25,000 of taxable income, 30 percent
On the next $25,000 of taxable income, 40 percent
On all income above $100,000, 46 percent

Some types of income receive special tax treatment. For example, gains and losses on the sale of some assets, such as investments in securities, may be taxed at a rate of no more than 28 percent if the assets are held for more than 12 months. Interest received on state and local bonds held for investment is not taxed at all. Some types of expenses are also given special tax treatment. For example, straight-line depreciation may be deducted for financial accounting purposes while accelerated cost recovery system (ACRS) deductions are taken on the tax return. In addition, the period for deducting expenses or the time of reporting income may differ between the tax return and the financial statements. Income received in advance is almost always taxed in the year received, while for financial accounting purposes, it is reported as income only over the periods to which it applies. Thus the net income reported for federal income tax purposes and for financial accounting purposes may differ greatly. The result may be that the income tax paid in a period may not reflect the tax that must ultimately be paid on the income reported to shareholders in that period.

Deferred Income Taxes

In order to present fairly to users of the corporation's financial statements the ultimate tax liability for the net income shown on the income statement, accountants have developed the concept of *deferred income taxes*. In accordance with this concept, they show as an expense on the income statement the ultimate tax liability for the income presented. The difference between the tax actually paid during the period and the amount that will ultimately be paid for the income is recorded as the deferred tax amount. This process is very complicated and is discussed in detail in all intermediate accounting textbooks. For our purposes we shall assume that the income shown on the income statement and the income reported on the tax return are essentially the same, which makes deferred taxes immaterial.

Recording the Estimated Tax on the Worksheet

The amount of the estimated tax is entered on the worksheet as a debit in the Income Statement section and a credit in the Balance Sheet section. The self-explanatory title, Provision for Income Taxes, is recorded in the Account Name column. Then the net income after income taxes is entered in the same columns, and the worksheet is completed. The illustration below shows how the last step would appear on the worksheet of the Duncan Lawn Furniture Corporation at the end of its first year of operations. It assumes that Duncan's accountant estimated the income tax liability at $12,800.

ACCOUNT NAME	INCOME STATEMENT		BALANCE SHEET	
	DEBIT	CREDIT	DEBIT	CREDIT
	429,358 36	494,653 08	377,884 72	312,590 00
Provision for Income Taxes	12,800 00			12,800 00
Net Income After Income Taxes	52,494 72			52,494 72
	494,653 08	494,653 08	377,884 72	377,884 72

STATEMENT PRESENTATION

A corporation's financial statements ordinarily include an income statement, a balance sheet, and a statement of retained earnings. The net income and income tax items affect each statement. Other types of presentations can be made, but the methods described and illustrated here are typical.

Income Statement

Income taxes are usually deducted at the bottom of the income statement from the figure entitled Net Income Before Income Taxes. This deduction is illustrated below for the Duncan Lawn Furniture Corporation.

Net Income Before Income Taxes	$65,294.72
Provision for Income Taxes	12,800.00
Net Income After Income Taxes	$52,494.72

As you saw in the income statement on page 691, any income tax reduction or addition resulting from extraordinary gains or losses should be matched with the gain or loss to which it applies. Only the income tax that applies to operating income should be deducted from the operating income figure. Sometimes income taxes are listed with operating expenses such as salaries, depreciation, and other routine items.

Balance Sheet

The partial balance sheet shown below lists the provision for income taxes figure of $12,800 as a current liability called Estimated Income Taxes Payable. The amount of retained earnings appearing on the balance sheet is ordinarily the balance in the Retained Earnings account after all adjusting and closing entries have been posted. This is also the final amount shown on the statement of retained earnings on page 700.

Liabilities and Stockholders' Equity

Current Liabilities			
Accounts Payable		$ 36,000.00	
Dividends Payable—Preferred		16,800.00	
Dividends Payable—Common		8,000.00	
Accrued Expenses Payable		4,300.00	
Estimated Income Taxes Payable		12,800.00	
Total Liabilities			$ 77,900.00
Stockholders' Equity			
Preferred Stock (12%, $100 par value, 2,000 shares authorized)			
At Par Value (1,400 shares issued)	$140,000.00		
Paid-in Capital in Excess of Par Value	6,000.00	$146,000.00	
Common Stock (no-par value, stated value of $50, 10,000 shares authorized)			
At Stated Value (2,000 shares issued)	$100,000.00		
Paid-in Capital in Excess of Stated Value	800.00	100,800.00	
Retained Earnings		27,694.72	
Total Stockholders' Equity			274,494.72
Total Liabilities and Stockholders' Equity			$352,394.72

Statement of Retained Earnings

The statement of retained earnings starts with the balance of the Retained Earnings account at the beginning of the period and shows all the changes that have taken place during the period. In the case of the Duncan Lawn Furniture Corporation, one of these changes is the addition of the $52,494.72 net income figure previously illustrated. The statement of retained earnings prepared for the Duncan Lawn Furniture Corporation is presented later in this chapter.

ENTERING INCOME TAXES AND TRANSFERRING NET INCOME

After the adjusting entries have been recorded and posted, the closing entries are prepared for the corporation from the information assembled on the worksheet. The recording procedure is the same as that used for a sole proprietorship or a partnership, except for the last entry. The final closing entry for a corporation closes out the balance of the Income Summary account, sets up the liability for Estimated Income Taxes Payable, and transfers the net income after income taxes to Retained Earnings.

The partial worksheet illustrated on page 692 would result in the final closing entry shown below.

19 X2				
Dec. 31	Income Summary	399	65,294 72	
	Estimated Income Taxes Payable	219		12,800 00
	Retained Earnings	381		52,494 72
	To set up estimated income taxes and close net income after income taxes to Retained Earnings.			

PRIOR PERIOD ADJUSTMENTS

Earlier in this chapter it was explained that today an all-inclusive concept is used to determine corporate net income. Under the "pure" all-inclusive concept, no direct entries are made in Retained Earnings for any items of gain or loss recognized during the year. The only entries made in the Retained Earnings account are for the transfer of the net income or net loss after income taxes at the end of the year, for dividends declared, and for setting up and closing out reserves of retained earnings. (In older terminology this was called the *clean surplus concept.*) As you have learned, however, authoritative bodies today favor a modified version of the all-inclusive concept. Under this version a very limited number of items, primarily prior period adjustments, can be entered directly in the Retained Earnings account.

The procedure for handling prior period adjustments can be illustrated with an example of a correction relating to a prior period. Suppose a used truck having an estimated life of five years and a salvage value of $1,000 was purchased on January 2, 19X1, for $7,000. Its purchase was erroneously charged to Delivery Expense instead of Delivery Equipment. The error was discovered at the end of October of the current year, 19X2. How should it be corrected?

Actually, there are two errors involved. One is the charge of $7,000 to the Delivery Expense account on January 2, 19X1, instead of the correct charge to the Delivery Equipment account (overstating expenses and understating assets). The second error is that no depreciation was taken on the truck in 19X1, since the entire cost was written off as an expense when the truck was purchased. Thus expenses were overstated in one respect and understated in another.

If the amount to be corrected is substantial, it should be entered in the Retained Earnings account. The procedure calls for the following steps.

1. Recording the original cost of the truck in the proper asset account.
2. Crediting Accumulated Depreciation—Delivery Equipment for the amount that should have been entered in 19X1.
3. Entering the difference as a direct adjustment to Retained Earnings.

In the journal entry shown below, straight-line depreciation is assumed. Depreciation for 19X2 will be recorded among the usual end-of-year adjustments.

19 X2					
Oct. 31	Delivery Equipment	146	7,000 00		
	Accumulated Depreciation—Delivery				
	Equipment	147		1,200 00	
	Retained Earnings	381		5,800 00	
	To correct error made January 2, 19X1, when truck was charged to Delivery Expense instead of Delivery Equipment; and to credit Accumulated Depreciation for last year's depreciation on a straight-line basis, five-year life, $1,000 salvage value.				

$$\frac{\$7,000 - \$1,000}{5} = \$1,200 \text{ per year}$$

If the prior period error to be corrected is not substantial and is therefore to be shown on the income statement, the accountant records the facts by using this procedure.

1. Recording the asset at original cost by debiting the asset account.
2. Crediting a special revenue account called Gain From Correction of Prior Year's Delivery Expense for the cost of the asset.

The accountant then corrects the depreciation omission for the prior year (19X1) by doing the following.

1. Debiting a special expense account called Correction of Prior Year's Depreciation Expense—Delivery Equipment for $1,200, the amount of depreciation not recorded in 19X1. (Alternatively, the prior year's depreciation could have been debited to the current year's depreciation expense account.)
2. Crediting Accumulated Depreciation—Delivery Equipment for the amount that should have been entered in 19X1.

The illustration on page 696 shows how these corrections would be recorded in one compound entry.

19X2					
Oct. 31	Delivery Equipment		146	7,000 00	
	Correction of Prior Year's Depreciation				
	Expense—Delivery Equipment		646	1,200 00	
	Accumulated Depreciation—				
	Delivery Equipment		147		1,200 00
	Gain From Correction of Prior				
	Year's Delivery Expense		432		7,000 00
	To record correction of error made				
	when January 2, 19X1 purchase of				
	truck was charged to Delivery Expense.				

Depreciation for the current year (19X2) will be recorded in the usual manner at the close of the period. Over the two-year interval, the total depreciation expense will be found by adding together the amounts in the Depreciation Expense—Delivery Equipment account and the Correction of Prior Year's Depreciation Expense—Delivery Equipment account.

APPROPRIATIONS OF RETAINED EARNINGS

The amount in the Retained Earnings account provides one indication of a corporation's ability to pay dividends because ordinary dividends to stockholders are generally distributions of retained earnings. However, all or part of retained earnings is usually reinvested in plant assets or working capital rather than distributed as dividends. In some cases, distribution of dividends may be restricted by contract—for example, in connection with a bond issue. How can these limitations be indicated on the financial statements?

One way of presenting such information is by adding a footnote to the balance sheet. The footnote states that management's plans or contractual obligations will probably affect the dividends that will be declared. A more formal way for the board of directors to show this intention is to *appropriate* part of the retained earnings by resolution at a formal meeting.

Suppose, for example, that after several years of successful operations, the directors of the Duncan Lawn Furniture Corporation foresee the need to build a warehouse costing $200,000 within the next five years. Construction of the new building will put a financial strain on the corporation. The directors therefore wish to restrict dividend payments and to notify the stockholders that the new storage facility is to be built and that dividends are to be restricted. A resolution is passed at a board meeting in November 19X4 to order the transfer of $40,000 from Retained Earnings to a Retained Earnings Appropriated for Warehouse Construction account. Similar appropriations will be made during each of the next four years. (Appropriations of retained earnings are sometimes called *reserves*. For example, an account showing appropriated amounts might be called Reserve for Warehouse Construction.)

The resolution appropriating $40,000 in 19X4 for the warehouse would be recorded in the minutes and would serve as the accountant's authorization to make the general journal entry shown on page 697. A similar entry is made during each of the succeeding four years.

	19	X4					
Nov.	5	Retained Earnings	381	40,000	00		
		Retained Earnings Appropriated for					
		Warehouse Construction	382			40,000	00
		To set up an appropriation for					
		construction of a new warehouse as					
		ordered by board of directors in					
		meeting of November 5.					

The balance sheet presentation of Retained Earnings indicates the amounts appropriated and unappropriated. The specific reserves are listed under the Appropriated heading. Assume that Retained Earnings for the Duncan Lawn Furniture Corporation amounted to $135,290.50 before the first appropriation was made. The following illustration shows how the figures would appear on a balance sheet prepared immediately thereafter.

Retained Earnings
  Appropriated
    Appropriated for Warehouse Construction $40,000.00
  Unappropriated   95,290.50

      Total Retained Earnings $135,290.50

Notice that the Total Retained Earnings figure is the same as before, but it is now divided into two parts—the appropriated portion from which dividends cannot, for the moment at least, be declared and the unappropriated balance available for any purpose. Remember, however, that retained earnings do not represent cash balances. Nor does reserving retained earnings provide the cash for any desired purpose. The availability of cash therefore influences the timing of the actual work of building the new warehouse.

Assume that cash is available and that the previously mentioned warehouse construction project is completed in 19X9 at a cost of $223,000. The effect of the project has been to increase plant assets by $223,000 and to decrease Cash by that amount. (The balance in the Retained Earnings Appropriated for Warehouse Construction account has not been affected.) Now that the project is finished, the board of directors can pass another resolution to return the amount of the reserve to unappropriated retained earnings. When such a resolution has been adopted, the entry shown below is made in the general journal. (The board of directors may prefer to wait until some future time to eliminate the appropriation.)

	19	X9					
Aug.	7	Retained Earnings Appropriated for					
		Warehouse Construction	382	200,000	00		
		Retained Earnings	381			200,000	00
		To return to Retained Earnings the					
		balance in Retained Earnings Appro-					
		priated for Warehouse Construction as					
		ordered by board of directors in					
		its meeting of August 7, following					
		completion of the new building.					

The board can use the reserve technique to notify stockholders of its intention to undertake virtually any type of activity that will affect the amount and probability of dividends. When the purpose for which retained earnings have been appropriated is attained, the board can direct that the reserve be closed and that the amount be transferred back to Retained Earnings.

The board of directors of a large corporation that has many geographically scattered and uninformed stockholders may regard appropriations of retained earnings as an extremely important precaution. These appropriations may not be so necessary in a small corporation whose few stockholders are fully informed about daily operations.

DIVIDENDS

The board of directors of a corporation has broad powers in declaring and paying dividends (which are ordinarily distributions of earnings). The board must weigh two basic considerations in connection with ordinary dividends—their legality and their financial feasibility.

Legality

State laws differ with respect to the conditions under which a board of directors can declare a dividend. In some states, the corporation must have accumulated earnings. In other states, dividends can be declared out of contributed capital or other nonoperating sources of stockholders' equity. Laws limiting the payment of dividends to stockholders are generally intended to protect the corporation's creditors by preventing an impairment of the corporation's capital.

Financial Feasibility

Even if a corporation has accumulated earnings, the earnings may have been invested in plant and equipment, inventories, or other assets. Although payment of dividends is sometimes made in other property or obligations of the corporation, dividend payments usually require cash. Ordinarily the board of directors examines the corporation's position and does not declare a dividend that would lead to financial difficulties.

Dividend Policy

In some corporations the board of directors tries to establish a policy of regular dividend distributions to stockholders, perhaps at the same amount per share each year. In years when net income is large, some of the earnings are retained for use in the corporation or for distribution as dividends in years when net income is small. A regular dividend policy tends to make the stock more attractive to investors and may help avoid sharp fluctuations in the stock's market price.

DECLARATION OF A CASH DIVIDEND

Three dates are involved in declaring dividends. The first is the *declaration date*—the date of the board of directors' meeting at which formal action is taken to declare the dividend. The dividend declaration and other actions taken by the board are recorded in the corporation's minute book. Once notice of the board's action in declaring a dividend has been given to the stockholders (for example, by an announcement in the newspapers), the corporation has a liability to the stockholders for the amount of the declared dividend. If statements are prepared before the dividend is paid, the amount appears on the balance sheet as a current liability.

The second date is the *record date*. This is the date on which the capital stock ledger is analyzed and a list is made of the stockholders (called *stockholders of record*) to whom dividends will be paid on a still later date, the *payment date*.

Suppose that the board of directors of the Duncan Lawn Furniture Corporation meets on December 1, 19X2, after 11 months of operation. The accounting records and interim financial reports indicate that the corporation will show a comfortable profit for its first year. Therefore, the board declares cash dividends of 12 percent on the preferred stock and $4 a share on the common stock. The dividends are payable the following January 15 to stockholders of record on December 31. On the declaration date (December 1, 19X2), there are 1,400 shares of preferred stock and 2,000 shares of common stock outstanding. The dividend liability is recorded as shown below. Notice that Retained Earnings is debited and that separate liability accounts are credited for the dividends payable to each class of stockholders.

19 X2					
Dec.	1	Retained Earnings	381	16,800 00	
		Dividends Payable—Preferred	208		16,800 00
		To record dividend payable on Jan. 15 to preferred stockholders of record Dec. 31 (1,400 shares of $100 par value at 12%).			
	1	Retained Earnings	381	8,000 00	
		Dividends Payable—Common	209		8,000 00
		To record dividend payable on Jan. 15 to common stockholders of record Dec. 31 (2,000 shares at $4 a share).			

The dividends payable accounts will appear on the balance sheet as current liabilities on December 31, as shown on page 693.

Treatment of Dividends on the Statements

The declared dividends will also be reported on the statement of retained earnings for the period as deductions from retained earnings.

The statement of retained earnings prepared by the Duncan Lawn Furniture Corporation for the year ended December 31, 19X2, is shown on page 700. Since this is the first year of operations, there is no opening balance for retained earnings and there are no prior period adjustments. The net income after taxes for the current year is the only source of retained earnings. The declared dividends reduce the retained earnings, leaving the balance shown on the statement.

PAYMENT OF A CASH DIVIDEND

On the record date, December 31, the accounts in the capital stock ledger of the Duncan Lawn Furniture Corporation are analyzed, and a list is made of the stockholders on that date and the number of shares each owns. Then the amount

DUNCAN LAWN FURNITURE CORPORATION
Statement of Retained Earnings
Year Ended December 31, 19X2

Balance, Jan. 1		$ -0-
Additions		
Net Income After Income Taxes		52,494.72
Deductions		
Dividend on Preferred Stock	$16,800.00	
Dividend on Common Stock	8,000.00	
Total Deductions		24,800.00
Balance, Dec. 31		$27,694.72

of the dividend due each investor is computed. On January 15, the payment date, the dividend checks are issued to the stockholders on the list. Large corporations with many stockholders may set up a separate bank account for dividend payments, or they may have a transfer agent make the payments from funds provided by the corporation. Since the Duncan Lawn Furniture Corporation is a small firm, it issues its own dividend checks, drawn on its regular bank account. The total effect of these checks is shown below.

19 X3					
Jan. 15	Dividends Payable—Preferred	208	16,800 00		
	Dividends Payable—Common	209	8,000 00		
	Cash	101		24,800 00	
	To record payment of dividends				
	declared on Dec. 1 to stockholders				
	of record on Dec. 31.				

STOCK DIVIDENDS

A corporation that has accumulated profits may actually be short of cash or may prefer to reinvest earnings permanently in the business. In this case the board of directors may reward stockholders by declaring a *stock dividend,* which is a distribution of the corporation's own stock on a pro rata basis. The following paragraph contains an example of a pro rata distribution of stock.

Suppose that in the second year of its operations, the Duncan Lawn Furniture Corporation continues to be profitable and that on December 3, 19X3, the board of directors declares a 12 percent dividend payable to the preferred stockholders in cash. (The corporation would make entries similar to those just illustrated.) Suppose also that at the same meeting, the board declares a stock dividend payable the following January 20 to common stockholders of record on December 28, at the rate of one new share of common stock for each ten shares held. There are presently 2,000 shares outstanding, so 200 additional shares will be issued.

When a stock dividend is declared, the total amount charged to Retained Earnings is the estimated market value of the shares to be issued.[4] Assuming that each share of Duncan stock is expected to have a market value of $54, a total of $10,800 would be charged against Retained Earnings. The stated value of the shares, $10,000, is credited to a new account entitled Common Stock Dividend Distributable. The $800 excess of the market value over the stated value is credited to Paid-in Capital in Excess of Stated Value of Common Stock. (Some companies credit this excess to a new capital account entitled Paid-in Capital From Common Stock Dividends.) The entry that records the corporation's obligation to issue the new shares of common stock is shown below.

19 X3					
Dec.	3	Retained Earnings	381	10,800 00	
		Common Stock Dividend Distributable	310		10,000 00
		Paid in Capital in Excess of Stated			
		Value of Common Stock	307		800 00
		To record declaration of common stock			
		dividend distributable on Jan. 20 to			
		common stockholders of record on			
		Dec. 28 at the rate of one share for			
		each ten held (200 shares at stated			
		value of $50 a share). Expected			
		market value, $54 a share.			

The balance in the Common Stock Dividend Distributable account appears on the December 31 balance sheet. It is shown not as a current liability (as was the case with the cash dividends payable), but in the Stockholders' Equity section with the common stock.

On December 28 the capital stock ledger is closed, and the stockholders' names are listed with the number of shares they own and the number of shares each is to receive as the stock dividend. For example, James Duncan, who owns 800 shares of common stock, will receive 80 new shares as his stock dividend.

On January 20 stock certificates are prepared for each stockholder on the list, and the 200 shares are distributed as a stock dividend. This issue of stock is recorded by the general journal entry shown below.

19 X4					
Jan.	20	Common Stock Dividend Distributable	310	10,000 00	
		Common Stock (200 shares)	301		10,000 00
		To record distribution of common stock			
		as dividend to stockholders of record			
		on Dec. 28.			

The effect of issuing a stock dividend is to convert a portion of the firm's retained earnings to permanent capital. Since no assets leave the corporation or

---

[4]"Restatement and Revision of Accounting Research Bulletins Nos. 1-42," *Accounting Research Bulletin, No. 43* (New York: American Institute of Certified Public Accountants, 1953), Chapter 7, par. 10.

enter the corporation, the total book value belonging to the stockholders is the same as it was before. However, the book value of each share is less because there are now more shares of stock outstanding. Each stockholder has the same total book value after the stock dividend as before, but each owns more shares of stock.

STOCK SPLITS

In recent years an increasing number of corporations have declared true *stock splits* or *split-ups*. Under this procedure the corporation issues two or more shares of new stock to replace each share outstanding without making any changes in the capital accounts. This might be done because the market price of the stock has increased to such a point that it is relatively difficult to sell and the market is slow, or merely to provide a more flexible capital structure. Stock splits ordinarily involve no-par value stock, but they can be made with par value stock. However, if par value stock is split, the corporation's charter is amended to change the par value.

To understand a stock split involving no-par value stock, assume that the Carson Corporation is authorized to issue 2,000 shares of no-par value stock that the directors have assigned a stated value of $100 a share. The number of shares actually issued and outstanding is 300. On December 1, 19X1, the market price of the stock is $330 a share. The board of directors feels that if the price of the stock were lower, the shares would have a wider market. Accordingly, on that date, the board declares a 4-for-1 split and reduces the stated value to $25 a share. The result is that a stockholder who formerly owned 1 share of stock with a stated value of $100 a share now owns 4 shares of stock with a stated value of $25 a share. Theoretically, the market price will also decrease to one-fourth of the original market value, or to $82.50 a share. However, as in the case of stock dividends, the new price will probably be a little higher than the theoretical price. Stockholders realize no income from the stock split, and the capital accounts of the corporation are unaffected.

The only record made by the Carson Corporation of the stock split is a memorandum notation in the general journal, as shown below.

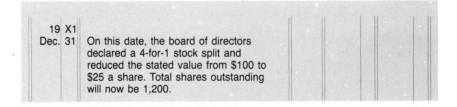

19 X1		
Dec. 31	On this date, the board of directors declared a 4-for-1 stock split and reduced the stated value from $100 to $25 a share. Total shares outstanding will now be 1,200.	

At the same time, an entry is made in the stock account in the general ledger to indicate that the stated value is now $25 a share and that 1,200 shares are outstanding instead of the original 300 shares. Of course, it will be necessary to change the various stockholders' records to reflect the number of shares now held by each stockholder.

OTHER STOCKHOLDERS' EQUITY ACCOUNTS

The American Institute of Certified Public Accountants has urged that the terminology related to stockholders' equity be clarified and that in accounting for corporate capital a clear distinction be made between (1) legal capital, (2) capital in excess of legal capital, and (3) undivided net income. The term *retained earnings* has already been used to describe net income not distributed to shareholders. *Legal capital* is the par value or stated value of the shares of stock issued. Capital in excess of legal capital is explained below.

ADDITIONAL PAID-IN CAPITAL

There are several additional types of paid-in capital arising from various sources. It is a good practice to identify the sources of the capital in the titles of the separate accounts used for each type of capital. Examples of such titles are discussed in the following sections.

Premium on Capital Stock

It has already been explained how capital stock can be issued at a premium above par value or at an amount above stated value. The descriptive titles of the accounts credited for a premium on the capital stock issued by the Duncan Lawn Furniture Corporation are consistent with current terminology. The specific account names used are Paid-in Capital in Excess of Par Value of Preferred Stock for the preferred stock and Paid-in Capital in Excess of Stated Value of Common Stock for the no-par value common stock. The amounts in these accounts are shown on the balance sheet as additions to the credits in the Preferred Stock account and the Common Stock account. (Many corporate balance sheets use the titles Premium on Common Stock and Premium on Preferred Stock.)

Treasury Stock Transactions

Another source of paid-in capital is gains on treasury stock transactions. These gains might arise from selling donated treasury stock or from selling purchased treasury stock for more than it cost. The account titles Donated Capital From Treasury Stock Transactions and Paid-in Capital From Treasury Stock Transactions are typical of titles now used. On the balance sheet the amounts relating to each class of stock are grouped with and added to the credits in the respective capital stock accounts.

Stock Dividends

This chapter has shown that when stock dividends are declared, an amount equal to the estimated market value of the new shares should be transferred from Retained Earnings to paid-in capital. The excess of market value over stated value (or over par value) is credited to Paid-in Capital From Stock Dividends, another part of paid-in capital.

Capital From Redemption of Stock Below Issue Price

Chapter 29 indicated that preferred stock may sometimes be redeemed at a price below the issue price. For example, a share of $100 par value preferred stock originally issued at par might be repurchased in the open market at $94 and canceled. The general journal entry to record this transaction is shown on page 704.

    Notice that the $6 difference between the issue price of the stock redeemed and canceled and the amount paid for it is credited to the Paid-in Capital From

19	X1						
May	19	Preferred Stock (1 share)	311	100	00		
		Cash	101			94	00
		Paid-in Capital From Redemption of					
		Preferred Stock	318			6	00
		To record redemption of 1 share for $94;					
		issue price $100.					

Redemption of Preferred Stock account. In the Stockholders' Equity section of the balance sheet, this account is grouped with the preferred stock and items related to it.

Another source of paid-in capital is the receipt of a gift of valuable property. For example, a community that wishes to attract new industry may offer a plant site as an inducement for a corporation to move there. This gift of property is recorded in the accounting records of the corporation at its estimated or appraised current value. The offsetting credit is made to a paid-in capital account, which is called Donated Capital. On the balance sheet Donated Capital is shown as a part of paid-in capital. The general journal entry below indicates how a gift of a plant site valued at $25,000 is recorded by a corporation.

19	X1					
June	2	Land	140	25,000	00	
		Donated Capital	371			25,000	00
		To record appraised value of plant site				
		donated to corporation by city.				

Sometimes stockholders also donate assets to a corporation. These assets should be recorded in the firm's accounting records at the fair market value on the date of the gift.

EQUITY INCREASE FROM APPRAISALS

Before 1940, corporations commonly revalued their property, plant, and equipment upward or downward to reflect substantial changes in value. In the 1920s, upward revaluation was common. In the 1930s, downward revaluations were generally made. It is no longer considered proper to increase the book value of assets, nor in most cases is it proper to reappraise them downward. Corporations whose accounting records still reflect the results of earlier upward revaluations should use an informative account to record the credit arising from the reappraisal. For example, Appraisal Capital, Appraisal Increase, or Excess of Appraised Value of Property Over Cost might be used. Where upward revaluations have been recorded, depreciation should be computed on the basis of the increased valuation. This complex problem is treated in detail in most intermediate accounting textbooks.

PRINCIPLES AND PROCEDURES SUMMARY

It is now generally accepted that all items of profit and loss except prior period adjustments should be included on the income statement. However, a few unusual and nonrecurring items may be shown separately in a section of the income statement called Extraordinary Gains and Losses. This section separates the unusual and nonrecurring items from the normal recurring operating items.

Corporate income is subject to federal income tax and to the income taxes of many states. The estimated taxes are credited to an account such as Estimated Income Taxes Payable. Net income after income taxes is credited to Retained Earnings in the final closing entry when the Income Summary account is closed. Net income is distributed to stockholders as dividends at the discretion of the board of directors.

Retained earnings reflect the accumulated, undistributed profits of the corporation. The board of directors may transfer amounts from the Retained Earnings account to appropriated retained earnings accounts (sometimes referred to as reserve accounts) to indicate restrictions on the distribution of retained earnings as dividends. Retained Earnings and the various appropriated accounts do not represent cash on hand. Thus when the purpose for which an appropriation of retained earnings was originally set up has been fulfilled, the directors may transfer the balance of the appropriated account back to Retained Earnings.

Paid-in capital represents capital arising from contributions for shares or from other dealings with stockholders.

MANAGERIAL IMPLICATIONS

Managers must understand just what enters into corporate net income—especially the difference between the all-inclusive and current operating concepts of income reporting. Otherwise, managers may not interpret the statement figures correctly and may make unwise decisions.

Managers must also be thoroughly familiar with the provisions of law and the principles of accounting that relate to dividends. It is especially important that they understand the nature of stock dividends since such dividends permit the business to retain its cash for operations and to invest a portion of the retained earnings in the firm's permanent capital.

Managers should know about the use of appropriated accounts to inform stockholders about restrictions on retained earnings. At the same time, they should realize that the mere appropriation of retained earnings does not in any way guarantee that the necessary cash will be on hand.

REVIEW QUESTIONS

1. Define the term *prior period adjustments*.
2. Explain the current operating concept. Is this concept usually followed today?

3. What is the all-inclusive concept?
4. What criteria must be met for an item to be classified as extraordinary?
5. What information is shown on the statement of retained earnings?
6. In 19X1 a corporation charged to expense a building addition. The cost of this addition should have been capitalized. In 19X4 the error was discovered. How should this prior period adjustment be accounted for?
7. What is an appropriation of retained earnings?
8. Does an appropriation of retained earnings include a transfer of cash to a restricted account? Explain.
9. Several years ago a corporation made an appropriation of retained earnings because of a building project. The building project was completed in the current year. What accounting entry will probably be made with respect to the appropriation?
10. What effect does an appropriation have on total retained earnings? Explain.
11. What is a stock dividend?
12. When a stock dividend is declared, what journal entry is made? How is the amount measured?
13. How would the Common Stock Dividend Distributable account be classified on the balance sheet?
14. Explain the difference between a stock split and a stock dividend.
15. What effect does a stock split have on retained earnings? Explain.
16. What does the term *legal capital* mean?
17. The Orion Corporation repurchased on the open market shares of its own $75 par value preferred stock at $90 a share and retired them. The stock had an original issue price of $96 a share. How is the transaction accounted for?
18. A stockholder of the Penrol Corporation gave the firm a building site with a fair market value of $100,000. How is the gift accounted for?
19. What is meant by the date of record? By the declaration date?
20. When a cash dividend is declared, what amounts are debited and credited?
21. Compare the effects on stockholders' equity of a cash dividend and a stock dividend.
22. Is it generally appropriate for a corporation to record an upward revaluation of its property, plant, and equipment? Explain.

MANAGERIAL DISCUSSION QUESTIONS

1. Why would managers be interested in establishing a policy of regular dividend payments?
2. Why might a lack of understanding about how corporate net income is calculated lead to unwise decisions?
3. Explain what powers a board of directors has to declare dividends.
4. Why might a board of directors want to declare a stock dividend for the preferred stockholders in the early stages of the corporation's development?
5. Assume that you are the controller of a corporation. Some members of the board of directors have asked you how the firm can have a large balance in the

Retained Earnings account but no cash with which to pay dividends. Explain.

6. How can management indicate that it intends to reinvest some of the firm's retained earnings in property, plant, and equipment?

7. Assume that a director of a corporation where you work has asked you how an appropriation of retained earnings will help the corporation accumulate funds to achieve a specific purpose. What explanation would you give to the director?

8. Suppose that the management of your company wishes to improve the firm's permanent capital position by making a transfer from retained earnings to paid-in capital. The president suggests that this might be accomplished by a stock split. React to his suggestion, and state your opinion about how the aim should be carried out.

9. How would you explain to management why it is important to distinguish between paid-in capital and retained earnings?

EXERCISES

EXERCISE 30-1   **Computing federal income taxes.** The Sherwood Corporation's Income Summary account has a credit balance of $41,000 on December 31, 19X1, before income taxes have been recorded. Using the tax rates given in this chapter, compute the corporation's federal income taxes payable for 19X1. (Assume that the firm's taxable income is the same as its income for financial accounting purposes.)

EXERCISE 30-2   **Recording income taxes payable and closing the income summary.** Using the data for the Sherwood Corporation from Exercise 30-1, give the general journal entry to close the firm's Income Summary account for 19X1.

EXERCISE 30-3   **Recording the correction of an error.** The Painter Corporation spent $3,000 for office supplies in 19X1. This amount was charged to Advertising Expense instead of Office Supplies Expense. The error was discovered in March 19X3. Give the general journal entry, if any, required in 19X3 to correct the error.

EXERCISE 30-4   **Recording the correction of an error.** On July 1, 19X1, the Rossiter Corporation purchased a new delivery truck for $10,000. That amount was charged to Delivery Expense. On January 10, 19X3, the error was discovered. Depreciation on the truck should be $150 a month. Give the general journal entry, if any, required to correct the error in 19X3. (Assume that the error is a significant prior period error.)

EXERCISE 30-5   **Recording the appropriation of retained earnings.** On December 31, 19X1, the board of directors of the Schuman Corporation voted to appropriate $50,000 of retained earnings each year for five years to establish a reserve for contingencies. Give the general journal entry on December 31, 19X1, to record the appropriation.

EXERCISE 30-6   **Reporting retained earnings on the balance sheet.** The following are selected accounts from the general ledger of the Torres Corporation on December 31, 19X1. Show how the data related to retained earnings would appear on the corporation's balance sheet for December 31, 19X1.

Allowance for Uncollectible Accounts	$ 12,000
Retained Earnings Appropriated for Contingencies	63,000
Common Stock Dividend Distributable	20,000
Retained Earnings Appropriated for Plant Expansion	100,000
Retained Earnings, Unappropriated	343,000

EXERCISE 30-7   **Recording the declaration and payment of a cash dividend.** On November 30, 19X1, the board of directors of the United Corporation declared a cash dividend of $1 a share on its 300,000 outstanding shares of common stock. The dividend is payable on December 31, 19X1, to stockholders of record on December 8, 19X1. Give any general journal entries necessary on November 30, December 8, and December 31.

EXERCISE 30-8   **Reporting dividends payable on the balance sheet.** Based on the facts given in Exercise 30-7, indicate how the declaration of the dividend by the United Corporation would affect a balance sheet prepared on December 7, 19X1.

EXERCISE 30-9   **Recording a stock dividend.** The Venito Corporation had outstanding 100,000 shares of $5 par value common stock on December 3, 19X1. At that date, it declared a 10 percent common stock dividend distributable on December 30 to stockholders of record on December 15. The estimated market value of the shares at the time of their issue is $12 a share. Give any general journal entries necessary on December 3, December 15, and December 30.

EXERCISE 30-10   **Recording a stock split.** The Allied Corporation had outstanding 100,000 shares of no-par value common stock, with a stated value of $10, on December 1, 19X1. The company voted to split the stock on a 3-for-1 basis, issuing two new shares to stockholders for each share presently owned. The estimated market value of the new shares will be $14.50. Give any general journal entry required in this situation.

EXERCISE 30-11   **Recording the donation of land to a corporation.** The city of Oakville contributed to the Van Ness Corporation a tract of land on which to build a plant. When the contribution was made on August 10, 19X1, the land's fair market value was $80,000. Give the general journal entry, if any, necessary to record the contribution.

EXERCISE 30-12   **Recording the repurchase and retirement of preferred stock.** On August 31, 19X1, the Donahue Corporation had outstanding 100,000 shares of 9 percent preferred stock with a par value of $10. The stock was originally issued for $10.40 a share. On that date the corporation repurchased and retired all the preferred stock for $8 a share. Give the general journal entry to record the repurchase and retirement of the preferred stock.

PROBLEMS

PROBLEM 30-1   **Preparing a worksheet and financial statements for a corporation.** The Boyd Corporation has been authorized to issue 5,000 shares of 14 percent noncumulative, nonparticipating preferred stock with a par value of $100 a share and 5,000 shares of common stock with a stated value of $100 a share. As of December 31, 19X1, 400 shares of preferred stock and 200 shares of common stock have been issued. A condensed trial balance as of December 31, 19X1, is provided below. Assume that all necessary adjusting entries, except those given in the instructions, have been made.

BOYD CORPORATION
Trial Balance (Condensed)
December 31, 19X1

Account Name	Debit	Credit
Cash	$ 10,265	
Notes Receivable	12,460	
Accounts Receivable (Net)	27,130	
Land	18,000	
Building	44,000	
Accumulated Depreciation—Building		$ 4,000
Equipment	39,000	
Accumulated Depreciation—Equipment		11,000
Notes Payable		5,000
Accounts Payable		6,325
Dividends Payable—Preferred		
Dividends Payable—Common		
Common Stock Dividend Distributable		
Common Stock		20,000
Paid-in Capital in Excess of Stated Value—Common		1,000
Discount on Common Stock	400	
Preferred Stock—14%		40,000
Paid-in Capital in Excess of Par Value—Preferred		3,000
Paid-in Capital From Treasury Stock Transactions—Preferred		600
Retained Earnings		26,225
Sales (Net Total)		206,840
Expenses (Total)	173,185	
Gain on Sales of Securities		2,400
Loss on Condemnation of Building	3,200	
Refund on Prior Year's Income Tax		1,250
Totals	$327,640	$327,640

Instructions

1. Prepare a condensed ten-column worksheet as of December 31, 19X1. Enter the trial balance accounts and amounts shown. (Provide three lines for the Retained Earnings account.) Total and rule the Trial Balance columns.

2. On the worksheet, record the results of the board of directors' action in declaring the following dividends payable on January 31, 19X2, to stockholders of record on December 31, 19X1. (Debit the Retained Earnings account for these amounts.)

   a. The normal annual 14 percent dividend on the preferred stock (Adjustment a).

   b. A cash dividend of $5 a share on the common stock (Adjustment b).

   c. An additional common stock dividend of one share for each four shares held. The current market value of the common stock is $108 a share (Adjustment c).

3. Extend the combined Trial Balance and Adjustments figures into the Adjusted Trial Balance columns. Then total and balance these columns.

4. Extend the Adjusted Trial Balance figures into the appropriate columns of the Income Statement and Balance Sheet sections. Then total both sections. The company uses the all-inclusive concept of income reporting. The tax refund is to be included on the income statement.

5. Enter the provision for income taxes, estimated to be $8,280.

6. Determine and enter the amount of net income after income taxes, total and balance all columns, and rule the columns.

7. Prepare a condensed income statement for the year, using the all-inclusive concept of reporting. The tax refund is to be included in the Revenue section of the income statement. The gain on the sale of securities resulted in an income tax of $528, while the loss on condemnation of the building resulted in a tax saving of $704. (Both of these items are nonrecurring and unusual and are to be considered as extraordinary gains and losses.) The income tax applicable to operating income was $8,456.

8. Prepare a statement of retained earnings for the year, assuming that no entries were made in the Retained Earnings account during the year.

9. Prepare a balance sheet as of December 31, 19X1.

PROBLEM 30-2

Recording dividend transactions and preparing a statement of retained earnings. The Retained Earnings account of the Garcia Chemical Corporation had a credit balance of $16,800 before closing entries were made on December 31, 19X1. The worksheet prepared at the end of 19X1 showed estimated income taxes of $3,700 and net income after income taxes of $21,300. The worksheet prepared at the end of 19X2 showed estimated income taxes of $4,500 and net income after income taxes of $25,100. The selected transactions shown on page 711 took place during 19X2.

Instructions

1. Set up a ledger account for Retained Earnings 381, and record the December 31, 19X1, balance.

2. Give the general journal entry as of December 31, 19X1, to set up the income tax liability and close the balance of the Income Summary account to the Retained Earnings account.
3. Record the transactions shown below in general journal form. Use the account titles illustrated in the textbook. Post these entries to the Retained Earnings account only.
4. Give the general journal entry as of December 31, 19X2, to record the income tax liability and close the balance of the Income Summary account to the Retained Earnings account. Post to the Retained Earnings account.
5. Analyze the Retained Earnings account, and prepare a statement of retained earnings for the year 19X2.

TRANSACTIONS FOR 19X2

Nov.   15 The board of directors declared an annual 12 percent cash dividend on 500 shares of $100 par value preferred stock and a cash dividend of $3 a share on 2,000 shares of no-par value common stock, with a stated value of $50. Both dividends are payable December 15 to stockholders of record on December 1. (Use a compound entry.)
       15 The board of directors declared a 10 percent common stock dividend to be distributed on December 20 to common stockholders of record on December 1. The common stock is expected to have a market value of $58 a share when issued.
Dec.   15 Paid the cash dividends declared on November 15.
       20 Issued common stock for the stock dividend declared on November 15.

PROBLEM 30-3   **Recording a variety of corporate transactions.** The Stockholders' Equity section of the Curtis Corporation's balance sheet on December 31, 19X1, is given below.

Stockholders' Equity

Preferred Stock (10%, $50 par value, 1,000 shares authorized)		
At Par Value (500 shares issued)	$25,000	
Paid-in Capital in Excess of Par Value	2,000	$ 27,000
Common Stock (no-par value, stated value of $50, 1,000 shares authorized)		
At Stated Value (900 shares issued)	$45,000	
Paid-in Capital in Excess of Stated Value	1,500	46,500
Retained Earnings		32,475
Total Stockholders' Equity		$105,975

Some of the corporation's transactions that took place during 19X2 are shown on page 712.

Instructions   1. Set up general ledger accounts for the stockholders' equity items, and enter the given balances. Use the account titles and numbers illustrated in the textbook.

2. Record the transactions listed below in general journal form.
3. Post the general journal entries to the stockholders' equity accounts only. (Set up new accounts as required.)
4. Prepare the Stockholders' Equity section of the Curtis Corporation's balance sheet as of December 31, 19X2.

TRANSACTIONS FOR 19X2

Jan.   15 Received land valued at $40,000 as a gift from a neighboring city. The corporation has agreed to build a new factory in this location.

Feb.   6 The corporation reacquired 60 shares of preferred stock, paying $56 a share. (Record at cost.)

Mar.   12 Sold, for $58 a share, 10 shares of the corporation's preferred treasury stock.

Apr.   19 Paid $54 a share to redeem and cancel 30 shares of the corporation's preferred stock.

May   28 Sold, for $47 a share, 10 shares of the corporation's preferred treasury stock.

June   10 Office equipment costing $6,000 that was paid for on January 2, 19X1, was charged in error to Office Supplies Expense 523 rather than to Office Equipment 153. The equipment is expected to have a useful life of 10 years and no salvage value. The corporation uses the straight-line method of depreciation for all of its office equipment. (Make the necessary correction for 19X1. Record the correction through retained earnings.)

Nov.   20 The board of directors declared an annual 10 percent cash dividend on the preferred stock issued and outstanding and a $4 a share cash dividend on the common stock issued and outstanding. Both dividends are payable January 15, 19X3, to stockholders of record on December 20.

Dec.   31 The board of directors instructed that $14,000 be appropriated from Retained Earnings. This appropriation is for an expansion of the firm's warehouse that is needed.

           31 The accountant is instructed to amortize $400 of goodwill (debit Goodwill Written Off 690, credit Goodwill 190) and $200 of organization costs.

           31 The worksheet prepared at the end of the year shows estimated income taxes of $4,400 and net income after income taxes of $23,750. (Make the appropriate closing entry in the general journal.)

PROBLEM 30-4   **Reporting stockholders' equity on the balance sheet.** On December 31, 19X1, the general ledger accounts of the Rosenberg Furniture Corporation included the balances shown on page 713. According to its charter, the corporation is authorized to issue 10,000 shares of $10 par value, 11 percent cumulative preferred stock and 5,000 shares of $50 par value common stock. Dividends are in arrears for two years on the preferred shares.

Instructions Prepare the Stockholders' Equity section of the balance sheet as of December 31, 19X1.

ACCOUNTS	BALANCES
Retained Earnings Appropriated for Contingencies	$ 10,000
Paid-in Capital From Treasury Stock Transactions	3,000
Retained Earnings—Unappropriated	524,625
Accumulated Depreciation—Buildings	1,800
Preferred Stock Subscribed (1,200 shares)	12,000
Subscriptions Receivable on Preferred Stock	8,000
Preferred Stock—11%	82,000
Treasury Stock—Preferred (200 shares at cost)	1,600
Common Stock	200,000
Treasury Stock—Common (100 shares at cost)	5,000
Common Stock Subscribed (1,000 shares)	50,000
Paid-in Capital in Excess of Par Value—Common Stock	6,000
Subscriptions Receivable on Common Stock	20,000
Organization Costs	2,280
Paid-in Capital in Excess of Par Value—Preferred Stock	1,000
Retained Earnings Appropriated for Treasury Stock—Common	5,000
Retained Earnings Appropriated for Treasury Stock—Preferred	1,600

ALTERNATE PROBLEMS

PROBLEM 30-1A **Preparing a worksheet and financial statements for a corporation.** The Harris Corporation has been authorized to issue 3,000 shares of 13 percent noncumulative, nonparticipating preferred stock with a par value of $100 a share and 200,000 shares of common stock with a par value of $10 a share. As of December 31, 19X1, 800 shares of preferred stock and 28,600 shares of common stock have been issued. A condensed trial balance as of December 31, 19X1, is provided on page 714. Assume that all necessary adjusting entries, except those given in the instructions, have been made.

Instructions
1. Prepare a condensed ten-column worksheet as of December 31, 19X1. Enter the trial balance accounts and amounts shown. (Provide three lines for the Retained Earnings account.) Total and rule the Trial Balance columns.
2. On the worksheet, record the results of the board of directors' action in declaring the following dividends payable on January 31, 19X2, to stockholders of record on December 31, 19X1. (Debit Retained Earnings for these amounts.)
   a. The normal annual 13 percent dividend on the preferred stock (Adjustment a).
   b. A cash dividend of $0.20 a share on the common stock (Adjustment b).
   c. An additional common stock dividend of 1 share for each 20 shares owned. The current market value of the common stock is $12 a share (Adjustment c).
3. Extend the combined Trial Balance and Adjustments figures into the Adjusted Trial Balance columns. Then total and balance these columns.

4. Extend the Adjusted Trial Balance figures into the appropriate columns of the Income Statement and Balance Sheet sections. Then total both sections. The company uses the all-inclusive concept of income reporting.
5. Enter the provision for income taxes, which the accountant estimates to be $39,200.
6. Determine and enter the amount of net income after income taxes, total and balance all columns, and rule the columns.
7. Prepare a condensed income statement for the year, using the all-inclusive concept of reporting. The gain on the sale of securities resulted in an income tax of $1,050, while the loss from earthquake damage resulted in a tax reduction of $3,800. (Both items are deemed to be unusual and nonrecurring and are to be classified as extraordinary gains and losses.) The income tax applicable to operating income was $41,950.
8. Prepare a statement of retained earnings for the year, assuming that no entries were made in the Retained Earnings account during the year.
9. Prepare a balance sheet as of December 31, 19X1.

HARRIS CORPORATION
Trial Balance (Condensed)
December 31, 19X1

Account Name	Debit	Credit
Cash	$ 11,745	
Notes Receivable	2,500	
Accounts Receivable (Net)	134,740	
Receivable From Insurance Company	71,400	
Land	50,000	
Buildings	250,000	
Accumulated Depreciation—Buildings		$25,000
Equipment	125,000	
Accumulated Depreciation—Equipment		20,000
Notes Payable		20,000
Accounts Payable		24,900
Accrued Expenses Payable		7,110
Dividends Payable—Preferred		
Dividends Payable—Common		
Common Stock Dividend Distributable		
Common Stock		286,000
Preferred Stock—13%		80,000
Paid-in Capital in Excess of Par Value—Preferred		8,000
Retained Earnings		50,000
Sales (Net Total)		560,275
Expenses (Total)	431,400	
Loss From Earthquake Damage	8,000	
Gain on Sale of Securities		3,500
	$1,084,785	$1,084,785

Recording dividend transactions and preparing a statement of retained earnings. The stockholders' equity accounts of Durable Metal Products Inc. on January 1, 19X1, contained the balances shown below.

Preferred Stock (10%, $50 par value,		
2,000 shares authorized)		
At Par Value (600 shares issued)	$30,000	
Paid-in Capital in Excess of Par Value	1,200	$ 31,200
Common Stock ($20 par value, 10,000		
shares authorized)		
At Par Value (5,000 shares issued)		100,000
Total Capital Stock		$131,200
Retained Earnings		320,000
Total Stockholders' Equity		$451,200

The corporation's transactions affecting stockholders' equity during 19X1 are given below. The worksheet that the accountant prepared at the end of 19X1 showed estimated income taxes of $7,300 and net income after taxes of $37,700.

Instructions

1. Set up a ledger account for Retained Earnings 381, and record the January 1, 19X1, balance.
2. Record the transactions given below in general journal form. Use the account titles illustrated in the textbook. Post these entries to the Retained Earnings account only.
3. Give the general journal entry as of December 31, 19X1, to record the income tax liability and close the balance of the Income Summary account to the Retained Earnings account. Post to the Retained Earnings account.
4. Analyze the Retained Earnings account, and prepare a statement of retained earnings for the year 19X1.

TRANSACTIONS FOR 19X1

June 15 The board of directors declared a semiannual dividend of 5 percent on the preferred stock, payable on July 15 to stockholders of record on July 1.

July 15 Paid the dividend on the preferred stock.

Dec. 15 The board of directors declared a semiannual dividend of 5 percent on the preferred stock, payable on January 15, 19X2, to stockholders of record on December 31, 19X1.

15 The board of directors declared a 12 percent common stock dividend to be distributed to the common stockholders of record on December 31, 19X1. The new shares are to be issued on January 15, 19X2. A market price of $30 a share is expected for the new shares of common stock that the corporation will issue.

Recording a variety of corporate transactions. The Stockholders' Equity section of the Alto Corporation's balance sheet on December 31, 19X2, is given on page 716.

Stockholders' Equity

Preferred Stock (13%, $100 par value,
   2,000 shares authorized)

At Par Value (1,200 shares issued)	$120,000	
Paid-in Capital in Excess of Par Value	2,400	$122,400

Common Stock (no-par value, stated value of $20,
   10,000 shares authorized)

At Stated Value (7,000 shares issued)	$140,000	
Paid-in Capital in Excess of Stated Value	21,000	161,000
Retained Earnings		135,000
Total Stockholders' Equity		$418,400

Some of the corporation's transactions that took place during 19X3 are given below.

Instructions

1. Set up general ledger accounts for the stockholders' equity items, and enter the given balances. Use the account titles and numbers illustrated in the textbook.
2. Record the transactions listed below in general journal form.
3. Post the general journal entries to the stockholders' equity accounts only. (Set up new accounts as required.)
4. Prepare the Stockholders' Equity section of the Alto Corporation's balance sheet as of December 31, 19X3.

TRANSACTIONS FOR 19X3

Jan.   3 Received land valued at $10,000 for location of a new plant. The land was a gift from a group of citizens.

Feb.   8 The corporation reacquired 100 shares of preferred stock, paying $105 a share.

Mar. 13 Sold, for $106 a share, 30 shares of preferred treasury stock.

Apr. 19 Paid $105.50 a share to redeem and cancel 50 shares of preferred stock.

May 30 Sold, for $102 a share, 20 shares of preferred treasury stock.

July 18 Discovered that office equipment purchased on January 5, 19X2, costing $2,000, was incorrectly charged to Office Supplies Expense 681 instead of to Office Equipment 136. The equipment was estimated to have a useful life of 8 years from the date of purchase and no salvage value. The corporation uses the straight-line method of depreciation. (Make the necessary correction for 19X2, recording the correction through retained earnings.)

Dec. 10 The board of directors declared an annual 13 percent cash dividend on the outstanding preferred stock and a $2 a share cash dividend on the outstanding common stock. Both dividends are payable on January 20, 19X4, to stockholders of record on December 31.

         31 The board of directors voted that $25,000 of retained earnings be appropriated for plant expansion.

31 Amortization for the year: $500 of goodwill (debit Goodwill Written Off 690, credit Goodwill 190) and $300 of organization costs. The amortization is to appear on the income statement.

31 The worksheet prepared at the end of the year shows estimated income taxes of $6,980 and net income of $27,020 after income taxes. (Make the appropriate closing entry in the general journal.)

PROBLEM 30-4A   **Reporting stockholders' equity on the balance sheet.** On December 31, 19X1, the ledger accounts of Superior Medical Supplies, Inc., included the balances shown below. The corporation is authorized to issue 20,000 shares of $20 par value, 12 percent cumulative preferred stock and 10,000 shares of $100 par value common stock. Dividends are in arrears for two years on the preferred stock.

Instructions   Prepare the Stockholders' Equity section of the balance sheet as of December 31, 19X1, using the cost basis to account for treasury stock.

ACCOUNTS	BALANCES
Retained Earnings Appropriated for Contingencies	$ 20,000
Paid-in Capital From Treasury Stock Transactions	6,000
Retained Earnings—Unappropriated	49,250
Accumulated Depreciation—Buildings	3,600
Preferred Stock Subscribed (1,200 shares)	24,000
Subscriptions Receivable on Preferred Stock	16,000
Preferred Stock	164,000
Treasury Stock—Preferred (200 shares at cost)	3,200
Common Stock	400,000
Treasury Stock—Common (100 shares at cost)	10,000
Common Stock Subscribed (1,000 shares)	100,000
Paid-in Capital in Excess of Par Value—Common Stock	12,000
Subscriptions Receivable on Common Stock	40,000
Organization Costs	4,560
Paid-in Capital in Excess of Par Value—Preferred Stock	2,000
Retained Earnings Appropriated for Treasury Stock—Common	10,000
Retained Earnings Appropriated for Treasury Stock—Preferred	3,200

CHAPTER

As you have seen, corporations may obtain needed funds by selling stock. However, there are also other ways for a corporation to obtain the money it requires for expansion and other purposes. In this chapter we will discuss the use of bonds as a means of raising additional funds.

BONDS AND OTHER LONG-TERM LIABILITIES

THE NEED TO BORROW MONEY

Suppose that after several years, the operations of the Duncan Lawn Furniture Corporation have been successful and that a minimum of $100,000 is now needed to expand the business. The directors wonder how best to raise the additional money. They can, of course, issue more stock. However, James Duncan and the other stockholders are not in a position to buy more stock themselves. They are also reluctant to sell stock to outsiders because it might mean sharing managerial control of the business with the new stockholders.

The finance committee discusses the problem with the firm's banker, who suggests that it would be wise to borrow the needed funds. The company could probably borrow money at a rate of interest lower than the rate of return it could earn by using the funds. Furthermore, the banker points out that interest on the loan would be deductible for income tax purposes. Thus the government would, in effect, pay part of the cost of the borrowed money. The banker then outlines various ways to obtain credit.

SHORT-TERM AND LONG-TERM CREDIT

The manner of borrowing depends somewhat on the length of time for which credit is required.

Short-Term Notes

The procedure for discounting a note payable was discussed in Chapter 20. The bank lends the face amount of the note, less interest. The note is paid in full at maturity, which is usually a few months after the issue date.

Banks and other lending agencies may also advance sums that are secured by a pledge of inventories or accounts receivable. Control of the inventories, such as goods stored in a public warehouse, may be transferred to the lender for collection. Although these arrangements may continue over fairly long periods of time, they are classified as short-term credit.

Long-Term Notes

Loans for what might be called an intermediate period (two to five years) can sometimes be obtained with long-term notes. The accounting procedures for such notes may differ from those used for ordinary short-term bank notes because the interest is often paid periodically over the life of the note instead of being deducted in advance. A special problem may arise if a noninterest-bearing note is issued for assets other than cash. This problem is discussed later in the present chapter.

Mortgage Loans

Loans for periods of five or more years are often secured by a mortgage on property—land, buildings, equipment, or even trucks. The mortgage ordinarily gives the lender the right to seize and sell the property pledged as security if either the principal or the current interest is not paid when due. Interest may be payable annually, but it is usually paid at shorter intervals over the life of the loan. Repayment of the principal may be in a lump sum at a future date or in installments over the life of the loan.

Bonds

Corporations may also borrow for a long term by issuing *bonds,* which are written promises to pay the principal borrowed at a specified future date. Interest is due at a fixed rate that is payable annually or at shorter intervals over the life of the bond.

TYPES OF BONDS

Since borrowing by issuing bonds seems to be the best method for the Duncan Lawn Furniture Corporation, the banker supplies information on the various types of bonds: secured, unsecured, registered, and coupon.

Secured Bonds

Bonds are called *secured* when property of value is pledged for the benefit of the bondholders. A *bond contract,* or *bond indenture,* is prepared with a trustee who acts to protect the bondholders' interest when necessary. In the case of default, for example, the trustee takes legal steps to sell the pledged property and pay off the bonds. The bonds may be identified according to the nature of the property pledged and the year of maturity—for example, First Mortgage 10 Percent Real Estate Bonds Payable, 19X5; or Collateral Trust 14 Percent Bonds Payable, 19X2. A *collateral trust* involves the pledge of securities, such as the stocks or bonds of other companies.

Unsecured Bonds

Bonds issued on the general credit of the corporation (often called *debenture* bonds) are *unsecured.* They involve no pledge of specific property that the bondholders can seize to satisfy their claims. However, the bondholders do have some protection in case of liquidation because the claims of creditors, including bondholders, rank above those of stockholders. Creditors must be paid in full before stockholders can receive anything.

Registered Bonds

Bonds issued to a particular individual whose name is listed in the corporation's records are *registered* bonds. Ownership is transferred by completing an assignment form and having the change of ownership entered in the corporation's records. Interest is paid by check to each registered bondholder. The corporation must maintain a detailed subsidiary ledger, similar to the stockholders' ledger, for registered bonds. This ledger lets the corporation know at all times who owns the bonds and is therefore entitled to receive interest payments.

Coupon Bonds

Some bonds are issued with individual coupons attached for each interest payment. These coupons are in the form of a check payable to the bearer. On or after each interest date, the bondholder detaches the coupon from the bond and presents it to a bank for payment. *Coupon* bonds are transferred by delivery, and no record of the owner's identity is kept by the corporation. Because of the need to identify payees of interest for federal income tax purposes, coupon bonds are much less common today than in former years.

Other Characteristics of Bonds

Bonds are issued in various denominations, but a face value of $1,000 is typical. Some bonds offer special privileges, such as convertibility into common stock at the option of the bondholder under specified conditions. These privileges are discussed in most intermediate accounting textbooks.

ENTRIES FOR BOND ISSUE AND INTEREST

Suppose that the finance committee of the Duncan Lawn Furniture Corporation recommends the authorization of $100,000 of 11 percent bonds, maturing in 10 years, with interest payment dates on April 1 and October 1. Suppose also that the board of directors approves the plan. The bonds are then registered with the Securities and Exchange Commission so they can be sold outside the state in which they are issued. Half the authorized bonds are to be sold immediately. The remainder are to be held for possible future needs. The bonds are in coupon form and are unsecured.

Bonds Issued at Par

On April 1, 19Y1, the issue date, Duncan sells $50,000 of its bonds at par value for cash. The corporation records this transaction by debiting Cash and crediting an account called 11% Bonds Payable, 19Z1 (indicating the maturity date 10 years later). After the entry is posted, the ledger account for the bonds appears as shown below.

<table>
<tr><td colspan="7" align="center">11% Bonds Payable, 19Z1
(Authorized $100,000; Interest April 1, October 1)   No. 261</td></tr>
<tr><td>DATE</td><td>EXPLANATION</td><td>POST. REF.</td><td>DEBIT</td><td>CREDIT</td><td>BALANCE</td><td>DR. CR.</td></tr>
<tr><td>19 Y1
Apr. 1</td><td></td><td>J4</td><td></td><td>50,000 00</td><td>50,000 00</td><td>Cr.</td></tr>
</table>

Notice that the amount of bonds authorized is recorded as a memorandum item in the ledger account. On financial statements the bonds payable are listed as long-term liabilities. Both the amount authorized and the amount issued are shown. One of two methods is generally used to present the bonds on the balance sheet.

1. The par value of the bonds authorized is shown. The amount unissued is deducted to arrive at the par value of the bonds issued. This presentation is illustrated in the section of the balance sheet shown below.

Long-Term Liabilities

11% Bonds Payable, due April 1, 19Z1		
Authorized	$100,000	
Less Unissued	50,000	
Issued		$50,000

2. The par value of the bonds authorized is shown as a parenthetical note. Only the par value of the bonds issued is extended to the money columns of the balance sheet.

Long-Term Liabilities

11% Bonds Payable, due April 1, 19Z1. (Bonds with a par value of $100,000 are authorized, of which bonds with a par value of $50,000 are unissued)	$50,000

most common →

The second method of presentation is the one more commonly used.

Payment of Interest

On October 1 the interest for six months at 11 percent becomes due on the $50,000 of bonds issued. Since some interest checks may not be presented promptly by the bondholders, it is convenient to transfer the amount of cash needed to pay the interest to a special account in the bank. The entry to record this transfer of funds is illustrated in general journal form below.

19 Y1					
Oct.	1	Bond Interest Expense	692	2,750 00	
		Cash	101		2,750 00
		To record transfer of funds to special account to pay semiannual interest on $50,000 of bonds issued.			

Accrual of Interest

D – Bond Interest Expense

C – Bond Interest Payable

On December 31, when the fiscal year ends for the Duncan Lawn Furniture Corporation, bond interest of $1,375 has accrued for three months ($50,000 × 0.11 × 3/12). An adjusting entry is made debiting Bond Interest Expense and crediting Bond Interest Payable.

When the adjusting entry has been posted, the Bond Interest Expense account has a balance of $4,125 ($2,750 + $1,375)—the correct amount of interest for the nine months since the bonds have been issued. The Bond Interest Expense account is listed under nonoperating expenses on the income statement.

Entries for Interest— Second Year

Assuming that the same bonds remain outstanding during all of the second year, 19Y2, the following entries would be required to record bond interest transactions.

1. January 1: Reverse the $1,375 entry for accrued interest made on December

31. Record a reversing entry in the general journal, debiting Bond Interest Payable and crediting Bond Interest Expense.

2. April 1: Record the payment of interest for six months, $2,750, by debiting Bond Interest Expense and crediting Cash.

3. October 1: Record the payment of interest for six months, $2,750, by debiting Bond Interest Expense and crediting Cash.

4. December 31: Record accrued interest for three months, $1,375, by debiting Bond Interest Expense and crediting Bond Interest Payable. After these four entries have been posted, the Bond Interest Expense account will look like this.

Bond Interest Expense					No.	692

DATE	EXPLANATION	POST. REF.	DEBIT	CREDIT	BALANCE	DR. CR.
19 Y2						
Jan. 1	Reversing Entry	J1		1,375 00	1,375 00	Cr.
Apr. 1		J4	2,750 00		1,375 00	Dr.
Oct. 1		J10	2,750 00		4,125 00	Dr.
Dec. 31	Adjusting Entry	J12	1,375 00		5,500 00	Dr.

Notice that the balance in the Bond Interest Expense account on December 31 is $5,500, which is the correct amount of interest incurred for one year on the $50,000 of bonds issued.

BONDS ISSUED AT A PREMIUM

Two years after the first bonds were sold, the Duncan Lawn Furniture Corporation decides to issue another $20,000 of the $100,000 authorized. Although interest rates have fallen to 10 percent in the two years since the first bonds were issued, the bond interest remains fixed at 11 percent. Each $1,000 bond will therefore earn $110 interest a year. Bondholders will naturally be attracted by the favorable interest rate offered and will probably be willing to pay more than $1,000 for each bond. Under these conditions the $20,000 of bonds are sold on April 1, 19Y3, at a market quotation of 105.4 ($1,054 each: 105.4 percent of $1,000 par), yielding $21,080 in cash. The $1,080 above the face amount of the bonds is a premium paid by investors because the contract rate of interest on the bonds is above the market rate of interest at the time they are sold. This transaction is recorded in general journal form as shown below.

19 Y3				
Apr. 1	Cash	101	21,080 00	
	Premium on Bonds Payable	251		1,080 00
	11% Bonds Payable, 19Z1	261		20,000 00
	To record issuance of bonds at 105.4.			

Amortization of Bond Premium

(handwritten in margin: 1080 ÷ 8 = $135 ; also "months" written beside text)

The issuing corporation must write off, or amortize, the premium paid by the bond purchasers over the period from the issue date to maturity. In this case the bonds are ten-year bonds sold two years after their issue date, leaving an eight-year period over which to amortize the premium. On a straight-line basis, the amortization amounts to $135 a year, or $11.25 a month ($135 ÷ 12). A common method of handling the amortization is to use the straight-line method, amortizing an equal part of the premium at each interest payment date. (A preferable method, the effective interest method, is discussed later in this chapter.) Under the straight-line amortization method, the following entries are made by Duncan on October 1 to record the interest on the $70,000 of bonds outstanding and the amortization of the premium on $20,000 of these bonds. The bond interest paid is $3,850 ($70,000 × 0.11 × 6/12).

	19 Y3				
Oct.	1	Bond Interest Expense	692	3,850 00	
		Cash	101		3,850 00
		To record payment of semiannual interest on $70,000 of bonds issued.			
	1	Premium on Bonds Payable	251	67 50	
		Bond Interest Expense	692		67 50
		To record amortization of premium for six months on $20,000 of bonds issued.			

The amount of bond interest paid includes $2,750 for the $50,000 of bonds first issued and $1,100 for the $20,000 issued two years later. The $67.50 amortization of bond premium is for six months at $11.25 a month.

Adjusting and Reversing Entries

On December 31 an adjusting entry is required for three months' interest on $70,000 of bonds and for amortization of the three months' premium on $20,000 of bonds. Interest payable on the $70,000 of bonds is $1,925 ($70,000 × 0.11 × 3/12). The amortization of the premium amounts to $33.75 ($11.25 × 3). In the entry shown below, Premium on Bonds Payable is debited for $33.75 and Bond Interest Payable is credited for $1,925. The difference of $1,891.25 is charged to Bond Interest Expense.

	19 Y3				
Dec.	31	Bond Interest Expense	692	1,891 25	
		Premium on Bonds Payable	251	33 75	
		Bond Interest Payable	232		1,925 00
		To record accrued interest on $70,000 of bonds and to amortize premium on $20,000 of bonds for three months.			

On January 1 of the following year, this adjusting entry will be reversed. The entries on each April 1 and October 1 for interest and amortization will be the same as the one previously illustrated for October 1, 19Y3. The adjusting and reversing entries will be repeated at the end of each year.

BONDS ISSUED AT A DISCOUNT

Suppose that the Duncan Lawn Furniture Corporation decides to issue another $20,000 of bonds on April 1, 19Y4, a year after the preceding issue. If the prevailing interest rates on other investments have risen to 12 percent since the last sale of bonds, investors will no longer be willing to pay a premium for an investment paying only 11 percent. In fact, they will not be interested in buying the bonds at par value either. Instead, they may offer only $953.17, or 95.317, for each $1,000, 11 percent bond. Assuming that the Duncan Lawn Furniture Corporation sells the bonds at 95.317, the cash it receives for the $20,000 par value bonds is $19,063.40 and there is a $936.60 discount, as shown by this entry.

19 Y4				
Apr. 1	Cash	101	19,063 40	
	Discount on Bonds Payable	151	936 60	
	11% Bonds Payable, 19Z1	261		20,000 00
	To record issuance of bonds at 95.317.			

Amortization of Bond Discount

The bonds in question have seven years to run, and the $936.60 discount must be amortized over this period. On a straight-line basis, the amortization will thus be $133.80 a year ($936.60 ÷ 7). The October 1 interest payment will be made on the $90,000 of bonds outstanding for a total of $4,950 cash. The premium on the bonds issued in 19Y3 will be amortized as previously illustrated. A new entry is required to amortize $66.90 of the discount for a half a year. This entry debits Bond Interest Expense (since the discount increases the actual cost of borrowing) and credits Discount on Bonds Payable for $66.90. (The effective interest method of amortizing a discount is discussed later in this chapter.)

Adjusting and Reversing Entries

On December 31 an adjusting entry is made to accrue interest payable for three months on $90,000 of bonds at 11 percent, or $2,475. Bond discount amortized for three months, $33.45 (3/12 × $133.80), is added, and bond premium amortized for three months, $33.75, is subtracted from this figure. What remains is a debit of $2,474.70 to Bond Interest Expense. The adjusting entry is illustrated below. This entry is, of course, reversed on the first day of the following year.

19 Y4				
Dec. 31	Bond Interest Expense	692	2,474 70	
	Premium on Bonds Payable	251	33 75	
	Discount on Bonds Payable	151		33 45
	Bond Interest Payable	232		2,475 00
	To record accrued interest on $90,000 of bonds, to amortize premium on $20,000 of bonds, and to amortize discount on $20,000 of bonds for three months.			

BALANCE SHEET PRESENTATION OF PREMIUM AND DISCOUNT

The Premium on Bonds Payable account has a credit balance that should be shown on the balance sheet under the heading Long-Term Liabilities, as an addition to the par value of bonds payable. The Discount on Bonds Payable account has a debit balance that should be subtracted from the par value of the bonds payable. If there are both a discount and a premium on a bond issue, the two are combined and shown on the balance sheet as a single net figure. The method of reporting bonds payable and the related discount or premium on the balance sheet is illustrated below for the Duncan Lawn Furniture Corporation on December 31, 19Y4.

Long-Term Liabilities

11% Bonds Payable, due April 1, 19Z1 (Authorized $100,000 par value, less $10,000 par value unissued)	$90,000.00	
Net Premium on Bonds Payable	7.50	
Net Liability		$90,007.50

Book value of Bonds

The balance of the Bonds Payable account plus that of the Premium on Bonds Payable account (or minus that of the Discount on Bonds Payable account) is referred to as the *book value* or the *carrying value* of the bonds.

BONDS ISSUED BETWEEN INTEREST DATES

The preceding examples were for bonds that were issued on interest dates. In practice, however, bonds are often issued between interest dates. The new owner is nevertheless entitled to be paid for the entire interest period when he or she receives the interest check on the interest payment date. Consequently, when bonds are sold between interest dates, the purchaser pays the seller for the interest accrued to the day of purchase.

Recording Issuance of the Bonds

Suppose that the Duncan Lawn Furniture Corporation sells its remaining $10,000 par value bonds on July 1, 19Y5. At this time the prevailing interest rate has again changed. Purchasers of the bonds are now willing to pay face value for the bonds, $10,000, plus accrued interest from April 1 to July 1, 19Y5—a period of three months. Interest for three months at 11 percent on $10,000 is $275, and the total cash actually collected is $10,275. The required entry is presented in general journal form below.

19 Y5					
July	1	Cash	101	10,275 00	
		Bond Interest Expense	692		275 00
		11% Bonds Payable, 19Z1	261		10,000 00
		To record issuance of bonds at par plus accrued interest for three months.			

Notice that the $275 received for accrued interest is credited to the Bond Interest Expense account. When the interest is paid in October, the purchasers of the $10,000 of bonds will receive $550. Of this amount, $275 is a return of what they paid for accrued interest and the remaining $275 is interest actually earned for the three months (July, August, and September) during which they have owned the bonds. In the accounting records of the corporation, the final result is a net interest expense of $275 on these bonds.

Amortization of Discount or Premium

If bonds are issued at a discount or a premium between interest dates, the discount or premium is amortized over the time remaining from the date of issue to the date of maturity. Suppose, for example, that on March 1, 19X4, a corporation issues $100,000 par value, 9 percent, 10-year bonds, dated January 1, 19X1, and maturing January 1, 19Y1, with interest payments due on January 1 and July 1 of each year. The bonds are issued at 102.5, plus accrued interest. The necessary entry is shown in general journal form below.

19X4					
Mar.	1	Cash	101	104,000 00	
		Bond Interest Expense ($100,000			
		× 9% × 2/12)	692		1,500 00
		9% Bonds Payable, 19Y1	261		100,000 00
		Premium on Bonds Payable	251		2,500 00
		To record issuance of $100,000 of 9%			
		bonds at 102.5 plus accrued interest			
		for two months.			

On July 1, 19X4, the date of the first interest payment, the amount of the bond premium to amortize is $121.95, assuming that the straight-line method of amortization is used.

Total premium	$2,500
Number of months from date of issue	
to date of maturity (March 1,	
19X4, to January 1, 19Y1)	82
Amortization each month = $2,500 ÷ 82 =	$30.488
Amortization from March 1, 19X4, to	
July 1, 19X4 = $30.488 × 4 =	$121.95

The entry to record payment of the interest and amortization of the premium on July 1, 19X4, is shown below.

19X4					
July	1	Bond Interest Expense	692	4,378 05	
		Premium on Bonds Payable	251	121 95	
		Cash	101		4,500 00
		To record semiannual interest on 9%			
		bonds and to amortize bond premium			
		for four months.			

Present Value of $1

PERIODS	4%	5%	6%	7%	8%	10%	12%	14%	16%	18%
1	.962	.952	.943	.935	.926	.909	.893	.877	.862	.847
2	.925	.907	.890	.873	.857	.826	.797	.769	.743	.718
3	.889	.864	.840	.816	.794	.751	.712	.675	.641	.609
4	.855	.823	.792	.763	.735	.683	.636	.592	.552	.516
5	.822	.784	.747	.713	.681	.621	.567	.519	.476	.437
6	.790	.746	.705	.666	.630	.564	.507	.456	.410	.370
7	.760	.711	.665	.623	.583	.513	.452	.400	.354	.314
8	.731	.677	.627	.582	.540	.467	.404	.351	.305	.266
9	.703	.645	.592	.544	.500	.424	.361	.308	.263	.225
10	.676	.614	.558	.508	.463	.386	.322	.270	.227	.191
11	.650	.585	.527	.475	.429	.350	.287	.237	.195	.162
12	.625	.557	.497	.444	.397	.319	.257	.208	.168	.137
13	.601	.530	.469	.415	.368	.290	.299	.182	.145	.116
14	.577	.505	.442	.388	.340	.263	.205	.160	.125	.099
15	.555	.481	.417	.362	.315	.239	.183	.140	.108	.084
16	.534	.458	.394	.339	.292	.218	.163	.123	.093	.071
17	.513	.436	.371	.317	.270	.198	.146	.108	.080	.060
18	.494	.416	.350	.296	.250	.180	.130	.095	.069	.051
19	.475	.396	.331	.277	.232	.164	.116	.083	.060	.043
20	.456	.377	.312	.258	.215	.149	.104	.073	.051	.037
21	.439	.359	.294	.242	.199	.135	.093	.064	.044	.031
22	.422	.342	.278	.226	.184	.123	.083	.056	.038	.026
23	.406	.326	.262	.211	.170	.112	.074	.049	.033	.022
24	.390	.310	.247	.197	.158	.102	.066	.043	.028	.019
25	.375	.295	.233	.184	.146	.092	.059	.038	.024	.016

THE EFFECTIVE INTEREST METHOD OF AMORTIZATION

As pointed out previously, a premium or a discount on bonds arises because the *contractual rate* of interest on the bonds is not the same as the *market rate* of interest at the time the bonds are issued. The amount that an investor is willing to pay for bonds depends on the market rate of interest, the principal amount of the bonds, the contractual interest to be received each period, and the length of time until maturity.

For example, assume that the current rate of interest in the financial markets is approximately 10 percent a year, compounded semiannually, and that an individual wishes to invest an amount in 11 percent bonds (5½ percent each six months) with a face value of $20,000, maturing eight years (16 interest periods) from the date of purchase. This individual is in reality making two investments—one in the principal amount of $20,000 to be received eight years later and a second in the right to receive $1,100 interest each six months for 16 periods. In order to find the amount that the investor will be willing to pay for the two future cash flows, two financial tables called *present value tables* are used.

In determining the amount to be paid for the principal amount of the bonds, a table showing the present value of $1 is used. This table, a portion of which is reproduced above, indicates that in order to earn 10 percent a year compounded semiannually (5 percent for each six-month period) on an amount due eight years later, the investor should pay 0.458 (or 45.8 percent) of the maturity value. Thus, the amount to be paid for the face value of bonds with a maturity value of $20,000 is $9,160 ($20,000 × 0.458).

Present Value of an Annuity of $1 per Period

PERIODS	4%	5%	6%	7%	8%	10%	12%	14%	16%	18%
1	0.962	0.952	0.943	0.935	0.926	0.909	0.893	0.877	0.862	0.847
2	1.886	1.859	1.833	1.808	1.783	1.736	1.690	1.647	1.605	1.566
3	2.775	2.723	2.673	2.624	2.577	2.487	2.402	2.322	2.246	2.174
4	3.630	3.546	3.465	3.387	3.312	3.170	3.037	2.914	2.798	2.690
5	4.452	4.330	4.212	4.100	3.993	3.791	3.605	3.433	3.274	3.127
6	5.242	5.076	4.917	4.767	4.623	4.355	4.111	3.889	3.685	3.498
7	6.002	5.786	5.582	5.389	5.206	4.868	4.564	4.288	4.039	3.812
8	6.733	6.463	6.210	5.971	5.747	5.335	4.968	4.639	4.344	4.078
9	7.435	7.108	6.802	6.515	6.247	5.759	5.328	4.946	4.607	4.303
10	8.111	7.722	7.360	7.024	6.710	6.145	5.650	5.216	4.833	4.494
11	8.760	8.306	7.887	7.499	7.139	6.495	5.938	5.453	5.029	4.656
12	9.385	8.863	8.384	7.943	7.536	6.814	6.194	5.660	5.197	4.793
13	9.986	9.394	8.853	8.356	7.904	7.103	6.424	5.842	5.342	4.910
14	10.563	9.899	9.294	8.746	8.244	7.367	6.628	6.002	5.468	5.008
15	11.118	10.380	9.712	9.108	8.559	7.606	6.811	6.142	5.575	5.092
16	11.652	10.837	10.106	9.447	8.851	7.824	6.974	6.265	5.669	5.162
17	12.166	11.274	10.477	9.763	9.122	8.022	7.120	6.373	5.749	5.222
18	12.659	11.690	10.828	10.059	9.372	8.201	7.250	6.467	5.818	5.273
19	13.134	12.085	11.158	10.336	9.604	8.365	7.366	6.550	5.877	5.316
20	13.590	12.462	11.470	10.594	9.818	8.514	7.469	6.623	5.929	5.353
21	14.029	12.821	11.764	10.836	10.017	8.649	7.562	6.687	5.973	5.384
22	14.451	13.163	12.042	11.061	10.201	8.772	7.645	6.743	6.011	5.410
23	14.857	13.489	12.303	11.272	10.371	8.883	7.718	6.792	6.044	5.432
24	15.247	13.799	12.550	11.469	10.529	8.985	7.784	6.835	6.073	5.451
25	15.622	14.094	12.783	11.654	10.675	9.077	7.843	6.873	6.097	5.467

The second computation requires the use of a table showing the present value of an annuity of $1. This table, a portion of which is reproduced above, indicates that the amount to be invested today for a fixed amount to be received at the end of each of 16 periods, at an effective rate of 5 percent for each period, is 10.837 times the fixed amount to be received each period. Thus, in order to earn an annual rate of 10 percent (5 percent for each six-month period) from the receipt of $1,100 each period, an individual must invest $11,920 ($1,100 × 10.837).

The total amount to be invested for 11 percent bonds with a par value of $20,000 is thus $21,080 ($9,160 + $11,920) if the effective rate is to be 10 percent compounded semiannually. As you saw on page 722, this is the amount paid by investors on April 1, 19Y3, for $20,000 par value of the Duncan Lawn Furniture Corporation's 11 percent bonds.

Clearly, the premium is an adjustment of interest expense over the period the bonds are to be outstanding. Thus even though the straight-line method of amortization previously illustrated is often used because of its simplicity, the *effective interest method* of amortization should be used if the amounts are material. Under this method the interest expense for each period (in this case, six months) is computed by multiplying the book value of the bonds (the maturity value plus the premium or minus the discount) by the effective interest rate. The amount of premium to be amortized each period is the difference between the interest expense as computed above and the contractual amount of interest for the period.

Using the data given for the $20,000 of 11 percent bonds issued at a premium by Duncan on April 1, 19Y3, the following table can be set up with the information needed for amortization at each of the first four interest payment dates.

PARTIAL AMORTIZATION TABLE

(1) Interest Date	(2) Book Value at Start of Period	(3) Interest Expense (Col. 2 × 5%)	(4) Premium Amortized ($1,100 − Col. 3)	(5) Unamortized Premium at End of Period	(6) Book Value at End of Period
Oct. 1, 19Y3	$21,080.00	$1,054.00	— $46.00 =	$1,034.00	$21,034.00
Apr. 1, 19Y4	21,034.00	1,051.70	48.30	985.70	20,985.70
Oct. 1, 19Y4	20,985.70	1,049.29	50.71	934.99	20,934.99
Apr. 1, 19Y5	20,934.99	1,046.75	53.25	881.74	20,881.70

From the information in the amortization table, the entry shown below is made at the time of the interest payment on October 1, 19Y3. Similar entries involving the amortization of the premium will be recorded at each succeeding interest payment date.

19 Y3					
Oct. 1	Bond Interest Expense	692	1,054 00		
	Premium on Bonds Payable	251	46 00		
	Cash	101		1,100 00	
	To record interest and to amortize premium on $20,000 of bonds for six months.				

Year-End Adjustments

When the effective interest method of amortization is used, year-end amortization is recorded at the time the adjustment for accrued interest is made. The amount to be amortized is a pro rata portion of the total amortization for the interest period in which the adjustment is made. For example, on December 31, 19Y3, the following entry would be made by Duncan to amortize the bond premium for the three-month period from October 1 through December 31.

19 Y3					
Dec. 31	Bond Interest Expense (3/6 × $1,051.70)	692	525 85		
	Premium on Bonds Payable (3/6 of $48.30)	251	24 15		
	Bond Interest Payable (11% × $20,000 × 3/6)	232		550 00	
	To record accrued interest and to amortize premium on $20,000 of bonds for three months.				

On January 1, 19Y4, the above entry is reversed so that the entry at the next interest payment date of April 1, 19Y4, can be made in the usual manner. The entry of April 1 will be a debit to Bond Interest Expense for $1,051.70, a debit to Premium on Bonds Payable for $48.30, and a credit to Cash for $1,100.

Amortization of Discount

Let us turn now to the $20,000 par value bonds issued by the Duncan Lawn Furniture Corporation on April 1, 19Y4 (discussed on page 724). At the time, the market rate of interest was 12 percent. Thus, since the bonds carry an interest rate of 11 percent, they were issued for $19,063.40, a discount of $936.60. This issue price was again based on figures obtained from the two present value tables shown on pages 727–728. The present value of the face amount was found by multiplying the maturity value of $20,000 by 0.442, the present value of $1 due 14 periods later with a discount rate of 6 percent a period. The present value of the face amount of the bonds is therefore $8,840. Similarly, the present value of the semiannual interest of $1,100 was found by multiplying that amount by the present value factor of 9.294 (based on 14 periods and an effective interest rate of 6 percent each period). The present value of the interest payments is $10,223.40. The total present value of the bonds is therefore $19,063.40 ($8,840 + $10,223.40), which was the issue price of the bonds.

Amortization of a discount is computed in the same way as amortization of a premium—by comparing the effective interest with the contractual interest each period. The following table shows the amortization of the discount on Duncan's bonds for the first four interest periods.

PARTIAL AMORTIZATION TABLE

(1) Interest Date	(2) Book Value at Start of Period	(3) Interest Expense (Col. 2 × 6%)	(4) Discount Amortized (Col. 3 − $1,100)	(5) Unamortized Discount at End of Period	(6) Book Value at End of Period
Oct. 1, 19Y4	$19,063.40	$1,143.80	$43.80	$892.80	$19,107.20
Apr. 1, 19Y5	19,107.20	1,146.32	46.32	846.48	19,153.52
Oct. 1, 19Y5	19,153.52	1,149.21	49.21	797.27	19,202.73
Apr. 1, 19Y6	19,202.73	1,152.16	52.16	745.11	19,254.89

The entry made by Duncan on October 1, 19Y4, to record the interest and the amortization of the discount on its $20,000 of bonds is shown below. The amount credited to Discount on Bonds Payable comes from the amortization table.

19 Y4					
Oct. 1	Bond Interest Expense	692	1,143 80		
	Cash	101		1,100 00	
	Discount on Bonds Payable	151		43 80	
	To record interest and to amortize discount on $20,000 of bonds for six months.				

Year-end adjustments and beginning-of-year reversals are made in the same manner as previously discussed for the bond premium.

BOND SINKING FUND AND APPROPRIATION OF RETAINED EARNINGS

At the maturity of the bond issue on April 1, 19Z1, the Duncan Lawn Furniture Corporation will have to pay bondholders the face amount of their bonds, a total of $100,000 in cash. (The premium and discount are completely amortized with the last interest payment on April 1, 19Z1.) Careful planning is needed to make sure that the required money will be available on the maturity date. In order to ensure the availability of cash, the corporation may voluntarily set up a *bond sinking fund* or it may be required to do so by its contract with the bondholders. Here is how the plan might work.

Bond Sinking Fund

Suppose that the corporation is to accumulate $20,000 a year in the bond sinking fund for each of the last five years that the bonds are outstanding. The cash put into the fund will be invested, and the net earnings of the fund will reduce the amount that the corporation will have to add each year after the first. For example, the bond sinking fund is started on April 1, 19Y6, by transferring $20,000 in cash to it. This $20,000 is immediately invested to earn interest. During the next year $2,800 is earned on the investments made by the sinking fund, and a $50 expense is incurred in operating the fund. This leaves net earnings of $2,750 for the year. On April 1 of the second year, only $17,250 need be added to the fund. This procedure is repeated each year, so that at the end of the fifth year the fund should have accumulated the $100,000 needed to pay off the bonds.

Entries for the first two transfers to the fund, the first year's net earnings, and the final retirement of the bonds at the end of the fifth year are given in general journal form on page 732.

In order to simplify the illustration, it is assumed that the sinking fund is handled by an outside trustee, who makes the necessary detailed entries to record the fund transactions. If the corporation handled the bond sinking fund itself, additional entries would be required to show the investment of the fund's cash, the receipt of earnings, and the payment of fund expenses.

Other procedures may be used to finance the sinking fund. For example, an assumption may be made about the rate of earnings of the sinking fund and a constant amount contributed each period, which when added to the earnings will equal the required balance. If earnings exceed or are less than the rate assumed, the periodic contributions will be adjusted.

The bond sinking fund is reported as an investment in the Assets section of the balance sheet.

Retained Earnings Appropriated for Bond Retirement

As further protection for the bondholders and as a clear indication to the stockholders that retained earnings are being held in the business to pay the bonds at maturity, the bond contract may require that dividend payments be restricted by appropriations of retained earnings while the bonds are outstanding. Even if the bond contract does not require the appropriation, retained earnings may be appropriated by order of the board of directors.

19 Y6					
Apr.	1	Bond Sinking Fund	138	20,000 00	
		Cash	101		20,000 00
		To record transfer of first of five annual			
		installments to bond sinking fund.			
19 Y7					
Apr.	1	Bond Sinking Fund	138	2,750 00	
		Income From Sinking Fund			
		Investments	493		2,750 00
		To record net income earned by bond			
		sinking fund during the year.			
	1	Bond Sinking Fund	138	17,250 00	
		Cash	101		17,250 00
		To record transfer of second annual			
		installment to bond sinking fund, $20,000			
		less $2,750 net earned on fund			
		investments during the year.			
19 Z1					
Apr.	1	11% Bonds Payable, 19Z1	261	100,000 00	
		Bond Sinking Fund	138		100,000 00
		To record retirement of bonds with cash from			
		bond sinking fund.			

If such an appropriation is decided on at the Duncan Lawn Furniture Corporation, an entry might be made to appropriate $20,000 a year during each of the last five years of the life of the bonds. The firm might also adopt some other "schedule of appropriations." When the bonds have been paid off, the appropriated retained earnings are returned to the Retained Earnings account. The entries shown below are to make an appropriation on April 1, 19Y6 (similar entries would be made each year for the next four years), and to remove the appropriation when the bonds have been paid. The Retained Earnings Appropriated for Bond Retirement account would be shown under the heading Appropriated Retained Earnings on the balance sheet.

19 Y6					
Apr.	1	Retained Earnings	381	20,000 00	
		Retained Earnings Appropriated for			
		Bond Retirement	383		20,000 00
		To set up appropriation for bond sinking fund.			
19 Z1					
Apr.	1	Retained Earnings Appropriated for			
		Bond Retirement	383	100,000 00	
		Retained Earnings	381		100,000 00
		To close out appropriation for bond			
		sinking fund on retirement of bonds.			

The Retained Earnings Appropriated for Bond Retirement account is sometimes referred to as the Reserve for Bond Sinking Fund, even though the account has nothing to do with a sinking fund.

RETIREMENT OF BONDS

There are several different ways that corporations can retire the bonds they issue.

Retirement on Due Date

The retirement of Duncan's bonds by payment from the sinking fund illustrates one method of bond retirement. Of course, if there had been no bond sinking fund, the corporation would have recorded the retirement on the maturity date by debiting 11% Bonds Payable, 19Z1, and crediting Cash.

Early Retirement

Under certain circumstances a corporation may retire some or all of its bonds before maturity by purchasing them on the open market. This may be done because the corporation has surplus cash, because it wants to save interest costs, because it expects interest rates to decrease, or for other reasons. When bonds are retired prior to maturity, the bondholders are paid the agreed-upon price for the bonds plus the accrued interest to the date of purchase. The following steps are taken to record the purchase and retirement.

1. The corporation records the amortization of the discount or premium from the date of the last amortization entry to the current date on the bonds being retired.
2. The corporation removes the par value of the bonds from the Bonds Payable account and removes the unamortized discount or premium applicable to the retired bonds from the Discount on Bonds Payable account or the Premium on Bonds Payable account. The purchase price is credited to Cash (or Accounts Payable), and the difference between the purchase price and the book value of the bonds is recorded as a gain or loss. Interest Expense is debited and Cash is credited for the accrued interest paid.

On the income statement, any significant gain or loss on early retirement of bonds is always shown as an extraordinary gain or loss.[1]

To illustrate the early retirement of bonds, we will assume that on January 1, 19X1, the Drake Corporation issued $1,000,000 par value of its 15 percent, 20-year bonds, maturing January 1, 19Z1, with interest payable on January 1 and July 1 of each year. The bonds were issued at 102.4, so a premium of $24,000 was recorded. The premium is being amortized on a straight-line basis at $100 a month ($600 for each interest payment period).

On July 1, 19X6, after the interest was paid and the premium was amortized, the account balances related to the bonds were as follows: 15% Bonds Payable, 19Z1, $1,000,000; Premium on Bonds Payable, $17,400 ($24,000 − $6,600).

On September 1, 19X6, the corporation decided to purchase on the open market at 101 plus accrued interest $300,000 par value of the bonds—30 percent of the total outstanding. The bondholders were paid $303,000 for the bonds, plus $7,500 accrued interest for two months, and the bonds were retired. The necessary entries are given on page 734.

---

[1] "Reporting Gains and Losses From Extinguishment of Debt," *Statement of Financial Accounting Standards, No. 4* (Stamford, Conn.: Financial Accounting Standards Board, 1975), par. 8.

1. The amortization on the bonds being retired is recorded as shown in the general journal entry below.

19 X6				
Sept. 1	Premium on Bonds Payable (30% × $100 × 2)	251	60 00	
	Bond Interest Expense	692		60 00
	To amortize premium for two months on bonds being retired.			

$$\$24{,}000 \times \frac{\$300{,}000}{\$1{,}000{,}000} \times \frac{2\ mos.}{240\ mos.} = \$60$$

2. The par value and unamortized premium are removed. The cash payment for the bonds and the accrued interest are recorded. The unamortized premium is computed as follows.

Unamortized premium after July 1, 19X6, amortization:	
30% × $17,400	$5,220
Less Amortization for July and August	60
Balance	$5,160

The entry to record the retirement of the bonds is shown in general journal form below.

19 X6				
Sept. 1	15% Bonds Payable, 19Z1	261	300,000 00	
	Premium on Bonds Payable	251	5,160 00	
	Bond Interest Expense ($300,000 × 15% × 2/12)	692	7,500 00	
	Cash	101		310,500 00
	Gain on Early Retirement of Bonds	496		2,160 00
	To record retirement of bonds at 101 plus accrued interest and to write off unamortized premium.			

$$\$24{,}000 \times \frac{\$300{,}000}{\$1{,}000{,}000} \times \frac{172\ mos.}{240\ mos.} = \$5{,}160$$

On the income statement, the gain of $2,160 less the related income tax is shown as an extraordinary gain.

MORTGAGE LIABILITIES

If long-term borrowing is arranged through a mortgage loan instead of by issuing bonds, the following entries are required.

1. When cash is received, debit Cash and credit Mortgage Payable. Ordinarily there is no premium or discount on a mortgage loan.
2. When interest payments are made, debit Mortgage Interest Expense and credit Cash. Payments on the principal are of course debited to Mortgage

Payable. These payments are usually made in equal installments. A schedule of amortization shows what part of each payment is applied to interest and what part is applied to principal.

3. Accrue interest at the end of each year, and reverse the adjustment at the beginning of the next year.

4. When the mortgage is paid at maturity, debit Mortgage Payable and credit Cash.

ISSUANCE OF NONINTEREST-BEARING NOTES FOR NONCASH ASSETS

Although most notes payable bear interest, and almost invariably notes issued in return for cash do so, sometimes noninterest-bearing notes are issued to obtain assets other than cash. For example, a person may purchase land for $50,000, giving the seller a two-year noninterest-bearing note for $50,000. A transaction such as this suggests that the land is "overpriced" and that in reality the purchaser is paying less than $50,000 for the property. The difference between $50,000 and the true value of the property is considered the interest charge. (If interest is specified but the rate is unreasonably low, there may also be a presumption that the face value of the note does not reflect the true purchase price of the asset.)

Generally accepted accounting principles require that if the fair market value of the acquired property is known, the asset should be recorded at its fair market value. The Notes Payable account should then be credited for the face value of the note, and the difference should be debited to an account called Discount on Notes Payable. For example, the acquisition of land with a fair market value of $40,000 by the issuance of a two-year noninterest-bearing note payable for $50,000 is recorded as shown below.

19 X1					
May	1	Land	141	40,000 00	
		Discount on Notes Payable	252	10,000 00	
		Notes Payable	251		50,000 00
		To record issuance of a two-year noninterest-bearing note for $50,000 to purchase land with a fair market value of $40,000.			

The discount should be amortized according to the effective interest method. However, because transactions of this type are rare and the amounts involved are small, it is customary to use the straight-line method to amortize the discount.

If the value of the asset acquired cannot be determined, its present value must be imputed. This is done by calculating the present value of the note, using an interest rate that seems reasonable under the circumstances, given the financial condition of the debtor.[2]

---

[2]"Interest on Receivables and Payables," *Opinions of the Accounting Principles Board, No. 2* (New York: American Institute of Certified Public Accountants, 1971), pars. 12–13.

For example, assume that the debtor issues a $100,000 noninterest-bearing note in return for used machinery whose market value cannot be determined. Assume also that an interest rate of 10 percent is reasonable under the circumstances. By referring to a present value table, you would find that the present value of $1 due two years from now is 0.82645. This means that $0.82645 would have to be invested today to accumulate $1 two years from now if the amount invested today were to earn interest of 10 percent a year, compounded annually. Thus the present value of $100,000 due two years from now is $82,645. The entry to record the purchase in the general journal is shown below.

19 X1				
June 1	Machinery and Equipment	131	82,645 00	
	Discount on Notes Payable	252	17,355 00	
	Notes Payable	251		100,000 00
	To record issuance of a two-year noninterest-bearing note for $100,000 to purchase machinery. Present value of $100,000 at 10% discount rate used to establish value.			

The amount shown in the Discount on Notes Payable account would be subtracted from the face value of the long-term notes payable on the balance sheet. This amount would be amortized over the period to maturity in much the same way as discounts on bonds payable are amortized. The exact sums to be amortized over the two-year period are shown below. Note that the amortization for the second year would be limited to the balance of $9,090.50 remaining in the discount account ($17,355 − $8,264.50).

Year 1: $8,264.50 (10% of $82,645)
Year 2: $9,090.95 (10% of $90,909.50 [$82,645 + $8,264.50])

PRINCIPLES AND PROCEDURES SUMMARY

Long-term borrowing may be accomplished through the issuance of bonds. A bond is a written promise to repay a certain sum at a future date. It bears interest that is usually payable annually or semiannually at a specified rate. Bonds may be secured or unsecured and may be registered or may be bearer bonds with interest coupons attached.

Bonds may be issued at par, at a premium, or at a discount. The premium and the discount are amortized over the life of the bonds as an adjustment of the interest expense. When bond interest dates do not coincide with the fiscal year, an adjustment is made for accrued bond interest at the end of the year. The adjustment is reversed at the beginning of the next year. When bonds are issued between interest dates, the purchaser pays for the accrued interest to the date of purchase.

A bond sinking fund may be used to accumulate the cash required to pay bonds at maturity. In addition, an appropriation of retained earnings for bond retirement may be established by transfers from retained earnings. This appropriation indicates that the earnings are not available for dividends because of the need to accumulate funds with which to pay the bonds.

When bonds are retired prior to maturity, a gain or loss results if the repurchase price differs from the book value of the bonds. The gain or loss is shown as an extraordinary item on the income statement.

If noninterest-bearing notes are issued for assets other than cash, it may be appropriate to record the assets at fair market value or imputed value, giving rise to a discount on the notes payable.

MANAGERIAL IMPLICATIONS

Managers should be aware of the possibility of using bonds as a means of obtaining long-term financing. They should understand the different types of bonds and bond retirement funds, the provisions relating to interest, and the appropriations of retained earnings. Managers should also appreciate and understand the advantages and disadvantages of using bonds so that they can raise capital under terms and conditions most favorable to the firm.

REVIEW QUESTIONS

1. What is meant by the term *collateral trust*?
2. Distinguish between secured bonds and debenture bonds.
3. What is a bond indenture?
4. What are registered bonds? Coupon bonds?
5. How is the Bonds Payable account classified on the balance sheet?
6. Are authorized, unissued bonds shown on the balance sheet? If so, where?
7. Why might a company use a special bank account for paying bond interest?
8. What factor or factors would account for the fact that bonds are issued at a premium?
9. Explain the straight-line method of amortizing a premium on bonds payable.
10. Why is a bond premium or discount amortized as part of the adjustment process at the end of the year?
11. Why is the year-end adjusting entry for amortization of a bond premium reversed at the start of the new year?
12. How is a discount on bonds payable shown on the balance sheet?
13. Explain how bond interest is handled when bonds are issued between interest payment dates.
14. Explain the effective interest method of amortizing a premium on bonds payable.
15. Why is the effective interest method preferable to the straight-line method of amortizing a bond premium or discount?

16. Explain how the issue price of bonds is determined.
17. What is a bond sinking fund?
18. What purpose does an appropriation of retained earnings for bond retirement serve?
19. What entry or entries would be made when bonds are retired at maturity?
20. Explain the accounting treatment necessary when bonds are retired before maturity.
21. Explain how to record a transaction in which a noncurrent asset is acquired through the issuance of a noninterest-bearing, three-year note payable.

MANAGERIAL DISCUSSION QUESTIONS

1. Under what circumstances would it be wise for corporate management to borrow needed long-term funds instead of selling stock?
2. Which type of bonds would give management greater flexibility in formulating and controlling a corporation's financial affairs?
3. If registered bonds are safer than coupon bonds, why are coupon bonds still used?
4. Over what period of time must a premium on bonds payable be amortized? What impact does this premium have on the effective cost of borrowing?
5. Why would management repurchase and retire a corporation's bonds prior to their maturity?
6. What are the major advantages of bonds that should be considered by management?

EXERCISES

EXERCISE 31-1 **Recording the issuance of bonds at par.** The Webster Corporation issued $500,000 of its 14 percent bonds payable on March 1, 19X1. The bonds were issued at par. Interest is payable semiannually on September 1 and March 1. Give the entry in general journal form to record the issuance of the bonds.

EXERCISE 31-2 **Recording the payment of bond interest.** Refer to Exercise 31-1. Give the entry in general journal form to record the payment of the bond interest on September 1, 19X1.

EXERCISE 31-3 **Computing accrued bond interest.** Refer to Exercise 31-1. What amount of bond interest will be accrued on December 31, 19X1?

EXERCISE 31-4 **Computing bond interest for a year.** Refer to Exercises 31-1, 31-2, and 31-3. What amount of interest expense will the Webster Corporation have for 19X1?

EXERCISE 31-5 **Computing the proceeds from bonds issued at a discount.** The Krause Corporation was authorized to issue $1,000,000 of its 12 percent bonds. On April 1,

19X2, the corporation issued bonds with a par value of $350,000 at a price of 96.4. The bonds mature 10 years from the date of issue. Interest is payable semiannually on October 1 and April 1. What amount of cash did the corporation receive from the bonds issued on April 1, 19X2?

EXERCISE 31-6 **Computing the amortization of a bond discount on a straight-line basis.** Refer to Exercise 31-5. What amount of discount will be amortized on October 1, 19X2, assuming that straight-line amortization is used?

EXERCISE 31-7 **Recording the adjusting entry for bond interest and discount.** Refer to Exercises 31-5 and 31-6. Give the adjusting entry that would be made on December 31, 19X2, to record accrued interest and to amortize the discount.

EXERCISE 31-8 **Computing net bond interest.** Refer to Exercises 31-5, 31-6, and 31-7. What will be the Krause Corporation's net bond interest expense for 19X2?

EXERCISE 31-9 **Presenting bonds and a discount on the balance sheet.** Refer to Exercises 31-5 through 31-8. Prepare the Long-Term Liabilities section of the Krause Corporation's balance sheet for December 31, 19X2.

EXERCISE 31-10 **Computing the present value of a future amount.** Refer to the table on page 727 that gives the present value of $1. What amount would an investor pay today for the right to receive $500,000, due 10 years from now, in order to earn a 12 percent annual rate of interest, compounded semiannually? To earn 16 percent annually, compounded semiannually?

EXERCISE 31-11 **Computing the present value of an annuity.** Refer to the table on page 728 that gives the present value of an annuity of $1. What amount would an investor pay today for the right to receive $35,000 at the end of each six-month period for 10 years, with the first payment due six months from today, if the effective interest rate is to be 12 percent a year, compounded semiannually? If the effective interest rate is to be 16 percent a year, compounded semiannually?

EXERCISE 31-12 **Computing the issue price of bonds needed to yield a specified rate.** Refer to the two present value tables on pages 727 and 728. On July 1, 19X1, the Ruffino Corporation issued $500,000 of its 14 percent 10-year bonds. Interest is payable semiannually on January 1 and July 1. The bonds mature 10 years from the date of issue. Assuming that the bonds are issued to yield 12 percent a year, compounded semiannually, what will be the issue price of the bonds? Assuming that the bonds are issued to yield 16 percent a year, compounded semiannually, what will be the issue price of the bonds?

EXERCISE 31-13 **Computing the amortization of a bond discount under the effective interest method.** On March 1, 19X1, the Argus Corporation issued $1,000,000 of its 13 percent bonds. Interest is payable semiannually on September 1 and March 1. The bonds were issued at 96.8, a price that will yield an effective annual interest rate of 14 percent, compounded semiannually. Using the effective interest method of amortization, compute the amount of discount that will be amortized on September 1, 19X1. Then determine the amount that will be charged to Bond Interest Expense on that date.

EXERCISE 31-14 **Computing the amortization of a bond premium under the effective interest method.** On March 1, 19X3, the Lopez Corporation issued $1,000,000 of its 13 percent bonds. Interest is payable semiannually on September 1 and March 1. The bonds were issued at 103.6, a price that will yield an effective annual interest rate of 12 percent, compounded semiannually. Using the effective interest method of amortization, compute the amount of premium that will be amortized on September 1, 19X3. Then determine the total amount that will be charged to Bond Interest Expense on that date.

EXERCISE 31-15 **Recording the retirement of bonds before maturity.** On March 1, 19X3, the Lawrence Corporation issued $1,000,000 of its 12 percent bonds, maturing 10 years later on September 1, 19Y3. Interest is payable semiannually on September 1 and March 1. The issue price was 96.4. Interest and amortization have been recorded through March 1, 19X7, four years after the bonds were issued. On June 1, 19X7, the corporation repurchased and retired $400,000 par value of the bonds at a purchase price of 99.8, plus accrued interest. Give the entry in general journal form to record the repurchase and retirement.

EXERCISE 31-16 **Recording the purchase of an asset for a noninterest-bearing note payable.** On May 1, 19X3, the Thornton Corporation purchased a tract of land for a future building site by issuing a three-year noninterest-bearing note payable for $350,000. The land had a fair market value of $250,000 on that date. Give the entry in general journal form to record the purchase.

PROBLEMS

PROBLEM 31-1 **Recording bond transactions involving bonds issued at par.** The board of directors of the Rainbow Paint Corporation authorized the issuance of $300,000 par value, 10-year, 12 percent bonds dated April 1, 19X1, and maturing on April 1, 19Y1. Interest is payable semiannually on April 1 and October 1. The Rainbow Paint Corporation uses the calendar year as its fiscal year. The bond transactions that occurred in 19X1 and 19X2 are shown below and on page 741.

Instructions Record the given transactions in general journal form. (Use the account titles illustrated in the textbook.)

TRANSACTIONS FOR 19X1

Apr. 1 Issued $80,000 of bonds at par value.
Oct. 1 Paid the semiannual interest on the bonds issued.
Dec. 31 Recorded the adjusting entry for the accrued bond interest.
31 Closed the Bond Interest Expense account into the Income Summary account.

TRANSACTIONS FOR 19X2

Jan.   1 Reversed the adjusting entry made on December 31, 19X1.

Apr.   1 Issued $20,000 of bonds at par value.

        1 Paid the interest for six months on the bonds previously issued.

Oct.   1 Paid the interest for six months on the outstanding bonds.

Dec. 31 Recorded the adjusting entry for the accrued bond interest.

      31 Closed the Bond Interest Expense account into the Income Summary account.

PROBLEM 31-2 **Recording bond transactions involving bonds issued at a premium.** Sun-King Solar Energy Systems, Inc., was authorized by its board of directors to issue $700,000 of 10-year, 14 percent bonds dated April 1, 19X1, and maturing on April 1, 19Y1. Interest is payable semiannually on April 1 and October 1. The corporation did not immediately issue the bonds because funds were not currently needed. The transactions that took place in 19X3 and 19X4 are shown below.

Instructions 1. Record the given transactions in general journal form. (Use the account titles illustrated in the textbook.)

      2. Prepare the Long-Term Liabilities section of the corporation's balance sheet on December 31, 19X3.

TRANSACTIONS FOR 19X3

Feb.   1 Issued $20,000 par value bonds for $20,196, plus accrued interest.

Apr.   1 Paid the semiannual interest on the outstanding bonds and amortized the bond premium. (Make two entries.) Use the straight-line method to compute the amortization.

Oct.   1 Paid the semiannual interest on the outstanding bonds and amortized the bond premium.

Dec. 31 Recorded the adjusting entry for accrued interest and amortization of the bond premium for three months. (Make one entry.)

      31 Closed the Bond Interest Expense account into the Income Summary account.

TRANSACTIONS FOR 19X4

Jan.   1 Reversed the adjusting entry made on December 31, 19X3.

PROBLEM 31-3 **Recording bond transactions involving bonds issued at a discount.** The board of directors of the Marcus Corporation authorized the issuance of $400,000 par value, 10-year, 15 percent bonds, dated March 1, 19X1, and maturing on March 1, 19Y1. The interest is payable semiannually on September 1 and March 1. The transactions that occurred in 19X1 and 19X2 are shown below and on page 742.

Instructions 1. Record the given transactions in general journal form. (Use the account titles illustrated in the textbook.)

      2. Prepare the Long-Term Liabilities section of the corporation's balance sheet on December 31, 19X1.

TRANSACTIONS FOR 19X1

May   1 Issued bonds with a par value of $200,000 for $195,280, plus accrued interest.
Sept.   1 Paid the semiannual bond interest and amortized the discount for four months. (Make two entries.) Use the straight-line method to compute the amortization.
Dec.   31 Recorded an adjusting entry to accrue the interest and to amortize the discount. (Make one entry.)
       31 Closed the Bond Interest Expense account into the Income Summary account.

TRANSACTIONS FOR 19X2

Jan   1 Reversed the adjusting entry made on December 31, 19X1.
Mar.   1 Paid the semiannual bond interest and amortized the discount on the outstanding bonds.

PROBLEM 31-4   **Using the effective interest method of amortization and determining bond prices.** This problem has two parts.

1. The O'Connor Corporation is authorized to issue $10,000,000 par value of 12 percent bonds. The bonds are dated June 1, 19X1, and mature 15 years later on June 1, 19Y6. The interest is payable semiannually on June 1 and December 1. Since funds were not needed for five years, none of the bonds were issued until June 1, 19X6. On that date the corporation issued $1,000,000 par value of the bonds at 89.364, a price that provides an effective yield of 14 percent a year, compounded semiannually.

Instructions   Give the general journal entries needed to record the following.

A. The issuance of the bonds on June 1, 19X6.
B. The payment of the bond interest and the amortization of the discount on December 1, 19X6, using the effective interest method.
C. The adjusting entry for the accrued bond interest and the amortization of the discount on December 31, 19X6.
D. The entry to close the Bond Interest Expense account into the Income Summary account on December 31, 19X6.

2. On June 1, 19X8, when the bond issue had eight years left until maturity, the O'Connor Corporation issued an additional $600,000 par value of the 12 percent bonds. The bonds were issued at a price that yields an effective annual interest rate of 10 percent, compounded semiannually.

Instructions   A. Compute the amount received for the bonds.
B. Give the general journal entry to record the issuance of the bonds.

PROBLEM 31-5   **Recording bond sinking fund transactions.** Advanced Technology, Inc., a manufacturer of robots, has outstanding $1,000,000 of 14 percent bonds payable, dated January 1, 19X1, and maturing on January 1, 19Z1, 20 years later. The corporation is required under the bond contract to transfer $37,400 to a sinking fund each year. The directors have also voted to restrict retained earnings by transferring $50,000 each year to a Retained Earnings Appropriated for Bond Retirement account. The pertinent account balances on January 1, 19X5, are Bond Sinking Fund, $158,500, and Retained Earnings Appropriated for Bond Retirement, $200,000. Transactions that took place at the end of 19X5 are shown below.

Instructions
1. Prepare entries in general journal form to record the end-of-year transactions.
2. Show how the Bond Sinking Fund account and the Retained Earnings Appropriated for Bond Retirement account would be presented on the balance sheet as of December 31, 19X5. (Assume that the ending balance of the Retained Earnings—Unappropriated account was $455,720.)
3. Assuming that the Bond Sinking Fund account had a balance of $1,000,000 on January 1, 19Z1, give the entry in general journal form to record the payment of the amount due and the retirement of the bonds.

TRANSACTIONS FOR 19X5

Dec. 31 The annual bond sinking fund deposit was made.
      31 The annual appropriation of retained earnings was recorded.
      31 The bond sinking fund trustee reported $18,900 of net income on the sinking fund investments for the year.

PROBLEM 31-6 **Recording the retirement of bonds prior to maturity.** On April 1, 19X1, the Santana Corporation issued $1,000,000 par value, 14 percent bonds at 98.8. The bonds have a life of 20 years. The discount was to be amortized on each interest payment date. The interest is payable semiannually on April 1 and October 1. On March 1, 19X6, the corporation purchased one-half of the outstanding bonds from the bondholders and retired them. The purchase price was 99.2, plus accrued interest for five months.

Instructions Give the entries in general journal form for the following.

1. To amortize the discount on the bonds being retired (five months' amortization). Use the straight-line method.
2. To record the repurchase and retirement of the bonds. (Use the Loss on Early Retirement of Bonds 693 account.)

ALTERNATE PROBLEMS

PROBLEM 31-1A **Recording bond transactions involving bonds issued at par.** The Handy Tool Corporation obtained authorization from its board of directors to issue $800,000 of 14 percent bonds dated May 1, 19X1. The bonds will mature in 19Y1. The interest is payable semiannually on May 1 and November 1. The bond transactions shown on page 744 occurred in 19X1 and 19X2.

Instructions Record the given transactions in general journal form. (Use the account titles illustrated in the textbook.)

TRANSACTIONS FOR 19X1

May	1	Issued $300,000 of bonds at par value.
Nov.	1	Paid the semiannual bond interest on the outstanding bonds.
Dec.	31	Recorded the adjusting entry to accrue the interest on the bonds issued.
	31	Closed the Bond Interest Expense account into the Income Summary account.

TRANSACTIONS FOR 19X2

Jan.	1	Reversed the adjusting entry of December 31, 19X1
May	1	Paid the semiannual bond interest.
Nov.	1	Paid the semiannual bond interest.
	1	Issued $50,000 of bonds at par value.
Dec.	31	Recorded the adjusting entry to accrue the interest on the bonds.
	31	Closed the Bond Interest Expense account into the Income Summary account.

PROBLEM 31-2A   **Recording bond transactions involving bonds issued at a premium.** Creative Ceramics, Inc., obtained authorization from its board of directors to issue $600,000 of 12 percent bonds. Each bond has a face value of $1,000 and is in registered form. The interest is payable semiannually on May 1 and November 1. The bonds mature in 10 years from the issue date (May 1, 19X1). Because the funds to be raised were not immediately needed, no bonds were issued until 19X3. The transactions that occurred in 19X3 and 19X4 are shown below.

Instructions   1. Record the given transactions in general journal form. (Use the account titles illustrated in the textbook.)
2. Prepare the Long-Term Liabilities section of the corporation's balance sheet on December 31, 19X3.

TRANSACTIONS FOR 19X3

Feb.	1	Issued $50,000 of bonds at par value, plus accrued interest.
May	1	Paid the semiannual interest on the bonds issued.
	1	Issued $100,000 of bonds at 102.
Nov.	1	Paid the semiannual interest on the bonds.
	1	Recorded the amortization of the premium on the bonds sold on May 1, using the straight-line method.
Dec.	31	Recorded the adjusting entry to accrue interest on the bonds issued and to amortize the premium for two months.
	31	Closed the Bond Interest Expense account into the Income Summary account.

TRANSACTIONS FOR 19X4

Jan.	1	Reversed the adjusting entry of December 31, 19X3.

PROBLEM 31-3A   **Recording bond transactions involving bonds issued at a discount.** The Pacelli Corporation obtained authorization from its board of directors to issue

$500,000 of 13 percent bonds. The bonds mature 10 years from their issue date of May 1, 19X1. The interest is payable semiannually on May 1 and November 1. Because the funds were not immediately needed, no bonds were issued until 19X4. The transactions that occurred in 19X4 and 19X5 are shown below.

Instructions
1. Record the given transactions in general journal form. (Use the account titles illustrated in the textbook.)
2. Prepare the Long-Term Liabilities section of the corporation's balance sheet on December 31, 19X4.

TRANSACTIONS FOR 19X4

May	1	Issued $100,000 of bonds at 98.
Nov.	1	Paid the semiannual bond interest.
	1	Amortized the discount on the bonds issued. Use the straight-line method to compute the amortization.
Dec.	31	Recorded the adjusting entry to accrue the interest on the bonds issued and to amortize the discount for two months. (Make one entry.)
	31	Closed the Bond Interest Expense account into the Income Summary account.

TRANSACTIONS FOR 19X5

Jan.   1 Reversed the adjusting entry of December 31, 19X4.

PROBLEM 31-4A   **Using the effective interest method of amortization and determining bond prices.** This problem has two parts.

1. The Ivy Corporation is authorized to issue $2,500,000 par value of its 13 percent bonds. The bonds are dated May 1, 19X1, and mature 12 years later on May 1, 19Y3. The interest is payable semiannually on November 1 and May 1. On May 1, 19X2, bonds with a par value of $1,000,000 were issued at 105.9665, a price that provides an effective yield of 12 percent a year, compounded semiannually.

Instructions   Give the general journal entries needed to record the following.

A. The issuance of the bonds on May 1, 19X2.
B. The payment of the bond interest and the amortization of the premium on November 1, 19X2, using the effective interest method.
C. The adjusting entry for the accrued bond interest and the amortization of the bond premium on December 31, 19X2.
D. The entry to close the Bond Interest Expense account into the Income Summary account on December 31, 19X2.

2. On May 1, 19X4, the Ivy Corporation issued an additional $1,000,000 par value of the 13 percent bonds. The bonds were issued at a price that yields an effective annual interest rate of 14 percent, compounded semiannually.

Instructions   A. Compute the amount received for the bonds.
B. Give the general journal entry to record the issuance of the bonds.

PROBLEM 31-5A **Recording sinking fund transactions.** Graphic Effects, Inc., a printing company, has outstanding $6,000,000 of 12 percent bonds payable dated January 1, 19X1, and maturing January 1, 19Y3, 12 years later. The corporation is required under the bond contract to transfer $410,000 each year to a sinking fund. The directors have also voted to restrict retained earnings by transferring $500,000 each year to a Retained Earnings Appropriated for Bond Retirement account. On January 1, 19X6, the pertinent account balances are Bond Sinking Fund, $2,210,000, and Retained Earnings Appropriated for Bond Retirement, $2,500,000. Transactions that took place at the end of 19X6 are given below.

Instructions
1. Prepare entries in general journal form to record the end-of-year transactions.
2. Show how the Bond Sinking Fund account and the Retained Earnings Appropriated for Bond Retirement account would appear on the balance sheet as of December 31, 19X6. (Assume that the ending balance of the Retained Earnings—Unappropriated account was $8,495,670.)
3. Assuming that the Bond Sinking Fund account had a balance of $6,000,000 on January 1, 19Y3, give the entry in general journal form to record payment of the amount due and the retirement of the bonds.

TRANSACTIONS FOR 19X6

Dec.   31 The annual bond sinking fund deposit was made.
       31 The annual appropriation of retained earnings was recorded.
       31 The bond sinking fund trustee reported a net income of $288,400 on the sinking fund investments for the year.

PROBLEM 31-6A **Recording the retirement of bonds prior to maturity.** On February 1, 19X1, the McDowell Corporation issued $600,000 par value, 12 percent bonds at 98.2. The bonds were to have a life of 20 years. The discount was to be amortized on each interest payment date. The interest is payable semiannually on February 1 and August 1. On September 1, 19X4, the corporation purchased $300,000 par value of the bonds from the bondholders and retired them. The purchase price was 98.

Instructions Give the entries in general journal form for the following.

1. To amortize the discount on the bonds being retired (one month's amortization). Use the straight-line method.
2. To record the repurchase and retirement of the bonds. (Use the Gain on Early Retirement of Bonds 496 account.)

CHAPTER

32

TEMPORARY AND LONG-TERM INVESTMENTS

The last several chapters showed that corporate capital can be obtained by issuing stocks or bonds. Each of the corporation's transactions involved someone who was willing to buy the stocks or bonds as an investment. However, investors are not always individuals. Corporations may also invest part of their funds in the stocks and bonds of other firms. This chapter discusses the accounting treatment needed to record investment transactions by a business.

TYPES OF BUSINESS INVESTMENTS

Investments by business firms can be broadly divided into two classes—temporary and long-term. Some firms have enough capital to meet their busy-season needs and therefore have idle funds in the slack season. They may invest these funds in government bonds, U.S. Treasury certificates of indebtedness, bank certificates of deposit, or other obligations that will earn them interest and that they can easily convert into cash when they again need the funds. These seasonal investments are known as *temporary investments*. In order to be classified as temporary, an investment must meet two tests. First, the investment must be easily marketable. Second, the investing firm must intend to convert the investment into cash within one year from the balance sheet date. Clearly, the investments named above are highly marketable. In addition, corporations sometimes make temporary investments in the bonds of other corporations or in high-grade stocks of other corporations.

There are also situations in which business firms have funds in excess of all current needs and can invest them for a longer period of time. This type of investment, which is known as a *long-term investment,* may be made because the firm is attempting to accumulate money for some specific future purpose, such as building a new factory, or it may be made simply because the investment represents a profitable use of the funds available. In still other cases, the investor may be seeking to assure a source of supply of product or may be using the investment as a means of diversifying the scope of its operations. The investing corporation may even purchase a majority of another company's voting stock so that it controls the second corporation. The purchaser of a majority of another company's voting stock is called the *parent company,* or *holding company*. The corporation that has had the majority of its stock purchased by another corporation is called the *subsidiary company*. Because of the economic control of a subsidiary by a parent company, it is necessary to prepare consolidated financial statements for the two entities. *Consolidated financial statements* combine information from the statements of the parent and subsidiary companies and treat the two firms as though they were one economic unit. (Consolidated financial statements are discussed in Chapter 33.)

Assets—such as land, buildings, and machinery—that are owned but are not used in business operations are also considered investments. Similarly, funds such as the bond sinking fund described in the preceding chapter are classified as investments.

TEMPORARY INVESTMENTS

As pointed out previously, in order to be classified as temporary, an investment must be easily marketable and the firm must also intend to convert the investment into cash within one year from the balance sheet date. In this section we shall discuss the basic principles of accounting for temporary investments in both bonds and stocks.

Bonds as a Temporary Investment

Because they are easily marketable and safe, government bonds are a popular investment for funds that are temporarily available.

Purchase of Bonds Suppose that the Duncan Lawn Furniture Corporation finds itself with idle funds available for temporary investment. The board of directors authorizes the firm's treasurer to buy U.S. government bonds. On August 1 the treasurer purchases $10,000 face value 10 percent bonds at 92. Interest is payable on May 1 and November 1. A broker's fee of $45 is incurred in making the purchase. The broker's fee and any other acquisition costs are considered part of the cost of the bonds, as shown below.

Price of $10,000 bonds at 92	$9,200
Plus broker's fee	45
Total cost of bonds	$9,245
Plus accrued interest (May 1 to	
August 1 = $10,000 \times 0.10 \times \frac{3}{12}$)	250
Total cash paid	$9,495

These facts are now recorded in a compound entry that debits U.S. 10% Bonds, 19Z4, for $9,245, debits Interest Income for $250, and credits Cash for $9,495. The accrued interest is debited to the Interest Income account so that when the check representing interest for May 1 to November 1 is received on November 1, the entire amount can be credited to the Interest Income account. Note that the purchase price is debited to the investment account. Any discount or premium is not shown in a separate account.

Interest Income Received On November 1 the Duncan Lawn Furniture Corporation receives interest for six months, amounting to $500 ($10,000 \times 0.10 \times \frac{6}{12}$). The firm debits Cash and credits Interest Income. The $500 credit to Interest Income is partially offset by the $250 debit to Interest Income for accrued interest that was recorded at the time of purchase. This leaves a net credit of $250, the amount of interest earned for the three months that the bonds have been owned.

Accrued Interest Income at the End of the Year When the corporation's fiscal year ends on a date other than an interest date for the bonds it holds, accrued interest income will have to be recorded by an adjusting entry. Thus when Duncan closes its accounting records on December 31, interest of $166.67 has accrued for two months. The adjusting entry debits Interest Receivable and credits Interest Income, as shown below.

19 Y7					
Dec. 31	Interest Receivable	116	166 67		
	Interest Income	492			166 67
	To record accrued interest for two months on U.S. 10% Bonds, 19Z4.				

Statement Presentation The Interest Receivable of $166.67 is shown as a current asset on the balance sheet. The cost of the bonds, including the broker's fee, also appears as a current asset. If the market price changes materially by the balance sheet date, it can be noted in parentheses after the account title on the statement. If the price has fallen and the decline is expected to be permanent, many accountants would reduce the figure shown on the balance sheet to the market price. Accountants who handle the situation this way are following the lower of cost or market concept discussed in connection with inventory valuation. (However, this loss is not deductible by the corporation for income tax purposes until the bonds are sold.)

The $416.67 balance of Interest Income is shown near the bottom of the income statement as nonoperating income.

Reversing Entry for Accrued Interest On January 1 a reversing entry is made debiting Interest Income and crediting Interest Receivable. This entry allows the firm to record the receipt of interest on the next interest date (May 1) as it was handled on November 1. Cash is debited and Interest Income is credited for the entire $500 received.

Sale of Temporary Investment Suppose that shortly after the first of the year, the Duncan Lawn Furniture Corporation's busy season begins and the treasurer is instructed to sell the temporary investment in order to raise extra funds. On February 1 the $10,000 bonds are sold at 93 plus accrued interest, less a broker's fee of $46. The transaction is analyzed below.

Price of $10,000 bonds at 93	$9,300
Less broker's fee	46
Net proceeds from sale of bonds	$9,254
Accrued interest (Nov. 1 to Feb. 1—	
$10,000 \times 0.10 \times 3/12)	250
Total cash received	$9,504

The gain on the sale of the bonds is determined by comparing the net proceeds (excluding interest) of $9,254 with the cost of $9,245, which appears in the ledger account. The gain is $9, as shown below in general journal form.

19	Y8					
Feb.	1	Cash	101	9,504 00		
		U.S. 10% Bonds, 19Z4	119		9,245 00	
		Interest Income	492		250 00	
		Gain or Loss on Sale of Investments	495		9 00	
		To record sale of bonds at 93 plus				
		accrued interest and less broker's fee				
		of $46.				

When this entry has been posted, the bond investment account is closed. Interest Income shows a balance of $83.33 ($250 less $166.67 debited in the reversing entry on January 1), which is the interest for one month in the current year. The gain realized on the sale is reflected in the Gain or Loss on Sale of Investments account, which is reported on the income statement as a nonoperating income item. If a loss had been incurred, the account would have shown a debit balance and would have appeared as a nonoperating expense on the income statement.

Although the example given above illustrates the accounting treatment of an investment in government bonds, temporary investments in bonds of corporations are accounted for in exactly the same manner. Note that any discount or premium (difference between maturity value and purchase price) on bonds acquired as a temporary investment is not amortized. This is because the bonds will not be held to maturity and the sales price to be realized on their disposition is unknown, so there is no basis for determining the proper amount of amortization.

Equity Securities (Stock) as a Temporary Investment

Because temporary investments should have easy marketability and low risk, most corporations prefer to invest temporarily idle funds in U.S. government bonds and corporate bonds. However, a corporation may wish to make temporary investments in equity securities (shares of stock of other corporations) because of high dividends being paid on the stock or because of favorable market conditions. A major benefit of stock investments is that only 15 percent of the dividends received by a corporation on stock of another corporation is subject to the federal income tax. Stock acquired as a short-term investment should be of high quality with little risk involved and with a stable market value.

Purchase of Stock for a Temporary Investment Stock acquired as a temporary investment is accounted for on the cost basis. (As we shall see later, this is actually on the basis of the lower of cost or market.) Under the cost basis, the investment account is not adjusted to reflect the net income or net loss of the investee corporation, nor is it affected by dividends received. All costs incurred in purchasing shares of stock are treated as part of the asset's cost. This cost includes the purchase price, the broker's fee, transfer taxes, and any other incidental acquisition cost. For example, assume that on June 12, 19Y5, the Duncan Lawn Furniture Corporation purchases 200 shares of the 100,000 shares of outstanding common stock of the Harpool Corporation at a price of $60 a share. The broker's fee and transfer taxes are $200. The entry for this transaction is shown below.

19 Y5				
June 12	Temporary Investment in Harpool			
	Corporation Common Stock		12,200 00	
	Cash			12,200 00
	To record purchase of 200 shares of			
	Harpool Corporation common			
	stock at $60 a share, plus incidental			
	costs of $200.			

Decline in Market Value Under generally accepted accounting principles, a portfolio of temporary investments in marketable equity securities should be reported on the balance sheet at the lower of its aggregate (total) cost or its aggregate market value as of the balance sheet date. When aggregate market value falls below aggregate cost, a valuation account (with a credit balance) is set up to reduce the total carrying value of the portfolio to its total market value.[1] Any amount that must be credited to the allowance account in order to reduce the carrying value of the securities is debited to an "unrealized loss" account, which appears on the income statement for the period. Assume, for example, that on December 31, 19Y5, the Duncan Lawn Furniture Corporation has the temporary investments in common stock shown below. The market value on December 31, 19Y5, and the original cost are also shown.

Security	Cost	Market Value December 31, 19Y5
200 shares, Harpool Corp. common stock	$12,200	$11,600
100 shares, Dane Corp. common stock	8,700	8,800
Aggregate (total)	$20,900	$20,400

Excess of cost over market value: $500

On December 31, 19Y5, Duncan must provide an allowance account of $500. The necessary entry is shown on page 752 in general journal form.

On the income statement, the unrealized loss is shown as an ordinary loss or an extraordinary loss, depending on whether or not the holding of securities is an

[1] "Accounting for Certain Marketable Securities," *Statement of Financial Accounting Standards, No. 12* (Stamford, Conn.: Financial Accounting Standards Board, 1975).

19 Y5			
Dec. 31	Unrealized Loss on Valuation of Temporary Investment in Equity Securities	500 00	
	Allowance to Reduce Temporary Investment in Equity Securities to Market Value		500 00
	To reduce carrying value of marketable short-term securities to market value.		

unusual and nonrecurring event for the investor. The allowance account is shown on the balance sheet as a deduction from the cost of temporary investments, as illustrated below.

Temporary Investments

Investment in Marketable Equity Securities, at Cost	$20,900
Less Allowance to Reduce Securities to Market Value	500
Marketable Securities at Lower of Cost or Market	$20,400

Subsequent Recovery of Market Value Assume that at the next balance sheet date the allowance necessary to reduce the carrying value of Duncan's temporary investment in equity securities from cost to market value is less than $500. In this situation the allowance account is debited to reduce it, and the amount of the necessary adjustment is credited as unrealized income. For example, suppose that Duncan still holds both the Dane Corporation stock and the Harpool Corporation stock on December 31, 19Y6 (even though it had been management's plan to sell the stock prior to this date), and the shares are still classified as temporary investments. Suppose further that the market price of the Harpool stock is $60 a share and the market price of the Dane stock is $86 a share. The necessary balance in the allowance account is thus $300, as shown below.

Security	Cost	Market Value December 31, 19Y6
200 shares, Harpool Corp. common stock	$12,200	$12,000
100 shares, Dane Corp. common stock	8,700	8,600
Aggregate (total)	$20,900	$20,600

Excess of cost over market value: $300

The adjusting entry to reduce the allowance account to the desired balance is shown on page 753. The unrealized gain is reported on the income statement as other income (or, if nonrecurring and unusual, as an extraordinary gain).

19 Y6				
Dec. 31	Allowance to Reduce Temporary Investment in Equity Securities to Market Value	200 00		
	Unrealized Gain on Recovery in Market Value of Temporary Investment in Equity Securities		200 00	
	To reduce allowance account to required balance.			

An unrealized gain resulting from recovery of market value is recorded only to the point that the allowance account is reduced to zero. In other words, the investment carrying value is never more than aggregate cost. Suppose that the aggregate market value of the Harpool Corporation stock and the Dane Corporation stock on December 3, 19Y6, is $30,000, the allowance account will be eliminated and an unrealized gain of only $500 will be recorded.

Sale of Temporary Investments in Equity Securities When temporary investments in marketable equity securities are sold, the difference between the amount realized from the sale and the *recorded cost* of the securities is recorded as a gain or loss. For example, assume that on January 3, 19Y7, the Duncan Lawn Furniture Corporation sells 50 shares of Dane Corporation stock for $4,225. The entry to record the sale is shown below in general journal form.

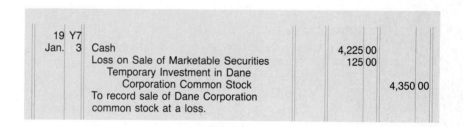

19 Y7				
Jan. 3	Cash	4,225 00		
	Loss on Sale of Marketable Securities	125 00		
	Temporary Investment in Dane Corporation Common Stock		4,350 00	
	To record sale of Dane Corporation common stock at a loss.			

Obviously, the sale of the Dane Corporation stock will affect the amount that must be in the allowance account on the next balance sheet date. However, this will be taken care of automatically in the routine entry made to adjust the allowance account to the proper balance at that time.

Cash Dividends on Stock Under the lower of cost or market method of recording investments in equity securities, the investing company does *not* record its share of the net income reported by the corporations that issued the securities. Only when dividends are declared or paid by these corporations does the investor record income. For example, if at the end of 19Y5 the Dane Corporation reports a net income of $1,000,000, the Duncan Lawn Furniture Corporation will make no entry. If, however, on January 10, 19Y6, Dane declares a dividend of $1 a share, payable on February 10 to stockholders of record on January 25, Duncan will make the entry shown on page 754.

19 Y6			
Jan. 10	Dividend Receivable—Dane Corporation	100 00	
	Dividend Income		100 00
	To record declaration of dividend		
	by Dane Corporation of $1 a share		
	(100 shares).		

Duncan makes no entry on January 25, the date of record of the Dane dividend. When it receives cash in payment of the dividend, it will record the facts as shown below in general journal form.

19 Y6			
Feb. 10	Cash	100 00	
	Dividend Receivable—Dane		
	Corporation		100 00
	To record receipt of dividend from		
	Dane Corporation.		

Many investors prefer to make no entry on the declaration date of a dividend. Instead, they wait until they receive the cash, at which time they debit Cash and credit Dividend Income for the amount received.

LONG-TERM INVESTMENTS

The most common types of long-term investments for corporations are the bonds and stocks of other corporations. The methods used to account for such investments are discussed in this section.

Bonds as Long-Term Investments

Bonds purchased for long-term investment are initially recorded at cost. However, when such bonds are purchased at a price that is more or less than the face value, the premium or discount is amortized over the remaining life of the bonds. (In the case of a short-term investment, the discount or premium is not amortized because the buyer does not intend to hold the bonds until maturity.)

Purchase of Bonds at a Discount Assume that on May 1, 19Z1, the Duncan Lawn Furniture Corporation buys bonds with a face value of $20,000. They are the Wayne Corporation's 11 percent bonds, which have a cost to Duncan of 95.1766, a price that will yield an effective annual interest rate of 12 percent, compounded semiannually. The bonds mature on September 1, 19Z9, eight years and four months later. Interest is payable on March 1 and September 1. The amount of cash to be paid for the bonds is $19,401.99, as analyzed below.

Purchase price of bonds ($20,000 at 95.1766)	$19,035.32
Accrued interest ($20,000 × 0.11 × $\frac{2}{12}$)	366.67
Total cash paid	$19,401.99

The entry required to record the purchase is shown below in general journal form.

	19	Z1							
May	1		Wayne Corporation 11% Bonds, 19Z9	132	19,035	32			
			Interest Income	492	366	67			
			Cash	101			19,401	99	
			To record purchase of $20,000 of bonds at 95.1766 plus accrued interest for two months.						

Interest Income Received On September 1, 19Z1, the $1,100 interest on the bonds for six months is received by the Duncan Lawn Furniture Corporation. The amount is recorded by a debit to Cash and a credit to Interest Income. With the $366.67 debit to Interest Income at the time of purchase, this account now shows a net credit balance of $733.33, the interest actually earned on the bonds for four months.

Amortization of the Discount The bonds were purchased at a discount that must be amortized over the remaining life of the investment. As in the case of a discount or premium on bonds payable, a discount or premium on long-term bond investments should be amortized under the effective interest method. Because of its simplicity, however, the straight-line method of amortization is commonly used unless the amounts involved are material. Assume that Duncan has decided to use the straight-line method. (The effective interest method is illustrated later in this chapter.) Since the bonds mature eight years and four months (100 months) from the date of their purchase, the discount of $964.68 ($20,000 face value − $19,035.32 cost) will be amortized at the rate of $9.65 a month ($964.68 ÷ 100). For the four months from May 1 to September 1, the amount to be amortized is $38.60 ($9.65 × 4).

The bond investment account is debited and Interest Income is credited because the discount is assumed to be an adjustment of the face rate of interest on the bonds to the market rate. The periodic debits will gradually increase the investment account to $20,000 (the face amount of the bonds) by the maturity date. The two entries required to record the receipt of interest and the amortization of the discount are shown below in general journal form.

	19	Z1							
Sept.	1		Cash	101	1,100	00			
			Interest Income	492			1,100	00	
			To record receipt of interest on Wayne Corporation bonds for six months.						
	1		Wayne Corporation 11% Bonds, 19Z9	132	38	60			
			Interest Income	492			38	60	
			To record amortization of discount on bonds at $9.65 a month for four months.						

Accrued Interest Income at the End of the Year On December 31, 19Z1, interest must be accrued on the bonds for the four months since September 1, and the discount must be amortized for the same period, as shown below.

19 Z1				
Dec. 31	Interest Receivable	116	733 33	
	Wayne Corporation 11% Bonds, 19Z9	132	38 60	
	Interest Income	492		771 93
	To record accrued interest and to amortize discount on bonds for four months.			

Statement Presentation Interest Receivable appears on the balance sheet as a current asset. The account Wayne Corporation 11% Bonds, 19Z9, is shown under Investments at $19,112.52, the original cost plus the amount of discount amortized ($19,035.32 + $77.20). Interest Income appears as a nonoperating income item on the income statement.

Reversing Entry for Accrued Interest The adjusting entry is completely reversed on January 1, 19Z2. Then on March 1, when the full six-month interest payment is received, Cash is debited and Interest Income is credited for $1,100, as was done on September 1. The accountant also makes another entry to amortize the six months' discount. This entry debits Wayne Corporation Bonds, 19Z9, and credits Interest Income for $57.90 ($9.65 × 6).

Interest and amortization entries similar to these are made each year as long as the bonds are held. At maturity the investment account will have a balance of $20,000. This balance will be credited and closed out when the bonds are paid off by the Wayne Corporation and the Duncan Lawn Furniture Corporation receives the face value in cash.

Use of the Effective Interest Method of Amortization for Bond Investments As noted previously, discounts and premiums on bond investments should be amortized under the effective interest method because they represent an adjustment of contractual interest to the market rate. The procedure to be followed is identical to that used for amortizing a discount or premium on bonds payable, which was discussed in Chapter 31.

The $20,000 of Wayne Corporation 11% bonds, maturing in 19Z9, purchased for $19,035.32, will provide an example of how a discount on a bond investment is amortized under the effective interest method. The price of $19,035.32 will yield an effective interest rate of 12 percent, compounded semiannually, until maturity. Thus the amount of interest income to be reported each interest period should be 6 percent of the book value of the investment at the start of that period. The amount of discount to be amortized should be the difference between the amount of effective interest income earned and the contractual interest earned during the period. An amortization table for the Wayne Corporation bonds for the years 19Z1 and 19Z2 is shown on page 757. (Notice that this table

PARTIAL AMORTIZATION TABLE

(1) Interest Date	(2) Book Value at Start of Period	(3) Effective Interest (Col. 2 × 6%)	(4) Contractual Interest ($1,100 each 6 mos.)	(5) Discount Amortized (Col. 3 − Col. 4)	(6) Book Value at End of Period (Col. 2 + Col. 5)
Sept. 1, 19Z1	$19,035.32	$ 761.41	$ 733.33	$28.08	$19,063.40
Mar. 1, 19Z2	19,063.40	1,143.80	1,100.00	43.80	19,153.52
Sept. 1, 19Z2	19,153.52	1,149.21	1,100.00	49.21	19,202.73

corresponds exactly to the one on page 759 for the 11 percent bonds payable issued to yield 12 percent, except that the table above has an extra four months added to it.)

The interest and amortization for the interest payment date of September 1, 19Z1, cover the four months that the bonds were actually held (May 1 to September 1).

Effective interest ($19,035.32 × 0.06 × ⁴⁄₆)	$761.41
Contractual interest ($20,000 × 0.055 × ⁴⁄₆)	733.33
Discount amortized	$ 28.08

All entries related to the interest and amortization on these bonds from September 1, 19Z1, through March 1, 19Z2, are shown below and on page 758 in general journal form. The entries are based on the data in the amortization table. (Remember that at the time the bonds were purchased, the accrued interest of $366.67 from March 1 to May 1 was debited to Interest Income. As a result, the net credit to Interest Income as of September 1 is $761.41. This represents the cash interest of $733.33 for four months plus the discount amortized of $28.08 for four months.)

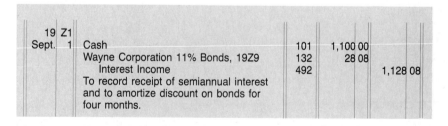

19 Z1						
Sept.	1	Cash	101	1,100 00		
		Wayne Corporation 11% Bonds, 19Z9	132	28 08		
		Interest Income	492		1,128 08	
		To record receipt of semiannual interest and to amortize discount on bonds for four months.				

19 Z1						
Dec.	31	Interest Receivable ($20,000 × 11% × ⁴⁄₁₂)	116	733 33		
		Wayne Corporation 11% Bonds, 19Z9				
		($43.80 × ⁴⁄₆)	132	29 20		
		Interest Income	492		762 53	
		To record accrued interest and to amortize discount on bonds for four months.				

	19 Z2						
	Jan.	1	Interest Income	492	762	53	
			Interest Receivable	116			733 33
			Wayne Corporation 11% Bonds, 19Z9	132			29 20
			To reverse adjusting entry of Dec. 31.				

	19 Z2						
	May	1	Cash	101	1,100	00	
			Wayne Corporation 11% Bonds, 19Z9	132	43	80	
			Interest Income	492			1,143 80
			To record receipt of interest and to				
			amortize discount on bonds for six months.				

Purchase of Bonds at a Premium If a long-term investment in bonds is made at a premium, the purchase is recorded at full cost, including broker's fees. The interest is recorded in the usual manner. The premium is amortized over the remaining life of the bonds. The principles and computations are the same as those applied to investments purchased at a discount. However, the effect of the premium amortization is to reduce interest income. This reduction is accomplished by a periodic debit to Interest Income and a credit to the bond investment account for the amortization. By maturity the balance of the investment account is reduced to the face value of the bonds. This amount is also the amount of cash to be received when the bonds are redeemed by the issuing corporation.

For example, suppose that a corporation purchases $100,000 par value of the 12 percent bonds of the Ames Corporation on June 1, 19X1, for $111,000 plus accrued interest. The bonds are due on August 1, 19Y0, nine years and two months (110 months) later. Interest is payable on August 1 and February 1. The entry to record this purchase is as follows.

	19 X1						
	June	1	Ames Corporation 12% Bonds, 19Y0	134	111,000	00	
			Interest Income	492	4,000	00	
			Cash	101			115,000 00
			To record purchase of $100,000 of bonds				
			at 111 plus accrued interest for four				
			months.				

If straight-line amortization is used, when the bond interest is received on August 1, 19X1, a premium of $200 ($11,000 × 2/110) will be amortized. The entry to record receipt of the interest and amortization of the premium will be as shown on page 759.

Sale of Long-Term Bond Investment When bonds being held as a long-term investment are sold, amortization of the discount or premium must be

19 X1						
Aug.	1	Cash ($100,000 × 6%)	101	6,000 00		
		Ames Corporation 12% Bonds, 19Y0,				
		($11,000 × 2/110)	134		200 00	
		Interest Income	492		5,800 00	
		To record receipt of semiannual				
		interest and to amortize premium on				
		bonds for two months.				

brought up to date. Then the difference between the sale price and the book value after amortization is recognized as a gain or loss. For example, let us return again to the investment in Wayne Corporation bonds held by the Duncan Lawn Furniture Corporation. Suppose that Duncan has been using the straight-line method to amortize the discount on the Wayne Corporation bonds purchased on May 1, 19Z1 (see pages 754–756). On June 1, 19Z5, four years and one month after purchasing the bonds, Duncan sells the bonds at 99 plus accrued interest and pays a broker's fee of $65. The first step in recording this transaction is to amortize the discount from the last interest date, March 1, to the date of sale—a period of three months. The amortization for this period amounts to $28.95 ($9.65 × 3). The entry is shown below.

19 Z5						
June	1	Wayne Corporation 11% Bonds, 19Z9	132	28 95		
		Interest Income	492		28 95	
		To record amortization of discount for				
		three months at $9.65 a month to date				
		of sale of bonds.				

When the amortization is brought up to date, the Wayne Corporation 11% Bonds, 19Z9 account has a debit balance of $19,508.17, which is explained below.

Cost recorded on date of purchase	$19,035.32
Discount amortized: 49 months at $9.65 each month	472.85
Balance of asset account	$19,508.17

The next step is to compute accrued interest on these bonds for a period of three months (March 1 to June 1). The interest amounts to $550 ($20,000 × 0.11 × 3/12). Finally, the sale is analyzed, as illustrated below.

Price of $20,000 bonds at 99	$19,800
Less broker's fee	65
Net proceeds from sale of bonds	$19,735
Accrued interest for 3 months	550
Total cash received	$20,285

The previous entries and calculations now make it possible to determine the gain or loss. In this instance the gain on the sale is $226.83. It is determined by comparing the net proceeds from the sale of the bonds with the book value shown in the investment account ($19,735.00 − $19,508.17). The entry to record the sale of this bond investment is given below in general journal form.

19 Z5						
June	1	Cash	101	20,285 00		
		Wayne Corporation 11% Bonds, 19Z9	132		19,508 17	
		Interest Income	492		550 00	
		Gain or Loss on Sale of Investments	495		226 83	
		To record sale of bonds at 99 plus accrued interest for three months, less $65 broker's fee.				

Equity Securities (Stock) as Long-Term Investments

Investors purchase the stock of other corporations for a variety of reasons. In some cases the purchase is made solely for investment purposes—for the stock's dividends or for its expected appreciation in value. In other cases the purchase is made for "political" reasons—for example, to gain a measure of control over a corporation that is a source of supply or is a major customer of the investor. The proper accounting for a long-term investment in the stock of another corporation depends on whether the investor exercises "significant influence" over the *investee* (the company that issued the stock).[2]

Accounting for Long-Term Investments in Equity Securities When the Investor Does Not Exercise Significant Influence Over the Investee In general, if the investor owns less than 20 percent of the voting stock of the investee, the investor is presumed to be incapable of exercising significant influence over the investee. In that event the long-term investment in the stock is accounted for at the lower of cost or market value. The method is much the same as that used for short-term investments in stock.

Recording a Stock Purchase The entry to record the purchase of a long-term investment in stock is almost identical to that previously illustrated for short-term investments. The only difference is that the account indicates a long-term investment.

Recording a Decline in Value If at a balance sheet date the aggregate market value of long-term investments in stock is less than the aggregate cost, an allowance account is set up to reduce the carrying value to market price. This is done in much the same way as previously illustrated for short-term investments. However, for long-term investments, adjustments to the allowance account are not reported on the income statement. Instead, they are accumulated in an account that is shown in the Stockholders' Equity section of the balance sheet.[3]

---

[2]"The Equity Method of Accounting for Investments in Common Stock," *Opinions of the Accounting Principles Board, No. 18* (New York: American Institute of Certified Public Accountants, 1971).

[3]"Accounting for Certain Marketable Securities," *Statement of Financial Accounting Standards, No. 12* (Stamford, Conn.: Financial Accounting Standards Board, 1975).

This procedure can be illustrated as follows. Assume that on December 31, 19Y5, the portfolio of long-term investments in marketable equity securities of the Duncan Lawn Furniture Corporation includes the stocks shown below. All have been purchased during 19Y5.

Security	Cost	Market Value Dec. 31, 19Y5
300 shares, Glenn Corp. common stock	$44,000	$36,000
200 shares, Klammer Corp. common stock	30,000	33,000
Aggregate (total)	$74,000	$69,000

Excess of cost over market value: $5,000

Duncan has not previously set up an allowance account to reduce the carrying value of its securities. The entry to record the decline in market value and establish the allowance account on December 31, 19Y5, is shown below.

19 Y5				
Dec. 31	Cumulative Unrealized Net Loss on Long-Term Equity Securities		5,000 00	
	Allowance to Reduce Long-Term Equity Securities to Market Value			5,000 00
	To set up allowance account for decline in market value of long-term equity securities.			

On the December 31, 19Y5, balance sheet, the allowance account is offset against the long-term investments as shown below.

Long-Term Investments

Marketable Equity Securities, at Cost	$74,000
Less Allowance to Reduce Equity Securities to Market Value	5,000
Marketable Equity Securities at the Lower of Cost or Market Value	$69,000

The Cumulative Unrealized Net Loss account is shown in the Stockholders' Equity section below.

Stockholders' Equity

Common Stock	$200,000
Retained Earnings	250,000
	$450,000
Less Cumulative Unrealized Net Loss on Long-Term Equity Securities	5,000
Total Stockholders' Equity	$445,000

Recording a Recovery of Market Value At the time a balance sheet is prepared, a comparison is made of the cost and the market value of the portfolio of long-term equity securities. Suppose that the comparison reveals that all or part of the allowance account previously established is no longer needed. In this situation the allowance account is reduced to the appropriate balance. The entry required is a debit to the allowance account and a credit to the Cumulative Unrealized Net Loss account. For example, assume that the market value of Duncan's portfolio of long-term investments in equity securities on December 31, 19Y6, is as shown below.

Security	Cost	Market Value December 31, 19Y6
300 shares, Glenn Corp. common stock	$44,000	$36,000
200 shares, Klammer Corp. common stock	30,000	35,000
Aggregate (total)	$74,000	$71,000

Excess of cost over market value: $3,000

The recovery is recorded by a $2,000 debit to the Allowance to Reduce Long-Term Equity Securities to Market Value account and a $2,000 credit to the Cumulative Unrealized Net Loss on Long-Term Equity Securities account.

Recording a Sale of Stock The sale of shares of stock held for long-term investment and accounted for at the lower of cost or market value is handled in the same way as the sale of shares held for temporary investment. The difference between the amount realized from the sale and the original cost of the shares is recorded as a realized gain or loss (see page 753).

Recording Cash Dividends Cash dividends on long-term investments in marketable equity securities accounted for at the lower of cost or market value are handled in the same way as those on short-term investments in equity securities (see pages 753 and 754).

Accounting for Long-Term Investments in Equity Securities When the Investor Exercises Significant Influence Over the Investee If the investor owns 20 percent or more of the voting stock of the issuing company (the *investee*), the investor is considered to be capable of exercising significant influence over the investee. (Significant influence can also be exercised in other ways. Interlocking members of boards of directors and long-term purchase or sales contracts, for example, are considered to have such influence.) The investor is generally required to show the economic results of this influence by recording the investment using the *equity method* of accounting. Under this method the investor records in each period its proportionate share of the net income or net loss reported by the investee. The following procedures illustrate this method of accounting for stock investments.

Recording a Stock Purchase As with other methods of accounting, the stock investment is initially recorded at total cost under the equity method. This cost includes purchase price, brokers' fees, transfer taxes, and other incidental acquisition costs.

Recording a Share of the Investee's Net Income If the investee reports net income at the end of the fiscal year, the investor records its proportionate share under the equity method of accounting. It does so by debiting the investment account and crediting a revenue account.

For example, suppose that on January 12, 19Y5, the Duncan Lawn Furniture Corporation purchases 10,000 shares of the 40,000 shares of outstanding common stock of the Newmont Company. Duncan pays a total of $245,000 for the stock and charges this amount to an account called Long-Term Investment in Newmont Company Common Stock. At the end of 19Y5, Newmont reports a net income of $120,000. Since Duncan owns 25 percent of the common stock of Newmont, Duncan records $30,000 of Newmont's net income. The entry is shown below.

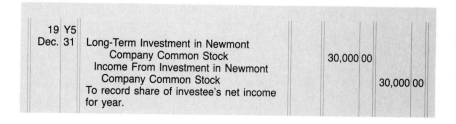

19 Y5			
Dec. 31	Long-Term Investment in Newmont Company Common Stock	30,000 00	
	Income From Investment in Newmont Company Common Stock		30,000 00
	To record share of investee's net income for year.		

Recording Cash Dividends Under the equity method of accounting for investments in stock, cash dividends are treated as a reduction of the investment account. In effect, the dividends represent a return of part of the investment's cost. For example, suppose that on February 10, 19Y6, Newmont pays a cash dividend of $1 a share, and Duncan receives $10,000. The dividend is recorded by the entry shown below, assuming that Duncan records dividends only when they are received.

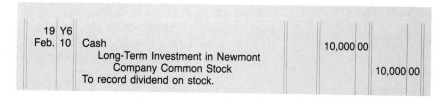

19 Y6			
Feb. 10	Cash	10,000 00	
	Long-Term Investment in Newmont Company Common Stock		10,000 00
	To record dividend on stock.		

Recording a Share of the Investee's Net Loss If the investee reports a net loss for the period, the investor using the equity method records its proportionate share of the loss. For example, if at the end of 19Y6, Newmont reports a net loss of $50,000, Duncan records its 25 percent share of the loss as shown below.

19 Y6			
Dec. 31	Loss From Investment in Newmont Company Common Stock	12,500 00	
	Long-Term Investment in Newmont Company Common Stock		12,500 00
	To record 25 percent of loss reported by Newmont Company.		

Carrying Value of Investment Under the equity method, the investment in common stock is carried at its original cost plus the investor's share of cumulative net income or less the investor's share of cumulative net loss and less the dividends received by the investor. The Long-Term Investment in Newmont Company Common Stock account is shown below as it appears in Duncan's general ledger on December 31, 19Y6.

Long-Term Investment in
Newmont Company Common Stock   No.   136

DATE	EXPLANATION	POST. REF.	DEBIT	CREDIT	BALANCE	DR. CR.
19 Y5						
Jan. 12		J1	245,000 00		245,000 00	Dr.
Dec. 31		J12	30,000 00		275,000 00	Dr.
19 Y6						
Feb. 10		J2		10,000 00	265,000 00	Dr.
Dec. 31		J12		12,500 00	252,500 00	Dr.

Recording Amortization of Goodwill Under the equity method, any amount by which the cost of the stock investment exceeds the investor's share of the value of the investee's net assets (the fair market value of the total assets minus the total liabilities) at the date the stock is purchased is considered to be attributable to the unrecorded intangible asset of goodwill. Like all intangibles, goodwill is amortized over its useful life, which cannot exceed 40 years.

Using a highly simplified illustration, assume that on January 2, 19X4, an investor purchases 30 percent of the outstanding stock of an investee for $600,000. At that time the book value and the fair market value of the investee's assets are $2,500,000 and its liabilities are $700,000. Its net assets, therefore, are $1,800,000. The purchase price of $600,000 is thus $60,000 more than the actual value of the net assets purchased, as shown below.

Purchase price of 30 percent interest	$600,000
Value of 30 percent of net assets ($1,800,000 × 0.30)	540,000
Excess	$ 60,000

Assume also that the investor decides that the $60,000 should be amortized over a period of 20 years. The amount paid for goodwill is included in the investment account. Therefore, the entry shown below is made by the investor on December 31, 19X4, to amortize the goodwill for that year.

19 X4				
Dec. 31	Income From Investment in Investee		3,000 00	
	Investment in Investee			3,000 00
	To amortize goodwill included in			
	purchase price of stock of investee			
	($60,000 ÷ 20 years).			

Recording a Sale of Stock No unusual problems arise from the sale of stock under the equity method of accounting. The portion of the investment account balance that applies to the shares sold is removed from the account by a credit. Cash is debited for the amount realized from the sale, and the difference is recorded as a gain or loss.

Stock Dividends The procedures to be followed when the investor receives a stock dividend are the same no matter which method of accounting for the investment is used. When a stock dividend is received, only a memorandum entry is made in the general journal and a notation is made in the investment account. The notation shows the number of shares received as a dividend and the total number of shares now held. The cost of the original shares is assumed to apply to all shares owned, including those received as a dividend. If shares are later sold, the cost of each share to be removed from the investment account is found by dividing the total shares (both old and new) into the total cost.

Assume that on January 3, 19X1, the Felton Company purchases 1,000 shares of Acme Unlimited common stock for a total price of $7,040. In July Acme Unlimited declares and issues a 10 percent stock dividend, and Felton receives 100 shares of common stock. The memorandum entry to be made is shown below.

19 X1	
July 15	On this date, 100 shares of Acme
	Unlimited common stock have been
	received as a 10 percent dividend on
	the 1,000 shares owned. Total cost is
	$7,040; the cost for each share is now
	$6.40 ($7,040 ÷ 1,100 shares).

When a stock investment is sold, the gain or loss is determined by comparing the net proceeds with the recorded cost. If Felton later sells Acme's common stock for $9 a share, the recognized gain to be reported is $2.60 a share ($9 selling price − $6.40).

PRINCIPLES AND PROCEDURES SUMMARY

Short-term or temporary investments (classified on the balance sheet as current assets) are often made to use temporarily idle funds. If bonds are purchased as temporary investments, they are recorded at cost. Interest income is recorded when it is received, and it is accrued at the end of the fiscal year. Short-term investments in stock are recorded at cost initially, but if the aggregate (total) market value on the balance sheet date is less than the aggregate cost, an allowance account is used to reduce the carrying value to the market value. On the income statement, declines in aggregate market value to below cost are shown as unrealized losses and recoveries of previous declines in aggregate market value are shown as unrealized income. The difference between the amount realized from the sale of stock and the original cost of the shares is recognized as a realized gain or loss.

Long-term investments in bonds usually involve a discount or premium. Interest is recorded as it is received, and it is accrued at the end of each fiscal year. The original cost of the bonds is adjusted at the time of each interest entry to amortize the premium or discount over the remaining life of the investment. The adjusted cost is shown in the investment section of the balance sheet. Interest Receivable is a current asset. Bonds can, of course, be sold at a gain or loss before maturity. The discount or premium must be amortized up to the date of sale.

Long-term investments in stock are accounted for on the basis of the lower of cost or market value if the investor owns less than 20 percent of the investee's voting stock. An allowance account is used to reduce the carrying value to the market value. Under this method, declines in market value to below cost and recoveries of previous declines in value are recorded as adjustments of a Cumulative Unrealized Net Loss account. This account does not appear on the income statement, but it is a deduction from stockholders' equity.

If the investor owns 20 percent or more of the investee's voting stock, the investment is usually accounted for under the equity method. Using this method, the investor debits its share of the investee's net income to the investment account and credits it to a revenue account. Similarly, the investor charges its share of the investee's net losses to a loss account and credits them to the investment account. It also credits any dividends to the investment account.

Stock dividends distributed do not represent income under either method of accounting for stock investments. The new shares are added to the old shares, and their total is divided into the balance of the investment account to get the cost for each share.

MANAGERIAL IMPLICATIONS

Corporate managers must be alert to the possibility of investing idle funds for short periods of time in order to earn income until the money is required in business operations. In addition, managers may want to make investments for long periods of time to gain long-term earnings or fixed income, to acquire an interest in another business, or to establish goodwill with a supplier or customer.

Managers must keep a close watch over investments in securities by appraising any changes in market conditions. Such changes may require prompt action. Managers must also be sure that all of the firm's investment transactions are properly accounted for. Income must be accurately recorded. Gains and losses must be carefully recognized on sales of investments for both financial and tax reporting purposes.

REVIEW QUESTIONS

1. What are the requirements for an investment to be classified as temporary?
2. What specific types of investments are customarily made if funds are available for only a short period? Why?
3. What is a parent company? A subsidiary?
4. What are consolidated financial statements? Why are they prepared?
5. When a business purchases bonds at a discount, how is the discount reflected in the firm's accounts?
6. When a business purchases bonds with interest accrued on them, how does it account for the accrued interest at the time of purchase? Why?
7. Why would a business not amortize a discount or premium on bonds acquired as a short-term investment?
8. Explain the steps necessary to account for the sale of bonds acquired at a discount and held as a short-term investment.
9. Assume that the current year is the first year that a corporation has owned shares of stock as a short-term investment. At the end of the year, the fair market value of the shares owned is less than the original cost. Explain how this decline in value is accounted for and shown in the financial statements.
10. At the end of one year, the value of stock held by a firm as a short-term investment was $2,200 less than cost. Then at the end of the second year, the value of the shares on hand was $300 greater than cost. Explain the proper method of accounting for the investment at the end of the second year.
11. Explain the straight-line method of amortizing the discount on long-term bond investments.
12. Explain the steps necessary to account for the sale of a long-term bond investment when the bonds were originally purchased at a premium.
13. Assume that a corporation owns 8 percent of the common stock of another corporation and is holding it as a long-term investment. Explain how the investor would account for (a) a loss of $30,000 reported by the investee, (b) a profit of $50,000 reported by the investee, and (c) a dividend of $900 received from the investee.
14. In 19X1 a corporation acquired small numbers of shares in several other corporations, which are to be held as long-term investments. At the end of 19X1, the shares had a fair market value of $82,000 and a cost of $94,000. Explain how these facts would be accounted for and shown in the firm's financial statements at the end of 19X1.

15. Under what circumstances should the equity method of accounting for stock investments be used?
16. Explain the equity method of accounting.
17. Explain how stock dividends received on stock investments are accounted for.
18. Explain how to compute amortization of the discount on bond investments under the effective interest method.
19. If a business acquires bonds between interest dates, how would the firm compute amortization of a discount or premium for the period from the date of purchase until the first interest date under the effective interest method?

MANAGERIAL DISCUSSION QUESTIONS

1. For what reasons would managers choose to make a long-term investment in another company instead of using the funds to expand their own business?
2. Why would directors consider a short-term bond investment for the use of excess funds when they know that the bonds are subject to market fluctuations?
3. One of the directors of a corporation asks why a stock dividend on the firm's long-term stock investment was not entered as an increase in the investment account. How would you explain the reason behind the recording procedure?
4. Why would a corporation buy bonds at a premium for a long-term investment, knowing that the premium will have to be amortized?
5. A corporation's balance sheet shows its long-term investment in marketable equity securities at cost even though the market value far exceeds cost. A manager wants to know why the securities are not shown at their market value. Explain this situation.

EXERCISES

EXERCISE 32-1 **Recording the purchase of bonds at a premium for a temporary investment.** On May 1, 19X3, the Rand Company purchased $20,000 par value of the Lee Corporation's 15 percent bonds at 102.7 plus accrued interest. Interest is payable on July 1 and January 1. The broker's fee was $116. The bonds mature on January 1, 19X9, and are being held as a temporary investment. Give the entry in general journal form to record the purchase of the bonds.

EXERCISE 32-2 **Recording the receipt of interest on bonds held as a temporary investment.** Refer to Exercise 32-1. Give the entry in general journal form to record the receipt of the interest on July 1, 19X3, from the bonds of the Lee Corporation.

EXERCISE 32-3 **Recording accrued interest on a bond investment.** Refer to Exercise 32-1. Give the entry in general journal form on December 31, 19X3, to record the accrued interest on the $20,000 of Lee Corporation bonds.

EXERCISE 32-4 **Recording the sale of bonds held as a temporary investment.** Refer to Exercise 32-1. On February 1, 19X4, the Rand Company sold the bonds of the Lee Corporation at 102.8 plus accrued interest. The brokerage fee was $97. Give the entry in general journal form to record the sale.

EXERCISE 32-5 **Recording a decline in value of a short-term equity investment.** The Tivelli Corporation first purchased stock as a short-term investment in 19X1. On December 31 of that year, the cost of the shares on hand was $31,000 and the fair market value was $27,000. Give the necessary general journal entry to record the decline in value.

EXERCISE 32-6 **Recording the adjustment for a decline in the value of an equity investment.** Refer to Exercise 32-5. On December 31, 19X2, the cost of the Tivelli Corporation's temporary investment in equity securities was $26,000 and the fair market value was $25,000. Give the general journal entry to adjust the allowance account.

EXERCISE 32-7 **Recording the purchase of bonds for a long-term investment.** On July 1, 19X1, the Alvarez Company purchased $60,000 par value of the March Corporation's 12 percent bonds at 97.5 plus accrued interest. The interest is payable on April 1 and October 1. The bonds mature on October 1, 19X7, six years and three months after the purchase. Give the entry in general journal form to record the purchase of the bonds.

EXERCISE 32-8 **Recording the receipt of the interest and the amortization of a discount on bonds under the straight-line method.** Refer to Exercise 32-7. Give the entry in general journal form on October 1, 19X1, to record the receipt of the interest and the amortization of the discount, using the straight-line method.

EXERCISE 32-9 **Recording the accrual of the interest and the amortization of a discount under the straight-line method.** Refer to Exercise 32-7. Give the entry in general journal form on December 31, 19X1, to record the accrual of the bond interest and the amortization of the discount, using the straight-line method.

EXERCISE 32-10 **Closing the account for interest income.** Refer to Exercise 32-7. Give the general journal entry to close the Interest Income account on December 31, 19X1.

EXERCISE 32-11 **Reversing an accrual of interest and the amortization of a discount.** Refer to Exercise 32-9. Give the necessary reversing entry on January 1, 19X2.

EXERCISE 32-12 **Recording the purchase of stock for a long-term investment.** On July 1, 19X1, the Hardee Corporation purchased as a long-term investment 2,000 of the 100,000 outstanding shares of common stock of the Joyner Corporation for $18.25 a share. On October 31 Hardee received a cash dividend of $1 a share. On November 18, 19X1, Hardee sold 500 shares of the Joyner Corporation's stock for $21.75 a share. On December 31, 19X1, the Joyner Corporation reported a net income of $6 a share. Give the entry in general journal form to record the purchase of the stock.

EXERCISE 32-13   **Recording the receipt of a cash dividend.** Refer to Exercise 32-12. Give the entry in general journal form to record the receipt of the dividend on October 31, 19X1.

EXERCISE 32-14   **Recording the sale of stock held as a long-term investment.** Refer to Exercise 32-12. Give the entry in general journal form to record the sale of the 500 shares on November 18, 19X1.

EXERCISE 32-15   **Recording the net income reported by an investee.** Refer to Exercise 32-12. Give any entry required on December 31, 19X1, to record Hardee's share of Joyner's net income.

EXERCISE 32-16   **Computing interest income under the effective interest method.** On June 1, 19X1, the Farrell Company purchased $100,000 par value of the May Corporation's 12 percent bonds at 106.1. The bonds were purchased to yield a 10 percent annual rate, compounded semiannually. The interest is payable on March 1 and September 1. What amount of interest income will be recorded for the period of June 1, 19X1, to September 1, 19X1, if the effective interest method of amortization is used?

EXERCISE 32-17   **Computing the amortization of a premium under the effective interest method.** Refer to Exercise 32-16. What amount of the premium on the bonds will be amortized on September 1, 19X1, if the effective interest method of amortization is used?

EXERCISE 32-18   **Computing the amortization of a premium under the effective interest method.** Refer to Exercise 32-16. What amount of the premium on the bonds will be amortized on December 31, 19X1, if the effective interest method of amortization is used?

EXERCISE 32-19   **Recording the purchase of stock as a long-term investment under the equity method.** On August 1, 19X1, the Delmar Corporation purchased as a long-term investment 25,000 shares of the 100,000 outstanding shares of common stock of the Hale Corporation for $21 a share. On November 10, 19X1, Delmar received a cash dividend of $1 a share. On December 12, 19X1, Delmar sold 1,000 shares of the Hale Corporation's stock for $24 a share. On December 31, 19X1, Hale reported a net income of $200,000 for the year. Give the entry in general journal form to record the purchase of the stock.

EXERCISE 32-20   **Recording the receipt of a cash dividend under the equity method.** Refer to Exercise 32-19. Give the entry in general journal form to record the receipt of the dividend on November 10, 19X1.

EXERCISE 32-21 **Recording the sale of stock under the equity method.** Refer to Exercise 32-19. Give the entry in general journal form to record the sale of the 1,000 shares on December 12, 19X1.

EXERCISE 32-22 **Recording the net income of an investee under the equity method.** Refer to Exercise 32-19. Give the entry in general journal form to record Delmar's share of Hale's net income on December 31, 19X1.

EXERCISE 32-23 **Recording the net loss of an investee under the equity method.** Assume the same facts as in Exercises 32-19 through 32-22, except that at the end of 19X1 Hale reported a net loss of $80,000 instead of a net income of $200,000. Give the entry in general journal form required at Delmar to record its share of Hale's net loss under the equity method of accounting.

EXERCISE 32-24 **Determining the gain or loss from a sale of stock obtained through a stock dividend.** On September 1, 19X1, the general ledger of the Kline Company showed a balance of $36,000 in an account called Investment in Common Stock of the Hill Company. This amount was the book value of 4,000 shares. On September 1 Kline received a stock dividend of 10 percent (400 new shares). On September 26 the new shares and 600 of the old shares were sold for $8.99 a share. What amount of gain or loss will result from the sale?

PROBLEMS

PROBLEM 32-1 **Recording transactions involving temporary investments in bonds.** The Town Real Estate Corporation had excess cash on hand between development projects and decided to invest the funds temporarily. Selected transactions for 19X1 are shown below.

Instructions Record each of the transactions in general journal form. (Use the account titles given in the related textbook illustrations.)

TRANSACTIONS FOR 19X1

Jan. 1 Purchased $100,000 face value of U.S. Treasury 10 percent bonds, maturing in 19Y1. The price was 97. The interest is payable on Apr. 1 and Oct. 1. Paid a $220 broker's fee.

Mar. 1 Purchased 25 Lincoln Bank Company 14 percent, $1,000 bonds, maturing in 19Y1. The price was 99. The interest is payable on Jan. 1 and July 1. Paid a $70 broker's fee.

Apr. 1 Received a check for the semiannual interest on the government bonds.

July 1 Received a check for the semiannual interest on the bank bonds.

Oct. 1 Received a check for the semiannual interest on the government bonds.

Nov. 1 Sold all the Lincoln Bank Company bonds at 98 plus accrued interest. Paid a $68 broker's fee.

Dec. 1 Sold all the government bonds at 98 plus accrued interest. Paid a $205 broker's fee.

PROBLEM 32-2 **Recording transactions involving temporary investments in stocks.** The transactions shown below are for the Schorr Company. They relate to its temporary investments in common stock in 19X1 and 19X2.

Instructions
1. Record each of the transactions in general journal form. Include any entries necessary to properly value the securities at the end of 19X1 and 19X2.
2. Show how the short-term investments will appear on the balance sheet as of December 31, 19X1.

TRANSACTIONS FOR 19X1

Nov.   1 Purchased 100 shares of Zeno Corporation common stock for $42 a share, plus a $45 broker's fee.

Nov.   8 Purchased 200 shares of Bay Corporation common stock for $36 a share, plus a $65 broker's fee.

Dec.   31 On this date the market values of the stock investments were Zeno Corporation, $42 a share; Bay Corporation, $32 a share.

TRANSACTIONS FOR 19X2

June   18 The Zeno Corporation declared a cash dividend of $1 a share payable on July 10 to stockholders of record as of June 30. (The Schorr Company records dividend income when dividends are declared.)

July   10 Received the cash dividend on the Zeno Corporation stock.

Dec.   31 On this date the market values of the stock investments were Zeno Corporation, $43 a share; Bay Corporation, $41 a share.

PROBLEM 32-3 **Recording long-term bond investments under straight-line amortization.** The Bio-Medical Products Corporation makes certain long-term investments to earn income. The selected transactions shown below and on page 773 took place during the years 19X1 and 19X2. The firm uses the straight-line method to amortize bond premiums and discounts.

Instructions   Record the transactions in general journal form.

TRANSACTIONS FOR 19X1

Jan.   1 Purchased as a long-term investment $30,000 par value of AB Corporation 12 percent bonds at a price of $30,795 for the bonds, plus accrued interest and an $85 broker's fee. The bonds pay interest on Apr. 30 and Oct. 31. They mature on Oct. 31, 19X7.

Apr.   30 Received the interest on the AB Corporation bonds. Amortized the premium for four months.

Oct.   31 Received the interest on the AB Corporation bonds. Amortized the premium for six months.

Dec.   31 Made an adjusting entry for the accrued interest on the AB Corporation bonds. Amortized the premium for two months.

       31 Made an entry to close the Interest Income account into the Income Summary account.

TRANSACTIONS FOR 19X2

Jan.   1 Reversed the adjusting entry prepared on Dec. 31.

Apr. 30 Received the interest on the AB Corporation bonds. Amortized the premium for six months.

Oct. 31 Received the interest on the AB Corporation bonds. Amortized the premium for six months.

Nov. 30 Because cash was needed unexpectedly for use in the business, sold the AB Corporation bonds for $30,300 less a broker's fee of $110 plus accrued interest. (Amortize the premium for one month. Then determine and record the gain or loss on the sale.)

Dec. 31 Closed the Interest Income and Gain or Loss on Sale of Investments accounts into the Income Summary account.

PROBLEM 32-4

Recording long-term bond investments under the effective interest method of amortization. The Easy-Stride Shoe Corporation has long-term investments in bonds of other corporations. It uses the effective interest method to amortize premiums and discounts. Selected transactions for 19X1 are given below.

Instructions

1. Prepare a table showing the amortization on the Voss Corporation bonds for the first four interest payment dates.
2. Give entries in general journal form to record each of the transactions.

TRANSACTIONS FOR 19X1

Mar.   1 Purchased 100 of the Voss Corporation's $1,000 par value, 14 percent bonds, maturing March 1, 19Y1. Interest is payable on Sept. 1 and Mar. 1. The purchase price was 111.183, plus a $200 broker's fee. The total cost will yield an effective rate of 12 percent a year, compounded semiannually.

Sept. 1 Received interest on the Voss Corporation bonds, and amortized the premium.

Oct.   1 Purchased $200,000 par value of the Reiman Corporation's 11 percent bonds at 96.24, plus a broker's fee of $400 and interest accrued to date. The interest is payable on Jan. 1 and July 1. The total purchase price, including the broker's fee, will yield an effective rate of 12 percent, compounded semiannually. The bonds mature in 19Y1.

Dec. 31 Recorded the accrued interest on the Voss Corporation bonds, and amortized the premium.

     31 Recorded the accrued interest on the Reiman Corporation bonds, and amortized the discount.

PROBLEM 32-5

Recording long-term stock investments. The data shown on page 774 relates to long-term investments in stock made by the Pacific Shipping Corporation in 19X1 and 19X2.

Instructions

1. Record all transactions in general journal form. Include any entries necessary to properly value the investments at the end of 19X1 and 19X2.

2. Show how the investments will appear on the balance sheet as of December 31, 19X1.
3. Explain how the Cumulative Unrealized Net Loss account will be reported on the balance sheet as of December 31, 19X1.

TRANSACTIONS FOR 19X1

July   10 Purchased 2,000 shares of Welt Company common stock for $11.75 a share plus a $100 broker's fee. The Welt Company has outstanding 50,000 shares of common stock.

Aug.   30 Received 200 shares of Welt Company common stock, representing a 10 percent dividend on the 2,000 shares owned.

Sept.   18 Purchased 500 shares of Veno Corporation common stock for $42 a share plus a $100 broker's fee.

Dec.   31 On this date the values of the shares held for investment were Welt Company, $10 a share; Veno Corporation, $40 a share.

TRANSACTIONS FOR 19X2

June   10 Sold 1,100 shares of Welt Company common stock for $13.50 a share, less an $85 broker's fee.

Dec.   31 On this date the values of the shares held for investment were Welt Company, $12 a share; Veno Corporation, $40 a share.

PROBLEM 32-6   **Recording long-term stock investments under the equity method.** Selected transactions relating to long-term stock investments of the Freeway Motorcycle Company are given below.

Instructions   Record all the transactions in general journal form.

TRANSACTIONS FOR 19X1

Jan.   6 Purchased 1,000 of the 3,000 outstanding common shares of the Thiro Corporation for $22 a share plus a $100 broker's fee.

Dec.   31 The Thiro Corporation reported a net income of $12,000 for the year ended Dec. 31, 19X1.

TRANSACTIONS FOR 19X2

June   10 Received $1,000 representing a cash dividend of $1 a share on the outstanding common stock of the Thiro Corporation.

Dec.   31 The Thiro Corporation reported a net loss of $6,000 for the year ended Dec. 31, 19X2.

TRANSACTIONS FOR 19X3

Feb.   10 Received 100 shares of Thiro Corporation common stock, representing a 10 percent dividend on the shares owned.

Mar.   20 Sold the 100 shares of Thiro Corporation common stock received as a dividend on Feb. 10. The stock was sold for $21.50 a share less a $108 broker's fee.

ALTERNATE PROBLEMS

PROBLEM 32-1A   **Recording transactions involving temporary investments in bonds.** The Green Acres Farm Equipment Company had idle funds that it decided to invest temporarily in marketable securities. Selected transactions for 19X1 are given below.

Instructions   Record each of the transactions in general journal form. (Use the account titles shown in the related textbook illustrations.)

TRANSACTIONS FOR 19X1

Feb.   1   Purchased $40,000 face value of U.S. Treasury 10 percent bonds, maturing Oct. 1, 19Y1. The price was 101 plus accrued interest. The interest is payable on Apr. 1 and Oct. 1. Paid a $125 broker's fee.

Apr.   1   Received a check for the semiannual interest on the U.S. Treasury bonds.

May   1   Purchased 50 University Corporation 14 percent, $1,000 bonds, maturing Mar. 1, 19Y1. The price was 101.6 plus accrued interest. The interest is payable on Mar. 1 and Sept. 1. Paid a $185 broker's fee.

Sept.   1   Received a check for the semiannual interest on the 14 percent University Corporation bonds.

Oct.   1   Received a check for the semiannual interest on the U.S. Treasury bonds.

Nov.   1   Sold all the U.S. Treasury bonds at 100.9 plus accrued interest. Paid a $128 broker's fee.

Dec.   1   Sold all the University Corporation bonds at 102 plus accrued interest. Paid a $180 broker's fee.

PROBLEM 32-2A   **Recording transactions involving temporary investments in stocks.** The transactions shown below and on page 776 are for the Valenza Corporation. They relate to its temporary investments in common stock in 19X1 and 19X2.

Instructions   1. Record each of the transactions in general journal form. Include any entries necessary to properly value the investments at the end of 19X1 and 19X2.
2. Show how the short-term investments will appear on the balance sheet as of December 31, 19X1.

TRANSACTIONS FOR 19X1

Nov.   12   Purchased 500 shares of Howe Corporation common stock for $26 a share plus a $60 broker's fee.

19   Purchased 300 shares of Belmo Corporation common stock for $38 a share plus a $94 broker's fee.

Dec.   31   On this date the market values of the stock investments were Howe Corporation, $24 a share; Belmo Corporation, $39 a share.

Apr. 17 The Howe Corporation declared a cash dividend of $1 a share, payable on May 15 to stockholders of record as of April 30. (Valenza records dividend income when dividends are declared.)

May 15 Received the cash dividend on the Howe Corporation stock.

Dec. 31 On this date the market values of the stock investments were Howe Corporation, $25 a share; Belmo Corporation, $39 a share.

PROBLEM 32-3A **Recording long-term bond investments under straight-line amortization.** The Micro Software Corporation makes certain long-term investments to earn income. The selected transactions shown below took place during 19X1 and 19X2. The firm uses the straight-line method to amortize bond premiums and discounts.

Instructions Record the transactions in general journal form.

TRANSACTIONS FOR 19X1

Jan. 1 As a long-term investment, purchased $25,000 par value of Martin Corporation 13 percent bonds at a price of $23,870 for the bonds, plus accrued interest and a $107 broker's fee. The bonds pay interest on Mar. 31 and Sept. 30. They mature on Sept. 30, 19X8.

Mar. 31 Received the interest on the Martin Corporation bonds. Amortized the discount for three months.

Sept. 30 Received the interest on the Martin Corporation bonds. Amortized the discount for six months.

Dec. 31 Made an adjusting entry for the accrued interest on the Martin Corporation bonds. Amortized the discount for three months.

31 Made an entry to close the Interest Income account into the Income Summary account.

TRANSACTIONS FOR 19X2

Jan. 1 Reversed the adjusting entry prepared on Dec. 31.

Mar. 31 Received the interest on the Martin Corporation bonds. Amortized the discount for six months.

Sept. 30 Received the interest on the Martin Corporation bonds. Amortized the discount for six months.

Nov. 30 Because cash was needed unexpectedly for use in the business, sold the Martin Corporation bonds for $24,400 plus accrued interest, less a $135 broker's fee. (Amortize the discount for two months. Then determine and record the gain or loss on the sale.)

Dec. 31 Closed the Interest Income and Gain or Loss on Sale of Investments accounts into the Income Summary account.

PROBLEM 32-4A **Recording long-term bond investments under the effective interest method of amortization.** The True-Fit Clothing Corporation has long-term investments in bonds of other corporations. It uses the effective interest method to amortize premiums and discounts. Selected transactions for the year 19X1 are given below.

Instructions

1. Prepare a table showing the amortization of the Ruiz Corporation bonds for the first four interest payment dates.
2. Give entries in general journal form to record each of the transactions.

TRANSACTIONS FOR 19X1

Apr. 1 Purchased 100 of the Ruiz Corporation's $1,000 par value, 13 percent bonds, maturing April 1, 19Y3. The interest is payable on Apr. 1 and Oct. 1. The purchase price was 93.945, plus a $300 broker's fee. The total cost will yield an effective rate of 14 percent a year, compounded semiannually.

Sept. 1 Purchased $50,000 par value of the Dufour Corporation's 15 percent bonds at 105.72, plus a broker's fee of $168 and accrued interest. The interest is payable on Aug. 1 and Feb. 1. The purchase price plus the broker's fee will yield an effective rate of 14 percent a year, compounded semiannually. The bonds mature in 19Y1.

Oct. 1 Received the interest on the Ruiz Corporation bonds, and amortized the discount.

Dec. 31 Recorded the accrued interest on the Ruiz Corporation bonds, and amortized the discount.

      31 Recorded the accrued interest on the Dufour Corporation bonds, and amortized the premium.

PROBLEM 32-5A

Recording long-term stock investments. The data shown below and on page 778 relates to long-term investments in stock by the Horizon Air Freight Company in 19X1 and 19X2.

Instructions

1. Record all the transactions in general journal form. Include any entries necessary to properly value the securities at the end of 19X1 and 19X2.
2. Show how the investments will appear on the balance sheet as of December 31, 19X1.
3. Explain how the Cumulative Unrealized Net Loss account will be reported on the balance sheet as of December 31, 19X1.

TRANSACTIONS FOR 19X1

June   8 Purchased 1,500 shares of Dentex Corporation common stock for $20 a share, plus a $195 broker's fee. The Dentex Corporation has outstanding 60,000 shares of common stock.

Sept. 10 Received 150 shares of Dentex Corporation common stock, representing a 10 percent dividend on the 1,500 shares owned.

Oct. 18 Purchased 400 shares of Ervin Corporation common stock for $62 a share, plus a $125 broker's fee.

Dec. 31 On this date the values of the shares held for investment were Dentex Corporation, $20 a share; Ervin Corporation, $49 a share.

Apr. 12 Sold 200 shares of Dentex Corporation common stock for $19 a share, less a $45 broker's fee.

Dec. 31 On this date the values of the shares held for investment were Dentex Corporation, $20 a share; Ervin Corporation, $53 a share.

PROBLEM 32-6A **Recording long-term stock investments under the equity method.** Selected transactions relating to long-term stock investments of the Harmony Record and Tape Corporation are given below.

Instructions Record all the transactions in general journal form.

TRANSACTIONS FOR 19X1

Feb. 10 Purchased 2,000 of the 8,000 outstanding common shares of the Gestic Corporation for $49.75 a share, plus a $100 broker's fee.

Dec. 31 The Gestic Corporation reported a net income of $56,000 for the year ended Dec. 31, 19X1.

TRANSACTIONS FOR 19X2

July 5 Received $4,000, representing a cash dividend of $2 a share on the outstanding common stock of the Gestic Corporation.

Dec. 31 The Gestic Corporation reported a net loss of $8,000 for the year ended Dec. 31, 19X2.

TRANSACTIONS FOR 19X3

Mar. 8 Received 200 shares of Gestic Corporation common stock, representing a 10 percent dividend on the shares owned. (Compute the new cost for each share to the nearest tenth of a cent.)

June 8 Sold the 200 shares of Gestic Corporation common stock received as a stock dividend on Mar. 8. The stock was sold for $49.50 a share less transfer taxes of $49.50 and a $65 broker's fee.

CHAPTER 33

Financial statements are merely summaries of a corporation's activities. They cannot explain in detail the vast number of transactions that the corporation engages in. For this reason, corporations must provide additional information to help readers understand the basic financial statements. In the next chapter we shall discuss the statement of changes in financial position, a required financial statement that supports the balance sheet and the income statement and helps explain why the balance sheet presented on a given date differs from the last one presented. In this chapter we shall examine certain other aspects of corporate reporting designed to help users understand and interpret financial reports. Three topics will be covered: (1) consolidated financial statements, (2) supplemental disclosures, and (3) inflation disclosures.

CORPORATE REPORTING

CONSOLIDATED FINANCIAL STATEMENTS

Corporations often invest in the stock of other corporations in order to acquire control of them. Ownership of more than one-half the voting stock will give the investor the desired control. In other situations a corporation may form a new corporation to carry on specific types of activities or to engage in different types of businesses. For example, an oil-producing company may form a new corporation to carry on pipeline operations or to operate a refinery. As pointed out previously, the corporation owning a majority of the voting stock of another corporation is called the *parent corporation,* while the investee is referred to as a *subsidiary* of the parent corporation. A parent corporation and its subsidiaries are known as *affiliated companies*.

Although financial statements are prepared for each corporation because each is a separate legal entity, separate statements by themselves do not give a complete and accurate picture of the economic effects of the parent corporation's ownership and control of the subsidiary. For this reason, *consolidated financial statements* are prepared for affiliated companies. In the consolidated statements the companies are treated as if they are a single economic enterprise. The consolidated statements will thus give an overall view of the parent corporation and its subsidiaries. In certain cases, where the activities of the parent and the subsidiaries are dissimilar, it may be undesirable to prepare consolidated statements. For example, it is commonly agreed that if one of the corporations is a financial institution and the other is a manufacturing business, consolidated statements would be inappropriate.

The preparation of consolidated statements is very complex and technical when there are many transactions between the affiliated companies. In this chapter we shall examine simple situations that illustrate the general nature of consolidated statements.

Consolidated Balance Sheet at the Date of Acquisition

The preparation of a consolidated balance sheet involves the combining of similar types of asset accounts and similar types of liability accounts of the parent corporation and its subsidiary or subsidiaries. For example, the total cash of the two or more companies is determined by adding together the amounts shown as

Cash on the separate balance sheets. Similarly, the accounts payable of the two or more companies are added together. However, some of the accounts on the separate statements of the affiliated companies reflect the same equity. For example, if a parent corporation has a single subsidiary and owns 100 percent of its stock, the stock is shown on the parent corporation's balance sheet as Investment in Common Stock of Subsidiary. This account reflects the parent corporation's ownership of the net assets of the subsidiary. Since the actual asset and liability accounts of the subsidiary will appear on the consolidated balance sheet, inclusion of the investment account would have the effect of reporting the subsidiary's assets and liabilities twice. Thus the investment account must be eliminated when the consolidated balance sheet is prepared.

Since the removal of the asset account Investment in Common Stock of Subsidiary from the consolidated balance sheet reduces the total assets of the two companies, it is also necessary to reduce the total stockholders' equity. This is done by eliminating the stockholders' equity of the subsidiary corporation because it is reflected in the combined assets and liabilities of the parent and its subsidiary. The investment account of the parent and the stockholders' equity accounts of the subsidiary are known as *reciprocal accounts* because they show opposite sides of the same thing.

There may be other reciprocal accounts, and they, too, must be eliminated when the consolidated balance sheet is prepared. For example, if the parent corporation lends $100,000 to its subsidiary and the transaction is evidenced by a note, the transaction will result in Notes Payable of $100,000 on the balance sheet of the subsidiary and Notes Receivable of $100,000 on the balance sheet of the parent. If the two corporations are viewed as a single economic entity, as is done in consolidated statements, there is no asset and no liability arising from the transaction. The economic entity simply owes itself $100,000. The transaction creates no receivable from an outside party and no payable to an outside party. Thus, in the process of preparing a consolidated balance sheet, these two reciprocal accounts are eliminated.

The preparation of a consolidated balance sheet is facilitated by the use of a special worksheet called a *consolidation worksheet*. To illustrate the handling of the consolidation worksheet at the date of purchase of the controlling interest in a subsidiary, three situations are presented here.

Acquisition of 100 Percent of a Subsidiary's Stock at Book Value

Assume that on January 1, 19X1, a corporation purchases 100 percent of the common stock of another corporation for $300,000. Information from the balance sheets of the two firms just after the acquisition is shown on page 781.

In this case the purchase price of $300,000 for the subsidiary corporation's common stock was exactly equal to the stock's book value. The consolidation worksheet presented on page 781 therefore involves only one elimination—the elimination of the parent's investment account and the subsidiary's stockholders' equity accounts. The items in the last column of the worksheet will appear on the consolidated balance sheet.

Eliminations are purely worksheet entries. They are not recorded in the accounts of either the parent corporation or the subsidiary corporation.

	Parent Corporation	Subsidiary Corporation
Assets		
Cash	$ 100,000	$ 20,000
Land		50,000
Other Assets	600,000	350,000
Investment in Subsidiary	300,000	
Total Assets	$1,000,000	$420,000
Liabilities and Stockholders' Equity		
Accounts Payable	$ 80,000	$ 70,000
Other Liabilities	220,000	50,000
Common Stock	100,000	200,000
Retained Earnings	600,000	100,000
Total Liabilities and Stockholders' Equity	$1,000,000	$420,000

PARENT CORPORATION AND SUBSIDIARY CORPORATION
Worksheet for Consolidated Balance Sheet
January 1, 19X1

	JAN. 1 BALANCES		ELIMINATIONS		CONSOLI-DATED BALANCE SHEET
	PARENT	SUBSIDIARY	DEBIT	CREDIT	
Assets					
Cash	100,000 00	20,000 00			120,000 00
Land		50,000 00			50,000 00
Other Assets	600,000 00	350,000 00			950,000 00
Investment in Subsidiary	300,000 00			(a)300,000 00	
Totals	1,000,000 00	420,000 00			1,120,000 00
Liab. and Stockholders' Equity					
Accounts Payable	80,000 00	70,000 00			150,000 00
Other Liabilities	220,000 00	50,000 00			270,000 00
Common Stock	100,000 00	200,000 00	(a)200,000 00		100,000 00
Retained Earnings	600,000 00	100,000 00	(a)100,000 00		600,000 00
Totals	1,000,000 00	420,000 00	300,000 00	300,000 00	1,120,000 00

Acquisition of 100 Percent of a Subsidiary's Stock for More Than Book Value It is unusual for the parent corporation to acquire the stock of a subsidiary for an amount exactly equal to its book value. The assets of the subsidiary almost always are worth more or less than their book value. In addition, the subsidiary may be a going concern and the parent is therefore willing to pay more than book value for the subsidiary's stock in order to obtain the organization, the assets in place, and the goodwill of the subsidiary. To the extent that the difference between the purchase price of the stock and its underlying book value can be attributed to specific identifiable assets, the difference between the book value of each such asset and its market value should be recorded as an adjustment on the consolidation worksheet (but not in the accounts). The market value of these assets when the stock is purchased should appear on the consolidated balance sheet prepared as of the date of purchase. Any excess of the purchase price of the subsidiary's stock over its revised book value is treated as an intangible asset, goodwill, that has been acquired.

For example, assume the same facts as in the preceding case, except that the parent corporation paid $350,000 for the subsidiary corporation's common stock and that the subsidiary corporation's land had a fair market value of $80,000 on the date the stock was purchased. Thus the $50,000 paid for the stock in excess of its book value includes $30,000 attributable to the land and $20,000 to goodwill. The worksheet for the consolidated balance sheet appears as follows in this situation.

PARENT CORPORATION AND SUBSIDIARY CORPORATION
Worksheet for Consolidated Balance Sheet
January 1, 19X1

| | JAN. 1 BALANCES | | ELIMINATIONS | | CONSOLIDATED BALANCE SHEET |
	PARENT	SUBSIDIARY	DEBIT	CREDIT	
Assets					
Cash	50,000 00	20,000 00			70,000 00
Land		50,000 00	(a)30,000 00		80,000 00
Other Assets	600,000 00	350,000 00			950,000 00
Investment in Subsidiary	350,000 00			(a)30,000 00 (b)300,000 00	*20,000 00
Totals	1,000,000 00	420,000 00			1,120,000 00
Liab. and Stockholders' Equity					
Accounts Payable	80,000 00	70,000 00			150,000 00
Other Liabilities	220,000 00	50,000 00			270,000 00
Common Stock	100,000 00	200,000 00	(b)200,000 00		100,000 00
Retained Earnings	600,000 00	100,000 00	(b)100,000 00		600,000 00
Totals	1,000,000 00	420,000 00	330,000 00	330,000 00	1,120,000 00

*Goodwill

Acquisition of Less Than 100 Percent of a Subsidiary's Stock It is apparent from the examples above that consolidated balance sheets are prepared to emphasize the ownership of the stockholders of the parent corporation. In many cases the parent corporation does not purchase 100 percent of the subsidiary's stock. In that event the ownership of the outside stockholders in the subsidiary is shown on the consolidated balance sheet as a minority interest, usually located between the Liabilities section and the Stockholders' Equity section. An adjustment is recorded on the consolidation worksheet to account for the minority interest. The remainder of the consolidation process is carried out in the normal way.

For example, assume that in the case discussed on page 780, the parent corporation acquired only 75 percent, rather than 100 percent, of the subsidiary corporation's stock and that the purchase price was $235,000. The consolidation worksheet at the date of the acquisition would appear as shown on page 783.

PARENT CORPORATION AND SUBSIDIARY CORPORATION
Worksheet for Consolidated Balance Sheet
January 1, 19X1

	JAN. 1 BALANCES		ELIMINATIONS		CONSOLI-DATED BALANCE SHEET
	PARENT	SUBSIDIARY	DEBIT	CREDIT	
Assets					
Cash	165,000 00	20,000 00			185,000 00
Land		50,000 00			50,000 00
Other Assets	600,000 00	350,000 00			950,000 00
Investment in Subsidiary	235,000 00			(a)225,000 00	*10,000 00
Totals	1,000,000 00	420,000 00			1,195,000 00
Liab. and Stockholders' Equity					
Accounts Payable	80,000 00	70,000 00			150,000 00
Other Liabilities	220,000 00	50,000 00			270,000 00
Common Stock—Parent	100,000 00				100,000 00
Common Stock—Subsidiary		200,000 00	(a)150,000 00		**50,000 00
Retained Earnings—Parent	600,000 00				600,000 00
Retained Earnings—Subsidiary		100,000 00	(a)75,000 00		**25,000 00
Totals	1,000,000 00	420,000 00	225,000 00	225,000 00	1,195,000 00

*Goodwill
**Minority Interest

The consolidated balance sheet prepared from the preceding worksheet is shown below. Notice how the minority interest is presented on this statement.

PARENT CORPORATION AND SUBSIDIARY CORPORATION
Consolidated Balance Sheet
January 1, 19X1

Assets

Cash	$185,000	
Land	50,000	
Other Assets	950,000	
Intangible Assets—Goodwill	10,000	
Total Assets		$1,195,000

Liabilities and Stockholders' Equity

Liabilities		
Accounts Payable	$150,000	
Other Liabilities	270,000	
Total Liabilities		$ 420,000
Minority Interest in Subsidiary Corporation		75,000
Stockholders' Equity		
Common Stock	$100,000	
Retained Earnings	600,000	
Total Stockholders' Equity		700,000
Total Liabilities and Stockholders' Equity		$1,195,000

Consolidated statements are prepared only when a corporation owns more than 50 percent of the voting stock of another corporation. As discussed in Chapter 32, when the investor owns more than 20 percent of the investee, it is proper to use the equity method of accounting for the investment. Thus, following the date of acquisition of control of a subsidiary, the investment account of the parent corporation will be increased by the parent's share of the subsidiary's profits and by additional investments. Similarly, the investment account will be reduced by dividends received by the parent and by the parent's share of the subsidiary's losses. Thus, in periods after the acquisition date, the parent's share of changes in the subsidiary's equity will be reflected in both the parent's investment account and the subsidiary's equity accounts.

To illustrate the eliminations necessary to prepare a consolidated balance sheet at a date after acquisition, assume that a parent corporation purchased 75 percent of a subsidiary corporation's stock for $235,000 on January 1, 19X1. At the date of purchase, the subsidiary corporation's Common Stock account had a balance of $200,000 and its Retained Earnings account had a balance of $100,000. All of the excess of the purchase price over the stock's book value was attributed to goodwill. In the year following the purchase, the subsidiary's net income was $50,000 and it paid dividends of $20,000. Information from the balance sheets of the two corporations on December 31, 19X1, is given on the consolidation worksheet below. Included in the accounts receivable of the parent corporation is $10,000 due from the subsidiary corporation. The same amount is also reflected in the accounts payable of the subsidiary corporation. The following consolidation worksheet shows how these items would be eliminated.

PARENT CORPORATION AND SUBSIDIARY CORPORATION
Worksheet for Consolidated Balance Sheet
December 31, 19X1

	DEC. 31 BALANCES		ELIMINATIONS		CONSOLI-DATED BALANCE SHEET
	PARENT	SUBSIDIARY	DEBIT	CREDIT	
Assets					
Cash	142,500 00	75,000 00			217,500 00
Accounts Receivable	100,000 00	55,000 00		(b)10,000 00	145,000 00
Land		50,000 00			50,000 00
Other Assets	500,000 00	250,000 00			750,000 00
Investment in Subsidiary	257,500 00			(a)247,500 00	*10,000 00
Totals	1,000,000 00	430,000 00			1,172,500 00
Liab. and Stockholders' Equity					
Accounts Payable	110,000 00	60,000 00	(b)10,000 00		160,000 00
Other Liabilities	40,000 00	40,000 00			80,000 00
Common Stock—Parent	400,000 00				400,000 00
Common Stock—Subsidiary		200,000 00	(a)150,000 00		**50,000 00
Retained Earnings—Parent	450,000 00				450,000 00
Retained Earnings—Subsidiary		130,000 00	(a)97,500 00		**32,500 00
Totals	1,000,000 00	430,000 00	257,500 00	257,500 00	1,172,500 00

* Goodwill
** Minority Interest

Consolidated Income Statement

Preparation of a consolidated income statement presents far more challenge than does preparation of a consolidated balance sheet. This is especially true when the parent corporation owns less than 100 percent of the subsidiary's stock. The minority stockholders own a share of the net income reported by the subsidiary, and that share must be carefully computed and allocated. To illustrate the preparation of a simple consolidated income statement, assume that a parent corporation owns 80 percent of the stock of a subsidiary corporation. Information from the income statements of the two corporations is shown in condensed form in the first two columns of the following consolidation worksheet. (On the worksheet for a consolidated income statement, it is customary to first list all revenues and other credit items and then to list all costs and expenses.)

PARENT CORPORATION AND SUBSIDIARY CORPORATION
Worksheet for Consolidated Income Statement
Year Ended December 31, 19X1

	DEC. 31 BALANCES		ELIMINATIONS		CONSOLIDATED INCOME STATEMENT
	PARENT	SUBSIDIARY	DEBIT	CREDIT	
Revenues					
Sales	1,000,000 00	600,000 00	(a)100,000 00		1,500,000 00
Interest Income	40,000 00	20,000 00	(b)20,000 00		40,000 00
Share of Income of Subsidiary	80,000 00		(c)80,000 00		
Management Fee Income	25,000 00		(d)25,000 00		
Totals	1,145,000 00	620,000 00			1,540,000 00
Costs and Expenses					
Cost of Goods Sold	600,000 00	400,000 00		(a)100,000 00	900,000 00
Management Fee Expense		25,000 00		(d)25,000 00	
Other Operating Expenses	300,000 00	89,000 00			389,000 00
Interest Expense	20,000 00	6,000 00		(b)20,000 00	6,000 00
Totals	920,000 00	520,000 00			
Net Income—Parent	225,000 00				225,000 00
Net Income—Subsidiary		100,000 00		(c)80,000 00 (e)20,000 00	
Minority Interest in Net Income			(e)20,000 00		20,000 00
Totals			245,000 00	245,000 00	1,540,000 00

The following eliminations were made on the consolidation worksheet illustrated above.

a. The subsidiary corporation's cost of goods sold includes $100,000 of merchandise purchased from the parent corporation. The same amount is shown as part of the sales reported on the parent corporation's income statement. The subsidiary resold all of this merchandise. The intercompany purchase and sale were eliminated on the consolidation worksheet.

b. The interest income of the subsidiary corporation consists of $20,000 paid by the parent corporation on a loan made by the subsidiary to the parent. The payment is shown as interest expense on the parent corporation's income statement. The reciprocal amounts were eliminated on the consolidation worksheet.

c. The parent corporation has recorded its $80,000 share of the subsidiary corporation's net income as a debit to the investment account. Since all the sales and expenses of the subsidiary will be included in the consolidated income statement, this duplicate reporting of income must be eliminated. The net income amount reported by the subsidiary was therefore eliminated on the worksheet to the extent that it belonged to the parent corporation.

d. The management fee income shown on the income statement of the parent corporation and the management fee expense shown on the income statement of the subsidiary corporation are reciprocal amounts and were thus eliminated on the worksheet. Because the amounts did not result from transactions outside the economic unit, they should not appear on the consolidated income statement. After all eliminations are recorded and the worksheet is completed, the following consolidated income statement is prepared from it.

e. Of the subsidiary corporation's $100,000 net income, $20,000 belongs to the minority stockholders of the subsidiary. Since all the sales and expenses of the subsidiary will be included in the consolidated income statement, the minority share of $20,000 was deducted from the combined total income of the two corporations on the worksheet and allocated to the minority interest.

PARENT CORPORATION AND SUBSIDIARY CORPORATION
Consolidated Income Statement
Year Ended December 31, 19X1

Revenue		
Net Sales		$1,500,000
Cost of Goods Sold		900,000
Gross Profit on Sales		$ 600,000
Operating Expenses		389,000
Net Income From Operations		$ 211,000
Other Income		
Interest Income	$40,000	
Other Expense		
Interest Expense	6,000	
Net Other Income		34,000
Total Combined Income		$ 245,000
Less Minority Interest in Net Income		20,000
Consolidated Net Income		$ 225,000

When there are sales of property, plant, and equipment at a profit or when there is merchandise inventory sold by one of the affiliated companies to the other and there is an ending inventory of unsold merchandise, special problems are created in preparing a consolidated income statement. These problems are treated in intermediate and advanced accounting textbooks.

SUPPLEMENTAL DISCLOSURES

It is generally accepted that the preparer of financial statements must disclose all information that might affect the statement users' interpretation of the statements. This may require the disclosure of supplemental financial data or statistics, or it may require disclosure of nonfinancial data essential to a proper understanding of the statements. Many of the *Statements of Financial Accounting Standards* issued by the Financial Accounting Standards Board include requirements for disclosures that are related to the accounting standards laid down. Similarly, the *Opinions* issued by the American Institute of Certified Public Accountants often require disclosures. One of the most important aspects of financial reporting, in the judgment of the Securities and Exchange Commission, is the disclosure of all pertinent facts. Many of the SEC's pronouncements therefore relate to disclosures. A few of the disclosures normally found in published financial statements are summarized below to illustrate the types of information that are involved.

Comparative Statements

Published financial reports must always include the statements of at least the preceding year in addition to those of the current year. Most corporations present comparative statements for at least three years. This gives the reader an opportunity to easily detect trends over the periods of time covered by the statements.

Comparative Statistical Data

Most annual reports issued by public corporations contain comparative data for key statistics or financial items for at least five years and often for 10 to 15 years. Such information as earnings per share, sales, net income, and stockholders' equity over a number of years can be very useful to the analyst in detecting trends.

Accounting Policies

The footnotes to the financial statements must include a summary of major accounting policies. The inventory valuation method being used, the method of accounting for sales, depreciation methods, policies for capitalizing expenditures, and other accounting methods that are used when there are alternative methods available are essential disclosures.

Summaries of Selected Information

A number of supplemental analyses or summaries of information must be presented. For example, an analysis of the property, plant, and equipment accounts is required, including the beginning balances, purchases, retirements and sales, and the ending balances. Similar data is required for the related depreciation, depletion, and amortization.

Another required analysis is of long-term debt. This analysis must show details about the corporation's outstanding debt, such as maturity dates, interest rates, assets pledged to guarantee payment, and similar information that will be useful to readers of the firm's statements.

Still another type of required supplemental analysis involves disclosure by a corporation that has leased property, plant, or equipment of the amounts of rent owed under its rental contracts. The total amount due during each of the following five years and a total figure for all sums due after five years are generally required. The corporation that provides the leased items must also show this same information.

Information About Long-Term Commitments and Contracts

There are numerous requirements for information about specific long-term commitments or contracts. For example, if the corporation has a pension plan, such information as the following must be disclosed.

1. A statement that the plan exists, identifying or describing the employee groups covered.
2. A statement of the company's accounting and funding policies for the plan.
3. The provision made for the pension costs incurred during the period.
4. An explanation of significant matters affecting comparability for all the periods presented in the financial report.
5. Various other types of data whose disclosure is called for by the FASB in numerous *Statements of Financial Accounting Standards.*

If the corporation has a stock option plan for employees, a detailed analysis of this plan is also required. Some of the information that must be disclosed is as follows.

1. The status of the plan at the end of the period, including the number of shares under option, the option price, and the number of shares on which options were exercisable.
2. For options exercised during the period, the number of shares involved and the option price for those shares.

Other Disclosure Requirements

As pointed out earlier, there are literally hundreds of specific disclosure requirements imposed by various authoritative bodies. Some of these requirements apply to all audited companies, others apply only to corporations that are publicly held and are under the regulatory authority of the Securities and Exchange Commission, and others apply only to enterprises engaged in specific business activities. These disclosure requirements are examined in detail in intermediate and advanced accounting texts.

INFLATION ACCOUNTING DISCLOSURES

Throughout this book it has been emphasized that business transactions are recorded on the historical-cost basis. Thus, for example, buildings and equipment are recorded in a firm's accounts at their cost when purchased. As a result, asset accounts commonly reflect a variety of purchases made at different times with dollars of different purchasing power. None of the dollars making up the account balance may reflect the same purchasing power as dollars at the date the asset is presented on a current financial statement. This sometimes causes severe difficulty in measuring the firm's financial condition and its true profitability.

The nature of the problem may be illustrated by a simple example. Assume that a business purchased land at a cost of $1,000 in 1935 and that the land is still owned at the end of the current year. The Land account will continue to reflect the original entry of $1,000 made in 1935. Yet the land may actually be worth many times the original cost, or it may have declined to less than the $1,000 book value. In any event, because of general price inflation, the $1,000 in the Land account represents dollars spent in 1935 with far greater purchasing power than $1,000 would have today.

In recent years, concern has been growing over the impact of inflation on financial reports and the fact that statements based on historical costs may be misleading. Actually, there are two types of inflation that concern accountants and statement users. One is the increase in the general price level (changes in the general purchasing power of the dollar). The other is the change in prices of specific assets in comparison to general changes in prices. For example, suppose a building is purchased in 19X1 for $1,000,000. In 19X6, five years later, the general price level has increased by 25 percent. If the price of the asset involved has changed in direct proportion to the increase in the general price level, the purchase price of a new identical asset would be $1,250,000. However, the price of this specific asset may have behaved differently from the general price level, so that a replacement for the old asset might cost, for example, $1,800,000.

Accountants have often suggested that the financial statements based on historical costs should be "restated" to reflect the changes in the general purchasing power of the dollar and also to reflect changes in the prices or value of specific assets.

General Price-Level Changes

The general level of prices is often expressed by a *price index*. This is found by comparing the prices of an assortment of goods and services at a particular point with the price of those goods and services in a base period. The base period is given an index of 100, and the prices of other periods are expressed in terms of a percentage of the base period amount. For example, assume that 19W7 is the base period and that the price of the collection of goods and services included in the index for that year was $1,000. Assume also that in 19X3 the price of the goods and services in the collection is $1,500. Thus the index of 19X3 compared with the index of 19W7 is 150 ($1,500 ÷ $1,000). Conversely, it may be said that the value of the dollar in 19X3 is only 66 ⅔ percent ($1,000 ÷ $1,500) of its value in 19W7.

A number of general price-level indexes are available. A common one widely used by the public and also by accountants is the *Consumer Price Index* (*CPI*), which is published by the Bureau of Labor Statistics. This index reflects the price of a "market basket" of goods and services bought by the typical consumer. The individual prices of these goods and services are measured monthly, and a monthly index is then calculated. An average annual index is also computed and published. The CPI uses 1967 as its base period, and the prices for that year are expressed as 100 percent. The average CPI for selected years is given below.

YEAR	CPI	YEAR	CPI
1967	100.0	1979	217.4
1970	116.3	1980	246.8
1975	161.2	1981	271.5
1976	170.5	1982	287.8
1977	181.5	1983	296.6
1978	195.4		

Specific Price Changes

The change in the prices of specific assets may be expressed in various ways. The most common approach is the use of *current costs*. The current cost of an asset may be measured by the cost of acquiring an identical asset today, or the current cost may represent *replacement cost*—the cost of acquiring an asset with the same productive capacity. If the replacement cost of an individual asset is not easily determinable, a *specific price-level index* is often used to measure the current cost. For example, specific price-level indexes are available for various types of factory equipment. These indexes are prepared in the same way as general price-level indexes except that the prices measured are restricted to a specific type of asset rather than covering a broad collection of goods and services.

Requirements for Disclosure of the Effects of Inflation

The Financial Accounting Standards Board requires very large corporations to disclose the effects of inflation on certain aspects of their financial statements.[1] This includes the impact of inflation on inventories of goods and materials; on property, plant, and equipment; and on income from current operations. The data for income from current operations must include adjustments for the constant-dollar cost of goods sold, depreciation, and amortization. Separate disclosure must be made of the purchasing power gains and losses on net monetary assets.

The FASB's requirements include the impact of *both* general price-level changes and current costs; however, our discussion will be limited to general price-level effects. Although the FASB's requirements for inflation disclosures apply only to very large corporations, the same general approach may be used for a business of any size.

The process of restating the items on financial statements to reflect general price-level changes is very complicated, and the detailed techniques are beyond the scope of this book. Nevertheless, every student of accounting should have some familiarity with this topic. The following sections therefore present the basic concepts of general price-level adjustments to the financial statements (also called *constant-dollar accounting*). The techniques of current-cost restatements are similar to those of constant-dollar accounting.

Constant-dollar accounting involves the restatement of certain items on the financial statements. These are items that reflect historical costs. Several approaches may be used in making such restatements. In the discussion that follows, it is assumed that all items are restated to reflect the year-end price levels.

Restatement of Items Related to Nonmonetary Assets

It is easy to understand why the recorded costs of assets may be misleading. For example, assume that the Smith Corporation bought a building five years ago, at the beginning of 19X2, and recorded it at cost expressed in dollars with the purchasing power of that time. Similarly, depreciation of the building reflects dollar amounts that are based on the cost incurred when the building was acquired. Since the reader of the current year's statements thinks in terms of "today's dollars," constant-dollar adjustments are needed to restate the items into

---

[1]"Financial Reporting and Changing Prices," *Statement of Financial Accounting Standards, No. 33* (Stamford, Conn.: Financial Accounting Standards Board, 1979).

dollars with end-of-year purchasing power. Both the historical-cost amount for the building and the related depreciation must be restated into dollars of year-end value.

The conversion process is quite simple. The price index at the end of the current year is divided by the price index at the time of purchase to find the restatement ratio. The asset's cost and its related depreciation based on historical cost are then multiplied by the restatement ratio. Using the example given above for the Smith Corporation, assume that the price index at the end of the current year, 19X6, is 250 percent of the base period on which the index is computed and that the index at the time of the building's purchase was 200 percent of the base period. The building cost $1,000,000 and is being depreciated according to the straight-line method over a period of 20 years at $50,000 each year. Thus, the accumulated depreciation at the end of 19X6, the fifth year, is $250,000.

On a balance sheet restated to a constant-dollar basis, the building would be shown at $1,250,000 in terms of 19X6 dollars, as computed below.

$$\frac{\text{Original}}{\text{Cost}} \times \frac{\text{Price Index at End of Current Year}}{\text{Price Index at Date of Purchase}} = \frac{\text{Restated}}{\text{Amount}}$$

$$\$1,000,000 \times \frac{250}{200} = \$1,250,000$$

Similarly, the accumulated depreciation of $250,000 would be restated at $312,500.

$$\$250,000 \times \frac{250}{200} = \$312,500$$

The current year's depreciation for the building on the income statement of the Smith Corporation would be restated from $50,000 to $62,500.

$$\$50,000 \times \frac{250}{200} = \$62,500$$

Similar restatements must be made for other types of property, plant, and equipment such as land, machinery, furniture, trucks, fixtures, and so on. Procedures for restating merchandise inventory will depend on whether the LIFO, FIFO, average cost, or specific identification method is being used. Restatements of assets must also be reflected in the related expenses such as depreciation, depletion, amortization, and cost of goods sold. In addition, the paid-in capital accounts, which reflect the investments of shareholders at the date when the stock was issued, must be restated since they reflect dollars received with a purchasing power that is different from today's dollars.

The constant-dollar balance sheet of the Smith Corporation for December 31, 19X6, is shown on page 792. Notice that the historical-cost amounts are given in one column, the restatement ratios in the next column, and the constant-dollar amounts in the final column. An explanation of the restatement ratios is provided in footnotes to the balance sheet.

SMITH CORPORATION
Constant-Dollar Balance Sheet
December 31, 19X6

	Historical-Cost Amounts	Restatement Ratio	Constant-Dollar Amounts
Assets			
Cash	$ 30,000	Not restated (1)	$ 30,000
Accounts Receivable	80,000	Not restated (1)	80,000
Merchandise Inventory	150,000	250/245 (2)	153,061
Equipment	100,000	250/210 (3)	119,048
Less Accumulated Depreciation	(60,000)	250/210 (3)	(71,429)
Building	1,000,000	250/200 (3)	1,250,000
Less Accumulated Depreciation	(250,000)	250/200 (3)	(312,500)
Total Assets	$1,050,000		$1,248,180
Liabilities and Stockholders' Equity			
Liabilities			
Accounts Payable and Accrued Liabilities	$ 300,000	Not restated	$ 300,000
Stockholders' Equity			
Common Stock	325,000	250/150 (4)	541,667
Retained Earnings	425,000	(5)	406,513
Total Stockholders' Equity	$ 750,000		$ 948,180
Total Liabilities and Stockholders' Equity	$1,050,000		$1,248,180

Notes to Constant-Dollar Balance Sheet:
(1) The monetary assets and liabilities are not restated because they are already expressed in dollars that reflect year-end purchasing power.
(2) The ending inventory is based on average costing and is assumed to have been acquired throughout the year. Thus the restatement ratio is the ratio of the ending price index to the average price index for the year. The average price index is assumed to be 245.
(3) The items of property, plant, and equipment and the related accumulated depreciation are restated based on the ratio of the year-end price index to the price index at the date of acquisition of each asset.
(4) The common stock is restated based on the ratio of the year-end price index to the price index at the date when the stock was issued.
(5) Under this procedure the constant-dollar retained earnings amount is a balancing figure.

Purchasing Power Gains and Losses on Monetary Items

Monetary assets and liabilities represent assets and liabilities that are in the form of cash or that are receivable or payable in specific dollar amounts. Thus they do not require restatement because they already reflect end-of-year purchasing power. Cash, accounts receivable, notes receivable, accounts payable, and bonds payable are typical examples of monetary assets and liabilities.

The holders of monetary assets and liabilities do, however, lose or gain purchasing power as a result of changes in the value of the dollar. For example, if $1,000 is placed in a checking account in 19X1 when the price-level index is 200, the depositor will still have $1,000 in 19X6 if the money has not been withdrawn. However, if the price-level index has increased to 250, the $1,000 will buy far fewer goods and services than it would have bought in 19X1. The holder of this monetary asset has therefore lost purchasing power because of inflation. On the other hand, an individual who borrows $10,000 in 19X1 when the price-level index is 200 and still owes that amount in 19X6 when the price-level index has advanced to 250 has had a gain in real purchasing power. To repay the $10,000 debt will require far less purchasing power than was obtained when the $10,000 was borrowed. Thus the debtor gains by borrowing dollars and then repaying the loan with dollars of lesser value.

Determining the amount of gain or loss in purchasing power for each year in the above cases is a simple matter. It involves comparing the purchasing power of the monetary asset or liability at the start of the year with the purchasing power of the monetary asset or liability at the end of the year. Because most companies have both monetary assets and monetary liabilities, it is easier to work with the *net monetary assets* or *net monetary liabilities* than with both elements separately. For example, assume that in the above two examples, the price-level index at the start of 19X6 was 240 and at the end of that year it was 250. The purchasing power gain on the net monetary liabilities of $9,000 during 19X6 is computed as follows.

Net monetary liabilities (in absolute dollars)	$9,000
Net monetary liabilities owed for entire year, expressed in year-end purchasing power	
$9,000 \times \dfrac{250}{240} =$	9,375
Net gain in purchasing power	$ 375

In the above example, it was assumed that the same net monetary liabilities existed throughout the year. This would almost never be true in an actual business because there is a constant inflow and outflow of monetary assets and liabilities during the year. Conceptually, to measure the exact gain or loss in purchasing power, it would be necessary to measure the price level at the time of each change in net monetary position and compute the gain or loss until the next change. This obviously is not practical. A compromise is to identify large changes and compute the gain or loss on these changes and to assume that other changes took place ratably (proportionately) throughout the year. In this way the ratio of the end-of-year price index to the average price index for the year can be applied to the net change deemed to have occurred ratably throughout the year.

For example, the Smith Corporation's balance sheet for December 31, 19X6, given on page 792, shows that the net monetary liabilities of the firm on that date are $190,000 (monetary liabilities of $300,000 minus monetary assets of $110,000). Assume that on January 1, 19X6, the firm had net monetary liabilities of $107,000, so that during the year there was a net increase of

$83,000 in these liabilities ($190,000 − $107,000). Assume further that the increase can logically be interpreted to have occurred ratably throughout the year. In this case the firm's net gain in purchasing power for the year is $6,152. The necessary computations are shown below.

Net monetary liabilities on Jan. 1, expressed in year-end purchasing power	
$107,000 \times \dfrac{250}{240} =$	$111,458
Increase in monetary liabilities during year, expressed in year-end purchasing power	
$83,000 \times \dfrac{250}{245} =$	84,694
Net restated monetary liabilities if there is no gain or loss in purchasing power	$196,152
Net monetary liabilities at end of year (in absolute dollars)	190,000
Net gain in purchasing power from net monetary liabilities	$ 6,152

Under the inflation rules imposed by the FASB on large corporations, this gain of $6,152 would be included as an income item at the bottom of the constant-dollar income statement.

Restatement of the Income Statement

The historical-cost income statement may be restated to end-of-year price levels. In doing so, it is customary to assume that sales and other revenue transactions occur ratably throughout the year so that the restatement to reflect year-end price levels is achieved by applying to each item a ratio equal to the relationship between the year-end price index and the average price index during the year. It is also customary to assume that operating expenses involving cash or other monetary assets or liabilities have been incurred ratably throughout the year, so that the same ratio is applied to them. However, some expense items such as depreciation, depletion, and amortization must be restated based on the ratio of the end-of-year index at the time the related assets were purchased. Restatement of the cost of goods sold is based on an analysis of the elements of the beginning and ending inventories.

The constant-dollar income statement of the Smith Corporation for the year ended December 31, 19X6, is shown on page 795. Notice that this statement includes the unadjusted historical-cost figures, the restatement ratios, and the amounts adjusted for general price-level changes (the constant-dollar amounts). The gain in purchasing power on the net monetary liabilities, which was previously computed, appears at the bottom of the constant-dollar income statement.

Comparative Constant-Dollar Statements

It is customary for very large corporations to present comparative statements with price-level adjustments for two or more years. When this is done, the constant-dollar data for prior years is again restated to reflect the change in price level for the current year. This procedure and other information about inflation accounting are discussed in intermediate accounting textbooks.

SMITH CORPORATION
Constant-Dollar Income Statement
Year Ended December 31, 19X6

	Historical-Cost Amounts	Restatement Ratio	Constant-Dollar Amounts
Revenue			
Net Sales	$1,050,000	250/245 (1)	$1,071,429
Cost of Goods Sold			
Merchandise Inventory, Jan. 1	$ 100,000	250/234 (2)	$ 106,838
Net Purchases	700,000	250/245 (3)	714,286
Total Merchandise Available for Sale	$ 800,000		$ 821,124
Merchandise Inventory, Dec. 31	150,000	250/245 (4)	153,061
Cost of Goods Sold	$ 650,000		$ 668,063
Gross Profit on Sales	$ 400,000		$ 403,366
Operating Expenses			
Salaries and Wages	$ 125,000	250/245 (3)	$ 127,551
Other Operating Expenses	160,000	250/245 (3)	163,265
Depreciation of Building	50,000	250/200 (5)	62,500
Depreciation of Equipment	10,000	250/210 (5)	11,905
Total Operating Expenses	$ 345,000		$ 365,221
Net Income From Operations	$ 55,000		$ 38,145
Gain in Purchasing Power		(6)	6,152
Net Income—Constant-Dollar Basis			$ $44,297

Notes to Constant-Dollar Income Statement:

(1) Sales are assumed to have been made ratably throughout the year so that the restatement ratio is the ratio of the year-end price index to the average price index of the year.

(2) The restated amount of the beginning inventory is based on the assumption that its historical cost was at the average of the preceding year's price index of 234. The restatement ratio is thus the ratio of the year-end price index for the current year to the average price index of the preceding year.

(3) The amounts for these costs and expenses are assumed to have been incurred ratably throughout the year.

(4) The ending inventory was computed by the average costing method. It is assumed that this inventory is made up of items acquired throughout the year.

(5) The restatement ratio for each of the depreciation amounts is the ratio of the price index at the end of the year to the price index at the date the asset was purchased.

(6) The purchasing power gain was computed as shown on page 794.

PRINCIPLES AND PROCEDURES SUMMARY

When one corporation owns a majority of the stock in another corporation, the investor is said to be the parent corporation and the investee is said to be a subsidiary. Even though separate statements are prepared for each corporation, it is necessary to prepare consolidated statements for the two corporations in order to show their combined financial condition and the results of their operations as a single economic unit. All intercompany items are eliminated, so that only the results of transactions with parties outside the corporation are reflected in the statements. A minority share of ownership in the subsidiary is shown on the balance sheet between the Liabilities section and the Stockholders' Equity section. Similarly, the minority interest in the net income is subtracted from the total combined income to arrive at the consolidated net income.

In order to help users understand its financial statements, a corporation should disclose all factors that might affect the users' interpretation of the figures in the statements. For example, accounting policies should be explained. Similarly, transactions involving agreements such as pension plans and stock option plans that might affect the corporation's future earnings or future financial condition should be analyzed and explained.

Because accounting is based on historical costs, changes in prices over a period of years may make the financial statements difficult to understand or even misleading. Large corporations are required to show the impact of inflation on their statements, with specific attention being called to the impact on inventories, on property, plant, and equipment, on depreciation, on cost of goods sold, and on net income from operations. In addition, the gain or loss in purchasing power resulting from net monetary assets or liabilities must be shown. Many corporations prepare constant-dollar statements in which all items are restated to reflect a dollar unit with constant purchasing power, as measured by a general price-level index.

MANAGERIAL IMPLICATIONS

It is not enough for management and other users to know how each separate corporation in an affiliated group performed. The affiliated companies represent a single economic unit, and their overall performance can be measured only if a consolidated income statement is prepared. Similarly, their overall financial position can be determined only if a consolidated balance sheet is prepared.

If financial statements are to be useful, the reader must know exactly what accounting policies are being followed. There are alternative methods that may be chosen in accounting, and the financial results will vary widely depending on the method used. Similarly, management can make decisions only if all pertinent facts are known. That is why it is important that all material factors affecting the figures shown on the statements be disclosed.

Because historical costs incurred at different times are mixed together in the financial accounts and because the recorded costs do not reflect current values, they may be misleading. For example, if the balance sheet shows a building at a cost of $100,000, it is very important for management to know when the building was purchased. A building that cost $100,000 in 1955 and a building that cost $100,000 in 1985 are likely to have a completely different economic value. Thus statements that show price-level adjustments are useful to management in better understanding the economic health and operations of the business.

REVIEW QUESTIONS

1. If consolidated statements are prepared, will separate statements be prepared for each affiliated company? Why?
2. What is the purpose of consolidated financial statements?
3. Why is the Investment in Common Stock of Subsidiary account eliminated when a consolidated balance sheet is prepared?
4. What are reciprocal accounts? How are they handled in consolidations?
5. If the purchase price of a subsidiary's stock is greater than the stock's underlying book value, how is the excess treated in consolidated statements?
6. Are the eliminations shown on a consolidation worksheet entered in the accounts of the parent corporation? Explain.
7. How is the minority interest in a subsidiary's common stock shown on the consolidated balance sheet?
8. Under what conditions should consolidated financial statements be prepared?
9. What items should be eliminated in preparing a consolidated income statement?
10. How is the minority interest in the net income of a subsidiary shown on the consolidated income statement?
11. What are comparative statements? Why are they used?
12. What is the purpose of supplemental disclosures?
13. Why is it necessary for a corporation to disclose the major accounting policies it uses in footnotes to its financial statements?
14. What are general price-level changes?
15. What is a price index? How is it computed?
16. Distinguish between a general price-level index and a specific price index.
17. What disclosures about inflation does the FASB require of large companies?
18. How are items of property, plant, and equipment restated on constant-dollar financial statements?
19. What is meant by the term *purchasing power gain or loss on monetary items?*
20. Does a debtor have a purchasing power gain or purchasing power loss during a period of increasing prices?
21. Which paid-in capital accounts are restated on constant-dollar financial statements?
22. Why are monetary assets and liabilities not restated on a constant-dollar balance sheet?
23. How are sales restated on a constant-dollar income statement?

MANAGERIAL DISCUSSION QUESTIONS

1. What are some reasons why the managers of a corporation might want to purchase a majority interest in another corporation?
2. Assume that you are a member of the controller's staff at a corporation that has several subsidiaries. One of the vice presidents asks you why it is necessary to prepare consolidated statements when separate statements are available for all the affiliated companies. How would you explain the value of the consolidated statements?
3. The managers of a corporation are studying the financial statements of another company that they are interested in purchasing. Why would they pay careful attention to footnotes disclosing accounting policies such as the inventory valuation method used and the depreciation method used?
4. Why are constant-dollar statements useful to management?

EXERCISES

EXERCISE 33-1 **Eliminating a 100 percent investment in stock purchased for book value.** On July 1, 19X1, the Patrick Corporation acquired all the common stock of the Stevens Corporation for $280,000. On that date the Common Stock account of the Stevens Corporation had a balance of $150,000 and its Retained Earnings account had a balance of $130,000. What will be the eliminating entry on the consolidation worksheet?

EXERCISE 33-2 **Eliminating a 100 percent investment in stock purchased for more than book value.** On July 1, 19X1, the Patrick Corporation acquired all the common stock of the Stevens Corporation for $350,000. On that date the Common Stock account of the Stevens Corporation had a balance of $150,000 and its Retained Earnings account had a balance of $130,000. The entire excess of purchase price over book value can be attributed to the fact that the Stevens Corporation has land with a fair market value of $70,000 in excess of its book value. Explain how these facts will be handled on the consolidation worksheet.

EXERCISE 33-3 **Eliminating a 100 percent interest in stock purchased for more than book value.** Assume the same facts as in Exercise 33-2, except that $20,000 of the excess of the purchase price over the book value of the Stevens Corporation's stock can be attributed to the excess of the fair market value of the Stevens Corporation's land over its book value, while the remainder is attributable to goodwill. Explain how these facts will be handled on the consolidation worksheet.

EXERCISE 33-4 **Eliminating a 70 percent investment in stock purchased for book value.** On July 1, 19X1, the Patrick Corporation purchased 70 percent of the common stock of the Stevens Corporation for $210,000. On that date the Stevens Corporation's

Common Stock account had a balance of $200,000 and its Retained Earnings account had a balance of $100,000. How would these facts be handled on the consolidation worksheet?

EXERCISE 33-5   **Eliminating a 70 percent investment in stock purchased for more than book value.** Assume the same facts as in Exercise 33-4, except that the purchase price of the stock was $260,000. Explain how these facts would be handled on the consolidation worksheet.

EXERCISE 33-6   **Eliminating a 70 percent investment in stock after purchase for more than book value.** Assume the same facts as in Exercise 33-5. In addition, during the six-month period from July 1, 19X1, to December 31, 19X1, the Stevens Corporation reported a net income of $50,000. The Patrick Corporation records its investment in the Stevens Corporation on the equity basis. Explain how these facts would be reflected on the consolidation worksheet on December 31, 19X1.

EXERCISE 33-7   **Eliminating intercompany transactions.** On December 1, 19X1, the Patrick Corporation, the parent company, sold merchandise for $1,600,000 to the Stevens Corporation, its subsidiary. The Patrick Corporation recorded the transaction by a debit to Accounts Receivable and a credit to Sales. The Stevens Corporation debited Purchases and credited Accounts Payable. All of the merchandise was sold by the Stevens Corporation during December, but payment was not made by Stevens to Patrick. Describe how these facts would be treated on the consolidation worksheet.

EXERCISE 33-8   **Restating land on a constant-dollar balance sheet.** The Chavez Corporation purchased land in 19X1 when the general price-level index was 164. In 19X4 when the index was 205, the company prepared a constant-dollar balance sheet. What ratio will be used in restating the land?

EXERCISE 33-9   **Restating depreciation expense.** On January 1, 19X2, the Blaine Corporation purchased a building for $150,000. On that date the general price-level index was 124. At the end of four years on December 31, 19X5, the index was 160. The building is expected to have a useful life of 25 years and no salvage value. The firm uses straight-line depreciation for the building. What amount of depreciation expense will be shown on the constant-dollar income statement of the Blaine Corporation for 19X5?

EXERCISE 33-10   **Restating a building.** Refer to Exercise 33-9. At what amount will the building be shown on the constant-dollar balance sheet of the Blaine Corporation on December 31, 19X5?

EXERCISE 33-11   **Restating accumulated depreciation.** Refer to Exercise 33-9. At what amount will the accumulated depreciation for the building be shown on the constant-dollar balance sheet of the Blaine Corporation on December 31, 19X5?

EXERCISE 33-12   **Computing a gain or loss in purchasing power on monetary items.** An investor purchased a corporate bond on January 1, 19X1, for $1,000. On that date the general price-level index was 160. On December 31, 19X1, the index was 168. Compute the amount (if any) of purchasing power gain or loss on the bond. (Indicate whether the amount is a gain or loss.)

EXERCISE 33-13   **Computing a gain or loss in purchasing power on net monetary items.** The Rizzoli Corporation's monetary assets and liabilities on January 1, 19X1, and December 31, 19X1, are given below.

	January 1, 19X1	December 31, 19X1
Monetary Assets	$80,000	$100,000
Monetary Liabilities	20,000	25,000

The general price-level index on January 1 was 120. On December 31 the index was 130. The average index for the year was 125. Changes in monetary assets and liabilities occurred ratably throughout the year. Compute the amount of gain or loss in purchasing power during the year. Indicate whether the amount is a gain or a loss.

EXERCISE 33-14   **Applying constant-dollar restatement to sales.** During 19X1 the McFee Corporation's sales were $1,000,000. The general price-level index was 210 on January 1 and 231 on December 31. The average index during the year was 220. At what amount will sales be shown on a constant-dollar income statement?

EXERCISE 33-15   **Applying constant-dollar restatement to the cost of goods sold.** The Fenn Corporation's historical cost of goods sold schedule for 19X2 shows the following amounts.

Merchandise Inventory, January 1, 19X2	$ 2,000,000
Purchases (Net)	9,000,000
Total Merchandise Available for Sale	$11,000,000
Less Merchandise Inventory, Dec. 31, 19X2	2,500,000
Cost of Goods Sold	$ 8,500,000

The average costing method was used for inventory valuation, and the inventories are assumed to be composed of items acquired throughout the year. Certain price indexes are given below.

Average Price Index, 19X1	160.0
Price Index, January 1, 19X2	168.0
Average Price Index, 19X2	176.4
Price Index, December 31, 19X2	184.8

Compute the cost of goods sold under constant-dollar accounting.

EXERCISE 33-16   **Applying constant-dollar restatement to expenses.** Two expense accounts of the Routh Corporation for the year ended December 31, 19X8, are shown below.

Amortization of Goodwill	$ 10,000
Salaries and Wages	392,600

The amortization covers goodwill of $100,000 recorded in January 19X1, when another corporation was acquired. At that time the general price-level index was 124. The goodwill is being amortized over 10 years. The index on January 1, 19X8, was 206. The average index for 19X8 was 214. The index on December 31, 19X8, was 226. At what amounts would these two expenses be shown on a constant-dollar income statement prepared for 19X8?

PROBLEMS

PROBLEM 33-1 **Preparing a consolidated balance sheet at the date of acquisition of 100 percent of the stock.** On January 1, 19X1, the Avanti Corporation, which distributes designer jeans, acquired 100 percent of the stock of the Flair Corporation, a small firm that sells highly styled shirts and blouses. Information from the balance sheets of the two corporations just after the acquisition is shown below.

	Avanti Corporation		Flair Corporation	
Assets				
Current Assets				
Cash	$230,000		$20,000	
Accounts Receivable (Net)	188,000		30,000	
Merchandise Inventory	170,000		32,000	
Prepaid Expenses	4,500		1,000	
Total Current Assets		$592,500		$ 83,000
Property, Plant, and Equipment				
Plant and Equipment	$190,000		$30,000	
Less Accumulated Depreciation	40,000	150,000	8,000	22,000
Long-Term Investments				
Common Stock of Flair Corporation		109,000		
Total Assets		$851,500		$105,000
Liabilities and Stockholders' Equity				
Current Liabilities				
Accounts Payable	$215,000		$18,000	
Notes Payable	20,000		7,000	
Total Current Liabilities		$235,000		$ 25,000
Stockholders' Equity				
Common Stock	$400,000		$50,000	
Retained Earnings	216,500		30,000	
Total Stockholders' Equity		616,500		80,000
Total Liabilities and Stockholders' Equity		$851,500		$105,000

Instructions 1. Prepare a worksheet for a consolidated balance sheet as of January 1, 19X1. Any excess of the purchase price over the underlying book value is attributable to goodwill.

2. Prepare a consolidated balance sheet as of January 1, 19X1.

PROBLEM 33-2 **Preparing a consolidated balance sheet at the date of acquisition of less than 100 percent of the stock.** Refer to the information from the balance sheets of the Avanti Corporation and the Flair Corporation given in Problem 33-1. Assume, however, that the $109,000 paid by the Avanti Corporation was for only 80 percent of the stock of the Flair Corporation. A part of the excess paid by Avanti over the book value of the stock was because Flair's land, included in its plant and equipment, had a fair market value of $9,000 more than its book value.

Instructions 1. Prepare a worksheet for a consolidated balance sheet as of January 1, 19X1.
2. Prepare a consolidated balance sheet as of January 1, 19X1.

PROBLEM 33-3 **Preparing a consolidated balance sheet after an acquisition.** On January 2, 19X1, the Lee Corporation, a distributor of snack foods, acquired 80 percent of the common stock of the Kroll Corporation, a distributor of candy, for $300,000. At that date the balance of the Retained Earnings account of the Kroll Corporation was $30,000. Information from the balance sheets of the two corporations on December 31, 19X1, is as follows.

	Lee Corporation	Kroll Corporation
Assets		
Current Assets		
Cash	$ 48,000	$ 40,000
Accounts Receivable (Net)	122,000	72,000
Merchandise Inventory	140,000	98,000
Total Current Assets	$310,000	$210,000
Property, Plant, and Equipment		
Land	$122,000	$ 68,000
Buildings (Net)	152,000	90,000
Total Property, Plant, and Equipment	$274,000	$158,000
Long-Term Investments		
Common Stock of Kroll Corporation	$314,400	
Total Assets	$898,400	$368,000
Liabilities and Stockholders' Equity		
Liabilities		
Accounts Payable	$154,000	$ 20,000
Stockholders' Equity		
Common Stock	$500,000	$300,000
Retained Earnings	244,400	48,000
Total Stockholders' Equity	$744,400	$348,000
Total Liabilities and Stockholders' Equity	$898,400	$368,000

The accounts receivable of the Kroll Corporation include $18,400 owed by the Lee Corporation. This amount is included in the accounts payable of the Lee Corporation. Any excess of the purchase price of the stock over its book value is due to goodwill.

Instructions Prepare a worksheet for a consolidated balance sheet as of December 31, 19X1.

PROBLEM 33-4 **Preparing a consolidated income statement.** Information from the income statements of the Adelphi Corporation and the Zumwalt Corporation for the year ended December 31, 19X3, is given below. The Adelphi Corporation owns 80 percent of the outstanding stock of the Zumwalt Corporation. Both firms produce uniforms for nurses and other medical personnel.

	Adelphi Corporation	Zumwalt Corporation
Revenues		
Sales	$5,000,000	$2,400,000
Service Income	100,000	
Income From Investment in Zumwalt Corp.	320,000	
Interest Income	160,000	80,000
Total Revenues	$5,580,000	$2,480,000
Costs and Expenses		
Cost of Goods Sold	$2,400,000	$1,400,000
Management Fee Expense		100,000
Other Operating Expenses	1,200,000	276,000
Interest Expense	80,000	24,000
Total Costs and Expenses	$3,680,000	$1,800,000
Net Income Before Income Taxes	$1,900,000	$ 680,000
Provision for Income Taxes	700,000	280,000
Net Income After Income Taxes	$1,200,000	$ 400,000

Additional Information The Adelphi Corporation sold merchandise to the Zumwalt Corporation for $800,000 during the year. All this merchandise was in turn resold by Zumwalt. The $100,000 service income on Adelphi's income statement represents a management fee charged to Zumwalt and is reported by Zumwalt as a management fee expense. Included in Adelphi's interest income is $24,000 interest received from Zumwalt and shown as a deduction on Zumwalt's income statement.

Instructions 1. Prepare a worksheet for a consolidated income statement for 19X3.
2. Prepare a consolidated income statement for 19X3.

PROBLEM 33-5 **Preparing a constant-dollar balance sheet.** A comparative balance sheet for the Industrial Tool Corporation as of December 31, 19X2, and December 31, 19X1, is given on page 804.

Additional Information 1. The general price-level index on January 1, 19X1, was 200; on December 31, 19X1, it was 210; and on December 31, 19X2, it was 225. The average index during 19X1 was 205, and during 19X2 it was 218.

INDUSTRIAL TOOL CORPORATION
Comparative Balance Sheet
December 31, 19X2, and December 31, 19X1

	19X2	19X1
Assets		
Current Assets		
Cash	$173,550	$124,050
Accounts Receivable (Net)	207,000	183,000
Merchandise Inventory	360,000	375,000
Prepaid Insurance	6,300	7,800
Total Current Assets	$746,850	$689,850
Property, Plant, and Equipment		
Plant and Equipment	$134,250	$126,000
Less Accumulated Depreciation	40,950	31,500
Total Property, Plant, and Equipment	$ 93,300	$ 94,500
Total Assets	$840,150	$784,350
Liabilities and Stockholders' Equity		
Current Liabilities		
Accounts Payable	$187,950	$177,600
Estimated Taxes Payable	39,000	25,500
Other Payables	27,300	21,900
Total Current Liabilities	$254,250	$225,000
Long-Term Liabilities		
12% Bonds Payable	90,000	90,000
Total Liabilities	$344,250	$315,000
Stockholders' Equity		
14% Preferred Stock ($100 par value)	$150,000	$150,000
Common Stock ($100 par value)	225,000	225,000
Retained Earnings	120,900	94,350
Total Stockholders' Equity	$495,900	$469,350
Total Liabilities and Stockholders' Equity	$840,150	$784,350

2. The inventory valuation was based on average cost. The ending inventory each year is assumed to have been acquired ratably throughout the year.

3. The plant and equipment is made up of assets costing $126,000, purchased in 19W5, when the general price-level index was 160, and assets costing $8,250, purchased on January 2, 19X2. Accumulated depreciation on the assets acquired in 19W5 was $39,950 on December 31, 19X2, and accumulated depreciation on the assets acquired during 19X2 was $1,000.

4. Both the preferred stock and the common stock were issued in 19W5, when the general price-level index was 160.

Instructions Prepare a balance sheet for the Industrial Tool Corporation as of December 31, 19X2, restated on a constant-dollar basis.

Computing a gain or loss in purchasing power and preparing a constant-dollar income statement. This problem involves the Industrial Tool Corporation, which was discussed in Problem 33-5. The firm's income statement for the year ended December 31, 19X2, is given below.

INDUSTRIAL TOOL CORPORATION
Income Statement
Year Ended December 31, 19X2

Revenue		
Sales		$1,950,000
Cost of Goods Sold		
Merchandise Inventory, Jan. 1		$ 375,000
Purchases (Net)		1,349,400
Total Merchandise Available for Sale		$1,724,400
Less Merchandise Inventory, Dec. 31		360,000
Cost of Goods Sold		$1,364,400
Gross Profit on Sales		$ 585,600
Operating Expenses		
Selling Expenses		
Sales Salaries Expense		$ 184,800
Rent Expense		19,800
Delivery Expense		13,500
Advertising Expense		15,300
Depreciation Expense		5,000
Other Selling Expenses		59,200
Total Selling Expenses		$ 297,600
Administrative Expenses		
Officers' Salaries Expense		$ 90,000
Office Salaries Expense		20,000
Loss From Uncollectible Accounts		14,550
Rent Expense		4,000
Depreciation Expense		4,450
Other Administrative Expenses		53,450
Total Administrative Expenses		$ 186,450
Total Operating Expenses		$ 484,050
Net Income From Operations		$ 101,550
Other Expenses		
Bond Interest Expense		10,800
Net Income Before Income Taxes		$ 90,750
Provision for Income Taxes		32,700
Net Income After Income Taxes		$ 58,050

Instructions   1. Using the information given in Problem 33-5, compute the gain or loss in purchasing power on the firm's net monetary assets or liabilities for the year

19X2. Assume that changes in monetary assets and liabilities occurred ratably throughout the year.

2. Using the information given in Problem 33-5 and the income statement given on page 805, prepare a constant-dollar income statement for the Industrial Tool Corporation for the year 19X2. (The equipment purchased in 19X2 was office equipment. Depreciation on this equipment is included in the administrative expenses.)

ALTERNATE PROBLEMS

PROBLEM 33-1A **Preparing a consolidated balance sheet at the date of acquisition of 100 percent of the stock.** On January 1, 19X4, the Everglow Corporation, which distributes low-priced lamps, acquired 100 percent of the stock of the Starlite Corporation, a small firm that sells a line of expensive lamps. Information from the balance sheets of the two corporations just after the acquisition is shown below.

	Everglow Corporation		Starlite Corporation	
Assets				
Current Assets				
Cash		$160,000		$ 5,000
Accounts Receivable (Net)		98,000		15,200
Merchandise Inventory		80,000		10,000
Prepaid Expenses		2,000		800
Total Current Assets		$340,000		$31,000
Property, Plant, and Equipment				
Plant and Equipment	$160,000		$24,000	
Less Accumulated Depreciation	40,000	120,000	6,000	18,000
Long-Term Investments				
Common Stock of Starlite Corporation		45,000		
Total Assets		$505,000		$49,000
Liabilities and Stockholders' Equity				
Current Liabilities				
Accounts Payable	$125,000		$ 5,000	
Accrued Expenses Payable	10,000		1,500	
Total Current Liabilties		$135,000		$ 6,500
Stockholders' Equity				
Common Stock	$200,000		$30,000	
Retained Earnings	170,000		12,500	
Total Stockholders' Equity		370,000		42,500
Total Liabilities and Stockholders' Equity		$505,000		$49,000

Instructions
1. Prepare a worksheet for a consolidated balance sheet as of January 1, 19X4. A part of the excess of the purchase price over the book value of the Starlite Corporation's stock is attributable to the fact that Starlite's merchandise inventory was undervalued by $1,000 at the date of the stock's purchase.
2. Prepare a consolidated balance sheet as of January 1, 19X4.

PROBLEM 33-2A **Preparing a consolidated balance sheet at the date of acquisition of less than 100 percent of the stock.** Refer to the information from the balance sheets of the Everglow Corporation and the Starlite Corporation given in Problem 33-1A. Assume, however, that the $45,000 paid by the Everglow Corporation was for only 75 percent of the stock of the Starlite Corporation. A part of the excess paid by Everglow over the book value of the stock was due to the fact that Starlite's merchandise inventory was worth $5,000 more than its book value. The remaining excess was due to goodwill.

Instructions
1. Prepare a worksheet for a consolidated balance sheet as of January 1, 19X4.
2. Prepare a consolidated balance sheet as of January 1, 19X4.

PROBLEM 33-3A **Preparing a consolidated balance sheet after an acquisition.** On January 1, 19X1, the Lawrence Corporation, an importer of tea, purchased 90 percent of the common stock of the Perez Corporation, an importer of coffee, for $84,000. At that date the balance of the Retained Earnings account of the Perez Corporation

	Lawrence Corporation	Perez Corporation
Assets		
Current Assets		
Cash	$ 13,000	$ 21,000
Accounts Receivable (Net)	19,000	
Merchandise Inventory	20,000	27,000
Total Current Assets	$ 52,000	$ 48,000
Property, Plant, and Equipment		
Plant and Equipment (Net)	79,000	60,000
Long-Term Investments		
Common Stock of Perez Corporation	93,000	
Total Assets	$224,000	$108,000
Liabilities and Stockholders' Equity		
Current Liabilities		
Accounts Payable	$ 48,000	$ 17,000
Stockholders' Equity		
Common Stock	$120,000	$ 60,000
Retained Earnings	56,000	31,000
Total Stockholders' Equity	$176,000	$ 91,000
Total Liabilities and Stockholders' Equity	$224,000	$108,000

was $21,000. Information from the balance sheets of the two corporations on December 31, 19X1, is given on page 807.

Additional Information   The accounts receivable of the Lawrence Corporation include $9,600 owed by the Perez Corporation. The excess paid by Lawrence over the book value of Perez's stock is due in part to the fact that the fair market value of land owned by Perez (which is included in its property, plant, and equipment) is $8,000 greater than the book value of the land. The remaining excess is due to goodwill.

Instructions   Prepare a worksheet for a consolidated balance sheet as of December 31, 19X1.

PROBLEM 33-4A   **Preparing a consolidated income statement.** Information from the income statements of the Baker Corporation and the Donahue Corporation for the year ended December 31, 19X1, is given below. The Baker Corporation owns 90 percent of the outstanding stock of the Donahue Corporation. Both firms make parts for motorcycles.

	Baker Corporation	Donahue Corporation
Revenues		
Sales	$6,000,000	$1,800,000
Management Fee Income	90,000	
Income From Investment in Donahue Corp.	81,000	
Interest Income	40,000	6,000
Total Revenues	$6,211,000	$1,806,000
Costs and Expenses		
Cost of Goods Sold	$4,000,000	$1,350,000
Management Fee Expense		90,000
Other Operating Expenses	1,000,000	210,000
Interest Expense		30,000
Total Costs and Expenses	$5,000,000	$1,680,000
Net Income Before Income Taxes	$1,211,000	$ 126,000
Provision for Income Taxes	471,000	36,000
Net Income After Income Taxes	$ 740,000	$ 90,000

Additional Information   The Donahue Corporation sold merchandise to the Baker Corporation for $700,000 during the year. This amount is included in Donahue's sales and in Baker's cost of goods sold. Baker charged Donahue a management fee of $90,000 during the year. Included in the interest income of Baker is $30,000 paid by Donahue. The same amount is shown by Donahue as interest expense.

Instructions   1. Prepare a worksheet for a consolidated income statement for 19X1.
2. Prepare a consolidated income statement for 19X1.

PROBLEM 33-5A   **Preparing a constant-dollar balance sheet.** A comparative balance sheet for the Snow Togs Corporation as of December 31, 19X3, and December 31, 19X2, is shown on page 809. This firm sells down coats and jackets.

SNOW TOGS CORPORATION
Comparative Balance Sheet
December 31, 19X3, and December 31, 19X2

	19X3	19X2
Assets		
Current Assets		
Cash	$ 55,000	$ 60,000
Accounts Receivable (Net)	104,000	85,000
Merchandise Inventory	182,000	160,000
Prepaid Expenses	9,500	11,000
Total Current Assets	$350,500	$316,000
Property, Plant, and Equipment		
Land	$150,000	$150,000
Building	$250,000	$250,000
Less Accumulated Depreciation	167,000	157,000
Net Book Value	$ 83,000	$ 93,000
Equipment	$ 65,000	$ 65,000
Less Accumulated Depreciation	48,000	46,000
Net Book Value	$ 17,000	$ 19,000
Total Property, Plant, and Equipment	$250,000	$262,000
Total Assets	$600,500	$578,000
Liabilities and Stockholders' Equity		
Current Liabilities		
Accounts Payable	$ 70,000	$ 95,000
Accrued Liabilities	18,000	25,000
Total Current Liabilities	$ 88,000	$120,000
Long-Term Liabilities		
15% Bonds Payable	$100,000	$100,000
Total Liabilities	$188,000	$220,000
Stockholders' Equity		
Common Stock, no-par value	$300,000	$300,000
Retained Earnings	112,500	58,000
Total Stockholders' Equity	$412,500	$358,000
Total Liabilities and Stockholders' Equity	$600,500	$578,000

Additional Information

1. The general price-level index at the beginning of 19X2 was 180; at the end of 19X2 it was 190; and at the end of 19X3 it was 200. The average index for 19X3 was 195; for 19X2 it was 184.
2. The land and building were acquired in 19W0, when the general price-level index was 95. The equipment was acquired in 19W5, when the index was 145.

3. The inventory valuation was based on average costing. The beginning inventory for each year is assumed to be representative of the average price level for the preceding year. The ending inventory is assumed to have been acquired ratably throughout the year.
4. The stock was issued in 19W0, when the general price-level index was 95.

Instructions Prepare a balance sheet for the Snow Togs Corporation as of December 31, 19X3, restated on a constant-dollar basis.

PROBLEM 33-6A **Computing a gain or loss in purchasing power and preparing a constant-dollar income statement.** This problem involves the Snow Togs Corporation, which was discussed in Problem 33-5A. The firm's income statement for the year ended December 31, 19X3, is given below.

SNOW TOGS CORPORATION
Income Statement
Year Ended December 31, 19X3

Revenue		
Sales		$490,000
Cost of Goods Sold		
Merchandise Inventory, Jan. 1	$160,000	
Purchases (Net)	350,000	
Total Merchandise Available for Sale	$510,000	
Less Merchandise Inventory, Dec. 31	182,000	
Cost of Goods Sold		328,000
Gross Profit on Sales		$162,000
Operating Expenses		
Selling Expenses	$ 42,000	
Administrative Expenses	31,000	
Depreciation Expense	12,000	
Total Operating Expenses		85,000
Net Income From Operations		$ 77,000
Other Expenses		
Interest Expense		15,000
Net Income Before Income Taxes		$ 62,000
Provision for Income Taxes		9,500
Net Income After Income Taxes		$ 52,500

Instructions
1. Using the information given in Problem 33-5A, compute the gain or loss in purchasing power on the firm's net monetary assets or liabilities for the year 19X3. Assume that changes in monetary assets and liabilities occurred ratably throughout the year.
2. Using the information given in Problem 33-5A and the income statement given above, prepare a constant-dollar income statement for the Snow Togs Corporation for the year ended December 31, 19X3.

In the previous chapters of this book, three major financial statements were explained and illustrated. These are the income statement, the balance sheet, and the statement of retained earnings (or the statement of partners' equities). One additional statement is required to complete the set of annual financial statements. This is the statement of changes in financial position.

ANALYZING THE FLOW OF FUNDS, AND REPORTING CHANGES IN FINANCIAL POSITION

THE NEED FOR A STATEMENT OF CHANGES IN FINANCIAL POSITION

The purpose of the *statement of changes in financial position* is to show where a company's financial resources were obtained from during the year and how they were used.[1] As the title suggests, this statement essentially reports why the balance sheet at the end of the year differs from the balance sheet at the start of the year. To prepare the statement of changes in financial position, it is necessary to have the income statement for the year, the statement of retained earnings for the year, and balance sheets for both the beginning and the end of the year. In addition, it is necessary to have available information about all entries made in the accounts during the year.

To illustrate preparation of the statement of changes in financial position, data for the Duncan Lawn Furniture Corporation for the year 19Y3 will be used. Most of this data comes from the financial statements shown on pages 812–815.

THE NATURE OF FUNDS

The statement of changes in financial position centers on the inflow and outflow of (1) working capital or (2) cash. Either of these may be considered the *funds* of a corporation. For many businesses the statement of changes in financial position will consist solely of an analysis of the sources and uses of working capital or cash because the company has no transaction involving financial resources that does not fit into one category or the other.

---

[1]Requirements for the statement of changes in financial position are found in "Reporting Changes in Financial Position," *Opinions of the Accounting Principles Board, No. 19* (New York: American Institute of Certified Public Accountants, 1971).

DUNCAN LAWN FURNITURE CORPORATION
Comparative Income Statement
Years Ended December 31, 19Y3 and 19Y2

	19Y3	19Y2
Revenue		
Sales	$3,241,578	$2,970,530
Less Sales Returns and Allowances	22,496	19,390
Net Sales	$3,219,082	$2,951,140
Cost of Goods Sold		
Merchandise Inventory, Jan. 1	$ 285,100	$ 253,700
Merchandise Purchases (Net)	1,982,488	1,808,270
Freight In	15,000	13,000
Total Merchandise Available for Sale	$2,282,588	$2,074,970
Less Merchandise Inventory, Dec. 31	300,000	285,100
Cost of Goods Sold	$1,982,588	$1,789,870
Gross Profit on Sales	$1,236,494	$1,161,270
Operating Expenses		
Selling Expenses (Schedule A)	$ 719,346	$ 706,032
Administrative Expenses (Schedule B)	288,952	260,501
Total Operating Expenses	$1,008,298	$ 966,533
Net Income From Operations	$ 228,196	$ 194,737
Other Income		
Gain on Sale of Equipment	$ 1,000	$ -0-
Interest Income	355	722
Total Other Income	$ 1,355	$ 722
Total Income for Year	$ 229,551	$ 195,459
Other Expenses		
Bond Interest Expense	$ 7,049	$ 5,500
Other Interest Expense	200	$ 1,200
Total Other Expenses	$ 7,249	$ 6,700
Net Income Before Income Taxes	$ 222,302	$ 188,759
Provision for Income Taxes	82,250	66,160
Net Income After Income Taxes	$ 140,052	$ 122,599

DUNCAN LAWN FURNITURE CORPORATION — *Schedule A*
Comparative Schedule of Selling Expenses
Years Ended December 31, 19Y3 and 19Y2

	19Y3	19Y2
Sales Salaries	$385,600	$378,200
Sales Commissions	42,000	38,000
Payroll Taxes—Sales Staff	38,600	34,300
Employee Fringe Benefits	31,600	38,300
Freight Out and Deliveries	28,870	22,750
Advertising	99,630	103,100
Sales Supplies	10,307	13,960
Rent	22,000	22,000
Utilities	9,039	7,820
Insurance	9,800	9,300
Repairs and Maintenance	1,800	3,102
Depreciation	8,300	6,200
Travel and Entertainment	12,000	9,600
Other Taxes	7,800	7,600
Miscellaneous	12,000	11,800
Total Selling Expenses	$719,346	$706,032

DUNCAN LAWN FURNITURE CORPORATION — *Schedule B*
Comparative Schedule of Administrative Expenses
Years Ended December 31, 19Y3 and 19Y2

	19Y3	19Y2
Officers' Salaries	$165,759	$150,000
Office Employees' Salaries	57,000	49,500
Payroll Taxes—Administrative Staff	16,800	16,655
Office Supplies	15,633	14,726
Postage, Copying, and Miscellaneous	3,800	3,700
Loss From Uncollectible Accounts	5,360	4,800
Rent	8,000	7,500
Depreciation	6,400	4,800
Other Taxes	4,800	4,200
Utilities	5,400	4,620
Total Administrative Expenses	$288,952	$260,501

Although either working capital or cash may be classified as funds, customarily accountants and financial analysts use the term *funds* to refer to *working capital,* the excess of a company's current assets over its current liabilities. (It should be noted that the term *working capital* is sometimes used to indicate total current assets, while the excess of current assets over current liabilities is referred to as *net working capital.*) At this point we will assume that working capital is

DUNCAN LAWN FURNITURE CORPORATION
Comparative Balance Sheet
December 31, 19Y3 and 19Y2

	19Y3	19Y2
Assets		
Current Assets		
Cash	$ 72,860	$100,187
Accounts Receivable (Net)	198,184	168,184
Merchandise Inventory	300,000	285,000
Prepaid Insurance	5,700	2,700
Other Prepayments	5,500	2,500
Total Current Assets	$582,244	$558,571
Property, Plant, and Equipment		
Land	$ 30,000	$ 30,000
Building	$120,000	-0-
Less Accumulated Depreciation	2,000	-0-
Net Book Value—Building	$118,000	$ -0-
Equipment and Fixtures	$103,200	$ 83,600
Less Accumulated Depreciation	54,300	44,000
Net Book Value—Equipment and Fixtures	$ 48,900	$ 39,600
Total Property, Plant, and Equipment	$196,900	$ 69,600
Total Assets	$779,144	$628,171
Liabilities and Stockholders' Equity		
Current Liabilities		
Accounts Payable	$ 89,201	$ 85,000
Estimated Income Taxes Payable	41,125	21,300
Accrued Liabilities	14,446	17,530
Total Current Liabilities	$144,772	$123,830
Long-Term Liabilities		
11% Bonds Payable, 19Z1	$ 70,000	$ 50,000
Premium on Bonds Payable	979	-0-
Total Long-Term Liabilities	$ 70,979	$ 50,000
Total Liabilities	$215,751	$173,830
Stockholders' Equity		
12% Preferred Stock, $100 Par Value	$100,000	$100,000
Paid-in Capital in Excess of Par Value	6,000	6,000
Common Stock, $50 Stated Value	160,000	150,000
Paid-in Capital in Excess of Stated Value	29,000	19,000
Retained Earnings (Schedule C)	268,393	179,341
Total Stockholders' Equity	$563,393	$454,341
Total Liabilities and Stockholders' Equity	$779,144	$628,171

DUNCAN LAWN FURNITURE CORPORATION   *Schedule C*
Comparative Statement of Retained Earnings
Years Ended December 31, 19Y3 and 19Y2

	19Y3	19Y2
Balance, Jan. 1	$179,341	$114,742
Additions		
Net Income After Income Taxes	140,052	122,599
Total	$319,393	$237,341
Deductions		
Dividends—Preferred Stock	$ 12,000	$ 12,000
Dividends—Common Stock	39,000	46,000
Total	$ 51,000	$ 58,000
Balance, Dec. 31	$268,393	$179,341

the central element in the statement of changes in financial position. Then, later in the chapter, we will examine the procedure for building the statement of changes in financial position around cash flow.

FUNDS FLOW

Working capital is a basic measure of a company's ability to pay its current obligations, and it shows the margin of security provided to short-term creditors. The day-to-day activities of a business involve the flow of working capital through the operating cycle. Merchandise is purchased on credit, goods are sold on credit, cash is received from customers, payments are made on accounts payable and for operating expenses, and more merchandise is purchased to renew the cycle.

The working capital for the Duncan Lawn Furniture Corporation on December 31, 19Y3, and December 31, 19Y2, can be computed from the comparative balance sheet shown on page 814.

	19Y3	19Y2
Current Assets	$582,244	$558,571
Current Liabilities	144,772	123,830
Working Capital	$437,472	$434,741

According to these figures, Duncan's working capital increased from $434,741 in 19Y2 to $437,472 in 19Y3. However, users of the firm's financial statements are concerned with more than merely the dollar amount of working capital. They are also interested in the relationships between various working capital items, and, as you will see in the next two chapters, they will compute certain ratios and proportions in order to analyze the working capital. To provide more information about this area, it is customary to prepare a schedule showing the details of working capital changes. This schedule indicates the increase or

DUNCAN LAWN FURNITURE CORPORATION
Schedule of Working Capital Changes
Year Ended December 31, 19Y3

	Amounts on December 31		Working Capital Increase or (Decrease)
	19Y3	19Y2	
Current Assets			
Cash	$ 72,860	$100,187	$(27,327)
Accounts Receivable (Net)	198,184	168,184	30,000
Merchandise Inventory	300,000	285,000	15,000
Prepaid Insurance	5,700	2,700	3,000
Other Prepayments	5,500	2,500	3,000
Total Current Assets	$582,244	$558,571	
Current Liabilities			
Accounts Payable	$ 89,201	$ 85,000	(4,201)
Estimated Income Taxes Payable	41,125	21,300	(19,825)
Accrued Liabilities	14,446	17,530	3,084
Total Current Liabilities	$144,772	$123,830	
Working Capital	$437,472	$434,741	$ 2,731

decrease in each specific current asset and current liability. The schedule of working capital changes prepared at the Duncan Lawn Furniture Corporation for 19Y3 is shown above. The necessary information was taken from the comparative balance sheet illustrated on page 814.

Notice that the column on the right shows the effect on working capital of an increase or decrease in the balance of each current asset and current liability. An increase in a current asset, such as the $30,000 increase in Accounts Receivable, represents an increase in working capital. A decrease in a current asset, such as the $27,327 decrease in Cash, represents a decrease in working capital. On the other hand, a decrease in a current liability, such as the $3,084 decrease in Accrued Liabilities, means an increase in working capital. An increase in a current liability, such as the $4,201 increase in Accounts Payable, means a decrease in working capital.

Let us now turn to the *flow of working capital*—the determination of where working capital came from and how it was used during the year. This information is determined by analyzing transactions and changes in account balances that took place during the year.

SOURCES OF FUNDS

There are four principal sources of working capital for a business: the net income that results from operations, investments by the owners, long-term borrowing, and sales of long-lived assets.

Net Income From Operations	Net income from current operations is a major source of working capital. Most revenue transactions increase either Cash or Accounts Receivable, both current assets, thereby increasing the amount of working capital. For example, during 19Y3 the Duncan Lawn Furniture Corporation had sales of $3,241,578. Cash and Accounts Receivable were debited for amounts that equaled this total, and Sales was credited for the total. The result was an increase in working capital.

Most expense transactions involve cash payments (a decrease in current assets), the incurring of payables (an increase in current liabilities), or the use of prepaid expenses (a decrease in current assets). These transactions decrease the amount of working capital. For example, payment of advertising costs by Duncan would result in a debit to Advertising Expense and a credit to Cash, thus decreasing current assets.

There are certain revenue items that do not bring about an increase in working capital and certain expense items that do not cause a decrease in working capital. Because of this, a difference often exists between the amount of net income and the amount of working capital from operations. However, in computing the working capital provided by operations, the starting point is the net income after income taxes, as shown on the income statement. This starting point is used so that the relationship between the net income reported and the actual working capital resulting from operations can be clearly indicated. This very logical approach often helps owners and managers to understand why working capital may decrease even though the income statement shows a net income.

Expense Items Not Decreasing Working Capital As noted already, not all expense items actually affect working capital. For example, depreciation expense does not decrease a current asset or increase a current liability. It causes a decrease in the book value of plant and equipment through credits to the accumulated depreciation accounts, but it does not decrease working capital.

In 19Y3 Duncan recorded depreciation of $14,700. Of this amount, $8,300 was charged to selling expenses and $6,400 was charged to administrative expenses (see Schedules A and B on page 813). This $14,700 represents an expense not requiring working capital. Hence the net income after income taxes of $140,052, shown on the income statement on page 812, does not truly measure the working capital provided by operations. Depreciation and any other charges not resulting from changes in current assets or current liabilities should be added to the net income shown on the income statement in order to measure the actual working capital provided by operations.

Revenue Items and Other Items Not Increasing Working Capital
Similar but opposite adjustments are necessary if items that do not increase working capital have been included as revenue or as credits to expense accounts. For example, if merchandise is sold and a long-term note receivable is obtained for the sale instead of cash or an account receivable or a short-term note receivable, the amount shown as sales revenue on the income statement would overstate the inflow of current assets from sales activities.

Another item that can cause a difference between the net income reported by a company and the true amount of working capital generated by the firm's operations is the amortization of a premium on bonds payable. For example, during 19Y3 the Duncan Lawn Furniture Corporation issued bonds payable at a premium of $1,080. However, by the end of 19Y3, a total of $101 of this premium had been amortized by debits to Premium on Bonds Payable and credits to Bond Interest Expense. As a result, the income statement for 19Y3 shows Bond Interest Expense of only $7,049 even though the actual cash paid for interest expense during the year was $7,150. Hence the expense charge of $7,049 does not show the total outflow for interest, and the net income figure overstates the working capital inflow from operations by $101. This amount must be deducted from net income to arrive at the working capital from operations, as shown on page 819.

Gains and Losses on Sales of Noncurrent Assets Duncan's income statement for 19Y3 includes under Other Income an item entitled Gain on Sale of Equipment. The amount of this gain should be removed from the net income figure in order to arrive at the working capital provided by operations. An analysis of the transaction shows that Duncan sold some equipment for $2,700 in April 19Y3. The original cost of the equipment was $4,100, and the accumulated depreciation until the date of the sale was $2,400. Thus the cash sales price of $2,700 exceeded the book value of $1,700 by $1,000, which resulted in a gain to the business. The final figure shown on the income statement does not truly represent working capital provided by operations because the $1,000 gain on the sale of equipment did not come from operations. Therefore, as illustrated on page 819, the $1,000 item should be deducted from the net income figure in arriving at the working capital provided by operations. (The entire $2,700 increase in Cash resulting from the sale of the equipment is shown in the sources of working capital section of the statement of changes in financial position, as discussed on page 821.)

A loss on the sale of a noncurrent asset that was included in the determination of net income should be added to the net income figure in order to arrive at the true working capital provided by operations. Again, the entire sales price is shown as a source of working capital on the statement of changes in financial position.

Summary of the Funds Provided by Duncan's Operations The working capital provided by Duncan's operations for the year 19Y3 is summarized in the schedule shown on page 819.

Investments by Owners

When a corporation sells stock to its shareholders, the transaction usually brings working capital into the corporation in the form of cash. In the entry made to record the sale of stock, the current asset Cash is increased by the amount received for the stock, and no change is made in current liabilities. The same is true of an investment of cash by the owner of a sole proprietorship or by partners. Such investments by owners represent an important source of working capital. The Duncan Lawn Furniture Corporation's capital accounts show an increase in

DUNCAN LAWN FURNITURE CORPORATION
Schedule of Working Capital From Operations
Year Ended December 31, 19Y3

Net income, per income statement		$140,052
Add charges not requiring working capital:		
Depreciation expense		14,700
		$154,752
Deduct credits not providing working capital:		
Bond premium amortized	$ 101	
Gain on sale of equipment	1,000	1,101
Total working capital provided by operations		$153,651

Common Stock of $10,000 and an increase in Paid-in Capital in Excess of Stated Value of $10,000. An analysis of these two accounts shows that the increases resulted from the issue of 200 shares of common stock on October 1, 19Y3, for $100 a share. The entire $20,000 received for this stock represents an increase in working capital.

Long-Term Borrowing

When a corporation borrows money by issuing bonds or long-term notes, working capital is increased. In the entry made to record the transaction, the current asset Cash is increased by the amount received and Bonds Payable or Long-Term Notes Payable is increased. No change is made in current liabilities. For example, during 19Y3 Duncan issued $20,000 par value of its 11 percent bonds at a premium of $1,080 for a total issue price of $21,080. The entry to record this issue was a debit to Cash for $21,080 and offsetting credits to 11% Bonds Payable, 19Z1 for $20,000 and to Premium on Bonds Payable for $1,080. Since both of the latter amounts are classified as long-term liabilities, the result of this transaction was to increase working capital by $21,080. (As we have already seen, $101 of this premium was amortized during 19Y3 by a debit to Premium on Bonds Payable and a credit to Bond Interest Expense. Thus the entire change of $979 in the Premium on Bonds Payable account during 19Y3 has now been explained.)

Sale of Long-Term Assets

When a noncurrent asset, such as equipment or an investment, is sold for cash, the result is an increase in the current asset Cash with no offsetting effects on other current assets or current liabilities. Thus the price received for such assets represents an increase in working capital. Similarly, if a short-term receivable results from the sale, working capital is increased.

Earlier we analyzed the item Gain on Sale of Equipment shown on the income statement of the Duncan Lawn Furniture Corporation for 19Y3. That gain resulted from the sale of some equipment for $2,700. The equipment had a cost of $4,100 and accumulated depreciation of $2,400 at the date of sale. The gain was removed as a source of working capital from operations because the entire sales price of $2,700 is to be shown as working capital provided from the sale.

Summary of Duncan's Sources of Funds	The sources of working capital that the Duncan Lawn Furniture Corporation had for the year 19Y3 are summarized below.

SOURCES OF WORKING CAPITAL

Funds provided by operations (from schedule)	$153,651
Funds provided by issue of common stock	20,000
Funds provided by long-term borrowing	21,080
Funds provided by sale of equipment	2,700
Total working capital provided during year	$197,431

USES OF FUNDS	There are also four major uses of working capital: withdrawals by owners (including dividends and treasury stock purchases), purchases of noncurrent assets, payments of long-term liabilities, and losses from operations. The nature and effect of each use is explained in the paragraphs that follow.
Withdrawals by Owners	When the owners of a business withdraw cash, working capital is reduced. In corporations these withdrawals usually take the form of dividends paid to stockholders. The statement of retained earnings for the Duncan Lawn Furniture Corporation illustrated on page 815 shows that during 19Y3 Duncan paid dividends of $12,000 on preferred stock and $39,000 on common stock. Both dividend payments represent the use of working capital.
Purchase of Noncurrent Assets	The purchase of noncurrent assets for cash or by incurring short-term liabilities results in a decrease in working capital. An analysis of the property, plant, and equipment accounts of the Duncan Lawn Furniture Corporation for 19Y3 shows that the corporation constructed a new building at a cost of $120,000, paying cash. In addition, the corporation purchased new equipment and fixtures at a cost of $23,700, paying cash. Thus the corporation's statement of changes in financial position will reflect a total use of $143,700 for the purchase of property, plant, and equipment.
Payment of Long-Term Liabilities	When long-term liabilities are paid, working capital is used. Specifically, the current asset Cash is decreased without any change in current liabilities. Similarly, contributions to a bond sinking fund would involve a use of working capital. During 19Y3 Duncan did not retire any long-term debt or make payments to a bond sinking fund.
Net Loss From Operations	If the business suffers a loss from operations, working capital is decreased because the outflow of working capital for expenses exceeds the inflow from revenues. The loss, adjusted for any nonworking capital items such as depreciation and amortization, will be shown as a negative figure in the sources of working capital section rather than the uses of working capital section.
Summary of Duncan's Uses of Funds	The uses of working capital by the Duncan Lawn Furniture Corporation during 19Y3 are summarized on page 821.

USES OF WORKING CAPITAL

Funds used to pay dividends		$ 51,000
Funds used to purchase property, plant, and equipment		143,700
Total working capital used		$194,700

THE FORMAL STATEMENT OF CHANGES IN FINANCIAL POSITION

After all the changes in the noncurrent asset accounts, the long-term liability accounts, and the stockholders' equity accounts have been analyzed and explained, a formal statement of changes in financial position can be prepared. The formal statement completed by the Duncan Lawn Furniture Corporation for the year 19Y3 is presented below.

NONWORKING CAPITAL RESOURCES

Notice that on the statement of changes in financial position for Duncan all changes in the noncurrent assets were explained in the process of analyzing the sources and uses of working capital. This is not true for every corporation each year. Sometimes a corporation has changes in noncurrent assets that do not affect working capital. Yet these changes may represent important sources and uses of financial resources for the business and should be reported.

Prior to the issue in 1971 of *APB Opinion No. 19, Reporting Changes in Financial Position,* by the American Institute of Certified Public Accountants, it

DUNCAN LAWN FURNITURE CORPORATION
Statement of Changes in Financial Position
Year Ended December 31, 19Y3

Working capital was obtained from the following sources:			
Current operations			
Net income (from income statement)		$140,052	
Add: Depreciation expense		14,700	
		$154,752	
Less: Bond premium amortized	$ 101		
Gain on sale of equipment	1,000	1,101	
Net working capital provided by current operations			$153,651
Issue of common stock			20,000
Issue of bonds payable			21,080
Sale of equipment			2,700
Total working capital provided			$197,431
Working capital was used for the following purposes:			
Payment of dividends		$ 51,000	
Purchase of property, plant, and equipment		143,700	
Total working capital used			194,700
Net increase in working capital			$ 2,731

was possible for significant sources and uses of financial resources to go unreported on the statement of changes in financial position. This statement reflected only items involving working capital; it ignored transactions that did not involve working capital. For example, a corporation's issuance of capital stock in exchange for land and buildings or conversion of bonds into common stock would not appear on the statement of changes in financial position.

Recognizing the importance of such transactions to analysts seeking to interpret the affairs of a business, *Opinion No. 19* requires that *all* sources and uses of financial resources be shown on the statement of changes in financial position. Although no particular form or method of presentation is specified, the nonworking capital items have typically been treated as though they were both sources and uses of funds. *Opinion No. 19* does require that the statement show clearly the funds produced by operations.

To see how such transactions might be handled on the statement of changes in financial position, suppose that in addition to all the transactions that we have previously examined for the Duncan Lawn Furniture Corporation in 19Y3, the firm had also issued 500 shares of common stock to a landowner in return for some land. The transaction was recorded by a debit to Land for $50,000, the estimated fair market value of the asset, a credit to Common Stock for $25,000, the stated value of the shares, and a credit to Paid-in Capital in Excess of Stated Value for the balance of $25,000. This transaction did not cause an inflow or outflow of working capital. Nevertheless, it is an important source and use of financial resources. The transaction might be reflected in the statement of changes in financial position as shown on page 823.

STATEMENT OF CHANGES IN FINANCIAL POSITION BASED ON CASH FLOW

The examples of the statement of changes in financial position shown up to this point have emphasized working capital flow—the sources and uses of working capital. However, some companies prefer to emphasize *cash flow*—the sources and uses of cash. To quickly illustrate preparation of a statement of changes in financial position based on cash flow for the Duncan Lawn Furniture Corporation, we will take information from the statement of changes in financial position based on working capital flow that appears on page 821 and the schedule of working capital changes that appears on page 816.

In preparing the statement of changes in financial position based on cash flow, the starting point again is net income as shown on the income statement. In addition to the adjustments previously made for items affecting net income that did not result in changes in working capital, all items affecting working capital but not cash that are included in the net income must be treated as adjustments. Under a shortcut method commonly used, this is done by adding or subtracting from net income the increases or decreases in working capital accounts other than Cash.

For example, the schedule of working capital changes on page 816 shows that accounts receivable (net) increased by $30,000 during 19Y3. Obviously, this increase reflects sales included in the income statement for which cash has not yet been received. Thus the net income for 19Y3 overstates the amount of

DUNCAN LAWN FURNITURE CORPORATION
Statement of Changes in Financial Position
Year Ended December 31, 19Y3

Financial Resources Provided
  Working capital was obtained from the following sources:
  Current operations

Net income (from income statement)		$140,052	
Add: Depreciation expense		14,700	
		$154,752	
Less: Bond premium amortized	$ 101		
Gain on sale of equipment	1,000	1,101	
Net working capital provided by current operations			$153,651
Issue of common stock			20,000
Issue of bonds payable			21,080
Sale of equipment			2,700
Total working capital provided			$197,431
Financial resources not affecting working capital:			
Issue of common stock for land			50,000
Total financial resources provided			$247,431

Financial Resources Used
  Working capital was used for the following purposes:

Payment of dividends		$ 51,000	
Purchase of property, plant, and equipment		143,700	
Total working capital used			$194,700
Uses of resources not affecting working capital:			
Acquisition of land for common stock			50,000
Total financial resources used			$244,700
Net increase in working capital			$ 2,731

cash produced by sales. The opposite effect on cash flow is caused by Duncan's estimated income taxes payable. This item increased by $19,825 during the year, which means that part of the income tax expense reported on the income statement has not yet been paid in cash. Thus the cash outflow for taxes is less than the amount deducted from net income. To this extent, the net cash generated from operations exceeds the amount shown as net income.

The general rule to remember is that any decrease in working capital that results from a change in a current asset other than cash or a current liability represents an addition to net income in arriving at the cash provided by operations. Similarly, any increase in working capital resulting from a change in a current asset other than cash or a current liability represents a deduction that must be made from net income to arrive at the amount of cash provided by operations. This type of analysis was made for the noncash current assets and the current liabilities of the Duncan Lawn Furniture Corporation in 19Y3. The results are reflected in the statement changes in financial position on page 824.

DUNCAN LAWN FURNITURE CORPORATION
Statement of Changes in Financial Position
Year Ended December 31, 19Y3

Sources of cash:		
Current operations:		
Net income (from income statement)		$140,052
Add:		
Depreciation expense	$14,700	
Increase in accounts payable	4,201	
Increase in income taxes payable	19,825	38,726
		$178,778
Deduct:		
Bond premium amortized	$ 101	
Gain on sale of equipment	1,000	
Increase in accounts receivable	30,000	
Increase in merchandise inventory	15,000	
Increase in prepaid insurance	3,000	
Increase in other prepayments	3,000	
Decrease in accrued liabilities	3,084	55,185
Total cash provided by operations		$123,593
Other sources:		
Issue of common stock	$ 20,000	
Issue of bonds payable	21,080	
Sale of equipment	2,700	43,780
Total cash provided		$167,373
Uses of cash:		
Payment of dividends	$ 51,000	
Purchase of property, plant, and equipment	143,700	
Total cash used		194,700
Net decrease in cash		$ 27,327

PRINCIPLES AND PROCEDURES SUMMARY

A complete set of annual financial statements must include a statement of changes in financial position. This statement shows the sources and uses made of all financial resources during the year. It emphasizes the inflow and outflow of funds, beginning with the funds provided by the firm's operations.

The term *funds* usually refers to *working capital*, which is the excess of current assets over current liabilities. There are four major sources of working capital: the net income from operations, investments by owners, long-term borrowing, and the sale of long-term assets. Net income represents a source of funds because revenue and expense transactions generally involve current assets and current liabilities. However, some expenses, such as depreciation, do not require the use of funds. These nonfund expenses are added to net income to compute the funds produced by operations. Similarly, some revenues and other income credits do not result in funds being acquired. These items are deducted from net income to compute the funds from operations.

There are also four major uses of funds: withdrawals by owners (including dividends and treasury stock purchases), purchases of noncurrent assets, payment of long-term liabilities, and the net loss from operations. The formal statement of changes in financial position lists the sources and uses of funds and then shows the net increase or decrease in working capital during the period. It also shows sources and uses of financial resources not involving working capital.

The term *funds* is also used sometimes to mean *cash*. In this event the statement of changes in financial position emphasizes the inflow and outflow of cash for the year, especially the cash provided or used by operations.

MANAGERIAL IMPLICATIONS

The analysis of funds flow is a tremendous help to managers in planning future operations, in judging the status of working capital, in forecasting cash flow and cash needs, in arranging proper financing, and in planning dividend payments. It is also extremely useful in determining how well the company will be able to meet its currently maturing obligations.

REVIEW QUESTIONS

1. What is the purpose of the statement of changes in financial position?
2. What information is needed to prepare the statement of changes in financial position?
3. How does the statement of changes in financial position differ from a balance sheet?
4. Define the term *working capital*.
5. Why does *APB Opinion No. 19* require that all financial resources, not merely working capital, be included in the statement of changes in financial position?
6. Why is depreciation expense added to net income in arriving at the funds provided by operations?
7. What are the two major sections of a statement of changes in financial position?
8. Of what value to financial analysts is the detailed breakdown of changes in working capital?
9. A truck that cost $12,000 and had accumulated depreciation of $8,000 was sold for $2,600. The loss of $1,400 was shown on the income statement. How would these facts be reflected in the statement of changes in financial position?
10. A corporation retired bonds payable with a book value of $100,000, paying $98,000 for them. A gain of $2,000 was shown on the income statement.

How would these facts be reflected in the statement of changes in financial position?

11. How would amortization of a discount on bonds payable be reflected in the statement of changes in financial position?

12. A corporation issued bonds with a par value of $100,000 for land with a value of $100,000. How would this transaction be reflected in the statement of changes in financial position?

13. A company has prepared a statement of changes in financial position based on working capital flow. It wishes to also have a statement of changes in financial position based on cash flow. What additional information is needed?

14. Why must all changes in noncurrent assets and noncurrent liabilities be analyzed before the statement of changes in financial position is prepared?

15. A corporation has a net loss for the year. In preparing the statement of changes in financial position, this loss is shown as a negative figure under sources of funds. Why, in your opinion, was this rule developed?

16. What are the two meanings given to the term *funds*?

17. Name four common uses of funds.

18. Name three sources of funds in addition to net income from operations.

19. In arriving at the cash provided by operations, would an increase in merchandise inventory be added to or subtracted from net income?

MANAGERIAL DISCUSSION QUESTIONS

1. How can funds flow analysis help managers to arrange for proper financing?
2. A director of a corporation asks why depreciation is added to net income from operations as a source of working capital. How would you explain it?
3. Why would the management of a business want a statement of changes in financial position based on cash flow?
4. Of what importance to management might a net decrease in working capital be?

EXERCISES

EXERCISE 34-1   **Preparing a schedule of working capital changes.** Shown below are the current assets and current liabilities of the Bailey Corporation on December 31, 19X2, and December 31, 19X1. From this data prepare a schedule of working capital changes.

	Dec. 31, 19X2	Dec. 31, 19X1
Cash	$ 80,000	$ 60,000
Accounts Receivable (Net)	110,000	85,000
Prepaid Expenses	12,000	14,000
Merchandise Inventory	92,000	76,000
Accounts Payable	104,000	100,000

EXERCISE 34-2   **Preparing a schedule of working capital from operations.** The following data is taken from the income statement of the Varjac Corporation for the year ended December 31, 19X1. Use this data to prepare a schedule of working capital from operations.

Sales		$2,000,000
Cost of Goods Sold		1,200,000
Gross Profit on Sales		$ 800,000
Operating Expenses		
Depreciation	$ 31,000	
Other Selling Expenses	560,000	
Other Administrative Expenses	220,000	811,000
Net Loss From Operations		($ 11,000)
Bond Interest Expense		
Cash Interest	$ 30,000	
Amortization of Discount	1,500	31,500
Net Loss for Year		($ 42,500)

EXERCISE 34-3   **Determining the effects of transactions on working capital from operations.** The Ridolfi Corporation had the following three transactions during 19X1. What is the effect of each of these transactions on working capital from operations?

1. The sum of $3,000 was paid for a two-year insurance policy. (Prepaid Insurance was debited and Accounts Payable credited for the $3,000.)
2. A $12,000 short-term note payable was given for a purchase of merchandise.
3. A $4,000 short-term note payable was given for a purchase of equipment.

EXERCISE 34-4   **Determining the effects of transactions on the statement of changes in financial position.** What effect would each of the following transactions have on the statement of changes in financial position?

1. The sum of $8,000 was received for used office equipment that originally cost $18,000 and has accumulated depreciation of $12,000. The $2,000 gain was shown on the income statement.
2. The sum of $97,000 was received from the sale of investments in stock with a book value of $108,000. The $11,000 loss was shown on the income statement.

EXERCISE 34-5   **Determining the effects of bond interest income transactions on the statement of changes in financial position.** What effect would each of the following transactions have on the statement of changes in financial position?

1. The income statement reports $34,200 in interest income. This amount includes interest of $30,000 received in cash, interest receivable of $4,000 accrued at year end, and a bond discount of $200 that was amortized.
2. The income statement reports $19,000 in interest income. This amount represents interest of $20,000 received in cash and a bond premium of $1,000 that was amortized.

EXERCISE 34-6 **Determining the effects of a conversion of bonds into stock on the statement of changes in financial position.** The Lindsey Corporation issued 1,000 shares of common stock in return for outstanding convertible bonds. The entry made was a debit to Bonds Payable for $86,000, a credit to Common Stock for $60,000, and a credit to Paid-in Capital in Excess of Par Value for $26,000. What effect would this transaction have on the statement of changes in financial position?

EXERCISE 34-7 **Computing the working capital provided by operations.** The following information comes from the financial records of the Montez Corporation. Select the facts that are needed, and compute the amount of working capital provided by operations for the year.

1. Net income of $34,500 shown on the income statement.
2. Common stock issued for $31,000 during the year.
3. Depreciation expense of $13,000 shown on the income statement.
4. Loss of $4,000 on sales of equipment (selling price, $8,000; cost, $22,000; accumulated depreciation, $10,000).

EXERCISE 34-8 **Reporting the cash provided by operations.** Refer to Exercise 34-1. Assume that the Bailey Corporation had a net income of $80,000 for 19X2 and that its depreciation expense was $12,200. Using this data and the data from Exercise 34-1, prepare the section of the statement of changes in financial position that reports the sources of cash from current operations. (Assume that this firm bases the statement of changes in financial position on cash flow.)

EXERCISE 34-9 **Computing the cash provided by operations.** The income statement of the Dennis Corporation showed net income of $68,000 for 19X2. The firm's beginning inventory was $42,000, and its ending inventory was $48,000. Accounts payable totaled $31,000 on January 1 and $23,000 on December 31. Ignoring all other factors, compute the amount of cash provided by the firm's operations for the year.

EXERCISE 34-10 **Computing the cash provided by operations.** The income statement of the Muller Corporation showed net income of $30,000 for 19X1. The firm's accounts receivable totaled $21,000 on January 1 and $32,000 on December 31. Ignoring all other factors, compute the amount of cash provided by the firm's operations for the year.

EXERCISE 34-11 **Reporting the cash provided by operations.** The following information is taken from the income statement of the DeMaris Corporation for 19X1.

Sales		$650,000
Cost of Goods Sold		400,000
Gross Profit on Sales		$250,000
Depreciation	$ 10,000	
Other Operating Expenses	180,000	190,000
Net Income From Operations		$ 60,000

Additional information relating to account balances at the beginning and end of the year appears below.

	Jan. 1, 19X1	Dec. 31, 19X1
Accounts Receivable	$54,000	$60,000
Merchandise Inventory	28,000	33,000
Accrued Expenses	6,000	2,500
Accounts Payable	18,000	12,000

From the above data, prepare the section of the statement of changes in financial position that reports the sources of cash from current operations. (Assume that this firm bases its statement of changes in financial position on cash flow.)

PROBLEMS

PROBLEM 34-1   **Computing working capital changes and preparing a statement of changes in financial position.** A condensed comparative balance sheet for the Malaga Corporation on December 31, 19X3, appears below along with some additional information about the firm's financial activities during 19X3.

Instructions   1. Compute the amount of increase or decrease in working capital during 19X3.
2. Prepare a statement of changes in financial position for 19X3, using the working capital approach to funds.

MALAGA CORPORATION
Comparative Balance Sheet
December 31, 19X3 and 19X2

	19X3	19X2
Assets		
Cash	$ 30,000	$ 25,000
Accounts Receivable (Net)	50,000	40,000
Merchandise Inventory	80,000	75,000
Property, Plant, and Equipment	90,000	80,000
Less Accumulated Depreciation	(26,000)	(20,000)
Total Assets	$224,000	$200,000
Liabilities and Stockholders' Equity		
Liabilities		
Accounts Payable	$ 55,000	$ 40,000
Bonds Payable	90,000	80,000
Total Liabilities	$145,000	$120,000
Stockholders' Equity		
Common Stock, No-Par Value	$ 62,000	$ 50,000
Retained Earnings	17,000	30,000
Total Stockholders' Equity	$ 79,000	$ 80,000
Total Liabilities and Stockholders' Equity	$224,000	$200,000

Additional information for 19X3 follows.

1. Had a $13,000 net loss.
2. Recorded $6,000 in depreciation.
3. Issued bonds payable with a par value of $10,000 at par.
4. Received $12,000 for the issue of an additional 1,000 shares of no-par value common stock.
5. Purchased equipment for $10,000.

PROBLEM 34-2   **Reporting changes in working capital and preparing a statement of changes in financial position.** The Star Video Products Corporation sells equipment to television stations. Postclosing trial balance data and other financial data for the firm as of December 31, 19Y6 and 19Y7, appear below.

Instructions   1. Prepare a schedule of working capital changes for the year ended December 31, 19Y7.
2. Prepare a summary of the sources of working capital.
3. Prepare a summary of the uses of working capital.
4. Prepare a statement of changes in financial position, assuming that all financial resources are to be included. Base this statement on working capital flow.
5. Prove the accuracy of your work by reconciling the two summaries with the schedule prepared in Instruction 1. (Sources − Uses = Net Change.)

POSTCLOSING TRIAL BALANCE DATA

Account Name	December 31, 19Y6 Debit	December 31, 19Y6 Credit	December 31, 19Y7 Debit	December 31, 19Y7 Credit
Cash	$ 150,000		$ 210,000	
Accounts Receivable (Net)	193,500		195,700	
Inventory	410,525		419,250	
Prepaid Expenses	4,000		5,500	
Land	17,500		29,500	
Building	210,000		230,000	
Accum. Depr.—Building		$ 75,000		$ 82,500
Patents	20,000		18,000	
Notes Payable—Trade		30,000		20,000
Accounts Payable		150,000		138,250
Payroll Taxes Payable		17,500		19,875
Estimated Income Taxes Payable		55,000		15,000
Mortgage Payable, 19Y9		120,000		130,000
13% Bonds Payable, 19Z5		230,000		270,000
Common Stock		240,000		320,000
Retained Earnings		88,025		112,325
Totals	$1,005,525	$1,005,525	$1,107,950	$1,107,950

Additional information for 19Y7 follows.

1. Sold common stock for $80,000 in cash.
2. Had a net income of $28,200 after income taxes.

3. Sold additional bonds payable for $40,000 cash at par.
4. Completed a major addition to the building, costing $20,000 cash.
5. Bought additional land for $12,000. Paid $2,000 in cash. The balance is a mortgage.
6. Paid common stock dividends of $3,900 in cash.

PROBLEM 34-3   **Preparing a statement of changes in financial position based on cash flow.** Use the information given in Problem 34-2 to prepare a statement of changes in financial position for the Star Video Products Corporation for the year ended December 31, 19Y7. Take the cash flow approach.

PROBLEM 34-4   **Preparing a statement of changes in financial position based on working capital flow.** Use the information given in Problem 35-1 for the Golden West Corporation (pages 851 and 852) to prepare a statement of changes in financial position for 19X2. Take the working capital approach.

ALTERNATE PROBLEMS

PROBLEM 34-1A   **Computing working capital changes and preparing a statement of changes in financial position.** A condensed comparative balance sheet for the Osage Corporation on December 31, 19X2, appears below along with some additional information about the firm's financial activities during 19X2.

OSAGE CORPORATION
Comparative Balance Sheet
December 31, 19X2 and 19X1

	19X2	19X1
Assets		
Cash	$ 7,000	$13,000
Accounts Receivable (Net)	20,000	17,000
Merchandise Inventory	23,000	25,000
Property, Plant, and Equipment	70,000	60,000
Less Accumulated Depreciation	(25,000)	(20,000)
Total Assets	$95,000	$95,000
Liabilities and Stockholders' Equity		
Liabilities		
Accounts Payable	$20,000	$16,000
Stockholders' Equity		
Common Stock, No-Par Value	$55,000	$45,000
Retained Earnings	20,000	34,000
Total Stockholders' Equity	$75,000	$79,000
Total Liabilities and Stockholders' Equity	$95,000	$95,000

Instructions   1. Compute the amount of increase or decrease in working capital during 19X2.
2. Prepare a statement of changes in financial position for 19X2, using the working capital approach to funds.

Additional information for 19X2 follows.

1. Sold used machinery for $9,000 in cash. The original cost was $10,000, and the accumulated depreciation was $3,000. Included the gain of $2,000 in net income.
2. Purchased new machinery for $20,000. Of this amount, $10,000 was paid in cash. The balance of $10,000 is carried in Accounts Payable and falls due in January 19X3.
3. Had a net loss of $4,000.
4. Paid cash dividends of $10,000.
5. Recorded $8,000 in depreciation.

PROBLEM 34-2A   **Reporting changes in working capital and preparing a statement of changes in financial position.** The Diagnostic Equipment Corporation sells medical testing devices to hospitals. Postclosing trial balance data and other financial data for the firm as of December 31, 19X8 and 19X9, appear below.

POSTCLOSING TRIAL BALANCE DATA

Account Name	December 31, 19X8 Debit	December 31, 19X8 Credit	December 31, 19X9 Debit	December 31, 19X9 Credit
Cash	$ 152,400		$ 253,500	
Accounts Receivable (Net)	188,700		196,300	
Inventory	395,000		381,000	
Prepaid Expenses	4,800		6,200	
Land	50,000		40,000	
Buildings	200,000		250,000	
Accum. Depr.—Buildings		$ 60,000		$ 65,000
Patents	30,000		28,000	
Notes Payable—Short-Term		50,000		-0-
Accounts Payable		162,500		137,300
Payroll Taxes Payable		15,800		17,200
Estimated Income Taxes Payable		23,100		25,400
Mortgages Payable—Long-Term		80,000		110,000
12% Bonds Payable, 19Y8		200,000		250,000
Common Stock		220,000		290,000
Retained Earnings		209,500		260,100
Totals	$1,020,900	$1,020,900	$1,155,000	$1,155,000

Instructions   1. Prepare a schedule of working capital changes for the year ended December 31, 19X9.
2. Prepare a summary of the sources of working capital.
3. Prepare a summary of the uses of working capital.

4. Prepare a statement of changes in financial position, assuming that all financial resources are to be included. Base this statement on working capital flow.
5. Prove the accuracy of your work by reconciling the two summaries with the schedule prepared in Instruction 1. (Sources − Uses = Net Change.)

Additional information for 19X9 follows.

1. Sold an unused building lot for $15,000 in cash. The lot originally cost $10,000.
2. Constructed a new building for $50,000, of which $20,000 was paid in cash. The balance of $30,000 is a long-term mortgage payable.
3. Issued $50,000 of 12 percent bonds payable, maturing in 19Y8, for cash at par.
4. Sold common stock for $70,000 in cash.
5. Had a net income of $63,600 after income taxes.
6. Paid common stock dividends of $13,000 in cash.

PROBLEM 34-3A **Preparing a statement of changes in financial position based on cash flow.** Use the information given in Problem 34-2A to prepare a statement of changes in financial position for the Diagnostic Equipment Corporation for the year ended December 31, 19X9. Take the cash flow approach.

PROBLEM 34-4A **Preparing a statement of changes in financial position based on working capital flow.** Use the information given in Problem 35-1A for the Convenience Products Corporation (pages 855 and 856) to prepare a statement of changes in financial position for 19X2. Take the working capital approach. (The equipment disposed of at a loss of $4,000 was scrapped before it was fully depreciated. No cash or other asset was received.)

The preceding chapters discussed the application of accounting principles to the periodic financial statements. These statements are designed to help owners, managers, creditors, and other interested parties make intelligent business decisions. Obviously, the statement reader must know what the figures on the statements mean and how to analyze and interpret the data in a logical and systematic manner. For example, does a net income of X dollars mean a good, poor, or average performance? Do the results represent an improvement over the last period? Do the figures indicate that the firm is being run efficiently?

STATEMENT ANALYSIS—
COMPARATIVE STATEMENTS

THE NATURE OF STATEMENT ANALYSIS

Sound conclusions can be drawn from financial statements only when the meaning of their figures is completely understood. A detailed analysis must be made of every item and every relationship before the results can be evaluated. The figures are usually analyzed in a two-step procedure, as follows.

1. Differences, percentages, and ratios are computed.
2. The findings are interpreted.

The Computation Phase

The required computations are made by using simple arithmetic processes. The techniques can be learned rather quickly in actual practice.

Comparison With Prior Periods A very common procedure is to compare data for the current period with the same data of the company for previous periods. This comparison often reveals significant changes that need to be investigated. If comparisons are made with several prior periods, a trend is often revealed. This comparison technique is called *horizontal analysis*.

Percentage Analysis Most analysts determine percentage relationships between certain items on the financial statements. For example, it is customary to express each item on the income statement as a percentage of net sales. Similarly, on the balance sheet each item is expressed as a percentage of total assets. This technique is called *vertical analysis*.

Ratio Analysis Two individual items on the financial statements can be compared with one another and the relationship expressed as a ratio. Ratios are computed for items on the same financial statement or on different statements. These ratios are compared with those of prior years and with those of other companies to make them more meaningful.

Comparison With Industry Averages Comparison of a firm's financial statement ratios and percentages with those of its competitors often reveals important differences or similarities. Such comparisons are based on published reports of other companies in the industry or on the industry averages made available by trade associations, private financial services, or government agencies.

Comparison With Budgets or Standards The management of a company normally establishes budgets or goals that it expects the company to attain. Sometimes standards, representing highly efficient operating conditions, are also established. In both cases, actual results are compared with the budget or the standards, and the reasons for variations are analyzed.

The Interpretation Phase

The second step in statement analysis is much more difficult. It requires considerable experience to become proficient at interpreting financial statements. This is also the more important step because it is necessary for an understanding of the significance of the figures. Yardsticks against which appraisals can be made help to provide an understanding of the results of operations. As already noted, budgets or standards developed within the company are useful here; so also is industry data compiled by trade associations, government agencies, or others. Some guidelines for interpretation are suggested in this text, but there is no substitute for practice and experience.

In this chapter we shall examine comparative statements. The discussion will center on horizontal analysis and vertical analysis of the income statement, the balance sheet, and various supporting schedules. In the following chapter, we will look at ratio analysis and discuss the most widely used techniques for computing ratios between financial statement items.

ANALYSIS OF INCOME STATEMENTS

Both horizontal analysis and vertical analysis can be used to study income statements. These two techniques are valuable tools for assessing the results of operations.

Horizontal Analysis

Income statements for two periods may be evaluated by a horizontal analysis in which the items on each line are compared to determine the change in dollar amounts. In addition, the percentage of the change may be shown (with the earlier figures used as 100 percent or the *base*). The comparative income statement for the Duncan Lawn Furniture Corporation shown on page 836 is analyzed in this manner. For purposes of analysis, the figures on financial statements are often rounded to the nearest dollar or even to the nearest hundred dollars.

Notice the new descriptive heading on the comparative statement. Its third line indicates the periods covered by the statement. The year 19Y3 is the more recent year and is presented in the column to the left, with the figures for the earlier year, 19Y2, in the column to the right. The presentation is made in condensed form. The details of the selling expenses and administrative expenses are shown in separate schedules, which are discussed later in this chapter.

The two columns at the right of the comparative income statement give the

DUNCAN LAWN FURNITURE CORPORATION
Comparative Income Statement
Years Ended December 31, 19Y3 and 19Y2

	Amounts 19Y3	Amounts 19Y2	Increase or (Decrease) During 19Y3 Amount	Increase or (Decrease) During 19Y3 Percent
Revenue				
Sales	$3,241,578	$2,970,530	$271,048	9.1
Less Sales Returns and Allowances	22,496	19,390	3,106	16.0
Net Sales	$3,219,082	$2,951,140	$267,942	9.1
Cost of Goods Sold				
Merchandise Inventory, Jan. 1	$ 285,100	$ 253,700	$ 31,400	12.4
Merchandise Purchases (Net)	1,982,488	1,808,270	174,218	9.6
Freight In	15,000	13,000	2,000	15.4
Total Merchandise Available for Sale	$2,282,588	$2,074,970	$207,618	10.0
Less Merchandise Inventory, Dec. 31	300,000	285,100	14,900	5.2
Cost of Goods Sold	$1,982,588	$1,789,870	$192,718	10.8
Gross Profit on Sales	$1,236,494	$1,161,270	$ 75,224	6.5
Operating Expenses				
Selling Expenses (Schedule A)	$ 719,346	$ 706,032	$ 13,314	1.9
Administrative Expenses (Schedule B)	288,952	260,501	28,451	10.9
Total Operating Expenses	$1,008,298	$ 966,533	$ 41,765	4.3
Net Income From Operations	$ 228,196	$ 194,737	$ 33,459	17.2
Other Income				
Gain on Sale of Equipment	$ 1,000	$ -0-	$ 1,000	
Interest Income	355	722	(367)	(50.8)
Total Other Income	$ 1,355	$ 722	$ 633	87.7
Total Income for Year	$ 229,551	$ 195,459	$ 34,092	17.4
Other Expenses				
Bond Interest Expense	$ 7.049	$ 5,500	$ 1,549	28.2
Other Interest Expense	200	1,200	(1,000)	(83.3)
Total Other Expenses	$ 7,249	$ 6,700	$ 549	8.2
Net Income Before Income Taxes	$ 222,302	$ 188,759	$ 33,543	17.8
Provision for Income Taxes	82,250	66,160	16,090	24.3
Net Income After Income Taxes	$ 140,052	$ 122,599	$ 17,453	14.2

amount and percentage of increase or decrease during 19Y3. Decreases are shown in parentheses as they probably would be shown in a typed report. They might be presented in italics or parentheses in a printed report.

Notice that the amounts of increase or decrease can be added or subtracted in the column from top to bottom and will give correct subtotals at each point.

However, the percentages of change cannot be added or subtracted from top to bottom. Each percentage relates only to the line on which it appears. If the amount of change is zero, there is no percentage of change.

A study of each item quickly reveals the changes that occurred between the two years. It appears at a glance that business improved for the Duncan Lawn Furniture Corporation in 19Y3.

1. Gross sales and net sales were both up 9.1 percent.
2. Cost of goods sold increased 10.8 percent.
3. Gross profit on sales increased 6.5 percent.
4. Operating expenses increased 4.3 percent.
5. Net income from operations increased 17.2 percent.
6. Income taxes were up by 24.3 percent.
7. Net income after income taxes was 14.2 percent higher.

Horizontal analysis is especially useful in calling attention to relationships that bear further investigation. For example, although the increase in net sales for 19Y3 over 19Y2 was only 9.1 percent, the increase in cost of goods sold was 10.8 percent. An alert manager would call for pertinent facts to determine the reasons for the disproportionate increase in cost of goods sold. Questions such as the following would be asked. Is the firm's pricing policy being followed? Have prices not been revised to reflect cost increases? Is merchandise being stolen or damaged? Are sound purchasing policies being followed?

Management would be especially interested in learning in greater detail why administrative expenses showed an increase of 10.9 percent during 19Y3, while selling expenses increased only 1.9 percent. This would call for an analysis of each selling expense and each administrative expense shown in the schedules on page 840.

It should be kept in mind that percentages of increase or decrease can be misleading when small amounts are involved. For example, Duncan's interest income decreased from $722 in 19Y2 to $355 in 19Y3, a decrease of 50.8 percent. However, in terms of actual dollars, the amount is immaterial. On the other hand, even a small percentage change for an item involving many dollars is important because of the sizable amount. No percentage change is computed when there is no amount for the base period, as happened with the gain on the sale of equipment that is reported for 19Y3 on Duncan's comparative income statement. Actually, some analysts prefer to omit extraordinary items like this gain from their computations even if data for a base period is available because the changes are usually not meaningful for such items.

As noted previously, the process of interpretation is easier if some basis of comparison is available, such as a company budget, standard costs, or industry average data. Significant, or out-of-line, changes should be investigated in detail and the reasons evaluated.

Vertical Analysis of Income Statements

The figures on a firm's comparative income statement may also be analyzed by the completion of various vertical comparisons, as shown on page 838. Notice that the amounts for the two years are presented in parallel money columns exactly as in the preceding illustration. However, this time the two columns at

Base

DUNCAN LAWN FURNITURE CORPORATION
Comparative Income Statement
Years Ended December 31, 19Y3 and 19Y2

	Amounts 19Y3	Amounts 19Y2	Percent of Net Sales 19Y3	Percent of Net Sales 19Y2
Revenue				
Sales	$3,241,578	$2,970,530	100.7	100.7
Less Sales Returns and Allowances	22,496	19,390	0.7	0.7
Net Sales	$3,219,082	$2,951,140	100.0	100.0
Cost of Goods Sold				
Merchandise Inventory, Jan. 1	$ 285,100	$ 253,700	8.8*	8.6
Merchandise Purchases (Net)	1,982,488	1,808,270	61.6	61.3
Freight In	15,000	13,000	0.5	0.4
Total Merchandise Available for Sale	$2,282,588	$2,074,970	70.9	70.3
Less Merchandise Inventory, Dec. 31	300,000	285,100	9.3	9.6*
Cost of Goods Sold	$1,982,588	$1,789,870	61.6	60.7
Gross Profit on Sales	$1,236,494	$1,161,270	38.4	39.3
Operating Expenses				
Selling Expenses (Schedule A)	$ 719,346	$ 706,032	22.3	23.9
Administrative Expenses (Schedule B)	288,952	260,501	9.0	8.8
Total Operating Expenses	$1,008,298	$ 966,533	31.3	32.7*
Net Income From Operations	$ 228,196	$ 194,737	7.1	6.6
Other Income				
Gain on Sale of Equipment	$ 1,000	$ -0-		
Interest Income	355	722		
Total Other Income	$ 1,355	$ 722		
Total Income for Year	$ 229,551	$ 195,459	7.1	6.6
Other Expenses				
Bond Interest Expense	$ 7.049	$ 5,500	0.2	0.2
Other Interest Expense	200	1,200		
Total Other Expenses	$ 7,249	$ 6,700	0.2	0.2
Net Income Before Income Taxes	$ 222,302	$ 188,759	6.9	6.4
Provision for Income Taxes	82,250	66,160	2.5*	2.2
Net Income After Income Taxes	$ 140,052	$ 122,599	4.4	4.2

*Adjusted.

the right present each item for each year as a percentage of net sales. The later year is on the left and the earlier year on the right, as usual.

In each column the net sales figure is used as the base, or 100 percent. Then every figure in the column is expressed as a percentage of net sales (Amount ÷ Net Sales = Percentage of Net Sales). Note that gross sales is larger than 100 percent) $3,241,578 ÷ $3,219,082 = 100.7% in 19Y3, for example).

In making computations such as these, it is customary to carry the division one place further than needed to show the answer and then round off. In the examples given here, the percentages are shown to one decimal place. Thus the calculations are carried out to two decimal places. Then if the last digit on the right is 5 or over, the next to last digit is increased by one. If the last digit on the right is 4 or less, the next to last digit remains as originally computed. (The computation of the percentage of gross sales to net sales, described in the preceding paragraph, actually resulted in 100.69 percent. Since the last digit is 9, the next to last digit is raised by one, and the result appears as 100.7 percent.) Because of the procedure used for rounding off, the individual items may not add up to 100 percent. In this case one or more percentages are usually adjusted arbitrarily until the total equals 100 percent. However, if the difference is more than a very slight amount, there is a possibility that an error has been made, and all the computations should be checked before adjusting any of the figures.

Also note that the percentage figures may be added and subtracted, giving highly informative subtotals and final total percentages of change.

As you have seen, with vertical analysis of the income statement, each item is expressed as a percentage of net sales, which may have considerable significance in itself. For example, the ratio of gross profit to net sales indicates the efficiency of purchasing to a merchant or of manufacturing to a manufacturer and the adequacy of the markup of sales price over cost. The final figure of net income after income taxes is also an important measure of success in operations. Other items of income and expense may be of particular interest in a given situation, or they may be compared with similar items in the statements of competitors or with industry average data. When industry averages are expressed as percentages, the result is called a *common-size statement*. Some accountants also use this term for the type of vertical analysis illustrated on page 838.

Vertical analysis percentages are especially useful when they are compared with the percentages of the same company for prior years. It is helpful to make comparisons with several years in order to detect trends, but even year-to-year comparisons are useful. For example, the comparative income statement of the Duncan Lawn Furniture Corporation shows that gross profit on sales was 39.3 percent in 19Y2, but decreased to 38.4 percent in 19Y3. This decrease probably resulted from problems with pricing policies or with purchasing procedures. A comparison with the industry average might be very revealing. For example, if trade association publications reveal that the average gross profit for the industry is 43 percent, a more detailed analysis of Duncan's business activities would certainly be justified. Of course, the corporation's lower-than-average margin of gross profit may be attributed to peculiarities of its operations, its local competition, or other factors. However, the unfavorable comparison with the industry average is at least an indication of the need for further examination.

ANALYSIS OF OPERATING EXPENSES

Two supporting schedules for the income statement present details of the selling and administrative expenses, as shown on page 840. Again, comparative figures for two years are given.

DUNCAN LAWN FURNITURE CORPORATION

Comparative Schedule of Selling Expenses
Years Ended December 31, 19Y3, and December 31, 19Y2

	Amounts		Percent of Net Sales		Increase or (Decrease) During 19Y3	
	19Y3	19Y2	19Y3	19Y2	Amount	Percent
Sales Salaries	$385,600	$378,200	12.0	12.8	$ 7,400	2.0
Sales Commissions	42,000	38,000	1.3	1.3	4,000	10.5
Payroll Taxes—Sales Staff	38,600	34,300	1.2	1.2	4,300	12.5
Employee Fringe Benefits	31,600	38,300	1.0	1.3	(6,700)	(17.5)
Freight Out and Deliveries	28,870	22,750	0.9	0.8	6,120	26.9
Advertising	99,630	103,100	3.1	3.5	(3,470)	(3.4)
Sales Supplies	10,307	13,960	0.3	0.5	3,653	26.2
Rent	22,000	22,000	0.7	0.7	-0-	
Utilities	9,039	7,820	0.3	0.3	1,219	15.6
Insurance	9,800	9,300	0.3	0.3	500	5.4
Repairs and Maintenance	1,800	3,102	0.1	0.1	(1,302)	(42.0)
Depreciation	8,300	6,200	0.2	0.2	2,100	33.9
Travel and Entertainment	12,000	9,600	0.3	0.3	2,400	25.0
Other Taxes	7,800	7,600	0.2	0.3	200	2.6
Miscellaneous	12,000	11,800	0.4	0.4	200	1.7
Total Selling Expenses	$719,346	$706,032	22.3	23.9	$13,314	1.9

DUNCAN LAWN FURNITURE CORPORATION

Comparative Schedule of Administrative Expenses
Years Ended December 31, 19Y3, and December 31, 19Y2

	Amounts		Percent of Net Sales		Increase or (Decrease) During 19Y3	
	19Y3	19Y2	19Y3	19Y2	Amount	Percent
Officers' Salaries	$165,759	$150,000	5.1	5.1	$15,759	10.5
Office Employees' Salaries	57,000	49,500	1.8	1.7	7,500	15.2
Payroll Taxes—Administrative Staff	16,800	16,655	0.5	0.6	145	0.9
Office Supplies	15,633	14,726	0.5	0.5	907	6.2
Postage, Copying, and Miscellaneous	3,800	3,700	0.1	0.1	100	2.7
Loss From Uncollectible Accounts	5,360	4,800	0.2	0.2	560	11.7
Rent	8,000	7,500	0.2	0.3	1,100	14.7
Depreciation	6,400	4,800	0.2	0.2	1,600	33.3
Other Taxes	4,800	4,200	0.1	0.1	600	14.3
Utilities	5,400	4,620	0.2	0.2	780	16.9
Total Administrative Expenses	$288,952	$260,501	9.0	8.8	$28,451	10.9

Combined Horizontal and Vertical Analysis

On the income statement previously illustrated, the operating expenses were shown as two subtotals and a group total. In order to make analysis meaningful, the individual items are now presented as shown above.

Notice that the results of both horizontal and vertical analysis are given in each report. The vertical analysis percentages relate to net sales, as they would if the details of these expenses had been presented on the income statement. The horizontal analysis is completed in the usual manner. The arithmetic follows the pattern previously discussed, as does the interpretation of these figures.

Certain of the percentages resulting from the vertical analysis of the income statement are especially important and are discussed further in Chapter 36.

ANALYSIS OF BALANCE SHEETS

Balance sheets may be subjected to horizontal analysis and vertical analysis. Both types of analysis for balance sheet items are discussed in this section.

Horizontal Analysis

Data from a firm's balance sheets for two periods can be presented in comparative form to permit a detailed horizontal analysis. A comparative balance sheet showing the Duncan Lawn Furniture Corporation's financial position on December 31 of 19Y3 and 19Y2 is illustrated on page 842.

The amounts are presented in the first two money columns, with the later year at the left, as usual. Increases or decreases are recorded in the two columns at the right, first in dollar amounts and then in percentages. The earlier year serves as the base year for comparisons.

The arithmetic involved is the same as that for a horizontal analysis of income statements. The amounts are compared line by line. For example, the accountant computes the difference between the amounts for cash ($100,187 − $72,860) and finds that there is a decrease of $27,327. The accountant then determines the percentage of change by dividing the amount of change by the base year (19Y2) amount: $27,327 ÷ $100,187 = 27.3%. Every line is analyzed in the same manner.

Notice that the amounts of increase or decrease may be added or subtracted down the column. The change in total assets must always equal the change in total liabilities and stockholders' equity. On the other hand, the percentages of increase or decrease for each item cannot be added and subtracted. Each applies only to its own line. However, the percentage change in total assets must be the same as the percentage change in total liabilities and stockholders' equity.

Large changes should be analyzed to determine whether they are reasonable or reflect abnormal operations that require special managerial attention. A comparison with several preceding years may point out significant trends or patterns in a company's financial position. In the case of the Duncan Lawn Furniture Corporation, for example, the increase in merchandise inventory reflects good control of this asset because it increased by a smaller percentage than did the corporation's sales. A large increase in the goods on hand would call for examination and explanation. Suppose, for example, that the inventory had increased by 25 percent. Obsolete goods, special quantity purchases, the introduction of new product lines, and other unusual operating situations might explain such a large increase. Similarly, a large growth in accounts receivable might be explained by changes in credit policies, terms of sale, types of customers, size of orders, and other factors arising from changes in business conditions.

DUNCAN LAWN FURNITURE CORPORATION
Comparative Balance Sheet
December 31, 19Y3 and 19Y2

	Amounts on December 31		Increase or (Decrease) During 19Y3	
	19Y3	19Y2	Amount	Percent
Assets				
Current Assets				
Cash	$ 72,860	$100,187	$ (27,327)	(27.3)
Accounts Receivable (Net)	198,184	168,184	30,000	17.8
Merchandise Inventory	300,000	285,000	15,000	5.3
Prepaid Insurance	5,700	2,700	3,000	111.1
Other Prepayments	5,500	2,500	3,000	120.0
Total Current Assets	$582,244	$558,571	$ 23,673	4.2
Property, Plant, and Equipment				
Land	$ 30,000	$ 30,000	$ -0-	
Building	$120,000	-0-	$120,000	
Less Accumulated Depreciation	2,000	-0-	2,000	
Net Book Value—Building	$118,000	$ -0-	$118,000	
Equipment and Fixtures	$103,200	$ 83,600	$ 19,600	23.4
Less Accumulated Depreciation	54,300	44,000	10,300	23.4
Net Book Value—Equipment and Fixtures	$ 48,900	$ 39,600	$ 9,300	23.5
Total Property, Plant, and Equipment	$196,900	$ 69,600	$127,300	182.9
Total Assets	$779,144	$628,171	$150,973	24.0
Liabilities and Stockholders' Equity				
Current Liabilities				
Accounts Payable	$ 89,201	$ 85,000	$ 4,201	4.9
Estimated Income Taxes Payable	41,125	21,300	19,825	93.1
Accrued Liabilities	14,446	17,530	(3,084)	(17.6)
Total Current Liabilities	$144,772	$123,830	$ 20,942	16.9
Long-Term Liabilities				
11% Bonds Payable, 19Z1	$ 70,000	$ 50,000	$ 20,000	40.0
Premium on Bonds Payable	979	-0-	979	
Total Long-Term Liabilities	$ 70,979	$ 50,000	$ 20,979	42.0
Total Liabilities	$215,751	$173,830	$ 41,921	24.1
Stockholders' Equity				
12% Preferred Stock, $100 Par Value	$100,000	$100,000	$ -0-	
Paid-in Capital in Excess of Par Value	6,000	6,000	-0-	
Common Stock, $50 Stated Value	160,000	150,000	$ 10,000	6.7
Paid-in Capital in Excess of Stated Value	29,000	19,000	10,000	52.6
Retained Earnings (Schedule C)	268,393	179,341	89,052	49.7
Total Stockholders' Equity	$563,393	$454,341	$109,052	24.0
Total Liabilities and Stockholders' Equity	$779,144	$628,171	$150,973	24.0

DUNCAN LAWN FURNITURE CORPORATION
Comparative Balance Sheet
December 31, 19Y3 and 19Y2

	Amounts on December 31		Percent of Total Assets	
	19Y3	19Y2	19Y3	19Y2
Assets				
Current Assets				
Cash	$ 72,860	$100,187	9.4	15.9
Accounts Receivable (Net)	198,184	168,184	25.4	26.8
Merchandise Inventory	300,000	285,000	38.5	45.4
Prepaid Insurance	5,700	2,700	0.7	0.4
Other Prepayments	5,500	2,500	0.7	0.4
Total Current Assets	$582,244	$558,571	74.7	88.9
Property, Plant, and Equipment				
Land	$ 30,000	$ 30,000	3.9	4.8
Building	$120,000	-0-	15.4	
Less Accumulated Depreciation	2,000	-0-	0.3	
Net Book Value—Building	$118,000	$ -0-	15.1	
Equipment and Fixtures	$103,200	$ 83,600	13.3*	13.3
Less Accumulated Depreciation	54,300	44,000	7.0	7.0
Net Book Value—Equipment and Fixtures	$ 48,900	$ 39,600	6.3	6.3
Total Property, Plant, and Equipment	$196,900	$ 69,600	25.3	11.1
Total Assets	$779,144	$628,171	100.0	100.0
Liabilities and Stockholders' Equity				
Current Liabilities				
Accounts Payable	$ 89,201	$ 85,000	11.4	13.5
Estimated Income Taxes Payable	41,125	21,300	5.3	3.4
Accrued Liabilities	14,446	17,530	1.9	2.8
Total Current Liabilities	$144,772	$123,830	18.6	19.7
Long-Term Liabilities				
11% Bonds Payable, 19Z1	$ 70,000	$ 50,000	9.0	8.0
Premium on Bonds Payable	979	-0-	0.1	
Total Long-Term Liabilities	$ 70,979	$ 50,000	9.1	8.0
Total Liabilities	$215,751	$173,830	27.7	27.7
Stockholders' Equity				
12% Preferred Stock, $100 Par Value	$100,000	$100,000	12.8	15.9
Paid-in Capital in Excess of Par Value	6,000	6,000	0.8	1.0
Common Stock, $50 Stated Value	160,000	150,000	20.5	23.9
Paid-in Capital in Excess of Stated Value	29,000	19,000	3.7	3.0
Retained Earnings (Schedule C)	268,393	179,341	34.5*	28.5
Total Stockholders' Equity	$563,393	$454,341	72.3	72.3
Total Liabilities and Stockholders' Equity	$779,144	$628,171	100.0	100.0

*Adjusted.

A comparative balance sheet for the Duncan Lawn Furniture Corporation is presented on page 843 with the results of vertical analysis shown. Notice the use of the same general heading as in the preceding illustration. Amounts are shown in the first two money columns. The pair of columns on the right is used to record each item as a percentage of total assets for each year, the later year on the left and the earlier year on the right.

Each item is divided by the total assets appearing on the statement to find its percentage of that total. For instance, in 19Y3 cash amounted to $72,860 and the total assets were $779,144. When these two amounts are divided, cash is found to be 9.4 percent of total assets in 19Y3. The same procedure is applied to each item in turn.

A characteristic of the vertical process is that the percentages can be added and subtracted down the column to give 100 percent on the line for total assets and also on the line for the total liabilities and stockholders' equity. In making the computations and rounding off percentages, it may be necessary, as with vertical analysis of income statements, to adjust one or more of the figures to obtain an even 100 percent for each total.

The advantage of vertical analysis is that it shows the relationship of items and groups of items on the balance sheet to the total assets. In 19Y3 Duncan's current assets were 74.7 percent of its total assets, and its property, plant, and equipment accounted for the remaining 25.3 percent. Its current liabilities were 18.6 percent, and its long-term liabilities were 9.1 percent, resulting in total liabilities of 27.7 percent. In contrast, stockholders' equity provided 72.3 percent of total assets. Some relationships are also studied by computing ratios, as described in the next chapter.

Vertical analysis percentages are more useful when they are compared with the percentages of the same company for previous years and with those of other companies in the same industry. Changes in the percentages may reveal situations that need investigation. For example, the comparative balance sheet of the Duncan Lawn Furniture Corporation shows that cash has decreased from 15.9 percent of total assets in 19Y2 to 9.4 percent of total assets in 19Y3. The accountant would be quick to realize that this decline may mean a future problem, and the accountant would take steps to find out exactly why the decrease occurred.

ANALYSIS OF RETAINED EARNINGS

Retained earnings may be analyzed by both horizontal and vertical methods. Changes in retained earnings are presented in a supporting schedule covering the same two years as the comparative balance sheet.

Combined Horizontal and Vertical Analysis

Both horizontal and vertical techniques are used in preparing the comparative statement of retained earnings, as shown on page 845. Notice the heading, which describes it as a comparative statement and indicates the years covered.

As with all comparative statements, the amounts are entered in the first two money columns, and the figures for the later year are placed on the left. The two columns in the center present the results of the vertical analysis, with each item converted to a percentage of total assets. The pair of columns on the right shows

	Amounts on December 31		Percent of Total Assets		Increase or (Decrease) During 19Y3	
	19Y3	19Y2	19Y3	19Y2	Amount	Percent
Balance, Jan. 1	$179,341	$114,742	23.0	18.3	$64,599	56.3
Additions						
Net Income After Income Taxes	140,052	122,599	18.0	19.5	17,453	14.2
Total	$319,393	$237,341	41.0	37.8	$82,052	34.6
Deductions						
Dividends—Preferred	$ 12,000	$ 12,000	1.5	1.9		
Dividends—Common	39,000	46,000	5.0	7.3	(7,000)	(15.2)
Total	$ 51,000	$ 58,000	6.5	9.2	$(7,000)	(12.1)
Balance, Dec. 31	$268,393	$179,341	34.5*	28.6*	$89,052	49.7

*Adjusted.

the results of the horizontal analysis. Amounts of increase or decrease are given in the left column, and percentage changes appear in the column to the right. Any decreases are shown in parentheses.

The arithmetic follows the pattern used in applying both forms of analysis to the balance sheet. Amounts of increase or decrease may be added and subtracted down a column to compute subtotals and totals. However, the percentages of change calculated in the horizontal analysis cannot be added and subtracted. Each percentage relates only to the item on that line.

The analysis is interpreted in the same manner as previously described for the balance sheet. Duncan's net income in 19Y3 was 18.0 percent of its total assets, slightly lower than in 19Y2. Total dividends were 1.5 percent of total assets in 19Y3, as compared with 1.9 percent in 19Y2. Retained earnings increased by 49.7 percent during 19Y3.

SOME PRECAUTIONARY NOTES ON STATEMENT ANALYSIS

An analyst of financial statements must keep in mind a number of significant points that to some extent limit the benefits of the analysis. One of the most important points is that financial statements reflect book values, not current market values. The significance of this fact cannot be overemphasized. Book values depend on original cost and on the accounting policies followed. For example, suppose that one mineral producer decides to capitalize as an asset cost the amount spent for developing its mineral properties. Thus, its asset accounts will include all these capitalized costs less depletion taken. Another mineral producer decides to charge all such costs to expense, showing none as an asset.

Obviously, the statements of the two companies are not comparable. Similarly, differences in depreciation policies—including useful life and methods of computing depreciation—will produce widely varying book values. In many cases the market values of assets, especially of land and buildings, are quite different from the book values. For example, suppose a corporation purchased land for $50,000 a number of years ago and still carries the land in its accounting records at that amount. However, the land is worth $500,000 on the date of the balance sheet. Obviously, an analyst's interpretation of this statement would be considerably different if the land was carried at its current market value of $500,000 rather than $50,000.

Another point is that accounting assumes that the dollar is a stable monetary unit, although this is far from a correct assumption. The financial statements of all but the newest firms actually contain a mixture of dollars with different purchasing power. Changes in the general price level mean that the recorded book values of assets represent dollars with different purchasing power and do not represent dollars with today's purchasing power. Therefore, the significance of the dollar amounts is somewhat uncertain.

If these limitations arising from accounting policies and methods are understood, statement analysis can be helpful in evaluating the financial affairs of a business.

PRINCIPLES AND PROCEDURES SUMMARY

The two steps in financial statement analysis are computation and interpretation. The computation process includes direct comparison with other figures (prior statements, budgets, or industry averages) and calculation of percentages and ratios. The interpretation phase of analysis involves recognizing the meaning of the results of operations for the period and the financial position of the business at the end of the period.

The comparative statement is a convenient form for the presentation of figures for analysis and appraisal. Amount and percentage comparisons can be made both horizontally and vertically. Horizontal analysis involves the comparison of an item from one year to the next. Vertical analysis involves expressing each item on the statement as a percentage of some base amount. The amount of net sales is used as the base for all income statement items, while the amount of the total assets serves as the base for all balance sheet items.

MANAGERIAL IMPLICATIONS

Statement analysis is extremely important to managers in detecting problem areas in a business. Comparison of current data with the data of prior years indicates trends that may be either favorable or unfavorable. Percentage analysis figures can be compared with industry percentages and with percentages of prior years to detect variations that require prompt investigation. Judgment and experience are necessary for competent interpretation of financial statements.

REVIEW QUESTIONS

1. How does vertical analysis differ from horizontal analysis?
2. When a vertical analysis is made of the income statement, what item serves as the base for the percentage calculations?
3. How is a vertical analysis of the balance sheet prepared?
4. Why are the financial statement items of one period compared with those of the prior period?
5. What is ratio analysis?
6. Why is comparison with industry averages important in analyzing financial statements?
7. How does the computational phase of statement analysis differ from the interpretation phase?
8. In horizontal analysis it is common to exclude any calculation of percentage change when there was no amount for the base period. Why?
9. What is a common-size statement?
10. Why does the fact that accounting records are kept on the basis of historical cost sometimes cause difficulties for an analyst of financial statements?
11. How does the choice of accounting methods by a company sometimes cause difficulties in comparing the company's statements with those of other companies?

MANAGERIAL DISCUSSION QUESTIONS

1. Why is it important that all business managers understand financial statements and how to analyze them?
2. Suppose that in the vertical analysis of the income statement an item is found to be 18 percent of net sales. How would this information be used in order to make it meaningful? (What would it be compared with?)
3. For 19X3 a company's cost of goods sold was 66 percent of its net sales. For 19X2 the same item was 63 percent, and for 19X1 it was 60 percent. How should an analyst view this trend? What factors might the analyst wish to investigate further?
4. Would an analyst prefer to see an increase or a decrease in the trend of the percentage of cost of goods sold to net sales? Why?
5. In deciding whether an increase in accounts receivable is desirable or undesirable, what factors should an analyst consider?
6. Over a three-year period a company's balance sheets show that the total stockholders' equity has changed from 56 percent to 51 percent to 43 percent of total assets. What factors might explain this trend?
7. A company's income statements reveal that its net income after taxes has been 4.3 percent of net sales for each of the past three years. During that time the industry average has been about 7 percent. What types of questions would an analyst ask in seeking an explanation for this difference?

8. Many companies place great emphasis on the computation of the percentage of gross profit on sales. Why?

9. Would you, as an analyst, be satisfied with comparative percentages for only two years? Why?

10. Does an analyst inside a company have an advantage over analysts outside the company? Why?

11. A company's net sales increased by 35 percent from one year to the next year. During that period selling expenses increased by 41 percent. Is this desirable? Explain.

12. Why would a short-term creditor be interested in the analysis of a company's income statement?

13. Why might an analyst wish to exclude extraordinary gains and losses in analyzing the financial statements? Why would the analyst wish to include these items?

14. Why is it difficult to compare the statements of different companies in different industries?

15. Why is it difficult to compare the statements of different companies in the same industry?

EXERCISES

EXERCISE 35-1   **Preparing a horizontal analysis of income statement items.** A condensed comparative income statement for the Blue Ridge Corporation for the years 19X2 and 19X3 is shown below. Based on this information, prepare a horizontal analysis of all items from sales through gross profit on sales for 19X3 as compared with 19X2.

BLUE RIDGE CORPORATION
Comparative Income Statement
Years Ended December 31, 19X3 and 19X2

	19X3	19X2
Sales	$1,240,000	$1,020,000
Less Sales Returns and Allowances	40,000	20,000
Net Sales	$1,200,000	$1,000,000
Cost of Goods Sold	900,000	700,000
Gross Profit on Sales	$ 300,000	$ 300,000
Selling Expenses	$ 145,000	$ 130,000
General Expenses	85,000	80,000
Total Expenses	$ 230,000	$ 210,000
Net Income Before Income Taxes	$ 70,000	$ 90,000
Provision for Income Taxes	23,000	37,500
Net Income After Income Taxes	$ 47,000	$ 52,500

EXERCISE 35-2   **Preparing a vertical analysis of income statement items.** Based on the information given for the Blue Ridge Corporation in Exercise 35-1, prepare a vertical analysis of all items from sales through gross profit on sales for the years 19X3 and 19X2.

EXERCISE 35-3   **Interpreting the horizontal and vertical analysis of income statement items.** Based on the data computed in Exercises 35-1 and 35-2, make an evaluation of the changes in the income statement of the Blue Ridge Corporation for all items from sales through gross profit on sales. Write a brief explanation of your conclusions.

EXERCISE 35-4   **Interpreting the vertical analysis of gross profit on sales.** Suppose that industry statistics show that companies in the same line of business as the Blue Ridge Corporation had an average gross profit on sales of 36 percent in 19X2 and 37 percent in 19X3. Evaluate the Blue Ridge Corporation's gross profit on sales for the two years, using the data computed in Exercises 35-1 through 35-3. Write a brief explanation of your conclusions.

EXERCISE 35-5   **Preparing a horizontal and a vertical analysis of income statement items.** Using the data previously given for the Blue Ridge Corporation for 19X3 and 19X2, prepare both a vertical and a horizontal analysis of all income statement items from selling expenses through net income after income taxes.

EXERCISE 35-6   **Interpreting the vertical analysis of federal income taxes.** As a financial analyst, how would you evaluate the change in the percentage of the provision for federal income taxes to net sales from 19X2 to 19X3? Write a brief explanation of your conclusions.

EXERCISE 35-7   **Interpreting the vertical analysis of net income after taxes.** Suppose that you, as a financial analyst, found that for companies in the same industry and of the same general size as the Blue Ridge Corporation, net income after income taxes averaged 7 percent of net sales. Evaluate the Blue Ridge Corporation's net income after taxes in both 19X2 and 19X3. Write a brief explanation of your conclusions.

EXERCISE 35-8   **Interpreting the horizontal and vertical analysis of income statement items.** Write a brief explanation of why the Blue Ridge Corporation's net sales showed an increase of 20 percent in 19X3 over 19X2, while its net income showed both a percentage decrease and an actual dollar amount decrease.

EXERCISE 35-9   **Preparing a horizontal analysis of balance sheet items.** A condensed comparative balance sheet for the Niagara Corporation as of December 31, 19X2, and December 31, 19X1, is shown on page 850. Based on this information, prepare a horizontal analysis of all items for 19X2 as compared with 19X1.

NIAGARA CORPORATION
Comparative Balance Sheet
December 31, 19X2 and 19X1

	19X2	19X1
Assets		
Cash	$ 50,000	$ 78,000
Accounts Receivable (Net)	180,000	135,000
Inventory	300,000	237,000
Buildings (Net)	95,000	100,000
Equipment (Net)	85,000	80,000
Land	20,000	20,000
Total Assets	$730,000	$650,000
Liabilities and Stockholders' Equity		
Accounts Payable	$180,000	$140,000
Other Current Liabilities	20,000	20,000
Bonds Payable	100,000	80,000
Common Stock	200,000	200,000
Retained Earnings	230,000	210,000
Total Liabilities and Stockholders' Equity	$730,000	$650,000

EXERCISE 35-10   **Interpreting the horizontal analysis of balance sheet items.** Based on the horizontal analysis of the Niagara Corporation's balance sheet prepared in Exercise 35-9, write brief comments about any significant changes in the firm's current assets and current liabilities.

EXERCISE 35-11   **Preparing a vertical analysis of balance sheet items.** Based on the information given for the Niagara Corporation in Exercise 35-9, prepare a vertical analysis of all items for the years 19X2 and 19X1.

EXERCISE 35-12   **Interpreting the vertical analysis of balance sheet items.** Based on the vertical analysis of the Niagara Corporation's balance sheet prepared in Exercise 35-11, write brief comments about the percentage change of each current asset and each current liability in relation to total assets.

EXERCISE 35-13   **Interpreting the vertical analysis of inventory.** Assume that industry statistics show that for companies in the same line of business as the Niagara Corporation inventory averaged 20 percent of total assets in 19X1 and 18 percent of total assets in 19X2. Write brief comments about the Niagara Corporation's inventory position each year in comparison with the industry figures.

EXERCISE 35-14   **Interpreting the vertical analysis of stockholders' equity.** Assume that for companies in the same industry and of the same general size as the Niagara Corporation, stockholders' equity was 55 percent of total assets in 19X1 and 53 percent of total assets in 19X2. Write brief comments about the percentage of stockholders' equity to total assets at the Niagara Corporation each year in comparison with the industry figures.

PROBLEMS

PROBLEM 35-1   **Preparing a horizontal and a vertical analysis of financial statements and interpreting the results.** The Golden West Corporation sells high-quality leather boots, vests, and jackets. Its comparative income statement, balance sheet, and statement of retained earnings for the years 19X2 and 19X1 are given below and on page 852.

Instructions   1. Prepare both a horizontal and a vertical analysis of the three statements. Carry

GOLDEN WEST CORPORATION
Comparative Income Statement
Years Ended December 31, 19X2 and 19X1

	19X2	19X1
Revenue		
Net Sales	$1,950,000	$1,770,000
Cost of Goods Sold		
Merchandise Inventory, Jan. 1	$ 375,000	$ 390,000
Merchandise Purchases	1,349,400	1,257,600
Total Merchandise Available for Sale	$1,724,400	$1,647,600
Less Merchandise Inventory, Dec. 31	360,000	375,000
Cost of Goods Sold	$1,364,400	$1,272,600
Gross Profit on Sales	$ 585,600	$ 497,400
Operating Expenses		
Selling Expenses		
Sales Salaries Expense	$ 184,800	$ 158,850
Rent Expense	19,800	18,000
Delivery Expense	13,500	12,300
Advertising Expense	15,300	10,800
Depreciation Expense	5,000	4,800
Other Selling Expense	59,200	53,100
Total Selling Expenses	$ 297,600	$ 257,850
Administrative Expenses		
Officers' Salaries Expense	$ 90,000	$ 75,000
Office Employees' Salaries Expense	20,000	20,000
Loss From Uncollectible Accounts	14,550	12,600
Rent Expense	4,000	4,000
Depreciation Expense	4,450	4,200
Other Administrative Expenses	53,450	45,750
Total Administrative Expenses	$ 186,450	$ 161,550
Total Operating Expenses	$ 484,050	$ 419,400
Net Income From Operations	$ 101,550	$ 78,000
Other Expenses		
Bond Interest Expense	9,000	9,000
Net Income Before Income Taxes	$ 92,550	$ 69,000
Provision for Income Taxes	22,550	7,500
Net Income After Income Taxes	$ 70,000	$ 61,500

all calculations to two decimal places, and then round to one decimal place. (Leave all vertical analysis percentages unadjusted in this problem.)

2. Make written comments about any of the results that seem worthy of investigation.

GOLDEN WEST CORPORATION
Comparative Balance Sheet
December 31, 19X1 and 19X2

	19X2	19X1
Assets		
Current Assets		
Cash	$173,550	$124,050
Accounts Receivable (Net)	207,000	183,000
Merchandise Inventory	360,000	375,000
Prepaid Insurance	6,300	7,800
Total Current Assets	$746,850	$689,850
Property, Plant, and Equipment		
Plant and Equipment	$134,250	$126,000
Less Accumulated Depreciation	40,950	31,500
Total Property, Plant, and Equipment	$ 93,300	$ 94,500
Total Assets	$840,150	$784,350
Liabilities and Stockholders' Equity		
Current Liabilities		
Accounts Payable	$187,950	$177,600
Estimated Income Taxes Payable	39,000	25,500
Other Payables	27,300	21,900
Total Current Liabilities	$254,250	$225,000
Long-Term Liabilities		
10% Bonds Payable	90,000	90,000
Total Liabilities	$344,250	$315,000
Stockholders' Equity		
6% Preferred Stock ($100 par value)	$150,000	$150,000
Common Stock ($100 par value)	225,000	225,000
Retained Earnings	120,900	94,350
Total Stockholders' Equity	$495,900	$469,350
Total Liabilities and Stockholders' Equity	$840,150	$784,350

GOLDEN WEST CORPORATION
Comparative Statement of Retained Earnings
Years Ended December 31, 19X1 and 19X2

	19X2	19X1
Balance, Jan. 1	$ 94,350	$ 64,350
Additions		
Net Income for Year	70,000	61,500
Total	$164,350	$125,850
Deductions		
Dividends—Preferred Stock	$ 9,000	$ 9,000
Dividends—Common Stock	34,450	22,500
Totals	$ 43,450	$ 31,500
Balance, Dec. 31	$120,900	$ 94,350

Preparing a horizontal and a vertical analysis of financial statements and interpreting the results. The Sanchez Corporation sells office supplies and business forms through a retail store that it operates. The firm's comparative income statement and balance sheet for the years 19X3 and 19X2 are presented below and on page 854.

Instructions

1. Prepare both a horizontal and a vertical analysis of the two statements. Carry all calculations to two decimal places and then round to one place. (Leave all vertical analysis percentages unadjusted in this problem.)

2. Make written comments about any of the results that seem worthy of investigation.

SANCHEZ CORPORATION
Comparative Income Statement
Years Ended December 31, 19X3 and 19X2

	19X3	19X2
Revenue		
Sales	$385,196	$317,630
Less Sales Returns and Allowances	1,847	1,655
Net Sales	$383,349	$315,975
Cost of Goods Sold		
Merchandise Inventory, Jan. 1	$ 30,112	$ 42,560
Merchandise Purchases	249,879	207,422
Total Merchandise Available for Sale	$279,991	$249,982
Less Merchandise Inventory, Dec. 31	34,396	30,112
Cost of Goods Sold	$245,595	$219,870
Gross Profit on Sales	$137,754	$ 96,105
Operating Expenses		
Selling Expenses		
Sales Salaries Expense	$ 22,729	$ 20,750
Depreciation Expense	2,156	1,720
Delivery Expense	2,511	2,115
Sales Supplies Expense	2,372	1,915
Advertising Expense	12,693	10,480
Total Selling Expenses	$ 42,461	$ 36,980
Administrative Expenses		
Officers' Salaries Expense	$ 20,000	$ 18,000
Office Employees' Salaries Expense	12,920	9,360
Payroll Taxes Expense	3,713	3,575
Depreciation Expense	752	683
Office Supplies Expense	1,625	1,435
Loss From Uncollectible Accounts	337	240
Total Administrative Expenses	$ 39,347	$ 33,293
Total Operating Expenses	$ 81,808	$ 70,273
Net Income From Operations	$ 55,946	$ 25,832
Other Income		
Interest Income	275	385
Total Income for Year	$ 56,221	$ 26,217
Other Expense		
Organization Costs Written Off	800	800
Net Income Before Income Taxes	$ 55,421	$ 25,417
Provision for Income Taxes	11,650	4,200
Net Income After Income Taxes	$ 43,771	$ 21,217

SANCHEZ CORPORATION
Comparative Balance Sheet
December 31, 19X3 and 19X2

	19X3	19X2
Assets		
Current Assets		
Cash	$ 74,997	$ 52,833
Notes Receivable	6,000	8,000
Accounts Receivable (Net)	54,327	40,909
Interest Receivable	120	240
Merchandise Inventory	34,396	30,112
Prepaid Insurance	2,177	2,640
Supplies on Hand	725	628
Total Current Assets	$172,742	$135,362
Property, Plant, and Equipment		
Land	$ 35,000	$ 15,000
Building	$ 98,450	$ 98,450
Less Accumulated Depreciation	28,286	26,218
Net Book Value	$ 70,164	$ 72,232
Store Equipment	$ 58,900	$ 51,700
Less Accumulated Depreciation	30,575	25,045
Net Book Value	$ 28,325	$ 26,655
Office Equipment	$ 7,351	$ 6,895
Less Accumulated Depreciation	4,411	3,659
Net Book Value	$ 2,940	$ 3,236
Total Property, Plant, and Equipment	$136,429	$117,123
Intangible Assets		
Organization Costs	$ 1,600	$ 2,400
Total Assets	$310,771	$254,885
Liabilities and Stockholders' Equity		
Current Liabilities		
Accounts Payable	$ 32,336	$ 17,235
Dividends Payable—Preferred Stock	4,500	4,500
Dividends Payable—Common Stock	3,000	2,000
Estimated Income Taxes Payable	11,650	4,200
Salaries Payable	3,126	1,353
Employee Income Tax Payable	1,244	1,390
Payroll Taxes Payable	1,175	217
Total Liabilities	$ 57,031	$ 30,895
Stockholders' Equity		
Preferred Stock (6%, noncumulative, non-participating, $75 par value, 1,000 shares authorized)		
At Par Value (1,000 shares issued)	$ 75,000	$ 75,000
Common Stock ($25 par value, 1,000 shares authorized)		
At Par Value (1,000 shares issued)	$ 25,000	$ 25,000
Retained Earnings		
Appropriated for Purchase of New Building	$ 25,000	$ 20,000
Unappropriated	128,740	103,990
Total Retained Earnings	$153,740	$123,990
Total Stockholders' Equity	$253,740	$223,990
Total Liabilities and Stockholders' Equity	$310,771	$254,885

PROBLEM 35-1A

Preparing a horizontal and a vertical analysis of financial statements. The Convenience Products Corporation sells paper plates, napkins, and other supplies to fast-food restaurants. Its comparative income statement, schedule of selling expenses, balance sheet, and statement of retained earnings for the years 19X2 and 19X1 are given below and on page 856.

Instructions

1. Prepare both a horizontal and a vertical analysis of the statements. Carry all calculations to two decimal places, and then round to one decimal place. (Leave all vertical analysis percentages unadjusted in this problem.)
2. Make comments about any of the results that seem worthy of investigation.

CONVENIENCE PRODUCTS CORPORATION
Comparative Income Statement
Years Ended December 31, 19X2 and 19X1

	19X2	19X1
Revenue		
Sales	$6,530,000	$5,932,000
Less Sales Returns and Allowances	30,000	32,000
Net Sales	$6,500,000	$5,900,000
Cost of Goods Sold	4,548,000	4,242,000
Gross Profit on Sales	$1,952,000	$1,658,000
Operating Expenses		
Selling Expenses (Schedule A)	$ 992,000	$ 859,500
Administrative Expenses (Schedule B)	621,500	538,500
Total Operating Expenses	$1,613,500	$1,398,000
Net Operating Income	$ 338,500	$ 260,000
Other Income		
Gain on Sale of Investments	4,000	-0-
Total Income for Year	$ 342,500	$ 260,000
Other Deductions		
Interest Expense	$ 45,000	$ 45,000
Loss on Disposal of Equipment	4,000	-0-
Total Other Deductions	$ 49,000	$ 45,000
Net Income Before Income Taxes	$ 293,500	$ 215,000
Provision for Income Taxes	121,000	71,000
Net Income After Income Taxes	$ 172,500	$ 144,000

CONVENIENCE PRODUCTS CORPORATION *Schedule A*
Comparative Schedule of Selling Expenses
Years Ended December 31, 19X1 and 19X2

	19X2	19X1
Sales Salaries	$616,000	$529,500
Sales Commissions	214,000	193,000
Rent	66,000	60,000
Deliveries	45,000	41,000
Advertising	51,000	36,000
Total Selling Expenses	$992,000	$859,500

Note: Schedule B does not appear in this problem.

CONVENIENCE PRODUCTS CORPORATION
Comparative Balance Sheet
December 31, 19X2 and 19X1

	19X2	19X1
Assets		
Current Assets		
Cash	$ 389,000	$ 413,500
Accounts Receivable (Net)	817,500	610,000
Merchandise Inventory	1,500,000	1,250,000
Prepaid Insurance	21,000	26,000
Total Current Assets	$2,727,500	$2,299,500
Property, Plant, and Equipment		
Plant and Equipment	$ 447,500	$ 420,000
Less Accumulated Depreciation	136,500	105,000
Total Property, Plant, and Equipment	$ 311,000	$ 315,000
Investments	-0-	$ 100,000
Total Assets	$3,038,500	$2,714,500
Liabilities and Stockholders' Equity		
Current Liabilities		
Accounts Payable	$ 755,500	$ 622,000
Estimated Income Taxes Payable	121,000	71,000
Other Payables	91,000	73,000
Total Current Liabilities	$ 967,500	$ 766,000
Long-Term Liabilities		
15% Bonds Payable	$ 300,000	$ 300,000
Total Liabilities	$1,267,500	$1,066,000
Stockholders' Equity		
9% Preferred Stock	$ 500,000	$ 500,000
Common Stock ($50 par value)	800,000	750,000
Premium on Common Stock	10,000	-0-
Retained Earnings (Schedule C)	461,000	398,500
Total Stockholders' Equity	$1,771,000	$1,648,500
Total Liabilities and Stockholders' Equity	$3,038,500	$2,714,500

CONVENIENCE PRODUCTS CORPORATION   *Schedule C*
Comparative Statement of Retained Earnings
Years Ended December 31, 19X2 and 19X1

	19X2	19X1
Balance, Jan. 1	$398,500	$359,500
Additions		
Net Income After Extraordinary Items	172,500	144,000
Total	$571,000	$503,500
Deductions		
Dividends—Preferred Stock	$ 45,000	$ 45,000
Dividends—Common Stock	65,000	60,000
Total	$110,000	$105,000
Balance, Dec. 31	$461,000	$398,500

PROBLEM 35-2A

Preparing a horizontal and a vertical analysis of financial statements and interpreting the results. The Garrett Corporation sells auto parts through a retail store that it operates. The firm's comparative income statement and balance sheet for the years 19X2 and 19X1 are presented below and on page 858.

Instructions

1. Prepare both a horizontal and a vertical analysis of the two statements. Carry all calculations to two decimal places, and then round to one decimal place. (Leave all vertical analysis percentages unadjusted in this problem.)
2. Make written comments about any of the results that seem worthy of investigation.

GARRETT CORPORATION
Comparative Income Statement
Years Ended December 31, 19X2 and 19X1

	19X2	19X1
Revenue		
Sales	$258,475	$253,475
Less Sales Returns and Allowances	1,405	1,325
Net Sales	$257,070	$252,150
Cost of Goods Sold		
Merchandise Inventory, Jan. 1	$ 21,100	$ 20,000
Merchandise Purchases	146,785	145,376
Total Merchandise Available for Sale	$167,885	$165,376
Less Merchandise Inventory, Dec. 31	22,985	21,100
Cost of Goods Sold	$144,900	$144,276
Gross Profit on Sales	$112,170	$107,874
Operating Expenses		
Selling Expenses		
Sales Salaries Expense	$ 38,054	$ 39,965
Payroll Taxes Expense—Sales	925	1,000
Sales Supplies Expense	3,300	2,450
Total Selling Expenses	$ 42,279	$ 43,415
Administrative Expenses		
Officers' Salaries Expense	$ 28,000	$ 27,500
Office Employees' Salaries Expense	9,000	8,000
Payroll Taxes Expense—Administrative	2,925	3,300
Depreciation Expense	2,550	2,430
Loss From Uncollectible Accounts	828	914
Total Administrative Expenses	$ 43,303	$ 42,144
Total Operating Expenses	$ 85,582	$ 85,559
Net Income Before Income Taxes	$ 26,588	$ 22,315
Provision for Income Taxes	5,000	3,100
Net Income After Income Taxes	$ 21,588	$ 19,215

GARRETT CORPORATION
Comparative Balance Sheet
December 31, 19X2 and 19X1

	19X2	19X1
Assets		
Current Assets		
Cash	$ 53,972	$ 41,789
Accounts Receivable (Net)	32,457	30,424
Merchandise Inventory	22,985	21,100
Prepaid Insurance	2,000	1,990
Supplies on Hand	210	185
Total Current Assets	$111,624	$ 95,488
Property, Plant, and Equipment		
Land	$ 15,200	$ 5,200
Building and Equipment	$ 41,500	$ 41,500
Less Accumulated Depreciation	16,065	11,915
Net Book Value	$ 25,435	$ 29,585
Total Property, Plant, and Equipment	$ 40,635	$ 34,785
Total Assets	$152,259	$130,273
Liabilities and Stockholders' Equity		
Current Liabilities		
Accounts Payable	$ 22,023	$ 17,708
Salaries Payable	680	560
Payroll Taxes Payable	1,326	1,263
Estimated Income Taxes Payable	5,000	3,100
Total Liabilities	$ 29,029	$ 22,631
Stockholders' Equity		
Common Stock (6,000 shares outstanding)	$ 60,000	$ 60,000
Retained Earnings	63,230	47,642
Total Stockholders' Equity	$123,230	$107,642
Total Liabilities and Stockholders' Equity	$152,259	$130,273

The relationship between two selected items on a company's financial statements is often very meaningful. In some cases both items are found on the income statement. For example, the relationship between net income after income taxes and net sales is a highly useful measure of managerial performance. In other cases both items appear on the balance sheet. For example, the relationship between current assets and current liabilities is an important measure of liquidity. In still other cases one of the items is found on the income statement and the other is found on the balance sheet. For example, the relationship between net income after income taxes and stockholders' equity is a significant measure of earning power.

STATEMENT ANALYSIS— MEASURING PROFITABILITY, FINANCIAL STRENGTH, AND LIQUIDITY

RATIO ANALYSIS

The relationship between two items is expressed as a *ratio* (the division of one number by another), as a *rate* (the ratio between two numerical facts over a period of time), or as a *percentage* (a special rate in hundredths). The major purpose of ratio analysis is to give the statement reader a clear idea of the relationship between the two items and to eliminate some of the difficulty that the reader may find in grasping the significance of the dollar amounts.

A tremendously large number of ratios can be computed—so many that if all possible relationships were measured, the sheer number of ratios would confuse the reader. Since many ratios are not meaningful, the accountant or analyst should present only those ratios that are of real significance to the statement reader. The ratios discussed in this text are the most important ones used by investors, creditors, and managers. Although all the ratios presented here are of concern to the three groups, each group will give more attention to certain ratios that are of special importance for its purposes. The selection and classification of ratios is somewhat arbitrary. However, many analysts find it useful to divide financial ratios into the following three classes.

- Ratios measuring profitability and operating results
- Ratios measuring financial strength and equity protection
- Ratios measuring current position and liquidity

MEASURING PROFITABILITY AND OPERATING RESULTS

The profitability of a corporation is, of course, measured by net income. However, a dollar figure for net income is not a sufficiently revealing yardstick. The analyst needs to consider the sales of the company, the nature of its operations, the assets used in earning the income, the stockholders' equity, and many other factors in determining whether the net income is adequate. A number of ratios have been developed for testing the adequacy of a company's profit and in measuring the efficiency of its management.

Ratio of Net Income to Net Sales

The *ratio of net income to net sales* measures the rate of return on net sales and is widely used as a means of judging managerial efficiency and profitability. This rate is computed by dividing net income by net sales. Often the figure for net income before taxes is used because income taxes depend on factors that are not related to sales. However, because the Duncan Lawn Furniture Corporation has relatively little other income and other expense and few items affecting the tax liability, net income after income taxes is used in making the computation. In 19Y2, the ratio of net income after income taxes to net sales at Duncan was 4.2 percent. The figure increased to 4.4 percent in 19Y3.

	19Y3	19Y2
$\dfrac{\text{Net Income After Income Taxes}}{\text{Net Sales}}$	$\dfrac{\$140,052}{\$3,219,082} = 4.4\%$	$\dfrac{\$122,599}{\$2,951,140} = 4.2\%$

Two cautions should be kept in mind when using this ratio. It does not consider the investment necessary to earn the sales, and even though the rate of return on sales is important, the volume of sales is also important. A larger volume of sales at a smaller percentage of profit can yield more income.

Generally, the higher the rate of return on sales, the more satisfactory is the operation of the business. A comparison with the rates of past years can reveal a trend. For example, the improvement in the ratio of net income after income taxes to net sales from 4.2 percent in 19Y2 to 4.4 percent in 19Y3 for the Duncan Lawn Furniture Corporation indicates a small but favorable change. A comparison with the industry average can also be quite helpful because it places the company's figures in perspective. For example, if the industry average is 7.4 percent, management should make a detailed analysis to determine why Duncan's rate of 4.4 percent is so much less. This task would probably involve examining the other vertical analysis percentages of the income statement, along with considering some of the other ratios discussed in this chapter.

Ratio of Net Income to Stockholders' Equity

The *ratio of net income to stockholders' equity* measures the rate of return on the owners' investments and is extremely important in evaluating profitability. This rate is computed by dividing net income by total stockholders' equity. Some analysts use only the stockholders' equity shown on the balance sheet at the end of the year. Other analysts take an average of the beginning and ending stockholders' equity, so that changes in the stock outstanding, dividend payments, and other equity items are considered in the computation. The analyst can even compute an average stockholders' equity based on the amount at the end of each month if the necessary figures are available. Duncan uses the net income after income taxes figure and the total stockholders' equity at the end of the year to compute the rate of return on stockholders' equity.

	19Y3	19Y2
$\dfrac{\text{Net Income After Income Taxes}}{\text{Total Stockholders' Equity}}$	$\dfrac{\$140,052}{\$563,393} = 24.9\%$	$\dfrac{\$122,599}{\$454,341} = 27.0\%$

A comparison with rates of prior years can indicate a significant trend. For example, a constantly decreasing rate over a period of years would be cause for alarm. Similarly, a comparison with the industry average can indicate whether the firm's rate of return is in line with that of other companies in the industry. For example, if the average rate of return on stockholders' equity in the industry is 20.2 percent, Duncan's performance is very good.

<table>
<tr><td>Earnings Per Share of Common Stock</td><td>*Earnings per share of common stock* is an especially important computation to the stockholders because it measures the amount of profit accruing to each share of stock owned. Since corporations today issue a wide variety of securities that may be converted into common stock at a later date, two different earnings-per-share figures are calculated. The first of these is *primary earnings per share*. In a corporation like Duncan, the primary earnings per share can easily be computed by dividing the earnings available to the owners of the common stock by the weighted average number of shares outstanding during the year.</td></tr>
</table>

An analysis of Duncan's common stock account reveals that 3,000 shares were outstanding throughout the year 19Y3 and that 200 shares were issued on October 1, 19Y3. Thus, the weighted average number of shares outstanding for 19Y3 was 3,050 shares. This amount was calculated as follows.

3,000 shares × 12 months = 36,000 shares
200 shares × 3 months =   600 shares
Total   36,600 shares

$$\text{Average} = \frac{36,600}{12} = 3,050 \text{ shares}$$

A total of 3,000 shares were outstanding throughout 19Y2, so the average for that year was 3,000 shares. The average amounts for 19Y3 and 19Y2 are used to compute earnings per share as shown below. However, any dividend requirements on preferred stock must first be deducted in order to arrive at the income available to the owners of the common stock.

	19Y3	19Y2
Net Income After Income Taxes	$140,052	$122,599
Less Dividend Requirements on Preferred Stock	12,000	12,000
Income Available to Common Stock	$128,052	$110,599
Average Number of Common Shares Outstanding	3,050 shares	3,000 shares
Earnings per Share	$\frac{\$128,052}{3,050} = \$41.98$	$\frac{\$110,599}{3,000} = \$36.87$

When there is outstanding convertible preferred stock, outstanding convertible bonds, stock options held by officers and others, or other contractual obligations involving the firm's stock, the computation of primary earnings per share becomes more complex. In addition, it may be necessary to compute a figure known as *fully diluted earnings per share*. Such calculations are beyond the scope of this book and are discussed in intermediate accounting texts.

The earnings per share for the year is of importance to stockholders, especially when compared with their investment in each share of stock and the current market value of each share. A comparison with other companies in the industry is relatively meaningless because of the differences in par value, market value, and other factors. A comparison with earnings per share for the same company in prior years can be meaningful because it may show a trend, but changes in the number of shares outstanding and other elements that might lead to distortions in the ratio must be considered.

Price-Earnings Ratio of Common Stock

The *price-earnings ratio* is a measure that is widely used by investors. It compares the earnings per share of a corporation's common stock with the present market value of that stock. This comparison is one indicator of the attractiveness of the stock as an investment at its present market value. For example, if a corporation's common stock is selling at $44 a share and its earnings are $4 a share for the year, the price-earnings ratio is 11 to 1. Investors' interpretations of price-earnings ratios are largely dependent on their expectations about the future and on the amount that they are willing to pay for stock because of those expectations. For privately held companies (those companies whose shares are not traded in the financial markets), price-earnings ratios are not relevant because there is no readily available market value for the shares.

Yield on Common Stock

Although the price-earnings ratio is valuable in helping the investor measure the return on the current value of the stock investment, it does not measure the relationship between the cash income realized (as dividends) by the stockholder and the market value of each share. For a publicly held corporation, whose market value is easily determined and whose stock may be freely bought and sold, this is important. The *yield on common stock* is computed by dividing the dividend paid on each share by the current market value of the share. For example, if the price of a share of common stock is $60 and the corporation is paying an annual dividend of $6, the yield is 10 percent ($6 ÷ $60).

Ratio of Net Income to Total Assets

The *ratio of net income to total assets* measures the rate of return on the assets used by a company. In recent years this ratio has become an important tool in judging managerial performance, in measuring the effectiveness of the assets used, and in evaluating proposed capital expenditures. The rate is normally computed by dividing net income by total assets. Some analysts use the average of the assets at the beginning and end of the year in making the computation. If monthly figures are available, the average assets based on the monthly figures can be used. Other analysts use only the ending amount of assets or only the beginning amount of assets in the computation.

If the amounts are large, it is preferable to exclude from the net income figure revenue arising from nonoperating sources, such as dividend income and interest income, so that only the net income from normal business operations is used. In this case the assets used in earning the nonoperating income, investments, are excluded from the asset base. In evaluating the profitability of assets, the most desirable basis to use is net income before taxes and before nonrecurring items. In this way, comparative rates are not affected by nonrecurring items, tax-law changes, or managerial decisions that have an impact on income taxes but are not related to assets. Once again, the resulting computations are meaningful only if compared with rates of prior years and with the industry average.

The Duncan Lawn Furniture Corporation uses net income before income taxes and year-end total assets to compute the rate of return on its assets.

	19Y3	19Y2
$\dfrac{\text{Net Income Before Income Taxes}}{\text{Total Assets (end of year)}}$	$\dfrac{\$222,302}{\$779,144} = 28.5\%$	$\dfrac{\$188,759}{\$628,171} = 30.0\%$

Turnover of Assets

The *ratio of net sales to total assets* measures the effective use of assets in making sales. This ratio, sometimes called the *turnover of assets,* is computed by dividing net sales by total assets. In this computation, assets that are not used in producing sales, primarily investments, are excluded from total assets. Again, some analysts use average assets based on beginning and ending totals. If monthly amounts are available, they can be used in computing an average asset figure. Duncan uses its net sales and its total assets at the end of each year to compute the asset turnover rate.

	19Y3	19Y2
$\dfrac{\text{Net Sales}}{\text{Total Assets}}$	$\dfrac{\$3,219,082}{\$779,144} = 4.1 \text{ to } 1$	$\dfrac{\$2,951,140}{\$628,171} = 4.7 \text{ to } 1$

Generally, the higher the asset turnover rate, the more effectively the assets of the company are being used. A low turnover in comparison with the industry average shows that the assets are too great for the sales volume of the company. Once again, the trend of this ratio is of interest primarily because it indicates whether asset growth is accompanied by corresponding sales growth. If sales increase proportionately more than total assets, this ratio increases (a generally favorable indication). However, the question of whether the increased sales are profitable must be asked. Other types of analysis are required to answer this question, such as the ratio of net income to net sales, discussed earlier in this chapter.

One additional caution is needed in interpreting this ratio. Sales are measured in terms of current-year dollars. Total assets reflect costs incurred over a period of years. In times of rising prices, this ratio may increase because of price changes rather than because of an increased volume of sales.

MEASURING FINANCIAL STRENGTH AND EQUITY PROTECTION

A number of ratios are useful in measuring the financial strength of a corporation and the protection afforded to long-term creditors and owners. Some of the ratios involve profitability, and other ratios indicate relationships between balance sheet accounts.

Both the bondholders and the stockholders of a corporation are interested in the margin of safety that net income provides for the required bond interest payments. The *times bond interest earned ratio* is widely used to measure this safety. Since bond interest is a deduction made before income taxes are computed, the starting point for this computation is net income before taxes. To this amount, the bond interest paid during the year is added, and the resulting sum is divided by the total annual interest payable on the bonds outstanding at the end of the year.

In 19Y3 the income statement of the Duncan Lawn Furniture Corporation shows an interest deduction of $7,049. (This is a combination of $7,150 interest paid less $101 bond premium amortized during the year on the $20,000 of bonds issued on April 1.) The cash required for bond interest is $7,700, which is 11 percent of the $70,000 of bonds outstanding at the end of the year.

	19Y3	19Y2
Net Income		
Before Income Taxes	$222,302	$188,759
Add Bond		
Interest Deducted	7,049	5,500
Total Available		
for Bond Interest	$229,351	$194,259
$\dfrac{\text{Total Available for Bond Interest}}{\text{Bond Interest Requirement}}$	$\dfrac{\$229{,}351}{\$7{,}700} = 29.8$ times	$\dfrac{\$194{,}259}{\$5{,}500} = 35.3$ times

Duncan's bondholders apparently had little to worry about in either year as far as their interest was concerned. In 19Y3 the total available for bond interest was 29.8 times the sum required. This is less than the 19Y2 ratio of 35.3 times but still a very comfortable margin of safety.

The owners of preferred stock are also interested in the probable regularity of their dividend payments. This can be measured to some extent by the *times preferred dividends earned ratio*, which is computed by dividing net income after taxes by the amount required to pay the preferred dividends. At Duncan the dividends on the preferred stock totaled $12,000 for both 19Y3 and 19Y2.

	19Y3	19Y2
$\dfrac{\text{Net Income After Income Taxes}}{\text{Preferred Dividends}}$	$\dfrac{\$140{,}052}{\$12{,}000} = 11.7$ times	$\dfrac{\$122{,}599}{\$12{,}000} = 10.2$ times

The times preferred dividends earned ratio increased from 10.2 times in 19Y2 to 11.7 times in 19Y3, giving the preferred stockholders an even wider margin of protection. A comparison of this ratio with the industry average would be of relatively little value, but a comparison with prior years at the same company would be very useful.

The liabilities and stockholders' equity of a corporation are referred to as its *total equities* or *total capital*. The *ratio of stockholders' equity to total equities* measures the portion of total capital provided by the stockholders against possible losses. For obvious reasons, creditors are particularly interested in this cushion.

Since total equities and total assets are the same, the ratio is also called the *portion of assets provided by stockholders*. This ratio is computed by dividing stockholders' equity by total equities, as shown below for the Duncan Lawn Furniture Corporation.

	19Y3		19Y2	
$\dfrac{\text{Stockholders' Equity}}{\text{Total Equities}}$	$\dfrac{\$563,393}{\$779,144}$	$= 0.72 \text{ to } 1$	$\dfrac{\$454,341}{\$628,171}$	$= 0.72 \text{ to } 1$

In both 19Y3 and 19Y2, Duncan's stockholders were providing 72 cents of each dollar of total equities. Clearly, the more capital provided by the stockholders, the greater the protection to creditors. The ratio of stockholders' equity to total equities varies widely from industry to industry, and a comparison with the industry average is very important in determining a desirable ratio for a particular company.

Ratio of Stockholders' Equity to Total Liabilities

Another way of expressing the same relationship as in the preceding ratio is to compute the *ratio of stockholders' equity to total liabilities,* which is also known as the *ratio of owned capital to borrowed capital.* It is determined by dividing the stockholders' equity by the total liabilities, as shown below for the Duncan Lawn Furniture Corporation.

	19Y3		19Y2	
$\dfrac{\text{Total Stockholders' Equity}}{\text{Total Liabilities}}$	$\dfrac{\$563,393}{\$215,751}$	$= 2.61 \text{ to } 1$	$\dfrac{\$454,341}{\$173,830}$	$= 2.61 \text{ to } 1$

This ratio reveals that in both 19Y3 and 19Y2 Duncan's stockholders were providing $2.61 of capital for each dollar provided by creditors. Again, the more capital provided by stockholders, the less risk for creditors.

Ratio of Property, Plant, and Equipment to Long-Term Liabilities

The *ratio of property, plant, and equipment to long-term liabilities* measures the security afforded holders of long-term debts if assets are pledged as collateral for the debts. When the assets are not pledged as collateral, this ratio indicates the potential ability to borrow on the assets in the future. The ratio is computed by dividing the book value of property, plant, and equipment by total long-term liabilities.

Ideally, the present sound value or market value of the property, plant, and equipment rather than its book value should be used in the computation since these amounts more adequately measure the protection afforded long-term creditors in the event of liquidation. However, sound value or market value is almost never available to the financial statement reader outside the company, so the book value must be used in most cases. The ratio for the Duncan Lawn Furniture Corporation was 2.8 to 1 for 19Y3 and 1.4 to 1 for 19Y2, as shown below.

	19Y3		19Y2	
$\dfrac{\text{Property, Plant, and Equipment}}{\text{Long-Term Liabilities}}$	$\dfrac{\$196,900}{\$70,979}$	$= 2.8 \text{ to } 1$	$\dfrac{\$69,600}{\$50,000}$	$= 1.4 \text{ to } 1$

The large increase from 19Y2 to 19Y3 was due mostly to the fact that Duncan constructed a new building in 19Y3 at a cost of $120,000, while increasing its long-term liabilities only $20,000 through the issue of bonds payable. Comparisons with the ratios of prior years and with the industry average can be helpful because they place the company's figures in perspective.

In some cases the analyst is interested in measuring the protection afforded to one particular group of long-term creditors whose claim is secured by certain specified items of property, plant, and equipment. In this case the particular debt involved and the specific asset pledged are used in the computation.

Book Value Per Share of Stock

Book value per share of stock is a commonly used measure of the financial strength underlying each share of stock, and it is often computed by analysts and reported in financial journals. It represents the amount that each share would receive in case of liquidation if the assets were sold for exactly the book value. Obviously, book value has relatively little meaning in many cases because the recorded value of assets may be quite different from the market value.

If there is only one class of stock outstanding, the book value of each share is found by simply dividing total stockholders' equity by the number of shares outstanding. If more than one class of stock is outstanding, the relative rights of the various classes must be considered in computing the book value of each. The book value of preferred stock is computed first; then any remaining balance of stockholders' equity is divided by the number of common shares. Several special considerations must be given to preferred stock.

- If the preferred stock has a liquidation value assigned to it in the contract, this amount of stockholders' equity must be allocated to the preferred stock. If there is no liquidation value, the par value of each class of preferred stock is allocated to that class.
- Preferred stock can have special dividend rights. Dividends in arrears on cumulative preferred stock must be assigned to the preferred stock if retained earnings are available. If the preferred stock is participating, the portion of retained earnings properly belonging to preferred stock as dividends must be computed and allocated to these shares.

The Duncan Lawn Furniture Corporation has outstanding both preferred stock and common stock. The preferred stock involves no cumulative dividends. In case of liquidation, the owner of a share of this preferred stock will receive only its par value. Its book value is therefore the same as its par value, $100 a share. The common stock is entitled to receive all the difference between the total stockholders' equity and the portion related to the preferred stock. Book value per share of common stock is determined by dividing this difference by the number of common shares outstanding, as shown below.

	19Y3	19Y2
Stockholders' Equity	$563,393	$454,341
Less Preferred Stock Equity	100,000	100,000
To Common Stockholders	$463,393	$354,341
Common Shares Outstanding	$\dfrac{\$463,393}{3,200} = \$144.81$	$\dfrac{\$354,341}{3,000} = \$118.11$

This computation indicates that the book value of Duncan's common stock increased in 19Y3 by $26.70 a share, from $118.11 to $144.81.

MEASURING LIQUIDITY AND SOLVENCY

The ability of a company to pay its currently maturing debts is of critical importance to long-term creditors and stockholders as well as to short-term creditors. Many companies have failed because they lacked this ability, known as *liquidity*, even though they were profitable and had long-term financial strength. The analyst therefore computes various ratios to evaluate a company's present liquidity. Some ratios measure the relationship between current assets and current liabilities, and other ratios indicate the normal ability of the company to convert its current assets into cash.

Amount of Working Capital

As discussed in Chapter 34, working capital is a fundamental measure of the ability of a company to meet its current obligations and represents the margin of security afforded short-term creditors. The term *working capital* is used in this text to describe the excess of current assets over current liabilities. As we have seen in Chapter 34, Duncan's working capital in 19Y3 was $437,472, an increase of $2,731 over 19Y2. The statement of changes in financial position helps to explain increases and decreases in working capital.

Current Ratio

Although working capital is a very important element in the analysis of liquidity, the absolute amount of working capital has little meaning by itself. For example, the dollar amount of working capital for a large corporation obviously will be far greater than that for a small business, but it is difficult to judge how adequate the amount is without more information. The *current ratio,* the ratio of current assets to current liabilities, is a key measure in determining a firm's ability to pay current debts and therefore the adequacy of its working capital. The computation of the current ratio for the Duncan Lawn Furniture Corporation is shown below.

	19Y3	19Y2
$\dfrac{\text{Current Assets}}{\text{Current Liabilities}}$	$\dfrac{\$582,244}{\$144,772} = 4 \text{ to } 1$	$\dfrac{\$558,571}{\$123,830} = 4.5 \text{ to } 1$

Duncan had $4 of current assets for each dollar of current liabilities in 19Y3 compared with $4.50 for each dollar in 19Y2. Analysts assume that a current ratio of at least 2 to 1 is generally necessary for most merchandising and manufacturing businesses. However, it must be clearly understood that the 2-to-1 ratio is merely a rule of thumb, and the size of a desirable ratio varies widely from industry to industry and even from company to company within an industry. From the viewpoint of a short-term creditor, the higher the current ratio is, the greater the protection afforded. However, a company can easily have too high a current ratio. A very high ratio usually results from having idle cash on hand that is not earning income, large sums of money tied up in accounts receivable that may prove uncollectible, or inventories that contain many obsolete items or are greater than required to conduct normal operations.

Maintaining more working capital than is actually needed is not only unprofitable, but it can also be financially dangerous. It leads to long-run profit strains because funds are tied up in nonproducing current assets. Of course, the analyst should give adequate consideration to the procedures used for the valuation of inventories, marketable securities, and accounts receivable when judging the firm's working capital position.

Acid-Test Ratio

Although the current ratio measures a company's ability to meet current liabilities out of existing current assets, it is not a measure of immediate liquidity. For example, a considerable period of time may be necessary to sell the inventories and convert them into cash in the normal course of business operations. Immediate liquidity is measured by the *acid-test ratio*, sometimes called the *quick assets ratio*. This ratio is computed by dividing the total of the quick assets—cash, receivables, and marketable securities—by the current liabilities. Duncan's calculations for 19Y3 and 19Y2 are given below.

	19Y3		19Y2	
Cash	$ 72,860		$100,187	
Accounts Receivable	198,194		168,184	
Total Quick Assets	$271,054	= 1.87 to 1	$268,371	= 2.17 to 1
Current Liabilities	$144,772		$123,830	

The acid-test ratio shows that Duncan had $1.87 of quick assets for each dollar of current liabilities in 19Y3 compared with $2.17 for each dollar in 19Y2. Although a general rule of thumb is that the acid-test ratio should be at least 1 to 1, the preferred ratio varies widely from industry to industry. Such factors as due dates of current liabilities, composition of quick assets, and various operating factors must be considered in evaluating the adequacy of the ratio. Comparisons with the industry average and with the company's ratio in prior years can be helpful.

Inventory Turnover

It is important that a firm's inventory be turned over rapidly, so that excess amounts of working capital are not tied up in unnecessary merchandise. Since the cost of the merchandise that has been moved during the year is shown on the income statement as the cost of goods sold, the inventory turnover is easily determined. The ratio is computed by dividing the cost of goods sold during the period by the average inventory on hand. This ratio measures the number of times that the average inventory had to be replaced during the period. Obviously, the higher the turnover, the less time that has elapsed between the date of purchase and the date of sale.

Ideally, the average inventory amount should be based on monthly figures. However, the outside analyst usually has available only the inventory figures for the beginning and end of the fiscal year. In using the end-of-year inventory figure, the analyst must remember that usually the inventory at that time is near the lowest level of the entire year. Hence, using the beginning and ending inventory figures for the year produces an inventory average that may not be at all typical of the inventory during the other months. As a result, the inventory turnover computed is very likely to be higher than the actual turnover. The calculations for the Duncan Lawn Furniture Corporation are as follows.

	19Y3	19Y2
Inventory, Jan. 1	$285,100	$253,700
Inventory, Dec. 31	300,000	285,100
Totals	$585,100	$538,800
Average	$\dfrac{\$585,100}{2} = \$292,550$	$\dfrac{\$538,800}{2} = \$269,400$
$\dfrac{\text{Cost of Goods Sold}}{\text{Average Inventory}}$	$\dfrac{\$1,982,588}{\$292,550} = 6.8 \text{ times}$	$\dfrac{\$1,789,870}{\$269,400} = 6.6 \text{ times}$

Obviously, the inventory turnover ratio varies widely between industries. A bakery, for example, would expect to have an almost daily turnover; whereas, dealers in certain types of durable goods might have a turnover of only two times a year. Thus comparisons with the industry average and the company's ratio in prior years are very important.

Accounts Receivable Turnover

A company should collect its accounts and notes receivable as quickly as possible. Not only does prompt collection reduce the amount of working capital tied up in receivables, but it also reduces the likelihood that accounts will become uncollectible. The *accounts receivable turnover ratio* is a measure of the reasonableness of the accounts outstanding and of the approximate average collection time. This ratio is computed by dividing net credit sales by the average trade receivables, including notes arising from sales transactions. As in the case of the inventory turnover, it is desirable to use monthly balances in computing the average receivables, but analysts outside the company usually do not have access to monthly figures and must rely on an average of the balances at the beginning and end of the fiscal year. Also, analysts outside the company normally must use the net amount of all sales since they have no way of telling what part of the sales were on credit. The computations for the Duncan Lawn Furniture Corporation are shown below. (It is assumed that the accounts receivable on January 1, 19Y2, were $158,000 and that net credit sales were $1,910,812 in 19Y3 and $1,645,800 in 19Y2.)

	19Y3	19Y2
Accounts Receivable, Jan. 1	$168,184	$158,000
Accounts Receivable, Dec. 31	198,184	168,184
Totals	$366,368	$326,184
Average	$\dfrac{\$366,368}{2} = \$183,184$	$\dfrac{\$326,184}{2} = \$163,092$
$\dfrac{\text{Net Credit Sales}}{\text{Average Accounts Receivable}}$	$\dfrac{\$1,910,812}{\$183,184} = 10.4$	$\dfrac{\$1,645,800}{\$163,092} = 10.1$

The accounts receivable turnover is often expressed in a more meaningful and useful way as the *average collection period of accounts receivable*. The computation is quite simple. First, the average amount of net credit sales per day is computed. Then the number of days' sales in the accounts receivable is determined by dividing the average accounts receivable by the average daily net credit sales.

	19Y3	19Y2
$\dfrac{\text{Net Credit Sales}}{365}$	$\dfrac{\$1,910,812}{365} = \dfrac{\$5,235}{\text{per day}}$	$\dfrac{\$1,645,800}{365} = \dfrac{\$4,509}{\text{per day}}$
$\dfrac{\text{Average Accounts Receivable}}{\text{Average Daily Net Credit Sales}}$	$\dfrac{\$183,184}{\$5,235} = 35.0 \text{ days}$	$\dfrac{\$163,092}{\$4,509} = 36.2 \text{ days}$

The Duncan Lawn Furniture Corporation required approximately 35 days to collect accounts during 19Y3 compared with 36 days in 19Y2. As a rule of thumb, the average collection period should not exceed the net credit period plus one-third. Since Duncan's terms are net 30 days, the figures show that it is on the borderline of the 40 days suggested by the general rule.

One reason that the age of the accounts receivable is important is the need for cash to carry on business operations. The longer that receivables remain uncollected, the less cash is available. Another important consideration is that the older an account becomes, the less likely it is to be collected. (Aging the accounts receivable, which was discussed in Chapter 22, is a more direct method of studying a company's efficiency in making collections.)

OTHER RATIOS

By definition, a ratio is computed by dividing one number by another. Since there are a great many numbers on financial statements, there is almost no limit to the ratios that might be developed. Each analyst has his or her own set of preferred ratios to follow, and financial writers use many more than have been presented here. However, the ratios discussed in this chapter are among the most commonly used by accountants. As you have seen, the arithmetic is simple, but the interpretation depends largely on practice and on having suitable yardsticks that serve as a basis for judgment.

PRINCIPLES AND PROCEDURES SUMMARY

Stockholders, creditors, management, financial analysts, and many other groups have a keen interest in the financial affairs of a corporation. They are interested in the company's profitability, its long-term financial strength and equity protection, and its current position and liquidity. To help in measuring these important factors, many comparisons can be made between items on the financial statements. The resulting ratios can be compared with ratios for prior years in order to observe trends. Similarly, comparison with the same ratios for other companies in the industry will help reveal strengths and weaknesses of the company being analyzed.

MANAGERIAL IMPLICATIONS

Statement analysis assists management in identifying areas of operations that are weak and need management's attention. For example, a low inventory turnover compared with the industry average may reflect obsolete goods, overstocking of merchandise, poor purchasing procedures, or other operating inefficiencies. As another example, a low current ratio should serve as a warning that the company is facing a liquidity problem. In addition, a low current ratio combined with a low ratio of stockholders' equity to total equities may mean that the company is undercapitalized. Similarly, many other ratios taken alone or in combination can be of great use to the skillful manager in detecting and correcting problems.

REVIEW QUESTIONS

1. Why does working capital represent the margin of security afforded short-term creditors?
2. How is the current ratio computed? What information does this ratio provide?
3. How is immediate liquidity measured? Why does management keep a close watch on liquidity?
4. How is inventory turnover computed?
5. Why is the inventory turnover computed by an analyst outside the company likely to be higher than actual turnover? Does this distort the meaningfulness of the computation?
6. What are the procedures for determining the average collection period of accounts receivable?
7. How does the acid-test ratio differ from the current ratio?
8. Name three ratios that are often used in evaluating profitability.
9. Explain what the ratio of net income to stockholders' equity measures.
10. What is the procedure for measuring earnings per share of common stock?
11. What does the times bond interest earned ratio measure?
12. What is meant by yield on common stock? Why is this ratio not meaningful for most small companies?
13. Why would an analyst be interested in a firm's turnover of assets?
14. Explain how to compute the times preferred dividends earned ratio.
15. Explain how to compute the ratio of owned capital to borrowed capital.
16. Explain how to compute the book value per share of common stock. What are some of the limitations on the usefulness of this figure?

17. Define the term *liquidity*.
18. Why is it useful to know the inventory turnover of a company?
19. What does the accounts receivable turnover measure?
20. Why is it more useful to know the number of days' sales in receivables than the turnover of receivables?

MANAGERIAL DISCUSSION QUESTIONS

1. Why are ratios that measure profitability and operating results so important to management?
2. In general, a higher current ratio is favorable because it reflects a greater ability to meet currently maturing obligations. However, management should become concerned if the current ratio becomes too high. Why?
3. Suppose that you are the controller for a company that has an inventory turnover of eight times a year while the industry average is only six times a year. One of the officers asks you whether this is a favorable situation for the company. How would you evaluate the situation?
4. Why would an analyst be interested in a firm's ratio of owned capital to borrowed capital?
5. Assume that a director of a corporation where you work asks why the rate of return on assets is considered an important tool for judging managerial effectiveness. What explanation would you provide?
6. How does an analyst evaluate the composition of a firm's current assets?
7. As the accountant for a small company, you have just supplied the president with the firm's current ratio and acid-test ratio. The president wants to know why he cannot obtain sufficient information about the firm's liquidity by simply looking at the amount of working capital. What answer would you give?
8. Assume that you are the controller of the Vista Electronics Corporation, a firm that has expanded rapidly in the last few years. Your analysis of the corporation's latest financial statements shows that it is developing a shortage of working capital. To alert top management to the problem, you immediately wrote a memorandum explaining the situation. The president now wants recommendations from you about how to solve the problem. What are some ways that the corporation might obtain additional working capital?

EXERCISES

EXERCISE 36-1   **Analyzing the effects of transactions on financial statement items and ratios.**
For each of the transactions listed on page 873, decide what effect or effects it would have on a corporation's financial statements or ratios. Select the letter or letters that apply. If there is no appropriate response among the effects listed,

write "none." If more than one effect is applicable to a particular transaction, be sure to list all applicable letters. (Assume that state laws do not permit declaration of nonliquidating dividends except from earnings.)

TRANSACTION	EFFECT
1. Declaration of a cash dividend due in one month on noncumulative preferred stock.	A. Reduces the working capital.
	B. Increases the working capital.
	C. Reduces the current ratio.
2. Declaration and payment of an ordinary stock dividend.	D. Increases the current ratio.
	E. Reduces the dollar amount of the total capital stock.
3. Receipt of a cash dividend, not previously recorded, on stock of another corporation.	F. Increases the dollar amount of the total capital stock.
4. Omitting the payment of a dividend on cumulative preferred stock.	G. Reduces the total retained earnings.
	H. Increases the total retained earnings.
5. Receipt of preferred shares as a dividend on stock held as a temporary investment. This is not a regularly recurring dividend.	I. Reduces the equity per share of common stock.
	J. Reduces the equity of each common stockholder.
6. Issue of new common shares in a 5-for-1 stock split-up.	

EXERCISE 36-2 **Computing the ratio of net income to net sales.** Financial data for the Bradley Corporation for the years 19X1, 19X2, and 19X3 is given below. Using this data, compute its ratio of net income to net sales for each year.

	19X3	19X2	19X1
Net Sales	$600,000	$560,000	$500,000
Net Income	24,000	22,000	17,000
Total Assets	200,000	180,000	150,000
Stockholders' Equity	150,000	120,000	80,000

EXERCISE 36-3 **Computing the ratio of net income to stockholders' equity.** Using the data given in Exercise 36-2 for the Bradley Corporation, compute its ratio of net income to average stockholders' equity for 19X3 and 19X2.

EXERCISE 36-4 **Computing the ratio of net income to total assets.** Using the data given in Exercise 36-2 for the Bradley Corporation, compute its ratio of net income to total assets for 19X1, 19X2, and 19X3. (Base the calculation on total ending assets for each year.)

EXERCISE 36-5 **Computing the turnover of assets.** Using the data given in Exercise 36-2 for the Bradley Corporation, compute its turnover of assets for 19X1, 19X2, and 19X3. (Base the calculation on total ending assets for each year.)

EXERCISE 36-6 **Computing the ratio of stockholders' equity to total equities.** Using the data given in Exercise 36-2 for the Bradley Corporation, compute its ratio of stockholders' equity to total equities for 19X1, 19X2, and 19X3.

EXERCISE 36-7 **Computing the ratio of stockholders' equity to total liabilities.** Using the data given in Exercise 36-2 for the Bradley Corporation, compute its ratio of stockholders' equity to total liabilities for 19X1, 19X2, and 19X3.

EXERCISE 36-8 **Computing the earnings per share of common stock.** Financial data for the Myers Corporation for 19X1 is given below. Using this data, compute its earnings per share of common stock for the year.

1. Net income after income taxes for the year, $100,000.
2. Bonds outstanding (all year), $500,000 par value, 10 percent interest.
3. Preferred stock outstanding (all year), 20,000 shares, $20 par, 10 percent dividends.
4. Common stock outstanding (all year), 50,000 shares, $25 par value.
5. Market price of common stock on December 31, $30 a share.
6. Total federal and state income taxes paid, $50,000.
7. Dividends paid on common stock, $1 a share.

EXERCISE 36-9 **Computing the times bond interest earned ratio.** Using the data given in Exercise 36-8 for the Myers Corporation, compute its times bond interest earned ratio for 19X1.

EXERCISE 36-10 **Computing the times preferred dividends earned ratio.** Using the data given in Exercise 36-8 for the Myers Corporation, compute its times preferred dividends earned ratio for 19X1.

EXERCISE 36-11 **Computing the price-earnings ratio of common stock.** Using the data given in Exercise 36-8 for the Myers Corporation, compute the price-earnings ratio of its common stock on December 31, 19X1.

EXERCISE 36-12 **Computing the yield on common stock.** Using the data given in Exercise 36-8 for the Myers Corporation, compute the yield on each share of its common stock for 19X1.

EXERCISE 36-13 **Computing the current ratio.** Selected data from the financial statements of the Todd Corporation for 19X1 and 19X2 is given below. Using this data, compute the firm's current ratio for each year.

	19X2	19X1
Ending Merchandise Inventory	$ 120,000	$ 100,000
Accounts Receivable (Net)	180,000	150,000
Cash	30,000	40,000
Other Current Assets (Prepayments)	10,000	10,000
Current Liabilities	240,000	250,000
Net Sales	1,200,000	1,000,000
Cost of Goods Sold	720,000	580,000

EXERCISE 36-14 **Computing the acid-test ratio.** Using the data given in Exercise 36-13 for the Todd Corporation, compute its acid-test ratio for each year.

EXERCISE 36-15　**Computing the amount of working capital.** Using the data given in Exercise 36-13 for the Todd Corporation, compute its working capital for each year.

EXERCISE 36-16　**Computing the inventory turnover.** Using the data given in Exercise 36-13 for the Todd Corporation, compute its inventory turnover for each year. (Assume that the beginning inventory in 19X1 was $92,000.)

EXERCISE 36-17　**Computing the accounts receivable turnover.** Using the data given in Exercise 36-13 for the Todd Corporation, compute its accounts receivable turnover. (Assume that the beginning amount of accounts receivable in 19X1 was $140,000.)

EXERCISE 36-18　**Computing the average collection period.** Using the data given in Exercise 36-13, compute the number of days' sales in the accounts receivable.

PROBLEMS

PROBLEM 36-1　**Preparing a ratio analysis of financial statements.** Using the financial statements for the Golden West Corporation given in Problem 35-1 on pages 851 and 852, calculate each of the following ratios or measures for 19X2 and 19X1.

1. The ratio of net income after income taxes to net sales.
2. The ratio of net income to ending stockholders' equity.
3. The earnings per share of common stock, assuming that the preferred stock is nonparticipating and noncumulative.
4. The dividend yield per share of common stock. A dividend of $15.31 a share was paid on each share outstanding all year in 19X2, and a dividend of $10 a share was paid in 19X1. The market values were $74 a share in 19X2 and $69 a share in 19X1.
5. The ratio of net income to total assets.
6. The ratio of net sales to total assets other than investments.
7. The ratio of net sales to total property, plant, and equipment.
8. The times bond interest earned ratio.
9. The times preferred dividends earned ratio.
10. The ratio of stockholders' equity to total equities.
11. The ratio of stockholders' equity to total liabilities.
12. The book value per share of common stock, assuming that the preferred stock is noncumulative, nonparticipating, and has no liquidation premium.
13. The ratio of property, plant, and equipment (net) to long-term liabilities.
14. The current ratio.
15. The acid-test ratio.
16. The number of days' sales in receivables. The net accounts receivable totaled $177,000 on December 31, 19X0.
17. The merchandise inventory turnover.

PROBLEM 36-2　**Preparing a ratio analysis of financial statements.** Using the financial statements for the Sanchez Corporation, given in Problem 35-2 on pages 853 and

854, calculate each of the following ratios or measures for the years 19X3 and
19X2.

1. The ratio of net income after income taxes to net sales.
2. The ratio of net income to ending stockholders' equity.
3. The earnings per share of common stock, assuming that the preferred stock
   is noncumulative and nonparticipating.
4. The dividend yield per share of common stock. A dividend of $38.24 a share
   was paid in 19X3, and a dividend of $22.30 a share was paid in 19X2. The
   market values were $400 a share in 19X3 and $320 a share in 19X2.
5. The ratio of net income to total assets.
6. The ratio of net sales to total assets.
7. The ratio of net sales to total property, plant, and equipment.
8. The times preferred dividends earned ratio.
9. The ratio of stockholders' equity to total equities.
10. The ratio of stockholders' equity to total liabilities.
11. The book value per share of common stock, assuming that the preferred
    stock has no liquidation premium.
12. The current ratio.
13. The acid-test ratio.
14. The number of days' sales in receivables. The net accounts receivable to-
    taled $38,743 on December 31, 19X1.
15. The merchandise inventory turnover.

PROBLEM 36-3   **Interpreting the results of ratio analysis.** Selected ratios for other companies in
the same industry as the Sanchez Corporation are given below. Using these ratios
and the ratios you computed in Problem 36-2, make brief written comments
about any areas of Sanchez's operations that should be examined by management.

1. Net income to net sales, 8.1 percent.
2. Net sales to total assets, 2.4 to 1.
3. Days' sales in accounts receivable, 22.1 days.
4. Merchandise inventory turnover, 5.8 times.
5. Current ratio, 1.8 to 1.
6. Net sales to total property, plant, and equipment, 4.3 to 1.

ALTERNATE PROBLEMS

PROBLEM 36-1A   **Preparing a ratio analysis of financial statements.** Using the financial statements for the Convenience Products Corporation in Problem 35-1A on pages 855
and 856, calculate each of the following ratios or measures for 19X2 and 19X1.

1. The ratio of net income after income taxes to net sales.
2. The ratio of net income to ending stockholders' equity.
3. The earnings per share of common stock, assuming that the preferred stock
   is nonparticipating and noncumulative.
4. The dividend yield per share of common stock. A dividend of $4.25 a share
   was paid on each share outstanding all year in 19X2, and a dividend of $4 a

share was paid in 19X1. The market values were $52 a share in 19X2 and $51 a share in 19X1.

5. The ratio of net income to total assets.
6. The ratio of net sales to total assets other than investments.
7. The ratio of net sales to total property, plant, and equipment.
8. The times bond interest earned ratio.
9. The times preferred dividends earned ratio.
10. The ratio of stockholders' equity to total equities.
11. The ratio of stockholders' equity to total liabilities.
12. The book value per share of common stock, assuming that the preferred stock is noncumulative, nonparticipating, and has no liquidation premium.
13. The ratio of property, plant, and equipment (net) to long-term liabilities.
14. The current ratio.
15. The acid-test ratio.
16. The number of days' sales in receivables. The net accounts receivable totaled $554,000 on December 31, 19X0.
17. The merchandise inventory turnover. The merchandise inventory on January 1, 19X1, was $1,385,000.

PROBLEM 36-2A **Preparing a ratio analysis of financial statements.** Using the financial statements for the Garrett Corporation given in Problem 35-2A on pages 857 and 858, calculate each of the following ratios or measures for the years 19X2 and 19X1.

1. The ratio of net income after income taxes to net sales.
2. The ratio of net income to total stockholders' equity.
3. The dividend yield per share of common stock. A dividend of $1 a share was paid in 19X2, and a dividend of $1.30 a share was paid in 19X1. The market values were $18 a share in 19X2 and $18.50 a share in 19X1.
4. The ratio of net income to total assets.
5. The ratio of net sales to total assets.
6. The ratio of net sales to total property, plant, and equipment.
7. The ratio of stockholders' equity to total equities.
8. The ratio of stockholders' equity to total liabilities.
9. The book value per share of common stock.
10. The current ratio.
11. The acid-test ratio.
12. The number of days' sales in receivables. The net accounts receivable totaled $28,662 on December 31, 19X0.
13. The merchandise inventory turnover.

PROBLEM 36-3A **Interpreting the results of ratio analysis.** Selected ratios for other companies in the same industry as the Garrett Corporation are given below. Using this data and the ratios you computed in Problem 36-2A, make brief written comments or suggestions about any areas of strength or weakness for Garrett.

1. Net income to stockholders' equity, 21.4 percent.
2. Stockholders' equity to total liabilities, 2.2 to 1.
3. Net sales to total assets, 3.1 to 1.
4. Merchandise inventory turnover, 3.2 times.

*The ability to analyze financial data is highly important because so many
business decisions are based on the results of financial analysis. As you have
seen, financial analysis involves both the computation of percentages and
ratios and the interpretation of these percentages and ratios to discover
trends and assess profitability, financial strength, and liquidity. This project
will give you an opportunity to gain more practice in both aspects of financial analysis.*

FINANCIAL ANALYSIS AND
DECISION MAKING

INTRODUCTION

Assume that you are a loan officer at a bank. The Marshall Corporation, a
distributor of computer software, has approached the bank for a substantial loan.
You have been asked to analyze the financial statements of the firm for the last
two years and make a recommendation to the bank's loan committee.

The Marshall Corporation's income statement and balance sheet for 19X5
and 19X4 are shown on pages 879 and 880. When the vice president gave you
these reports, he made the following remarks.

- There has been a steady increase in sales and net income since the firm was
  established five years ago. Total assets have also increased every year.
- The firm recently constructed an addition to its building and purchased new
  warehouse equipment.
- The firm was able to pay a large dividend to stockholders during the year.
- The loan is needed to acquire a broader product line and add to the sales staff.

INSTRUCTIONS

Complete the following work in order to analyze the financial statements of the
Marshall Corporation.

1. Prepare a horizontal and a vertical analysis of the two statements. Carry
   computations to four decimal places and then round to three places. (Leave all
   vertical analysis percentages unadjusted.)
2. Make written comments about any results of the horizontal and vertical analysis that you might want to point out to the loan committee.
3. Compute the following ratios.
   a. The ratio of net income after income taxes to net sales
   b. The ratio of net income after income taxes to stockholders' equity
   c. The earnings per share of common stock
   d. The ratio of net income before income taxes to total assets

e. The ratio of net sales to total assets
f. The ratio of stockholders' equity to total equities
g. The ratio of stockholders' equity to total liabilities
h. The book value per share of common stock
i. The current ratio
j. The acid-test ratio
k. The inventory turnover ratio

4. Make written comments about any results of the ratio analysis that you might want to point out to the loan committee.

5. Would you recommend that the loan committee approve the loan to the Marshall Corporation? Prepare brief written comments stating the reasons behind the decision that you are recommending.

MARSHALL CORPORATION
Comparative Income Statement
Years Ended December 31, 19X5 and 19X4

	19X5	19X4
Revenue		
Net Sales	$2,859,000	$2,313,000
Cost of Goods Sold		
Merchandise Inventory, Jan. 1	$ 189,000	$ 180,000
Merchandise Purchases	1,186,290	1,005,000
Total Merchandise Available for Sale	$1,375,290	$1,185,000
Less Merchandise Inventory, Dec. 31	207,000	189,000
Cost of Goods Sold	$1,168,290	$ 996,000
Gross Profit on Sales	$1,690,710	$1,317,000
Operating Expenses		
Selling Expenses	$ 473,890	$ 390,600
Administrative Expenses	652,920	378,900
Total Operating Expenses	$1,126,810	$ 769,500
Net Income Before Income Taxes	$ 563,900	$ 547,500
Provision for Income Taxes	221,000	215,250
Net Income After Income Taxes	$ 342,900	$ 332,250

MARSHALL CORPORATION
Comparative Balance Sheet
December 31, 19X5 and 19X4

	19X5	19X4
Assets		
Current Assets		
Cash	$ 73,800	$ 216,450
Marketable Securities	25,000	175,000
Accounts Receivable (Net)	295,200	282,600
Merchandise Inventory	207,000	189,000
Prepaid Expenses	21,900	20,700
Total Current Assets	$ 622,900	$ 883,750
Property, Plant, and Equipment		
Building and Equipment	$ 851,200	$ 420,300
Less Accumulated Depreciation	120,600	108,000
Total Property, Plant, and Equipment	$ 730,600	$ 312,300
Total Assets	$1,353,500	$1,196,050
Liabilities and Stockholders' Equity		
Current Liabilities		
Notes Payable	$ 35,000	
Accounts Payable	285,000	$ 190,900
Other Payables	36,000	25,500
Estimated Income Taxes Payable	221,000	215,250
Total Liabilities	$ 577,000	$ 431,650
Stockholders' Equity		
Common Stock (50,000 shares outstanding)	$ 500,000	$ 500,000
Retained Earnings	276,500	264,400
Total Stockholders' Equity	$ 776,500	$ 764,400
Total Liabilities and Stockholders' Equity	$1,353,500	$1,196,050

ACCT 3 —>

PART 3
MANAGERIAL ACCOUNTING: BASIC PRINCIPLES

In Parts 1 and 2 of this book we examined financial accounting concepts and procedures. Emphasis was placed on the analysis and accumulation of accounting data and the reporting of this data in financial statements. Four basic financial statements were presented: the income statement, the balance sheet, the statement of retained earnings (for a corporation), and the statement of changes in financial position. All of these statements are historical in nature. They report the results of financial transactions that occurred in the past. However, if management is to properly carry out the functions of planning and control, it must have forward-looking information and analyses in addition to historical data. Historical data alone will not be enough.

COST CENTERS AND PROFIT CENTERS; DEPARTMENTALIZATION

THE NEED FOR MANAGERIAL ACCOUNTING

Basic financial statements are also limited in that they summarize the activities and financial position of a business as a whole. However, most management decisions are made about individual activities or segments of a business. For example, the income statement, although useful, is inadequate to answer questions such as these.

- Should a machine be replaced?
- How much profit was made on an order from a certain customer?
- Is a particular department of the business operating profitably?
- Should the firm discontinue a certain product?
- What price should be set for a new product?

The answers to such questions are provided by an area of accounting that is usually known as *managerial accounting*. In Part 3 of this book we will examine a number of topics that illustrate the broad scope of managerial accounting. First, the measurement of profit for individual segments of a business will be covered. Two common types of business segments—departments and branches—will be discussed. Next we will examine the methods used to determine and analyze the costs involved in the manufacture of products. Then the budgeting process—the planning of profits, financial position, capital outlays, and cash flow—will be illustrated. Finally, we will discuss the basic principles that underlie internal reports to management, and we will study some of the most common types of internal reports.

Although management is interested in the results of past operations, it is even more interested in the future. Typically, a forecast or estimate for the future begins with an analysis of what occurred in the past. For example, an estimate of future sales usually begins with an analysis of past sales. Similarly, an estimate of future expenses begins with an analysis of past expenses. Decisions about such matters as pricing also make use of information from past accounting records as a basis for future action. Thus, Part 3 of this book deals with the use of historical data in decision making and in controlling costs and profits.

PROFIT CENTERS AND COST CENTERS

As noted already, managerial accounting is usually concerned with the segments of a business. These segments are often referred to as *centers*. The accounting information related to each center is accumulated and analyzed separately from the information for other centers. There are two types of centers for accounting purposes—profit centers and cost centers. The two are similar with one important exception. For a *profit center*, both revenue and cost data are accumulated in order to measure profit; whereas for a *cost center*, only cost data is accumulated and no attempt is made to ascribe profit to the center.

ex. coat, dress, shoe departments

Typically, profit centers are revenue-producing segments that sell products or services to customers outside the business. For example, in a clothing store the coat, dress, suit, and shoe departments may all be separate profit centers. Sales and costs related to each department are accumulated and matched, and a "profit" is computed for the center. Similarly, each store in a chain of stores owned by one company or each branch sales office may be treated as a profit center. Sometimes a segment of a company is considered a profit center even though it does not sell products or services to an outside customer. For example, the producing segment of an oil company may be treated as a profit center even though the oil it produces is merely transferred to the company's refinery and is not sold directly to outside customers. In cases such as this, the revenue from the segment's activities is the *transfer price* of its product—the price at which the segment's goods are transferred to another segment of the company. In this chapter, we will examine the methods used to measure the profitability of revenue-producing departments, which are a very common type of profit center.

ex. purchasing department

Cost centers are those segments of a business that do not directly earn revenue. Often, cost centers represent areas of a business that merely provide services to other segments of the firm. The emphasis in accounting for cost centers is therefore on cost control rather than on profit measurement. For example, the purchasing department of a company does not produce revenue directly; it merely performs a service for other departments that do earn revenue. The purpose of accounting for the purchasing department as a separate unit is to measure the costs of its operations and to provide a basis for controlling those costs. Other typical cost centers of a company might be the data processing department, the maintenance department, the storeroom, the research laboratory, and the accounting department. In later chapters we will examine how costs are accumulated and analyzed for service departments such as these.

RESPONSIBILITY ACCOUNTING

A common theme underlying both profit centers and cost centers is the idea of responsibility accounting. The basic principle of *responsibility accounting* is that management should be able to evaluate the performance of each segment of the business and pinpoint responsibility for its financial results. With this type of system, internal accounting reports provide detailed data for each cost center and profit center so that management can determine how efficiently the individual segments are functioning. This type of information is essential if management is to control current operations effectively and develop sound plans for the future.

DEPARTMENTALIZED OPERATIONS

When the operations of a business include more than one type of sales or service activity, managers and owners want to know how much each activity is contributing to the firm's net income or net loss. If all sales are combined, information on revenue by type of activity will not be available unless each sales transaction is analyzed and the results of each activity are summarized whenever such data is needed. Obviously, this is a tedious and inefficient procedure.

Experienced accountants plan in advance to meet requests for such information. They first determine what data will be required. Then they set up a system for gathering the information. If management wants a detailed record of the profits provided by the different types of merchandise handled, accounts must be set up to departmentalize the related revenue and expenses. This is done when the accountant plans the business's chart of accounts.

For example, suppose that the Style Clothing Store decides to departmentalize revenues and expenses starting on February 1, 19X2, when its shoe department opens. After studying the planned organizational structure and operations of the expanded business, the accountant realizes that the firm's system of financial records must be redesigned to gather departmentalized data concerning the following items.

- Operating Revenues
- Cost of Goods Sold
- Gross Profit on Sales
- Operating Expenses (Direct Expenses and Indirect Expenses)
- Net Income From Operations

REVENUE SECTION

Now we will discuss how the accountant would plan the new departmentalized accounting system. Let's start with the accounts that will appear in the Revenue section of the income statement.

Sales

Separate records are established to accumulate sales data for each department. Accounts entitled Sales—Clothing and Sales—Shoes are opened. Separate account numbers, such as 401 and 402, might be assigned to each departmental sales account. However, many accountants prefer to use the procedure followed by the Style Clothing Store, which is to assign one basic number to all departmental sales accounts and to distinguish between the different departments by adding a separate digit for each department to the right of the basic account number. In this case, the clothing department will be identified by .1 and the shoe department by .2. The account numbers then are 401.1 for Sales—Clothing and 401.2 for Sales—Shoes.

Recording Credit Sales by Departments At the Style Clothing Store, sales on credit are recorded in a sales journal. At the end of each month, this journal is totaled and the sales for the month are posted in one summary figure to the Sales account. When the Sales account is departmentalized, the sales journal must show information for the separate departments. This can be done by setting up a separate column in the sales journal for each type of sale. The sales slips must be examined to identify the department to which a sale should be credited.

For example, suppose that on February 1, 19X2, Sales Slip 2178 covers a sale of clothing for $23.70 to Lois Adams. Sales Slip 2179 covers a sale of shoes for $18 to Joseph Burke. Sales Slip 2180 covers a sale of clothing for $21.40 and a sale of shoes for $16.50 to George Clay. Here is the way these sales slips are entered in the newly rearranged sales journal.

SALES JOURNAL for Month of February 19X2 — Page 1

DATE	SALES SLIP NO.	CUSTOMER'S NAME	✓	ACCOUNTS RECEIVABLE DEBIT	SALES TAX PAYABLE CREDIT	SALES— CLOTHING CREDIT	SALES— SHOES CREDIT
Feb. 1	2178	Lois Adams	✓	24 41	71	23 70	
1	2179	Joseph Burke	✓	18 54	54		18 00
1	2180	George Clay	✓	39 04	1 14	21 40	16 50
28		Totals		17,304 00	504 00	14,500 00	2,300 00
				(111)	(231)	(401.1)	(401.2)

Posting From the Sales Journal The posting procedure is similar to the procedure you learned about previously. Each day, postings are made to the individual customer accounts in the accounts receivable ledger. At the end of the month, postings of the column totals are made to the general ledger. For example, in the preceding illustration, the debits to the individual accounts for Adams, Burke, and Clay are posted immediately. At the end of February, the totals of the Accounts Receivable column, the Sales Tax Payable column, and the two Sales columns are posted.

Use of Analysis Ledger Sheets When the accounts for sales and other items are departmentalized, it may be convenient to use analysis ledger sheets rather than many different ledger accounts. Under this system, one Sales account is kept in the general ledger with separate analysis columns for recording the sales figures of each department. The posting of the Style Clothing Store's monthly sales from the sales journal to such an analysis ledger sheet results in the entry shown below.

Sales — No. 401

CLOTHING CR. 401.1	SHOES CR. 401.2	DATE	EXPLANATION	POST. REF.	DEBIT	CREDIT	BALANCE	DR. CR.
14,500 00	2,300 00	19 X2 Feb. 28		S1		16,800 00	16,800 00	Cr.

Notice that this analysis ledger sheet is almost identical to the one you learned about in Chapter 25.

Recording Cash Sales by Departments At the Style Clothing Store, sales slips are prepared for cash sales to show the type of merchandise sold. At the end of the day, the slips are analyzed to determine the total cash sales of each department. (Some firms obtain departmental totals for their cash sales from cash registers.) The totals are recorded in a cash receipts journal that has been rearranged to provide separate Sales columns for the different departments. When the volume of transactions does not justify separate departmental columns, as with Cash Short or Over, a department identification column is provided to the left of the amount. The cash receipts journal now used by the Style Clothing Store is shown below with the cash sales of February 1 entered.

The journal is totaled at the end of the month in the usual way. Totals accumulated in subdivided columns such as Cash Short or Over are analyzed by department as shown.

CASH RECEIPTS JOURNAL for Month of February 19X2 Page 1

DATE	EXPLANATION	√	ACCTS. REC. CREDIT	SALES TAX PAYABLE CREDIT	SALES— CLOTHING CREDIT	SALES— SHOES CREDIT	CASH SHORT OR OVER DEPT.	CASH SHORT OR OVER DEBIT	CASH DEBIT
Feb. 1	Cash sales			6 75	160 00	65 00	.1	40	231 35
28	Totals		14,500 00	301 50	8,000 00	2,050 00		5 00	24,846 50
			(111)	(231)	(401.1)	(401.2)	.1	3 00	(101)
							.2	2 00	
								5 00	
								(529)	

Posting From the Cash Receipts Journal Individual postings are made daily to the accounts receivable ledger. Column totals are posted at the end of the month. The only new procedure involved is the posting of the sales data to the departmental columns of the analysis ledger sheet. The Sales account appears below with both credit and cash sales for February posted.

Sales No. 401

CLOTHING CR. 401.1	SHOES CR. 401.2	DATE	EXPLANATION	POST. REF.	DEBIT	CREDIT	BALANCE	DR. CR.
		19 X2						
14,500 00	2,300 00	Feb. 28		S1		16,800 00	16,800 00	Cr.
8,000 00	2,050 00	28		CR1		10,050 00	26,850 00	Cr.
22,500 00	4,350 00							

Sales Returns and Allowances

When sales are departmentalized, the records for sales returns and allowances should also be separate. Departmental accounts for these transactions may easily be arranged by adding subaccount digits to the main account number, as was done with the Sales account. The accountant for the Style Clothing Store has therefore set up the following accounts: Sales Returns and Allowances—Clothing 452.1 and Sales Returns and Allowances—Shoes 452.2.

The new account titles and numbers are used to establish separate columns in an analysis ledger sheet kept for the main account. Separate columns are also provided in the sales returns and allowances journal. This journal, as illustrated below, shows entries for a return of shoes purchased by Angela Clark and an allowance made to Kenneth Davis on some clothing that was flawed but wearable.

SALES RETURNS AND ALLOWANCES JOURNAL for Month of February 19X2   Page 1

DATE		SALES SLIP NO.	CUSTOMER'S NAME	√	ACCOUNTS RECEIVABLE CREDIT	SALES TAX PAYABLE DEBIT	SALES RET. & ALLOW.— CLOTHING DEBIT	SALES RET. & ALLOW.— SHOES DEBIT
Feb.	2	2156	Angela Clark	√	15 45	45		15 00
	6	2183	Kenneth Davis	√	5 15	15	5 00	
	28		Totals		540 75	15 75	450 00	75 00
					(111)	(231)	(452.1)	(452.2)

If a firm has only a few sales returns and allowances, they are recorded in the general journal and posted individually.

Sales Discounts

Sales discounts that are treated as other expense need not be departmentalized because they appear after net income from operations on the income statement. However, if sales discounts are treated as deductions from sales, they must be departmentalized for presentation as part of the Revenue section of the income statement. Determining the exact amount to apply to each department is difficult if a customer receives a discount for goods sold in more than one department. To avoid this problem, some firms simply divide the total sales discounts for an accounting period in proportion to the credit sales of each department. No attempt is made to record sales discounts by department during the period. The Style Clothing Store, like most retail businesses, does not offer sales discounts.

COST OF GOODS SOLD SECTION

The accountant's next task is to revise the accounts that appear in the Cost of Goods Sold section of the income statement.

Merchandise Inventory

In order to determine the gross profit by departments, both the beginning and ending merchandise inventories must be departmentalized. The needed data can easily be obtained at the time the inventory is being counted because items are

VOUCHER REGISTER for Month of February 19X2

DATE	VOU. NO.	PAYABLE TO	PAID DATE	PAID CHECK NO.	ACCTS. PAY. CREDIT	FICA TAX PAY. CREDIT	EMPL. INC. TAX PAY. CREDIT
Feb. 1	2-01	Bay Clothing Company	Can.	V2-10	4,750 00		
1	2-02	Ward Express Company			45 00		
1	2-03	Craft Shoe Company	Can.	V2-11	1,650 00		
8	2-10	Bay Clothing Company			4,700 00		
12	2-11	Craft Shoe Company			1,630 00		
28		Totals			39,770 00	30 00	90 00
					(205)	(221)	(222)

recorded and priced on inventory sheets by departments. At the end of the period, after the count is completed, the departmental inventory totals are recorded in departmental Income Statement columns on the worksheet, as you will observe later in this chapter. Separate Income Statement columns are required for the departments to summarize the revenue and expenses relating to each. When the closing entries are posted, the departmental inventory figures are recorded in the analysis columns of the Merchandise Inventory account in the general ledger under 121.1 for clothing and 121.2 for shoes.

Merchandise Purchases

A separate column might be provided in the voucher register for the purchases of each department. However, in an expanding business, adding so many columns will soon make the voucher register unwieldy. Instead, a divided column can be used for merchandise purchases. The first subcolumn shows the department by its subcode number (in this case, .1 for clothing and .2 for shoes). The second subcolumn shows the amount, as usual. At the end of the month, the figures in the column are analyzed, and the total for each department is determined and posted.

Freight In

A similar arrangement can be used for Freight In and any other account to be departmentalized. To illustrate this technique, a portion of the rearranged voucher register for February is shown above with the merchandise purchases and freight transactions entered. In some cases, one freight bill will be paid on merchandise purchased and shipped together for two or more departments. In this event, the freight costs may be allocated to departments on the basis of the weight or cost of the merchandise purchased for each department.

MERCHANDISE PURCHASES		FREIGHT IN		STORE SUP. DEBIT	OTHER ACCOUNTS			
DEPT.	DEBIT	DEPT.	DEBIT		ACCOUNT TITLE	POST. REF.	DEBIT	CREDIT
.1	4,750 00	.1	45 00					
.2	1,650 00							
					Accounts Payable	205	4,750 00	
					Pur. Ret. and Allow.–Clothing	511.1		50 00
					Accounts Payable	205	1,650 00	
					Pur. Ret. and Allow.—Shoes	511.2		20 00
	31,425 00		300 00	315 00			7,920 00	70 00
.1	16,425 00	.1	175 00	(129)			(X)	(X)
.2	15,000 00	.2	125 00					
	31,425 00		300 00					
	(501)		(506)					

At the end of the month, the amounts in the Freight In column of the voucher register are analyzed by department and the totals are then posted to an analysis ledger account sheet, like the one for Sales illustrated previously.

Purchases Returns and Allowances

must be departmentalized

Purchases returns and allowances must also be related to departmental operations. The Style Clothing Store records these transactions in the voucher register by canceling the original voucher, as first discussed in Chapter 11. However, this time the name of the departmental subaccount is noted in the Account Title column of the Other Accounts section to relate the return or allowance to the department involved. The illustration on page 888 and above shows the procedure for recording an allowance of $50 against the $4,750 invoice issued by the Bay Clothing Company, originally entered as Voucher 2-01, and for recording an allowance of $20 against the Craft Shoe Company's $1,650 invoice, entered as Voucher 2-03. After the credits (assuming that there are only two) are posted from the Other Accounts section of the voucher register, the Purchases Returns and Allowances account as of February 28 appears as shown below.

CLOTHING CR. 511.1	SHOES CR. 511.2	DATE	EXPLANATION	POST. REF.	DEBIT	CREDIT	BALANCE	DR. CR.
		Purchases Returns and Allowances					No. 511	
		19 X2						
50 00		Feb. 8		VR1		50 00	50 00	Cr.
	20 00	12		VR1		20 00	70 00	Cr.

Purchase Discounts

The Style Clothing Store treats purchase discounts as deductions from purchases. It is therefore necessary to show the separate total of discounts that is applicable to the purchases of each department. When a voucher is prepared authorizing payment of an invoice, the amount of discount and the department for which the purchase was made are shown. The check register is modified to provide a divided column for recording purchase discounts. Again, the first subcolumn indicates the department by its subaccount digit number (in this case, *.1* for clothing and *.2* for shoes). The second subcolumn lists the amount, as usual. The following partial check register for the month of February shows this method of handling purchase discounts.

CHECK REGISTER for Month of February 19X2 — Page 1

DATE	CHECK NO.	PAYABLE TO	VOU. NO.	ACCTS. PAYABLE DEBIT	PURCHASES DISCOUNT DEPT.	PURCHASES DISCOUNT CREDIT	CASH CREDIT
Feb. 10	2106	Delta Shirt Co.	2-04	750 00	.1	15 00	735 00
28		Totals		23,831 00		206 00	23,625 00
				(205)	.1	160 00	(101)
					.2	46 00	
						206 00	
						(512)	

At the end of the month, the column total is analyzed and the total amount for each department is determined. These amounts are then posted to the analysis columns of the Purchases Discount account.

OPERATING EXPENSES SECTION: DIRECT EXPENSES

Some operating expenses can be identified directly with an individual department and are therefore referred to as *direct expenses*. In many cases, it is possible to charge direct expenses to the appropriate departments at the time the expenses are incurred. For example, at the Style Clothing Store, each salesclerk works in only one department. Thus the salaries expense for such employees can be charged directly to the proper departments throughout the fiscal year. Similarly, advertising costs at the Style Clothing Store are identified with specific departments and charged directly to those departments throughout the fiscal year. Other direct expenses, such as cash short and over and delivery expense, can also be charged to the departments as they are incurred.

INDIRECT AND SEMIDIRECT EXPENSES

All the accounts that have been adapted for departmental treatment in the discussion so far have one important common characteristic. These revenue and expense items can be easily and directly assigned to a specific department when a transaction is initially recorded.

Unfortunately, not all operating expenses are direct expenses. Other operating expenses cannot be easily assigned to particular departments when the transactions occur and are recorded. These operating expenses are referred to as *indirect expenses* and are so identified on the income statement. Some indirect expenses are closely related to departmental activities and can be allocated among the departments on a very meaningful basis at the end of the accounting period.

For example, the cost of depreciation for store equipment and the cost of insurance for store equipment and merchandise inventory bear a close relationship to individual sales departments and can be allocated to each of these departments. Some accountants consider costs such as depreciation and insurance direct expenses. Others consider them indirect expenses. Still others feel it more appropriate to set up a completely new category known as *semidirect expenses.*

Some expenses are neither closely related nor easily assignable to individual departments. At the end of the accounting period, these expenses are allocated on the most logical basis possible. For example, items such as postage and stationery used in the office are an operating expense, but if they are allocated to sales departments, the allocation must be done on a somewhat arbitrary basis. Later in this chapter you will see how indirect and semidirect expenses are allocated to permit the calculation of a net income from operations for each sales department.

Other accounts involve items that do not relate to store operations and are not allocated to departments. Some examples are Interest Income, Miscellaneous Income, and Interest Expense. These items appear under Other Income and Other Expenses on the income statement.

RECORDING INDIRECT AND SEMIDIRECT EXPENSES

Indirect and semidirect expenses are usually first entered in the voucher register. No attempt is made to allocate them to a sales department at that time. In accordance with usual procedures, the amount is charged to an expense account with an offsetting credit to Accounts Payable. If justified by frequent transactions, a special column might be provided in the voucher register for recording the indirect expense involved. Otherwise, the debit would be entered in the Other Accounts Debit column. Any expense items appearing in this column are then posted daily to their general ledger accounts. An expense for which a separate column is provided in the voucher register is posted as a total debit figure at the end of the month. A balance ledger sheet without analysis columns is used for each of these expense accounts.

The process of allocating indirect or semidirect items takes place after all regular journalizing and posting work is completed and a trial balance has been prepared. The trial balance and adjustment data for the Style Clothing Store as of January 31, 19X3, the end of the firm's fiscal year, is used to illustrate the entire departmental allocation process.

THE DEPARTMENTAL WORKSHEET

A redesigned worksheet is used in the departmentalized accounting system of the Style Clothing Store. This 16-column form includes the usual sections for Trial Balance, Adjustments, Adjusted Trial Balance, Income Statement, and Balance Sheet. However, the two-column Income Statement section used before is now expanded to an eight-column section that has Debit and Credit columns headed Total, Clothing Department, Shoe Department, and Nondepartmental. The first pair of Income Statement columns (headed Total) is used in the same way as the previous two-column Income Statement section. The balances of all income statement accounts are extended from the Adjusted Trial Balance section to these columns. The other new columns in the Income Statement section serve only for analysis to help the accountant prepare a departmental income statement.

In the rest of this chapter you will see how the accountant completes each section of the departmentalized worksheet and financial statements. Refer to the January 31, 19X3, worksheet of the Style Clothing Store shown on pages 894 and 895 as you read this material.

Adjustments

The adjustments, with one exception, are almost identical to those you have previously learned. The one exception is an adjustment that involves a departmentalized expense. On January 31, 19X3, the Store Supplies account at the Style Clothing Store contains a balance of $4,363.75. This balance represents the cost of supplies available for use during the year. On January 31, 19X3, the firm's accountant must make an adjustment to transfer the amount of supplies actually used during the fiscal year from this asset account to the Store Supplies Expense account. The firm treats the cost of store supplies used as a departmentalized expense and uses an analysis ledger sheet for it.

The count of store supplies made at the end of the fiscal year shows that supplies costing $110 are on hand, which means that supplies costing $4,253.75 were used during the year. Records of the supplies issued to the sales departments throughout the year indicate that $3,133.75 of the total used should be charged to the clothing department and $1,120 should be charged to the shoe department. In order to simplify the adjusting entry, each departmental amount is shown as a debit in the Adjustments section of the worksheet. These amounts are identified by the departmental numbers *.1* (clothing) and *.2* (shoes). When the adjusting entries are later journalized and posted, each analysis column in the ledger account will contain a debit for the proper departmental share. Here is how the Store Supplies Expense account will look after the adjusting entry has been posted.

CLOTHING DR. 523.1	SHOES DR. 523.2	DATE	EXPLANATION	POST. REF.	DEBIT	CREDIT	BALANCE	DR. CR.
			Store Supplies Expense					No.523
3,133 75	1,120 00	19 X3 Jan. 31	Adjusting	J1	4,253 75		4,253 75	Dr.

This is the only adjustment involving a departmentalized account that must be made at the Style Clothing Store as of January 31, 19X3. However, if adjustments were required for other accounts using departmental analysis sheets, the same type of procedures would be followed.

The remaining adjustments, similar to those illustrated in previous chapters, are listed here.

a. Estimated loss from uncollectible accounts for the period
b. Depreciation expense for store furniture and fixtures
c. Depreciation expense for office equipment
d. Prepaid property taxes transferred to expense
e. Accrued salaries and wages
f. Accrued payroll taxes
g. Accrued interest on notes payable
h. Store supplies used
i. Expired insurance
j. Prepaid interest transferred to expense
k. Accrued interest on notes receivable
l. Accrued commission on sales taxes

Adjusted Trial Balance Section

The Adjusted Trial Balance section is similar to that appearing previously in the nondepartmentalized worksheet in Chapter 16.

Extending Balance Sheet Items

The balances of the balance sheet accounts (101–399) are extended to the Balance Sheet section of the worksheet in the usual way, except for the $65,000 balance for Merchandise Inventory. As you learned in earlier chapters, the beginning inventory will be extended later with the income statement items. However, at this time the closing inventory of $66,000 ($56,000 clothing, $10,000 shoes) is recorded in the following way.

1. As an asset totaling $66,000 by an entry in the Debit column of the Balance Sheet section.
2. As a $66,000 reduction in the total cost of goods sold by an entry in the Total Credit column of the Income Statement section.
3. As a $56,000 reduction in the cost of goods sold of the clothing department by an entry in the Clothing Department Credit column of the Income Statement section.
4. As a $10,000 reduction in the cost of goods sold of the shoe department by an entry in the Shoe Department Credit column of the Income Statement section.

Extending Income Statement Items

The $65,000 balance in the Merchandise Inventory account (representing beginning inventory) should now be recorded in the Income Statement section in the following way.

1. As a major element in the total cost of goods sold by an entry for $65,000 in the Total Debit column.
2. As a major element in the cost of goods sold of the clothing department by an entry for $65,000 in the Clothing Department Debit column.

Because the February 1, 19X2, inventory consisted entirely of clothing, no extension is required to the Shoe Department Debit column at this time. How-

STYLE CLOTHING STORE
Departmental Worksheet
Year Ended January 31, 19X3

	ACCT. NO.	ACCOUNT NAME	TRIAL BALANCE DEBIT	TRIAL BALANCE CREDIT	ADJUSTMENTS DEBIT	ADJUSTMENTS CREDIT	ADJUSTED TRIAL BALANCE DEBIT	ADJUSTED TRIAL BALANCE CREDIT
1	101	Cash	14,320 89				14,320 89	
2	105	Petty Cash Fund	25 00				25 00	
3	106	Change Fund	100 00				100 00	
4	109	Notes Receivable	800 00				800 00	
5	110	Notes Receivable Discounted						
6	111	Accounts Receivable	28,067 35				28,067 35	
7	112	Allowance for Uncollectible Accounts		7 06		(a)669 15		676 21
8	116	Interest Receivable			(k)9 00		9 00	
9	121	Merchandise Inventory	65,000 00				65,000 00	
10	126	Prepaid Insurance	3,390 00			(i)3,090 00	300 00	
11	127	Prepaid Interest Expense	120 00			(j)60 00	60 00	
12	128	Prepaid Property Taxes	600 00			(d)120 00	480 00	
13	129	Stores Supplies	4,363 75			(h)4,253 75	110 00	
14	131	Furniture and Fixtures	4,600 00				4,600 00	
15	132	Accum. Depreciation—Furn. and Fixtures		360 00		(b)460 00		820 00
16	133	Office Equipment	2,750 00				2,750 00	
17	134	Accum. Depreciation—Office Equipment		215 00		(c)215 00		430 00
18	201	Notes Payable—Trade		2,000 00				2,000 00
19	203	Notes Payable—Bank		12,000 00				12,000 00
20	205	Accounts Payable		4,854 65				4,854 65
21	216	Interest Payable				(g)26 67		26 67
22	221	FICA Tax Payable		189 80				189 80
23	222	Employee Income Tax Payable		216 00				216 00
24	225	Salaries and Wages Payable				(e)80 00		80 00
25	226	Payroll Taxes Payable				(f)510 00		510 00
26	231	Sales Tax Payable		825 28		(l)16 50		808 78
27	301	Linda Hanson, Capital		29,000 00				29,000 00
28	302	Linda Hanson, Drawing	7,800 00				7,800 00	
29	311	Steven Casey, Capital		28,000 00				28,000 00
30	312	Steven Casey, Drawing	7,800 00				7,800 00	
31	321	Janet Miller, Capital		28,500 00				28,500 00
32	322	Janet Miller, Drawing	7,800 00				7,800 00	
33	401	Sales		395,797 80				395,797 80
34	452	Sales Returns and Allowances	6,041 25				6,041 25	
35	491	Interest Income		226 00		(k)9 00		235 00
36	493	Miscellaneous Income		218 60		(l)16 50		235 10
37	501	Merchandise Purchases	255,350 00				255,350 00	
38	506	Freight In	3,590 00				3,590 00	
39	511	Purchases Returns and Allowances		1,065 00				1,065 00
40	512	Purchases Discount		5,048 30				5,048 30
41	521	Sales Salaries Expense	42,800 00				42,800 00	
42	522	Advertising Expense	6,893 30				6,893 30	
43	523	Store Supplies Expense			(h).1 3,133 75		4,253 75	
44					.2 1,120 00			
45	529	Cash Short or Over	72 00				72 00	
46	532	Delivery Expense	3,860 00				3,860 00	
47	536	Insurance Expense			(i)3,090 00		3,090 00	
48	541	Custodial Wages Expense	5,040 00		(e)80 00		5,120 00	
49	542	Rent Expense	6,000 00				6,000 00	
50	543	Utilities Expense	5,944 05				5,944 05	
51	551	Office Salaries Expense	16,800 00				16,800 00	
52	552	Payroll Tax Expense	5,168 40		(f)510 00		5,678 40	
53	553	Other Office Expenses	804 50				804 50	
54	554	Professional Services Expense	775 00				775 00	
55	555	Taxes and Licenses	1,206 00		(d)120 00		1,326 00	
56	561	Loss From Uncollectible Accounts			(a)669 15		669 15	
57	562	Depreciation Expense—Furn. and Fixtures			(b)460 00		460 00	
58	563	Depreciation Expense—Office Equipment			(c)215 00		215 00	
59	591	Interest Expense	642 00		(g)26 67		728 67	
60					(j)60 00			
61		Totals	508,523 49	508,523 49	9,510 07	9,510 07	510,493 31	510,493 31
62		Net Income for Year						
63								

	INCOME STATEMENT								BALANCE SHEET		
	TOTAL		CLOTHING DEPT.		SHOE DEPT.		NONDEPARTMENTAL				
	DEBIT	CREDIT	DEBIT	CREDIT	DEBIT	CREDIT	DEBIT	CREDIT	DEBIT	CREDIT	
1									14,320 89		1
2									25 00		2
3									100 00		3
4									800 00		4
5											5
6									28,067 35		6
7										676 21	7
8									9 00		8
9	65,000 00	66,000 00	65,000 00	56,000 00		10,000 00			66,000 00		9
10									300 00		10
11									60 00		11
12									480 00		12
13									110 00		13
14									4,600 00		14
15										820 00	15
16									2,750 00		16
17										430 00	17
18										2,000 00	18
19										12,000 00	19
20										4,854 65	20
21										26 67	21
22										189 80	22
23										216 00	23
24										80 00	24
25										510 00	25
26										808 78	26
27										29,000 00	27
28									7,800 00		28
29										28,000 00	29
30									7,800 00		30
31										28,500 00	31
32									7,800 00		32
33		395,797 80		284,182 82		111,614 98					33
34	6,041 25		4,582 50		1,458 75						34
35		235 00						235 00			35
36		235 10						235 10			36
37	255,350 00		183,175 00		72,175 00						37
38	3,590 00		2,735 00		855 00						38
39		1,065 00		825 00			240 00				39
40		5,048 30		4,349 60			698 70				40
41	42,800 00		24,800 00		18,000 00						41
42	6,893 30		5,235 00		1,658 30						42
43	4,253 75		3,133 75		1,120 00						43
44											44
45	72 00		45 00		27 00						45
46	3,860 00		2,840 00		1,020 00						46
47	3,090 00		2,607 96		482 04						47
48	5,120 00		4,608 00		512 00						48
49	6,000 00		5,400 00		600 00						49
50	5,944 05		5,349 65		594 40						50
51	16,800 00		12,062 40		4,737 60						51
52	5,678 40		3,638 53		2,039 87						52
53	804 50		577 63		226 87						53
54	775 00		556 45		218 55						54
55	1,326 00		1,119 14		206 86						55
56	669 15		522 61		146 54						56
57	460 00		360 00		100 00						57
58	215 00		154 37		60 63						58
59	728 67						728 67				59
60											60
61	435,471 07	468,381 20	328,502 99	345,357 42	106,239 41	122,553 68	728 67	470 10	141,022 24	108,112 11	61
62	32,910 13		16,854 43		16,314 27			258 57		32,910 13	62
63	468,381 20	468,381 20	345,357 42	345,357 42	122,553 68	122,553 68	728 67	728 67	141,022 24	141,022 24	63

ever, it will be necessary at the end of future periods, when this department will have a beginning inventory.

Once the beginning inventory figures have been recorded, the balances of all income statement accounts (401–599) are extended from the Adjusted Trial Balance section to the Total columns of the Income Statement section.

After the balances have been extended, each figure in the Total columns must be analyzed to determine the amounts to be allocated to the clothing department, the shoe department, and nondepartmental operations. The gross profit accounts (revenue and cost of goods sold) and the direct expenses can easily be analyzed by referring to the departmental analysis ledger sheets maintained for this purpose in the general ledger. The subdigit columns on each ledger sheet indicate the departmental breakdown of the total shown in the Trial Balance section of the worksheet. Of course, the trial balance figures must be updated to reflect any entries appearing in the Adjustments section of the worksheet that relate to departmentalized accounts. Then, it is necessary to extend the amounts of the gross profit items and the direct expenses for each department to the departmental columns of the Income Statement section and to extend the "other income" items, Interest Income and Miscellaneous Income, neither of which is departmentalized, to the Nondepartmental columns.

The next step in preparing the departmentalized worksheet is to allocate the indirect expense items and record these items in the proper columns of the Income Statement section.

Allocating Indirect Expense Items As explained earlier in this chapter, some expenses cannot be related directly to particular departments. Instead, they must be allocated according to some reasonable basis. The procedures for allocating indirect expenses will now be considered by using the figures from the Adjusted Trial Balance section of the January 31, 19X3, worksheet.

Insurance Expense Insurance premiums are allocated to separate departments in proportion to the value of the furniture, fixtures, and inventory that are directly involved in the unit's operations. In order to simplify the computations, the Style Clothing Store's accountant uses the ending inventory amount and the cost (before depreciation) of the furniture and fixtures. On January 31, 19X3, the clothing department had furniture and fixtures that cost $3,600 and inventory of $56,000—a total of $59,600. The shoe department had furniture and fixtures of $1,000 and inventory of $10,000—a total of $11,000. On the basis of the total assigned asset value of $70,600, the accountant allocates insurance expense of $3,090 for the year to each department as shown below.

ASSET ITEM	CLOTHING DEPARTMENT	SHOE DEPARTMENT	PER-CENT	TOTAL INSURANCE EXPENSE	ALLOCATED TO EACH DEPARTMENT
Merchandise Inventory	$56,000.00	$10,000.00			
Furniture and Fixtures	3,600.00	1,000.00			
Total Clothing	$59,600.00		84.4 ×	$3,090 =	$2,607.96
Total Shoes	11,000.00	$11,000.00	15.6 ×	$3,090 =	482.04
Combined Totals	$70,600.00		100.0		$3,090.00

When this allocation is completed, the departmental shares of the $3,090 debit balance now appearing in the Adjusted Trial Balance Debit and Total Debit columns are entered in the departmental Income Statement Debit columns: $2,607.96 for clothing, $482.04 for shoes.

Custodial Wages Expense The cost of the work of the custodian is closely related to the space occupied by each department. Therefore, the custodian's wages are allocated to the two operating departments according to their floor area. The data and computations are as follows.

DEPARTMENT	BASIS: SQ. FT.	PER-CENT	TOTAL CUSTODIAL WAGES EXPENSE		ALLOCATED TO EACH DEPARTMENT
Clothing	3,600	90	× $5,120	=	$4,608
Shoes	400	10	× $5,120	=	512
Totals	4,000	100			$5,120

The worksheet treatment is the same as for insurance expense. The amount apportioned to each department is shown in the departmental Debit columns of the Income Statement section: $4,608 for clothing, $512 for shoes.

Rent Expense Rent expense is also allocated to the two departments in proportion to the space occupied by each. Thus, 90 percent of the $6,000 in rent expense, or $5,400, is shown in the Income Statement Debit column for the clothing department, and 10 percent, or $600, is shown in the Income Statement Debit column for the shoe department.

Utilities Expense Again, space occupied is a logical basis to use for allocating the utilities expense. Thus, $5,349.65 (90 percent of $5,944.05) is assigned to the clothing department, and $594.40 (10 percent of $5,944.05) is assigned to the shoe department. Both items are recorded as debits in the departmental Income Statement columns.

Office Salaries Expense Office salaries expense is allocated according to the total sales made by each department. The data and computations are shown below.

DEPARTMENT	BASIS: TOTAL SALES	PER-CENT	TOTAL OFFICE SALARIES EXPENSE		ALLOCATED TO EACH DEPARTMENT
Clothing	$284,182.82	71.8	× $16,800	=	$12,062.40
Shoes	111,614.98	28.2	× $16,800	=	4,737.60
Totals	$395,797.80	100.0			$16,800.00

Payroll Tax Expense Payroll tax expense is allocated on the basis of the total salaries and wages (including allocated custodial wages and office salaries) assigned to each department. This procedure is illustrated on page 898.

SCHEDULE OF SALARIES AND WAGES

	TOTAL	CLOTHING DEPARTMENT	SHOE DEPARTMENT
Sales Salaries	$42,800.00	$24,800.00	$18,000.00
Custodial Wages (allocated)	5,120.00	4,608.00	512.00
Office Salaries (allocated)	16,800.00	12,062.40	4,737.60
Totals	$64,720.00	$41,470.40	$23,249.60

$$\text{Average Payroll Tax Rate} = \frac{\$5,678.40}{\$64,720.00} = 8.7738\%$$

ALLOCATION OF PAYROLL TAX EXPENSE

DEPARTMENT	TOTAL SALARIES AND WAGES		AVERAGE PAYROLL TAX RATE		ALLOCATED TO EACH DEPARTMENT
Clothing	$41,470.40	×	8.7738%	=	$3,638.53
Shoe	$23,249.60	×	8.7738%	=	2,039.87
Total					$5,678.40

The procedure used by the Style Clothing Store to allocate payroll tax expense results in an approximation because not all salaries and wages are fully subject to payroll taxes. If it is considered necessary to have more precise tax figures for each department, the accountant must analyze the earnings of each employee to determine the exact amount of payroll taxes on that employee's earnings. Then, by identifying the department to which the employee's earnings were charged, the precise amount of payroll tax expense applicable to each department can be determined.

Other Office Expenses At the Style Clothing Store, postage, stationery, and a variety of other small items for office use are debited to an account called Other Office Expenses. The proportion of total sales in each department is used as the basis for allocating the $804.50 balance of Other Office Expenses. Of this amount, 71.8 percent, or $577.63, is assigned to clothing and 28.2 percent, or $226.87 is assigned to shoes. Both amounts are, of course, recorded as debits in the departmental Income Statement columns.

Professional Services Expense Total sales are used as a basis for allocating the balance of Professional Services Expense, which amounts to $775. Of this figure, 71.8 percent, or $556.45, is assigned to the clothing department and 28.2 percent, or $218.55, is assigned to the shoe department. The amounts are recorded as debits in the departmental Income Statement columns.

Taxes and Licenses This item has not previously been departmentalized. The most significant tax for the Style Clothing Store is the property tax, which is levied on merchandise inventory and other assets. Allocation can therefore be reasonably based on the combined total value of the ending merchandise inventory and the furniture and fixtures in each of the operating departments. As you saw when insurance expense was allocated, 84.4 percent of the total asset value is in the clothing department and 15.6 percent is in the shoe department. Thus, the $1,326 balance of the Taxes and Licenses account is allocated as follows: $1,119.14 to the clothing department and $206.86 to the shoe department.

Loss From Uncollectible Accounts The loss from uncollectible accounts for the year is estimated at 0.3 percent of credit sales. An analysis of the sales journal shows that credit sales were $174,300 for the clothing department and $48,750 for the shoe department. The amount of the projected loss from uncollectible accounts that should be allocated to each department is therefore computed as follows.

DEPARTMENT	BASIS: CREDIT SALES	PERCENT		TOTAL LOSS FROM UNCOLLECTIBLE ACCOUNTS		ALLOCATED TO EACH DEPARTMENT
Clothing	$174,300.00	78.1	×	$669.15	=	$522.61
Shoes	48,750.00	21.9	×	$669.15	=	146.54
Totals	$223,050.00	100.0				$669.15

Depreciation Expense—Furniture and Fixtures The assets used to compute depreciation for furniture and fixtures are departmentalized, and the depreciation expense is departmentalized in the same way in making the worksheet entries. Accordingly, $360 is extended to the Income Statement Debit column for the clothing department, and $100 is extended to the Income Statement Debit column for the shoe department.

Depreciation Expense—Office Equipment Depreciation on the office equipment is allocated according to each department's total sales—the basis already used for allocating office salaries and other office expenses. The amount of depreciation on the office equipment is $215, of which 71.8 percent, or $154.37, is extended to the Income Statement Debit column for the clothing department, and 28.2 percent, or $60.63, is extended to the Income Statement Debit column for the shoe department.

Nondepartmentalized Expense—Interest Interest Expense is not departmentalized. The amount shown in the Adjusted Trial Balance section, a debit of $728.67, is extended to the Debit column of the section headed Income Statement—Nondepartmental.

Completing the Income Statement Columns

The beginning and ending merchandise inventories and the sales, purchases, and operating expenses have now been departmentalized on the worksheet. Other revenue and expense (nonoperating) items have been extended to the Nondepartmental Income Statement columns.

Total Net Income or Loss After all revenue and expense items have been extended and analyzed, the Total columns in the Income Statement section of the worksheet are added in the usual way to determine the firm's net income or loss for the year.

Departmental Net Income or Loss In order to determine each department's net income or loss, the columns for the operating departments are now totaled.

Clothing Department The debits in the Income Statement—Clothing Department section total $328,502.99. The credits total $345,357.42. Since the credits exceed the debits, the difference of $16,854.43 represents a net income for the clothing department.

Shoe Department In the same manner, the debits are totaled for the shoe department, giving $106,239.41, and the credits are totaled, giving $122,533.68. Again, since the credits exceed the debits, the difference of $16,314.27 represents a net income for the shoe department.

Nondepartmental Net Income or Loss The total of the nondepartmental revenue as shown in the Credit column is $470.10. The nondepartmental expense, shown in the Debit column, totals $728.67. This net excess of expense over revenue ($258.57) is entered in the Credit column so that the two columns will balance.

The sum of the net income or loss figures in the three analysis sections must equal the net income figure listed in the Total Debit column, as shown below.

NET INCOME OR LOSS

Clothing Department	$16,854.43
Shoe Department	16,314.27
Nondepartmental	(258.57)
Total	$32,910.13

Completing the Balance Sheet Columns

The balance sheet accounts are extended to the Balance Sheet columns in the usual way, and the net income of $32,910.13 is entered in the Credit column in order to balance the column totals.

PREPARING THE INCOME STATEMENT

The financial statements are prepared from the information assembled on the worksheet. The departmentalized income statement is prepared from figures in the Income Statement section of the worksheet. This income statement contains separate columns for the figures pertaining to each department and a total column for the combined results. The departmental breakdown on the worksheet enables the accountant to show on the income statement the net income from operations for each department. The other revenue and expense items in the Nondepartmental columns of the worksheet are presented below the Net Income From Operations figures to arrive at the net income for the business as a whole. The completed income statement is shown on page 902.

| Net Income Analysis | The departmentalized income statement is sometimes called a *net income analysis* because a final net income is computed for each department, just as it is for the business as a whole.

There are two principal objections to using the net income analysis to decide whether a particular department should be retained or eliminated. One objection is the difficulty of determining the department's fair share of indirect or general expense items. The second objection is more important: if the particular department were eliminated, the indirect expenses allocated to it would not be eliminated. They would have to be absorbed by the remaining departments. Actually, in making managerial decisions, more attention should be paid to contribution margin figures and less to net income by departments. |

Contribution Margin

Contribution margin is the difference between a department's gross profit on sales and its direct expenses. It is the amount that the department has earned or produced above its own direct costs. This amount is available to help meet the indirect or general expenses of running the business and to provide a net income from operations. A department that more than meets its direct expenses (or has a positive contribution margin) is contributing something toward increasing the net income of the business (or decreasing its net loss). As already noted, if the department were eliminated, other departments would have to absorb all the indirect expenses without the help provided by the positive contribution margin of the department. On the other hand, if the direct expenses of a department exceed its gross profit on sales, the unit is reducing the net income of the business as a whole (or increasing its net loss). The business would then be more profitable if the department with the negative contribution margin were eliminated.

As can readily be seen, the concept of the contribution margin is important to business owners and managers because it provides them with valuable assistance in making decisions. Unfortunately, contribution margin figures are not provided in many traditional accounting reports.

Statement of Partners' Equities

The figures for the statement of partners' equities are, as usual, contained in the Balance Sheet section of the worksheet. The statement of partners' equities in a departmentalized firm is exactly like the one for a nondepartmentalized business illustrated in earlier chapters.

Balance Sheet

The balance sheet of a departmentalized firm is prepared from the Balance Sheet section of the worksheet in exactly the same manner as was shown in previous chapters.

ADJUSTING AND CLOSING PROCEDURES

After the worksheet and the financial statements have been completed, the accountant journalizes and posts the adjusting entries and then closes the financial records for the period, using the standard procedures.

Journalizing the Adjusting Entries

The adjusting entries are again journalized directly from the Adjustments columns of the worksheet. The procedure is exactly the same as the one you have

STYLE CLOTHING STORE
Income Statement
Year Ended January 31, 19X3

	Clothing	Shoes	Total
Operating Revenues			
Sales	$284,182.82	$111,614.98	$395,797.80
Less Sales Returns and Allowances	4,582.50	1,458.75	6,041.25
Net Sales	$279,600.32	$110,156.23	$389,756.55
Cost of Goods Sold			
Merchandise Inventory, Feb. 1, 19X2	$ 65,000.00	$ -0-	$ 65,000.00
Purchases	$183.175.00	$ 72,175.00	$255.350.00
Freight In	2,735.00	855.00	3,590.00
Delivered Cost of Purchases	$185,910.00	$ 73,030.00	$258,940.00
Less: Purchases Returns and Allowances	$ 825.00	$ 240.00	$ 1,065.00
Purchases Discount	4,349.60	698.70	5,048.30
Total Deductions	$ 5,174.60	938.70	$ 6,113.30
Net Delivered Cost of Purchases	$180,735.40	$ 72,091.30	$252,826.70
Total Merchandise Available for Sale	$245,735.40	$ 72,091.30	$317,826.70
Less Merchandise Inventory, Jan. 31, 19X3	56,000.00	10,000.00	66,000.00
Cost of Goods Sold	$189,735.40	$ 62,091.30	$251,826.70
Gross Profit on Sales	$ 89,864.92	$ 48,064.93	$137,929.85
Operating Expenses			
Direct Expenses			
Sales Salaries Expense	$ 24,800.00	$ 18,000.00	$ 42,800.00
Advertising Expense	5,235.00	1,658.30	6,893.30
Store Supplies Expense	3,133.75	1,120.00	4,253.75
Cash Short or Over	45.00	27.00	72.00
Delivery Expense	2,840.00	1,020.00	3,860.00
Total Direct Expenses	$ 36,053.75	$ 21,825.30	$ 57,879.05
Contribution Margin	$ 53,811.17	$ 26,239.63	$ 80,050.80
Indirect Expenses			
Insurance Expense	$ 2,607.96	$ 482.04	$ 3,090.00
Custodial Wages Expense	4,608.00	512.00	5,120.00
Rent Expense	5,400.00	600.00	6,000.00
Utilities Expense	5,349.65	594.40	5,944.05
Office Salaries Expense	12,062.40	4,737.60	16,800.00
Payroll Tax Expense	3,638.53	2,039.87	5,678.40
Other Office Expenses	577.63	226.87	804.50
Professional Services Expense	556.45	218.55	775.00
Taxes and Licenses	1,119.14	206.86	1,326.00
Loss From Uncollectible Accounts	522.61	146.54	669.15
Depreciation Expense—Furniture and Fixtures	360.00	100.00	460.00
Depreciation Expense—Office Equipment	154.37	60.63	215.00
Total Indirect Expenses	$ 36,956.74	$ 9,925.36	$ 46,882.10
Net Income From Operations	$ 16,854.43	$ 16,314.27	$ 33,168.70
Other Income			
Interest Income			$ 235.00
Miscellaneous Income			235.10
Total Other Income			$ 470.10
Other Expense			
Interest Expense			728.67
Net Nonoperating Expense			$ 258.57
Net Income for Year			$ 32,910.13
Distribution of Net Income			
Linda Hanson ⅓			$ 10,970.04
Steven Casey ⅓			10,970.04
Janet Miller ⅓			10,970.05
Total			$ 32,910.13

already learned, except that when an adjustment affects a departmentalized account, complete details are shown in the Explanation column of the journal.

19 X3		(Adjustment h)			
Jan. 31	Store Supplies Expense		523	4,253 75	
		Store Supplies	129		4,253 75
	To transfer cost of supplies used				
	to expense account as follows:				
	Clothing Dept.	$3,133.75			
	Shoe Dept.	1,120.00			
		$4,253.75			

The remaining adjusting entries are identical to those you studied previously.

Posting the Adjusting Entries

Next, the adjusting entries must be posted from the general journal to the general ledger accounts. As you saw on page 892, when departmentalized adjustments are posted to the analysis accounts, both the separate departmental adjustment amounts and the total adjustment amounts are entered.

Journalizing the Closing Entries

The closing entries are exactly the same as those you learned about in earlier chapters. The data for the entries closing the revenue and expense accounts is taken from the Total columns of the Income Statement section of the worksheet. The Income Summary account is credited for the total of the Total Credit column, $468,381.20, and the individual revenue accounts are debited for the amounts shown in the Total Credit column. Similarly, the Income Summary account is debited for the total of the Total Debit column, $435,471.07, and the individual expense accounts are credited for the amounts shown in the same column. The Income Summary account and the drawing accounts are closed in the usual way.

Posting the Closing Entries

After the closing entries have been journalized, they are posted to the general ledger accounts in the normal manner. However, the departmental items are first entered in *total* in the regular Debit or Credit columns, and then in the analysis columns. The following account illustrates the posting technique.

Store Supplies Expense   No. 523

CLOTHING DR. 523.1	SHOES DR. 523.2	DATE	EXPLANATION	POST. REF.	DEBIT	CREDIT	BALANCE	DR. CR.
3,133 75	1,120 00	19 X3 Jan. 31	Adjusting	J1	4,253 75		4,253 75	Dr.
3,133 75	1,120 00	31	Closing	J1		4,253 75	–0–	

PRINCIPLES AND PROCEDURES SUMMARY

When a business becomes departmentalized, separate accounts for sales, inventory, and other elements of the cost of goods sold are established because separate information is needed for each department. This may be done by setting up departmental accounts in the ledger or by using analysis ledger account sheets having separate columns for each department. The sales journal, voucher register, and other records of original entry must also be arranged to gather transaction data by departments.

In addition, separate accounts or departmental analysis ledger sheets may be set up for those expenses that can be assigned directly to a specific department. Other expenses must be allocated to the departments on some predetermined basis at the end of the accounting period. Expenses that are allocated on a logical basis closely related to use are sometimes referred to as semidirect expenses. Those expenses that must be allocated on an arbitrary basis are called indirect expenses. Most accountants consider both types to be indirect expenses.

On the departmentalized worksheet, the beginning trial balance, the adjustments, and the adjusted trial balance are entered in the usual way, and items are extended to the Total columns of the Income Statement section and to the Balance Sheet section. Data must also be extended to the departmental Income Statement columns.

Analysis ledger accounts provide the amounts for some items to be entered in the departmental Income Statement columns. Accounts that are not analyzed in the ledger must be analyzed in the course of completing the worksheet so that the appropriate departmental amounts can be applied to each income statement item.

When all items in the Adjusted Trial Balance columns have been extended to the proper statement section, the net income or net loss for the business as a whole is determined in the Total columns of the Income Statement section. Then the departmental Income Statement columns are totaled, and the net income or net loss of each department is determined. Finally, the total net income or net loss for the business is extended to the Balance Sheet section. At this point, the total debits must equal the total credits in the Balance Sheet columns.

Next, financial statements are prepared from the information contained in the worksheet. A departmentalized income statement, a statement of partners' equities, and a balance sheet were prepared for the Style Clothing Store. The income statement shows the contribution margin of each department as well as a final net income figure after allocation of all expenses.

MANAGERIAL IMPLICATIONS

It is essential for managers to know not only the total gross profit of a business but also the gross profit for each department. Departmentalized data shows managers which departments are most profitable and which are losing money or have low profit margins. Once alerted, managers can take proper steps to improve the profit picture. Department heads can then be told specifically what revenue or expense items should receive special attention.

Managers are keenly interested in the operations of each department. Departments that are less profitable may undergo policy changes or may be closed, and profitable departments may be expanded. The data shown on the departmentalized income statement helps managers to evaluate and control the operations of each unit. Similarly, managers are very much interested in prompt preparation of the balance sheet, which shows the financial condition of the business. Current statements and supporting schedules provide up-to-date information that managers need to run a company.

The contribution margin is very important in making managerial decisions. This figure is the amount by which the gross profit of a department exceeds its direct expenses and contributes toward the indirect expenses and net income from operations. Decisions to retain, eliminate, expand, or contract a segment of the business are properly based on the contribution margin analysis of the department or product involved.

Net income analysis has many shortcomings and should only be used with the greatest care in making decisions. The net income figure for a department is, at best, an estimate. Furthermore, managers must consider that many of the indirect expenses would not be eliminated by the decision to curtail or discontinue the operations of a department.

REVIEW QUESTIONS

1. How does managerial accounting differ from financial accounting?
2. Why does managerial accounting focus on the future?
3. What is a profit center? What is a cost center?
4. How could a segment of a business that does not sell products or services be considered a profit center?
5. In a retail store, what would be the logical profit centers?
6. What is responsibility accounting?
7. Why would a company prefer to use an analysis ledger sheet for recording sales, rather than use separate accounts for the sales of each department?
8. Why would a retail store such as a clothing store departmentalize its records?
9. Explain two ways by which sales returns and allowances might be journalized in a departmentalized business.
10. What are direct expenses?
11. How does the recording process for most direct expenses differ from that for indirect expenses?
12. Why are indirect expenses allocated to departments?
13. Why is interest expense not allocated to departments?
14. What is contribution margin?
15. How does a departmentalized income statement differ from one that is not departmentalized?
16. What is a logical basis for allocating property insurance expense to departments?

17. The Style Clothing Store, which was discussed in this chapter, allocates payroll tax expense on the basis of the total payroll for each department. What is the weakness of this method? What is its advantage?

MANAGERIAL DISCUSSION QUESTIONS

1. How can managers use departmentalized gross profit data to improve a firm's profit picture?
2. Of what value in managerial control is the identification of purchases returns and allowances by department?
3. If one department consistently has a comparatively large amount of cash short in its operations, what management action might be appropriate?
4. Why can't all operating expenses be charged directly to sales departments in order to achieve better managerial control?
5. Why is contribution margin analysis a better tool than net income analysis for managers to use when deciding whether to retain, expand, or contract operations?
6. How does a firm's accountant determine the reasonable basis to be used in allocating a specific indirect expense? Should management be concerned about the basis used?
7. The management of a store with three sales departments plans to install a bonus system for department managers. Do you think the bonus system should be based on each department's contribution margin or on the department's net income after allocating all administrative expenses? Explain.

EXERCISES

EXERCISE 37-1 **Recording the adjustment for store supplies used.** On December 31, 19X5, the Store Supplies account at the Lewis Home Center had a balance of $16,384. An inventory at that date showed supplies of $1,094 actually on hand. The firm's records indicate the following usage of store supplies by its three departments during the year: furniture department, $3,600; rug department, $5,990; and appliance department, $5,700. Give the general journal entry to record the adjustment for supplies used. The business has an analysis ledger sheet for Store Supplies Expense, which contains a column for each department as well as a Balance column. In the Explanation column of the journal, show the amount applicable to each department.

EXERCISE 37-2 **Closing a departmentalized expense account.** Using the information from Exercise 37-1, prepare a general journal entry to close the Store Supplies Expense account. In the explanation for the journal entry, show the amount applicable to each department.

EXERCISE 37-3 **Allocating insurance expense.** Selected financial data for E–Z Fashions, a retail store, on December 31, 19X6, is given on page 907. The firm's insurance expense for the year totaled $4,500 and is to be allocated on the basis of the book value of the inventory and equipment in each department. Compute the amount to be allocated to each department.

Credit Sales
   Women's Clothing, $320,000
   Men's Clothing, $484,000
Total Sales
   Women's Clothing, $400,000
   Men's Clothing, $600,000
Sales Returns and Allowances
   Women's Clothing
      Credit Sales, $3,200
      Cash Sales, $600
   Men's Clothing
      Credit Sales, $1,800
      Cash Sales, $340
Floor Space Occupied
   Women's Clothing, 6,400 sq ft
   Men's Clothing, 3,600 sq ft
Book Value of Inventory and Equipment
   Women's Clothing, $120,000
   Men's Clothing, $60,000

EXERCISE 37-4   **Allocating custodial expense.** The total custodial expense for the year at E–Z Fashions was $9,200. Compute the amount to be allocated to each department, using floor space occupied as the basis for the allocation. Obtain any necessary data from Exercise 37-3.

EXERCISE 37-5   **Allocating office expense.** The total office expense for the year at E–Z Fashions was $61,000. Compute the amount to be allocated to each department, using total sales as the basis for the allocation. Obtain any necessary data from Exercise 37-3.

EXERCISE 37-6   **Allocating the estimated loss from uncollectible accounts.** The loss from uncollectible accounts at E–Z Fashions is estimated to be ½ of 1 percent of net credit sales. Compute the amount to be allocated to each department. Obtain any necessary data from Exercise 37-3.

EXERCISE 37-7   **Allocating rent expense.** Rent expense for the year at E–Z Fashions is $24,000. Compute the amount to be allocated to each department, using floor space occupied as the basis for the allocation. Obtain any necessary data from Exercise 37-3.

EXERCISE 37-8   **Analyzing a departmentalized income statement.** Data from the departmentalized income statement of the Thorp Company for the year ended December 31, 19X4, is given on page 908. Assuming that a department's direct expenses can be eliminated if it is closed, what factors should management consider when deciding whether to close Department 1?

	DEPT. 1	DEPT. 2	TOTAL
Net Sales	$400,000	$600,000	$1,000,000
Cost of Goods Sold	250,000	350,000	600,000
Gross Profit on Sales	$150,000	$250,000	$ 400,000
Direct Expenses	120,000	190,000	310,000
Contribution Margin	$ 30,000	$ 60,000	$ 90,000
Indirect Expenses	50,000	20,000	70,000
Net Income (or Loss)	$(20,000)	$ 40,000	$ 20,000

EXERCISE 37-9 **Making a decision based on a departmentalized income statement.** Using the data given in Exercise 37-8, would you recommend closing Department 1? Why or why not?

PROBLEMS

PROBLEM 37-1 **Journalizing and posting departmental transactions.** The Midtown Book and Software Center is a retail store that specializes in business and technical books, microcomputer software, and microcomputer supplies such as blank disks and ribbons for printers. The firm has been organized into three departments—books (.1), supplies (.2), and software (.3)—as an aid in controlling operations and increasing profitability. Most sales are for cash, but a few customers are extended credit on terms of net due within 30 days of billing. Selected transactions for June 19X1 are given on pages 909 and 910. (The transactions have been minimized to conserve time and reduce repetition.)

Instructions 1. The following accounts are to be opened in the general ledger. Use analysis-type ledger forms for accounts whose titles are followed by the letter A in parentheses.

101	Cash	501	Merchandise Purchases (A)
111	Accounts Receivable	506	Freight In (A)
202	Accounts Payable	511	Purchases Ret. and Allow. (A)
221	FICA Tax Payable	527	Sales Salaries Expense (A)
222	Employee Income Tax Payable	528	Advertising Expense (A)
231	Sales Tax Payable	529	Cash Short or Over (A)
401	Sales (A)	541	Rent Expense
402	Sales Ret. and Allow. (A)	542	Utilities Expense

2. Analyze and record each of the transactions listed.
   a. Enter all credit sales in a sales journal with columns for Accounts Receivable (✓, Debit), Sales Tax Payable Credit, Sales—Books Credit, Sales—Supplies Credit, and Sales—Software Credit.
   b. Enter all cash sales and collections in a cash receipts journal with columns for Accounts Receivable (✓, Credit), Sales Tax Payable Credit, Sales (Books Credit, Supplies Credit, and Software Credit), Cash Short or Over (Dept., Debit), and Cash Debit.

c. Enter all approved vouchers in a voucher register with the same column heads as shown in the illustration on pages 262–263. Purchases returns and allowances that take place within the month of the original voucher should be recorded by circled entries just above the original voucher amount in the Accounts Payable and Merchandise Purchases columns, as illustrated in Chapter 11.

d. Enter other transactions, including sales returns and allowances, in the general journal.

3. Make any daily postings as required.

4. Foot and prove the money columns of the sales journal, cash receipts journal, and voucher register. Then enter the totals, and rule these records. Analyze the totals by department wherever necessary.

5. Make all summary postings as required.

TRANSACTIONS FOR JUNE 19X1

June 1 Prepared Voucher 6-01 for $600 owed to the Hill Real Estate Company for rent on the store for June.

2 Prepared Voucher 6-02 for $1,234.50 owed to Business Programs Inc. for software.

3 Summary of cash sales for June 1–3: Books, $890 plus 5 percent sales tax. No cash short or over. Supplies, $329 plus 5 percent sales tax. No cash short or over. Software, $441.50 plus 5 percent sales tax. Cash short, $1.

5 Sale to Susan Becker on credit: books, $21 plus 5 percent sales tax; software, $85.88 plus 5 percent sales tax (Sales Slip 601).

6 Gave Susan Becker a credit for the return of a book she purchased on June 5 for $7.95 plus sales tax of 5 percent.

9 Prepared Voucher 6-03 for $100 owed to the Daily News for advertising, chargeable as follows: books, $16; software, $84.

10 Summary of cash sales for week: Books, $920 plus 5 percent sales tax. Cash overage, $2. Supplies, $308 plus 5 percent sales tax. Cash shortage, $0.80. Software, $755 plus 5 percent sales tax. Cash shortage, $1.40.

13 Prepared Voucher 6-04 for $933.40 owed to the Apex Systems Company for software.

15 Returned software costing $39 to the Apex Systems Company. The purchase was recorded on Voucher 6-04.

17 Summary of cash sales for week: Books, $940 plus 5 percent sales tax. Cash shortage, $0.45. Supplies, $368 plus 5 percent sales tax. Cash shortage, $0.80. Software, $760 plus 5 percent sales tax. No cash short or over.

20 Sale to Patrick Foley on credit: software, $121.50 plus 5 percent sales tax (Sales Slip 602).

21 Prepared Voucher 6-05 for $308 owed to Martin Distributors for books.

21 Prepared Voucher 6-06 for $21 owed to the United Trucking Company for freight on books purchased from Martin Distributors.

24 Summary of cash sales for week: Books, $850 plus 5 percent sales tax. No cash short or over. Supplies, $448 plus 5 percent sales tax. Cash shortage, $1. Software, $664 plus 5 percent sales tax. Cash shortage, $1.50.

26 Prepared Voucher 6-07 for $65 owed to the Sanders Company for book purchases.

30 Prepared Voucher 6-08 for $1,010 owed to John Petrocelli, sales-clerk, for his salary, as follows: gross earnings (book department), $1,200; FICA, $84; income tax withheld, $106.

30 Prepared Voucher 6-09 for $957 to Donna Cole, salesclerk, for her salary as follows: gross earnings, $1,100 (supplies department, $750; software department, $350); FICA, $77; income tax withheld, $66.

30 Prepared Voucher 6-10 for $145 owed to City Utilities for utility bill.

30 Summary of cash sales for June 26 through June 30: Books, $885 plus 5 percent sales tax. No cash short or over. Supplies, $310 plus 5 percent sales tax. Cash shortage, $0.50. Software, $775 plus 5 percent sales tax. Cash shortage, $0.30.

30 Received a check from Susan Becker for $103.87 as payment on account.

PROBLEM 37-2   **Preparing a departmentalized worksheet.** The Glendale Shoe Emporium, a retail store, has two sales departments—one for dress shoes and the other for casual shoes. The store's trial balance for December 31, 19X1, is shown on page 911. Note that it contains departmentalized balances for revenue items and direct expense items. Data for adjustments is given below and on page 912.

Instructions   1. Enter the trial balance on a departmentalized worksheet with 16 columns.
2. Complete the worksheet. Allocate the indirect expenses as described on page 912. On an attached sheet, show all computations for the allocated amounts. (Save the completed worksheet for use in Problem 37-3.)

DATA FOR ADJUSTMENTS

a. Loss from uncollectible accounts, ½ of 1 percent of net sales.
b. Insurance expired during the year, $3,000.
c. Store supplies used:
   Department A: $3,832
   Department B: __1,606__
   Total $5,438

d. Depreciation of furniture and fixtures:
   Department A: 10 percent of $11,200 = $1,120
   Department B: 10 percent of $4,300 = __430__
   Total $1,550

e. Depreciation of office equipment:
   10 percent of $3,200 = $320
f. Custodial wages payable, $200.

GLENDALE SHOE EMPORIUM
Trial Balance
December 31, 19X1

101	Cash	$ 10,000	
106	Accounts Receivable	28,800	
107	Allowance for Uncollectible Accounts		$ 60
121	Merchandise Inventory, Jan. 1		
	Dept. A	$ 50,000	
	Dept. B	10,000	60,000
126	Prepaid Insurance	3,800	
129	Store Supplies	5,700	
131	Furniture and Fixtures	15,500	
132	Accumulated Depr.—Furniture and Fixtures		2,600
141	Office Equipment	3,200	
142	Accumulated Depr.—Office Equipment		1,900
201	Notes Payable		3,000
202	Accounts Payable		16,200
211	Salaries and Wages Payable		
212	Payroll Taxes Payable		212
221	Interest Payable		
301	Ellen Lord, Capital		42,234
302	Ellen Lord, Drawing	9,000	
401	Sales		
	Dept. A	$240,000	
	Dept. B	274,618	514,618
402	Sales Returns and Allowances		
	Dept. A	$ 400	
	Dept. B	200	600
491	Interest Income		96
501	Merchandise Purchases		
	Dept. A	$161,420	
	Dept. B	163,000	324,420
506	Freight In		
	Dept. A	$ 12,450	
	Dept. B	3,650	16,100
511	Purchases Returns and Allowances		
	Dept. A	-0-	
	Dept. B	$ 1,500	1,500
521	Sales Salaries Expense		
	Dept. A	$ 24,000	
	Dept. B	25,600	49,600
522	Advertising Expense		
	Dept. A	$ 10,000	
	Dept. B	8,000	18,000
523	Store Supplies Expense		
	Dept. A	-0-	
	Dept. B	-0-	-0-
529	Cash Short or Over		
	Dept. A	$ 40	
	Dept. B	80	120
536	Insurance Expense	-0-	
541	Custodial Wages Expense	6,300	
542	Rent Expense	7,500	
543	Utilities Expense	3,600	
551	Office Salaries Expense	11,800	
552	Payroll Tax Expense	6,770	
553	Other Office Expenses	1,400	
561	Loss From Uncollectible Accounts	-0-	
562	Depr. Expense—Furniture and Fixtures	-0-	
563	Depr. Expense—Office Equipment	-0-	
591	Interest Expense	210	

g. Payroll taxes payable:
10 percent of $200 custodial wages payable = $20.
h. Interest due on notes payable, $30.
i. Ending merchandise inventory, December 31, 19X1.

Department A:	$48,000
Department B:	10,500
Total	$58,500

The bases for allocating indirect expenses are given below. (**Note:** Because allocations are not precise, round each allocated amount to the nearest whole dollar.)

1. Insurance Expense—in proportion to the total of the furniture and fixtures (the gross assets before depreciation) and the ending inventory in the departments. These totals are as follows.

Department A:	$59,200
Department B:	14,800
Total	$74,000

2. Rent Expense, Custodial Wages Expense, and Utilities Expense—on the basis of floor space occupied, as follows.

Department A:	3,000 sq ft
Department B:	1,000 sq ft
Total	4,000 sq ft

3. Office Salaries Expense, Other Office Expenses, and Depreciation Expense for Office Equipment—on the basis of the gross sales in each department.
4. Loss From Uncollectible Accounts—½ of 1 percent of net sales, as computed in Adjustment a.
5. Payroll Tax Expense—on the basis of the total salaries and wages (including allocated salaries and wages) of each department.
6. Depreciation Expense for Furniture and Fixtures—as computed in Adjustment d.

PROBLEM 37-3 **Preparing a departmentalized income statement.** This problem is a continuation of Problem 37-2.

Instructions Prepare a departmentalized income statement for the Glendale Shoe Emporium for the year ended December 31, 19X1. Use the departmentalized worksheet that you completed in Problem 37-2.

PROBLEM 37-4 **Adjusting and closing departmental accounts.** The Discount Photographic Center has two departments: Cameras (.1) and Film (.2). Selected account balances and adjustment data appear on page 913.

Instructions 1. Open general ledger accounts for the four items listed. Use departmental analysis accounts for the expenses. Enter the balances as of December 31, writing "Balance" in the Explanation column and placing a check mark in the Posting Reference column.

2. In general journal form, record the necessary adjusting entries.
3. Post the adjusting entries to the accounts.
4. In general journal form, record one entry to close the two expense accounts.
5. Post the closing entry to the expense accounts.

SELECTED ACCOUNT BALANCES AS OF DECEMBER 31, 19X1

ACCT. NO	ACCOUNT NAME	BALANCE
129	Store Supplies	$ 8,000
211	Salaries and Wages Payable	-0-
521	Sales Salaries Expense	$39,300
	Cameras $25,700	
	Film 13,600	
523	Store Supplies Expense	-0-
	Cameras -0-	
	Film -0-	

ADJUSTMENT DATA FOR DECEMBER 31, 19X1

(a) Store supplies used: $7,320
     Cameras $3,900
     Film   3,420
(b) Accrued sales salaries payable: $950
     Cameras $600
     Film   350

ALTERNATE PROBLEMS

PROBLEM 37-1A   **Journalizing and posting departmental transactions.** The Learning Tree is a retail store that sells children's books, educational software, and school supplies. It is organized into three departments—books (.1), supplies (.2), and software (.3). Most sales are for cash, but a few customers are extended credit on terms of net due within 30 days of billing. Selected transactions for May 19X1 are given below and on page 914. (The transactions have been minimized to conserve time and reduce repetition.)

Instructions   Refer to the instructions given for Problem 37-1. Carry out these instructions for The Learning Tree for the month of May 19X1.

TRANSACTIONS FOR MAY 19X1

May   1 Prepared Voucher 5-01 for $750 owed to the Ward Real Estate Company for rent on the store for May.
       2 Prepared Voucher 5-02 for $820 owed to Selby Publishers for books.
       2 Prepared Voucher 5-03 for $384 owed to Educational Programs, Inc. for software.
       2 Sale to Paul Goldman on credit: books, $16 plus sales tax of 5 percent; software, $52 plus sales tax of 5 percent (Sales Slip 208).
       2 Prepared Voucher 5-04 for $26 owed to Allied Transport Company for freight on books purchased from Selby Publishers.

3 Gave Paul Goldman credit for $24 plus sales tax of 5 percent on software returned on the sale of May 2 (Sales Slip 208).

4 Prepared Voucher 5-05 for $422 owed to the Durable Notebook Company for a purchase of school supplies.

6 Summary of cash sales for week ended May 6: Books, $820.80 plus sales tax of 5 percent. No cash short or over. Supplies, $412.50 plus sales tax of 5 percent. Cash shortage, $1.85. Software, $620 plus sales tax of 5 percent. Cash shortage, $1.

10 Prepared Voucher 5-06 for $185 owed to City Utilities for utility bill.

11 Sale to Claire Chase on credit: supplies, $5.50 plus 5 percent sales tax; software, $63.10 plus 5 percent sales tax (Sales Slip 209).

13 Prepared Voucher 5-07 for $910 owed to the Ryan Publishing Company for books.

13 Summary of cash sales for week: Books, $825.30 plus 5 percent sales tax. Cash shortage, $2. Supplies, $620 plus 5 percent sales tax. Cash overage, $0.95. Software, $580 plus 5 percent sales tax. Cash shortage, $0.65.

15 Returned books and received credit of $64 from the Ryan Publishing Company. The purchase was recorded on Voucher 5-07.

20 Summary of cash sales for week: Books, $910 plus sales tax of 5 percent. No cash short or over. Supplies, $618 plus sales tax of 5 percent. Cash shortage, $0.30. Software, $509 plus sales tax of 5 percent. Cash overage, $1.25.

24 Prepared Voucher 5-08 for $125 owed to the Daily Clarion for advertising. The departmental breakdown is as follows: book department, $35; supplies department, $10; and software department, $80.

27 Summary of cash sales for week: Books, $980 plus 5 percent sales tax. No cash short or over. Supplies, $678.30 plus 5 percent sales tax. No cash short or over. Software, $620 plus 5 percent sales tax. Cash shortage, $0.90.

27 Received a check for $46.20 from Paul Goldman in payment of his account.

31 Prepared Voucher 5-09 for $937 owed to Carol Miller, salesclerk, for her salary, as follows: gross earnings (book department), $1,100, less FICA, $77; less income tax withheld, $86.

31 Prepared Voucher 5-10 for $866 owed to George McCann, salesclerk, for his salary as follows: gross earnings (supplies department), $350, and (software department), $650; less FICA, $70; less income tax withheld, $64.

31 Summary of cash sales for May 29 through 31: Books, $285 plus 5 percent sales tax. No cash short or over. Supplies, $106 plus 5 percent sales tax. Cash shortage, $1.20. Software, $455 plus 5 percent sales tax. Cash overage, $1.

PROBLEM 37-2A **Preparing a departmentalized worksheet.** In this problem use the trial balance of the Glendale Shoe Emporium as of December 31, 19X1, which is shown on page 911. Adjustment data is given on page 915.

Instructions

1. Enter the trial balance in the first two columns of a 16-column departmentalized worksheet.

2. Complete the worksheet. Allocate the indirect expenses as described below. On an attached sheet, show all computations for the allocated amounts. (Save the completed worksheet for use in Problem 37-3A.)

DATA FOR ADJUSTMENTS

a. Loss from uncollectible accounts, $4/10$ of 1 percent of gross sales.
b. Insurance expired during the year, $2,500.
c. Store supplies used:

Department A:	$3,800
Department B:	1,650
Total	$5,450

d. Depreciation of furniture and fixtures:

Department A:	12 percent of $11,200 =	$1,344
Department B:	12 percent of $4,300 =	516
Total		$1,860

e. Depreciation of office equipment:
   12 percent of $3,200 = $384
f. Custodial wages payable, $100.
g. Payroll taxes of $10 payable (10 percent of custodial wages payable).
h. Interest of $45 due on notes payable.
i. Ending merchandise inventory, December 31, 19X1:

Department A:	$48,800
Department B:	10,700
Total	$59,500

The bases for allocating indirect expenses are given below. (**Note:** Because allocations are not precise, round each allocated amount to the nearest whole dollar.)

1. Insurance Expense—in proportion to the total of the furniture and fixtures (the gross assets before depreciation) and the ending inventory in the departments. These totals are as follows.

Department A:	$60,000
Department B:	15,000
Total	$75,000

2. Rent Expense, Custodial Wages Expense, and Utilities Expense—on the basis of floor space occupied, as follows.

Department A:	2,000 sq ft
Department B:	2,000 sq ft
Total	4,000 sq ft

3. Office Salaries Expense, Other Office Expenses, and Depreciation Expense for Office Equipment—on the basis of the gross sales in each department.

4. Loss From Uncollectible Accounts—$\frac{4}{10}$ of 1 percent of gross sales, as computed in Adjustment a.
5. Payroll Tax Expense—on the basis of the total salaries and wages of each department, including allocated salaries and wages.
6. Depreciation Expense for Furniture and Fixtures—as computed in Adjustment d.

PROBLEM 37-3A

Preparing a departmentalized income statement. This problem is a continuation of Problem 37-2A.

Instructions

Prepare a departmentalized income statement for the Glendale Shoe Emporium for the year ended December 31, 19X1. Use the departmentalized worksheet that you completed in Problem 37-2A.

PROBLEM 37-4A

Adjusting and closing departmental accounts. The Focus Camera Shop has two departments: Cameras (.1) and Film (.2). Selected account balances and adjustment data appear below.

Instructions

1. Open general ledger accounts for the four items listed. Use departmental analysis accounts for the expenses. Enter the balances as of December 31, writing "Balance" in the Explanation column and placing a check mark in the Posting Reference column.
2. In general journal form, record the necessary adjusting entries.
3. Post the adjusting entries to the accounts.
4. In general journal form, record one entry to close the two expense accounts.
5. Post the closing entry to the expense accounts.

SELECTED ACCOUNT BALANCES AS OF DECEMBER 31, 19X1

ACCT. NO.	ACCOUNT NAME	BALANCE
129	Store Supplies	$ 7,900
211	Salaries and Wages Payable	-0-
521	Sales Salaries Expense	40,000
	Cameras $22,000	
	Film 18,000	
523	Store Supplies Expense	-0-
	Cameras -0-	
	Film -0-	

ADJUSTMENT DATA FOR DECEMBER 31, 19X1

(a) Store supplies used: $6,980
    Cameras $4,450
    Film   2,530
(b) Accrued sales salaries payable: $1,200
    Cameras $900
    Film   300

Firms that seek to grow must exerci[se]
their sales. Old customers must be ret[ained]
more purchases through attractive price[s]
service. At the same time, new customers
ness's enlarged capacity and to keep sale[s]
this chapter you will see how some firms inc[rease]
decentralized sales operations. You will also
cedures and records used for such operations.

HOME OFFICE AND BRANCH ACCOUNTING

SALES AGENCIES

One way to intensify sales efforts and increase sales is to obtain better local representation. Salespeople can make more frequent calls, customers can place orders more easily, and deliveries can be greatly speeded up with effective local representation. There are two common plans for conducting decentralized sales operations—sales agencies and sales branches. Each plan involves special accounting procedures.

A *sales agency* may be established by setting up a field office as headquarters for the salespeople serving a particular territory. The salespeople and employees in the agency accept orders, but the agency does not ordinarily keep stock on hand. Shipments are made from a central warehouse or shipping point. The agency ordinarily does not bill customers or keep accounts receivable records. Customers send their payments on account to the home office.

The sales agency may pay some or all of its own bills, such as office rent, salaries, supplies, and utilities. However, it is far more common for the home office to pay all the agency's bills and payroll and for the agency to make only very small payments. A petty cash fund is used for this purpose.

SALES BRANCHES

In contrast to a sales agency operation, a *sales branch* ordinarily carries an inventory of products and makes deliveries from stock. The system of record-keeping used varies with each situation.

The simplest plan avoids branch recordkeeping; the branch's bills and payroll are paid by the home office, and the branch's accounts receivable are maintained in the records of the home office. The branch may have a petty cash fund for making minor payments. Any cash received by such a branch would be sent directly to the home office or deposited in a bank account on which only home office personnel can write checks.

Often, however, a sales branch maintains accounts receivable with customers and receives collections from them on account. It also pays its own bills and payroll. In short, it keeps a complete set of accounting records with general and subsidiary ledgers, a general journal, and special journals for sales, purchases, cash receipts, and cash payments. In addition, the branch may operate a voucher system for its cash payments. There are also various in-between arrangements in use with respect to handling cash and recordkeeping in a branch. For example, the salaries of branch employees might be paid by the home office, although the branch makes other types of payments itself.

THE DIXON MERCHANDISING COMPANY SALES BRANCH

To illustrate the accounting procedures necessary for branch operations, the transactions of the Dixon Merchandising Company will be studied. The company, a partnership of Joan and Rita Dixon, has its home office in Chicago. It decides to open a sales branch in Denver on December 1, 19Y5. The branch will occupy rented office and warehouse space, carry a merchandise inventory, make deliveries to customers, bill the customers and collect from them, and pay all its expenses except payroll. It will maintain a complete set of accounting records, including a general journal, special journals, a general ledger, and an accounts receivable subsidiary ledger.

Since the routine preparation of accounting records is now familiar, none of the local operating details will be discussed at length. This presentation will explain the accounting procedure through which the two sets of records, those of the Denver branch and those of the home office, are linked together.

1. Certain branch transactions require entries in both sets of records.
2. Many other transactions require only routine entries in the records of the branch.
3. At the end of the period, financial statements can be prepared for the branch separately from the home office.
4. Or, the figures from both sets of accounting records can be combined to present a set of financial statements for company operations as a whole, including both the home office and the branch.

RECIPROCAL ACCOUNTS

The connecting link between the home office records and the branch records is provided by two reciprocal accounts, one in each set of records. The nature of the reciprocal accounts can best be understood by examining the accounting treatment given by both the home office and the branch to several transactions that commonly occur. These are transactions between the home office and the branch. They do not involve outside parties.

Cash Advanced by the Home Office to the Branch

When a new branch is established, the home office usually advances cash to it so that the branch can function until it begins to produce cash from its own operations.

Home Office Records An advance of cash to a new branch is considered an investment of the home office and is debited to an account bearing the name of the branch, such as Denver Branch, as shown below. This account is presented on the home office balance sheet under Investments.

	19 Y5					
Dec.	1	Denver Branch	171	5,000 00		
		Cash	101		5,000 00	
		Sent cash to Denver branch.				

Branch Office Records As the Denver branch receives cash from the home office, it records the transaction by debiting Cash and crediting an account entitled Home Office, which is the owner's equity account in the records of the branch.

	19 Y5					
Dec.	1	Cash	101	5,000 00		
		Home Office	331		5,000 00	
		Received cash from home office.				

Remittance of Cash to the Home Office

After a branch begins operations, sells merchandise to customers, collects accounts receivable, pays expenses, and so on, the branch will remit to the home office any cash not needed in its day-to-day operations. For example, the Denver branch periodically sends cash to the home office. Suppose that a remittance of $6,000 is sent at the end of December.

Home Office Records The home office enters the cash received from the branch by debiting Cash and crediting the Denver Branch account.

	19 Y5					
Dec.	31	Cash	101	6,000 00		
		Denver Branch	171		6,000 00	
		Received cash from Denver branch.				

Branch Office Records The branch enters the cash remittance to the home office by debiting the Home Office account and crediting Cash.

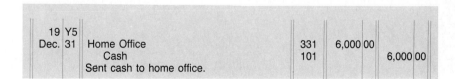

	19 Y5					
Dec.	31	Home Office	331	6,000 00		
		Cash	101		6,000 00	
		Sent cash to home office.				

Note that the reciprocal accounts always reflect the branch/home office transactions and must always be in balance.

The home office ships merchandise to the branch for stock. This movement is not a sale by the home office but a transfer that reduces the goods available for sale at the central warehouse. Shipments also increase the investment of the home office in the branch.

Home Office Records The home office enters each transfer of merchandise by a debit to Denver Branch and a credit to an account entitled Shipments to Branch.

19Y5					
Dec.	1	Denver Branch	171	20,000 00	
		Shipments to Branch or inventory	582		20,000 00
		Shipped merchandise to Denver branch.			

Branch Office Records The branch may receive all its inventory by transfer from the home office, or it may receive some by transfer and purchase the rest. In either case, transfers from the home office are recorded in the records of the branch by a debit to an account entitled Shipments From Home Office and a credit to the Home Office account.

19Y5					
Dec.	1	Shipments From Home Office	581	20,000 00	
		Home Office	331		20,000 00
		Received merchandise from home office.			

The two accounts affected by transfers of merchandise—the Shipments to Branch account of the home office and the Shipments From Home Office account of the branch—are temporary accounts. They are closed at the end of each fiscal period when the firm's other temporary accounts are formally closed.

Upon inspection of the merchandise received on December 1 from the home office, the Denver branch finds that items valued at $350 are different from those ordered. The branch therefore returns the items on December 4. In the accounting records of both the home office and the branch the return is treated as a reduction or reversal of a part of the entry made on December 1, when the merchandise was received by the branch.

Home Office Records The home office debits Shipments to Branch and credits Denver Branch for the amount of goods returned.

19Y5					
Dec.	4	Shipments to Branch	582	350 00	
		Denver Branch	171		350 00
		Received merchandise returned to home office by Denver branch.			

Branch Office Records The branch enters the return by a debit to Home Office and a credit to Shipments From Home Office.

19 Y5					
Dec.	4	Home Office	331	350 00	
		Shipments From Home Office	581		350 00
		Returned merchandise to home office.			

Other Branch/Home Office Transactions

There are obviously many other transactions that could occur between the home office and the branch. For example, items of property, plant, and equipment may be transferred between the two offices. Another very common type of transaction involves the payment of expenses by the home office on behalf of the branch. It is especially common for the home office to pay the salaries of branch personnel. The treatment of this transaction is illustrated by the following example.

At the end of December, the home office of the Dixon Merchandising Company pays the salaries of the branch salespeople and office workers. Checks are sent directly to the employees, and all payroll recordkeeping is done at the home office. The branch is notified of salary payments of $2,800 to the salespeople and $1,525 to the office workers. The employer's payroll taxes total $277.80 on sales salaries and $147.28 on office salaries.

Home Office Records The payroll amounts are entered in the accounting records of the home office as follows. (Payroll deductions have been ignored to simplify the illustration.)

19 Y5					
Dec.	31	Denver Branch	171	4,750 08	
		Wages Payable	215		4,325 00
		Payroll Taxes Payable	226		425 08
		To charge Denver branch for payroll and taxes.			

Branch Office Records The branch enters the payroll amounts in its records as debits to the various expense accounts and offsets the debits by one combined credit to the Home Office account.

19 Y5					
Dec.	31	Sales Salaries Expense	601	2,800 00	
		Payroll Taxes Expense—Sales	603	277 80	
		Office Salaries Expense	652	1,525 00	
		Payroll Taxes Expense—Office	653	147 28	
		Home Office	331		4,750 08
		To record payroll and payroll taxes paid or accrued by home office.			

The branch carries on the routine business activities of any merchandising firm and accounts for these transactions in the usual way. For example, sales on credit are recorded by debits to Accounts Receivable and credits to Sales. Similarly, expenses are recorded by the usual debits to expense accounts and credits to Accounts Payable or Cash.

DENVER BRANCH WORKSHEET AND STATEMENTS

Once the journal entries discussed previously are posted to the general ledger of the Denver branch, the end-of-period work progresses according to the familiar pattern.

1. A trial balance of the general ledger is taken to check the equality of the debits and credits.
2. Data for the adjustments is gathered, and the adjusting entries are recorded on the worksheet (as illustrated on page 923).
3. The adjusted trial balance figures are computed and entered on the worksheet.
4. The ending merchandise inventory is recorded directly on the worksheet, as a debit in the Balance Sheet section and a credit in the Income Statement section.
5. All items in the Adjusted Trial Balance section are extended to the appropriate statement columns, the net income is calculated, and the worksheet is completed.

Income Statement

The income statement of the Denver branch for December is prepared in the usual form as shown below, using the information on the worksheet. However, note that Shipments From Home Office replaces Purchases in the Cost of Goods Sold section.

DIXON MERCHANDISING COMPANY—DENVER BRANCH
Income Statement
Month Ended December 31, 19Y5

Revenue		
Sales		$24,000.00
Less Sales Returns and Allowances		130.00
Net Sales		$23,870.00
Cost of Goods Sold		
Merchandise Inventory, Dec. 1	$ -0-	
Shipments From Home Office *(purchases)*	19,650.00	
Total Merchandise Available for Sale	$19,650.00	
Less Merchandise Inventory, Dec. 31	8,800.00	
Cost of Goods Sold		10,850.00
Gross Profit on Sales		$13,020.00
Total Operating Expenses*		7,067.82
Net Income From Operations		$ 5,952.18

*Details omitted.

DIXON MERCHANDISING COMPANY—DENVER BRANCH
Worksheet
Month Ended December 31, 19Y5

ACCT. NO.	ACCOUNT NAME	TRIAL BALANCE DEBIT	TRIAL BALANCE CREDIT	ADJUSTMENTS DEBIT	ADJUSTMENTS CREDIT	ADJUSTED TRIAL BALANCE DEBIT	ADJUSTED TRIAL BALANCE CREDIT	INCOME STATEMENT DEBIT	INCOME STATEMENT CREDIT	BALANCE SHEET DEBIT	BALANCE SHEET CREDIT
101	Cash	11,550 00				11,550 00				11,550 00	
111	Accounts Receivable	9,870 00				9,870 00				9,870 00	
112	Allowance for Uncollectible Accts.				(a)47 74		47 74				47 74
126	Merchandise Inventory								8,800 00	8,800 00	
202	Accounts Payable		880 00				880 00				880 00
331	Home Office		23,340 08				23,340 08				23,340 08
401	Sales		24,000 00				24,000 00		24,000 00		
452	Sales Returns and Allowances	130 00				130 00		130 00			
581	Shipments From Home Office	19,650 00				19,650 00		19,650 00			
601	Sales Salaries Expense	2,800 00				2,800 00		2,800 00			
603	Payroll Taxes Expense—Sales	277 80				277 80		277 80			
621	Delivery Expense	280 00				280 00		280 00			
629	Sales Supplies and Other Selling Exp.	300 00				300 00		300 00			
631	Advertising Expense	500 00				500 00		500 00			
641	Rent Expense	800 00				800 00		800 00			
652	Office Salaries Expense	1,525 00				1,525 00		1,525 00			
653	Payroll Taxes Expense—Office	147 28				147 28		147 28			
669	Office Supplies and Other Office Exp.	390 00				390 00		390 00			
671	Loss From Uncollectible Accounts			(a)47 74		47 74		47 74			
	Totals	48,220 08	48,220 08	47 74	47 74	48,267 82	48,267 82	26,847 82	32,800 00	30,220 00	24,267 82
	Net Income							5,952 18			5,952 18
								32,800 00	32,800 00	30,220 00	30,220 00

Balance Sheet

The balance sheet of the Denver branch is also prepared in the usual form, using the information on the worksheet. However, in place of the owners' equity accounts, the branch shows the Home Office account, with the balance increased by the net income for the period.

DIXON MERCHANDISING COMPANY—DENVER BRANCH
Balance Sheet
December 31, 19Y5

Assets

Current Assets		
Cash		$11,550.00
Accounts Receivable	$ 9,870.00	
Less Allowance for Uncollectible Accounts	47.74	9,822.26
Merchandise Inventory		8,800.00
Total Assets		$30,172.26

Liabilities and Owners' Equity

Current Liabilities		
Accounts Payable		$ 880.00
Owners' Equity		
Home Office Account Balance Before Closing	$23,340.08	
Net Income From Operations	5,952.18	
Home Office Account Balance, Dec. 31		29,292.26
Total Liabilities and Owners' Equity		$30,172.26

BRANCH ADJUSTING AND CLOSING ENTRIES

As soon as the branch statements have been prepared, the adjusting and closing entries are entered in the branch's general journal and posted to its general ledger. With one exception, the adjusting and closing entries for a branch are exactly like those you have learned about in previous chapters. The exception is the entry to transfer the net income of the branch into owners' equity. This entry is made by closing the balance of the Income Summary account into the Home Office account. For example, the Income Summary account of the Denver branch, which contains a balance of $5,952.18 after the revenue and expense accounts have been closed into it, will be closed by the following entry.

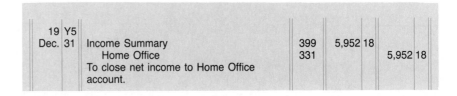

19 Y5				
Dec. 31	Income Summary	399	5,952 18	
	Home Office	331		5,952 18
	To close net income to Home Office account.			

Reversing entries would be made in the accounting records of the branch at the beginning of the next year as necessary.

RECORDING BRANCH PROFITS AND LOSSES IN THE HOME OFFICE ACCOUNTS

At the end of each fiscal period, the branch profit or loss must be recorded in the home office accounts. A branch profit is recorded by the home office as a debit to the Branch account and a credit to Income From Branch. Similarly, a loss would be recorded by a credit to the Branch account and a debit to Loss From Branch or some similar account. Note that this process is exactly like that used in the equity method of accounting for stock investments, which was discussed in Chapter 32.

The following entry is made in the home office accounts of the Dixon Merchandising Company to record the net income of $5,952.18 reported by its Denver branch on December 31, 19Y5.

19 Y5					
Dec. 31	Denver Branch	171	5,952 18		
	Income From Denver Branch	411		5,952 18	
	To record net income reported by				
	Denver branch.				

HOME OFFICE FINANCIAL STATEMENTS

Routine transactions of the home office are recorded in the usual way and are therefore not illustrated here. Similarly, at the end of the fiscal period, the usual steps are followed to take a trial balance, record adjustments on the worksheet, complete the worksheet, prepare financial statements, and make adjusting and closing entries.

The accounts involving transactions with the branch require special attention when preparing financial statements for the home office.

Income Statement

The income statement shown on page 926 for the home office is in the customary form, with two exceptions. Notice that in the Cost of Goods Sold section, the $19,650 representing shipments to the branch is deducted in order to determine the total merchandise available for sale by the home office. The net income of the Denver branch, $5,952.18, is added to the home office's net income from operations to obtain the total net income from operations.

Balance Sheet

The only new feature on the home office balance sheet is the listing of the balance of the Denver Branch account as an investment item among the assets. The net income of the branch is included in the partners' capital accounts along with other net income. The balance sheet of the home office appears on the worksheet illustrated on page 930. The statement of partners' equities is shown on page 931.

COMBINED STATEMENTS

The separate income statements and balance sheets for the branch and the home office are useful to management. However, it is also important to show how the company has performed as a whole and how it stands at the end of the year. This information is presented by combining the results given on the separate income statements into one report and by combining the figures shown on the separate balance sheets into another report.

DIXON MERCHANDISING COMPANY—HOME OFFICE
Income Statement
Year Ended December 31, 19Y5

Revenue		
Sales		$2,024,789.40
Less Sales Returns and Allowances		14,271.30
Net Sales		$2,010,518.10
Cost of Goods Sold		
Merchandise Inventory, Jan. 1	$ 92,000.00	
Merchandise Purchases (Net)	1,150,246.30	
Total	$1,242,246.30	
Less Shipments to Branch	19,650.00	
Total Merchandise Available for Sale	$1,222,596.30	
Less Merchandise Inventory, Dec. 31	90,000.00	
Cost of Goods Sold		1,132,596.30
Gross Profit on Sales		$ 877,921.80
Total Operating Expenses*		641,358.85
Net Income From Operations		
Home Office		$ 236,562.95
Income From Denver Branch		5,952.18
Total Net Income From Operations		$ 242,515.13
Other Income		
Interest Income		346.00
Total Income for Year		$ 242,861.13
Other Expense		
Interest Expense		14,730.00
Net Income for Year		$ 228,131.13

handwritten annotation: inventory in branch → (pointing to "Less Shipments to Branch")

*Details omitted.

Worksheet for Combined Income Statement

Branch and home office income statements can be most conveniently combined by using a worksheet like the one illustrated on page 928. Notice that the items listed on this special worksheet are set up in regular income statement order.

The procedure for completing the worksheet for the combined income statement is as follows.

1. The home office figures are entered in the first money column of the worksheet, and the branch office figures are entered in the second money column. (The figures are taken from the separate income statements, which were previously prepared.)

2. In the Eliminations columns, the balance of Shipments to Branch is offset against the balance of Shipments From Home Office. (At the end of each period, these accounts must have equal and opposite balances.) Shipments to

Branch has a credit balance and is therefore debited in making the elimination. Shipments From Home Office has a debit balance and is therefore credited. The effect of the two entries is to cancel out the balances of these reciprocal items.

3. After the reciprocal items are eliminated, the remaining figures for each item on each line are added across and entered in the column to the right, called Combined Income Statement.

4. The final combined net income for the year must be the same amount as was shown on the home office income statement on page 926, which included the branch net income. After this verification is made, the accountant can prepare the combined income statement.

Combined Income Statement

The combined income statement prepared from the worksheet on page 928 is illustrated on page 929. This income statement shows the results of operations for the business as a whole.

Worksheet for Combined Balance Sheet

A worksheet may also be used for combining home office and branch office balance sheet figures. Such a worksheet is illustrated on page 930. Notice that the items on this special worksheet are set up in regular balance sheet order.

The procedure for completing the worksheet for the combined balance sheet is as follows.

1. The home office figures are entered in the first money column of the worksheet, and the branch office figures are entered in the second money column. (The figures are taken from the individual balance sheets.)

2. In the Eliminations columns, the debit balance of the Denver Branch account in the home office records is offset against the credit balance of the Home Office account in the branch records. At the end of each fiscal period, the balances of these two reciprocal items must be equal and opposite. The effect of the two entries in the Eliminations columns is to cancel out the balances.

3. After the reciprocal items are eliminated, the remaining figures for each item on each line are added across and entered in the column at the right, called Combined Balance Sheet.

4. The total assets must equal the total liabilities and owners' equity. After this verification, the accountant can prepare the combined balance sheet.

Combined Balance Sheet

The resulting combined balance sheet prepared from the figures on the worksheet is given on page 931. This balance sheet shows the financial position of the entire business and is supported by the statement of partners' equities, which is also illustrated on page 931.

VARIATIONS FROM ILLUSTRATED PROCEDURES

As indicated earlier in this chapter, there are many possible variations in the accounting records maintained by a sales branch. An accountant who specializes in systems development is usually asked to devise procedures best suited to the firm's needs. For example, the home office of a firm might bill the branch at selling price for inventory transfers. This does not necessitate any procedural differences in making entries in the branch records. However, the branch income

DIXON MERCHANDISING COMPANY AND DENVER BRANCH
Worksheet for Combined Income Statement
Year Ended December 31, 19Y5

	DEC. 31 BALANCES		ELIMINATIONS		COMBINED INCOME STATEMENT
	HOME OFFICE	DENVER BRANCH	DEBIT	CREDIT	
Sales	2,024,789 40	24,000 00			2,048,789 40
Less Sales Returns and Allowances	14,271 30	130 00			14,401 30
Net Sales	2,010,518 10	23,870 00			2,034,388 10
Cost of Goods Sold					
Merchandise Inv., Jan. 1	92,000 00				92,000 00
Merchandise Purchases (Net)	1,150,246 30				1,150,246 30
Total	1,242,246 30				1,242,246 30
Less Shipments to Branch	19,650 00		(a)19,650 00		
Shipments From Home Office		19,650 00		(a)19,650 00	
Total Mdse. Available for Sale	1,222,596 30	19,650 00			1,242,246 30
Less Mdse. Inv., Dec. 31	90,000 00	8,800 00			98,800 00
Cost of Goods Sold	1,132,596 30	10,850 00			1,143,446 30
Gross Profit on Sales	877,921 80	13,020 00			890,941 80
Operating Expenses					
Selling Expenses					
Sales Salaries Expense	280,000 00	2,800 00			282,800 00
Payroll Taxes Expense—Sales	27,460 00	277 80			27,737 80
Delivery Expense	62,947 80	280 00			63,227 80
Sales Supplies and Other Exp.	37,511 10	300 00			37,811 10
Advertising Expense	60,015 30	500 00			60,515 30
Depreciation Expense	4,000 00				4,000 00
Rent Expense		800 00			800 00
Total Selling Expenses	471,934 20	4,957 80			476,892 00
Administrative Expenses					
Office Salaries Expense	87,700 00	1,525 00			89,225 00
Payroll Taxes Expense—Office	8,210 00	147 28			8,357 28
Office Supplies and Other Exp.	38,814 65	390 00			39,204 65
Depreciation Expense	11,000 00				11,000 00
Loss From Uncollectible Accts.	3,700 00	47 74			3,747 74
Rent Expense	20,000 00				20,000 00
Total Admin. Expenses	169,424 65	2,110 02			171,534 67
Total Operating Expenses	641,358 85	7,067 82			648,426 67
Net Income From Operations	236,562 95	5,952 18			242,515 13
Other Income					
Interest Income	346 00				346 00
Total Income for Year	236,908 95	5,952 18			242,861 13
Other Expense					
Interest Expense	14,730 00				14,730 00
Net Income for Year	222,178 95	5,952 18	19,650 00	19,650 00	228,131 13

DIXON MERCHANDISING COMPANY AND DENVER BRANCH
Combined Income Statement
Year Ended December 31, 19Y5

Revenue			
Sales			$2,048,789.40
Less Sales Returns and Allowances			14,401.30
Net Sales			$2,034,388.10
Cost of Goods Sold			
Merchandise Inventory, Jan. 1		$ 92,000.00	
Merchandise Purchases (Net)		1,150,246.30	
Total Merchandise Available for Sale		$1,242,246.30	
Less Merchandise Inventory, Dec. 31		98,800.00	
Cost of Goods Sold			1,143,446.30
Gross Profit on Sales			$ 890,941.80
Operating Expenses			
Selling Expenses			
Sales Salaries Expense	$282,800.00		
Payroll Taxes Expense—Sales	27,737.80		
Delivery Expense	63,227.80		
Sales Supplies and Other Selling Exp.	37,811.10		
Advertising Expense	60,515.30		
Depreciation Expense	4,000.00		
Rent Expense	800.00		
Total Selling Expenses		$ 476,892.00	
Administrative Expenses			
Office Salaries Expense	$ 89,225.00		
Payroll Taxes Expense—Office	8,357.28		
Office Supplies and Other Office Exp.	39,204.65		
Depreciation Expense	11,000.00		
Loss From Uncollectible Accounts	3,747.74		
Rent Expense	20,000.00		
Total Administrative Expenses		171,534.67	
Total Operating Expenses			648,426.67
Net Income From Operations			$ 242,515.13
Other Income			
Interest Income			346.00
Total Income for Year			$ 242,861.13
Other Expense			
Interest Expense			14,730.00
Net Income for Year			$ 228,131.13

DIXON MERCHANDISING COMPANY AND DENVER BRANCH
Worksheet for Combined Balance Sheet
December 31, 19Y5

	DEC. 31 BALANCES		ELIMINATIONS		COMBINED BALANCE SHEET
	HOME OFFICE	DENVER BRANCH	DEBIT	CREDIT	
Assets					
Current Assets					
Cash	88,369 80	11,550 00			99,919 80
Accounts Receivable	247,206 60	9,870 00			257,076 60
Allowance for Uncollectible Accts.	(3,825 00)	(47 74)			(3,872 74)
Merchandise Inventory	90,000 00	8,800 00			98,800 00
Prepaid Insurance	2,950 00				2,950 00
Supplies on Hand	1,120 00				1,120 00
Total Current Assets	425,821 40	30,172 26			455,993 66
Property, Plant, and Equipment					
Furniture and Fixtures	28,000 00				28,000 00
Accumulated Depreciation	(3,600 00)				(3,600 00)
Building	120,000 00				120,000 00
Accumulated Depreciation	(12,000 00)				(12,000 00)
Land	40,000 00				40,000 00
Total Prop., Plant, and Equip.	172,400 00				172,400 00
Investments					
Denver Branch	29,292 26			(a)29,292 26	
Total Assets	627,513 66	30,172 26			628,393 66
Liabilities and Owners' Equity					
Current Liabilities					
Accounts Payable	98,605 00	880 00			99,485 00
Accrued Expenses Payable	10,244 00				10,244 00
Total Current Liabilities	108,849 00	880 00			109,729 00
Long-Term Liabilities					
Mortgage Notes Payable	80,105 00				80,105 00
Total Liabilities	188,954 00	880 00			189,834 00
Owners' Equity					
Joan Dixon, Capital	224,279 83				224,279 83
Rita Dixon, Capital	214,279 83				214,279 83
Home Office		29,292 26	(a)29,292 26		
Total Owners' Equity	438,559 66	29,292 26			438,559 66
Total Liab. and Owners' Equity	627,513 66	30,172 26	29,292 26	29,292 26	628,393 66

DIXON MERCHANDISING COMPANY
Statement of Partners' Equities
Year Ended December 31, 19Y5

	Joan Dixon, Capital	Rita Dixon, Capital	Total Capital
Capital Balances, Jan. 1, 19Y5	$140,214.26	$130,214.27	$270,428.53
Net Income for Year	114,065.57	114,065.56	228,131.13
Totals	$254,279.83	$244,279.83	$498,559.66
Less Withdrawals	30,000.00	30,000.00	60,000.00
Capital Balances, Dec. 31, 19Y5	$224,279.83	$214,279.83	$438,559.66

DIXON MERCHANDISING COMPANY AND DENVER BRANCH
Combined Balance Sheet
December 31, 19Y5

Assets

Current Assets			
Cash			$ 99,919.80
Accounts Receivable		$257,076.60	
Less Allowance for Uncollectible Accounts		3,872.74	253,203.86
Merchandise Inventory			98,800.00
Prepaid Insurance			2,950.00
Supplies on Hand			1,120.00
Total Current Assets			$455,993.66
Property, Plant, and Equipment			
Furniture and Fixtures	$ 28,000.00		
Less Accumulated Depreciation	3,600.00	$ 24,400.00	
Building	$120,000.00		
Less Accumulated Depreciation	12,000.00	108,000.00	
Land		40,000.00	
Total Property, Plant, and Equip.			172,400.00
Total Assets			$628,393.66

Liabilities and Owners' Equity

Current Liabilities			
Accounts Payable			$ 99,485.00
Accrued Expenses Payable			10,244.00
Total Current Liabilities			$109,729.00
Long-Term Liabilities			
Mortgage Notes Payable			80,105.00
Total Liabilities			$189,834.00
Owners' Equity			
Joan Dixon, Capital		$224,279.83	
Rita Dixon, Capital		214,279.83	
Total Owners' Equity			438,559.66
Total Liabilities and Owners' Equity			$628,393.66

statement shows no gross profit on sales. Furthermore, the branch's ending inventory is valued at selling price, and this must be reduced to cost when the branch's statements are combined with those of the home office.

The property, plant, and equipment used by the branch may be carried either in the home office records or in the branch records. In each case the depreciation expense for these items is treated as an operating expense of the branch and appears on its income statement.

In some firms the branch pays its own employees. Payroll deductions and taxes might be handled separately by the branch. This procedure would involve entries in both sets of records to complete the transfer of payroll deductions and payroll taxes.

The details of these and other possible variations in home office/branch accounting procedures are beyond the scope of this chapter and are usually discussed in intermediate or advanced accounting textbooks. However, keep in mind that no matter what procedures are used, the accounting system of a firm that has one or more branches must meet certain objectives. The most important of these objectives is that the system provide timely, informative data about the operations of each segment of the business. Management needs such data in order to measure the profitability and efficiency of the individual branches and to make decisions about their future activities.

PRINCIPLES AND PROCEDURES SUMMARY

In an effort to increase business, firms may set up sales agencies or sales branches. An agency ordinarily carries no stock and keeps a minimum of accounting records. Orders are sent to the home office, and accounts receivable are maintained there. The home office usually pays agency operating expenses. A sales branch, however, usually has an inventory of merchandise from which it fills orders. The accounting work may be done at the home office, or the branch may keep a complete set of records, maintain accounts receivable with customers, and pay its own operating expenses.

Reciprocal accounts link the home office financial records and the branch financial records. The Branch Office account of the home office represents an investment and is appropriately listed on the balance sheet with other investments. The Home Office account of the branch represents the owners' equity in the branch operations. These two accounts normally have equal but opposite balances.

Temporary accounts are set up by the home office and the branch to record the shipment of merchandise to the branch for stock. The account at the home office, which has a credit balance, is called Shipments to Branch, while the account at the branch, which has a debit balance, is called Shipments From Home Office. These accounts also have equal but opposite balances during the fiscal period. They are closed out at the end of each period.

The closing process for a branch also includes the transfer of its net income to the Home Office account. The home office records the net income of the branch by an offsetting entry in the Branch account.

Separate financial statements are prepared for the home office and the branch. In addition, combined statements for the business as a whole are prepared. On the worksheet for the combined income statement, the temporary accounts used to record shipments of merchandise from the home office to the branch are offset and eliminated. On the worksheet for the combined balance sheet, the reciprocal accounts, Branch Office and Home Office, are offset. All like items from the separate statements are then drawn together into the combined statements.

MANAGERIAL IMPLICATIONS

In many cases a firm can grow and increase its profits best by establishing branches. However, adequate accounting records must be maintained so that the profitability and financial condition of each branch can be closely watched. Management's problem of control is complicated by the physical distance between the branches and the home office. Accounting records and reports help to bridge this gap.

It is essential that the home office know the financial condition of the branches at all times and also whether they have been profitable or unprofitable. Only if these facts are known can the home office take any necessary steps to improve branch operations. Since management is responsible for the entire business, the home office must also know the overall condition of the firm and its profitability. Managers therefore rely on combined statements, as do outsiders such as creditors who are interested in the financial affairs of the entire business rather than of the individual parts.

REVIEW QUESTIONS

1. What is a sales agency?
2. How does a sales branch differ from a sales agency?
3. Why are branch and home office reciprocal accounts needed?
4. What entries are made to record the advance of cash by the home office to a branch?
5. Would you classify the Home Office account in the records of the branch as a liability account or an owner's equity account, or would you select some other classification? Explain.
6. What accounting treatment is given by the home office to expenses that it pays on behalf of a branch?
7. How would a branch account for the sale of merchandise to a customer on credit?
8. How is the account Shipments From Home Office treated in the financial statements of the branch?
9. What method is used to report the profit or loss of a branch in the home office's separate financial statements?
10. How is the profit or loss of a branch recorded in the home office's accounts?
11. What is the purpose of combined statements?

12. How are the Home Office and Branch Office accounts handled on the worksheet for the combined balance sheet?
13. Where does the account Income From Branch appear on the combined income statement, if at all?
14. Where does the account Branch Office appear on the combined balance sheet?
15. Suppose that the home office transferred merchandise to a branch at the home office's cost plus 15 percent. How would the gross profit on sales and the ending inventory be handled in the financial statements of the branch? How would the ending inventory be handled when combined statements are prepared?
16. Suppose that the accounts of the home office include the equipment of a branch. How would the depreciation on this equipment be handled in the financial statements?
17. Give the titles of two sets of reciprocal accounts.
18. What reason might be given for the home office to ship merchandise to a branch at more than the home office's cost?
19. Where is the account Home Office presented in the financial statements of the branch?
20. How is the account Shipments to Branch handled in the financial statements of the home office?

MANAGERIAL DISCUSSION QUESTIONS

1. How can a firm maintain effective financial controls over the operations of distant sales agencies and branches?
2. How does branch accounting simplify the management of far-flung operations?
3. Assume that you are working for a firm that has a sales branch. The managers of your company are discussing billing procedures for merchandise shipments from the home office to the branch. One officer suggests that all merchandise should be billed at the marked selling price rather than at cost. What merit can you see in this suggestion?
4. Assume that you are employed by a company that operates three sales branches. Each branch has a petty cash fund for paying small items. Otherwise, all bills for merchandise, rent, salaries, and so on are paid by the home office. What benefits do you see in this procedure?
5. Assume that you work for a retail clothing company that operates several branch stores in different parts of the country. Management has been discussing whether all merchandise should be purchased by the home office and handled through a single warehouse or whether each store manager should be allowed to purchase merchandise. What is your opinion?
6. How does a branch accounting system keep management informed of the profitability of branch operations and the overall condition of the firm's operations?
7. Why would management want to have separate statements for the branch and the home office as well as combined statements?

EXERCISES

EXERCISE 38-1   **Recording cash advanced to a branch by the home office.** The Riggs Corporation advanced $10,000 to its Chicago branch on August 21, 19X2. In general journal form, give the entry that the home office would make to record the advance.

EXERCISE 38-2   **Recording cash received by a branch from the home office.** Refer to Exercise 38-1. In general journal form, give the entry that the Chicago branch would make to record receipt of the $10,000 cash from the home office.

EXERCISE 38-3   **Recording merchandise shipped by the home office to a branch.** On August 25, 19X2, the Riggs Corporation transferred merchandise costing $56,000 to its Chicago branch. In general journal form, give the entry that the home office would make to record the transfer.

EXERCISE 38-4   **Recording merchandise received by a branch from the home office.** Refer to Exercise 38-3. In general journal form, give the entry that the Chicago branch would make to record receipt of the $56,000 of merchandise shipped by the home office.

EXERCISE 38-5   **Recording the return of merchandise to the home office by a branch.** On September 8, 19X2, the Chicago branch of the Riggs Corporation returned part of the merchandise received in August from the home office. The cost of the merchandise involved in the return was $895. In general journal form, give the entry that the branch would make to record the return.

EXERCISE 38-6   **Recording the receipt by the home office of merchandise returned by a branch.** Refer to Exercise 38-5. In general journal form, give the entry that the home office would make to record the receipt of the merchandise returned by the branch.

EXERCISE 38-7   **Recording a cash remittance by a branch to the home office.** On August 31, 19X2, the Chicago branch of the Riggs Corporation remitted to the home office $2,500 cash. In general journal form, give the entry that the branch would make to record the remittance.

EXERCISE 38-8   **Recording cash received by the home office from a branch.** Refer to Exercise 38-7. In general journal form, give the entry that the home office would make to record receipt of the $2,500 cash remitted by the branch.

EXERCISE 38-9   **Recording the payment of an expense by the home office for a branch.** On September 1, 19X2, the home office of the Riggs Corporation paid rent of $1,000 for its Chicago branch. In general journal form, give the entry that the home office would make to record this payment.

EXERCISE 38-10 **Recording the payment of an expense by the home office for a branch.** Refer to Exercise 38-9. In general journal form, give the entry that the Chicago branch would make to record payment by the home office of the branch's rent.

EXERCISE 38-11 **Reporting shipments to a branch on the income statement of the home office.** On July 31, 19X2, the financial records at the home office of the Gonzalez Corporation included the following data. Prepare the Cost of Goods Sold section of the home office's income statement for the year ended July 31, 19X2.

Merchandise Inventory, Aug. 1, 19X1	$ 100,000
Merchandise Purchases (Net)	1,890,000
Shipments to San Diego Branch	500,000
Merchandise Inventory, July 31, 19X2	90,000

EXERCISE 38-12 **Closing a branch's income summary.** After all revenue and expense accounts were closed on December 31, 19X2, the Income Summary account of the Seattle Branch of the Ling Company had a debit balance of $35,000. In general journal form, give the entry that would be made at the branch to close the Income Summary account.

EXERCISE 38-13 **Recording a branch's net loss in the accounts of the home office.** Refer to Exercise 38-12. In general journal form, give the entry that the home office of the Ling Company would make to record the $35,000 loss of the Seattle branch for the year ended December 31, 19X2.

EXERCISE 38-14 **Reporting shipments from the home office on a branch's income statement.** Data for the Houston branch of the Allen Company is shown below. Prepare the Cost of Goods Sold section of the branch's income statement for the year ended December 31, 19X1.

Shipments From Home Office	$145,000
Merchandise Purchases (Net)	124,000
Merchandise Inventory, January 1, 19X1	41,000
Merchandise Inventory, December 31, 19X1	39,500

PROBLEMS

PROBLEM 38-1 **Recording transactions for a branch and a home office.** The Royal Cosmetics Company opened a branch in Atlanta on January 2, 19X2. Transactions during the month of January are summarized on page 937.

Instructions 1. Record the transactions in general journal form. Give the entries that would appear in the accounting records of the branch and the entries that would appear in the accounting records of the home office.
2. Give the entries to close the accounting records of the branch and to record the net income or net loss of the branch at the home office. The ending inventory of the branch on January 31 was $4,590.

Jan. 2 The home office shipped merchandise costing $5,000 to the branch.

2 The home office sent $2,600 in cash to the branch.

31 The home office paid administrative expenses of the branch totaling $2,200. (Debit Administrative Expenses.)

31 The branch made purchases of $6,000 on credit.

31 The branch made sales of $10,200 on credit.

31 The branch collected $8,000 on account.

31 The branch made payments of $3,700 on account.

31 The branch paid selling expenses of $2,900 in cash. (Debit Selling Expenses.)

31 The branch had accrued selling expenses of $350. (Credit Accounts Payable.)

31 The home office recorded accrued office salaries (Administrative Expense) of $100 applicable to the branch.

PROBLEM 38-2 **Recording transactions and preparing financial statements for a branch.** The Webb Electronics Company opened a sales branch in Boston on March 1, 19X1. The accounts of the branch and its transactions for March appear below and on page 938.

Instructions

1. Set up the general ledger accounts for the branch.

2. Record the given transactions in general journal form, and post them to the general ledger accounts.

3. Set up a ten-column worksheet, and take a trial balance of the general ledger accounts as of March 31.

4. Record on the worksheet the adjustment for uncollectible accounts, which is determined to be 1 percent of net sales. Then record the ending merchandise inventory of $14,000, and complete the worksheet. Identify the amount of the adjustment with the letter (a).

5. Prepare the following financial statements for the branch: an income statement for March and a balance sheet as of March 31, 19X1.

6. Prepare entries in general journal form to adjust and close the accounting records of the branch and to transfer the branch's net income to the home office. Post these entries to the general ledger accounts.

7. Prepare a postclosing trial balance.

GENERAL LEDGER ACCOUNTS OF BRANCH

101	Cash	581	Shipments From Home Office
111	Accounts Receivable	601	Sales Salaries Expense
112	Allowance for Uncollectible Accounts	603	Other Selling Expenses
121	Merchandise Inventory	631	Advertising Expense
202	Accounts Payable	641	Rent Expense
331	Home Office	652	Office Salaries Expense
399	Income Summary	653	Other Office Expenses
401	Sales	661	Payroll Taxes Expense
452	Sales Returns and Allowances	671	Loss From Uncollectible Accounts

TRANSACTIONS FOR MARCH 19X1

Mar. 1 Received $5,000 in cash from the home office.
2 Received $30,000 of merchandise from the home office.
3 Recorded rent expense of $400 as an account payable.
4 Returned merchandise costing $800 to the home office.
20 Recorded sales of $24,000 on credit.
24 Recorded expenses and charged them to the following accounts: Other Selling Expenses, $710; Advertising Expense, $1,000; and Other Office Expenses, $370. (Credit Accounts Payable for all the expenses.)
27 Collected $14,400 on accounts receivable.
27 Sent $8,000 in cash to the home office.
28 Paid $1,850 on accounts payable.
30 Some branch customers returned $200 of merchandise for credit against their accounts.
31 The home office sent payroll checks to branch employees: Sales Salaries Expense, $1,400; and Office Salaries Expense, $550. (Ignore taxes withheld.)
31 The home office notified the branch that it has accrued payroll taxes of $197 on branch payrolls.

PROBLEM 38-3 **Recording transactions at a home office.** This problem is a continuation of Problem 38-2. It involves the home office of the Webb Electronics Company, which is located in Sunnyvale, California.

Instructions 1. Prepare entries in general journal form for any transactions listed in Problem 38-2 that occurred between the home office and the Boston branch and would appear in the accounting records of the home office.
2. Record the net income of the Boston branch for the month of March 19X1. Obtain the amount from the income statement prepared in Problem 38-2.

PROBLEM 38-4 **Preparing combined statements for a branch and a home office.** The Ace Tennis Shop is owned by two partners—Ruth Levitt and Paul Ryan. At the beginning of 19X1, the firm established a branch in Dallas in order to expand its operations. Adjusted trial balance data for both the home office and the branch as of December 31, 19X1, is presented on page 939.

Instructions 1. Prepare a worksheet for a combined income statement for the home office and the Dallas branch of the Ace Tennis Shop.
2. Prepare the combined income statement. This statement is for the fiscal year ended December 31, 19X1.
3. Prepare a worksheet for a combined balance sheet for the home office and the Dallas branch of the Ace Tennis Shop. Adjust the two reciprocal accounts— Dallas Branch and Home Office—to reflect the branch net income for the year. Adjust the partners' capital accounts to include the combined net income. (Levitt and Ryan share net income in the ratio of 50:50.)
4. Prepare the combined balance sheet as of December 31, 19X1.

ACE TENNIS SHOP AND DALLAS BRANCH
Adjusted Trial Balance
December 31, 19X1

Acct. No.	Account Name	Home Office Debit	Home Office Credit	Dallas Branch Debit	Dallas Branch Credit
101	Cash	$ 86,455		$11,118	
111	Accounts Receivable	64,750		3,865	
112	Allowance for Uncollectible Accts.		$ 1,460		$ 248
121	Mdse. Inventory, Jan. 1	33,000		3,500	
131	Furniture and Equipment	17,400			
132	Accum. Depreciation		3,240		
171	Dallas Branch	14,275			
202	Accounts Payable		22,100		155
205	Accrued Expenses Payable		3,150		
331	Home Office				14,275
351	Ruth Levitt, Capital		75,000		
352	Paul Ryan, Capital		59,450		
401	Sales		611,200		67,850
452	Sales Returns and Allowances	1,745		520	
501	Merchandise Purchases	437,550			
581	Shipments From Home Office			47,500	
582	Shipments to Branch		47,500		
601	Sales Salaries Expense	71,200		7,300	
603	Sales Supplies and Other Selling Exp.	16,150		520	
631	Advertising Expense	24,820		830	
641	Rent Expense	8,000		1,800	
652	Office Salaries Expense	21,400		3,000	
653	Office Supplies and Other Office Exp.	18,130		1,225	
661	Payroll Taxes Expense	5,500		640	
671	Loss From Uncollectible Accounts	2,725		710	
	Totals	$823,100	$823,100	$82,528	$82,528

Ending Merchandise Inventory, Dec. 31:

Home Office	$35,000
Branch	4,000
Total	$39,000

ALTERNATE PROBLEMS

PROBLEM 38-1A   **Recording transactions for a branch and a home office.** The Continental Lamp Company opened a branch in Detroit on January 2, 19X1. Transactions during the month of January are summarized on page 940.

Instructions   1. Record the transactions in general journal form. Give the entries that would appear in the accounting records of the branch and the entries that would appear in the accounting records of the home office.

2. Give the entries to close the accounting records of the branch and to record the net income or net loss of the branch at the home office. The ending inventory of the branch on January 31 was $8,000.

TRANSACTIONS FOR JANUARY 19X1

Jan. 2 The home office sent $3,000 in cash to the branch.
      2 The home office shipped merchandise costing $3,800 to the branch.
      31 The branch made purchases of $8,500 on credit.
      31 The home office paid selling expenses of $450 for the branch. (Debit Selling Expenses.)
      31 The branch made sales of $9,200 on credit.
      31 The branch paid selling expenses of $2,400 in cash.
      31 The branch had accrued selling expenses of $285. (Credit Accounts Payable.)
      31 The home office recorded accrued office expenses of $300 applicable to the branch. (Credit Accounts Payable.)

PROBLEM 38-2A **Recording transactions and preparing financial statements for a branch.** The Storm King Coat Company has its home office in Minneapolis and maintains a sales branch in New York. The balances of the branch's general ledger accounts on November 30, 19X3, are shown on the postclosing trial balance given on page 941, followed by transactions that took place in December 19X3. The temporary accounts of the branch are listed below.

Instructions   1. Open general ledger accounts for the branch, and enter the postclosing trial balance amounts. Total the debit and credit balances to prove equality.
        2. Record the given transactions in general journal form.
        3. Post the general journal entries to the general ledger accounts.
        4. Set up a ten-column worksheet, and take a trial balance of the general ledger accounts in the first two columns.
        5. Make an adjustment on the worksheet to bring the balance of Allowance for Uncollectible Accounts to $500. Label this adjustment with the letter *a*.
        6. Enter the ending merchandise inventory of $12,000 on the worksheet. Then complete the worksheet.
        7. Prepare the following financial statements for the branch: an income statement for the month of December and a balance sheet as of December 31, 19X3.
        8. Journalize and post the necessary adjusting and closing entries.
        9. Prepare a postclosing trial balance.

TEMPORARY ACCOUNTS OF NEW YORK BRANCH

399	Income Summary	631	Advertising Expense
401	Sales	641	Rent Expense
452	Sales Returns and Allowances	652	Office Salaries Expense
581	Shipments From Home Office	653	Payroll Taxes Expense
601	Sales Salaries Expense	669	Office Expense
621	Delivery Expense	671	Loss From Uncollectible Accounts
629	Other Selling Expenses		

NEW YORK BRANCH
Postclosing Trial Balance
November 30, 19X3

Acct. No.	Account Name	Debit	Credit
101	Cash	$12,000	
111	Accounts Receivable	38,000	
112	Allowance for Uncollectible Accounts		$ 300
121	Merchandise Inventory	10,000	
202	Accounts Payable		1,650
331	Home Office		58,050
	Totals	$60,000	$60,000

TRANSACTIONS FOR DECEMBER 19X3

Dec. 1 Received $4,000 in cash from the home office.
     5 Received merchandise costing $32,000 from the home office.
    10 Returned merchandise costing $400 to the home office.
    31 Recorded cash sales of $22,000 and credit sales of $29,000 for the month.
    31 Recorded collections of $24,000 on accounts receivable.
    31 Recorded sales returns and allowances of $200, all from credit sales.
    31 The voucher register column totals for operating expenses were:

Delivery Expense	$ 250
Other Selling Expenses	300
Advertising Expense	800
Rent Expense	750
Office Expense	300
Total (credited to Accounts Payable)	$2,400

    31 Issued checks totaling $3,200 to pay approved vouchers.
    31 Recorded salaries and payroll taxes accrued by the home office:

Sales Salaries Expense	$6,750
Office Salaries Expense	1,350
Payroll Taxes Expense	875
Total	$8,975

       (Ignore taxes withheld from employee earnings.)
    31 Sent $40,000 in cash to the home office.

PROBLEM 38-3A

Recording transactions at a home office. This problem is a continuation of Problem 38-2A. It involves the home office of the Storm King Coat Company, which is located in Minneapolis.

Instructions

1. Prepare entries in general journal form for any transactions listed in Problem 38-2A that occurred between the home office and the New York branch and would appear in the accounting records of the home office.

2. Record the net income of the New York branch for the month of December 19X3. Obtain the amount from the income statement prepared in Problem 38-2A.

PROBLEM 38-4A **Preparing combined statements for a branch and a home office.** The Scandia Glassware Company has established a sales branch in Miami. Adjusted trial balance data for the home office and the branch as of December 31, 19X1, is given below.

Instructions
1. Prepare a worksheet for a combined income statement for the home office and the branch.
2. Prepare the combined income statement for the fiscal year ended December 31, 19X1.
3. Prepare a worksheet for a combined balance sheet for the home office and the branch. Adjust the two reciprocal accounts—Miami Branch and Home Office—to reflect the branch's net income for the year. Then adjust the Carl Olafson, Capital account to include the combined net income.
4. Prepare the combined balance sheet as of December 31, 19X1.

SCANDIA GLASSWARE COMPANY AND MIAMI BRANCH
Adjusted Trial Balance
December 31, 19X1

Acct. No.	Account Name	Home Office Debit	Home Office Credit	Miami Branch Debit	Miami Branch Credit
101	Cash	$ 419,133		$ 55,975	
111	Accounts Receivable	337,290		15,330	
112	Allowance for Uncollectible Accts.		$ 5,784		$ 1,569
121	Merchandise Inventory, Jan. 1	144,000		15,900	
131	Furniture and Equipment	63,750			
132	Accumulated Depreciation		14,250		
171	Miami Branch	61,401			
202	Accounts Payable		368,560		555
331	Home Office				61,401
351	Carl Olafson, Capital		379,500		
401	Sales		2,798,550		301,875
501	Merchandise Purchases	1,740,750			
581	Shipments to Branch		213,000		
582	Shipments From Home Office			213,000	
601	Selling Expenses	573,685		35,300	
651	Administrative Expenses	439,635		29,895	
		$3,779,644	$3,779,644	$365,400	$365,400

Ending Merchandise Inventory, Dec. 31:

Home Office	$135,000
Branch	16,500
Total	$151,500

Previous chapters explained and illustrated the accounting principles and procedures used by businesses engaged in the sale of services and merchandise. In those chapters it was assumed that the merchandising firms purchased their inventories from manufacturers or wholesalers. If a business— corporation, partnership, or sole proprietorship—engages in manufacturing as well as selling activities, additional accounts are needed to classify the cost elements involved in manufacturing operations.

ACCOUNTS AND RECORDS FOR A MANUFACTURING BUSINESS

STATEMENT OF COST OF GOODS MANUFACTURED

The Woodcraft Manufacturing Corporation was organized to acquire the business of Richard Strauss, a manufacturer of furniture. The company specializes in the production of wooden tables, and its manufacturing process therefore involves the acquisition and use of raw materials such as lumber, nails, glue, paint, and varnish. These materials are cut, shaped, assembled, painted, and polished in the factory, finally emerging as finished products ready for sale. With so many operations going on, management must maintain a close watch to see that the work is done carefully and efficiently and at a reasonable cost.

Special manufacturing records provide the essential continuous financial control. Periodically these records are summarized in an overall financial report called a *statement of cost of goods manufactured,* which supports the income statement. The statement of cost of goods manufactured of the Woodcraft Manufacturing Corporation for the year ended December 31, 19X3, is on page 944. This chapter will explain the meaning of the new account titles used on the statement of cost of goods manufactured and will show how the data is compiled.

BASIC COMPONENTS OF MANUFACTURING COST

Refer to the statement of cost of goods manufactured shown on page 944. The three essential components of the total manufacturing cost (d) are the raw materials used (a), the direct labor (b), and the manufacturing overhead (c). Each category of expense will be examined in detail.

Raw Materials

The presentation of data in the Raw Materials section of the statement is much like the presentation previously used in the Cost of Goods Sold section of the income statement for a merchandising business. The computation starts with the beginning inventory of raw materials. Then the amount of net purchases of raw

Subsidary Schedule
↓

WOODCRAFT MANUFACTURING CORPORATION
Statement of Cost of Goods Manufactured
Year Ended December 31, 19X3

Raw Materials

Raw Materials Inventory, Jan. 1			$ 10,000.00
Materials Purchases		$94,950.00	
Freight In		2,650.00	
Total Delivered Cost of Purchases		$97,600.00	
Less Purchases Ret. and Allow.	$860.00		
Purchases Discount	625.00	1,485.00	
Net Purchases		96,115.00	
Total Materials Available		$106,115.00	
Less Raw Materials Inventory, Dec. 31 *Balance sheet* ⟶		8,575.00	
Raw Materials Used			(a) $ 97,540.00
Direct Labor			(b) 76,350.90

Manufacturing Overhead

Indirect Labor	$ 12,275.00
Payroll Taxes—Factory	7,810.00
Indirect Materials and Supplies	2,210.35
Utilities—Factory	5,320.40
Repairs and Maintenance—Factory	2,715.65
Depreciation—Factory Plant and Equipment	2,850.00
Insurance—Factory	3,134.00
Property Taxes—Factory	3,170.20

Total Manufacturing Overhead	(c) 39,485.60
Total Manufacturing Cost	(d) $213,376.50
Add Work in Process Inventory, Jan. 1	7,000.00
	$220,376.50
Less Work in Process Inventory, Dec. 31 *Balance sheet* ⟶	7,500.00
Cost of Goods Manufactured *Income statement* ⟶	(e) $212,876.50

materials is determined by adding purchases and freight in and subtracting purchases returns and allowances and purchases discounts. The next step is to add the beginning inventory of raw materials and the net purchases in order to find the total materials available. Finally, the ending inventory is subtracted to determine the raw materials used. Although the routine looks familiar, there are some important points of difference.

1. The beginning and ending inventories consist of raw materials rather than merchandise.
2. All references to materials in this section (raw materials, materials purchases, and materials available) are related to direct materials only. *Direct materials* are all the items that go into a product and become part of it. For example, the direct materials in a table would include the wood, hardware, glue, and paint or varnish.

3. Other materials such as sandpaper and steel wool may be used in the manufacturing process, but these do not become part of the product. Therefore, they are called *indirect materials and supplies* and are listed in the Manufacturing Overhead section of the statement. Cleaning materials, lubricants, and other supplies used in general factory operations and maintenance are also treated as indirect materials and supplies on the statement of cost of goods manufactured. Some firms treat insignificant direct materials, such as glue, as indirect materials.

Direct Labor

On the statement, direct labor appears as a single total, $76,350.90 (b). This figure is obtained from the Direct Labor account, based upon payroll records and procedures similar to those described in Chapters 13 and 14. *Direct labor* includes the personnel who work directly on the product as it is being manufactured. In the factory operated by the Woodcraft Manufacturing Corporation, such personnel would include workers who saw and shape the lumber, assemble the pieces into tables, and finish or paint them.

All other factory labor is listed in the Manufacturing Overhead section of the statement. This *indirect labor* includes the wages of the following personnel.

1. Workers who transport materials from one place to another or are employed in the raw materials storeroom.
2. Repair and maintenance workers and janitorial workers.
3. Supervisors who see that the work is done properly but do not work directly on the product.

Manufacturing Overhead

Manufacturing overhead includes all the costs of manufacturing operations that are not classified as direct materials (Raw Materials section) or direct labor. In addition to indirect materials and indirect labor, manufacturing overhead might include utilities, depreciation of factory buildings and equipment, insurance, property taxes, and payroll taxes on factory wages. The Manufacturing Overhead section of Woodcraft's statement of cost of goods manufactured contains a listing of typical overhead costs.

Work in Process

The total manufacturing cost shown on the statement of cost of goods manufactured (page 944) includes all raw materials used, all direct labor costs incurred, and all manufacturing overhead applicable to the current production period. However, this figure does not represent the total cost of goods manufactured because it does not reflect the following two essential facts.

1. Not all products finished during the period are started from raw materials during the period. There is usually a carry-over of partially completed units from the previous period.
2. Not all products that enter the manufacturing process during the period are fully completed at the end of the period. Products that are only partially completed are called *work in process*.

At the end of each accounting period, an inventory of work in process must be taken by making an estimate of the costs that have been incurred for raw materials, direct labor, and manufacturing overhead. On the statement of cost of goods manufactured, the value of the work in process inventory at the beginning of the period is added to the total manufacturing cost, and the value of the work in process inventory at the end of the period is subtracted. The result, indicated by (e) on the statement shown on page 944, is the cost of all goods on which manufacturing was completed during the period.

COST OF GOODS SOLD

The cost of goods manufactured that is explained in detail in the statement of cost of goods manufactured becomes, in turn, one of the key figures required in the Cost of Goods Sold section of the income statement, as illustrated below.

The cost of goods sold is not the same as the cost of goods manufactured because two additional facts must be taken into account.

1. Not all finished products sold are actually made during the period. There is usually a carry-over of finished stock from the previous period.
2. Not all products made during the period are actually sold during the period.

At the end of each accounting period, an inventory of the finished goods on hand is taken. When the beginning and ending inventories of finished goods are known, it is then possible to complete the Cost of Goods Sold section of the income statement. The cost of goods manufactured is added to the beginning inventory to obtain the total finished goods available for sale. Then the ending inventory is subtracted, and the difference (which has obviously been used to fill customers' orders) represents the cost of goods sold. This figure is labeled (f) in the condensed income statement illustrated below.

subsidiary schedules

WOODCRAFT MANUFACTURING CORPORATION
Condensed Income Statement
Year Ended December 31, 19X3

Revenue		
* Sales		$357,249.60
Less Sales Returns and Allowances		2,120.40
Net Sales		$355,129.20
Cost of Goods Sold		
Finished Goods Inventory, Jan. 1	$ 23,250.00	
See schedule on 944 → Cost of Goods Manufactured *	212,876.50	
Total Goods Available for Sale	$236,126.50	
Balance sheet → Less Finished Goods Inventory, Dec. 31	24,175.00	
Cost of Goods Sold		(f) 211,951.50
Gross Profit on Sales		$143,177.70
Operating Expenses		
* Selling Expenses	$ 52,950.30	
* Administrative Expenses	58,770.65	111,720.95
Net Income Before Income Taxes		$ 31,456.75
Provision for Income Taxes		5,000.00
Net Income After Income Taxes		$ 26,456.75

When all transactions have been posted to the general ledger accounts at the end of the period, the usual trial balance is taken to prove the equality of the debits and credits. In the adjusting entries, there are accruals for the various manufacturing costs. The closing entries include three inventory accounts this time—Raw Materials, Work in Process, and Finished Goods—instead of the single Merchandise Inventory account that was used by the merchandising firms discussed in previous chapters.

The financial statements of a corporation that manufactures goods include the usual balance sheet, income statement, and statement of retained earnings. These statements may be slightly more elaborate than those discussed in previous chapters, but there are no new principles involved. In addition, there is a statement of cost of goods manufactured, as you have seen. This statement explains the total cost of goods manufactured figure that appears in the Cost of Goods Sold section of the income statement. End-of-period procedures for a manufacturing business are discussed in greater detail in Chapter 40.

PRINCIPLES AND PROCEDURES SUMMARY

The costs of manufacturing operations are recorded in new accounts that fall into three classifications: raw materials, direct labor, and manufacturing overhead. Inventory accounts are required for raw materials, work in process, and finished goods. The Finished Goods Inventory account shows the cost of the completed products ready for sale and thus corresponds to the Merchandise Inventory account of a merchandising business.

A corporation that manufactures goods prepares a balance sheet, income statement, and statement of retained earnings similar to that of any other corporation. In addition, a statement of cost of goods manufactured is prepared to show the results of the manufacturing activities. The total cost of goods manufactured appears on the income statement as part of the cost of goods sold, corresponding to the merchandise purchases on the income statement of a merchandising business.

MANAGERIAL IMPLICATIONS

In order for managers to plan and control operations, they need reliable accounting data about the costs of doing business. In a manufacturing firm, managers must be alert to control the costs involved in producing goods. The periodic statement of cost of goods manufactured provides detailed information about both the total cost of manufacturing and individual cost elements. Managers use this data to evaluate past performance and to guide future operations so that the firm can obtain the greatest profit.

REVIEW QUESTIONS

1. What does the statement of cost of goods manufactured show?
2. How do the accounting problems of a manufacturing business differ from

those of a merchandising business? In what ways does this difference affect the chart of accounts?

3. What procedure is used on the statement of cost of goods manufactured to arrive at the cost of raw materials used?
4. Define the term *direct materials*.
5. Define the term *indirect materials*.
6. What is direct labor?
7. What is indirect labor?
8. It is possible that one company might consider an item, such as paint, as one of its direct materials, while another company with identical manufacturing processes might classify the item as one of its indirect materials. Why?
9. How would the wages of the employee who issues materials from the factory storeroom be classified?
10. What is manufacturing overhead?
11. Why does the figure for total manufacturing cost not equal the cost of goods manufactured?
12. What is meant by work in process?
13. How does the work in process inventory enter into the computation of the cost of goods manufactured?
14. How does the cost of goods manufactured figure differ from the cost of goods sold figure?
15. How does the cost of goods manufactured relate to the income statement?
16. Name the three inventory accounts found in the chart of accounts of a manufacturing business and explain each one.
17. How is the work in process inventory determined?
18. Give five examples of manufacturing overhead items.

MANAGERIAL DISCUSSION QUESTIONS

1. Why do managers need special manufacturing records and a separate end-of-period statement reporting the costs involved in producing goods?
2. Assume that a director of a firm where you work asks you to explain the difference between cost of goods sold and cost of goods manufactured. She points out that the firm sells its own products exclusively. What explanation would you provide?
3. How can an inventory be taken if work in process items are in varying stages of completion at the end of the accounting period?
4. Why might management want direct labor costs separated from indirect labor costs?
5. Assume that you work for a merchandising company that has decided to manufacture its own products. What additional records will be necessary?
6. Why should management not use the statement of cost of goods manufactured alone as a means of measuring efficiency and controlling manufacturing costs?

EXERCISES

EXERCISE 39-1   **Computing the cost of materials used.** The Howard Company's beginning raw materials inventory was $109,600. Its net purchases for the period were $216,590, and its ending raw materials inventory was $93,700. What was its cost of raw materials used?

EXERCISE 39-2   **Determining an element of the cost of materials used.** During one month the O'Sullivan Company used $83,450 of raw materials. Its ending inventory of raw materials was $32,700. What was the total of the raw materials that it had available for use during the month?

EXERCISE 39-3   **Determining an element of the cost of materials used.** Refer to Exercise 39-2. The O'Sullivan Company's net purchases for the month totaled $79,850. What was its beginning raw materials inventory?

EXERCISE 39-4   **Determining an element of the cost of goods manufactured.** The Danville Company's total manufacturing cost for a year was $1,844,530. Its manufacturing overhead was $300,000, and its cost of raw materials used was $833,560. What was its direct labor cost for the year?

EXERCISE 39-5   **Determining an element of the cost of goods manufactured.** Refer to Exercise 39-4. The Danville Company's beginning work in process inventory was $237,600. Its cost of goods manufactured was $1,823,300. What was its ending work in process inventory?

EXERCISE 39-6   **Determining an element of the cost of goods sold.** The LeMay Company's cost of goods sold was $933,040 for one month. Its inventory of finished goods at the end of the month was $82,345. What was its total cost of goods available for sale during the month?

EXERCISE 39-7   **Determining an element of the cost of goods sold.** Refer to Exercise 39-6. Assume that the LeMay Company's beginning inventory of finished goods was $79,670. What was its cost of goods manufactured for the month?

EXERCISE 39-8   **Computing the cost of goods sold.** During one year the Todd Company had net sales of $1,620,000. Its gross profit was $460,000. What was its cost of goods sold?

EXERCISE 39-9   **Determining an element of the cost of goods sold.** Refer to Exercise 39-8. Assume that the Todd Company's ending inventory of finished goods was $32,600. What was its cost of goods available for sale?

EXERCISE 39-10   **Determining an element of the cost of goods sold.** Refer to Exercises 39-8 and 39-9. Assume that the Todd Company's beginning inventory of finished goods was $38,454. What was its cost of goods manufactured?

EXERCISE 39-11 **Determining an element of the cost of goods manufactured.** Refer to Exercises 39-8, 39-9, and 39-10. Assume that the Todd Company's beginning inventory of work in process was $60,020 and that its ending inventory of work in process was $57,980. What was its total manufacturing cost for the year?

EXERCISE 39-12 **Identifying items that are reported on the statement of cost of goods manufactured.** Which of the following items is least likely to appear on the statement of cost of goods manufactured?

1. Amortization of organization costs
2. Amortization of patents
3. Taxes on factory building

EXERCISE 39-13 **Identifying items that are reported on the statement of cost of goods manufactured.** Which of the following items would not be shown on the statement of cost of goods manufactured?

1. Finished goods inventory
2. Raw materials inventory
3. Work in process inventory

EXERCISE 39-14 **Identifying items that are classified as manufacturing overhead.** Which of the following items should not be included in the Manufacturing Overhead section of the statement of cost of goods manufactured?

1. Factory insurance
2. Payroll taxes on the wages of factory employees
3. Freight charges on purchases of raw materials

PROBLEMS

PROBLEM 39-1 **Preparing a statement of cost of goods manufactured.** Information about the Amtech Company, a maker of digital clocks, is given below and on page 951.

Instructions Prepare a statement of cost of goods manufactured for the month ended December 31, 19X4.

	DEC. 1, 19X4	DEC. 31, 19X4
Finished Goods Inventory	$16,200	$ 33,620
Raw Materials Inventory	8,000	7,300
Work in Process Inventory	6,200	5,100
Direct Labor		64,500
Freight In		1,612
Indirect Labor		24,020
Indirect Materials and Supplies		1,819
Insurance—Factory		2,937
Depreciation—Factory Building and Equipment		3,501
Materials Purchases		130,000

	DEC. 31, 19X4
Payroll Taxes—Factory	7,600
Utilities—Factory	4,725
Property Taxes—Factory	4,220
Materials Purchases Ret. and Allow.	310
Repairs and Maintenance—Factory	3,016

PROBLEM 39-2 **Preparing a statement of cost of goods manufactured and an income statement.** The Glenbrook Manufacturing Company makes tents and other camping equipment. Selected account balances for this firm on December 31, 19X2, the end of its fiscal year, are given below. Data about the beginning and ending inventories is also shown.

Instructions **1.** Prepare a statement of cost of goods manufactured for 19X2.
2. Prepare an income statement for 19X2.

ACCOUNTS	BALANCES
Sales	$495,138.35
Sales Returns and Allowances	3,782.15
Interest Income	240.00
Materials Purchases	141,092.30
Direct Labor	80,870.25
Indirect Labor	16,763.35
Payroll Taxes—Factory	9,435.40
Utilities—Factory	8,433.50
Repairs and Maintenance—Factory	11,391.80
Indirect Materials and Supplies	6,808.50
Depreciation—Factory Building	750.00
Depreciation—Factory Equipment	2,400.00
Insurance—Factory	4,530.20
Property Taxes—Factory	6,217.30
Sales Salaries Expense	26,225.00
Payroll Taxes Expense—Selling	2,210.30
Delivery Expense	21,240.60
Sales Supplies and Expense	31,248.75
Advertising Expense	11,710.20
Officers' Salaries Expense	55,000.00
Office Salaries Expense	17,325.00
Payroll Taxes Expense—Administrative	6,615.10
Office Supplies and Expense	6,310.20
Organization Costs Written Off	100.00

INVENTORY DATA	JAN. 1, 19X2	DEC. 31, 19X2
Finished Goods Inventory	$34,500	$33,600
Work in Process Inventory	25,400	24,950
Raw Materials Inventory	27,300	26,980

PROBLEM 39-3 **Preparing a statement of cost of goods manufactured and an income statement.** The data given below is for the Petrocelli Corporation, which makes toys.

Instructions 1. Prepare a statement of cost of goods manufactured for the year ended December 31, 19X1.

2. Prepare an income statement for the same period.

	JAN. 1, 19X1	DEC. 31, 19X1
Finished Goods Inventory	$35,000	$ 33,500
Raw Materials Inventory	19,500	18,800
Work in Process Inventory	14,500	14,300
Delivery Expense		14,000
Depreciation—Factory Building and Equipment		6,135
Direct Labor		142,735
Freight In		4,250
Indirect Labor		24,620
Indirect Materials and Supplies		4,287
Insurance—Factory		4,335
Materials Purchases		177,500
Payroll Taxes—Factory		16,862
Payroll Taxes Expense—Selling		2,785
Payroll Taxes Expense—Administrative		4,750
Officers' Salaries Expense		30,000
Office Salaries Expense		18,000
Office Supplies and Expense		21,000
Sales Salaries Expense		28,000
Sales Supplies and Expense		20,000
Utilities—Factory		8,841
Property Taxes—Factory		6,178
Materials Purchases Ret. and Allow.		610
Repairs and Maintenance—Factory		11,233
Sales		593,400
Sales Returns and Allowances		2,745
Estimated Income Taxes		12,500

ALTERNATE PROBLEMS

PROBLEM 39-1A **Preparing a statement of cost of goods manufactured.** The Music Masters Corporation makes electric guitars. Information about the company's operations appears below and on page 953.

Instructions Prepare a statement of cost of goods manufactured for the year ended December 31, 19X2.

	JAN. 1, 19X2	DEC. 31, 19X2
Finished Goods Inventory	$618,000	$ 531,000
Raw Materials Inventory	304,500	368,200
Work in Process Inventory	103,000	88,750
Direct Labor		1,444,000

DEC. 31, 19X2

Freight In	33,940
Indirect Labor	416,500
Indirect Materials and Supplies	67,340
Insurance—Factory	18,550
Depreciation—Factory Building and Equipment	116,800
Materials Purchases	2,040,000
Payroll Taxes—Factory	179,000
Utilities—Factory	83,010
Property Taxes—Factory	42,700
Materials Purchases Ret. and Allow.	2,720
Repairs and Maintenance—Factory	61,400
Patent Amortization	1,600
Waste Removal—Factory	16,800

PROBLEM 39-2A **Preparing a statement of cost of goods manufactured and an income statement.** The Highland Manufacturing Company makes small tools. Selected account balances for this firm on December 31, 19X1, the end of its fiscal year, are given below. Data about the beginning and ending inventories is on page 954.

Instructions 1. Prepare a statement of cost of goods manufactured for 19X1.
2. Prepare an income statement for 19X1.

ACCOUNTS	BALANCES
Depreciation—Factory Building and Equipment	$ 113,000
Depreciation Expense—Office Furniture and Equipment	4,500
Depreciation Expense—Delivery Equipment	9,000
Direct Labor	1,200,000
Freight In	31,000
Indirect Labor	216,000
Indirect Materials and Supplies	83,000
Insurance—Factory	12,600
Materials Purchases	1,628,000
Payroll Taxes—Factory	136,000
Payroll Taxes Expense—Administrative	15,800
Payroll Taxes Expense—Selling	9,000
Officers' Salaries Expense	90,000
Office Salaries Expense	72,000
Other Administrative Expenses	75,000
Sales Salaries Expense	92,000
Other Selling Expenses	63,000
Utilities—Factory	28,000
Property Taxes—Factory	13,900
Property Taxes Expense—Administrative	3,000
Materials Purchases Ret. and Allow.	39,000
Repairs and Maintenance—Factory	19,380
Repairs and Maintenance Expense—Office	3,200
Sales	4,395,000
Sales Returns and Allowances	8,430
Estimated Income Taxes	187,000

INVENTORY DATA	JAN. 1, 19X1	DEC. 31, 19X1
Finished Goods Inventory	$722,000	$704,000
Work in Process Inventory	101,600	93,800
Raw Materials Inventory	163,000	171,300

PROBLEM 39-3A   **Preparing a statement of cost of goods manufactured and an income statement.** The data given below is for the Segundo Corporation, which makes shirts.

Instructions   1. Prepare a statement of cost of goods manufactured for the year ended December 31, 19X1.
2. Prepare an income statement for the same period.

	JAN. 1, 19X1	DEC. 31, 19X1
Finished Goods Inventory	$40,000	$ 35,000
Raw Materials Inventory	20,000	20,500
Work in Process Inventory	11,000	11,200
Depreciation—Factory Building and Equipment		4,420
Direct Labor		109,875
Freight In		5,510
Indirect Labor		20,125
Indirect Materials and Supplies		3,470
Insurance—Factory		5,120
Materials Purchases		130,000
Office Salaries Expense		18,000
Officers' Salaries Expense		30,000
Other Office Expenses		21,000
Payroll Taxes Expense—Administrative		5,100
Payroll Taxes—Factory		12,870
Payroll Taxes Expense—Selling		4,960
Utilities—Factory		7,963
Property Taxes—Factory		5,220
Materials Purchases Discount		2,010
Materials Purchases Ret. and Allow.		400
Repairs and Maintenance—Factory		8,145
Sales		501,000
Sales Salaries Expense		50,080
Other Selling Expenses		20,600
Estimated Income Taxes		4,400
Other Administrative Expenses		8,000

CHAPTER 40

In earlier chapters you learned about the end-of-period procedures for service businesses and merchandising businesses. The end-of-period procedures for manufacturing businesses are similar but do involve certain differences. These differences are explained and illustrated in the present chapter. The discussion is based on the end-of-year activities of the Woodcraft Manufacturing Corporation on December 31, 19X5. This corporation was founded three years earlier when it purchased the assets of a company owned by Richard Strauss.

END-OF-PERIOD WORK FOR A MANUFACTURING BUSINESS

THE WORKSHEET FOR A MANUFACTURING BUSINESS

The worksheet for a manufacturing business is like that prepared for a merchandising firm, with one basic difference. There is an additional pair of columns in which to assemble the figures needed for the statement of cost of goods manufactured. Refer to the worksheet for the Woodcraft Manufacturing Corporation illustrated on pages 960 and 961 to see the arrangement of the columns.

When the original trial balance is entered on the worksheet, all the general ledger accounts except the summary accounts are listed. In this way, accounts that have no balances will be in the proper order when the adjustments are recorded later.

Adjustments

Adjusting entries are made in the Adjustments columns as before. Each part of an adjusting entry is identified by a letter for cross-reference. Examination of the trial balance figures and related information for the Woodcraft Manufacturing Corporation shows the need for some entries peculiar to manufacturing operations, as well as for a number of standard adjustments. The adjustments for Woodcraft are illustrated on page 956 and explained below and on pages 957 and 958. Carefully follow each item discussed, and trace its treatment on the worksheet.

Uncollectible Accounts The firm's accountant estimates that its uncollectible accounts will run about 0.2 percent of net sales. (Woodcraft makes all sales on credit.) The net sales figure is determined from the trial balance data as shown below.

Sales	$495,138.35
Less Sales Returns and Allowances	3,782.15
Net Sales	$491,356.20

Estimated Uncollectible Accounts: $491,356.20 \times 0.002 = \$982.71$

WOODCRAFT MANUFACTURING CORPORATION
Worksheet (Partial)
Year Ended December 31, 19X5

	ACCT. NO.	ACCOUNT NAME	TRIAL BALANCE DEBIT	TRIAL BALANCE CREDIT	ADJUSTMENTS DEBIT	ADJUSTMENTS CREDIT
1	101	Cash	41,196 87			
2	111	Accounts Receivable	55,375 15			
3	112	Allowance for Uncollectible Accounts		135 00		(a)982 71
4	116	Interest Receivable			(b)133 33	
5	121	Raw Materials Inventory	26,000 00			
6	122	Work in Process Inventory	10,500 00			
7	126	Finished Goods Inventory	28,700 00			
8	128	Prepaid Insurance	2,200 00			(c)380 00
9	129	Supplies on Hand			(d)800 00	
10	135	MNO Corporation 16% Bonds, 19Y2	5,400 00			(b)10 00
11	140	Land	7,500 00			
12	141	Factory Building	30,500 00			
13	142	Accumulated Depreciation—Factory Building		2,000 00		(e)750 00
14	143	Factory Equipment	38,500 00			
15	144	Accumulated Depreciation—Factory Equipment		5,300 00		(f)2,400 00
16	191	Organization Costs	200 00			(g)100 00
17	202	Accounts Payable		27,505 45		
18	208	Dividends Payable—Preferred		5,600 00		
19	209	Dividends Payable—Common		5,000 00		
20	215	Salaries and Wages Payable				(h)990 00
21	221	FICA Tax Payable		415 35		(i)74 25
22	222	Employee Income Tax Payable		673 20		
23	226	Unemployment Taxes Payable		1,500 00		
24	301	Common Stock		50,000 00		
25	305	Paid-in Capital in Excess of Stated Value		400 00		
26	311	Preferred Stock—8%		70,000 00		
27	315	Premium on Preferred Stock		3,000 00		
28	381	Retained Earnings		27,672 70		
29	382	Retained Earnings Appropriated for Plant Expansion		10,000 00		
30	401	Sales		495,138 35		
31	452	Sales Returns and Allowances	3,782 15			
32	492	Interest Income		616 67		(b)123 33
33	501	Materials Purchases	144,092 30			
34	502	Purchases Returns and Allowances		380 00		
35	503	Purchases Discount		2,620 00		
36	511	Direct Labor	80,050 25		(h)820 00	
37	521	Indirect Labor	16,593 35		(h)170 00	
38	523	Payroll Taxes—Factory	7,680 20		(i)74 25	
39	531	Utilities—Factory	8,433 50			
40	532	Repairs and Maintenance—Factory	11,391 80			
41	539	Indirect Materials and Supplies	7,608 50			(d)800 00
42	541	Depreciation—Factory Building			(e)750 00	
43	542	Depreciation—Factory Equipment			(f)2,400 00	
44	551	Insurance—Factory	4,150 20		(c)380 00	
45	552	Property Taxes—Factory	6,217 30			
46	601	Sales Salaries Expense	25,625 00			
47	603	Payroll Taxes Expense—Sales	1,810 30			
48	621	Delivery Expense	21,240 60			
49	629	Sales Supplies and Other Selling Expenses	28,248 75			
50	631	Advertising Expense	11,710 20			
51	651	Officers' Salaries Expense	55,000 00			
52	652	Office Salaries Expense	16,225 00			
53	653	Payroll Taxes Expense—Administrative	5,715 10			
54	669	Office Supplies and Other Office Expenses	6,310 20			
55	671	Loss From Uncollectible Accounts			(a)982 71	
56	691	Organization Costs Written Off			(g)100 00	
57		Totals	707,956 72	707,956 72	6,610 29	6,610 29
58		Cost of Goods Manufactured				
59						
60		Provision for Income Taxes				
61		Net Income After Income Taxes				

Therefore, Adjustment (a) for $982.71 is recorded on the worksheet as a debit to Loss From Uncollectible Accounts and a credit to Allowance for Uncollectible Accounts.

Interest Receivable The records show that the long-term investment in MNO Corporation 16% Bonds, 19Y2, has a face value of $5,000. These bonds pay interest semiannually on May 1 and November 1. Two months' interest, $133.33 ($5,000 × 0.16 × 2/12), has accrued and must be recorded. The firm's records also show that the bonds were purchased at a premium amounting to $5 a month over the remaining life of the bonds. Consequently, two months' premium, $10, must be amortized. The adjusting entry required, Adjustment (b), debits Interest Receivable for $133.33, credits MNO Corporation 16% Bonds, 19Y2, for $10, and credits Interest Income for $123.33.

Expired Insurance When insurance premiums are paid, the asset account Prepaid Insurance is debited. The amount of the expired premium must be transferred to Insurance—Factory each month. During the month of December 19X5, $380 of the insurance premium has expired. Adjustment (c) debits Insurance—Factory for $380 and credits Prepaid Insurance for the same amount.

Supplies on Hand At the Woodcraft Manufacturing Corporation, supplies are charged to an expense account when purchased. At the end of December, there are factory supplies on hand that cost $800 and small amounts of sales supplies and office supplies. Adjustment (d) debits the asset account Supplies on Hand for $800 and credits the expense account Indirect Materials and Supplies for the same amount. The value of the sales supplies and office supplies is considered too small to justify an adjusting entry.

Depreciation Each month during the year, the amount of depreciation for the current year to date is recorded on the firm's worksheet by an adjusting entry. However, depreciation charges are not actually recorded in the ledger until the end of the year. On December 31 a full year's depreciation is recorded. On the factory building, this amounts to $750. Accordingly, Adjustment (e) is made, debiting Depreciation—Factory Building and crediting Accumulated Depreciation—Factory Building for $750. Depreciation on the factory equipment for the year amounts to $2,400. Adjustment (f) debits Depreciation—Factory Equipment and credits Accumulated Depreciation—Factory Equipment for $2,400.

Organization Costs Written Off Costs amounting to $500 were incurred in organizing the Woodcraft Manufacturing Corporation. These were debited to an intangible asset account called Organization Costs. Following income tax accounting procedures, $100 of this amount is charged to expense each year. Adjustment (g) debits Organization Costs Written Off and credits Organization Costs for $100.

Accrued Payroll Woodcraft's officers and sales and office personnel are paid monthly salaries and have no accrued amounts due them. However, the factory workers are paid weekly and, on December 31, have worked three days since the end of their last pay period. Of the amount owed to the factory employees, $820 was earned by direct labor and $170 by indirect labor. Adjustment (h) debits Direct Labor for $820, debits Indirect Labor for $170, and credits Salaries and Wages Payable for $990.

Payroll Taxes on Accrued Payroll Payroll taxes are computed and recorded each pay period as salaries and wages are paid. These taxes must also be calculated on the $990 of accrued wages for the factory workers. The amount of taxes due is estimated to be only $74.25 for FICA tax because all of the workers have already earned the maximum amount subject to federal and state unemployment tax rules. Adjustment (i) debits Payroll Taxes—Factory and credits FICA Tax Payable for $74.25.

Adjusted Trial Balance

After the adjustments discussed above are entered on the worksheet, the Adjustments columns must be totaled and the equality of the debits and credits must be verified. Then the original trial balance figures are combined with the adjustments, and the new amounts are extended to the third pair of money columns, headed Adjusted Trial Balance. When this has been done, the figures in both columns are added to prove the equality of the debits and credits, as is shown in the illustration on pages 960 and 961.

Entering Ending Inventories on the Worksheet

Whenever financial statements are to be prepared, the ending inventories must be determined for the raw materials, work in process, and finished goods. As of December 31, the inventories of the Woodcraft Manufacturing Corporation were valued as follows: raw materials inventory, $25,000; work in process inventory, $10,000; and finished goods inventory, $27,500.

These ending inventories are recorded directly in the related statement columns of the worksheet. Remember that on the worksheet for a merchandising firm the merchandise inventory is entered directly in the Balance Sheet Debit column and the Income Statement Credit column. The same treatment is given the ending finished goods inventory of a manufacturing business. It is entered in the Balance Sheet Debit column and the Income Statement Credit column (where it is needed for determining the cost of goods sold).

The ending inventories of raw materials and work in process are also entered in the Balance Sheet Debit column. However, these figures are needed to determine the cost of goods manufactured, so they are entered in the Cost of Goods Manufactured Credit column of the worksheet (see page 961).

Completing the Worksheet

The account numbers in the chart of accounts of the Woodcraft Manufacturing Corporation are grouped according to the financial statements on which the accounts will appear. Accounts in the 100, 200, and 300 blocks appear on the balance sheet.

The 400 group includes revenue and revenue deductions that appear on the income statement. The 500 group covers manufacturing costs associated with the statement of cost of goods manufactured. The 600 group is used for selling and administrative expenses appearing on the income statement. These groupings should be kept in mind as the figures are carried across the worksheet from the Adjusted Trial Balance columns to the statement columns. Remember that balances never change sides when they are extended across the worksheet. Debits in the Adjusted Trial Balance section appear in the proper statement columns as debits, and credits in the Adjusted Trial Balance section appear in the proper statement columns as credits.

The three beginning inventory amounts need special attention. The debits for the beginning inventories of raw materials (Line 5) and work in process (Line 6) are extended from the Adjusted Trial Balance section to the Debit column of the Cost of Goods Manufactured section for use in the statement of cost of goods manufactured. The debit for the beginning inventory of finished goods is extended to the Income Statement Debit column since it must be used to determine the cost of goods sold.

	ACCT. NO.	ACCOUNT NAME	COST OF GOODS MANUFACTURED		INCOME STATEMENT		BALANCE SHEET		
			DEBIT	CREDIT	DEBIT	CREDIT	DEBIT	CREDIT	
5	121	Raw Materials Inventory	26,000 00	25,000 00			25,000 00		5
6	122	Work in Process Inventory	10,500 00	10,000 00			10,000 00		6
7	126	Finished Goods Inventory			28,700 00	27,500 00	27,500 00		7

After each of the figures has been carried from the Adjusted Trial Balance section to the appropriate financial statement column, the worksheet is completed by following the procedures discussed below.

Totaling and Balancing the Statement Columns

Cost of Goods Manufactured When the Cost of Goods Manufactured section is totaled, the Debit column amounts to $326,511.65 and the Credit column amounts to $38,000, as shown in the completed worksheet on pages 960–961. The difference of $288,511.65 is identified as Cost of Goods Manufactured and is entered as a debit in the Income Statement section and as a credit in the Cost of Goods Manufactured section. After this transfer is recorded, both columns of the Cost of Goods Manufactured section total $326,511.65 and are ruled with double lines.

Income Statement The Income Statement columns are now totaled. The debits amount to $493,961.66; the credits amount to $523,378.35. The excess of credits, $29,416.69, indicates a net income.

Next the income taxes payable on the net income are estimated. The estimate—$4,633.34—is entered as a debit in the Income Statement section and as a credit in the Balance Sheet section. It is labeled Provision for Income Taxes. The remaining $24,783.35 is labeled Net Income After Income Taxes and is entered as a debit in the Income Statement section and as a credit in the Balance Sheet section. The Income Statement columns, which now both total $523,378.35, are ruled.

Balance Sheet The worksheet is completed by adding the Debit and Credit columns in the Balance Sheet section. Since each column totals $244,200.35, the equality of the debits and credits is proved.

	ACCT. NO.	ACCOUNT NAME	TRIAL BALANCE DEBIT	TRIAL BALANCE CREDIT	ADJUSTMENTS DEBIT	ADJUSTMENTS CREDIT
1	101	Cash	41,196 87			
2	111	Accounts Receivable	55,375 15			
3	112	Allowance for Uncollectible Accounts		135 00		(a)982 71
4	116	Interest Receivable			(b)133 33	
5	121	Raw Materials Inventory	26,000 00			
6	122	Work in Process Inventory	10,500 00			
7	126	Finished Goods Inventory	28,700 00			
8	128	Prepaid Insurance	2,200 00			(c)380 00
9	129	Supplies on Hand			(d)800 00	
10	135	MNO Corporation 16% Bonds, 19Y2	5,400 00			(b)10 00
11	140	Land	7,500 00			
12	141	Factory Building	30,500 00			
13	142	Accumulated Depreciation—Factory Building		2,000 00		(e)750 00
14	143	Factory Equipment	38,500 00			
15	144	Accumulated Depreciation—Factory Equipment		5,300 00		(f)2,400 00
16	191	Organization Costs	200 00			(g)100 00
17	202	Accounts Payable		27,505 45		
18	208	Dividends Payable—Preferred		5,600 00		
19	209	Dividends Payable—Common		5,000 00		
20	215	Salaries and Wages Payable				(h)990 00
21	221	FICA Tax Payable		415 35		(i)74 25
22	222	Employee Income Tax Payable		673 20		
23	226	Unemployment Taxes Payable		1,500 00		
24	301	Common Stock		50,000 00		
25	305	Paid-in Capital in Excess of Stated Value		400 00		
26	311	Preferred Stock—8%		70,000 00		
27	315	Premium on Preferred Stock		3,000 00		
28	381	Retained Earnings		27,672 70		
29	382	Retained Earnings Appropriated for Plant Expansion		10,000 00		
30	401	Sales		495,138 35		
31	452	Sales Returns and Allowances	3,782 15			
32	492	Interest Income		616 67		(b)123 33
33	501	Materials Purchases	144,092 30			
34	502	Purchases Returns and Allowances		380 00		
35	503	Purchases Discount		2,620 00		
36	511	Direct Labor	80,050 25		(h)820 00	
37	521	Indirect Labor	16,593 35		(h)170 00	
38	523	Payroll Taxes—Factory	7,680 20		(i)74 25	
39	531	Utilities—Factory	8,433 50			
40	532	Repairs and Maintenance—Factory	11,391 80			
41	539	Indirect Materials and Supplies	7,608 50			(d)800 00
42	541	Depreciation—Factory Building			(e)750 00	
43	542	Depreciation—Factory Equipment			(f)2,400 00	
44	551	Insurance—Factory	4,150 20		(c)380 00	
45	552	Property Taxes—Factory	6,217 30			
46	601	Sales Salaries Expense	25,625 00			
47	603	Payroll Taxes Expense—Sales	1,810 30			
48	621	Delivery Expense	21,240 60			
49	629	Sales Supplies and Other Selling Expenses	28,248 75			
50	631	Advertising Expense	11,710 20			
51	651	Officers' Salaries Expense	55,000 00			
52	652	Office Salaries Expense	16,225 00			
53	653	Payroll Taxes Expense—Administrative	5,715 10			
54	669	Office Supplies and Other Office Expenses	6,310 20			
55	671	Loss From Uncollectible Accounts			(a)982 71	
56	691	Organization Costs Written Off			(g)100 00	
57		Totals	707,956 72	707,956 72	6,610 29	6,610 29
58		Cost of Goods Manufactured				
59		Provision for Income Taxes				
60		Net Income After Income Taxes				
61						
62						

Handwritten annotations: "given" (above Cost of Goods Manufactured), "given" (above Income Statement).

	ADJUSTED TRIAL BALANCE		COST OF GOODS MANUFACTURED		INCOME STATEMENT		BALANCE SHEET		
	DEBIT	CREDIT	DEBIT	CREDIT	DEBIT	CREDIT	DEBIT	CREDIT	
	41,196 87						41,196 87		1
	55,375 15						55,375 15		2
		1,117 71						1,117 71	3
	133 33						133 33		4
	26,000 00		26,000 00	25,000 00			25,000 00		5
	10,500 00		10,500 00	10,000 00			10,000 00		6
	28,700 00				28,700 00	27,500 00	27,500 00		7
	1,820 00						1,820 00		8
	800 00						800 00		9
	5,390 00						5,390 00		10
	7,500 00						7,500 00		11
	30,500 00						30,500 00		12
		2,750 00						2,750 00	13
	38,500 00						38,500 00		14
		7,700 00						7,700 00	15
	100 00						100 00		16
		27,505 45						27,505 45	17
		5,600 00						5,600 00	18
		5,000 00						5,000 00	19
		990 00						990 00	20
		489 60						489 60	21
		673 20						673 20	22
		1,500 00						1,500 00	23
		50,000 00						50,000 00	24
		400 00						400 00	25
		70,000 00						70,000 00	26
		3,000 00						3,000 00	27
		27,672 70						27,672 70	28
		10,000 00						10,000 00	29
		495,138 35				495,138 35			30
	3,782 15				3,782 15				31
		740 00				740 00			32
	144,092 30		144,092 30						33
		380 00		380 00					34
		2,620 00		2,620 00					35
	80,870 25		80,870 25						36
	16,763 35		16,763 35						37
	7,754 45		7,754 45						38
	8,433 50		8,433 50						39
	11,391 80		11,391 80						40
	6,808 50		6,808 50						41
	750 00		750 00						42
	2,400 00		2,400 00						43
	4,530 20		4,530 20						44
	6,217 30		6,217 30						45
	25,625 00				25,625 00				46
	1,810 30				1,810 30				47
	21,240 60				21,240 60				48
	28,248 75				28,248 75				49
	11,710 20				11,710 20				50
	55,000 00				55,000 00				51
	16,225 00				16,225 00				52
	5,715 10				5,715 10				53
	6,310 20				6,310 20				54
	982 71				982 71				55
	100 00				100 00				56
	713,277 01	713,277 01	326,511 65	38,000 00	288,511 65				57
				288,511 65					58
			326,511 65	326,511 65	493,961 66	523,378 35			59
					4,633 34			4,633 34	60
					24,783 35			24,783 35	61
					523,378 35	523,378 35	244,200 35	244,200 35	62

Handwritten annotations:
- Closing entry #1 closed to Manufacturing Summary (circling Cost of Goods Manufactured debit column)
- Closing Entry #2 – also closed to manufacturing Summary (circling Cost of Goods Manufactured credit column)
- Closing entry #3 closed to Inc. Summary (circling Income Statement credit column)
- Closing entry #4 closed to Inc. Summary includes a credit to manufact. Summary (circling Income Statement debit column)

As soon as the worksheet is completed, the following four financial statements are prepared: a balance sheet (Exhibit A), an income statement (Exhibit B), a schedule of cost of goods manufactured (Schedule B-1), and a statement of retained earnings (Exhibit C).

Notice that this listing of financial reports identifies the three main statements as exhibits and the new statement of cost of goods manufactured as a schedule related to the income statement (to which its final figure is carried). In the illustrations that follow, all figures that are carried from one statement to another are labeled with the related exhibit or schedule designation for easy cross-reference. Although the balance sheet usually appears as the first statement in published reports, it cannot be completed until Schedule B-1, Exhibit B, and Exhibit C have been prepared in turn.

Statement of Cost of Goods Manufactured

The figures for the statement of cost of goods manufactured all appear on the worksheet. This statement is presented below in the form used in the previous chapter. Notice the reference showing that the final figure is transferred to the income statement.

WOODCRAFT MANUFACTURING CORPORATION Statement of Cost of Goods Manufactured Year Ended December 31, 19X5			Schedule B-1
Raw Materials			
Raw Materials Inventory, Jan. 1			$ 26,000.00
Materials Purchases		$144,092.30	
Less Purchases Returns and Allowances	$ 380.00		
Purchases Discount	2,620.00	3,000.00	
Net Purchases			141,092.30
Total Materials Available			$167,092.30
Less Raw Materials Inventory, Dec. 31			25,000.00
Raw Materials Used			$142,092.30
Direct Labor *- actual account*			80,870.25
Manufacturing Overhead			
Indirect Labor		$ 16,763.35	
Payroll Taxes—Factory		7,754.45	
Utilities—Factory		8,433.50	
Repairs and Maintenance—Factory		11,391.80	
Indirect Materials and Supplies		6,808.50	
Depreciation—Factory Building		750.00	
Depreciation—Factory Equipment		2,400.00	
Insurance—Factory		4,530.20	
Property Taxes—Factory		6,217.30	
Total Manufacturing Overhead			65,049.10
Total Manufacturing Cost			$288,011.65
Add Work in Process Inventory, Jan. 1			+10,500.00
			$298,511.65
Less Work in Process Inventory, Dec. 31			−10,000.00
Cost of Goods Manufactured (to Exhibit B)			$288,511.65

Income Statement

All the figures needed for the income statement are available on the worksheet, including the total cost of goods manufactured (which is supported by the detailed statement of cost of goods manufactured). The income statement of the Woodcraft Manufacturing Corporation for the year ended December 31, 19X5, is shown below. Reference is made on the income statement to Schedule B-1 for the details of the cost of goods manufactured figure. The final net income after income taxes figure is transferred from the income statement to the statement of retained earnings. (Notice the reference at the bottom of the income statement explaining that this last figure is carried over to Exhibit C.)

WOODCRAFT MANUFACTURING CORPORATION			Exhibit B
Income Statement			
Year Ended December 31, 19X5			
Revenue			
Sales			$495,138.35
Less Sales Returns and Allowances			3,782.15
Net Sales			$491,356.20
Cost of Goods Sold			
Finished Goods Inventory, Jan. 1		$ 28,700.00	
Cost of Goods Manufactured (Schedule B-1)		288,511.65	
Total Goods Available for Sale		$317,211.65	
Less Finished Goods Inventory, Dec. 31		27,500.00	
Cost of Goods Sold			289,711.65
Gross Profit on Sales			$201,644.55
Operating Expenses			
Selling Expenses			
Sales Salaries Expense	$25,625.00		
Payroll Taxes Expense—Sales	1,810.30		
Delivery Expense	21,240.60		
Sales Supplies and Other Selling Expenses	28,248.75		
Advertising Expense	11,710.20		
Total Selling Expenses		$ 88,634.85	
Administrative Expenses			
Officers' Salaries Expense	$55,000.00		
Office Salaries Expense	16,225.00		
Payroll Taxes Expense—Administrative	5,715.10		
Office Supplies and Other Office Expenses	6,310.20		
Loss From Uncollectible Accounts	982.71		
Total Administrative Expenses		84,233.01	
Total Operating Expenses			172,867.86
Net Income From Operations			$ 28,776.69
Other Income			
Interest Income			740.00
Total Income for Year			$ 29,516.69
Other Expense			
Organization Costs Written Off			100.00
Net Income Before Income Taxes			$ 29,416.69
Provision for Income Taxes			4,633.34
Net Income After Income Taxes (to Exhibit C)			$ 24,783.35

Statement of Retained Earnings

The only statement for which all the needed figures are not supplied by the worksheet is the statement of retained earnings. Reference must be made to the general ledger to find the balance of the Retained Earnings account at the beginning of the period and to find the entries made in the account during the period. In this case, inspection of the ledger account reveals that on December 5, 19X5, the board of directors declared yearly dividends of 8 percent on the $70,000 par value of preferred stock outstanding and $5 a share on the 1,000 shares of common stock outstanding. On the same date, the board also ordered $5,000 transferred from Retained Earnings to the Retained Earnings Appropriated for Plant Expansion account. The Retained Earnings account with the entries just described is shown below.

		Retained Earnings				No.	381
DATE	EXPLANATION	POST. REF.	DEBIT	CREDIT	BALANCE	DR. CR.	
19 X5							
Jan. 1	Balance	✓			43,272 70	Cr.	
Dec. 5	Preferred Dividend	J12	5,600 00		37,672 70	Cr.	
5	Common Dividend	J12	5,000 00		32,672 70	Cr.	
5	Appropriated for Plant Expansion	J12	5,000 00		27,672 70	Cr.	

The one other figure needed, the net income after income taxes, is obtained from the worksheet. Then the statement of retained earnings can be prepared in the form shown below. The final balance is carried over to the balance sheet.

WOODCRAFT MANUFACTURING CORPORATION		Exhibit C
Statement of Retained Earnings		
Year Ended December 31, 19X5		
Balance, January 1		$43,272.70
Additions:		
Net Income After Income Taxes (Exhibit B)		24,783.35
		$68,056.05
Deductions:		
Dividends on Preferred Stock	$5,600.00	
Dividends on Common Stock	5,000.00	
Retained Earnings Appropriated for Plant Expansion	5,000.00	
Total Deductions		15,600.00
Balance, December 31 (to Exhibit A)		$52,456.05

Balance Sheet

The final balance of the Retained Earnings account appears on the balance sheet, with a reference to Exhibit C, which contains the details supporting that final balance. The Woodcraft Manufacturing Corporation's balance sheet as of December 31, 19X5, is shown on page 965. Notice that the estimated income tax recorded as a credit in the Balance Sheet section of the worksheet appears as a liability, Estimated Income Taxes Payable, on the balance sheet. This liability is recorded as explained in Chapter 30.

(4)

WOODCRAFT MANUFACTURING CORPORATION
Balance Sheet
December 31, 19X5

remember

Assets

Current Assets			
Cash			$ 41,196.87
Accounts Receivable		$55,375.15	
Less Allowance for Uncollectible Accounts		1,117.71	54,257.44
Interest Receivable			133.33
Inventories			
Raw Materials		$25,000.00	
Work in Process		10,000.00	
Finished Goods		27,500.00	62,500.00
Prepaid Expenses			
Prepaid Insurance		$ 1,820.00	
Supplies on Hand		800.00	2,620.00
Total Current Assets			$160,707.64
Long-Term Investments			
MNO Corporation 16% Bonds, 19Y2			5,390.00
Property, Plant, and Equipment			
Land		$ 7,500.00	
Factory Building	$30,500.00		
Less Accumulated Depreciation	2,750.00	27,750.00	
Factory Equipment	$38,500.00		
Less Accumulated Depreciation	7,700.00	30,800.00	
Total Property, Plant, and Equipment			66,050.00
Intangible Assets			
Organization Costs			100.00
Total Assets			$232,247.64

Liabilities and Stockholders' Equity

Current Liabilities			
Accounts Payable			$ 27,505.45
Dividends Payable—Preferred			5,600.00
Dividends Payable—Common			5,000.00
Salaries and Wages Payable			990.00
Estimated Income Taxes Payable			4,633.34
FICA Tax Payable			489.60
Employee Income Tax Payable			673.20
Unemployment Taxes Payable			1,500.00
Total Liabilities			$ 46,391.59
Stockholders' Equity			
Preferred Stock (8%, $100 par value,			
1,000 shares authorized)			
At Par Value (700 shares issued)	$70,000.00		
Premium on Preferred Stock	3,000.00	$73,000.00	
Common Stock (no-par value,			
5,000 shares authorized)			
At Stated Value (1,000 shares issued)	$50,000.00		
Paid-in Capital in Excess of Stated Value	400.00	50,400.00	
Retained Earnings			
Appropriated for Plant Expansion	$10,000.00		
Unappropriated (Exhibit C)	52,456.05	62,456.05	
Total Stockholders' Equity			185,856.05
Total Liabilities and Stockholders' Equity			$232,247.64

As soon as the financial statements have been prepared, the accountant completes the final phase of the accounting cycle. Four steps must be taken.

1. Adjusting entries must be recorded in the general journal and posted to the general ledger.
2. Closing entries must also be recorded in the general journal and posted to the general ledger.
3. A postclosing trial balance must be prepared.
4. Reversing entries must be recorded at the beginning of the next period of operations.

These procedures, discussed before in connection with merchandising businesses, will be adapted here to the operations of the Woodcraft Manufacturing Corporation.

Adjusting Entries

The adjustments that were recorded on the worksheet on pages 960–961 must now be journalized and posted. The procedures are almost exactly the same as those previously used for merchandising firms. The nine adjusting entries required at the Woodcraft Manufacturing Corporation are shown in the general journal on the next page.

Pay particular attention to the system used for entry identification and to the completeness of the explanations provided. The identification letter accompanying each adjusting entry is the same as the letter used for the adjustment on the worksheet on pages 960–961. These letters help to distinguish the various entries. The full explanation is important because it facilitates future reference by auditors and others.

Closing Entries

Since Woodcraft is engaged in manufacturing operations, the process of journalizing and posting its closing entries differs slightly from the method used by the types of businesses previously discussed. A second summary account is required in addition to the Income Summary account. The new summary account, called Manufacturing Summary, draws together all the elements of manufacturing cost. Its balance (actually the cost of goods manufactured) is then transferred to the Income Summary account. Next the estimated income taxes payable are recorded, and the balance of the Income Summary account, reflecting net income or net loss after taxes, is transferred to Retained Earnings. Note that the steps are performed in the same order that was used in totaling, balancing, and transferring the figures in the special statement columns of the worksheet. Here is a more detailed explanation of the procedure.

Manufacturing Summary Refer to the Cost of Goods Manufactured section of the worksheet on pages 960–961.

1. The Credit column serves as a guide for the first closing entry. The subtotal, $38,000, represents the sum of two ending inventories (Raw Materials and Work in Process), Purchases Returns and Allowances, and Purchases Dis-

19 X5					
Dec. 31	(Adjustment a)				
	Loss From Uncollectible Accounts	671	982 71		
	Allowance for Uncollectible Accounts	112		982 71	
	To record increase of allowance account				
	balance by 0.2% of net sales as follows:				
	Sales $495,138.35				
	Less: Returns				
	and Allow. 3,782.15				
	Net Sales $491,356.20				
	0.2% of Net Sales $982.71				
31	(Adjustment b)				
	Interest Receivable	116	133 33		
	MNO Corp. 16% Bonds, 19Y2	135		10 00	
	Interest Income	492		123 33	
	To record accrued interest for 2 months				
	($5,000 × 0.16 × 2/12 = $133.33) and				
	amortize premium for 2 months				
	at $5 a month.				
31	(Adjustment c)				
	Insurance—Factory	551	380 00		
	Prepaid Insurance	128		380 00	
	To transfer expired insurance for				
	December to expense.				
31	(Adjustment d)				
	Supplies on Hand	129	800 00		
	Indirect Materials and Supplies	539		800 00	
	To set up ending inventory of supplies.				
31	(Adjustment e)				
	Depreciation—Factory Building	541	750 00		
	Accum. Depr.—Factory Building	142		750 00	
	To record depreciation on building				
	for the year.				
31	(Adjustment f)				
	Depreciation—Factory Equipment	542	2,400 00		
	Accum. Depr.—Factory Equipment	144		2,400 00	
	To record depreciation on equipment				
	for the year.				
31	(Adjustment g)				
	Organization Costs Written Off	691	100 00		
	Organization Costs	191		100 00	
	To write off a portion of organization				
	costs.				
31	(Adjustment h)				
	Direct Labor	511	820 00		
	Indirect Labor	521	170 00		
	Salaries and Wages Payable	215		990 00	
	To record accrued factory payroll				
	to December 31.				
31	(Adjustment i)				
	Payroll Taxes—Factory	523	74 25		
	FICA Tax Payable	221		74 25	
	To record employer's taxes on				
	accrued payroll.				

count. A compound entry is made to debit each of these individual accounts and to credit the combined sum to Manufacturing Summary, as shown below.

19 X5				
Dec. 31	Raw Materials Inventory } *ending inv.*	121	25,000 00	
	Work in Process Inventory }	122	10,000 00	
	Purchases Returns and Allowances	502	380 00	
	Purchases Discount	503	2,620 00	
	Manufacturing Summary	398		38,000 00
	To record ending inventories of raw materials and work in process and to close the accounts for returns and discounts on purchases.			

2. The Debit column is the guide for the second closing entry. The total of $326,511.65 is debited to Manufacturing Summary, and each account in the column is credited, as shown below.

#2 →

19 X5				
Dec. 31	Manufacturing Summary	398	326,511 65	
	Raw Materials Inventory } *beg. inv.*	121		26,000 00
	Work in Process Inventory }	122		10,500 00
	Materials Purchases	501		144,092 30
	Direct Labor	511		80,870 25
	Indirect Labor	521		16,763 35
	Payroll Taxes—Factory	523		7,754 45
	Utilities—Factory	531		8,433 50
	Repairs and Maintenance—Factory	532		11,391 80
	Indirect Materials and Supplies	539		6,808 50
	Depreciation—Factory Building	541		750 00
	Depreciation—Factory Equipment	542		2,400 00
	Insurance—Factory	551		4,530 20
	Property Taxes—Factory	552		6,217 30
	To close beginning inventories of raw materials and work in process and manufacturing cost accounts.			

The posting of these two entries closes all the manufacturing cost accounts, and the Manufacturing Summary account reflects the net result—a debit balance of $288,511.65.

Manufacturing Summary					No. 398	
DATE	EXPLANATION	POST. REF.	DEBIT	CREDIT	BALANCE	DR. CR.
19 X5						
Dec. 31		J12		38,000 00	38,000 00	Cr.
31		J12	326,511 65		288,511 65	Dr.

The Manufacturing Summary remains open only for a brief time. What happens to it is discussed in the next section.

Revenue and Expense Accounts Refer to the Income Statement section of the Woodcraft Manufacturing Corporation's worksheet. Again, consider the Credit column first.

1. A compound entry is made debiting all the items appearing in the Credit column and crediting Income Summary for the total, $523,378.35. Note that this entry includes the ending amount for Finished Goods Inventory.

19 X5						
Dec. 31	Finished Goods Inventory	126	27,500 00		
	Sales	401	495,138 35		
	Interest Income	492	740 00		
	Income Summary	399		523,378 35
	To record ending inventory of finished goods and to close revenue accounts.				

2. The items in the Debit column receive the opposite treatment. Each account is credited for the amount listed. Included among the credits are the beginning amount for Finished Goods Inventory and the balance of Manufacturing Summary, which represents the cost of goods manufactured. The offsetting debit to Income Summary totals $493,961.66.

19 X5				
Dec. 31	Income Summary	399	493,961 66	
	Finished Goods Inventory	126		28,700 00
	Sales Returns and Allowances	452		3,782 15
	Sales Salaries Expense	601		25,625 00
	Payroll Taxes Expense—Sales	603		1,810 30
	Delivery Expense	621		21,240 60
	Sales Supplies and Other Selling Exp.	629		28,248 75
	Advertising Expense	631		11,710 20
	Officers' Salaries Expense	651		55,000 00
	Office Salaries Expense	652		16,225 00
	Payroll Taxes Expense—Administrative	653		5,715 10
	Office Supplies and Other Office Exp.	669		6,310 20
	Loss From Uncollectible Accounts	671		982 71
	Organization Costs Written Off	691		100 00
	Manufacturing Summary	398		288,511 65
	To close beginning finished goods inventory, operating expense accounts, and Manufacturing Summary.			

At this point all revenue accounts and all expense accounts—both manufacturing and nonmanufacturing—have been closed. The balance in the Income

Summary account, $29,416.69, therefore represents the net income before income taxes.

				Income Summary			No. 399	
DATE		EXPLANATION	POST. REF.	DEBIT	CREDIT	BALANCE		DR. CR.
19 X5 Dec.	31		J12		523,378 35	523,378 35		Cr.
	31		J12	493,961 66		29,416 69		Cr.

 Income Summary The figures that appear at the bottom of the Debit column in the Income Statement section of the worksheet provide the basis for the final closing entry. A debit of $29,416.69 to Income Summary closes that account. Estimated Income Taxes Payable (a new account) is credited for $4,633.34, thus creating a liability for the taxes owed. Retained Earnings is credited for $24,783.35, thus transferring the net income after income taxes to Retained Earnings. When this last closing entry is posted, both summary accounts have zero balances.

POSTCLOSING TRIAL BALANCE

A postclosing trial balance is taken to prove that the adjusting and closing entries were posted correctly. The ledger account balances should agree completely with those listed in the Balance Sheet section of the worksheet, with one exception—the Retained Earnings figure.

REVERSING ENTRIES

In Chapter 17 it was explained that it is efficient and convenient to reverse certain adjusting entries at the beginning of a new accounting period. The same reversing procedures will be followed with the accounts of the Woodcraft Manufacturing Corporation. Remember that, in most cases, only those adjusting entries for accrued expenses and accrued income that involve later payments and receipts of cash must be reversed.

Refer again to the adjusting entries on page 967. Consider the effect of each in turn.

1. Adjustment (a) for uncollectible accounts involves neither an accrued expense nor accrued income and therefore does not require reversing.
2. Adjustment (b) involves accrued income and must be reversed by a debit to MNO 16% Bonds, 19Y2, for $10, a debit to Interest Income for $123.33, and a credit to Interest Receivable for $133.33.
3. Adjustment (c) transfers expired insurance from Prepaid Insurance to the expense account. No accrued item is involved in this entry; therefore, it is not reversed.
4. Adjustment (d) records the ending inventory of manufacturing supplies. Although this adjustment does not involve an accrued item, it must be reversed

by a debit to Indirect Materials and Supplies and a credit to Supplies on Hand for $800. Because the firm initially records purchases of supplies as an expense, the asset account Supplies on Hand should not have a balance during a fiscal period.

5. Adjustments (e) and (f) for depreciation involve no accrued expenses or income. Thus, they are not reversed.

6. Adjustment (g) writes off a portion of Organization Costs to current expense. No accrued item is involved, and no reversal is needed.

7. Adjustment (h) for the accrued factory wages is reversed by a debit to Salaries and Wages Payable for $990 and credits to Direct Labor for $820 and to Indirect Labor for $170.

8. Adjustment (i) for the accrued payroll taxes on the accrued factory wages is reversed by debiting FICA Tax Payable and crediting Payroll Taxes—Factory for $74.25.

After these reversing entries have been posted, the transactions of the new period can be recorded as usual without having to consider the effect of the adjustments made in the prior period. The use of reversing entries therefore saves time and helps to prevent errors in the new period.

PRINCIPLES AND PROCEDURES SUMMARY

The worksheet for a manufacturing business is similar to one for a merchandising firm in most respects, but it has an additional pair of columns in which to record the figures for the cost of goods manufactured.

The three ending inventories are entered as debits in the Balance Sheet columns. Ending inventory figures for raw materials and work in process are entered as credits in the Cost of Goods Manufactured columns. The ending inventory of finished goods is entered as a credit in the Income Statement columns. Beginning inventory figures for raw materials and work in process are carried into the Debit column of the Cost of Goods Manufactured section. The beginning finished goods inventory appears in the Debit column of the Income Statement section.

In completing the worksheet, the Cost of Goods Manufactured columns are totaled, and the net cost of goods manufactured is transferred to the Debit column of the Income Statement section. The difference between the Debit and Credit column totals of this section gives a net income or net loss figure. If there is a net income (credits exceeding debits), the next step is to estimate the income taxes payable. Finally, the figures for the estimated income taxes payable and the net income remaining after income taxes are transferred to the Balance Sheet Credit column.

The worksheet supplies all the information needed to prepare the four financial statements, except for some of the figures needed for the statement of retained earnings. The Retained Earnings account in the general ledger must be analyzed to obtain these figures.

All accounts relating to the cost of goods manufactured are closed into a summary account called Manufacturing Summary. Its final balance, representing the cost of goods manufactured, is closed into the Income Summary account. All items in the Income Statement section of the worksheet are closed, as usual, into Income Summary. The final closing entry sets up the liability for estimated income taxes payable and transfers the net income after income taxes to the Retained Earnings account.

After the accounting records are adjusted and closed, a postclosing trial balance is prepared. At the beginning of the new period, certain adjusting entries are reversed.

MANAGERIAL IMPLICATIONS

Efficient procedures must be used in preparing financial statements for a manufacturing business if management is to be promptly provided with the information necessary to make wise and timely decisions. The worksheet allows the accountant to summarize and classify information so that the formal statements can be drawn up more easily. If the cost of goods manufactured figures are needed by management even before the statements are completed, they are readily available in the Cost of Goods Manufactured section of the worksheet.

The use of reversing entries enables accounting personnel to handle later transactions in the normal manner without regard to any adjustments made at the end of the preceding period. This decreases the possibility of oversight or error.

REVIEW QUESTIONS

1. What column headings are found on the worksheet for a manufacturing business?
2. How does the worksheet for a manufacturing business differ from one for a merchandising firm?
3. What is the purpose of the adjusted trial balance?
4. How are the beginning and ending inventories of raw materials handled on the worksheet?
5. How are the beginning and ending inventories of work in process handled on the worksheet?
6. How are the beginning and ending inventories of finished goods handled on the worksheet?
7. Where on the worksheet is the cost of goods manufactured figure found, and how is it handled?
8. What is the source of information for the statement of cost of goods manufactured?
9. What is the relationship between the cost of goods manufactured and the income statement?
10. Explain the source of the entries to close the various manufacturing cost accounts.
11. What is the source of the information for preparing the journal entry to close the Manufacturing Summary account?

12. Which of the various adjusting entries would normally be reversed?
13. How are the estimated income taxes payable handled on the worksheet of a manufacturing business?
14. Are the financial statements prepared after the closing entries are posted? Explain.
15. Does the Manufacturing Summary account have a balance during the fiscal period? Explain.
16. Is it necessary to prepare a postclosing trial balance? Explain.
17. Is the statement of cost of goods manufactured prepared before or after the income statement? Explain.

MANAGERIAL DISCUSSION QUESTIONS

1. How does the Cost of Goods Manufactured section of the worksheet help the accountant tell managers what they want to know about the firm's manufacturing operations?
2. On page 957 you are told that the value of the sales supplies and office supplies on hand at the end of the period is considered too small to justify an adjusting entry. If a director were to question the omission as a matter of policy (i.e., the accounting records should show everything), what would you say?
3. On page 957 it was stated that during each month of the year depreciation was entered on the worksheet but not actually recorded in the ledger. What is the purpose of this procedure?
4. Why would management want a statement of cost of goods manufactured?
5. A manager asks, "If the Manufacturing Summary account is only going to be closed into the Income Summary account, why not use one summary account for all items?" How would you explain the need for the Manufacturing Summary account?
6. Why is the balance of the Manufacturing Summary account transferred to the Income Summary account and not vice versa?
7. In what way does the postclosing trial balance improve efficiency?

EXERCISES

EXERCISE 40-1 **Recording the adjustment for manufacturing supplies used.** On December 31, 19X1, the Indirect Materials and Supplies account at the Beck Corporation showed a balance of $16,345.43. A physical count of the manufacturing supplies on that date revealed an inventory on hand costing $857.45. Give the general journal entry to record the necessary adjustment. Where would the cost of manufacturing supplies used appear in the financial statements?

EXERCISE 40-2 **Recording the adjustment for patent amortization.** In 19X1 the Willow Corporation paid $120,000 for a patent. The patent is being amortized at the rate of $1,000 a month. On January 1, 19X5, the balance of the Patent account was $72,000. Give the general journal entry to record amortization of the patent on

December 31, 19X5. Where would the related expense appear in the financial statements?

EXERCISE 40-3 **Recording the adjustment for amortization of organization costs.** The Marinelli Corporation was organized in 19X1, and organization costs of $30,000 were capitalized at that time. On January 1, 19X4, the balance of the Organization Costs account was $14,000. These costs are being amortized over a period of 60 months. Give the general journal entry to record amortization of organization costs on December 31, 19X4. Where would the related expense appear in the financial statements?

EXERCISE 40-4 **Closing the accounts with credit balances related to manufacturing.** On December 31, 19X1, the Credit column of the Cost of Goods Manufactured section of the worksheet for the Powell Corporation contained the following items. Give the general journal entry to record the ending inventories and to close the Purchases Returns and Allowances account.

Work in Process Inventory	$160,000.00
Raw Materials Inventory	193,000.00
Purchases Returns and Allowances	8,600.00
Total	$361,600.00

EXERCISE 40-5 **Recording estimated taxes and closing the income summary.** After the worksheet of the McDuff Corporation was completed and ruled, the lower portion of the Income Statement columns appeared as follows. Give the general journal entry to record the estimated income taxes and to close the Income Summary account.

	DEBIT	CREDIT
Totals	$2,931,712.20	$3,329,614.01
Provision for Income Taxes	172,000.00	
Net Income After Income Taxes	225,901.81	
	$3,329,614.01	$3,329,614.01

EXERCISE 40-6 **Computing the cost of raw materials used.** The following selected items appeared on the worksheet of the Lonberg Company on December 31, 19X4. From this information, prepare the section of the statement of cost of goods manufactured relating to the cost of raw materials used.

	DEBIT	CREDIT
Finished Goods Inventory	85,984.37	78,435.67
Work in Process Inventory	183,450.00	191,235.60
Raw Materials Inventory	86,546.90	93,421.67
Materials Purchases	994,567.30	
Purchases Returns and Allowances		1,454.78
Freight In (on Materials Purchases)	34,346.73	

EXERCISE 40-7 **Presenting inventory information on the balance sheet.** Using the information given in Exercise 40-6, show how the ending inventories of the Lonberg Company would be presented on its balance sheet as of December 31, 19X4.

EXERCISE 40-8 **Identifying items included in the cost of goods manufactured section of the worksheet.** Which of the following account balances would be extended to the Cost of Goods Manufactured section of the worksheet?

1. Insurance on Factory Building
2. Payroll Taxes on Factory Wages
3. Utilities for Factory
4. Salary of Factory Storeroom Clerk
5. Insurance on Raw Materials in Factory Storeroom
6. Insurance on Finished Goods
7. Salary of Factory Superintendent

EXERCISE 40-9 **Identifying items included in manufacturing overhead.** Which of the following items would be included in the Manufacturing Overhead section of the statement of cost of goods manufactured?

1. Raw Materials Used
2. Indirect Materials and Supplies
3. Direct Labor
4. Amortization of Patent
5. Advertising Expense
6. Delivery Expense
7. Depreciation of Factory Equipment
8. Repairs to Delivery Equipment

PROBLEMS

PROBLEM 40-1 **Preparing a worksheet for a manufacturing business.** The Neptune Manufacturing Corporation produces high-quality fishing rods, reels, and lines. The Trial Balance section of its worksheet and other year-end data are given below and on the next page.

Instructions
1. Prepare a 12-column manufacturing worksheet for the fiscal year ended December 31, 19X2. Enter the trial balance in the first two columns.
2. Using the data given, enter the adjustments, the ending inventories, and the estimated income taxes. Then complete the worksheet. (Keep this worksheet for use in Problems 40-2 and 40-3.)

YEAR-END DATA

a. Estimated uncollectible accounts: increase Allowance for Uncollectible Accounts to 3 percent of Accounts Receivable.
b. Expired insurance, $205. (Debit the Insurance—Factory account for the amount of the necessary adjustment.)

c. Indirect materials and supplies on hand, $185.

d. Depreciation of factory building and equipment, $3,775 for the year.

e. Accrued factory wages: direct labor, $425; indirect labor, $135. Accrued payroll (FICA) taxes, $40. (Make a compound entry for the accrued wages and payroll taxes.)

f. Ending inventories: finished goods, $21,100; work in process, $10,250; and raw materials, $13,300.

g. Federal income tax rates:

15 percent of first $25,000 of net income

20 percent of next $25,000 of net income

30 percent of next $25,000 of net income

40 percent of next $25,000 of net income

46 percent of all remaining net income

NEPTUNE MANUFACTURING CORPORATION
Worksheet (Partial)
Year Ended December 31, 19X2

| | | Trial Balance | |
		Debit	Credit
Acct. No.	Account Name		
101	Cash	$ 18,239.00	
111	Accounts Receivable	51,365.00	
112	Allowance for Uncollectible Accounts		$ 27.35
121	Raw Materials Inventory	12,000.00	
122	Work in Process Inventory	10,000.00	
126	Finished Goods Inventory	20,000.00	
131	Prepaid Insurance	2,195.00	
133	Supplies on Hand		
140	Land	5,200.00	
141	Factory Building and Equipment	41,500.00	
142	Accum. Depr.—Factory Bldg. and Equip.		8,140.00
202	Accounts Payable		16,345.00
215	Salaries and Wages Payable		
225	FICA Tax Payable		1,222.65
301	Common Stock		60,000.00
381	Retained Earnings		29,790.00
401	Sales		369,475.00
452	Sales Returns and Allowances	1,325.00	
501	Materials Purchases	72,250.00	
502	Purchases Ret. and Allow.		650.00
511	Direct Labor	81,245.00	
521	Indirect Labor	7,987.00	
525	Payroll Taxes—Factory	8,915.00	
531	Utilities—Factory	8,286.00	
532	Repairs and Maintenance—Factory	4,742.00	
537	Indirect Materials and Supplies	3,795.00	
541	Depr.—Factory Bldg. and Equip.		
551	Insurance—Factory	1,736.00	
552	Property Taxes—Factory	3,225.00	
601	Sales Salaries Expense	32,450.00	
603	Payroll Taxes Expense—Sales	3,000.00	
605	Sales Supplies and Expense	29,965.00	
651	Officers' Salaries Expense	37,500.00	
661	Office Salaries Expense	18,000.00	
662	Payroll Taxes Expense—Admin.	5,300.00	
663	Other Office Expenses	5,430.00	
671	Loss From Uncollectible Accounts		
	Totals	$485,650.00	$485,650.00

PROBLEM 40-2   **Preparing financial statements for a manufacturing business.** For this problem, use the worksheet completed for the Neptune Manufacturing Corporation in Problem 40-1.

Instructions   1. Prepare a statement of cost of goods manufactured.
2. Prepare an income statement.
3. Prepare a statement of retained earnings. Additional data needed is as follows.
    a. Balance of Retained Earnings, January 1, $36,790
    b. Dividends on common stock, $6,000
    c. Correction of prior year's error charged to Retained Earnings (resulting from understatement of Repairs and Maintenance—Factory for prior year), $1,000
4. Prepare a balance sheet.

PROBLEM 40-3   **Recording adjusting, closing, and reversing entries for a manufacturing business.** For this problem, use the worksheet completed for the Neptune Manufacturing Corporation in Problem 40-1.

Instructions   1. Open the following two general ledger accounts: Manufacturing Summary (398) and Income Summary (399).
2. Record the adjusting entries shown on the worksheet in general journal form. For each journal entry, use the letter that identifies the adjustment on the worksheet.
3. Prepare the closing entries for all accounts involved in the cost of goods manufactured.
4. Post the entries in Instruction 3 to the Manufacturing Summary account.
5. Prepare the closing entries for all revenue and expense accounts, the finished goods inventory, and the Manufacturing Summary account.
6. Prepare the closing entry to record the estimated income tax liability and close the Income Summary account.
7. Post the entries in Instructions 5 and 6 to the Manufacturing Summary account and the Income Summary account.
8. Journalize the reversing entries. Date all the reversing entries January 1, 19X3.

ALTERNATE PROBLEMS

PROBLEM 40-1A   **Preparing a worksheet for a manufacturing business.** The Skyway Products Corporation manufactures parts for airplanes. The Trial Balance section of its worksheet and other year-end data appear on pages 978 and 979.

Instructions   1. Prepare a 12-column manufacturing worksheet for the fiscal year ended December 31, 19X2. Enter the trial balance in the first two columns.
2. Using the data given, enter the adjustments, the ending inventories, and the estimated income taxes of $5,200. Then complete the worksheet. (Keep this worksheet for use in Problems 40-2A and 40-3A.)

SKYWAY PRODUCTS CORPORATION
Worksheet (Partial)
Year Ended December 31, 19X2

Acct. No.	Account Name	Trial Balance Debit	Trial Balance Credit
101	Cash	$ 24,650	
110	Notes Receivable	8,000	
111	Accounts Receivable	41,225	
112	Allowance for Uncollectible Accounts		$ 76
116	Interest Receivable		
121	Raw Materials Inventory	11,725	
122	Work in Process Inventory	16,000	
126	Finished Goods Inventory	42,560	
128	Prepaid Insurance	3,320	
129	Supplies on Hand		
140	Land	15,000	
141	Factory Building	98,450	
142	Accum. Depr.—Factory Building		24,150
143	Factory Machines	51,700	
144	Accum. Depr.—Factory Machines		19,875
145	Office Furniture and Equipment	6,895	
146	Accum. Depr.—Office Furn. and Equip.		2,976
191	Organization Costs	3,200	
202	Accounts Payable		15,235
208	Dividends Payable—Preferred		4,500
209	Dividends Payable—Common		2,000
215	Salaries and Wages Payable		
221	FICA Tax Payable		126
222	Employee Income Tax Payable		1,390
301	Common Stock		25,000
311	Preferred Stock		75,000
381	Retained Earnings—Unappropriated		84,773
382	Retained Earnings Appropriated for Plant Expansion		20,000
401	Sales		354,630
452	Sales Returns and Allowances	1,655	
492	Interest Income		145
501	Materials Purchases	91,000	
502	Purchases Ret. and Allow.		380
506	Freight In	1,225	
511	Direct Labor	76,000	
521	Indirect Labor	7,250	
523	Payroll Taxes—Factory	8,710	
531	Heat, Light, and Power—Factory	4,275	
532	Repairs and Maintenance—Factory	1,025	
539	Indirect Materials and Supplies	3,870	
541	Depr.—Factory Building		
542	Depr.—Factory Machines		
551	Insurance—Factory	5,321	
552	Property Taxes—Factory	2,850	
601	Sales Salaries Expense	26,750	
602	Payroll Taxes Expense—Sales	2,720	
621	Delivery Expense	4,115	
629	Sales Supplies and Expense	3,915	
631	Advertising Expense	10,480	
651	Officers' Salaries Expense	28,000	
652	Office Salaries Expense	19,360	
653	Payroll Taxes Expense—Admin.	7,575	
663	Depr. Expense—Office Furn. and Equip.		
669	Office Supplies and Other Office Expenses	1,435	
671	Loss From Uncollectible Accounts		
691	Organization Costs Written Off		
	Totals	$630,256	$630,256

YEAR-END DATA

a. A schedule of accounts receivable by age shows that $916 of the accounts receivable may not be collectible.

b. Interest income on notes receivable amounts to 9 percent on $8,000 for four months.

c. Of the prepaid insurance, $680 has expired. (Debit the expired amount to Insurance—Factory.)

d. A physical inventory discloses $628.50 of manufacturing supplies unused at the end of the period.

e. Depreciation expense for the year is as follows: $2,068 on the factory building, $5,170 on the factory machines, and $683.25 on the office furniture and equipment. (Make a compound entry.)

f. Organization costs of $800 should be written off.

g. Payroll accruals at the end of the period are as follows: $1,265.30 of direct labor, $88.25 of indirect labor, and $75 of payroll (FICA) taxes. (Include all elements in one compound entry.)

Physical inventories taken on December 31, 19X2, show $14,982.50 of raw materials on hand and $30,112.40 of finished goods on hand. The work in process inventory is estimated to be $13,200 on the same date.

PROBLEM 40-2A   **Preparing financial statements for a manufacturing business.** For this problem, use the worksheet completed for the Skyway Products Corporation in Problem 40-1A.

Instructions   1. Prepare a statement of cost of goods manufactured.
2. Prepare an income statement.
3. Prepare a statement of retained earnings. Additional data needed is as follows.
   a. Balance of Retained Earnings, January 1, $109,650.20
   b. Dividends declared during the year:
      (1) On preferred stock, $4,500.00
      (2) On common stock, $2,000.00
   c. Refund received on prior year's taxes, credited to Retained Earnings, $1,622.80
   d. Transfer to Retained Earnings Appropriated for Plant Expansion, $20,000.00
4. Prepare a balance sheet.

PROBLEM 40-3A   **Recording adjusting, closing, and reversing entries for a manufacturing business.** For this problem, use the worksheet completed for the Skyway Products Corporation in Problem 40-1A.

Instructions   1. Open the following two general ledger accounts: Manufacturing Summary (398) and Income Summary (399).
2. Record the adjusting entries shown on the worksheet in general journal form.

For each journal entry, use the letter that identifies the adjustment on the worksheet.

3. Prepare the closing entries for all accounts involved in the cost of goods manufactured.
4. Post the entries in Instruction 3 to the Manufacturing Summary account.
5. Prepare the closing entries for all revenue and expense accounts, the finished goods inventory, and the Manufacturing Summary account.
6. Prepare the closing entry to record the estimated income tax liability and close the Income Summary account.
7. Post the entries in Instructions 5 and 6 to the Manufacturing Summary account and the Income Summary account.
8. Journalize the reversing entries. Date all of these entries January 1, 19X3.

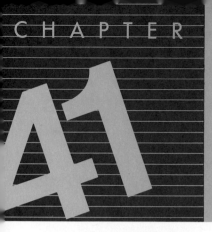

41

Up to this point we have discussed the basic accounting records and financial statements used by manufacturing businesses. These firms must also have other types of records that allow them to gather detailed information about the costs involved in making each product. In this chapter and later chapters, you will see how cost accounting systems are set up to provide such data.

JOB ORDER COST ACCOUNTING

THE NEED FOR A COST ACCOUNTING SYSTEM

The procedures illustrated in the previous two chapters are useful to a manufacturing business in computing the overall cost of making its products during the period. However, they have two shortcomings. First, unless a single product is manufactured and unless all goods worked on during the period are completed, the procedures described do not make it possible to determine the cost of each unit produced. Second, since costs are assembled and classified only at the end of the accounting period, the procedures described do not help in keeping a close watch on cost behavior and in controlling costs when they get out of line. Since the Woodcraft Manufacturing Corporation makes several products and since the company normally has work in process at the end of the accounting period, a more specialized accounting system must be installed in order to determine the cost of each unit produced.

TYPES OF COST ACCOUNTING SYSTEMS

There are two principal systems of cost accounting that the accountant would consider at this time: *job order cost accounting* and *process cost accounting*. A third type, *standard cost accounting,* may be used with either of the other two systems as a control on the efficiency of performance.

Job Order Cost Accounting

With the job order cost accounting system, unit costs of production are determined for each separate production order. Specifically, unit costs are determined by dividing the total costs incurred on a particular order by the number of units produced. This system is a logical choice for businesses that produce what each customer wants on special order or that produce more than one product in batches rather than on a continuous basis.

Process Cost Accounting

With the process cost accounting system, the total cost of a unit of product is found by adding the unit costs in each department through which the product passes while it is being manufactured. This type of cost accounting system resembles a departmentalized accounting system for a merchandising business. Separate cost records are kept for the various producing departments and service departments. *Producing departments,* such as woodworking and finishing, perform work directly on the product. *Service departments,* such as maintenance and materials distribution, assist in production but do not perform work on the actual product. The process cost accounting system is usually applied to situations in which there are continuous operations on standard types of products.

Standard Cost Accounting

The development of standard costs permits a firm to determine what its costs should be. Managers can then compare actual costs with predetermined standard costs that reflect the efficient performance expected. As previously mentioned, standard costs may be incorporated into either a job order cost accounting system or a process cost accounting system.

SETTING UP A COST ACCOUNTING SYSTEM

Since the Woodcraft Manufacturing Corporation makes several types of tables and customers order the various types in different quantities, Woodcraft does not have a continuous manufacturing process. Therefore, the accountant decides to use the job order cost system. She installs this system as soon as possible, deferring consideration of standard costs for the time being. Assume that changes in production are made during a general plant shutdown between Christmas Day and New Year's Day, 19Y1. All work in process is completed before the shutdown so that the new year starts with no beginning inventory of work in process. The new system of cost accounting is established and ready to function on January 2, 19Y2.

Installation of Perpetual Inventories

The accountant quickly realizes that taking physical inventories of raw materials, work in process, and finished goods before financial statements are prepared at the end of the accounting period is too difficult and expensive a process for large-scale operations. In addition, she knows that close control over inventories will assure that just the right amount of stock is kept on hand. Therefore, she explains to the directors and managers that the three principal inventories of a manufacturing business are generally maintained on a *perpetual inventory basis.* This inventory system includes the following typical procedures.

Raw Materials Inventory Raw materials and supplies of all kinds are to be recorded in one inventory account called Raw Materials Inventory (or Stores Inventory) in the following manner.

1. Purchases of materials and manufacturing supplies will be debited to the inventory account by means of a total posting from a Raw Materials Inventory Debit column in the voucher register.
2. As materials are used, a record will be kept of the amounts issued and the accounts that should be charged.
3. The records of materials usage will be summarized periodically, and appropriate entries will be made debiting work in process or expense accounts and crediting the Raw Materials Inventory account.

As a result of these debits and credits, the balance of the Raw Materials Inventory account at the end of any accounting period should reflect the cost of materials and supplies on hand. (At least once a year, a physical inventory should be taken to check the accuracy of the recorded inventory. In the event of a difference, the figure in the records should be adjusted to agree with the physical inventory figure.)

Work in Process Inventory The Work in Process Inventory account will be debited for materials issued for production. It will also be debited for labor and for manufacturing overhead charged to production. As work is completed, its cost will be transferred to the Finished Goods Inventory account. The balance in the Work in Process Inventory account at the end of the period should reflect the cost of work still incomplete at that time.

Finished Goods Inventory As goods are completed, they are moved from the producing departments to the finished goods storeroom. Their cost will be debited to the Finished Goods Inventory account and credited to the Work in Process Inventory account. As goods are sold, their cost will be determined and credited to the Finished Goods Inventory account with a corresponding debit to an account called Cost of Goods Sold. The balance of the Finished Goods Inventory account at the end of the period should equal the cost of the finished goods on hand. This balance should be checked by taking a physical inventory at least once a year.

Flow of Costs Illustrated

The flow of costs through the perpetual inventory accounts in the proposed cost accounting system is illustrated in the flowchart shown below.

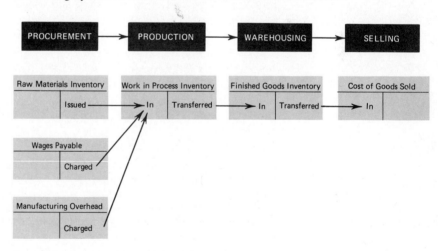

INSTALLATION OF A JOB ORDER COST SYSTEM

Installing the job order cost system includes setting up the three required inventory accounts and appropriate subsidiary accounts. It also requires the development of procedures to record costs incurred, costs of items placed in production, and the transfer of products to finished goods.

Perpetual Inventory Accounts

Each of the three inventory accounts—Raw Materials, Work in Process, and Finished Goods—serves as a perpetual inventory record, and each is supported by a subsidiary ledger. The *raw materials subsidiary ledger* contains a record for each of the different types of raw materials and manufacturing supplies that the firm uses. The *work in process subsidiary ledger* includes a job order cost sheet for each job being worked on. The *finished goods subsidiary ledger* contains a perpetual record for each of the different types of finished products.

ACCOUNTING FOR MATERIALS

Purchases of raw materials and supplies are debited to the Raw Materials Inventory account. As the materials and supplies are issued for production, Raw Materials Inventory is credited. The balance in this account at the end of each period represents the cost of materials and supplies on hand.

It is apparent that receipts and issues of raw materials and manufacturing supplies must be carefully controlled to prevent losses and to obtain reliable figures for cost accounting purposes. The system used at Woodcraft for controlling the receipt and issue of these items is as follows.

Raw Materials Ledger

Woodcraft orders all materials through the use of prenumbered purchase orders. When the materials and supplies are received, they are checked, counted, and weighed. They are then sent to the storeroom with a report showing what was received. A copy of this *receiving report* is compared with the supplier's invoice and with the purchase order that was issued by Woodcraft before the invoice is approved for payment. Data regarding prices and the quantities received is obtained from these two records for entry in the individual *raw materials ledger card* that is kept for each item. A typical raw materials ledger card with several transactions posted to it is shown below. The purchase order number (PO) listed in the Reference column identifies the source of the receipt.

RAW MATERIALS LEDGER CARD
(FIFO Cost Method)

ITEM: *Brace*   NUMBER: XTO-14

DATE	REF.	RECEIVED UNITS	PRICE	AMOUNT	ISSUED UNITS	PRICE	AMOUNT	BALANCE UNITS	PRICE	AMOUNT
19X2										
Jan. 3	PO-3	150	1 00	150 00				150	1 00	150 00
8	R-24				100	1 00	100 00	50	1 00	50 00
12	PO-14	150	1 10	165 00				{50 / 150}	{1 00 / 1 10}	215 00
17	R-51				{50 / 50}	{1 00 / 1 10}	105 00	100	1 10	110 00
24	PO-32	100	1 15	115 00				{100 / 100}	{1 10 / 1 15}	225 00
29	R-90				100	1 10	110 00	100	1 15	115 00

Materials Requisition

The costs of factory materials are distributed between direct materials (work in process) and indirect materials (manufacturing overhead). Materials or supplies are issued by the storeroom only upon presentation of a *materials requisition* signed by someone authorized to withdraw such items. The materials requisition describes the item needed and the quantity and shows the job or purpose for which it is needed. (Jobs are ordinarily identified by a job order number, assigned when production on the job begins.) The materials requisition is used by the stores clerk in recording issues on the individual raw materials ledger cards. The requisition covering the ledger card entry of January 8 appears below. (The requisition number R-24 is shown in the Reference column of the ledger card.)

Goto 984

MATERIALS REQUISITION			No. R-24	
Charge to Account No. _122_				
Job No. _J-8_		Date _Jan. 8,_ 19 _Y2_		
Quantity	Description		Unit Cost	Total Cost
100	Brace XTO-14		$1 00	$100 00
Authorized by: J. Kelly		Issued by: T. Santos		Received by: R. Adams

The raw materials ledger clerk prices the items listed on the materials requisitions and later summarizes the requisitions issued during a week or other operating period. This summary of requisitions issued classifies the direct material costs by jobs and identifies the supplies and indirect materials. It is also the basis for charges to the job order cost sheets (described later) and for a journal entry. ✳This entry debits Work in Process Inventory and Manufacturing Overhead (a new account that is explained later) and credits Raw Materials Inventory.

Pricing Basis

In Chapter 23 you learned that there are a number of different methods of pricing merchandise inventory, each of which yields significantly different total figures. Similarly, the pricing method used in charging materials requisitions can have a very important effect on the final product cost figures obtained. Each company establishes a definite pricing policy after discussion by the accountant with the officers and other members of top management.

Recording Materials Issued

Suppose that the management of the Woodcraft Manufacturing Corporation decides to use the first in, first out (FIFO) method of pricing materials issued. Also assume that at the end of January, purchases of materials for the month (as shown by the total of the Raw Materials Inventory Debit column in the voucher register) amounted to $12,000 and that total issues of materials and supplies for the month were $9,500 ($9,000 direct materials, $500 supplies). Entries to record these transactions appear in general journal form on page 986.

19 Y2						
Jan. 31	Raw Materials Inventory		121	12,000 00		
	Accounts Payable		202			12,000 00
	To record cost of materials and supplies purchased during January.					
31	Work in Process Inventory		122	9,000 00		
	Manufacturing Overhead		500	500 00		
	Raw Materials Inventory		121			9,500 00
	To record cost of materials issued for use in jobs and indirect materials and supplies consumed during January, as shown in summary of materials requisitions.					

supplies (actual)

Purchase Discounts

When a perpetual inventory system is used for raw materials, the accountant must decide whether the cost of these materials is to be entered in the inventory accounts at the invoice price or at the net invoice price after purchase discounts are deducted.

If the net invoice price after discount is used, the net amount is entered in the purchases journal or voucher register in the manner discussed in Chapter 11. It is then necessary to compute the amount of discount applicable to each item on the invoice so that the net cost of each item can be identified. This procedure is usually rather time consuming.

In order to avoid computing the amount of discount applicable to each item, the accountant at the Woodcraft Manufacturing Corporation decides to record raw materials at their gross invoice price. This method of treatment requires a slight modification in statement presentation. When raw materials are recorded at gross price under the perpetual inventory system, the purchase discounts may be treated either as other income or as a reduction in the cost of goods sold for the period. Woodcraft chooses the latter procedure, which is the preferred method. Thus discounts are reported as shown on page 962.

ACCOUNTING FOR LABOR

The same payroll accounting procedures that you studied previously in this book are used by Woodcraft. However, factory labor costs are distributed between direct labor (Work in Process Inventory) and indirect labor (Manufacturing Overhead). Payrolls are summarized and recorded weekly or monthly. Each summary includes a breakdown of labor costs for the payroll period. The labor costs that Woodcraft incurred during January are illustrated below.

PAYROLL PERIOD	DIRECT LABOR	INDIRECT LABOR	TOTAL LABOR COSTS
Jan. 8	$1,200	$200	$1,400
15	1,300	250	1,550
22	1,200	225	1,425
29	1,100	150	1,250
Totals for January	$4,800	$825	$5,625

The monthly entry to record this payroll data is shown below as it would appear in general journal form.

labor (actual)

19	Y2					
Jan.	31	Work in Process Inv. (Direct Labor)	122	4,800 00		
		Mfg. Overhead (Indirect Labor)	500	825 00		
		FICA Tax Payable	221		337 50	
		Employee Income Tax Payable	222		610 00	
		Salaries and Wages Payable	215		4,677 50	
		To record total labor costs for January, as shown in payroll summary.				

Time Tickets

In addition to recording the time when they enter and leave the plant, workers who perform direct labor prepare a series of *time tickets* to account for all time spent in the plant. Each such worker completes a separate time ticket indicating the starting and stopping time for any job on which he or she works. If the worker is idle for part of the day, a time ticket designating ''idle time'' is prepared so that the cost of this time can be charged appropriately. (Idle time is generally charged to manufacturing overhead, but under certain circumstances, it may be charged to the job on which a delay occurs.) A typical time ticket appears below.

LABOR TIME TICKET

Name _Frank Wilson_   Date _Jan. 7_ , 19 _Y2_

Description of work:
Assembling Tables

Time Started _8:00_

Time Stopped _10:20_

Hours Worked _2 1/3_

Rate of Pay _$6.00_

Charge Job No. _J-5_

Total Charge _$14.00_ — *cost of labor*

Approval of Supervisor _J. Kelly_

A cost clerk computes the total time shown on the time ticket and applies the worker's rate to obtain the cost of the labor. Labor time tickets are sorted by jobs and summarized at the end of each payroll period for entry on the individual job order cost sheets (as illustrated on page 990). The total charged to all the cost sheets must agree with the amounts debited to Work in Process Inventory for direct labor as the payrolls are recorded.

ACCOUNTING FOR MANUFACTURING OVERHEAD

Manufacturing overhead may be entered in the accounting records in various ways. One common method is to set up a control account called Manufacturing Overhead in the general ledger and have a subsidiary ledger containing a sheet for each type of overhead item. The actual overhead costs are then debited to the control account, and the details are posted to the appropriate individual subsidiary ledger accounts.

In January Woodcraft incurred overhead costs amounting to $2,425 in addition to indirect materials and indirect labor. The monthly entry to record these costs is illustrated below in general journal form.

actual →

19 Y2				
Jan. 31	Manufacturing Overhead	500	2,425 00	
	Accounts Payable and Other Accounts	XXX		2,425 00
	To record overhead for January.			

Applying Overhead to Jobs

Under the job order cost system, the manufacturing overhead cannot be assigned to a product by simply dividing the total overhead by units of product because each job may cover a different kind of product and should, therefore, have different amounts of overhead assigned to it.

Methods for the application of overhead vary. Under one widely used method, an estimate is made of the overhead costs for the coming year. A similar estimate is also made of the direct labor costs for the coming year. Estimated total overhead is divided by estimated total direct labor costs to get a *predetermined overhead application rate.* As direct labor is charged to jobs from summaries of labor time tickets, the overhead rate is applied to the labor costs. The resulting figure is the amount of overhead to be charged to each job.

For example, suppose that estimates for the coming year indicate expected total direct labor costs of $60,000 and total manufacturing overhead costs of $45,000. The predetermined overhead application rate is computed to be 75 percent of direct labor costs.

$$\frac{\text{Estimated overhead costs}}{\text{Estimated direct labor costs}} = \frac{\$45,000}{\$60,000} = 75\% \text{ application rate}$$

In January direct labor costs charged to jobs totaled $4,800. Applying overhead to jobs at the rate of 75 percent of direct labor costs results in charges of $3,600. This data is recorded in general journal form below.

budget →

19 Y2				
Jan. 31	Work in Process Inventory	122	3,600 00	
	Manufacturing Overhead Applied	501		3,600 00
	To apply overhead to jobs in January			
	at 75% of direct labor costs.			

Notice that the entry recording the application of overhead to jobs debits Work in Process Inventory and credits Manufacturing Overhead Applied. At the end of each month, the credit balance in the applied account is compared with the debit balance in Manufacturing Overhead, the control account. If the credit balance of the applied account is larger, overhead has been overapplied. In January the debit balance of the control account is larger, reflecting an underapplied amount of $150, as shown below.

Manufacturing Overhead (Debit)		
Indirect Materials and Supplies	$ 500	
Indirect Labor	825	
Other Overhead Costs	2,425	
Total Charged to Manufacturing Overhead		$3,750
Manufacturing Overhead Applied (Credit)		3,600
Underapplied Overhead in January (Net Debit Balance)		$ 150

At the end of each month during the year, any underapplied amount is shown on the balance sheet as a deferred charge. Any overapplied amount is shown as a deferred credit. This is done because the application rate is an average based on estimates for the year and may not balance precisely from month to month. If any difference remains at the end of the year, it is usually closed out as an adjustment to the Cost of Goods Sold account on the income statement.

JOB ORDER COST SHEET

Each new job started in production is assigned a number for identification and reference. A *job order cost sheet* is also set up for the job at this time. The cost sheets for all jobs currently in production constitute a subsidiary ledger that supports the Work in Process Inventory account in the general ledger. The recording procedure gathers together all cost elements.

1. Charges for direct materials are posted to the Materials section of the job order cost sheet from summaries of materials requisitions.
2. Charges for direct labor are posted to the Labor section from summaries of the labor time tickets.
3. As labor costs are posted, overhead is computed at the established application rate and recorded in the Overhead Applied section.
4. When the job is completed, the costs are totaled and divided by the number of units produced to determine the unit cost.

The job order cost sheet for Job J-5, started and completed during the month of January, is illustrated on page 990. Notice that the information at the top of the sheet shows the job number and the nature of the product being manufactured, its starting and completion dates, and the number of units produced. Woodcraft's costs for materials and direct labor are posted weekly, and overhead is applied weekly on the basis of 75 percent of direct labor costs. All three costs are then summarized and divided by the units produced to determine the unit cost, as shown in the Summary section.

ACCOUNTING FOR WORK COMPLETED

As each job is completed during the month, the product involved is transferred to finished goods. When the related job order cost sheet is totaled, it supplies the data about quantity, unit cost, and total cost required for posting to the appropriate card in the finished goods subsidiary ledger. This ledger uses the same ledger card forms as the raw materials subsidiary ledger previously illustrated.

JOB ORDER COST SHEET

For Stock __X__

Customer's Name _____

Address _____

Item __X123 - Tables__

Job. No. __J-5__   Date __—__
Started __Jan. 3, 19Y2__
Completed __Jan. 15, 19Y2__
Quantity __25__ (ordered)   __25__ (completed)

MATERIALS		LABOR		OVERHEAD APPLIED			SUMMARY	
Date	Amount	Date	Amount	Date	Rate	Amount	Item	Amount
Jan. 8	200 00	Jan. 8	116 00	Jan. 8	75%	87 00	Materials	$250 00
15	50 00	15	55 10	15	75%	41 33	Labor	171 10
							Overhead	128 33
							Total	$549 43
							Unit Cost	$ 21 977
							Comments:	
Totals	250 00		171 10			128 33		

At the end of the month, a summary of completed jobs is prepared and an entry is made to transfer the total cost from the Work in Process Inventory account to the Finished Goods Inventory account, as shown below in general journal form.

19 Y2					
Jan. 31	Finished Goods Inventory	126	14,200 00		
	Work in Process Inventory	122		14,200 00	
	To transfer cost of jobs completed during January.				

ACCOUNTING FOR COST OF GOODS SOLD

As goods are sold, sales invoices are prepared for the customers. The cost of each order is entered as a memorandum on the office copy of the invoice. (This cost information comes from the finished goods ledger card for each item.) Later the information noted on the invoice copy is used to record credits on the finished goods ledger cards for quantities sold and their costs. At the end of the month, the total cost of goods sold is determined from a summary of the information entered on the invoice copies. This figure is then recorded as shown below in general journal form.

At the end of the year, underapplied or overapplied overhead for the year is normally closed out to the Cost of Goods Sold account. On the income statement

19 Y2					
Jan. 31	Cost of Goods Sold	560	12,000 00		
	Finished Goods Inventory	126		12,000 00	
	To record cost of goods sold during January.				

the balance of the Cost of Goods Sold account and the adjustment for underapplied or overapplied overhead are shown as illustrated below.

Sales		$200,000
Cost of Goods Sold (per ledger account)	$148,000	
Add Underapplied Manufacturing Overhead	2,100	
Cost of Goods Sold (adjusted)		150,100
Gross Profit on Sales		$ 49,900

The accountant may prefer to show all the details of actual manufacturing cost, including the actual overhead incurred, on the statement of cost of goods manufactured rather than treat the underapplied or overapplied overhead as an adjustment of cost of goods sold.

LEDGER ACCOUNTS ILLUSTRATED

The Woodcraft Manufacturing Corporation had inventories of raw materials and finished goods on January 1, 19Y2. There was, however, no beginning inventory of work in process. The three perpetual inventory accounts and the Cost of Goods Sold account are shown below and on page 992 as they appear at the end of January. The entries discussed in this chapter have been posted.

Raw Materials Inventory   No. 121

DATE		EXPLANATION	POST. REF.	DEBIT	CREDIT	BALANCE	DR. CR.
19 Y2							
Jan.	1	Balance	✓			22,340 00	Dr.
	31		J1	12,000 00		34,340 00	Dr.
	31		J1		9,500 00	24,840 00	Dr.

Work in Process Inventory   No. 122

DATE		EXPLANATION	POST. REF.	DEBIT	CREDIT	BALANCE	DR. CR.
19 Y2							
Jan.	31	Materials	J1	9,000 00		9,000 00	Dr.
	31	Direct Labor	J1	4,800 00		13,800 00	Dr.
	31	Mfg. Overhead Applied	J1	3,600 00		17,400 00	Dr.
	31	To Finished Goods	J1		14,200 00	3,200 00	Dr.

Finished Goods Inventory   No. 126

DATE		EXPLANATION	POST. REF.	DEBIT	CREDIT	BALANCE	DR. CR.
19 Y2							
Jan.	1	Balance	✓			16,000 00	Dr.
	31		J1	14,200 00		30,200 00	Dr.
	31		J1		12,000 00	18,200 00	Dr.

Cost of Goods Sold						No.	560
DATE	EXPLANATION	POST. REF.	DEBIT	CREDIT	BALANCE	DR. CR.	
19 Y2 Jan. 31		J1	12,000 00		12,000 00	Dr.	

PRINCIPLES AND PROCEDURES SUMMARY

Under the job order cost system, each of three inventory accounts—Raw Materials Inventory, Work in Process Inventory, and Finished Goods Inventory—is operated as a perpetual inventory record. Job cost sheets function as a subsidiary ledger supporting the Work in Process Inventory account in the general ledger.

Materials are issued upon presentation of a written requisition that shows the number of the job for which the materials will be used, and that job is charged with the proper cost. Time tickets provide a basis for charging direct labor to the specific job. Manufacturing overhead is assigned to jobs on the basis of an application rate that is commonly related to direct labor costs. Underapplied or overapplied overhead is carried forward from month to month. The net underapplied or overapplied overhead at the end of the year is closed out, often as an adjustment to the cost of goods sold.

As each job is completed, the cost sheet furnishes data needed for transferring costs from the Work in Process Inventory account to the Finished Goods Inventory account. The cost of each order is also entered on the office copy of the sales invoice. At the end of the month, the cost of goods sold is determined by summarizing this data. Then the transfer entry is recorded in the general journal.

MANAGERIAL IMPLICATIONS

The job order cost system keeps managers informed of the cost of manufacturing specific orders or batches of goods and serves as a basis for setting prices. The use of an overhead application rate helps to develop a more consistent unit cost from month to month because the effects of unusual expenses or variations in monthly volume of output are averaged over the entire year.

Perpetual inventory procedures help in keeping management informed about the exact amounts tied up in inventories. In this way they serve as useful tools for inventory control.

REVIEW QUESTIONS

1. Why is a cost accounting system needed?
2. What is a job order cost accounting system? When is a job order cost accounting system appropriate?

3. What is a process cost accounting system? Under what conditions would a process cost accounting system be appropriate?
4. Explain the standard cost system.
5. What is a producing department? A service department?
6. What does the Raw Materials Inventory account show?
7. Describe the entries made in the Raw Materials Inventory account.
8. What does the balance of the Work in Process Inventory account represent?
9. What information does a job order cost sheet contain?
10. When direct materials are issued from the storeroom, what entries are made in the subsidiary records?
11. What is a receiving report?
12. What is a raw materials ledger card?
13. What entry is made for indirect materials issued from the storeroom?
14. What is a time ticket? Why are time tickets important under the job order cost accounting system?
15. What is idle time? How is the cost of idle time accounted for?
16. What is an overhead application rate?
17. Why is an overhead application rate necessary under the job order cost accounting system?
18. What is a materials requisition?
19. Name the sources of postings to the job order cost sheet.
20. How is underapplied or overapplied manufacturing overhead disposed of at the end of the year?
21. Under the perpetual inventory method, what journal entries are made for sales and cost of goods sold?

MANAGERIAL DISCUSSION QUESTIONS

1. Why should management insist that all materials requisitions be signed by an authorized individual?
2. Assume that you are an accountant at a manufacturing firm. At the end of one year, there is a large overapplied overhead amount. How would you explain to management why this balance might exist?
3. How do perpetual inventory procedures help managers to obtain tighter internal control over materials and supplies?
4. Why should management insist that a physical inventory be taken once a year even though perpetual inventory records are kept?
5. Assume that a director of the firm where you work asks why you record raw materials at their gross price even though it is the firm's policy to pay suppliers within the discount period. What would you say?
6. From an administrative standpoint, why is direct labor cost a simple basis to use for the application of manufacturing overhead?
7. Why would managers want the overapplied or underapplied overhead figure to appear in the Cost of Goods Sold section of the income statement?
8. In general, would managers prefer to see overapplied or underapplied overhead? Why?

EXERCISES

EXERCISE 41-1 **Recording the purchase of direct materials.** During October 19X6 the Nash Manufacturing Company purchased and issued the following materials and supplies. Give the entry in general journal form to record the cost of the direct materials purchased. (Use Oct. 31, 19X6, as the date of the entry.)

Purchases:		Issues from storeroom:	
Direct materials	$36,900	Direct materials	$34,725
Manufacturing supplies	2,050	Manufacturing supplies	1,018

EXERCISE 41-2 **Recording the purchase of manufacturing supplies.** Refer to Exercise 41-1. Give the entry in general journal form to record the cost of the manufacturing supplies purchased during October.

EXERCISE 41-3 **Recording the issue of direct materials.** Refer to Exercise 41-1. Give the entry in general journal form to record the cost of the direct materials issued during October.

EXERCISE 41-4 **Recording the issue of manufacturing supplies.** Refer to Exercise 41-1. Give the entry in general journal form to record the cost of the manufacturing supplies issued during October.

EXERCISE 41-5 **Recording the factory payroll.** A payroll summary prepared at the Nash Manufacturing Company showed the following figures for October 19X6. Give the entry in general journal form to record the labor costs incurred. (Use Oct. 31, 19X6, as the date of the entry.)

Direct labor costs incurred	$16,412
Indirect labor costs incurred	2,060
FICA tax withheld	1,108
Income tax withheld	2,032

EXERCISE 41-6 **Recording labor costs in subsidiary records.** Refer to Exercise 41-5. Explain how the direct labor costs incurred during October at the Nash Manufacturing Company should be entered in the subsidiary ledger accounts of its job order cost system.

EXERCISE 41-7 **Computing the overhead application rate.** The McNulty Corporation bases its manufacturing overhead rate on the ratio of estimated overhead costs to estimated direct labor costs for each year. Data about the firm's estimated manufacturing costs for the coming year, 19X2, is given below. What is McNulty's overhead application rate for 19X2?

Estimated direct labor costs	$ 837,584.00
Estimated overhead costs	268,026.88
Estimated costs of direct materials	1,675,168.00

EXERCISE 41-8   **Recording applied overhead for a period.** Assume that the McNulty Corporation's actual direct labor costs were $901,600 in 19X2. Using the overhead application rate computed in Exercise 41-7, give the general journal entry summarizing the overhead applied by McNulty during 19X2. (Use Dec. 31, 19X2, as the date of the entry.)

EXERCISE 41-9   **Computing the overhead applicable to a job.** During 19X2 the McNulty Corporation began and completed Job SO-465. Costs entered on the job order cost sheet for this job were $9,810 for materials and $6,950 for labor. Using the overhead rate determined in Exercise 41-7, compute the amount of overhead that should be applied to the job. Then compute the total cost of the job.

EXERCISE 41-10   **Determining whether overhead is overapplied or underapplied.** For the year 19X2 the McNulty Corporation's actual overhead costs were $263,610, and its applied overhead was $264,820. Did the firm have overapplied or underapplied overhead for the year? What amount was overapplied or underapplied?

EXERCISE 41-11   **Recording the cost of goods completed and the cost of goods sold.** The records of the Gulfport Corporation for 19X3 show that it completed goods costing $1,208,500 and that it had a cost of goods sold of $1,364,300. Give the entries in general journal form to record the cost of goods completed and the cost of goods sold for the year. (Use Dec. 31, 19X3, as the date of the entries.)

EXERCISE 41-12   **Computing alternative overhead rates.** The Granville Corporation is considering two methods for applying overhead. One method is based on direct labor costs, and the other method is based on the number of direct labor hours worked. Estimated data for the next year, 19X4, is shown below. What would be the overhead application rate based on direct labor costs? What would be the overhead application rate based on direct labor hours? (Divide the estimated overhead costs by the estimated number of direct labor hours to obtain this rate.)

Estimated direct labor costs	$1,200,000
Estimated direct labor hours	150,000 hours
Estimated overhead costs	$ 600,000

EXERCISE 41-13   **Applying overhead on the basis of direct labor costs.** During 19X4 the Granville Corporation began and completed Job A4-21. The direct labor costs incurred on the job were $4,950 (600 hours at $8.25 an hour). The direct materials used had a cost of $7,230. If the overhead rate is based on direct labor costs, what amount of overhead should be applied to the job? (Use the first rate determined in Exercise 41-12.) What is the total cost of the job?

EXERCISE 41-14   **Applying overhead on the basis of direct labor hours.** Refer to the information given in Exercise 41-13 for the Granville Corporation. What amount of overhead should be applied to Job A4-21 if the overhead rate is based on direct labor hours? (Use the second rate determined in Exercise 41-12. Multiply this rate by the number of direct labor hours involved in the job.) What is the total cost of the job?

EXERCISE 41-15   **Computing the cost of each unit manufactured.** Refer to Exercise 41-13. Assuming that 500 units are completed on Job A4-21, what would be the total cost of each unit if overhead is applied on the basis of direct labor costs?

EXERCISE 41-16   **Computing the cost of each unit manufactured.** Refer to Exercise 41-14. Assuming that 500 units are completed on Job A4-21, what would be the total cost of each unit if overhead is applied on the basis of direct labor hours?

EXERCISE 41-17   **Comparing unit costs under different overhead application methods.** Refer to your solutions for Exercises 41-15 and 41-16. Compute the difference in the unit cost of the goods produced on Job A4-21 under the two overhead application methods used. Which method resulted in a higher unit cost?

PROBLEMS

PROBLEM 41-1   **Recording transactions under the job order cost system.** The cost data given below is for the Harbor Rainwear Company, a maker of raincoats. This data covers the month of January 19X8.

Instructions
1. Prepare general journal entries to record each item of cost data given. Use the account titles listed in the textbook.
2. Compute the amount of overapplied or underapplied overhead for the month.
3. Prepare a partial income statement for the month of January, adjusted for any overapplied or underapplied overhead.

COST DATA FOR JANUARY 19X8

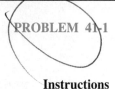

a. Raw materials and supplies costing $30,000 were purchased.
b. The summary of materials requisitions shows that materials and supplies valued at $24,000 were issued for use in jobs. Direct materials accounted for $22,400, and the balance consisted of indirect materials and supplies.
c. The payroll summary shows that direct labor amounted to $11,000, indirect labor amounted to $1,500, FICA tax deductions were $625, and income tax deductions were $1,225.
d. Manufacturing overhead of $5,625 was incurred in addition to indirect materials and indirect labor. (Credit to Accounts Payable.)
e. The predetermined overhead application rate is 80 percent of direct labor costs.
f. The summary of completed jobs shows that the cost of these jobs amounted to $35,500.
g. The summary of sales invoices shows that goods costing $28,800 were sold on credit for $46,000.

PROBLEM 41-2   **Recording transactions under the job order cost system.** In June 19X5 the Executive Desk Corporation had the transactions given on page 997 in connection with its manufacturing operations.

Instructions
1. Prepare general journal entries to record each item of cost data given. Use the account titles listed in the textbook.
2. Compute the amount of overapplied or underapplied overhead for the month.
3. Prepare a partial income statement for the month of June, adjusted for any overapplied or underapplied overhead.

COST DATA FOR JUNE 19X5

a. Raw materials costing $62,700 were purchased.
b. Raw materials costing $56,000 were used: direct materials, $52,400; indirect materials, $3,600.
c. Factory wages of $64,000 were incurred: direct labor, $45,270; indirect labor, $18,730. FICA tax deductions were $4,480, and income tax deductions were $6,800.
d. Other overhead costs of $12,210 were incurred. (Credit to Accounts Payable.)
e. Estimated manufacturing overhead costs were applied to jobs in production at the rate of 70 percent of direct labor costs.
f. Finished goods costing $124,564 were transferred to the warehouse.
g. Finished goods costing $127,555 were sold and shipped to customers.
h. Finished goods sold for $181,452 were billed to customers.

PROBLEM 41-3 **Preparing job order cost sheets and making journal entries to transfer costs.** The Sanger Woodworking Shop builds custom-made cabinets and shelves. On January 1, 19X1, one job (X0-59) was in progress. The costs accumulated to date on that job were materials, $3,750; labor, $1,720; and overhead, $860. During January the following costs were incurred in production work on Job X0-59 and on Jobs X1-1 and X1-2, which were started on January 5, 19X1.

	MATERIALS	LABOR	ITEMS	QUANTITY
Job X0-59	$1,080	$1,380	X123 Cabinets	120
Job X1-1	6,020	3,100	X456 Shelves	200
Job X1-2	4,050	840	X078 Cabinets	80

Manufacturing overhead is applied at the rate of 50 percent of direct labor costs. During January actual manufacturing overhead costs of $2,990 were incurred. Job X0-59 was completed on January 18 and was delivered to the customer. The sales price was $16,800.

Instructions
1. Prepare job order cost sheets for the three jobs. Enter the beginning balances applicable to Job X0-59.
2. Post the costs of the materials and labor for January to the job order cost sheets.
3. Compute the overhead amounts that should be applied to the three jobs worked on during the month, and enter these amounts on the job cost sheets.
4. Give the entry in general journal form to transfer the cost of the job completed from work in process to finished goods.
5. Compute the amount of underapplied or overapplied overhead for January.

ALTERNATE PROBLEMS

PROBLEM 41-1A

Recording transactions under the job order cost system. The cost data given below is for Rio Grande Leather Products Inc., a maker of shoes and boots. This data covers the month of December 19X4.

Instructions

1. Prepare general journal entries to record each item of cost data given. Use the account titles listed in the textbook.
2. Compute the amount of overapplied or underapplied overhead for the month.
3. Prepare a partial income statement for the month of December, adjusted for any overapplied or underapplied overhead.

COST DATA FOR DECEMBER 19X4

a. Materials purchases, $36,500.
b. Materials issued to production, $30,500: direct materials, $29,900; indirect materials, $600.
c. Payroll: direct labor, $12,000; indirect labor, $2,600; FICA tax deducted, $1,600; income tax deducted, $1,300.
d. Manufacturing overhead of $6,000 was incurred in addition to indirect materials and indirect labor. (Credit to Accounts Payable.)
e. Manufacturing overhead is applied to production at a predetermined rate of 75 percent of direct labor costs.
f. Jobs costing $41,000 were completed and transferred to finished goods.
g. Finished goods costing $37,000 were sold and billed to customers at $48,000.

PROBLEM 41-2A

Recording transactions under the job order cost system. In June 19X5 the Classical Piano Company had the transactions given below in connection with its manufacturing operations.

Instructions

1. Prepare general journal entries to record each item of cost data given. Use the account titles listed in the textbook.
2. Compute the amount of overapplied or underapplied overhead for the month.
3. Prepare a partial income statement for the month of June, adjusted for any overapplied or underapplied overhead.

COST DATA FOR JUNE 19X5

a. Raw materials costing $57,700 were purchased.
b. Raw materials costing $60,900 were used: direct materials, $57,875; indirect materials, $3,025.
c. Factory wages of $57,065 were incurred: direct labor, $39,570; indirect labor, $17,495. FICA tax deducted, $3,450; income tax deducted, $6,080.
d. Other overhead costs amounting to $11,570 were incurred. (Credit to Accounts Payable.)
e. Estimated manufacturing overhead costs were applied to jobs in production at the rate of 85 percent of direct labor costs.
f. Finished goods costing $127,035 were transferred to the warehouse.

g. Finished goods costing $125,295 were sold and shipped to customers.

h. Finished goods sold for $160,745 were billed to customers.

PROBLEM 41-3A **Preparing job order cost sheets and making journal entries to transfer costs.** The Kreeger Corporation makes water tanks for high-rise buildings. On January 1, 19X4, two jobs, X3-108 and X3-109, were in progress. The costs accumulated to date on these jobs are shown below. Job X3-108 involves three A200 water tanks, and Job X3-109 involves two A500 water tanks.

	JOB X3-108	JOB X3-109
Materials	$18,500	$14,100
Labor	4,100	2,650
Overhead	2,460	1,590

During January the following costs were incurred in production work on the two existing jobs and on a new job, X4-1, which involves two A300 water tanks.

	JOB X3-108	JOB X3-109	JOB X4-1
Materials	$1,300	$2,640	$13,670
Labor	1,800	1,750	1,060

Manufacturing overhead is applied at the rate of 60 percent of direct labor costs. During January actual manufacturing overhead costs of $3,067 were incurred. Jobs X3-108 and X3-109 were completed on January 15, 19X4. The sales price of Job X3-108 was $41,300, and the sales price of Job X3-109 was $37,600.

Instructions
1. Prepare job order cost sheets for the three jobs. Enter the beginning balances applicable to Jobs X3-108 and X3-109.
2. Post the costs of the materials and labor for January to the job order cost sheets.
3. Compute the overhead amounts that should be applied to the three jobs worked on during January, and enter these amounts on the job order cost sheets.
4. Give the entry in general journal form to transfer the costs of the two jobs completed from work in process to finished goods.
5. Compute the amount of underapplied or overapplied overhead for January.

CHAPTER 42

In the previous chapter the basic principles and procedures of job order cost accounting were discussed. You saw how such a system is used to gather and determine the cost of each item produced. In this chapter you will learn how a process cost accounting system operates.

PROCESS COST ACCOUNTING

THE NEED FOR A PROCESS COST ACCOUNTING SYSTEM

Some time after the job order cost accounting system was installed at the Woodcraft Manufacturing Corporation, the firm again broadened the scope of its activities. One specific product, a table, had proved very popular, and large orders were being received from several customers. Some of the tables of this type were being sold unpainted. Others were fully finished. The management of Woodcraft considered the possibility of expanding the existing plant in order to produce more of the tables, but found that there was inadequate room. The company then decided to construct a completely new plant for the manufacture of the table. Since the new plant will produce a single product and production will be continuous, the accountant decides to use a process cost accounting system.

SETTING UP THE PROCESS COST ACCOUNTING SYSTEM

The process cost accounting system has many of the same features as the job order cost accounting system. The flow of costs is exactly like that shown on page 983, and the same inventory accounts are used. There are, however, several significant differences. For example, there is no need to maintain job order cost sheets when a process cost accounting system is used because products are not made in batches or by order. In addition, there is increased emphasis on departmentalization. Under the system proposed by Woodcraft's accountant, all costs for materials, labor, and overhead will be identified with departments. The monthly cost of each department will then be allocated to the units of product worked on in the department that month. Thus a process cost accounting system may be viewed as a monthly average cost system. As products are transferred from one department to another, the related costs are also transferred.

The accountant at Woodcraft consults the factory supervisors to find out how various manufacturing activities will be organized and assigned to departmental units. Suppose that two producing departments are established—the woodworking department and the finishing department. All products go through the woodworking department. Then tables to be sold unpainted are moved directly to the finished goods storeroom and recorded in the Finished Goods Inventory account. Other tables go to the finishing department and then to the finished goods storeroom. Knowledge of this flow of operations helps the accountant plan the necessary recording procedures for all producing and service activities. (Service department costs must be allocated as manufacturing overhead to the producing units that benefit.)

Let us see how the process cost accounting system developed for the Woodcraft Manufacturing Corporation is put into effect. To do this, we will examine the data for the first month's operation under the new system.

DATA FOR THE FIRST MONTH

The transactions for January have been recorded and departmentalized. Service department costs have been assigned to the two producing departments. Materials, labor, and manufacturing overhead have been charged to the work in process accounts of the producing departments. A record has been kept of the products started, completed, and still in process in each department. The stage of completion of the ending work in process has been estimated. The illustration below tells the story in summary form, using three headings—Costs, Quantities, and Stage of Completion.

DEPARTMENTAL COST DATA FOR JANUARY 19Y4

	WOODWORKING DEPT.	FINISHING DEPT.
Costs		
Materials	$13,000.00	$ 910.00
Labor	6,240.00	2,340.00
Manufacturing Overhead	4,875.00	1,690.00
Total Costs	$24,115.00	$4,940.00
Quantities		
Started in Production	4,000	-0-
Transferred In From Prior Department	-0-	2,700
Transferred Out to Next Department	2,700	-0-
Transferred Out to Finished Goods	1,000	2,500
Work in Process—Ending	300	200
Stage of Completion—Ending Work in Process		
Materials	Complete	½
Labor	⅔	½
Manufacturing Overhead	⅔	½

In the Quantities section, note that of the 4,000 units started in production in the woodworking department, 2,700 were transferred to the finishing department and 1,000 to finished goods for sale as unpainted tables. This leaves 300 tables still in process. The Stage of Completion section indicates that all the required materials have been issued and that two-thirds of the work has been done on these 300 tables.

A similar review of the data in the column for the finishing department reveals that of the 2,700 units transferred in from the woodworking department, only 2,500 were completed and transferred, in turn, to finished goods. This left

200 tables in process at the end of the period, half of which were complete as to materials, labor, and overhead.

Now that the total costs and the number of units of each product are known, it might seem that the cost for each type of table could be determined by dividing the total cost for each cost element by the number of units. However, this calculation would not be correct because some of the units are only partly complete. The *equivalent production* must be established before meaningful unit costs can be computed.

Equivalent Production Computations

The equivalent production technique shows the amount of work accomplished in terms of equivalent whole units. These computations are illustrated below.

EQUIVALENT PRODUCTION COMPUTATIONS—JANUARY 19Y4

Woodworking Department

Materials: Units Transferred Out		
To Next Department	2,700	
To Finished Goods	1,000	3,700
(a) Work in Process—100% × 300 units =		300
Equivalent Production for Materials		4,000
Labor and Manufacturing Overhead:		
Units Transferred Out		
To Next Department	2,700	
To Finished Goods	1,000	3,700
(b) Work in Process—⅔ × 300 units =		200
Equivalent Production for Labor and Overhead		3,900

Finishing Department

Materials, Labor, and Manufacturing Overhead:	
Units Transferred Out	2,500
(c) Work in Process—½ × 200 units =	100
Equivalent Production for Materials, Labor, and Overhead	2,600

The 300 units in process in the woodworking department are two-thirds completed as to labor and manufacturing overhead (b). They are equivalent to 200 completed units in this respect (⅔ × 300 = 200). The *total equivalent production* (fully completed units + partially completed units) is determined by adding the 200 units to the 3,700 units completed and transferred out of the department. On this basis, equivalent production is 3,900 units for labor and manufacturing overhead. However, for materials (a), the equivalent production is 4,000 units (3,700 + 300 = 4,000) because all the materials have been issued for the 300 tables in process.

In the finishing department, the 200 tables that are half completed (c) as to materials, labor, and manufacturing overhead are equivalent to 100 completed units (½ × 200 = 100). This figure is then added to the 2,500 units actually completed to obtain a total equivalent production of 2,600 units for each of the three elements of cost.

With the basic data on costs, quantities, and equivalent production assembled, a cost of production report can be prepared. One form of this report provides separate sections to summarize quantities and costs. In turn, each section is composed of two parts that reconcile the totals of the quantities and costs to be accounted for with the totals accounted for.

Woodworking Department A cost of production report for the woodworking department is illustrated below.

COST OF PRODUCTION REPORT—JANUARY 19Y4
Woodworking Department

Quantity Schedule	Units	
(a) Quantity To Be Accounted For:		
Started in Production	4,000	*800*
Total To Be Accounted For	4,000	
(b) Quantity Accounted For:		
Transferred Out to Next Department	2,700	*500*
Transferred Out to Finished Goods	1,000	
Work in Process—Ending	300	*300*
Total Accounted For	4,000	

Cost Schedule	Total Cost	E.P. Units	Unit Cost
(c) Costs To Be Accounted For:			
Costs in Current Department			
Materials	$13,000.00 ÷ 4,000 =		$3.25
Labor	6,240.00 ÷ 3,900 =		1.60
Manufacturing Overhead	4,875.00 ÷ 3,900 =		1.25
Cumulative Cost Total	$24,115.00		$6.10
(d) Costs Accounted For:			
Transferred Out to Next Department	$16,470.00 = 2,700 × $6.10		
Transferred Out to Finished Goods	6,100.00 = 1,000 × 6.10		
Total Costs Transferred Out	$22,570.00		
Work in Process—Ending			
Materials	$ 975.00 =	300 ×	$3.25
Labor	320.00 =	200 ×	1.60
Manufacturing Overhead	250.00 =	200 ×	1.25
Total Work in Process	$ 1,545.00		
Total Costs Accounted For	$24,115.00		

The first section, called the Quantity Schedule, requires little explanation. Its first part (a) shows the units to be accounted for, and its second part (b) explains what happened to these units. To simplify the procedure, all units started in process are assumed to be completed or still in process. (In practice, units may be spoiled or lost, causing additional complications in the determination of costs.)

The second section is entitled Cost Schedule. Its first part (c) shows the total cost of each cost element, the unit cost that results from dividing the total cost of each element by the appropriate equivalent production units, and the cumulative cost total. (In practice, the equivalent production units and computations are not shown. The report has only two columns, Total Cost and Unit Cost.)

The second part of the Cost Schedule section (d) accounts for the various costs in two groups. First it shows the cost of units completed through this department and transferred out. Then it presents the cost of the ending inventory of work in process. The sum of these two amounts equals the cumulative cost total shown in the top part of the Cost Schedule section. Refer to the figures given in the cost of production report for the woodworking department, which is illustrated on page 1003. The ending work in process cost is computed as follows.

1. By multiplying the units in process by the stage of completion for each cost element to get the equivalent production units.
2. By multiplying the equivalent units for each cost element by the unit cost for that element.
3. By adding the total costs by elements to get the total cost of work in process.

As an example, there are 300 equivalent units for materials and the unit cost is $3.25. Multiplying these figures gives the total materials cost in the ending work in process inventory—$975 (300 × $3.25). For labor, the equivalent units total 200 (300 × ⅔). Multiplying 200 equivalent units by the unit cost of $1.60 gives a total cost for labor of $320. For manufacturing overhead, 200 equivalent units are multiplied by the $1.25 unit cost to get a total of $250. When the three cost elements are added, the result is a value of $1,545 for the total ending work in process inventory of the department, as shown on page 1003.

Finishing Department A cost of production report for the second producing unit, the finishing department, is shown on the next page.

In the Quantity Schedule section, the quantity to be accounted for (a) consists of units transferred in from the prior department. In turn, these units are accounted for (b) as transferred to finished goods or still in process at the end of the month. Note that there is a new item in the first part (c) of the Cost Schedule section. Under Costs To Be Accounted For, the figure called Costs in Prior Department brings forward from the woodworking department the cost of the 2,700 tables transferred in, $16,470. Costs in the current department (finishing) are listed next, and each is divided by the 2,600 equivalent units (see page 1002) to obtain the unit cost figures. Total costs in the current department are then added to total costs in the prior department to get the cumulative cost total. Unit costs are added in the same manner to obtain the figure of $8 for the cumulative unit cost of both departments.

Again, the costs are accounted for in two groups. The first item shows the cost of 2,500 units completed and transferred out to finished goods. These are valued at $20,000 ($8 a unit × 2,500 units). The next computation shows the cost elements relating to the work in process inventory. A new element appears in this computation—the costs in the prior department of $6.10 a unit. Applying this cost to the ending inventory of 200 units (all complete with respect to the work of the prior department) results in a total value of $1,220 ($6.10 × 200). Current department costs are determined by multiplying the equivalent units for each cost element (200 × ½, or 100, in each case) by the unit cost, as shown. The total work in process inventory plus the costs transferred out equals the total cost accounted for. This figure, in turn, equals the cumulative cost total, determined in the first part of the Cost Schedule section. Refer to the figures given in the cost of production report below.

COST OF PRODUCTION REPORT—JANUARY 19Y4
Finishing Department

Quantity Schedule	Units
(a) Quantity To Be Accounted For:	
Transferred In From Prior Department	2,700
Total To Be Accounted For	2,700
(b) Quantity Accounted For:	
Transferred Out to Finished Goods	2,500
Work in Process—Ending	200
Total Accounted For	2,700

Cost Schedule	Total Cost	E.P. Units	Unit Cost
(c) Costs To Be Accounted For:			
Costs in Prior Department	$16,470.00 ÷ 2,700 =		$6.10
Costs in Current Department			
Materials	$ 910.00 ÷ 2,600 =		$ .35
Labor	2,340.00 ÷ 2,600 =		.90
Manufacturing Overhead	1,690.00 ÷ 2,600 =		.65
Total Current Department Costs	$ 4,940.00		$1.90
Cumulative Cost Total	$21,410.00		$8.00

(d) Costs Accounted For:		
Transferred Out to Finished Goods	$20,000.00 =	2,500 × $8.00
Work in Process—Ending		
Costs in Prior Department	$ 1,220.00 =	200 × $6.10
Costs in Current Department		
Materials	35.00 =	100 × $ .35
Labor	90.00 =	100 × .90
Manufacturing Overhead	65.00 =	100 × .65
Total Work in Process	$ 1,410.00	
Total Costs Accounted For	$21,410.00	

Debits to the departmental work in process accounts are made during the month as follows.

1. Materials issued to production are recorded by debiting the departmental work in process accounts and crediting Raw Materials Inventory, as shown below.

19 Y4				
Jan. 31	Work in Process—Woodworking Dept.	122	13,000 00	
	Work in Process—Finishing Dept.	123	910 00	
	Raw Materials Inventory	121		13,910 00
	To charge materials to production in January.			

2. Labor is debited to the departmental work in process accounts and credited to Salaries and Wages Payable, as shown below.

19 Y4				
Jan. 31	Work in Process—Woodworking Dept.	122	6,240 00	
	Work in Process—Finishing Dept.	123	2,340 00	
	Salaries and Wages Payable	215		8,580 00
	To distribute factory payroll for January.			

3. Manufacturing overhead is debited to the departmental work in process accounts and credited to the Manufacturing Overhead account, as shown below. (Remember that Manufacturing Overhead is a control account with a supporting subsidiary ledger that shows the details of overhead items. Manufacturing Overhead is charged with overhead costs as they are actually incurred during the month.)

19 Y4				
Jan. 31	Work in Process—Woodworking Dept.	122	4,875 00	
	Work in Process—Finishing Dept.	123	1,690 00	
	Manufacturing Overhead	500		6,565 00
	To distribute overhead for January.			

Data is posted to the departmental work in process accounts. In turn, these accounts supply the data needed for the cost of production reports. After these reports have been prepared, an entry is recorded in the general journal to transfer costs from the woodworking department to the finishing department and to the Finished Goods Inventory account. Another entry shows the transfer from the finishing department to the Finished Goods Inventory account. These entries are illustrated on page 1007.

		19 Y4					
Jan.	31	Work in Process—Finishing Dept.	123	16,470 00		
		Finished Goods Inventory	126	6,100 00		
		Work in Process—Woodworking Dept.	122		22,570 00
		To transfer cost of goods completed during January out of woodworking department.			
	31	Finished Goods Inventory	126	20,000 00		
		Work in Process—Finishing Dept.	123		20,000 00
		To transfer cost of goods completed during January out of finishing department.			

After the above entries have been posted, the departmental work in process accounts appear as shown below. Note that each ending balance agrees with the amount shown in the departmental cost of production report.

Work in Process—Woodworking Department   No. 122

DATE		EXPLANATION	POST. REF.	DEBIT	CREDIT	BALANCE	DR. CR.
19 Y4							
Jan.	31	Materials	J1	13,000 00		13,000 00	Dr.
	31	Labor	J1	6,240 00		19,240 00	Dr.
	31	Mfg. Overhead	J1	4,875 00		24,115 00	Dr.
	31	Transferred Out	J1		22,570 00	1,545 00	Dr.

Work in Process—Finishing Department   No. 123

DATE		EXPLANATION	POST. REF.	DEBIT	CREDIT	BALANCE	DR. CR.
19 Y4							
Jan.	31	Materials	J1	910 00		910 00	Dr.
	31	Labor	J1	2,340 00		3,250 00	Dr.
	31	Mfg. Overhead	J1	1,690 00		4,940 00	Dr.
	31	From Prior Department	J1	16,470 00		21,410 00	Dr.
	31	Transferred Out	J1		20,000 00	1,410 00	Dr.

Entries for Sale of Finished Goods

The final step in the month's flow of costs relates to the sale of finished goods. Suppose that Woodcraft's sales during January totaled $29,500 and that the cost of the goods sold amounted to $18,750. The entry for the sales involves a debit to Accounts Receivable and a credit to Sales at the selling price. A second entry is made to transfer the cost, debiting Cost of Goods Sold and crediting Finished Goods Inventory for $18,750. These entries are illustrated on page 1008 in general journal form, and the postings to the ledger accounts for Finished Goods Inventory and Cost of Goods Sold also appear on page 1008. (Assume a beginning balance of $32,000 for Finished Goods Inventory.)

19 Y4						
Jan. 31	Accounts Receivable	111	29,500 00			
	Sales	401			29,500 00	
	To record sales on credit for January.					
31	Cost of Goods Sold	560	18,750 00			
	Finished Goods Inventory	126			18,750 00	
	To record cost of goods sold in January.					

Finished Goods Inventory   No. 126

DATE	EXPLANATION	POST. REF.	DEBIT	CREDIT	BALANCE	DR. CR.
19 Y4						
Jan. 1	Balance	✓			32,000 00	Dr.
31		J1	6,100 00		38,100 00	Dr.
31		J1	20,000 00		58,100 00	Dr.
31		J1		18,750 00	39,350 00	Dr.

Cost of Goods Sold   No. 560

DATE	EXPLANATION	POST. REF.	DEBIT	CREDIT	BALANCE	DR. CR.
19 Y4						
Jan. 31		J1	18,750 00		18,750 00	Dr.

DATA FOR THE SECOND MONTH

In January there were no beginning inventories of work in process. In the second month and later months, such beginning inventories are recorded as a normal part of business operations. Data covering the performance of both producing departments for the second month is summarized on page 1009. Note that the costs of the beginning work in process inventory are shown first, broken down by department and cost element.

Equivalent Production Computations

The equivalent production computations for the second month are worked out just as they were for January. The beginning inventory does not complicate the situation at all since the *average method* is used here. (This method simply combines the beginning inventory figures with the current period figures.) The computations are summarized on page 1009.

Cost of Production Report—February

With the data for February assembled and the equivalent production figures worked out, the next step is to prepare the cost of production report. This report is illustrated on page 1011 as it would normally be prepared, showing both departments in one presentation. (The total cost and unit cost figures appear without the computations that were shown in the January reports.)

DEPARTMENTAL COST DATA FOR FEBRUARY 19Y4

	WOODWORKING DEPT.	FINISHING DEPT.
Costs		
Work in Process—Beginning		
Costs in Prior Department	$ -0-	$1,220.00
Costs in Current Department		
Materials	975.00	35.00
Labor	320.00	90.00
Manufacturing Overhead	250.00	65.00
Current Department Costs—February		
Materials	13,380.00	1,130.50
Labor	6,565.00	2,839.50
Manufacturing Overhead	4,850.00	1,919.50
Total Costs	$26,340.00	$7,299.50
Quantities		
Work in Process—Beginning	300	200
Started in Production	4,050	-0-
Transferred In From Prior Department	-0-	3,000
Transferred Out to Next Department	3,000	-0-
Transferred Out to Finished Goods	1,200	3,100
Work in Process—Ending	150	100
Stage of Completion—Work in Process		
Beginning Inventory		
Materials	Complete	½
Labor	⅔	½
Manufacturing Overhead	⅔	½
Ending Inventory		
Materials	Complete	½
Labor	⅓	½
Manufacturing Overhead	⅓	½

EQUIVALENT PRODUCTION COMPUTATIONS FOR FEBRUARY 19Y4

Woodworking Department

Materials: Units Transferred Out
To Next Department	3,000	
To Finished Goods	1,200	4,200
Work in Process—Ending 100% × 150 units =		150
Equivalent Production for Materials		4,350

Labor and Manufacturing Overhead:
Units Transferred Out
To Next Department	3,000	
To Finished Goods	1,200	4,200
Work in Process—Ending ⅓ × 150 units =		50
Equivalent Production for Labor and Overhead		4,250

Finishing Department

Materials, Labor, and Manufacturing Overhead:
Units Transferred Out	3,100
Work in Process—Ending ½ × 100 units =	50
Equivalent Production for Materials, Labor, and Overhead	3,150

Quantity Schedule Again, the Quantity Schedule section is almost self-explanatory. The beginning inventory of work in process plus the units started in production or received from the prior department make up the total to be accounted for (a). These are either transferred out or remain in process at the end of the period (b). Once again, it is assumed that no units were spoiled or lost.

Cost Schedule For the first time, a beginning inventory (c) appears for the woodworking department. The unit costs in this department are determined by adding the beginning inventory and the current period costs for each cost element and then dividing the total by the equivalent production. For instance, materials costs are computed by adding $975 (d) and $13,380 (f) to obtain $14,355. Dividing this by 4,350 equivalent units gives the unit cost of $3.30. For labor, $320 (e) is added to $6,565 (g) to get $6,885. Dividing by 4,250 equivalent units gives the unit cost of $1.62. The same procedure is followed for manufacturing overhead. The total unit cost for the department is $6.12.

The last part of the Cost Schedule section for the woodworking department appears exactly as it did in January. Quantities transferred (h) to the finishing department or to finished goods are multiplied by the $6.12 unit cost figure to get the total cost transferred out. The ending work in process inventory (i) is computed by multiplying the equivalent production units for each cost element by the unit cost for that element, as shown below.

Woodworking Department

Materials:	150 units fully completed × $3.30 = $495
Labor:	150 units × ⅓ completed × $1.62 = $81
Manufacturing Overhead:	150 units × ⅓ completed × $1.20 = $60

For the finishing department, two items are shown under Costs in Prior Department. The beginning inventory amount is added to the cost transferred in during the current period, and this total is divided by the total units to get an average unit cost for the work in the prior department. Specifically, the total cost of $19,580 is divided by the 3,200 total units, giving an average cost of $6.11875.

Current department unit costs are computed as they were for the woodworking department. Consider the cost of materials first. The beginning inventory figure, $35, is added to the current period amount, $1,130.50, to obtain a total materials cost of $1,165.50. This total is divided by the 3,150 equivalent units to obtain the unit cost of $0.37. Labor and manufacturing overhead computations are handled in the same manner. The procedure used to account for the costs of the finishing department is the same as the procedure used for the woodworking department.

Entries to Record February Costs

Entries for the February cost charges and transfers are shown on page 1012, along with the departmental work in process accounts as they appear after these entries are posted. Note that the beginning balances in the work in process accounts are the same as the ending balances for January. The figures shown in the accounts at the end of February correspond with those recorded on the February cost of production report. (Refer to the illustration on page 1011.)

COST OF PRODUCTION REPORT—FEBRUARY 19Y4

	Woodworking Department			Finishing Department	
Quantity Schedule	Units			Units	
(a) Quantity To Be Accounted For:					
Work in Process—Beginning	300			200	
Started in Production	4,050			-0-	
Transferred In From Prior Department	-0-			3,000	
Total To Be Accounted For	4,350			3,200	
(b) Quantity Accounted For:					
Transferred Out to Next Department	3,000			-0-	
Transferred Out to Finished Goods	1,200			3,100	
Work in Process—Ending	150			100	
Total Accounted For	4,350			3,200	

Cost Schedule	Total Cost	Unit Cost		Total Cost	Unit Cost
Costs To Be Accounted For:					
Costs in Prior Department					
Work in Process—Beginning	-0-			$ 1,220.00	$6.10
Transfers In—Current Month	-0-			18,360.00	6.12
Total Prior Department				$19,580.00	$6.11875
Costs in Current Department					
(c) Work in Process—Beginning					
(d) Materials	$ 975.00			$ 35.00	
(e) Labor	320.00			90.00	
Manufacturing Overhead	250.00			65.00	
Current Period Costs					
(f) Materials	13,380.00	$3.30		1,130.50	$0.37
(g) Labor	6,565.00	1.62		2,839.50	0.93
Manufacturing Overhead	4,850.00	1.20		1,919.50	0.63
Total Current Department	$26,340.00	$6.12		$ 6,079.50	$1.93
Cumulative Cost Total	$26,340.00	$6.12		$25,659.50	$8.04875
Costs Accounted For:					
(h) Transferred Out to Next Department	$18,360.00	$6.12		$ -0-	
Transferred Out to Finished Goods	7,344.00	6.12		24,951.13	$8.04875
Total Costs Transferred Out	$25,704.00			$24,951.13	
(i) Work in Process—Ending					
Costs in Prior Department	$ -0-			$ 611.87*	$6.11875
Costs in Current Department					
Materials	495.00	3.30		18.50	0.37
Labor	81.00	1.62		46.50	0.93
Manufacturing Overhead	60.00	1.20		31.50	0.63
Total Work in Process	$ 636.00			$ 708.37	
Total Costs Accounted For	$26,340.00			$25,659.50	

*Adjusted.

19 Y4					
Feb. 28	Work in Process—Woodworking Dept.	122	13,380 00	
	Work in Process—Finishing Dept.	123	1,130 50	
	Raw Materials Inventory	121		14,510 50
	To charge materials to production in			
	February.			
28	Work in Process—Woodworking Dept.	122	6,565 00	
	Work in Process—Finishing Dept.	123	2,839 50	
	Salaries and Wages Payable	215		9,404 50
	To distribute factory payroll for			
	February.			
28	Work in Process—Woodworking Dept.	122	4,850 00	
	Work in Process—Finishing Dept.	123	1,919 50	
	Manufacturing Overhead	500		6,769 50
	To distribute overhead for February.			
28	Work in Process—Finishing Dept.	123	18,360 00	
	Finished Goods Inventory	126	7,344 00	
	Work in Process—Woodworking Dept.	122		25,704 00
	To transfer cost of goods completed			
	during February out of woodworking			
	department.			
28	Finished Goods Inventory	126	24,951 13	
	Work in Process—Finishing Dept.	123		24,951 13
	To transfer cost of goods completed			
	during February out of finishing			
	department.			

Work in Process—Woodworking Department   No. 122

DATE	EXPLANATION	POST. REF.	DEBIT	CREDIT	BALANCE	DR. CR.
19 Y4						
Jan. 31	Balance	✓			1,545 00	Dr.
Feb. 28	Materials	J2	13,380 00		14,925 00	Dr.
28	Labor	J2	6,565 00		21,490 00	Dr.
28	Mfg. Overhead	J2	4,850 00		26,340 00	Dr.
28	Transferred Out	J2		25,704 00	636 00	Dr.

Work in Process—Finishing Department   No. 123

DATE	EXPLANATION	POST. REF.	DEBIT	CREDIT	BALANCE	DR. CR.
19 Y4						
Jan. 31	Balance	✓			1,410 00	Dr.
Feb. 28	Materials	J2	1,130 50		2,540 50	Dr.
28	Labor	J2	2,839 50		5,380 00	Dr.
28	Mfg. Overhead	J2	1,919 50		7,299 50	Dr.
28	Prior Department	J2	18,360 00		25,659 50	Dr.
28	Transferred Out	J2		24,951 13	708 37	Dr.

Assume that sales totaling $40,000 are made during February and that the cost of goods sold is $25,500. Entries in general journal form recording the sales and the transfer of costs from Finished Goods Inventory to Cost of Goods Sold are shown below. The ledger accounts for Finished Goods Inventory and Cost of Goods Sold are also illustrated below with the February entries posted.

19 Y4					
Feb. 28	Accounts Receivable	111	40,000 00	
	Sales	401		40,000 00
	To record sales on credit for February.			
28	Cost of Goods Sold	560	25,500 00	
	Finished Goods Inventory	126		25,500 00
	To record cost of goods sold in February.			

Finished Goods Inventory   No. 126

DATE	EXPLANATION	POST. REF.	DEBIT	CREDIT	BALANCE	DR. CR.
19 Y4						
Jan. 31	Balance	✔			39,350 00	Dr.
Feb. 28		J2	7,344 00		46,694 00	Dr.
28		J2	24,951 13		71,645 13	Dr.
28		J2		25,500 00	46,145 13	Dr.

Cost of Goods Sold   No. 560

DATE	EXPLANATION	POST. REF.	DEBIT	CREDIT	BALANCE	DR. CR.
19 Y4						
Jan. 31	Balance	✔			18,750 00	Dr.
Feb. 28		J2	25,500 00		44,250 00	Dr.

PRINCIPLES AND PROCEDURES SUMMARY

Two principal types of cost accounting systems are used to determine the unit costs of products: the process cost system and the job order cost system.

A perpetual inventory procedure is generally used in cost accounting. There are separate inventory accounts for raw materials, work in process, and finished goods. Costs flow through these inventory accounts and into the Cost of Goods Sold account. The balances in the inventory accounts at the end of the accounting period represent the cost of the items on hand.

In the process cost system, costs for materials, labor, and manufacturing overhead are charged to the work in process accounts of the producing departments. At the end of the period, a cost of production report is prepared to give full details about costs and quantities. The equivalent production unit technique is used to convert ending work in process to equivalent finished production. Then the costs for each equivalent unit of materials, labor, and manufacturing overhead are computed. The value of goods transferred out of the department, as well as of work in process inventories, is determined on the basis of the equivalent units of production for each cost element. The costs of the goods transferred from one department to another are charged to the receiving department and removed from the work in process account of the first department.

Even if there is a beginning work in process inventory, the same basic process cost accounting procedures are followed. When the average cost method is used, the beginning inventory elements are added to the costs incurred during the current period. For example, the beginning inventory of materials is added to the cost of materials put into production during the current period. The equivalent units of production are then computed for each element in the same manner as when there was no beginning inventory of work in process. Other methods of handling the beginning work in process do exist and are treated in detail in cost accounting textbooks.

MANAGERIAL IMPLICATIONS

Managers must be provided with accurate and up-to-date cost data about the products manufactured so that they can determine prices, appraise efficiency, and make appropriate operating decisions. A firm should probably seek the aid of a specially trained cost accountant to develop a cost accounting system that will accurately and speedily yield the required data. Use of the process cost system provides an average manufacturing cost for each unit, which is useful in pricing products, controlling costs, and making decisions.

REVIEW QUESTIONS

1. Why are job order cost sheets not used in the process cost accounting system?
2. Why may a process cost accounting system be referred to as an average cost system?
3. What are equivalent units of production?
4. What information is contained in the Quantity Schedule section of a cost of production report?
5. In a cost of production report, what other amount must be equal to the Costs To Be Accounted For amount?
6. How is the ending inventory of work in process computed?
7. Why might the equivalent units for materials differ from the equivalent units for labor and overhead?
8. In one firm, goods are transferred from the cleaning department to the mixing department. The costs transferred from the cleaning department in April 19X1 totaled $86,000. What will be the journal entry to record the transfer?

9. What entry is made to transfer costs from the final processing department to finished goods?
10. How does a cost of production report with a beginning inventory of work in process differ from a report that shows no beginning inventory?
11. How is the cost of an equivalent unit for labor determined when there is a beginning inventory and the average method of handling the beginning inventory is used?
12. Will the same equivalent units normally be used for materials, labor, and overhead? Explain.
13. How are the costs transferred from a prior department treated in the cost of production report?
14. What is the source of the information in the Costs To Be Accounted For section of the cost of production report?
15. Will the amount shown as a department's ending inventory of work in process on the cost of production report agree with the work in process account for the department in the general ledger after adjusting and closing entries have been posted? Explain.
16. A company uses the process cost accounting system. It has two service departments. How will the cost of the service departments enter into the cost of an equivalent unit for the producing departments?
17. Why was it not necessary for the Woodcraft Manufacturing Corporation to use an overhead application rate under its process cost accounting system?
18. In one company some of the units processed in a department are sold without further processing. Other units, which are identical, are transferred to a second department for further processing. How will this affect the computations on the cost of production report?
19. Why would the process cost accounting system not be satisfactory when several products are being manufactured in the same department?
20. How does accounting for the raw materials inventory and the finished goods inventory differ under the process cost accounting system and the job order cost accounting system?

MANAGERIAL DISCUSSION QUESTIONS

1. What kinds of operating decisions can be made more accurately if cost data is available?
2. Assume that the directors of a firm where you work ask you to explain the difference between the job order cost accounting system and the process cost accounting system. They want to know which system provides the most accurate costs for each unit of product. What would you tell them?
3. The accountant for the Woodcraft Manufacturing Corporation installed the perpetual inventory system for keeping track of major inventories. How does this inventory system work?
4. How could managers use the cost of labor for each equivalent unit to help control costs?

5. Management has observed that labor costs for each equivalent unit have increased substantially in each of the past several months. What steps will management probably take?

6. While examining the cost of production report shown on page 1011, one of Woodcraft's directors asks how the materials cost of $3.30 in the woodworking department was calculated. Explain.

7. From the cost of production report on page 1011, determine the cost of a completely finished unit of goods. How does this cost compare with the figure shown on the January report?

8. In what ways is a process cost accounting system superior to the manufacturing cost system described in Chapter 41?

EXERCISES

EXERCISE 42-1 **Computing equivalent units for prior department costs.** Information about production in the mixing department of the Sandberg Corporation during March 19X1 is given below. Compute the equivalent units of production for the prior department costs for March.

Beginning inventory, work in process	-0-
Transferred in from prior department	6,000 units
Transferred out to next department	4,200 units
Ending inventory, work in process	1,800 units
Stage of completion of ending work in process	
Prior department costs	100%
Materials	60%
Labor and overhead	60%

EXERCISE 42-2 **Computing equivalent units for materials.** Refer to Exercise 42-1. Compute the equivalent units of production for materials for March.

EXERCISE 42-3 **Computing equivalent units for labor and overhead.** Refer to Exercise 42-1. Compute the equivalent units of production for labor and overhead for March.

EXERCISE 42-4 **Computing the cost of an equivalent unit for materials and the cost of the materials transferred out and in process.** On February 1, 19X1, there was no beginning inventory in the cooking department of the Ellis Corporation. During the month, production was started on 2,000 units. The total cost of materials was $18,400. All materials were placed in production at the start of the manufacturing process in the cooking department. By the end of the month, 1,600 units had been transferred to the next department and 400 units were still in process.

1. What is the cost of an equivalent unit for materials in the department?
2. What is the cost of materials in the goods transferred to the next department?
3. What is the cost of materials in the ending work in process inventory?

EXERCISE 42-5 **Computing the cost of an equivalent unit for labor and overhead.** On April 1, 19X4, the forming department of the DeCarlo Corporation had no work in process inventory. During the month of April, labor costs of $64,000 and overhead costs of $16,000 were incurred in the department. Production was started on 3,000 units, of which 2,000 were completed and transferred to finished goods during the month. At the end of the month, there were 1,000 units in process to which 40 percent of the labor and overhead had been added.

1. What is the cost of an equivalent unit for labor?
2. What is the cost of an equivalent unit for overhead?

EXERCISE 42-6 **Determining the labor costs in the work in process inventory and the goods transferred out.** Refer to Exercise 42-5, and answer the following questions.

1. What is the amount of labor costs for the 2,000 units transferred to the next department?
2. What is the amount of labor costs for the 1,000 units in process?

EXERCISE 42-7 **Determining the overhead costs in the work in process inventory and the goods transferred out.** Refer to Exercise 42-5, and answer the following questions.

1. What is the amount of overhead costs for the 2,000 units transferred to the next department?
2. What is the amount of overhead costs for the 1,000 units in process?

EXERCISE 42-8 **Computing equivalent units for prior department costs.** On January 1, 19X2, the beginning inventory in the finishing department of the Gilmore Company was 2,000 units in the following stages of completion.

Prior department costs	100%
Materials	100%
Labor and overhead	80%

During the month 5,000 units were transferred in from the prior department, and 6,000 units were completed and transferred to finished goods. At the end of the month, 1,000 units were in process in the following stages of completion. Compute the equivalent units of production for the prior department costs for January.

Prior department costs	100%
Materials	90%
Labor and overhead	70%

EXERCISE 42-9 **Computing equivalent units for materials.** Refer to Exercise 42-8. Compute the equivalent units of production for materials in the finishing department for January.

EXERCISE 42-10 **Computing equivalent units for labor and overhead.** Refer to Exercise 42-8. Compute the equivalent units of production for labor and overhead in the finishing department for January.

EXERCISE 42-11 **Computing equivalent units for materials.** The grinding department is the first manufacturing department of the Wyatt Corporation. On January 1, 19X1, the beginning inventory in this department consisted of 1,000 units. Costs for the work in process were as follows.

Materials (100% complete)	$15,000
Labor (75% complete)	9,000
Overhead (75% complete)	3,000

During the month 5,000 units were started in production with the following costs: materials, $75,300; labor, $61,664; and overhead, $20,555. By the end of the month, 5,200 units had been completed and transferred to the next department, and there were 800 units in the ending work in process inventory. To these 800 units, all materials had been added and 80 percent of the labor and overhead had been added. Compute the equivalent units of production for materials in the grinding department for January.

EXERCISE 42-12 **Computing the cost of an equivalent unit for materials.** Refer to Exercise 42-11. Compute the cost of an equivalent unit for materials for January.

EXERCISE 42-13 **Computing the cost of materials transferred to the next department.** Refer to Exercises 42-11 and 42-12. Compute the cost of the materials transferred to the next department in January.

EXERCISE 42-14 **Computing the cost of materials in the ending work in process inventory.** Refer to Exercises 42-11 and 42-12. Compute the cost of materials in the ending work in process inventory on January 31.

EXERCISE 42-15 **Computing equivalent units for labor and overhead.** Refer to Exercise 42-11. Compute the equivalent units of production for labor and overhead for January.

EXERCISE 42-16 **Computing the cost of an equivalent unit for labor.** Refer to Exercises 42-11 and 42-15. Compute the cost of an equivalent unit for labor for January.

EXERCISE 42-17 **Computing the cost of an equivalent unit for overhead.** Refer to Exercises 42-11 and 42-15. Compute the cost of an equivalent unit for overhead for January.

EXERCISE 42-18 **Computing labor costs in the ending work in process inventory.** Refer to Exercises 42-11 and 42-16. Compute the labor costs in the ending work in process inventory on January 31.

EXERCISE 42-19 **Computing labor costs in work transferred to the next department.** Refer to Exercises 42-11 and 42-16. Compute the labor costs in the work transferred to the next department in January.

EXERCISE 42-20 **Computing overhead costs in the ending work in process inventory.** Refer to Exercises 42-11 and 42-17. Compute the overhead costs in the ending work in process inventory on January 31.

EXERCISE 42-21 **Computing overhead costs in the work transferred to the next department.** Refer to Exercises 42-11 and 42-17. Compute the overhead costs in the work transferred to the next department in January.

EXERCISE 42-22 **Reconciling costs to be accounted for and costs accounted for.** Using the data from Exercises 42-11 through 42-21, prepare a schedule summarizing the costs to be accounted for and how these costs were accounted for.

PROBLEMS

PROBLEM 42-1 **Making equivalent production computations.** The Early American Chair Company manufactures a single type of wooden chair, which is a reproduction of an antique. The departmental supervisors of this firm have submitted the monthly production reports for April 19X6. These reports have been summarized, and the results are shown below.

Instructions Prepare the equivalent production computations for each department.

EARLY AMERICAN CHAIR COMPANY
DATA FROM COST OF PRODUCTION REPORTS FOR APRIL 19X6

	CUTTING DEPARTMENT	ASSEMBLING DEPARTMENT	FINISHING DEPARTMENT
Quantities			
Started In Production— Current Month	1,620	-0-	-0-
Transferred In From Prior Department	-0-	1,500	1,420
Transferred Out to Next Department	1,500	1,420	-0-
Transferred Out to Finished Goods	-0-	-0-	1,360
Work in Process—Ending	120	80	60
Stage of Completion of Ending			
Work in Process			
Materials	Complete	Complete	25%
Labor	50%	75%	25%
Overhead	50%	75%	25%

PROBLEM 42-2 **Recording transactions under a process cost system.** The Security Lock Corporation has two producing departments—the fabricating department and the assembling department. The data given on page 1020 is from the firm's records for the month of January 19X4. There were no beginning inventories.

Instructions 1. In general journal form, record the flow of costs that follow.
  a. The issuance of materials to each department.

b. The distribution of payroll to each department.

c. The distribution of manufacturing overhead to each department.

Date all entries January 31, 19X4.

2. Prepare equivalent production computations for each department.

3. Prepare a cost of production report for each department.

4. Use the same procedure as in Instruction 1, and record the following in general journal form.

   a. The transfer of goods from the fabricating department to the assembling department.

   b. The transfer of completed goods from the assembling department to the finished goods storeroom.

   c. Credit sales of $12,000 for finished goods that cost $8,000.

   (Keep all your working papers for use in Problem 42-5.)

SECURITY LOCK CORPORATION
DATA FOR JANUARY 19X4

	FABRICATING DEPT.	ASSEMBLING DEPT.
Costs		
Materials	$4,080	$ 950
Labor	2,420	2,220
Manufacturing Overhead	1,210	1,110
Total Costs	$7,710	$4,280
Quantities		
Beginning Inventories	-0-	-0-
Started in Production	2,400	-0-
Transferred In From Prior Department	-0-	2,000
Transferred Out to Next Department	2,000	-0-
Transferred Out to Finished Goods	-0-	1,800
Work in Process—Ending	400	200
Stage of Completion—Ending Work in Process		
Materials	Complete	½
Labor	½	¼
Manufacturing Overhead	½	¼

PROBLEM 42-3 **Making equivalent production computations.** Newport Industries manufactures a line of plastic toys in one of its factories. All materials in the first department (molding) of this factory are added at the start of production. Raw materials put into production in the second department (finishing) are added in proportion to labor and manufacturing overhead. Data for the month of February 19X1 appears on page 1021.

Instructions Prepare equivalent production computations for each department.

NEWPORT INDUSTRIES
DATA FOR FEBRUARY 19X1

	MOLDING DEPARTMENT	FINISHING DEPARTMENT
Quantities		
Beginning Work in Process	1,500	2,400
Started in Production	21,000	-0-
Transferred In From Prior Department	-0-	20,700
Transferred Out to Next Department	20,700	-0-
Transferred Out to Finished Goods	-0-	21,000
Ending Work in Process	1,800	2,100
Stage of Completion—Work in Process		
Beginning		
Materials	Complete	75%
Labor and Manufacturing Overhead	40%	75%
Ending		
Materials	Complete	50%
Labor and Manufacturing Overhead	33⅓%	50%

PROBLEM 42-4

Preparing a cost of production report. The Variety Paint Corporation adds all materials at the beginning of production. On January 1, 19X1, 2,000 gallons of its product were in production in the first department. During the month of January, 24,000 gallons were put into production. On January 31, 4,000 gallons were still in production. The ending inventory is estimated to be complete as to materials and 60 percent complete as to labor and overhead. Cost data for the month is as follows.

	MATERIALS	LABOR	OVERHEAD
Beginning Inventory of Work in Process	$ 8,100	$ 1,704	$ 3,440
Added During January	101,100	23,916	47,800

Instructions   Prepare a cost of production report for the month of January, assuming that the average cost method is used.

PROBLEM 42-5

Preparing a cost of production report. This is a continuation of Problem 42-2. The data shown on page 1022 appears in the records of the Security Lock Corporation for the month of February 19X4.

Instructions   1. Prepare equivalent production computations for each department.
2. Prepare a cost of production report for both departments in a form similar to the one on page 1009. Carry the unit cost computations to six places when necessary, and round off to five places.

SECURITY LOCK CORPORATION
DATA FOR FEBRUARY 19X4

	FABRICATING DEPT.	ASSEMBLING DEPT.
Costs		
Work in Process—Beginning		
Costs in Prior Department	$ -0-	$ 670
Costs in Current Department		
Materials	680	50
Labor	220	60
Manufacturing Overhead	110	30
Current Department Costs—February		
Materials	5,100	1,718
Labor	3,410	3,716
Manufacturing Overhead	1,870	1,890
Total Costs	$11,390	$8,134
Quantities		
Work in Process—Beginning	400	200
Started in Production	3,000	-0-
Transferred In From Prior Department	-0-	3,200
Transferred Out to Next Department	3,200	-0-
Transferred Out to Finished Goods	-0-	2,600
Work in Process—Ending	200	800
Stage of Completion—Work in Process		
Beginning Inventory		
Materials	Complete	½
Labor	½	¼
Manufacturing Overhead	½	¼
Ending Inventory		
Materials	Complete	Complete
Labor	½	¾
Manufacturing Overhead	½	¾

ALTERNATE PROBLEMS

PROBLEM 42-1A   **Making equivalent production computations.** The New Look Cabinet Company manufactures a popular type of wooden cabinet for kitchens. The departmental supervisors of this firm have submitted the monthly production reports for November 19X6. These reports have been summarized, and the results are shown on page 1023.

Instructions   Prepare the equivalent production computations for each department.

NEW LOOK CABINET COMPANY
DATA FROM COST OF PRODUCTION REPORTS FOR NOVEMBER 19X6

	CUTTING DEPARTMENT	ASSEMBLING DEPARTMENT	FINISHING DEPARTMENT
Quantities			
Started in Production—Current Month	1,800	-0-	-0-
Transferred In From Prior Department	-0-	1,500	1,400
Transferred Out to Next Department	1,500	1,400	-0-
Transferred Out to Finished Goods	-0-	-0-	1,325
Work in Process—Ending	300	100	75
Stage of Completion—Ending Work in Process			
Materials	Complete	Complete	66⅔%
Labor	50%	75%	66⅔%
Overhead	50%	75%	66⅔%

PROBLEM 42-2A   **Recording transactions under a process cost system.** The Major League Products Corporation began business in January 19X1. It manufactures a single product—baseball bats. The product is started in the cutting and shaping department and is completed in the sanding and finishing department. Data for the month of January, the first month of operations, is given on page 1024.

Instructions   1. In general journal form, record the flow of costs indicated below.
   a. The issuance of materials to each department.
   b. The distribution of payroll to each department.
   c. The distribution of manufacturing overhead to each department.
   Date all entries January 31, 19X1.
2. Prepare equivalent production computations for each department.
3. Prepare a cost of production report for each department.
4. Use the same procedure as in Instruction 1, and record the following in general journal form.
   a. The transfer of goods from the cutting and shaping department to the sanding and finishing department.
   b. The transfer of completed goods from the sanding and finishing department to the finished goods storeroom.
   c. Credit sales of $90,000 for finished goods that cost $65,000.

MAJOR LEAGUE PRODUCTS CORPORATION
DATA FOR JANUARY 19X1

	CUTTING AND SHAPING DEPT.	SANDING AND FINISHING DEPT.
Costs		
Materials	$32,800	$ 4,550
Labor	15,600	11,700
Manufacturing Overhead	12,168	8,450
Total Costs	$60,568	$24,700
Quantities		
Started in Production	8,200	-0-
Transferred In From Prior Department	-0-	7,200
Transferred Out to Next Department	7,200	-0-
Transferred Out to Finished Goods	-0-	6,200
Work in Process—Ending	1,000	1,000
Stage of Completion—Ending Work in Process		
Materials	Complete	30%
Labor	60%	30%
Manufacturing Overhead	60%	30%

PROBLEM 42-3A   **Making equivalent production computations.** The Modern Optics Company manufactures a line of high-quality camera lenses in one of its factories. All materials in the first department (grinding) of this factory are added at the start of production. Raw materials put into production in the second department (finishing) are added in proportion to labor and manufacturing overhead. Data for the month of January 19X1 is given below.

Instructions   Prepare equivalent production computations for each department.

MODERN OPTICS COMPANY
DATA FOR JANUARY 19X1

	GRINDING DEPARTMENT	FINISHING DEPARTMENT
Quantities		
Beginning Work in Process	100	75
Started in Production	1,250	-0-
Transferred In From Prior Department	-0-	1,225
Transferred Out to Next Department	1,225	-0-
Transferred Out to Finished Goods	-0-	1,200
Ending Work in Process	125	100
Stage of Completion—Work in Process		
Beginning		
Materials	Complete	66⅔%
Labor and Manufacturing Overhead	25%	66⅔%
Ending		
Materials	Complete	75%
Labor and Manufacturing Overhead	60%	75%

PROBLEM 42-4A **Preparing a cost of production report.** The Columbus Fertilizer Company adds all materials at the beginning of production. On January 1, 19X1, 8,000 pounds of the product were in production in the first department. During the month of January, 72,000 pounds were put into production. On January 31, 12,000 pounds were still in production. The ending inventory is estimated to be complete as to materials and two-thirds complete as to labor and overhead. Cost data for the month is as follows.

	MATERIALS	LABOR	OVERHEAD
Beginning Inventory of			
Work in Process	$ 16,000	$ 7,200	$ 3,600
Added During January	144,000	66,520	34,400

Instructions Prepare a cost of production report for the month of January, assuming that the average cost method is used.

PROBLEM 42-5A **Preparing a cost of production report.** The Marshall Manufacturing Company uses a process cost system. Data from this system for July 19X4 is shown below.

Instructions 1. Prepare equivalent production computations for both departments.
2. Prepare a cost of production report for the two departments, using the average cost basis. Carry the unit cost computations to five places when necessary, and round off to four places.

MARSHALL MANUFACTURING COMPANY
COST DATA FOR JULY 19X4

Costs	FORMING DEPT.	FINISHING DEPT.
Work in Process—Beginning		
Costs in Prior Department	$ -0-	$21,815.00
Costs in Current Department		
Materials	5,400.00	2,225.00
Labor	1,800.00	1,825.00
Manufacturing Overhead	1,425.00	1,450.00
Current Department Costs—July		
Materials	77,100.00	25,337.50
Labor	63,875.00	20,225.00
Manufacturing Overhead	51,825.00	16,925.00
Total Costs	$201,425.00	$89,802.50

Quantities		
Work in Process—Beginning	2,500	4,000
Started in Production	35,000	-0-
Transferred In From Prior Department	-0-	34,500
Transferred Out to Next Department	34,500	-0-
Transferred Out to Finished Goods	-0-	35,000
Work in Process—Ending	3,000	3,500

Stage of Completion—Work in Process		
Beginning Inventory		
Materials	Complete	¾
Labor	⅔	¾
Manufacturing Overhead	⅔	¾
Ending Inventory		
Materials	Complete	½
Labor	⅓	½
Manufacturing Overhead	⅓	½

Traditionally, manufacturing firms have used either the job order cost system or the process cost system to determine the unit cost of the goods they produce. Cost accounting has been regarded as a means of measuring the historical costs of goods manufactured. However, in recent years, accountants have become increasingly concerned about the control of manufacturing costs and the development of cost data that will provide more useful information for making managerial decisions. In this chapter, two such developments are considered.

STANDARD COSTS; DIRECT COSTING

USE OF CONTROL STANDARDS

The use of standards as a cost control device is examined first in this chapter. Then the concept of *direct costing,* often called *variable costing,* is discussed as a technique for determining more useful "costs" of goods manufactured. Both of these techniques are based on the relationship between volume of production and the behavior of costs. The presentations in this chapter are very basic; cost accounting textbooks provide a much more thorough discussion of both topics.

The manager in charge of the Woodcraft Manufacturing Corporation plant that uses the job order cost accounting system discussed in Chapter 41 wants to operate the plant as efficiently and economically as possible without sacrificing product quality. As each job is completed, the manager studies the job order cost sheet to be sure that the job was done properly. He also watches for any clues to the need for improvement of plant operations.

Although the manager's sense of responsibility is commendable, the practical results might leave something to be desired. For example, if the accountant shows the manager Job Order Cost Sheet J-79 covering 25 Style X-167 tables at a total cost of $858.82 and at a unit cost of $34.353, what conclusions can the manager draw about efficiency and economy? Does $34.353 represent an excellent performance or a poor one? Concrete facts about what it *should cost* to build 25 tables of this type are needed. This is exactly the kind of information that control standards are designed to supply. Suppose that, to get this information, the Woodcraft Manufacturing Corporation decides to use standard costs.

SETTING STANDARDS

Standards are set for the quantities and costs of materials and for the labor required to manufacture a given product. In turn, manufacturing overhead standards may be set by use of an application rate based on labor costs, or the allocation may be related to labor hours. The latter is probably a more common practice when standard costs are used, although Woodcraft applies overhead as a percent of direct labor cost.

Materials Standards

The quantity of each kind of material required for a product is determined by the engineers who designed the item and prepared its specifications. The cost of each kind of required material can be determined by the purchasing department, whose personnel should be familiar with market sources and prices. The account-ant can combine both types of information (quantity and price) to develop stand-ard costs for materials.

Labor Standards

The labor time and the kind of labor required to make a product can be deter-mined by production engineers through time and motion studies. Approximate data can be developed from experience if records are kept of what was produced and what labor was required. Wage rate information can be furnished by the personnel department or obtained from contracts with unions. The accountant can apply the wage rates to the quantities of labor specified in order to develop the standard costs for the labor involved in each product.

Manufacturing Overhead Standards

When standard costs are used, the amount of overhead that should be charged to each unit of product is worked out in advance, in the same manner as the stand-ards for materials and labor are developed. The result may be stated in terms of dollars for each unit or in terms of a relationship to labor dollars, labor hours, or some other basis. For control purposes, standards are set for each item or activity contributing to overhead, such as electricity, repairs, maintenance, and factory supplies.

STANDARD COST CARD

After standards are established, a *standard cost card* is set up for each product. This card indicates in detail the standard quantities and costs involved in the manufacturing process. A standard cost card such as the one shown below might be set up at Woodcraft for the Style X-167 table.

STANDARD COST CARD

ITEM: Table X-167

Materials

1 Top: 6 board feet at $1.20	$ 7.20
4 Legs: 4 board feet at $1.20	4.80
4 Braces: N-176 at $0.60	2.40
16 Screws: 1″ No. 8 flat head steel	0.48
Finishing Materials: ½ pint T-18	1.20
Total Materials	$16.08

Labor

Cutting and Shaping: ½ hour at $9	$ 4.50
Assembling: ¼ hour at $8	2.00
Finishing: ¼ hour at $10	2.50
Total Labor	9.00

Manufacturing Overhead

$9 (direct labor cost) × 0.75	6.75
Total Standard Cost per Unit	$31.83

Notice the breakdown of costs under the three main classifications—materials, labor, and manufacturing overhead. Under the heading Materials the quantity and cost of each type of material required are listed, and the total standard materials cost is determined. Under the heading Labor the hours required for each of three different operations are shown, and the rate per hour for that kind of labor is applied to find the total standard labor cost. Using an overhead application rate of 75 percent of direct labor costs, the standard overhead for each table is determined. The total standard labor cost is multiplied by the overhead application rate ($9.00 \times 0.75 = 6.75).

COMPARING ACTUAL AND STANDARD COSTS

If the plant manager had this information on the standard cost of the Style X-167 table, he would be able to compare the actual cost of Job J–79 with the standard to see how efficiently the job was carried out. Since 25 of these tables were produced, each item on the standard cost card is multiplied by 25 and is then compared with the actual cost recorded on the job order cost sheet. If the actual cost exceeds the standard cost, the variance is unfavorable. If the actual cost is less than the standard cost, the variance is favorable. The analysis in this case shows an unfavorable variance.

ANALYSIS OF COSTS FOR JOB J–79

| Cost Element | Standard | | Actual Cost | Variance |
	Quantity	Cost		
Materials	25 × $16.08	$402.00	$419.83	$17.83
Labor	25 × 9.00	225.00	250.85	25.85
Overhead	25 × 6.75	168.75	188.14	19.39
Totals	25 × $31.83	$795.75	$858.82	$63.07

With this data the plant manager is much better informed than before. He now knows that the standard cost for making the 25 tables is $795.75, but that costs charged to the job amounted to $858.82, an unfavorable variance of $63.07. The manager can also see that each cost element was charged in excess of standard: $17.83 for materials, $25.85 for labor, and $19.39 for overhead. This helps pinpoint the nature of the difficulty. The next question is: Why were these costs all higher than standard?

Analysis of Materials Variance

By referring to the materials requisitions charged to Job Order Cost Sheet J–79, the manager can find out exactly what types of materials were used and what each type cost. This information can be compared with what should have been used and what the cost should have been. Differences in each item may be the result of a difference in quantities used, a difference in unit cost, or a combination of both.

What this analysis reveals for the materials used in Job J-79 is illustrated on page 1029. (Favorable variances in this and following illustrations are shown in parentheses.)

ANALYSIS OF MATERIALS VARIANCE

Cost Elements	Standard Cost	Actual Cost	Quantity Variance	Price Variance
Lumber for tops and legs				
Standard: 250 bd ft at $1.20	$300.00			
Actual: 260 bd ft at $1.22		$317.20		
Quantity variance: 10 bd ft at $1.20			$12.00	
Price variance: 260 bd ft at $0.02				$5.20
Braces	60.00	60.00		
Screws	12.00	12.00		
Finishing materials				
Standard: 12½ pints at $2.40	30.00			
Actual: 12¼ pints at $2.50		30.63		
Quantity variance: ¼ pint at $2.40			(0.60)	
Price variance: 12¼ pints at $0.10				1.23
Totals	$402.00	$419.83	$11.40	$6.43

The computations involved in determining the variances are quite simple. For example, the lumber cost variances are calculated as follows.

1. The *quantity variance* for an item is the difference between its actual quantity and its standard quantity multiplied by the standard cost of the item. Thus the quantity variance for the lumber is 260 board feet (bd ft) − 250 board feet = 10 board feet × $1.20 = $12.00.
2. The *price variance* for an item is the difference between its actual price and its standard price multiplied by the actual quantity. Thus the price variance for the lumber is $1.22 − $1.20 = $0.02 × 260 board feet = $5.20.

The example of variance analysis shown in the table above indicates that the use of excess quantities of materials on Job J–79 cost $11.40 and the payment of prices higher than standard accounted for the remaining $6.43 of the unfavorable variance of $17.83 for materials. Specifically, braces and screws were used in the expected quantities and cost the standard amount. Lumber was used in excess of the standard quantity, and its cost exceeded the standard price. Finishing materials were used in quantities slightly below standard, but their unit cost was above standard.

Analysis of Labor Variance

Labor time tickets can be analyzed in detail to discover the causes of the labor cost variance of $25.85. Again, the difference may be the result of using a different quantity of labor hours from standard, of paying for labor at a rate different from standard, or a combination of both. What the analysis of Job J–79 reveals is indicated in the table on page 1030.

This table shows that more labor hours were worked than is standard for each operation, making for unfavorable quantity variances. On the other hand, all the labor was paid at a rate lower than standard, making for favorable price variances in each operation. (The labor used on this job may have been some-

ANALYSIS OF LABOR VARIANCE

Cost Elements	Standard Cost	Actual Cost	Quantity Variance	Price Variance
Cutting and Shaping				
Standard: 12.5 hr at $9	$112.50			
Actual: 14 hr at $8.80		$123.20		
Quantity variance: 1.5 hr at $9			$13.50	
Price variance: 14 hr at ($0.20)				($2.80)
Assembling				
Standard: 6.25 hr at $8	50.00			
Actual: 8.5 hr at $8.10		68.85		
Quantity variance: 2.25 hr at $8			18.00	
Price variance: 8.5 hr at $0.10				0.85
Finishing				
Standard: 6.25 hr at $10	62.50			
Actual: 6 hr at $9.80		58.80		
Quantity variance: (0.25) hr at $10			(2.50)	
Price variance: 6 hr at ($0.20)				(1.20)
Totals	$225.00	$250.85	$29.00	($3.15)

what below the normal level in experience or training, which may be part of the reason more hours were required to get the work done.) At another time, labor market conditions or wage scales set in union contracts may make it difficult to hire workers below the standard rates.

Analysis of Manufacturing Overhead Variance

The manufacturing overhead variance cannot be analyzed in quite the same manner as that for materials and labor. Since the predetermined overhead application rate used on Job J–79 was 75 percent of direct labor cost, the variance in labor cost is reflected in the overhead applied to the job. If the overhead variance were analyzed in the same way, the results shown below would be obtained.

ANALYSIS OF MANUFACTURING OVERHEAD VARIANCE

Cost Elements	Standard Cost	Applied Cost	Quantity Variance	Price Variance
Standard: $225 × 0.75	$168.75			
Actual: $250.85 × 0.75		$188.14		
Quantity variance				
Cutting and Shaping: $9 × 0.75 × 1.5 hr			$10.13	
Assembling: $8 × 0.75 × 2.25 hr			13.50	
Finishing: $10 × 0.75 × (0.25) hr			(1.88)	
Price variance				
Cutting and Shaping: ($0.20) × 0.75 × 14 hr				($2.10)
Assembling: $0.10 × 0.75 × 8.5 hr				0.64
Finishing: ($0.20) × 0.75 × 6 hr				(0.90)
Totals	$168.75	$188.14	$21.75	($2.36)

This analysis simply shows why the *applied* overhead charged to Job J–79 was $19.39 more than standard. Since the total labor cost for the job exceeded the standard by $25.85 and overhead is applied at the rate of 75 percent of direct labor cost, the job is automatically charged for $19.39 ($25.85 × 0.75) more than standard. The analysis does indicate the amounts by which overhead was applied in excess of standard because of the variance for each type of labor.

Obviously, the above analysis is of little help to management in controlling overhead costs. Management is far more interested in comparing the *actual* overhead costs incurred with what the overhead costs *should be* than comparing applied overhead with the standard. Each specific element of actual overhead must be compared with expectations of costs if the costs are to be properly controlled. Action can be taken only if it is known what specific overhead items are out of line. The comparison of actual overhead costs with budgeted amounts gives this information and is discussed in Chapter 47.

A more elaborate standard cost system involves the incorporation of standard costs into the regular accounting records. This approach is discussed in cost accounting textbooks.

DIRECT COSTING

As the use of accounting data in making business decisions has increased, accountants have become more and more concerned with developing meaningful cost information. One aspect of manufacturing costs that has received special attention is the relationship between fixed manufacturing costs and the volume of goods produced. Similar attention has also been given to the relationship between selling and administrative expenses and the volume of sales.

Some manufacturing costs are *fixed;* that is, they do not vary in total during a period even though the volume of goods manufactured may be higher or lower than anticipated. For example, if the depreciation of factory machinery and equipment is $20,000 a year, the depreciation for each unit of goods produced will be $4 if 5,000 units are produced ($20,000 ÷ 5,000 units). On the other hand, if the volume of output increases to 20,000 units of goods, the unit cost for depreciation will be only $1 ($20,000 ÷ 20,000 units). Other manufacturing costs that tend to remain constant in total regardless of the volume of output are insurance and taxes on factory property, plant, and equipment; salaries, fringe benefits, and payroll taxes for factory managers and supervisors; and other "costs of occupancy." Similarly, some selling and administrative expenses are fixed. Examples are depreciation of office equipment, rent on the office building, salaries and related expenses for officers, and many other office expenses.

As might be expected, some manufacturing costs tend to vary in total directly with the volume of manufacturing activity. These are referred to as *variable* costs. Direct materials, direct labor, and some manufacturing supplies are typical examples of costs that tend to vary directly with the volume of output. For example, if the cost of direct materials in a unit of product is $10, the total cost of the materials needed to produce 10,000 units should be $100,000 and the total cost of the materials needed to produce 12,500 units should be $125,000. Similarly, some selling and administrative expenses tend to vary in direct proportion to the sales volume (expressed either in units or in dollars). Sales commissions, delivery expense, the loss from uncollectible accounts, and certain other expenses are variable.

Many manufacturing costs are *semivariable;* that is, they have characteristics of fixed costs and also characteristics of variable costs. The cost of utilities in a factory is a typical example of a semivariable cost. There is a minimum cost necessary for lighting, heating, and cooling merely because the factory is open. This is a fixed element. As the volume of production increases, however, additional power is required to operate machinery and equipment. That portion of the cost tends to be variable in its behavior. Many other manufacturing costs, as well as selling and administrative expenses, are semivariable. There are several techniques for estimating the fixed portion and the variable portion per unit for semivariable costs. As a result, semivariable costs can be separated into fixed and variable parts, and these parts can be combined with other fixed and variable costs. Some of the procedures involved are briefly examined in Chapter 47. Others are discussed in detail in cost accounting textbooks.

Some accountants contend that fixed costs are not dependent on the quantity of goods produced and therefore should not be applied to any specific units. Fixed costs generally relate to the development of the capacity to produce goods, not to the actual production. Therefore, these accountants argue that fixed manufacturing costs should be written off as current expenses of the period in which they are incurred and should not be included as part of the cost of goods manufactured during the period. Only variable costs—those that vary in total with the volume of production—should be considered in computing the costs of goods manufactured. This procedure is referred to as *direct costing,* or *variable costing.*

DIRECT COSTING ILLUSTRATED

To illustrate the use of direct costing, assume that the Davis Manufacturing Corporation has divided all its manufacturing costs into fixed and variable elements. Data pertaining to the firm's operations for its first year of business is summarized below.

Beginning inventory of finished goods	-0-
Units produced (no work in process inventories)	10,000
Units sold	7,000
Units in ending inventory of finished goods	3,000
Sales price for each unit	$30
Variable manufacturing costs (materials, labor, and variable overhead)	$12 per unit manufactured
Variable selling and administrative expenses	$2 per unit sold
Fixed manufacturing costs for the year	$60,000
Fixed selling and administrative expenses	$50,000

When this information is used with traditional or so-called *absorption costing procedures,* a condensed income statement, including the cost of goods manufactured, appears as illustrated on page 1033.

DAVIS MANUFACTURING CORPORATION
Income Statement
Year Ended December 31, 19X1
(Absorption Costing)

Sales (7,000 units at $30)		$210,000
Cost of Goods Sold		
Variable Manufacturing Costs (10,000 × $12)	$120,000	
Fixed Manufacturing Costs	60,000	
Total Cost of Goods Manufactured (10,000 × $18)	$180,000	
Less Finished Goods Inventory, Dec. 31 (3,000 × $18)	54,000	
Cost of Goods Sold		126,000
Gross Profit on Sales		$ 84,000
Selling and Administrative Expenses		
Variable (7,000 × $2)	$ 14,000	
Fixed	50,000	64,000
Net Income for Year		$ 20,000

The statement shown below reflects the same data but uses a direct costing approach. Notice that in this statement only the variable manufacturing costs are reflected in the cost of goods sold. The excess of sales over the variable cost of goods sold is referred to as the *manufacturing margin*. Next, the variable operating expenses are deducted to arrive at the *marginal income on sales*. Then the fixed manufacturing costs and the fixed selling and administrative expenses are deducted to arrive at the net income for the year. (This is only one of several different arrangements of the statement that might be used.)

DAVIS MANUFACTURING CORPORATION
Income Statement
Year Ended December 31, 19X1
(Direct Costing)

Sales (7,000 units at $30)		$210,000
Cost of Goods Sold		
Variable Manufacturing Costs (10,000 × $12)	$120,000	
Less Finished Goods Inventory, Dec. 31 (3,000 × $12)	36,000	
Cost of Goods Sold		84,000
Manufacturing Margin		$126,000
Variable Selling and Administrative Expenses (7,000 × $2)		14,000
Marginal Income on Sales		$112,000
Fixed Costs and Expenses		
Fixed Manufacturing Costs	$ 60,000	
Fixed Selling and Administrative Expenses	50,000	110,000
Net Income for Year		$ 2,000

The net income is higher under absorption costing than under direct costing, due to the higher value of the finished goods inventory. When absorption costing is used, a portion of the fixed manufacturing overhead is deferred to future periods as part of the inventory value. However, under direct costing, all the fixed overhead is charged off as a current expense. In a period when the inventory level decreases, a smaller net income will be reported under absorption costing. This effect of inventory changes on net income is the main argument used by those who prefer direct costing over absorption costing. They point out that under absorption costing, fixed manufacturing costs are being deferred as an asset (inventory). However, the fixed costs incurred during a period do not in any way benefit the future (because future fixed costs must nevertheless be incurred in the future).

USE OF DIRECT COSTING IN DECISION MAKING

Direct costing helps to clarify cost-volume-profit relationships that assist management in making operating decisions and controlling costs. For example, direct costing is often useful in setting prices, especially when special offers to buy or sell a product are being considered. Direct costing is also helpful in deciding whether to buy or manufacture an item or a part, in scheduling production, and in making many other decisions.

To illustrate one use of direct costing, we will assume that the Davis Manufacturing Corporation receives an offer from a foreign customer to purchase 1,000 units of its product at $20 a unit. In addition to the usual manufacturing costs and selling and administrative expenses, there would be packaging and shipping costs of $1 a unit. The company has adequate manufacturing capacity to take the special order without endangering its regular production and its ability to take care of steady customers. Management must now analyze the financial aspects of the special order.

In most managerial decisions of this type, consideration must be given to the *marginal revenues* and *incremental costs* rather than to total average cost. A review of the data illustrated on page 1033 shows that the total average unit cost of Davis's product is currently $27.14.

Manufacturing costs ($180,000 ÷ 10,000 units)	$18.00
Selling and administrative expenses ($64,000 ÷ 7,000 units)	9.14
Total average unit cost	$27.14

The first reaction of many business managers to an offer of $20 would be to compare the suggested sales price of $20 with an average total cost of $27.14 plus the additional packaging and shipping costs of $1 a unit and conclude that a loss of $8.14 a unit would be incurred. However, closer consideration must be given to the marginal revenues and incremental costs. The use of direct costing clarifies the situation considerably, since the incremental (variable) costs are already computed under this method. Although the present total average manufacturing, selling, and administrative cost is $27.14, the additional incremental cost of each of the 1,000 units under the special order would be only $15.

Variable manufacturing costs	$12
Variable selling and administrative expenses	2
Additional packaging and shipping costs	1
Total incremental cost for each unit	$15

Thus the acceptance of the special order would result in an estimated additional profit to the firm of $5 a unit ($20 − $15), or a total of $5,000 for the 1,000 units.

Such analysis must be approached very carefully and consideration given to all relevant factors. In the above example the special order could be taken only if sufficient capacity were available and if the special price on the order did not jeopardize sales to other customers. Furthermore, federal laws that prohibit price differentials, unless they can be justified by cost savings, must not be violated.

Although direct costing is beneficial in making operating decisions, it is not used for financial reporting. It is not acceptable for federal income tax purposes and for financial accounting purposes because it is at variance with the basic rule that all costs incurred in getting products ready for sale to customers should be considered as inventory costs.

PRINCIPLES AND PROCEDURES SUMMARY

Standard costs serve as a measure of operating efficiency and economy. Materials standards are developed by design engineers. Labor time standards are based on time and motion studies, and labor rates are determined by union contracts or wage levels in the local labor market. Manufacturing overhead is stated in relation to labor dollars, labor hours, or units of product. Actual costs are ultimately compared with standard costs to evaluate performance, and variances are analyzed to identify cause and responsibility.

When direct costing is used, only the variable manufacturing costs are considered as part of the cost of goods manufactured. Fixed overhead costs are charged off as expenses in the period in which they are incurred. Direct costing is often used for internal analysis and in decision making, but it is not acceptable for income tax reporting or in published financial statements.

MANAGERIAL IMPLICATIONS

Standard costs are extremely useful tools that help management to control manufacturing activities. The comparison of standard costs with actual results provides managers with a measure of the total cost of inefficient operations or gives an indication of the contribution of efficient operations. A further breakdown of total variances from standards pinpoints the responsibility for inefficient operations. The analysis of materials and labor variances is especially helpful. Manufacturing overhead variances can also be analyzed. However, a comparison of actual overhead costs with the overhead budget is a more meaningful tool for controlling overhead costs.

In deciding how to set prices, whether to buy or manufacture parts or products, whether to close a segment of the business, and so on, managers must give primary consideration to incremental costs and marginal revenues. Direct costing provides much of the information necessary in making such decisions. Since only variable costs are treated as product costs under direct costing, it is easy to tell at a glance the incremental costs incurred in manufacturing a unit of product.

REVIEW QUESTIONS

1. What are standard costs?
2. How are standards set for materials?
3. Who provides information about wage rates in setting labor standards?
4. What is a standard cost card?
5. Explain how to compute the quantity variance for materials.
6. What does the price variance for materials show?
7. How is the price variance for labor computed?
8. What information is revealed by the quantity variance for labor?
9. Why is a comparison of applied overhead, based on direct labor cost, and standard overhead not a useful procedure in controlling costs?
10. What two variances make up the total labor variance?
11. What is a fixed cost?
12. Explain the relationship between the total of a variable cost and the volume of output.
13. What are semivariable costs?
14. Name two fixed manufacturing costs.
15. What is direct costing?
16. How are fixed manufacturing costs handled under direct costing?
17. What is absorption costing?
18. What is the major difference between direct costing and absorption costing?
19. What is the manufacturing margin?
20. Explain the meaning of the term *marginal income on sales*.
21. In a period when the finished goods inventory decreases, will the reported profit be greater under absorption costing or under direct costing? Explain.
22. What are marginal revenues? incremental costs?

MANAGERIAL DISCUSSION QUESTIONS

1. Explain how determination of standard costs enables managers to pinpoint responsibility for inefficient performance.
2. A director of a manufacturing firm asks what can be done to correct a price variance. Are all variances controllable by the immediate production-line supervisor?
3. A general pay increase is granted to factory employees by a firm using an overhead application rate based on direct labor cost. What other cost element will be indirectly affected? Will it increase or decrease?

4. In a large company the overall wage structure is determined by the personnel department. However, the manager of each producing department has limited control over the rates paid individual workers. Who would be responsible for labor price variances?
5. Which manager would generally be responsible for labor quantity variances?
6. In what circumstances would direct costing be of help to management in setting the prices of products?
7. Explain why direct costing might be an inappropriate basis for management to use in setting prices.

EXERCISES

EXERCISE 43-1   **Computing the total variance for a product.** The standard cost card for a unit of product at the Leslie Corporation shows the following information.

Budget ↙

Materials: 16 gallons at $1 a gallon	$16
Labor: 1/2 hour at $8 an hour ↗	4
Overhead: 50% of direct labor	2
Total	$22

stand

During the month of February 19X1, 4,000 units were produced. The actual costs were as shown below. Calculate the total variance between the actual cost and the standard cost in February.

Materials: 65,000 gallons at $0.99 a gallon	$64,350
Labor: 1,900 hours at $8.20 an hour	15,580 — *direct labor*
Overhead: $15,580 × 0.50	7,790
Total	$87,720

actual

EXERCISE 43-2   **Computing the total variance for materials.** Refer to Exercise 43-1. Calculate the total variance for materials in February.

EXERCISE 43-3   **Computing the quantity variance for materials.** Refer to Exercise 43-1. Calculate the quantity variance for materials in February.

EXERCISE 43-4   **Computing the price variance for materials.** Refer to Exercise 43-1. Calculate the price variance for materials in February.

EXERCISE 43-5   **Computing the total variance for labor.** Refer to Exercise 43-1. Calculate the total variance for labor in February.

EXERCISE 43-6   **Computing the quantity variance for labor.** Refer to Exercise 43-1. Calculate the quantity variance for labor in February.

EXERCISE 43-7   **Computing the rate variance for labor.** Refer to Exercise 43-1. Calculate the rate variance for labor in February.

EXERCISE 43-8   **Computing the total variance for overhead.** Refer to Exercise 43-1. Calculate the total variance for overhead in February.

EXERCISE 43-9   **Computing the quantity variance for overhead.** Refer to Exercise 43-1. Calculate the quantity variance for overhead in February.

EXERCISE 43-10   **Computing total variable manufacturing costs.** The Jacobs Corporation has divided all of its costs and expenses into fixed and variable components. Data for the company's first year of operations is given below. Calculate the variable manufacturing costs for the year.

No beginning inventory of finished goods
Units produced (no work in process), 6,000
Units sold, 4,000
Ending inventory of finished goods, 2,000
Sales price, $100 a unit
Variable manufacturing costs, $40 for each unit manufactured
Variable selling and administrative expenses, $16 for each unit sold
Fixed manufacturing costs for year, $112,000
Fixed selling and administrative expenses for year, $100,000

EXERCISE 43-11   **Computing the cost of goods manufactured under absorption costing.** Refer to Exercise 43-10. Calculate the cost of goods manufactured for the year, assuming that the company uses absorption costing.

EXERCISE 43-12   **Computing ending inventory under absorption costing.** Refer to Exercise 43-10. Calculate the ending inventory of finished goods, assuming that the company uses absorption costing.

EXERCISE 43-13   **Computing the cost of goods sold under absorption costing.** Refer to Exercise 43-10. Calculate the cost of goods sold for the year, assuming that the company uses absorption costing.

EXERCISE 43-14   **Computing net income under absorption costing.** Refer to Exercise 43-10. Calculate the net income for the year, assuming that the company uses absorption costing.

EXERCISE 43-15   **Computing ending inventory under direct costing.** Refer to Exercise 43-10. Calculate the ending inventory of finished goods, assuming that the company uses direct costing.

EXERCISE 43-16   **Computing the manufacturing margin.** Refer to Exercise 43-10. Calculate the manufacturing margin for the year, assuming that the company uses direct costing.

EXERCISE 43-17   **Computing net income under direct costing.** Refer to Exercise 43-10. Calculate the net income for the year, assuming that the company uses direct costing.

EXERCISE 43-18 **Analyzing data about a special order.** Refer to Exercise 43-10. Assume that the Jacobs Corporation has an opportunity to sell 1,000 units in a foreign country for $68 a unit. The order will not affect its current sales, all of which are domestic. Freight and shipping costs of $10 a unit would be incurred on the foreign order. What would be the effect on profits if the special order is taken? Show all calculations.

PROBLEMS

PROBLEM 43-1 **Analyzing materials variances.** The Charleston Plastics Company manufactures a product called Merlex, which requires three raw materials. Production is in batches of 2,000 pounds of materials. Waste occurs sometimes and is thrown away. The firm uses standard costs as a control device. Its standard costs for materials for each batch of Merlex have been established as follows.

MATERIAL	QUANTITY	STANDARD COST PER POUND	STANDARD COST PER BATCH
Plastic base	1,800 lb	$0.15	$270
Tint	100 lb	0.20	20
Hardener	100 lb	0.25	25
Totals	2,000 lb		$315

The output is packaged in containers of 25 pounds each. During the month of February 19X1, 2,400 containers of Merlex were produced. There was no beginning or ending inventory of work in process. The materials actually used during February are listed below.

MATERIAL	QUANTITY	TOTAL COST
Plastic base	55,296 lb	$8,441
Tint	3,012 lb	592
Hardener	3,072 lb	781

Instructions 1. Compute the total variance between the actual cost of the materials used during February and the standard cost of the materials. Also compute the total variance for each type of material.
2. Analyze the variances for each type of material for the month.

PROBLEM 43-2 **Analyzing labor variances.** The finishing department of the Great Lakes Tool Corporation uses two classes of direct labor in the manufacturing process. Standard labor costs have been established for each unit of the product, as follows.

LABOR CLASS	STANDARD HOURS	STANDARD RATE PER HOUR
Class FL-3	¼	$8.00
Class FL-4	2	7.50

During the month of May 19X1, a total of 2,836 units were produced. Actual labor costs, by class, are shown below. _actual_

LABOR CLASS	HOURS	COST
Class FL-3	716	$ 5,685.04
Class FL-4	5,512	42,442.40

Instructions

1. Compute the total labor cost variance for the month and the total variance for each class of labor.
2. Analyze the variance for each class of labor.

PROBLEM 43-3   **Analyzing materials and labor variances.** The Atlantic Manufacturing Company makes a product that is processed through two departments: cutting and assembling. All materials are added in the cutting department (the first department). During the month of May 19X1, 4,500 units of the product were made. Data about standard costs and actual costs of materials and labor are shown below.

Instructions

1. Prepare a comparison of the actual cost of materials with the standard cost of materials for the 4,500 units of product. Then prepare an analysis of the materials variances.
2. Prepare a comparison of the actual cost of labor with the standard cost of labor for the 4,500 units of product. Then prepare an analysis of the labor variances.

STANDARD COSTS

Raw Materials
Panel Units: 4 units at $2.10 a unit	$8.40
Assembly Sets: 4 sets at $0.06 a set	0.24
Standard materials cost per unit	$8.64

Direct Labor
Cutting Dept.: ⅙ hour at $7.20 an hour	$1.20
Assembling Dept.: ¼ hour at $8.00 an hour	2.00
Standard direct labor cost per unit	$3.20

ACTUAL COSTS

Raw Materials
Panel Units: 18,100 at $2.12 a unit	$38,372.00
Assembly Sets: 18,050 at $0.055 a set	992.75
Total actual materials cost	$39,364.75

Direct Labor
Cutting Dept.: 752 hours at $7.30 an hour	$5,489.60
Assembling Dept.: 1,100 hours at $7.90 an hour	8,690.00
Total actual direct labor cost	$14,179.60

PROBLEM 43-4   **Analyzing materials, labor, and overhead variances.** The Shannon Company makes several different types of wooden furniture. Standard cost data for the manufacture of its Style M-241 cedar chest appears below. During June 19X5, 20 cedar chests were produced. Data for the actual costs is also shown below.

Instructions
1. Prepare a comparison of the actual costs with the standard costs for the 20 chests.
2. Prepare the following:
   a. An analysis of materials variance.
   b. An analysis of labor variance.
   c. An analysis of manufacturing overhead variance.
3. Determine the grand totals of all analyses prepared in Instruction 2, and check them against the totals shown in the comparison prepared in Instruction 1.

STANDARD COST DATA

Materials

50 linear feet 3- × 3-inch dressed cedar at $0.52 a foot	$26.00
10 linear feet ¾- × ¾-inch dressed cedar at $0.18 a foot	1.80
2 hammered brass hinges H-112 at $0.75 a hinge	1.50
1 hammered brass lock L-216 at $1.00 a lock	1.00
30 screws ¾-inch flat head brass at $0.02 a screw	0.60
¾ pint clear shellac S-20 at $3.20 a pint	2.40
Total materials	$33.30

Labor

Layout: ¼ hour at $6 an hour	$1.50
Cutting: ¼ hour at $6 an hour	1.50
Assembling: ¾ hour at $6 an hour	4.50
Finishing: 1 hour at $6 an hour	6.00
Total Labor	13.50

Manufacturing Overhead

2¼ hours (80% of $13.50 direct labor cost)	10.80
Total Standard Cost per Unit	$57.60

ACTUAL COSTS

a. The cost of materials was at standard, except as noted in Items d, e, and f below.
b. The cost of labor was at standard, except as noted in Items g and h below.
c. The manufacturing overhead applied was at 80 percent of direct labor cost.
d. For each chest 47½ linear feet of 3- × 3-inch dressed cedar were used at $0.50 a linear foot.
e. The actual cost of hinges was $0.76 each.
f. One-half pint of shellac was required for finishing each chest.
g. The layout work required ⅜ hour for each chest, and the worker received $6.50 an hour.
h. Finishing required only ¾ hour for each chest.

PROBLEM 43-5 **Preparing an income statement based on direct costing.** The information shown below relates to the operations of the Viking Products Corporation for the year ended December 31, 19X1. This company makes sails for small sailboats.

Instructions Using the direct costing approach, prepare an income statement for the year ended December 31, 19X1.

DATA FOR 19X1

Do both Abs & Dir; reconcile diff.

Sales: 10,000 units at $50 a unit.
Variable manufacturing costs: 12,000 units at $25 a unit.
Variable selling and administrative expenses: 10,000 units at $5 a unit.
Fixed manufacturing costs: $50,000.
Fixed selling and administrative expenses: $40,000.
Finished goods inventory, January 1, 19X1: None.
Finished goods inventory, December 31, 19X1: 2,000 units.

During period produced 12000

PROBLEM 43-6 **Preparing an income statement based on direct costing, and making a pricing decision.** The Vargas Company began operations in 19X5 to manufacture small motors for lawn mowers, garden tractors, and other equipment. Relevant data for the first year of operations appears below. There are no work in process inventories.

Instructions 1. Prepare an income statement for 19X5, using direct costing.
2. Assume that the company has an opportunity to sell 10,000 units of the product to a firm in another state for $18 a unit. No fixed or variable selling and administrative expenses would be incurred in connection with these units except shipping costs of 50 cents a unit and extra recordkeeping costs of 25 cents a unit. The company has idle capacity, and the order would not affect present markets. Would it be profitable for the company to accept the order? Show all computations.

OPERATIONS DATA FOR 19X5

Quantities

Beginning inventories, finished goods	-0-	units
Units produced during the year	60,000	
Units sold during the year	45,000	

Costs

Direct materials ($10 a unit)	$600,000
Direct labor ($4 a unit)	240,000
Variable factory overhead ($1 a unit)	60,000
Fixed factory overhead	180,000
Variable selling and administrative expenses ($1 a unit)	45,000
Fixed selling and administrative expenses	100,000
Selling price for each unit	26

ALTERNATE PROBLEMS

PROBLEM 43-1A

Analyzing materials variances. The Regis Chemical Company manufactures a product called Kalene, which requires three raw materials. Production is in batches of 1,040 gallons of raw materials that yield only 1,000 gallons of finished product. (Some evaporation of the base occurs, but the amount of evaporation varies slightly from batch to batch.) The firm uses standard costs as a control device. Its standard costs for materials for each batch of Kalene have been established as follows.

MATERIAL	QUANTITY	STANDARD COST PER GALLON	STANDARD COST PER BATCH
Inert base	840 gal	$ 0.20	$168.00
Acid	160 gal	1.60	256.00
Activator	40 gal	10.25	410.00
Total	1,040 gal	$12.05	$834.00

The output is packaged in 50-gallon drums. During the month of July 19X1, 300 drums of Kalene were produced. There was no beginning or ending inventory of work in process. The materials actually used during July are listed below.

MATERIAL	QUANTITY	COST PER GALLON
Inert base	12,840 gal	$ 0.21
Acid	2,390 gal	1.56
Activator	612 gal	10.10

Instructions

1. Compute the total variance between the actual cost of the materials used during July and the standard cost of the materials. Also compute the total variance for each type of material.
2. Analyze the variances for each type of material for the month.

PROBLEM 43-2A

Analyzing labor variances. The assembling department of the United Appliance Company uses two classes of direct labor in the manufacturing process. Standard labor costs have been established for each unit of the product as follows.

LABOR CLASS	STANDARD HOURS	STANDARD RATE PER HOUR
Class DL-1	½	$7.50
Class DL-2	1	6.80

During the month of June 19X1, a total of 4,040 units were produced. Actual labor costs, by class, are shown below.

LABOR CLASS	HOURS	COST
Class DL-1	2,106	$16,110.90
Class DL-2	4,010	27,468.50

Instructions 1. Compute the total labor cost variance for the month and the total variance for each class of labor.
2. Analyze the variance for each class of labor.

PROBLEM 43-3A **Analyzing materials and labor variances.** The Chesapeake Manufacturing Company makes a product that is processed through two departments: assembling and finishing. All materials are added in the first department. During the month of May 19X1, 10,000 units of the product were made. Standard costs and actual costs for materials and labor are given below.

Instructions 1. Prepare a comparison of the actual cost of materials with the standard cost of materials for the 10,000 units of product. Then prepare an analysis of the materials variances.
2. Prepare a comparison of the actual cost of labor with the standard cost of labor for the 10,000 units of product. Then prepare an analysis of the labor variances.

STANDARD COSTS

Raw Materials

Framing: 10 square feet at $0.20 a square foot	$2.00
Filler: 14 pounds at $0.06 a pound	0.84
Standard materials cost per unit	$2.84

Direct Labor

Assembling Dept.: ¼ hour at $6.80 an hour	$1.70
Finishing Dept.: ⅒ hour at $8.00 an hour	0.80
Standard direct labor cost per unit	$2.50

ACTUAL COSTS

Raw Materials

Framing: 100,500 square feet at $0.196 a square foot	$19,698.00
Filler: 138,970 pounds at $0.061 a pound	8,477.17
Total actual materials cost	$28,175.17

Direct Labor

Assembling Dept.: 2,580 hours at $7.00 an hour	$18,060.00
Finishing Dept.: 987 hours at $8.05 an hour	7,945.35
Total actual direct labor cost	$26,005.35

PROBLEM 43-4A **Analyzing materials, labor, and overhead variances.** The Good Earth Company makes fertilizers and other agricultural products. On the basis of past experience, this firm has established standards for each type of product. The standards for one unit of a certain product as well as the actual results of operations for the product in January 19X1 are shown on page 1045.

Instructions 1. Compute the total variance between the actual cost of materials and the standard cost of materials. Then compute the portion of this variance resulting from (a) the quantity of the materials used and (b) the unit price of the materials.

2. Compute the total variance between the actual cost of labor and the standard cost of labor. Then compute the portion of this variance resulting from (a) the number of hours worked and (b) the labor rate per hour.

3. Compute the total variance between manufacturing overhead applied and the standard overhead. Then compute the portion of this variance resulting from (a) the number of hours worked and (b) the labor price factor.

4. Compute the grand total of all the analyses.

STANDARD COSTS

Materials: 5 pounds at $6 a pound	$30.00
Labor: 3 hours at $8 an hour	24.00
Manufacturing overhead: 50% of direct labor	12.00

ACTUAL COSTS

Units of product manufactured	10,500
Pounds of materials used	53,025
Labor hours worked	32,550
Cost per pound of materials used	$5.96
Cost per hour of labor	$8.10

PROBLEM 43-5A **Preparing an income statement based on direct costing.** The data shown below pertains to the operations of the Reliable Products Corporation for the year ended December 31, 19X2. The firm makes auto parts.

Instructions Using the direct costing approach, prepare an income statement for the year ended December 31, 19X2.

DATA FOR 19X2

Sales: 20,000 units at $60 a unit.
Variable manufacturing costs: 24,000 units at $30 a unit.
Variable selling and administrative expenses: $5 a unit.
Fixed manufacturing costs: $200,000.
Fixed selling and administrative expenses: $180,000.
Finished goods inventory, January 1, 19X2: None.
Finished goods inventory, December 31, 19X2: 4,000 units.
Produced 24000 units

PROBLEM 43-6A **Preparing an income statement based on direct costing, and making a pricing decision.** The Valtec Corporation began operations in 19X1 to manufacture disk drives for microcomputers. Relevant data for the year appears on page 1046. There are no work in process inventories.

Instructions 1. Prepare an income statement for 19X1, using direct costing.

2. Assume that the company has an opportunity to sell 2,000 units of the product in a foreign country for $60 a unit. No fixed or variable selling and administrative expenses would be incurred in connection with these units except shipping costs of $1 a unit and extra recordkeeping costs of $0.25 a unit. The company has idle capacity, and the order would not affect present markets.

Would it be profitable for the company to accept the order? Show all computations.

OPERATIONS DATA FOR 19X1

Quantities

Beginning inventories, finished goods	–0–	units
Units produced during the year	5,000	
Units sold during the year	1,200	

Costs

Direct materials ($20 a unit)	$100,000
Direct labor ($24 a unit)	120,000
Variable factory overhead ($6 a unit)	30,000
Fixed factory overhead	60,000
Variable selling and administrative expenses ($10 a unit)	12,000
Fixed selling and administrative expenses	32,000
Selling price for each unit	100

Managers are constantly making business decisions, and most of these decisions rely heavily on financial information and analyses. In many instances accountants play a key role in the decision-making process. Managers require as much measurable data, properly analyzed, as is possible to handle. It is the accountant's job to gather the necessary financial data, analyze it, and present it to management in a manner that will permit effective and efficient decision making.

COST-REVENUE ANALYSIS FOR DECISION MAKING

THE DECISION PROCESS

Normally, the decision process used in business involves the following six steps.

1. Defining the problem.
2. Identifying workable alternatives.
3. Determining relevant cost and revenue data.
4. Evaluating the cost and revenue data.
5. Considering any nonfinancial factors that should be taken into account.
6. Making a decision.

When the cost and revenue data is evaluated, management must attempt to measure the difference in profitability among the various alternatives that have been identified. Many types of decisions that must be made in business are most efficiently handled through the process outlined above. One of these, special pricing of products, was discussed in Chapter 43. Four other common situations requiring cost-revenue analysis in order to make a decision have been chosen for illustration in this chapter. The decisions involved are as follows.

1. Purchasing new equipment.
2. Retaining or discontinuing a product.
3. Making or buying a part.
4. Replacing old equipment.

CONCEPTS OF COST-REVENUE ANALYSIS

Before these four specific situations are examined, certain concepts underlying cost-revenue analysis will be discussed.

The Concept of Contribution Margin

Most cost-revenue analysis involves the contribution approach to profitability. You have already seen an application of this approach in analyzing departmental profitability in Chapter 37. Similarly, direct costing, discussed in Chapter 43, makes use of the contribution approach. Most decisions concerning segments of a business (such as branches, products, machines, and so on) also involve contribution analysis. One of the advantages of this approach is that it avoids arbitrary and often meaningless allocations of common costs. (*Common costs* are those not directly traceable to a segment.) The profitability of a segment is judged by its contribution toward covering the common costs of the business and producing a profit.

A *contribution margin* (revenue less variable costs) is calculated for each segment of a business. The controllable fixed costs of the segment are deducted from this margin to determine the segment's contribution to the overall profit of the business. (The *controllable fixed costs* are those that the segment manager can control.) The company's common costs are not allocated. They are deducted from the total of all segment contributions to determine the company's profit.

Sound decisions about adding, keeping, or eliminating a particular segment of the business can be made more easily by using the contribution approach. If a segment produces a contribution margin, it is helping to meet companywide fixed costs as well as providing part of the firm's profit. Failure of the segment to generate a contribution margin would certainly cause management to consider eliminating it from the business. Plans for any new segment should show that it can produce a contribution margin if it is to be considered favorably by management.

In addition to the concept of contribution margin, there are certain cost concepts that are very important in analyzing the facts that pertain to a decision-making situation. These concepts provide ways of classifying costs that are useful for decision making.

The Concept of Relevant Costs

As pointed out in Chapter 37, for planning purposes, relevant costs are future or expected costs. Historical costs are irrelevant except to the extent that they serve as a basis for estimating future outlays. In addition, only those costs that will change as a result of a decision are relevant.

If a decision must be made to replace a machine, the book value of the existing machine is a historical cost and therefore irrelevant. The cost of the new machine, however, is relevant. If a decision must be made to close a warehouse, the salaries of the warehouse personnel are relevant if these workers will be terminated when the warehouse closes. The nonrefundable prepaid rent on the warehouse for the remainder of the year is irrelevant since it has been paid and cannot be recovered.

A historical cost that has been incurred and thus is irrelevant for decision-making purposes is called a *sunk cost*. The prepaid rent on the warehouse and the cost of the existing machine discussed above are both sunk costs.

The Concept of Differential Costs

In decision making, management always compares two or more alternatives. Even in deciding on the acquisition of a machine where only one bid has been received from possible suppliers, management has two alternatives: to accept the bid or to reject it. A *differential cost* is the difference in cost between one alternative and another. For example, the difference in cost between using a hand-operated press and an automated press would be a differential cost. While the term *incremental cost* is often used interchangeably with differential cost, incremental cost actually means only an *increase* in cost from one alternative to another. For example, if it costs $6,000 to produce 20 units and $7,800 to produce 30 units, the incremental cost of producing the additional 10 units is $1,800.

The Concept of Opportunity Costs

Not all costs used in decision making appear in the accounting records of a business. *Opportunity costs* are earnings or potential benefits foregone because a certain course of action is taken. For example, assume that the management of a firm must decide between purchasing additional equipment and investing in top-grade securities. The opportunity cost of a decision to purchase the equipment is the estimated amount of the interest or dividends lost on the securities when the funds are applied to the purchase of the equipment.

In the following illustrative cases, the concepts of contribution margin, relevant costs, differential costs, and opportunity costs are examined.

DECISION ANALYSIS— PURCHASING NEW EQUIPMENT

The management of the Logan Manufacturing Company is considering the purchase of a new machine that will improve the productivity of its factory employees. The machine has an estimated useful life of ten years and no anticipated salvage value. The firm's accountant has gathered the following relevant data about the two alternatives.

COST AND REVENUE DATA NEEDED FOR AN ANALYSIS OF THE EFFECTS OF PURCHASING A NEW MACHINE

	If Machine Is Not Bought	If Machine Is Bought
Annual Sales (in units)	8,000	8,000
Sales Price (per unit)	$ 30.00	$ 30.00
Cost of Machine		22,500.00
Other Cost Data:		
Materials (per unit)	12.00	12.00
Labor (per unit)	9.00	8.25
Variable Overhead (per unit)	3.00	3.00
Fixed Overhead (per year)	18,000.00	19,800.00*

*Includes depreciation of $1,800 a year for the machine.

In evaluating the proposed purchase, one method is to estimate the net income under each alternative and compute the difference. Another method is for management to look only at the differential cost and revenue data. Using a contribution approach, the net income under each alternative is determined as shown on page 1050.

ANALYSIS OF THE EFFECTS OF PURCHASING A NEW MACHINE
(BASED ON ANNUAL INCOME)

	If Machine Is Not Bought	If Machine Is Bought	Difference
Annual Sales	$240,000	$240,000	
Variable Costs			
Materials	$ 96,000	$ 96,000	
Labor	72,000	66,000	$6,000
Manufacturing Overhead	24,000	24,000	
Total Variable Costs	$192,000	$186,000	
Contribution Margin	$ 48,000	$ 54,000	
Fixed Costs	18,000	19,800	(1,800)
Net Income	$ 30,000	$ 34,200	$4,200

The analysis shows that there is an annual savings of $4,200 each year if the machine is bought. Notice that the sales revenue, the cost of materials, and the variable overhead costs remain the same for both alternatives. However, the cost of labor and the fixed overhead costs change. The results of this analysis would seem to indicate that the company should purchase the new machine, but other factors, such as employee morale and the quality of the product, must be considered before making a final decision. In this case a study of the situation leads to the conclusion that employee morale will improve and that there will be no change in product quality. Management therefore decides to purchase the new machine.

DECISION ANALYSIS—RETAINING OR DISCONTINUING A PRODUCT

After reviewing the firm's income statement for 19X1, the management of the Logan Manufacturing Company had to decide whether to discontinue Product C. This product incurred a loss of $7,050 in 19X1, as shown below.

LOGAN MANUFACTURING COMPANY
Income Statement
Year Ended December 31, 19X1
(Absorption Costing)

	Product A	Product B	Product C	Total
Sales	$15,000	$27,000	$33,000	$75,000
Cost of Goods Sold	7,125	9,900	33,750	50,775
Gross Profit on Sales	$ 7,875	$17,100	$ (750)	$24,225
Operating Expenses	4,000	4,050	6,300	14,350
Net Income or (Loss)	$ 3,875	$13,050	$(7,050)	$ 9,875

Other relevant data about the three products made by the Logan Manufacturing Company is as follows.

	PRODUCT A	PRODUCT B	PRODUCT C
Units Sold	1,000	1,200	2,000
Sales Price (per unit)	$ 15.00	$ 22.50	$ 16.50
Variable Manufacturing Costs (per unit)	3.75	4.50	12.00
Variable Operating Expenses (per unit)	2.25	1.50	1.80
Fixed Manufacturing Costs (per year)	3,375.00	4,500.00	9,750.00
Fixed Operating Expenses (per year)	750.00	2,250.00	2,700.00

In analyzing the profitability of Product C, it is useful to prepare an income statement based on direct costing, an approach that you first studied in Chapter 43. This income statement would show the following data.

LOGAN MANUFACTURING COMPANY
Income Statement
Year Ended December 31, 19X1
(Direct Costing)

	Product A	Product B	Product C	Total
Sales	$15,000	$27,000	$33,000	$75,000
Variable Costs				
Manufacturing	$ 3,750	$ 5,400	$24,000	$33,150
Operating	2,250	1,800	3,600	7,650
Total Variable Costs	$ 6,000	$ 7,200	$27,600	$40,800
Contribution Margin	$ 9,000	$19,800	$ 5,400	$34,200
Fixed Costs				
Manufacturing	$ 3,375	$ 4,500	$ 9,750	$17,625
Operating	750	2,250	2,700	5,700
Total Fixed Costs	$ 4,125	$ 6,750	$12,450	$23,325
Net Income or (Loss)	$ 4,875	$13,050	($7,050)	$10,875

The analysis given above indicates that since Product C contributes $5,400 toward the firm's fixed costs and net income, discontinuing it will reduce the net income by $5,400 if all fixed costs that have been allocated to the product continue. An income statement based on direct costing, showing the net income of the Logan Company if Product C is discontinued, is on page 1052.

LOGAN MANUFACTURING COMPANY
Income Statement
Year Ended December 31, 19X1
(Direct Costing)

	Product A	Product B	Total
Sales	$15,000	$27,000	$42,000
Variable Costs			
Manufacturing	$ 3,750	$ 5,400	$ 9,150
Operating	2,250	1,800	4,050
Total Variable Costs	$ 6,000	$ 7,200	$13,200
Contribution Margin	$ 9,000	$19,800	$28,800
Fixed Costs*			
Manufacturing	$ 7,554	$10,071	$17,625
Operating	1,425	4,275	5,700
Total Fixed Costs	$ 8,979	$14,346	$23,325
Net Income	$ 21	$ 5,454	$ 5,475

*Allocated on the basis of the original departmental fixed costs.

While other relevant factors should be considered, the quantitative (measurable) analysis indicates that Product C should not be discontinued.

DECISION ANALYSIS—MAKING OR BUYING A PART

A manufacturing company is sometimes faced with a decision about whether to purchase an asset, such as a machine, from a supplier or to manufacture the asset in its own facilities. Similarly, it may be necessary for a company to decide whether it is cheaper to buy a part that enters into its finished product or to manufacture the part itself. For example, suppose that the Logan Manufacturing Company now purchases a part for $15 a unit. The company uses 12,000 of these items each year. The part could be made in the company's molding department.

The molding department has a capacity of 20,000 direct labor hours a year. This department has been operating at a level of 15,000 hours for several years. Its labor costs are $12 an hour, and its variable manufacturing overhead costs are $6 an hour. Annual fixed costs for the department total $90,000. The estimated cost of materials is $6.60 for each part. Four parts can be produced during each hour.

The data can be analyzed on the basis of unit cost or annual cost. If the unit cost approach is used, there is a savings of $3.90 a part if Logan manufactures the part itself. The total savings on a unit cost basis are $46,800 a year (12,000 parts × $3.90). The necessary computations are shown on page 1053.

 Notice that the fixed manufacturing overhead costs are not considered because these costs remain the same whether the part is bought or made.

ANALYSIS OF THE EFFECTS OF MAKING OR BUYING A PART

Cost to Purchase Part		$15.00
Cost to Manufacture Part		
Variable Costs Only		
Materials	$6.60	
Labor (¼ hour at $12 an hour)	3.00	
Manufacturing Overhead (¼ hour at $6 an hour)	1.50	11.10
Differential Cost (savings per unit if part is manufactured)		$ 3.90

DECISION ANALYSIS— REPLACING OLD EQUIPMENT

The process used to reach a decision about replacing old equipment is much like that used to evaluate a proposed purchase of new machinery. It is important to understand, however, that when a decision is made about whether to replace existing equipment, its book value is not considered because it is a sunk cost. (Book value equals the original cost less accumulated depreciation. As discussed previously in this chapter, sunk costs are costs that were incurred in the past and have no impact on future decisions.) Whether the existing equipment is replaced or not, its book value will be charged off against revenue. The only difference is whether it is charged off immediately or over a period of years. If the equipment is not replaced, the book value is written off against revenue over future years as depreciation. If the equipment is replaced, the book value is written off against revenue immediately.

Assume that the Logan Manufacturing Company purchased the factory machine discussed on pages 1049–1050. Five years later an equipment supplier tells the company that a new model is available. This model, which is priced at $18,750, has an estimated useful life of five years with no salvage value. The new machine is more efficient and should reduce labor costs at Logan from $8.25 to $7.125 a unit. It should also reduce variable manufacturing overhead costs from $3 to $2.625 a unit. The supplier is not offering a trade-in allowance for he old equipment, and the old equipment has no resale value on the market.

One useful method of evaluating the proposed replacement is to compare the net income that would be earned under the two alternatives during the next five years. This period represents the remaining useful life of the old machine and the estimated useful life of the new machine. The analysis on page 1054 assumes production and sale of 8,000 units a year at $30 a unit and shows net income of $171,000 if the machine is retained, compared with net income of $212,250 if the machine is replaced.

This analysis indicates a savings of $41,250 over the five-year period as a result of replacing the equipment. The change in the fixed costs represents the difference between the depreciation charge on the old machine ($11,250 over the next five years) and that on the new machine ($18,750 over the next five years). Of course, if the new machine is purchased, depreciation will be discontinued on the old machine and begun on the new one; and the book value of the old machine ($11,250) must be written off as a loss.

ANALYSIS OF THE EFFECTS OF REPLACING AN OLD MACHINE
(BASED ON FIVE-YEAR INCOME)

	If Machine Is Retained	If Machine Is Replaced	Difference
Sales	$1,200,000	$1,200,000	-0-
Variable Costs			
Materials	$ 480,000	$ 480,000	
Labor	330,000	285,000	$45,000
Manufacturing Overhead	120,000	105,000	15,000
Total Variable Costs	$ 930,000	$ 870,000	$60,000
Contribution Margin	$ 270,000	$ 330,000	$60,000
Fixed Costs	$ 99,000	$ 106,500	$ 7,500
Write-Off of Book Value of Old Machine		11,250	11,250
Total	$ 99,000	$ 117,750	$18,750
Net Income	$ 171,000	$ 212,250	$41,250

The savings from the replacement of the old machine can also be calculated on an annual basis by subtracting the depreciation on the new machine from the annual variable cost reductions in labor and overhead. The necessary computations are shown below.

ANALYSIS OF THE EFFECTS OF REPLACING AN OLD MACHINE
(BASED ON NET ANNUAL SAVINGS)

Variable Cost Reductions	
Labor ($8.25 − $7.125)	$1.125 per unit
Manufacturing Overhead ($3.00 − $2.625)	.375 per unit
Total	$1.500 per unit
Total Variable Cost Reduction (8,000 units × $1.50)	$12,000
Less Annual Depreciation on New Machine ($18,750 ÷ 5 years)	3,750
Net Annual Savings From Replacement of Old Machine	$ 8,250

Net Savings for Five Years: $8,250 × 5 = $41,250

The cases discussed in this chapter provide just a few examples of the many decision-making situations that occur in business each day. No matter what their size, most companies are faced with similar situations in the normal course of their operations. The accountant who understands cost-revenue analysis can greatly assist management in reaching logical decisions that will increase the company's profitability.

PRINCIPLES AND PROCEDURES SUMMARY

Management is constantly involved in decision making. Many of these decisions require financial data, which must be gathered and analyzed by the accountant. The decision process usually consists of the following steps: defining the problem, identifying workable alternatives, determining relevant cost and revenue data, evaluating the cost and revenue data, considering any nonfinancial factors that should be taken into account, and making a decision.

Relevant costs in decision analysis are usually future costs. Sunk costs are historical costs and are therefore not relevant to business decisions. An important part of decision analysis usually involves determining differential costs—the differences in cost among the various alternatives. Often the contribution approach is used in evaluating the data that results from the analysis

Typical business decisions involve purchasing new equipment; adding, retaining, or discontinuing a product; replacing old equipment; making or buying parts; and setting prices for products.

MANAGERIAL IMPLICATIONS

An understanding of cost and revenue behavior is critical in managerial decision making today. Although a firm's accountant usually gathers and analyzes the necessary data, management must be familiar with such concepts as sunk costs, relevant costs, differential costs, opportunity costs, and contribution margin in order to intelligently assess the data and reach a logical decision. Many business decisions involve large amounts of money and have a strong impact on the future success of the company. Cost-revenue analysis provides management with a highly useful tool for evaluating the financial effects of decisions before they are made.

REVIEW QUESTIONS

1. What is a contribution margin?
2. What are relevant costs?
3. What are differential costs?
4. Explain opportunity costs.
5. What are sunk costs?
6. Why are sunk costs ignored in most managerial decisions?
7. What is the contribution approach to management decision analysis?
8. Suggest some nonmeasurable data that might be considered in deciding to replace existing equipment with new equipment.
9. Is absorption costing or direct costing more useful in making decisions? Why?
10. In the make-or-buy decision on page 1052, fixed manufacturing overhead costs were not considered. Why?

11. Suppose that a company is considering the purchase of new equipment. The old equipment will be sold when the new equipment is acquired. How should the proceeds from the sale of the old equipment be considered in the analysis of the effects of the purchase?

12. Why do the analyses presented in this chapter focus on future costs rather than on past costs? Does this mean that historical costs are useless? Explain.

13. Give some reasons why a company might decide to purchase a part that is used in its finished product rather than manufacture the part.

MANAGERIAL DISCUSSION QUESTIONS

1. What types of information are needed to decide whether to discontinue or retain a product line that appears to be losing money because it is selling for less than its cost (computed under absorption costing)?

2. Assume that the company where you are employed has a substantial amount of unused plant capacity. A foreign company has offered to purchase a large quantity of your company's product, but at 10 percent less than the product's normal selling price. What types of information are needed to arrive at a decision about whether to accept the order?

3. Suppose that your company is considering the purchase of a new machine for use in its production process. The cost of the machine is $250,000. If the purchase is made, an old machine currently in use will be scrapped. It has no net salvage value because its removal cost is equal to its gross salvage amount. The old machine has a book value of $100,000, and management is reluctant to take the loss that would result if this machine is scrapped. Discuss the types of information that management would need to make a decision about purchasing the new asset. Give special attention to the problem of the old asset's book value.

4. Suppose that your company has been manufacturing a part used in its finished product. The total manufacturing cost of the part is $18.20. An outside supplier has offered to provide the part for $17. Describe the measurable data that management would need in making a decision about whether to accept the supplier's offer.

EXERCISES

EXERCISE 44-1   **Identifying relevant costs.** The Anderson Company is considering the replacement of existing equipment with new equipment. The old equipment has a book value of $60,000 and a remaining useful life of eight years. The new equipment would cost $220,000 and have a useful life of eight years with an estimated salvage value of $20,000. The annual production of 10,000 units would not be changed. The new equipment would reduce direct labor costs by $5 a unit and would reduce variable overhead costs by $1 a unit. Other fixed costs would increase by $30,000 a year. Of the information just given, what items are "relevant" to the decision to replace the equipment?

EXERCISE 44-2   **Deciding whether to purchase new equipment.** The Orlando Company is considering the purchase of a new factory machine at a cost of $50,000 to replace an existing fully depreciated machine. The new machine would have a life of five years and would produce 10,000 units a year (the current output). Direct labor costs would be reduced by $0.95 a unit and variable overhead costs would be reduced by $0.46 a unit. Other fixed costs would increase by $2,000 a year. Should the machine be purchased? What is the impact on net income of the decision?

EXERCISE 44-3   **Deciding whether to purchase new equipment.** Assume the same facts as in Exercise 44-2, except that the old factory machine has a book value of $16,000 and has no salvage value. Should the new machine be purchased? What is the impact on net income of the decision?

EXERCISE 44-4   **Deciding whether to make or buy a part.** The Keith Corporation is manufacturing a part used in its finished product. The costs for each unit of the part are as follows.

Direct Materials	$16.00
Direct Labor	12.00
Manufacturing Overhead	
Variable	2.00
Fixed	6.00

The fixed overhead is based on $600,000 of fixed costs to manufacture 100,000 parts a year. If the part is not manufactured, fixed costs will be reduced by approximately $140,000 a year. The firm has an opportunity to purchase the part from an outside company for $32 a unit. Should Keith accept the offer or should it continue to manufacture the part?

EXERCISE 44-5   **Deciding whether to make or buy a part.** Assume the same facts as in Exercise 44-4, except that the part can be purchased from an outside company for $34.20 a unit. What should the decision be?

EXERCISE 44-6   **Deciding whether to make or buy a part.** Assume the same facts as in Exercise 44-4, except that the part can be purchased from an outside company for $29.80. What should the decision be?

EXERCISE 44-7   **Deciding whether to discontinue a product.** The O'Mara Company provides the following data about one of its products.

Sales (30,000 units at $40)	$1,200,000	Variable Costs	
Cost of Goods Sold	1,125,000	Manufacturing	$30 per unit
Gross Profit on Sales	$ 75,000	Operating Expenses	5 per unit
Operating Expenses	225,000	Fixed Costs	
Net Loss	$ (150,000)	Manufacturing	$225,000
		Operating Expenses	75,000

If the product is discontinued, fixed manufacturing costs will decrease $100,000 a year. Fixed operating expenses will not change. Based on the information that has been given, would you suggest that O'Mara discontinue the product? By what amount would the company's overall net income or net loss change if the product is discontinued?

EXERCISE 44-8   **Deciding whether to discontinue a product.** Assume the same facts as in Exercise 44-7, except that fixed manufacturing costs will decrease by $150,000 and fixed operating expenses will decrease by $50,000 if the product is discontinued. Should the product be discontinued? By what amount will the company's net income or net loss change if the product is discontinued?

EXERCISE 44-9   **Deciding whether to accept an order at a special price.** The standard cost sheet for a product made by the Polanski Corporation shows the following data.

variable costs →

Direct Materials	$35.00
Direct Labor (2 hours at $10.50 an hour)	21.00
Manufacturing Overhead	
Variable (2 hours at $7 an hour)	14.00
Fixed	21.00
Total	$91.00

The product normally sells for $105. The company is presently operating at only slightly over 50 percent of capacity. A foreign chain of discount stores has offered to purchase 2,000 units of the product for $87 a unit. Shipping costs would be $1 a unit. Special packaging would be needed and would cost $2 a unit more than the normal packaging. Should the order be accepted? (Show all calculations.)

EXERCISE 44-10   **Deciding whether to accept an order at a special price.** Ignoring all factors except those given in Exercise 44-9, what is the least amount that the Polanski Corporation could profitably accept for a special order of 2,000 units?

PROBLEMS

PROBLEM 44-1   **Analyzing the effects of a decision to purchase equipment.** The Fairfield Company makes doors, which it sells to home builders. The firm's finishing department is not mechanized. Employees use hand tools to finish the product. The factory superintendent has proposed that the firm acquire an electric-powered machine to perform some of the finishing functions. Presently, 20,000 units a year are manufactured and sold. A summary of the manufacturing costs of the finishing department is shown below.

Direct Materials	$600,000
Direct Labor	400,000
Manufacturing Overhead	
Variable	40,000
Fixed	100,000

The machine being considered will cost $800,000 and have a useful life of five years, with no salvage value. The machine will cause the following changes in costs.

- Direct labor will decrease by $10 a unit.
- Indirect materials will decrease by $0.50 a unit.
- Power will increase by $0.80 a unit.
- Repairs will increase by $4,000 a year.
- Taxes and insurance will increase by $5,000 a year.
- Interest expense will increase by an average of $40,000 a year.

Instructions   1. Prepare an analysis showing the effect on net income of purchasing the equipment.
2. What other factors should be considered in making the decision?

PROBLEM 44-2   **Analyzing the effects of a decision to discontinue a product.** The following data is taken from the budgeted income statement of the Glickman Medical Technology Corporation for 19X1. It shows the projected net income or loss for each of the firm's three products. Management is concerned about the budgeted loss for Product C and wants to discontinue the product.

	PRODUCT A	PRODUCT B	PRODUCT C	TOTAL
Sales	$187,500	$675,000	$112,500	$975,000
Cost of Goods Sold				
Direct Materials	$ 22,500	$112,500	$ 15,000	$150,000
Direct Labor	37,500	150,000	30,000	217,500
Manufacturing Overhead	18,750	75,000	15,000	108,750
Total	$ 78,750	$337,500	$ 60,000	$476,250
Gross Profit on Sales	$108,750	$337,500	$ 52,500	$498,750
Operating Expenses	75,000	187,500	67,500	330,000
Net Income or (Loss)	$ 33,750	$150,000	($ 15,000)	$168,750

Materials and labor are variable costs. Manufacturing overhead is applied at 50 percent of the direct labor cost. Variable overhead is 10 percent of the direct labor cost. Fixed overhead totals $87,000 a year. Operating expenses include variable costs at 20 percent of sales dollars. Fixed operating expenses total $135,000. The fixed overhead costs and fixed operating expenses are expected to continue if Product C is eliminated.

Instructions   1. Prepare an analysis indicating the effects of discontinuing Product C.
2. What other factors should be considered in arriving at a decision to discontinue Product C?

PROBLEM 44-3   **Analyzing the effects of a decision to make or buy a part.** The Doyle Farm Equipment Company is currently manufacturing a part that goes into its main product. Each year 3,000 of these parts are used. Cost data for the past year that relates to the 3,000 parts is given on page 1060. Fixed costs are allocated on the basis of direct labor hours. An outside company has offered to supply the part at

$25.50 a unit, plus a shipping charge of $2.31 a unit. The plant capacity now used by Doyle to manufacture the part would not be used in the foreseeable future if the part is purchased outside.

Direct Materials	$159,000
Direct Labor	68,000
Indirect Labor	2,000
Other Variable Overhead Costs	6,000
Fixed Overhead Costs	15,000

Instructions
1. Prepare an analysis comparing the unit cost of manufacturing the part with the unit cost of purchasing it.
2. What other factors are important in making the decision to accept or reject the offer?

PROBLEM 44-4 **Analyzing the effects of a decision to replace an asset.** The Easy Rider Corporation makes automobile tires. The firm is considering the replacement of a machine used in its manufacturing operations with a new machine that will cost $300,000 and have an estimated life of ten years. The existing machine has a book value of $45,000 and could be used for ten more years. It has no salvage value. Operating costs related to the two machines are as follows.

	OLD MACHINE	NEW MACHINE
Direct Labor	$200,000	$175,000
Supervisory Labor	8,000	8,000
Power	195,000	180,000
Maintenance	20,000	12,000

Instructions
1. Compute the difference in income if the proposed change is made. Assume that sales will remain the same and that the only additional fixed cost will be the depreciation on the new machine.
2. What other factors should be considered in making the decision?

PROBLEM 44-5 **Analyzing the effects of a decision to accept a special order.** The Kitchen-Aide Company produces a small toaster oven. Annual production is 500,000 units, each of which regularly sells for $24. Information from the standard cost sheet for this product is as follows.

Direct Materials		$ 7.00
Direct Labor		3.00
Manufacturing Overhead		
Variable	$1.00	
Fixed	5.00	6.00
Total		$16.00

Nonmanufacturing costs are $2 a unit for variable items and $500,000 a year for fixed items. A foreign chain of stores has offered to buy 20,000 units at $17 a unit and will pay the shipping costs. This order will not affect Kitchen-Aide's

ability to serve its existing market, and it will not increase the firm's nonmanufacturing fixed costs. Its nonmanufacturing variable costs on the 20,000 units
will be reduced by $1 a unit.

Instructions
1. Prepare an analysis showing the net income or loss that would result from
accepting this order.
2. What other factors must be considered in deciding whether to accept or reject
the order?

ALTERNATE PROBLEMS

PROBLEM 44-1A
Analyzing the effects of a decision to purchase equipment. The Montvale
Company makes wooden furniture, which it sells to retail stores. The firm's
polishing department uses hand labor to perform its work on all products. A
proposal has been made by the company's vice president to acquire machinery
that will perform most of the functions of this department. The polishing department has consistently produced 100,000 units a year, and that is the estimated
production for the foreseeable future. A summary of the manufacturing costs of
the department is given below.

Direct Materials	$ 50,000
Direct Labor	2,000,000
Manufacturing Overhead	
Variable	300,000
Fixed	200,000

The machinery being considered will cost $3,000,000 and have an estimated
useful life of five years, with no salvage value. The machinery will cause the
following changes in costs.

- Direct labor will decrease by $7 a unit.
- Indirect materials will decrease by $0.30 a unit.
- Power will increase by $1.05 a unit.
- Repairs will increase by $6,000 a year.
- Taxes and insurance will increase by $14,000 a year.
- Departmental supervision will decrease by $18,000 a year.
- Interest expense will increase by an average of $110,000 a year.

Instructions
1. Prepare an analysis showing the effect on net income of purchasing the equipment.
2. What other factors should be considered in making the decision?

PROBLEM 44-2A
Analyzing the effects of a decision to discontinue a product. The data given
on page 1062 is taken from the budgeted income statement of the Jenson Spe-
cialty Tool Corporation for 19X2. It shows the projected net income or loss for
each of the firm's three products. Management is concerned about the budgeted
loss for Product Z and wants to discontinue it.

	PRODUCT X	PRODUCT Y	PRODUCT Z	TOTAL
Sales	$25,000	$90,000	$15,000	$130,000
Cost of Goods Sold				
Direct Materials	$ 3,000	$15,000	$ 2,000	$ 20,000
Direct Labor	5,000	20,000	4,000	29,000
Manufacturing Overhead	2,500	10,000	2,000	14,500
Total	$10,500	$45,000	$ 8,000	$ 63,500
Gross Profit on Sales	$14,500	$45,000	$ 7,000	$ 66,500
Operating Expenses	10,000	25,000	9,000	44,000
Net Income or (Loss)	$ 4,500	$20,000	($2,000)	$ 22,500

Materials and labor are variable costs. Manufacturing overhead is applied at 50 percent of the direct labor cost. Variable overhead is 10 percent of the direct labor cost. Fixed overhead totals $11,600 a year. Operating expenses include variable costs at 20 percent of sales dollars. Fixed operating expenses total $18,000. The fixed overhead costs and fixed operating expenses are expected to continue if Product Z is eliminated.

Instructions
1. Prepare an analysis indicating the effects of discontinuing Product Z.
2. What other factors should be considered in arriving at a decision to discontinue Product Z?

PROBLEM 44-3A **Analyzing the effects of a decision to make or buy a part.** The Antonelli Garden Equipment Corporation is currently manufacturing a part that goes into its main product. Each year 8,000 of these parts are used. Cost data for the past year that relates to the 8,000 parts is given below. Fixed costs are allocated on the basis of direct labor hours. An outside company has offered to supply the part for $22.20 a unit, plus a shipping charge of $0.50 a unit. The plant capacity now used by Antonelli to manufacture the part would not be used within the foreseeable future if the part is purchased outside.

Direct Materials	$ 94,000
Direct Labor	100,000
Indirect Labor	1,100
Other Variable Overhead Costs	3,200
Fixed Overhead Costs	8,000

Instructions
1. Prepare an analysis comparing the unit cost of manufacturing the part with the unit cost of purchasing it.
2. What other factors are important in making the decision to accept or reject the offer?

PROBLEM 44-4A **Analyzing the effects of a decision to replace an asset.** The Sunshine Products Corporation makes light bulbs. The firm is considering the replacement of a machine used in its factory. The new machine will cost $270,000 and have an estimated useful life of eight years. The existing machine has a book value of

$84,000 and could be used for eight more years. Operating costs related to the two machines are as follows.

	OLD MACHINE	NEW MACHINE
Direct Labor	$193,000	$157,000
Supervisory Labor	15,000	15,000
Power	197,000	184,000
Maintenance	19,000	10,000

Instructions

1. Compute the difference in income if the proposed change is made. Assume that sales will remain the same and that the only additional fixed cost will be the depreciation on the new machine.
2. What other factors should be considered in making the decision?

PROBLEM 44-5A

Analyzing the effects of a decision to accept a special order. The Perma-Frost Company makes a product used in the manufacture of air conditioners. Annual production totals 100,000 units, each of which sells for $60. Information from the standard cost sheet for this product is as follows.

Direct Materials		$12.00
Direct Labor		10.50
Manufacturing Overhead		
Variable	$4.50	
Fixed	9.60	14.10
Total		$36.60

Nonmanufacturing costs are $6 a unit for variable items and $500,000 a year for fixed items. A foreign manufacturer has offered to purchase 10,000 units at $36 a unit and will pay all shipping charges. This order will not affect Perma-Frost's ability to serve its existing market, and it will not increase the firm's nonmanufacturing fixed costs. Its nonmanufacturing variable costs on the 10,000 units will be $1 a unit less than on units sold at the normal price.

Instructions

1. Prepare an analysis showing the net income or loss that would result from accepting this offer.
2. What other factors should be considered in deciding whether to accept or reject this offer?

CHAPTER

45

The accounting procedures discussed so far have dealt with the analysis, recording, summarization, and evaluation of business transactions after they have taken place. However, the stakes in modern business are so high that an alert manager can hardly take the chance of just waiting to see what happens. Instead, a manager tries to plan operations in advance with trends and prospects clearly in mind and to control every step of the work so that maximum profits will be earned.

BUDGETING SALES AND EXPENSES

BUDGETING

The process of planning and controlling the future operations of a business is called *budgeting*. The budget computations may be made in units of production, in dollars, or in a combination of both.

The accountant assists managers in the budgeting process by preparing analyses and estimates upon which the budget may be planned. Later, in the control phase of the process, the accountant prepares reports and compares the company's actual results with the budget plan to guide managers in exercising control.

The budgeting process plays a vital role in modern business. It establishes overall goals for an organization and sets up detailed plans for achieving these goals. It also provides a means of measuring the performance of individual units of the business and assessing the effectiveness of the managers who run the units.

FACTORS FAVORING SUCCESSFUL BUDGETING

Successful budgeting does not just happen. It must be carefully developed by following a number of principles and procedures.

1. The budget must reflect reasonably attainable goals for sales and expenses. If a budget contains goals that are obviously unattainable, it will not motivate operating personnel to do their best work. The budget plan should demand good performance but not the impossible.
2. The budget should be prepared from basic data reflecting past results, modified by expected future changes. A study of past results is a logical starting point for the budget. Of course, these past results must be modified to reflect changes in conditions that are anticipated during the budget period.
3. The budget period must be of reasonable length. The length of the budget period should allow for management's needs for control data and for the practical limitations involved in planning very far ahead. For example, operating budgets for sales, expenses, and manufacturing costs may be prepared in broad outline for a year ahead and in much greater detail for a three-month period.

4. **Those responsible for operating results should have a part in developing the budget.** If operating personnel at all levels take part in budget planning and accept the figures that are finally developed, they will be much more cooperative and the budget program is likely to be much more successful.

5. **Thorough review should be given budget proposals at successive management levels.** The proposals made by operating personnel must, of course, be reviewed by managers at different levels to detect and adjust any shortcomings before the budget is adopted.

6. **The budget should be formally adopted by top management and specifically communicated to operating personnel.** When all parts of the budget have been formally accepted by top management as the operating plan for the company, each operating unit should receive appropriate budgetary data for information and guidance.

7. **Frequent reports comparing actual results with the budget should be made.** During the period covered by the budget, reports should be presented often, and in considerable detail, comparing actual results with the budget figures for each operating responsibility. This is a job that the accountant must perform. (Such reports are discussed and illustrated in Chapter 47.)

ORGANIZATION FOR EFFECTIVE BUDGETING

Responsibility for budgeting must be clearly defined and assigned. Many companies have a budget committee composed of top managers in the sales, production, and financial areas. Often the chief accountant is designated budget director and provided with a staff to help prepare and administer the budget. The budget director need not, of course, be an accountant; but in any event, the accountant has an important part to play in preparing analyses of past operations and projecting the effects of proposed future operations.

The financial statements prepared by the Woodcraft Manufacturing Corporation at the end of 19Y2 are shown on pages 1066–1068 to help you understand the budget for 19Y3. Many sources of information must be used in developing a budget. However, one of the most important starting points in the budget process is to examine and analyze the results of operations for prior periods.

The specific details of budget preparation vary somewhat from company to company, but the procedures described in this chapter and the next chapter are typical of those used in many firms. As you study the procedures, notice that budget figures are first developed for individual areas such as sales, inventory, purchases of raw materials, and operating expenses. Then these amounts are brought together in order to draw up budgeted financial statements for the coming period, such as a budgeted income statement and a budgeted statement of cost of goods manufactured.

When the planning process is completed, the firm has a budget package consisting of detailed projections for each area of the business and for the company as a whole.

The various projections for income statement elements such as sales and expenses are usually referred to as the *operating budget,* while the projections for cash and other balance sheet items are usually known as the *financial budget*. The preparation of an operating budget at the Woodcraft Manufacturing Corporation is discussed in this chapter, and the development of a financial budget for the firm is covered in the next chapter. Keep in mind that the operating budget must be created first.

WOODCRAFT MANUFACTURING CORPORATION
Income Statement
Year Ended December 31, 19Y2

Exhibit B

Revenue			
Sales		$1,485,265.00	
Less Sales Returns and Allowances		10,195.00	
Net Sales			$1,475,070.00
Cost of Goods Sold			
Finished Goods Inventory, Jan. 1		$ 86,000.00	
Cost of Goods Manufactured (Schedule B-1)		895,244.29	
Total Goods Available		$ 981,244.29	
Less Finished Goods Inventory, Dec. 31		80,000.00	
Cost of Goods Sold			901,244.29
Gross Profit on Sales			$ 573,825.71
Operating Expenses			
Selling Expenses			
Sales Salaries Expense	$144,230.00		
Payroll Taxes Expense—Sales	12,615.85		
Delivery Expense	44,260.25		
Sales Supplies and Other Selling Expenses	23,710.15		
Advertising Expense	25,015.40		
Total Selling Expenses		$ 249,831.65	
Administrative Expenses			
Officers' Salaries Expense	$153,000.00		
Office Salaries Expense	49,500.00		
Payroll Taxes Expense—Administrative	17,655.30		
Office Supplies and Other Office Expenses	11,725.75		
Loss From Uncollectible Accounts	2,450.00		
Total Administrative Expenses		234,331.05	
Total Operating Expenses			484,162.70
Net Income From Operations			$ 89,663.01
Other Income			
Interest Income			265.00
Total Income for Year			$ 89,928.01
Other Expense			
Bond Interest Expense			6,000.00
Net Income Before Income Taxes			$ 83,928.01
Provision for Income Taxes			19,821.00
Net Income After Income Taxes (To Exhibit C)			$ 64,107.01

WOODCRAFT MANUFACTURING CORPORATION   *Exhibit C*
Statement of Retained Earnings
Year Ended December 31, 19Y2

Balance, Jan. 1		$152,192.35
Additions		
Net Income After Income Taxes (Exhibit B)		64,107.01
		$216,299.36
Deductions		
Dividends on Preferred Stock	$ 8,000.00	
Dividends on Common Stock	68,000.00	
Total Deductions		76,000.00
Balance, Dec. 31 (To Exhibit A)		$140,299.36

WOODCRAFT MANUFACTURING CORPORATION   *Schedule B-1*
Statement of Cost of Goods Manufactured
Year Ended December 31, 19Y2

Raw Materials			
Raw Materials Inventory, Jan. 1		$ 78,000.00	
Materials Purchases	$454,408.79		
Less Returns and Allowances	1,133.20		
Net Purchases		453,275.59	
Total Materials Available		$531,275.59	
Less Raw Materials Inventory, Dec. 31		75,000.00	
Raw Materials Used			$456,275.59
Direct Labor			250,140.65
Manufacturing Overhead			
Indirect Labor		$ 49,780.15	
Payroll Taxes—Factory		26,245.45	
Utilities—Factory		19,300.40	
Repairs and Maintenance—Factory		32,175.70	
Indirect Materials and Supplies		20,325.45	
Depreciation—Factory Bldg. and Equip.		12,000.00	
Insurance—Factory		13,350.60	
Property Taxes—Factory		13,650.30	
Total Manufacturing Overhead			186,828.05
Total Manufacturing Costs			$893,244.29
Add Work in Process Inventory, Jan. 1			32,000.00
			$925,244.29
Less Work in Process Inventory, Dec. 31			30,000.00
Cost of Goods Manufactured (To Exhibit B)			$895,244.29

WOODCRAFT MANUFACTURING CORPORATION
Balance Sheet
December 31, 19Y2

Assets

Current Assets			
Cash			$ 99,665.80
Accounts Receivable (Net)			168,184.25
Inventories			
Raw Materials		$ 75,000.00	
Work in Process		30,000.00	
Finished Goods		80,000.00	185,000.00
Prepaid Expenses			
Prepaid Insurance		$ 2,700.00	
Supplies on Hand		2,500.00	5,200.00
Total Current Assets			$458,050.05
Property, Plant, and Equipment			
Land		$ 30,000.00	
Factory Bldg. and Equipment	$233,600.00		
Less Accumulated Depreciation	44,000.00	189,600.00	
Total Prop., Plant, and Equip.			219,600.00
Total Assets			$677,650.05

Liabilities and Stockholders' Equity

Current Liabilities			
Accounts Payable		$ 85,220.79	
Income Taxes Payable		19,821.00	
Other Payables		7,308.90	
Total Current Liabilities			$112,350.69
Long-Term Liabilities			
12% Bonds Payable, 19Z4			50,000.00
Total Liabilities			$162,350.69
Stockholders' Equity			
8% Preferred Stock, $100 Par Value	$100,000.00		
Paid-in Capital in Excess of Par Value	6,000.00	$106,000.00	
Common Stock, No Par, $50 Stated Value	$250,000.00		
Paid-in Capital in Excess of Stated Value	19,000.00	269,000.00	
Retained Earnings (Exhibit C)		140,299.36	
Total Stockholders' Equity			515,299.36
Total Liabilities and Stockholders' Equity			$677,650.05

WOODCRAFT MANUFACTURING CORPORATION BUDGET FOR 19Y3

Suppose that the officers of the Woodcraft Manufacturing Corporation ask their budget director to prepare a budget covering operations and finances for the next year, 19Y3. The budget director begins by getting estimates of the firm's expected volume of sales from the sales managers. Then, once the sales budget is determined, the budget director is ready to help the production and operating managers draw up budgets for the manufacturing costs and operating expenses that will be incurred in obtaining these sales.

BUDGETING SALES

Developing a sales budget involves two elements: analysis of what has been done before and appraisal of future prospects.

Analyzing Prior Period Actual Sales

The accountant begins by preparing analyses of prior period sales. (In practice, this work is done toward the end of the current year before the final figures are known. The examples shown here are based on the figures for the full year, 19Y2.) Sales totals may be analyzed according to such aspects as individual salespeople, sales territories, customers, and products. A sales analysis by products is illustrated below.

info. from marketing department

WOODCRAFT MANUFACTURING CORPORATION
Analysis of Sales
Year Ended December 31, 19Y2

Product	Quantity Sold	Average Selling Price	Total Sales
Chairs			
Style D-11	6,000	$30	$ 180,000
Style D-12	15,000	28	420,000
Style D-15	17,500	26	455,000
Style D-21 (unpainted)	9,000	20	180,000
Total Chairs	47,500		$1,235,000
Tables and Desks*			250,265
Total Sales			$1,485,265

*Itemized data omitted.

The chair styles are listed in detail, and, in practice, the tables and desks would be also. However, in this illustration and in succeeding ones, information about the tables and desks is given in total only, to save space. The required data is obtained by analyzing sales invoices, which show all details of the products sold. If prices are stable during the year, the information can be assembled more easily from the finished goods inventory records, which would show the quantity of each item sold. These quantities can then be multiplied by the selling prices to get total sales values.

Forecasting Business Conditions for the Coming Period

While the accountant is analyzing past results, sales executives are weighing the business prospects for the coming period. In large firms the services of economists, statisticians, and market analysts may be obtained to help in this forecast.

Developing a Sales Budget

The managers of the sales department uses the analysis of past results and sales forecasts to prepare the sales budget. In the process they must decide upon the probable number of units of each product to be sold and the probable average unit selling price. The sales budget may be presented as shown below in a form resembling the analysis of sales for the past period.

WOODCRAFT MANUFACTURING CORPORATION
Sales Budget
Year 19Y3

Product	Quantity To Be Sold	Average Selling Price	Estimated Sales Revenue
Chairs			
Style D-11	7,500	$29.50	$ 221,250.00
Style D-12	16,500	27.80	458,700.00
Style D-15	18,500	26.20	484,700.00
Style D-21 (unpainted)	9,500	20.00	190,000.00
Total Chairs	52,000		$1,354,650.00
Tables and Desks*			300,000.00
Total Budgeted Sales			$1,654,650.00

*Itemized data omitted.

BUDGETING PRODUCTION

Before the factory budget can be prepared, the number of units to be produced must be determined. This total includes the number of units to be sold, plus or minus any desired change in the ending inventories of finished goods and work in process.

Analysis of the Beginning Finished Goods Inventory

When all entries have been posted, the accounting records show the balance of finished goods on hand at the end of each month during the previous year. Subsidiary ledger records for each item provide detailed information on quantities and costs by product. From this data the accountant prepares the analysis of the finished goods inventory. This analysis shows for each product the quantity in inventory, its unit cost, and the total cost of finished goods at the end of the previous year (which becomes the beginning inventory for the year being budgeted). The analysis of the finished goods inventory for the Woodcraft Manufacturing Corporation is shown on page 1071.

Budgeting the Ending Finished Goods Inventory

Next, management decides how many units of each item it would like to have in the finished goods inventory at the end of the period, after considering expected movements of costs and selling prices and the trend of future sales. These quantities are then multiplied by estimates of the cost of manufacturing the various products to determine the anticipated total cost of each item. Finally the individual totals are added together to find the expected overall cost of the ending

WOODCRAFT MANUFACTURING CORPORATION
Analysis of Finished Goods Inventory
December 31, 19Y2

Product	Quantity	Unit Cost	Total Cost
Chairs			
Style D-11	600	$17.50	$10,500.00
Style D-12	1,500	16.60	24,900.00
Style D-15	1,650	15.80	26,070.00
Style D-21 (unpainted)	750	12.10	9,075.00
Total Chairs	4,500		$70,545.00
Tables and Desks*			9,455.00
Total Finished Goods			$80,000.00

*Itemized data omitted.

comes from marketing dept.

finished goods inventory. The budget for the ending finished goods inventory that was prepared at the Woodcraft Manufacturing Corporation is illustrated below.

WOODCRAFT MANUFACTURING CORPORATION
Budgeted Finished Goods Inventory
December 31, 19Y3

Product	Quantity	Unit Cost	Total Cost
Chairs			
Style D-11	700	$17.36	$12,152.00
Style D-12	1,550	16.44	25,482.00
Style D-15	1,600	15.66	25,056.00
Style D-21 (unpainted)	600	11.96	7,176.00
Total Chairs	4,450		$69,866.00
Tables and Desks*			14,134.00
Total Finished Goods Budgeted			$84,000.00

*Itemized data omitted.

Budgeting the Ending Work in Process Inventory

Besides the number of finished units to be produced, the factory budget must also include changes in the work in process inventory that are expected between the beginning and end of the budget period. The beginning work in process inventory can be analyzed from process cost of production reports for each department and from job order cost sheets. The desired ending work in process inventory can be approximated by factory management. In Woodcraft's case, management decided to let the work in process inventory increase slightly, from $30,000 at the beginning of 19Y3 to $35,000 at the end of the year.

Determination of Budgeted Units To Be Produced

The next step in the budgeting procedure is to add the desired ending quantity of the finished goods inventory to the budgeted sales in units to get the total units required. The number of units in the beginning finished goods inventory is subtracted from this total to determine the number that must be produced. The computations for the four chair styles made by Woodcraft are illustrated below. Quantities for the tables and desks would be worked out in the same way.

After the company has determined the number of units to be produced in the coming period, the process of budgeting the cost of goods manufactured can begin. This process will now be described.

WOODCRAFT MANUFACTURING CORPORATION
Budgeted Quantities To Be Produced *in units*
Year Ending December 31, 19Y3

Finished Goods:	D-11	D-12	D-15	D-21
Desired Ending Inventory	700	1,550	1,600	600
Budgeted Sales	7,500	16,500	18,500	9,500
Total	8,200	18,050	20,100	10,100
Beginning Inventory	600	1,500	1,650	750
Quantity To Be Produced	7,600	16,550	18,450	9,350

consult w/ production

BUDGETING THE COST OF GOODS MANUFACTURED

The cost of goods manufactured budget is an important part of the operating budget and must be developed carefully. The accountant begins this process by analyzing the operations of prior periods.

Analysis of Operations for Prior Periods

The cost accounting records described in previous chapters are used in making analyses of prior period operations. These analyses serve as a guide for budgeting. For the chairs, process cost accounting records indicate the cost in each department broken down by cost elements—materials, labor, and manufacturing overhead. For the tables and desks, job order cost sheets are available showing the costs of each job. Finished goods inventory records for each product are also available and show the results for the entire period.

The Raw Materials Budget

Once the schedule of budgeted quantities to be produced and the budget of the ending work in process inventory have been prepared, the forecast of raw materials to be used is developed. Based on the analysis of the beginning raw materials inventory, the desired level of the ending raw materials inventory, and the raw materials to be used, the necessary net raw materials purchases can easily be estimated. Net purchases for 19Y3 are forecast to be $519,000. Purchases returns and allowances are estimated on the basis of past experience to be about ¼ of 1 percent of net purchases, or approximately $1,300. Thus gross purchases are estimated at $520,300 ($519,000 + $1,300). The raw materials budget of the Woodcraft Manufacturing Corporation is shown on page 1073.

WOODCRAFT MANUFACTURING CORPORATION
Raw Materials Budget
Year Ending December 31, 19Y3

production (handwritten, left margin)

last years actual bs (handwritten, right margin)

estimates (handwritten)

Raw Materials		
Raw Materials Inventory, Jan. 1		$ 75,000
Materials Purchases	$520,300	
Less Returns and Allowances	1,300	
Net Purchases		519,000
Total Materials Available		$594,000
Less Raw Materials Inventory, Dec. 31		82,000
Raw Materials To Be Used		$512,000

The Direct Labor Budget

Woodcraft's direct labor budget for 19Y3 is estimated at $284,000. This estimate is based on the scheduled production and the estimate of each type of labor required for each unit of product, along with the forecast of wage rates.

The Manufacturing Overhead Budget

The raw materials budget and the direct labor budget are prepared after the appropriate data concerning production totals and unit costs has been gathered. Since these costs are considered to be variable costs, the total of each of these two elements is in direct proportion to the production volume.

As you have already learned, however, not all manufacturing overhead cost items are variable. Some overhead costs, such as manufacturing supplies, vary substantially with production. Other overhead elements are fixed for the period, almost regardless of the volume of production. The accountant must carefully study the anticipated behavior of each cost item in order to assess its probable variability. The manufacturing overhead budget data for the Woodcraft Manufacturing Corporation for 19Y3 is shown below.

production (handwritten, left margin)

WOODCRAFT MANUFACTURING CORPORATION
Manufacturing Overhead Budget
Year Ending December 31, 19Y3

Manufacturing Overhead	
Indirect Labor	$ 55,400
Payroll Taxes—Factory	30,970
Utilities—Factory	21,500
Repairs and Maintenance—Factory	30,000
Indirect Materials and Supplies	23,300
Depreciation—Factory Bldg. and Equip.	15,500
Insurance—Factory	14,400
Property Taxes—Factory	19,700
Total Manufacturing Overhead	$210,770

Note that this budget is based on the assumption that a specific number of units of product will be manufactured. As such, it is a useful tool in planning for the future. However, if the actual volume of output is different from that anticipated, this fixed budget is not a good tool for measuring manufacturing costs. Another possibility is to work out a flexible budget, which consists of budgeted amounts for different possible volumes of production. The flexible budget has an advantage as a control device because the appropriate volume level figures from this budget can be used for comparison with actual results. The flexible budget is discussed briefly in Chapter 47 in connection with internal reports for management and is covered thoroughly in cost accounting textbooks.

Development of the Cost of Goods Manufactured Budget

When the estimates of materials, labor, and overhead for the anticipated production have been completed, the accountant summarizes them in the form of a budgeted statement of cost of goods manufactured. This type of statement is illustrated below.

Schedule B-1 represents the beginning of a report package of projected financial statements as they might appear at the end of the year if the budget

WOODCRAFT MANUFACTURING CORPORATION Schedule B-1
Budgeted Statement of Cost of Goods Manufactured
Year Ending December 31, 19Y3

Raw Materials		
Raw Materials Inventory, Jan. 1		$ 75,000
Materials Purchases	$520,300	
Less Returns and Allowances	1,300	
Net Purchases		519,000
Total Materials Available		$ 594,000
Less Raw Materials Inventory, Dec. 31		82,000
Raw Materials Used		$ 512,000
Direct Labor		284,000
Manufacturing Overhead		
Indirect Labor	$ 55,400	
Payroll Taxes—Factory	30,970	
Utilities—Factory	21,500	
Repairs and Maintenance—Factory	30,000	
Indirect Materials and Supplies	23,300	
Depreciation—Factory Bldg. and Equip.	15,500	
Insurance—Factory	14,400	
Property Taxes—Factory	19,700	
Total Manufacturing Overhead		210,770
Total Manufacturing Costs		$1,006,770
Add Work in Process Inventory, Jan. 1		30,000
		$1,036,770
Less Work in Process Inventory, Dec. 31		35,000
Cost of Goods Manufactured (To Exhibit B)		$1,001,770

plans are carried out exactly. Other statements are developed until the master budget is completed.

BUDGETED SCHEDULE OF OPERATING EXPENSES

The analysis of past operations provides a useful starting point for budgeting operating expenses as well as for budgeting manufacturing costs. Detailed departmental expense analyses are prepared for the sales and administrative department heads and supervisors.

Based on the sales and production budgets, the executives in charge of these operations consider the volume of sales and administrative work to be accomplished during the coming period. The amount of work to be done suggests the number of personnel required (such as salespeople and office workers). Salary scales are appraised and costs of proposed increases determined. Related supplies and other costs of selling, distributing, and accounting for the proposed activities are also estimated.

All this data is then combined into detailed budgets for the individual sales and administrative departments. The overall result is presented in schedules of selling and administrative expenses as a part of the budget report package. The figures determined by the Woodcraft Manufacturing Corporation for 19Y3 are shown below in a single schedule of budgeted operating expenses.

WOODCRAFT MANUFACTURING CORPORATION *Schedule B-2*
Budgeted Schedule of Operating Expenses
Year Ending December 31, 19Y3

Operating Expenses		
Selling Expenses		
Sales Salaries Expense	$160,000	
Payroll Taxes Expense—Sales	14,000	
Delivery Expense	49,000	
Sales Supplies and Other Selling Expenses	25,700	
Advertising Expense	27,000	
Total Selling Expenses		$275,700
Administrative Expenses		
Officers' Salaries Expense	$168,000	
Office Salaries Expense	52,000	
Payroll Taxes Expense—Admin.	18,100	
Office Supplies and Other Office Expenses	17,500	
Loss From Uncollectible Accounts	3,286	
Total Administrative Expenses		258,886
Total Operating Expenses (To Exhibit B)		$534,586

BUDGETED INCOME STATEMENT

In order to project the income statement as it might appear at the end of the coming year, 19Y3, estimates of sales returns and allowances, interest income, bond interest expense, and the required provision for income taxes are needed.

Sales Returns and Allowances

An analysis of records from prior years shows that there have been fewer merchandise returns but that sales allowances have been substantial. The analysis reveals that in prior years gross sales have been about 100.7 percent of net sales. Assuming that the same relationship will continue in 19Y3, the gross sales budgeted of $1,654,650 is divided by 100.7 percent to determine estimated net sales of $1,643,150. (This figure is rounded off to the nearest ten dollars for convenience.) The difference between gross and net sales, $11,500, is the estimated amount of sales returns and allowances for the year.

Interest Income

The amount of interest income is so small at Woodcraft that little time is spent in estimating it. A total of $300 is assumed to be a reasonable estimate of interest income for 19Y3.

Bond Interest Expense

On January 1, 19Y3, the face value of the 12 percent bonds outstanding is $50,000. Management plans to issue $20,000 more at par value on April 1, the

---

WOODCRAFT MANUFACTURING CORPORATION   *Exhibit B*
Budgeted Income Statement
Year Ending December 31, 19Y3

Revenue		
Sales — *Total of Sales budgets*		$1,654,650
Less Sales Returns and Allowances- *estimates*		11,500
Net Sales		$1,643,150
Cost of Goods Sold		
Finished Goods Inventory, Jan. 1 *(from last yrs. BS pg. 1074)*	$ 80,000	
Cost of Goods Manufactured (Schedule B-1)	1,001,770	
Total Goods Available	$1,081,770	
Less Finished Goods Inventory, Dec. 31 *(estimate)*	84,000	
Cost of Goods Sold		997,770
Gross Profit on Sales		$ 645,380
Operating Expenses		
Selling Expenses *(pg. 1075)*	$ 275,700	
Administrative Expenses	258,886	
Total Operating Expenses (Schedule B-2)		534,586
Net Income From Operations		$ 110,794
Other Income		
Interest Income		300
Total Income for Year		$ 111,094
Other Expense		
Bond Interest Expense		7,800
Net Income Before Income Taxes		$ 103,294
Provision for Income Taxes		27,500
Net Income After Income Taxes (To Exhibit C)		$ 75,794

---

next interest date. Interest expense will be 12 percent of $50,000 for a year ($6,000) plus 12 percent of $20,000 for nine-twelfths of a year ($1,800). The total is $7,800 for the year.

Provision for Income Taxes

The last estimate required is that of income taxes. Assume that the budgeted income statement shows net income before income taxes of $103,294. When the accountant makes the tax estimate—$27,500 in this case—the budgeted income statement can be completed, as shown on page 1076.

PRINCIPLES AND PROCEDURES SUMMARY

The preparation of the operating budget begins with an estimate of sales. Managers analyze past operations and forecast expected future business conditions. In large firms, economists, statisticians, market analysts, and others help managers make such forecasts. From this data, sales managers develop a budget of sales for the coming year.

Next, estimates are made for the desired inventories of finished goods and work in process. Again, the accountant's analyses of past results provide information used by managers to reach decisions.

After sales and inventory estimates are decided on, manufacturing costs are determined through analyses of past results and expected cost factors. Records of selling and administrative expenses are studied to obtain detailed information on past performance, and future needs are estimated. Detailed departmental budgets are then prepared for selling and administrative activities.

The final step is the preparation of a projected income statement for the coming year, reflecting the results of the budget plan.

MANAGERIAL IMPLICATIONS

Few tools are as useful to managers as budgets. Budgets force everyone in the organization to look ahead. In this way, managers can make definite plans, see possible problems, and take corrective action if necessary. Budgets also provide a means for coordinating activities and plans so that every department in the organization knows what the other departments are doing. This aids each department in recognizing what the common objectives and goals are. The sales and expense budgets also lay the groundwork for planning the acquisition of plant and equipment, providing for cash that will be needed, and arranging for new capital.

REVIEW QUESTIONS

1. What is budgeting?
2. Should the budget represent an ideal goal or one that can reasonably be attained?
3. Why is an analysis of past results necessary in preparing a budget?

4. What should be the length of the budget period?
5. Why is it necessary for various levels of management to review the budget?
6. Who is responsible for preparing reports comparing actual performance with the budget?
7. Should operating personnel play a role in developing the budget? Explain.
8. What is a financial budget?
9. What is an operating budget?
10. Why is the sales budget the first budget to be prepared?
11. How is the number of units to be produced determined?
12. Explain how the finished goods inventory budget is prepared.
13. What general approach is used to budget manufacturing overhead?
14. What is a flexible budget?
15. How would a firm budget sales salaries?
16. Suppose that you are asked to compute the budget for next year's factory repairs and maintenance. Explain how you would go about doing so.
17. How would a firm budget depreciation of its factory equipment for the next year?
18. How would a firm estimate the budgeted amount of direct labor for the next year?

MANAGERIAL DISCUSSION QUESTIONS

1. Explain how managers use budgeting procedures as an aid in coordinating activities.
2. At a meeting of a firm's budget committee, one of the directors says that it is time to set some unusually high performance goals in order to provide "plenty of challenge" to the employees. What do you think of this approach to standard setting?
3. "Once the firm's budget is adopted, the employees should be told what the company expects everyone to accomplish." Do you agree or disagree with this statement? Why?
4. In an effort to reduce the amount of time required to prepare a budget, someone has proposed that top management have confidence in its experience and judgment and eliminate reviews at every management level. Is this a sound proposal? Why or why not?
5. How do managers arrive at a sales budget for the year?
6. Evaluate the operating budget prepared in this chapter as a useful tool for management in controlling costs.

EXERCISES

EXERCISE 45-1 **Budgeting sales.** During 19X2 the Merrill Company sold 3,000 units of a product for $18.20 a unit. It is estimated that during 19X3 the price will increase by 6 percent and the number of units sold will decrease by 4 percent. What is the expected sales volume (number of units) and the expected sales revenue of the product for 19X3?

EXERCISE 45-2   **Budgeting the number of units to be produced.** During 19X1 the Hadley Corporation sold 3,000 units of a product. The ending inventory on December 31, 19X1, was 263 units. It is expected that the number of units sold will increase by 20 percent in 19X2. Management wants to have an ending inventory of units that is in proportion to the changes in the sales of units during 19X2. How many units of the product should Hadley plan to produce in 19X2?

EXERCISE 45-3   **Budgeting direct labor.** During 19X1 the assembling department of the Martinez Company produced 100,000 units of product and had direct labor costs of $400,000. During 19X2 estimated production will be 109,000 units. Wage rates are expected to increase by 5 percent. Compute the direct labor budget for this department for 19X2.

EXERCISE 45-4   **Budgeting the salaries of factory clerks.** During 19X4 the salaries of the factory clerks at the McKenzie Corporation amounted to $116,000. A total of 20,000 units were produced. Production for 19X5 is budgeted at 23,000 units. As a result, one additional factory clerk will be employed at a salary of $14,000, beginning July 1, 19X5. Salaries of the other factory clerks will be increased by 8 percent. Compute the firm's budgeted salaries for factory clerks for 19X5.

EXERCISE 45-5   **Budgeting depreciation.** During 19X1 the Gilbert Company had depreciation of $60,000 on its factory equipment. This amount represented straight-line depreciation at a rate of 10 percent on a total equipment cost of $600,000. Included in the $600,000 total for equipment is the $80,000 cost of a machine that will be fully depreciated on May 1, 19X2. New equipment costing $120,000 will be purchased and put into use on July 1, 19X2. Compute the total budgeted depreciation for 19X2.

EXERCISE 45-6   **Budgeting indirect labor.** During 19X1 the Thunder Bay Corporation had indirect labor totaling $264,000. Of that amount, $104,000 represented the fixed costs of supervisors, timekeepers, and similar types of employees. The other $160,000 represented variable costs. During 19X2 the volume of units produced is expected to increase by 5 percent over 19X1. All wages and salaries will increase by an average of 8 percent for the year. Compute the budget for indirect labor for 19X2.

EXERCISE 45-7   **Budgeting federal income taxes.** The Landis Corporation is expected to have a net income of $609,000 for 19X3. Its federal income taxes will be computed at the following rates: 15 percent on the first $25,000 of net income, 20 percent on the next $25,000, 30 percent on the next $25,000, 40 percent on the next $25,000, and 46 percent on all net income in excess of $100,000. How much should the firm budget for federal income taxes for 19X3?

EXERCISE 45-8   **Budgeting direct materials.** During 19X1 the Hart Company produced 100,000 units of a product at a total cost of $750,000 for direct materials. It is forecast that during 19X2, 108,000 units will be produced. The prices of the raw materials are expected to increase by 9 percent for each unit, but it is also expected that more efficient production will reduce the quantity of materials needed for each unit by 2 percent. Compute the direct materials budget for 19X2.

EXERCISE 45-9   **Budgeting the loss from uncollectible accounts.** During 19X2 the Thurgood Company had a loss of $16,000 from uncollectible accounts. Sales were $3,200,000. During 19X3 sales are expected to be $3,520,000. The company estimates that its rate of uncollectible accounts will decrease by 10 percent because of improved credit procedures. Compute the budget for the loss from uncollectible accounts for 19X3.

EXERCISE 45-10   **Budgeting the expense for advertising.** During 19X1 the Greenwald Company had advertising expense totaling $160,000. Of this amount, $120,000 represented contractual advertising with a national magazine. The contract covers 19X1 and 19X2 and requires payment of $120,000 each year. The other $40,000 spent in 19X1 was for completely discretionary advertising. Greenwald plans to increase its discretionary advertising by 25 percent during 19X2. Compute the advertising expense budget for 19X2.

PROBLEMS

PROBLEM 45-1   **Preparing a schedule of budgeted quantities to be produced and a budget of raw materials purchases.** The Durabilt Company manufactures a single product. Each unit requires the following raw materials.

ITEM	QUANTITY	UNIT COST	TOTAL
Frames	1	$4.00	$4.00
Panels	4	1.50	6.00
Assembly Units	1	2.85	2.85

Beginning inventories on January 1, 19X2, are expected to be as follows.

Raw Materials
  Frames, 2,200 at $4.00 a frame
  Panels, 8,800 at $1.50 a panel
  Assembly Units, 2,200 at $2.85
  a unit

Finished Goods, 3,000 units
Work in Process, 2,000 units
  (all materials added)

Estimated sales for the month of January 19X2 are 3,000 units; for February, 2,200 units; and for March, 1,600 units. Management wants to have enough units on hand in the finished goods inventory to meet expected sales for the following month. Management also wants to have raw materials on hand equal to the following month's production requirements. Work in process should remain almost constant.

Instructions   1. Prepare a schedule of budgeted quantities to be produced for the months of January and February 19X2.
2. Prepare a budget of raw materials purchases for January. Include both quantities and costs, and show the purchases in total and for each type of material.

PROBLEM 45-2

Preparing a schedule of budgeted quantities to be produced and a raw materials budget. The Eagle Corporation manufactures a single product. Information about the raw materials required and the expected beginning inventories on February 1, 19X2, appears below. The following sales forecast has been made for the months of February through April 19X2: February, 4,000 units; March, 3,500 units; and April, 3,000 units. Each month the firm needs to have enough units on hand in the finished goods inventory to meet expected sales for the following month. The firm also needs to have raw materials on hand that are equal to the following month's production requirements. Work in process should remain almost constant.

RAW MATERIALS REQUIRED (PER UNIT)

ITEM	QUANTITY	UNIT COST	TOTAL
Frames	2	$3.40	$6.80
Walls	3	0.80	2.40
Finishing Units	1	6.00	6.00

EXPECTED BEGINNING INVENTORIES ON FEBRUARY 1, 19X2

Raw Materials
   Frames, 7,000 at $3.40 a frame
   Walls, 10,500 at $0.80 a wall
   Finishing Units, 3,500 at $6.00 a unit
Finished Goods, 4,000 units
Work in Process, 2,000 units (all materials added)

Instructions

1. Prepare a schedule of budgeted quantities to be produced for the months of February and March 19X2.
2. Prepare a raw materials budget for February 19X2. Use one column for each type of material and one column for the total.

PROBLEM 45-3

Preparing a budgeted income statement. The New Image Corporation sells high-quality film and video tape for use by professional photographers. The firm's income statement for the year ended December 31, 19X3, and estimated changes for 19X4 appear below and on page 1082.

Instructions

Prepare a budgeted income statement for the New Image Corporation for 19X4. Round off each item to the nearest dollar.

ESTIMATES OF PROBABLE CHANGES IN 19X4

a. Sales are expected to increase 6 percent in physical volume at an average increase in price of 5 percent.
b. Merchandise purchases are expected to increase 6 percent in physical volume at an average increase in cost of 3 percent. Ending merchandise inventory is estimated at $1,212,000.
c. Sales salaries are expected to increase 6 percent, other selling expenses 5 percent, and delivery expense 4 percent. Rent expense is expected to be the same as in 19X3, and advertising expense is budgeted at $36,000.

d. Officers' salaries are expected to remain the same as in 19X3; office salaries and other office expenses are expected to increase 6 percent. The loss from uncollectible accounts is estimated at the same percentage of net sales as in 19X3 (0.6359 percent).

e. Bond interest expense will remain the same as in 19X3.

f. Income taxes are expected to be 15 percent of the first $25,000 of net income before taxes, 20 percent of the next $25,000, 30 percent of the next $25,000, 40 percent of the next $25,000, and 46 percent of all net income above $100,000.

NEW IMAGE CORPORATION
Income Statement
Year Ended December 31, 19X3

Revenue			
Net Sales			$5,520,000
Cost of Goods Sold			
Merchandise Inventory, Jan. 1		$1,125,000	
Merchandise Purchases		4,176,000	
Total Merchandise Available		$5,301,000	
Less Merchandise Inventory, Dec. 31		1,170,000	
Cost of Goods Sold			4,131,000
Gross Profit on Sales			$1,389,000
Operating Expenses			
Selling Expenses			
Sales Salaries Expense	$472,800		
Rent Expense	43,200		
Delivery Expense	29,280		
Advertising Expense	33,120		
Other Selling Expenses	117,600		
Total Selling Expenses		$ 696,000	
Administrative Expenses			
Officers' Salaries Expense	$150,000		
Office Salaries and Other Office Expenses	255,900		
Loss From Uncollectible Accounts	35,100		
Total Administrative Expenses		441,000	
Total Operating Expenses			1,137,000
Net Income From Operations			$ 252,000
Other Expense			
Bond Interest Expense			12,000
Net Income Before Income Taxes			$ 240,000
Provision for Income Taxes			60,600
Net Income After Income Taxes			$ 179,400

PROBLEM 45-4 **Preparing a budgeted statement of cost of goods manufactured and a budgeted income statement.** The Gold Seal Products Corporation manufactures three types of ladders. A condensed income statement and a condensed statement of cost of goods manufactured, both for the year ended December 31, 19X5, are shown below and on page 1084. Budget schedules and other supplementary data for 19X6 appear on pages 1084 and 1085.

Instructions Prepare the following schedule and statements for the year 19X6.

1. Budgeted schedule of quantities to be produced.
2. Budgeted statement of cost of goods manufactured (condensed).
3. Budgeted income statement (condensed).

GOLD SEAL PRODUCTS CORPORATION
Condensed Income Statement
Year Ended December 31, 19X5

Revenue		
Sales		$787,800
Less Sales Returns and Allowances		7,800
Net Sales		$780,000
Cost of Goods Sold		
Finished Goods Inventory, Jan. 1	$ 62,400	
Cost of Goods Manufactured	538,600	
Total Goods Available	$601,000	
Less Finished Goods Inventory, Dec. 31	71,000	
Cost of Goods Sold		530,000
Gross Profit on Sales		$250,000
Operating Expenses		
Selling Expenses	$ 98,000	
Administrative Expenses	82,000	
Total Operating Expenses		180,000
Net Income From Operations		$ 70,000
Other Income		
Interest Income		4,000
Total Income for Year		$ 74,000
Other Expense		
Organization Costs Written Off		2,000
Net Income Before Income Taxes		$ 72,000
Provision for Income Taxes		21,400
Net Income After Income Taxes		$ 50,600

GOLD SEAL PRODUCTS CORPORATION
Condensed Statement of Cost of Goods Manufactured
Year Ended December 31, 19X5

Raw Materials		
Raw Materials Inventory, Jan. 1	$ 43,400	
Materials Purchases	266,600	
Total Materials Available	$310,000	
Less Raw Materials Inventory, Dec. 31	45,000	
Raw Materials Used		$265,000
Direct Labor		179,500
Manufacturing Overhead		96,300
Total Manufacturing Costs		$540,800
Add Work in Process Inventory, Jan. 1		22,000
		$562,800
Less Work in Process Inventory, Dec. 31		24,200
Cost of Goods Manufactured		$538,600

GOLD SEAL PRODUCTS CORPORATION
Analysis of Finished Goods Inventory
December 31, 19X5

Product	Quantity	Unit Cost	Total Cost
Ladders			
Type 112	5,750	$ 5.26	$30,250*
Type 224	2,500	7.90	19,750
Type 336	1,750	12.00	21,000
Total Ladders	10,000		
Total Finished Goods Inventory			$71,000

*Rounded off.

GOLD SEAL PRODUCTS CORPORATION
Budgeted Finished Goods Inventory
December 31, 19X6

Product	Quantity	Unit Cost	Total Cost
Ladders			
Type 112	6,500	$ 5.60	$36,400
Type 224	2,500	8.40	21,000
Type 336	1,500	12.60	18,900
Total Ladders	10,500		
Total Finished Goods Budgeted			$76,300

GOLD SEAL PRODUCTS CORPORATION
Sales Budget
Year 19X6

Product	Quantity To Be Sold	Average Selling Price	Estimated Sales Revenue
Ladders			
Type 112	51,250	$ 8.00	$410,000
Type 224	20,000	12.00	240,000
Type 336	12,000	18.00	216,000
Total Ladders	83,250		
Total Budgeted Sales			$866,000

SUPPLEMENTARY DATA FOR 19X6

a. Total selling expenses are expected to increase 6 percent over 19X5.
b. Total administrative expenses are expected to increase 4 percent over 19X5.
c. Sales returns and allowances are expected to amount to 1 percent of budgeted gross sales.
d. Interest income is estimated to be $2,700.
e. Organization costs written off will be the same as in 19X5.
f. Net purchases of raw materials for 19X6 are estimated at $303,900; and purchases returns and allowances are estimated at $1,200.
g. Estimated direct labor to be used in 19X6 is $201,300; and estimated manufacturing overhead is $109,500.
h. It is expected that the cost of the raw materials inventory as of December 31, 19X6, will be $3,000 more than the cost as of December 31, 19X5.
i. It is expected that the number of units in the work in process inventory as of December 31, 19X6, will remain the same as the number of units on December 31, 19X5, but the cost will increase $1,800.
j. The provision for federal income taxes should be based on 15 percent of the first $25,000 of net income before taxes, 20 percent of the next $25,000, 30 percent of the next $25,000, 40 percent of the next $25,000, and 46 percent of all net income above $100,000.

ALTERNATE PROBLEMS

PROBLEM 45-1A **Preparing a schedule of budgeted quantities to be produced and a budget of raw materials purchases.** The Russell Company manufactures a single product. Each unit requires the following raw materials.

ITEM	QUANTITY	UNIT COST	TOTAL
Material K-4	2	$3.40	$6.80
Material K-12	3	0.80	2.40
Material L-4	1	6.00	6.00

Beginning inventories on January 1, 19X2, are expected to be as follows.

Raw Materials
  K-4, 7,000 at $3.40 each
  K-12, 10,500 at $0.80 each
  L-4, 3,500 at $6.00 each
Finished Goods, 4,000 units
Work in Process, 2,000 units (all materials added)

Estimated sales for the month of January 19X2 are 4,000 units; for February, 3,500 units; and for March, 3,000 units. Management wants to have enough units on hand in the finished goods inventory to meet expected sales for the following month. Management also wants to have raw materials on hand equal to production requirements for the following month. Work in process should remain almost constant.

Instructions
1. Prepare a schedule of budgeted quantities to be produced for the months of January and February 19X2.
2. Prepare a budget of raw materials purchases for January. Include both quantities and costs, and show the purchases in total and for each type of material.

PROBLEM 45-2A **Preparing a schedule of budgeted quantities to be produced and a raw materials budget.** The Fox Corporation manufactures a single product. The raw materials required for each unit and the beginning inventories on January 1, 19X2, are shown below. The following sales forecast has been made for the first quarter of 19X2: January, 3,000 units; February, 2,200 units; and March, 1,600 units. Each month the firm needs to have enough units on hand in the finished goods inventory to meet expected sales for the following month. The firm also needs to have raw materials on hand that are equal to the following month's production requirements. Work in process should remain almost constant.

RAW MATERIALS REQUIRED (PER UNIT)

ITEM	QUANTITY	UNIT COST	TOTAL
Frames	1	$4.00	$4.00
Walls	4	1.50	6.00
Assembly Units	1	2.85	2.85

EXPECTED BEGINNING INVENTORIES ON JANUARY 1, 19X2

Raw Materials
  Frames, 2,200 at $4.00 a frame
  Walls, 8,800 at $1.50 a wall
  Assembly Units, 2,200 at $2.85 a unit
Finished Goods, 3,000 units
Work in Process, 2,000 units (all materials added)

Instructions
1. Prepare a schedule of budgeted quantities to be produced for the months of January and February 19X2.
2. Prepare a raw materials budget for January 19X2. Use one column for each type of material and one column for the total.

Preparing a budgeted income statement. The Vitality Corporation sells exercise bicycles and other fitness equipment. The firm's income statement for the year ended December 31, 19X1, and estimated changes for 19X2 appear below and on page 1088.

Instructions Prepare a budgeted income statement for the Vitality Corporation for 19X2. Round off each item to the nearest dollar.

VITALITY CORPORATION
Income Statement
Year Ended December 31, 19X1

Revenue			
Net Sales			$1,840,000
Cost of Goods Sold			
Merchandise Inventory, Jan. 1		$ 375,000	
Merchandise Purchases		1,392,000	
Total Merchandise Available for Sale		$1,767,000	
Less Merchandise Inventory, Dec. 31		390,000	
Cost of Goods Sold			1,377,000
Gross Profit on Sales			$ 463,000
Operating Expenses			
Selling Expenses			
Sales Salaries Expense	$157,600		
Rent Expense	14,400		
Delivery Expense	9,760		
Advertising Expense	11,040		
Other Selling Expenses	39,200		
Total Selling Expenses		$ 232,000	
Administrative Expenses			
Officers' Salaries Expense	$ 50,000		
Office Salaries and Other Office Expenses	85,300		
Loss From Uncollectible Accounts	11,700		
Total Administrative Expenses		147,000	
Total Operating Expenses			379,000
Net Income From Operations			$ 84,000
Other Expense			
Bond Interest Expense			4,000
Net Income Before Income Taxes			$ 80,000
Provision for Income Taxes			20,200
Net Income After Income Taxes			$ 59,800

ESTIMATES OF PROBABLE CHANGES IN 19X2

a. Sales are expected to increase 6 percent in physical volume at an average increase in price of 5 percent.

b. Merchandise purchases are expected to increase 6 percent in physical volume at an average increase in cost of 4 percent. Ending merchandise inventory is estimated at $405,000.

c. Sales salaries are expected to increase 7 percent, other selling expenses 5 percent, and delivery expense 4 percent. Rent expense is expected to be the same as in 19X1, and advertising expense is budgeted at $12,000.

d. Officers' salaries are expected to remain the same as in 19X1; office salaries and other office expenses are expected to increase 6 percent. The loss from uncollectible accounts is estimated at the same percentage of net sales as in 19X1 (0.6359 percent).

e. Bond interest expense will remain the same as in 19X1.

f. Income taxes are expected to be 15 percent of the first $25,000 of net income before taxes, 20 percent of the next $25,000, 30 percent of the next $25,000, 40 percent of the next $25,000, and 46 percent of all net income over $100,000.

PROBLEM 45-4A **Preparing a budgeted statement of cost of goods manufactured and a budgeted income statement.** The Silver Star Products Corporation manufactures three types of tool chests. A condensed income statement and a condensed statement of cost of goods manufactured, both for the year ended December 31, 19X5, are shown on page 1089. Budget schedules and other supplementary data for 19X6 appear below and on page 1090.

Instructions Prepare the following schedule and statements for the year 19X6.

1. Budgeted schedule of quantities to be produced.
2. Budgeted statement of cost of goods manufactured (condensed).
3. Budgeted income statement (condensed).

SUPPLEMENTARY DATA FOR 19X6

a. Total selling expenses are expected to increase 5 percent over 19X5.
b. Total administrative expenses are expected to increase 4 percent over 19X5.
c. Sales returns are expected to amount to 1 percent of budgeted gross sales.
d. Interest income is estimated to be $8,100.
e. Organization costs written off will be the same as in 19X5.
f. Net purchases of raw materials for 19X6 are estimated at $911,700, and purchases returns and allowances are estimated at $3,600.
g. Estimated direct labor to be used in 19X6 is $603,900, and estimated manufacturing overhead is $328,500.
h. It is expected that the cost of the raw materials inventory as of December 31, 19X6, will be $9,000 more than the cost as of December 31, 19X5.
i. It is expected that the number of units in the work in process inventory as of December 31, 19X6, will remain the same as the number of units on December 31, 19X5, but the cost will increase $5,400.
j. The provision for federal income taxes should be based on 15 percent of the first $25,000 of net income before taxes, 20 percent of the next $25,000, 30 percent of the next $25,000, 40 percent of the next $25,000, and 46 percent of all net income above $100,000.

SILVER STAR PRODUCTS CORPORATION
Condensed Income Statement
Year Ended December 31, 19X5

Revenue		
Sales		$2,361,000
Less Sales Returns and Allowances		21,000
Net Sales		$2,340,000
Cost of Goods Sold		
Finished Goods Inventory, Jan. 1	$ 187,200	
Cost of Goods Manufactured	1,615,800	
Total Goods Available	$1,803,000	
Less Finished Goods Inventory, Dec. 31	213,000	
Cost of Goods Sold		1,590,000
Gross Profit on Sales		$ 750,000
Operating Expenses		
Selling Expenses	$ 294,000	
Administrative Expenses	246,000	
Total Operating Expenses		540,000
Net Income From Operations		$ 210,000
Other Income		
Interest Income		12,000
Total Income for Year		$ 222,000
Other Expense		
Organization Costs Written Off		6,000
Net Income Before Income Taxes		$ 216,000
Provision for Income Taxes		97,200
Net Income After Income Taxes		$ 118,800

SILVER STAR PRODUCTS CORPORATION
Condensed Statement of Cost of Goods Manufactured
Year Ended December 31, 19X5

Raw Materials		
Raw Materials Inventory, Jan. 1	$130,200	
Materials Purchases	799,800	
Total Materials Available	$930,000	
Less Raw Materials Inventory, Dec. 31	135,000	
Raw Materials Used		$ 795,000
Direct Labor		538,500
Manufacturing Overhead		288,900
Total Manufacturing Costs		$1,622,400
Add Work in Process Inventory, Jan. 1		66,000
		$1,688,400
Less Work in Process Inventory, Dec. 31		72,600
Cost of Goods Manufactured		$1,615,800

SILVER STAR PRODUCTS CORPORATION
Analysis of Finished Goods Inventory
December 31, 19X5

Product	Quantity	Unit Cost	Total Cost
Tool Chests			
Style AXY	17,250	$ 5.26	$ 90,750
Style POQ	7,500	7.90	59,250
Style AOZ	5,250	12.00	63,000
Total Tool Chests	30,000		
Total Finished Goods Inventory			$213,000

SILVER STAR PRODUCTS CORPORATION
Budgeted Finished Goods Inventory
December 31, 19X6

Product	Quantity	Unit Cost	Total Cost
Tool Chests			
Style AXY	19,500	$ 5.60	$109,200
Style POQ	7,500	8.40	63,000
Style AOZ	4,500	12.60	56,700
Total Tool Chests	31,500		
Total Finished Goods Budgeted			$228,900

SILVER STAR PRODUCTS CORPORATION
Sales Budget
Year 19X6

Product	Quantity To Be Sold	Average Selling Price	Estimated Sales Revenue
Tool Chests			
Style AXY	153,750	$ 8.00	$1,230,000
Style POQ	60,000	12.00	720,000
Style AOZ	36,000	18.00	648,000
Total Tool Chests	249,750		
Total Budgeted Sales			$2,598,000

After the operating budget has been completed, attention must be given to the development of a plan for managing the firm's financial resources during the budget period. The end result of this process is a budgeted balance sheet, but its focal point is the projection of cash inflow and outflow. Routine business operations, which are reflected in the operating budget, are an important source and use of cash. However, there are also other important needs for financial resources. A critical use of these resources is the acquisition of property, plant, and equipment. For that reason we will begin our discussion of financial planning by examining the procedures used for budgeting capital expenditures.

CAPITAL BUDGETING AND FINANCIAL PLANNING

BUDGETING CAPITAL EXPENDITURES

A *capital expenditure* is involved when the item purchased has a useful life of more than one year and is an item of property, plant, or equipment. With many possible projects competing for the limited funds available, a problem of selection arises.

Selection of Projects

Decisions about investments in business assets are strongly influenced by the profits that these investments can be expected to produce for the owners and by the amount of funds available for capital outlays. All projects are carefully appraised to determine their relative necessity and profitability. In some firms the projects are then listed for consideration in the order of their attractiveness. With this guide and with knowledge of the amount of money available for capital expenditures, management approves items in order on the list until the limit is reached. Other organizations approach the problem in a somewhat different manner. They first determine an acceptable standard for the rate of return on investment and then undertake to provide funds for all projects that meet or exceed this standard.

Several approaches may be used by management in evaluating and ranking investments. Three common methods are described in this chapter.

Payback Period

One simple approach to capital budgeting involves computation of the *payback period* for each new asset that is being considered. The accountant estimates the number of years that it will take to recover the proposed outlay for the asset from the net cash flow resulting from the asset's use. For example, assume that a new machine can be purchased for $10,000 and has a useful life of 5 years. Also assume that the firm's cash earnings will be increased by an estimated $3,000 a year because of the machine (ignoring depreciation). The payback period is thus 3.3 years, as computed below.

$$\frac{\$10,000 \text{ cost}}{\$3,000 \text{ cash earnings a year}} = 3.3 \text{ years}$$

Obviously, a shorter payback period tends to reduce the risk inherent in buying a new asset. Other things being equal, a project with a short payback period is generally ranked above projects with long payback periods. For example, assume that three new assets are being considered for purchase and each costs $10,000. If one asset has a payback period of 3.3 years, the second a payback period of 4.5 years, and the third a payback period of 4 years, the asset with a payback period of 3.3 years would be favored. On the other hand, a payback period of 3 years for an asset with a life of 4 years is not as favorable as a payback period of 6 years for an asset with a life of 15 years.

Simple Rate of Return on Investment

Proposed capital expenditures are also commonly evaluated by estimating the rate of profit that the investment will earn. *Return on investment* may be based either on the original investment in the asset or on the average investment.

For example, suppose that an asset can be purchased for $10,000 and that it is expected to earn a net income of $2,000 a year after deducting all expenses (including depreciation). The rate of return on the original investment is 20 percent, as computed below.

$$\frac{\$2,000 \text{ annual net income}}{\$10,000 \text{ original investment}} = 20\%$$

Assuming that straight-line depreciation is used and that the asset has no salvage value, the average investment or book value would be approximately $5,000 ($10,000 + 0 ÷ 2). Thus the rate of return on average investment would be 40 percent.

$$\frac{\$2,000 \text{ annual net income}}{\$5,000 \text{ average investment}} = 40\%$$

Obviously, the higher the rate of return on investment, the more desirable the project. If three projects had rates of return of 20, 25, and 18 percent on original investment, the project with a return of 25 percent would be ranked first.

The method illustrated here is called the *simple rate of return method* because it does not consider the time value of money. The rate computed is not a *discounted rate*.

Discounted Cash Flow

The analytical procedures discussed above ignore the fact that the increased cash flow from a new asset is spread over a period of years. Obviously, a cash flow of $1,000 to be received 20 years from now is not worth as much, and should not be given the same consideration, as a cash flow of $1,000 during the current year. Thus analytical procedures that consider the timing of cash flow are commonly used to assess the financial benefits of proposed new assets. These techniques involve the present value tables that you first learned about in Chapter 31. There are many sophisticated models based on present value tables that are used in evaluating capital expenditures. The two procedures discussed below are quite simple but provide an illustration of the techniques involved.

Net Present Value Method

Under the net present value method, a firm compares the present value of all future net cash inflows from a capital project with the present cash outlay needed to acquire the asset. The greater the excess of present value over the asset's cost, the greater its desirability.

For example, assume that the management of a company is considering the two capital projects described below.

	PROJECT A
Cost	$10,000
Expected cash flow each year	$ 3,000
Estimated useful life	6 years
Estimated salvage value	None

	PROJECT B
Cost	$20,000
Expected cash flow each year	$ 7,000
Estimated useful life	5 years
Estimated salvage value	$ 2,000

Assume also that the cost of capital (or interest rate) is 12 percent. The present value of the future cash flow can be determined by referring to the table giving the present value of an annuity of $1, which appears on page 728. This table shows that the present value of an annuity of $1 at 12 percent a year for 6 years is 4.111 times the annual cash inflow. Thus the total present value of Project A is $12,333 ($3,000 × 4.111). The net present value of this project is $2,333, as shown below.

Present value of future cash flow	$12,333
Less cash outlay needed to acquire asset	10,000
Net present value	$ 2,333

For Project B there are two types of cash flow. The first type is the annual cash flow of $7,000 from operations. The second type is the cash flow of $2,000 expected from salvage (the sale of the item for secondhand use or for scrap). The present value of the second type of cash flow is found by multiplying the present value of $1 due 5 years later, based on a discount rate of 12 percent, by the expected cash proceeds from salvage. (The necessary table appears on page 727.) All the necessary computations for Project B are shown below. They indicate that its total present value is $26,369 and its net present value is $6,369.

Present value of cash flow from operations:		
Annual cash flow	$7,000	
Present value factor (from table for present value of an annuity of $1 at 12% for 5 periods)	× 3.605	$25,235
Present value of cash flow from salvage:		
Gross amount expected from salvage	$2,000	
Present value factor (from table for present value of $1 at 12% due 5 periods later)	× 0.567	1,134
Total present value		$26,369
Less cash outlay needed to acquire asset		20,000
Net present value		$ 6,369

The net present value of Project B is $4,036 higher than that of Project A ($6,369 − $2,333), which suggests that it is the preferred investment. However, other factors, such as relative total cost, need for the asset, and availability of substitute assets must also be considered.

If there is no net present value, the cash flow from the project will not yield a rate of return equal to the cost of capital.

Effective Rate of Return

A procedure based on the same present value tables involved in the previous example can be used to approximate the *effective rate of return* or *discounted rate of return* on a capital project. This approach overcomes the objections to the undiscounted rate of return on investment technique illustrated on page 1092. For example, suppose that a firm wants to compute the discounted rate of return on an asset that costs $10,000 and will yield a net cash flow of $3,000 a year for 5 years. In the previous example, you saw that the present value of an annual cash flow (an annuity) was computed as follows.

Present Value = Present Value Factor x Annual Cash Flow

In this case, we know that the present value is $10,000 and that the annual cash flow is $3,000. Thus the present value factor can be computed as follows.

$$\text{Present Value Factor} = \frac{\text{Present Value}}{\text{Annual Cash Flow}}$$

$$\text{Present Value Factor} = \frac{\$10,000}{\$3,000} = 3.333$$

We also know that the useful life is 5 years. Thus we can estimate the effective interest rate by consulting the table for the present value of an annuity of $1 and finding (or approximating) the interest rate which, based on a 5-year cash flow, gives a factor of 3.333. The table on page 728 shows that if the interest rate is 14 percent and the annuity period is 5 years, the factor is 3.433. For a 16 percent rate, the factor is 3.274. Thus the effective rate lies between 14 percent and 16 percent. We can estimate the rate more closely by using ratio and proportion, as follows.

Factor at rate of 14%	3.433
Factor at rate of 16%	3.274
Difference	0.159

Factor computed for asset involved	3.333
Factor at 16%	3.274
Difference	0.059

The factor that has been computed is 0.371 (0.059 ÷ 0.159) of the 2 percent difference between 16 percent and 14 percent (using 16 percent as the base). The estimated effective rate of return is 15.258 percent (16% − [0.371 × 2%]). The importance of the discounted rate of return is obvious when it is compared with the simple rate of return. The simple rate of return may be completely misleading, especially when assets have long estimated lives.

Planning Period

Capital expenditures determine the location and nature of a business for many years to come. Therefore, they must be undertaken with great care. Changes in products or production methods often require planning ahead for long periods. Capital expenditures may be planned in broad outline for five, ten, or more years in advance. Detailed plans are prepared for shorter periods, such as a year ahead.

Control of Expenditures

The list of projects budgeted becomes the plan. As the plan is put into effect during the year, specific expenditures must be authorized. The accountant records the actual expenditures and compares them periodically with the budget and with the specific authorizations to help management control the various activities. If a project involves construction work, it may be accounted for on what amounts to a job order cost basis. Materials, labor, and overhead are charged to the project as it progresses. Total cost is then transferred to the appropriate asset account when the project is completed.

Capital Expenditures Budget for 19Y3

Suppose that, after using evaluation procedures similar to those outlined above, the management of the Woodcraft Manufacturing Corporation decides to spend $55,000 on capital items during 19Y3 and prepares the capital expenditures budget shown below.

WOODCRAFT MANUFACTURING CORPORATION
Capital Expenditures Budget
Year Ending December 31, 19Y3

Item	Priority	
Addition to Factory Building	A	$22,000
Cutting Machinery	B	8,000
Shaping Machinery	C	5,000
Computer	D	10,000
Materials Handling Equipment	E	10,000
Total Capital Expenditures Budgeted		$55,000

FINANCIAL BUDGETING

The next step in the budgeting process is to see how the proposed budgets for sales, expenses, and capital expenditures will affect the financial position of the business.

Property, Plant, and Equipment

Additions to plant and equipment amounting to $55,000 are shown in the capital expenditures budget prepared at the Woodcraft Manufacturing Corporation. No assets are to be disposed of during the coming year. Depreciation of $15,500 on plant and equipment has already been estimated for the year in the manufacturing overhead budget (page 1073). Starting with the figures from the balance sheet of December 31, 19Y2, and giving consideration to the changes budgeted for 19Y3, the ending balances can be computed as shown on page 1096.

	BALANCES DEC. 31, 19Y2	BUDGETED CHANGES IN 19Y3	BALANCES DEC. 31, 19Y3
Property, Plant, and Equipment			
Land	$ 30,000	$ -0-	$ 30,000
Factory Bldg. and Equipment	$233,600	$55,000	$288,600
Less Accumulated Depreciation	44,000	15,500	59,500
Net Book Value	$189,600	$39,500	$229,100
Total Prop., Plant, and Equip.	$219,600	$39,500	$259,100

Long-Term Liabilities

Woodcraft's management plans to sell an additional $20,000 of authorized bonds at par value on the next interest date, April 1, 19Y3. Thus the bonds expected to be outstanding on December 31, 19Y3, total $70,000, as shown below.

Bonds Outstanding, Dec. 31, 19Y2	$50,000
Bonds To Be Issued, April 1, 19Y3	20,000
Bonds Outstanding, Dec. 31, 19Y3	$70,000

Stockholders' Equity

All of Woodcraft's authorized stock has already been issued. No changes are being considered for any stockholders' equity item except retained earnings. The budgeted net income after income taxes was determined in the preceding chapter to be $75,794. The only other item expected to affect retained earnings during the year is dividends. Management proposes to pay the 8 percent preferred stock dividend of $8,000 and to reduce the dividend on the common stock to $12 a share, or $60,000 in total, with payment to be made in December. Starting with the balance on December 31, 19Y2 (rounded off to the nearest dollar), the budgeted statement of retained earnings for 19Y3 can be prepared as shown below.

WOODCRAFT MANUFACTURING CORPORATION   *Exhibit C*
Budgeted Statement of Retained Earnings
Year Ending December 31, 19Y3

Balance, January 1		$140,299
Additions		
Net Income After Income Taxes (Exhibit B)		75,794
		$216,093
Deductions		
Dividends on Preferred Stock	$ 8,000	
Dividends on Common Stock	60,000	
Total Deductions		68,000
Balance, December 31 (to Exhibit A)		$148,093

With this final estimate of retained earnings on December 31, 19Y3, the Stockholders' Equity section of the balance sheet projected for that date appears as shown below.

Stockholders' Equity

8% Preferred Stock, $100 Par Value	$100,000
Paid-in Capital in Excess of Par Value	6,000
Common Stock, $50 Stated Value	250,000
Paid-in Capital in Excess of Stated Value	19,000
Retained Earnings	148,093
Total Stockholders' Equity	$523,093

Analysis of Working Capital Changes

A careful study of expected changes in working capital is of particular importance, especially in relation to the company's most vital asset, cash. The timing of changes must be studied to be sure that funds will be available as needed for the budget plans. Therefore, each current asset and current liability is reviewed to determine the changes expected in these items during the year and to estimate the account balances at the end of the period. A detailed monthly cash budget may be prepared (see pages 1102–1103) to reflect changes in working capital items and all other changes that will affect cash specifically. The detailed projection of cash flow is useful, indeed, almost essential in any business. The techniques and procedures are therefore treated in some detail in this chapter.

Cash Receipts From Accounts Receivable

The major source of cash receipts in many businesses is the collection of accounts receivable from sales. Estimating these collections on a monthly basis first requires projecting the net sales by month. The budgeted net sales for the Woodcraft Manufacturing Corporation for 19Y3 are broken down as shown below.

January	$130,000	July	$ 142,000
February	132,000	August	145,000
March	135,000	September	151,000
April	134,000	October	142,000
May	136,000	November	128,000
June	141,000	December	127,150
Total Budgeted Net Sales for 19Y3			$1,643,150

Next the accountant studies the pattern of payment expected from customers. Woodcraft offers sales terms of net 30 days. An analysis of its recent experience with collections shows average collection periods of 39.2 days in 19Y1 and 41.6 days in 19Y2. Assuming that the average collection period for 19Y3 will be about 40 days, roughly 75 percent of the accounts receivable at the beginning of each month will be collected by the end of that month.

Expected collections for Woodcraft's accounts receivable can be determined on this basis from month to month. The accountant can therefore estimate the balance of the Accounts Receivable account at the beginning of each successive month during the year, as shown on page 1098. (Figures are rounded off to the nearest dollar.)

	JANUARY	FEBRUARY	MARCH
Accounts Receivable, First of Month	$168,184	$172,046	$175,011
Collections: 75% of Beginning Balance	126,138	129,035	131,258
Remaining Balance	$ 42,046	$ 43,011	$ 43,753
Sales on Credit During Month	130,000	132,000	135,000
Accounts Receivable, End of Month	$172,046	$175,011	$178,753

Carrying out these computations for the remaining months of 19Y3 results in an ending balance of $171,135 for Accounts Receivable. The $3,286 estimated for uncollectible accounts must be subtracted from this amount, leaving a balance sheet figure of $167,849 for Accounts Receivable on December 31, 19Y3.

Other Cash Receipts

The only other cash receipts expected are $300 from interest income and $20,000 from the sale of bonds on April 1. These receipts are shown for the appropriate months in the Receipts section of the budgeted cash flow report illustrated at the bottom of this page and the next page.

Changes in Inventories and Prepaid Expense Items

The budgeted ending inventories were determined in the previous chapter in the course of preparing the budgeted income statement and its related schedules. Changes in inventories, revealed by a comparison of beginning and ending figures, are taken into consideration in analyzing the accounts payable and the payments on these accounts.

For the Woodcraft Manufacturing Corporation, the balance of Prepaid Insurance at the end of the year is estimated to be $3,350, an increase of $650 from the $2,700 balance at the beginning of the year. The balance of Supplies on Hand is estimated to be $2,575 at the end of the year, an increase of $75 from the $2,500 balance at the beginning of the year. These changes are also provided for in connection with the analysis of accounts payable.

Cash Payments on Accounts Payable

With the exception of payrolls, which are treated separately because of their size and complexity, most cash expenditures of the typical business relate to the Accounts Payable account. The expense budgets of the Woodcraft Manufactur-

WOODCRAFT MANUFACTURING CORPORATION
Budgeted Cash Flow
Year Ending December 31, 19Y3

	Jan.	Feb.	March	Apr.	May
Balance, First of Month	$ 99,666				
Receipts					
Collections on Accts. Rec.	$126,138	$129,035	$131,258	$134,065	$134,016
Interest Income					
Sale of Bonds				20,000	
Total Receipts	$126,138	$129,035	$131,258	$154,065	$134,016

ing Corporation (page 1075) provide the information on items (other than payrolls) to be handled through Accounts Payable in 19Y3. The accountant uses this data to prepare an analysis of the accounts payable transactions budgeted, as shown on the next page.

The figures in the Manufacturing section for Raw Materials Purchases, Utilities—Factory, Repairs and Maintenance—Factory, Indirect Materials and Supplies, and Insurance—Factory appear on the budgeted statement of cost of goods manufactured that is given on page 1074.

The figures listed in the Selling section for Delivery Expense, Sales Supplies and Other Selling Expenses, and Advertising Expense are included under Selling Expenses in the budgeted schedule of operating expenses on page 1075. The $17,500 for Office Supplies and Other Office Expenses shown in the Administrative section appears in the same schedule.

Notice that the first portion of this analysis indicates the nature of the items involved and shows the effect of proposed changes in the inventory of indirect materials and supplies and in prepaid insurance. The second portion of the analysis indicates the firm's projected pattern for paying accounts payable. For example, the accountant estimates that 70 percent of the balance of the Accounts Payable account at the beginning of any month will be paid during that month. Expected payments can be determined on this basis from month to month. The balance of Accounts Payable at the beginning of each successive month during the year can then be estimated as shown below, rounded off to the nearest dollar.

	JANUARY	FEBRUARY	MARCH
Accounts Payable, First of Month	$85,221	$82,566	$80,770
Payments: 70% of Beginning Balance	59,655	57,796	56,539
Remaining Balance	$25,566	$24,770	$24,231
Accounts Payable Incurred During Month	57,000	56,000	59,000
Accounts Payable, End of Month	$82,566	$80,770	$83,231

Each monthly payments figure for Accounts Payable is recorded in the Payments section of the budgeted cash flow report shown on pages 1102–1103 (see

June	July	Aug.	Sept.	Oct.	Nov.	Dec.	Total
$135,504	$139,626	$141,407	$144,101	$149,276	$143,819	$131,954	$1,640,199
	50	100	100	50			300
							20,000
$135,504	$139,676	$141,507	$144,201	$149,326	$143,819	$131,954	$1,660,499

WOODCRAFT MANUFACTURING CORPORATION
Analysis of Accounts Payable Transactions Budgeted
Year Ending December 31, 19Y3

Payments To Be Made Through Accounts Payable:

Manufacturing

Raw Materials Purchases (Net)		$519,000
Utilities—Factory		21,500
Repairs and Maintenance—Factory	$30,000	
Less Labor Paid Through Payrolls	20,000	10,000
Indirect Materials and Supplies	$23,300	
Add Increase in Inventory	75	23,375
Insurance—Factory	$14,400	
Add Increase in Prepaid Insurance	650	15,050
Total Manufacturing		$588,925

Selling

Delivery Expense	$49,000	
Sales Supplies and Other Selling Expenses	25,700	
Advertising Expense	27,000	
Total Selling		101,700

Administrative

Office Supplies and Other Office Expenses		17,500
Total Accounts Payable Transactions		$708,125

Planned Credits to Accounts Payable by Months:

January	$ 57,000
February	56,000
March	59,000
April	60,000
May	60,000
June	62,000
July	64,000
August	63,000
September	60,000
October	57,000
November	55,000
December	55,125
Total	$708,125

Item 1). Carrying out these computations for the remaining months of 19Y3 results in an ending balance of $74,275 for Accounts Payable.

Payment of Income Taxes

The income taxes shown on the December 31, 19Y2, balance sheet ($19,821) are payable in two equal installments, on March 15 and June 15, and are so budgeted. Refer to Item 2 in the budgeted cash flow report on pages 1102–1103. Income taxes payable for 19Y3 were estimated at $27,500 when the budgeted income statement was being prepared (page 1076).

Payment of Other Payables	The balance of $7,308.90 in Other Payables at the end of 19Y2 includes the three items shown below.

Salaries and Wages Payable	$3,150.60
Payroll Taxes Payable	2,658.30
Bond Interest Payable	1,500.00
Total	$7,308.90

Salaries and Wages Payable will be paid with the first payroll payment in January. Payroll Taxes Payable will also be paid in January. Bond Interest Payable will be paid on the regular interest date, April 1. All these payments are included in the budgeted cash flow.

Analyses projected to the end of 19Y3 indicate that the balance of Other Payables at that time will be $9,001, as shown below.

Salaries and Wages Payable	$4,201
Payroll Taxes Payable	2,700
Bond Interest Payable	2,100
Total	$9,001

Cash Payments on Payrolls

Selling and administrative salaries are paid each month as they are earned. The manufacturing payroll is paid weekly, and a balance payable of $3,150.60 existed at the beginning of the year. The above analysis shows an expected balance payable of $3,200 at the end of the year, an increase of about $50. The analysis of payroll payments by months is shown as Item 3 in the budgeted cash flow report under the three headings Manufacturing, Selling, and Administrative. The Manufacturing section includes a total of $20,000 that will be charged to Repairs and Maintenance—Factory for the year; the Administrative section includes the salaries that will be paid to the officers and office workers of the firm during 19Y3.

Cash Payments on Payroll Taxes

The employer's FICA taxes are deposited each month for the previous month. State unemployment taxes are paid quarterly, and federal unemployment taxes are also paid on a quarterly basis. Estimates of tax-exempt wages are prepared and correlated with the expected monthly payroll payments in determining these payroll taxes. Their payment is indicated under the appropriate months in Item 4 of the budgeted cash flow report, as is shown on pages 1102–1103.

Other Cash Payments

In addition to the cash payments previously discussed, the budgeted cash flow report shows that Woodcraft must also make other types of payments. Property taxes (Item 5) for 19Y3 are estimated at $19,700, payable in December. Bond interest (Item 6) is paid on April 1 and October 1. At the opening of business on April 1, there will be $50,000 of bonds outstanding, and interest at 12 percent for six months amounts to $3,000. On October 1 there will be $70,000 of bonds outstanding ($50,000 + $20,000 issued on April 1), and interest at 12 percent for six months amounts to $4,200. Dividend payments (Item 7) totaling $68,000 will be made in December. Payments on projected purchases of plant and equipment (Item 8) are shown in the months in which the payments are planned.

WOODCRAFT MANUFACTURING CORPORATION
Budgeted Cash Flow
Year Ending December 31, 19Y3

	Jan.	Feb.	Mar.	Apr.	May
Balance, First of Month	$ 69,995	$106,491	$105,645	$106,568	$120,709
Receipts					
Collections on Accts. Rec.	$126,138	$129,035	$131,258	$134,065	$134,016
Interest Income					
Sale of Bonds				20,000	
Total Receipts	$126,138	$129,035	$131,258	$154,065	$134,016
Total Cash Available	$225,804	$235,526	$236,903	$260,633	$254,725
Payments					
(1) Payment of Accts. Pay.	$ 59,655	$ 57,796	$ 56,539	$ 58,262	$ 59,478
(2) Income Taxes			9,911		
(3) Payroll Payments					
Manufacturing	26,000	27,000	28,000	29,000	31,000
Selling	13,000	13,000	13,000	13,200	13,500
Administrative	18,000	18,000	18,500	18,500	18,500
(4) Payroll Taxes	2,658	4,085	4,385	7,962	4,005
(5) Property Taxes					
(6) Bond Interest				3,000	
(7) Dividends					
(8) Plant and Equipment		10,000		10,000	10,000
Total Payments	$119,313	$129,881	$130,335	$139,924	$136,483
Balance, End of Month	$106,491	$105,645	$106,568	$120,709	$118,242

Budgeted Cash Flow

The accountant brings together all the estimates of cash flow for individual items in a comprehensive month-by-month analysis. This budgeted cash flow report provides an estimate of the cash balance at the end of each month. For example, the cash balance on December 31, 19Y3, is expected to be $69,995 (see page 1104).

If this analysis had shown that a shortage of cash would develop during the year, management would have planned to borrow cash or rearrange the pattern of expenditures so that the available cash would be adequate. Such information is important for every business and absolutely essential for one that has a weak cash position. If an excess of cash is expected during part of the year, it may be invested temporarily to earn interest and thus increase the profits of the firm.

Budgeted Balance Sheet

The activities discussed previously provide the end-of-year estimates for each item on the balance sheet. A final budgeted balance sheet can now be prepared for December 31, 19Y3, as illustrated on page 1104. This statement shows how the balance sheet will appear if all the budget plans work out.

With the completion of the budgeted balance sheet, the Woodcraft Manufacturing Corporation has a *master budget* for 19Y3 that includes both a detailed operating budget and a detailed financial budget.

June	July	Aug.	Sept.	Oct.	Nov.	Dec.	Total
$118,242	$114,937	$113,424	$109,466	$120,894	$134,735	$155,529	$ 99,666
$135,504	$139,626	$141,407	$144,101	$149,276	$143,819	$131,954	$1,640,199
	50	100	100	50			300
							20,000
$135,504	$139,676	$141,507	$144,201	$149,326	$143,819	$131,954	$1,660,499
$253,746	$254,613	$254,931	$253,667	$270,220	$278,554	$287,483	$1,760,165
$ 59,844	$ 61,353	$ 63,206	$ 63,062	$ 60,918	$ 60,276	$ 58,682	$ 719,071
9,910							19,821
32,000	34,000	35,000	33,000	30,000	27,000	26,350	358,350
13,500	13,500	13,500	13,800	13,500	13,500	13,000	160,000
19,000	19,000	19,000	18,000	18,000	18,000	17,500	220,000
4,555	8,336	4,759	4,911	8,867	4,249	4,256	63,028
						19,700	19,700
				4,200			7,200
						68,000	68,000
	5,000	10,000				10,000	55,000
$138,809	$141,189	$145,465	$132,773	$135,485	$123,025	$217,488	$1,690,170
$114,937	$113,424	$109,466	$120,894	$134,735	$155,529	$69,995	$69,995

PRINCIPLES AND PROCEDURES SUMMARY

The capital expenditures budget lists approved projects and the expected cost of each. The projected cash flow report summarizes expected cash receipts and payments during the same future accounting period. These projections are based on an analysis of the firm's past experience in paying accounts payable and collecting cash from customers. Past experience is also applied to budgeted sales and costs of the future period to determine cash flow. Based on the projected pattern of sales, purchases, and other costs, the ending balance of cash and the expected balances of accounts payable and accounts receivable can be determined. The final step in the budget process is to prepare the expected balance sheet for the end of the period.

MANAGERIAL IMPLICATIONS

The financial budget is of crucial importance to management. The monthly projections of cash flow assist management in planning ahead to arrange for short-term or long-term financing as needed or to put excess funds to work earning income. The projected balance sheet indicates potential problems to be overcome. The budget provides a tool for advance planning and, later, for evaluating actual results so that managerial effectiveness and efficiency can be measured.

WOODCRAFT MANUFACTURING CORPORATION
Budgeted Balance Sheet
December 31, 19Y3

Exhibit A

Assets

Current Assets			
Cash			$ 69,995
Accounts Receivable		$171,135	
Less Allowance for Uncollectible Accounts		3,286	167,849
Inventories			
Raw Materials		$ 82,000	
Work in Process		35,000	
Finished Goods		84,000	201,000
Prepaid Expenses			
Prepaid Insurance		$ 3,350	
Supplies on Hand		2,575	5,925
Total Current Assets			$444,769
Property, Plant, and Equipment			
Land		$ 30,000	
Factory Building and Equipment	$288,600		
Less Accumulated Depreciation	59,500	229,100	
Total Prop., Plant, and Equip.			259,100
Total Assets			$703,869

Liabilities and Stockholders' Equity

Current Liabilities		
Accounts Payable		$ 74,275
Income Taxes Payable		27,500
Other Payables		9,001
Total Current Liabilities		$110,776
Long-Term Liabilities		
12% Bonds Payable, 19Z1		70,000
Total Liabilities		$180,776
Stockholders' Equity		
8% Preferred Stock, $100 Par Value	$100,000	
Paid-in Capital in Excess of Par Value	6,000	
Common Stock, $50 Stated Value	250,000	
Paid-in Capital in Excess of Stated Value	19,000	
Retained Earnings (Exhibit C)	148,093	
Total Stockholders' Equity		523,093
Total Liabilities and Stockholders' Equity		$703,869

REVIEW QUESTIONS

1. What is capital budgeting?
2. What is a payback period? How is it computed?
3. Would a shorter or longer payback period be desirable? Explain.
4. What is the basis used in computing the rate of return on an investment?
5. What is the shortcoming of the simple rate of return on investment as a basis for judging capital projects?
6. Explain the net present value approach to evaluating capital investments.
7. Explain the effective rate of return approach to evaluating capital investments.
8. Why is it necessary to rank capital projects?
9. How does salvage value affect the net present value?
10. Explain how to estimate monthly cash collections on accounts receivable.
11. Where is information obtained for forecasting cash expenditures for manufacturing overhead?
12. Where is information obtained for budgeting cash outlays for bond interest?
13. What are the major sources of cash receipts for a manufacturing company?
14. Would the estimate of the total cash needed for dividends be one of the first or one of the last computations made in preparing the budgeted cash flow report? Explain.
15. Suppose that in preparing its financial budget the Woodcraft Manufacturing Corporation had found that there would be a period of several months in which the cash available would not be adequate to pay current accounts and that money would have to be borrowed. Would this affect the operating budget? Explain.
16. Why is it desirable to prepare a budgeted balance sheet?
17. Why are monthly forecasts of cash receipts and cash payments made?
18. How does depreciation enter into the cash flow forecast?
19. How does the estimate of uncollectible accounts affect the cash flow forecast?
20. What is the source of the estimate of the cash that will be needed to pay for direct labor?

MANAGERIAL DISCUSSION QUESTIONS

1. Assume that the management of a company where you work has asked you to recommend procedures for evaluating proposed capital outlays. They wish to know about the ease of the computations involved in the different methods and how reliable and useful these methods are. They also want you to recommend which methods should be used. What would your response be?
2. Why is a month-by-month cash flow analysis useful to management?
3. Management has asked you if the financial budget is useful in controlling costs. How would you respond?
4. Suppose that during the last part of 19X1 you prepared an operating budget and a financial budget for 19X2, including a projected income statement and

a projected balance sheet. In February of 19X2 it has become apparent that your budget will be considerably below actual results. What should you do to be of assistance to management?

5. Assume that you have just been hired as the budget director of a large company. The president of the company took an elementary accounting course in college. In that course he learned about the payback method for evaluating capital projects. At a meeting with you, he states that this method is adequate, by itself, as a tool for evaluating proposed capital investments. Would you agree with him? Why or why not?

6. Of what use to management is a budgeted balance sheet?

EXERCISES

EXERCISE 46-1 **Computing a payback period.** The Springfield Corporation is considering the purchase of two new machines to perform a manufacturing function. Data relating to the two machines is given below. Calculate the payback period for Machine 1.

MACHINE 1

Cost	$270,000
Cash savings per year	30,000
Estimated useful life	12 years
Estimated salvage value	-0-

MACHINE 2

Cost	$270,000
Cash savings per year	20,000
Estimated useful life	18 years
Estimated salvage value	-0-

EXERCISE 46-2 **Computing a payback period.** Refer to Exercise 46-1. Calculate the payback period for Machine 2.

EXERCISE 46-3 **Computing the simple rate of return on an original investment.** Refer to Exercise 46-1. Assume that the company uses straight-line depreciation. Calculate the simple rate of return on Machine 1, using the original investment as the base.

EXERCISE 46-4 **Computing the simple rate of return on an original investment.** Refer to Exercise 46-1. Assume that the company uses straight-line depreciation. Calculate the simple rate of return on Machine 2, using the original investment as the base.

EXERCISE 46-5 **Computing the simple rate of return on an average investment.** Refer to Exercise 46-1. Assume that the company uses straight-line depreciation. Calculate the simple rate of return on Machine 1, using the average investment as the base.

EXERCISE 46-6	**Computing the simple rate of return on an average investment.** Refer to Exercise 46-1. Assume that the company uses straight-line depreciation. Calculate the simple rate of return on Machine 2, using the average investment as the base.
EXERCISE 46-7	**Computing present value.** Refer to Exercise 46-1. Assuming that the company's cost of capital is 10 percent, calculate the present value of the savings from Machine 1. (Use the table on page 728.)
EXERCISE 46-8	**Computing present value.** Refer to Exercise 46-1. Assuming that the company's cost of capital is 10 percent, calculate the present value of the savings from Machine 2. (Use the table on page 728.)
EXERCISE 46-9	**Computing net present value.** Using the present value determined in Exercise 46-7, calculate the net present value, if any, of Machine 1.
EXERCISE 46-10	**Computing net present value.** Using the present value determined in Exercise 46-8, calculate the net present value, if any, of Machine 2.
EXERCISE 46-11	**Computing a discounted rate of return.** Using the data in Exercise 46-1 and the table on page 728, estimate the discounted rate of return on the investment in Machine 1.
EXERCISE 46-12	**Computing a discounted rate of return.** Using the data in Exercise 46-1 and the table on page 728, estimate the discounted rate of return on the investment in Machine 2.
EXERCISE 46-13	**Comparing investment opportunities.** Using the computations from Exercises 46-1 through 46-12, make an analysis comparing the relative merits of buying Machine 1 and buying Machine 2.
EXERCISE 46-14	**Computing estimated cash payments for salaries.** On January 1, 19X3, the Lindberg Company had accrued salaries of $16,300. Total direct and indirect labor costs budgeted for the year are $1,080,000. Expected year-end accrued salaries are $12,200. Calculate the estimated cash payments for salaries in 19X3.
EXERCISE 46-15	**Computing estimated collections on accounts receivable.** The Kelly Corporation's actual and budgeted credit sales for certain months are as follows: December 19X2 (actual), $340,000; January 19X3 (budgeted), $280,000; February 19X3 (budgeted), $260,000; and March 19X3 (budgeted), $300,000. The firm's records show that typically 10 percent of credit sales are collected in the month of sale, 80 percent in the second month after sale, and 10 percent in the third month after sale. Calculate the estimated collections on the accounts receivable in March 19X3.
EXERCISE 46-16	**Computing estimated cash payments on accounts payable.** The Leonard Corporation has analyzed its records and finds that typically it pays 60 percent of its

invoices for purchases in the month the purchases are made and the remainder in the following month. The records also show that 80 percent of all its accounts payable are subject to cash discounts of 2 percent. Estimated credit purchases for selected months of 19X1 are $600,000 for March and $650,000 for April. Calculate the estimated cash payments on accounts payable in April 19X1.

EXERCISE 46-17 **Computing estimated cash payments for payroll taxes.** On January 1, 19X1, the Slater Corporation had accrued payroll taxes payable of $12,920. Budgeted payroll taxes for the year are $84,300. Expected year-end taxes will be $13,200. Calculate the estimated cash payments for payroll taxes in 19X1.

PROBLEMS

PROBLEM 46-1 **Using the payback period and the simple rate of return in evaluating capital investments.** The Cortez Chemical Company has $500,000 to invest in capital projects during 19X2. It is considering three projects, each costing $250,000. Relevant information about each project is given below.

	PROJECT A	PROJECT B	PROJECT C
Investment Required	$250,000	$250,000	$250,000
Annual Net Income			
(Ignoring Depreciation)	48,000	34,000	35,000
Depreciable Life (in Years)	10	25	20

The company's president suggests that projects should be chosen on the basis of payback period. However, the controller suggests that projects should be chosen on the basis of rate of return on original investment.

Instructions 1. Compute the payback period for each proposal. Round off your answer to one decimal place. Rank the projects in order of payback period.
2. Compute the simple rate of return on investment for each project, using the original investment as a base. (Carry your answer to four decimal places and then round off.) Rank the projects in order of return on investment.
3. Which ranking would you prefer? Why?
4. What shortcoming do you see in both of these methods?

PROBLEM 46-2 **Using the net present value and the effective rate of return in evaluating capital investments.** Refer to the data given in Problem 46-1 for the Cortez Chemical Company. Assume that its internal rate of return (cost of capital) is 12 percent.

Instructions 1. Compute the net present value of the three projects.
2. Compute the estimated effective rate of return for the three projects.
3. Based on these analyses, rank the projects in order of preference.

PROBLEM 46-3 **Budgeting cash receipts from sales.** The monthly sales forecast for the first quarter of 19X1 for the Wayne Steel Products Corporation is as follows.

MONTH	ESTIMATED CASH SALES	ESTIMATED CREDIT SALES	TOTAL SALES
January	$18,240	$133,860	$152,100
February	19,500	144,300	163,800
March	21,120	153,480	174,600

The balance of Accounts Receivable on December 31, 19X0, is composed of sales made in the months shown below.

MONTH	TOTAL CREDIT SALES IN MONTH	PERCENT UNCOLLECTED ON DEC. 31	BALANCE UNCOLLECTED ON DEC. 31
December	$198,600	100%	$198,600
November	212,400	10%	21,240
October	178,500	4%	7,140
Prior months			4,272
Balance of Accounts Receivable, Dec. 31, 19X0			$231,252

Invoices for the prior month's sales are mailed to credit customers on the first day of each month. A 2 percent discount is allowed for payments made by the 11th of the month. Past records show that discounts are taken on approximately 75 percent of credit sales. An additional 15 percent of credit sales will be collected by the end of the month following the sale, 6 percent during the second month, and 3 percent during the third month. One percent will never be collected.

Instructions Prepare a schedule of monthly cash receipts for the first quarter of 19X1. Disregard receipts from sources other than sales.

PROBLEM 46-4 **Budgeting cash payments for materials purchases.** About one-half of the purchases of raw materials made by the Wayne Steel Products Corporation are subject to a cash discount of 2 percent if paid by the 10th day of the following month. Other purchases are not subject to a discount, and payment is usually made by the last day of the following month. As of December 31, 19X0, the balance of Accounts Payable was $96,000, of which $66,000 was for purchases of raw materials. The remaining $30,000 represents purchases of items that have been vouchered and are not subject to cash discounts. The schedule of estimated purchases of raw materials for the first quarter of 19X1 is as follows.

MONTH	ESTIMATED MATERIALS PURCHASES
January	$72,000
February	78,300
March	54,600

Instructions Prepare a forecast of monthly cash payments for materials purchases for the first quarter of 19X1.

PROBLEM 46-5 **Assembling a capital budget.** The Wong Ceramics Company has decided to buy the following property, plant, and equipment during the year ending December 31, 19X2.

MONTH	DESCRIPTION OF ASSET	COST
Jan.	Land for parking lot	$ 15,000
May	New factory machine	12,000
June	New maintenance building	30,000
Sept.	Addition to dry kiln building	120,000
Oct.	Computer for factory	16,000

Instructions Prepare a capital expenditures budget for the year. Group like items (equipment and so on) together. (Keep all papers for use in Problem 46-8.)

PROBLEM 46-6 **Budgeting cash receipts from accounts receivable.** The budgeted net credit sales for the Wong Ceramics Company for each month of 19X2 are shown below. Assuming that the average collection period for 19X2 will be about 37 days, approximately 80 percent of the accounts receivable at the beginning of any month will be collected by the end of that month.

Instructions Prepare a schedule of accounts receivable collections. Round off your computations to the nearest dollar. (Keep all papers for use in Problem 46-8.)

WONG CERAMICS COMPANY
Schedule of Accounts Receivable Collections
Year Ending December 31, 19X2

Month	Accts. Rec. Balance First of Mo.	Collections 80% of Begin. Bal.	Remaining Balance	Sales on Credit During Mo.	Accts. Rec. Balance End of Mo.
Jan.	$240,000			$156,000	
Feb.				160,000	
Mar.				162,000	
Apr.				158,000	
May				146,000	
June				150,000	
July				148,000	
Aug.				144,000	
Sept.				164,000	
Oct.				168,000	
Nov.				180,000	
Dec.				202,000	

PROBLEM 46-7 **Budgeting accounts payable payments and balances.** The expected credits to accounts payable by month for the Wong Ceramics Company for 19X2 are shown on page 1111. It is estimated that 90 percent of the balance of accounts payable at the beginning of any month will be paid during that month.

Instructions Prepare a schedule of accounts payable payments. Round off your computations to the nearest dollar. (Keep all papers for use in Problem 46-8.)

WONG CERAMICS COMPANY
Schedule of Accounts Payable Payments
Year Ending December 31, 19X2

Month	Accts. Pay. Balance First of Mo.	Payments 90% of Begin. Bal.	Remaining Balance	Accts. Pay. Incurred During Mo.	Accts. Pay. Balance End of Mo.
Jan.	$124,000			$ 80,000	
Feb.				84,000	
Mar.				86,000	
Apr.				82,000	
May				76,000	
June				78,000	
July				74,000	
Aug.				78,000	
Sept.				88,000	
Oct.				96,000	
Nov.				104,000	
Dec.				110,000	

PROBLEM 46-8

Budgeting cash flow. This problem is a continuation of Problems 46-5 through 46-7. The data given below and on page 1112 is needed in the analysis of budgeted cash flow for the Wong Ceramics Company for the year ending December 31, 19X2.

Instructions

1. Prepare a budgeted cash flow report similar to the one illustrated on pages 1102 and 1103.
2. Enter the capital expenditures from the information and budget prepared in Problem 46-5.
3. Enter the collections on accounts receivable computed in Problem 46-6
4. Enter the payments on accounts payable computed in Problem 46-7.
5. Enter the data contained in Items a through j below.
6. Complete the calculations for the analysis.

DATA FOR CASH FLOW ANALYSIS

a. The cash balance as of January 1, 19X2, is $218,600.
b. Payment of payrolls and payroll taxes by month is estimated as shown in the table on page 1112.
c. Monthly interest income of $100 is expected except for March, June, September, and December, when the monthly amount should be $150.
d. The company expects to receive $25,000 from the issuance of bonds in February and $40,000 from the issuance of bonds in October.
e. Federal income taxes will be $30,000 in March and $30,000 in June.
f. State income taxes of $5,000 will be payable in April.
g. Property taxes of $10,500 will be payable in December.
h. Bond interest payable will be $6,250 in February and $7,250 in October.
i. Dividends of $20,000 will be payable in January.
j. The company expects to receive $50,000 in July from the sale of surplus land.

| | Payrolls | | | |
	Manufacturing	Selling	Administrative	Payroll Taxes
Jan.	$ 24,000	$ 14,000	$ 15,000	$ 5,240
Feb.	23,000	14,000	15,000	5,160
Mar.	22,500	13,500	15,000	5,080
Apr.	23,000	13,500	15,000	5,120
May	22,000	13,000	14,000	4,920
June	22,000	12,500	14,000	4,880
July	23,000	12,500	14,000	4,960
Aug.	23,000	12,000	13,000	4,200
Sept.	23,500	13,000	13,000	4,610
Oct.	24,000	13,500	13,000	4,500
Nov.	25,000	14,000	13,500	4,480
Dec.	25,000	14,000	14,000	4,400
Totals	$280,000	$159,500	$168,500	$57,550

ALTERNATE PROBLEMS

PROBLEM 46-1A   **Using the payback period and the simple rate of return in evaluating capital investments.** The DeVoe Paper Company has $1,100,000 to invest in capital projects during 19X2. It is considering three projects. Relevant information about each project is given below.

	PROJECT A	PROJECT B	PROJECT C
Investment Required	$510,000	$600,000	$480,000
Annual Net Income			
(Ignoring Depreciation)	100,000	90,000	120,000
Depreciable Life (in Years)	12	25	8

The firm's president suggests that projects should be chosen on the basis of payback period. However, the controller suggests that projects should be chosen on the basis of rate of return on original investment.

Instructions   1. Compute the payback period for each project. Round off your answer to one decimal place. Rank the projects in order of payback period.
2. Compute the simple rate of return on investment for each project, using the original investment as a base. (Carry your answer to five decimal places and then round off.) Rank the projects in order of return on investment.
3. Which ranking would you prefer? Why?
4. What shortcoming do you see in both of these methods?

PROBLEM 46-2A   **Using the net present value and the effective rate of return in evaluating capital investments.** Refer to the data given in Problem 46-1A for the DeVoe Paper Company. Assume that its internal rate of return (cost of capital) is 12 percent and that the present value factor at 20 percent for 8 years is 3.837.

Instructions

1. Compute the net present value of the three projects.
2. Compute the estimated effective rate of return for the three projects.
3. Based on these analyses, rank the projects in order of preference.

PROBLEM 46-3A

Budgeting cash receipts from sales. The monthly sales forecast for the third quarter of 19X6 for the Marathon Shoe Manufacturing Company is as follows.

MONTH	ESTIMATED CASH SALES	ESTIMATED CREDIT SALES	TOTAL SALES
July	$6,080	$44,620	$50,700
August	6,500	48,100	54,600
September	7,040	51,160	58,200

The balance of Accounts Receivable on June 30, 19X6, is composed of credit sales made in the months shown below.

MONTH	TOTAL CREDIT SALES IN MONTH	PERCENT UNCOLLECTED ON JUNE 30	BALANCE UNCOLLECTED ON JUNE 30
June	$66,200	100%	$66,200
May	70,800	10%	7,080
April	59,500	4%	2,380
Prior months			1,424
Balance of Accounts Receivable, June 30, 19X6			$77,084

On the first day of each month, invoices for the prior month's sales are mailed to credit customers. A 2 percent cash discount is allowed if the customer pays by the 10th of the month. The invoice balance is due in full by the last day of the month. Past records show that discounts are taken on about 75 percent of credit sales. An additional 15 percent of credit sales are collected by the end of the month following the sale, 6 percent during the second month, and 3 percent during the third month. One percent will never be collected.

Instructions

Prepare a schedule of monthly cash receipts for the third quarter of 19X6. Disregard receipts from sources other than sales.

PROBLEM 46-4A

Budgeting cash payments for materials purchases. About one-half of the purchases of raw materials made by the Marathon Shoe Manufacturing Company are subject to a cash discount of 2 percent if payment is made by the 10th of the following month. Other purchases are not subject to a discount, and payment is usually made by the last day of the following month. As of June 30, 19X6, the balance of Accounts Payable is $32,000, of which $22,000 is for purchases of raw materials. The remaining $10,000 represents other bills that have been vouchered and are not subject to cash discounts. The schedule of estimated purchases of raw materials for the third quarter of 19X6 is as follows.

MONTH	ESTIMATED MATERIALS PURCHASES
July	$24,000
August	26,100
September	18,200

Instructions   Prepare a forecast of monthly cash payments for materials purchases for the third quarter of 19X6.

PROBLEM 46-5A   **Assembling a capital budget.** The management of the Johnson Plastic Products Company plans to buy the following plant and equipment during the year ending December 31, 19X5.

MONTH	DESCRIPTION OF ASSET	COST
Jan.	Addition to garage	$ 10,000
Mar.	New materials handling equipment	50,000
May	New tool shed	1,000
July	New factory machines	100,000
Sept.	New storage warehouse	70,000
Oct.	Expansion of factory storeroom	20,000
		$251,000

Instructions   Prepare a capital expenditures budget for the year. Group like items (equipment and so on) together. (Keep all papers for use in Problem 46-8A.)

PROBLEM 46-6A   **Budgeting cash receipts from accounts receivable.** The budgeted net credit sales for the Johnson Plastic Products Company for each month of 19X5 are shown below. Assuming that the average collection period for 19X5 will be 37 days, approximately 80 percent of the accounts receivable at the beginning of any month will be collected by the end of that month.

Instructions   Prepare a schedule of accounts receivable collections. Round off your computations to the nearest dollar. (Keep all papers for use in Problem 46-8A.)

JOHNSON PLASTIC PRODUCTS COMPANY
Schedule of Accounts Receivable Collections
Year Ending December 31, 19X5

Month	Accts. Rec. Balance First of Mo.	Collections 80% of Begin. Bal.	Remaining Balance	Sales on Credit During Mo.	Accts. Rec. Balance End of Mo.
Jan.	$200,000			$180,000	
Feb.				190,000	
Mar.				200,000	
Apr.				225,000	
May				100,000	
June				150,000	
July				250,000	
Aug.				300,000	
Sept.				300,000	
Oct.				200,000	
Nov.				190,000	
Dec.				180,000	

Budgeting accounts payable payments and balances. The expected credits to accounts payable by month for the Johnson Plastic Products Company for 19X5 are shown below. It is estimated that 90 percent of the balance of accounts payable at the beginning of any month will be paid during the month.

Instructions Prepare a schedule of accounts payable payments. Round off your computations to the nearest dollar. (Keep all papers for use in Problem 46-8A.)

JOHNSON PLASTIC PRODUCTS COMPANY
Schedule of Accounts Payable Payments
Year Ending December 31, 19X5

Month	Accts. Pay. Balance First of Mo.	Payments 90% of Begin. Bal.	Remaining Balance	Accts. Pay. Incurred During Mo.	Accts. Pay. Balance End of Mo.
Jan.	$110,000			$ 90,000	
Feb.				95,000	
Mar.				105,000	
Apr.				125,000	
May				60,000	
June				70,000	
July				120,000	
Aug.				140,000	
Sept.				150,000	
Oct.				110,000	
Nov.				90,000	
Dec.				95,000	

PROBLEM 46-8A **Budgeting cash flow.** This problem is a continuation of Problems 46-5A through 46-7A. The data given below and on page 1116 is needed in the analysis of budgeted cash flow for the Johnson Plastic Products Company for the year ending December 31, 19X5.

Instructions 1. Prepare a budgeted cash flow report similar to the one illustrated on pages 1102 and 1103.
2. Enter the capital expenditures from the information and budget prepared in Problem 46-5A.
3. Enter the collections on accounts receivable computed in Problem 46-6A.
4. Enter the payments on accounts payable computed in Problem 46-7A.
5. Enter the data given in Items a through j below.
6. Complete the calculations for the analysis.

DATA FOR CASH FLOW ANALYSIS

a. The cash balance as of January 1, 19X5, is $201,000.
b. Payment of payrolls and payroll taxes by month is estimated as shown in the table on page 1116.

	Payrolls			
	Manufacturing	Selling	Administrative	Payroll Taxes
Jan.	$ 30,000	$ 15,000	$ 10,000	$ 5,100
Feb.	32,000	18,000	10,000	5,500
Mar.	35,000	20,000	10,000	5,900
Apr.	30,000	20,000	12,000	5,700
May	25,000	17,000	12,000	4,900
June	30,000	16,000	11,000	5,200
July	35,000	15,000	11,000	5,600
Aug.	40,000	22,000	14,000	6,500
Sept.	35,000	21,000	14,000	6,000
Oct.	30,000	18,000	12,000	4,800
Nov.	20,000	17,000	12,000	4,400
Dec.	25,000	15,000	12,000	4,500
Totals	$367,000	$214,000	$140,000	$64,100

c. Monthly interest income of $200 is expected during January through August. The amount will increase to $250 monthly for the rest of the year.

d. The company expects to receive $40,000 from the sale of bonds in March.

e. Bond interest payable will be $3,000 on March 1 and $3,000 on September 1.

f. Federal income taxes will be $35,000 in March and $35,000 in June.

g. State income taxes will be $2,000 in March and $2,000 in June.

h. Property taxes of $15,000 will be due in November.

i. Dividends payable will be $12,500 in January and $12,500 in July.

j. The company expects to obtain $10,000 from the sale of surplus equipment in April.

Financial statements, such as the balance sheet, the income statement, and the statement of retained earnings, are called general purpose reports because they must serve many purposes for many people. In addition to such reports, the accountant prepares internal reports to meet the special needs of the company's managers. These reports may cover any phase of operations and may be in any form that best serves the objective.

INTERNAL REPORTS FOR MANAGEMENT

PRINCIPLES OF GOOD INTERNAL REPORTING

Effective internal reporting demands a great deal of judgment and initiative on the part of accountants. In fact, whenever possible, accountants must anticipate managerial needs rather than wait passively for requests to be made. As they work continuously to improve the firm's reporting procedures, they will follow a number of well-established reporting principles.

The old selling adage about having the right thing, in the right place, at the right time applies with equal effectiveness to internal reporting.

Timeliness

To be useful, a report must be presented while it can provide the information needed to influence action. Some reports are prepared on a daily basis. These should be in the hands of the user on the following day. Similar speed is desirable in the presentation of weekly and monthly reports.

Accuracy

Accounting records and reports must be accurate. A single careless error in a report will make the reader suspect all the other figures, and repeated errors could well destroy an accountant's usefulness to management. However, when managers want to reach a quick decision and ask for approximate figures, the accountant should not hesitate to provide such figures, with the understanding that they are subject to later correction.

Brevity

Most managerial personnel receive more reports and information than they can digest and use effectively. Accountants preparing internal reports should find out just what is needed and summarize the results of their work to emphasize the more useful parts. Complete information may be presented in an appendix to the report or be made available only to those who want it.

Clarity

The report must be clear not only to the accountant who prepared it but also to the reader for whom it was prepared. Most users of reports are not accountants, and few have had much training in accounting. The accountant should design internal reports to fit the readers' abilities and preferences.

REPORTING TO DIFFERENT LEVELS OF MANAGEMENT

Experience shows that the potential reader's managerial level has a direct bearing on the type of data needed and the way it can be presented most effectively.

Production Supervisors

Costs can be controlled only by people, and production supervisors are the people in the best position to control such critical costs as labor and materials. Reports to this first level of management should contain only information of immediate usefulness in supervision. The data may be more understandable if presented in physical terms rather than in dollar terms. For instance, the number of hours of labor or pieces or pounds of material may provide more guidance at this level than the number of dollars involved. Daily reports are most essential here because corrective action must be taken promptly, while the facts are in the supervisor's mind and before losses from inefficiencies mount.

Departmental supervisors responsible for several lower-level supervisors may receive the same reports that their subordinates receive along with summaries covering the operations of all the supervisors under their control. This pattern is followed as reports are prepared for succeedingly higher levels of management. Thus persons at higher levels ordinarily receive summarized information covering a broad area as well as the supporting detailed reports originally prepared for the next lower level of management.

Plant Management

When there are separate plants (or other operating subdivisions) within a business, the plant managers should receive in suitable summarized form all information pertaining to their operations. In addition, they should receive copies of the more detailed reports provided to department heads and other managerial personnel below them.

Major Executives

Major executives, such as the president and vice presidents, should receive reports covering the activities for which they are responsible. These reports are ordinarily in summary form and are supported by many detailed reports that are consulted as required.

ORAL AND WRITTEN REPORTS

Accountants may be called upon to make either oral or written reports to managerial personnel. The ability to think and speak quickly and clearly is thus as important as the ability to write correctly and clearly.

Oral Reports

In the course of their work, accountants gather many facts relating to a business. Some of these facts are so important that management should be informed of them immediately. A simple oral report, in person or by telephone, may serve the purpose. On some occasions, an accountant is also called upon to speak at a meeting, perhaps of a management committee or of the board of directors.

Written Reports

In many firms, accountants are expected to do more than merely present lists of figures. They are often asked to analyze and interpret the figures and to report this analysis in writing. It may be desirable to present the essential findings in a summary section and then to provide the supporting details in the main body of the report. Accountants use four basic techniques of presentation to communicate this information.

Summaries of Accounting Records Accountants present summaries of the data in accounting records, such as lists of accounts receivable, accounts payable, and inventories. Financial statements, such as the balance sheet and the income statement, are examples of more formal summaries.

Horizontal Analysis of Data The various financial statements can be presented in comparative form and analyzed horizontally, with dollar and percentage differences shown for the items on each line. Examples of horizontal analysis are illustrated in budget reports presented later in this chapter. (The horizontal analysis technique was explained in Chapter 35.)

Vertical Analysis of Data Accounting data may also be analyzed vertically by presenting each item as a percentage of some base figure. (This technique was also discussed in Chapter 35.) Income statements are analyzed in percentages of net sales; balance sheets are analyzed in percentages of total assets. The same method can be used to analyze any list of items vertically.

Graphic Presentation of Data Numerical reports may be confusing to some people. Graphic presentation of data—use of charts, for example—is an effective method of making the information more understandable. Normally, these techniques are taught in a statistics course; however, some graphic techniques are presented in many cost accounting and managerial accounting textbooks.

TYPICAL INTERNAL REPORTS

In reaching most vital decisions, alert and efficient managers rely heavily on the facts and figures supplied by internal reports. Thus accountants may prepare a great variety of regular and special internal reports. The following examples illustrate some of the possibilities.

Budget Reports

The use of budgets as control tools requires comparison of the actual results of operations with the budget plan. There are many possible ways of reporting such comparisons.

Budgeted Data by Months To be most effective, budget comparison reports should be prepared often—in most cases at least monthly. This requires that the budget totals for the year be broken down, item by item, by months. (In some cases it is better to build up the annual total by first developing the figures for each month and then adding them together to get the total for the year.) In the report shown on page 1120, budgeted data for a firm's manufacturing overhead for three months of 19Y3 is compared with the actual results for the first two months.

WOODCRAFT MANUFACTURING CORPORATION
Budgeted and Actual Manufacturing Overhead
For Selected Months, 19Y3

	Budgeted			Actual	
	January	February	March	January	February
Item					
Indirect Labor	$ 4,170	$ 4,170	$ 4,200	$ 4,140	$ 4,200
Payroll Taxes—Factory	2,374	2,374	2,412	2,380	2,496
Utilities—Factory	1,500	1,500	1,575	1,375	1,460
Repairs and Maintenance—Factory	2,500	2,500	2,600	2,604	2,460
Indirect Materials and Supplies	1,800	1,800	1,850	1,820	1,813
Depr.—Factory Bldg. and Equipment	1,250	1,250	1,250	1,250	1,250
Insurance—Factory	1,200	1,200	1,200	1,200	1,200
Property Taxes—Factory	1,642	1,642	1,642	1,642	1,642
Totals	$16,436	$16,436	$16,729	$16,411	$16,521

Current Month Comparison Another form of budget comparison report presents actual data and budget estimates for the current month and then indicates the amount by which the actual result for each item is under or over the budget. When expense data is presented, amounts over the budget are usually shown in parentheses or italics. In the report illustrated below, the amounts over the budget are given in parentheses.

WOODCRAFT MANUFACTURING CORPORATION
Budget Comparison Report—Manufacturing Overhead
Month of January 19Y3

	Actual— January	Budget— January	Actual Under (Over) Budget
Item			
Indirect Labor	$ 4,140	$ 4,170	$ 30
Payroll Taxes—Factory	2,380	2,374	(6)
Utilities—Factory	1,375	1,500	125
Repairs and Maintenance—Factory	2,604	2,500	(104)
Indirect Materials and Supplies	1,820	1,800	(20)
Depr.—Factory Bldg. and Equip.	1,250	1,250	-0-
Insurance—Factory	1,200	1,200	-0-
Property Taxes—Factory	1,642	1,642	-0-
Totals	$16,411	$16,436	$ 25

Year-to-Date Comparisons A report like the one just illustrated may be prepared for any month. However, in months after the first, a budget comparison report is usually prepared to show the actual amounts and the amounts over or under the budget for both the month and the year to date. An example of this type of budget comparison report is shown below.

WOODCRAFT MANUFACTURING CORPORATION
Budget Comparison Report—Manufacturing Overhead
Two Months Ended February 28, 19Y3

Item	Month of February Actual	Month of February Under (Over) Budget	Year to Date Actual	Year to Date Under (Over) Budget
Indirect Labor	$ 4,200	$(30)	$ 8,340	$ -0-
Payroll Taxes—Factory	2,496	(122)	4,876	(128)
Utilities—Factory	1,460	40	2,835	165
Repairs and Maintenance—Factory	2,460	40	5,064	(64)
Indirect Materials and Supplies	1,813	(13)	3,633	(33)
Depr.—Factory Bldg. and Equip.	1,250	-0-	2,500	-0-
Insurance—Factory	1,200	-0-	2,400	-0-
Property Taxes—Factory	1,642	-0-	3,284	-0-
Totals	$16,521	$ (85)	$32,932	$ (60)

Comparison of Budgeted and Actual Statements for Year The budgeted financial statements reflect management's hopes and plans for the year. It is no wonder that managers are eager to compare actual and planned results as soon as possible and to seek explanations in those cases when actual results are substantially out of line with plans. Reports comparing Woodcraft's actual income statement, statement of cost of goods manufactured, and balance sheet at the end of the year 19Y3 with the budgeted statements appear on pages 1122–1123 (rounded off to the nearest dollar). Similar comparative reports would be prepared for operating expenses and for retained earnings.

Reports comparing budgeted figures and actual amounts are a highly important control device in modern business. These reports alert management to deviations from the company's plans and provide an opportunity to take corrective action.

No matter how well a firm prepares its budgets, constant monitoring of performance is required to achieve success. Effective managers examine budget comparison reports carefully, investigate the problems that they reveal, and develop strategies for dealing with these problems.

A good internal reporting system and timely action by management are two essential elements in making budgets work. Fortunately, the spread of computers is helping accountants provide a broad range of detailed budget comparison reports to management quickly and efficiently.

WOODCRAFT MANUFACTURING CORPORATION

Comparison of Actual and Budgeted Cost of Goods Manufactured
Year Ended December 31, 19Y3

	Actual	Budget	Under (Over) Budget
Raw Materials			
Raw Materials Inventory, Jan. 1	$ 75,000	$ 75,000	$ -0-
Materials Purchases	$ 515,151	$ 520,300	$5,149
Less Returns and Allowances	1,208	1,300	92
Net Purchases	$ 513,943	$ 519,000	$5,057
Total Materials Available	$ 588,943	$ 594,000	$5,057
Less Raw Materials Inventory, Dec. 31	82,000	82,000	-0-
Raw Materials Used	$ 506,943	$ 512,000	$5,057
Direct Labor	$ 281,238	$ 284,000	$2,762
Manufacturing Overhead			
Indirect Labor	$ 54,328	$ 55,400	$1,072
Payroll Taxes—Factory	31,621	30,970	(651)
Utilities—Factory	21,200	21,500	300
Repairs and Maintenance—Factory	28,924	30,000	1,076
Indirect Materials and Supplies	23,164	23,300	136
Depr.—Factory Bldg. and Equip.	15,700	15,500	(200)
Insurance—Factory	14,430	14,400	(30)
Property Taxes—Factory	19,715	19,700	(15)
Total Manufacturing Overhead	$ 209,082	$ 210,770	$1,688
Total Manufacturing Costs	$ 997,263	$1,006,770	$9,507
Add Work in Process Inventory, Jan. 1	30,000	30,000	-0-
	$1,027,263	$1,036,770	$9,507
Less Work in Process Inventory, Dec. 31	35,000	35,000	-0-
Cost of Goods Manufactured (To Exhibit B)	$ 992,263	$1,001,770	$9,507

The Flexible Budget

You have now seen that a comparison of actual results with the amounts included in the budget helps managers determine how well the plan is being followed. However, to obtain maximum control over operations, management needs to know how actual results compare with the results that should have been achieved for the work actually performed. An invaluable tool for controlling the costs of materials and labor is the use of cost standards, which were discussed in Chapter 43. A technique commonly used for controlling manufacturing overhead costs is the *flexible budget*. Although comprehensive flexible budgeting procedures are quite complex, a brief description will be provided in this section in order to indicate their nature and scope. A detailed examination of flexible budgeting is presented in cost accounting textbooks.

When flexible budgeting is used, each element of manufacturing overhead is examined carefully to see if it is variable or fixed. As discussed in earlier chap-

WOODCRAFT MANUFACTURING CORPORATION   *Exhibit B*
Comparison of Actual and Budgeted Income Statement
Year Ended December 31, 19Y3

	Actual	Budget	Under (Over) Budget
Revenue			
Sales	$1,620,789	$1,654,650	$33,861
Less Sales Returns and Allowances	11,248	11,500	252
Net Sales	$1,609,541	$1,643,150	$33,609
Cost of Goods Sold			
Finished Goods Inventory, Jan. 1	$ 80,000	$ 80,000	$ -0-
Cost of Goods Mfd. (Schedule B-1)	992,263	1,001,770	9,507
Total Goods Available	$1,072,263	$1,081,770	$ 9,507
Less Finished Goods Inventory, Dec. 31	88,000	84,000	(4,000)
Cost of Goods Sold	$ 984,263	$ 997,770	$13,507
Gross Profit on Sales	$ 625,278	$ 645,380	$20,102
Operating Expenses			
Selling Expenses	$ 273,673	$ 275,700	$ 2,027
Administrative Expenses	255,476	258,886	3,410
Total Operating Expenses (Schedule B-2)	$ 529,149	$ 534,586	$ 5,437
Net Income From Operations	$ 96,129	$ 110,794	$14,665
Other Income			
Interest Income	293	300	7
Total Income	$ 96,422	$ 111,094	$14,672
Other Expense			
Bond Interest Expense	7,725	7,800	75
Net Income Before Income Taxes	$ 88,697	$ 103,294	$14,597
Provision for Income Taxes	21,700	27,500	5,800
Net Income After Income Taxes (To Exhibit C)	$ 66,997	$ 75,794	$ 8,797

ters, the total amount of cost for a variable item changes in proportion to the amount of work done. With fixed items, the total amount of cost remains constant regardless of the volume of work done. Other costs are semivariable—that is, they vary to some extent with the volume of work but do not vary in proportion. Clearly, some costs will usually be fixed; for example, depreciation on factory plant and equipment. Other costs, such as indirect materials and manufacturing supplies, will almost always be variable.

Once each overhead item has been analyzed to determine how it should behave in reaction to volume changes, it is possible to determine approximately what the costs *should be* at the level of output actually attained for the period. For this purpose, volume is often measured in terms of direct labor hours worked. However, if only one product is being manufactured, volume may be measured in units of product manufactured.

WOODCRAFT MANUFACTURING CORPORATION *Exhibit A*
Comparison of Actual and Budgeted Balance Sheet
December 31, 19Y3

	Actual	Budgeted	Under (Over) Budget
Assets			
Current Assets			
Cash	$ 52,860	$ 69,995	$17,135
Accounts Receivable (Net)	172,825	167,849	(4,976)
Raw Materials Inventory	82,000	82,000	-0-
Work in Process Inventory	35,000	35,000	-0-
Finished Goods Inventory	88,000	84,000	(4,000)
Prepaid Insurance	3,450	3,350	(100)
Supplies on Hand	2,375	2,575	200
Total Current Assets	$436,510	$444,769	$ 8,259
Property, Plant, and Equipment			
Land	$ 30,000	$ 30,000	$ -0-
Factory Bldg. and Equipment	$285,600	$288,600	$ 3,000
Less Accumulated Depreciation	59,700	59,500	(200)
Book Value	$225,900	$229,100	$ 3,200
Total Prop., Plant, and Equip.	$255,900	$259,100	$ 3,200
Total Assets	$692,410	$703,869	$11,459

	Actual	Budgeted	Under (Over) Budget
Liabilities and Stockholders' Equity			
Current Liabilities			
Accounts Payable	$ 77,859	$ 74,275	$(3,584)
Estimated Income Taxes Payable	21,700	27,500	5,800
Other Payables	7,829	9,001	1,172
Total Current Liabilities	$107,388	$110,776	$ 3,388
Long-Term Liabilities			
12% Bonds Payable, 19Z1	$ 70,000	$ 70,000	$ -0-
Premium on Bonds Payable	725	-0-	(725)
Total Long-Term Liabilities	$ 70,725	$ 70,000	$ (725)
Total Liabilities	$178,113	$180,776	$ 2,663
Stockholders' Equity			
8% Preferred Stock, $100 Par Value	$100,000	$100,000	$ -0-
Paid-in Capital in Excess of Par Value	6,000	6,000	-0-
Common Stock, $50 Stated Value	250,000	250,000	-0-
Paid-in Capital in Excess of Stated Value	19,000	19,000	-0-
Retained Earnings (Exhibit C)	139,297	148,093	8,796
Total Stockholders' Equity	$514,297	$523,093	$ 8,796
Total Liabilities and Stockholders' Equity	$692,410	$703,869	$11,459

To illustrate the general concept of flexible budgeting, suppose that the accountant for the Woodcraft Manufacturing Corporation has classified all of the firm's overhead items for 19Y4 as purely fixed costs or purely variable costs, as shown below. Also suppose that the accountant has determined appropriate cost behavior for each item.

OVERHEAD ITEM	COST BEHAVIOR
Variable Costs:	
Indirect Labor	$1.20 per direct labor hour
Payroll Taxes—Factory	0.70 per direct labor hour
Utilities—Factory	0.42 per direct labor hour
Repairs and Maintenance—Factory	0.64 per direct labor hour
Indirect Materials and Supplies	0.48 per direct labor hour
Fixed Costs:	
Depr.—Factory Bldg. and Equip.	$1,300 per month
Insurance—Factory	1,200 per month
Property Taxes—Factory	1,642 per month

The application of flexible budgeting is shown below, using actual data for January 19Y4. Assume that 3,900 direct labor hours were worked during the month. The flexible budget based on this volume is compared with the actual costs for the month. The differences are indicated in the last column of the report. Notice that six of the eight overhead items listed in the comparative analysis exceed the flexible budget. The total of the manufacturing overhead costs for January 19Y4 is also higher than the flexible budget.

OVERHEAD ITEM	FLEXIBLE BUDGET BASED ON 3,900 HRS.	ACTUAL COST	UNDER (OVER) BUDGET
Indirect Labor	$ 4,680	$ 4,725	$ (45)
Payroll Taxes—Factory	2,730	2,810	(80)
Utilities—Factory	1,638	1,710	(72)
Repairs and Maintenance—Factory	2,496	2,604	(108)
Indirect Materials and Supplies	1,872	1,870	2
Depr.—Factory Bldg. and Equip.	1,300	1,300	-0-
Insurance—Factory	1,200	1,210	(10)
Property Taxes—Factory	1,642	1,665	(23)
Total	$17,558	$17,894	$(336)

Management would take immediate steps to determine why so many overhead items exceed the budget. If budget estimates have been determined realistically and correctly, the flexible budget obviously is of great help in finding out how well costs are being controlled.

Manufacturing Cost Reports

The cost of production reports illustrated in the chapter on process cost accounting are examples of internal reports that are valuable to factory managers. Reports comparing actual costs with standards costs similar to those in Chapter 43 are especially useful in controlling costs and keeping watch over production efficiency.

Sales Management Reports

Accountants may prepare a variety of reports for sales managers. They may analyze sales by products and present reports like the one illustrated on page 1069. They may analyze the sales made by salespeople or by sales territories. They may also prepare reports similar to the studies of manufacturing overhead shown previously in this chapter, comparing actual selling expenses with the budget.

General Administrative Management Reports

The general administrative management of a firm is interested in the principal financial statements, such as the income statement and the balance sheet, which were analyzed in Chapters 35 and 36. Such managers may also be interested in a breakdown of revenue and expenses by departments, as illustrated in Chapter 37. In this connection the contribution margin of each department (the excess of its revenue over its direct expenses) serves as a guide in running the business.

If a firm consists of a home office and branches, management wants to have financial statements for each part of the business as well as for the firm as a whole. Statements of this type were illustrated in Chapter 38.

The age of the accounts receivable is important to credit managers and to general management because of its bearing on the financial health of the business. The procedures for aging the accounts receivable and reporting the results were discussed in Chapter 22. Many companies using computers prepare weekly or even daily reports in which the accounts receivable are analyzed by age.

Most reports to general administrative management are prepared on a monthly basis. However, one that is prepared daily is the cash balance report, an example of which is illustrated below.

WOODCRAFT MANUFACTURING CORPORATION

DAILY CASH REPORT

FOR January 23, 19Y3

BANK ACCOUNTS	Balance Yesterday	Receipts	Payments	Balance This Day
Undeposited Cash on Hand	$ 3,140.25	$2,870.60	$3,140.25	$ 2,870.60
First National Bank	63,267.20	-0-	3,410.35	59,856.85
City Trust Company	48,145.60	3,140.25	1,475.10	49,810.75
Totals	$114,553.05	$6,010.85	$8,025.70	$112,538.20

Last Deposit Date:

First National Bank __Jan. 22__

City Trust Company __Jan. 23__

Last Check Issued:

First National Bank __F-24 762__

City Trust Company __C-11 921__

Prepared on __January 24, 19Y3__   by __J.Q.P.__

Each bank account is shown on a separate line. The balance at the beginning of the day (from the day before) is shown in the left money column; then receipts (amounts deposited in the account) are added. Payments (checks written) are subtracted, and the day's ending balance is recorded in the column at the right.

Totals for each column are shown. The arithmetic for each line and the totals must prove out in this manner: Beginning Balance + Receipts − Payments = Ending Balance.

The first item on the daily cash report, Undeposited Cash on Hand, represents receipts that were not deposited in the bank in time to be credited that day. These funds may have been put in the bank's night depository and should be credited on the following day. For example, the $3,140.25 collected on January 22 and undeposited at the end of that day is shown as paid from Undeposited Cash on Hand and is then recorded as a receipt for the City Trust Company on January 23.

At the bottom part of this report, a record is made of the last deposit date for each bank account and the number of the last check written on that account. Other notations are self-explanatory.

PRINCIPLES AND PROCEDURES SUMMARY

In addition to the standard financial statements, most accountants are required to prepare internal reports to meet the special needs of management. These internal reports should be timely, accurate, brief, clear, and functional. Different levels of management require different types of data and different methods of presentation.

Internal reports may be oral or written. Typical written internal reports include comparisons between actual amounts and budgeted amounts, manufacturing cost reports, sales reports, and general administrative reports. The latter are prepared on a monthly basis to facilitate control.

MANAGERIAL IMPLICATIONS

The internal reporting system of a firm supplies managers with data about business operations that is essential to making intelligent decisions. Internal reports should therefore be designed so that they immediately call attention to problem areas and to deviations from plans. They should also provide a quickly and easily understood means of measuring performance.

As business operations change, management and the accountant should be alert to the need for new or improved internal reports. It is also important to watch for reports that are no longer necessary and should therefore be eliminated. Only useful reports should be prepared.

REVIEW QUESTIONS

1. Name four characteristics of good internal reporting.
2. Why is it important that internal reports be brief?
3. What is a timely report?

4. What types of reports would be prepared for production supervisors?
5. How do reports prepared for major executives normally differ from those prepared for lower-level management?
6. Why are oral reports usually not satisfactory for accounting matters?
7. What is horizontal analysis of data?
8. What is vertical analysis of data?
9. What are budget reports?
10. Why are monthly comparisons made between budgeted and actual amounts?
11. What is a flexible budget?
12. Do you think that a flexible budget would be as useful in controlling costs as the operating budget is? Explain.
13. Describe how a flexible budget is prepared.
14. What types of internal reports might be prepared for sales managers?
15. After the accountant prepares a comparison between actual results and the flexible budget, what use would be made of the comparison?
16. What is a daily cash report?
17. Why is the cash report prepared on a daily basis rather than on a weekly or monthly basis?
18. Why are graphs and charts useful in internal accounting reports?

MANAGERIAL DISCUSSION QUESTIONS

1. Why do managers prefer reports that are especially designed to call attention to problem areas?
2. Why are daily reports essential for effective use by first-level managers?
3. Many accountants confirm their oral reports by distributing written summaries. Why?
4. When comparing budgeted figures and actual figures, should a firm's accountant investigate all items that are over budget or under budget? Explain.
5. Why would management be interested in having the accountant set up a flexible budget?
6. The president of the Harvey Corporation examined a copy of a report comparing actual manufacturing costs for the first three months of 19X1 with the amounts estimated for those costs when the operating budget was prepared in 19X0. He was shocked to find that the budgeted cost of indirect labor for the quarter was $145,600, while the actual cost was $184,200. He asks you, the accountant, to explain to him why "costs are completely out of control." How would you begin your examination of the facts in order to make a report to the president?
7. As chief accountant of the McIntosh Company, you have prepared a report analyzing overhead costs for the first six months of 19X1. Your analysis shows that depreciation for the six-month period was $9.20 per unit produced, while in the same period last year the depreciation was $10.40 per unit. Management has asked you to explain why this decrease occurred. What factors might account for the decline?

EXERCISE 47-1 **Comparing budgeted and actual manufacturing overhead costs.** The manufacturing overhead budget of the Roberts Corporation for the month of January 19X3 included costs of $68,000 for indirect labor and $13,234 for payroll taxes. Actual costs for the month were $65,476 for indirect labor and $15,103 for payroll taxes. Compute the difference between the actual and budgeted costs for each of these items, compute the total actual costs and the total budgeted costs, and compute the difference between the totals.

EXERCISE 47-2 **Preparing a flexible budget for variable overhead costs.** The following information relates to the manufacturing overhead of the Grant Company.

OVERHEAD ITEM	COST BEHAVIOR
Variable Costs:	
Indirect Labor	$2.04 per direct labor hour
Payroll Taxes	0.64 per direct labor hour
Other Variable Costs	3.67 per direct labor hour
Fixed Costs:	
Supervisory Labor	$7,245 per month
Depreciation	3,987 per month
Property Taxes and Insurance	2,879 per month
Other Fixed Costs	3,458 per month

During the month of January 19X1 the direct labor hours worked at this firm totaled 3,285. Set up a flexible budget showing the amounts of the variable cost items for January.

EXERCISE 47-3 **Determining the total of the variable overhead costs in a flexible budget.** Refer to the work that you completed in Exercise 47-2. Compute the total of the variable overhead costs in the flexible budget for January 19X1.

EXERCISE 47-4 **Comparing the variable overhead costs in a flexible budget with the actual costs.** During January 19X1 the Grant Company had the actual overhead costs shown below. Refer to the flexible budget that you prepared in Exercises 47-2 and 47-3. Compute the difference between the budgeted amount for each variable item and the actual amount.

ACTUAL OVERHEAD COSTS FOR JANUARY 19X1

Indirect Labor	$ 5,554
Payroll Taxes	2,151
Other Variable Costs	12,122
Supervisory Labor	7,261
Depreciation	3,987
Property Taxes and Insurance	2,850
Other Fixed Costs	3,475

EXERCISE 47-5 **Comparing the total of the variable overhead costs in a flexible budget with the total of the actual costs.** Refer to the work that you completed in Exercise

47-4. Compute the difference between the total of the budgeted amounts for the variable items and the total of the actual amounts.

EXERCISE 47-6   **Completing a flexible budget.** Refer to the fixed overhead costs shown in Exercise 47-2. Complete the flexible budget that you began in Exercises 47-2 and 47-3 by entering the fixed overhead costs. Then compute the total of these costs and the total of all the budgeted overhead costs for January 19X1.

EXERCISE 47-7   **Comparing the fixed overhead costs in a flexible budget with the actual costs.** Refer to the actual overhead costs shown in Exercise 47-4 and to the flexible budget that you completed in Exercise 47-6. Compute the difference between the budgeted amount for each fixed item and the actual amount. Also compute the difference between the total budgeted costs for fixed overhead and the total actual costs.

EXERCISE 47-8   **Comparing the total manufacturing overhead costs in a flexible budget with the actual costs.** Refer to the work that you completed in Exercises 47-2 through 47-7. Compute the difference between the total of the budgeted costs for all overhead items and the total of the actual costs. How well did the Grant Company control its manufacturing overhead costs in January 19X1? Explain.

EXERCISE 47-9   **Determining the amount of a semivariable overhead item for a flexible budget.** At the Nicoletti Corporation, it is estimated that indirect labor costs are $15,000 a month plus $1.04 per direct labor hour. During August 19X2 the direct labor hours totaled 5,684. What amount would be shown for indirect labor in the firm's flexible budget for August?

EXERCISE 47-10   **Analyzing an increase in sales salaries.** A report on selling expenses prepared for the management of the Schmitt Corporation shows that the firm paid sales salaries of $346,800 in 19X2 and $397,600 in 19X3. Compute the percentage of increase from 19X2 to 19X3. Does this increase necessarily reflect a lack of control over sales salaries? Explain.

PROBLEMS

PROBLEM 47-1   **Comparing budgeted and actual costs.** The Winner's Circle Corporation is a manufacturing business that was recently set up to produce tennis rackets and other types of sporting goods. On March 31, 19X2, after the first three months of operations, the firm's trial balance includes the selected account balances shown on page 1131. The budgeted schedule of manufacturing overhead for the year ending December 31, 19X2, and the budgeted schedule of operating expenses for the same period are shown on pages 1131 and 1132.

Instructions   1. Prepare a budget comparison report for manufacturing overhead for the three months ended March 31, 19X2. Use the illustration on page 1121 as a guide. Assume that overhead costs will be evenly spread throughout the year.

2. Prepare a budget comparison report for operating expenses for the three months ended March 31, 19X2. Use the same columnar setup as in the report prepared for Instruction 1. Assume that expenses will be evenly distributed throughout the year.

WINNER'S CIRCLE CORPORATION
Selected Account Balances
March 31, 19X2

Indirect Labor	$11,230
Payroll Taxes—Factory	3,415
Indirect Materials and Supplies	9,615
Heat, Light, and Power—Factory	6,710
Repairs and Maintenance—Factory Building	1,570
Repairs and Maintenance—Factory Equipment	5,580
Depreciation—Factory Building	2,000
Depreciation—Factory Equipment	4,305
Insurance—Factory	3,440
Property Taxes—Factory	3,775
Sales Salaries Expense	47,320
Payroll Taxes Expense—Sales	4,250
Salespeople's Travel Expense	8,610
Delivery Expense	15,480
Sales Supplies and Other Selling Expenses	4,470
Advertising Expense	10,650
Officer's Salaries Expense	48,750
Office Salaries Expense	16,750
Payroll Taxes Expense—Administrative	5,835
Travel and Entertainment Expense	4,470
Office Supplies and Other Office Expenses	5,390
Loss From Uncollectible Accounts	1,320
Depreciation Expense—Office Equipment	1,500

WINNER'S CIRCLE CORPORATION
Budgeted Schedule of Manufacturing Overhead
Year Ending December 31, 19X2

Indirect Labor	$ 43,840
Payroll Taxes—Factory	12,880
Indirect Materials and Supplies	40,240
Heat, Light, and Power—Factory	26,400
Repairs and Maintenance—Factory Building	6,800
Repairs and Maintenance—Factory Equipment	23,800
Depreciation—Factory Building	8,000
Depreciation—Factory Equipment	16,480
Insurance—Factory	13,600
Property Taxes—Factory	14,880
Total Manufacturing Overhead	$206,920

WINNER'S CIRCLE CORPORATION
Budgeted Schedule of Operating Expenses
Year Ending December 31, 19X2

Operating Expenses

Selling Expenses

Sales Salaries Expense	$183,600	
Payroll Taxes Expense—Sales	18,480	
Salespeople's Travel Expense	33,420	
Delivery Expense	57,440	
Sales Supplies and Other Selling Expenses	18,200	
Advertising Expense	41,760	
Total Selling Expenses		$352,900

Administrative Expenses

Officers' Salaries Expense	$195,000	
Office Salaries Expense	68,000	
Payroll Taxes Expense—Administrative	26,580	
Travel and Entertainment Expense	16,440	
Office Supplies and Other Office Expenses	24,200	
Loss From Uncollectible Accounts	4,660	
Depreciation Expense—Office Equipment	6,000	
Total Administrative Expenses		340,880
Total Operating Expenses (To Exhibit B)		$693,780

PROBLEM 47-2   **Preparing a flexible budget.** The Cosmic Systems Corporation makes parts for satellites and other spacecraft. The firm's accountant has assembled the following information relating to its manufacturing overhead.

OVERHEAD ITEM	COST BEHAVIOR
Variable Costs:	
Indirect Labor	$2.03 per direct labor hour
Payroll Taxes	0.94 per direct labor hour
Indirect Materials and Supplies	0.18 per direct labor hour
Power for Equipment	0.75 per direct labor hour
Repairs and Maintenance	0.18 per direct labor hour
Other Variable Costs	1.22 per direct labor hour
Fixed Costs:	
Depreciation	$126,000 per year
Property Taxes and Insurance	30,000 per year
Heating and Lighting	27,000 per year
Supervisory Labor	60,000 per year
Other Fixed Costs	21,000 per year

Instructions   Prepare a flexible budget for manufacturing overhead for the month of January 19X3. Assume the following alternative situations.

1. A total of 9,300 direct labor hours are worked.
2. A total of 14,567 direct labor hours are worked.

Preparing a flexible budget and a budget comparison report. A schedule showing the expected behavior of manufacturing overhead costs at the Lenox Tile Company is given below, along with data about actual costs for January 19X1. During that month a total of 3,000 direct labor hours were worked in the factory.

Instructions

1. Prepare a flexible budget of manufacturing overhead for the month of January 19X1, based on the actual hours worked. Enter the budgeted amounts in the first money column of the form.
2. Prepare a comparison of actual and budgeted overhead for the month, using the format shown on page 1125.

EXPECTED COST

OVERHEAD ITEM	COST BEHAVIOR
Indirect Labor	$2.00 per direct labor hour
Payroll Taxes	1.25 per direct labor hour
Power	1.50 per direct labor hour
Repairs and Maintenance	0.20 per direct labor hour
Indirect Materials and Supplies	0.50 per direct labor hour
Heating and Lighting	$1,500 per month
Depreciation—Plant and Equipment	2,900 per month
Insurance	2,000 per month
Property Taxes	1,250 per month

ACTUAL COSTS

Indirect Labor	$5,860
Payroll Taxes	3,890
Power	4,820
Repairs and Maintenance	500
Indirect Materials and Supplies	1,600
Heating and Lighting	1,460
Depreciation—Plant and Equipment	2,900
Insurance	2,100
Property Taxes	1,250

ALTERNATE PROBLEMS

PROBLEM 47-1A **Comparing budgeted and actual costs.** The Safety Products Corporation was established several years ago to manufacture smoke detector alarms and other fire prevention equipment. On June 30, 19X4, after the first six months of the company's fiscal year, the trial balance includes the selected account balances shown on page 1134. The budgeted schedule of manufacturing overhead for the year ending December 31, 19X4, and the budgeted schedule of operating expenses for the same period are shown on pages 1134 and 1135.

Instructions

1. Prepare a budget comparison report for manufacturing overhead for the six months ended June 30, 19X4. Use the illustration on page 1121 as a guide.

Assume that overhead costs will be evenly spread throughout the year.

2. Prepare a budget comparison report for operating expenses for the six months ended June 30, 19X4. Use the same columnar setup as in the report prepared for Instruction 1. Assume that expenses will be evenly distributed throughout the year.

SAFETY PRODUCTS CORPORATION
Selected Account Balances
June 30, 19X4

Indirect Labor	$26,900
Payroll Taxes—Factory	8,795
Indirect Materials and Supplies	21,320
Heat, Light, and Power—Factory	9,895
Repairs and Maintenance—Factory Building	3,980
Repairs and Maintenance—Factory Equipment	5,715
Depreciation—Factory Building	5,000
Depreciation—Factory Equipment	7,705
Insurance—Factory	6,220
Property Taxes—Factory	6,000
Sales Salaries Expense	95,100
Payroll Taxes Expense—Sales	9,120
Salespeople's Travel Expense	32,800
Delivery Expense	14,900
Sales Supplies and Other Selling Expenses	7,840
Advertising Expense	26,375
Officers' Salaries Expense	75,000
Office Salaries Expense	37,800
Payroll Taxes Expense—Administrative	10,800
Travel and Entertainment Expense	14,300
Office Supplies and Other Office Expenses	15,650
Loss From Uncollectible Accounts	2,590
Depreciation Expense—Office Equipment	3,250

SAFETY PRODUCTS CORPORATION
Budgeted Schedule of Manufacturing Overhead
Year Ending December 31, 19X4

Indirect Labor	$ 54,100
Payroll Taxes—Factory	16,650
Indirect Materials and Supplies	39,570
Heat, Light, and Power—Factory	19,775
Repairs and Maintenance—Factory Building	7,840
Repairs and Maintenance—Factory Equipment	11,465
Depreciation—Factory Building	10,000
Depreciation—Factory Equipment	15,410
Insurance—Factory	12,385
Property Taxes—Factory	11,900
Total Manufacturing Overhead	$199,095

SAFETY PRODUCTS CORPORATION
Budgeted Schedule of Operating Expenses
Year Ending December 31, 19X4

Operating Expenses

Selling Expenses

Sales Salaries Expense	$190,000	
Payroll Taxes Expense—Sales	18,050	
Salespeople's Travel Expense	65,500	
Delivery Expense	25,800	
Sales Supplies and Other Selling Expenses	15,675	
Advertising Expense	53,295	
Total Selling Expenses		$351,320

Administrative Expenses

Officers' Salaries Expense	$150,000	
Office Salaries Expense	75,780	
Payroll Taxes Expense—Administrative	21,620	
Travel and Entertainment Expense	28,500	
Office Supplies and Other Office Expenses	25,450	
Loss From Uncollectible Accounts	5,270	
Depreciation Expense—Office Equipment	6,500	
Total Administrative Expenses		313,120
Total Operating Expenses (To Exhibit B)		$664,440

PROBLEM 47-2A **Preparing a flexible budget.** The Audio Technology Corporation makes high-quality stereo equipment. The firm's accountant has assembled the following information relating to its manufacturing overhead.

OVERHEAD ITEM	COST BEHAVIOR
Variable Costs:	
Indirect Labor	$1.87 per direct labor hour
Payroll Taxes	1.02 per direct labor hour
Indirect Materials and Supplies	0.18 per direct labor hour
Repairs and Maintenance	0.21 per direct labor hour
Fringe Benefits of Employees	1.17 per direct labor hour
Power for Equipment	0.98 per direct labor hour
Other Variable Costs	1.32 per direct labor hour
Fixed Costs:	
Depreciation	$96,000 per year
Property Taxes and Insurance	39,600 per year
Supervisory Labor	72,900 per year
Storeroom Costs	18,000 per year
Security Services	36,000 per year
Other Fixed Costs	21,900 per year

Instructions Prepare a flexible budget for the month of February 19X1. Assume the following alternative situations.

1. A total of 6,200 direct labor hours are worked.
2. A total of 4,900 direct labor hours are worked.

PROBLEM 47-3A   **Preparing a flexible budget and a budget comparison report.** A schedule showing the expected behavior of manufacturing overhead costs at the Deluxe Carpet Company is given below, along with data about actual costs for January 19X1. During that month a total of 4,000 direct labor hours were worked in the factory.

Instructions   1. Prepare a flexible budget of manufacturing overhead for the month of January 19X1, based on the actual hours worked. Enter the budgeted amounts in the first money column of the form.
2. Prepare a comparison of actual and budgeted overhead for the month, using the format shown on page 1125.

EXPECTED COSTS

OVERHEAD ITEM	COST BEHAVIOR
Indirect Labor	$1.00 per direct labor hour
Payroll Taxes	0.60 per direct labor hour
Power	0.70 per direct labor hour
Repairs and Maintenance	0.10 per direct labor hour
Indirect Materials and Supplies	0.25 per direct labor hour
Heating and Lighting	$ 880 per month
Depreciation—Plant and Equipment	1,500 per month
Insurance	1,000 per month
Property Taxes	600 per month

ACTUAL COSTS

Indirect Labor	$4,160
Payroll Taxes	2,508
Power	3,000
Repairs and Maintenance	370
Indirect Materials and Supplies	980
Heating and Lighting	1,100
Depreciation—Plant and Equipment	1,500
Insurance	1,000
Property Taxes	625

GLOSSARY

Absorption costing A system of reporting income from manufacturing operations in which all costs, both fixed and variable, are assigned to the cost of goods manufactured. This system is used for reporting under generally accepted accounting principles.

Accelerated cost recovery system (ACRS) A method of depreciation or cost recovery used for federal income tax purposes for long-term assets purchased after 1981. Under ACRS, long-term assets fall automatically into certain classes, and the costs of all assets in a class are charged to expense through a standard formula.

Account A separate record showing the increases and decreases in each asset, liability, owner's equity, revenue, and expense item of a business.

Account balance The difference between the total debits and the total credits in an account.

Account form of balance sheet The form of balance sheet in which assets are listed on the left side and liabilities and owner's equity are listed on the right side.

Accounting The process by which financial information about a business is recorded, classified, summarized, and interpreted and then communicated to owners, managers, and other interested parties.

Accounting cycle The series of steps performed during each accounting period to classify, record, and summarize financial data for a business and produce needed financial information.

Accounting equation An equation that expresses the relationship of the fundamental elements of accounting: Assets = Liabilities + Owner's Equity.

Accounting period The period of time covered by the income statement and other financial statements that report operating results.

Accounts payable Amounts that a business must pay its creditors in the future.

Accounts receivable Amounts owed to the business by its credit customers.

Accrual basis of accounting A generally accepted method of accounting in which all revenues and expenses are recognized on the income statement in the period when they are earned and incurred regardless of when the cash related to the transactions is received or paid.

Accrued expenses Expenses that have been incurred but have not yet been paid for and recorded.

Accrued income Income that has been earned but has not yet been received and recorded.

Adjustments Entries made at the end of an accounting period to update the general ledger accounts for previously unrecorded items. These entries are first listed on the worksheet and then journalized and posted.

All-inclusive concept This view of reporting the results of operations holds that every item of profit or loss should be shown on the income statement.

Amortization of bond premium or bond discount The process of systematically writing off the premium or discount on bonds as an adjustment to interest expense over the period that the bonds are outstanding.

Amortization of intangible assets The process of allocating the acquisition cost of an intangible asset to expense over its legal life or economic life, whichever is shorter.

Assets Items of value owned by a business.

Audit trail A chain of references that makes it possible to trace information about transactions through an accounting system.

Average cost method A method of valuing inventory that uses the weighted-average unit cost. This average cost is found by dividing the total cost of the goods available by the total number of units available.

Balance sheet The financial statement that shows the financial position of a business at a specific date by summarizing the business's assets, liabilities, and owner's equity.

Bonds A long-term, interest-bearing debt obligation issued by a corporation.

Book value of an asset The difference between the acquisition cost of an asset and the balance of the related contra account, such as Accumulated Depreciation or Accumulated Depletion.

Budgeting The process of planning and controlling the future operations of a business by developing a set of financial goals and evaluating performance in terms of these goals.

Business transaction A financial event that a firm is involved in.

Capital *See* Owner's equity.

Capital expenditure Expenditure for a purchase of an item of property, plant, or equipment that has a useful life of more than one year.

Cash In accounting, currency, coins, checks, money orders, and funds on deposit in a bank are all considered forms of cash.

Cash discount A discount offered by many wholesalers of goods to their credit customers to encourage quick payment by the customers. This type of price reduction is a sales discount to the seller and a purchase discount to the buyer.

Charge account *See* Open-account credit.

Chart of accounts A list of the numbers and titles of a firm's general ledger accounts.

Classified income statement An income statement in which items are divided into groups of similar accounts and a subtotal is given for each group. This form of income statement identifies revenues by source and expenses by type.

Clean surplus concept *See* All-inclusive concept.

Closing entries Entries made at the end of an accounting period to transfer the net income or net loss to owner's equity and to reduce the balances of the revenue and expense accounts to zero so that they are ready to receive data for the next period.

Common costs Costs that are not directly traceable to a segment of a business such as a department or branch.

Common stock A class of corporate stock that has the right to vote as well as other basic rights of ownership.

Common-size statement A financial statement in which all the items are expressed as a percentage of one of the items. For example, on a common-size income statement, all items are expressed as a percentage of net sales.

Comparative statements Financial statements that include information for two or more periods.

Compound entry A journal entry that contains several debits or several credits.

Consistency principle Under this principle, a business must use the same accounting methods from one period to the next. The application of this principle permits comparability of financial statements.

Consolidated financial statements Financial statements that combine information from the individual statements of parent and subsidiary companies and treat the firms as though they were one economic unit.

Constant-dollar accounting A method of demonstrating the impact of inflation on financial statements by restating certain historical cost items into dollars of equal purchasing power. A price index is used to determine the restated amounts.

Contingent liability A liability that is indefinite as to existence and amount. A future event, such as the settlement of a lawsuit, must take place before the existence of the liability and the amount can be determined.

Contra account An account with a balance opposite to the normal balance for that class of account. For example, a contra asset account such as Accumulated Depreciation has a credit balance rather than the normal debit balance for an asset account. A contra account serves to reduce the balance of a related account on a financial statement.

Contribution margin Revenue less variable costs.

Control account A general ledger account that serves as a link between a subsidiary ledger and the general ledger because its balance summarizes the individual balances of the accounts in the subsidiary ledger.

Corporation A business entity granted separate legal status under state law. Ownership in this type of entity is evidenced by shares of stock.

Cost centers Segments of a business that do not directly earn revenue. Accounting for cost centers emphasizes cost control.

Cost depletion A method of depletion in which the depletion charged each year is related to the units of the natural resource that are removed during the period.

Cost of goods sold The cost of goods sold is equal to the beginning inventory for an accounting period plus the net delivered cost of the purchases made during the period minus the ending inventory.

Cost principle Under this principle, assets are recorded on the basis of the original amount paid for them.

Credit An amount entered on the right side of an account.

Creditor A company or individual to whom a business owes money.

Cumulative preferred stock Preferred stock that has the right to receive a stated dividend for the current year and for any prior years in which the dividend was not paid. The amounts owed to such stockholders must be paid before the common stockholders receive any dividends.

Current assets Cash, assets that will be converted into cash within one year, and assets that will be used up within one year.

Current cost The value of an asset as measured by the cost of acquiring an identical asset today or the cost of replacing the asset with an asset that has the same productive capacity. *See* Replacement cost.

Current liabilities Liabilities that must be paid within one year.

Current operating concept This view of reporting the results of operations holds that only normally recurring items of profit and loss should appear on the income statement. Nonrecurring gains and losses should be shown on the statement of retained earnings.

Debit An amount entered on the left side of an account.

Debt securities Bonds and other debt instruments of a corporation.

Declining-balance method An accelerated method of depreciation in which the book value of an asset at the beginning of the year is multiplied by an appropriate percentage to obtain the depreciation charge for that year.

Deferred expenses *See* Prepaid expenses.

Deferred income *See* Unearned income.

Depletion The allocation of the cost of natural resources to expense over their useful lives.

Depreciable base of an asset The difference between the cost of an asset and its salvage value. This amount is used in the computation of the yearly depreciation charge.

Depreciation The process of allocating the cost of a long-term asset to operations during its expected useful life.

Differential cost The difference in cost between one alternative and another.

Direct costing A system of reporting income from manufacturing operations in which only variable costs are considered as part of the cost of goods manufactured. Fixed costs are charged as expenses in the period incurred. This system is used only for internal reporting purposes; it is not permitted for reporting under generally accepted accounting principles.

Direct expenses Operating expenses that can be identified specifically with individual departments.

Direct labor Wages of employees who work directly on a product as it is being manufactured.

Direct materials Items that go into a product during the manufacturing process and become part of that product.

Discount The difference between the par value of stocks and bonds and the amount at which they are actually issued.

Discounted rate of return *See* Effective rate of return.

Discounting An arrangement in which the bank deducts the interest on a note in advance, and the borrower receives only the difference between the face amount of the note and the interest on it to maturity.

Dividend A distribution of the earnings of a corporation to the stockholders (owners).

Double-entry system A system of accounting under which each transaction is recorded by means of counterbalancing debit and credit entries. At least one account must be debited and one account must be credited. However, no matter how many accounts are involved, the debit and credit totals for a transaction must be equal.

Effective interest method of amortizing bond premium or discount A method of amortizing bond premium or discount in which the interest expense is a constant percentage of the book value of the bonds.

Effective rate of return method An analytical procedure to compute a discounted rate of return on an investment. This procedure takes into consideration the time value of money.

Endorsement The legal process by which the payee of a check transfers ownership of the check to a bank or to another person or firm. This is accomplished by writing or stamping the payee's name on the back of the check.

Equity method A method used to record a long-term investment in equity securities when the investor exercises significant influence over the investee. Under this method, the investor records in each period its proportionate share of the net income or net loss of the investee. A receipt of a dividend by the investor is recorded as a decrease in the investment account.

Equity securities Shares of stock in a corporation.

Expenses The costs of the goods and services that are used to produce revenue.

Experience-rating system A method used by states to adjust an employer's SUTA tax rate because of a favorable or unfavorable employment record.

Extraordinary items Transactions and events that are both unusual in nature and infrequent in occurrence. They are reported net of taxes on the income statement following the figure for net income from operations after taxes.

Face value *See* Principal.

Fair market value method of recording trade-ins A method of recording the exchange of a business asset for a similar asset under APB Opinion No. 29, which requires that all losses on trade-ins be recorded.

Financial accounting The accumulation of data about a business's financial transactions and the reporting of this data to owners and other interested parties.

Financial Accounting Standards Board (FASB) The organization that now has primary responsibility for establishing financial accounting standards and principles.

Financial budget A budget containing projections for cash and other balance sheet items.

Financial statements The periodic reports that summarize the financial affairs of a business.

First in, first out method (FIFO) A method of valuing inventory which assumes that the first items purchased are the first items to be sold. Therefore, the cost of the ending inventory is computed by referring to the cost of the latest purchases.

Fiscal period *See* Accounting period.

Fiscal year Any 12-month accounting period used by a business.

Fixed costs Costs that do not vary in total during a period even though the volume of goods manufactured may be higher or lower than anticipated.

Flexible budget A projection that contains budgeted amounts at various levels of production. For example, budgeted amounts might be given for 80 percent, 100 percent, and 120 percent of capacity.

Full disclosure principle Under this principle, it is necessary to present on a financial statement all information that might affect the statement user's interpretation of the profitability and financial position of a business.

Funds A term that is normally used by accountants and financial analysts to refer to working capital. However, it is also sometimes used to mean cash. *See* Working capital.

General ledger The main ledger of a business; the ledger that contains the accounts that are reported on the financial statements.

Generally accepted accounting principles (GAAPs) The rules of accounting used by businesses in reporting their financial activities.

Going concern assumption The assumption that a business will continue to operate indefinitely.

Goodwill The value of a business in excess of the value of its identifiable assets. Goodwill usually arises when the profits of a business are greater than normal for the assets employed.

Gross profit method A method of estimating ending inventory based on the assumption that the rate of gross profit on sales is relatively constant from one period to another.

Gross profit on sales Gross profit is the difference between net sales and the cost of goods sold.

Horizontal analysis An analysis involving comparison of data for the current period with the same data of a company for previous periods. For example, this year's cash balance is presented as a percentage of last year's.

Income statement A financial statement that shows the revenue, expenses, and net income or net loss of a business for a specific period of time.

Income tax method of recording trade-ins A method of recording the exchange of a business asset for a similar asset for federal income tax purposes. No gain or loss is recorded on the transaction, and the cost of the new asset is the book value of the old asset plus the cash paid.

Incremental cost The increase in cost from one alternative to another.

Indirect expenses Operating expenses that cannot be easily assigned to a particular department when transactions occur and are recorded. Some indirect expenses, such as depreciation, have a meaningful relationship to individual departments and can be allocated based on this relationship. Other indirect expenses must be allocated on the most logical basis possible.

Indirect labor Wages of employees who work in a factory but are not directly involved in manufacturing the product such as factory supervisors and maintenance workers.

Indirect materials and supplies Items that are used in the manufacturing process but do not become part of the product. For example, cleaning supplies and oil for machinery fall into this category.

Intangible assets Noncurrent assets that are used in the operation of a business and have no physical characteristics. Patents, copyrights, franchises, trademarks, organization costs, and goodwill are examples of intangible assets.

Interest The price charged for the use of money or credit.

Inventory *See* Merchandise inventory.

Invoice A bill for goods purchased on credit. It is sent by the seller to the purchaser.

Job order cost accounting A system used to collect data about costs when goods are produced for specific orders or lots.

Journal A chronological (day-by-day) listing of the financial transactions of a business.

Journalizing The process of recording data in a journal.

Last in, first out method (LIFO) A method of valuing inventory which assumes that the last items purchased are the first items to be sold. Therefore, the cost of the ending inventory is computed by referring to the cost of the earliest purchases.

Ledger A record containing the separate accounts of a business. *See also* General ledger and Subsidiary ledger.

Legal capital An amount equal to the par value or stated value of the shares of stock outstanding.

Liabilities Amounts owed by a business to its creditors. The debts or obligations of a business.

Liquidity The ability of a company to pay its currently maturing debts.

List price The established retail price of merchandise.

Long-term liabilities Liabilities that are due more than a year in the future.

Managerial accounting The area of accounting that provides an internal reporting system. This system gives management financial information for use in decision making and long-range planning.

Manufacturing business A business that sells goods that it makes or assembles.

Manufacturing margin The difference between sales and the variable cost of goods sold.

Manufacturing overhead The cost of all manufacturing operations that are not classified as direct materials or direct labor.

Marginal income on sales The difference between manufacturing margin and variable operating expenses. *See also* Manufacturing margin.

Marginal revenue Revenue that changes as a result of a decision.

Master budget A projection that includes both a detailed operating budget and a detailed financial budget.

Matching principle Under this principle, the revenue earned during an accounting period should be compared, or matched, against the costs incurred in earning that revenue in order to properly measure the income for the period.

Maturity date The date on which a note becomes due and must be paid.

Maturity value The total amount that must be paid when a note is due. This amount is the sum of the principal plus the interest.

Merchandise inventory The stock of goods that a business has on hand for sale to customers.

Merchandising business A business that sells goods that it has purchased for resale.

Mill The typical unit of measure for property taxes. One mill is a thousandth part of a dollar, or $0.001.

Mixed accounts Accounts that contain elements of both assets and expenses or both liabilities and revenues.

Modified all-inclusive approach This view of reporting the results of operations holds that almost all items of profit or loss should be reported on the income statement but in two distinct parts. The first part should report the income arising from ordinary, recurring operations, and the second part should report gains or losses arising from extraordinary, nonrecurring items. Other items should appear on the statement of retained earnings. This is the generally accepted approach.

Monetary assets and liabilities Assets and liabilities that are in the form of cash or that are receivable or payable in specific dollar amounts.

Multiple-step income statement An income statement in which revenues and expenses are divided into groups, and several steps are therefore necessary to compute the net income or net loss for the period. *See also* Classified income statement.

Natural resources Assets such as timber, oil, and minerals, which are physically removed from the land in the process of production.

Negotiable A term that means ownership of a check, promissory note, or other financial instrument can be transferred from one person or firm to another. The transfer is made by endorsing and delivering the instrument.

Net income The amount by which revenue is greater than expenses.

Net income analysis A name for a departmentalized income statement that shows computation of a final net income for each department as well as for the business as a whole.

Net loss The amount by which expenses are greater than revenue.

Net present value method An analytical procedure that compares the present value of all future net cash inflows from a capital project with the present cash flow outlay needed to acquire the asset.

Net price The list price of an item minus all trade discounts.

Net sales Sales less sales returns and allowances and sales discounts.

Net worth *See* Owner's equity.

No-par value stock Stock that is not given a par value by the organizers of the corporation. The entire amount received from the issue of the stock is credited to the stock account, or the stock may be assigned a stated value, which is similar to par value for accounting purposes. *See also* Stated value.

Noncumulative preferred stock Preferred stock that has no continuing right to receive dividends for years in which none were declared.

Nonparticipating preferred stock Preferred stock that is entitled to only the dividend amount specified on the stock certificate. It does not share with common stock in any additional dividends.

Note A written promise to pay a debt.

Objectivity assumption The assumption that financial statement information is unbiased, fair, and verifiable.

Open-account credit The form of credit most commonly offered by professional people and small businesses. It permits the sale of services or goods with the understanding that the amount owed will be paid at a later date.

Operating expenses Expenses that arise from the normal activities of a business.

Opportunity costs Earnings or potential benefits foregone because a certain course of action is taken.

Other expenses Expenses that are not directly connected with operations.

Other income Income that is earned from nonoperating sources.

Owner's equity The financial interest of the owner of a business.

Par value A figure assigned by the organizers of a corporation to each share of stock for accounting purposes. It is the amount credited to the stock account for each share issued.

Parent company The purchaser of a majority of another company's voting stock.

Participating preferred stock Preferred stock that receives the dividend specified on the stock certificate and may also share in additional dividends with the common stock.

Partnership A form of business entity owned by two or more persons.

Payback period A calculation to determine the number of years it will take to recover the proposed outlay for an asset.

Payee The person or firm to whom a check or promissory note is payable.

Percentage depletion A depletion method based on a percentage of gross income from the sale of minerals from a property. This method is used for federal income tax purposes.

Periodicity of income assumption Under this assumption, the life of a business entity is arbitrarily divided into time periods, usually a year in length, for income determination. This is done to meet the need of owners and other statement readers for meaningful financial information at regular intervals.

Permanent account An account that continues from one accounting period to the next. Examples are asset and liability accounts and the owner's capital account.

Perpetual inventory basis A method of recording inventory in which items added to the inventory and items removed are recorded on a daily basis. Thus, the current balance on hand is always available.

Petty cash fund A cash fund of a limited amount used to make small expenditures for which it is not practical to write checks.

Postclosing trial balance A trial balance prepared as the last step in the end-of-period routine. Its purpose is to verify that the debits and credits in the general ledger are equal after the adjusting and closing entries have been posted.

Posting The process of transferring data from a journal to a ledger.

Preferred stock A class of corporate stock which has special preferences that set it apart from common stock. These preferences may include preferred claims on profits or on assets in the event of liquidation.

Premium The amount paid in excess of par value for securities such as stocks and bonds.

Prepaid expenses Expense items that are paid for and recorded prior to their use. Most firms treat these items as assets when they are first acquired and gradually transfer them to expense as they are used.

Principal The amount shown on the face of a note or a bond. This is the amount that must be paid to the holder when the note or bond matures.

Prior period adjustments These adjustments are primarily corrections of material errors made in prior accounting periods, which are reported on the statement of retained earnings.

Process cost accounting A system used to collect costs when similar goods are produced in a continuous flow.

Producing departments Departments in a manufacturing operation that work directly on products.

Profit centers Revenue-producing segments of a business that sell products or services to customers outside the business. Sales and cost data for each center are accumulated, and a "profit" is computed.

Promissory note A written promise to pay a specified amount of money on a specified date.

Property, plant, and equipment Assets, such as buildings, machinery, trucks, and land that will be used for a long time in the operation of a business. All assets in this category except land are subject to depreciation.

Purchase discount See Cash discount.

Ratio analysis An analysis involving the comparison of two individual items on financial statements in which one item is divided by the other to form a relationship that is expressed as a ratio.

Real property A category of property, plant, and equipment that includes land, land improvements, buildings, and other structures attached to the land.

Realization principle Under this principle, revenue is recorded and reported on the income statement only when earned. Thus, revenue is recognized when a sale is made or a service is provided to an outsider.

Reciprocal accounts Accounts that are used to record opposite sides of the same transaction.

Reconciling the bank statement The process used to determine why the balance shown on the bank statement differs from the balance shown in the Cash account and the checkbook and to bring the two sets of records into agreement.

Replacement cost The cost of acquiring an asset with the same productive capacity as an existing asset. This amount often represents the current cost of an asset that is like the existing asset. *See* Current cost.

Report form of balance sheet The form of balance sheet in which the liabilities and owner's equity are listed under the assets.

Responsibility accounting An accounting system designed to evaluate the performance of the various segments of a business such as departments and branches and assign responsibility for financial results.

Retail business A business that sells goods and services directly to individual consumers.

Retail method A method of estimating ending inventory based on the assumption that all items have the same rate of markon. Multiplying the retail value of the ending inventory by a cost to retail percentage converts the retail value to cost.

Retained earnings Earnings of a corporation that are kept in the business and not paid out in dividends. This amount represents the accumulated, undistributed profits of the corporation.

Return on investment The rate of profit that an investment will earn. This rate is equal to the annual net income divided by the original investment or the average investment.

Revenue The inflow of money or other assets that results from the sale of goods or services or from the use of money or property.

Reversing entries Journal entries made at the beginning of an accounting period that are the opposite of certain adjusting entries, particularly adjusting entries for accrued expenses and income.

Sales allowance A reduction in the price of goods or services that is given to a customer by the seller.

Sales discount *See* Cash discount.

Salvage value The amount an asset can be sold for when it is disposed of at the end of its useful life.

Semidirect expenses *See* Indirect expenses.

Semivariable costs Costs that have characteristics of both fixed costs and variable costs. For example, utility expense is a semivariable cost.

Separate entity assumption In accounting it is assumed that the financial affairs and records of a business are separate and distinct from the financial affairs and records of the owners.

Service business A business that provides services to its customers. Cleaning stores, hotels, airlines, and trucking companies are all examples of service businesses. The firms operated by doctors, lawyers, accountants, and other professionals are also classified as service businesses.

Service departments Departments in a manufacturing operation that assist in production but do not actually work on product.

Simple rate of return method A method of computing return on investment that does not consider the time value of money. *See* Return on investment.

Single-step income statement A form of income statement in which all revenues are listed in one section and all expenses are listed in another section. Thus, the net income or net loss can be determined in one step—by subtracting the total expenses from the total revenues.

Sole Proprietorship A business entity owned by one person.

Special journal A journal that is used to record only a specific type of transaction.

Specific identification method A method of valuing inventory that involves use of the actual purchase prices of the inventory items.

Stable monetary unit assumption The assumption that money is the unit of measurement in accounting and that money does not change in value significantly from one period to another.

Standard cost accounting A cost accounting system in which costs are measured on the basis of predetermined or budgeted amounts or standards.

Stated value A figure assigned to a share of no-par value stock by the organizers of a corporation. It is the amount credited to the stock account for each share of no-par value stock issued and sold. *See also* No-par value stock.

Statement of changes in financial position A financial statement showing the sources and uses of a company's financial resources during an accounting period.

Stockholders The owners of a corporation. Their investment in the corporation is evidenced by shares of stock.

Stockholders' equity The stockholders' investment in a corporation plus the profits that have been retained in the business.

Straight-line method of amortizing bond premium or discount A method of amortizing bond premium or discount in which the interest expense is a constant dollar amount for each accounting period that occurs while the bonds are outstanding.

Straight-line method of depreciation A method of writing off the cost of property, plant, and equipment that allocates the same amount of depreciation to each year of the useful life of an item.

Subsidiary company A corporation that has had a majority of its voting stock purchased by another corporation.

Subsidiary ledger A ledger that contains accounts of a single type and that is subordinate to the general ledger. For example, the accounts receivable ledger contains only accounts for credit customers.

Sum-of-the-years'-digits method An accelerated method of depreciation in which a fractional part of the depreciable cost of an asset is charged to expense each year. The denominator of the fraction is the sum of the numbers representing the years of the asset's useful life, and the numerator is the number of years remaining in the asset's useful life.

Sunk cost A historical cost that has already been incurred and is thus irrelevant for decision-making purposes.

Taking a physical inventory The process of counting the number of units of each type of goods on hand at the end of an accounting period and then multiplying that number by the appropriate cost per item.

Tangible personal property A category of property, plant, and equipment that includes machinery, equipment, furniture, and fixtures.

Temporary account An account whose balance is transferred to owner's equity at the end of each accounting period. Examples are revenue and expense accounts.

Total capital *See* Total equities.

Total equities Liabilities plus stockholders' equity.

Trade discount A discount or price adjustment granted by a wholesale business in order to reduce the list price or established retail price of the goods being sold.

Transfer price The price at which the goods of one segment of a business are transferred to another segment.

Treasury stock A corporation's own capital stock that has been reacquired. The balance of the Treasury Stock ac-

count is deducted from the sum of all items in the Stockholders' Equity section of the balance sheet.

Trial balance A listing of all the accounts in the general ledger and their balances. It is used to prove the equality of the debits and credits in the accounts.

Unearned income Income that has been received and recorded but not yet earned. Most businesses initially record these amounts as liabilities and then transfer portions to income as the sums are earned.

Units-of-output method A method of depreciation in which the depreciation charged each year is related to the number of units produced by the asset.

Variable costing *See* Direct costing.

Variable costs Costs that vary in total directly with the volume of manufacturing activity. For example, direct labor is a variable cost.

Vertical analysis Analysis that involves expressing each item on a financial statement as a percentage of some base amount. For example, net income is expressed as a percentage of net sales.

Voucher system A system used to control liabilities and cash payments. A form called a voucher is prepared to authorize payment of all obligations, and no check can be issued without a properly approved voucher.

Wholesale business A business that sells goods to retailers or large consumers such as hotels and hospitals.

Work in process Manufactured products that are only partially completed at the end of an accounting period.

Working capital Current assets minus current liabilities. This term is sometimes used to refer to the current assets of a company. Working capital is a basic measure of a company's ability to pay its current obligations.

Worksheet A columnar form used to gather all the data needed at the end of an accounting period to prepare the financial statements. This form is a handy device for recording adjustments and determining the updated account balances before the formal adjusting entries are journalized and posted.

INDEX

Stock (*see also* Capital stock transactions)
call price of, 676
common, 633, 634, 665
dividends (*see* Dividends)
as long-term investment, 760–765
no-par value, 635
par value, 635
preferred, 633–634, 676–677, 703–704
ratio analysis of, 861–867
stated value, 635
as temporary investment, 750–754
watered, 670
Stock dividends, 700–702, 765
Stock splits, 702
Stockholders, 631; *def.,* 5
characteristics of a corporation and, 631–632
meeting of, 662–663
Stockholders' equity, 632, 703
ratio analysis of, 860–865
Stockholders' ledger (*see* Capital stock ledger)
Stockholders of record, 699
Straight-line method of depreciation, 83, 357, 548, 549
Subscribers' ledger, 674
Subscription book, 674
Subsidiary company, 747, 779
financial statements of (*see* Consolidated financial statements)
Subsidiary ledgers, 126, 984
Sum-of-the-years'-digits method of depreciation, 549–550; *illus.,* 550
Sunk cost, 1048
Supplemental disclosures, 787–788

T account, *def.,* 35; *illus.,* 35
Tangible personal property, 544
Tax calendar, 583; *illus.,* 583
Taxes
business (*see* Business taxes)
income (*see* Income tax)
payroll (*see* Payroll taxes)
property (*see* Property taxes)
sales (*see* Sales tax)
Temporary accounts, *def.,* 47
Temporary investments, 748–754
Time-and-a-half pay, 299
Time draft, 494–495
Time tickets, 987; *illus.,* 987

Times bond interest earned ratio, 864
Times preferred dividends earned ratio, 864
Trade acceptance, 495; *illus.,* 495
Trade discounts, 141
Trade-in of an asset, 554–556
Trading on the equity, 638–639
Transfer price, 883
Transmittal of Income and Tax Statements (Form W-3), 333
Treasury stock, 674–676, 703
Trial balance, 77; *illus.,* 78
adjusted (*see* Adjusted trial balance)
errors
not revealed by, 79
revealed by, 78–79
postclosing, 110–111, 411, 970; *illus.,* 111, 412
preparing, 78
section of worksheet, 80; *illus.,* 80, 88, 366, 390, 894, 960
Turnover of assets, 863

Uncollectible accounts, 504–514
on the balance sheet, 510
charging off
allowance method, 505–508
direct method, 504
collecting on account that was written off, 509–510
estimating, 505–508
on the income statement, 510
internal control of, 514
other receivables and, 510
valuation account and, 506
recording losses from, 354, 356, 504, 508–509; *illus.,* 356, 508
on installment sales, 513–514
Unearned income, 364–365; *def.,* 364
Unemployment insurance, 334–335
Unincorporated business taxes, 575
Units-of-output method of depreciation, 550
Unsecured bonds, 719
Useful life, 357

Valuation account, 506
Valuation of inventory, 526–536
cost or market, whichever is lower, 531–533
costing methods, 526–531
average cost, 527–528
first in, first out, 528–529

Valuation of inventory, costing methods (*continued*)
last in, first out, 529
specific identification, 527
estimation procedures, 533–535
gross profit method, 533–534
retail method, 534–535
Variable costing (*see* Direct costing)
Variable costs, 1031–1032
Vertical analysis (percentage analysis), 834, 1119
of balance sheet, 843, 844
of income statement, 837–839
of operating expenses, 840–841
of retained earnings, 844–845
Voucher check, 239–240
Voucher system, 257–269

Wage and Tax Statement (Form W-2), 331–333; *illus.,* 332
Watered stock, 670
Wholesale business, 141–142
Work in process, 945–946, 983, 1071
Work in process ledger, 984
Worker's compensation insurance, 300, 340
Working capital, *def.,* 593, 813
amount of, 867
changes in, 1097
flow of, 816–821
net, 813; *def.,* 593
sources of, 816–820
uses of, 820–821
Worksheet, 79–87, 354–367, 384–396; *illus.,* 88–89, 390–391
for branch office, 922; *illus.,* 923
for combined home office/branch statements, 926–927; *illus.,* 928, 930
consolidation, 780; *illus.,* 781–785
for departmentalized business, 891–900; *illus.,* 894–895
ending merchandise inventory on, 365, 385–386; *illus.,* 386
estimated tax on, 692; *illus.,* 692
for a manufacturing business, 955–961; *illus.,* 956, 960–961
preparing financial statements from, 87–89, 389–396, 891–901, 924–931, 955–965

Yield on common stock, 862